MUSTANG 1989-93 REPAIR MANUAL

CHILTON'S

Covers all U.S. and Canadian models of Ford Mustang

by Kevin M. G. Maher, A.S.E.

PUBLISHED BY **HAYNES NORTH AMERICA, Inc.**

Manufactured in USA

ISBN 0-8019-8815-2
Library of Congress Catalog Card No. 96-84585
8901234567 9876543210

Haynes Publishing Group
Sparkford Nr Yeovil
Somerset BA22 7JJ England

Haynes North America, Inc
861 Lawrence Drive
Newbury Park
California 91320 USA

AB

Contents

Contents

SAFETY NOTICE

Proper service and repair procedures are vital to the safe, reliable operation of all motor vehicles, as well as the personal safety of those performing repairs. This manual outlines procedures for servicing and repairing vehicles using safe, effective methods. The procedures contain many NOTES, CAUTIONS and WARNINGS which should be followed, along with standard procedures to eliminate the possibility of personal injury or improper service which could damage the vehicle or compromise its safety.

It is important to note that repair procedures and techniques, tools and parts for servicing motor vehicles, as well as the skill and experience of the individual performing the work vary widely. It is not possible to anticipate all of the conceivable ways or conditions under which vehicles may be serviced, or to provide cautions as to all possible hazards that may result. Standard and accepted safety precautions and equipment should be used when handling toxic or flammable fluids, and safety goggles or other protection should be used during cutting, grinding, chiseling, prying, or any other process that can cause material removal or projectiles.

Some procedures require the use of tools specially designed for a specific purpose. Before substituting another tool or procedure, you must be completely satisfied that neither your personal safety, nor the performance of the vehicle will be endangered.

Although information in this manual is based on industry sources and is complete as possible at the time of publication, the possibility exists that some car manufacturers made later changes which could not be included here. While striving for total accuracy, the authors or publishers cannot assume responsibility for any errors, changes or omissions that may occur in the compilation of this data.

PART NUMBERS

Part numbers listed in this reference are not recommendations by Haynes North America, Inc. for any product brand name. They are references that can be used with interchange manuals and aftermarket supplier catalogs to locate each brand supplier's discrete part number.

SPECIAL TOOLS

Special tools are recommended by the vehicle manufacturer to perform their specific job. Use has been kept to a minimum, but where absolutely necessary, they are referred to in the text by the part number of the tool manufacturer. These tools can be purchased, under the appropriate part number, from your local dealer or regional distributor, or an equivalent tool can be purchased locally from a tool supplier or parts outlet. Before substituting any tool for the one recommended, read the SAFETY NOTICE at the top of this page.

ACKNOWLEDGMENTS

This publication contains material that is reproduced and distributed under a license from Ford Motor Company. No further reproduction or distribution of the Ford Motor Company material is allowed without the express written permission from Ford Motor Company.

1
GENERAL INFORMATION AND MAINTENANCE
HOW TO USE THIS BOOK 1-2
TOOLS AND EQUIPMENT 1-2
SERVICING YOUR VEHICLE SAFELY 1-4
FASTENERS, MEASUREMENTS AND CONVERSIONS 1-5
SERIAL NUMBER IDENTIFICATION 1-8
ROUTINE MAINTENANCE AND TUNE-UP 1-10
FLUIDS AND LUBRICANTS 1-34
TOWING THE VEHICLE 1-48
JUMP STARTING A DEAD BATTERY 1-49
JACKING AND HOISTING 1-50

HOW TO USE THIS BOOK

This Chilton's Total Car Care manual is intended to help you learn more about the inner workings of your Ford Mustang while saving you money on its upkeep and operation.

The beginning of the book will likely be referred to the most, since that is where you will find information for maintenance and tune-up. The other sections deal with the more complex systems of your vehicle. Systems (from engine through brakes) are covered to the extent that the average do-it-yourselfer can attempt. This book will not explain such things as rebuilding a differential because the expertise required and the special tools necessary make this uneconomical. It will, however, give you detailed instructions to help you change your own brake pads and shoes, replace spark plugs, and perform many more jobs that can save you money and help avoid expensive problems.

A secondary purpose of this book is a reference for owners who want to understand their vehicle and/or their mechanics better.

Where to Begin

Before removing any bolts, read through the entire procedure. This will give you the overall view of what tools and supplies will be required. So read ahead and plan ahead. Each operation should be approached logically and all procedures thoroughly understood before attempting any work.

If repair of a component is not considered practical, we tell you how to remove the part and then how to install the new or rebuilt replacement. In this way, you at least save labor costs.

Avoiding Trouble

Many procedures in this book require you to "label and disconnect . . ." a group of lines, hoses or wires. Don't be think you can remember where everything goes—you won't. If you hook up vacuum or fuel lines incorrectly, the vehicle may run poorly, if at all. If you hook up electrical wiring incorrectly, you may instantly learn a very expensive lesson.

You don't need to know the proper name for each hose or line. A piece of masking tape on the hose and a piece on its fitting will allow you to assign your own label. As long as you remember your own code, the lines can be reconnected by matching your tags. Remember that tape will dissolve in gasoline or solvents; if a part is to be washed or cleaned, use another method of identification. A permanent felt-tipped marker or a metal scribe can be very handy for marking metal parts. Remove any tape or paper labels after assembly.

Maintenance or Repair?

Maintenance includes routine inspections, adjustments, and replacement of parts which show signs of normal wear. Maintenance compensates for wear or deterioration. Repair implies that something has broken or is not working. A need for a repair is often caused by lack of maintenance. for example: draining and refilling automatic transmission fluid is maintenance recommended at specific intervals. Failure to do this can shorten the life of the transmission/transaxle, requiring very expensive repairs. While no maintenance program can prevent items from eventually breaking or wearing out, a general rule is true: MAINTENANCE IS CHEAPER THAN REPAIR.

Two basic mechanic's rules should be mentioned here. First, whenever the left side of the vehicle or engine is referred to, it means the driver's side. Conversely, the right side of the vehicle means the passenger's side. Second, screws and bolts are removed by turning counterclockwise, and tightened by turning clockwise unless specifically noted.

Safety is always the most important rule. Constantly be aware of the dangers involved in working on an automobile and take the proper precautions. Please refer to the information in this section regarding SERVICING YOUR VEHICLE SAFELY and the SAFETY NOTICE on the acknowledgment page.

Avoiding the Most Common Mistakes

Pay attention to the instructions provided. There are 3 common mistakes in mechanical work:

1. Incorrect order of assembly, disassembly or adjustment. When taking something apart or putting it together, performing steps in the wrong order usually just costs you extra time; however, it CAN break something. Read the entire procedure before beginning. Perform everything in the order in which the instructions say you should, even if you can't see a reason for it. When you're taking apart something that is very intricate, you might want to draw a picture of how it looks when assembled in order to make sure you get everything back in its proper position. When making adjustments, perform them in the proper order. One adjustment possibly will affect another.
2. Overtorquing (or undertorquing). While it is more common for overtorquing to cause damage, undertorquing may allow a fastener to vibrate loose causing serious damage. Especially when dealing with aluminum parts, pay attention to torque specifications and utilize a torque wrench in assembly. If a torque figure is not available, remember that if you are using the right tool to perform the job, you will probably not have to strain yourself to get a fastener tight enough. The pitch of most threads is so slight that the tension you put on the wrench will be multiplied many times in actual force on what you are tightening.

   There are many commercial products available for ensuring that fasteners won't come loose, even if they are not torqued just right (a very common brand is Loctite®). If you're worried about getting something together tight enough to hold, but loose enough to avoid mechanical damage during assembly, one of these products might offer substantial insurance. Before choosing a threadlocking compound, read the label on the package and make sure the product is compatible with the materials, fluids, etc. involved.
3. Crossthreading. This occurs when a part such as a bolt is screwed into a nut or casting at the wrong angle and forced. Crossthreading is more likely to occur if access is difficult. It helps to clean and lubricate fasteners, then to start threading the bolt, spark plug, etc. with your fingers. If you encounter resistance, unscrew the part and start over again at a different angle until it can be inserted and turned several times without much effort. Keep in mind that many parts have tapered threads, so that gentle turning will automatically bring the part you're threading to the proper angle. Don't put a wrench on the part until it's been tightened a couple of turns by hand. If you suddenly encounter resistance, and the part has not seated fully, don't force it. Pull it back out to make sure it's clean and threading properly.

Be sure to take your time and be patient, and always plan ahead. Allow yourself ample time to perform repairs and maintenance.

TOOLS AND EQUIPMENT

See Figures 1 thru 15

Without the proper tools and equipment it is impossible to properly service your vehicle. It would be virtually impossible to catalog every tool that you would need to perform all of the operations in this book. It would be unwise for the amateur to rush out and buy an expensive set of tools on the theory that he/she may need one or more of them at some time.

The best approach is to proceed slowly, gathering a good quality set of those tools that are used most frequently. Don't be misled by the low cost of bargain tools. It is far better to spend a little more for better quality. Forged wrenches, 6 or 12-point sockets and fine tooth ratchets are by far preferable to their less expensive counterparts. As any good mechanic can tell you, there are few worse experiences than trying to work on a vehicle with bad tools. Your monetary savings will be far outweighed by frustration and mangled knuckles.

Begin accumulating those tools that are used most frequently: those associated with routine maintenance and tune-up. In addition to the normal assortment of screwdrivers and pliers, you should have the following tools:

- Wrenches/sockets and combination open end/box end wrenches in sizes ⅛–¾ in. and/or 3mm–19mm 13⁄16in. or ⅝ in. spark plug socket (depending on plug type).

➡If possible, buy various length socket drive extensions. Universal-joint and wobble extensions can be extremely useful, but be careful when using them, as they can change the amount of torque applied to the socket.

- Jackstands for support.
- Oil filter wrench.
- Spout or funnel for pouring fluids.

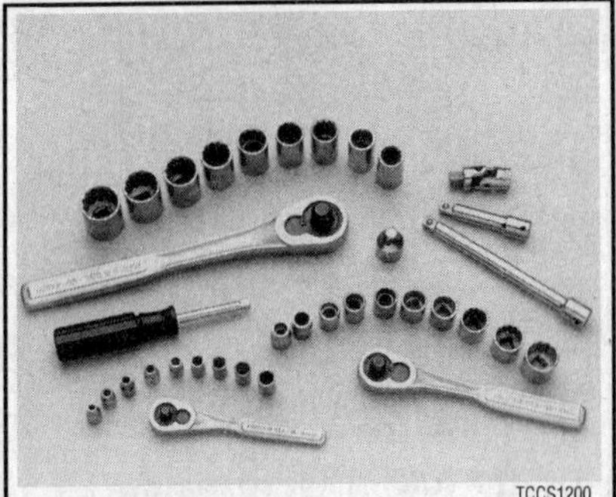

Fig. 1 All but the most basic procedures will require an assortment of ratchets and sockets

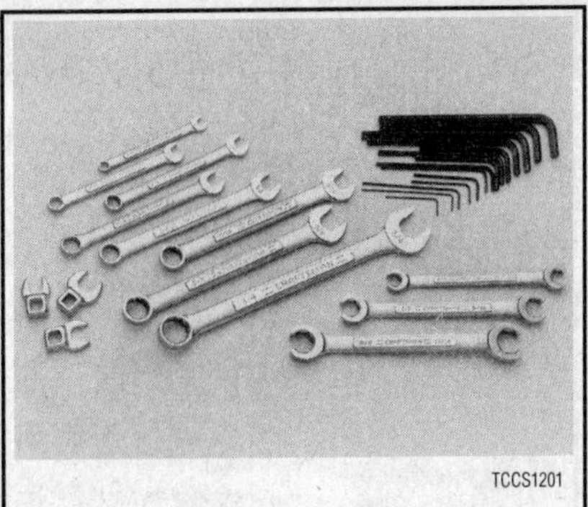

Fig. 2 In addition to ratchets, a good set of wrenches and hex keys will be necessary

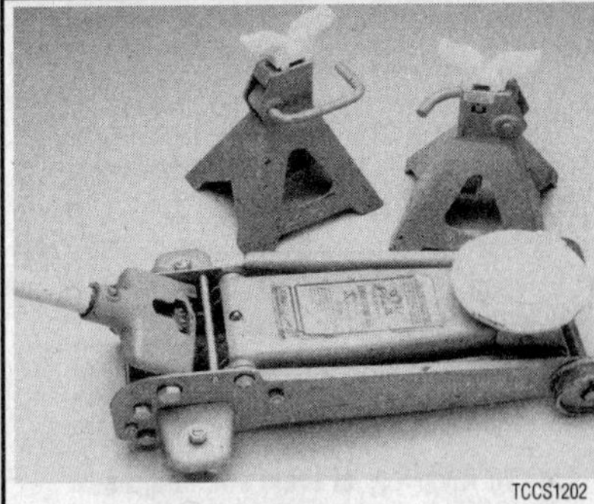

Fig. 3 A hydraulic floor jack and a set of jackstands are essential for lifting and supporting the vehicle

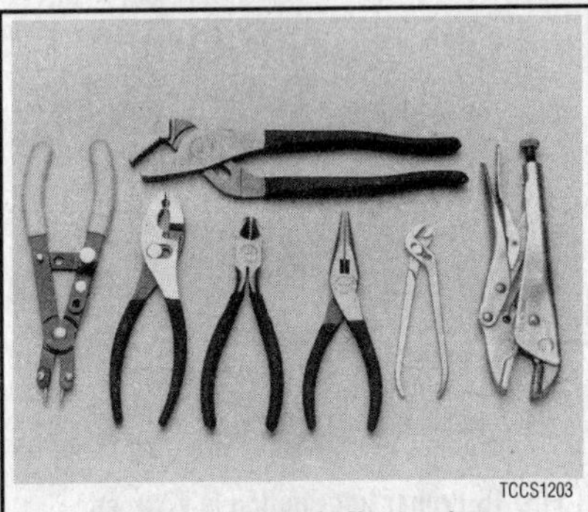

Fig. 4 An assortment of pliers, grippers and cutters will be handy for old rusted parts and stripped bolt heads

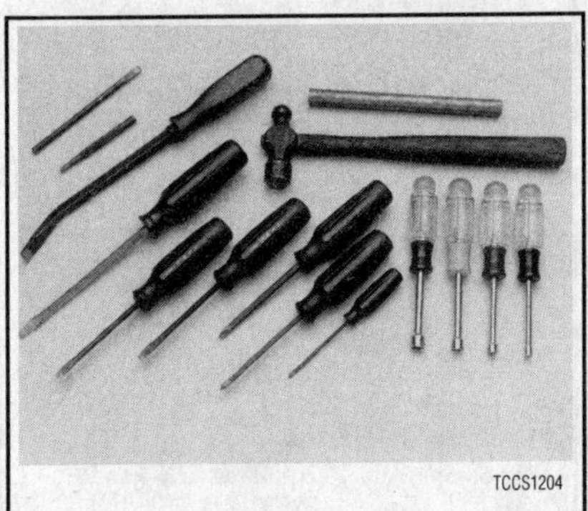

Fig. 5 Various drivers, chisels and prybars are great tools to have in your toolbox

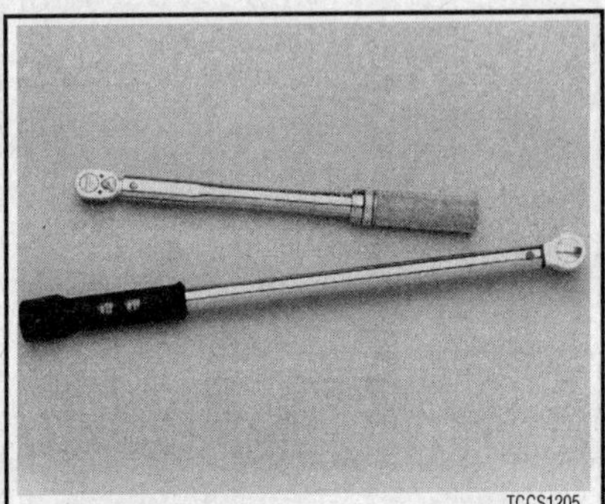

Fig. 6 Many repairs will require the use of a torque wrench to assure the components are properly fastened

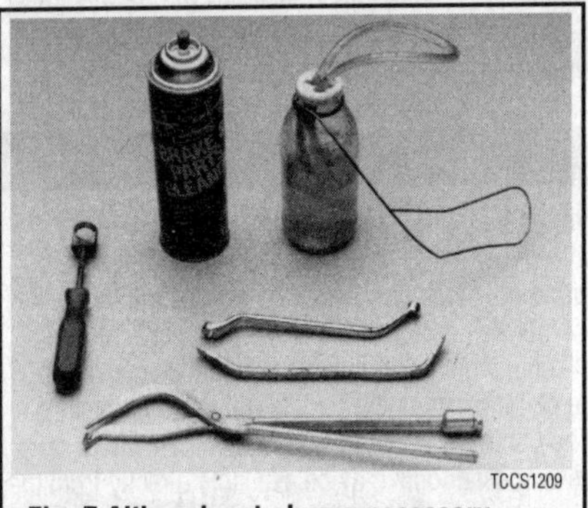

Fig. 7 Although not always necessary, using specialized brake tools will save time

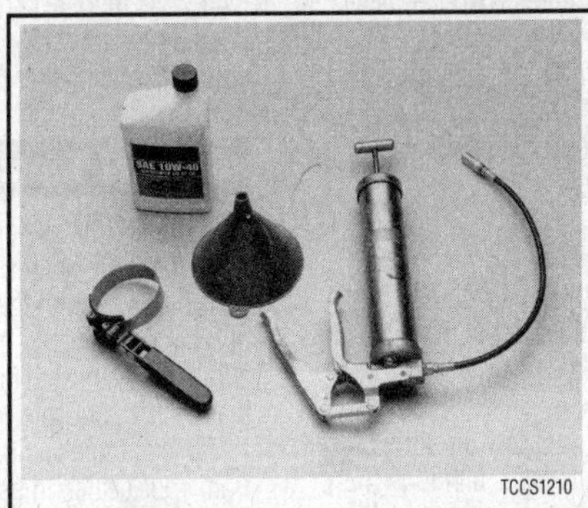

Fig. 8 A few inexpensive lubrication tools will make maintenance easier

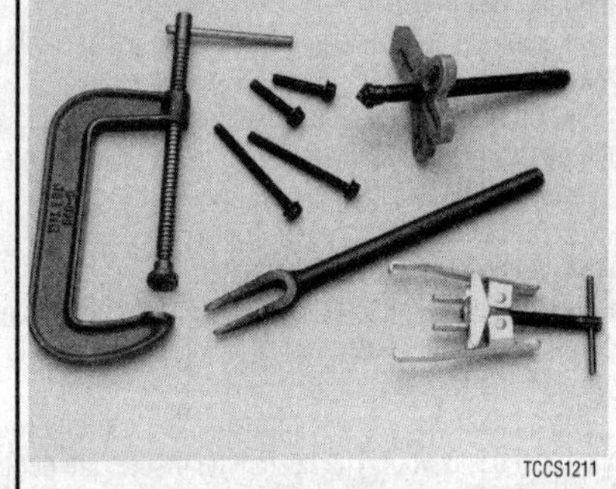

Fig. 9 Various pullers, clamps and separator tools are needed for many larger, more complicated repairs

- Grease gun for chassis lubrication (unless your vehicle is not equipped with any grease fittings)
- Hydrometer for checking the battery (unless equipped with a sealed, maintenance-free battery).
- A container for draining oil and other fluids.
- Rags for wiping up the inevitable mess.

In addition to the above items there are several others that are not absolutely necessary, but handy to have around. These include an equivalent oil absorbent gravel, like cat litter, and the usual supply of lubricants, antifreeze and fluids. This is a basic list for routine maintenance, but only your personal needs and desire can accurately determine your list of tools.

After performing a few projects on the vehicle, you'll be amazed at the other tools and non-tools on your workbench. Some useful household items are: a large turkey baster or siphon, empty coffee cans and ice trays (to store parts), a ball of twine, electrical tape for wiring, small rolls of colored tape for tagging lines or hoses, markers and pens, a note pad, golf tees (for plugging vacuum lines), metal coat hangers or a roll of mechanic's wire (to hold things out of the way), dental pick or similar long, pointed probe, a strong magnet, and a small mirror (to see into recesses and under manifolds).

A more advanced set of tools, suitable for tune-up work, can be drawn up easily. While the tools are slightly more sophisticated, they need not be outrageously expensive. There are several inexpensive tach/dwell meters on the market that are every bit as good for the average mechanic as a professional model. Just be sure that it goes to a least 1200–1500 rpm on the tach scale and that it works on 4, 6 and 8-cylinder engines. The key to these purchases is to make them with an eye towards adaptability and wide range. A basic list of tune-up tools could include:

- Tach/dwell meter.
- Spark plug wrench and gapping tool.
- Feeler gauges for valve adjustment.
- Timing light.

The choice of a timing light should be made carefully. A light which works on the DC current supplied by the vehicle's battery is the best choice; it should have a xenon tube for brightness. On any vehicle with an electronic ignition sys-

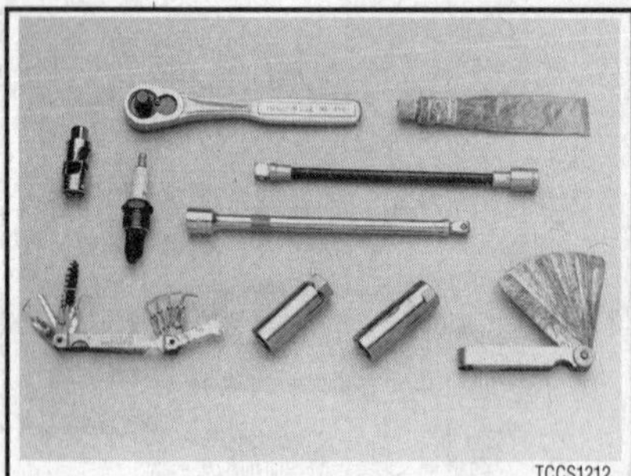
TCCS1212
Fig. 10 A variety of tools and gauges should be used for spark plug gapping and installation

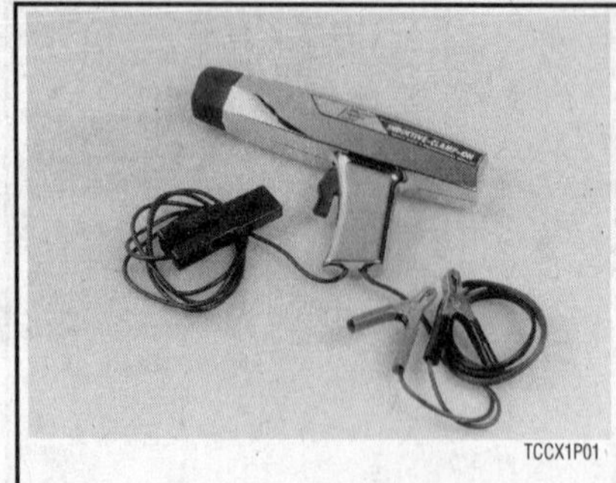
TCCX1P01
Fig. 11 Inductive type timing light

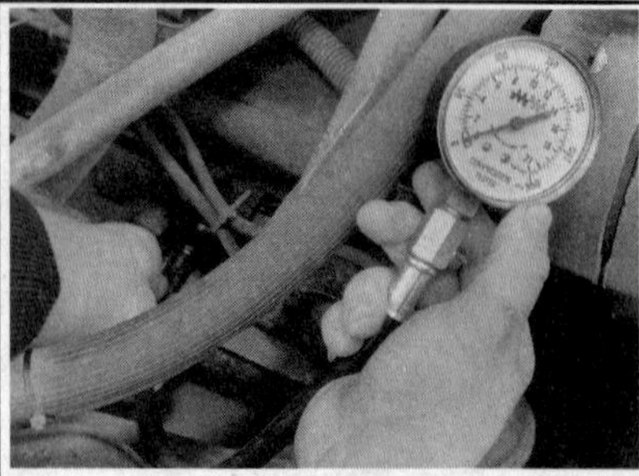
TCCX1P02
Fig. 12 A screw-in type compression gauge is recommended for compression testing

TCCX1P03
Fig. 13 A vacuum/pressure tester is necessary for many testing procedures

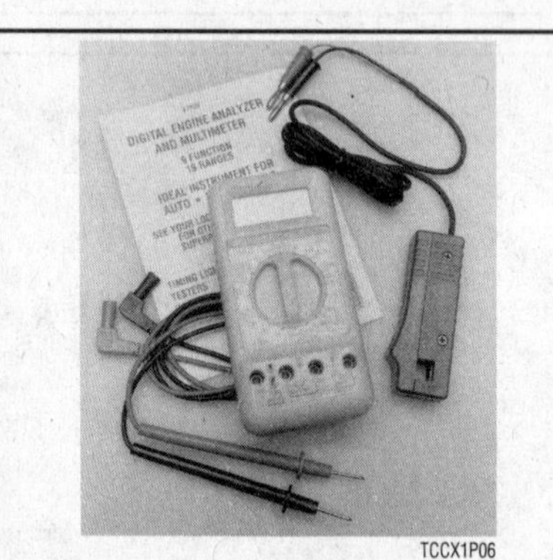

TCCX1P06
Fig. 14 Most modern automotive multimeters incorporate many helpful features

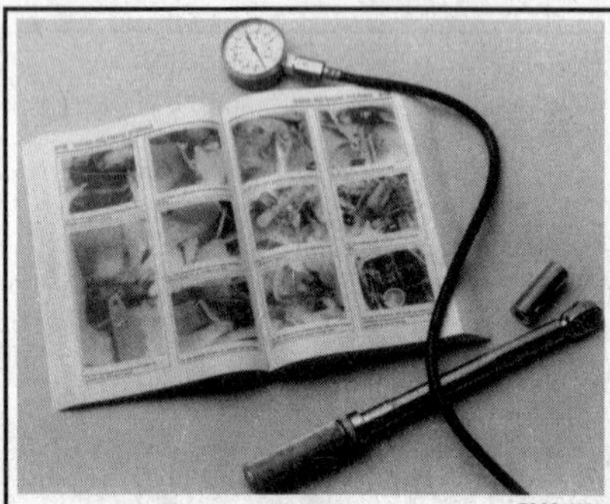
TCCS1213
Fig. 15 Proper information is vital, so always have a Chilton Total Car Care manual handy

tem, a timing light with an inductive pickup that clamps around the No. 1 spark plug cable is preferred.

In addition to these basic tools, there are several other tools and gauges you may find useful. These include:

- Compression gauge. The screw-in type is slower to use, but eliminates the possibility of a faulty reading due to escaping pressure.
- Manifold vacuum gauge.
- 12V test light.
- A combination volt/ohmmeter
- Induction Ammeter. This is used for determining whether or not there is current in a wire. These are handy for use if a wire is broken somewhere in a wiring harness.

As a final note, you will probably find a torque wrench necessary for all but the most basic work. The beam type models are perfectly adequate, although the newer click types (breakaway) are easier to use. The click type torque wrenches tend to be more expensive. Also keep in mind that all types of torque wrenches should be periodically checked and/or recalibrated. You will have to decide for yourself which better fits your pocketbook, and purpose.

Special Tools

Normally, the use of special factory tools is avoided for repair procedures, since these are not readily available for the do-it-yourself mechanic. When it is possible to perform the job with more commonly available tools, it will be pointed out, but occasionally, a special tool was designed to perform a specific function and should be used. Before substituting another tool, you should be convinced that neither your safety nor the performance of the vehicle will be compromised.

Special tools can usually be purchased from an automotive parts store or from your dealer. In some cases special tools may be available directly from the tool manufacturer.

SERVICING YOUR VEHICLE SAFELY

➧ **See Figures 16, 17 and 18**

It is virtually impossible to anticipate all of the hazards involved with automotive maintenance and service, but care and common sense will prevent most accidents.

The rules of safety for mechanics range from "don't smoke around gasoline," to "use the proper tool(s) for the job." The trick to avoiding injuries is to develop safe work habits and to take every possible precaution.

Do's

- Do keep a fire extinguisher and first aid kit handy.
- Do wear safety glasses or goggles when cutting, drilling, grinding or prying, even if you have 20–20 vision. If you wear glasses for the sake of vision, wear safety goggles over your regular glasses.
- Do shield your eyes whenever you work around the battery. Batteries contain sulfuric acid. In case of contact with, flush the area with water or a mixture of water and baking soda, then seek immediate medical attention.
- Do use safety stands (jackstands) for any undervehicle service. Jacks are for raising vehicles; jackstands are for making sure the vehicle stays raised until you want it to come down.
- Do use adequate ventilation when working with any chemicals or hazardous materials. Like carbon monoxide, the asbestos dust resulting from some brake lining wear can be hazardous in sufficient quantities.
- Do disconnect the negative battery cable when working on the electrical system. The secondary ignition system contains EXTREMELY HIGH VOLTAGE. In some cases it can even exceed 50,000 volts.
- Do follow manufacturer's directions whenever working with potentially hazardous materials. Most chemicals and fluids are poisonous.
- Do properly maintain your tools. Loose hammerheads, mushroomed punches and chisels, frayed or poorly grounded electrical cords, excessively worn screwdrivers, spread wrenches (open end), cracked sockets, slipping ratchets, or faulty droplight sockets can cause accidents.
- Likewise, keep your tools clean; a greasy wrench can slip off a bolt head, ruining the bolt and often harming your knuckles in the process.

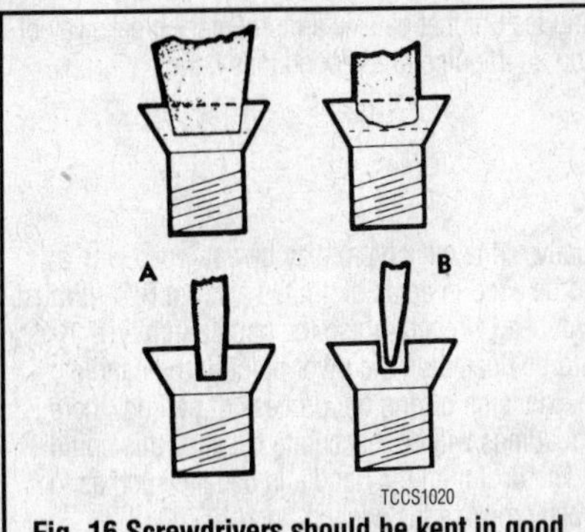

Fig. 16 Screwdrivers should be kept in good condition to prevent injury or damage which could result if the blade slips from the screw

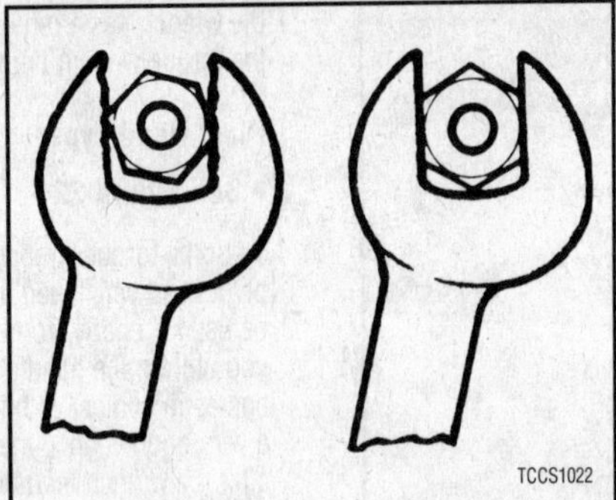

Fig. 17 Using the correct size wrench will help prevent the possibility of rounding off a nut

Fig. 18 NEVER work under a vehicle unless it is supported using safety stands (jackstands)

- Do use the proper size and type of tool for the job at hand. Do select a wrench or socket that fits the nut or bolt. The wrench or socket should sit straight, not cocked.
- Do, when possible, pull on a wrench handle rather than push on it, and adjust your stance to prevent a fall.
- Do be sure that adjustable wrenches are tightly closed on the nut or bolt and pulled so that the force is on the side of the fixed jaw.
- Do strike squarely with a hammer; avoid glancing blows.
- Do set the parking brake and block the drive wheels if the work requires a running engine.

Don'ts

- Don't run the engine in a garage or anywhere else without proper ventilation—EVER! Carbon monoxide is poisonous; it takes a long time to leave the human body and you can build up a deadly supply of it in your system by simply breathing in a little at a time. You may not realize you are slowly poisoning yourself. Always use power vents, windows, fans and/or open the garage door.
- Don't work around moving parts while wearing loose clothing. Short sleeves are much safer than long, loose sleeves. Hard-toed shoes with neoprene soles protect your toes and give a better grip on slippery surfaces. Watches and jewelry is not safe working around a vehicle. Long hair should be tied back under a hat or cap.
- Don't use pockets for toolboxes. A fall or bump can drive a screwdriver deep into your body. Even a rag hanging from your back pocket can wrap around a spinning shaft or fan.
- Don't smoke when working around gasoline, cleaning solvent or other flammable material.
- Don't smoke when working around the battery. When the battery is being charged, it gives off explosive hydrogen gas.
- Don't use gasoline to wash your hands; there are excellent soaps available. Gasoline contains dangerous additives which can enter the body through a cut or through your pores. Gasoline also removes all the natural oils from the skin so that bone dry hands will suck up oil and grease.
- Don't service the air conditioning system unless you are equipped with the necessary tools and training. When liquid or compressed gas refrigerant is released to atmospheric pressure it will absorb heat from whatever it contacts. This will chill or freeze anything it touches.
- Don't use screwdrivers for anything other than driving screws! A screwdriver used as an prying tool can snap when you least expect it, causing injuries. At the very least, you'll ruin a good screwdriver.
- Don't use an emergency jack (that little ratchet, scissors, or pantograph jack supplied with the vehicle) for anything other than changing a flat! These jacks are only intended for emergency use out on the road; they are NOT designed as a maintenance tool. If you are serious about maintaining your vehicle yourself, invest in a hydraulic floor jack of at least a 1Zx ton capacity, and at least two sturdy jackstands.

FASTENERS, MEASUREMENTS AND CONVERSIONS

Bolts, Nuts and Other Threaded Retainers

See Figures 19 and 20

Although there are a great variety of fasteners found in the modern car or truck, the most commonly used retainer is the threaded fastener (nuts, bolts, screws, studs, etc.). Most threaded retainers may be reused, provided that they are not damaged in use or during the repair. Some retainers (such as stretch bolts or torque prevailing nuts) are designed to deform when tightened or in use and should not be reinstalled.

Whenever possible, we will note any special retainers which should be replaced during a procedure. But you should always inspect the condition of a retainer when it is removed and replace any that show signs of damage. Check all threads for rust or corrosion which can increase the torque necessary to achieve the desired clamp load for which that fastener was originally selected. Additionally, be sure that the driver surface of the fastener has not been compromised by rounding or other damage. In some cases a driver surface may become only partially rounded, allowing the driver to catch in only one direction. In many of these occurrences, a fastener may be installed and tightened, but the driver would not be able to grip and loosen the fastener again.

If you must replace a fastener, whether due to design or damage, you must ALWAYS be sure to use the proper replacement. In all cases, a retainer of the same design, material and strength should be used. Markings on the heads of most bolts will help determine the proper strength of the fastener. The same material, thread and pitch must be selected to assure proper installation and safe operation of the vehicle afterwards.

Thread gauges are available to help measure a bolt or stud's thread. Most automotive and hardware stores keep gauges available to help you select the proper

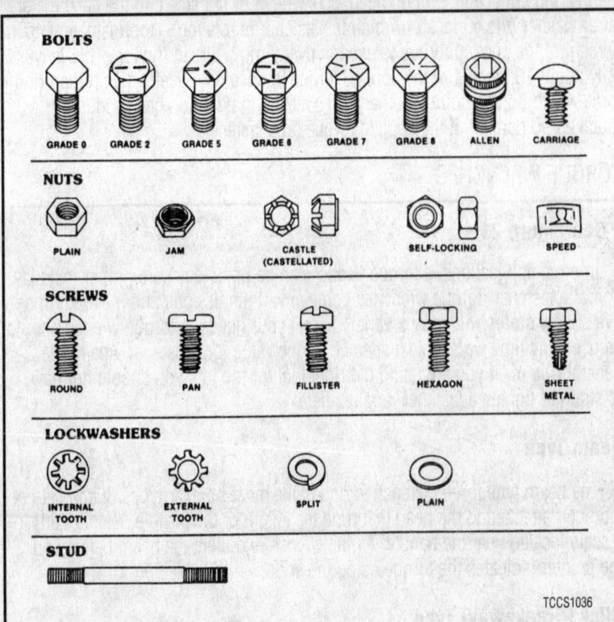

Fig. 19 There are many different types of threaded retainers found on vehicles

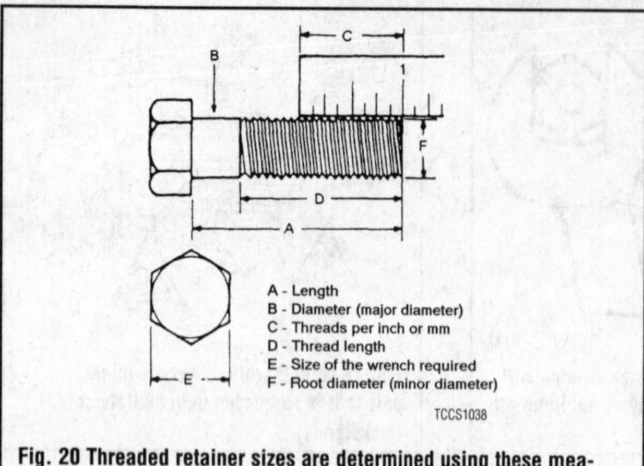

Fig. 20 Threaded retainer sizes are determined using these measurements

size. In a pinch, you can use another nut or bolt for a thread gauge. If the bolt you are replacing is not too badly damaged, you can select a match by finding another bolt which will thread in its place. If you find a nut which threads properly onto the damaged bolt, then use that nut to help select the replacement bolt.

***** WARNING**

Be aware that when you find a bolt with damaged threads, you may also find the nut or drilled hole it was threaded into has also been damaged. If this is the case, you may have to drill and tap the hole, replace the nut or otherwise repair the threads. NEVER try to force a replacement bolt to fit into the damaged threads.

Torque

Torque is defined as the measurement of resistance to turning or rotating. It tends to twist a body about an axis of rotation. A common example of this would be tightening a threaded retainer such as a nut, bolt or screw. Measuring torque is one of the most common ways to help assure that a threaded retainer has been properly fastened.

When tightening a threaded fastener, torque is applied in three distinct areas, the head, the bearing surface and the clamp load. About 50 percent of the measured torque is used in overcoming bearing friction. This is the friction between the bearing surface of the bolt head, screw head or nut face and the base material or washer (the surface on which the fastener is rotating). Approximately 40 percent of the applied torque is used in overcoming thread friction. This leaves only about 10 percent of the applied torque to develop a useful clamp load (the force which holds a joint together). This means that friction can account for as much as 90 percent of the applied torque on a fastener.

TORQUE WRENCHES

➧ See Figure 21

In most applications, a torque wrench can be used to assure proper installation of a fastener. Torque wrenches come in various designs and most automotive supply stores will carry a variety to suit your needs. A torque wrench should be used any time we supply a specific torque value for a fastener. Again, the general rule of "if you are using the right tool for the job, you should not have to strain to tighten a fastener" applies here.

Beam Type

The beam type torque wrench is one of the most popular types. It consists of a pointer attached to the head that runs the length of the flexible beam (shaft) to a scale located near the handle. As the wrench is pulled, the beam bends and the pointer indicates the torque using the scale.

Click (Breakaway) Type

Another popular design of torque wrench is the click type. To use the click type wrench you pre-adjust it to a torque setting. Once the torque is reached, the wrench has a reflex signaling feature that causes a momentary breakaway of the torque wrench body, sending an impulse to the operator's hand.

Pivot Head Type

➧ See Figure 22

Some torque wrenches (usually of the click type) may be equipped with a pivot head which can allow it to be used in areas of limited access. BUT, it must be used properly. To hold a pivot head wrench, grasp the handle lightly, and as you pull on the handle, it should be floated on the pivot point. If the handle comes in contact with the yoke extension during the process of pulling, there is a very good chance the torque readings will be inaccurate because this could alter the wrench loading point. The design of the handle is usually such as to make it inconvenient to deliberately misuse the wrench.

➡It should be mentioned that the use of any U-joint, wobble or extension will have an effect on the torque readings, no matter what type of wrench you are using. For the most accurate readings, install the socket directly on the wrench driver. If necessary, straight extensions (which hold a socket directly under the wrench driver) will have the least effect on the torque reading. Avoid any extension that alters the length of the wrench from the handle to the head/driving point (such as a crow's foot). U-joint or wobble extensions can greatly affect the readings; avoid their use at all times.

Rigid Case (Direct Reading)

A rigid case or direct reading torque wrench is equipped with a dial indicator to show torque values. One advantage of these wrenches is that they can be held at any position on the wrench without affecting accuracy. These wrenches are often preferred because they tend to be compact, easy to read and have a great degree of accuracy.

TORQUE ANGLE METERS

Because the frictional characteristics of each fastener or threaded hole will vary, clamp loads which are based strictly on torque will vary as well. In most applications, this variance is not significant enough to cause worry. But, in certain applications, a manufacturer's engineers may determine that more precise clamp loads are necessary (such is the case with many aluminum cylinder heads). In these cases, a torque angle method of installation would be specified. When installing fasteners which are torque angle tightened, a predetermined seating torque and standard torque wrench are usually used first to remove any compliance from the joint. The fastener is then tightened the specified additional portion of a turn measured in degrees. A torque angle gauge (mechanical protractor) is used for these applications.

Standard and Metric Measurements

➧ See Figure 23

Throughout this manual, specifications are given to help you determine the condition of various components on your vehicle, or to assist you in their installation. Some of the most common measurements include length (in. or cm/mm), torque (ft. lbs., inch lbs. or Nm) and pressure (psi, in. Hg, kPa or mm Hg). In most cases, we strive to provide the proper measurement as determined by the manufacturer's engineers.

Though, in some cases, that value may not be conveniently measured with what is available in your toolbox. Luckily, many of the measuring devices which are available today will have two scales so the Standard or Metric measurements may easily be taken. If any of the various measuring tools which are available to you do not contain the same scale as listed in the specifications, use the accompanying conversion factors to determine the proper value.

The conversion factor chart is used by taking the given specification and multiplying it by the necessary conversion factor. For instance, looking at the first line, if you have a measurement in inches such as "free-play should be 2 in." but your ruler reads only in millimeters, multiply 2 in. by the conversion factor of 25.4 to get the metric equivalent of 50.8mm. Likewise, if the specification was given only in a Metric measurement, for example in Newton Meters (Nm), then look at the center column first. If the measurement is 100 Nm, multiply it by the conversion factor of 0.738 to get 73.8 ft. lbs.

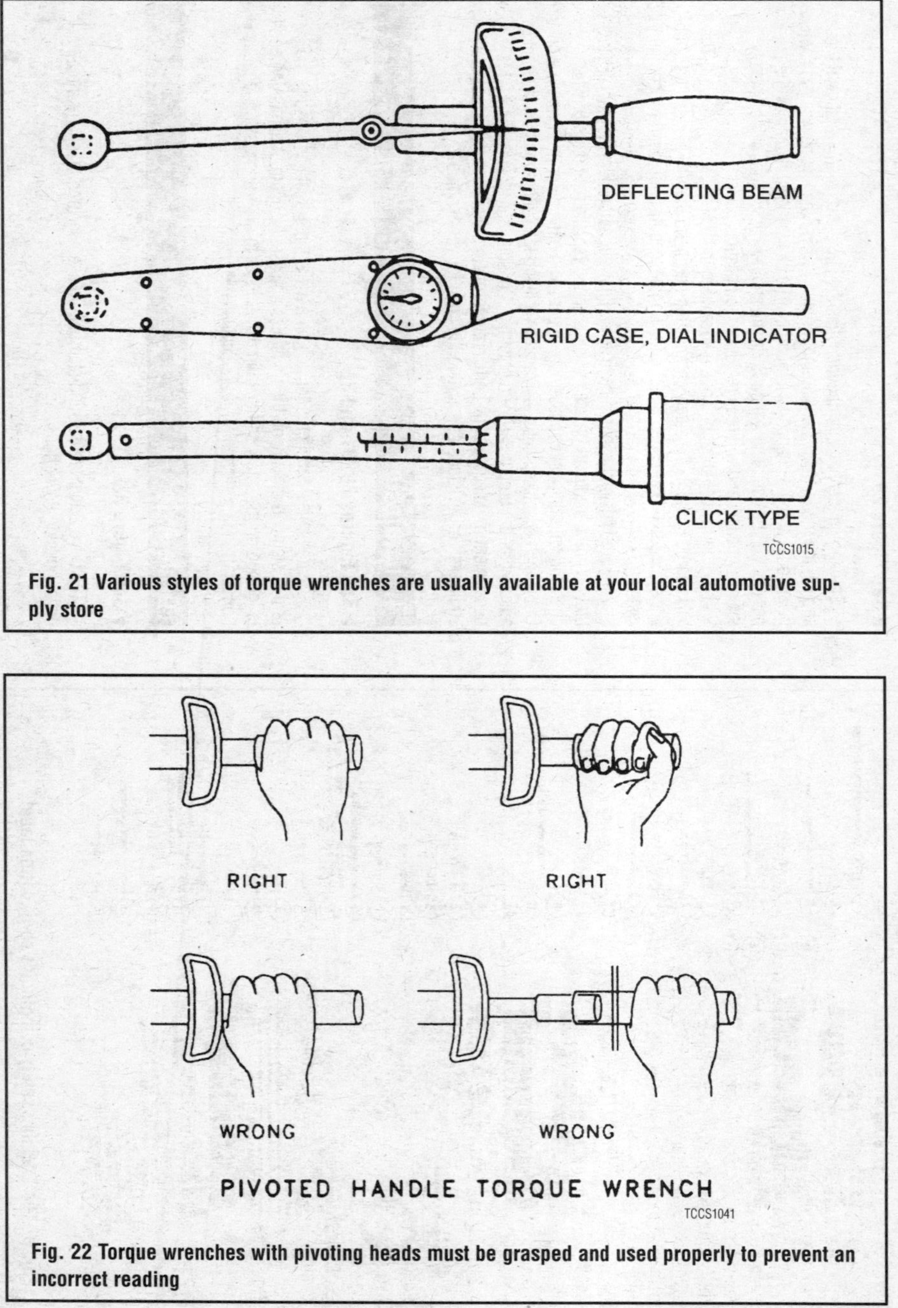

Fig. 21 Various styles of torque wrenches are usually available at your local automotive supply store

Fig. 22 Torque wrenches with pivoting heads must be grasped and used properly to prevent an incorrect reading

CONVERSION FACTORS

LENGTH–DISTANCE				
Inches (in.)	x 25.4	= Millimeters (mm)	x .0394	= Inches
Feet (ft.)	x .305	= Meters (m)	x 3.281	= Feet
Miles	x 1.609	= Kilometers (km)	x .0621	= Miles
VOLUME				
Cubic Inches (in3)	x 16.387	= Cubic Centimeters	x .061	= in3
IMP Pints (IMP pt.)	x .568	= Liters (L)	x 1.76	= IMP pt.
IMP Quarts (IMP qt.)	x 1.137	= Liters (L)	x .88	= IMP qt.
IMP Gallons (IMP gal.)	x 4.546	= Liters (L)	x .22	= IMP gal.
IMP Quarts (IMP qt.)	x 1.201	= US Quarts (US qt.)	x .833	= IMP qt.
IMP Gallons (IMP gal.)	x 1.201	= US Gallons (US gal.)	x .833	= IMP gal.
Fl. Ounces	x 29.573	= Milliliters	x .034	= Ounces
US Pints (US pt.)	x .473	= Liters (L)	x 2.113	= Pints
US Quarts (US qt.)	x .946	= Liters (L)	x 1.057	= Quarts
US Gallons (US gal.)	x 3.785	= Liters (L)	x .264	= Gallons
MASS–WEIGHT				
Ounces (oz.)	x 28.35	= Grams (g)	x .035	= Ounces
Pounds (lb.)	x .454	= Kilograms (kg)	x 2.205	= Pounds
PRESSURE				
Pounds Per Sq. In. (psi)	x 6.895	= Kilopascals (kPa)	x .145	= psi
Inches of Mercury (Hg)	x .4912	= psi	x 2.036	= Hg
Inches of Mercury (Hg)	x 3.377	= Kilopascals (kPa)	x .2961	= Hg
Inches of Water (H_2O)	x .07355	= Inches of Mercury	x 13.783	= H_2O
Inches of Water (H_2O)	x .03613	= psi	x 27.684	= H_2O
Inches of Water (H_2O)	x .248	= Kilopascals (kPa)	x 4.026	= H_2O
TORQUE				
Pounds–Force Inches (in–lb)	x .113	= Newton Meters (N·m)	x 8.85	= in–lb
Pounds–Force Feet (ft–lb)	x 1.356	= Newton Meters (N·m)	x .738	= ft–lb
VELOCITY				
Miles Per Hour (MPH)	x 1.609	= Kilometers Per Hour (KPH)	x .621	= MPH
POWER				
Horsepower (Hp)	x .745	= Kilowatts	x 1.34	= Horsepower
FUEL CONSUMPTION*				
Miles Per Gallon IMP (MPG)	x .354	= Kilometers Per Liter (Km/L)		
Kilometers Per Liter (Km/L)	x 2.352	= IMP MPG		
Miles Per Gallon US (MPG)	x .425	= Kilometers Per Liter (Km/L)		
Kilometers Per Liter (Km/L)	x 2.352	= US MPG		

*It is common to covert from miles per gallon (mpg) to liters/100 kilometers (1/100 km), where mpg (IMP) x 1/100 km = 282 and mpg (US) x 1/100 km = 235.

TEMPERATURE

Degree Fahrenheit (°F)	= (°C x 1.8) + 32
Degree Celsius (°C)	= (°F – 32) x .56

TCCS1044

Fig. 23 Standard and metric conversion factors chart

SERIAL NUMBER IDENTIFICATION

Vehicle

▸ See Figure 24

VIN PLATE

▸ See Figures 25 and 26

The vehicle identification number is located on the left side of the dash panel behind the windshield. It is also contained on various other labels and identifiers found throughout the vehicle.

A seventeen-digit combination of numbers and letters forms the Vehicle Identification Number (VIN). Each letter, number or combination represents different items and can be decoded using Ford factory information. Refer to the accompanying illustration for the VIN details or see your local Ford parts dealer.

VEHICLE SAFETY COMPLIANCE LABEL

▸ See Figures 27 and 28

The label is attached to the driver's door lock pillar. The label contains the name of the manufacturer, the month and year of the vehicle, certification statement and the VIN. The label also contains gross vehicle weight and tire data.

Fig. 24 Dealers will usually install underhood labels to indicate is special recall service has been performed

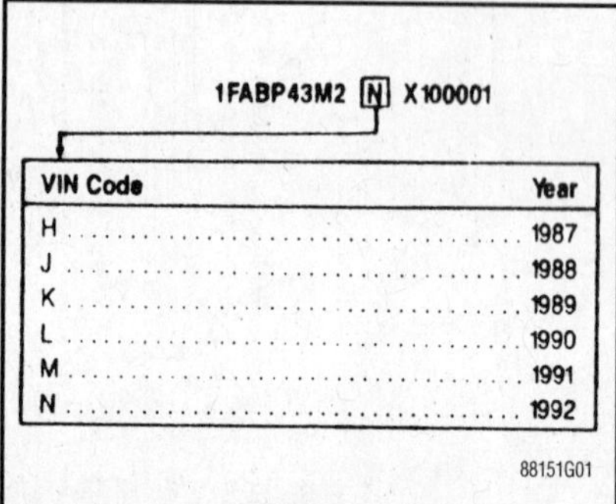

VIN Code	Year
H	1987
J	1988
K	1989
L	1990
M	1991
N	1992

Fig. 25 The 10th digit of the Vehicle Identification Number (VIN) represents the model year

Fig. 26 The VIN is located on a metallic plate fastened to the driver's side of the dash

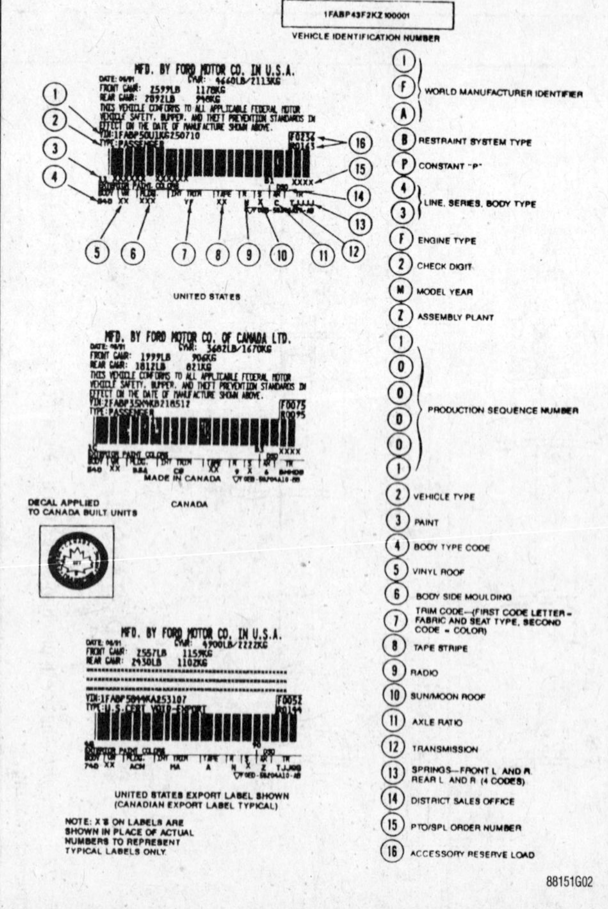

Fig. 27 The Mustang safety compliance certification label

Engine

▸ See Figure 29

The engine identification tag identifies the cubic inch displacement of the engine, the model year, the year and month in which the engine was built, where it was built and the change level number. The change level is usually the number one (1), unless there are parts on the engine that will not be completely interchangeable and will require minor modification.

The engine identification code is located in the VIN at the eighth digit. The VIN can be found in the safety certification decal and the VIN plate at the upper left side of the dash panel. Refer to the Engine Identification chart for engine VIN codes.

All Ford Mustangs should have an engine calibration number label. The calibration number should be used when ordering replacement parts or when checking calibrations. Because engine parts will often differ even within a given Cubic Inch Displacement (CID) family, verifying the calibration number will ensure that the proper parts are obtained. Consult your local dealer's parts department to determine any pertinent information regarding dates, optional equipment or revisions concerning the code for your engine.

Transmission

▸ See Figures 30, 31 and 32

The transmission letter is located on a metal tag or plate attached to the case, or it is stamped directly on the transmission case. Also, the transmission code is located on the safety certification decal. Refer to the Transmission Identification chart in this section for more details.

Drive Axle

▸ See Figure 33

The drive axle code is found stamped on a tag secured by one of the differential housing cover bolts.

VEHICLE IDENTIFICATION CHART

Engine Code					
Code	Liters	Cu. In. (cc)	Cyl.	Fuel Sys.	Eng. Mfg.
A	2.3	140 (2300)	4	MFI	Ford
M	2.3	140 (2300)	4	MFI	Ford
E	5.0 (HO)	302 (4949)	8	MFI	Ford

MFI - Multiport fuel injection
HO - High Output

Model Year	
Code	Year
K	1989
L	1990
M	1991
N	1992
P	1993

88151C01

ENGINE IDENTIFICATION

Year	Model	Engine Displacement Liters (cc)	Engine Series (ID/VIN)	Fuel System	No. of Cylinders	Engine Type
1989	Mustang	2.3 (2300)	A	MFI	4	SOHC
	Mustang 1	5.0 (4949)	E	MFI	8	OHV
1990	Mustang	2.3 (2300)	A	MFI	4	SOHC
	Mustang 1	5.0 (4949)	E	MFI	8	OHV
1991	Mustang	2.3 (2300)	M	MFI	4	SOHC
	Mustang 1	5.0 (4949)	E	MFI	8	OHV
1992	Mustang	2.3 (2300)	M	MFI	4	SOHC
	Mustang 1	5.0 (4949)	E	MFI	8	OHV
1993	Mustang	2.3 (2300)	M	MFI	4	SOHC
	Mustang 1	5.0 (4949)	E	MFI	8	OHV

MFI - Multiport fuel injection
SOHC - Single overhead camshaft
OHV - Overhead valve
1 High output

88151C02

TRANSMISSION IDENTIFICATION

Year	Model	Transmission Identification	Transmission Type
1989	Mustang	2	5-Speed T5OD Manual
	Mustang	L	A4LD Automatic
	Mustang	T	AOD Automatic
1990	Mustang	2	5-Speed T5OD Manual
	Mustang	L	A4LD Automatic
	Mustang	T	AOD Automatic
1991	Mustang	2	5-Speed T5OD Manual
	Mustang	L	A4LD Automatic
	Mustang	T	AOD Automatic
1992	Mustang	2	5-Speed T5OD Manual
	Mustang	L	A4LD Automatic
	Mustang	T	AOD Automatic
1993	Mustang	2	5-Speed T5OD Manual
	Mustang	L	A4LD Automatic
	Mustang	T	AOD Automatic

88151C03

REAR AXLE IDENTIFICATION

Year	Model	Axle Identification	Axle Type
1989	Mustang	8	2.73 Axle Ratio Conventional
	Mustang	M	2.73 Axle Ratio Limited-Slip
	Mustang	Y	3.08 Axle Ratio Conventional
	Mustang	Z	3.08 Axle Ratio Limited-Slip
	Mustang	F	3.45 Axle Ratio Conventional
	Mustang	R	3.45 Axle Ratio Limited-Slip
	Mustang	5	3.27 Axle Ratio Conventional
	Mustang	E	3.27 Axle Ratio Limited-Slip
	Mustang	6	3.73 Axle Ratio Conventional
	Mustang	W	3.73 Axle Ratio Limited-Slip
	Mustang	2	3.55 Axle Ratio Conventional
	Mustang	K	3.55 Axle Ratio Limited-Slip
1990	Mustang	8	2.73 Axle Ratio Conventional
	Mustang	M	2.73 Axle Ratio Limited-Slip
	Mustang	Y	3.08 Axle Ratio Conventional
	Mustang	Z	3.08 Axle Ratio Limited-Slip
	Mustang	F	3.45 Axle Ratio Conventional
	Mustang	R	3.45 Axle Ratio Limited-Slip
	Mustang	5	3.27 Axle Ratio Conventional
	Mustang	E	3.27 Axle Ratio Limited-Slip
	Mustang	6	3.73 Axle Ratio Conventional
	Mustang	W	3.73 Axle Ratio Limited-Slip
	Mustang	2	3.55 Axle Ratio Conventional
	Mustang	K	3.55 Axle Ratio Limited-Slip
1991	Mustang	8	2.73 Axle Ratio Conventional
	Mustang	M	2.73 Axle Ratio Limited-Slip
	Mustang	Y	3.08 Axle Ratio Conventional
	Mustang	Z	3.08 Axle Ratio Limited-Slip
	Mustang	F	3.45 Axle Ratio Conventional
	Mustang	R	3.45 Axle Ratio Limited-Slip
	Mustang	5	3.27 Axle Ratio Conventional
	Mustang	E	3.27 Axle Ratio Limited-Slip
	Mustang	6	3.73 Axle Ratio Conventional
	Mustang	W	3.73 Axle Ratio Limited-Slip
	Mustang	2	3.55 Axle Ratio Conventional
	Mustang	K	3.55 Axle Ratio Limited-Slip
1992	Mustang	8	2.73 Axle Ratio Conventional
	Mustang	M	2.73 Axle Ratio Limited-Slip
	Mustang	7	3.07 Axle Ratio Conventional
	Mustang	Y	3.08 Axle Ratio Conventional
	Mustang	Z	3.08 Axle Ratio Limited-Slip
	Mustang	F	3.45 Axle Ratio Conventional
	Mustang	R	3.45 Axle Ratio Limited-Slip
	Mustang	5	3.27 Axle Ratio Conventional
	Mustang	E	3.27 Axle Ratio Limited-Slip
	Mustang	6	3.73 Axle Ratio Conventional
	Mustang	W	3.73 Axle Ratio Limited-Slip
	Mustang	2	3.55 Axle Ratio Conventional
	Mustang	K	3.55 Axle Ratio Limited-Slip
1993	Mustang	8	2.73 Axle Ratio Conventional
	Mustang	M	2.73 Axle Ratio Limited-Slip
	Mustang	7	3.07 Axle Ratio Conventional
	Mustang	Y	3.08 Axle Ratio Conventional
	Mustang	Z	3.08 Axle Ratio Limited-Slip
	Mustang	F	3.45 Axle Ratio Conventional
	Mustang	R	3.45 Axle Ratio Limited-Slip
	Mustang	5	3.27 Axle Ratio Conventional
	Mustang	E	3.27 Axle Ratio Limited-Slip
	Mustang	6	3.73 Axle Ratio Conventional
	Mustang	W	3.73 Axle Ratio Limited-Slip
	Mustang	2	3.55 Axle Ratio Conventional
	Mustang	K	3.55 Axle Ratio Limited-Slip

88151C04

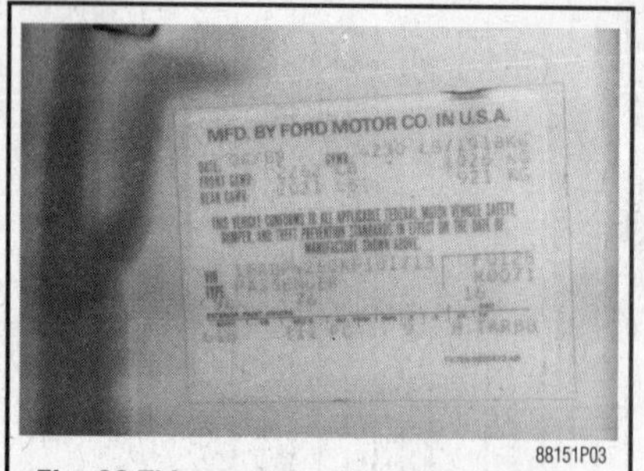

Fig. 28 This example of a safety compliance label is found on the driver's door of a 1988 Mustang GT

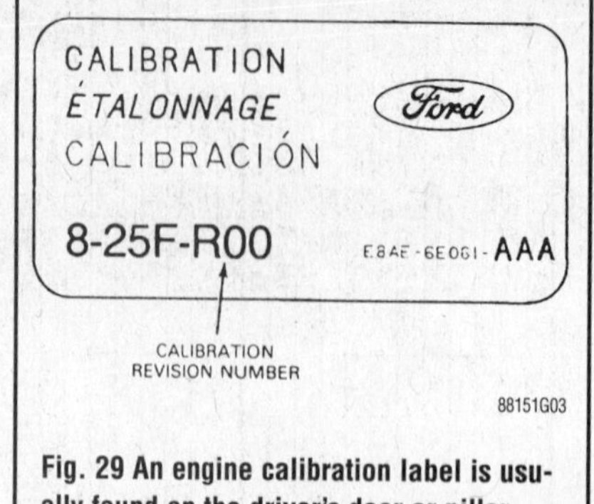

Fig. 29 An engine calibration label is usually found on the driver's door or pillar

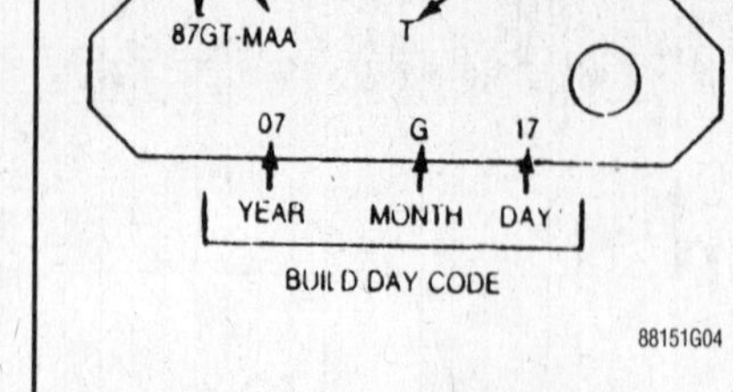

Fig. 30 Transmission identification tag—A4LD automatic

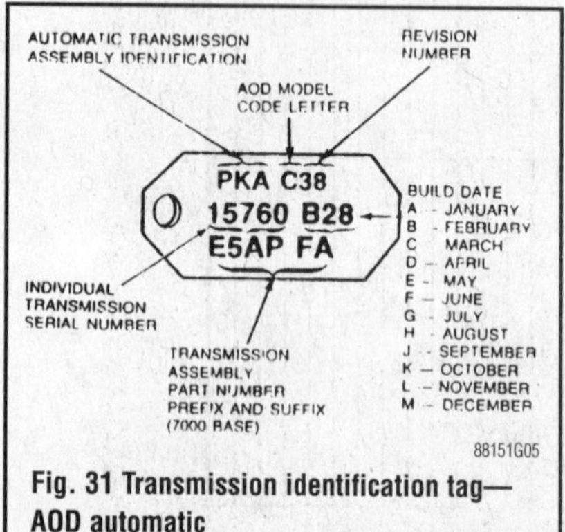

Fig. 31 Transmission identification tag—AOD automatic

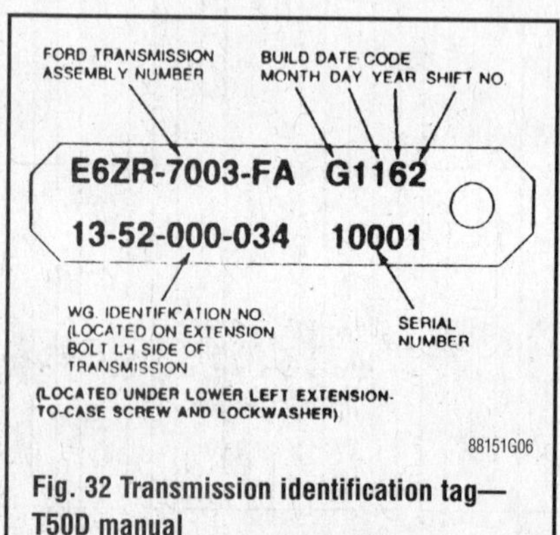

Fig. 32 Transmission identification tag—T50D manual

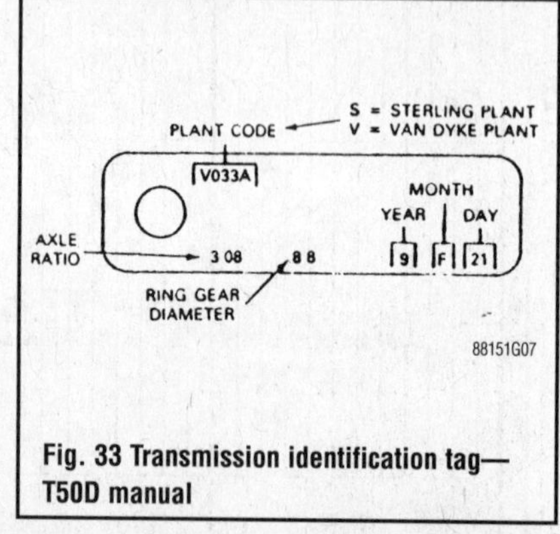

Fig. 33 Transmission identification tag—T50D manual

ROUTINE MAINTENANCE AND TUNE-UP

➧ See Figures 34, 35 and 36

Proper maintenance and tune-up is the key to long and trouble-free vehicle life, and the work can yield its own rewards. Studies have shown that a properly tuned and maintained vehicle can achieve better gas mileage than an out-of-tune vehicle. As a conscientious owner and driver, set aside a Saturday morning, say once a month, to check or replace items which could cause major problems later. Keep your own personal log to jot down which services you performed, how much the

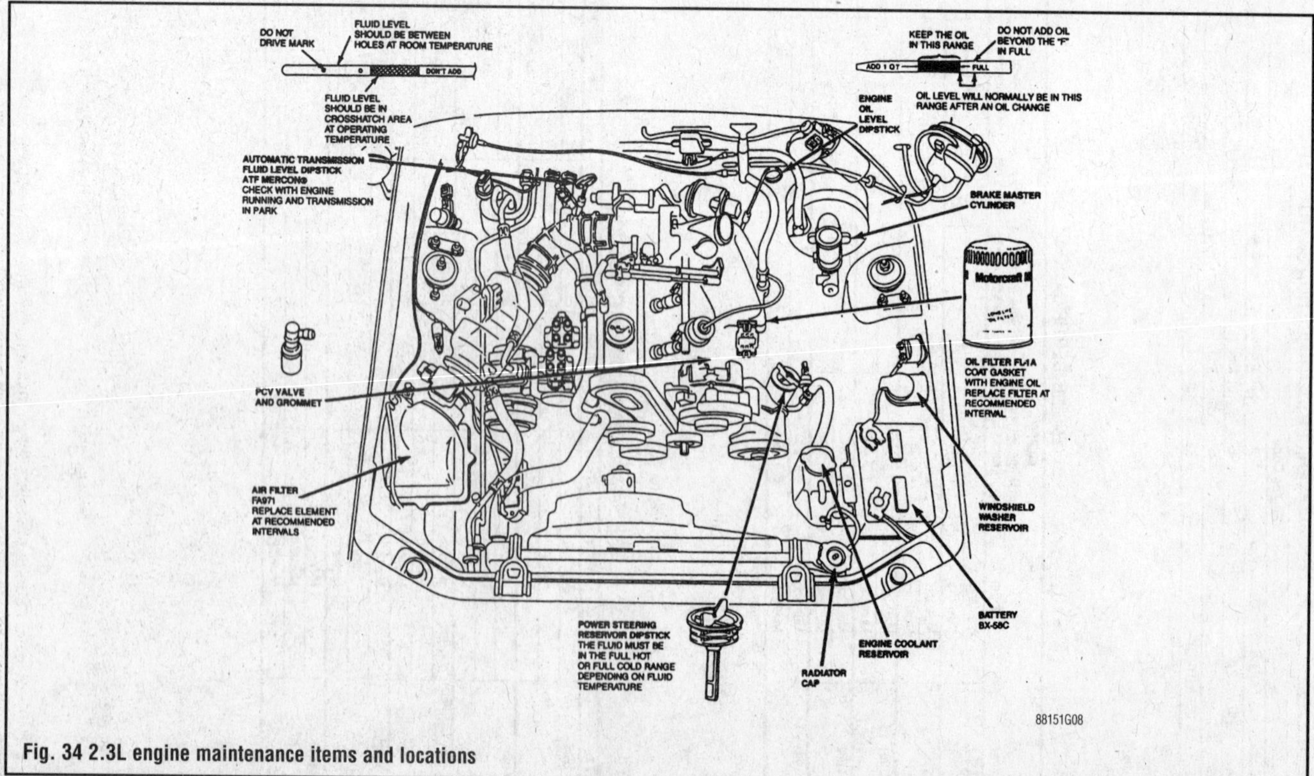

Fig. 34 2.3L engine maintenance items and locations

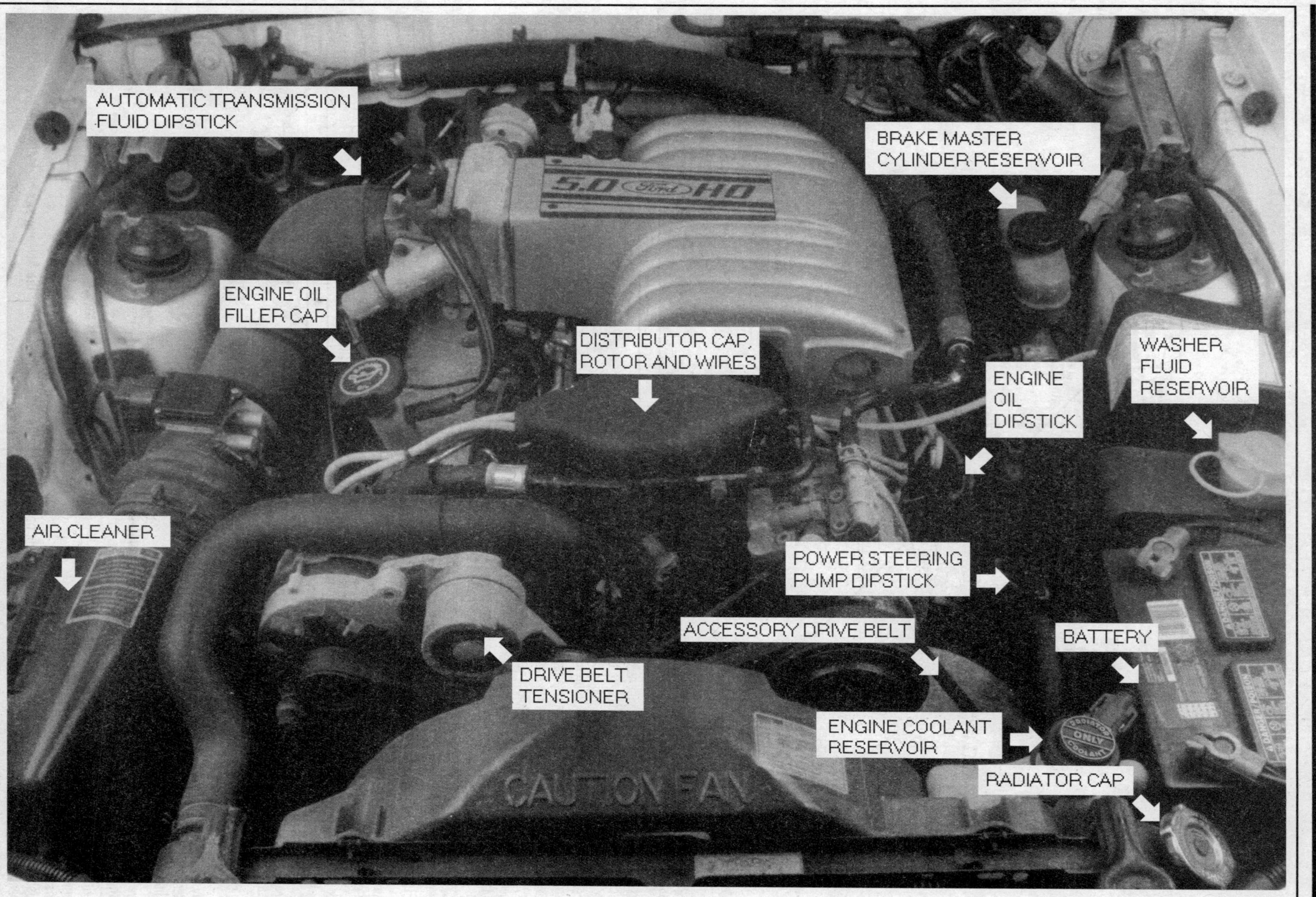

Fig. 35 Routine maintenance items and locations—5.0L engine shown

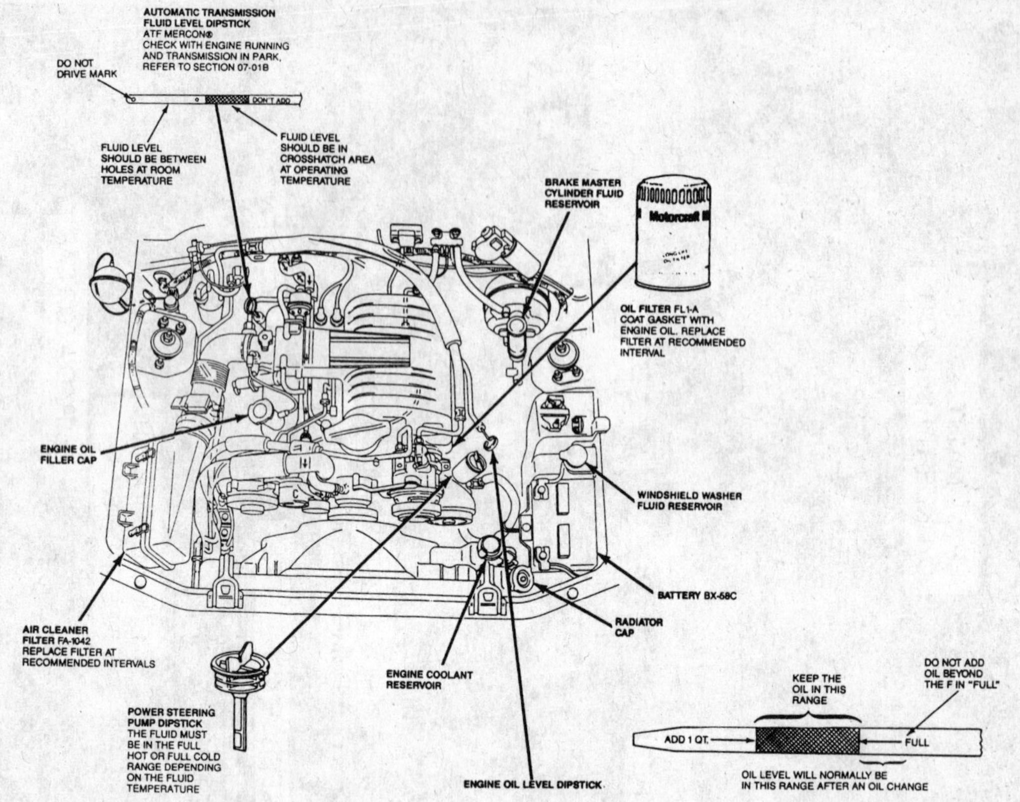

88151G09

Fig. 36 5.0L engine maintenance items and locations

parts cost you, the date, and the exact odometer reading at the time. Keep all receipts for such items as engine oil and filters, so that they may be referred to in case of related problems or to determine operating expenses. As a do-it-yourselfer, these receipts are the only proof you have that the required maintenance was performed. In the event of a warranty problem, these receipts will be invaluable.

The literature provided with your vehicle when it was originally delivered includes the factory recommended maintenance schedule. If you no longer have this literature, replacement copies are usually available from the dealer. A maintenance schedule is provided later in this section, in case you do not have the factory literature.

Air Cleaner (Element)

See Figures 37, 38, 39 and 40

The air cleaner is a paper element type. The paper cartridge should be replaced every 30,000 miles (48,000 km).

➡Check the air filter more often if the vehicle is operated under severe (especially dusty) conditions and replace or clean it as necessary.

REMOVAL & INSTALLATION

1. Disconnect the negative battery cable.
2. Label, then disconnect all hoses and tubes connected to the air filter assembly.
3. Remove the screws (2.3L) or release the clamps (5.0L) that attach the air cleaner lid to the housing.

➡Before removal, be sure to note the proper positioning of the element within the housing for installation purposes.

4. Lift the cover from the housing to expose the element, then remove the filter element.

To install:

5. Using a damp rag, clean all of the inside surfaces of the air cleaner body and cover.

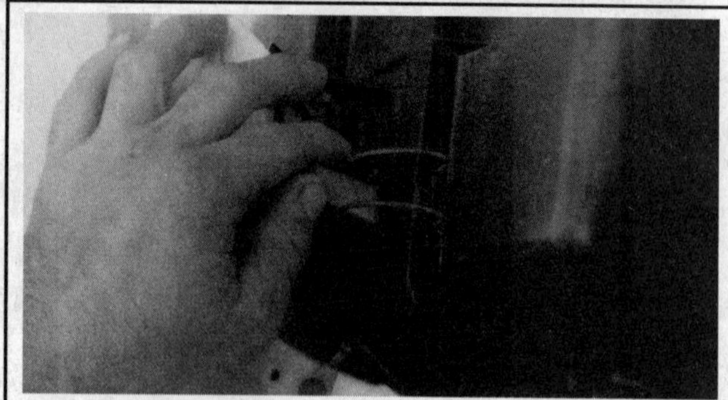

88151P05

Fig. 37 Release the clamps (or screws, as applicable) retaining the lid to the air filter housing

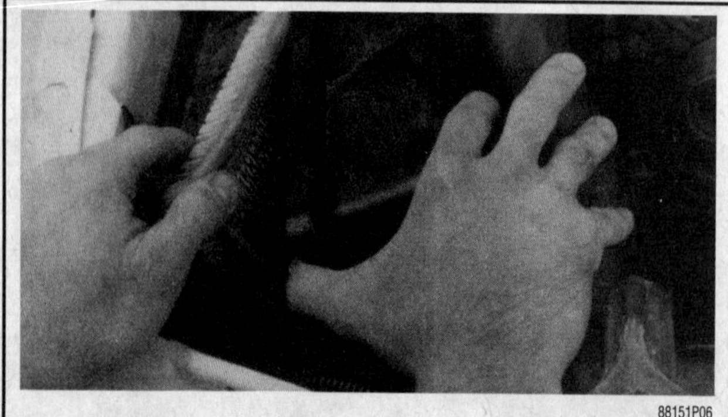

88151P06

Fig. 38 Lift the lid from the housing and carefully remove the filter element

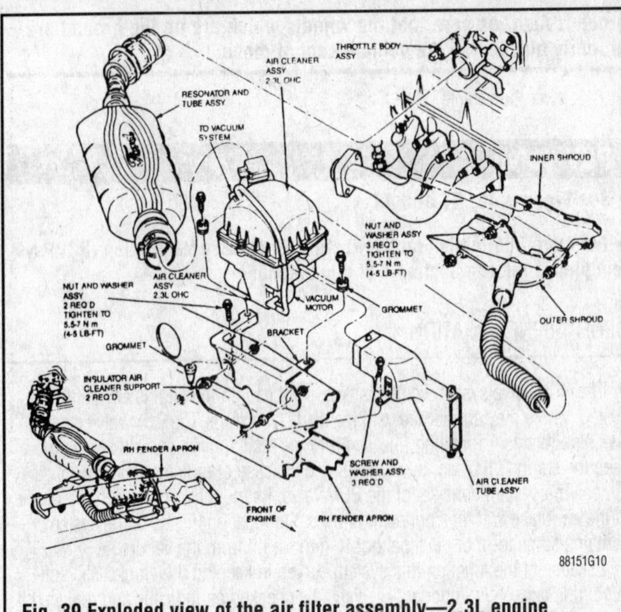

Fig. 39 Exploded view of the air filter assembly—2.3L engine

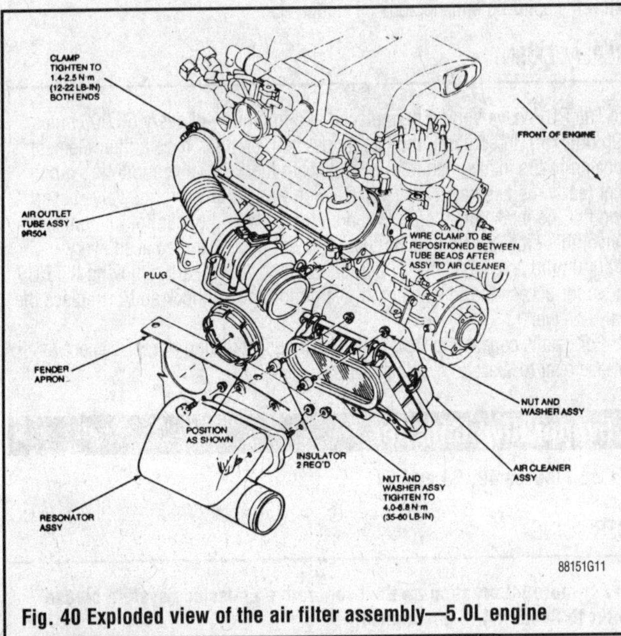

Fig. 40 Exploded view of the air filter assembly—5.0L engine

6. Install the air filter element (as noted during removal) and position the air cleaner cover on the housing.
7. Install the screws or clamps that attach the air cleaner lid to the housing.
8. Connect all hoses and tubes to the air filter assembly.
9. Connect the negative battery cable.

Fuel Filter

The fuel filter on the Mustang is normally found under-vehicle, near the fuel tank mounted to the rear crossmember.

DESCRIPTION

➧ See Figures 41 and 42

Fuel is filtered at 3 separate locations on these vehicles:

- Fuel pump inlet filter
- In-line fuel filter
- Injector filter screen

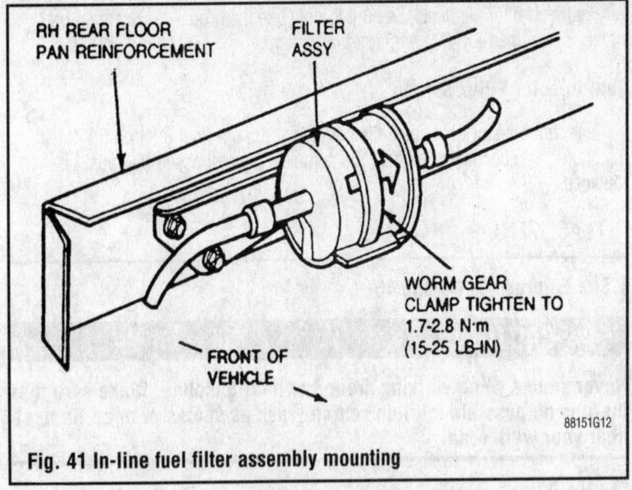

Fig. 41 In-line fuel filter assembly mounting

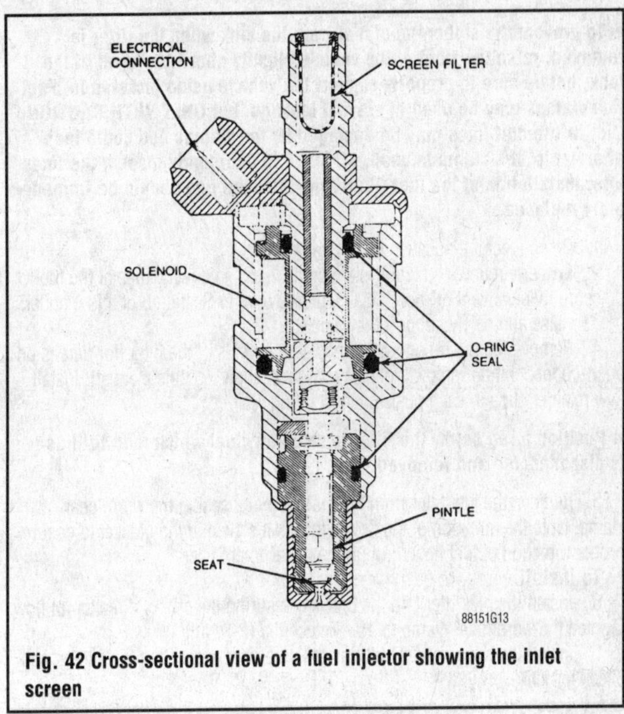

Fig. 42 Cross-sectional view of a fuel injector showing the inlet screen

Of these 3 fuel filters, only the in-line type has ever really been considered a maintenance item. The others are expected to serve the life of the components to which they are attached. But even the in-line fuel filters have become more efficient, so no periodic replacement interval is recommended by the manufacturer. It is never a bad idea to replace the filter on a older vehicle or a used vehicle where the quality of gasoline which may have been used in the car is not a known item. Likewise, any vehicle that shows signs of fuel filter clogging (such as hesitation or stumbling on acceleration which cannot be traced to the ignition system or other fuel system components) is a good candidate for an in-line filter replacement.

Fuel Pump Inlet Filter

A nylon filter element is attached to the electric fuel pump inlet inside the fuel tank. It is used to protect the fuel pump from possible tank contaminations.

In-Line Fuel Filter

The in-line fuel filter is designed to filter material which could damage the tiny metering orifices of the injector nozzles. The filter is located downstream of the electric fuel pump and is usually mounted to the rear crossmember. The in-line filter is of one-piece construction, meaning that it cannot be cleaned and must be replaced as an assembly should it become clogged. Because flow will vary between filter elements, be sure to only use the proper replacement part which is designed for your engine's fuel system.

Fuel Injector Filter Screen

Each fuel injector contains a filter screen at the top (fuel inlet point). If the injector screen becomes clogged, the complete injector assembly must be replaced.

REPLACEMENT

➧ See Figures 43, 44 and 45

⁂ CAUTION

Never smoke when working around or near gasoline. Make sure that there is no possible ignition source (such as sparks or open flames) near your work area.

In-Line Filter

➡To prevent the siphoning of fuel from the tank when the filter is removed, raise the front of the vehicle slightly above the level of the tank, but be sure to properly support the vehicle using jackstands. Fuel line clamps may be used to prevent leakage, but ONLY WITH CAUTION. Old, brittle fuel lines may be damaged by the clamps and could leak afterwards. If a clamp is used, BE SURE to thoroughly inspect the lines after installation of the fuel filter. Any damaged line should be immediately replaced.

1. Disconnect the negative battery cable.
2. Properly relieve the fuel system pressure using a test gauge at the fuel pressure relief valve. For more details, please refer to Section 5 of this manual.
3. Raise and safely support the vehicle.
4. Remove the push-connect fittings at both ends of the filter (for details on push-connect fitting removal, please refer to Section 5 of this manual). Install new retainer clips in each push-connect fitting.

➡Position a rag below the filter to catch any fuel which may spill as it is disconnected and removed.

5. Remove the fuel filter from the bracket by loosening the worm gear clamp. Note the direction of the flow arrow as installed in the bracket to ensure proper direction of fuel flow through the replacement filter.

To install:

6. Install the fuel filter into the bracket, ensuring the proper direction of flow. Tighten the worm gear clamp to 15–25 inch lbs (2-3 Nm).
7. Install the push connect fittings onto the filter ends. Start the engine and check for leaks.

⁂ CAUTION

Use extreme caution when starting and running an engine which is supported by jackstands. MAKE SURE no drive wheels are on the ground. Also, be sure that the wheels which are on the ground are properly blocked so the vehicle cannot move.

8. Lower the vehicle.

PCV Valve

➧ See Figures 46, 47 and 48

➡For more information on the Positive Crankcase Ventilation (PCV) system please refer to Section 4 of this manual.

GENERAL INFORMATION

The PCV valve system vents crankcase gases into the engine air/fuel intake system where they are burned with the air/fuel mixture. The PCV valve system keeps pollutants from being released into the atmosphere, and also helps to keep the engine oil clean, by ridding the crankcase of moisture and corrosive fumes. The system consists of the PCV valve, its mounting grommet, the nipple in the air intake and the connecting hoses. On most applications the system contains some form of oil separator to remove oil from the vapors.

Because of the function this system serves in keeping the crankcase ventilated, it is extremely important the valve be checked periodically and replaced if clogged. A restricted PCV valve will allow pressure to build in the crankcase, which can decrease gas mileage, cause gasket oil leaks and most importantly allow the build-up of dangerous oil sludge/acids.

REPLACEMENT

The PCV valve should be replaced at a minimum of every 60,000 miles (96,000 km). In addition, the late model 5.0L engines have a filter element located in the intake manifold, just beneath the PCV valve mounting grommet (early models had a PCV valve which was mounted in the valve cover and not the intake manifold). When equipped with the manifold mounted valve, this crankcase emission filter element should be replaced every 30,000 miles (48,000 km). Of course, as-long-as you are removing the PCV valve for access to the element, it is a good time to check and/or replace the valve as well.

For details concerning PCV system component testing or replacement, please refer to Section 4 of this manual.

Evaporative Canister

➧ See Figures 49, 50 and 51

SERVICING

➡For more information on the Evaporative Emissions system please refer to Section 4 of this manual.

The canister is located under the hood, to the right of the engine.

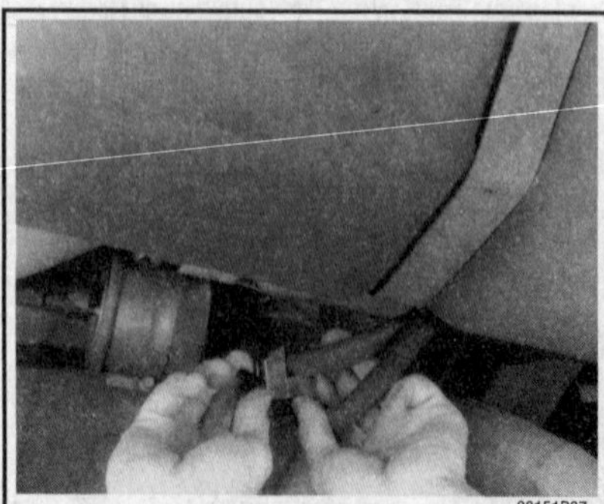
88151P07

Fig. 43 Though fuel line clamps can be used to prevent leakage, MAKE SURE the line is not damaged

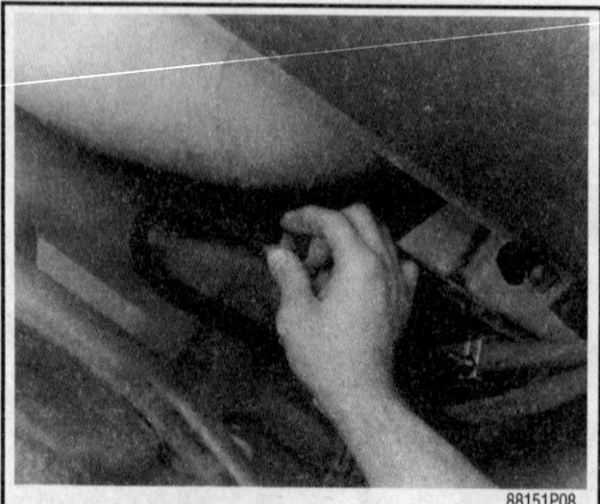
88151P08

Fig. 44 Once the hairpin clip is removed, the push-connect fitting may be disengaged from the filter

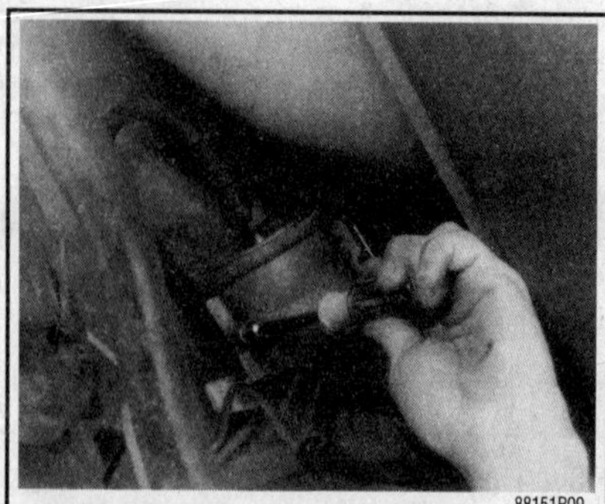
88151P09

Fig. 45 If you have trouble getting to the push-connect fittings, try loosening the worm clamp and repositioning the filter slightly for access

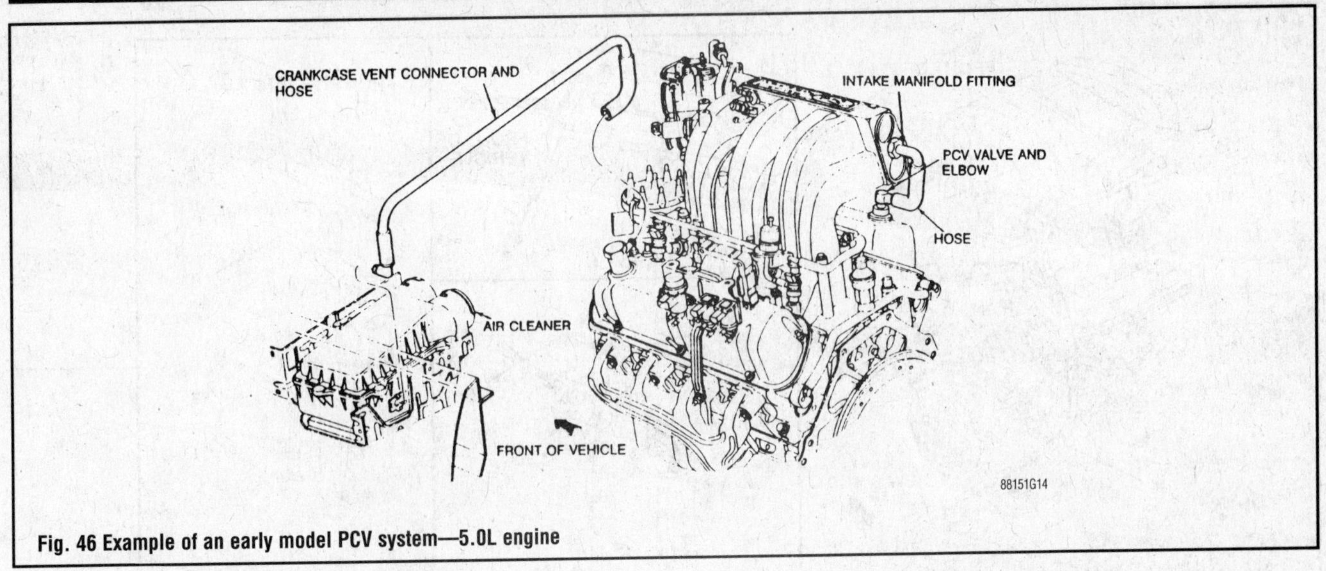

Fig. 46 Example of an early model PCV system—5.0L engine

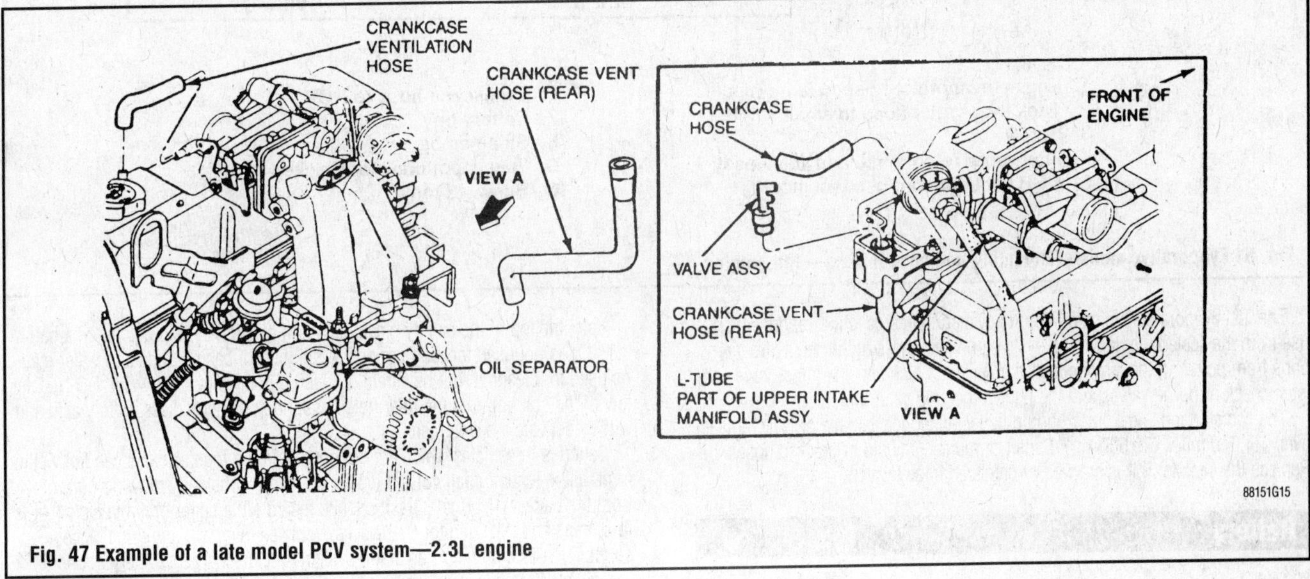

Fig. 47 Example of a late model PCV system—2.3L engine

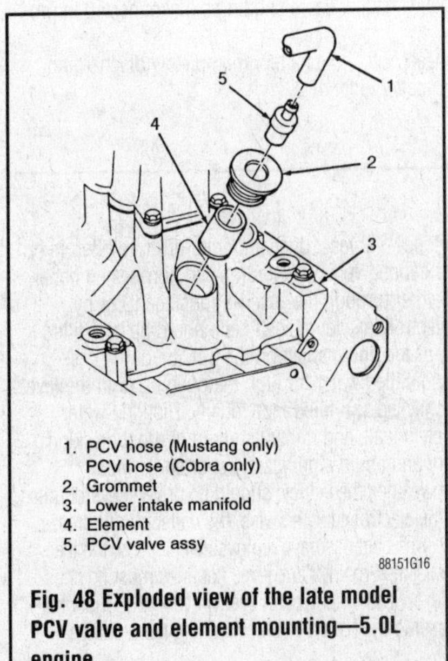

Fig. 48 Exploded view of the late model PCV valve and element mounting—5.0L engine

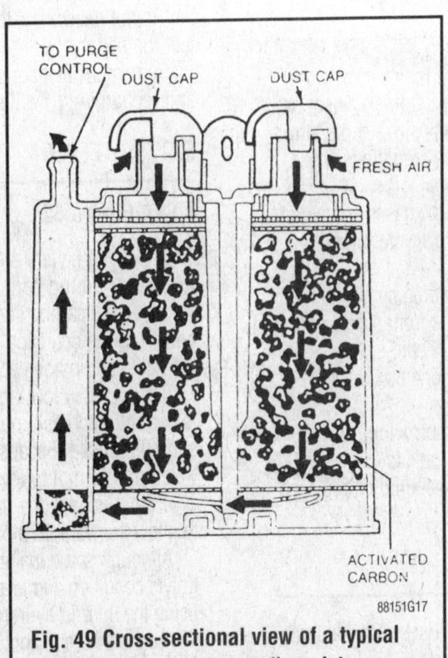

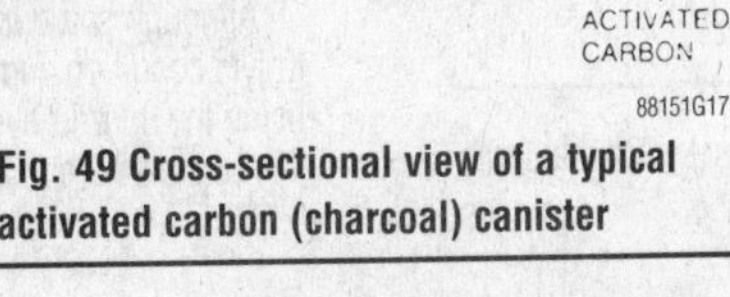

Fig. 49 Cross-sectional view of a typical activated carbon (charcoal) canister

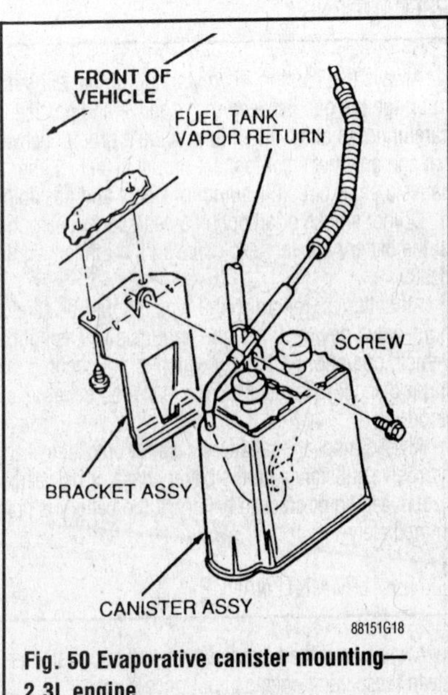

Fig. 50 Evaporative canister mounting—2.3L engine

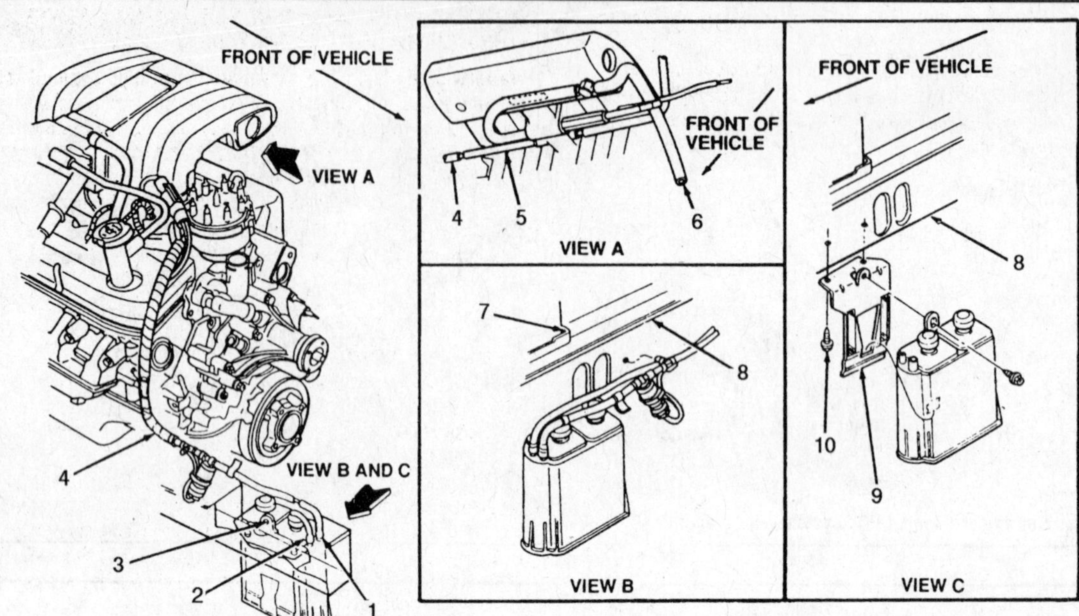

Fig. 51 Evaporative canister mounting and hose routing—5.0L engine

The fuel evaporative emission control system stores gasoline vapors which rise from the sealed fuel tank. The system prevents these unburned hydrocarbons from polluting the atmosphere. It consists of a charcoal vapor storage canister, check or purge valves and the interconnecting vapor lines.

The canister and vapor lines should be inspected for damage or leaks at least every 24,000 miles (38,500 km). Repair or replace any old or cracked hoses. Replace the canister if it is cracked or damaged in any way.

Battery

PRECAUTIONS

Always use caution when working on or near the battery. Never allow a tool to bridge the gap between the negative and positive battery terminals. Also, be careful not to allow a tool to provide a ground between the positive cable/terminal and any metal component on the vehicle. Either of these conditions will cause a short circuit, leading to sparks and possible personal injury.

Do not smoke or all open flames/sparks near a battery; the gases contained in the battery are very explosive and, if ignited, could cause severe injury or death.

All batteries, regardless of type, should be carefully secured by a battery hold-down device. If not, the terminals or casing may crack from stress during vehicle operation. A battery which is not secured may allow acid to leak, making it discharge faster. The acid can also eat away at components under the hood.

Always inspect the battery case for cracks, leakage and corrosion. A white corrosive substance on the battery case or on nearby components would indicate a leaking or cracked battery. If the battery is cracked, it should be replaced immediately.

GENERAL MAINTENANCE

Always keep the battery cables and terminals free of corrosion. Check and clean these components about once a year.

Keep the top of the battery clean, as a film of dirt can help discharge a battery that is not used for long periods. A solution of baking soda and water may be used for cleaning, but be careful to flush this off with clear water. DO NOT let any of the solution into the filler holes. Baking soda neutralizes battery acid and will de-activate a battery cell.

Batteries in vehicles which are not operated on a regular basis can fall victim to parasitic loads (small current drains which are constantly drawing current from the battery). Normal parasitic loads may drain a battery on a vehicle that is in storage and not used for 6–8 weeks. Vehicles that have additional accessories such as a phone or an alarm system may discharge a battery sooner. If the vehicle is to be stored for longer periods in a secure area and the alarm system is not necessary, the negative battery cable should be disconnected to protect the battery.

Remember that constantly deep cycling a battery (completely discharging and recharging it) will shorten battery life.

BATTERY FLUID

➧ **See Figure 52**

Check the battery electrolyte level at least once a month, or more often in hot weather or during periods of extended vehicle operation. On non-sealed batteries, the level can be checked either through the case (if translucent) or by removing the cell caps. The electrolyte level in each cell should be kept filled to the split ring inside each cell, or the line marked on the outside of the case.

If the level is low, add only distilled water through the opening until the level is correct. Each cell must be checked and filled individually. Distilled water should be used, because the chemicals and minerals found in most drinking water are harmful to the battery and could significantly shorten its life.

If water is added in freezing weather, the vehicle should be driven several miles to allow the water to mix with the electrolyte. Otherwise, the battery could freeze.

Although some maintenance-free batteries have removable cell caps, the electrolyte condition and level on all sealed maintenance-free batteries must be checked using the built-in hydrometer "eye." The exact type of eye will vary. But, most battery manufacturers, apply a sticker to the battery itself explaining the readings.

➡Although the readings from built-in hydrometers will vary, a green eye usually indicates a properly charged battery with sufficient fluid level. A dark eye is normally an indicator of a battery with sufficient fluid, but which is low in charge. A light or yellow eye usually indicates that electrolyte has dropped below the necessary level. In this last case, sealed batteries with an insufficient electrolyte must usually be discarded.

Checking the Specific Gravity

See Figures 53, 54 and 55

A hydrometer is required to check the specific gravity on all batteries that are not maintenance-free. On batteries that are maintenance-free, the specific gravity is checked by observing the built-in hydrometer "eye" on the top of the battery case.

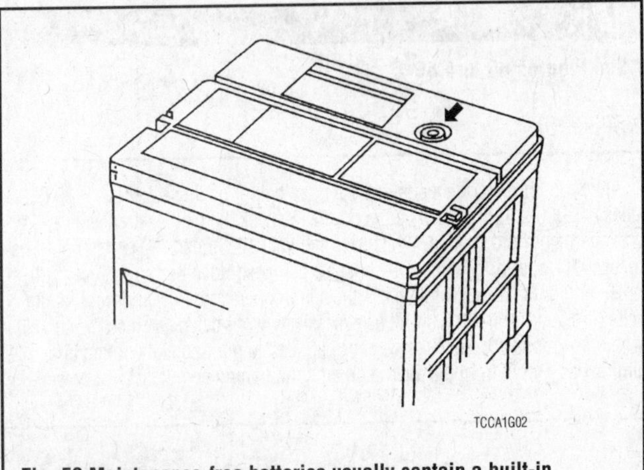

Fig. 52 Maintenance-free batteries usually contain a built-in hydrometer to check fluid level

CAUTION

Battery electrolyte contains sulfuric acid. If you should splash any on your skin or in your eyes, flush the affected area with plenty of clear water. If it lands in your eyes, get medical help immediately.

The fluid (sulfuric acid solution) contained in the battery cells will tell you many things about the condition of the battery. Because the cell plates must be kept submerged below the fluid level in order to operate, the fluid level is extremely important. And, because the specific gravity of the acid is an indication of electrical charge, testing the fluid can be an aid in determining if the battery must be replaced. A battery in a vehicle with a properly operating charging system should require little maintenance, but careful, periodic inspection should reveal problems before they leave you stranded.

At least once a year, check the specific gravity of the battery. It should be between 1.20 and 1.26 on the gravity scale. Most auto stores carry a variety of inexpensive battery hydrometers. These can be used on any non-sealed battery to test the specific gravity in each cell.

The battery testing hydrometer has a squeeze bulb at one end and a nozzle at the other. Battery electrolyte is sucked into the hydrometer until the float is lifted from its seat. The specific gravity is then read by noting the position of the float. If gravity is low in one or more cells, the battery should be slowly charged and checked again to see if the gravity has come up. Generally, if after charging, the specific gravity between any two cells varies more than 50 points (0.50), the battery should be replaced, as it can no longer produce sufficient voltage to guarantee proper operation.

CABLES

See Figures 56, 57, 58 and 59

Once a year (or as necessary), the battery terminals and the cable clamps should be cleaned. Loosen the clamps and remove the cables, negative cable first. On top post batteries, the use of a puller specially made for this purpose is

Fig. 53 On non-sealed batteries, the fluid level can be checked by removing the cell caps

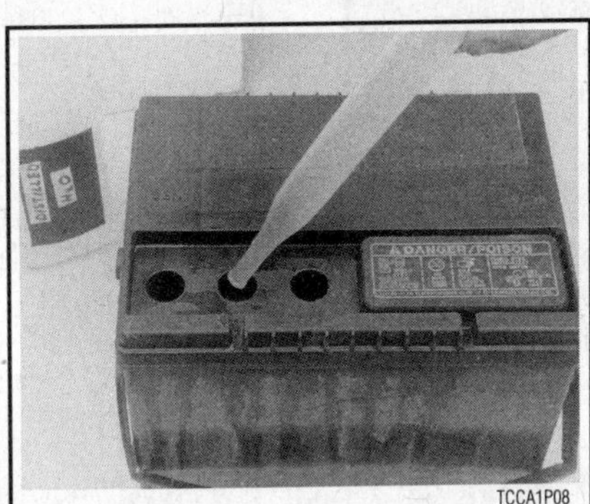

Fig. 54 If the fluid level is low, add only distilled water until the level is correct

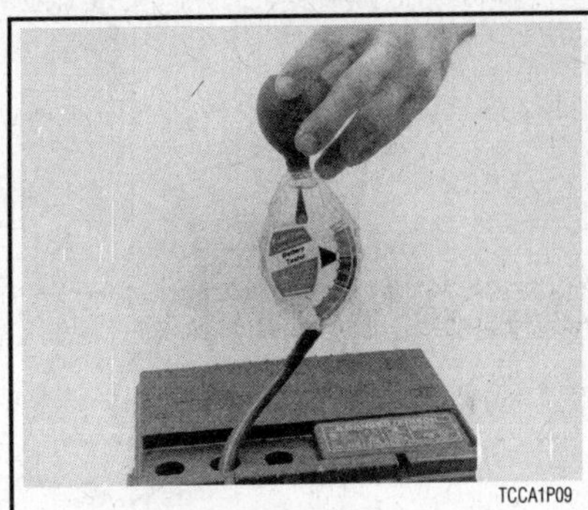

Fig. 55 Check the specific gravity of the battery's electrolyte with a hydrometer

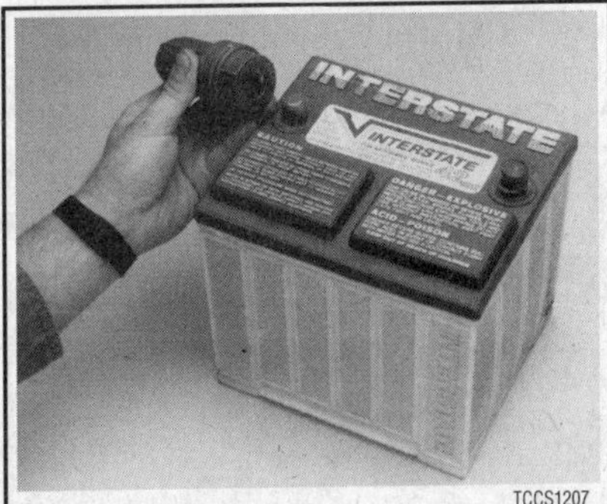

Fig. 56 The underside of this special battery tool has a wire brush to clean post terminals

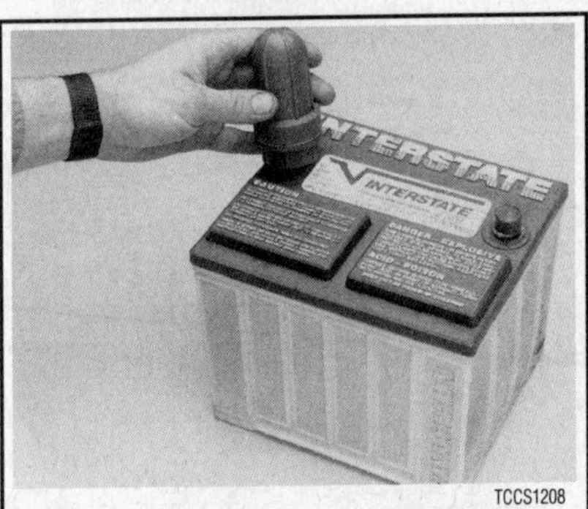

Fig. 57 Place the tool over the battery posts and twist to clean until the metal is shiny

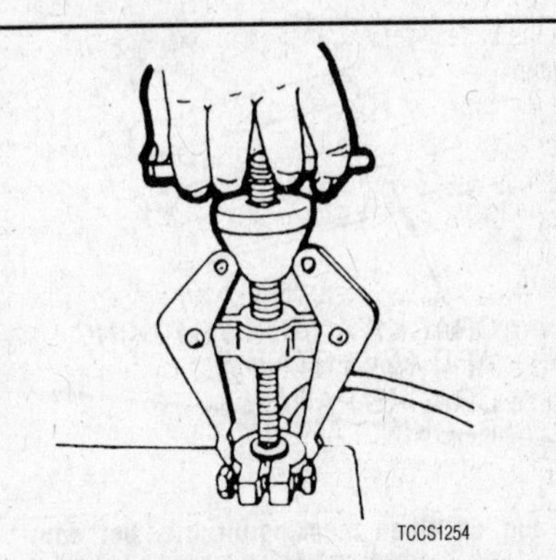

Fig. 58 A special tool is available to pull the clamp from the post

recommended. These are inexpensive and available in most parts stores. Side terminal battery cables are secured with a small bolt.

Clean the cable clamps and the battery terminal with a wire brush, until all corrosion, grease, etc., is removed and the metal is shiny. It is especially important to clean the inside of the clamp thoroughly (an old knife is useful here), since a small deposit of oxidation there will prevent a sound connection and inhibit starting or charging. Special tools are available for cleaning these parts, one type for conventional top post batteries and another type for side terminal batteries. It is also a good idea to apply some dielectric grease to the terminal, as this will aid in the prevention of corrosion.

After the clamps and terminals are clean, reinstall the cables, negative cable last; DO NOT hammer the clamps onto battery posts. Tighten the clamps securely, but do not distort them. Give the clamps and terminals a thin external coating of grease after installation, to retard corrosion.

Check the cables at the same time that the terminals are cleaned. If the cable insulation is cracked or broken, or if the ends are frayed, the cable should be replaced with a new cable of the same length and gauge.

CHARGING

**** CAUTION**

The chemical reaction which takes place in all batteries generates explosive hydrogen gas. A spark can cause the battery to explode and splash acid. To avoid personal injury, be sure there is proper ventilation and take appropriate fire safety precautions when working with or near a battery.

A battery should be charged at a slow rate to keep the plates inside from getting too hot. However, if some maintenance-free batteries are allowed to discharge until they are almost "dead," they may have to be charged at a high rate to bring them back to "life." Always follow the charger manufacturer's instructions on charging the battery.

REPLACEMENT

When it becomes necessary to replace the battery, select one with an amperage rating equal to or greater than the battery originally installed. Deterioration and just plain aging of the battery cables, starter motor, and associated wires makes the battery's job harder in successive years. This makes it prudent to install a new battery with a greater capacity than the old.

Belts

▸ See Figures 60 thru 65

INSPECTION

Although Ford recommends that the drive belt(s) be inspected every 30,000 miles (48,000 km), it is really a good idea to check them at least once a year, or at every major fluid change. Whichever interval you choose, the belts should be checked for wear or damage. Obviously, a damaged drive belt can cause problems should it give way while the vehicle is in operation. But, improper length belts (too short or long), as well as excessively worn belts, can also cause problems. Loose accessory drive belts can lead to poor engine cooling and diminished output from the alternator, air conditioning compressor or power

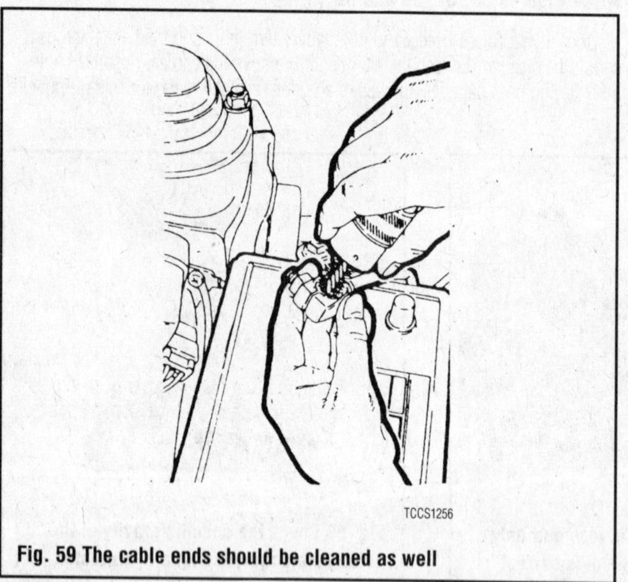

Fig. 59 The cable ends should be cleaned as well

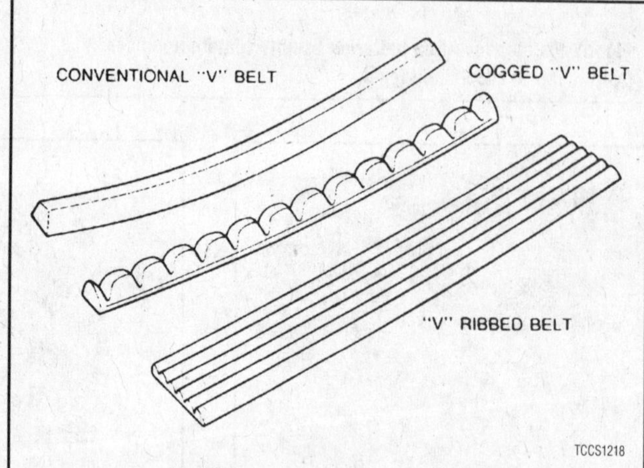

Fig. 60 There are typically 3 types of accessory drive belts found on vehicles today—the V-ribbed serpentine drive belt is found on vehicles covered by this manual

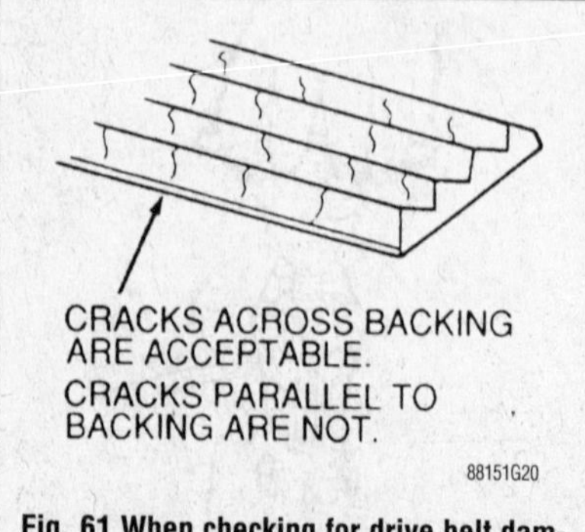

Fig. 61 When checking for drive belt damage, cracks across the backing are acceptable . . .

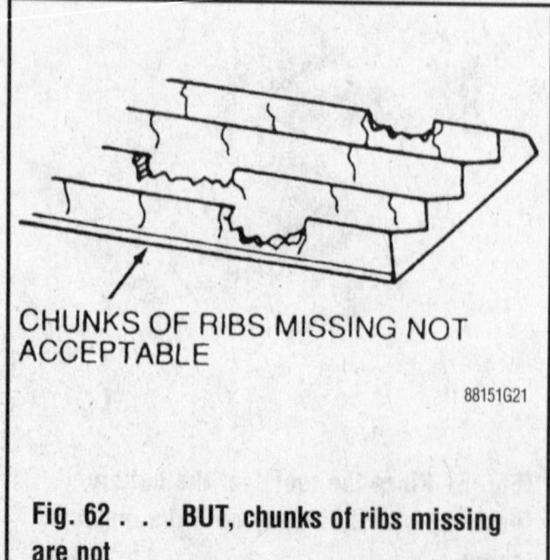

Fig. 62 . . . BUT, chunks of ribs missing are not

Fig. 63 Make sure the belt tensioner arrow falls within the range markings on the tensioner's face

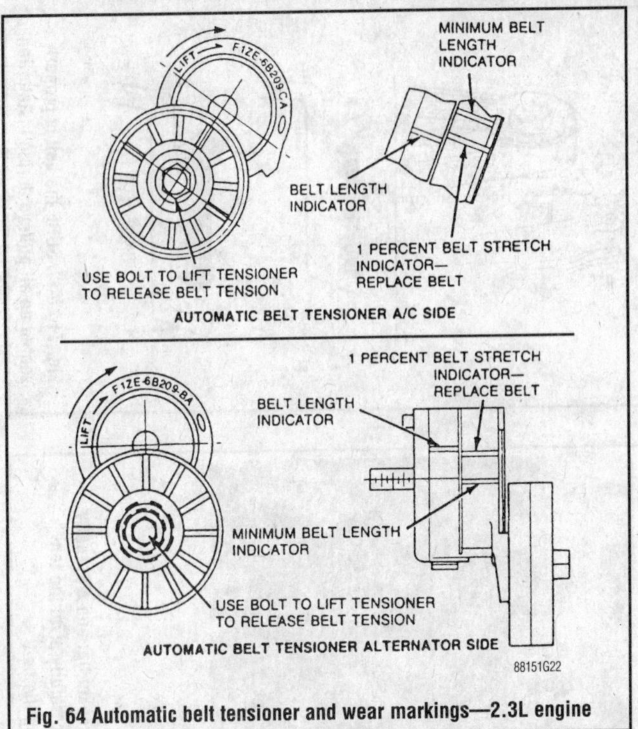

Fig. 64 Automatic belt tensioner and wear markings—2.3L engine

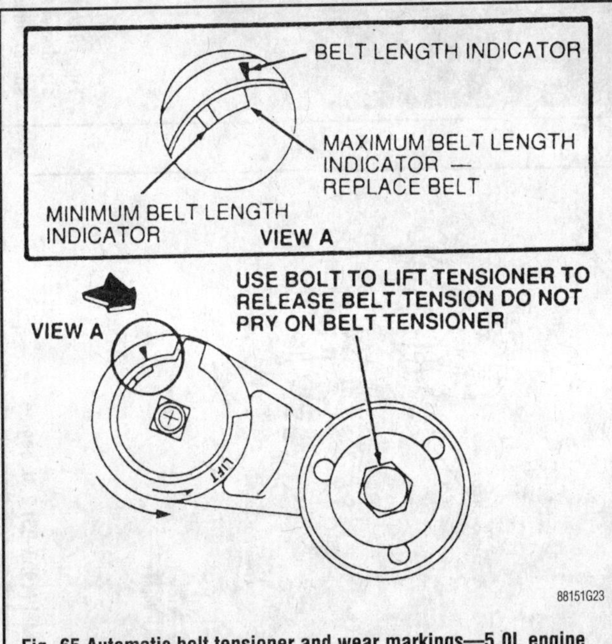

Fig. 65 Automatic belt tensioner and wear markings—5.0L engine

steering pump. A belt that is too tight places a severe strain on the driven unit and can wear out bearings quickly.

The V-ribbed serpentine drive belts used by these engines should be inspected for rib chunking, severe glazing, frayed cords or other visible damage. Any belt which is missing sections of 2 or more adjacent ribs which are ½ in. (13mm) or longer must be replaced. You might want to note that V-ribbed belts do tend to form small cracks across the backing. If the only wear you find is in the form of one or more cracks are across the backing and NOT parallel to the ribs, the belt is still good and does not need to be replaced.

As for belt tension, an automatic spring-loaded tensioner is used on these vehicles to keep the belt properly adjusted at all times. The tensioner is also useful as a wear indicator. When the belt is properly installed, the arrow on the tensioner housing must point within the acceptable range lines on the tensioner's face. If the arrow falls outside the range, either an improper belt has been installed or the belt is worn beyond its useful lifespan. In either case, a new belt must be installed immediately to assure proper engine operation and to prevent possible accessory damage.

REMOVAL & INSTALLATION

See Figures 66 thru 71

The 2.3L and 5.0L Mustang engines utilize one or more wide-ribbed V-belts to drive the engine accessories such as the water pump, alternator, air conditioner compressor, air pump, etc. Because these belts use a spring loaded tensioner for adjustment, belt replacement tends to be somewhat easier than it used to be on engines where accessories were pivoted and bolted in place for tension adjustment. Basically, all belt replacement involves is to pivot the tensioner to loosen the belt, then slide the belt off of the pulleys. The two most important points are to pay CLOSE attention to the proper belt routing (since serpentine belts tend to be "snaked" all different ways through the pulleys) and to make sure the V-ribbs are properly seated in all the pulleys.

Although belt routing diagrams have been included in this section, the first places you should check for proper belt routing are the labels in your engine compartment. These should include a belt routing diagram which may reflect changes made during a production run.

1. Disconnect the negative battery cable for safety. This will help assure that no-one mistakenly cranks the engine over with your hands between the pulleys.

➡Take a good look at the installed belt and make a note of the routing. Before removing the belt, make sure the routing matches that of the belt routing label or one of the diagrams in this book. If for some reason a diagram does not match (you may not have the original engine or it may have been modified) then carefully note the changes on a piece of paper.

2. Using the proper sized socket and breaker bar (or a large handled wrench), pivot the tensioner away from the belt. This will loosen the belt sufficiently that it can be pulled off of one or more of the pulleys. It is usually easiest to carefully pull the belt out from underneath the tensioner pulley itself.
3. Once the belt is off one of the pulleys, gently pivot the tensioner back into position. DO NOT allow the tensioner to snap back as this could damage the tensioner's components.
4. Now finish removing the belt from the components and remove it from the engine.

To install:

5. While referring to the proper routing diagram (which you identified earlier), begin to route the belt over the pulleys, leaving whatever pulley you first released it from for last.
6. Once the belt is mostly in place, carefully pivot the tensioner and position the belt over the final pulley. As you begin to allow the tensioner back into contact with the belt, run your hand around the pulleys and make sure the belt is properly seated in the ribs. If not, release the tension and seat the belt.

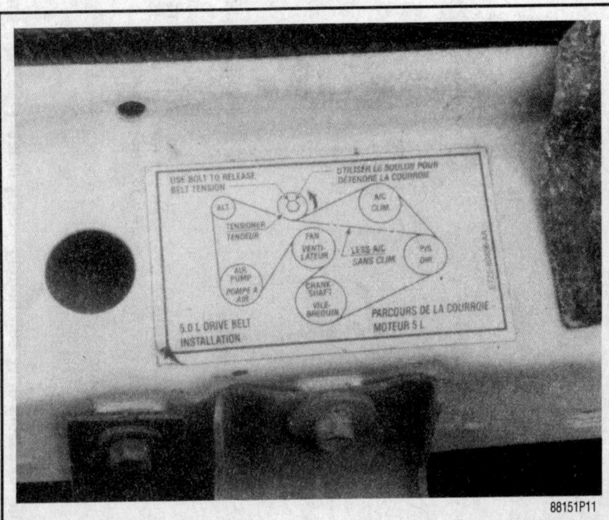

Fig. 66 Always check the engine compartment for belt routing labels

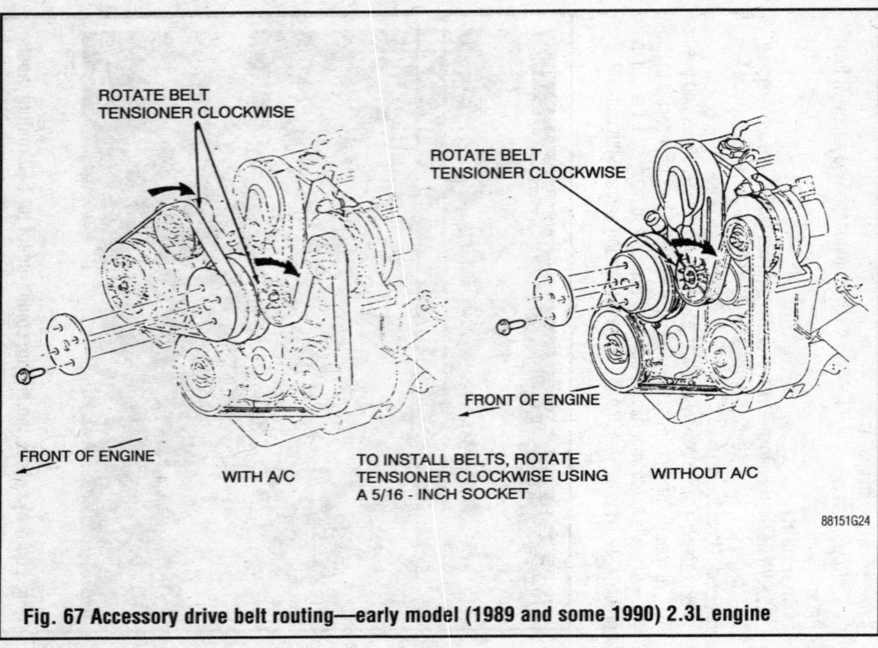

Fig. 67 Accessory drive belt routing—early model (1989 and some 1990) 2.3L engine

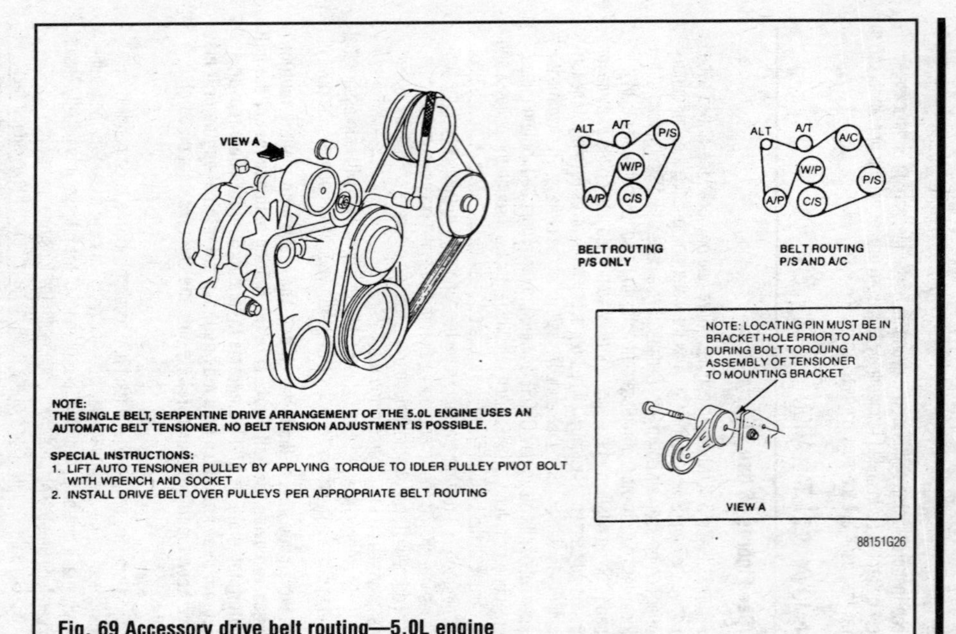

Fig. 69 Accessory drive belt routing—5.0L engine

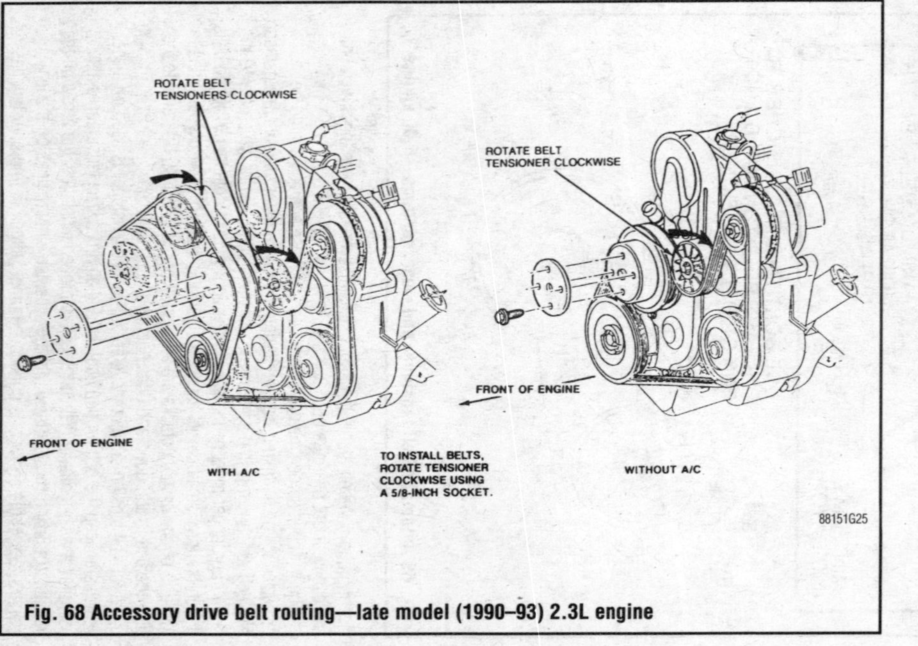

Fig. 68 Accessory drive belt routing—late model (1990–93) 2.3L engine

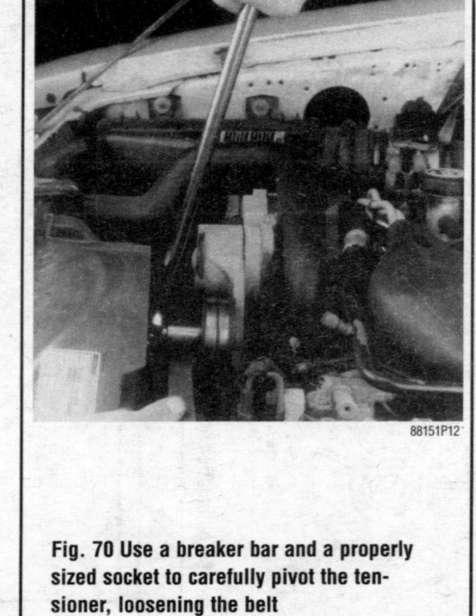

Fig. 70 Use a breaker bar and a properly sized socket to carefully pivot the tensioner, loosening the belt

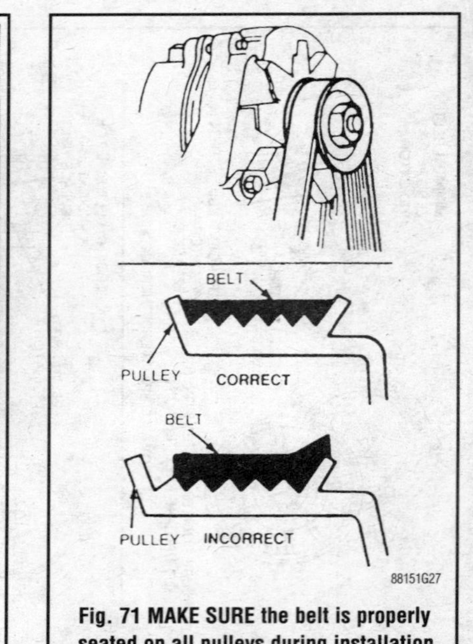

Fig. 71 MAKE SURE the belt is properly seated on all pulleys during installation

7. Once the belt is installed, take another look at all the pulleys to double check your installation. Connect the negative battery cable, then start and run the engine to check belt operation.

8. Once the engine has come up to normal operating temperature, shut the ignition **OFF** and check that the belt tensioner arrow aligns in the proper adjustment range.

Timing Belts

INSPECTION

➧ **See Figures 72 thru 78**

The 2.3L Mustang engine utilizes a timing belt to drive the camshaft from the crankshaft's turning motion and to maintain proper valve timing. Some manufacturer's schedule periodic timing belt replacement to assure optimum engine performance, to make sure the motorist is never stranded should the belt break (as the engine will stop instantly) and for some (manufacturer's with interference motors) to prevent the possibility of severe internal engine damage should the belt break.

Although the 2.3L engine is not listed as an interference motor (it is not listed by the manufacturer as a motor whose valves might contact the pistons if the camshaft was rotated separately from the crankshaft) the first 2 reasons for

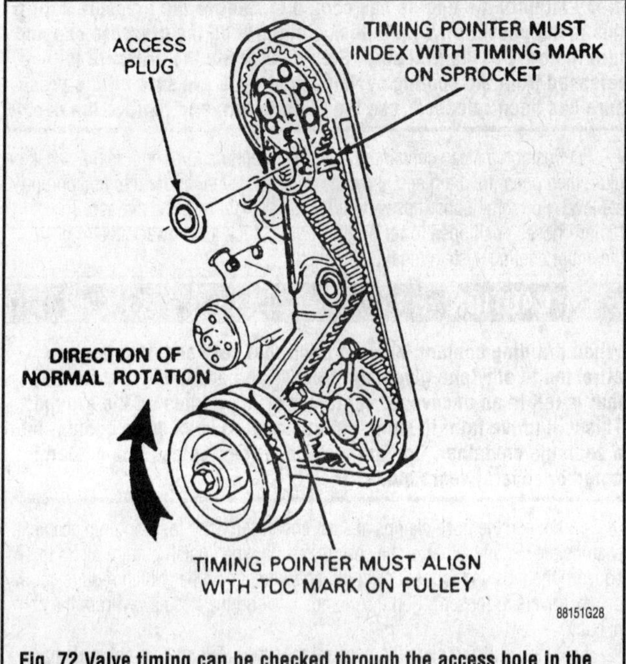

Fig. 72 Valve timing can be checked through the access hole in the timing cover

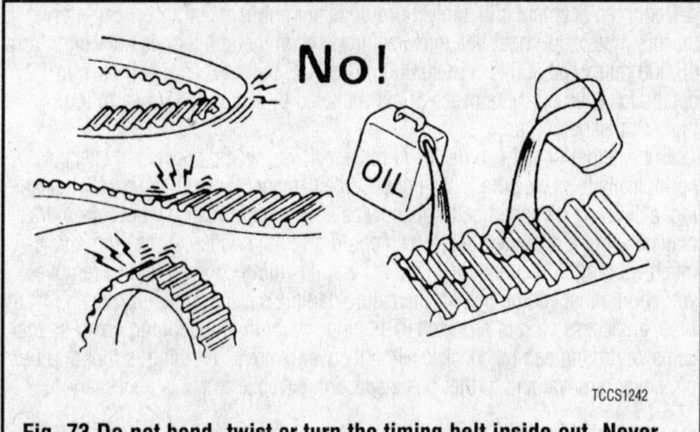

Fig. 73 Do not bend, twist or turn the timing belt inside out. Never allow oil, water or steam to contact the belt

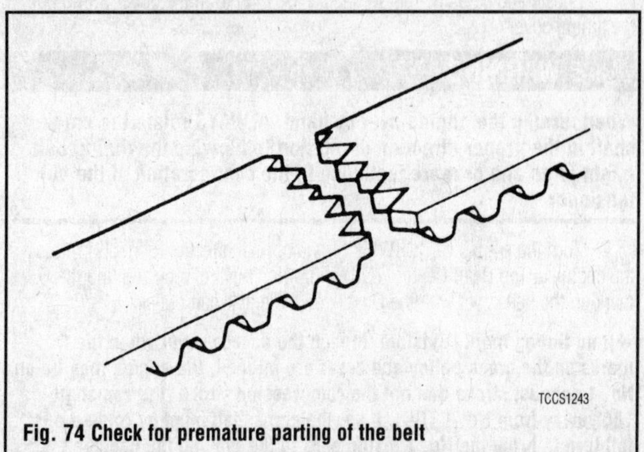

Fig. 74 Check for premature parting of the belt

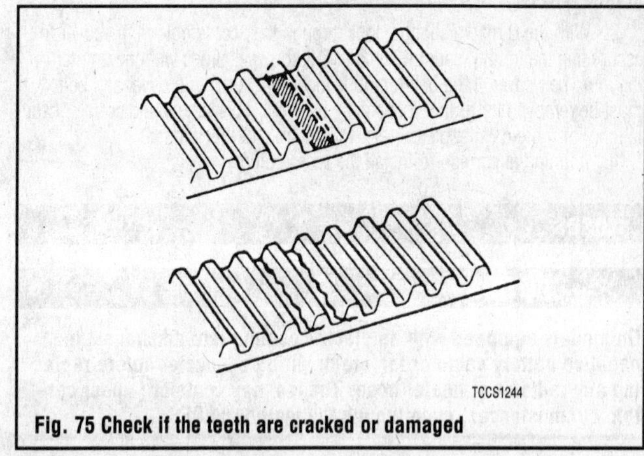

Fig. 75 Check if the teeth are cracked or damaged

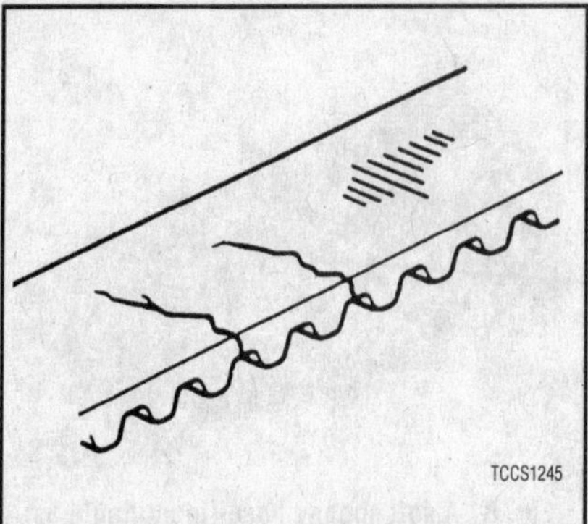

Fig. 76 Look for noticeable cracks or wear on the belt face

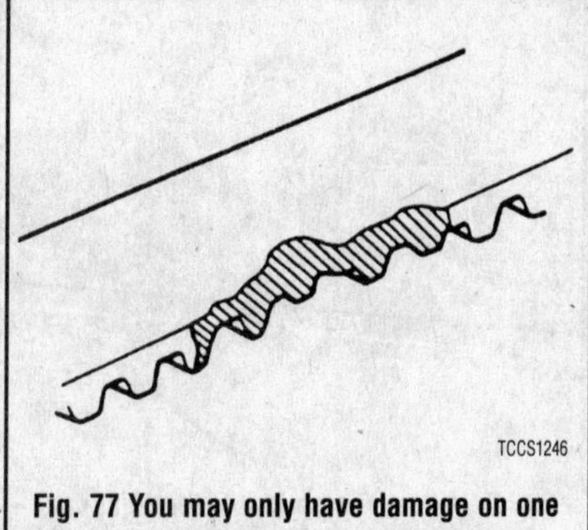

Fig. 77 You may only have damage on one side of the belt; if so, the guide could be the culprit

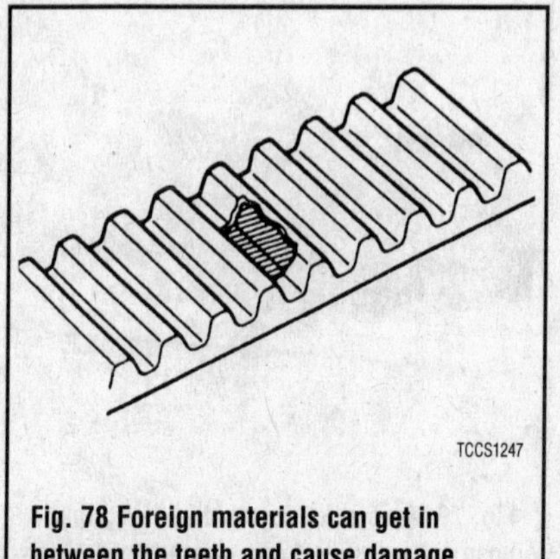

Fig. 78 Foreign materials can get in between the teeth and cause damage

periodic replacement still apply. Ford does not publish a replacement interval for this motor, but most belt manufacturers recommend intervals anywhere from 45,000 miles (72,500 km) to 90,000 miles (145,000 km). You will have to decide for yourself if the peace of mind offered by a new belt is worth it on higher mileage engines.

But whether or not you decide to replace it, you would be wise to check it periodically to make sure it has not become damaged or worn. Generally speaking, a severely damaged belt will show as engine performance would drop dramatically, but a damaged belt (which could give out suddenly) may not give as much warning. In general, any time the engine timing cover(s) is(are) removed you should inspect the belt for premature parting, severe cracks or missing teeth. Also, an access plug is provided in the upper portion of the timing cover so that camshaft timing can be checked without cover removal. If timing is found to be off, cover removal and further belt inspection or replacement is necessary.

CAMSHAFT TIMING INSPECTION

1. Locate and carefully remove the access plug from the upper portion of the timing cover.

✽✽ WARNING

When turning the engine over by hand, ALWAYS rotate the crankshaft in the proper direction of rotation, otherwise the timing belt might jump one or more teeth due to the configuration of the belt tensioner.

2. Turn the engine CLOCKWISE (in the normal direction of rotation) to set the engine at Top Dead Center (TDC) of the No. 1 cylinder by aligning the 0 mark on the belt cover with the 0 mark on the crankshaft pulley.

➡If no timing mark is visible through the access cover when the 0 marks on the crank pulley and cover are aligned, the engine may be on No. 1 exhaust stroke and not the compression stroke (the camshaft is 180° away from No. 1 TDC). If so, the crankshaft must be rotated one full turn to bring the No. 1 piston back to the top and the camshaft around to close the No. 1 intake and exhaust valves.

3. With the 0 marks aligned, look through the access hole in the cover to assure that the timing mark on he camshaft sprocket aligns with the pointer on the inner belt cover. If the belt timing is incorrect, the timing cover and belt must be removed for further inspection, possible replacement and correct installation. For more details, please refer to Section 3 of this manual.
4. If timing is correct, re-install the access plug.

Hoses

✽✽ CAUTION

On models equipped with an electric cooling fan, disconnect the negative battery cable or fan motor wiring connector before replacing any radiator or heater hose. The fan may come on, under certain circumstances, even though the ignition is OFF.

INSPECTION

➧ **See Figures 79, 80, 81 and 82**

Upper and lower radiator hoses along with the heater hoses should be checked for deterioration, leaks and loose hose clamps at least annually or every 12,000 miles (19,000 km), whichever comes first. It is also wise to check the hoses periodically in early spring and at the beginning of the fall or winter when you are performing other maintenance. A quick visual inspection could uncover a weakened hose which might have left you stranded if it had remained unrepaired.

Whenever you are checking the hoses, make sure the engine and cooling system are cold. Visually inspect for cracking, rotting or collapsed hoses, and replace as necessary. Run your hand along the length of the hose. If a weak or swollen spot is noted when squeezing the hose wall, the hose should be replaced.

REMOVAL & INSTALLATION

➧ **See Figure 83**

1. Disconnect the negative battery cable for safety.
2. Remove the radiator pressure cap.

✽✽ CAUTION

Never remove the pressure cap while the engine is running, or personal injury from scalding hot coolant or steam may result. If possible, wait until the engine has cooled to remove the pressure cap. If this is not possible, wrap a thick cloth around the pressure cap and turn it slowly to the first stop. Step back while the pressure is released from the cooling system. When you are sure all the pressure has been released, use the cloth to turn and remove the cap.

3. Position a clean container under the radiator and/or engine draincock or plug, then open the drain and allow the cooling system to drain to an appropriate level. For some upper hoses, only a little coolant must be drained. To remove hoses positioned lower on the engine, such as a lower radiator hose, the entire cooling system must be emptied.

✽✽ CAUTION

When draining coolant, keep in mind that cats and dogs are attracted to ethylene glycol antifreeze, and are likely to drink any that is left in an uncovered container or in puddles on the ground. This will prove fatal in sufficient quantity. Always drain coolant into a sealable container. Coolant may be reused unless it is contaminated or several years old.

4. Loosen the hose clamps at each end of the hose requiring replacement. Clamps are usually either of the spring tension type (which require pliers to squeeze the tabs and loosen) or of the screw tension type (which require screw or hex drivers to loosen). Pull the clamps back on the hose away from the connection.
5. Twist, pull and slide the hose off the fitting, taking care not to damage the neck of the component from which the hose is being removed.

TCCS1219

Fig. 79 The cracks developing along this hose are a result of age-related hardening

TCCS1220

Fig. 80 A hose clamp that is too tight can cause older hoses to separate and tear on either side of the clamp

TCCS1221

Fig. 81 A soft spongy hose (identifiable by the swollen section) will eventually burst and should be replaced

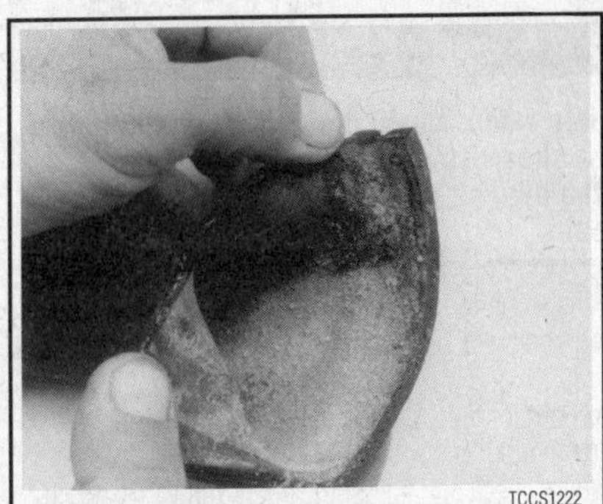

Fig. 82 Hoses are likely to deteriorate from the inside if the cooling system is not periodically flushed

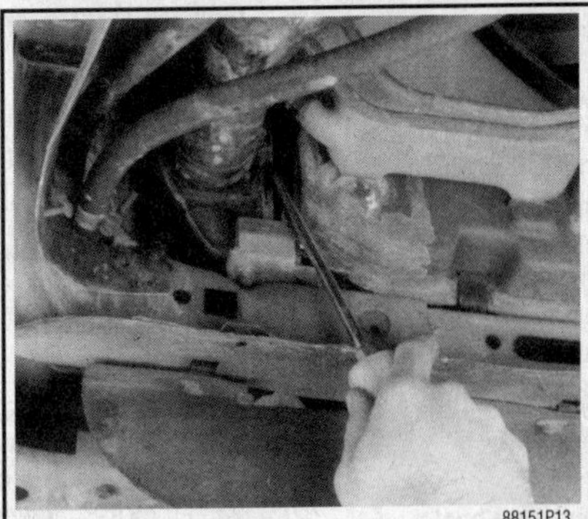

Fig. 83 To remove this lower radiator hose, you must first loosen the retaining clamp

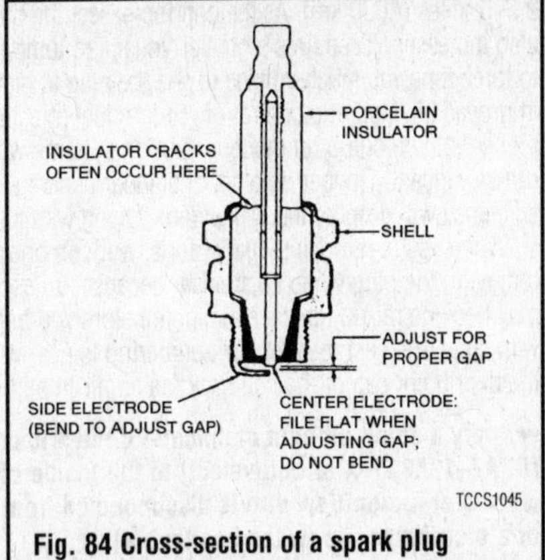

Fig. 84 Cross-section of a spark plug

➡If the hose is stuck at the connection, do not try to insert a screwdriver or other sharp tool under the hose end in an effort to free it, as the connection and/or hose may become damaged. Heater connections especially may be easily damaged by such a procedure. If the hose is to be replaced, use a single-edged razor blade to make a slice along the portion of the hose which is stuck on the connection, perpendicular to the end of the hose. Do not cut deep so as to prevent damaging the connection. The hose can then be peeled from the connection and discarded.

6. Clean both hose mounting connections. Inspect the condition of the hose clamps and replace them, if necessary.

To install:

7. Dip the ends of the new hose into clean engine coolant to ease installation.
8. Slide the clamps over the replacement hose, then slide the hose ends over the connections into position.
9. Position and secure the clamps at least 1/4 in. (6.35mm) from the ends of the hose. Make sure they are located beyond the raised bead of the connector. If you are using screw tension type clamps, tighten them to 20–30 inch lbs. (2–4 Nm). Do not overtighten hose clamps as they will cut into the hose (possibly causing a leak).
10. Close the radiator or engine drains and properly refill the cooling system with the clean engine coolant drained earlier or a suitable mixture of fresh coolant and water.
11. If available, install a pressure tester and check for leaks. If a pressure tester is not available, run the engine until normal operating temperature is reached (allowing the system to naturally pressurize), then check for leaks.

⁂ CAUTION

If you are checking for leaks with the system at normal operating temperature, BE EXTREMELY CAREFUL not to touch any moving or hot engine parts. Once the temperature has been reached, shut the engine OFF, and check for leaks around the hose fittings and connections which were removed earlier.

Spark Plugs

See Figure 84

A typical spark plug consists of a metal shell surrounding a ceramic insulator. A metal electrode extends downward through the center of the insulator and protrudes a small distance. Located at the end of the plug and attached to the side of the outer metal shell is the side electrode. The side electrode bends in at a 90° angle so that its tip is just past and parallel to the tip of the center electrode. The distance between these two electrodes (measured in thousandths of an inch or hundredths of a millimeter) is called the spark plug gap.

The spark plug does not produce a spark but instead provides a gap across which the current can arc. The coil produces anywhere from 20,000 to 50,000 volts (depending on the type and application) which travels through the wires to the spark plugs. The current passes along the center electrode and jumps the gap to the side electrode, and in doing so, ignites the air/fuel mixture in the combustion chamber.

SPARK PLUG HEAT RANGE

See Figure 85

Spark plug heat range is the ability of the plug to dissipate heat. The longer the insulator (or the farther it extends into the engine), the hotter the plug will operate; the shorter the insulator (the closer the electrode is to the block's cooling passages) the cooler it will operate. A plug that absorbs little heat and remains too cool will quickly accumulate deposits of oil and carbon since it is not hot enough to burn them off. This leads to plug fouling and consequently to misfiring. A plug that absorbs too much heat will have no deposits but, due to the excessive heat, the electrodes will burn away quickly and might possibly lead to preignition or other ignition problems. Preignition takes place when plug tips get so hot that they glow sufficiently to ignite the air/fuel mixture before the actual spark occurs. This early ignition will usually cause a pinging during low speeds and heavy loads.

The general rule of thumb for choosing the correct heat range when picking a spark plug is: if most of your driving is long distance, high speed travel, use a colder plug; if most of your driving is stop and go, use a hotter plug. Original equipment plugs are generally a good compromise between the 2 styles and most people never have the need to change their plugs from the factory-recommended heat range.

REMOVAL & INSTALLATION

See Figures 86, 87, 88 and 89

A standard set of spark plugs usually requires replacement after about 20,000–30,000 miles (32,000–48,000 km), depending on your style of driving. In normal operation plug gap increases about 0.001 in (0.025 mm) for every

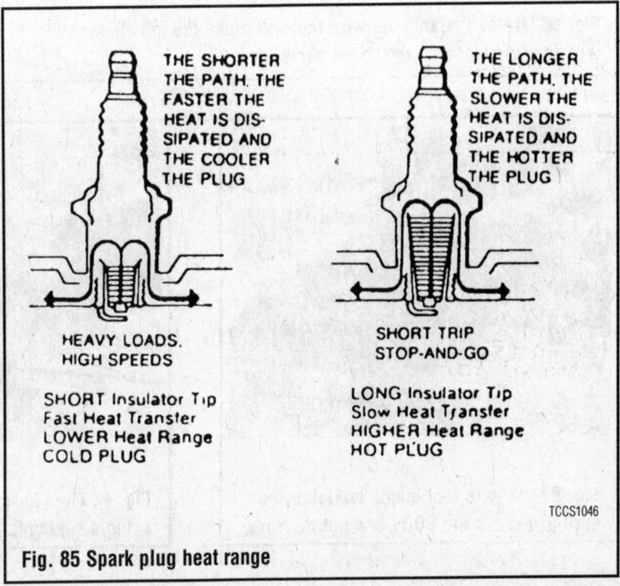

Fig. 85 Spark plug heat range

2,500 miles (4000 km). As the gap increases, the plug's voltage requirement also increases. It requires a greater voltage to jump the wider gap and about two to three times as much voltage to fire the plug at high speeds than at idle. The improved air/fuel ratio control of modern fuel injection combined with the higher voltage output of modern ignition systems will often allow an engine to run significantly longer on a set of standard spark plugs, but keep in mind that efficiency will drop as the gap widens (along with fuel economy and power).

When you're removing spark plugs, work on one at a time. Don't start by removing the plug wires all at once, because, unless you number them, they may become mixed up. Take a minute before you begin and number the wires with tape. The best location for numbering is near where the wires come out of the distributor cap or the coil pack (as applicable).

➡Apply a small amount of silicone dielectric compound (D7AZ–19A331–A or equivalent) to the inside of the terminal boots whenever an ignition wire is disconnected from the plug, ignition coil, or a distributor cap (when applicable).

1. Disconnect the negative battery cable, and if the vehicle has been run recently, allow the engine to thoroughly cool.
2. Carefully twist the spark plug wire boot to loosen it, then pull upward and remove the boot from the plug. Be sure to pull on the boot and not on the wire, otherwise the connector located inside the boot may become separated.
3. Using compressed air, blow any water or debris from the spark plug well to assure that no harmful contaminants are allowed to enter the combustion chamber when the spark plug is removed. If compressed air is not available, use a rag or a brush to clean the area.

➡Remove the spark plugs when the engine is cold, if possible, to prevent damage to the threads. If removal of the plugs is difficult, apply a few drops of penetrating oil or silicone spray to the area around the base of the plug, and allow it a few minutes to work.

4. Using a spark plug socket that is equipped with a rubber insert to properly hold the plug, turn the spark plug counterclockwise to loosen and remove the spark plug from the bore. Be sure to hold the socket straight on the plug; this will avoid breaking the plug or rounding off the hex flats on the plug.

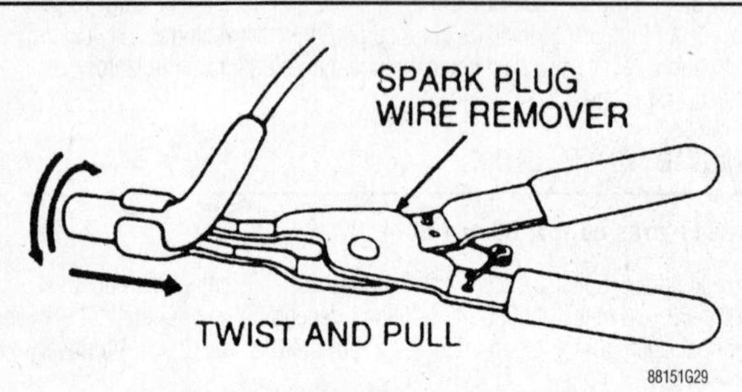

Fig. 86 Use of a spark plug wire tool will make the job easier and will help prevent damage to the wires

✱✱ WARNING

Be sure not to use a flexible extension on the socket. Use of a flexible extension may allow a shear force to be applied to the plug. A shear force could break the plug off in the cylinder head, leading to costly and frustrating repairs.

5. Once the plug is out, inspect it for signs of wear, fouling or damage. This is crucial, since plug readings are a vital sign of internal engine condition.

To install:

6. Inspect the spark plug boot for tears or damage. If a damaged boot is found, the spark plug wire must be replaced.
7. Using a wire feeler gauge, check and adjust the spark plug gap. When using a gauge, the proper size should pass between the electrodes with a slight drag. The next larger size should not be able to pass while the next smaller size should pass freely.
8. Squirt a drop of penetrating oil on the threads (don't oil it too heavily) of the new plug, then carefully thread the plug into the bore by hand. If resistance is felt before the plug is almost completely threaded, back the plug out and begin threading again. In small, hard to reach areas, an old spark plug wire and boot could be used as a threading tool. The boot will hold the plug while you twist the end of the wire and the wire is supple enough to twist before it would allow the plug to crossthread.

✱✱ WARNING

Do not use the spark plug socket to thread the plugs. Always thread the plug carefully by hand or using an old plug wire to prevent the possibility of crossthreading and damaging the cylinder head bore.

9. Carefully tighten the spark plug. If the plug you are installing is equipped with a crush washer, seat the plug, then tighten about 1/4 turn to crush the washer. If you are installing a tapered seat plug, tighten the plug to specifications provided by the vehicle or plug manufacturer.
10. Apply a small amount of silicone dielectric compound to the end of the spark plug lead or inside the spark plug boot to prevent sticking, then install the boot to the spark plug and push until it clicks into place. The click may be felt or heard, then gently pull back on the boot to assure proper contact.

INSPECTION & GAPPING

▸ See Figures 90, 91, 92 and 93

Check the plugs for deposits and wear. If they are not going to be replaced, clean the plugs thoroughly. Remember that any kind of deposit will decrease the efficiency of the plug. Plugs can be cleaned on a spark plug cleaning machine, which can sometimes be found in service stations, or you can do an acceptable job of cleaning with a stiff brush. If the plugs are cleaned, the electrodes must be filed flat. Use an ignition points file, not an emery board or the like, which will leave deposits. The electrodes must be filed perfectly flat with sharp edges; rounded edges reduce the spark plug voltage by as much as 50%.

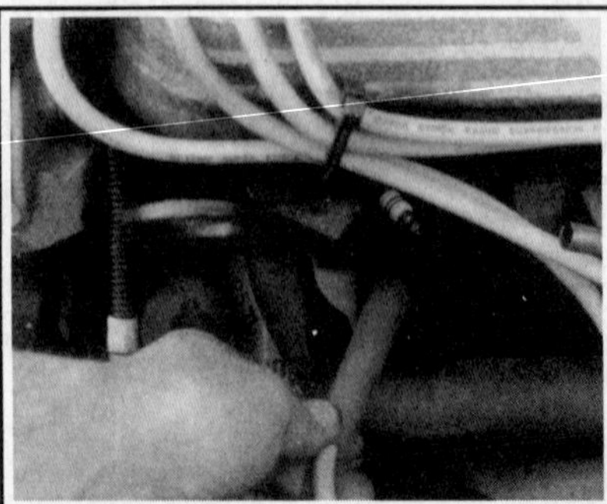

Fig. 87 If a wire tool is not available, be sure you grasp the BOOT and not the wire

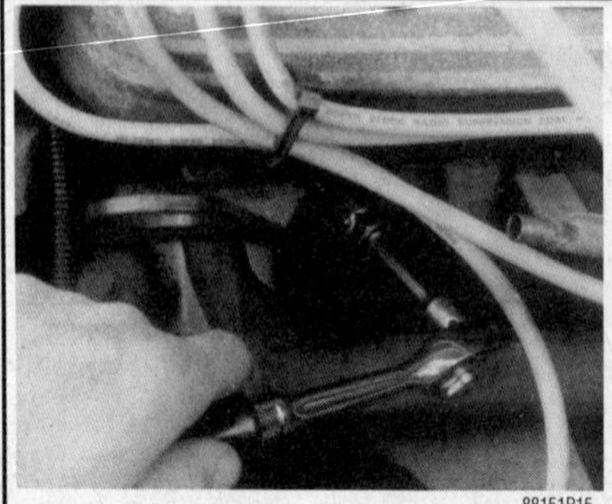

Fig. 88 Then loosen and remove the plug using a spark plug socket

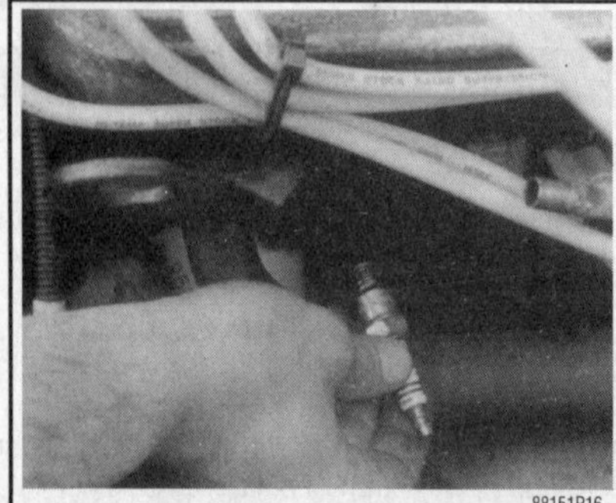

Fig. 89 During installation ALWAYS start the plug by hand to help prevent crossthreading

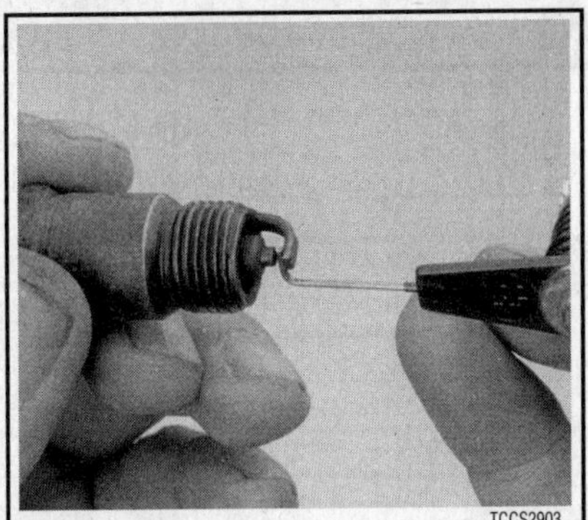

Fig. 90 Checking the spark plug gap with a feeler gauge

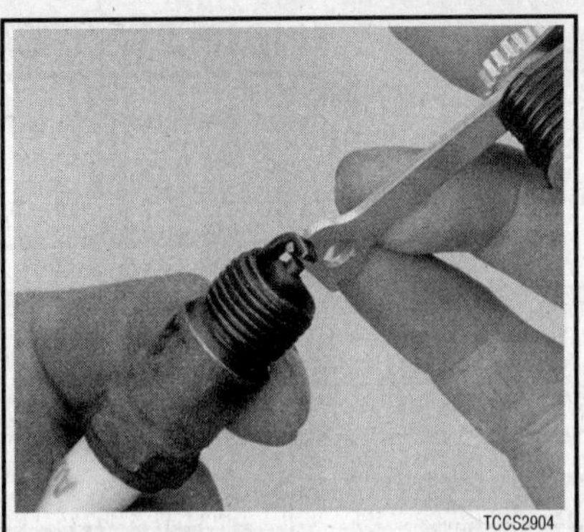

Fig. 91 Adjusting the spark plug gap

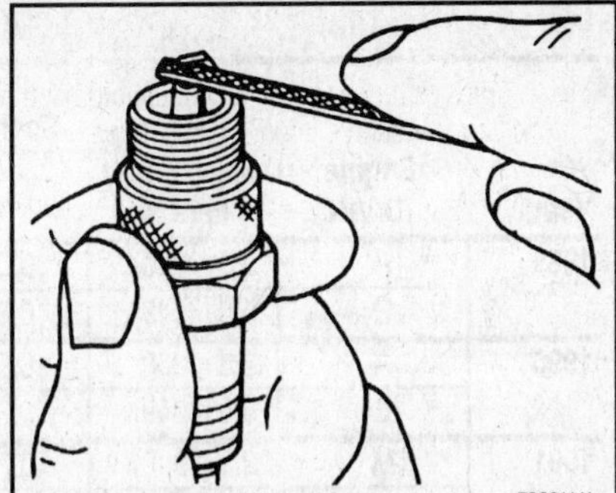

Fig. 92 If the standard plug is in good condition, the electrode may be filed flat—WARNING: do not file platinum plugs

A normally worn spark plug should have light tan or gray deposits on the firing tip.

A carbon fouled plug, identified by soft, sooty, black deposits, may indicate an improperly tuned vehicle. Check the air cleaner, ignition components and engine control system.

This spark plug has been **left in the engine too long,** as evidenced by the extreme gap- Plugs with such an extreme gap can cause misfiring and stumbling accompanied by a noticeable lack of power.

An oil fouled spark plug indicates an engine with worn poston rings and/or bad valve seals allowing excessive oil to enter the chamber.

A physically damaged spark plug may be evidence of severe detonation in that cylinder. Watch that cylinder carefully between services, as a continued detonation will not only damage the plug, but could also damage the engine.

A bridged or almost bridged spark plug, identified by a build-up between the electrodes caused by excessive carbon or oil build-up on the plug.

TCCA1P40

Fig. 93 Inspect the spark plug to determine engine running conditions

GASOLINE ENGINE TUNE-UP SPECIFICATIONS

Year	Engine ID/VIN	Engine Displacement Liters (cc)	Spark Plugs Gap (in.)	Ignition Timing (deg.)[4] MT	Ignition Timing (deg.)[4] AT	Fuel Pump (psi)	Idle Speed (rpm) MT	Idle Speed (rpm) AT	Valve Clearance In.	Valve Clearance Ex.
1989	A	2.3 (2300)	0.044 [1]	10B [1]	10B [1]	30-45 [2]	850 [3]	750 [3]	HYD	HYD
	E	5.0 (4949)	0.044 [1]	10B [1]	10B [1]	30-45 [2]	700 [3]	700 [3]	HYD	HYD
1990	A	2.3 (2300)	0.044 [1]	10B [1]	10B [1]	30-45 [2]	850 [3]	750 [3]	HYD	HYD
	E	5.0 (4949)	0.044 [1]	10B [1]	10B [1]	30-45 [2]	700 [3]	700 [3]	HYD	HYD
1991	M	2.3 (2300)	0.044 [1]	10B [1]	10B [1]	30-45 [2]	975 [3]	975 [3]	HYD	HYD
	E	5.0 (4949)	0.054 [1]	10B [1]	10B [1]	30-45 [2]	700 [3]	700 [3]	HYD	HYD
1992	M	2.3 (2300)	0.044 [1]	10B [1]	10B [1]	30-45 [2]	975 [3]	975 [3]	HYD	HYD
	E	5.0 (4949)	0.054 [1]	10B [1]	10B [1]	30-45 [2]	700 [3]	700 [3]	HYD	HYD
1993	M	2.3 (2300)	0.044 [1]	10B [1]	10B [1]	30-45 [2]	975 [3]	975 [3]	HYD	HYD
	E	5.0 (4949)	0.054 [1]	10B [1]	10B [1]	30-45 [2]	700 [3]	700 [3]	HYD	HYD

NOTE: The Vehicle Emission Control Information label often reflects specification changes made during production. The figures on the label must always be used if they differ from those in this chart.

B - Before top dead center

HYD - Hydraulic

1 Check the underhood label for calibration variations. Timing is preset at the factory and is not adjustable on non-distributor ignition models.

2 Specification is for engine running; Key on, engine off is 35-40 psi.

3 Calibrations vary depending upon the model: refer to the underhood label.

4 Timing is preset at the factory and is not adjustable on non-distributor ignition models.

88151C05

Check spark plug gap before installation. The ground electrode (the L-shaped one connected to the body of the plug) must be parallel to the center electrode and the specified size wire gauge (please refer to the Tune-Up Specifications chart for details) must pass between the electrodes with a slight drag.

➡**NEVER adjust the gap on a used platinum type spark plug.**

Always check the gap on new plugs as they are not always set correctly at the factory. Do not use a flat feeler gauge when measuring the gap on a used plug, because the reading may be inaccurate. A round-wire type gapping tool is the best way to check the gap. The correct gauge should pass through the electrode gap with a slight drag. If you're in doubt, try one size smaller and one larger. The smaller gauge should go through easily, while the larger one shouldn't go through at all. Wire gapping tools usually have a bending tool attached. Use that to adjust the side electrode until the proper distance is obtained. Absolutely never attempt to bend the center electrode. Also, be careful not to bend the side electrode too far or too often as it may weaken and break off within the engine, requiring removal of the cylinder head to retrieve it.

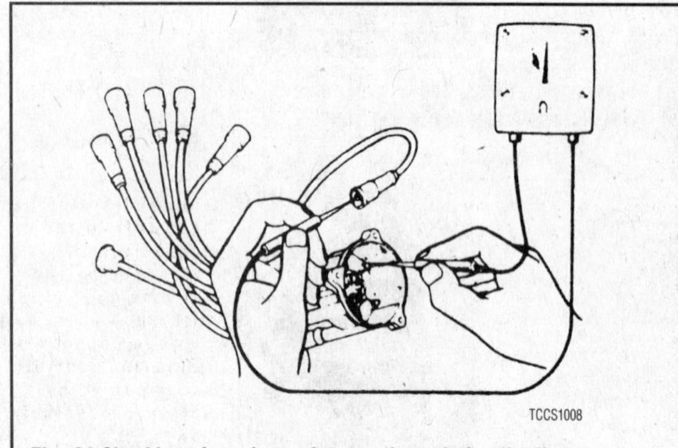

TCCS1008

Fig. 94 Checking plug wire resistance through the distributor cap with an ohmmeter

Spark Plug Wires

TESTING & REPLACEMENT

See Figures 94 and 95

At every tune-up/inspection, visually check the spark plug cables for burns, cuts, or breaks in the insulation. Start by wiping the wires with a clean, damp cloth. The carefully inspect the surface of the wires. Check the boots and the nipples on the distributor cap and/or ignition coil (as applicable). Replace any damaged wiring.

Every 50,000 miles (80,000 km) or 60 months, the resistance of the wires should be checked with an ohmmeter. Wires with excessive resistance will cause misfiring, and may make the engine difficult to start in damp weather. To check resistance on the distributorless 2.3L (VIN M) engine, remove a wire from the both the spark plug and the ignition coil pack tower, then use an ohmmeter probe at each end. On the 2.3L (VIN A) and on 5.0L engines, remove the distributor cap, then unplug only 1 wire at a time from the spark plug. Check resistance from the inside terminal of the distributor cap to the spark plug end of the cable. In both cases, resistance of any given spark plug wire should be LESS than 7000 ohms per foot of wire. Therefore a 2 foot long spark plug wire with 10,000 ohms of resistance would be acceptable (less than the 14,000 ohm max.), while the same wire should be discarded if resistance is 15,000 ohms.

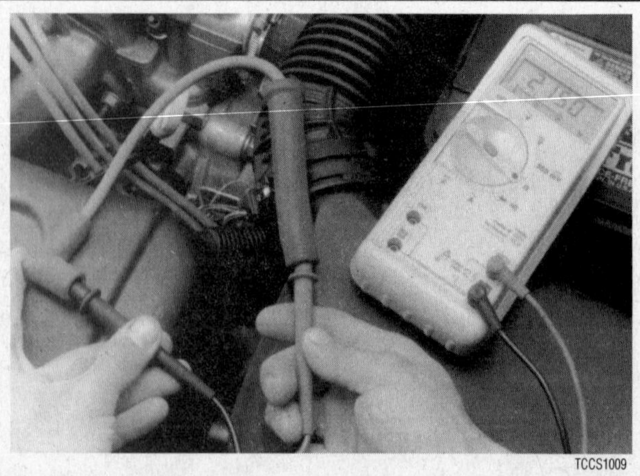

TCCS1009

Fig. 95 Checking individual plug wire resistance with a digital ohmmeter

➡If all of the wires must be disconnected from the spark plugs, coil packs or distributor cap at one time, be sure to tag the wires to assure proper installation.

The best possible method for installing a new set of wires is to replace ONE AT A TIME so there can be no mix-up. On distributor equipped engines, don't rely on wiring diagrams or sketches, since the position of the distributor can be changed (unless the distributor is keyed for installation in only one direction). Start by replacing the longest wire first. Install the boot firmly over the spark plug. Route the wire in exactly the same path as the original and connect it to the distributor or coil pack (as applicable). Repeat the process for each shorter wire.

Distributor Cap and Rotor

Of the engines covered by this manual, only the 2.3L (VIN A) and 5.0L engines utilize a distributor ignition system. The 2.3L (VIN M) engine uses a distributorless electronic ignition system where separate ignition coils fire the spark plugs directly through the secondary ignition wires.

It is normally a good idea to inspect the distributor cap and rotor any time you perform a tune-up which includes checking the spark plug wires for wear, damage or excessive resistance.

REMOVAL & INSTALLATION

See Figures 96 thru 101

1. Disconnect the negative battery cable for safety.
2. If equipped, remove the protective rubber boot from the distributor assembly by carefully lifting at the edges.

➡Depending on the reason you have for removing the distributor cap, it may (in some cases) make more sense to leave the spark plug wires attached. This is handy if you are testing spark plug wires or if removal was necessary to access other components (and wire play allows you to reposition the cap out of the way).

3. Tag and disconnect the spark plug wires from the distributor cap towers. THIS STEP IS CRITICAL. Do not attempt to rewire the cap based only on a diagram, this too often leads to confusion and miswiring.
4. Disconnect the ignition coil lead from the distributor cap.
5. Loosen the distributor cap hold-down screws and/or release the hold-down clamps. Most original equipment distributors and caps utilize the hold-down screws.
6. Carefully lift the distributor cap STRAIGHT up and off the distributor in order to prevent damage to the rotor blade and spring.
7. If necessary, grasp the rotor by hand and pull upward to remove it from the distributor shaft and armature.
8. Inspect both the distributor cap and rotor for damage (replace as necessary).

To install:

9. Align the locating boss on the rotor with the hole on the armature, then carefully seat the rotor on the distributor shaft. Make sure the rotor is fully seated, but do not force it as the plastic components often break easily.
10. Position the distributor cap on the base, noting the square alignment locator.
11. Secure the cap using the hold-down screws and/or the release clamps. If used, tighten the cap hold-down screws to 18–23 inch lbs. (2.0–2.6 Nm).
12. Connect the ignition coil lead to the center tower of the distributor cap.
13. If removed, connect the spark plug wire leads as tagged during removal.
14. If equipped, reposition and seat the protective rubber boot over the distributor assembly.
15. Connect the negative battery cable.

INSPECTION

See Figures 102 and 103

After removing the distributor cap and rotor, clean the components (both inside and outside of the cap) using soap and water. If compressed air is available, carefully dry the components (wearing safety goggles) or allow the parts to air dry. You can dry them with a clean, soft cloth, just don't leave any lint or moisture behind.

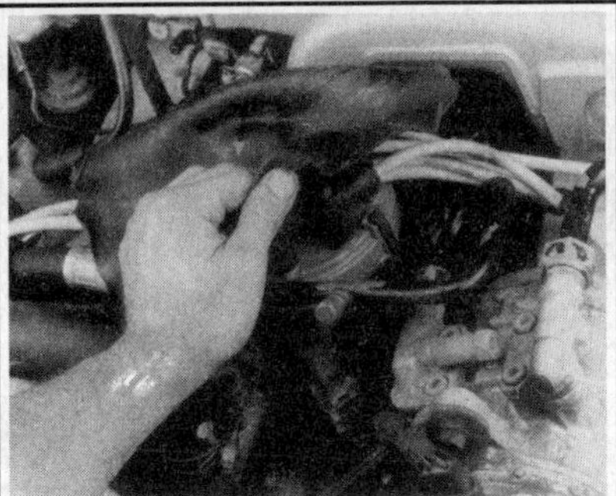

88151P17

Fig. 96 If equipped, remove the protective rubber boot from the top of the distributor assembly

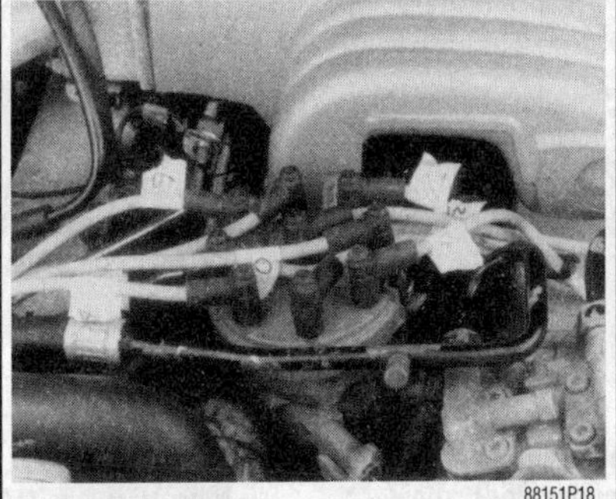

88151P18

Fig. 97 Tag ALL of the spark plug wires before disconnecting them

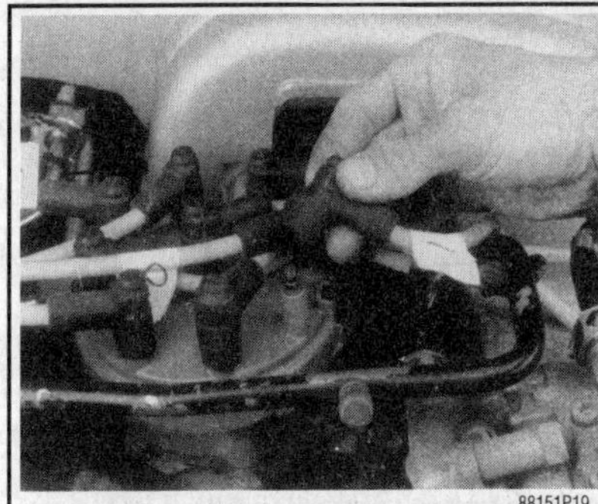

88151P19

Fig. 98 Disconnect some or all of the wires (as necessary for the job) from the cap

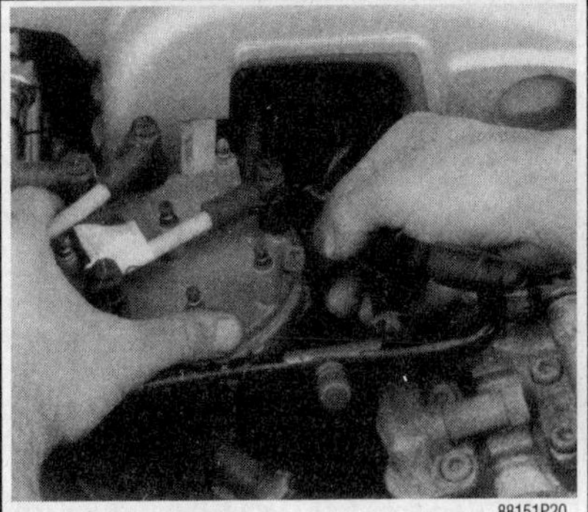

88151P20

Fig. 99 Release the cap hold-down screws and/or (in this case) the retaining clamps

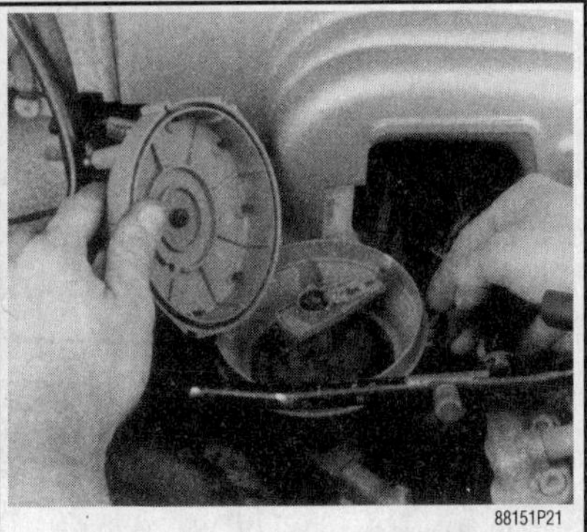

88151P21

Fig. 100 Lift the cap from the distributor assembly

88151P22

Fig. 101 If necessary, grasp and pull the rotor from the distributor shaft

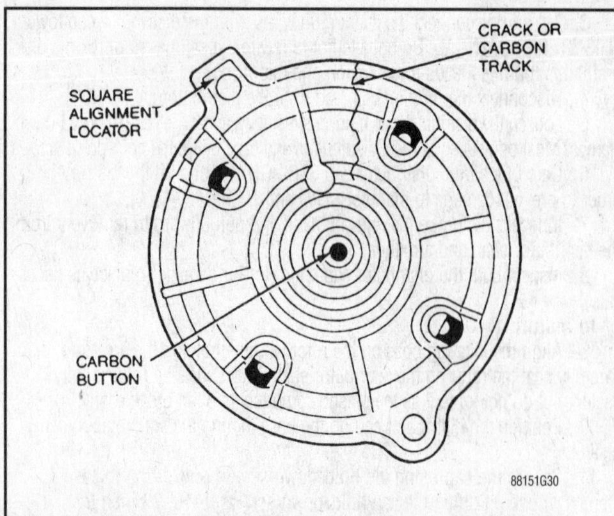

Fig. 102 Check the distributor cap for cracks, a damaged carbon button or carbon tracks

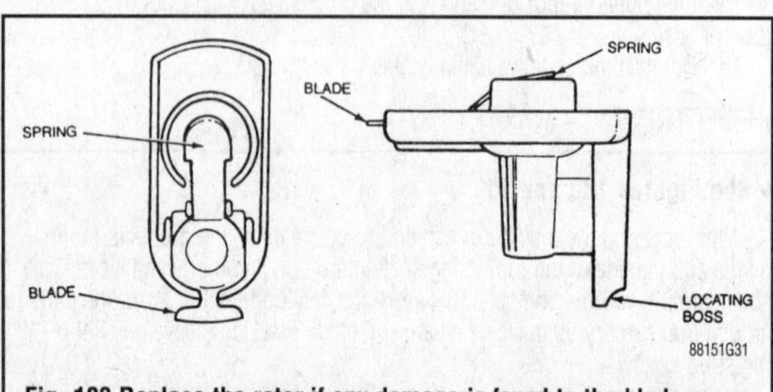

Fig. 103 Replace the rotor if any damage is found to the blade or spring

Once the cap and rotor have been thoroughly cleaned, check for cracks, carbon tracks, burns or other physical damage. Make sure the distributor cap's carbon button is free of damage. Check the cap terminals for dirt or corrosion. Always check the rotor blade and spring closely for damage. Replace any components where damage is found.

Ignition Timing

➡**No periodic checking or adjustment of the ignition timing is necessary for any of the vehicles covered by this manual. However, the distributor ignition system used by the 2.3L (VIN A) and 5.0L engines does allow for both, should the distributor be removed and installed or otherwise disturbed.**

GENERAL INFORMATION

Ignition timing is the measurement, in degrees of crankshaft rotation, of the point at which the spark plugs fire in each of the cylinders. It is measured in degrees before or after Top Dead Center (TDC) of the compression stroke.

Because it takes a fraction of a second for the spark plug to ignite the mixture in the cylinder, the spark plug must fire a little before the piston reaches TDC. Otherwise, the mixture will not be completely ignited as the piston passes TDC and the full power of the explosion will not be used by the engine.

The timing measurement is given in degrees of crankshaft rotation before the piston reaches TDC (BTDC). If the setting for the ignition timing is 5° BTDC, the spark plug must fire 5° before each piston reaches TDC. This only holds true, however, when the engine is at idle speed.

As the engine speed increases, the pistons go faster. The spark plugs have to ignite the fuel even sooner if it is to be completely ignited when the piston reaches TDC. On all engines covered by this manual, spark timing changes are accomplished electronically by the engine and ignition control computers.

If the ignition is set too far advanced (BTDC), the ignition and expansion of the fuel in the cylinder will occur too soon and tend to force the piston down while it is still traveling up. This causes engine ping. If the ignition spark is set too far retarded, after TDC (ATDC), the piston will have already passed TDC and started on its way down when the fuel is ignited. This will cause the piston to be forced down for only a portion of its travel. This will result in poor engine performance and lack of power.

Timing marks consisting of O marks or scales can be found on the rim of the crankshaft pulley and the timing cover. The mark(s) on the pulley correspond(s) to the position of the piston in the number 1 cylinder. A stroboscopic (dynamic) timing light is used, which is hooked into the circuit of the No. 1 cylinder spark plug. Every time the spark plug fires, the timing light flashes. By aiming the timing light at the timing marks while the engine is running, the exact position of the piston within the cylinder can be easily read since the stroboscopic flash makes the pulley appear to be standing still. Proper timing is indicated when the mark and scale are in proper alignment.

Because these vehicles utilize high voltage, electronic ignition systems, only a timing light with an inductive pickup should be used. This pickup simply clamps onto the No. 1 spark plug wire, eliminating the adapter. It is not susceptible to cross-firing or false triggering, which may occur with a conventional light, due to the greater voltages produced by electronic ignition.

CHECKING & ADJUSTING

2.3L (VIN A) and 5.0L Engines

➧ **See Figures 104, 105, 106 and 107**

SETTING INITIAL (BASE) TIMING

➡**Specific instructions and specifications for setting initial timing can be found in the Vehicle Emission Control Information (VECI) label in the engine compartment. Because this label contains information regarding any specific calibration requirements for YOUR vehicle, those instructions and specifications should be followed if they differ from the following.**

This procedure should not be used as a periodic maintenance adjustment. Timing should only be set after the distributor has been disturbed (removed and re-installed) in some way. If problems are encountered setting the initial timing with this procedure and no mechanical causes are found, follow the spark timing advance check procedure found later in this section.

➡**Do not change the ignition timing by the use of a different octane rod without having the proper authority to do so. Federal emission requirements will be affected.**

1. Start the engine and allow it to run until it reaches normal operating temperature.

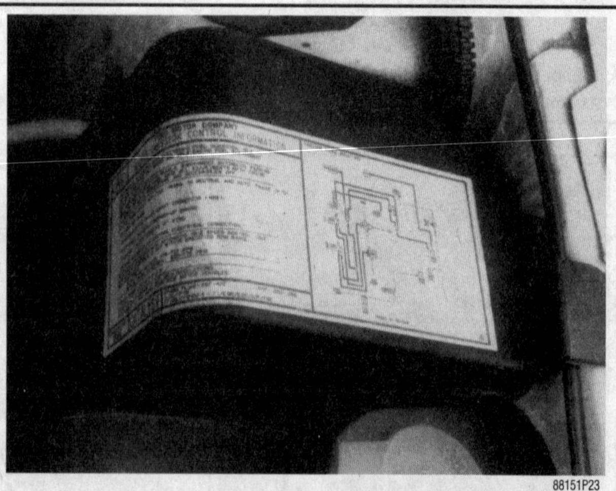

Fig. 104 The information found on the VECI is specific to YOUR car and should always be used if it differs from another source

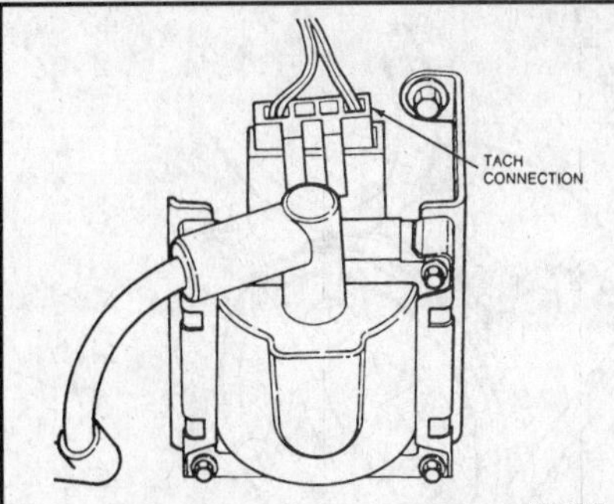

Fig. 105 Using an alligator clip a tachometer may be hooked-up to the ignition cold connector

Fig. 106 If adjustment is necessary, loosen the distributor hold-down bolt

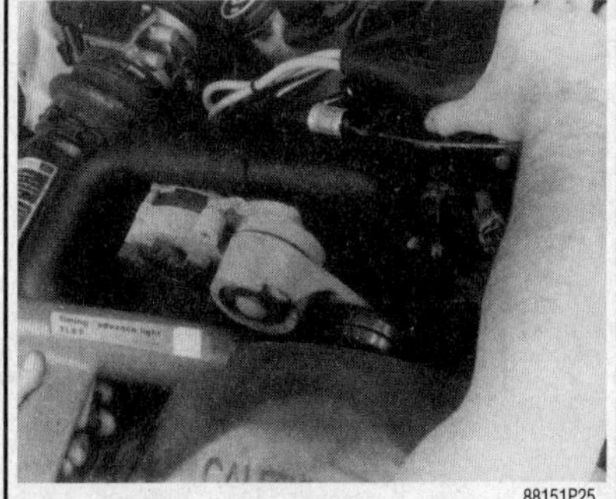

Fig. 107 Adjust the timing by rotating the distributor while watching the timing marks

⁂ CAUTION

NEVER run an engine in a garage or building without proper ventilation. Carbon monoxide will quickly enter the body, excluding oxygen from the blood stream. This condition will cause dizziness, sleepiness and eventually death.

2. Once normal operating temperature has been reached, shut the engine **OFF**.
3. Firmly apply the parking brake and block the drive wheels. Place the transmission in **P** (A/T) or **NEUTRAL** (M/T, as applicable.
4. Make sure heater and A/C, along with all other accessories are in the OFF position.
5. Connect an inductive timing light, such as the Rotunda 059-00006 or equivalent, to the No. 1 spark plug wire, according the tool manufacturer's instructions.
6. Connect a tachometer to the ignition coil connection using an alligator clip. This can be done by inserting the alligator clip into the back of the connector, onto the dark green/yellow dotted wire.

➡DO NOT allow the alligator clip to accidentally ground to a metal surface while attached to the coil connector as that could permanently damage the ignition coil.

7. Disconnect the single wire in-line SPOUT connector which connect the control computer (usually terminal 36) to the ignition control module. This will prevent the electronic ignition from advancing the timing during the set procedure.
8. Using a suitable socket or wrench, loosen the distributor hold-down bolt slightly at this time, BUT DO NOT ALLOW THE DISTRIBUTOR TO MOVE or timing will have to be set regardless of the current conditions.

➡A remote starter must NOT be used to start the vehicle when setting the initial ignition timing. Disconnecting the start wire at the starter relay will cause the ignition control module to revert to Start Mode timing after the vehicle is started. Reconnecting the start wire after the vehicle is running WILL NOT correct the timing.

9. Start the engine (using the ignition key and NOT a remote starter to assure timing will be set correctly) and allow the engine to return to normal operating temperature.
10. With the engine running at the specified rpm, check the initial timing. If adjustments must be made, rotate the distributor while watching the timing marks. Once proper adjustment has been reached, make sure the distributor is not disturbed until the hold-down bolt can be secured.
11. Reconnect the single wire in-line SPOUT connector and check the timing to verify that the distributor is now advancing beyond the initial setting.
12. Shut the engine **OFF** and tighten the distributor bolt while CAREFULLY holding the distributor from turning. If the distributor moves, you will have to start the engine and reset the timing.
13. Restart the engine and repeat the procedure to check the timing and verify that it did not change
14. Shut the engine **OFF**, then disconnect the tachometer and timing light.

CHECKING SPARK TIMING ADVANCE

Spark timing advance is controlled by the EEC system. This procedure checks the capability of the ignition module to receive the spark timing command from the EEC module. The use of a volt/ohmmeter is required.

1. Turn the ignition switch **OFF.**
2. Disconnect the pin-in-line connector (SPOUT connector) near the TFI module.
3. Start the engine and measure the voltage, at idle, from the SPOUT connector to the distributor base. The reading should equal battery voltage.
4. If the result is okay, the problem lies within the EEC-IV system.
5. If the result was not satisfactory, separate the wiring harness connector from the ignition module. Check for damage, corrosion or dirt. Service as necessary.
6. Measure the resistance between terminal No. 5 and the pin-in-line connector. This test is done at the ignition module connector only. The reading should be less than 5 ohms.
7. If the reading is okay, replace the TFI module.
8. If the result was not satisfactory, service the wiring between the pin in-line connector and the TFI connector.

2.3L (VIN M) Engine

The 2.3L (VIN M) engine utilizes a Distributorless Ignition System (DIS). On this system, ignition coil packs fire the spark plugs directly through the spark plug wires. All spark timing and advance is determined by the ignition control module and engine control computer. No ignition timing adjustments are necessary or possible.

Valve Lash

No periodic valve lash adjustments are necessary or possible on these engines. Both the 2.3L and 5.0L engines utilize hydraulic valvetrains to automatically maintain proper valve lash. If an engine is determined to have a valve tap, the following inspection procedures can help determine if the hydraulic adjuster is to blame.

INSPECTION

2.3L Engine

➧ See Figures 108 and 109

1. Turn the ignition **OFF** and disconnect the negative battery cable.
2. Remove the valve cover.
3. Position the camshaft so that the base circle of the lobe is facing the cam follower of the valve to be checked.
4. Using valve spring compressor tool T88T–6565–BH or equivalent, slowly apply pressure to the cam follower until the lash adjuster is completely collapsed.
5. With the follower collapsed, insert a feeler gauge between the base circle of the camshaft and the follower. The clearance should be 0.040–0.050 in. (1.0–1.3 mm).
6. If the clearance is excessive, remove the cam follower and inspect for damage.

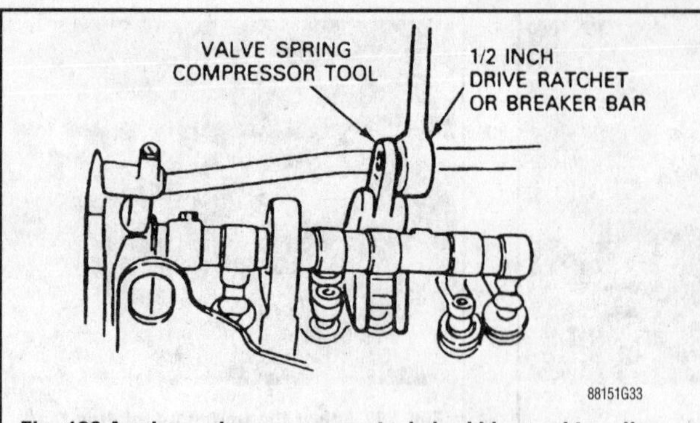

Fig. 108 A valve spring compressor tool should be used to collapse the lash adjuster—2.3L

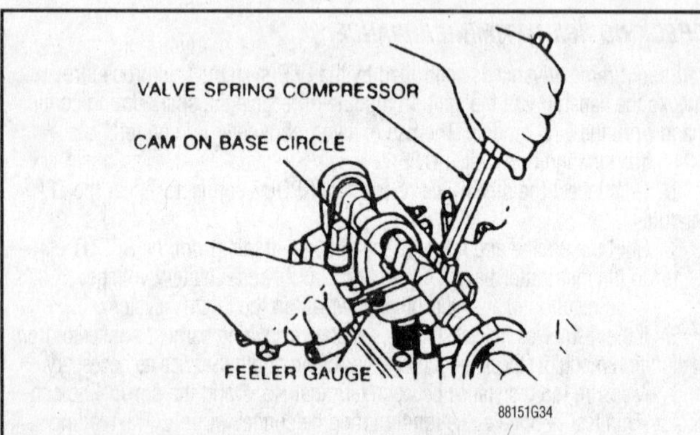

Fig. 109 With the adjuster collapsed, use a feeler gauge to check for proper valve clearance

7. If the cam follower appears to be intact and not excessively worn, measure the assembled height of the valve spring to make sure the valve is not sticking.

8. If the assembled height of the valve spring is correct, check the camshaft for wear. If the camshaft dimensions are correct, replace the lash adjuster.

9. Install the valve cover and any other removed components.

5.0L Engine

See Figures 110 and 111

The valve lash is not adjustable. If the collapsed lifter clearance is incorrect, different length replacement pushrods are available to compensate.

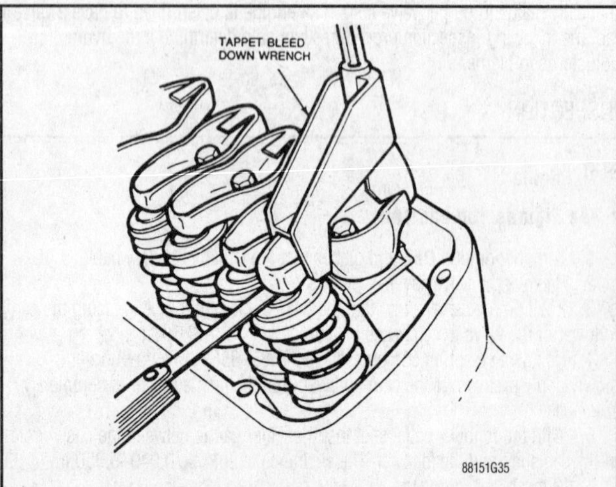

Fig. 110 Use a tappet bleed down wrench and a feeler gauge to check valve clearance

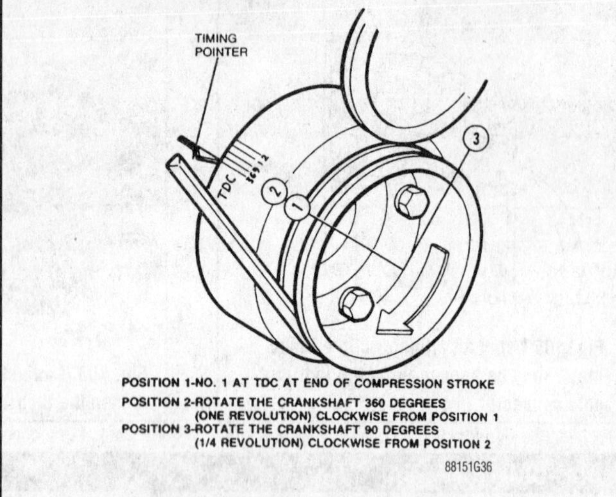

Fig. 111 To check all of the valves, the crankshaft must be turned to 3 different positions

1. Remove the valve cover(s) for access to the valves whose lash is being checked.

2. Either have an assistant help by cranking the engine or install a remote starter switch. Crank the engine with the ignition switch **OFF** until No.1 piston is at TDC on the compression stroke.

➡Follow the tool manufacturer's instructions when installing the remote starter switch. In most cases, the BROWN lead (terminal I) and the RED/BLUE lead (terminal S) at the starter relay should be disconnected. Then, install the remove starter switch between the battery and terminal S of the relay.

3. With the crankshaft in the positions designated in the steps below, piston lifter bleed-down wrench T71P–6513–B, or equivalent, on the rocker arm. Slowly apply pressure to bleed down the lifter until the plunger is completely bottomed. Hold the lifter in this position and check the available clearance between the rocker arm and the valve stem tip with a feeler gauge.

4. The clearance should be 0.123–0.146 in (3.1–3.7mm). If the clearance is less than specified, install a shorter pushrod to compensate. If the clearance is greater than specified, install a longer pushrod.

➡An easy way to tell if a cylinder is at TDC of the compression stroke is to watch that cylinder's valves as the engine is cranked or rotated. If the valves remain closed (the rockers don't move) as the piston approaches the top of it's travel, that piston is on its compression stroke (the closed valves were allowing compression to build). If instead, a valve opens as the piston travels upward (releasing compression in that cylinder) then that piston is on its exhaust stroke.

5. The following valves can be checked with the engine in position No. 1, with the No. 1 piston at TDC on the compression stroke:
- No. 1 intake and No. 1 exhaust
- No. 4 intake and No. 3 exhaust
- No. 8 intake and No. 7 exhaust

6. Rotate the engine 360° (1 full revolution) from the 1st position (No. 1 is now on its exhaust stroke) and check the following valves:
- No. 3 intake and No. 2 exhaust
- No. 7 intake and No. 6 exhaust

7. Rotate the engine 90° (¼ revolution) from the 2nd position and check the following valves:
- No. 2 intake and No. 4 exhaust
- No. 5 intake and No. 5 exhaust
- No. 6 intake and No. 8 exhaust

Idle Speed and Mixture Adjustments

The engines covered by this manual utilize sophisticated multi-port fuel injection systems in which an engine control computer utilizes information from various sensors to control idle speed and air fuel mixtures. No periodic adjustments are either necessary or possible on these systems. If a problem is suspected, please refer to Sections 4 and 5 of this manual for more information on electronic engine controls and fuel injection.

Air Conditioning System

SYSTEM SERVICE & REPAIR

➡It is recommended that the A/C system be serviced by an EPA Section 609 certified automotive technician utilizing a refrigerant recovery/recycling machine.

The do-it-yourselfer should not service his/her own vehicle's A/C system for many reasons, including legal concerns, personal injury, environmental damage and cost.

According to the U.S. Clean Air Act, it is a federal crime to service or repair (involving the refrigerant) a Motor Vehicle Air Conditioning (MVAC) system for money without being EPA certified. It is also illegal to vent R-12 refrigerant into the atmosphere. State and/or local laws may be more strict than the federal regulations, so be sure to check with your state and/or local authorities for further information.

➡Federal law dictates that a fine of up to $25,000 may be levied on people convicted of venting refrigerant into the atmosphere.

When servicing an A/C system you run the risk of handling or coming in contact with refrigerant, which may result in skin or eye irritation or frostbite. Although low in toxicity (due to chemical stability), inhalation of concentrated refrigerant fumes is dangerous and can result in death; cases of fatal cardiac arrhythmia have been reported in people accidentally subjected to high levels of refrigerant. Some early symptoms include loss of concentration and drowsiness.

Also, some refrigerants can decompose at high temperatures (near gas heaters or open flame), which may result in hydrofluoric acid, hydrochloric acid and phosgene (a fatal nerve gas).

It is usually more economically feasible to have a certified MVAC automotive technician perform A/C system service on your vehicle.

PREVENTIVE MAINTENANCE

Although the A/C system should not be serviced by the do-it-yourselfer, preventive maintenance should be practiced to help maintain the efficiency of the vehicle's A/C system. Be sure to perform the following:

- The easiest and most important preventive maintenance for your A/C system is to be sure that it is used on a regular basis. Running the system for five minutes each month (no matter what the season) will help ensure that the seals and all internal components remain lubricated.

➡Some vehicles automatically operate the A/C system compressor whenever the windshield defroster is activated. Therefore, the A/C system would not need to be operated each month if the defroster was used.

- In order to prevent heater core freeze-up during A/C operation, it is necessary to maintain proper antifreeze protection. Be sure to properly maintain the engine cooling system.
- Any obstruction of or damage to the condenser configuration will restrict air flow which is essential to its efficient operation. Keep this unit clean and in proper physical shape.

➡Bug screens which are mounted in front of the condenser (unless they are original equipment) are regarded as obstructions.

- The condensation drain tube expels any water which accumulates on the bottom of the evaporator housing into the engine compartment. If this tube is obstructed, the air conditioning performance can be restricted and condensation buildup can spill over onto the vehicle's floor.

SYSTEM INSPECTION

Although the A/C system should not be serviced by the do-it-yourselfer, system inspections should be performed to help maintain the efficiency of the vehicle's A/C system. Be sure to perform the following:

The easiest and often most important check for the air conditioning system consists of a visual inspection of the system components. Visually inspect the system for refrigerant leaks, damaged compressor clutch, abnormal compressor drive belt tension and/or condition, plugged evaporator drain tube, blocked condenser fins, disconnected or broken wires, blown fuses, corroded connections and poor insulation.

A refrigerant leak will usually appear as an oily residue at the leakage point in the system. The oily residue soon picks up dust or dirt particles from the surrounding air and appears greasy. Through time, this will build up and appear to be a heavy dirt impregnated grease.

For a thorough visual and operational inspection, check the following:

- Check the surface of the radiator and condenser for dirt, leaves or other material which might block air flow.
- Check for kinks in hoses and lines. Check the system for leaks.
- Make sure the drive belt is properly tensioned. During operation, make sure the belt is free of noise or slippage.
- Make sure the blower motor operates at all appropriate positions, then check for distribution of the air from all outlets.

➡Remember that in high humidity, air discharged from the vents may not feel as cold as expected, even if the system is working properly. This is because moisture in humid air retains heat more effectively than dry air, thereby making humid air more difficult to cool.

Windshield Wipers

ELEMENT (REFILL) CARE & REPLACEMENT

See Figures 112, 113 and 114

For maximum effectiveness and longest element life, the windshield and wiper blades should be kept clean. Dirt, tree sap, road tar and so on will cause streaking, smearing and blade deterioration if left on the glass. It is advisable to wash the windshield carefully with a commercial glass cleaner at least once a month. Wipe off the rubber blades with the wet rag afterwards. Do not attempt to move wipers across the windshield by hand; damage to the motor and drive mechanism will result.

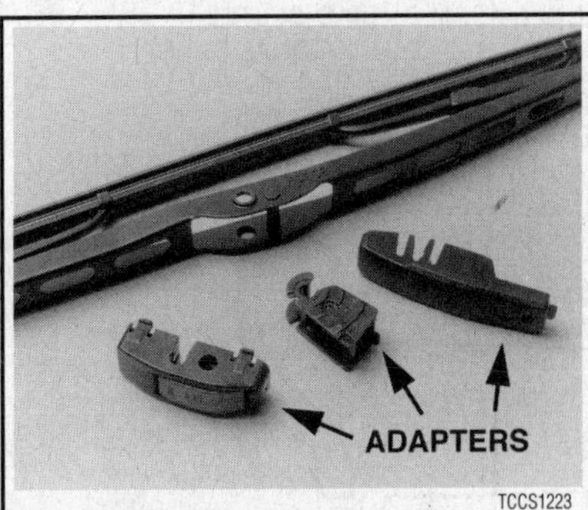

Fig. 112 Most aftermarket blades are available with multiple adapters to fit different vehicles

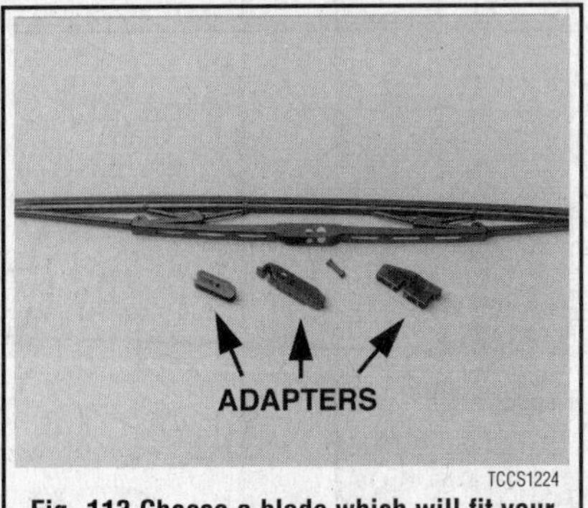

Fig. 113 Choose a blade which will fit your vehicle, and that will be readily available next time you need blades

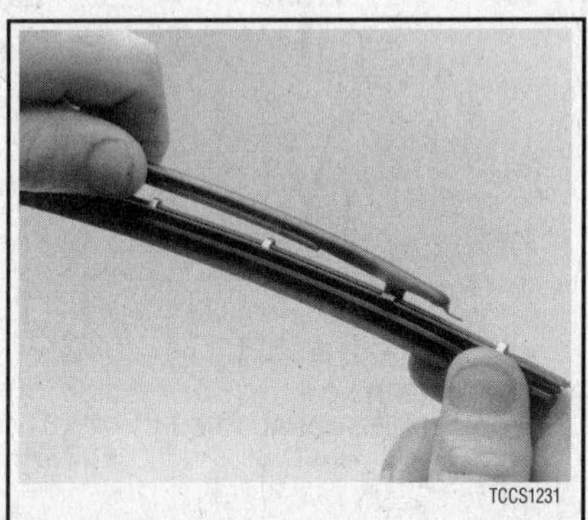

Fig. 114 When installed, be certain the blade is fully inserted into the backing

To inspect and/or replace the wiper blade elements, place the wiper switch in the **LOW** speed position and the ignition switch in the **ACC** position. When the wiper blades are approximately vertical on the windshield, turn the ignition switch to **OFF**.

Examine the wiper blade elements. If they are found to be cracked, broken or torn, they should be replaced immediately. Replacement intervals will vary with usage, although ozone deterioration usually limits element life to about one year. If the wiper pattern is smeared or streaked, or if the blade chatters across the glass, the elements should be replaced. It is easiest and most sensible to replace the elements in pairs.

If your vehicle is equipped with aftermarket blades, there are several different types of refills and your vehicle might have any kind. Aftermarket blades and arms rarely use the exact same type blade or refill as the original equipment.

Regardless of the type of refill used, be sure to follow the part manufacturer's instructions closely. Make sure that all of the frame jaws are engaged as the refill is pushed into place and locked. If the metal blade holder and frame are allowed to touch the glass during wiper operation, the glass will be scratched.

Tires and Wheels

Common sense and good driving habits will afford maximum tire life. Make sure that you don't overload the vehicle or run with incorrect pressure in the tires. Either of these will increase tread wear. Fast starts, sudden stops and sharp cornering are hard on tires and will shorten their useful life span.

➡For optimum tire life, keep the tires properly inflated, rotate them often and have the wheel alignment checked periodically.

Inspect your tires frequently. Be especially careful to watch for bubbles in the tread or sidewall, deep cuts or underinflation. Replace any tires with bubbles in the sidewall. If cuts are so deep that they penetrate to the cords, discard the tire. Any cut in the sidewall of a radial tire renders it unsafe. Also look for uneven tread wear patterns that may indicate the front end is out of alignment or that the tires are out of balance.

TIRE ROTATION

➧ See Figure 115

Tires must be rotated periodically to equalize wear patterns that vary with a tire's position on the vehicle. Tires will also wear in an uneven way as the front steering/suspension system wears to the point where the alignment should be reset.

Rotating the tires will ensure maximum life for the tires as a set, so you will not have to discard a tire early due to wear on only part of the tread. Regular rotation is required to equalize wear.

When rotating "unidirectional tires," make sure that they always roll in the same direction. This means that a tire used on the left side of the vehicle must not be switched to the right side and vice-versa. Such tires should only be rotated front-to-rear or rear-to-front, while always remaining on the same side of the vehicle. These tires are marked on the sidewall as to the direction of rotation; observe the marks when reinstalling the tire(s).

Some styled or "mag" wheels may have different offsets front to rear. In these cases, the rear wheels must not be used up front and vice-versa. Furthermore, if these wheels are equipped with unidirectional tires, they cannot be rotated unless the tire is remounted for the proper direction of rotation.

➡The compact or space-saver spare is strictly for emergency use. It must never be included in the tire rotation or placed on the vehicle for everyday use.

Front

Front

(FOR NON-DIRECTIONAL TIRES AND WHEELS)

(FOR DIRECTIONAL TIRES AND WHEELS)

TCCS1260

Fig. 115 Compact spare tires must NEVER be used in the rotation pattern

TIRE DESIGN

➧ See Figure 116

For maximum satisfaction, tires should be used in sets of four. Mixing of different brands or types (radial, bias-belted, fiberglass belted) should be avoided. In most cases, the vehicle manufacturer has designated a type of tire on which the vehicle will perform best. Your first choice when replacing tires should be to use the same type of tire that the manufacturer recommends.

When radial tires are used, tire sizes and wheel diameters should be selected to maintain ground clearance and tire load capacity equivalent to the original specified tire. Radial tires should always be used in sets of four.

⁂ CAUTION

Radial tires should never be used on only the front axle.

When selecting tires, pay attention to the original size as marked on the tire. Most tires are described using an industry size code sometimes referred to as P-Metric. This allows the exact identification of the tire specifications, regardless of the manufacturer. If selecting a different tire size or brand, remember to check the installed tire for any sign of interference with the body or suspension while the vehicle is stopping, turning sharply or heavily loaded.

Snow Tires

Good radial tires can produce a big advantage in slippery weather, but in snow, a street radial tire does not have sufficient tread to provide traction and control. The small grooves of a street tire quickly pack with snow and the tire behaves like a billiard ball on a marble floor. The more open, chunky tread of a snow tire will self-clean as the tire turns, providing much better grip on snowy surfaces.

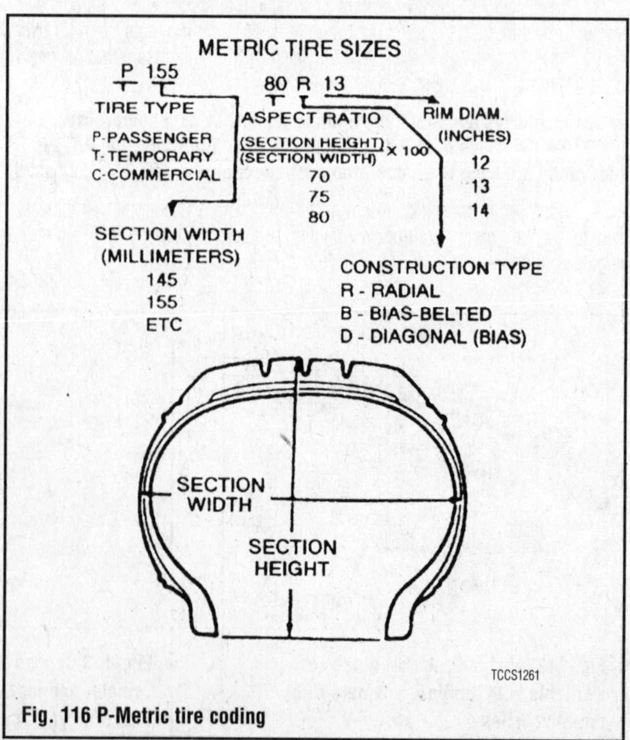

Fig. 116 P-Metric tire coding

To satisfy municipalities requiring snow tires during weather emergencies, most snow tires carry either an M + S designation after the tire size stamped on the sidewall, or the designation "all-season." In general, no change in tire size is necessary when buying snow tires.

Most manufacturers strongly recommend the use of 4 snow tires on their vehicles for reasons of stability. If snow tires are fitted only to the drive wheels, the opposite end of the vehicle may become very unstable when braking or turning on slippery surfaces. This instability can lead to unpleasant endings if the driver can't counteract the slide in time.

Note that snow tires, whether 2 or 4, will affect vehicle handling in all non-snow situations. The stiffer, heavier snow tires will noticeably change the turning and braking characteristics of the vehicle. Once the snow tires are installed, you must re-learn the behavior of the vehicle and drive accordingly.

➡Consider buying extra wheels on which to mount the snow tires. Once done, the "snow wheels" can be installed and removed as needed. This eliminates the potential damage to tires or wheels from seasonal removal and installation. Even if your vehicle has styled wheels, see if inexpensive steel wheels are available. Although the look of the vehicle will change, the expensive wheels will be protected from salt, curb hits and pothole damage.

TIRE STORAGE

If they are mounted on wheels, store the tires at proper inflation pressure. All tires should be kept in a cool, dry place. If they are stored in the garage or basement, do not let them stand on a concrete floor; set them on strips of wood, a mat or a large stack of newspaper. Keeping them away from direct moisture is of paramount importance. Tires should not be stored upright, but in a flat position.

INFLATION & INSPECTION

➧ See Figures 117 thru 122

The importance of proper tire inflation cannot be overemphasized. A tire employs air as part of its structure. It is designed around the supporting strength of the air at a specified pressure. For this reason, improper inflation drastically reduces the tire's ability to perform as intended. A tire will lose some air in day-to-day use; having to add a few pounds of air periodically is not necessarily a sign of a leaking tire.

Two items should be a permanent fixture in every glove compartment: an accurate tire pressure gauge and a tread depth gauge. Check the tire pressure (including the spare) regularly with a pocket type gauge. Too often, the gauge on the end of the air hose at your corner garage is not accurate because it suffers too much abuse. Always check tire pressure when the tires are cold, as pressure increases with temperature. If you must move the vehicle to check the tire inflation, do not drive more than a mile before checking. A cold tire is generally one that has not been driven for more than three hours.

A plate or sticker is normally provided somewhere in the vehicle (door post, hood, tailgate or trunk lid) which shows the proper pressure for the tires. Never counteract excessive pressure build-up by bleeding off air pressure (letting some air out). This will cause the tire to run hotter and wear quicker.

TCCS1095

Fig. 117 Tires with deep cuts, or cuts which bulge, should be replaced immediately

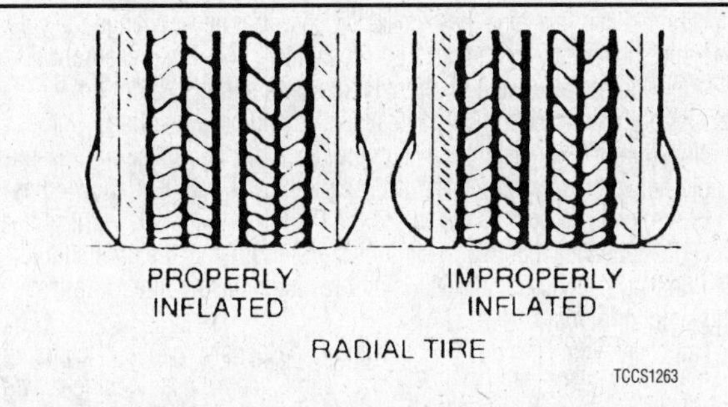

Fig. 118 Radial tires have a characteristic sidewall bulge; don't try to measure pressure by looking at the tire. Use a quality air pressure gauge

CONDITION	RAPID WEAR AT SHOULDERS	RAPID WEAR AT CENTER	CRACKED TREADS	WEAR ON ONE SIDE	FEATHERED EDGE	BALD SPOTS	SCALLOPED WEAR
EFFECT	1. 2.						
CAUSE	UNDER-INFLATION OR LACK OF ROTATION	OVER-INFLATION OR LACK OF ROTATION	UNDER-INFLATION OR EXCESSIVE SPEED*	EXCESSIVE CAMBER	INCORRECT TOE	UNBALANCED WHEEL OR TIRE DEFECT*	LACK OF ROTATION OF TIRES OR WORN OR OUT-OF-ALIGNMENT SUSPENSION.
CORRECTION	ADJUST PRESSURE TO SPECIFICATIONS WHEN TIRES ARE COOL ROTATE TIRES			ADJUST CAMBER TO SPECIFICATIONS	ADJUST TOE-IN TO SPECIFICATIONS	DYNAMIC OR STATIC BALANCE WHEELS	ROTATE TIRES AND INSPECT SUSPENSION

*HAVE TIRE INSPECTED FOR FURTHER USE.

TCCS1267

Fig. 119 Common tire wear patterns and causes

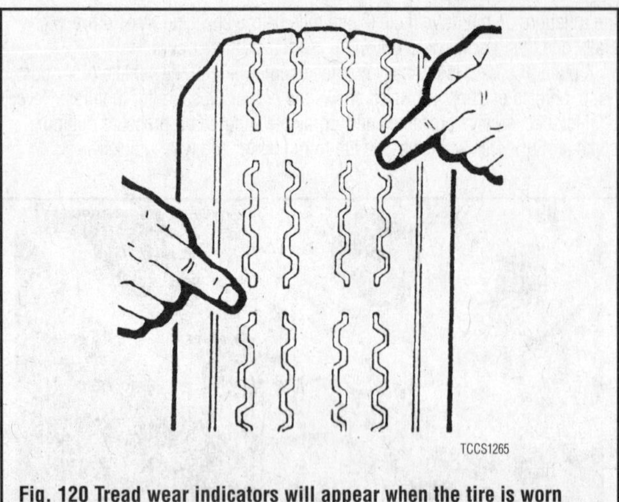

Fig. 120 Tread wear indicators will appear when the tire is worn

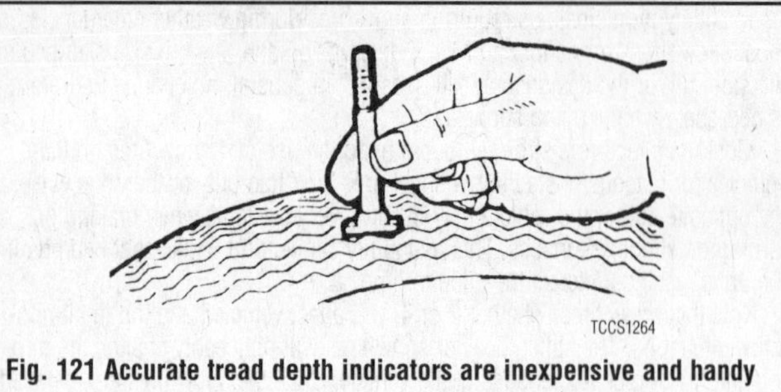

Fig. 121 Accurate tread depth indicators are inexpensive and handy

Fig. 122 A penny works well for a quick check of tread depth

CAUTION

Never exceed the maximum tire pressure embossed on the tire! This is the pressure to be used when the tire is at maximum loading, but it is rarely the correct pressure for everyday driving. Consult the owner's manual or the tire pressure sticker for the correct tire pressure.

Once you've maintained the correct tire pressures for several weeks, you'll be familiar with the vehicle's braking and handling personality. Slight adjustments in tire pressures can fine-tune these characteristics, but never change the cold pressure specification by more than 2 psi. A slightly softer tire pressure will give a softer ride but also yield lower fuel mileage. A slightly harder tire will give crisper dry road handling but can cause skidding on wet surfaces. Unless you're fully attuned to the vehicle, stick to the recommended inflation pressures.

All automotive tires have built-in tread wear indicator bars that show up as ½ in. (13mm) wide smooth bands across the tire when 1⁄16 in. (1.5mm) of tread remains. The appearance of tread wear indicators means that the tires should be replaced. In fact, many states have laws prohibiting the use of tires with less than this amount of tread.

You can check your own tread depth with an inexpensive gauge or by using a Lincoln head penny. Slip the Lincoln penny (with Lincoln's head upside-down) into several tread grooves. If you can see the top of Lincoln's head in 2 adjacent grooves, the tire has less than 1⁄16 in. (1.5mm) tread left and should be replaced. You can measure snow tires in the same manner by using the "tails" side of the Lincoln penny. If you can see the top of the Lincoln memorial, it's time to replace the snow tire(s).

Clutch

ADJUSTMENT

Mustangs equipped with a manual transmission utilize a self-adjusting clutch, but every 5000 miles (8000 km) you should make sure the clutch pedal and cable are adjusting themselves. To do this, place the transmission in 1st gear, then reach down, grab the clutch pedal and pull upward (very little effort, a force of 10 lbs/4.5 Kg should be sufficient) until it stops. Finally, depress the clutch pedal and listen for an audible "click." If you hear a sound, the clutch was in need of adjustment, and it has just adjusted itself.

FLUIDS AND LUBRICANTS

See Figures 123 and 124

General Information

FLUID DISPOSAL

Used fluids such as engine oil, transmission fluid, antifreeze and brake fluid are hazardous wastes and must be disposed of properly. Before draining any fluids, consult with your local authorities; in many areas waste oil, etc. is being accepted as a part of recycling programs. A number of service stations and auto parts stores are also accepting waste fluids for recycling.

Be sure of the recycling center's policies before draining any fluids, as many will not accept different fluids that have been mixed together.

FUEL AND ENGINE OIL RECOMMENDATIONS

Fuel

➡Some fuel additives contain chemicals that can damage the catalytic converter and/or oxygen sensor. Read all of the labels carefully before using any additive in the engine or fuel system.

All vehicles covered by this manual are designed to run on unleaded fuel. The use of a leaded fuel in a vehicle requiring unleaded fuel will plug the catalytic converter and render it inoperative. It will also increase exhaust backpressure to the point where engine output will be severely reduced. Obviously, use of leaded fuel should not be a problem, since most companies have stopped selling it for quite some time.

The minimum octane rating of the unleaded fuel being used must be at least 87 (as listed on the pumps), which usually means regular unleaded. Some areas may have 86 or even lower octanes available, which would make 87 midgrade or even premium. In these cases a minimum fuel octane of 87 should STILL be used.

Fuel should be selected for the brand and octane which performs best with your engine. Judge a gasoline by its ability to prevent pinging, its engine starting capabilities (cold and hot) and general all weather performance. The use of a fuel too low in octane (a measurement of anti-knock quality) will result in spark knock. Since many factors such as altitude, terrain, air temperature and humidity affect operating efficiency, knocking may result even though the recommended fuel is being used. If persistent knocking occurs, it may be necessary to switch to a different brand or grade of fuel. Continuous or heavy knocking may result in engine damage.

➡Your engine's fuel requirement can change with time, mainly due to carbon buildup, which will in turn change the compression ratio. If your engine pings or knocks switch to a higher grade of fuel. Sometimes just changing brands will cure the problem.

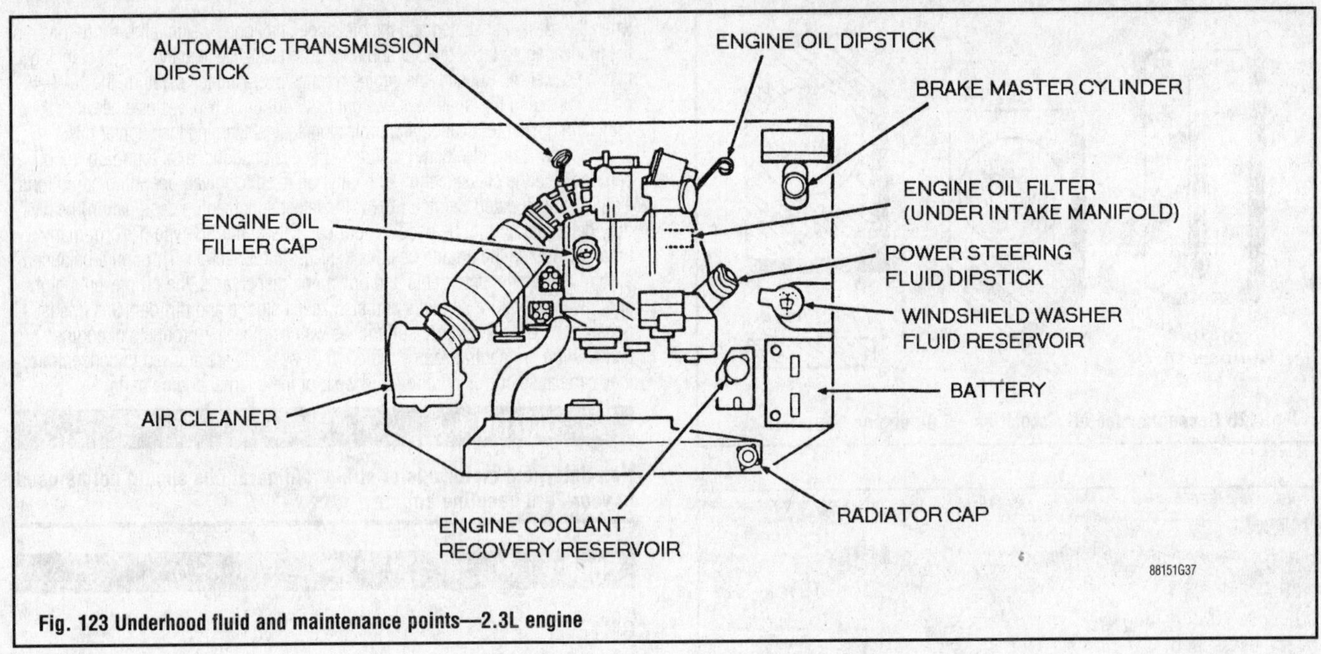

Fig. 123 Underhood fluid and maintenance points—2.3L engine

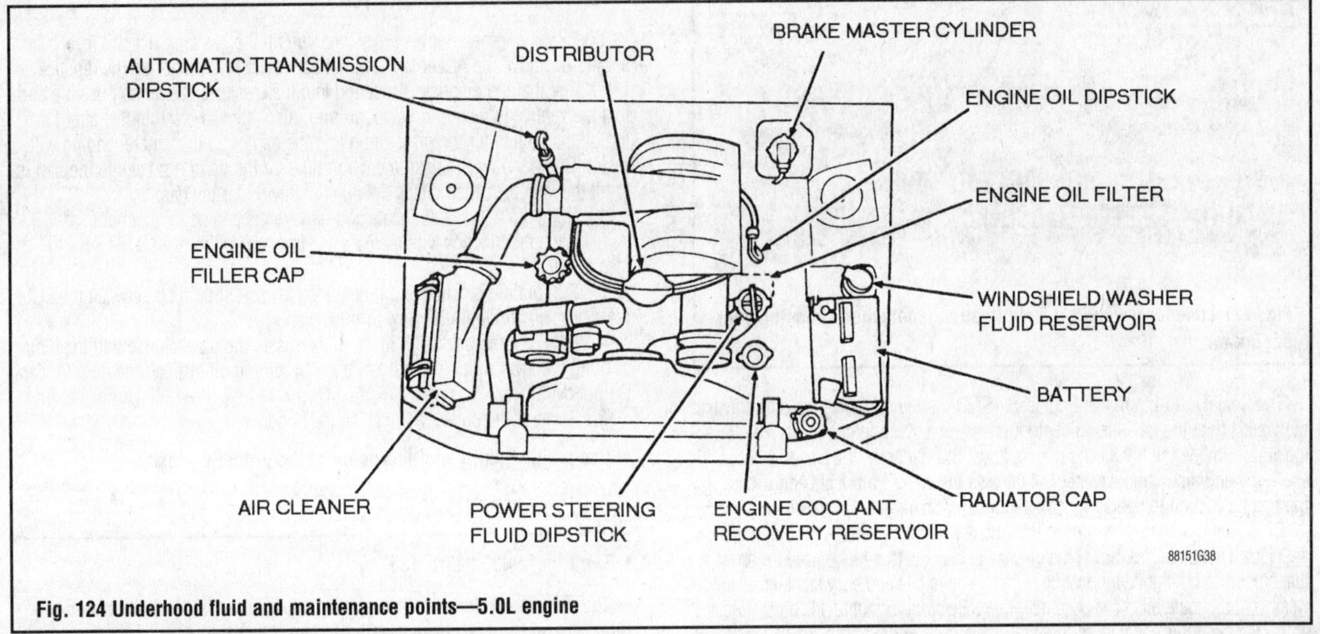

Fig. 124 Underhood fluid and maintenance points—5.0L engine

The other most important quality you should look for in a fuel is that it contains detergents designed to keep fuel injection systems clean. Many of the major fuel companies will display information right at the pumps telling you that their fuels contain these detergents. The use of a high-quality fuel which contains detergents will help assure trouble-free operation of your car's fuel system.

Oil

➧ See Figures 125, 126 and 127

The recommended oil viscosities for sustained temperatures ranging from below 0° (−18°C) to above 32°F (0°C) are listed in the section. They are broken down into multi-viscosities and single viscosities. Multi-viscosity oils are recommended because of their wider range of acceptable temperatures and driving conditions.

When adding oil to the crankcase or changing the oil and filter, it is important that oil of an equal quality to original equipment be used in your car. The use of inferior oils may void the warranty, damage your engine, or both.

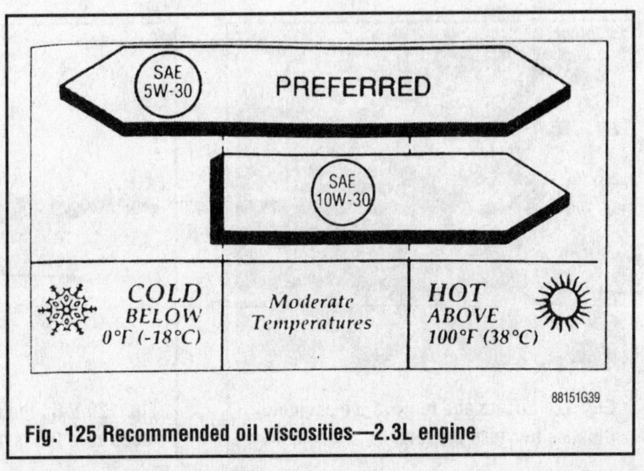

Fig. 125 Recommended oil viscosities—2.3L engine

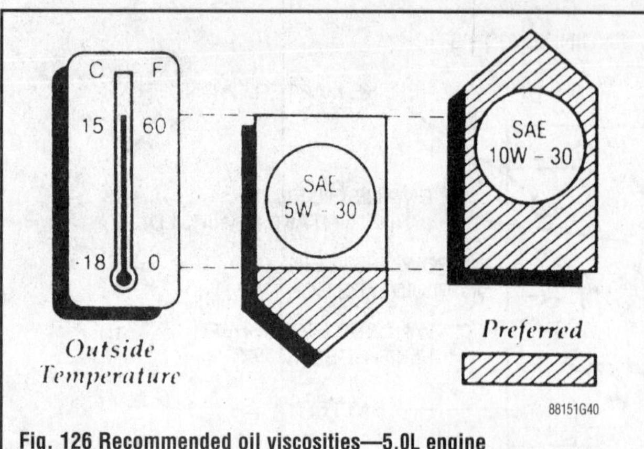

Fig. 126 Recommended oil viscosities—5.0L engine

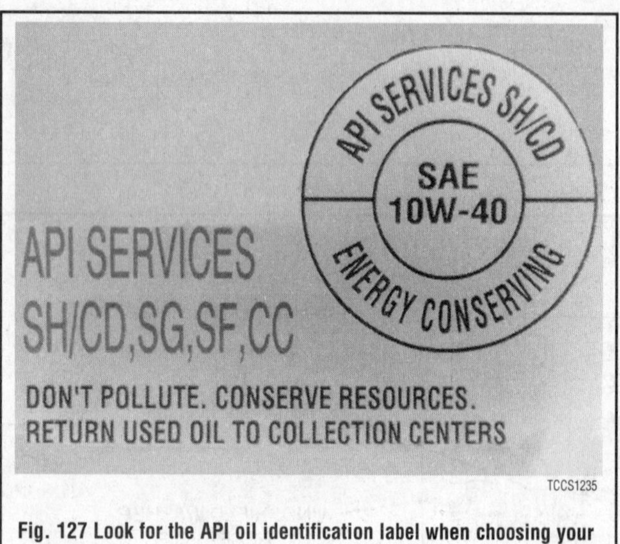

Fig. 127 Look for the API oil identification label when choosing your engine oil

The Society of Automotive Engineers (SAE) grade number of the oil indicates the viscosity of the oil—its ability to lubricate at a given temperature. The lower the SAE number, the lighter the oil; the lower the viscosity, the easier it is to crank the engine in cold weather but the less the oil will lubricate and protect the engine in high temperatures. This number is marked on every oil container.

Oil viscosities should be chosen from those oils recommended for the lowest anticipated temperatures during the oil change interval. Due to the need for an oil that embodies both good lubrication at high temperature and easy cranking in cold weather, multigrade oils have been developed. Basically, a multigrade oil is thinner at low temperatures and thicker at high temperatures. For example, a 10W–40 oil (the W stands for winter) exhibits the characteristics of a 10-weight (SAE 10) oil when the car is first started and the oil is cold. Its lighter weight allows it to travel to the lubricating surfaces quicker and offer less resistance to starter motor cranking than a heavier oil. But after the engine reaches operating temperature, the 10W–40 oil begins acting like straight 40-weight (SAE 40) oil. It behaves as a heavier oil, providing greater lubrication and protection against foaming than lighter oils.

The American Petroleum Institute (API) designations, also found on the oil can, indicate the classification of engine oil used for given operating conditions. Only oils designated Service SG (or the latest superceding designation) heavy-duty detergent should be used in your car. Oils of the SG-type perform many functions inside the engine besides their basic lubrication. Through a balanced system of metallic detergents and polymeric dispersants, the oil prevents high and low temperature deposits and also keeps sludge and dirt particles in suspension. Acids, particularly sulfuric, as well as other by-products of engine combustion are neutralized by the oil. If these acids are allowed to concentrate, they can cause corrosion and rapid wear of the internal engine parts.

**** CAUTION**

Non-detergent motor oils or straight mineral oils should not be used in your Ford gasoline engine

Engine

OIL LEVEL CHECK

See Figures 128, 129 and 130

Check the engine oil level every time you fill the gas tank. The oil level should be above the ADD mark and not above the FULL mark on the dipstick. Make sure that the dipstick is inserted into the crankcase as far as possible and that the vehicle is resting on level ground. Also, allow a few minutes after turning off the engine for the oil to drain into the pan or an inaccurate reading will result. One good way to assure enough time for the oil to run back to the pan is to fill the tank first, then check the oil after paying for the gas.

1. Open the hood, then locate and remove the engine oil dipstick.
2. Wipe the dipstick with a clean, lint-free rag and reinsert it. Be sure to insert it all the way.
3. Pull out the dipstick and note the oil level. It should be between the FULL (safe or max) and the ADD (low or min) marks.
4. If the level is below the lower mark, install the dipstick and add fresh oil to bring the level within the proper range by adding oil through the oil filler cap. Do not overfill.
5. Recheck the oil level and close the hood.

➡Use a high quality multigrade oil of the proper viscosity.

OIL AND FILTER CHANGE

See Figures 131 thru 137

➡The engine oil and oil filter should be changed at the recommended intervals on the Maintenance Chart. Though some manufacturer's have at times recommended changing the filter only at every other oil

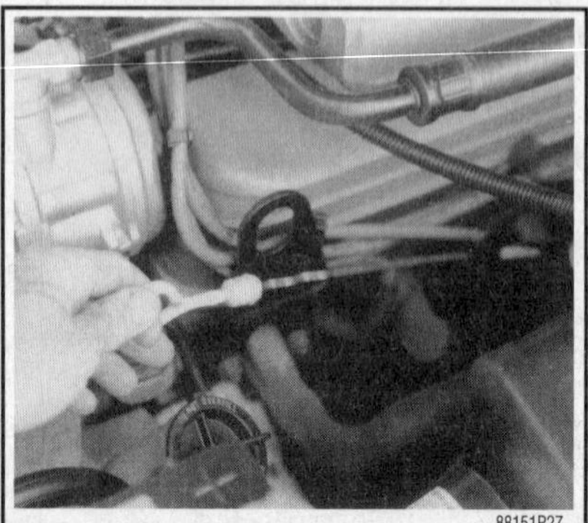

Fig. 128 Locate and remove the engine oil dipstick to check the level

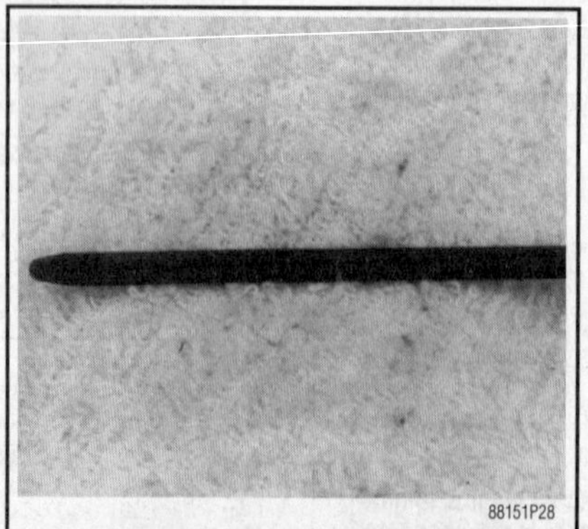

Fig. 129 Hold the dipstick horizontally and make sure the level is between the marks

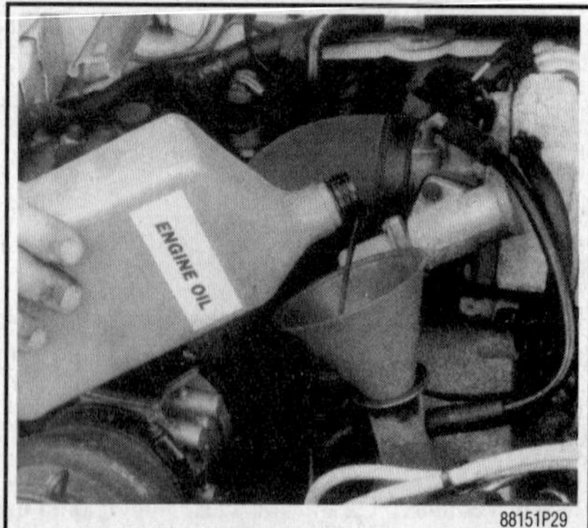

Fig. 130 If necessary add oil through the capped filler on the valve cover

88151P30

Fig. 131 Loosen the drain pan oil plug using a wrench or socket—front plug on 5.0L engine shown

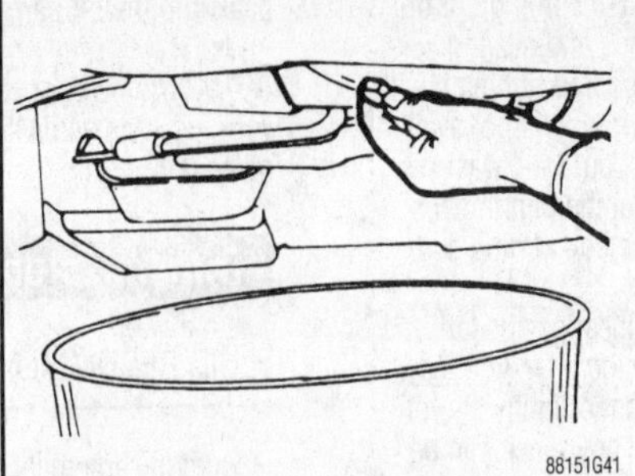
88151G41

Fig. 132 Unscrew the plug by hand, keeping inward pressure on the plug so oil won't escape and the plug won't fall out

88151P31

Fig. 133 Once the plug is unthreaded, pull it away quickly to help keep HOT oil off your hands

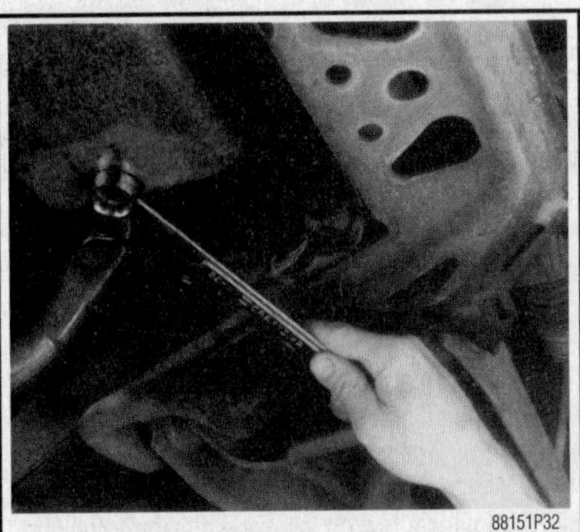
88151P32

Fig. 134 On 5.0L engines, don't forget the rear drain plug as well

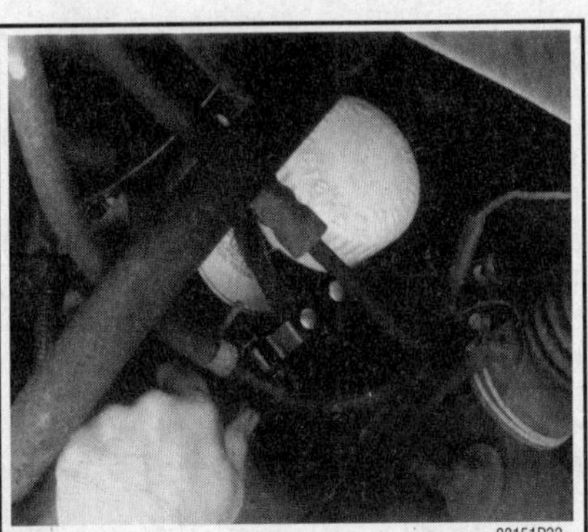
88151P33

Fig. 135 Use an oil filter wrench to loosen the old filter

TCCS1901

Fig. 136 Before installing a new oil filter, lightly coat the rubber gasket with clean oil

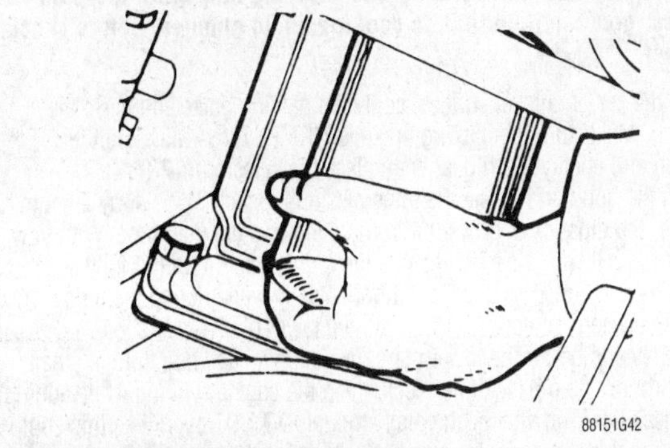
88151G42

Fig. 137 Always install the new filter by hand (an oil filter wrench will usually lead to overtightening)

change, we recommend that you always change the filter with the oil. The benefit of fresh oil is quickly lost if the old filter is clogged and unable to do its job. Also, leaving the old filter in place leaves a significant amount of dirty oil in the system.

The oil should be changed more frequently if the vehicle is being operated in very dusty area. Before draining the oil, make sure that the engine is at operating temperature. Hot oil will hold more impurities in suspension and will flow better, allowing the removal of more oil and dirt.

➡It is usually a good idea to place your ignition key in the box or bag with the bottles of fresh engine oil. In this way it will be VERY HARD to forget to refill the engine crankcase before you go to start the engine.

1. Raise and support the vehicle safely. Make sure the oil drain plug is at the lowest point on the oil pan. If not, you may have to raise the vehicle slightly higher on one jackstand (side) than the other.

2. Before you crawl under the car, take a look at where you will be working and gather all the necessary tools: such as a few wrenches or a strip of sockets, the drain pan, a clean rag . . . If the oil filter is more accessible from underneath the vehicle, you will also want to grab a bottle of oil, the new filter and a filter wrench at this time.

3. Position the drain pan underneath the drain plug in the oil pan. Keep in mind that the fast flowing oil which spill out as you pull the plug will come out with some force that it could miss the pan. Position the drain pan accordingly and be ready to move the pan more directly beneath the plug as the oil flow lessens to a trickle.

➡The Ford 5.0L engine is equipped with 2 drain plugs (one in front of the crossmember and one behind it, closer the transmission). Both should be removed to assure proper pan draining, but if the front end is raise and supported on ramps or jackstands, the oil may not fully drain from the front plug. The best way to assure all oil has been drained is to pull the plugs, then remove the jackstands and carefully lower the vehicle (make sure your drain pans are properly positioned because the relative positioning of the drain holes will change as the vehicle is lowered). Once you are sure the front portion of the oil pan has sufficiently drained, raise the vehicle and support it again with jackstands.

4. Loosen the drain plug with a wrench (or socket and driver), then carefully unscrew the plug with your fingers. Use a rag to shield your fingers from the heat. Push in on the plug as you unscrew it so you can feel when all of the screw threads are out of the hole (and so you will keep the oil from seeping past the threads until you are ready to pull the plug). You can then remove the plug quickly to avoid having hot oil run down your arm. This will also help assure that have the plug in your hand, not in the bottom of a pan of hot oil.

✲✲ CAUTION

Be careful of the oil; when at operating temperature, it is hot enough to cause a severe burn.

5. Allow the oil to drain until nothing but a few drops are coming out of the drain hole. Check the drain plug to make sure the threads and sealing surface are not damaged. Carefully thread the plug into position and tighten it with a torque wrench to 15–25 ft. lbs. (20–34 Nm). If a torque wrench is not available, snug the drain plug and give a slight additional turn. You don't want the plug to fall out (as you would quickly become stranded), but the pan threads are EASILY striped from overtighening (and this can be time consuming and/or costly to fix).

6. The oil filter is located on the left side of all the engines installed in these vehicles, position the drain pan beneath it. To remove the filter, you may need an oil filter wrench since the filter may have been fitted too tightly and/or the heat from the engine may have made it even tighter. A filter wrench can be obtained at any auto parts store and is well-worth the investment. Loosen the filter with the filter wrench. With a rag wrapped around the filter, unscrew the filter from the boss on the side of the engine. Be careful of hot oil that will run down the side of the filter. Make sure that your drain pan is under the filter before you start to remove it from the engine; should some of the hot oil happen to get on you, there will be a place to dump the filter in a hurry and the filter will usually spill a good bit of dirty oil as it is removed.

7. Wipe the base of the mounting boss with a clean, dry cloth. When you install the new filter, smear a small amount of fresh oil on the gasket with your finger, just enough to coat the entire contact surface. When you tighten the filter, rotate it about a half-turn after it contacts the mounting boss (or follow any instructions which came on the filter or parts box).

8. Remove the jackstands and carefully lower the vehicle, then IMMEDIATELY refill the engine crankcase with the proper amount of oil. DO NOT WAIT TO DO THIS because if you forget and someone tries to start the car . . . well you get the picture.

9. Refill the engine crankcase slowly, checking the level often. You may notice that it usually takes less than the amount of oil listed in the capacity chart to refill the crankcase. But, that is only until the engine is run and the oil filter is filled with oil. To make sure the proper level is obtained, run the engine to normal operating temperature, shut the engine **OFF**, allow the oil to drain back into the oil pan, and recheck the level. Top off the oil at this time to the fill mark.

10. Drain your used oil in a suitable container for recycling and clean-up your tools, as you will be needing them again in a couple of thousand more miles (kilometers?).

Fig. 138 Two ranges are included on most Mustang A/T dipsticks, one for normal operating temperature and one for overnight cold

Transmission

FLUID RECOMMENDATIONS

Both the automatic and manual transmissions covered by this manual use Mercon® automatic transmission fluid for lubrication. DO NOT use improper fluids such as Dexron® or gear oil. Use of improper fluids could lead to leaks or transmission damage.

On automatic transmissions the fluid type is normally stamped on the dipstick. Be sure to double check the dipstick before adding any fluid.

LEVEL CHECK

Automatic Transmission

➧ See Figures 138, 139, 140 and 141

It is very important to maintain the proper fluid level in an automatic transmission. If the level is either too high or too low, poor shifting operation and internal damage are likely to occur. For this reason, a regular check of the fluid level is essential.

Although it is best to check fluid at normal operating temperature, it can be checked overnight cold, if the ambient temperatures are 50–95°F (21–35°C). If so, refer to the dots on the transmission dipstick instead of the cross-hatched area and level marking lines.

1. Drive the vehicle for 15–20 minutes allowing the transmission to reach operating temperature.

➡If the car is driven at extended highway speeds, is driven in city traffic in hot weather or is being used to pull a trailer, fluid temperatures will likely exceed normal operating and checking ranges. In these circumstances, give the fluid time to cool (about 30 minutes) before checking the level.

2. Park the car on a level surface, apply the parking brake and leave the engine idling. Make sure the parking brake is FIRMLY ENGAGED. Shift the transmission and engage each gear, then place the selector in **P** (PARK).

3. Open the hood and locate the transmission dipstick. Wipe away any dirt in the area of the dipstick to prevent it from falling into the filler tube. Withdraw the dipstick, wipe it with a clean, lint-free rag and reinsert it until it fully seats.

4. Withdraw the dipstick and hold it horizontally while noting the fluid level. It should be between the upper (FULL) and the lower (ADD) marks.

5. If the level is below the lower mark, use a funnel and add fluid in small quantities through the dipstick filler neck. Keep the engine running while adding fluid and check the level after each small amount. DO NOT overfill as this could lead to foaming and transmission damage or seal leaks.

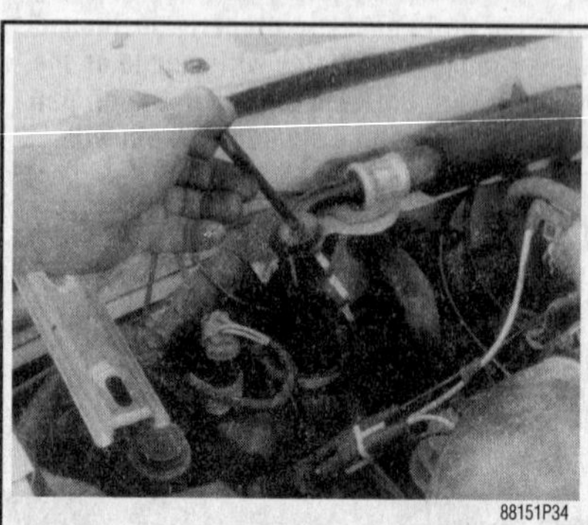

Fig. 139 Locate the automatic transmission dipstick (not the engine oil) and remove it from the guide tube

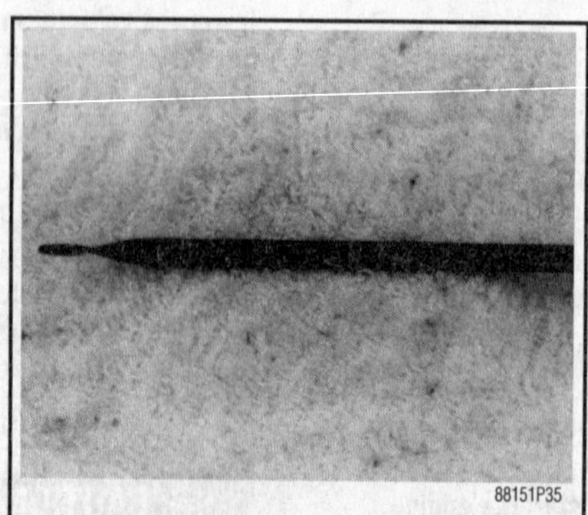

Fig. 140 When checking the transmission fluid level, be sure to hold the dispstick horizontally

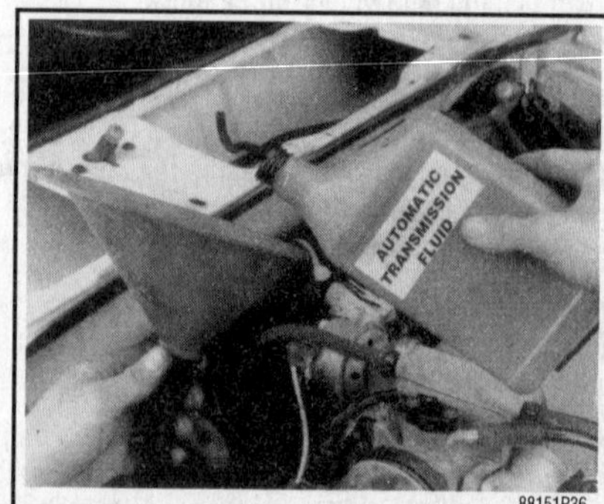

Fig. 141 If necessary, add fluid (in small increments) through the dipstick guide tube—a funnel with a flexible hose is really useful for this

Manual Transmission

➧ See Figure 142

The fluid level should be checked every six months or 6000 miles (9600 km), whichever comes first.

1. Park the car on a level surface, turn the engine **OFF**, FIRMLY apply the parking brake and block the drive wheels.

➡Ground clearance may make access to the transmission filler plug impossible without raising and supporting the vehicle, BUT if this is done the car MUST be supported at four corners and level. If only the front or rear is supported, an improper fluid level will be indicated. If you are going to place the car on four jackstands, this might be the perfect opportunity to rotate the tires as well.

2. Remove the filler plug from the side of the transmission case using a 3/8 in. drive ratchet and extension. The fluid level should be even with the bottom of the filler hole.
3. If additional fluid is necessary, add it through the filler hole using a siphon pump or squeeze bottle.
4. When you are finished, carefully install the filler plug, but DO NOT overtighten it and damage the housing.

DRAIN AND REFILL

Automatic Transmission

➧ See Figures 143 thru 155

Under normal service (moderate highway driving excluding excessive hot or cold conditions), the manufacturer feel that automatic transmission fluid should not need to be changed. However, if a major service is performed to the transmission, if transmission fluid becomes burnt or discolored through severe usage or if the vehicle is subjected to constant stop-and-go driving in hot weather, trailer towing, long periods of highway use at high speeds, fluid should be changed to prevent transmission damage. A preventive maintenance change is therefore recommended for most vehicles at least every 90,000 miles (145,000 km).

➡Although not a required service, transmission fluid changing can help assure a trouble-free transmission. Likewise, changing the transmission filter at this time is also added insurance.

1. Raise the car and support it on jackstands.

➡The torque converters on some transmissions are equipped with drain plugs. Because it may take some time to drain the fluid from the converter, you may wish to follow that procedure at this time, then come back to the pan and filter removal.

2. Place a drain pan under the transmission.
3. Loosen all of the pan attaching bolts to within a few turns of complete removal, then carefully break the gasket seal allowing most of the fluid to drain.

✱✱ CAUTION

DO NOT force the pan while breaking the gasket seal. DO NOT allow the pan flange to become bent or otherwise damaged.

4. When fluid has drained to the level of the pan flange, remove the pan bolts and carefully lower the pan doing your best to drain the rest of the fluid into the drain pan.
5. Clean the transmission oil pan thoroughly using a safe solvent, then allow it to air dry. DO NOT use a cloth to dry the pan which might leave behind bits of lint. Discard the old pan gasket.
6. Loosen and remove the oil filter screen retaining bolts, then carefully lower the filter from the transmission. Make sure any gaskets or seals are removed with the old filter. The A4LD transmission usually has an O-ring for each of the tubes connecting the filter to the valve body, while the AOD transmission usually has one round seal and a rectangular gasket.
7. Install the new oil filter screen making sure all gaskets or seals are in place, then secure using the retaining screws.

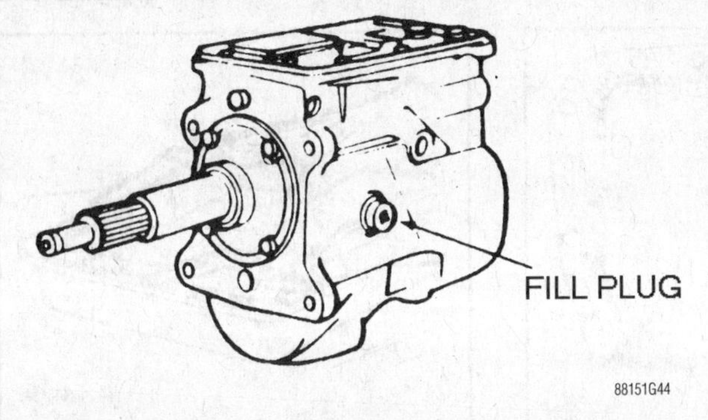

Fig. 142 The manual transmission filler/inspection plug is normally found on the middle to upper side of the housing

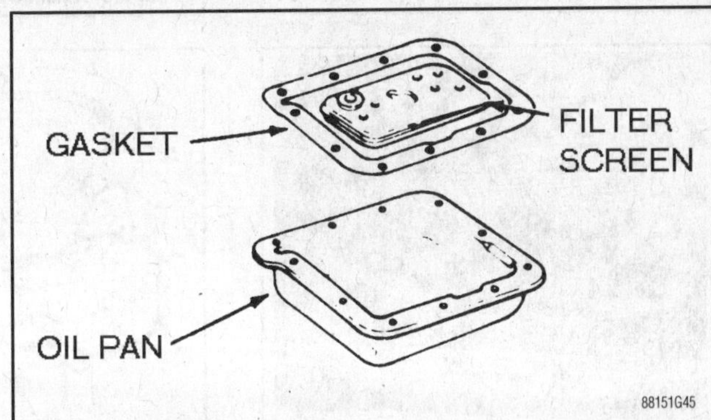

Fig. 143 The oil filter on automatic transmissions is mounted inside the fluid pan

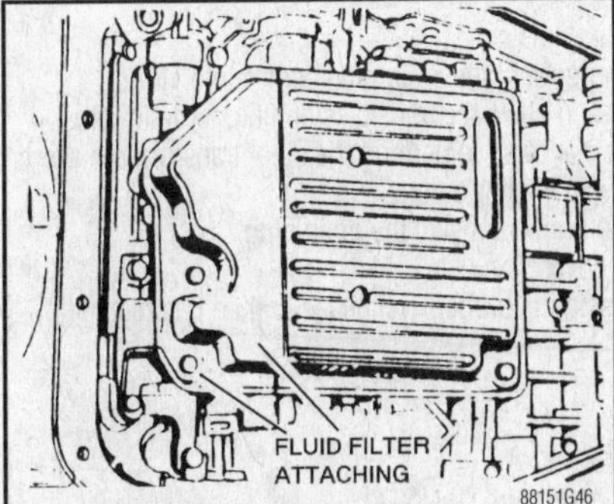

Fig. 144 The filter is usually attached to the transmission with bolts around the perimeter—AOD shown

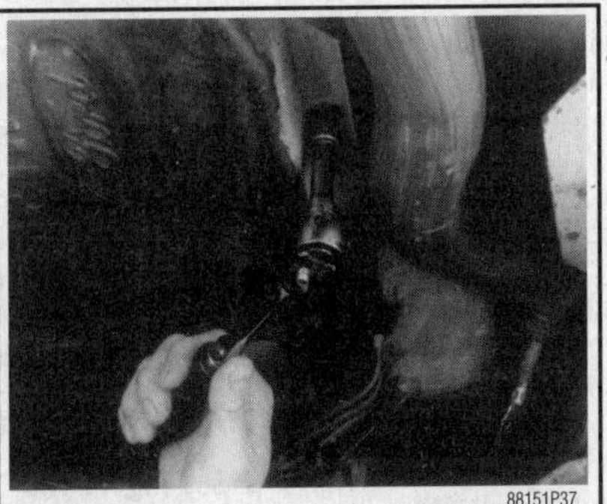

Fig. 145 Loosen all of the transmission fluid pan retaining bolts . . .

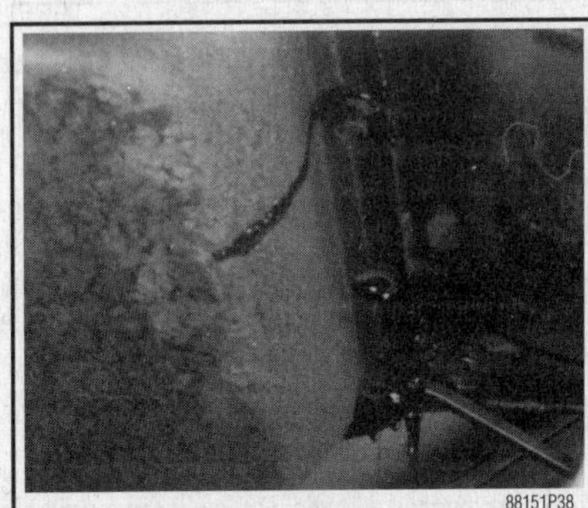

Fig. 146 . . . then carefully break the gasket seal and allow the fluid to drain

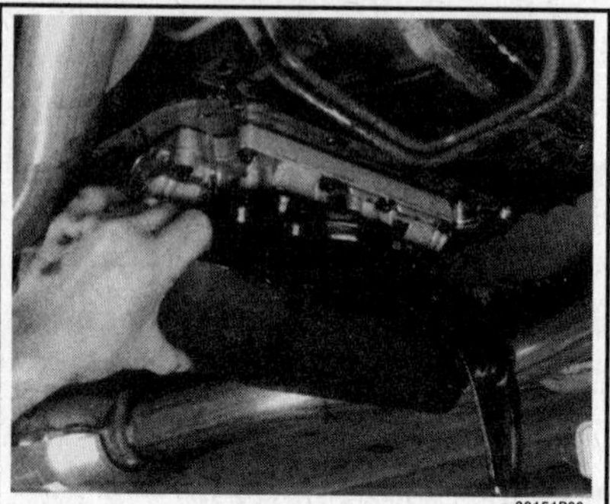
88151P39

Fig. 147 Remove the bolts and lower the transmission pan, allowing the remaining fluid to drain

88151P40

Fig. 148 Check the mating surfaces for traces of the old gasket—in this case, it is all left on the transmission

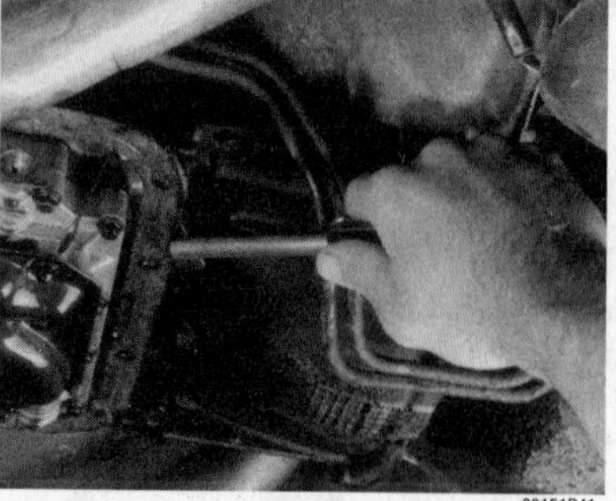
88151P41

Fig. 149 CAREFULLY clean the gasket mating surfaces—DO NOT allow pieces of the old gasket to remain on the valve body or in the pan

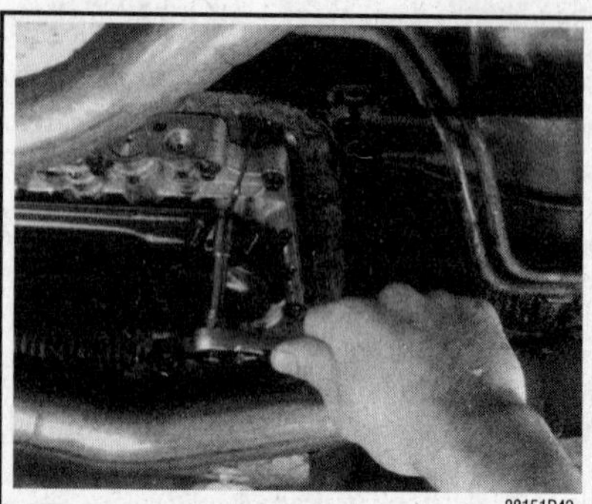
88151P42

Fig. 150 Loosen and remove the filter screen retaining bolts . . .

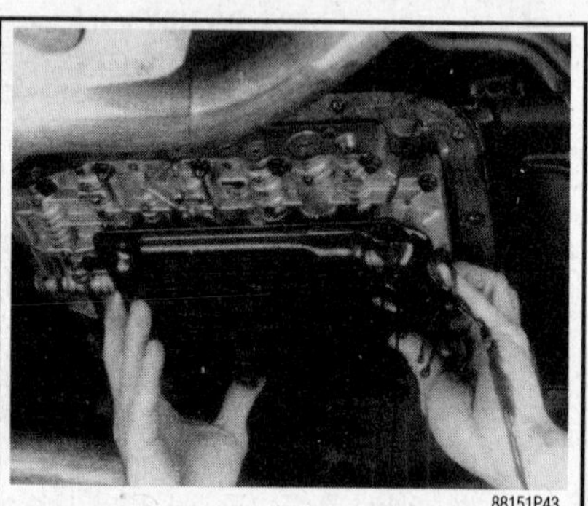
88151P43

Fig. 151 . . . then lower the filter screen from the transmission

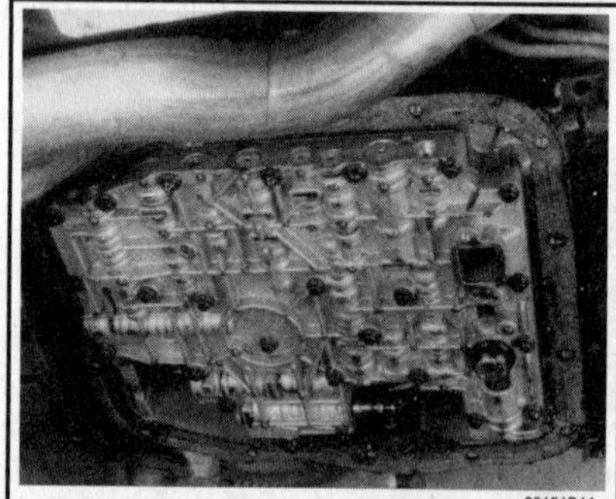
88151P44

Fig. 152 Inspect the transmission valve body for any seals or gaskets that the filter may have left behind

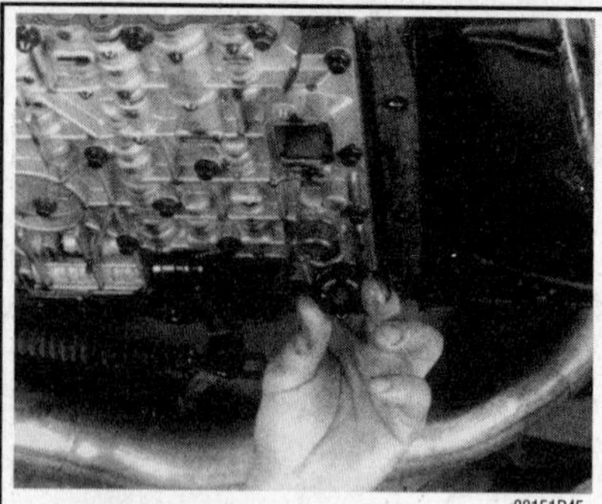
88151P45

Fig. 153 In this case an old seal was left on the valve body—it should be removed and discarded

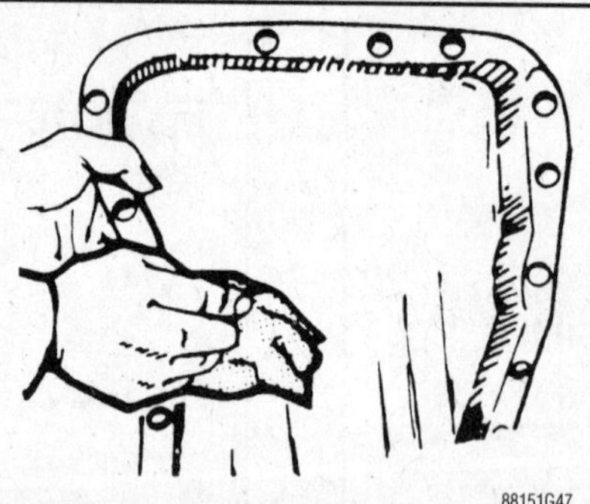
88151G47

Fig. 154 If a cloth is used to clean the oil pan MAKE SURE no bits of lint are left behind

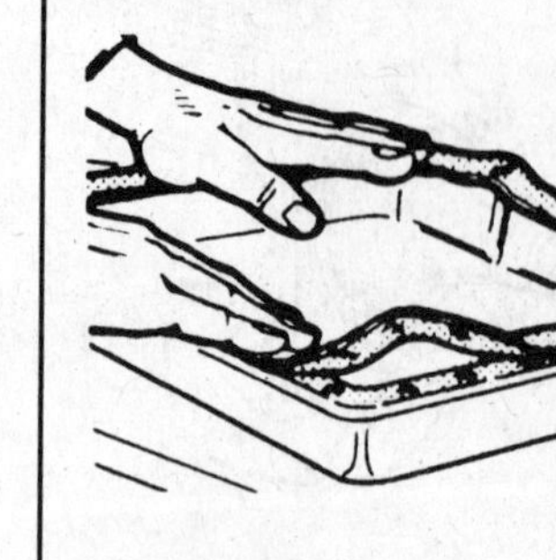
88151G48

Fig. 155 Position the new gasket on the pan to assure a proper fit before installation

8. Place a new gasket on the fluid pan, then install the pan to the transmission. Tighten the attaching bolts to 8–10 ft. lbs. (8–11 Nm) for the A4LD transmission or to 71–119 inch lbs. (8–13 Nm) for AOD transmissions.

9. Add three quarts of fluid to the transmission through the filler tube.

10. Remove the jackstands and carefully lower the vehicle.

11. Start the engine and move the gear selector through the shift pattern. Allow the engine to reach normal operating temperature.

12. Check the transmission fluid. Add fluid, as necessary to obtain the correct level.

TORQUE CONVERTER

Some torque converters, such as those usually used on the AOD transmission, are equipped with drain plugs, if so you will probably want to drain the fluid in the converter also at the time of a transmission pan fluid change. Just, make sure that you compensate for the additional fluid drained during the refilling process.

1. Remove the lower engine dust cover.

2. Rotate the torque converter until the drain plug comes into view.

3. Remove the drain plug and allow the transmission fluid to drain. This could take some time, so you may wish to perform the other transmission service (fluid pan and filter removal) while waiting.

4. Once the fluid has been drained, install the drain plug.

5. Install the engine dust cover.

6. Make sure the transmission is properly refilled with fluid before attempting to drive the vehicle.

Manual Transmission

➧ See Figure 156

Under normal conditions, the manufacturer feels that manual transmission fluid should not need to be changed. However, if the car is driven in deep water (as high as the transmission casing) it is a good idea to replace the fluid. Little

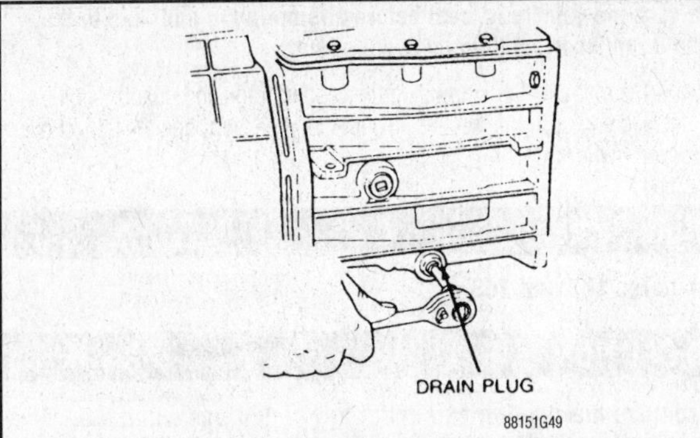

Fig. 156 The transmission fluid is removed through the drain plug in the lower portion of the housing

harm can come from a fluid change when you have just purchased a used vehicle, especially since the condition of the transmission fluid is usually not known.

If the fluid is to be drained, it is a good idea to warm the fluid first so it will flow better. This can be accomplished by 15–20 miles of highway driving. Fluid which is warmed to normal operating temperature will flow faster, drain more completely and remove more contaminants from the housing.

1. Drive the vehicle to assure the fluid is at normal operating temperature.
2. Raise and support the vehicle safely on jackstands. Remember that the vehicle must be supported level (usually at four points) so the proper amount of fluid can be added.
3. Place a drain pan under the transmission housing, below the drain plug. Remember that the fluid will likely flow with some force at first (arcing outward from the transmission), and will not just drip straight downward into the pan. Position the drain pan accordingly and move it more directly underneath the drain plug as the flow slows to a trickle.
4. Remove the drain plug and allow the transmission fluid to drain out.

➡The transmission drain plug is usually a square receiver which is designed to accept a ⅜ in. driver such as a ratchet or extension.

5. Once the transmission has drained sufficiently, install the the drain plug.
6. Remove the filler plug, and fill the transmission to the proper level with the required fluid.
7. Reinstall the filler plug once you are finished.
8. Remove the jackstands and carefully lower the vehicle.

Rear Axle

FLUID LEVEL CHECK

➧ See Figure 157

The fluid level in the rear axle should be checked at each oil change. Like the manual transmission which is available on the Mustang, the rear axle does not have a dipstick to check fluid level. Instead, a filler plug is located in the side of the housing (or in the side of the cover), at a level just barely above the level to which fluid should fill the housing. To check the fluid level:

1. Make sure the transmission is in **P** (A/T) or in gear on a manual, then FIRMLY set the parking brake and block the drive wheels.
2. Check under the vehicle is see if there is sufficient clearance for you to access the filler plug on the side of the differential housing. If not you will have to raise and support the vehicle using jackstands at four points to make sure it is completely level. Failure to support the vehicle level will prevent from properly checking or filling the rear axle fluid.
3. Thoroughly clean the area surrounding the fill plug. This will prevent any dirt from entering the housing and contaminating the gear oil.
4. Remove the fill plug and make sure that the gear oil is up to the bottom of the fill hole. If lubricant does not appear at the hole when the plug is removed, additional lubricant should be added. Use hypoid gear lubricant SAE 80 or 90.

➡If the differential is the limited-slip type, be sure to use special limited-slip additive with the lubricant.

5. Once you are finished, install the fill plug, then (if raised) remove the jackstands and lower the vehicle.

DRAIN AND REFILL

➧ See Figures 158, 159, 160 and 161

Drain and refill the rear axle housing every 100,000 miles (160,000 km) or any time the vehicle is driven in high water (up to the axle). Although some fluid can be removed using a suction gun, the best method is to remove the rear cover to make sure most all of any present contaminants are removed. As with any fluid change, the oil should be at normal operating temperature to assure the best flow and removal of fluid/contaminants.

1. Run the vehicle until the lubricant reaches operating temperature.
2. If necessary for access, raise and support the vehicle safely using jackstands; but make sure that the vehicle is level so you can properly refill the axle when you are finished.
3. Use a wire brush to clean the area around the differential. This will help prevent dirt from contaminating the differential housing while the cover is removed.

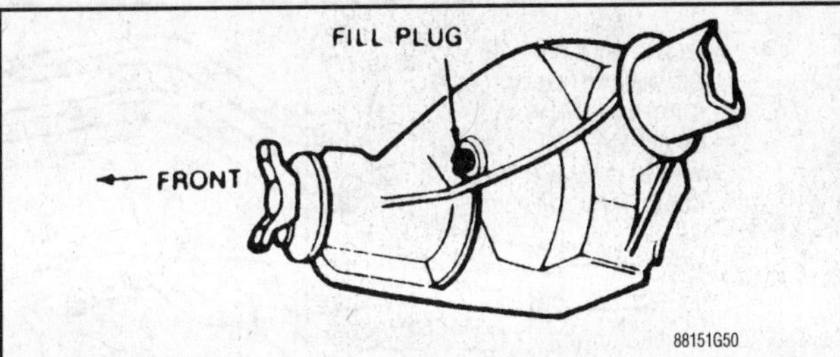

Fig. 157 Gear oil is checked or added through a fill plug in the differential housing or cover

Fig. 158 Thoroughly clean the axle housing of dirt, grease and mung (to prevent contaminating the differential)

Fig. 159 Loosen each of the cover bolts, then remove all but two . . .

Fig. 160 . . . then carefully break the gasket seal and allow the fluid to drain

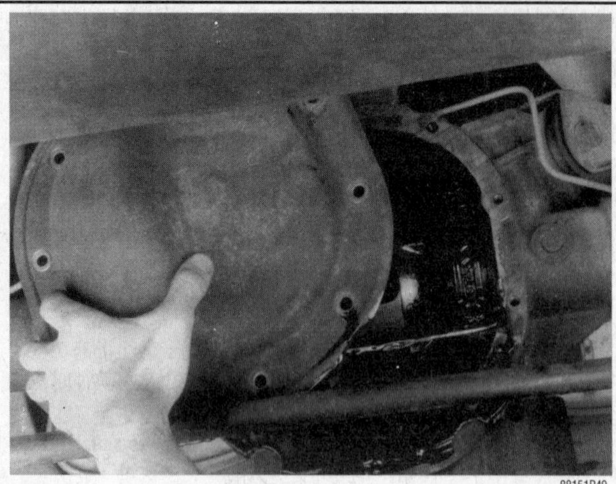

88151P49

Fig. 161 Remove the cover for cleaning and inspection once most of the fluid has drained

4. Position a drain pan under the rear axle.
5. Loosen and remove all but 2 of the rear cover upper or side retaining bolts. The remaining 2 bolts should then be loosened to within a few turns of complete removal. Use a small prytool to carefully break the gasket seal at the base of the cover and allow the lubricant to drain. Be VERY careful not to force or damage the cover and gasket mating surface.
6. Once most of the fluid has drained, remove the final retaining bolts, then separate the cover from the housing.

To install:

7. Carefully clean the gasket mating surfaces of the cover and axle housing of any remaining gasket or sealer. A putty knife is a good tool to use for this. You may want to cover the differential gears using a rag or piece of plastic to prevent contaminating them with dirt or pieces of the old gasket.
8. Install the rear cover using a new gasket and sealant. Tighten the retaining bolts using a crisscross pattern.

➡Make sure the vehicle is level before attempting to add fluid to the rear axle or an incorrect fluid level will result.

9. Refill the rear axle housing using the proper grade and quantity of lubricant as detailed earlier in this section. Install the filler plug, operate the vehicle and check for any leaks.

Cooling System

▸ **See Figures 162 and 163**

⁂ CAUTION

Never remove the radiator cap under any conditions while the engine is running! Failure to follow these instructions could result in damage to the cooling system and/or personal injury. To avoid having scalding hot coolant or steam blow out of the radiator, use extreme care when removing the radiator cap from a hot radiator. Wait until the engine has cooled, then wrap a thick cloth around the radiator cap and turn it slowly to the first stop. Step back while the pressure is released from the cooling system. When you are sure

88151P50

Fig. 162 ALWAYS heed warning labels found in the engine compartment—this one include suggestions for safe cooling system service

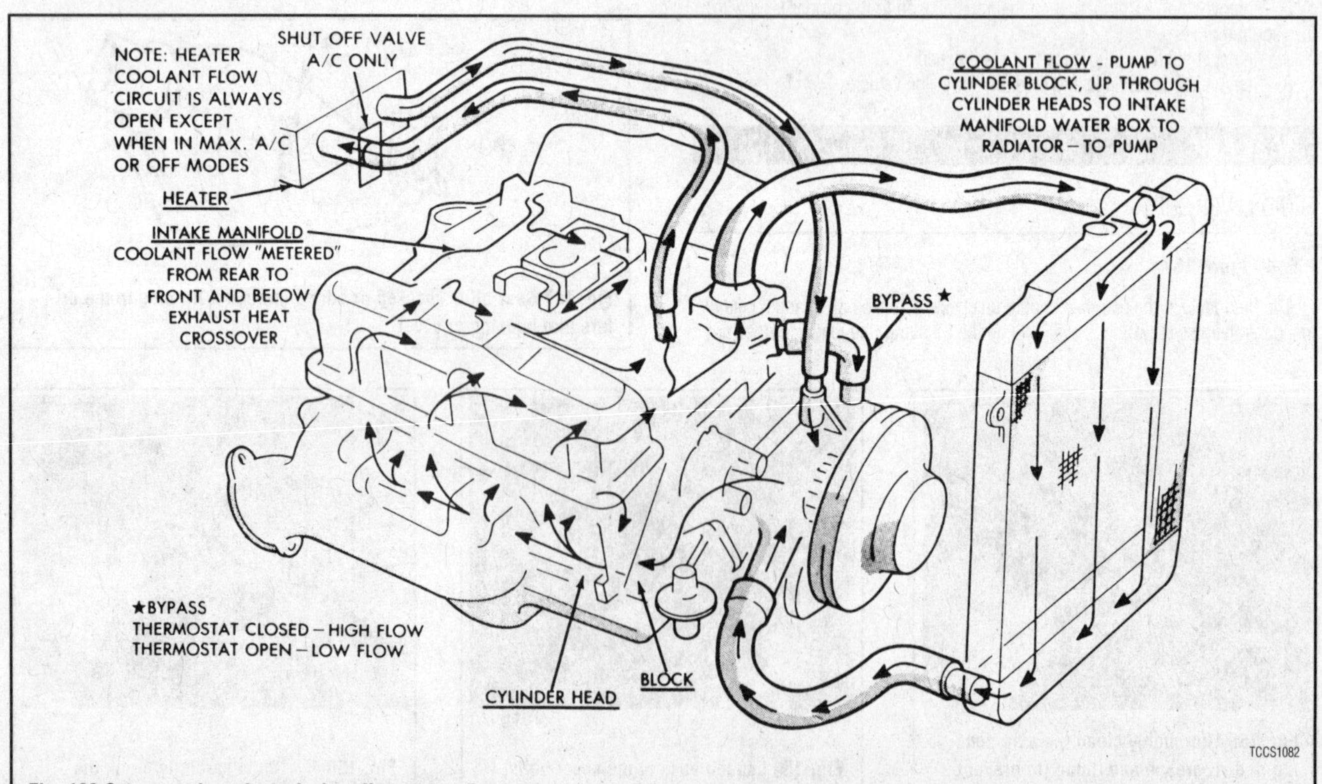

TCCS1082

Fig. 163 Cut-away view of a typical cooling system flow

the pressure has been released, press down on the radiator cap (with the cloth still in position), turn and remove the cap.

INSPECTION

See Figures 164, 165, 166, 167 and 168

Any time you have the hood open, glance at the coolant recovery tank to make sure it is properly filled. Top of the cooling system using the recovery tank and its markings as a guideline. If you top off the system, make a note of it to check again soon. A coolant level that consistently drops is usually a sign of small, hard to detect leak, though in the worst case it could be a sign of an internal engine leak (blown head gasket/cracked block? . . . check the engine oil for coolant contamination). In most cases, you will be able to trace the leak to a loose fitting or damaged hose (and you might solve a problem before it leaves you stranded). Evaporating ethylene glycol antifreeze will leave small, white (salt like) deposits, which can be helpful in tracing a leak.

At least annually or every 12,000 miles (19,000 km), all hoses, fittings and cooling system connections should be inspected for damage, wear or leaks. Hose clamps should be checked for tightness, and soft or cracked hoses should be replaced. Damp spots, or accumulations of rust or dye near hoses or fittings indicate possible leakage. These must be corrected before filling the system with fresh coolant. The pressure cap should be examined for signs of deterioration and aging. The fan belt and/or other drive belt(s) should be inspected and adjusted to the proper tension. Refer to the information on drive belts found earlier in this section. Finally, if everything looks good, obtain an antifreeze/coolant testing hydrometer in order to check the freeze and boil-over protection capabilities of the coolant currently in your engine. Old or improperly mixed coolant should be replaced.

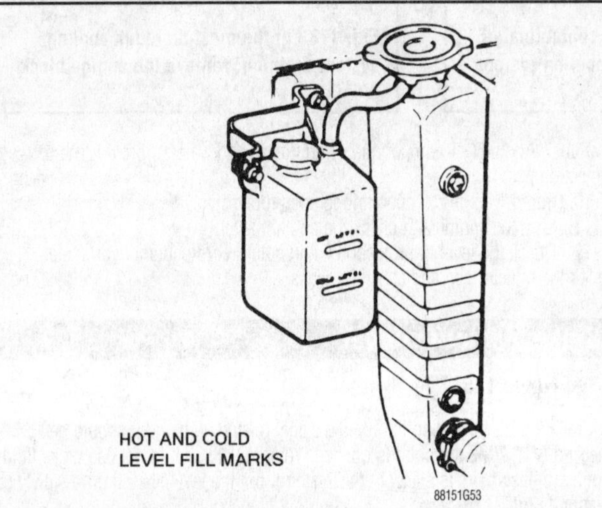

Fig. 164 Coolant level should be monitored by periodically checking the coolant recovery tank

CAUTION

When draining coolant, keep in mind that cats and dogs are attracted to ethylene glycol antifreeze, and are likely to drink any that is left in an uncovered container or in puddles on the ground. This will prove fatal in sufficient quantity. Always drain coolant into a sealable container. Coolant may be reused unless it is contaminated or several years old.

At least once every 3 years or 36,000 miles (48,000 km), the engine cooling system should be inspected, flushed and refilled with fresh coolant. If the coolant is left in the system too long, it loses its ability to prevent rust and corrosion. If the coolant has too much water, it won't protect against freezing.

If you experience problems with your cooling system, such as overheating or boiling-over, check the simple before expecting the complicated. Make sure the system can fully pressurize (are all the connections tight/is the radiator cap on properly, is the cap seal intact?). Ideally, a pressure tester should be connected to the radiator opening and the system should be pressurized and inspected for leaks. If no obvious problems are found, use a hydrometer antifreeze/coolant tester (available at most automotive supply stores) to check the condition and concentration of the antifreeze in your cooling system. Excessively old coolant or the wrong proportions of water and coolant will hurt the coolant's boiling and freezing points.

Check the Radiator Cap

See Figure 169

While you are checking the coolant level, check the radiator cap for a worn or cracked gasket. If the top doesn't seal properly, fluid will be lost and the engine will overheat. Worn caps should be replaced with a new one

Clean Radiator of Debris

See Figure 170

Periodically, clean any debris—leaves, paper, insects, etc.— from the radiator fins. Pick the large pieces off by hand. The smaller pieces can be washed away with water pressure from a hose.

Carefully straighten any bent radiator fins with a pair of needle-nosed pliers. Be careful; the fins are very soft. Don't wiggle the fins back and forth too much. Straighten them once and try not to move them again.

DRAINING AND REFILLING

See Figures 171, 172, 173 and 174

A complete drain and refill of the cooling system at least every 30,000 miles (48,000 km) or 3 years will remove the accumulated rust, scale and other deposits. The recommended coolant for most late model cars is a 50/50 mixture of ethylene glycol and water for year-round use. Choose a good quality antifreeze with water pump lubricants, rust inhibitors and other corrosion inhibitors along with acid neutralizers.

1. Drain the existing antifreeze and coolant. Open the radiator and engine drains (petcocks) or disconnect the bottom radiator hose at the radiator outlet. The engine block drain plugs can also be temporarily removed to

Fig. 165 Small amounts of coolant should be added to the coolant recovery tank . . .

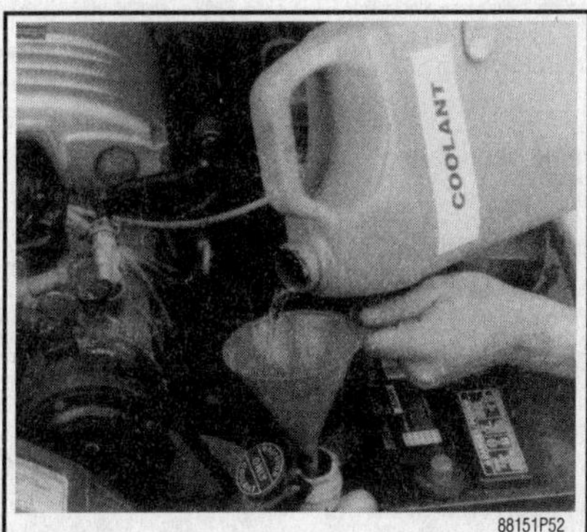

Fig. 166 . . . a funnel helps reduce the mess

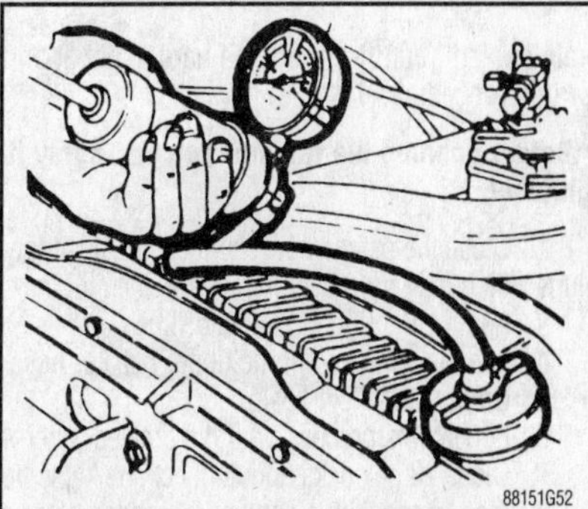

Fig. 167 If possible, pressure check the system at least once a year to help catch problems before something breaks

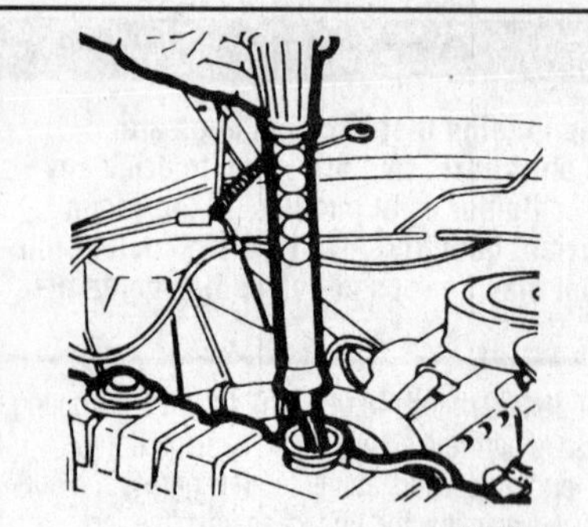
88151G51

Fig. 168 Use an antifreeze/coolant testing hydrometer to check the condition of the coolant in your engine

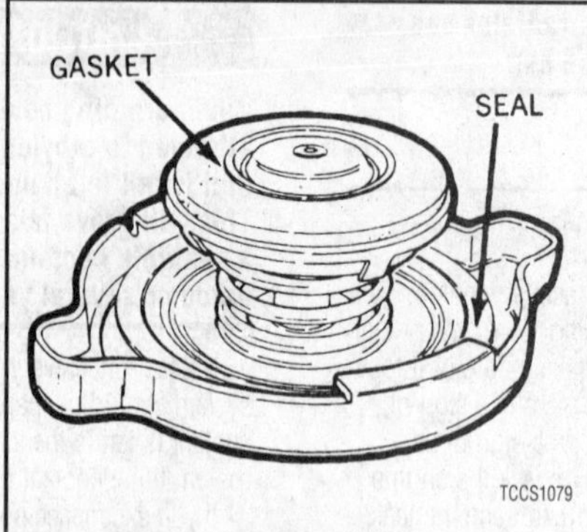

TCCS1079

Fig. 169 Be sure the rubber gasket on the radiator cap has a tight seal

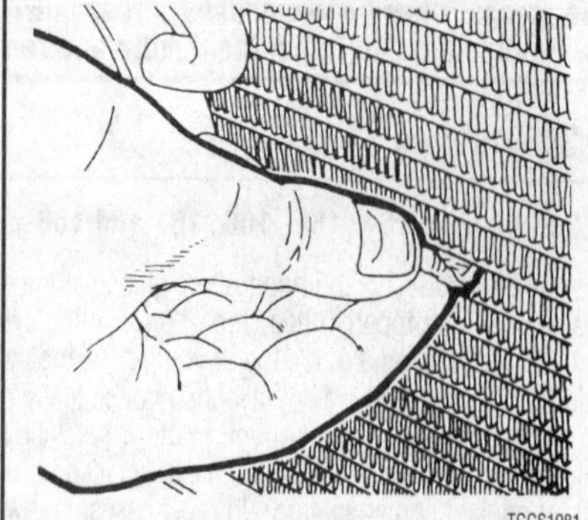
TCCS1081

Fig. 170 Periodically remove all debris from the radiator fins

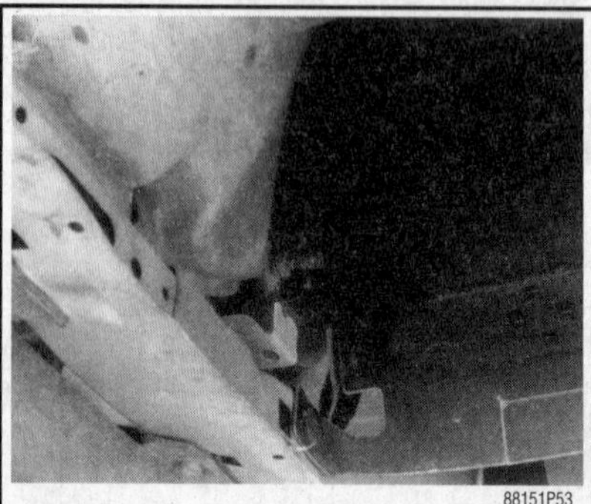
88151P53

Fig. 171 The radiator petcock is usually the easiest method of draining the cooling system

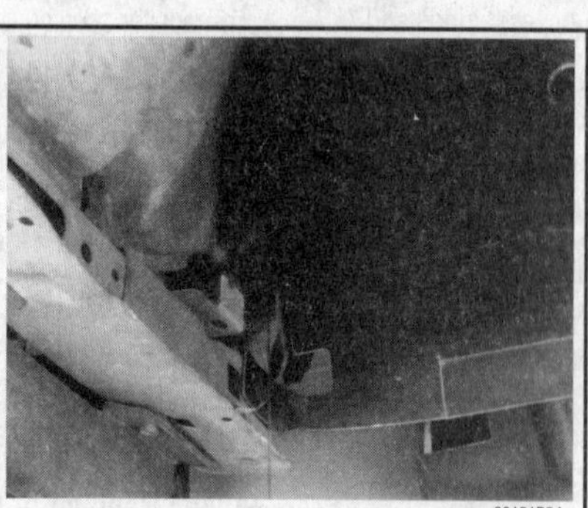
88151P54

Fig. 172 The trickle of rust contaminated coolant suggests that this cooling system was neglected

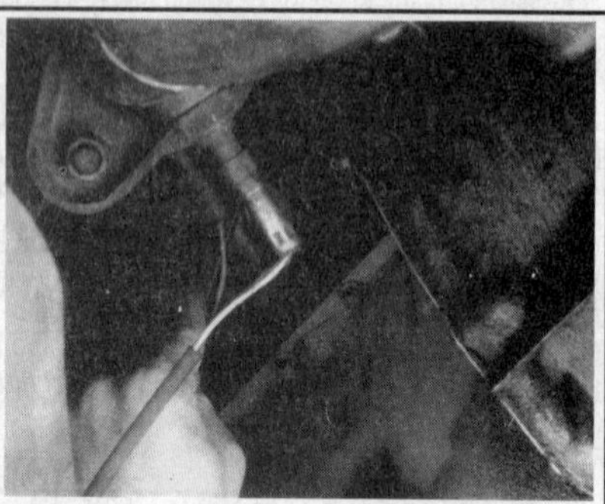
88151P55

Fig. 173 For the most thorough cooling system draining, remove the engine block plug(s)

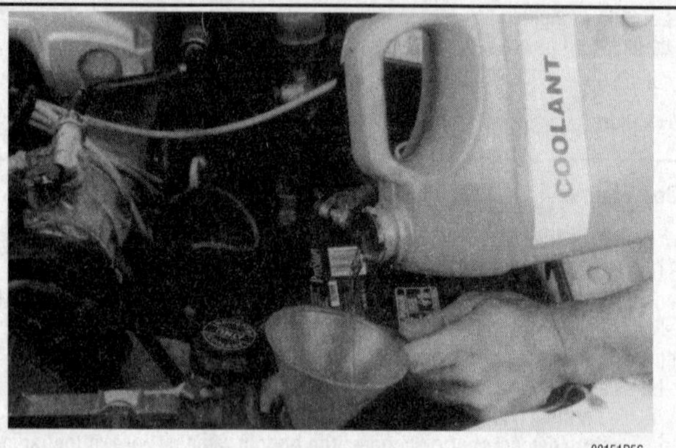

88151P56

Fig. 174 When the entire system is emptied, refilling must take place through the radiator opening (as opposed to the recovery tank)

drain coolant, but they are often hard to get at and it is not really necessary for this procedure.

➡Before opening the radiator petcock, spray it with some penetrating lubricant.

2. Close the petcock or reconnect the hose (and install any block drain plugs which may have been removed), then fill the system with water.
3. Add a can of quality radiator flush.
4. Idle the engine until the upper radiator hose gets hot.
5. Drain the system again.
6. Repeat this process until the drained water is clear and free of scale.
7. Close all petcocks and connect any loose hoses.
8. If equipped with a coolant recovery system, flush the reservoir with water and leave empty.
9. Determine the capacity of the coolant system. (See the Capacities Specifications). Add a 50/50 mix of quality antifreeze and water to provide the desired protection.
10. Run the engine to operating temperature.
11. Stop the engine and check the coolant level.
12. Check the level of protection with an antifreeze/coolant hydrometer. Install the radiator cap and check for leaks.

Brake Master Cylinder

➧ See Figure 175

Brake fluid level and condition is a safety related item and it should be checked ANY TIME the hood is opened. Your vehicle should not use brake fluid rapidly (unless there is a leak in the system), but the level should drop slowly in relation to brake pad wear.

✲✲ WARNING

BRAKE FLUID EATS PAINT. Take great care not to splash or spill brake fluid on painted surfaces. Should you spill a small amount on the car's finish, don't panic, just flush the area with plenty of water.

The master cylinder reservoir is located under the hood, on the left side firewall. All vehicles covered by this manual should be equipped with a see-through plastic reservoir. This makes checking the level easy and helps reduce the risk of fluid contamination (since you don't have to expose the fluid by opening the cap to check the level). Fluid should be kept near the FULL line or between the MIN and MAX lines, depending on how the reservoir is marked.

If it becomes necessary to add fluid to the system, take a moment to clean the area around the cap and reservoir. Use a clean rag to wipe away dust and dirt which could enter the reservoir after the cover is removed. If the level of the brake fluid is less than half the volume of the reservoir (and the brake pads are not approaching a replacement point), it is advised that you check the brake system for leaks. Leaks in the hydraulic system often occur at the wheel cylinders.

When adding fluid to the system ONLY use fresh DOT 3 brake fluid from a

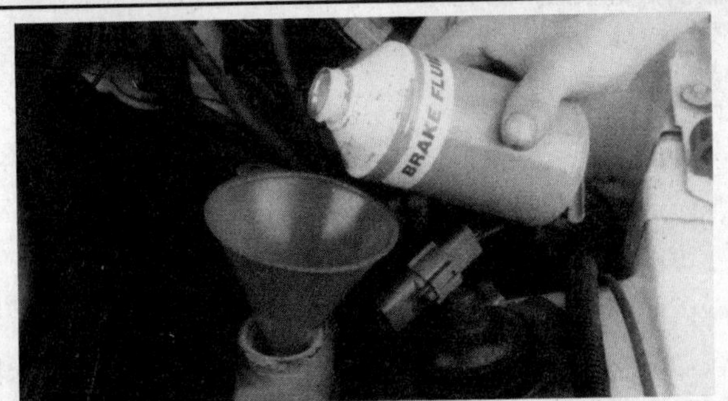

88151P57

Fig. 175 When adding brake fluid, only use FRESH fluid from a SEALED container (and make sure the funnel is clean too)

sealed container. DOT 3 brake fluid will absorb moisture when it is exposed to the atmosphere, this will lower its boiling point. A container that has been opened once, closed and placed on a shelf will allow enough moisture to enter over time to contaminate the fluid within. If your brake fluid is contaminated with water, you could boil the brake fluid under hard braking and loose all/some of the brake system. Don't take the risk, buy fresh brake fluid whenever you must add to the system.

Power Steering Pump Reservoir

♦ **See Figures 176, 177, 178 and 179**

The level of the power steering fluid should be checked in the reservoir periodically, at least once a year. Fluid is checked using the dipstick which is attached to the reservoir cap (which is highlighted in yellow on some Mustangs covered by this manual. Although the dipstick is equipped with range markings so that you can check the fluid hot or cold, it is recommended that you check the fluid at normal operating temperature (HOT).

**** WARNING**

Extensive driving with a low power steering fluid level can damage the power steering pump.

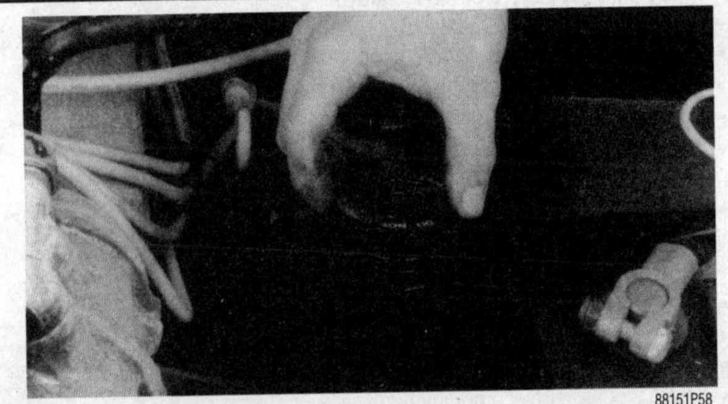
88151P58

Fig. 176 The power steering fluid is checked using a dipstick which is part of the cap

➡The power steering pump on your vehicle requires the use of power steering fluid that meets Ford's specification ESW-M2C33-F, or an equivalent Type F automatic transmission fluid.

1. Warm the fluid to normal operating temperature by driving for at least one mile, or start the engine and allow it to idle for five minutes.
2. With the engine idling, turn the steering wheel back-and-forth several times from lock-to-lock, then center the wheels and shut the engine **OFF**.
3. Locate the power steering pump reservoir, then remove the cap/dipstick and note the level as indicated by the markings. To be sure of your reading, put the cap back in position, remove it again and double check the level.
4. If the level is below the indicator markings, add fluid to bring it up to the proper level (a funnel is usually very helpful). If you are checking the level after running the engine or driving, make sure you add enough fluid to bring it to the FULL HOT range, but like most automotive fluids, DO NOT overfill.
5. When you are finished, install the dipstick and make sure it is secure.

Chassis Greasing

♦ **See Figure 180**

Chassis greasing should be performed every 12 months or 12,000 miles (19,000 km) for most cars. Greasing can be performed with a commercial pressurized grease gun or at home by using a hand-operated grease gun. Wipe the grease fittings clean before greasing in order to prevent the possibility of forcing any dirt into the component.

There are far less grease points on the modern automotive chassis than there were on cars of yesteryear. The tie rod ends on these vehicles should be checked and lubricated periodically, and the front suspension should be checked for grease fittings.

A water resistant long life grease that meets Ford's ESA-M1C75-B specification should be used for all chassis greasing applications.

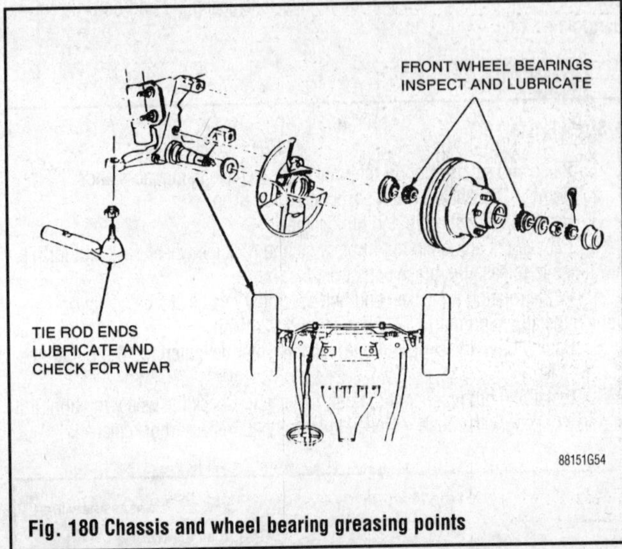

88151G54

Fig. 180 Chassis and wheel bearing greasing points

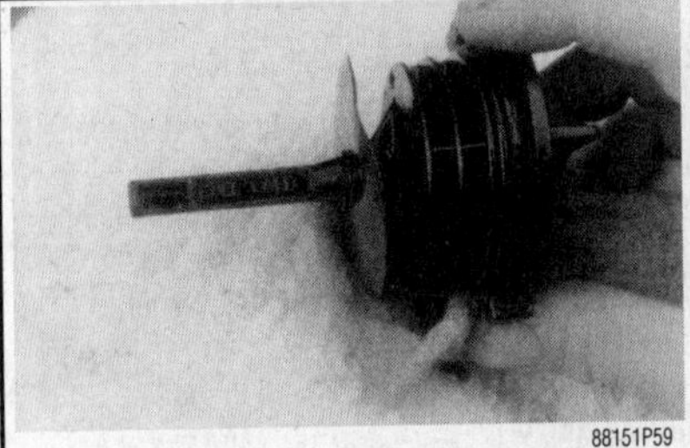
88151P59

Fig. 177 One side of the dipstick has markings towards the bottom for checking the level COLD . . .

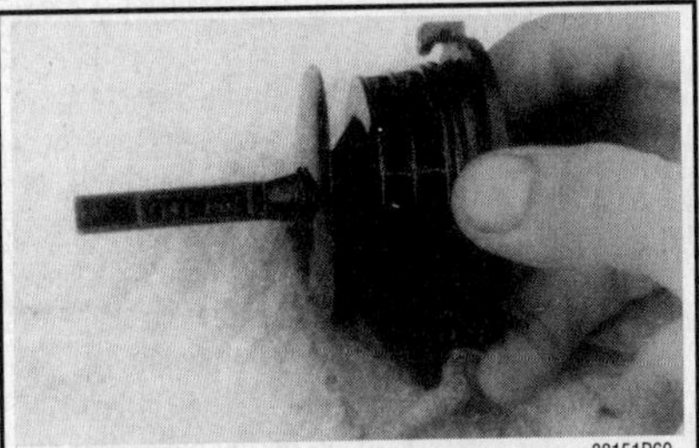
88151P60

Fig. 178 . . . the other side has a larger range, higher up, for checking the level of HOT fluid

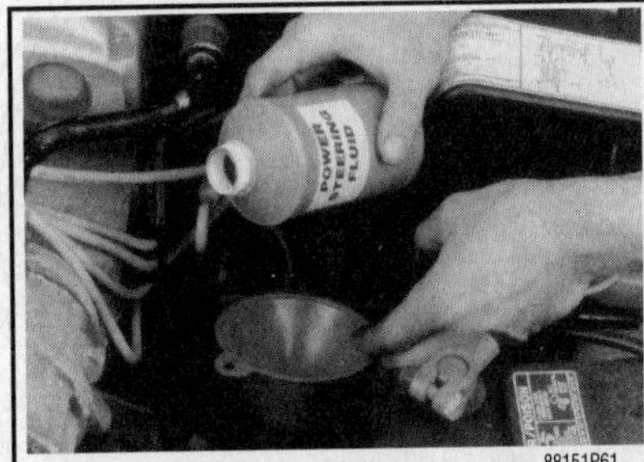

88151P61

Fig. 179 If necessary, add fresh fluid to the reservoir

Body Lubrication

Whenever you take care of chassis greasing it is also advised that you walk around the vehicle and give attention to a number of other surfaces which require a variety of lubrication/protection.

HOOD/DOOR LATCH AND HINGES

Wipe clean any exposed surfaces of the door hatches and hinges, hood latch and auxiliary catch. Then, treat the surfaces using a multi-purpose grease spray that meets Ford's ESR-M1C159-A specification.

LOCK CYLINDERS

Should be treated with Ford Lock Lubricant, part no. D8AZ-19587-AA or equivalent. Consult your local parts supplier for equivalent lubricants.

DOOR WEATHERSTRIPS

Spray the door weatherstripping using a silicone lubricant to help pressure the rubber.

CLUTCH, THROTTLE VALVE (TV) AND KICKDOWN LINKAGE

A water resistant long life grease that meets Ford's ESA-M1C75-B specification should be used for all linkages.

Wheel Bearings

See Figure 181

The front wheel bearings should be removed, cleaned, inspected, repacked, installed and adjusted at least every 30,000 miles (48,000 km). The rear wheel bearings are part of the rear axle assembly and do not require periodic service.

ADJUSTMENT

See Figure 182

1. Raise and safely support the front of the vehicle using jackstands.
2. Remove the wheel or hub cover and grease cap.
3. Remove the cotter pin and nut retainer.
4. Loosen the adjusting nut three turns and rock the wheel back and forth a few times to release the brake pads from the rotor.
5. While rotating the wheel and hub assembly in a clockwise direction, tighten the adjusting nut to 17–25 ft. lbs. (23–24 Nm).
6. Back off the adjusting nut one-half turn, then retighten to 10–28 inch lbs. (1.1–3.2 Nm).
7. Install the nut retainer and a new cotter pin. Check the wheel rotation. If it is noisy or rough, the bearings need to be cleaned, repacked or replaced.

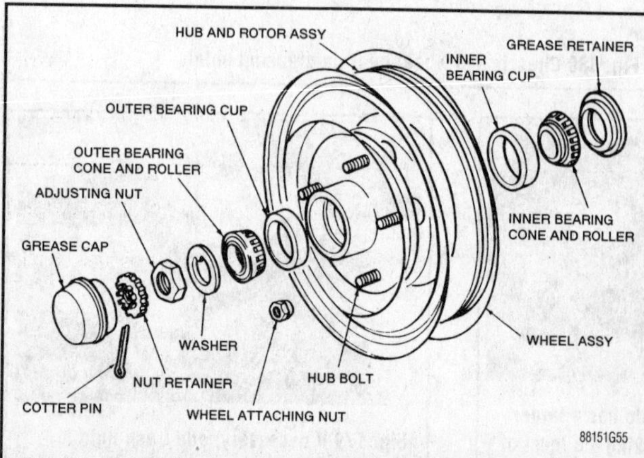

Fig. 181 Exploded view of the front wheel bearing assembly

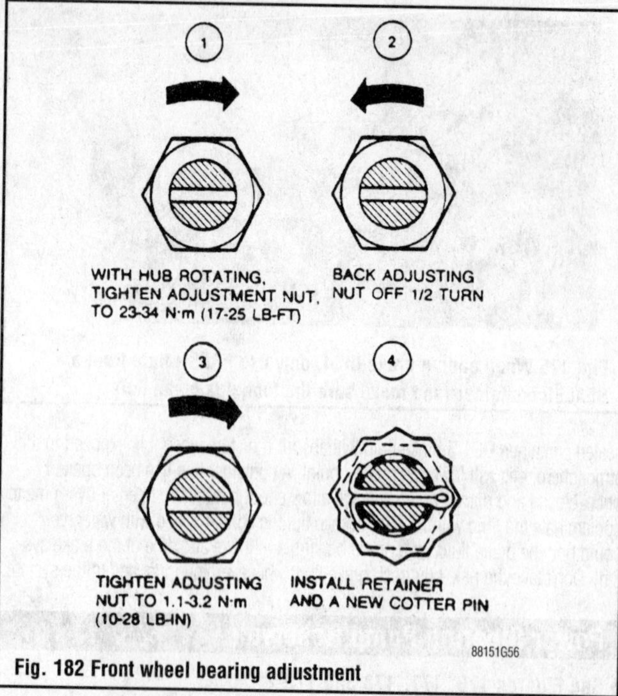

Fig. 182 Front wheel bearing adjustment

8. Lower the vehicle. Before driving, pump the brake pedal several times to restore the proper brake pedal travel.

REMOVAL & INSTALLATION

See Figures 183 thru 194

Before handling the bearings, learn these rules.

You should ALWAYS:

- Remove all dirt from the housing before exposing the bearing.
- Treat a used bearing as gently as you would a new one.
- Work with clean tools in clean surroundings.
- Use clean, dry canvas or plastic gloves.
- Always use clean, fresh solvents and lubricants.
- Place the bearings on clean paper to dry.
- Cover disassembled bearings to prevent rust and contamination by dirt.
- Use clean rags when necessary.
- Keep the bearings in oiled, moisture-proof paper when they are to be stored or out of service for more than a short period.
- Clean the inside of the housing before replacing the bearing.

You should NEVER:

- Work in dirty surroundings.
- Use dirty, chipped or damaged tools.
- Work on wooden surfaces or use wooden mallets.
- Handle the bearings with dirty or wet hands.
- Use gasoline for cleaning anything.
- Use compressed air to spin-dry the bearings. They will be damaged.
- Spin the bearings before cleaning them.
- Use dirty rags or cotton waste to wipe the bearings.
- Allow the bearing to be scratched, dropped or nicked during service.

1. Loosen the lugnuts on the wheel(s) being removed, then raise and support the vehicle safely using jackstands.
2. Remove the wheel and tire assembly. Remove the caliper and suspend it with a length of wire; do not allow it to hang by the hose.
3. CAREFULLY Pry off the dust cap, making sure not to distort the flange. Tap out and discard the cotter pin. Remove the nut retainer.
4. Loosen and remove the adjusting nut, along with the flat washer (the outer bearing cone and roller assembly may come off at this time.
5. Being careful not to drop the outer bearing (if it is still in the hub), pull off the brake disc and wheel hub assembly.
6. Remove the inner grease seal using a seal removal tool. If necessary, a small prybar may be used, but be VERY CAREFUL not to damage the bearing or the race. Remove the inner wheel bearing.

88151P62

Fig. 183 Carefully remove the grease cap from the wheel hub and disc

88151P63

Fig. 184 Straighten the ends of the cotter pin . . .

88151P64

Fig. 185 . . . then remove the cotter pin from the spindle

88151P65

Fig. 186 Remove the castellated nut retainer . . .

88151P66

Fig. 187 . . . then loosen and remove the wheel bearing and hub retaining nut

88151P67

Fig. 188 Once the flat washer is removed . . .

88151P68

Fig. 189 . . . the outer bearing is usually free for removal (or it sometimes just falls right out)

88151P69

Fig. 190 Remove the hub and disc assembly (along with the inner bearing) from the spindle

7. Clean the wheel bearings with solvent and inspect them for pits, scratches and excessive wear. Wipe all the old grease from the hub and inspect the bearing races. If either bearings or races are damaged, the bearing races must be removed; new bearings and races should then be installed as a set.

8. If the bearings are to be replaced, drive out the races from the hub using a brass drift.

9. Make certain the spindle, hub and bearing assemblies are clean prior to installation.

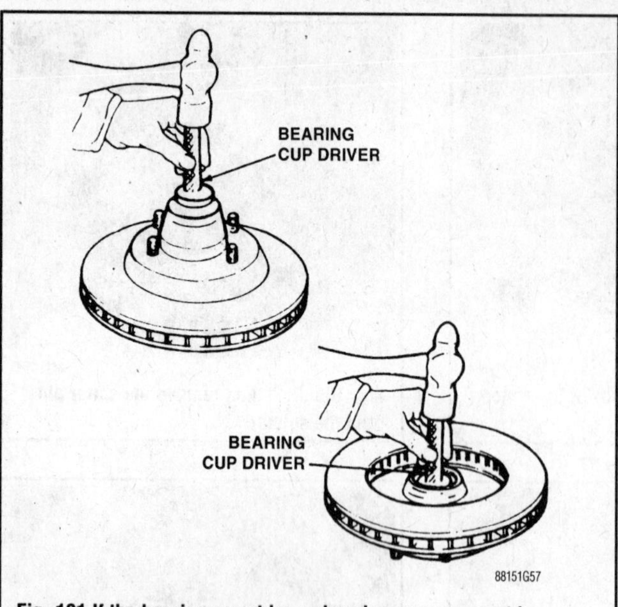

Fig. 191 If the bearings must be replaced, new races must be installed using appropriately sized drivers

To install:

10. If the bearing races were removed, install new ones using a bearing race installer (a suitably sized round driver).
11. Pack the bearings with a bearing packer. If done by hand, take great care to force as much grease as possible between the rollers and the cages, scoop the grease in from the top and bottom of the bearing cages.
12. Coat the inner surface of the hub and bearing races with grease.
13. Install the inner bearing in the hub. Lubricate the lip of the new seal with grease, then being careful not to distort it, install the oil seal with is lip facing the bearing. Drive the seal in until its outer edge is even with the edge of the hub. A seal installer is best to use for this, but any suitably sized and SMOOTH EDGED round driver can be used, including a piece of plastic pipe or a socket.
14. Install the hub/disc assembly on the spindle; being careful not to damage the oil seal.
15. Install the outer bearing, flat washer and spindle nut.
16. Properly adjust the wheel bearings. For details, refer to the procedure and the illustration found earlier in this section.
17. Install the grease cap, taking care not to distort and damage the cap, but also making sure it is fully seated.
18. Install the caliper, then install the wheel and tire assembly.
19. Remove the jackstands and carefully lower the vehicle.

CAUTION

BE SURE to pump the brake pedal to seat the pads before attempting to move the vehicle.

Fig. 192 Thoroughly pack the bearing with fresh, high temperature wheel bearing grease before installation

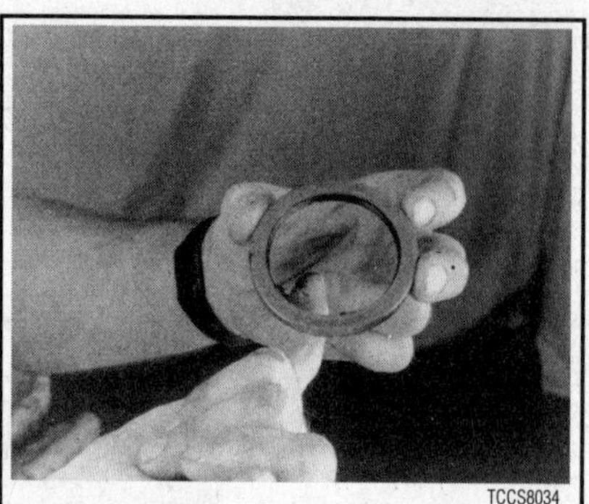

Fig. 193 Apply a thin coat of fresh grease to the new seal's inner bearing lip

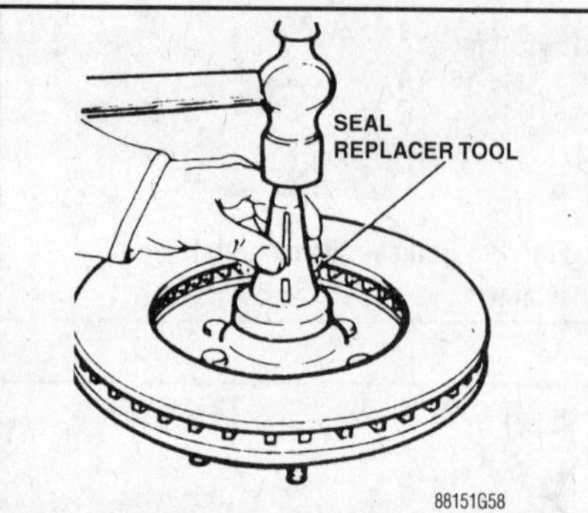

Fig. 194 The inner wheel bearing seal must also be driven in place using an installation tool

TOWING THE VEHICLE

See Figures 195 and 196

Preferred Method—Flatbed

For maximum safety to the components of your drivetrain and chassis, it is most desirable to have your vehicle towed by on a flatbed or whole car trailer. The only way to properly place the vehicle on a flatbed is to have it pulled on from the front.

WARNING

For the 1993 Cobra, a flatbed is a requirement as any other method will likely damage body components.

Alternate Method—T-hook

If a flatbed is available, your car (unless it is a Cobra) can be towed using a T-hook wrecker. In this case, it is best to tow from the rear, with the rear wheels off the ground, as this will prevent wear and tear on the drivetrain. Make sure the transmission is in N and that the parking brake is released. Tow vehicle speed should not exceed 35 mph (56 km/h) when using this method.

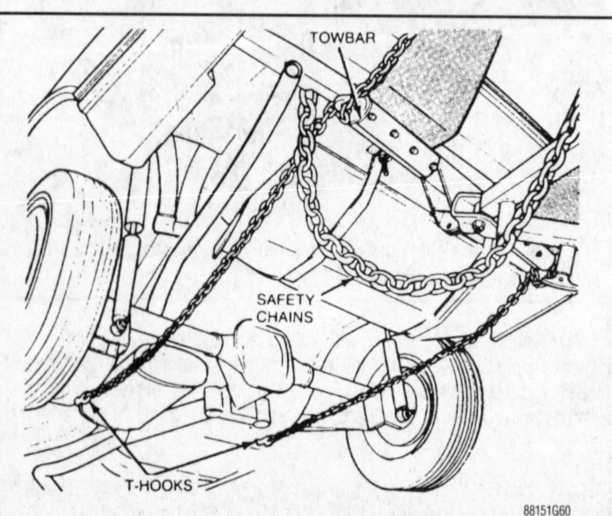

Fig. 195 When necessary, the car (unless it is a Cobra) can be towed from the rear (with the rear wheels off the ground) using a T-hook

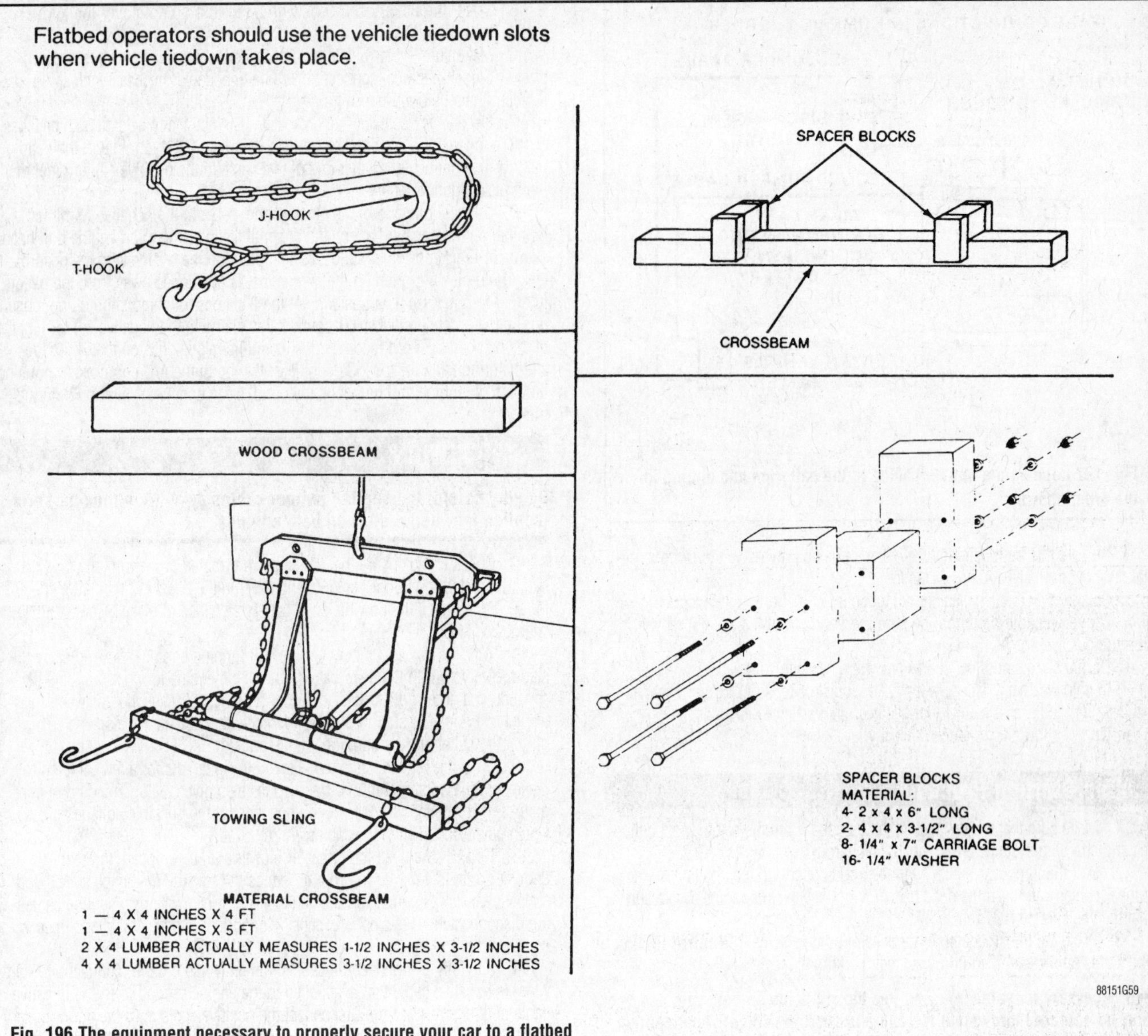

Fig. 196 The equipment necessary to properly secure your car to a flatbed

When necessary, you can tow using the T-hook in the front, with the rear wheel on the ground, BUT the all above conditions for rear towing are applicable AND the total distance towed should NOT EXCEED 50 miles (80 km) or transmission damage may occur unless the driveshaft is removed.

Last Chance Method—Dolly

If absolutely necessary, you can tow your vehicle with either the front or rear wheels on a dolly. Again the preferred method would be to leave the front wheels on the ground and the rear on the dolly so the drivetrain is not turning. All conditions which are applicable to the T-hook also apply to the dolly method.

JUMP STARTING A DEAD BATTERY

➧ **See Figure 197**

Whenever a vehicle is jump started, precautions must be followed in order to prevent the possibility of personal injury. Remember that batteries contain a small amount of explosive hydrogen gas which is a by-product of battery charging. Sparks should always be avoided when working around batteries, especially when attaching jumper cables. To minimize the possibility of accidental sparks, follow the procedure carefully.

✲✲ CAUTION

NEVER hook the batteries up in a series circuit or the entire electrical system will go up in smoke, especially the starter!

Vehicles equipped with a diesel engine may utilize two 12 volt batteries. If so, the batteries are connected in a parallel circuit (positive terminal to positive terminal, negative terminal to negative terminal). Hooking the batteries up in parallel circuit increases battery cranking power without increasing total battery voltage output. Output remains at 12 volts. On the other hand, hooking two 12 volt batteries up in a series circuit (positive terminal to negative terminal, positive terminal to negative terminal) increases total battery output to 24 volts (12 volts plus 12 volts).

Jump Starting Precautions

- Be sure that both batteries are of the same voltage. Vehicles covered by this manual and most vehicles on the road today utilize a 12 volt charging system.

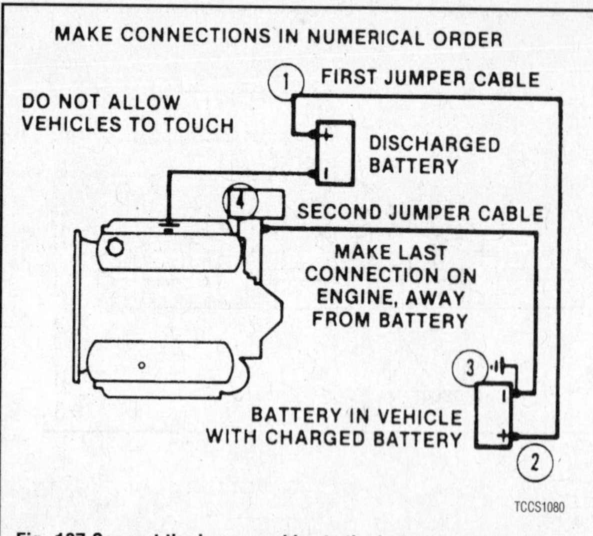

Fig. 197 Connect the jumper cables to the batteries and engine in the order shown

- Be sure that both batteries are of the same polarity (have the same terminal, in most cases NEGATIVE grounded).
- Be sure that the vehicles are not touching or a short could occur.
- On serviceable batteries, be sure the vent cap holes are not obstructed.
- Do not smoke or allow sparks anywhere near the batteries.
- In cold weather, make sure the battery electrolyte is not frozen. This can occur more readily in a battery that has been in a state of discharge.
- Do not allow electrolyte to contact your skin or clothing.

Jump Starting Procedure

1. Make sure that the voltages of the 2 batteries are the same. Most batteries and charging systems are of the 12 volt variety.
2. Pull the jumping vehicle (with the good battery) into a position so the jumper cables can reach the dead battery and that vehicle's engine. Make sure that the vehicles do NOT touch.
3. Place the transmissions/transaxles of both vehicles in **Neutral** (MT) or **P** (AT), as applicable, then firmly set their parking brakes.

➡If necessary for safety reasons, the hazard lights on both vehicles may be operated throughout the entire procedure without significantly increasing the difficulty of jumping the dead battery.

4. Turn all lights and accessories OFF on both vehicles. Make sure the ignition switches on both vehicles are turned to the **OFF** position.
5. Cover the battery cell caps with a rag, but do not cover the terminals.
6. Make sure the terminals on both batteries are clean and free of corrosion or proper electrical connection will be impeded. If necessary, clean the battery terminals before proceeding.
7. Identify the positive (+) and negative (−) terminals on both batteries.
8. Connect the first jumper cable to the positive (+) terminal of the dead battery, then connect the other end of that cable to the positive (+).terminal of the booster (good) battery.
9. Connect one end of the other jumper cable to the negative (−) terminal on the booster battery and the final cable clamp to an engine bolt head, alternator bracket or other solid, metallic point on the engine with the dead battery. Try to pick a ground on the engine that is positioned away from the battery in order to minimize the possibility of the 2 clamps touching should one loosen during the procedure. DO NOT connect this clamp to the negative (–) terminal of the bad battery. Ford recommends using the raised boss on the top of the alternator housing for the 2.3L engine or the top of the A/C compressor housing on the 5.0L engine, but in theory any good, clean engine metal should do the trick.

✲✲ CAUTION

Be very careful to keep the jumper cables away from moving parts (cooling fan, belts, etc.) on both engines.

10. Check to make sure that the cables are routed away from any moving parts, then start the donor vehicle's engine. Run the engine at moderate speed for several minutes to allow the dead battery a chance to receive some initial charge.
11. With the donor vehicle's engine still running slightly above idle, try to start the vehicle with the dead battery. Crank the engine for no more than 10 seconds at a time and let the starter cool for at least 20 seconds between tries. If the vehicle does not start in 3 tries, it is likely that something else is also wrong or that the battery needs additional time to charge.
12. Once the vehicle is started, allow it to run at idle for a few minuted to make sure that it is operating properly. This also gives the engine control computer time to "relearn" its idle conditions without the possible voltage spikes which could occur when the cables are removed.
13. Turn ON the headlights, heater blower and, if equipped, the rear defroster of both vehicles in order to reduce the severity of voltage spikes and subsequent risk of damage to the vehicles' electrical systems when the cables are disconnected. This step is especially important to any vehicle equipped with computer control modules.
14. Carefully disconnect the cables in the reverse order of connection. Start with the negative cable that is attached to the engine ground, then the negative cable on the donor battery. Disconnect the positive cable from the donor battery and finally, disconnect the positive cable from the formerly dead battery. Be careful when disconnecting the cables from the positive terminals not to allow the alligator clips to touch any metal on either vehicle or a short and sparks will occur.

JACKING AND HOISTING

➧ See Figures 198, 199, 200, 201 and 202

Your vehicle was supplied with a jack for emergency road repairs. This jack is fine for changing a flat tire or other short term procedures not requiring you to go beneath the vehicle. If it is used in an emergency situation, carefully follow the instructions provided either with the jack or in your owner's manual. Do not attempt to use the jack on any portions of the vehicle other than specified by the vehicle manufacturer. Always block the diagonally opposite wheel when using a jack.

✲✲ CAUTION

It is very important to be careful about running the engine on vehicles equipped with limited slip differentials while on a jack. When the drivetrain is engaged, power is transmitted to the wheel with the best traction. If one drive wheel is in contact with the ground, the vehicle will drive off the jack, possibly resulting in severe injury or damage.

Always raise a Ford car from under the axles, suspension arms or frame rails. Be sure to block the diagonally opposite wheel. Place jackstands under the vehicles at the points mentioned or directly under the frame when you are going to work under the vehicle.

With the exception of a hoist (which moist of us would love to have, but where would we put it?), the most convenient way of raising the vehicle is the use of a garage or floor jack. You may use the floor jack on any of the frame and suspension points illustrated.

Never place the jack under the radiator, engine or transmission components. Severe and expensive damage will result when the jack is raised. Additionally, never jack under the floorpan or bodywork; the metal will deform.

✲✲ CAUTION

NEVER WORK OR EVEN REACH UNDER A VEHICLE THAT IS NOT PROPERLY SUPPORTED. We are talking about your life here and the few minutes it takes to position a set of jackstands are precious little to ask to protect it.

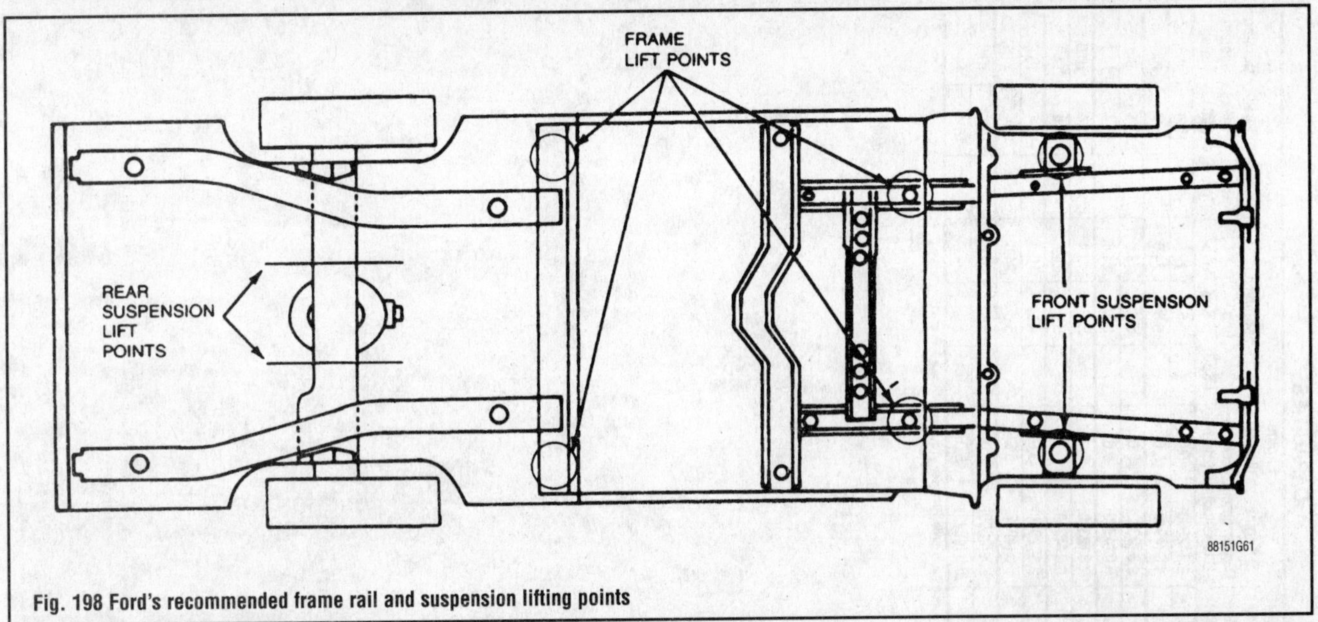

Fig. 198 Ford's recommended frame rail and suspension lifting points

Fig. 199 Though it is often done, Ford does not specifically recommend using the front cowl as a lifting point

Fig. 200 Jackstands should be placed under reinforced the side support bars which are available for the emergency jack

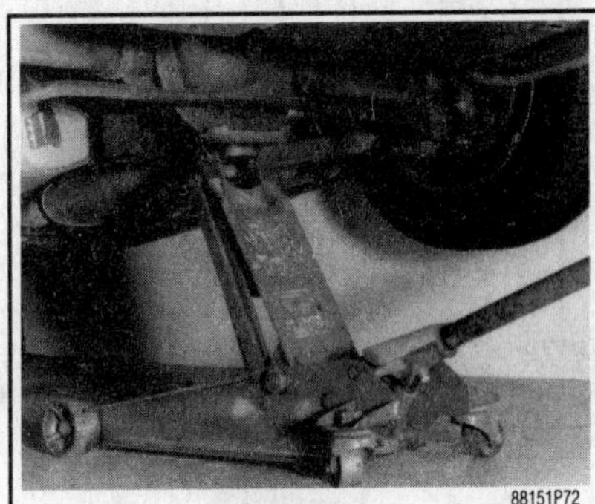

Fig. 201 The rear differential housing can be used as a lifting point for the entire rear end

Fig. 202 Jackstands can be placed under the axle housing or again under the reinforced side supports under the vehicle's body

Whenever you plan to work under the vehicle, you must support it on jackstands or ramps. NEVER use cinder blocks or stacks of wood to support the vehicle, even if you're only going to be under it for a few minutes. Never crawl under the vehicle when it is supported only by the tire-changing jack or other floor jack.

➡**Always position a block of wood or small rubber pad on top of the jack or jackstand to protect the lifting point's finish when lifting or supporting the vehicle.**

Small hydraulic, screw, or scissors jacks are satisfactory for raising the vehicle. Drive-on trestles or ramps are also a handy and safe way to both raise and support the vehicle. Be careful though, some ramps may be too steep to drive your vehicle onto without scraping the front bottom panels. The ground effects on many of the performance Mustang's will not easily clear the steep grade of the ramps. though one option might be to use the ramps like jackstands that you place under the tires once the vehicle is raised. Never support the vehicle on any suspension member (unless specifically instructed to do so by a repair manual) or by an underbody panel.

Jacking Precautions

The following safety points cannot be overemphasized:

- Always block the opposite wheel or wheels to keep the vehicle from rolling off the jack.
- When raising the front of the vehicle, firmly apply the parking brake.
- DON'T run the engine while the vehicle is on jackstands, ESPECIALLY if one or more drive wheels are remaining on the ground.
- When the drive wheels are to remain on the ground, leave the vehicle in gear to help prevent it from rolling.
- Always use jackstands to support the vehicle when you are working underneath. Place the stands beneath the vehicle's jacking brackets. Before climbing underneath, rock the vehicle a bit to make sure it is firmly supported.

CUSTOMER MAINTENANCE SCHEDULE A

Follow this Schedule if your driving habits MAINLY include one or more of the following conditions:

- Short trips of less than 10 miles (16 km) when outside temperatures remain below freezing.
- Operating during HOT WEATHER
  — Driving in stop-and-go "rush hour" traffic.
- Towing a trailer or using a car-top carrier.
- Operating in severe dust conditions.
- Extensive idling, such as police, taxi or door-to-door delivery service.

SERVICE INTERVAL Perform at the months or distances shown, whichever comes first. Miles × 1000	3	6	9	12	15	18	21	24	27	30	33	36	39	42	45	48	51	54	57	60
Kilometers × 1000	4.8	9.6	14.4	19.2	24	28.8	33.6	38.4	43.2	48	52.8	57.6	62.4	67.2	72	76.8	81.6	86.4	91.2	96
EMISSION CONTROL SERVICE																				
Change Engine Oil and Oil Filter Every 3 Months OR	X	X	X	X	X	X	X	X	X	X	X	X	X	X	X	X	X	X	X	X
Replace Spark Plugs										X										X
Inspect Accessory Drive Belt(s)										X										X
Replace PCV Valve																				X
Replace Air Cleaner Filter①										X										X
Replace Engine Coolant, EVERY 36 Months OR										X										X
Check Engine Coolant Protection, Hoses and Clamps	ANNUALLY																			
GENERAL MAINTENANCE																				
Inspect Exhaust Heat Shields										X										X
Change Automatic Transmission Fluid②										X										X
Lubricate Steering and/or Suspension Linkage										X										X
Inspect Brake Linings and Drums (Rear)③										X										X
Inspect and Repack Front Wheel Bearings										X										X

① If operating in severe dust, more frequent intervals may be required. Consult your dealer.
② Change automatic transmission fluid if your driving habits frequently include one or more of the following conditions:
- Operation during hot weather (above 32°C (90°F)) carrying heavy loads and in hilly terrain.
- Towing a trailer or using a car top carrier.
- Police, taxi or door to door delivery service.

③ If your driving includes continuous stop-and-go driving or driving in mountainous areas, more frequent intervals may be required.

88151G63

CUSTOMER MAINTENANCE SCHEDULE B

Follow Maintenance Schedule B if, generally, you drive your vehicle on a daily basis for several miles and NONE OF THE UNIQUE DRIVING CONDITIONS SHOWN IN SCHEDULE A APPLY TO YOUR DRIVING HABITS.

SERVICE INTERVALS Perform at the months or distances shown, whichever comes first. Miles x 1000	7.5	15	22.5	30	37.5	45	52.5	60
Kilometers x 1000	12	24	36	48	60	72	84	96
EMISSIONS CONTROL SERVICE								
Change Engine Oil and Filter (every 6 months) or 7,500 Miles Whichever Occurs First	X	X	X	X	X	X	X	X
Replace Spark Plugs				X				X
Change Crankcase Emission Filter①				X①				X①
Inspect Accessory Drive Belt(s)				X				X
Replace Air Cleaner Filter①				X①				X①
Replace PCV Valve								X
Change Engine Coolant Every 36 Months or				X				X
Check Engine Coolant Protection, Hoses and Clamps	ANNUALLY							
GENERAL MAINTENANCE								
Check Exhaust Heat Shields				X				X
Lube Steering and/or Suspension		X③		X		X③		X
Inspect Brake Linings and Drums (Rear)②				X				X
Inspect and Repack Front Wheel Bearings				X				X

① If operating in severe dust, more frequent intervals may be required. Consult your dealer.
② If your driving includes continuous stop-and-go driving or driving in mountainous areas, more frequent intervals may be required.
③ All vehicles.

88151G63

CAPACITIES

Year	Model	Engine ID/VIN	Engine Displacement Liters (cc)	Engine Oil with Filter (qts.)	Transmission (pts.) 4-Spd	5-Spd	Auto.	Drive Axle Rear (pts.)	Fuel Tank (gal.)	Cooling System (qts.)
1989	Mustang	A	2.3 (2300)	5.0	-	5.6	19.0	1	15.4	9.9
	Mustang	E	5.0 (4949)	5.0	-	5.6	24.6	1	15.4	14.1
1990	Mustang	A	2.3 (2300)	5.0	-	5.6	19.0	1	15.4	9.9
	Mustang	E	5.0 (4949)	5.0	-	5.6	24.6	1	15.4	14.1
1991	Mustang	M	2.3 (2300)	5.0	-	5.6	19.4	1	15.4	10.0
	Mustang	E	5.0 (4949)	5.0	-	5.6	24.6	1	15.4	14.1
1992	Mustang	M	2.3 (2300)	5.0	-	5.6	19.4	1	15.4	10.0
	Mustang	E	5.0 (4949)	5.0	-	5.6	24.6	1	15.4	14.1
1993	Mustang	M	2.3 (2300)	5.0	-	5.6	19.4	1	15.4	10.0
	Mustang	E	5.0 (4949)	5.0	-	5.6	24.6	1	15.4	14.1

Note: All capacities are approximate, use only as a guide. Refill slowly, checking the fluid level often

1 7.50" axle: 3.25 pts.
8.80" axle: 3.75 pts.

TCCS1C07

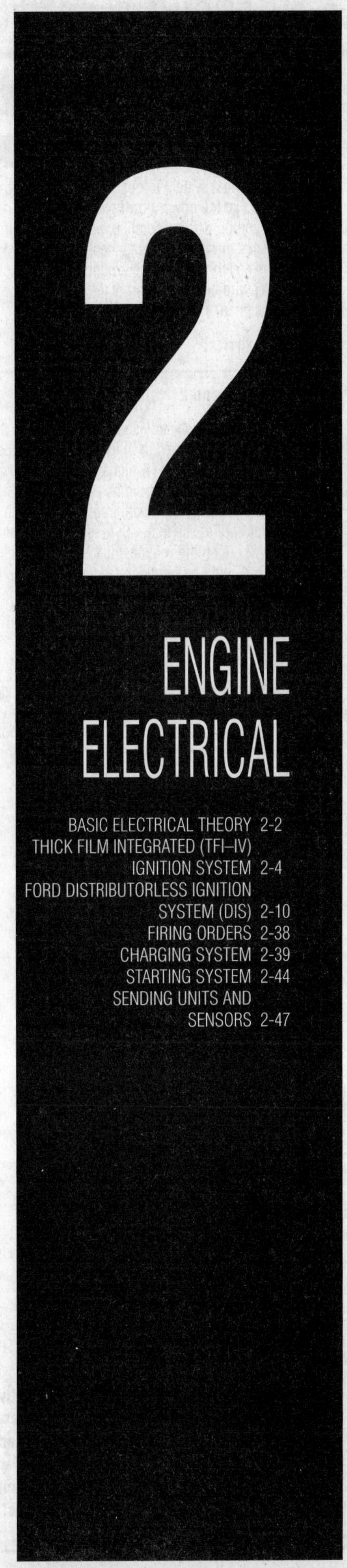
2
ENGINE ELECTRICAL
BASIC ELECTRICAL THEORY 2-2
THICK FILM INTEGRATED (TFI–IV) IGNITION SYSTEM 2-4
FORD DISTRIBUTORLESS IGNITION SYSTEM (DIS) 2-10
FIRING ORDERS 2-38
CHARGING SYSTEM 2-39
STARTING SYSTEM 2-44
SENDING UNITS AND SENSORS 2-47

BASIC ELECTRICAL THEORY

Understanding Electricity

For any electrical system to operate, there must be a complete circuit. This simply means that the power flow from the battery must make a full circle. When an electrical component is operating, power flows from the battery to the components, passes through the component (load) causing it to function, and returns to the battery through the ground path of the circuit. This ground may be either another wire or a metal part of the vehicle (depending upon how the component is designed).

BASIC CIRCUITS

➧ **See Figures 1 and 2**

Perhaps the easiest way to visualize a circuit is to think of connecting a light bulb (with two wires attached to it) to the battery. If one of the two wires was attached to the negative post (−) of the battery and the other wire to the positive post (+), the circuit would be complete and the light bulb would illuminate. Electricity could follow a path from the battery to the bulb and back to the battery. It's not hard to see that with longer wires on our light bulb, it could be mounted anywhere on the vehicle. Further, one wire could be fitted with a switch so that the light could be turned on and off. Various other items could be added to our primitive circuit to make the light flash, become brighter or dimmer under certain conditions, or advise the user that it's burned out.

Ground

Some automotive components are grounded through their mounting points. The electrical current runs through the chassis of the vehicle and returns to the battery through the ground (−) cable; if you look, you'll see that the battery ground cable connects between the battery and the body of the vehicle.

Load

Every complete circuit must include a "load" (something to use the electricity coming from the source). If you were to connect a wire between the two terminals of the battery (DON'T do this, but take out word for it) without the light bulb, the battery would attempt to deliver its entire power supply from one pole to another almost instantly. This is a short circuit. The electricity is taking a short cut to get to ground and is not being used by any load in the circuit. This sudden and uncontrolled electrical flow can cause great damage to other components in the circuit and can develop a tremendous amount of heat. A short in an automotive wiring harness can develop sufficient heat to melt the insulation on all the surrounding wires and reduce a multiple wire cable to one sad lump of plastic and copper. Two common causes of shorts are broken insulation

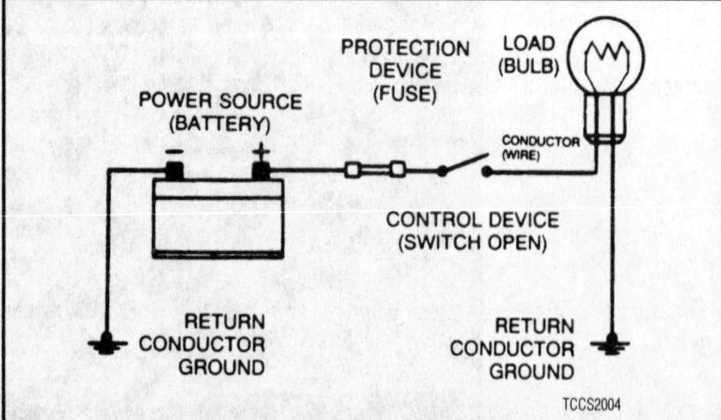

Fig. 1 Here is an example of a simple automotive circuit. When the switch is closed, power from the positive battery terminal flows through the fuse, then the switch and to the load (light bulb), the light illuminates and then, the circuit is completed through the return conductor and the vehicle ground. If the light did not work, the tests could be made with a voltmeter or test light at the battery, fuse, switch or bulb socket

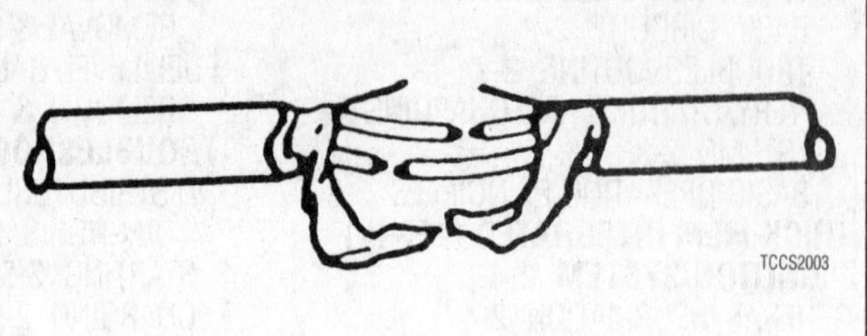

Fig. 2 Damaged insulation can allow wires to break (causing an open circuit) or touch (causing a short)

(thereby exposing the wire to contact with surrounding metal surfaces or other wires) or a failed switch (the pins inside the switch come out of place and touch each other).

Switches and Relays

Some electrical components which require a large amount of current to operate also have a relay in their circuit. Since these circuits carry a large amount of current (amperage or amps), the thickness of the wire in the circuit (wire gauge) is also greater. If this large wire were connected from the load to the control switch on the dash, the switch would have to carry the high amperage load and the dash would be twice as large to accommodate wiring harnesses as thick as your wrist. To prevent these problems, a relay is used. The large wires in the circuit are connected from the battery to one side of the relay and from the opposite side of the relay to the load. The relay is normally open, preventing current from passing through the circuit. An additional, smaller wire is connected from the relay to the control switch for the circuit. When the control switch is turned on, it grounds the smaller wire to the relay and completes its circuit. The main switch inside the relay closes, sending power to the component without routing the main power through the inside of the vehicle. Some common circuits which may use relays are the horn, headlights, starter and rear window defogger systems.

Protective Devices

It is possible for larger surges of current to pass through the electrical system of your vehicle. If this surge of current were to reach the load in the circuit, it could burn it out or severely damage it. To prevent this, fuses, circuit breakers and/or fusible links are connected into the supply wires of the electrical system. These items are nothing more than a built–in weak spot in the system. It's much easier to go to a known location (the fusebox) to see why a circuit is inoperative than to dissect 15 feet of wiring under the dashboard, looking for what happened.

When an electrical current of excessive power passes through the fuse, the fuse blows (the conductor melts) and breaks the circuit, preventing the passage of current and protecting the components.

A circuit breaker is basically a self repairing fuse. It will open the circuit in the same fashion as a fuse, but when either the short is removed or the surge subsides, the circuit breaker resets itself and does not need replacement.

A fuse link (fusible link or main link) is a wire that acts as a fuse. One of these is normally connected between the starter relay and the main wiring harness under the hood. Since the starter is usually the highest electrical draw on the vehicle, an internal short during starting could direct about 130 amps into the wrong places. Consider the damage potential of introducing this current into a system whose wiring is rated at 15 amps and you'll understand the need for protection. Since this link is very early in the electrical path, it's the first place to look if nothing on the vehicle works, but the battery seems to be charged and is properly connected.

TROUBLESHOOTING

➧ **See Figures 3, 4 and 5**

Electrical problems generally fall into one of three areas:

- The component that is not functioning is not receiving current.

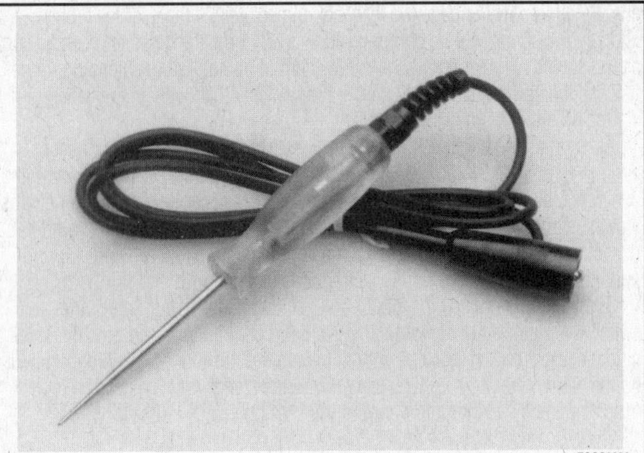

TCCS2006

Fig. 3 A 12 volt test light is useful when checking parts of a circuit for power

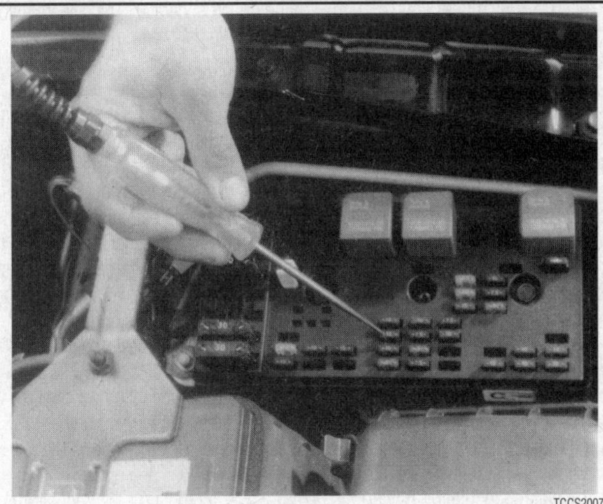

TCCS2007

Fig. 4 Here, someone is checking a circuit by making sure there is power to the component's fuse

- The component is receiving power but is not using it or is using it incorrectly (component failure).
- The component is improperly grounded.

The circuit can be can be checked with a test light and a jumper wire. The test light is a device that looks like a pointed screwdriver with a wire on one end and a bulb in its handle. A jumper wire is simply a piece of wire with alligator clips or special terminals on each end. If a component is not working, you must follow a systematic plan to determine which of the three causes is the villain.

1. Turn ON the switch that controls the item not working.

➡**Some items only work when the ignition switch is turned ON.**

2. Disconnect the power supply wire from the component.
3. Attach the ground wire of a test light or a voltmeter to a good metal ground.
4. Touch the end probe of the test light (or the positive lead of the voltmeter) to the power wire; if there is current in the wire, the light in the test light will come on (or the voltmeter will indicate the amount of voltage). You have now established that current is getting to the component.
5. Turn the ignition or dash switch **OFF** and reconnect the wire to the component.

If there was no power, then the problem is between the battery and the component. This includes all the switches, fuses, relays and the battery itself. The next place to look is the fusebox; check carefully either by eye or by using the test light across the fuse clips. The easiest way to check is to simply replace the fuse. If the fuse is blown, and upon replacement, immediately blows again, there is a short between the fuse and the component. This is generally (not always) a sign of an internal short in the component. Disconnect the power wire at the component again and replace the fuse; if the fuse holds, the component is the problem.

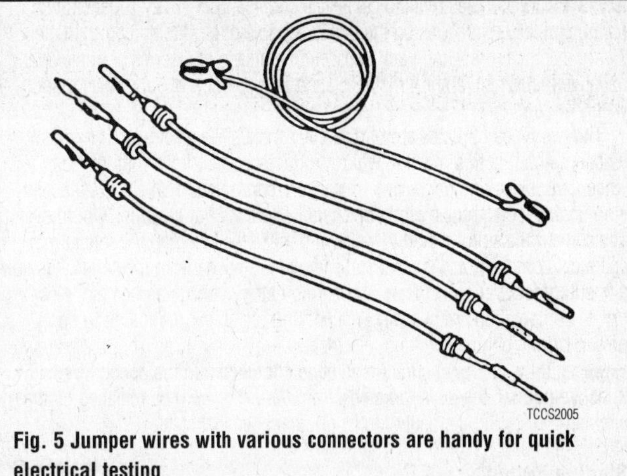

TCCS2005

Fig. 5 Jumper wires with various connectors are handy for quick electrical testing

**** WARNING**

DO NOT test a component by running a jumper wire from the battery UNLESS you are certain that it operates on 12 volts. Many electronic components are designed to operate with less voltage and connecting them to 12 volts could destroy them. Jumper wires are best used to bypass a portion of the circuit (such as a stretch of wire or a switch) that DOES NOT contain a resistor and is suspected to be bad.

If all the fuses are good and the component is not receiving power, find the switch for the circuit. Bypass the switch with the jumper wire. This is done by connecting one end of the jumper to the power wire coming into the switch and the other end to the wire leaving the switch. If the component comes to life, the switch has failed.

**** WARNING**

Never substitute the jumper for the component. The circuit needs the electrical load of the component. If you bypass it, you will cause a short circuit.

Checking the ground for any circuit can mean tracing wires to the body, cleaning connections or tightening mounting bolts for the component itself. If the jumper wire can be connected to the case of the component or the ground connector, you can ground the other end to a piece of clean, solid metal on the vehicle. Again, if the component starts working, you've found the problem.

A systematic search through the fuse, connectors, switches and the component itself will almost always yield an answer. Loose and/or corroded connectors, particularly in ground circuits, are becoming a larger problem in modern vehicles. The computers and on-board electronic (solid state) systems are highly sensitive to improper grounds and will change their function drastically if one occurs.

Remember that for any electrical circuit to work, ALL the connections must be clean and tight.

➡**For more information on Understanding and Troubleshooting Electrical Systems, please refer to Section 6 of this manual.**

Battery, Starting and Charging Systems

BASIC OPERATING PRINCIPLES

Battery

The battery is the first link in the chain of mechanisms which work together to provide cranking of the automobile engine. In most modern vehicles, the battery is a lead/acid electrochemical device consisting of six 2v subsections (cells) connected in series so the unit is capable of producing approximately 12v of electrical pressure. Each subsection consists of a series of positive and negative plates held a short distance apart in a solution of sulfuric acid and water.

The two types of plates are of dissimilar metals. This sets-up a chemical reaction, and it is this reaction which produces current flow from the battery when its positive and negative terminals are connected to an electrical accessory such as a lamp or motor. The continued transfer of electrons would eventually convert the sulfuric acid to water, and make the two plates identical in chemical composition. As electrical energy is removed from the battery, its voltage output tends to drop. Thus, measuring battery voltage and battery electrolyte composition are two ways of checking the ability of the unit to supply power. During engine cranking, electrical energy is removed from the battery. However, if the charging circuit is in good condition and the operating conditions are normal, the power removed from the battery will be replaced by the alternator, restoring the battery to its original chemical state.

Starting System

The battery and starting motor are linked by very heavy electrical cables designed to minimize resistance to the flow of current. Generally, the major power supply cable that leaves the battery goes directly to the starter, while other electrical system needs are supplied by a smaller cable. During starter operation, power flows from the battery to the starter and is grounded through the vehicle's frame/body or engine and the battery's negative ground strap.

The starter is a specially designed, direct current electric motor capable of producing a great amount of power for its size. One thing that allows the motor to produce a great deal of power is its tremendous rotating speed. It drives the engine through a tiny pinion gear (attached to the starter's armature), which drives the very large flywheel ring gear at a greatly reduced speed. Another factor allowing it to produce so much power is that only intermittent operation is required of it. Thus, little allowance for air circulation is necessary, and the windings can be built into a very small space.

The starter solenoid is a magnetic device which employs the small current supplied by the start circuit of the ignition switch. This magnetic action moves a plunger which mechanically engages the starter and closes the heavy switch connecting it to the battery. The starting switch circuit usually consists of the starting switch contained within the ignition switch, a neutral safety switch or clutch pedal switch, and the wiring necessary to connect these in series with the starter solenoid or relay.

The pinion, a small gear, is mounted to a one way drive clutch. This clutch is splined to the starter armature shaft. When the ignition switch is moved to the **START** position, the solenoid plunger slides the pinion toward the flywheel ring gear via a collar and spring. If the teeth on the pinion and flywheel match properly, the pinion will engage the flywheel immediately. If the gear teeth butt one another, the spring will be compressed and will force the gears to mesh as soon as the starter turns far enough to allow them to do so. As the solenoid plunger reaches the end of its travel, it closes the contacts that connect the battery and starter, then the engine is cranked.

As soon as the engine starts, the flywheel ring gear begins turning fast enough to drive the pinion at an extremely high rate of speed. At this point, the one-way clutch begins allowing the pinion to spin faster than the starter shaft so that the starter will not operate at excessive speed. When the ignition switch is released from the starter position, the solenoid is de–energized and a spring pulls the gear out of mesh, interrupting the current flow to the starter.

Some starters employ a separate relay, mounted away from the starter, to switch the motor and solenoid current on and off. The relay replaces the solenoid electrical switch, but does not eliminate the need for a solenoid mounted on the starter used to mechanically engage the starter drive gears. The relay is used to reduce the amount of current the starting switch must carry.

Charging System

The automobile charging system provides electrical power for operation of the vehicle's ignition system, starting system and all electrical accessories. The battery serves as an electrical surge or storage tank, storing (in chemical form) the energy originally produced by the engine driven generator. The system also provides a means of regulating output to protect the battery from being overcharged and to avoid excessive voltage to the accessories.

The storage battery is a chemical device incorporating parallel lead plates in a tank containing a sulfuric acid/water solution. Adjacent plates are slightly dissimilar, and the chemical reaction of the two dissimilar plates produces electrical energy when the battery is connected to a load such as the starter motor. The chemical reaction is reversible, so that when the generator is producing a voltage (electrical pressure) greater than that produced by the battery, electricity is forced into the battery, and the battery is returned to its fully charged state.

Newer automobiles use alternating current generators or alternators, because they are more efficient, can be rotated at higher speeds, and have fewer brush problems. In an alternator, the field usually rotates while all the current produced passes only through the stator winding. The brushes bear against continuous slip rings. This causes the current produced to periodically reverse the direction of its flow. Diodes (electrical one way valves) block the flow of current from traveling in the wrong direction. A series of diodes is wired together to permit the alternating flow of the stator to be rectified back to 12 volts DC for use by the vehicle's electrical system.

The voltage regulating function is performed by a regulator. The regulator is often built into the alternator; this system is termed an integrated or internal regulator.

THICK FILM INTEGRATED (TFI–IV) IGNITION SYSTEM

General Information

➧ **See Figure 6**

The Thick Film Integrated (TFI-IV) ignition system is used for all EEC-IV electronic fuel-injected vehicles. The TFI-IV system module has six pins and uses an E-core ignition coil, named after the shape of the laminations making up the core.

There are two types of TFI-IV systems:

- PUSH START– this first TFI-IV system featured a "push-start" mode which allowed manual transmission vehicles to be push started. Automatic transmission vehicles must not be push-started.
- COMPUTER CONTROLLED DWELL– This second TFI-IV system features an EEC-IV controlled ignition coil charge time.

The TFI-IV ignition system with the Universal distributor has a distributor base mounted TFI ignition module and a Hall-effect stator assembly. The distributor also contains a provision to change the basic distributor calibration with the use of a replaceable retard (or octane) rod. The standard 0° calibration may be changed to either 3° or 6° retard rods. No other calibration changes are possible.

➡Initial timing adjustments are not required unless the distributor has been removed from the engine or moved from its initial factory setting.

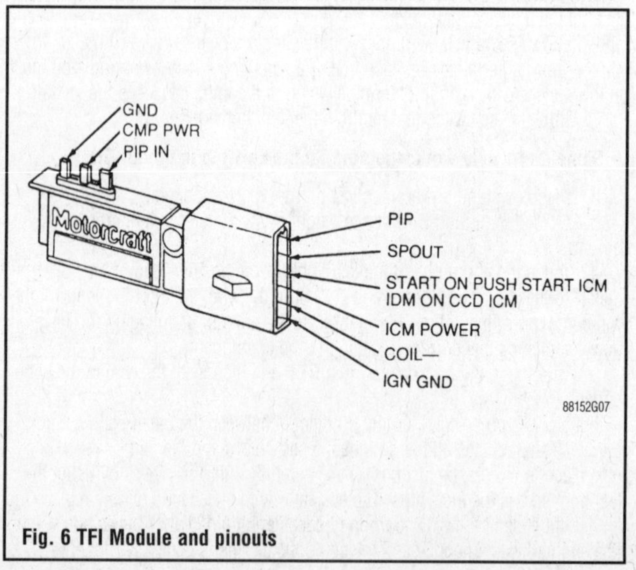

Fig. 6 TFI Module and pinouts

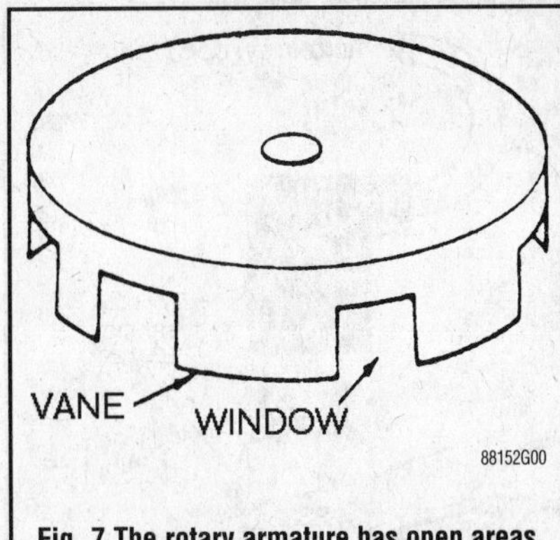

Fig. 7 The rotary armature has open areas called windows and tabs called vanes

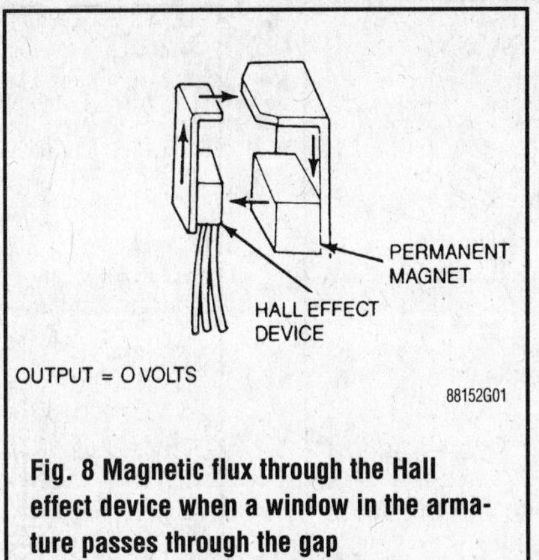

Fig. 8 Magnetic flux through the Hall effect device when a window in the armature passes through the gap

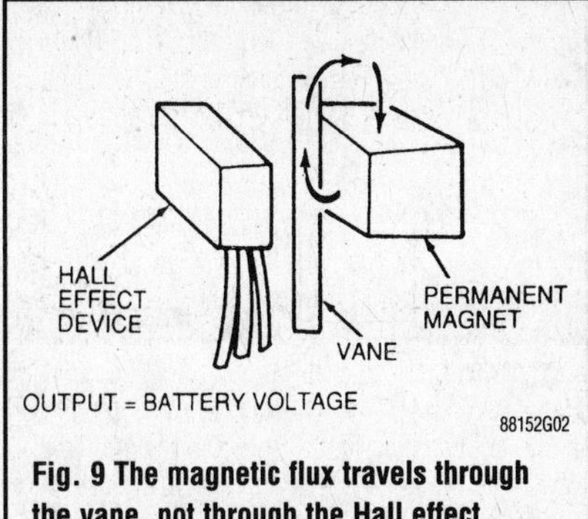

Fig. 9 The magnetic flux travels through the vane, not through the Hall effect device, when the vane passes through the gap

Both the PUSH START and COMPUTER CONTROLLED DWELL TFI-IV systems operate in the same manner. The TFI-IV module supplies voltage to the Profile Ignition Pickup (PIP) sensor, which sends crankshaft position information to the TFI-IV module. The TFI-IV module then sends this information to the EEC-IV module which determines the spark timing. The EEC-IV module sends an electronic signal to the TFI-IV module to turn off the coil and produce a spark to fire the spark plug.

SYSTEM OPERATION

See Figures 7, 8 and 9

The operation of the universal distributor is accomplished through the Hall-effect stator assembly, causing the ignition coil to be switched off and on by the EEC-IV computer and TFI-IV modules. The vane switch is an encapsulated package consisting of a Hall sensor on one side and a permanent magnet on the other side.

A rotary armature, made of ferrous metal, is used to trigger the Hall-effect switch. When the window of the armature is between the magnet and the Hall-effect device, a magnetic flux field is completed through the Hall-effect device and back to the magnet. As the vane passes through the opening, the flux lines are shunted through the vane and back to the magnet. A voltage is produced while the vane passes through the opening. When the vane clears the opening, the window causes the signal to go to 0 volts. The signal is then used by the EEC-IV system for crankshaft-position sensing and the computation of the desired spark advance based on the engine demand and calibration. The voltage distribution is accomplished through a conventional rotor, cap and ignition wires.

Diagnosis and Testing

SERVICE PRECAUTIONS

- Always turn the key **OFF** and isolate both ends of a circuit whenever testing for shorts or continuity.
- Never measure voltage or resistance directly at the processor connector.
- Always disconnect solenoids and switches from the harness before measuring for continuity, resistance or energizing by way of a 12-volt source.
- When disconnecting connectors, inspect for damaged or pushed-out pins, corrosion, loose wires, etc. Service if required.

PRELIMINARY CHECKS

1. Visually inspect the engine compartment to ensure that all vacuum lines and spark plug wires are properly routed and securely connected.
2. Examine all wiring harnesses and connectors for insulation damage, burned, overheated, loose or broken conditions. Check the the TFI module is securely fastened to the side of the distributor.
3. Be certain that the battery is fully charged and that all accessories are off during the diagnosis.

TFI–IV AND TFI–IV WITH CCD

Ignition Coil Secondary Voltage Test

CRANK MODE

1. Connect a spark tester between the ignition coil wire and a good engine ground.
2. Crank the engine and check for spark at the tester.
3. Turn the ignition switch **OFF.**
4. If no spark occurs, check the following:
   a. Inspect the ignition coil for damage or carbon tracking.
   b. Check that the distributor shaft is rotating when the engine is being cranked.
   c. If the results in Steps a and b are okay, go to Module Test.
5. If a spark did occur, check the distributor cap and rotor for damage or carbon tracking. Go to the Ignition Coil Secondary Voltage (Run Mode) Test

RUN MODE

1. Fully apply the parking brake. Place the gear shift lever in neutral (manual) or **P**(automatic).
2. Disconnect the S terminal wire at the starter relay. Attach a remote starter switch.
3. Turn the ignition switch to the **RUN** position.
4. Using the remote starter switch, crank the engine and check for spark.
5. Turn the ignition switch **OFF**.
6. If no spark occurred, go to the Wiring Harness test.
7. If a spark did occur, the problem is not in the ignition system.

Wiring Harness Test

See Figure 10

1. Push the connector tabs and separate the wiring harness connector from the ignition module. Check for dirt, corrosion or damage.
2. Check that the S terminal wire at the starter relay is disconnected.
3. Measure the battery voltage.
4. Carefully insert a small, straight pin in the appropriate terminal.

➡Do not allow the straight pin to contact electrical ground while performing this test.

5. Measure the voltage at the following points:
   a. TFI without CCD: Terminal No. 3 (Run circuit) with the ignition switch in **START** and **RUN.**
   b. TFI without CCD: Terminal No. 4 (Start circuit) with the ignition switch in **START.**
   c. TFI with CCD:Terminal No. 3 (Run circuit) with the ignition switch in **START** and **RUN.**
6. Turn the ignition switch **OFF** and remove the straight pin.
7. Reconnect the S terminal wire at the starter relay.
8. If the results are within 90% of battery voltage, replace the TFI module.

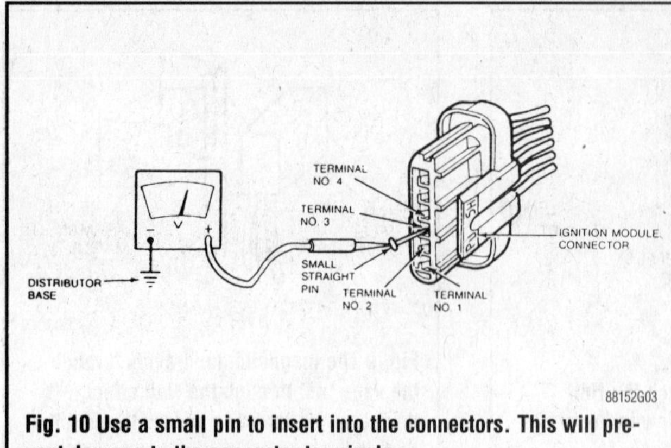

Fig. 10 Use a small pin to insert into the connectors. This will prevent damage to the connector terminals

9. If the results are not within 90% of battery voltage, inspect the wiring harness and connectors in the faulty circuit. Also, check for a faulty ignition switch.

Module Test

➧ **See Figure 11**

1. Remove the distributor from the engine. Remove the TFI module from the distributor.
2. Measure the resistance between the TFI module terminals as shown below:
   a. GID—PIP IN: should be greater than 500 ohms.
   b. PIP PWR—PIP IN: should be less than 2,000 ohms.
   c. PIP PWR—TFI PWR: should be less than 200 ohms.
   d. GND—IGN GND: should be less than 2 ohms.
   e. PIP IN—PIP: should be less than 200 ohms.

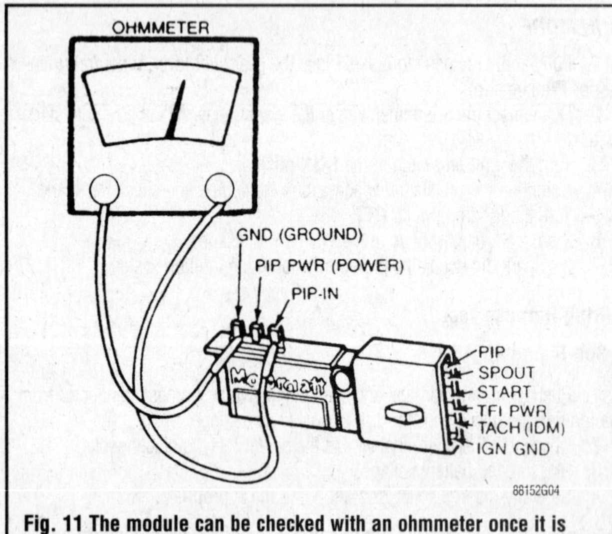

Fig. 11 The module can be checked with an ohmmeter once it is removed from the distributor

Coil Wire and Coil Test

➧ **See Figures 12 thru 17**

1. Disconnect the ignition coil connector and check for dirt, corrosion or damage.
2. Substitute a known-good coil and check for spark using the spark tester.

➡**Dangerous high voltage may be present when performing this test. Do not hold the coil while performing this test.**

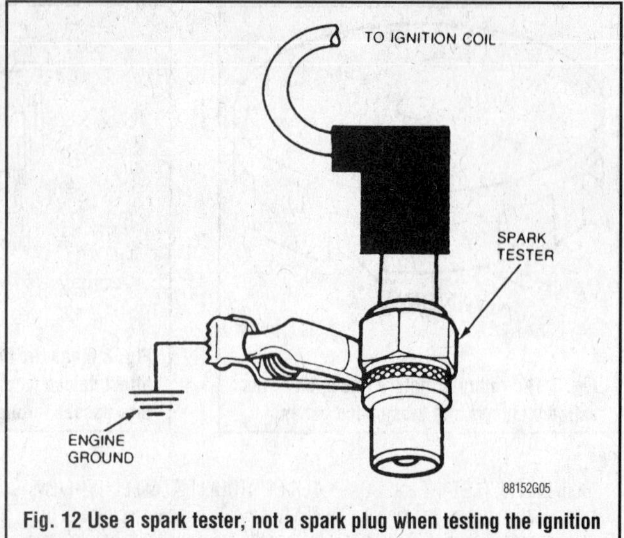

Fig. 12 Use a spark tester, not a spark plug when testing the ignition coil and wire

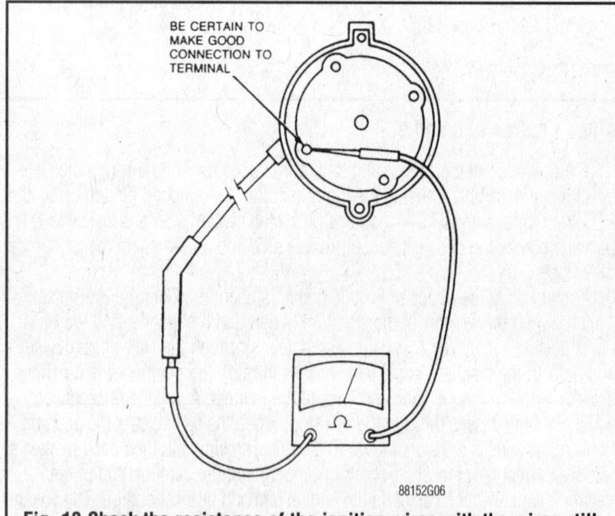

Fig. 13 Check the resistance of the ignition wires with the wires still attached to the cap

Fig. 14 The coil may reside under a cover at the fender well

Fig. 15 Remove the cover to access the coil for the tests

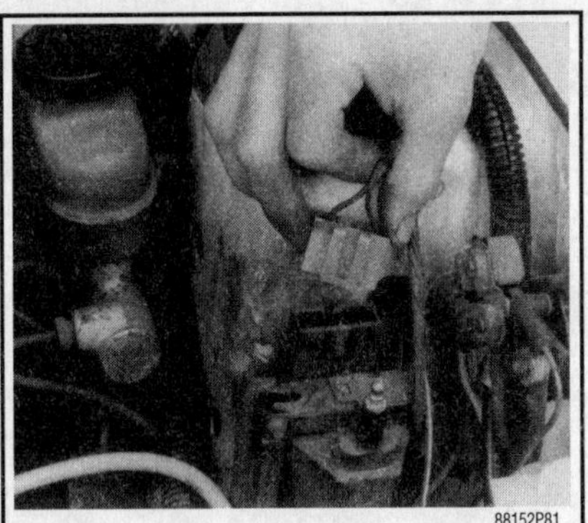

Fig. 16 Pull the connector off after releasing the clip at the front

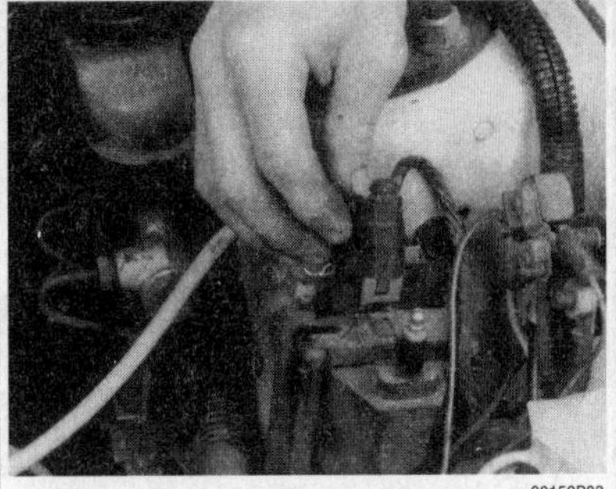

Fig. 17 Pull on the boot, not the wire, when removing the coil wire from the terminal

3. Crank the engine and check for spark.
4. Turn the ignition switch **OFF.**
5. If a spark did occur, measure the resistance of the ignition coil wire, replace it if the resistance is greater than 7000 ohms per foot. If the readings are within specification, replace the ignition coil.
6. If no spark occurs, the problem is not the coil. Go to the EEC-IV and TFI-IV system test.

EEC–IV and TFI–IV System Test

➧ See Figures 18 and 19

1. Disconnect the pin-in-line connector near the distributor.
2. Crank the engine
3. Turn the ignition switch **OFF**.
4. If a spark did occur, check the PIP and ignition ground wires for continuity. If okay, the problem is not in the ignition system.
5. If no spark occurs, check the voltage at the positive (+) terminal of the ignition coil with the ignition switch in **RUN**.
6. If the reading is not within battery voltage, check for a worn or damaged ignition switch.
7. If the reading is within battery voltage, check for faults in the wiring between the coil and TFI module terminal No. 2 or any additional wiring or components connected to that circuit.

Spark Timing Advance Test

Spark timing advance is controlled by the EEC system. This procedure checks the capability of the ignition module to receive the spark timing command from the EEC module. The use of a volt/ohmmeter is required.

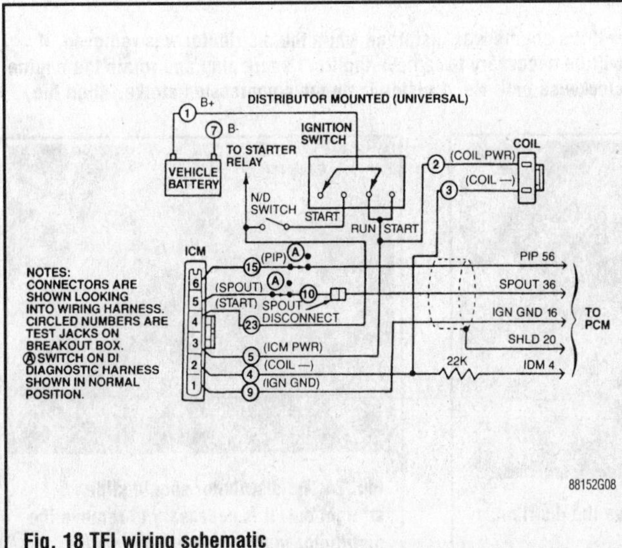

Fig. 18 TFI wiring schematic

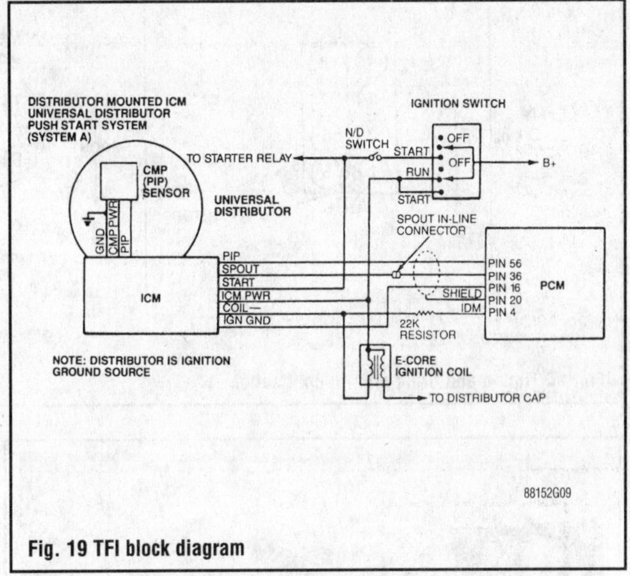

Fig. 19 TFI block diagram

1. Turn the ignition switch **OFF.**
2. Disconnect the pin-in-line connector (SPOUT connector) near the TFI module.
3. Start the engine and measure the voltage, at idle, from the SPOUT connector to the distributor base. The reading should equal battery voltage.
4. If the result is okay, the problem lies within the EEC-IV system.
5. If the result was not satisfactory, separate the wiring harness connector from the ignition module. Check for damage, corrosion or dirt. Service as necessary.
6. Measure the resistance between terminal No. 5 and the pin-in-line connector. This test is done at the ignition module connector only. The reading should be less than 5 ohms.
7. If the reading is okay, replace the TFI module.
8. If the result was not satisfactory, service the wiring between the pin inline connector and the TFI connector.

Distributor

REMOVAL & INSTALLATION

➧ See Figures 20, 21, 22, 23 and 24

1. Rotate the engine until the No. 1 piston is on top dead center of its compression stroke.
2. Disconnect the negative battery cable. Disconnect the vehicle wiring harness connector from the distributor. Before removing the distributor cap, mark the position of the No. 1 wire tower on the cap for reference.
3. Loosen the distributor cap hold-down screws and remove the cap. Mark

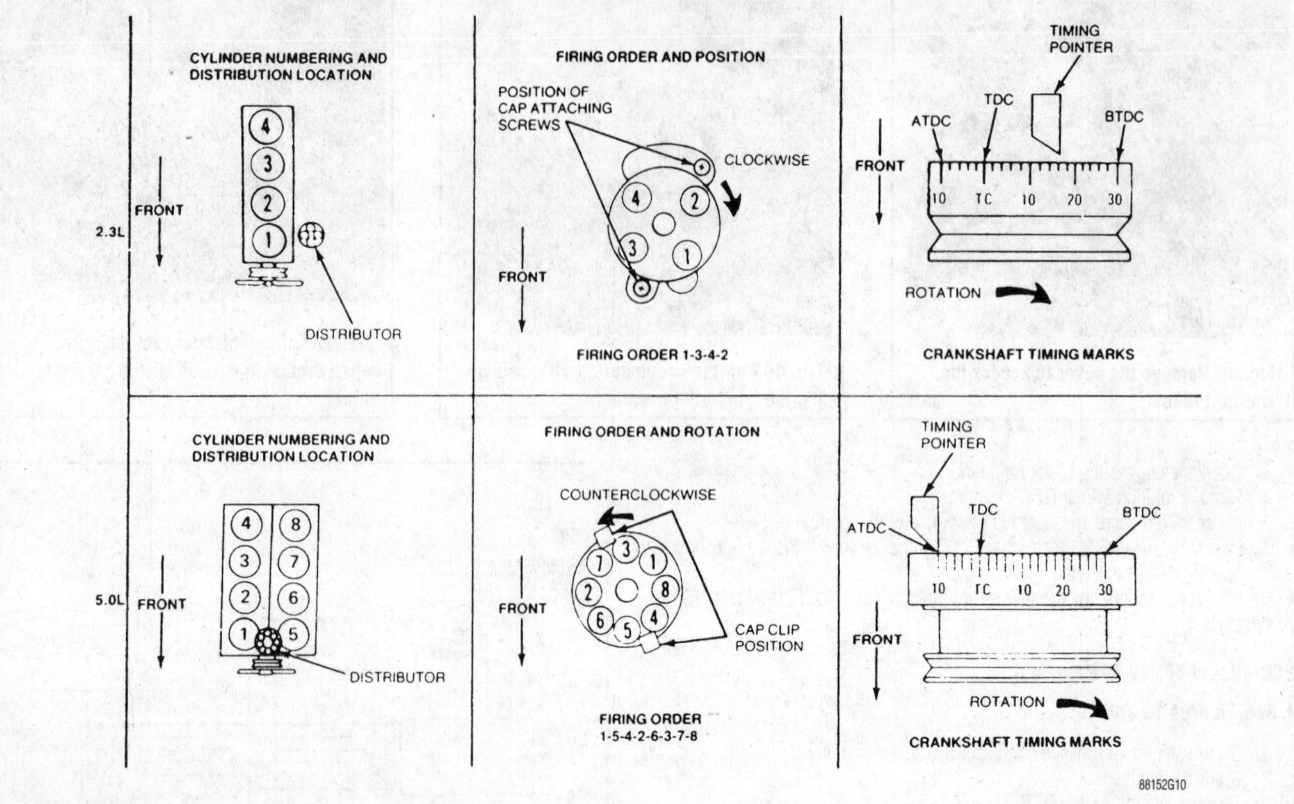

CYLINDER NUMBERING AND DISTRIBUTION LOCATION

2.3L FRONT

DISTRIBUTOR

FIRING ORDER AND POSITION

POSITION OF CAP ATTACHING SCREWS

CLOCKWISE

FRONT

FIRING ORDER 1-3-4-2

TIMING POINTER

TDC ATDC BTDC

FRONT

10 TC 10 20 30

ROTATION

CRANKSHAFT TIMING MARKS

CYLINDER NUMBERING AND DISTRIBUTION LOCATION

5.0L FRONT

DISTRIBUTOR

FIRING ORDER AND ROTATION

COUNTERCLOCKWISE

FRONT

CAP CLIP POSITION

FIRING ORDER 1-5-4-2-6-3-7-8

TIMING POINTER

TDC ATDC BTDC

10 TC 10 20 30

FRONT

ROTATION

CRANKSHAFT TIMING MARKS

88152G10

Fig. 20 Timing and firing order identification

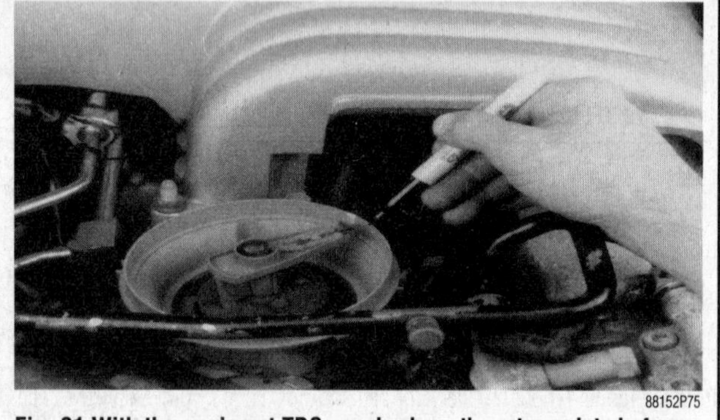

88152P75

Fig. 21 With the engine at TDC, mark where the rotor points before removing the distributor

the position of the rotor to the distributor housing. Position the cap and wires out of the way.

4. Scribe a mark in the distributor body and the engine block to indicate the position of the distributor in the engine.
5. Remove the distributor hold-down bolt and clamp.

➡Some engines may be equipped with a security-type distributor hold down bolt. If this is the case, use distributor wrench T82L–12270–A or equivalent, to remove the retaining bolt and clamp.

6. Remove the distributor assembly from the engine. Be sure not to rotate the engine while the distributor is removed.

To install:

7. Make sure that the engine is still with the No.1 piston up on top dead center of its compression stroke.

➡If the engine was disturbed while the distributor was removed, it will be necessary to remove the No.1 spark plug and rotate the engine clockwise until No. 1 piston is on the compression stroke. Align the

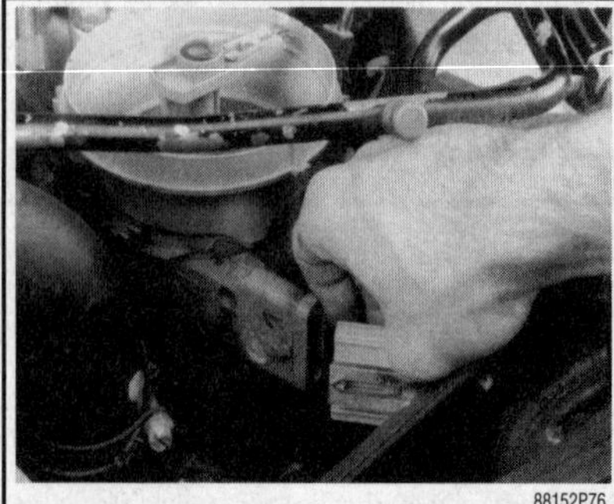

88152P76

Fig. 22 Disconnect the TFI module by pressing the catch and releasing the harness

88152P77

Fig. 23 Loosen and remove the distributor holddown

88152P78

Fig. 24 The distributor should slide straight out. It is necessary to remove the distributor to change the TFI module

timing pointer with TDC on the crankshaft damper or flywheel, as required.

8. Check that the O-ring is installed and in good condition on the distributor body.
9. On all vehicles:
   a. Rotate the distributor shaft so the rotor points toward the mark on the distributor housing made previously.
   b. Rotate the rotor slightly so the leading edge of the vane is centered in the vane switch state assembly.
   c. Rotate the distributor in the block to align the leading edge of the vane with the vane switch stator assembly. Make certain the rotor is pointing to the No. 1 mark on the distributor base.

➡If the vane and vane switch stator cannot be aligned by rotating the distributor in the cylinder block, remove the distributor enough to just disengage the distributor gear from the camshaft gear. Rotate the rotor enough to engage the distributor gear on another tooth of the camshaft gear. Repeat Step 9 if necessary.

10. Install the distributor hold-down clamp and bolt(s); tighten them slightly.
11. Install the cap and wires. Install the No. 1 spark plug, if removed.
12. Recheck the initial timing.
13. Tighten the hold-down clamp and recheck the timing. Adjust if necessary.

Stator

REMOVAL & INSTALLATION

See Figures 25, 26, 27 and 28

1. Disconnect the negative battery cable.
2. Remove the distributor assembly from the engine. Remove the rotor. Remove the ignition module from the base, if equipped.
3. Mark the armature and distributor gear for orientation during reassembly.
4. Hold the distributor drive gear and remove the armature retaining screws. Remove the armature.
5. Remove the distributor gear retaining pin and discard it.
6. Place the distributor assembly in an arbor press. Press off the distributor gear from the shaft, using bearing removal tool D84L–950–A or equivalent.

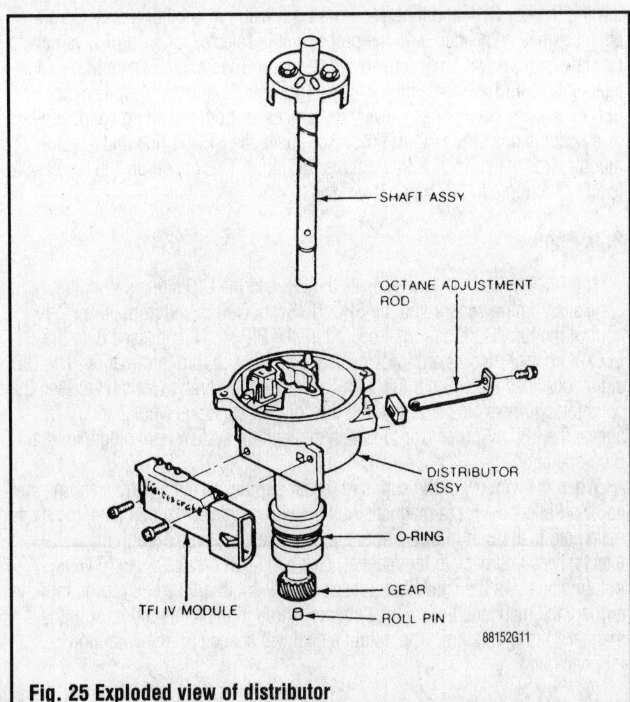

Fig. 25 Exploded view of distributor

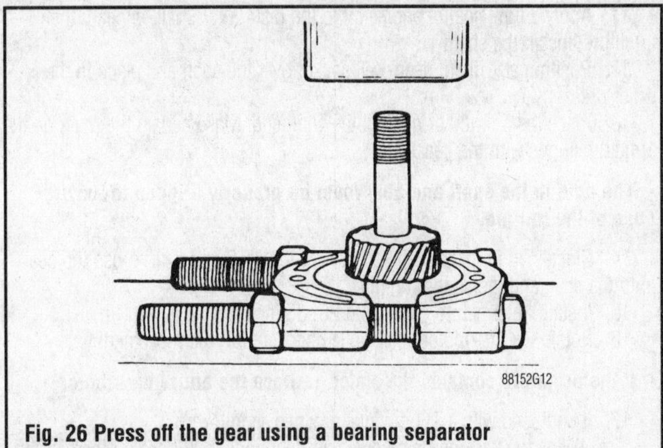

Fig. 26 Press off the gear using a bearing separator

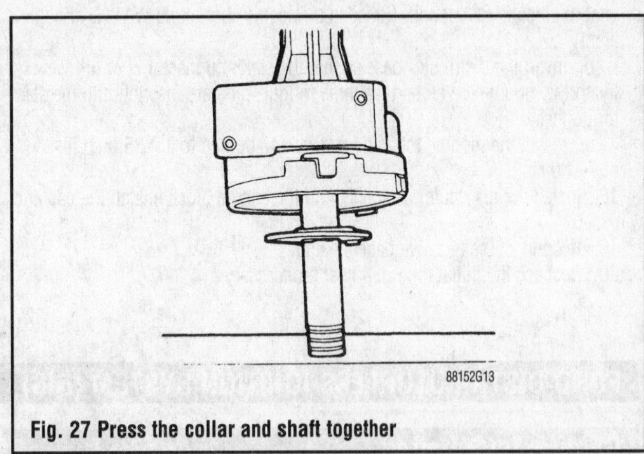

Fig. 27 Press the collar and shaft together

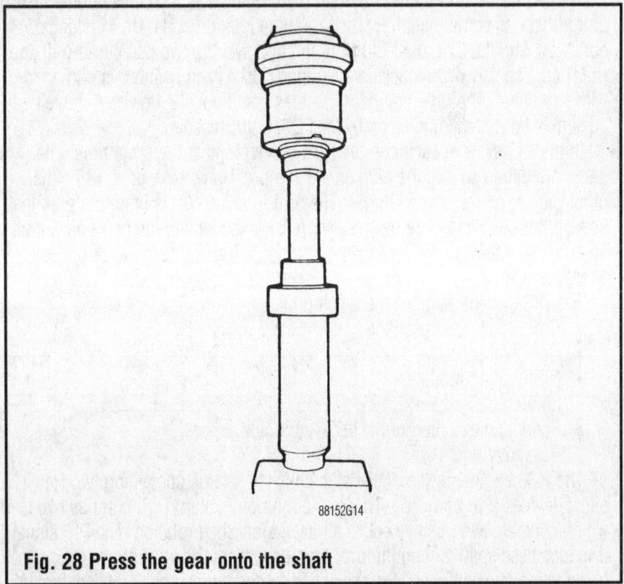

Fig. 28 Press the gear onto the shaft

7. Clean and polish the shaft with emery paper. Wipe clean so that the shaft slides out freely from the distributor base. Remove the shaft.
8. Remove the stator assembly retaining screws and remove the stator.

To install:

9. Position the stator assembly over the bushing and press to secure. Place the stator connector in position. The tab should fit in the notch on the base and the fastening eyelets should align with the screw holes. Be certain the wires are placed away from moving parts.
10. Install the stator retaining screws. Tighten to 15–35 inch lbs (1.7–4.0 Nm)

11. Apply a light coat of engine oil to the distributor shaft, beneath the armature. Install the shaft.
12. Position a ½ inch, deep-well socket over the shaft and place in the arbor press.
13. Place the distributor gear on the shaft end. Make certain the mark on the armature aligns with the gear.

➡The hole in the shaft and gear must be properly aligned to ensure ease of the roll pin.

14. Place a ⅝ in. deep-well socket over the shaft and gear; press the gear onto the shaft and install the roll pin.
15. Install the armature. Tighten to 25–35 inch lbs. (2.8–4.0 Nm)
16. Rotate the distributor shaft while checking for free movement

➡If the armature contacts the stator, replace the entire distributor

17. If equipped with a TFI module, proceed as follows:
    a. Wipe the back of the module and its mounting surface on the distributor clean. Coat the base of the TFI ignition module uniformly with a 1⁄32 inch coat of silicone compound. (Silicone di-electric compound WA–10 or equivalent)
    b. Invert the distributor base so that the stator connector is in full view. Insert the module. Be certain the three module pins are inserted into the stator connector.
    c. Install the module retaining screws and tighten to 15–35 inch lbs. (1.7–4.0 Nm).
18. Install the distributor assembly into the engine block. Install the cap and wires.
19. Reconnect the negative battery cable.
20. Recheck the initial timing. Adjust if necessary.

TFI Ignition Module

REMOVAL & INSTALLATION

➧ See Figure 25

1. Disconnect the negative battery cable.
2. Remove the distributor assembly from the engine.
3. Place the distributor on the workbench and remove the module retaining screws. Pull the right side of the module down the distributor mounting flange and back up to disengage the module terminal from the connector in the distributor base. The module may be pulled toward the flange and away from the distributor.

➡Do not attempt to lift the module from the mounting surface, except as explained above. The pins will break at the distributor module connector.

To install:

4. Coat the base plate of the TFI ignition module uniformly with 1⁄32 inch of silicone dielectric compound WA–10 or equivalent.
5. Position the module on the distributor base mounting flange. Carefully position the module toward the distributor bowl and engage the three connector pins securely.
6. Install the retaining screws. Tighten to 15–35 inch lbs (1.7–4.0 Nm), starting with the upper right screw.
7. Install the distributor into the engine. Install the cap and wires.
8. Reconnect the negative battery cable.
9. Recheck the initial timing. Adjust if necessary.

FORD DISTRIBUTORLESS IGNITION SYSTEM (DIS)

General Information

The Distributorless Ignition System (DIS) eliminates the conventional distributor and all its components by using multiple ignition coils. On Mustangs equipped with the 2.3L dual-plug DIS ignition system, two coil packs (left and right) are used. Two coil packs are required, since each cylinder is equipped with two plugs. The right coil pack operates continuously; however, the left coil pack may be switched on or off by the EEC-IV processor.

In the DIS system, each coil fires two spark plugs at the same time. The plugs are paired so that the plug on the compression stroke fires, while the other plug is on its exhaust stroke. The next time the coil is fired, the plug that was on the exhaust will be on the compression stroke and the first one will be on exhaust. The spark in the exhaust cylinder is wasted, but little of the coil energy is lost.

The DIS system includes these components:

- Crankshaft timing sensor
- Camshaft sensor
- DIS ignition module
- Ignition coil pack
- Spark angle portion of the EEC-IV module
- Related wiring

The 2.3L engine uses a dual-Hall crankshaft sensor, containing two Hall-effect devices (PIP and CID). The Profile Ignition Pickup (PIP) cup has two teeth which generate two positive edges for each crankshaft rotation. The PIP signal provides base spark timing information. The Cylinder Identification (CID) cup has one tooth which generates one positive edge during each crankshaft revolution. The CID is used by the DIS module to determine which coil should be fired. Despite the EEC-IV processor telling the DIS module when to fire, it's the job of the DIS module to decide which coils to fire based on the CID signal. The CID signal is also used by the EEC processor to know which bank of injectors to fire.

SYSTEM OPERATION

In the DIS system, the EEC-IV processor determines the spark angle using the PIP signal to establish base timing. Spark Output (SPOUT) is provided by the EEC-IV processor to the DIS module and serves two purposes. The leading edge fires the coil and the trailing edge controls the dwell time. This feature is referred to as Computer Controlled Dwell (CCD)

The DIS module incorporates an Ignition Diagnostics Monitor (IDM). This is an output signal that provides diagnostic information concerning the ignition system to the EEC-IV processor for self-test. It is also the input signal for the vehicle's tachometer.

If the CID circuit fails and an attempt to start the engine is made, the DIS module will randomly select one of the coils to fire. If hard starting results, turning the key **OFF** and trying to restart will result in another guess. Several attempts may be needed until the proper coil is selected, allowing the vehicle to be started and driven until repairs can be made. The Failure Effects Mode Management (FMEM) system will try to keep the vehicle drivable despite certain EEC-IV system failures that prevent the processor from providing spark angle or dwell commands. The EEC-IV processor opens the SPOUT line and the DIS module fires the coils directly from the PIP input. This condition will result in a fixed spark angle of 10° and a fixed dwell.

2.3L Engine

The DIS ignition module receives the PIP and the CID signals from the crankshaft timing sensor and the SPOUT (Spark Out) signal from the EEC-IV control module. During normal operation, the PIP signal is passed onto the EEC-IV control module and provides base timing and rpm information. The CID signal provides the DIS module with information required to switch between the coils for cylinders Nos. 1 and 4 and the coils for cylinders Nos. 2 and 3. DPI allows the EEC-IV processor to switch the ignition system from single to dual plug operation.

When the window of the cup is in the air gap between the permanent magnet and Hall-effect device, a magnetic flux field is completed. At this time, the magnetic field is allowed to travel from the permanent magnet through the Hall-effect device and back to the magnet. This condition creates a low (0 volts) output signal. As the crankshaft rotates and the tooth on the cup moves into the air gap, the magnetic field will be shunted through the tooth and back to the magnet. During this time, the output signal will change from low to high (source volts).

SYSTEM COMPONENTS

➧ See Figure 29

Dual Crank Sensor

The dual Hall crankshaft sensor on the 2.3L engine contains two Hall-effect devices, PIP and CID. The sensor is mounted on a bracket near the crankshaft damper.

Ignition Coil Pack

The ignition coil pack contains two separate coils. Each ignition coil fires two spark plugs simultaneously. The spark plug fired on the exhaust stroke uses very little of the ignition coil's stored energy.

DIS Ignition Module

The DIS ignition module receives the PIP signal from the crankshaft sensor. The CID signal provides the DIS ignition module with the information required to synchronize the ignition coils so that they are fired in the proper sequence.

Diagnosis and Testing

SERVICE PRECAUTIONS

- Always turn the ignition key **OFF** and isolate both ends of a circuit whenever testing for shorts or continuity.
- Never measure voltage or resistance directly at the processor connector.
- Always disconnect solenoids and switches from the harness before measuring for continuity, resistance or energizing by way of a 12-volt source.
- When disconnecting connectors, inspect for damaged or pushed-out pins, corrosion, loose wires, etc. Service if required.

Preliminary Checks

1. Visually inspect the engine compartment to ensure that all vacuum lines and spark plug wires are properly routed and securely connected.
2. Examine all wiring harnesses and connectors for insulation damage, burned, overheated, loose or broken connections.
3. Be certain that the battery is fully charged and that all accessories are **OFF** during the diagnosis.

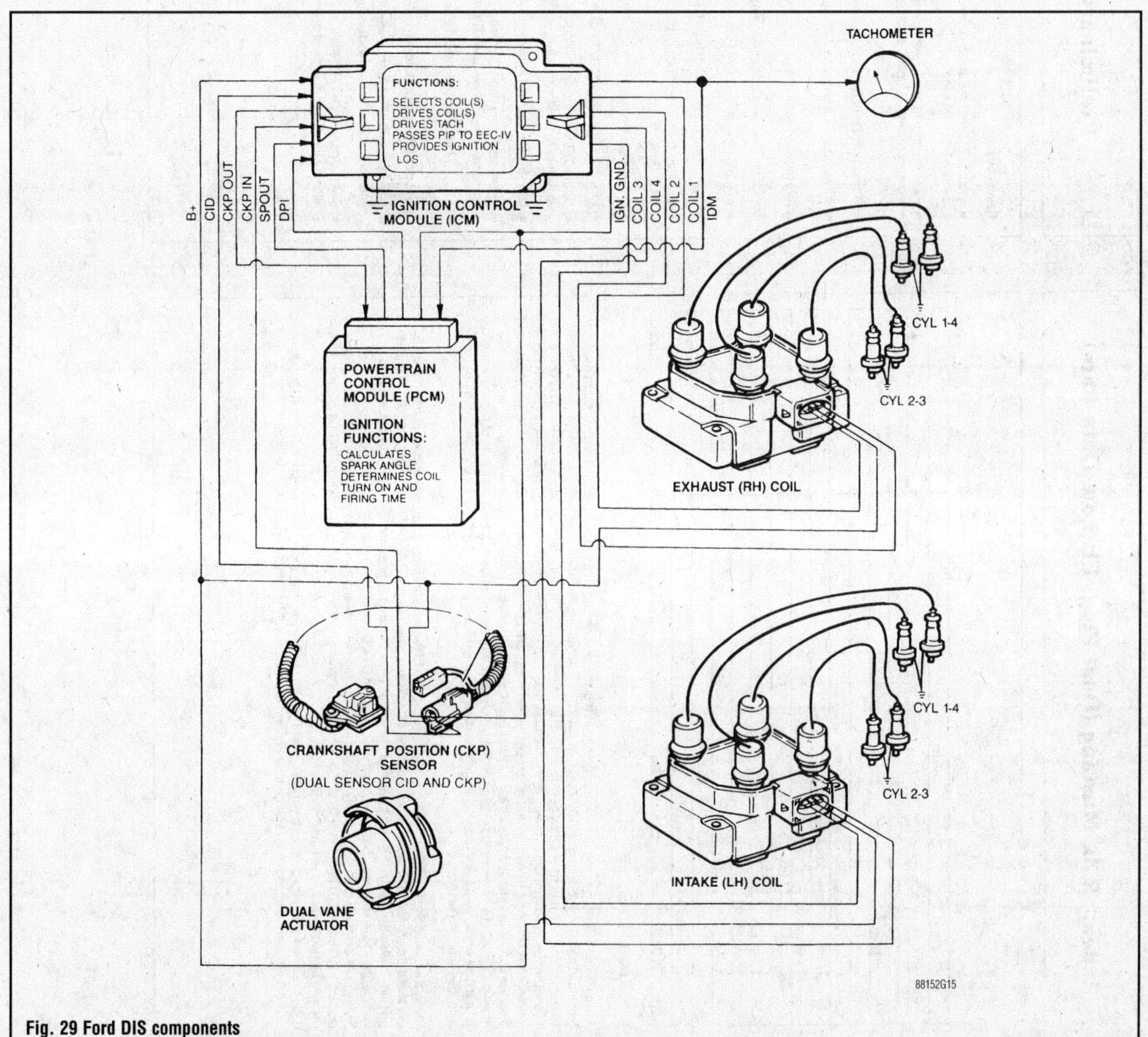

Fig. 29 Ford DIS components

Index: 2.3L Mustang (Dual Plug) EI (Low Data Rate)

IMPORTANT NOTE:

Most DVOM's used by auto technicians belong to a class or type known as "averaging". Examples are the Rotunda Digital Volt-Ohmmeter 007-0001, Fluke 70, 20 series and Fluke 88. Recently technicians have started to use DVOM'S of a different class (True RMS, DVOM's, Fluke 87, 8060A, 8062A, etc.). True RMS DVOM's should not be used with the Pinpoint Tests because they may display different voltage readings depending upon whether the DVOM is turned on first and then the test leads are connected, or if the leads are connected first and then the DVOM is turned on. Also they may not auto range to the same range every time and some display significantly different values depending on the range selected. It would be impossible to list all of the meters and how to use each, so we are requesting that you perform the following test to verify your DVOM is compatible with the Pinpoint Tests.

Using a known good Electronic Ignition vehicle, install the EI (Low Data Rate) diagnostic cable, connect the EEC Breakout Box to the diagnostic cable, start the vehicle and measure the AC voltage between J18 (RC1D) and ground. The battery should be charged and the engine must be idling between 700 and 900 rpm. On any EI vehicle the value should be between 1.0 and 2.0 volts AC (1.5 volts AC is typical).
If you have the hand held testers they may be used instead of the Diagnostic Cable / EEC Breakout Box to gain access to J18 (RC1D) and J31 (PIP EECI). Next, with the engine idling, measure between PIP and ground. This reading should be between 6 and 8 volts AC.
If the readings you get agree with our test, your DVOM is OK to use with the Ignition Pinpoint Tests. If not, do not use it, it will lead to false parts replacement and the root cause will be difficult or impossible to find.

88152G23

Preliminary Checkout, Equipment and Notes

Checkout

- Visually inspect the engine compartment to ensure all vacuum hoses and spark plug wires are properly and securely connected.
- Examine all wiring harnesses and connectors for damaged insulation, burned, overheated, damaged pins, loose or broken conditions. Check sensor shield connector. Make sure ICM mounting screws are clean and tight.
- Be certain the battery is fully charged.
- All accessories should be off during diagnosis.

Equipment (Required)

Obtain the following test equipment or an equivalent:

- EI (Low Data Rate) Diagnostic Harness (Rotunda 007-00044), (Figure 1).
- Spark Tester, Neon bulb type (Special Service Tool D89P-6666-A).
- Volt-Ohmmeter (Rotunda 007-00001, 105-00050, 105-00051, 105-00052, 105-00053 or Scan Tool (007-00500).
- Remote starter switch.
- EEC Breakout Box (Rotunda T83L-50-EEC-IV). Two may be required.
- Spark Tester, Gap type (Special Service Tool D81P-6666-A). A spark plug with a broken side electrode is not sufficient to check for spark and may lead to incorrect results.
- DIS / EDIS Adapter Tachometer—007-00061.
- Inductive Timing Light (Rotunda 059-00014). Do not use "advance knob" if timing light has one (it will not work correctly with EI (Low Data Rate) Ignition Systems).
- A 12 volt incandescent test lamp.

Equipment (Recommended)

- Module Tester (DMT) Rotunda 007-00071. This tester contains 12 LEDS, 12 Test Jacks and a built-in interface cable that allows the tester to monitor all DIS module signals.
- Coil / Sensor Tester (CST) Rotunda 007-00072. This tester is similar to the DIS Module Tester (DMT) except it allows monitoring of signals at the sensor and coils.

88152G24

Preliminary Checkout, Equipment and Notes

Notes

- When making measurements on a wiring harness, both a visual inspection and a continuity test should be performed. Inspect the connector pins for damage (corrosion, bent or spread pins, etc.) when directed to remove a connector.
- Spark timing adjustments are not possible.
- When making voltage checks a **LOW** reading means any value within a range of 0 to 1 volt. Also a **HIGH** reading means any value that falls within a range of B+ to 2 volts less than B+.
- When making voltage checks and a reference to ground is made, use the negative battery terminal. B+ means the positive battery cable at the battery.
- When using the spark plug firing indicator, place the grooved end as close as possible to the plug boot. Very weak flashing may be caused by a fouled plug.
- Do not use an incandescent test lamp to check the PIP, SPOUT, IDM or CID circuits. The lamp will prevent the circuit from operating.

88152G25

EI (Low Data Rate—Previously DIS) Diagnostic Harness

2.3L Mustang

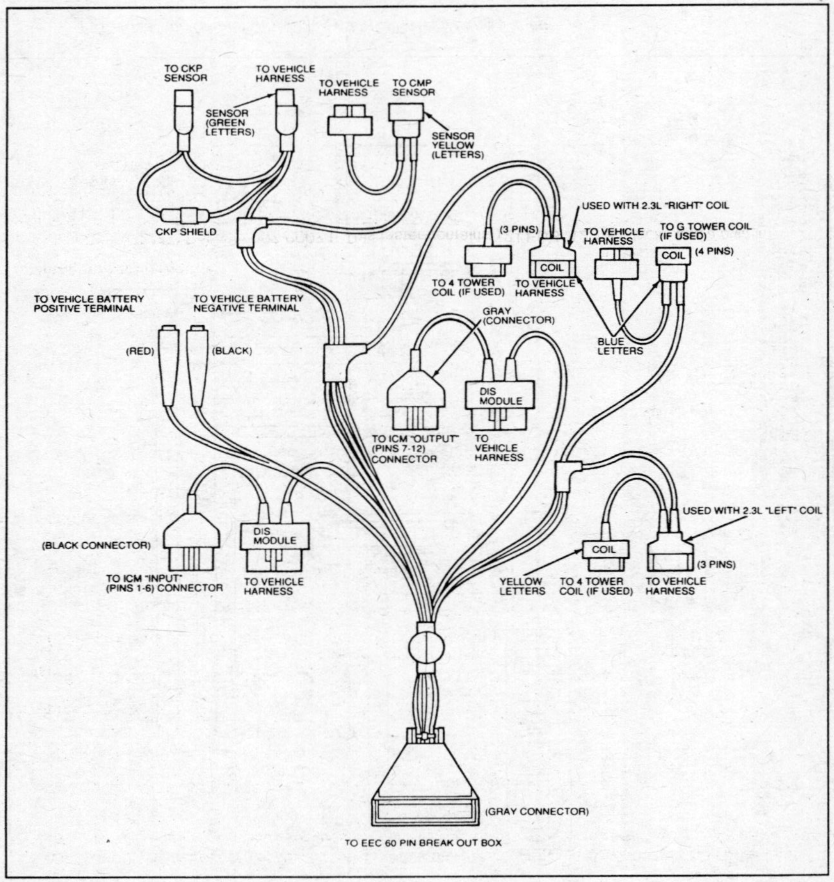

88152G26

2.3L Mustang (Dual Plug) EI (Low Data Rate—Previously DIS) Module and Pin-Out

2.3L Mustang

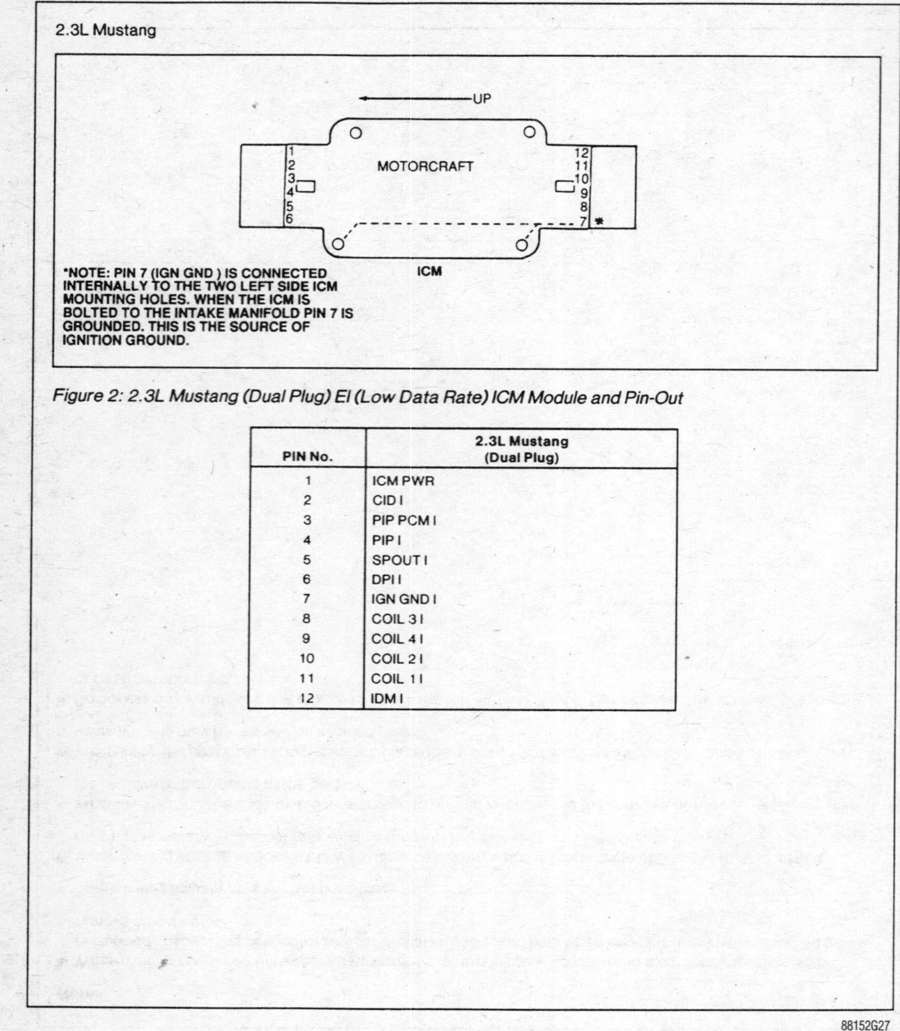

Figure 2: 2.3L Mustang (Dual Plug) EI (Low Data Rate) ICM Module and Pin-Out

PIN No.	2.3L Mustang (Dual Plug)
1	ICM PWR
2	CID I
3	PIP PCM I
4	PIP I
5	SPOUT I
6	DPI I
7	IGN GND I
8	COIL 3 I
9	COIL 4 I
10	COIL 2 I
11	COIL 1 I
12	IDM I

88152G27

2.3L Mustang (Dual Plug) EI (Low Data Rate—Previously DIS) Wiring Schematic

2.3L Mustang

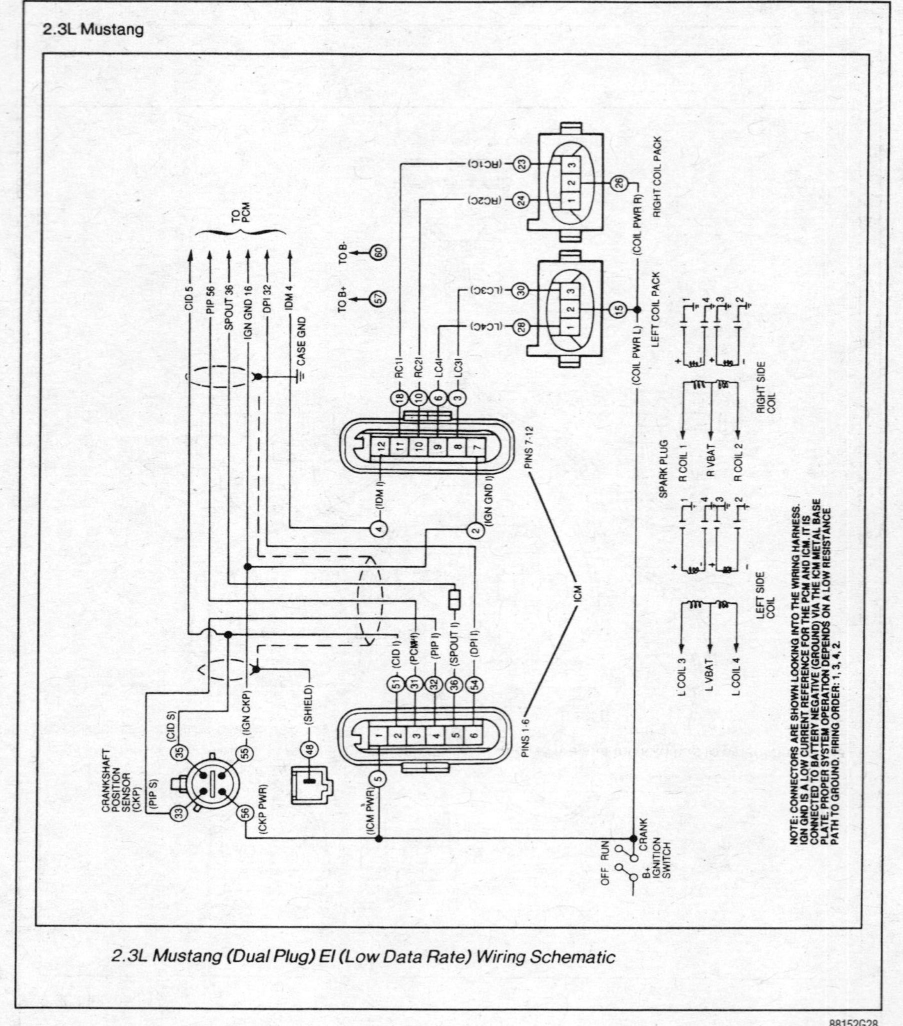

2.3L Mustang (Dual Plug) EI (Low Data Rate) Wiring Schematic

88152G28

EI (Low Data Rate—Previously DIS) Schematic and Breakout Box Overlay Acronyms

EI Acronyms

There is a logic to the names on the Schematic and Overlays for the DIAGNOSTIC HARNESS that will help you.

Acronym	Definition
PIP	Profile Ignition Pickup (Crankshaft Position Sensor signal).
CID	Cylinder Identification.
SPOUT	SPARK OUT (PCM Spark control signal).
IDM	Ignition Diagnostic Monitor (Diagnostic signal to PCM).
B+	Battery Positive.
B-	Battery Negative.
IGN GND or IGND	Low current ground reference.
DPI	Dual Plug Inhibit (High—Right Plugs fire; Low—Both Sides fire).
RC1, RC2	Right Coil Drive (For Coils 1 and 2 fires plugs on right side of engine).
LC1, LC2	Left Coil Drive (For Coils 1 and 2 fires plugs on left side of engine).
CID	Cylinder Identification Signal
CID PCMs	The CID signal being sent to the PCM measured at the sensor.

Overlay Designators

On the Schematic and Overlays, each of these signals is identified along with a suffix letter that tells you where the measurement is being taken. The key to these letters is:

Prefix / Suffix	Measurement Location
Prefix	"J" is a breakout box jack.
Suffix	"I" is at the ICM.
Suffix	"CKP" or "S" is at the sensor.
Suffix	"P" is at the PCM.
Suffix	"C" is at the coil.

A couple of examples:

Acronym	Definition
RC 1I	Right Coil, number "1", at the ICM Terminal.
RC 1C	Right Coil, number "1", at the Coil Terminal.
CKP PWR	Battery voltage at sensor.
ICM PWR	Battery voltage at ICM.

88152G29

CKP (Crankshaft Position Sensor) Description

The Dual Hall crankshaft sensor contains two Hall digital output devices (PIP, CID) in one package. The sensor is located on a bracket mounted near the crankshaft damper.

Two rotary vane cups (or wheels) are mounted on the damper and are used to trigger the Hall sensors. The vane cups are made of ferrous metal. When the window of a cup is in the air gap between the Hall device and the permanent magnet, a magnetic flux field is completed from the magnet through the Hall device and back to the magnet. This condition results in a low (0 volt) output signal As the crankshaft turns, a tooth on the cup will move into the air gap. The magnetic field will be shunted by the tooth preventing it from reaching the hall device and the output signal will change from a low to a high (B+).

The PIP cup has two teeth, resulting in two positive going edges each revolution of the crankshaft, and the CID cup has one tooth and generates one positive edge per revolution of the crankshaft. CID is used by the ICM to enable it to select the proper coil to fire. The PCM tells the ICM when to fire, but the ICM has to select one of the two coils based on CID signal (which two of four coils if in the DPI mode).

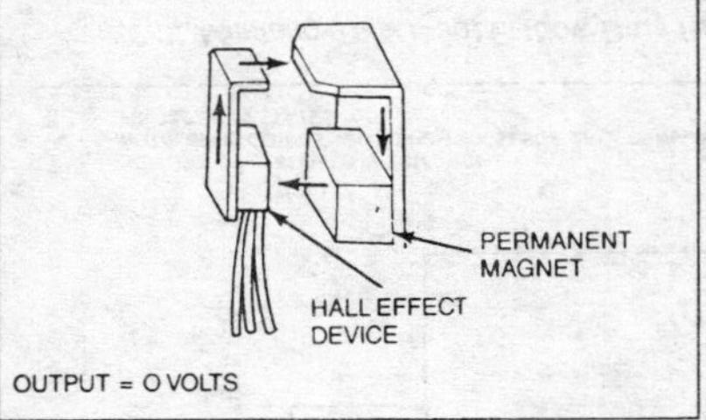

Magnetic Flux Field

HALL EFFECT DEVICE
PERMANENT MAGNET
VANE
OUTPUT = BATTERY VOLTAGE

Hall Effect Device Response to Vane

88152G30

2.3L Mustang (Dual Plug) EI (Low Data Rate—Previously DIS) System Description

The 2.3L Mustang (Dual Plug) EI (Electronic Ignition) System consists of a crankshaft-mounted Dual Hall Sensor, two 4-tower coil packs, and an ignition module (ICM).

The EI (Low Data Rate) system eliminates the need for a distributor by using multiple ignition coils. Each coil fires two spark plugs at the same time. The plugs are paired so that as one fires during the compression cycle, the other fires during the exhaust stroke. The next time the coil is fired, the plug that was on exhaust will be on compression, and the one that was on compression will be on exhaust (the spark in the exhaust cylinder is wasted but little of the coil energy is lost). Two coils are mounted together in a "coil pack". Each coil pack has two tach wires, one for each coil. Since there are two plugs per cylinder, two coil packs are required. One is called the Right Coil Pack and the other, the Left Coil Pack. The Right Coil Pack and right spark plugs operate continuously, but the Left Coil Pack and left spark plugs may be switched on or off by the PCM. The PCM computes the spark angle and dwell for the ignition system.

The Crankshaft Position (CKP) Sensor is a dual digital-output Hall device that responds to two rotating metallic shutters mounted together on the crankshaft. The PIP output is a 50-percent duty cycle signal that provides base spark timing information. The other signal (CID) is required so that the ICM "knows" which coil to fire. CID is high (B+) half of the crank revolution (180 degrees) and low (0 volts) for the other [illegible]. CID is also used by the PCM so it can select which bank of injectors to fire.

The PCM determines spark angle using the PIP signal to establish base timing. SPOUT is sent from the PCM to the ICM and serves two purposes: the leading edge fires the coil and the trailing edge controls the dwell time. This feature is called CCD or Computer-Controlled Dwell.

The Ignition Diagnostic Monitor (IDM) is an output from the ICM to the PCM that provides diagnostic information about the ignition system for Self-Test. IDM is also used by the vehicle tachometer.

Dual Plug Inhibit (DPI) allows the PCM to switch the ignition system from single to dual plug operation.

If the CID circuit fails, the ICM will randomly select one of the two coils to fire. If erratic starting results, turning the key off and then cranking again will result in another "guess." Several attempts may be needed until the proper coil is selected, allowing the vehicle to be started and driven until repairs can be made. The Failure Mode Effects Management (FMEM) system will keep the vehicle driveable in the event of EEC system or ignition failures that would otherwise prevent spark angle or dwell commands. The PCM opens the SPOUT line and the ICM fires the coils directly from the PIP output. This results in a fixed spark angle of 10 degrees and fixed dwell.

The Right Coil Pack fires the right side spark plugs

The Left Coil Pack fires the left side spark plugs.

88152G31

2.3L Mustang (Dual Plug) EI (Low Data Rate—Previously DIS) Block Diagram

Mustang

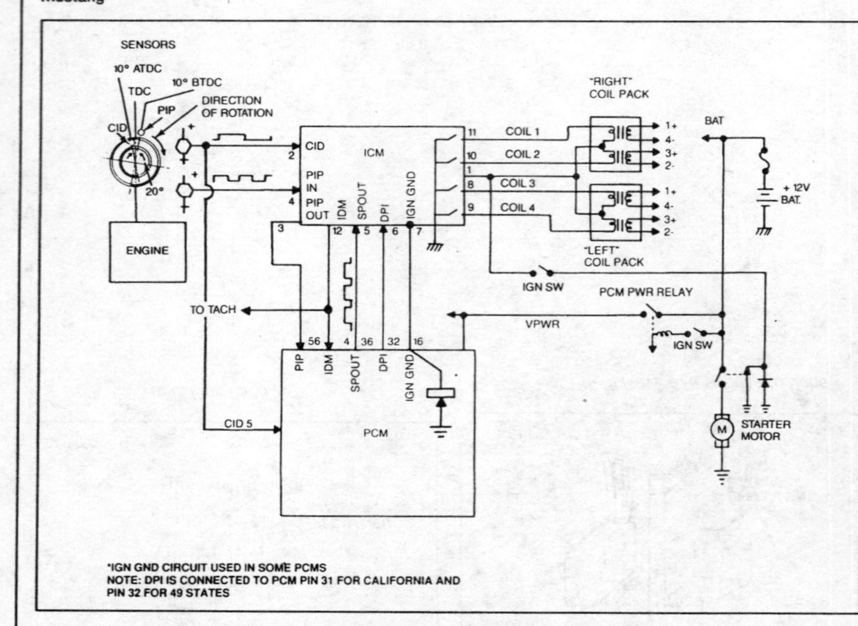

2.3L Mustang (Dual Plug) EI (Low Data Rate) Ignition System

88152G32

2.3L Mustang (Dual Plug) EI (Low Data Rate—Previously DIS) Waveforms

Timing Diagram

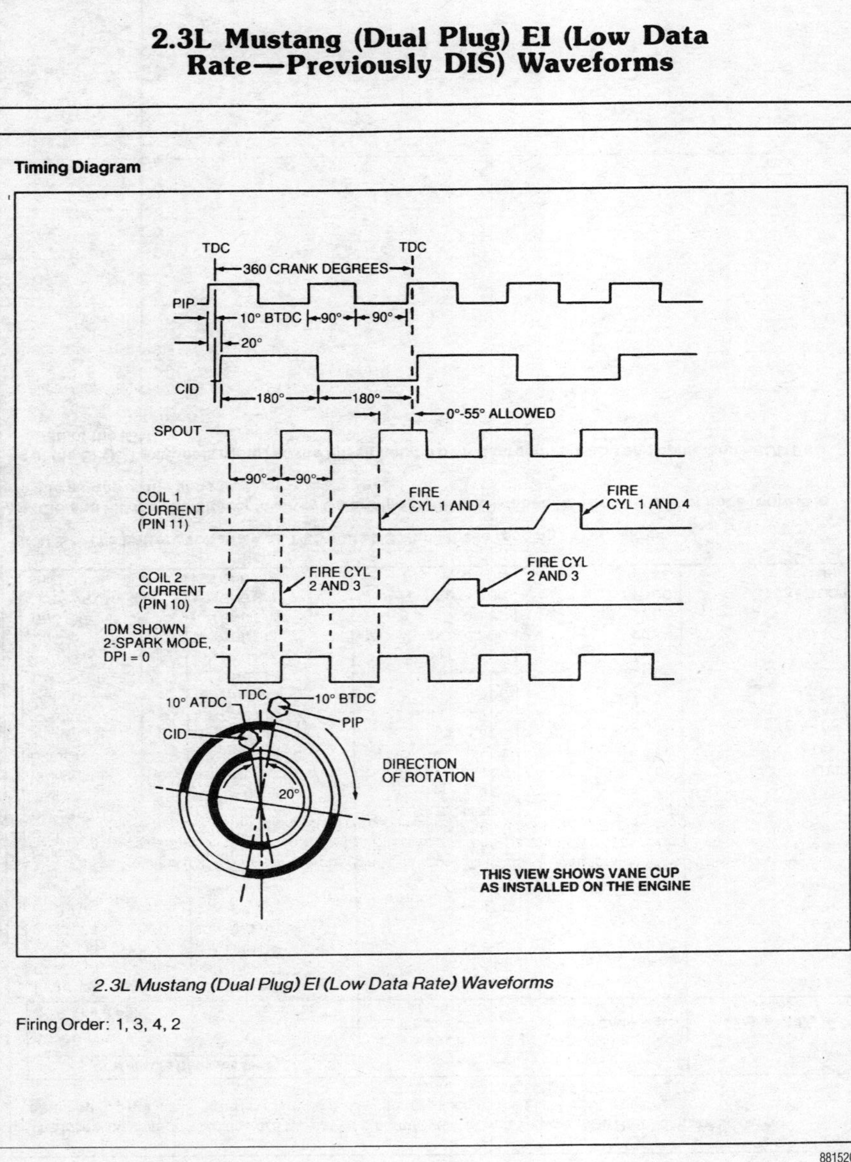

2.3L Mustang (Dual Plug) EI (Low Data Rate) Waveforms

Firing Order: 1, 3, 4, 2

88152G33

2.3L MFI Mustang (Dual Plug) EI (Low Data Rate—Previously DIS) Component Location

Mustang

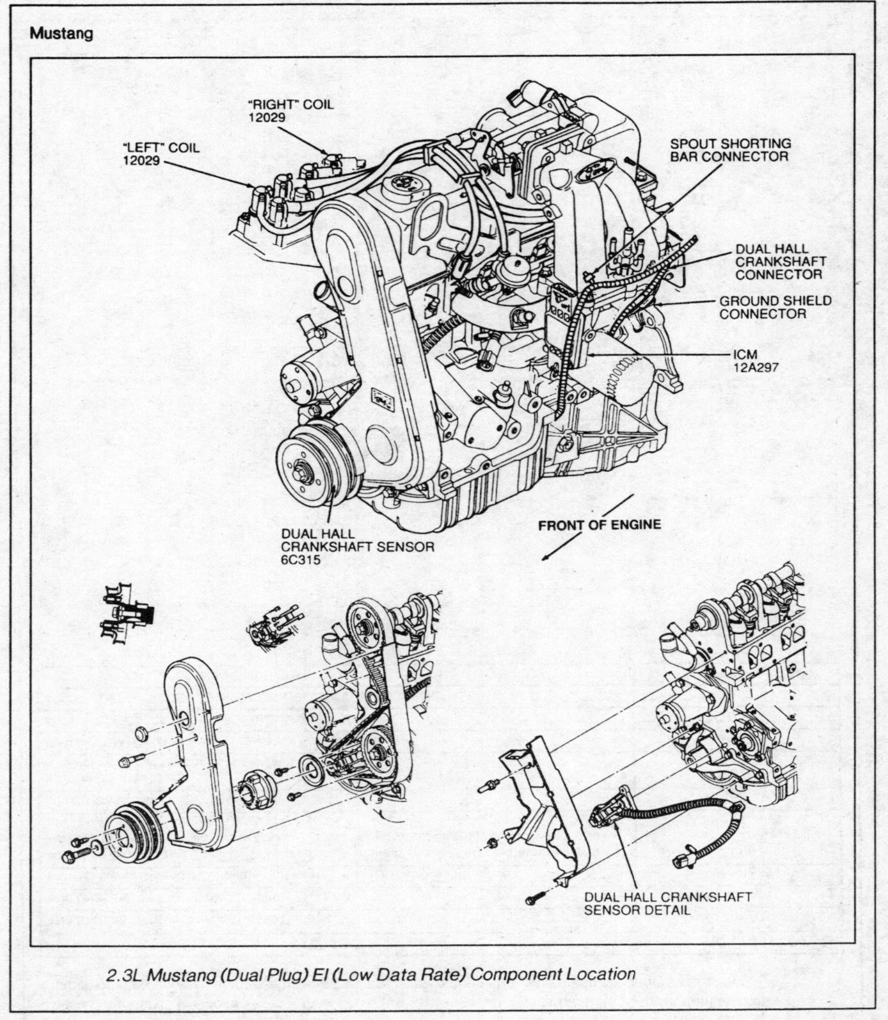

2.3L Mustang (Dual Plug) EI (Low Data Rate) Component Location

88152G34

2.3L Mustang (Dual Plug) EI (Low Data Rate—Previously DIS) Typical Values

The following voltage readings are typical for a normal vehicle with EI (Low Data Rate) diagnostic cable attached. Do not use a "true RMS" type A/C voltmeter such as the Fluke 8060a or 87.

Measure Between Pins		Key On Engine Off (volts)	Engine Cranking (volts)	Engine Idling (volts)
First Pin	Second Pin			
RC1C J23	IGN GND I J2	14.5 DC	1.2 AC	1.6 AC
RC2C J24	IGN GND I J2	14.5 DC	1.2 AC	1.6 AC
LC3C J30	IGN GND I J2	14.5 DC	1.2 AC	1.6 AC
LC4C J28	IGN GND I J2	14.5 DC	1.2 AC	1.6 AC
RC1I J18	IGN GND I J2	14.4 DC	1.2 AC	1.6 AC
RC2I J10	IGN GND I J2	14.4 DC	1.2 AC	1.6 AC
LC3I J3	IGN GND I J2	14.4 DC	1.2 AC	1.6 AC
LC4I J6	IGN GND I J2	14.6 DC	1.2 AC	1.6 AC
COIL PWR R J26	IGN GND I J2	14.6 DC	13.0 DC	14.8 DC
COIL PWR L J15	IGN GND I J2	14.6 DC	13.0 DC	14.8 DC
IDMI J4	IGN GND I J2	0.2 DC	4.9 AC	5.2 AC
IGN GND I J2	IGN GND I J2	0.1 DC	0.1 DC	0.1 DC
DPI J54	IGN GND I J2	0.1 DC	0.1 DC	0.1 DC
SPOUTI J36	IGN GND I J2	11.8 DC	0.1 AC	3.0 AC
PIPI J31	IGN GND I J2	11.8/0.2 DC	5.0 AC	6.8 AC
CIDI J51	IGN GND I J2	11.8/0.2 DC	4.0 AC	7.0 AC
ICM PWR J5	IGN GND I J2	14.7 DC	13.0 DC	14.8 DC
PIPS J33	IGN GND I J2	11.8/0.2 DC	5.0 AC	6.8 AC
CIDS J35	IGN GND I J2	11.8/0.2 DC	4.0 AC	7.0 AC
IGND CKP J55	IGN GND I J2	0.2 DC	0.2 DC	0.2 DC
CKP PWR J56	IGN GND I J2	14.7 DC	13.0 DC	14.8 DC
SHIELD J48	IGN GND I J2	0.1 DC	0.1 DC	0.1 DC

NOTE: **The battery voltage was 14.6 volts DC when these readings were taken.**

- **CID and PIP may be high or low Key On Engine Off (KOEO) depending on whether or not a tooth is in the air gap of the sensor.**
- **If the SPOUT jumper is removed the PIP signal will be fed through the ICM and appear on SPOUT at J36 of the ICM.**

88152G35

2.3L Mustang (Dual Plug) EI (Low Data Rate—Previously DIS) Diagnostics by Code and Symptom

These diagnostics (Pinpoint Tests A through G) are written to catch "Hard Faults"; intermittent failures will be difficult or impossible to diagnose unless they are present the entire time these procedures are used.

TEST STEP	ACTION TO TAKE
•No Start and No Diagnostic Trouble Codes.	GO to A1.
•No Start and 211 —PIP circuit fault.	GO to A3.
•No Start with Diagnostic Trouble Code not listed elsewhere in this index.	GO to A1.
•222 and Erratic Start (Engine will start normally at least once out of five attempts). When it fails to start, the cranking rpm is erratic (Ignition is firing out of time) but when it starts it starts normally — CID circuit fault.	GO to B1.
•214 CID open at PCM	GO to B20.
•222 and Normal Start. — IDM low circuit fault or right coil fault.	GO to B12.
•218 — IDM circuit fault high or open or left coil pack open.	GO to C1.
•224 — C1, C2, C3 or C4 circuit fault or 215, 216, 217.	GO to D1.
•223 — DPI circuit fault open or high. SPOUT circuit fault high.	GO to E1.
•213 — SPOUT circuit failure open or low.	GO to F1.

88152G36

2.3L Mustang (Dual Plug) EI (Low Data Rate—Previously DIS) Pinpoint Test Diagnostics	Pinpoint Test	Notes

CAUTION

A 12 volt incandescent test lamp should not be used to test CID, IDM, Spout or PIP circuit signals. It will load the circuit and may cause erroneous measurements or improper ICM/PCM operations (i.e. Engine stall). An incandescent test lamp is required to verify proper coil circuit operation in Section D.

Note

- When a DVOM is used on the DC range, correct Test Lead Polarity must be followed. The red lead is positive (+) and the black lead is negative (-).
- To check PIP or CID, the engine is "bumped" with the starter while watching the voltmeter. Both the CID and PIP signals are digital and should switch between B+ and ground as the engine turns. To see the signal change using the DVOM, the engine must be turned in very short bursts without starting the engine.
- Refer to the appropriate EVTM for wire colors.
- The 2.3L engine used in the Mustang has a bank-to-bank sequential fuel injection system. The CID signal is connected to the PCM as well as the ICM to allow the PCM to "fire" one or the other bank at the proper time.
- Both coils are activated during cranking and running except when the temperature is less than -7° C (20° F). Below -7° C (20° F) the engine cranks on the right coil then runs on both coils. However, the Ranger truck engine starts on right coil only and runs on both coils.
- The A/C voltage reading from a "true RMS" type DVOM (Fluke 87) may be significantly different taken from a "standard" or averaging DVOM (Rotunda Digital Volt Ohmmeter 007-0001, Fluke 88, 75, etc) leading to incorrect answer of Pinpoint Test Steps.

88152G37

2.3L Mustang (Dual Plug) EI (Low Data Rate—Previously DIS). Pinpoint Test Diagnostics	Pinpoint Test	Notes

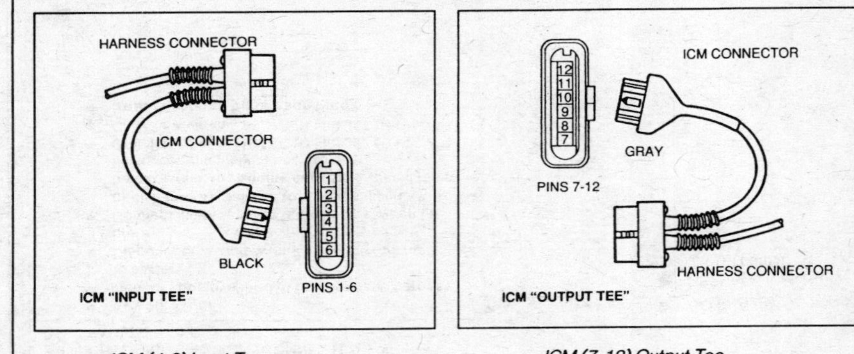

ICM (1-6) Input Tee

ICM (7-12) Output Tee

88152G38

2.3L Mustang (Dual Plug) EI (Low Data Rate—Previously DIS) No Start — Pinpoint Test A

TEST STEP		RESULT	▶ ACTION TO TAKE
A1	PERFORM EEC QUICK TEST		
	• perform EEC Quick Test. • **Are pass codes or no service codes present (KOEO, KOER or Continuous Memory)?**	Yes No	▶ GO to A2. ▶ SERVICE any PCM codes first. If still no start, GO to A2.
A2	CHECK FOR SPARK DURING CRANK		
	• Using a Neon Bulb Spark Tester (D89P6666-A) or Air Gap Spark Tester (D81P-6666-A), check for spark at each right side spark plug wire while cranking. • **Was spark present on all right side spark plug wires and consistent (one spark per crank revolution)?**	Yes No	▶ GO to A12. ▶ GO to A3.
A3	DETERMINE MISSING SPARK COMBINATION—SPARK FAULT		
	• **Was spark missing from both number 1 and number 4 plug wires but present at other plug wires?** or • **Was spark missing from both number 2 and number 3 plug wires but present at other plug wires?**	Yes No	▶ GO to A5. ▶ GO to A4.
A4	CHECK PLUGS AND WIRES—SPARK FAULT—KEY OFF		
	• Check spark plug wires for insulation damage, looseness, shorting or other damge. • Remove and check spark plugs for damage, wear, carbon deposits and proper plug gap. • **Are plugs and wires OK?**	Yes No	▶ REINSTALL plugs and wires. GO to A5. ▶ SERVICE or REPLACE damaged or worn spark plugs or plug wires.
A5	CHECK ICM PWR—SPARK FAULT—KOEO		
	• Connect EI Low Data Rate diagnostic harness to breakout box. • Use 2.3L overlay. • Connect EI diagnostic harness negative lead. • Install 1-6 ICM Tee. • DVOM on 20 volt DC scale. • Key on. • Measure voltage between (+)J5 (ICM PWR) and (-)J60 (B-). • **Is voltage greater than 10 volts DC?**	Yes No	▶ GO to A6. ▶ CHECK connectors, SERVICE or REPLACE harness. ICM PWR to ICM open. **CAUTION: Never connect the PCM and EI diagnostic harness to the EEC breakout box at the same time. If done with the key on it may damage the PCM.**

88152G39

2.3L Mustang (Dual Plug) EI (Low Data Rate—Previously DIS) No Start — Pinpoint Test A

TEST STEP		RESULT	▶ ACTION TO TAKE
A6	CHECK IGN GND AT ICM—SPARK FAULT—KEY OFF		
	• Key off. • Install 7-12 ICM Tee. • DVOM on 200 ohm scale. • **Is resistance between J2 (IGN GND I) and J60 (B-) less than 5.0 ohms?** NOTE: **If a negative resistance value is obtained, switch leads of DVOM and repeat measurements.**	Yes No	▶ GO to A7. ▶ GO to A17. IGN GND I open fault.
A7	CHECK FOR C1/C2 HIGH AT ICM—KOEO		
	• DVOM on 20 volt DC scale. • Key on. • Measure voltage between (+)J18 (RC1I) and (-)J60 (B-). • Measure voltage between (+)J10 (RC2I) and (-)J60 (B-). • **Is voltage greater than 10 volts DC in both tests?**	Yes No	▶ GO to A8. ▶ GO to A18. C1/C2 low fault.
A8	CHECK PIP AT ICM—SPARK FAULT—KOEC		
	• DVOM to 20 volt DC scale. • Connect leads of DVOM between (+)J32 (PIP I) and (-)J60 (B-). • Bump engine in short bursts with starter without starting engine for at least five engine revolutions and watch for change in DVOM reading. • **Does DVOM reading switch between low (less than 2.0 volts DC) and higher (more than 8.0 volts DC)?**	Yes No	▶ GO to A9. ▶ GO to A21. PIP fault.
A9	CHECK ICM—COIL DISCONNECTED—SPARK FAULT—KOEC		
	• Key off. • Connect positive lead of EI diagnostic harness to battery. • Disconnect vehicle wiring harness from right coil. • Connect incandescent test lamp between each if the two pairs of test points given below. Crank the engine each time. See if lamp blinks continuously during crank. • Check between J18 (RC1I) and J57 (B+). • Check between J10 (RC2I) and J57 (B+). • **Does test lamp blink each time?**	Yes No	▶ GO to A10. ▶ REPLACE ICM. No C1/C2 output.

88152G40

2.3L Mustang (Dual Plug) EI (Low Data Rate—Previously DIS) No Start	Pinpoint Test	A

	TEST STEP	RESULT ▶	ACTION TO TAKE
A10	CHECK RIGHT COIL PACK COIL PWR—SPARK FAULT—KOEO		
	• Key off. • DVOM on 20 volt DC scale. • Install the right 2.3L coil tee (the word "coil" is written in blue letters). • Key on. • Reconnect coil. • Measure voltage between (+)J26 (COIL PWR R) and (-)J60 (B-). • **Is voltage greater than 10 volts DC?**	Yes ▶ No ▶	GO to A11. CHECK connector, SERVICE or REPLACE harness. COIL PWR open.
A11	CHECK C1/C2 AT RIGHT COIL—SPARK FAULT—KOEC		
	• Connect incandescent test lamp between each of the two pairs of test points given below. Crank engine each time. See if lamp blinks continuously during crank. • Check between J23 (RC1C) and J57 (B+). • Check between J24 (RC2C) and J57 (B+). • **Does test lamp blink each time?**	Yes ▶ No ▶	REPLACE right coil pack. No ouput, input OK. CHECK connectors, SERVICE or REPLACE harness. One or both coil wires may be open. Coil pack may be damaged.
A12	CHECK PIP PCM AT ICM—KOEC		
	• Connect EI diagnostic harness to breakout box. • Use 2.3L overlay. • Install 1-6 ICM Tee. • DVOM to 20 volt DC scale. • Connect leads of DVOM between (+)J31 (PIP PCM I) and (-)J60 (B-). • Bump engine in short bursts with starter without starting engine for at least five engine revolutions and watch for change in DVOM reading. • **Does DVOM reading switch between low (less than 2.0 volts DC) and high (more than 8.0 volts DC)?**	Yes ▶ No ▶	GO to A13. REPLACE ICM. PIP open.
A13	CHECK PIP TO PCM CONTINUITY—KEY OFF		
	• Key off. • DVOM on 200 ohm scale. • Disconnect PCM. • Connect second breakout box to PCM vehicle harness connector. • Measure resistance between Pin 56 of second breakout box and J31 (PIP PCM I). • **Is resistance less than 5.0 ohms?**	Yes ▶ No ▶	GO to A14. SERVICE harness and connectors. PIP open.

88152G41

2.3L Mustang (Dual Plug) EI (Low Data Rate—Previously DIS) No Start	Pinpoint Test	A

	TEST STEP	RESULT ▶	ACTION TO TAKE
A14	CHECK IGN GND AT ICM—GND FAULT		
	• Key off. • Install 7-12 ICM tee. • Measure resistance between J2 (IGN GND I) and J60 (B-). • **Is resistance less than 5.0 ohms?**	Yes ▶ No ▶	GO to A16. GO to A15.
A15	CHECK ICM MOUNTING SCREWS FOR CORROSION OR LOOSENESS.		
	• Check ICM mounting screws for corrosion or looseness. • **Are mounting screws clean and tight?**	Yes ▶ No ▶	REPLACE ICM. Ignition ground is open. TIGHTEN, CLEAN or REPLACE mounting screws. CLEAN mounting area on ICM. Be sure to REPLACE any heat sink grease that is removed.
A16	CHECK IGN GND TO PCM CONTINUITY—KEY OFF		
	• Key off. • Set DVOM to 200 ohm scale. • Disconnect PCM and install the second EEC breakout box to the PCM vehicle harness connector. • Measure resistance between Pin 16 of second breakout box and J2 (IGN GND I). • **Is resistance less than 5.0 ohms?**	Yes ▶ No ▶	REFER to Section 2A. Ignition System OK. CHECK connectors, SERVICE or REPLACE harness IGN GND open between PCM and ICM.
A17	CHECK ICM MOUNTING SCREWS—GND FAULT—KEY OFF		
	• Check ICM mounting screws for corrosion or looseness. • **Are mounting screws clean and tight?**	Yes ▶ No ▶	REPLACE ICM. IGN GND open. TIGHTEN, CLEAN or REPLACE mounting screws. CLEAN mounting area on ICM.

88152G42

2.3L Mustang (Dual Plug) EI (Low Data Rate—Previously DIS) No Start — Pinpoint Test A

TEST STEP		RESULT ▶	ACTION TO TAKE
A18	CHECK FOR C1/C2 HIGH AT ICM CONNECTOR—ICM DISCONNECTED—C1/C2 LOW FAULT—KOEO		
	• Key off. • Set DVOM to 20 volt DC scale. • Disconnect EI diagnostic harness connector from ICM (Pins 7-12). Do not disconnect vehicle harness from other side of 7-12 ICM tee. • Key on. • Measure voltage between (+)J18 (RC1I) and (-) J60 (B-). • Measure voltage between (+)J10 (RC2I) and (-) J60 (B-). • **Is voltage greater than 10 volts DC in both tests?**	Yes ▶ No ▶	REPLACE ICM. C1 or C2 short to GND. Coil pack may be damaged. GO to A19. C1/C2 low fault.
A19	CHECK RIGHT COIL PACK VBAT—C1/C2 LOW FAULT—KEY OFF		
	• Key off. • DVOM on 20 volt DC scale. • Install right coil tee (The word "coil" is printed in blue letters and connectors have 3 pins). • Key on. • Measure voltage between (+)J26 (COIL PWR R) and (-)J60 (B-). • **Is voltage greater than 10 volts DC?**	Yes ▶ No ▶	GO to A20. CHECK connectors, SERVICE or REPLACE harness. COIL PWR open.
A20	CHECK FOR C1/C2 HIGH AT RIGHT COIL—C1/C2 LOW FAULT—KOEO		
	• DVOM on 20 volt DC scale. • Key on. • Measure voltage between (+)J23 (RC1C) and (-)J60 (B-). • Measure voltage between (+)J24 (RC2C) and (-)J60 (B-). • **Is voltage greater than 10 volts DC in both tests?**	Yes ▶ No ▶	SERVICE connectors and harness. One or both coil wires are open. REPLACE coil C1/C2 open.

88152G43

2.3L Mustang (Dual Plug) EI (Low Data Rate—Previously DIS) No Start — Pinpoint Test A

TEST STEP		RESULT ▶	ACTION TO TAKE
A21	CHECK PIP AT ICM—ICM DISCONNECTED—PIP FAILURE—KOEC		
	• Key off. • Disconnect EI diagnostic harness connector from ICM (Pins 1-6). Do not disconnect vehicle harness from ICM 1-6 tee. • DVOM to 20 volt DC scale. • Connect leads of DVOM between (+)J32 (PIP I) and (-)J60 (B-). • Bump engine in short bursts with starter without starting engine for at least five engine revolutions and watch for change in DVOM reading. • **Does DVOM reading switch between low (less than 2.0 volts DC) and high (more than 8.0 volts DC)?**	Yes ▶ No ▶	GO to A22. GO to A25. PIP circuit failure.
A22	CHECK FOR PCM SHORTING PIP—PCM DISCONNECTED—PIP FAULT—KOEC		
	• Key off. • Reconnect EI diagnostic harness connector to ICM (Pins 1-6). • Disconnect PCM. • DVOM on 20 volt DC scale. • Connect leads of DVOM between (+)J32 (PIP I) and (-)J60 (B-). • Bump engine in short bursts with starter without starting engine for at least five engine revolutions and watch for change in DVOM reading. • **Does DVOM reading switch between low (less than 2.0 volts DC) and high (more than 8.0 volts DC)?**	Yes ▶ No ▶	REPLACE PCM. PIP shorted. GO to A23.
A23	CHECK PIP P FOR SHORT HIGH—ICM AND PCM DISCONNECTED—PIP FAULT—KOEC		
	• Key off. • DVOM on 20 volt DC scale. • Disconnect EI diagnostic harness connector from ICM (Pins 1-6). Do not disconnect the vehicle harness from the other end of the TEE. • Key on. • Measure voltage between (+)J31 (PIP PCM I) and (-)J60 (B-). • **Is voltage less than 0.5 volts?**	Yes ▶ No ▶	GO to A24. CHECK connectors, SERVICE or REPLACE harness. PIP PCM is shorted high.

88152G44

2.3L Mustang (Dual Plug) EI (Low Data Rate—Previously DIS) No Start — Pinpoint Test A

	TEST STEP	RESULT ▶	ACTION TO TAKE
A24	CHECK PIP PCM FOR SHORT LOW—ICM AND PCM DISCONNECTED—PIP FAULT—KOEC		
	• Key off. • DVOM on 20K ohm scale. • Do not reconnect ICM or PCM. • Measure resistance between J31 (PIP PCM I) and J60 (B-). • **Is resistance more than 10K ohms?**	Yes ▶ No ▶	REPLACE ICM. No PIP EEC output. CHECK connectors, SERVICE or REPLACE harness. PIP PCM is shorted to ground.
A25	CHECK CKP PWR AT CRANKSHAFT SENSOR—PIP FAULT—KOEO		
	• Key off. • Reconnect the 1-6 ICM tee. • Install crankshaft sensor tee (The word "SENSOR" is printed in green letters). • DVOM on 20 volt DC scale. • Key on. • Measure the voltage between (+)J56 (CKP PWR) and (-)J2 (IGN GND I). • **Is voltage greater than 10 volts?**	Yes ▶ No ▶	GO to A26. CHECK connectors, SERVICE or REPLACE harness. CKP PWR to sensor open.
A26	CHECK IGN GND AT CRANKSHAFT SENSOR—PIP FAULT—KEY OFF		
	• Key off. • DVOM on 200 ohm scale. • **Is resistance between J55 (IGND CKP) and J60 (B-) less than 5.0 ohms?**	Yes ▶ No ▶	GO to A27. CHECK connectors, SERVICE or REPLACE harness. IGN GND to sensor open.
A27	CHECK PIP AT CRANKSHAFT SENSOR—PIP FAULT—KOEC		
	• DVOM on 20 volt DC scale. • Connect leads of DVOM between (+)J33 (PIP S) and (-)J60 (B-). • Bump engine in short bursts with starter without starting engine for at least five engine revolutions and watch for change in DVOM reading. • **Does DVOM reading switch between low (less than 2.0 volts DC) and high (more than 8.0 volts DC)?**	Yes ▶ No ▶	CHECK connectors, SERVICE or REPLACE harness. PIP is open between sensor and ICM. GO to A28. PIP fault.

88152G45

2.3L Mustang (Dual Plug) EI (Low Data Rate—Previously DIS) No Start — Pinpoint Test A

	TEST STEP	RESULT ▶	ACTION TO TAKE
A28	CHECK PIP CIRCUIT FOR SHORT HIGH—CRANKSHAFT SENSOR AND ICM DISCONNECTED—PIP FAULT—KEY ON		
	• Key off. • Disconnect EI diagnostic harness connector from crankshaft sensor. Do not disconnect vehicle harness from crankshaft sensor tee. • DVOM on 20 volt DC scale. • Disconnect EI diagnostic harness connector from ICM Pins 1-6. • Key on. • Measure voltage between (+)J33 (PIP S) and (-)J60 (B-). • **Is voltage less than 0.5 volts?**	Yes ▶ No ▶	GO to A29. CHECK connectors, SERVICE or REPLACE harness. PIP is shorted high between the sensor and ICM.
A29	CHECK PIP CIRCUIT FOR SHORT TO GROUND—CRANKSHAFT SENSOR AND ICM DISCONNECTED—PIP FAULT—KEY OFF		
	• Key off. • DVOM on 20K ohm scale. • Measure resistance between J33 (PIP S) and J60 (B-). • **Is resistance greater than 10K ohms?**	Yes ▶ No ▶	GO to A30. CHECK connectors, SERVICE or REPLACE harness. PIP is shorted to ground between the sensor and the ICM.
A30	CHECK CRANKSHAFT VANE—PIP FAULT—KEY OFF		
	• **Does crankshaft vane move through sensor air gap when the engine is cranked?**	Yes ▶ No ▶	REPLACE crankshaft sensor. No output. REFER to Service Manual, .to service vane damage.

88152G46

2.3L Mustang (Dual Plug) EI (Low Data Rate—Previously DIS)—Code 222 CID Failure, IDM Low Fault, DPI High Fault or Right Coil Pack Failure — Pinpoint Test B

	TEST STEP	RESULT ▶	ACTION TO TAKE
B1	CHECK FOR SPARK FROM RIGHT COIL—KOER		
	• Using a Neon Spark Tester Special Service Tool (D89P-6666-A) or Air Gap Spark Tester (D81P-6666-A), check for spark at each of the right side spark plug wires while cranking engine, or if engine will start, engine running. • **Is spark consistent on one or more plug wires (one spark per crank revolution)?**	Yes ▶ No ▶	GO to B2. GO to D1. Right coil pack failure.
B2	VERIFY ERRATIC START—KOEC		
	• Attempt to start vehicle five times. NOTE: **Engine will start normally at least once out of five attempts. When it fails to start, cranking rpm is erratic (ignition is firing out of time—CID circuit fault).** • **Does engine fail to start at least once?**	Yes ▶ No ▶	GO to B3. GO to B12. IDM low fault or DPI high fault.
B3	CID FAULT—CHECK CID AT ICM—KOER		
	• Key off. • Install diagnostic cable tee to Pins 1-6 side of ICM. • Connect EI diagnostic harness negative lead to battery. • Connect EI diagnostic harness to EEC breakout box. • Use 2.3L DP EI (Low Data Rate) overlay. • Set DVOM to 20 volt DC scale. • Measure voltage between (+)J51 (CID I) and (-)J60 (B-). • Bump engine in short bursts with starter without starting engine for at least ten engine revolutions. • **Does DVOM reading switch between low (less than 2.0 volts DC) and high (greater than 8.0 volts DC)?**	Yes ▶ No ▶	REPLACE ICM. Does not respond to CID input. REMOVE all test equipment. RECONNECT all components. CLEAR Continuous Memory. RERUN Quick Test. GO to B4.
B4	CID FAULT—CHECK CID AT CRANKSHAFT SENSOR—KOER		
	• Key off. • Connect crankshaft sensor tee (The word "SENSOR" is printed in green letters). • Set DVOM to 20 volt DC scale. • Measure voltage between (+)J35 (CIDS) and (-)J60 (B-). • Bump engine in short bursts with starter without starting engine for at least ten engine revolutions. • **Does DVOM reading switch between low (less than 2.0 volts DC) and high (greater than 8.0 volts DC)?**	Yes ▶ No ▶	CHECK connectors, SERVICE or REPLACE the harness. CID circuit is open. REMOVE all test equipment. RECONNECT all components. CLEAR Continuous Memory. RERUN Quick Test. GO to B5.

88152G47

2.3L Mustang (Dual Plug) EI (Low Data Rate—Previously DIS)—Code 222 CID Failure, IDM Low Fault, DPI High Fault or Right Coil Pack Failure — Pinpoint Test B

	TEST STEP	RESULT ▶	ACTION TO TAKE
B5	CID FAULT—CHECK CKP PWR AT CRANKSHAFT SENSOR—KOEO		
	• Set DVOM to 20 volt DC range. • Key on. • Measure voltage between (+)J56 (CKP PWR) and (-)J60 (B-). • **Is voltage greater than 10 volts?**	Yes ▶ No ▶	GO to B6. CHECK connectors, SERVICE or REPLACE harness. CKP PWR is open. REMOVE all test equipment. RECONNECT all components. CLEAR Continuous Memory. RERUN Quick Test.
B6	CID FAULT—CHECK IGN GND AT CRANKSHAFT SENSOR—KEY OFF		
	• Key off. • Set DVOM to 200 ohm range. • Measure resistance between J55 (IGN D CKP) and J60 (B-). • **Is resistance less than 5.0 ohms?** NOTE: **If a negative resistance valve is obtained, switch leads of the DVOM and repeat measurement.**	Yes ▶ No ▶	GO to B7. CHECK connectors, SERVICE or REPLACE the harness. IGND CKP is open. REMOVE all test equipment. RECONNECT all components. CLEAR Continuous Memory. RERUN Quick Test.
B7	CHECK CID AT CRANKSHAFT SENSOR—ICM DISCONNECTED—KOEC		
	• Key off. • Disconnect ICM tee 1-6 from ICM. Do not disconnect vehicle harness from other side of tee. • Set DVOM to 20 volt DC scale. • Measure voltage between (+)J35 (CID S) and (-)J60 (B-). • Bump engine in short bursts with starter without starting engine for at least ten engine revolutions. • **Does DVOM reading switch between low (less than 2.0 volts DC) and high (greater than 8.0 volts DC)?**	Yes ▶ No ▶	REPLACE ICM. CID shorted low. REMOVE all test equipment. RECONNECT all components. CLEAR Continuous Memory. RERUN Quick Test. GO to B8.

88152G48

2.3L Mustang (Dual Plug) EI (Low Data Rate—Previously DIS)—Code 222 CID Failure, IDM Low Fault, DPI High Fault or Right Coil Pack Failure — Pinpoint Test B

	TEST STEP	RESULT	► ACTION TO TAKE
B8	CHECK CID AT CRANKSHAFT SENSOR—ICM AND PCM DISCONNECTED—CID FAULT—KOEC		
	• Key off. • Disconnect PCM from vehicle harness. • Set DVOM to 20 volts DC scale. • Measure voltage between (+)J35 (CID S) and (-)J60 (B-). • Bump engine in short bursts with starter without starting engine for at least ten engine revolutions. • **Does DVOM reading switch between low (less than 2.0 volts DC) and high (greater than 8.0 volts DC)?**	Yes No	► REPLACE PCM. CID shorted. REMOVE all test equipment. RECONNECT all components. CLEAR Continuous Memory. RERUN Quick Test. ► GO to B9.
B9	CHECK FOR CID SHORT HIGH—ICM, PCM AND CRANKSHAFT SENSOR DISCONNECTED—CID FAULT—KEY ON		
	• Key off. • Disconnect EI diagnostic harness CKP sensor tee from sensor. Do not disconnect vehicle harness from other side of tee. • Key on. • Set DVOM to 20 volt DC scale. • Measure voltage between (+)J51 (CID I) and (-)J60 (B-). • **Is DVOM reading less than 0.5 volts DC?**	Yes No	► GO to B10. ► SERVICE connectors and harness. CID shorted high. REMOVE test equipment. RECONNECT all components. CLEAR Continuous Memory. RERUN Quick Test.
B10	CHECK FOR CID SHORT LOW—ICM, PCM AND CRANKSHAFT SENSOR DISCONNECTED—CID FAULT—KOEO		
	• Key off. • Set DVOM to 20K ohm scale. • Measure resistance between (+)J51 (CID I) and (-) J60 (B-). • **Is DVOM reading greater than 10K ohms?**	Yes No	► GO to B11. ► CHECK connectors, SERVICE or REPLACE harness. CID shorted low. REMOVE test equipment. RECONNECT all components. CLEAR Continuous Memory. RERUN Quick Test.

88152G49

2.3L Mustang (Dual Plug) EI (Low Data Rate—Previously DIS)—Code 222 CID Failure, IDM Low Fault, DPI High Fault or Right Coil Pack Failure — Pinpoint Test B

	TEST STEP	RESULT	► ACTION TO TAKE
B11	CHECK VANE—CID FAULT—KOEC		
	• **Does CID vane move through sensor air gap when engine is cranked or running?**	Yes No	► REPLACE crank sensor. No CID output. REMOVE test equipment. RECONNECT all components. CLEAR Continuous Memory. RERUN Quick Test. ► REFER to the Service Manual,
B12	CHECK DPI AT ICM—DPI HIGH FAULT OR IDM LOW FAULT—KOEO		
	• Key off. • Install ICM tee to Pins 1-6 side of ICM. • Connect EI diagnostic harness to EEC breakout box. • Use 2.3L DP EI (Low Data Rate) overlay. • Connect EI diagnostic harness negative lead to battery. • Set DVOM to 20 volt DC range. • Start engine. • Measure voltage between (+)J54 (DPI I) and (-)J60 (B-). • **Is voltage less than 1.0 volt DC?**	Yes No	► GO to B15. IDM low fault. ► GO to B13. DPI high fault.
B13	CHECK DPI—ICM DISCONNECTED—DPI HIGH FAULT—KOEO		
	• Key off. • Set DVOM to 20 volt DC scale. • Disconnect 1-6 ICM tee from ICM only. Do not disconnect vehicle harness from other side of tee. • Key on. • Measure voltage between (+)J54 (DPI I) and (-)J60 (B-). • **Is voltage greater than 1.0 volt DC?**	Yes No	► GO to B14. ► REPLACE ICM. DPI short high. REMOVE test equipment. RECONNECT all components. CLEAR Continuous Memory. RERUN Quick Test.

88152G50

2.3L Mustang (Dual Plug) EI (Low Data Rate—Previously DIS)—Code 222 CID Failure, IDM Low Fault, DPI High Fault or Right Coil Pack Failure — Pinpoint Test B

TEST STEP		RESULT	▶ ACTION TO TAKE
B14	CHECK FOR DPI SHORT HIGH—ICM AND PCM DISCONNECTED—DPI HIGH FAULT—KOEO		
	• Key off. • Disconnect PCM. • Set DVOM to 20 volt DC range. • Key on. • Measure voltage between (+)J54 (DPI I) and (-)J60 (B-). • **Is voltage less than 0.5 volts DC?**	Yes	▶ REPLACE PCM. DPI shorted high. REMOVE test equipment. RECONNECT all components. CLEAR Continuous Memory. RERUN Quick Test.
		No	▶ CHECK connectors, SERVICE or REPLACE harness. DPI shorted high. REMOVE test equipment. RECONNECT all components. CLEAR Continuous Memory. RERUN Quick Test.
B15	CHECK IDM AT ICM—IDM LOW FAULT—KOER		
	• Set DVOM to 20 volt AC range. • Install IDM output tee (Pins 7-12) between IDM and vehicle harness. • Start engine. • Measure voltage between J4 (IDM I) and J60 (B-). • **Is voltage greater than 2.0 volts AC?**	Yes	▶ GO to **B19**.
		No	▶ GO to **B16**.
B16	CHECK IDM AT ICM—PCM DISCONNECTED—IDM LOW FAULT—KOEC		
	• Key off. • Disconnect PCM. • Set DVOM to 20 volt AC range. • Measure voltage between J4 (IDM I) and J60 (B-) while cranking engine. • **Is settled voltage greater than 3.0 volts AC?**	Yes	▶ REPLACE PCM. IDM shorted. REMOVE test equipment. RECONNECT all components. CLEAR Continuous Memory. RERUN Quick Test.
		No	▶ GO to **B17**.
B17	CHECK FOR IDM SHORT LOW—ICM DISCONNECTED—IDM SHORT FAULT—KEY OFF		
	• Key off. • Disconnect EI diagnostic harness tee from Pins 7-12 side of ICM. Do not disconnect vehicle harness from other side of tee. • Set DVOM to 200 ohm range. • Measure resistance between J4 (IDM I) J60 (B-). • **Is resistance greater than 10K ohms?**	Yes	▶ GO to **B18**.
		No	▶ CHECK connectors, SERVICE or REPLACE harness. IDM shorted low. REMOVE all test equipment. RECONNECT all components. CLEAR Continuous Memory. RERUN Quick Test.

88152G51

2.3L Mustang (Dual Plug) EI (Low Data Rate—Previously DIS)—Code 222 CID Failure, IDM Low Fault, DPI High Fault or Right Coil Pack Failure — Pinpoint Test B

TEST STEP		RESULT	▶ ACTION TO TAKE
B18	CHECK FOR IDM SHORT HIGH—ICM DISCONNECTED—IDM SHORT LOW—KOEO		
	• Set DVOM to 20 volt DC range. • Key on. • Measure voltage between (+)J4 (IDM I) and (-)J60 (B-). • **Is voltage less than 0.5 volt?**	Yes	▶ REPLACE ICM. No IDM output. REMOVE test equipment. RECONNECT all components. CLEAR Continuous Memory. RERUN Quick Test.
		No	▶ CHECK connectors, SERVICE or REPLACE harness. IDM shorted high. REMOVE test equipment. RECONNECT all components. CLEAR Continuous Memory. RERUN Quick Test.
B19	CHECK FOR IDM OPEN—KEY OFF—IDM LOW FAULT		
	• Key off. • Disconnect PCM. • Connect the second EEC breakout box to PCM vehicle harness connector. • Measure resistance between J4 (IDM I) and Pin 4 (IDM) of second EEC breakout box. • **Is resistance less than 5.0 ohms?**	Yes	▶ REPLACE PCM. Does not respond to IDM input. REMOVE test equipment. RECONNECT all components. CLEAR Continuous Memory. RERUN Quick Test.
		No	▶ CHECK connectors, SERVICE or REPLACE harness. IDM open. REMOVE test equipment. RECONNECT all components. CLEAR Continuous Memory. RERUN Quick Test.

88152G52

2.3L Mustang (Dual Plug) EI (Low Data Rate—Previously DIS)—Code 222 CID Failure, IDM Low Fault, DPI High Fault or Right Coil Pack Failure — Pinpoint Test B

	TEST STEP	RESULT	▶	ACTION TO TAKE
B20	CHECK CID AT PCM CONNECTOR—PCM DISCONNECTED—KOEC			
	• Key off. • Disconnect PCM. • Connect EEC breakout box to PCM vehicle harness connector. • DVOM on 20 volt DC scale. • Connect DVOM lead between Pin 5 (CID) and -J60 ground. • Bump engine in short bursts with starter without starting the engine for at least five engine revolutions and watch for a change in DVOM reading. • **Does the DVOM reading switch between low (less than 2.0 volts DC) and high (greater than 8.0 volts DC)?**	Yes	▶	REPLACE PCM. Does not respond to CID input. REMOVE all test equipment. RECONNECT all components. CLEAR Continuous Memory. RERUN Quick Test.
		No	▶	CHECK connectors. SERVICE or REPLACE harness. CID open. REMOVE test equipment. RECONNECT all components. CLEAR Continuous Memory. RERUN Quick Test.

88152G53

2.3L Mustang (Dual Plug) EI (Low Data Rate—Previously DIS)—Code 218 IDM Open, IDM High or Left Coil Pack Failure — Pinpoint Test C

	TEST STEP	RESULT	▶	ACTION TO TAKE
C1	CHECK FOR ANY LEFT SIDE SPARK—IDM OPEN, IDM HIGH OR LEFT COIL PACK FAILURE—KOER			
	• Start engine. • Using a Neon Bulb Spark Tester (D89P-6666-A) or air gap spark tester, check for spark at each left spark plug wire. • **Is spark present at any left spark plug wire?**	Yes No	▶ ▶	GO to C2. GO to D1.
C2	CHECK IDM—IDM OPEN OR IDM HIGH FAULT—KOER			
	• Key off. • Install ICM tee to Pins 7-12 side of ICM. • Connect negative lead of EI diagnostic harness to battery. • Connect EI diagnostic harness to EEC breakout box. • Use 2.3L EI (Low Data Rate) overlay. • Set DVOM to 20 volt AC range. • Start engine. • Measure voltage between J4 (IDM I) and J60 (B-). • **Is voltage greater than 1.0 volt AC?**	Yes No	▶ ▶	GO to C3. GO to C4.
C3	CHECK IDM TO PCM CONTINUITY—IDM OPEN FAULT—KEY OFF			
	• Key off. • Set DVOM to 200 ohm range. • Disconnect PCM. • Connect second EEC breakout box to PCM vehicle harness connector. • Measure resistance between J4 (IDM I) and Pin 4 (IDM) of second breakout box. • **Is resistance less than 5.0 ohms?**	Yes	▶	REPLACE PCM. Does not respond to IDM input. REMOVE test equipment. RECONNECT all components. CLEAR Continuous Memory. RERUN Quick Test.
		No	▶	CHECK connectors. SERVICE or REPLACE harness. IDM open. REMOVE test equipment. RECONNECT all components. CLEAR Continuous Memory. RERUN Quick Test.

88152G54

2.3L Mustang (Dual Plug) EI (Low Data Rate—Previously DIS)—Code 218 IDM Open, IDM High or Left Coil Pack Failure — Pinpoint Test C

	TEST STEP	RESULT ▶	ACTION TO TAKE
C4	CHECK FOR IDM—PCM DISCONNECTED—IDM OPEN FAULT—KOEC		
	• Key off. • Disconnect PCM. • Set DVOM to 20 volt AC range. • Measure voltage between J4 (IDM I) and J60 (B-) while cranking engine. • **Is voltage greater than 1.0 volt AC?**	Yes ▶ No ▶	REPLACE PCM. IDM short high. REMOVE test equipment. RECONNECT all components. CLEAR Continuous Memory. RERUN Quick Test. GO to C5.
C5	CHECK IDM FOR SHORT HIGH—ICM AND PCM DISCONNECTED—IDM HIGH FAULT—KOEO		
	• Key off. • Disconnect 7-12 ICM tee from ICM only. Do not disconnect other side of tee from vehicle harness. • Set DVOM to 20 volt DC range. • Key on. • Measure voltage between (+)J4 (IDM I) and (-)J60 (B-). • **Is voltage less than 6.0 volt DC?** NOTE: **The tachometer circuit (if the vehicle has a tachometer in the dash panel) will feed +5 volts DC into the IDM circuit.**	Yes ▶ No ▶	GO to C6. CHECK connectors, SERVICE or REPLACE harness. IDM shorted high. REMOVE test equipment. RECONNECT all components. CLEAR Continuous Memory. RERUN Quick Test.
C6	CHECK IDMD FOR SHORT LOW—ICM AND PCM DISCONNECTED—IDM HIGH FAULT—KEY OFF		
	• Key off. • Set DVOM to 20K ohm range. • Measure resistance between J4 (IDM I) and J60 (B-). • **Is resistance greater than 10K ohms?**	Yes ▶ No ▶	REPLACE ICM. IDM shorted high. REMOVE all test equipment. RECONNECT all components. CLEAR Continuous Memory. RERUN Quick Test. CHECK connectors, SERVICE or REPLACE harness. No IDM input. REMOVE test equipment. RECONNECT all components. CLEAR Continuous Memory. RERUN Quick Test.

88152G55

2.3L Mustang (Dual Plug) EI (Low Data Rate—Previously DIS) No Start and/or Code 224 Coil Failure — Pinpoint Test D

	TEST STEP	RESULT ▶	ACTION TO TAKE
D1	CHECK FOR SPARK DURING CRANK		
	• Using a Neon Bulb Spark Tester (OTC D89P-6666-A) or Air Gap Spark Tester (D81P-6666-A), check for spark at all spark plug wires while cranking. • **Was spark consistent on all spark plug wires?**	Yes ▶ No ▶	Ignition system is OK. GO to D2.
D2	CHECK FOR SPARK AT RIGHT SPARK PLUG WIRES DURING CRANK—SPARK FAULT		
	• **Was spark consistent on all right spark plug wires (one spark per crankshaft revolution)?** NOTE: **Check spark at all spark plugs.**	Yes ▶ No ▶	GO to D3. GO to D19.
D3	CHECK LEFT SPARK PLUGS AND WIRES—LEFT SPARK FAULT		
	• Check left spark plug wires for insulation damage, looseness, shorting or other damage. • Remove and check left spark plugs for damage, wear, carbon deposits and proper plug gap. NOTE: **Left coil plugs and wires are attached to the left coil.** • **Are spark plugs and wires OK?**	Yes ▶ No ▶	REINSTALL plugs and wires. GO to D4. SERVICE or REPLACE damaged component. REMOVE all test equipment. RECONNECT all components. CLEAR Continuous Memory. RERUN Quick Test.
D4	CHECK COIL PWR AT LEFT COIL—LEFT SPARK FAULT		
	WARNING: NEVER CONNECT PCM TO THE EEC BREAKOUT BOX WHEN PERFORMING EI DIAGNOSTICS. • Key off. • Install left coil tee only at this time (The left coil tee has the word "COIL" printed in yellow letters). • Connect EI diagnostic harness B+ and B- leads to battery. • Use 2.3L EI (Low Data Rate) overlay. • DVOM on 20 volt DC scale. • Key on, engine off. • Measure voltage between (+)J15 (COIL PWR L) and (-)J60 (B-) at breakout box. • **Is DC voltage greater than 10 volts?**	Yes ▶ No ▶	GO to D5. SERVICE open circuit in harness. COIL PWR L is open. REMOVE all test equipment. RECONNECT all components. CLEAR Continuous Memory. RERUN Quick Test.

8152G56

2.3L Mustang (Dual Plug) EI (Low Data Rate—Previously DIS) No Start and/or Code 224 Coil Failure	Pinpoint Test	D

	TEST STEP	RESULT ▶	ACTION TO TAKE
D5	CHECK FOR C3 HIGH AT COIL PACK—COIL FAULT—KOEO		
	• DVOM on 20 volt DC scale. • Key on, engine off. • Measure voltage between (+)J30 (LC3C) and (-)J60 (B-) at breakout box. • **Is DC voltage reading greater than 10 volts DC?**	Yes ▶ No ▶	GO to D6. GO to D13.
D6	CHECK FOR C4 HIGH AT COIL PACK—COIL FAILURE—KOEO		
	• DVOM on 20 volt DC scale. • Key on, engine off. • Measure voltage between (+)J28 (LC4C) and (-)J60 (B-) at breakout box. • **Is DC voltage reading greater than 10 volts DC?**	Yes ▶ No ▶	GO to D7. GO to D11.
D7	CHECK FOR C3 HIGH AT ICM—COIL FAULT—KOEO		
	• Key off. • Connect ICM 7-12 tee to the ICM and vehicle harness connector. • DVOM on 20 volt DC scale. • Key on, engine off. • Measure voltage between (+)J3 (LC3I) and (-)J60 (B-) at breakout box. • **Is DC voltage reading greater than 10 volts DC?**	Yes ▶ No ▶	GO to D8. SERVICE open circuit. C3 open in harness. REMOVE all test equipment. RECONNECT all components. CLEAR Continuous Memory. RERUN Quick Test.
D8	CHECK FOR C4 HIGH AT ICM—COIL FAULT—KOEO		
	• DVOM on 20 volt DC scale. • Key on, engine off. • Measure voltage between (+)J6 (LC4 I) and (-)J60 (B-) at breakout box. • **Is DC voltage reading greater than 10 volts DC?**	Yes ▶ No ▶	GO to D9. SERVICE open circuit. C4 open in harness. REMOVE all test equipment. RECONNECT all components. CLEAR Continuous Memory. RERUN Quick Test.

88152G57

2.3L Mustang (Dual Plug) EI (Low Data Rate—Previously DIS) No Start and/or Code 224 Coil Failure	Pinpoint Test	D

	TEST STEP	RESULT ▶	ACTION TO TAKE
D9	CHECK FOR C3 LOW AT COIL PACK—COIL DISCONNECTED—KOEO		
	• Key off. • Disconnect left coil pack from coil tee, leave vehicle harness connected to coil tee (the word "COIL" is printed in yellow letters). • DVOM on 20 volt DC scale. • Key on, engine off. • Measure voltage between (+)J30 (LC3C) and (-)J60 (B-) at breakout box. • **Is DC voltage reading less than 0.5 volts DC?**	Yes ▶ No ▶	GO to D15. GO to D10.
D10	CHECK FOR C3 LOW—ICM AND LEFT COIL DISCONNECTED—COIL FAULT—KOEO		
	• Key off. • Disconnect ICM from the ICM 7-12 tee, leave vehicle harness connected to coil tee. • DVOM on 20 volt DC scale. • Key on, engine off. • Measure voltage between (+)J30 (LC3C) and (-)J60 (B-) at breakout box. • **Is DC voltage reading less than 1.0 volts DC?**	Yes ▶ No ▶	REPLACE ICM. C3 shorted high. REMOVE all test equipment. RECONNECT all components. CLEAR Continuous Memory. RERUN Quick Test. SERVICE short circuit. C3 shorted high in harness. REMOVE all test equipment. RECONNECT all components. CLEAR Continuous Memory. RERUN Quick Test.
D11	CHECK FOR C4 CIRCUIT SHORT TO GROUND COIL FAULT—KEY OFF		
	• Key off. • DVOM on 20K ohm scale. • Measure resistance between J60 (B-) and J28 (LC4C) at breakout box. • **Is resistance reading greater than 10K ohms?** NOTE: **If a negative resistance value is obtained, switch the leads of the DVOM and repeat measurement.**	Yes ▶ No ▶	REPLACE left coil pack. C4 open in coil. REMOVE all test equipment. RECONNECT all components. CLEAR Continuous Memory. RERUN Quick Test. GO to D12.

88152G58

2.3L Mustang (Dual Plug) EI (Low Data Rate—Previously DIS) No Start and/or Code 224 Coil Failure	Pinpoint Test	D

TEST STEP	RESULT ▶	ACTION TO TAKE
D12 CHECK FOR C4 SHORT TO GROUND IN HARNESS—ICM DISCONNECTED—COIL FAULT LOW		
• Key off. • Disconnect ICM from ICM 7-12 tee, leave vehicle harness connected to module tee. • DVOM on 20K ohm scale. • Measure resistance between J60 (B-) and J28 (LC4C) at breakout box. • **Is resistance reading greater than 10K ohms?**	Yes ▶	REPLACE ICM. C4 is shorted to ground. REMOVE all test equipment. RECONNECT all components. CLEAR Continuous Memory. RERUN Quick Test.
	No ▶	SERVICE short circuit. C4 is shorted to ground in harness. REMOVE all test equipment. RECONNECT all components. CLEAR Continuous Memory. RERUN Quick Test.
D13 CHECK FOR C3 SHORT TO GROUND—COIL FAULT LOW		
• Key off. • DVOM on 20K ohm scale. • Measure resistance between J60 (B-) and J30 (LC3C) at breakout box. • **Is resistance reading greater than 10K ohms?**	Yes ▶	REPLACE left coil pack. C3 open in coil. REMOVE all test equipment. RECONNECT all components. CLEAR Continuous Memory. RERUN Quick Test.
	No ▶	GO to D14.
D14 CHECK FOR C3 SHORT LOW—ICM DISCONNECTED—COIL FAULT		
• Key off. • Disconnect ICM from the ICM 7-12 tee, leave vehicle harness connected to module tee. • DVOM on 20K ohm scale. • Measure resistance between J60 (B-) and J30 (LC3C) at breakout box. • **Is resistance greater than 10K ohms?**	Yes ▶	REPLACE ICM. C3 shorted low. REMOVE all test equipment. RECONNECT all components. CLEAR Continuous Memory. RERUN Quick Test.
	No ▶	SERVICE short circuit. C4 shorted low in harness. REMOVE all test equipment. RECONNECT all components. CLEAR Continuous Memory. RERUN Quick Test.

88152G59

2.3L Mustang (Dual Plug) EI (Low Data Rate—Previously DIS) No Start and/or Code 224 Coil Failure	Pinpoint Test	D

TEST STEP	RESULT ▶	ACTION TO TAKE
D15 CHECK FOR C4 LOW—COIL DISCONNECTED—KOEO		
• DVOM on 20 volt DC scale. • Key on, engine off. • Measure voltage between (+)J28 (LC4C) and (-)J60 (B-) at breakout box. • **Is DC voltage reading less than 0.5 volts DC?**	Yes ▶ No ▶	GO to D17. GO to D16.
D16 CHECK FOR C4 SHORT HIGH—ICM AND COIL DISCONNECTED—COIL FAULT—KOEO		
• Key off. • Disconnect ICM from the ICM 7-12 tee, leave vehicle harness connected to module tee. • DVOM on 20 volt DC scale. • Key on, engine off. • Measure voltage between (+)J28 (LC4C) and (-)J60 (B-) at breakout box. • **Is DC voltage reading less than 1.0 volts DC?**	Yes ▶	REPLACE ICM. C4 is shorted high. REMOVE all test equipment. RECONNECT all components. CLEAR Continuous Memory. RERUN Quick Test.
	No ▶	SERVICE short circuit. C4 is shorted high in harness. REMOVE all test equipment. RECONNECT all components. CLEAR Continuous Memory. RERUN Quick Test.
D17 CHECK FOR C3 AT COIL PACK—COILS DISCONNECTED—KOEC		
• Key off. • Disconnect left and right coils. • Connect positive lead of diagnostic cable to battery. • Connect left coil tee to vehicle harness (the word "COIL" is printed in yellow letters). Do not connect left coil to tee. • Connect incandescent test lamp between J57 (B+) and J30 (LC3C). • Crank engine. • **Does test lamp blink during crank?**	Yes ▶ No ▶	GO to D18. REPLACE ICM. C3 open. REMOVE all test equipment. RECONNECT all components. CLEAR Continuous Memory. RERUN Quick Test.

88152G60

2.3L Mustang (Dual Plug) EI (Low Data Rate—Previously DIS) No Start and/or Code 224 Coil Failure	Pinpoint Test	D

	TEST STEP	RESULT	ACTION TO TAKE
D18	CHECK FOR C4 AT COIL PACK—COILS DISCONNECTED—KOEC		
	• Key off. • Connect incandescent test lamp between J57 (B+) and J28 (LC4C). • Crank engine. • **Does test lamp blink during crank?**	Yes ▶	REPLACE left coil pack. Input to coil pack is OK, but no high voltage output. REMOVE all test equipment. RECONNECT all components. CLEAR Continuous Memory. RERUN Quick Test.
		No ▶	REPLACE ICM. No C4 output. REMOVE all test equipment. RECONNECT all components. CLEAR Continuous Memory. RERUN Quick Test.
D19	CHECK RIGHT PLUGS AND WIRES—RIGHT SPARK FAULT		
	• Check right spark plug wires for insulation damage, looseness, shorting or other damage. • Remove and check right spark plugs for damage, wear, carbon deposits and proper plug gap. NOTE: **Right coil plugs and wires are attached to right coil.** • **Are spark plugs and wires OK?**	Yes ▶	REINSTALL plugs and wires. GO to D20.
		No ▶	SERVICE or REPLACE damaged component. REMOVE all test equipment. RECONNECT all components. CLEAR Continuous Memory. RERUN Quick Test.
D20	CHECK FOR COIL PWR R AT RIGHT COIL—RIGHT SPARK FAULT—KOEO		
	• Key off. • Connect negative lead to battery. • Install right coil tee (the word "COIL" is printed in blue letters and the tee connectors have 3 pins). • DVOM on 20 volt DC scale. • Key on, engine off. • Measure voltage between (+)J26 (COIL PWR R) and (-)J60 (B-) at breakout box. • **Is DC voltage greater than 10 volts DC?**	Yes ▶	GO to D21.
		No ▶	SERVICE open circuit in harness. COIL PWR R is open. REMOVE all test equipment. RECONNECT all components. CLEAR Continuous Memory. RERUN Quick Test.

88152G61

2.3L Mustang (Dual Plug) EI (Low Data Rate—Previously DIS) No Start and/or Code 224 Coil Failure	Pinpoint Test	D

	TEST STEP	RESULT	ACTION TO TAKE
D21	CHECK FOR C1 HIGH AT COIL PACK—COIL FAULT—KOEO		
	• DVOM on 20 volt DC scale. • Key on, engine off. • Measure voltage between (+)J23 (RC1C) and (-)J60 (B-) at breakout box. • Is DC voltage reading greater than 10 volts DC?	Yes ▶	GO to D22.
		No ▶	GO to D27. C1 low fault.
D22	CHECK FOR C2 HIGH—COIL FAULT—KOEO		
	• DVOM on 20 volt DC scale. • Key on, engine off. • Measure voltage between (+)J24 (RC2C) and (-)J60 (B-) at breakout box. • Is DC voltage reading greater than 10 volts DC?	Yes ▶	GO to D23.
		No ▶	GO to D29. C2 low fault.
D23	CHECK FOR C1 HIGH AT ICM—COIL FAULT—KOEO		
	• Key off. • Install ICM 7-12 tee. • DVOM on 20 volt DC scale. • Key on, engine off. • Measure voltage between (+)J18 (RC1I) and (-)J60 (B-) at breakout box. • Is DC voltage reading greater than 10 volts DC?	Yes ▶	GO to D24.
		No ▶	**SERVICE open circuit. C1 open in harness. REMOVE all test equipment. RECONNECT all components. CLEAR Continuous Memory. RERUN Quick Test.**
D24	CHECK FOR C2 HIGH AT ICM—COIL FAULT—KOEO		
	• DVOM on 20 volt DC scale. • Key on, engine off. • Measure voltage between (+)J10 (RC2I) and (-)J60 (B-) at breakout box. • Is DC voltage reading greater than 10 volts DC?	Yes ▶	GO to D25.
		No ▶	**SERVICE open circuit. C2 open in harness. REMOVE all test equipment. RECONNECT all components. CLEAR Continuous Memory. RERUN Quick Test.**
D25	CHECK FOR C1 LOW AT COIL PACK—COIL FAILURE—COIL DISCONNECTED—KOEO		
	• Key off. • Disconnect right coil from coil tee. Leave vehicle harness connected to coil tee. • DVOM on 20 volt DC scale. • Key on, engine off. • Measure voltage between (+)J23 (RC1C) and (-)J60 (B-) at breakout box. • Is DC voltage reading less than 0.5 volts DC?	Yes ▶	GO to D31.
		No ▶	GO to D26. C1 high fault.

88152G62

2.3L Mustang (Dual Plug) EI (Low Data Rate—Previously DIS) No Start and/or Code 224 Coil Failure — Pinpoint Test D

	TEST STEP	RESULT	▶ ACTION TO TAKE
D26	CHECK FOR C1 SHORT LOW AT COIL PACK—ICM AND COIL DISCONNECTED—COIL FAULT		
	• Key off. • Disconnected ICM from the ICM 7-12 tee, leave vehicle harness connected to module tee. • DVOM on 20 volt DC scale. • Key on, engine off. • Measure voltage between (+)J23 (RC1C) and (-)J60 (B-) at breakout box. • **Is DC voltage reading less than 1.0 volts DC?**	Yes	▶ REPLACE ICM. C1 shorted high. REMOVE all test equipment. RECONNECT all components. CLEAR Continuous Memory. RERUN Quick Test.
		No	▶ SERVICE short circuit. C1 shorted high in harness. REMOVE all test equipment. RECONNECT all components. CLEAR Continuous Memory. RERUN Quick Test.
D27	CHECK FOR C1 SHORT LOW—COIL FAULT LOW—KEY OFF		
	• Key off. • DVOM on 20K ohm scale. • Measure resistance between J60 (B-) and J23 (RC1C) at breakout box. • **Is resistance reading greater than 10K ohms?**	Yes	▶ REPLACE Right Coil Pack. C1 open in coil. REMOVE all test equipment. RECONNECT all components. CLEAR Continuous Memory. RERUN Quick Test.
		No	▶ GO to D28.
D28	CHECK FOR C1 SHORT TO GROUND IN ICM—ICM DISCONNECTED—COIL FAULT LOW		
	• Key off. • Disconnect ICM from ICM 7-12 tee, leave vehicle harness connected to module tee. • DVOM on 20K ohm scale. • Measure resistance between J60 (B-) and J23 (RC1C) at breakout box. • **Is resistance reading greater than 10K ohms?**	Yes	▶ REPLACE ICM. C1 is shorted to ground. REMOVE all test equipment. RECONNECT all components. CLEAR Continuous Memory. RERUN Quick Test.
		No	▶ SERVICE short circuit. C1 is shorted to ground in harness. REMOVE all test equipment. RECONNECT all components. CLEAR Continuous Memory. RERUN Quick Test.

88152G63

2.3L Mustang (Dual Plug) EI (Low Data Rate—Previously DIS) No Start and/or Code 224 Coil Failure — Pinpoint Test D

	TEST STEP	RESULT	▶ ACTION TO TAKE
D29	CHECK FOR C2 SHORT LOW—COIL FAULT LOW—KEY OFF		
	• Key off. • DVOM on 2K ohm scale. • Measure resistance between J60 (B-) and J24 (RC2C) at breakout box. • **Is resistance reading greater than 100 ohms?**	Yes	▶ REPLACE Right Coil Pack. C2 open in coil. REMOVE all test equipment. RECONNECT all components. CLEAR Continuous Memory. RERUN Quick Test.
		No	▶ GO to D30.
D30	CHECK FOR C2 SHORT LOW AT COIL PACK—ICM DISCONNECTED—COIL FAULT—KEY OFF		
	• Key off. • Disconnect ICM from ICM 7-12 tee, leave vehicle harness connected to module tee. • DVOM on 20K ohm scale. • Measure resistance between J24 (RC2C) and J60 (B-) at breakout box. • **Is resistance reading greater than 10K ohms?**	Yes	▶ REPLACE ICM. C2 shorted low. REMOVE all test equipment. RECONNECT all components. CLEAR Continuous Memory. RERUN Quick Test.
		No	▶ SERVICE short circuit. C2 shorted low in harness. REMOVE all test equipment. RECONNECT all components. CLEAR Continuous Memory. RERUN Quick Test.
D31	CHECK FOR C2 LOW AT COIL PACK—RIGHT COIL DISCONNECTED—KOEO		
	• DVOM on 20 volt DC scale. • Key on, engine off. • Measure voltage between (+)J24 (RC2C) and (-)J60 (B-) at breakout box. • **Is DC voltage reading less than 0.5 volts DC?**	Yes	▶ GO to D33.
		No	▶ GO to D32. C2 high fault.

88152G64

2.3L Mustang (Dual Plug) EI (Low Data Rate—Previously DIS) No Start and/or Code 224 Coil Failure — Pinpoint Test D

	TEST STEP	RESULT	▶ ACTION TO TAKE
D32	CHECK FOR SHORT HIGH IN ICM C2—ICM DISCONNECTED—COIL FAULT—KOEO		
	• Key off. • Disconnect ICM from ICM 7-12 tee, leave EI diagnostic harness connected to vehicle harness connector. • DVOM on 20 volt DC scale. • Key on, engine off. • Measure voltage between (+)J24 (RC2C) and (-)J60 (B-) at breakout box. • **Is DC voltage reading less than 0.5 volts DC?**	Yes	▶ REPLACE ICM. C2 shorted high. REMOVE all test equipment. RECONNECT all components. CLEAR Continuous Memory. RERUN Quick Test.
		No	▶ SERVICE short circuit. C2 shorted high in harness. REMOVE all test equipment. RECONNECT all components. CLEAR Continuous Memory. RERUN Quick Test.
D33	CHECK FOR C1 AT COIL PACK—COILS DISCONNECTED—KOEC		
	• Connect EI diagnostic harness positive lead to battery. • Connect incandescent test lamp between J57 (B+) and J23 (RC1C). • Disconnect left coil from vehicle harness. Do not install left coil tee. • Crank engine. • **Does test lamp blink during crank?**	Yes	▶ GO to D34.
		No	▶ REPLACE ICM. C1 driver damaged. REMOVE all test equipment. RECONNECT all components. CLEAR Continuous Memory. RERUN Quick Test.
D34	CHECK FOR C2 AT COIL PACK—COILS DISCONNECTED—COIL FAULT—KOEC		
	• Key off. • Connect incandescent test lamp between J57 (B+) and J24 (RC2C). • Crank engine. • **Does test lamp blink during crank?**	Yes	▶ REPLACE right coil pack. Input to coil pack is OK, but no high voltage output. REMOVE all test equipment. RECONNECT all components. CLEAR Continuous Memory. RERUN Quick Test.
		No	▶ SERVICE harness. C2 open in harness. REMOVE all test equipment. RECONNECT all components. CLEAR Continuous Memory. RERUN Quick Test.

88152G65

2.3L Mustang (Dual Plug) EI (Low Data Rate—Previously DIS) Code 223: DPI Open, DPI High or SPOUT High — Pinpoint Test E

	TEST STEP	RESULT	▶ ACTION TO TAKE
E1	CHECK SPOUT AT ICM		
	• Key off. • Connect EI diagnostic harness negative and positive lead to battery. • Install EI diagnostic harness to breakout box and the ICM (Pins 1-6). • Use 2.3L EI DP (Low Data Rate) overlay. • Connect DVOM between (+)36 (SPOUT) and (-)J60 (B-) • Set DVOM to 20 volt AC range. • Start engine. • **Is voltage greater than 2.0 volts AC?**	Yes	▶ GO to E2.
		No	▶ GO to E6. SPOUT high fault.
E2	DP FAULT—VERIFY DUAL PLUG OPERATION		
	• Using a Neon Spark Tester (D89P-6666-A) or Air Gap Spark Tester, check for spark at each left side plug wire with the engine running. • **Is spark present at one or more wires during dual plug operation?**	Yes	▶ REPLACE ICM. ICM not indicating dual plug operation. REMOVE all test equipment. RECONNECT all components. CLEAR Continuous Memory. RERUN Quick Test.
		No	▶ GO to E3.
E3	DP FAULT—CHECK DPI CONTINUITY—PCM AND ICM DISCONNECTED		
	• Key off. • Set DVOM to 200 ohm scale. • Disconnect PCM. • Disconnect ICM from ICM 1-6 tee. Leave vehicle harness connected to module tee. • Measure resistance between Test Pin 32 (DPI) at the PCM vehicle harness connector and J54 (DPI). • **Is resistance less than 5.0 ohms?**	Yes	▶ GO to E4.
		No	▶ CHECK connectors, SERVICE or REPLACE the harness. DPI is open between the ICM and the PCM. REMOVE all test equipment. RECONNECT all components. CLEAR Continuous Memory. RERUN Quick Test.
E4	DPI FAULT—CHECK FOR DPI SHORT HIGH—PCM AND ICM DISCONNECTED—KOEO		
	• Key on. • Set DVOM to 20 volt DC range. • Measure voltage between (+)J54 (DPI) and (-)J60 (B-). • **Is the voltage less than 0.5 volt DC?**	Yes	▶ GO to E5.
		No	▶ SERVICE harness. DPI short high. REMOVE all test equipment. RECONNECT all components. CLEAR Continuous Memory. RERUN Quick Test.

88152G66

2.3L Mustang (Dual Plug) EI (Low Data Rate—Previously DIS) Code 223: DPI Open, DPI High or SPOUT High — Pinpoint Test E

	TEST STEP	RESULT ▶	ACTION TO TAKE
E5	FORCE DUAL PLUG COMMAND AT ICM (DPI LOW)—DPI FAULT—KOER		
	• Connect an incandescent 12 volt test lamp between J54 (DPI) and J60 (B-). • Reconnect PCM. • Reconnect ICM tee (1-6) to ICM. **CAUTION: Do not Jumper J54 to VPWR+ or B+; the DPI circuit in the PCM may be damaged.** • Start engine. • **Is test lamp on?**	Yes ▶	REPLACE PCM. PCM DPI signal shorted high in PCM. REMOVE all test equipment. RECONNECT all components. CLEAR Continuous Memory. RERUN Quick Test.
		No ▶	REPLACE ICM. ICM not responding to DPI signal. REMOVE all test equipment. RECONNECT all components. CLEAR Continuous Memory. RERUN Quick Test.
E6	CHECK PCM SIDE OF SPOUT—SPOUT HIGH FAULT—ICM DISCONNECTED—KOEC		
	• Key off. • Set DVOM to 20 volt AC range. • Disconnect ICM (Pins 1-6) from ICM diagnostic harness tee. Do not disconnect vehicle wiring connector from the other end of the tee. • Crank engine. • Measure voltage between J36 (SPOUT) and J60 (B-). • **Is the voltage greater than 0.1 volts AC?**	Yes ▶	REPLACE ICM. SPOUT is shorted high in the ICM. REMOVE all test equipment. RECONNECT all components. CLEAR Continuous Memory. RERUN Quick Test.
		No ▶	GO to E7.

88152G67

2.3L Mustang (Dual Plug) EI (Low Data Rate—Previously DIS) Code 223: DPI Open, DPI High or SPOUT High — Pinpoint Test E

	TEST STEP	RESULT ▶	ACTION TO TAKE
E7	CHECK SPOUT FOR SHORT HIGH IN HARNESS—PCM AND ICM DISCONNECTED—KOEO		
	• Key off. • Set DVOM to 20 volt DC range. • Disconnect PCM. • Key on. • Measure voltage between J36 (SPOUT) and J60 (B-). • **Is voltage less than 0.5 volts DC?**	Yes ▶	REPLACE PCM. SPOUT is shorted high in the PCM. REMOVE all test equipment. RECONNECT all components. CLEAR Continuous Memory. RERUN Quick Test.
		No ▶	SERVICE harness and connectors. SPOUT is shorted high between ICM and PCM. REMOVE all test equipment. RECONNECT all components. CLEAR Continuous Memory. RERUN Quick Test.

88152G68

2.3L Mustang (Dual Plug) EI (Low Data Rate—Previously DIS) Code 213/412 or No Codes and Lack of Power—Spout Open or Low	Pinpoint Test	F

	TEST STEP	RESULT	▶	ACTION TO TAKE
F1	CHECK FOR BASE TIMING (10 BTDC)—SPOUT JUMPER DISCONNECTED			
	• Key off. • Install timing light. • Engine running at normal operating temperature. • Transmission out of gear. • Engine at idle rpm. • Remove SPOUT harness jumper plug from SPOUT vehicle harness connector. • Check timing. • **Is engine timing 10 ± 2 degrees BTDC or ADTC?**	Yes No	▶ ▶	GO to F2. GO to F4.
F2	CHECK FOR TIMING GREATER THAN 16 DEGREES BTDC AT IDLE			
	• Key off. • Reinstall SPOUT harness jumper to SPOUT vehicle harness connector. • Engine at idle rpm. • Check timing. • **Is timing greater than 16 degrees BTDC?**	Yes No	▶ ▶	Ignition System is OK. GO to F3.
F3	CHECK FOR SPOUT SHORT LOW—SPOUT FAULT—KEY OFF—ICM DISCONNECTED			
	• Key off. • Install 1-6 ICM tee. • Use 2.3L EI DP overlay. • Connect diagnostic harness negative and positive leads to the battery. • Set DVOM to 20K ohm range. • Measure resistance between J36 (SPOUT) and J60 (B-). • **Is resistance greater than 10K ohms?**	Yes No	▶ ▶	GO to F6. GO to F5.

88152G69

2.3L Mustang (Dual Plug) EI (Low Data Rate—Previously DIS) Code 213/412 or No Codes and Lack of Power—Spout Open or Low	Pinpoint Test	F

	TEST STEP	RESULT	▶	ACTION TO TAKE
F4	SPOUT FAULT—INSPECT SENSOR/TRIGGER WHEEL—KEY OFF			
	• **Is sensor or trigger wheel damaged?**	Yes	▶	REPLACE or SERVICE as required. REMOVE all test equipment. RECONNECT all components. CLEAR Continuous Memory. RERUN Quick Test.
		No	▶	REPLACE ICM. ICM not responding to input signals. REMOVE all test equipment. RECONNECT all components. CLEAR Continuous Memory. RERUN Quick Test.
F5	CHECK FOR SPOUT SHORT LOW—SPOUT FAULT—KEY OFF—PCM DISCONNECTED			
	• Key off. • Disconnect the PCM. • Set DVOM to 200 ohm range. • Measure resistance between J36 (SPOUT) and J60 (B-). • **Is resistance greater than 10 ohms?**	Yes	▶	REPLACE PCM. SPOUT shorted to ground. REMOVE all test equipment. RECONNECT all components. CLEAR Continuous Memory. RERUN Quick Test.
		No	▶	SERVICE harness and connectors. SPOUT shorted to ground between PCM and ICM. REMOVE all test equipment. RCONNECT all components. CLEAR Continuous Memory. RERUN Quick Test.

88152G70

2.3L Mustang (Dual Plug) EI (Low Data Rate—Previously DIS) Code 213/412 or No Codes and Lack of Power—Spout Open or Low	Pinpoint Test	F

TEST STEP		RESULT ▶	ACTION TO TAKE
F6	CHECK SPOUT CIRCUIT CONTINUITY—PCM DISCONNECTED—ICM DISCONNECTED		
	• Key off. • Disconnect PCM and install a second EEC breakout box at PCM vehicle harness connector. • Set DVOM to 200 ohm range. • Measure resistance between J36 (SPOUT) at the second breakout box and J36 (SPOUT) at the first breakout box. • **Is resistance less than 5.0 ohms?**	Yes ▶ No ▶	GO to F7. SERVICE open circuit in harness between PCM and ICM. REMOVE all test equipment. RECONNECT all components. CLEAR Continuous Memory. RERUN Quick Test.
F7	CHECK SPOUT TRANSMISSION FROM PCM TO ICM—SPOUT JUMPER DISCONNECTED		
	• Key off. • Reconnect PCM and ICM. • Remove SPOUT harness jumper plug from SPOUT vehicle harness connector. • Set DVOM to 20 volt AC range. • Start engine and measure voltage between J36 (SPOUT) at the second breakout box and J60 (B-). • **Is voltage greater than 2.0 volts AC?**	Yes ▶ No ▶	REPLACE ICM. ICM is short to ground or open. REMOVE all test equipment. RECONNECT all components. CLEAR Continuous Memory. RERUN Quick Test. REPLACE PCM. SPOUT not being transmitted. REMOVE all test equipment. RECONNECT all components. CLEAR Continuous Memory. RERUN Quick Test.

88152G71

Crankshaft Position Sensor

➧ See Figures 30, 31, 32 and 33

REMOVAL & INSTALLATION

1. Turn the ignition **OFF** and disconnect the negative battery cable.
2. Loosen the tensioner pulleys for the A/C compressor, if equipped.
3. Remove the belts from the crankshaft pulley.
4. Disconnect the sensor electrical connectors from the engine wiring harness.
5. Remove the connector from the sensor assembly by prying out the red clip and removing the wires. Note the positioning of the wires within the connector.
6. Raise and support the vehicle safely. Remove the crankshaft pulley assembly by loosening and removing the 4 bolts.
7. Remove the timing belt shield assemblies.
8. Turn the crankshaft so the keyway is in the 10 o'clock position. This will align the vane windows of the inner and outer cups.
9. Remove the two crankshaft sensor mounting bolts and the plastic wire retainer. Slide the wires out from behind the inner timing belt cover while removing the sensor.

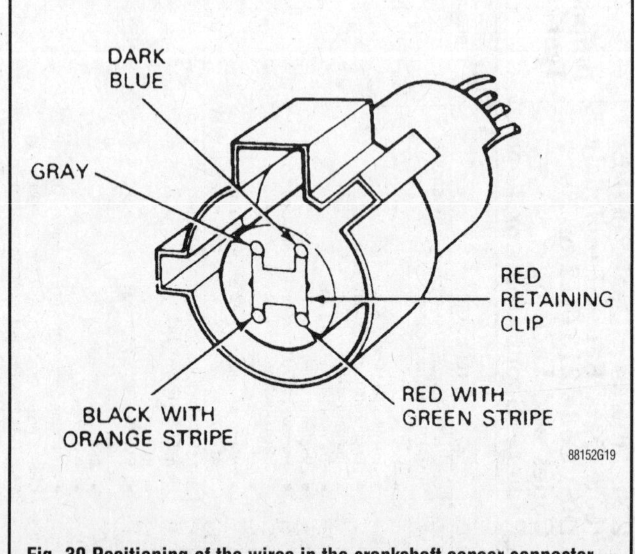

Fig. 30 Positioning of the wires in the crankshaft sensor connector

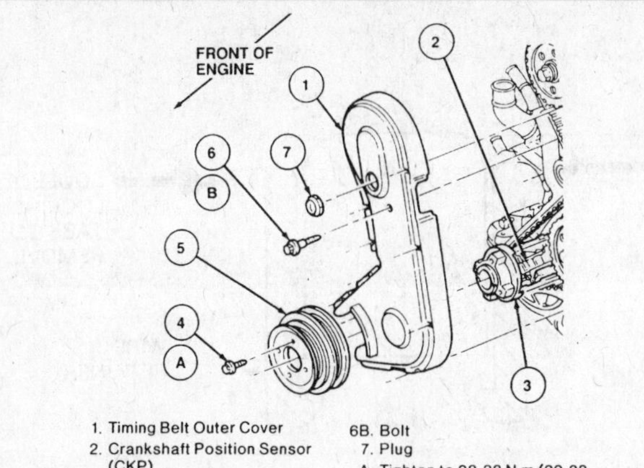

Fig. 31 Removal of the timing belt cover to access the crankshaft sensor

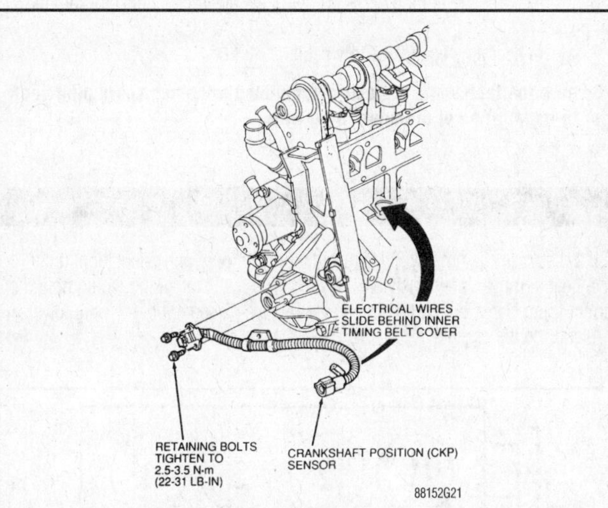

Fig. 32 Position the sensor harness behind the inner timing belt cover

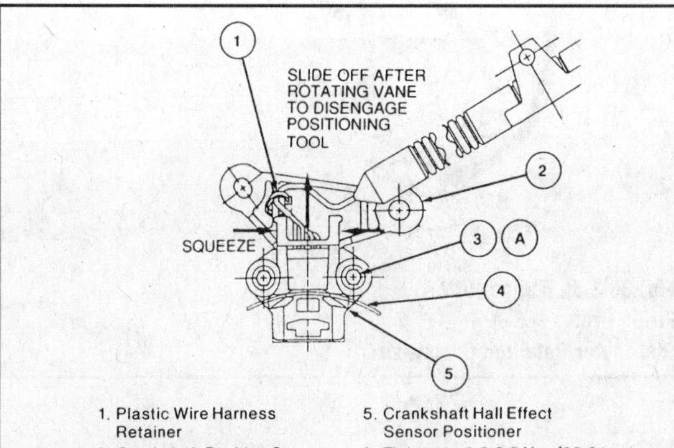

Fig. 33 The positioning tool must be used to align the vanes and sensor

To install:

10. Remove the connector from the new sensor and slide the assembly into place. Be sure to put the wires behind the inner timing belt cover.
11. Position the crankshaft sensor assembly on the bracket. Install the two sensor retaining bolts but do not torque them yet.
12. Replace the wires into the connector in the correct positions. Connect the sensor harness to the engine wiring harness.
13. Place the Crankshaft Sensor Positioning Tool T89P-6316-A or equivalent, into location. Rotate the crankshaft so the outer vane on the pulley hub engages both side of the tool. Torque the bolts to 22–31 inch lbs (2.5–3.5 Nm). Rotate the crankshaft so the vanes disengage from the tool and the tool can be removed.
14. Install the wiring harness retainer and trim off the excess length. Install the timing belt cover and torque the bolt to 6–9 ft. lbs. (8–12 Nm).
15. Install the crankshaft pulley and torque the bolts to 20–28 ft. lbs. (28–38 Nm). Lower the vehicle.
16. Install the A/C and power steering belts. Adjust as necessary. Reconnect the negative battery cable and perform a road test.

DIS Module

➧ See Figure 34

REMOVAL & INSTALLATION

1. Turn the ignition **OFF** and disconnect the negative battery cable.
2. Unplug both electrical connectors at the DIS module.
3. Remove the DIS module mounting bolts, then remove the module.

To install:

4. Apply a uniform coating of heat-sink grease ESF–M99G123–A or equivalent to the mounting surface of the DIS module.
5. Install the module and the mounting bolts. Torque the mounting bolts to 22–31 inch lbs (2.5–3.5 Nm).
6. Plug both electrical connectors into the module. Connect the negative battery cable.

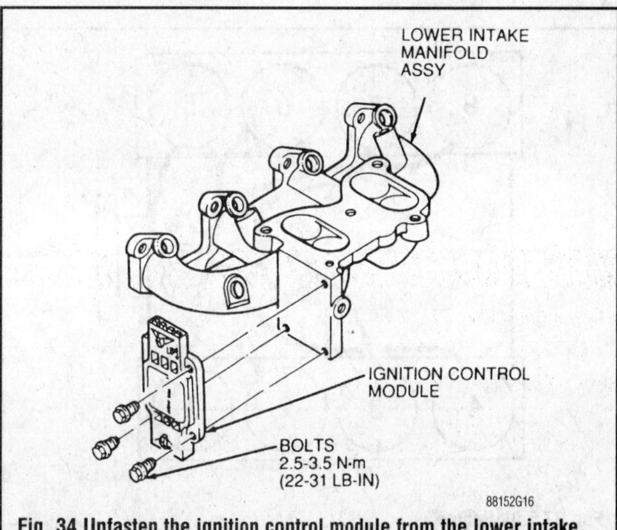

Fig. 34 Unfasten the ignition control module from the lower intake manifold

Ignition Coil Pack

➧ See Figures 35 and 36

REMOVAL & INSTALLATION

1. Turn the ignition **OFF** and disconnect the negative battery cable.
2. Unplug the electrical harness connector from the ignition coil pack.

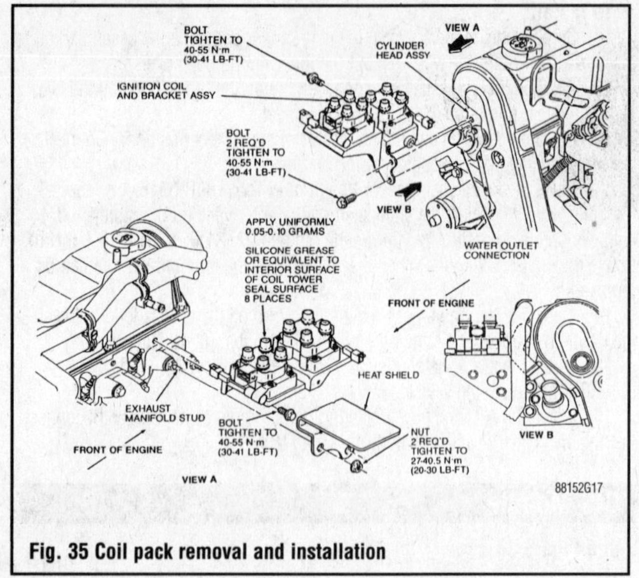

Fig. 35 Coil pack removal and installation

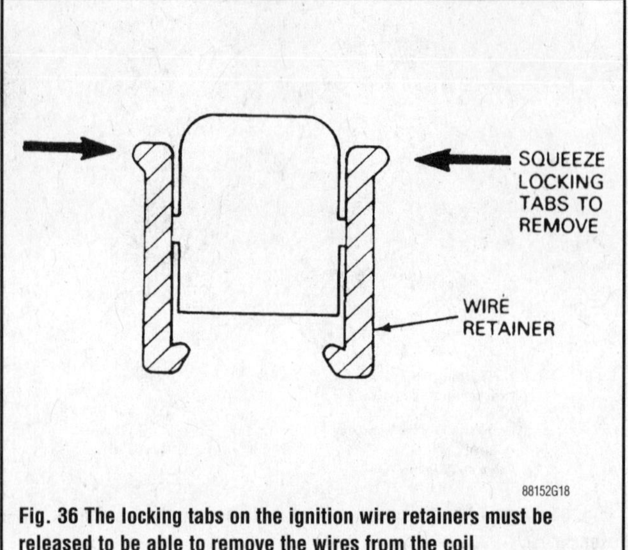

Fig. 36 The locking tabs on the ignition wire retainers must be released to be able to remove the wires from the coil

3. Remove the spark plug wires by squeezing the locking tabs to release the coil boot retainers.
4. Remove the coil pack mounting screws and remove the coil pack.

To install:

5. Install the coil pack and the retaining screws. Tighten the retaining screws to 40–62 inch lbs.
6. Connect the spark plug wires and plug the electrical connector into the coil pack.
7. Reconnect the negative battery cable.

➡Be sure to place some dielectric compound into each spark plug boot prior to installation of the spark plug wire.

FIRING ORDERS

See Figures 37, 38 and 39

➡To avoid confusion, remove and tag the wires one at a time, for replacement.

If a distributor is not keyed for installation with only one orientation, it could have been removed previously and rewired. The resultant wiring would hold the correct firing order, but could change the relative placement of the plug towers in relation to the engine.

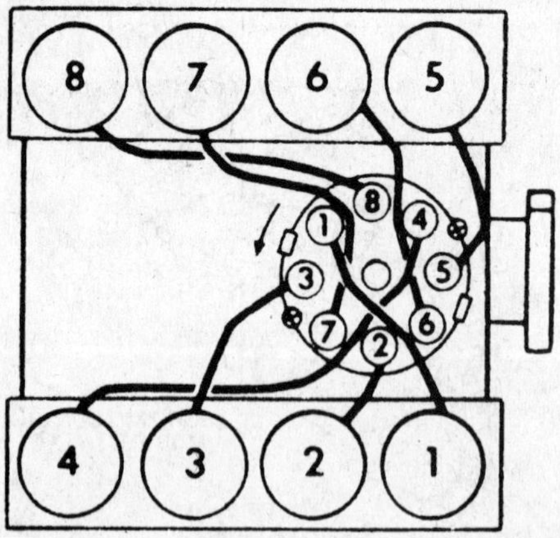

88152G72

Fig. 37 5.0L Engine
Firing Order: 1-3-7-2-6-5-4-8
Distributor Rotation: Counterclockwise

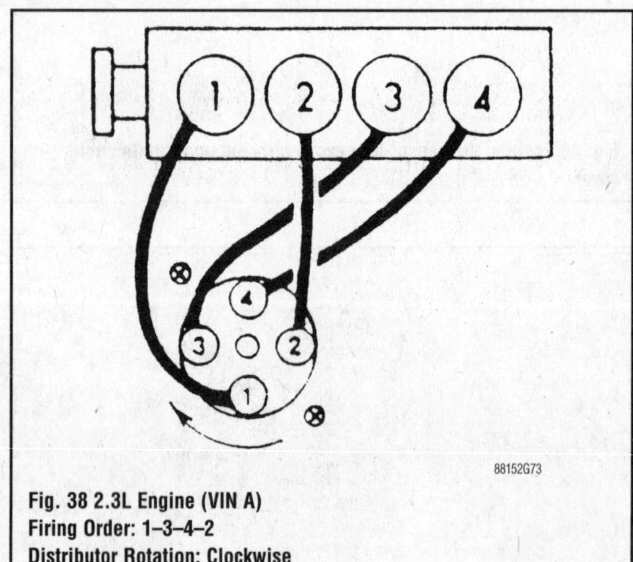

Fig. 38 2.3L Engine (VIN A)
Firing Order: 1-3-4-2
Distributor Rotation: Clockwise

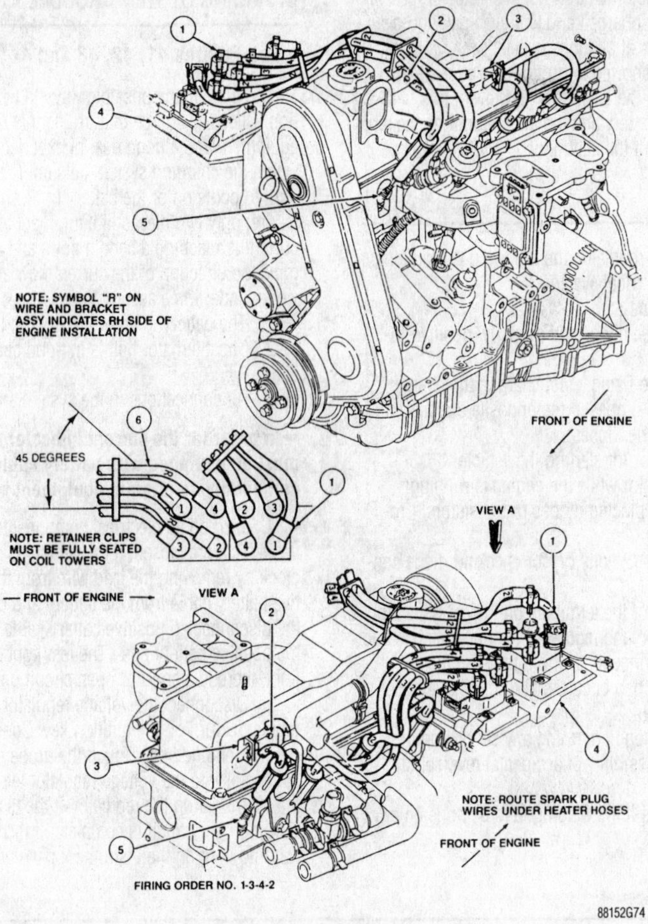

Fig. 39 2.3L Engine (VIN M)
Firing Order: 1–3–4–2
Distributorless Ignition

CHARGING SYSTEM

Description and Operation

OPERATION

▶ **See Figure 40**

The alternator charging system is a negative (–) ground system which consists of an alternator, a regulator, a charge indicator, a storage battery, wiring connecting the components, and fuse link wire.

The alternator is belt-driven from the engine. Energy is supplied from the alternator/regulator system to the rotating field through two brushes to two slip-rings. The slip-rings are mounted on the rotor shaft and are connected to the field coil. This energy supplied to the rotating field from the battery is called excitation current and is used to initially energize the field to begin the generation of electricity. Once the alternator starts to generate electricity, the excitation current comes from its own output rather than the battery.

The alternator produces power in the form of alternating current. The alternating current is rectified by 6 diodes into direct current. The direct current is used to charge the battery and power the rest of the electrical system.

When the ignition key is turned on, current flows from the battery, through the charging system indicator light on the instrument panel, to the voltage regulator, and to the alternator. Since the alternator is not producing any current, the alternator warning light comes on. When the engine is started, the alternator begins to produce current and turns the alternator light off. As the alternator turns and produces current, the current is divided in two ways: part to the battery to charge the battery and power the electrical components of the vehicle, and part is returned to the alternator to enable it to increase its output. In this situation, the alternator is receiving current from the battery and from itself. A voltage regulator is wired into the current supply to the alternator to prevent it from receiving too much current which would cause it to put out too much cur-

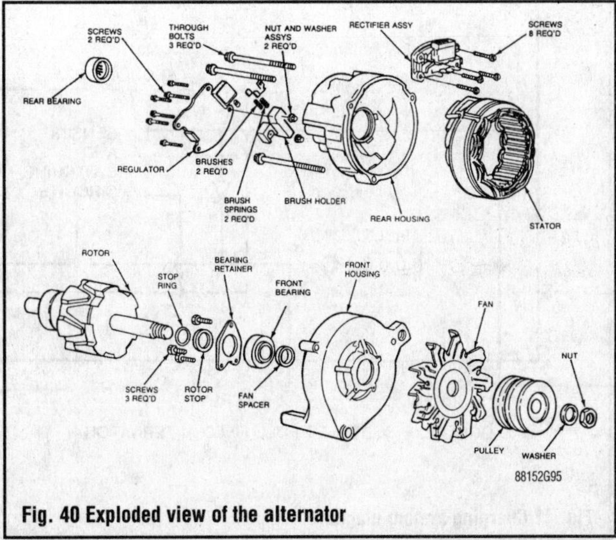

Fig. 40 Exploded view of the alternator

rent. Conversely, if the voltage regulator does not allow the alternator to receive enough current, the battery will not be fully charged and will eventually go dead.

The battery is connected to the alternator at all times, whether the ignition key is turned on or not. If the battery were shorted to ground, the alternator would also be shorted. This would damage the alternator. To prevent this, a fuse link is installed in the wiring between the battery and the alternator. If the battery is shorted, the fuse link is melted, protecting the alternator.

ALTERNATOR PRECAUTIONS

To prevent damage to the alternator and regulator, the following precautions should be taken when working with the electrical system.

1. Never reverse the battery connections.
2. Booster batteries for starting must be connected properly: positive-to-positive and negative-to-ground.
3. Disconnect the battery cables before using a fast charger; the charger has a tendency to force current through the diodes in the opposite direction for which they were designed. This burns out the diodes.
4. Never use a fast charger as a booster for starting the vehicle.
5. Never disconnect the voltage regulator while the engine is running.
6. Avoid long soldering times when replacing diodes or transistors. Prolonged heat is damaging to AC generators.
7. Do not use test lamps of more than 12 volts (V) for checking diode continuity.
8. Do not short across or ground any of the terminals on the AC generator.
9. The polarity of the battery, generator, and regulator must be matched and considered before making any electrical connections within the system.
10. Never operate the alternator on an open circuit. make sure that all connections within the circuit are clean and tight.
11. Disconnect the battery terminals when performing any service on the electrical system. This will eliminate the possibility of accidental reversal of polarity.
12. Disconnect the battery ground cable if arc welding is to be done on any part of the vehicle.

CHARGING SYSTEM TROUBLESHOOTING

➧ See Figures 41, 42, 43 and 44

There are many possible ways in which the charging system can malfunction. Often the source of a problem is difficult to diagnose, requiring special equipment and a good deal of experience. This is usually not the case, however, where the charging system fails completely and causes the dash board warning light to come on or the battery to discharge. To troubleshoot a complete system failure, only two pieces of equipment are needed: a test light, to determine that current is reaching a certain point and a current indicator (ammeter), to determine the direction of the current flow and its measurement in amps.This test works under three assumptions:

1. The battery is known to be good and fully charged.
2. The alternator belt is in good condition and adjusted to the proper tension.
3. All connections in the system are clean and tight.

➡In order for the current indicator to give a valid reading, the vehicle must be equipped with battery cables which are of the same gauge size and quality as original equipment battery cables.

4. Turn off all electrical components on the vehicle. Make sure the doors of the vehicle are closed. If the vehicle is equipped with a clock, disconnect the clock by removing the lead wire from the rear of the clock. Disconnect the positive battery cable from the battery and connect the ground wire on a test light to the disconnected positive battery cable. Touch the probe end of the test light to the positive battery post. The test light should not light. If the test light does light, there is a short or open circuit on the vehicle.
5. Disconnect the voltage regulator wiring harness connector at the voltage regulator. Turn on the ignition key. Connect the wire on a test light to a good ground (engine bolt). Touch the probe end of a test light to the ignition wire connector into the voltage regulator wiring connector. This wire corresponds to the **I** terminal on the regulator. If the test light goes on, the charging system warning light circuit is complete. If the test light does not come on and the warning light on the instrument panel is on, either the resistor wire, which is

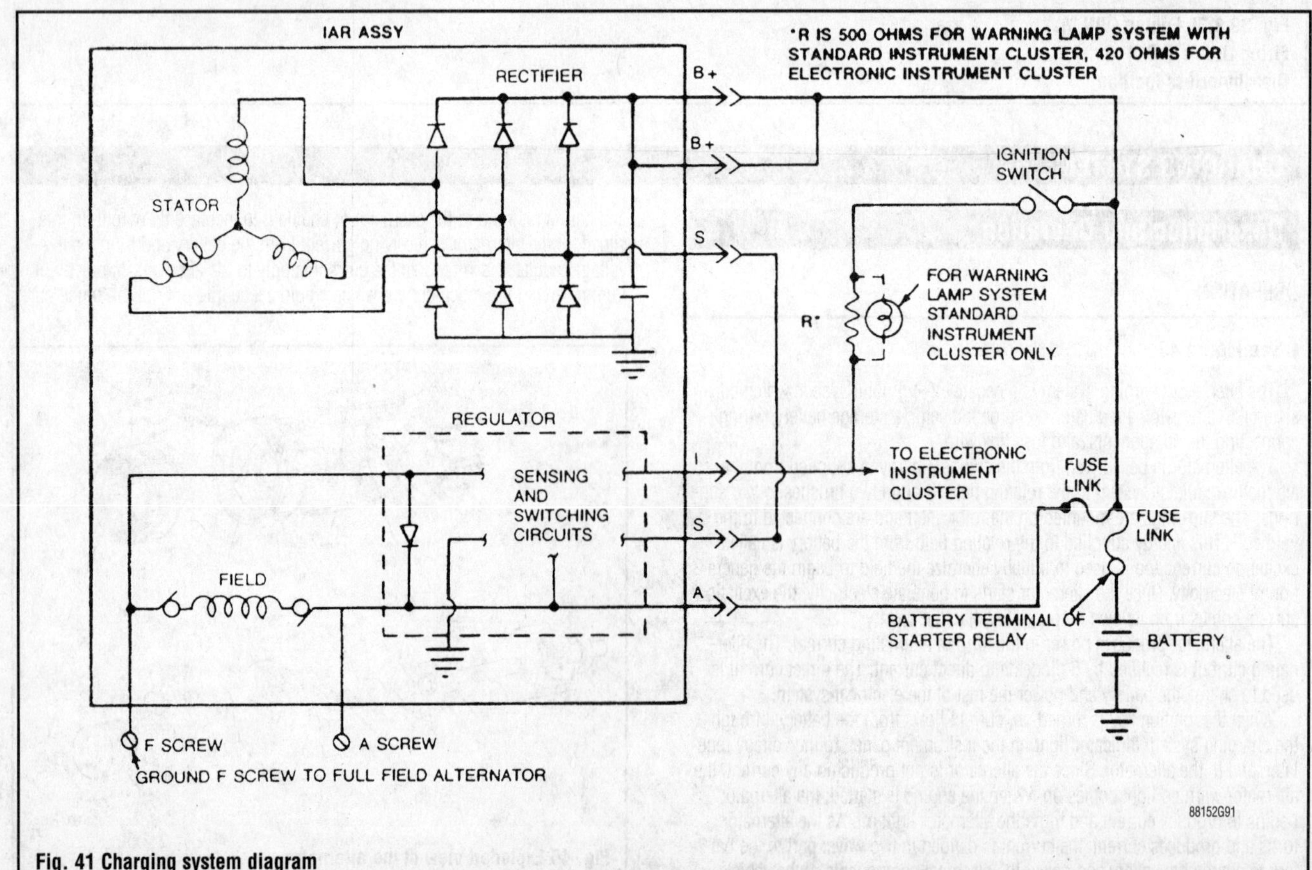

Fig. 41 Charging system diagram

CHARGING SYSTEM TEST — IAR ALTERNATOR

TEST STEP	RESULT	ACTION TO TAKE
B1 PRELIMINARY CHECKS		
Preliminary Checks — • Fuse Link • Battery Terminals and Cable Clamps • Wiring and Ground Connections to Alternator Regulator and Engine • Alternator Belt Tension	OK ▶	GO to **B2**.
	Ø(OK) ▶	SERVICE and/or REPLACE as necessary. GO to **B2**.
B2 BASE VOLTAGE AND NO LOAD TEST		
• Connect voltmeter to battery posts. Read battery voltage — this is base reading. • Start engine, run at 1500 rpm with no electrical load. Voltage should increase but not more than 2.0 V.	Increases, but not more than 2.0 V ▶	GO to **B3**.
	No increase ▶	GO to **B5**.
	Increases more than 2.0 V ▶	GO to **B12**.
B3 LOAD TEST		
• Increase engine speed to 2000 rpm. • Turn heater A/C, blower and headlamps on high. • Voltage should read a minimum of 1/2 V over base voltage.	Increases 1/2 V or more ▶	GO to **B4**.
	Increases less than 1/2 V ▶	GO to **B5**.
B4 BATTERY DRAIN TEST — KEY OFF		
Problem can still be battery drain. Turn Off ignition, install test lamp in series with positive battery cable and check to isolate problem circuit.	Battery drain ▶	CHECK vehicle circuits for drain.
	No battery drain ▶	REFER to BATTERY
B5 UNDER VOLTAGE TEST		
• Disconnect regulator. • Check resistance between regulator A and F terminals on regulator. • Resistance should be more than 2.4 ohms.	2.4 ohms or less ▶	CHECK alternator for shorted field circuit and service if required. REPLACE regulator — GO to **B2**.
	More than 2.4 ohms ▶	GO to **B6**.
B6 A TERMINAL VOLTAGE CHECK		
• Reconnect regulator. • Measure A terminal voltage.	No voltage ▶	SERVICE A circuit wiring.
	Battery voltage ▶	GO to **B7**.

88152G92

Fig. 42 Charging system diagnostics

CHARGING SYSTEM TEST — IAR ALTERNATOR — Continued

TEST STEP	RESULT	ACTION TO TAKE
B7 F TERMINAL VOLTAGE CHECK — IGNITION OFF		
• Measure regulator F terminal voltage with ignition off.	No voltage ▶	SERVICE IAR for open or grounded field circuit — GO to **B2**.
	Battery voltage ▶	GO to **B8**.
B8 F TERMINAL VOLTAGE CHECK — IGNITION ON		
• Turn ignition to RUN position (engine not running). • Measure regulator F terminal voltage.	More than 1.5V ▶	GO to **B9**.
	1.5V or less ▶	GO to **B10**.
B9 I CIRCUIT TESTS		
• Perform I Circuit tests.	OK ▶	REPLACE regulator — GO to **B2**.
	Ø(OK) ▶	SERVICE I Circuit wiring. GO to **B2**.
B10 JUMPERED LOAD TEST		
• Disconnect alternator plug. • Connect jumper wires between B + blades and wiring plug. • Repeat load test measuring voltage to jumper wires from battery negative clamp. • Voltage should rise 1/2V or more.	Voltage rise — 1/2V or more ▶	SERVICE alternator to starter relay wiring — GO to **B2**.
	Voltage rise — less than 1/2V ▶	GO to **B11**.
B11 LOAD TEST REPEAT — F TERMINAL		
• Keep B + jumper wires in place. • Connect another jumper wire from alternator rear housing to regulator F terminal. • Repeat load test measuring voltage at B + jumper wires. • Voltage should rise 1/2V or more.	Voltage rise 1/2V or more ▶	REPLACE regulator. GO to **B2**.
	Voltage rise less than 1/2V ▶	SERVICE alternator. GO to **B2**.
B12 OVER VOLTAGE TEST		
• Turn ignition to RUN position (engine not running). • Measure voltage at regulator A terminal and starter solenoid. • Voltage difference should be 1/2V or less.	Voltage difference 1/2V or less ▶	GO to **B13**.
	Voltage difference more than 1/2V ▶	SERVICE A Circuit wiring. GO to **B2**.
B13 REGULATOR GROUND CHECK		
Check for loose regulator ground screws.	OK ▶	GO to **B14**.
	Ø(OK) ▶	SERVICE ground screws. GO to **B2**.

88152G93

Fig. 43 Charging system diagnostics—continued

CHARGING SYSTEM TEST — IAR ALTERATOR — Continued

	TEST STEP	RESULT	▶	ACTION TO TAKE
B14	ENGINE GROUND CHECK			
	Check for bad engine ground.	(OK)	▶	GO to **B15**.
		(Ø OK)	▶	SERVICE engine ground. GO to **B2**.
B15	ALTERNATOR GROUND CHECK			
	Check alternator ground.	(OK)	▶	GO to **B16**.
		(Ø OK)	▶	SERVICE alternator ground. GO to **B2**.
B16	REPEAT NO LOAD TEST			
	• Start engine, run at 1500 rpm with no electrical load. Voltage should increase but not more than 2.0 V	Increases 2.0 V or less	▶	GO to **B3**.
		Increases more than 2.0 V	▶	GO to **B17**.
B17	A AND F VOLTAGE CHECKS			
	• Turn ignition off. • Measure voltage at regulator A and F terminals. • Terminal voltages should be the same. — Battery voltage	Battery voltage	▶	REPLACE regulator. GO to **B2**.
		Different than battery voltage	▶	SERVICE integral assembly for grounded field circuit or bad regulator. GO to **B2**.

88152G94

Fig. 44 Charging system diagnostics—continued

parallel with the warning light, or the wiring to the voltage regulator, is defective. If the test light does not come on and the warning light is not on, either the bulb is defective or the power supply wire from the battery through the ignition switch to the bulb has an open circuit. Connect the wiring harness to the regulator.

6. Examine the fuse link wire in the wiring harness from the starter relay to the alternator. If the insulation on the wire is cracked or split, the fuse link may be melted. Connect a test light to the fuse link by attaching the ground wire on the test light to an engine bolt and touching the probe end of the light to the bottom of the fuse link wire where it splices into the alternator output wire. If the bulb in the test light does not light, the fuse link is melted.

7. Start the engine and place a current indicator on the positive battery cable. Turn off all electrical accessories and make sure the doors are closed. If the charging system is working properly, the gauge will show a draw of less than 5 amps. If the system is not working properly, the gauge will show a draw of more than 5 amps. A charge moves the needle toward the battery, a draw moves the needle away from the battery. Turn the engine off.

8. Disconnect the wiring harness from the voltage regulator. Connect a male spade terminal (solderless connector) to each end of a jumper wire. Insert one end of the wire into the wiring harness connector which corresponds to the **A** terminal on the regulator. Insert the other end of the wire into the wiring harness connector which corresponds to the **F** terminal on the regulator. Position the connector with the jumper wire installed so that it cannot contact any metal surface under the hood. Position a current indicator gauge on the positive battery cable. Have an assistant start the engine. Observe the reading on the current indicator. Have your assistant slowly raise the speed of the engine to about 2,000 rpm or until the current indicator needle stops moving, whichever comes first. Do not run the engine for more than a short period of time in this condition. If the wiring harness connector or jumper wire becomes excessively hot during this test, turn off the engine and check for a grounded wire in the regulator wiring harness. If the current indicator shows a charge of about three amps less than the output of the alternator, the alternator is working properly. If the previous tests showed a draw, the voltage regulator is defective. If the gauge does not show the proper charging rate, the alternator is defective.

BELT TENSION ADJUSTMENT

All vehicles are equipped with an automatic belt tensioner. No adjustment is necessary or possible. The belt tensioner is equipped with a belt wear indicator; when 1 percent belt stretch is indicated, the drive belt must be replaced. If the wear indicator is difficult to see on the 5.0L HO engine, locate the tab on the tensioner face plate. The tab should be between the stops.

REMOVAL & INSTALLATION

See Figures 45 thru 52

1. Disconnect the negative battery cable. Rotate the belt tensioner clockwise and remove the belt from the pulley.
2. Tag and disconnect the wiring connectors from the rear of the alternator. To disconnect push-on type terminals, depress the lock tab and pull straight off.
3. Loosen the alternator pivot bolt and remove the adjusting bolt.
4. Remove the alternator pivot bolt and the alternator.
5. Installation is the reverse of the removal procedure.

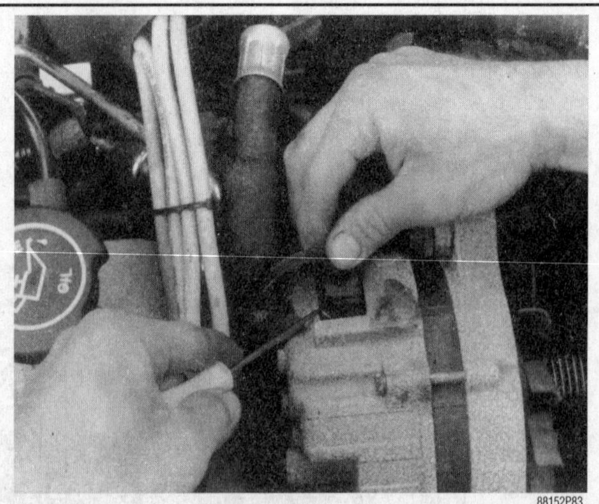

88152P83

Fig. 45 Use a pick to release the catches on the side of the connectors if you can't get your fingers down far enough

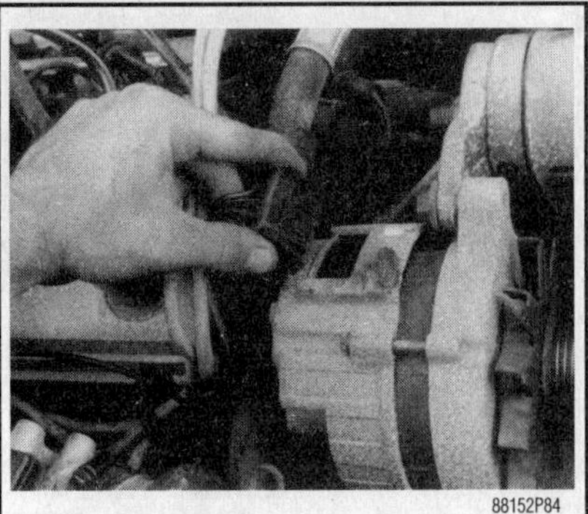
88152P84

Fig. 46 Squeeze the catches to gether and pull up to release the connector

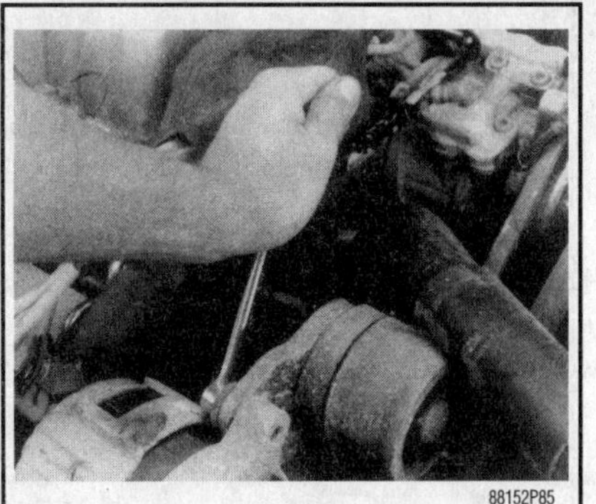
88152P85

Fig. 47 The adjustment arm bolt is the upper bolt

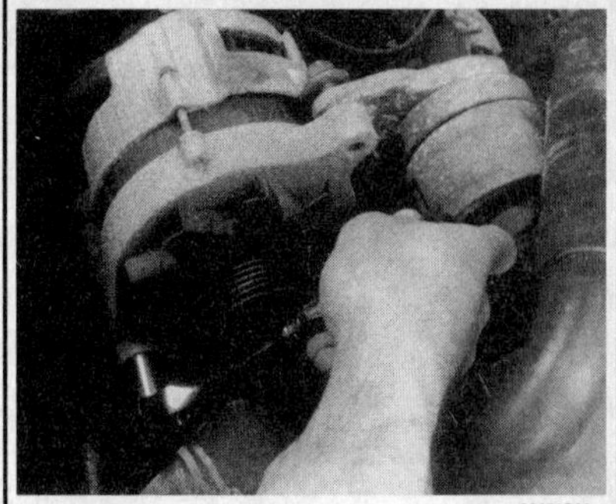
88152P86

Fig. 48 The pivot arm bolt is the lower of the two bolts and is longer

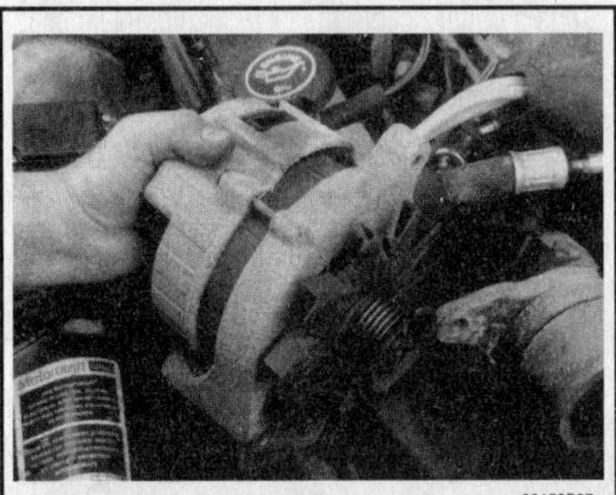
88152P87

Fig. 49 Rotate the alternator up to access the regulator wiring if it isn't already disconnected

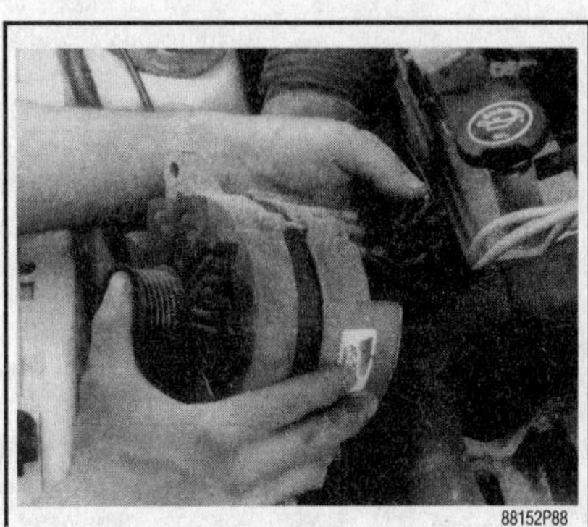
88152P88

Fig. 50 The regulator has a seperate connector

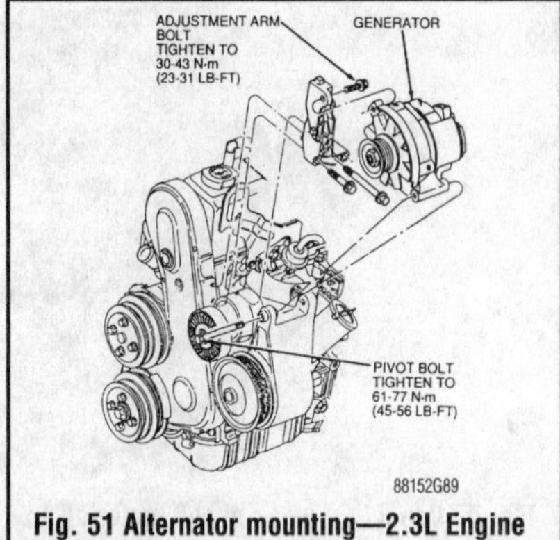

88152G89

Fig. 51 Alternator mounting—2.3L Engine

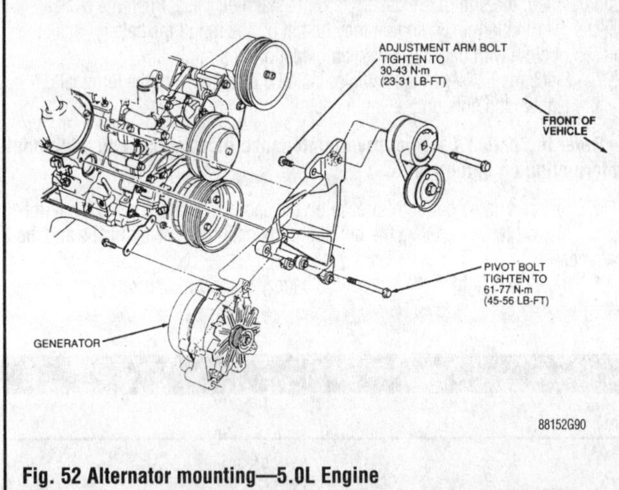

88152G90

Fig. 52 Alternator mounting—5.0L Engine

Voltage Regulator

REMOVAL & INSTALLATION

See Figures 53, 54, 55, 56 and 57

1. Disconnect the negative battery cable.
2. Remove 4 TORX® head screws holding the voltage regulator to the alternator rear housing. Remove the regulator, with the brush holder attached.
3. Hold the regulator in one hand and pry off the cap covering the **A** terminal screw head with a small prybar.
4. Remove 2 TORX® head screws retaining the regulator to the brush holder. Separate the regulator from the brush holder.

To install:

5. Install the brush holder on the regulator with 2 retaining screws. Tighten the screws to 25–35 inch lbs .(2.8–4.0 Nm).
6. Install the cap on the head of the **A** terminal screw.

88152P96

Fig. 53 The regulator and brush holder is mounted on the backside of the alternator

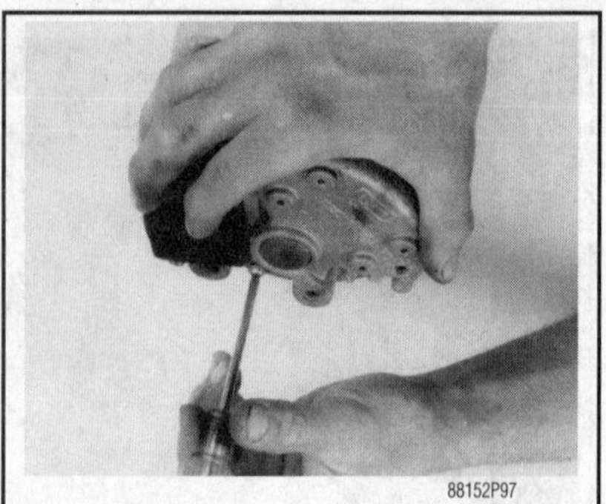

Fig. 54 Hold the regulator while removing the screws to prevent teh regulator from dropping out and damaging the brushes

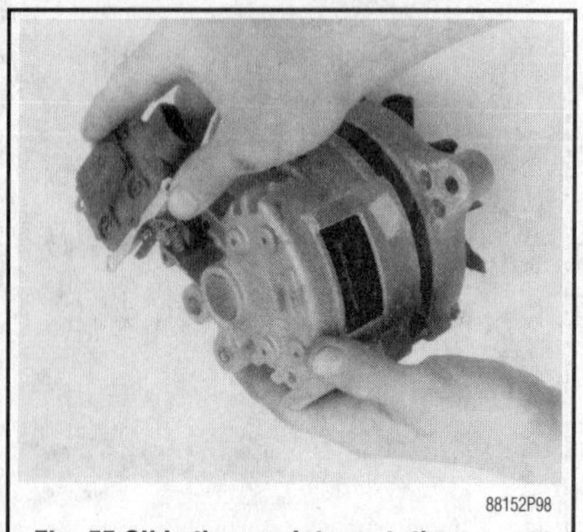

Fig. 55 Slide the regulator out. the brushes will move out of the holder

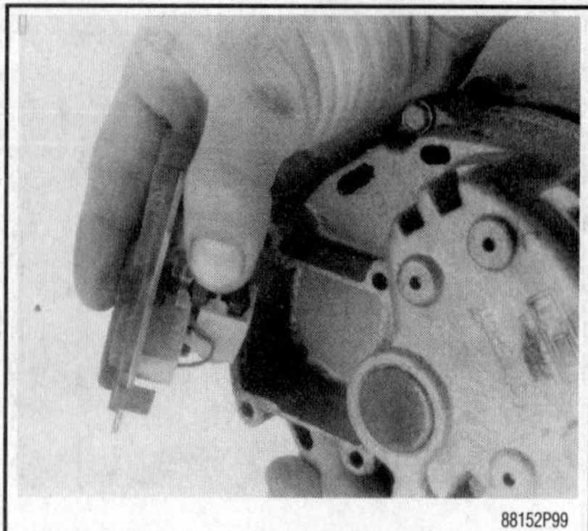

Fig. 56 When installing the regulator, press the brushes back into the housing

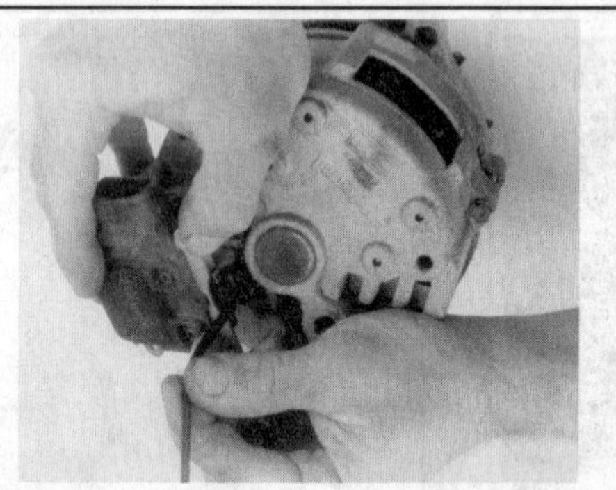

Fig. 57 Use a thin piece of soft material, like this plastice wire tie, to hold the brushes in position while replacing the regulator or use a paper clip inserted in the hole

7. Depress the brushes into the holder and hold the brushes in position by inserting a standard size paper clip, orequivalent tool, through both the location hole in the regulator and through the holes in the brushes.
8. Install the regulator/brush holder assembly and remove the paper clip. Install the attaching screws and tighten to 20–30 inch lbs. (2.3–3.4 Nm).

Battery

REMOVAL & INSTALLATION

1. Loosen the nuts which secure the cable ends to the battery terminals. Lift the negative battery cables from the terminals first with a twisting motion, then the positive cables. If there is a battery cable puller available, make use of it.
2. Remove the holddown nuts from the battery holddown bracket. Remove the bracket and the battery. Lift the battery straight up and out of the vehicle, being sure to keep it level to avoid spilling acid.
3. Before installing the battery in the vehicle, make sure that the battery terminals are clean and free from corrosion. Use a battery terminal cleaner on the terminals and on the inside of the battery cable ends. If a cleaner is not available, use coarse grade sandpaper to remove the corrosion. A mixture of baking soda and water poured over the terminals and cable ends will help remove and neutralize any acid buildup.

**** CAUTION**

Take great care to avoid getting any of the baking soda solution inside the battery. If any solution gets inside the battery a violent reaction will take place and/or the battery will be damaged.

4. Before installing the cables onto the terminals, cut a piece of felt cloth, or something similar into a circle about 3 in. (76mm) across. Cut a hole in the middle about the size of the battery terminals at their base. Push the cloth pieces over the terminals so that they lie flat on the top of the battery. Soak the pieces of cloth with oil. This will keep oxidation to a minimum.
5. Place the battery in the vehicle. Install the cables onto the terminals.
6. Tighten the nuts on the cable ends.

➡Refer to Section 1 for battery maintenance illustrations and additional information on battery care.

7. Smear a light coating of grease on the cable ends and tops of the terminals. This will further prevent the buildup of oxidation on the terminals and the cable ends.
8. Install and tighten the nuts of the battery holddown bracket.

STARTING SYSTEM

Testing

➧ See Figures 58, 59 and 60

Use the charts to help located and diagnosis starting system problems. Remember that the starter uses large amounts of current during operation, so use all appropriate precautions during testing.

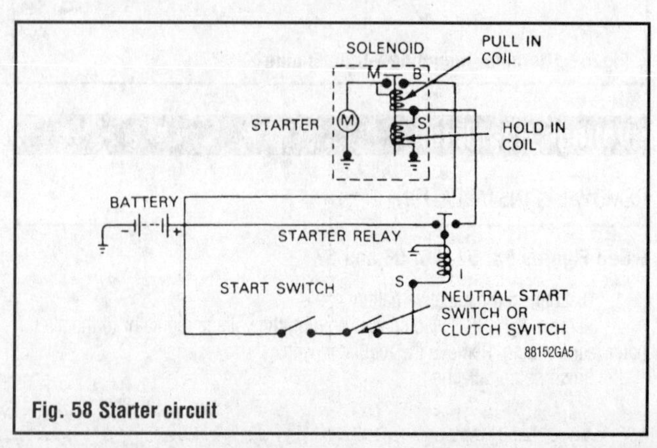

Fig. 58 Starter circuit

Starter Motor

REMOVAL & INSTALLATION

➧ See Figures 61, 62 and 63

1. Disconnect the negative battery cable.
2. Raise the front of the vehicle and install jackstands beneath the

System Inspection

CAUTION: When disconnecting the plastic hardshell connector at the solenoid "S" terminal, grasp the plastic connector and pull lead off. DO NOT pull separately on lead wire.

WARNING: WHEN SERVICING STARTER OR PERFORMING OTHER UNDERHOOD WORK IN THE VICINITY OF THE STARTER, BE AWARE THAT THE HEAVY GAUGE BATTERY INPUT LEAD AT THE STARTER SOLENOID IS "ELECTRICALLY HOT" AT ALL TIMES.

A protective cap or boot is provided over this terminal on all carlines and must be replaced after servicing. Be sure to disconnect battery negative cable before servicing starter.

1. Inspect starting system for loose connections.
2. If system does not operate properly, note condition and continue diagnosis using the symptom chart.

WARNING: WHEN WORKING IN AREA OF THE STARTER, BE CAREFUL TO AVOID TOUCHING HOT EXHAUST COMPONENTS.

CONDITION	POSSIBLE SOURCE	ACTION
Starter solenoid does not pull-in and starter does not crank (Audible click may or may not be heard).	• Open fuse. • Low battery. • Inoperative fender apron relay. • Open circuit or high resistance in external feed circuit to starter solenoid. • Inoperative starter.	• Check fuse continuity. • Refer to appropriate battery section in this manual. • Go to Evaluation Procedure 2. • Go to Test A. • Replace starter. See removal and installation procedure.
Unusual starter noise during starter overrun.	• Starter not mounted flush (cocked). • Noise from other components. • Ring gear tooth damage or excessive ring gear runout. • Defective starter.	• Realign starter on transmission bell housing. • Investigate other powertrain accessory noise contributors. • Refer to appropriate engine section in this manual. • Replace starter. See removal and installation procedure.
Starter cranks but engine does not start.	• Problem in fuel system. • Problem in ignition system. • Engine related concern.	• Refer to appropriate fuel system section in this manual. • Refer to appropriate ignition system section in this manual. • Refer to appropriate engine section in this manual.
Starter cranks slowly.	• Low battery. • High resistance or loose connections in starter solenoid battery feed or ground circuit. • Ring gear runout excessive. • Inoperative starter.	• Refer to appropriate battery section in this manual. • Check that all connections are secure. • Refer to appropriate engine section in this manual. • Replace Starter. See removal and installation procedure.
Starter remains engaged and runs with engine.	• Shorted ignition switch. • Battery cable touching solenoid 'S' terminal (inoperative or mispositioned cable). • Inoperative starter.	• Refer to appropriate ignition system section in this manual. • Replace or relocate cable and replace starter. • Replace starter. See removal and installation procedure.

88152GA6

Fig. 59 System inspection chart

Evaluation Procedure 1

NOTE: Hoist vehicle (if necessary) to access starter solenoid terminals.

CAUTION: Remove plastic safety cap on starter solenoid and disconnect hardshell connector at solenoid 'S' terminal

CHECK STARTER MOTOR — TEST A

	TEST STEP	RESULT ▶	ACTION TO TAKE
A1	CHECK FOR VOLTAGE TO STARTER • Key OFF. Transmission in Park or Neutral. • Check for voltage between starter B+ terminal and starter drive housing. • Is voltage OK? (12-12.45V)	Yes ▶ No ▶	GO to **A2**. CHECK wire connections between battery and starter solenoid and the ground circuit for open or short.
A2	CHECK STARTER MOTOR • Key OFF. Transmission in Park or Neutral. • Connect one end of a jumper wire to the starter B+ terminal and momentarily touch the other end to solenoid 'S' terminal. • Does starter crank?	Yes ▶ No ▶	CHECK connections from output of fender apron relay to 'S' terminal for open or short. Defective starter. REPLACE starter.

Evaluation Procedure 2

CHECK FENDER APRON RELAY — TEST B

	TEST STEP	RESULT ▶	ACTION TO TAKE
B1	CHECK FENDER APRON RELAY • Key in START. Transmission in Park or Neutral. • Is case ground OK?	Yes ▶ No ▶	GO to **B2**. SERVICE ground. GO to **B2**.
B2	CHECK VOLTAGE AT FENDER APRON RELAY START TERMINAL • Key in START. Transmission in Park or Neutral. • Check for voltage between fender apron relay start terminal and case ground. • Is voltage OK? (12-12.45 V)	Yes ▶ No ▶	GO to **B3**. Open circuit or high resistance exists in external circuit wiring or components. Check the following: • All circuit connections including plastic hardshell connector at solenoid 'S' terminal to make sure it is not broken or distorted. • Ignition switch. • Neutral switch or manual lever position sensor. • Anti-theft contact.
B3	CHECK OUTPUT TERMINAL VOLTAGE • Key in START. Transmission in Park or Neutral. • Check for voltage at output terminal of fender relay. • Is voltage OK?	Yes ▶ No ▶	REFER to Starter System Diagnosis in this section. Defective fender apron relay. REMOVE and REPLACE relay.

88152GA7

Fig. 60 Evaluations procedure charts

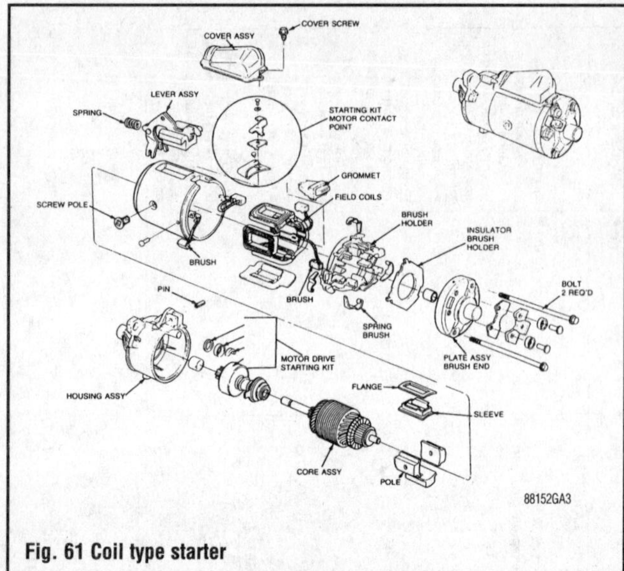

Fig. 61 Coil type starter

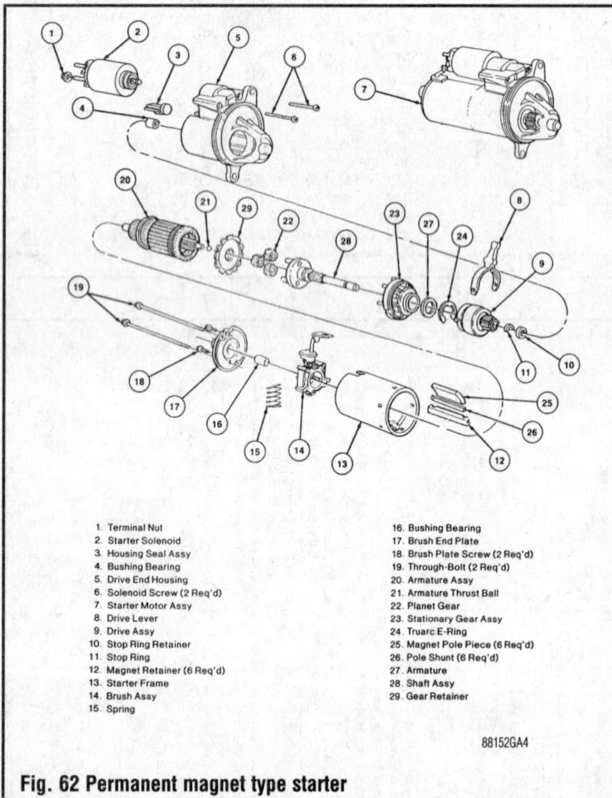

Fig. 62 Permanent magnet type starter

frame. Firmly apply the parking brake and place blocks in back of the rear wheels.

3. Tag and disconnect the wiring at the starter.
4. Remove the starter mounting bolts and remove the starter.
5. Reverse the above procedure to install. Observe the following torques:

- Mounting bolts: 12–15 ft. lbs. (16–21 Nm) on starters with 3 mounting bolts.

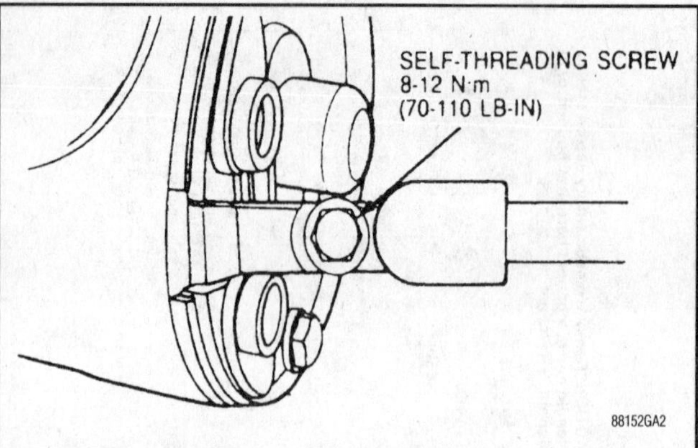

Fig. 63 Some starters use a self-threading bolt to hold the starter cable

- 15–20 ft. lbs. (21–27 Nm) on starters with two mounting bolts.
- Make sure that the nut or bolt securing the heavy cable to the starter is snugged down tightly.

Starter Relay

REMOVAL & INSTALLATION

See Figure 64

1. Disconnect the negative battery cable from the battery.
2. Disconnect the positive battery cable from the battery terminal.
3. Remove the nut securing the positive battery cable to the relay.
4. Remove the positive cable and any other wiring under that cable.
5. Tag and remove the push-on wires from the front of the relay.
6. Remove the nut and disconnect the cable from the starter side of the relay.
7. Remove the relay attaching bolts and remove the relay.
8. Installation is the reverse of removal.

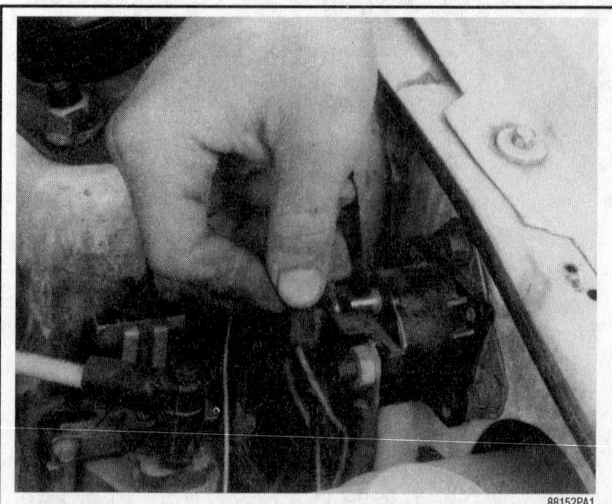

Fig. 64 Make sure the negative battery cable is disconnected before removing any of the relay wiring

SENDING UNITS AND SENSORS

The following sending units or sensors are used solely to provide information to the instrument panel gauges or warning lights. Sensors which provide information to the engine and emission control system can be found in Section 4.

Oil Pressure

See Figures 65, 66, 67, 68 and 69

REMOVAL & INSTALLATION

1. Disconnect the wiring at the unit.
2. Unscrew the unit.
3. Coat the threads with electrically conductive sealer and screw the unit into place. The torque should be 10–18 ft. lbs (13–24 Nm).

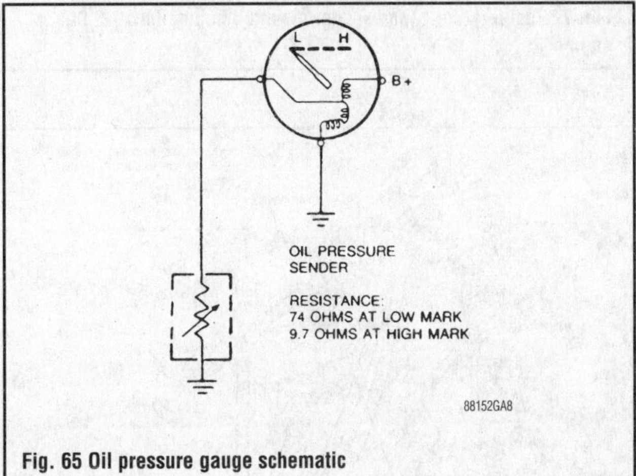

Fig. 65 Oil pressure gauge schematic

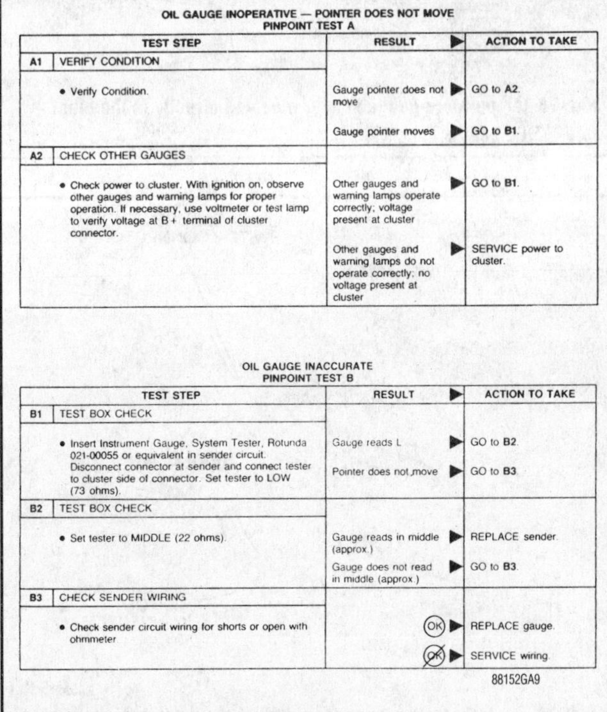

OIL GAUGE INOPERATIVE — POINTER DOES NOT MOVE
PINPOINT TEST A

	TEST STEP	RESULT	ACTION TO TAKE
A1	VERIFY CONDITION		
	• Verify Condition.	Gauge pointer does not move	GO to A2.
		Gauge pointer moves	GO to B1.
A2	CHECK OTHER GAUGES		
	• Check power to cluster. With ignition on, observe other gauges and warning lamps for proper operation. If necessary, use voltmeter or test lamp to verify voltage at B+ terminal of cluster connector.	Other gauges and warning lamps operate correctly; voltage present at cluster	GO to B1.
		Other gauges and warning lamps do not operate correctly; no voltage present at cluster	SERVICE power to cluster.

OIL GAUGE INACCURATE
PINPOINT TEST B

	TEST STEP	RESULT	ACTION TO TAKE
B1	TEST BOX CHECK		
	• Insert Instrument Gauge, System Tester, Rotunda 021-00055 or equivalent in sender circuit. Disconnect connector at sender and connect tester to cluster side of connector. Set tester to LOW (73 ohms).	Gauge reads L	GO to B2.
		Pointer does not move	GO to B3.
B2	TEST BOX CHECK		
	• Set tester to MIDDLE (22 ohms).	Gauge reads in middle (approx.)	REPLACE sender.
		Gauge does not read in middle (approx.)	GO to B3.
B3	CHECK SENDER WIRING		
	• Check sender circuit wiring for shorts or open with ohmmeter.	OK	REPLACE gauge.
		NOT OK	SERVICE wiring.

88152GA9

Fig. 66 Oil pressure gauge diagnostic chart

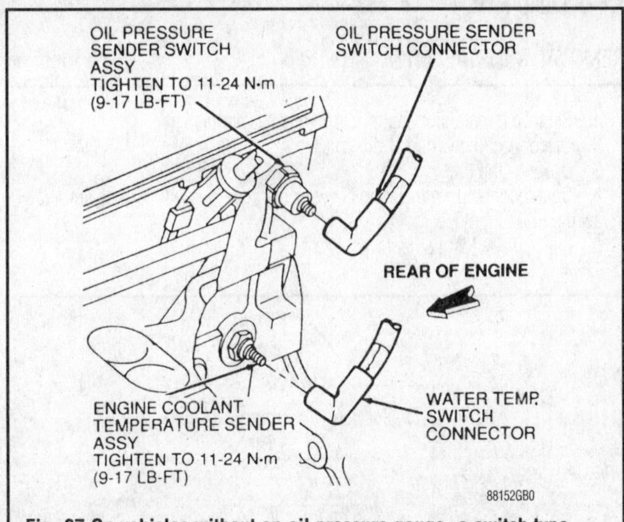

Fig. 67 On vehicles without an oil pressure gauge, a switch type sender is used to illuminate the oil light—2.3L engine

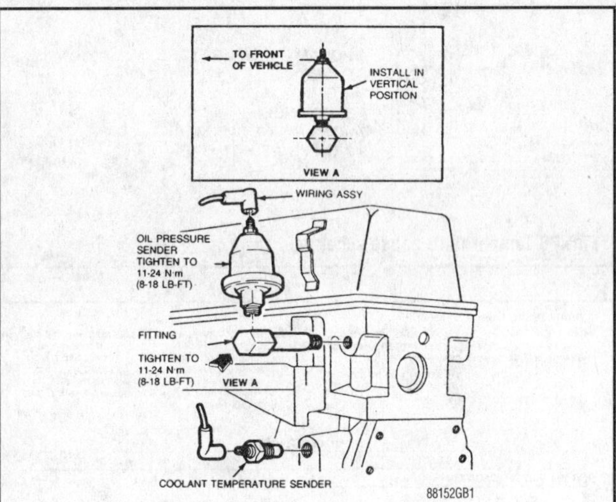

Fig. 68 The oil pressure gauge sender is screwed into an adapter on the side of the engine—2.3L engine

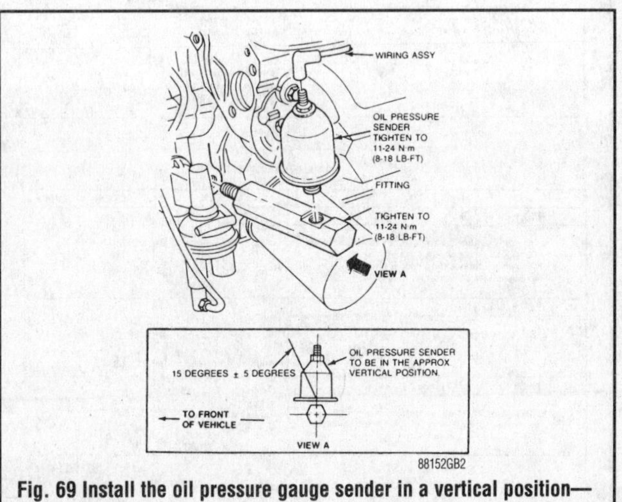

Fig. 69 Install the oil pressure gauge sender in a vertical position—5.0L engine

Coolant Temperature

See Figures 70, 71, 72, 73 and 74

REMOVAL & INSTALLATION

1. Remove the radiator cap to relieve any system pressure.
2. Disconnect the wiring at the unit.
3. Unscrew the unit.
4. Coat the threads with Teflon® tape or electrically conductive sealer and screw the unit into place.
5. Replace any lost coolant.

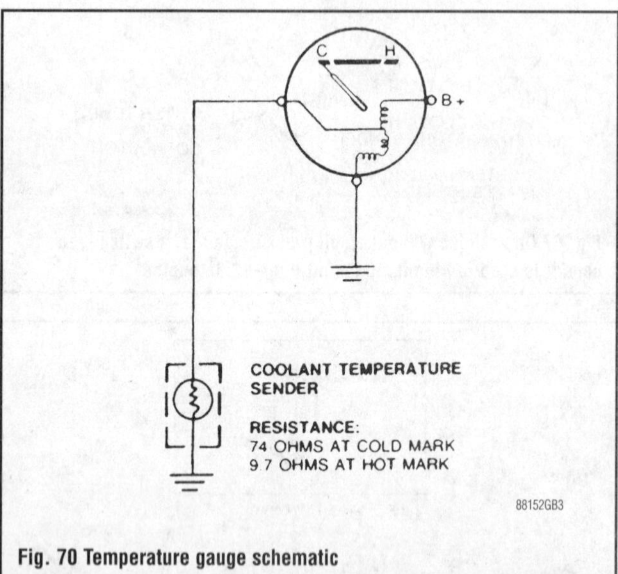

Fig. 70 Temperature gauge schematic

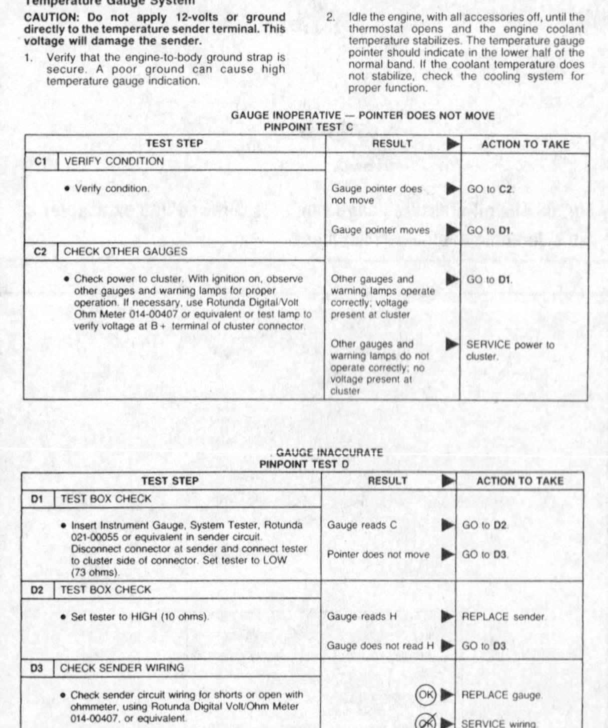

Temperature Gauge System

CAUTION: Do not apply 12-volts or ground directly to the temperature sender terminal. This voltage will damage the sender.

1. Verify that the engine-to-body ground strap is secure. A poor ground can cause high temperature gauge indication.
2. Idle the engine, with all accessories off, until the thermostat opens and the engine coolant temperature stabilizes. The temperature gauge pointer should indicate in the lower half of the normal band. If the coolant temperature does not stabilize, check the cooling system for proper function.

GAUGE INOPERATIVE — POINTER DOES NOT MOVE
PINPOINT TEST C

	TEST STEP	RESULT ▶	ACTION TO TAKE
C1	VERIFY CONDITION		
	• Verify condition.	Gauge pointer does not move ▶	GO to **C2**.
		Gauge pointer moves ▶	GO to **D1**.
C2	CHECK OTHER GAUGES		
	• Check power to cluster. With ignition on, observe other gauges and warning lamps for proper operation. If necessary, use Rotunda Digital/Volt Ohm Meter 014-00407 or equivalent or test lamp to verify voltage at B+ terminal of cluster connector.	Other gauges and warning lamps operate correctly; voltage present at cluster ▶	GO to **D1**.
		Other gauges and warning lamps do not operate correctly; no voltage present at cluster ▶	SERVICE power to cluster.

GAUGE INACCURATE
PINPOINT TEST D

	TEST STEP	RESULT ▶	ACTION TO TAKE
D1	TEST BOX CHECK		
	• Insert Instrument Gauge, System Tester, Rotunda 021-00055 or equivalent in sender circuit. Disconnect connector at sender and connect tester to cluster side of connector. Set tester to LOW (73 ohms).	Gauge reads C ▶	GO to **D2**.
		Pointer does not move ▶	GO to **D3**.
D2	TEST BOX CHECK		
	• Set tester to HIGH (10 ohms).	Gauge reads H ▶	REPLACE sender.
		Gauge does not read H ▶	GO to **D3**.
D3	CHECK SENDER WIRING		
	• Check sender circuit wiring for shorts or open with ohmmeter, using Rotunda Digital Volt/Ohm Meter 014-00407, or equivalent.	(OK) ▶	REPLACE gauge.
		(NOT OK) ▶	SERVICE wiring.

88152GB4

Fig. 71 Temperature gauge diagnostic chart

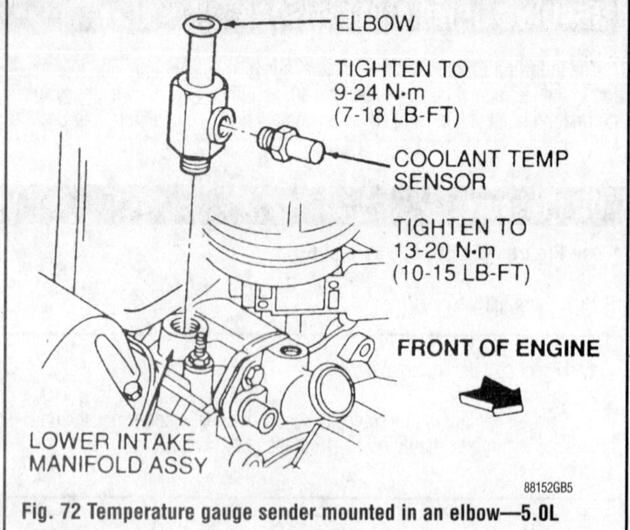

Fig. 72 Temperature gauge sender mounted in an elbow—5.0L engine

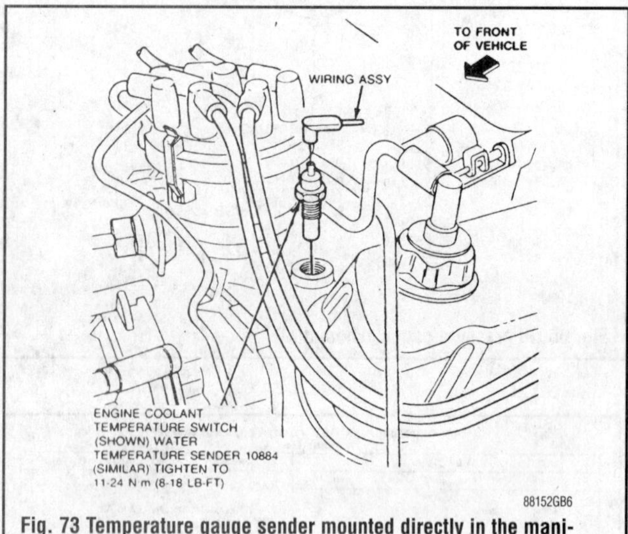

Fig. 73 Temperature gauge sender mounted directly in the manifold—5.0L engine

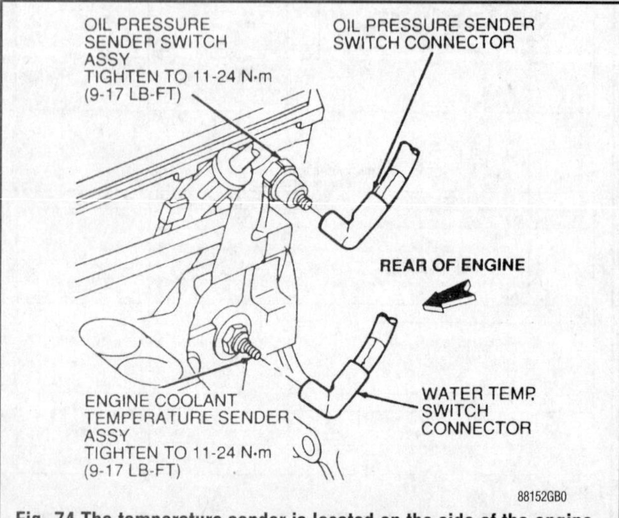

Fig. 74 The temperature sender is located on the side of the engine just below the oil pressure sender—2.3L engine

Fuel Level Gauge

➧ See Figures 75, 76, 77 and 78

REMOVAL & INSTALLATION

1. Disconnect the battery ground.
2. Remove the instrument cluster.
3. Remove the cluster mask and lens.
4. Remove the fuel/oil pressure gauge assembly.
5. Installation is the reverse of removal.

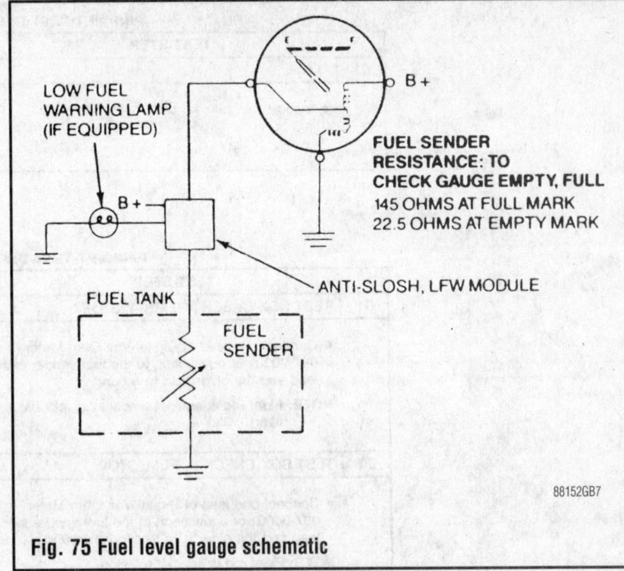

Fig. 75 Fuel level gauge schematic

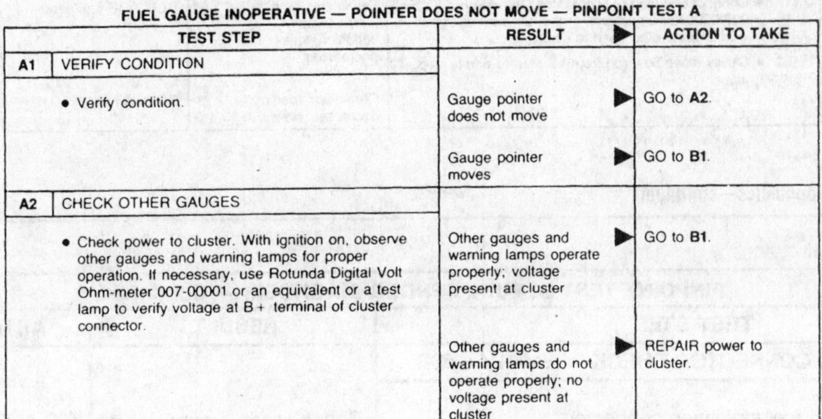

FUEL GAUGE INOPERATIVE — POINTER DOES NOT MOVE — PINPOINT TEST A

	TEST STEP	RESULT	ACTION TO TAKE
A1	VERIFY CONDITION		
	• Verify condition.	Gauge pointer does not move	GO to **A2**.
		Gauge pointer moves	GO to **B1**.
A2	CHECK OTHER GAUGES		
	• Check power to cluster. With ignition on, observe other gauges and warning lamps for proper operation. If necessary, use Rotunda Digital Volt Ohm-meter 007-00001 or an equivalent or a test lamp to verify voltage at B+ terminal of cluster connector.	Other gauges and warning lamps operate properly; voltage present at cluster	GO to **B1**.
		Other gauges and warning lamps do not operate properly; no voltage present at cluster	REPAIR power to cluster.

PINPOINT TEST B: FUEL GAUGE INACCURATE

	TEST STEP	RESULT	ACTION TO TAKE
B1	TEST BOX CHECK		
	• Turn ignition switch to the OFF position. • Insert Instrument Gauge System Tester, Rotunda 021-00038 or equivalent, in sender circuit. Disconnect Circuit 14405 connector under instrument panel and connect tester to cluster side of connector. Set tester to the 22 ohm position. • Turn ignition to the ON position. • Wait 60 seconds. • Read fuel gauge.	Gauge reads 1/8-3/8 or 5/8-7/8	REPLACE gauge.
		Gauge reads 3/8-5/8	REPLACE Anti-Slosh Module.
		Gauge reads E	GO to **B2**.
		Pointer past full	REPLACE Anti-Slosh Module.
		Pointer does not move	REPLACE fuel gauge.
B2	TEST BOX CHECK		
	• Turn ignition switch to the OFF position. • Insert Instrument Gauge System Tester, Rotunda 021-00038 or equivalent, in sender circuit. Disconnect Circuit 14405 connector under instrument panel and connect tester to cluster side of connector. Set tester to the 145 ohm position. • Turn ignition to the RUN position. • Wait 60 seconds. • Read fuel gauge.	Gauge reads full	GO to **B3**.
		Gauge reads less than 7/8	REPLACE fuel gauge.
B3	SENDER WIRING CHECK		
	• Check sender circuit wiring for shorts or open with ohmmeter.	Circuit OK	GO to **C1**.
		Circuit not OK	SERVICE wiring.

88152GB8

Fig. 76 Fuel level gauge diagnostics

PINPOINT TEST C: FUEL SENDER DIAGNOSIS

	TEST STEP	RESULT ▶	ACTION TO TAKE
C1			
	• Inspect fuel tank for distortion or damage.	Damaged ▶	REPLACE fuel tank.
		Not damaged ▶	GO to **D1**

PINPOINT TEST D: FUEL SENDER DIAGNOSIS

	TEST STEP	RESULT ▶	ACTION TO TAKE
D1	TEST BOX CHECK — EMPTY STOP		
	• Connect one lead of Digital Volt Ohm Meter 007-00001 or equivalent, to the fuel sender signal lead and the other lead to ground.	Ohmmeter reads 14-18 ohms ▶	GO to **D2**.
	NOTE: Float rod is against empty stop (closest to filter).	Ohmmeter reads less than 14 ohms or greater than 18 ohms ▶	REPLACE fuel sender.
D2	TEST BOX CHECK — FULL STOP		
	• Connect one lead of Digital Volt Ohm Meter 007-00001 or equivalent, to the fuel sender signal lead and the other lead to sender ground.	Ohmmeter reads 155-165 ohms ▶	GO to **D3**.
	NOTE: Float rod is against full stop.	Ohmmeter reads less than 155 ohms or greater than 165 ohms ▶	REPLACE fuel sender.
D3	TEST BOX CHECK — FLOAT ROD TRAVEL		
	• Connect one lead of Digital Volt Ohm Meter 007-00001 or equivalent, to the fuel sender signal lead and the other lead to sender ground. • Slowly move float rod from full stop to empty stop.	Ohmmeter reading jumps to open condition while decreasing ▶	REPLACE fuel sender.
		Ohmmeter reading decreases slowly ▶	GO to **D4**.

88152GB9

Fig. 77 Fuel level gauge diagnostics—continued

PINPOINT TEST D: FUEL SENDER DIAGNOSIS — Continued

	TEST STEP	RESULT ▶	ACTION TO TAKE
D4	HARNESS CONNECTOR CHECK — EMPTY STOP		
	• Attach all fuel indication connectors. • Move float rod stop to empty position. • Turn ignition to the RUN position. • Wait 60 seconds. • Read fuel gauge.	Gauge reads empty ▶ Gauge reads greater than empty ▶	GO to **D5**. GO to **B3**.
D5	HARNESS CONNECTOR CHECK — FULL STOP		
	• Attach all fuel indication connectors. • Move float rod to full stop position. • Turn ignition to the RUN position. • Wait 60 seconds. • Read fuel gauge.	Gauge reads full ▶ Gauge reads less than full ▶	GO to **D6**. GO to **B3**.
D6	FUEL SENDER INSPECTION		
	• Inspect fuel sender. • Inspect float and float rod.	Float rod is distorted ▶ Float is badly distorted/damaged hitting the filter. Loose on float rod. ▶	REPLACE sender. REPLACE sender.

88152GC0

Fig. 78 Fuel level gauge diagnostics—continued

Troubleshooting Basic Starting System Problems

Problem	Cause	Solution
Starter motor rotates engine slowly	• Battery charge low or battery defective	• Charge or replace battery
	• Defective circuit between battery and starter motor	• Clean and tighten, or replace cables
	• Low load current	• Bench-test starter motor. Inspect for worn brushes and weak brush springs.
	• High load current	• Bench-test starter motor. Check engine for friction, drag or coolant in cylinders. Check ring gear-to-pinion gear clearance.
Starter motor will not rotate engine	• Battery charge low or battery defective	• Charge or replace battery
	• Faulty solenoid	• Check solenoid ground. Repair or replace as necessary.
	• Damaged drive pinion gear or ring gear	• Replace damaged gear(s)
	• Starter motor engagement weak	• Bench-test starter motor
	• Starter motor rotates slowly with high load current	• Inspect drive yoke pull-down and point gap, check for worn end bushings, check ring gear clearance
	• Engine seized	• Repair engine
Starter motor drive will not engage (solenoid known to be good)	• Defective contact point assembly	• Repair or replace contact point assembly
	• Inadequate contact point assembly ground	• Repair connection at ground screw
	• Defective hold-in coil	• Replace field winding assembly
Starter motor drive will not disengage	• Starter motor loose on flywheel housing	• Tighten mounting bolts
	• Worn drive end busing	• Replace bushing
	• Damaged ring gear teeth	• Replace ring gear or driveplate
	• Drive yoke return spring broken or missing	• Replace spring
Starter motor drive disengages prematurely	• Weak drive assembly thrust spring	• Replace drive mechanism
	• Hold-in coil defective	• Replace field winding assembly
Low load current	• Worn brushes	• Replace brushes
	• Weak brush springs	• Replace springs

TCCS2C01

Troubleshooting Basic Charging System Problems

Problem	Cause	Solution
Noisy alternator	• Loose mountings • Loose drive pulley • Worn bearings • Brush noise • Internal circuits shorted (High pitched whine)	• Tighten mounting bolts • Tighten pulley • Replace alternator • Replace alternator • Replace alternator
Squeal when starting engine or accelerating	• Glazed or loose belt	• Replace or adjust belt
Indicator light remains on or ammeter indicates discharge (engine running)	• Broken belt • Broken or disconnected wires • Internal alternator problems • Defective voltage regulator	• Install belt • Repair or connect wiring • Replace alternator • Replace voltage regulator/alternator
Car light bulbs continually burn out—battery needs water continually	• Alternator/regulator overcharging	• Replace voltage regulator/alternator
Car lights flare on acceleration	• Battery low • Internal alternator/regulator problems	• Charge or replace battery • Replace alternator/regulator
Low voltage output (alternator light flickers continually or ammeter needle wanders)	• Loose or worn belt • Dirty or corroded connections • Internal alternator/regulator problems	• Replace or adjust belt • Clean or replace connections • Replace alternator/regulator

TCCS2C02

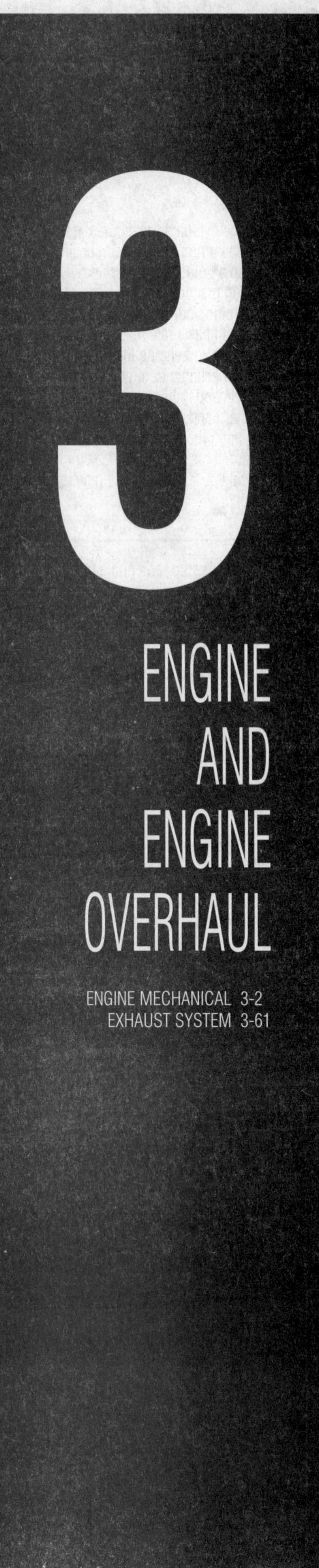

3 ENGINE AND ENGINE OVERHAUL

ENGINE MECHANICAL

Engine Overhaul Tips

See Figure 1

Most engine overhaul procedures are fairly standard. In addition to specific parts replacement procedures and specifications for your individual engine, this section is also a guide to acceptable rebuilding procedures. Examples of standard rebuilding practice are given and should be used along with specific details concerning your particular engine.

Competent and accurate machine shop services will ensure maximum performance, reliability and engine life. In most instances it is more profitable for the do-it-yourself mechanic to remove, clean and inspect the component, buy the necessary parts and deliver these to a shop for actual machine work.

On the other hand, much of the rebuilding work (crankshaft, block, bearings, piston rods, and other components) is well within the scope of the do-it-yourself mechanic's tools and abilities. You will have to decide for yourself the depth of involvement you desire in an engine repair or rebuild.

TOOLS

The tools required for an engine overhaul or parts replacement will depend on the depth of your involvement. With a few exceptions, they will be the tools found in a mechanic's tool kit (see Section 1 of this manual). More in-depth work will require some or all of the following:

- A dial indicator (reading in thousandths) mounted on a universal base
- Micrometers and telescope gauges
- Jaw and screw-type pullers
- Scraper
- Valve spring compressor
- Ring groove cleaner
- Piston ring expander and compressor
- Ridge reamer
- Cylinder hone or glaze breaker
- Plastigage®
- Engine stand

The use of most of these tools is illustrated in this chapter. Many can be rented for a one-time use from a local parts jobber or tool supply house specializing in automotive work.

Occasionally, the use of special tools is called for. See the information on Special Tools and the Safety Notice in the front of this book before substituting another tool.

INSPECTION TECHNIQUES

Procedures and specifications are given in this chapter for inspecting, cleaning and assessing the wear limits of most major components. Other procedures such as Magnaflux® and Zyglo® can be used to locate material flaws and stress cracks. Magnaflux® is a magnetic process applicable only to ferrous materials. The Zyglo® process coats the material with a fluorescent dye penetrant and can be used on any material.

Checking for suspected surface cracks can be more readily made using spot check dye. The dye is sprayed onto the suspected area, wiped off and the area sprayed with a developer. Cracks will show up brightly.

OVERHAUL TIPS

Aluminum has become extremely popular for use in engines, due to its low weight. Observe the following precautions when handling aluminum parts:

- Never hot tank aluminum parts (the caustic hot tank solution will eat the aluminum.
- Remove all aluminum parts (identification tag, etc.) from engine parts prior to the tanking.
- Always coat threads lightly with engine oil or anti-seize compounds before installation, to prevent seizure.
- Never overtorque bolts or spark plugs especially in aluminum threads.

Stripped threads in any component can be repaired using any of several commercial repair kits (Heli-Coil®, Microdot®, Keenserts®, etc.).

When assembling the engine, any parts that will be exposed to frictional contact must be prelubed to provide lubrication at initial start-up. Any product specifically formulated for this purpose can be used, but engine oil is not recommended as a prelube in most cases.

When semi-permanent (locked, but removable) installation of bolts or nuts is desired, threads should be cleaned and coated with Loctite® or another similar, commercial non-hardening sealant.

REPAIRING DAMAGED THREADS

See Figures 2, 3, 4, 5 and 6

Several methods of repairing damaged threads are available. Heli-Coil® (shown here), Keenserts® and Microdot® are among the most widely used. All involve basically the same principle—drilling out stripped threads, tapping the hole and installing a prewound insert—making welding, plugging and oversize fasteners unnecessary.

Two types of thread repair inserts are usually supplied: a standard type for most inch coarse, inch fine, metric course and metric fine thread sizes and a spark lug type to fit most spark plug port sizes. Consult the individual tool manufacturer's catalog to determine exact applications. Typical thread repair kits will contain a selection of prewound threaded inserts, a tap (corresponding to the outside diameter threads of the insert) and an installation tool. Spark plug inserts usually differ because they require a tap equipped with pilot threads and a combined reamer/tap section. Most manufacturers also supply blister-packed thread repair inserts separately in addition to a master kit containing a variety of taps and inserts plus installation tools.

Before attempting to repair a threaded hole, remove any snapped, broken or damaged bolts or studs. Penetrating oil can be used to free frozen threads. The offending item can usually be removed with locking pliers or using a screw/stud extractor. After the hole is clear, the thread can be repaired, as shown in the series of accompanying illustrations and in the kit manufacturer's instructions.

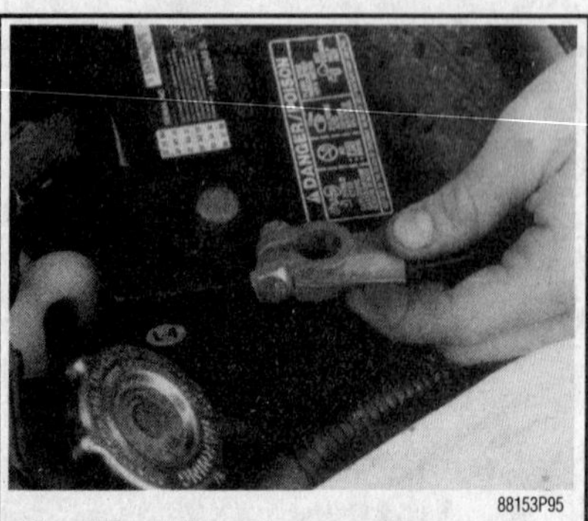
88153P95

Fig. 1 For safety, disconnect the negative battery cable before working in the engine compartment

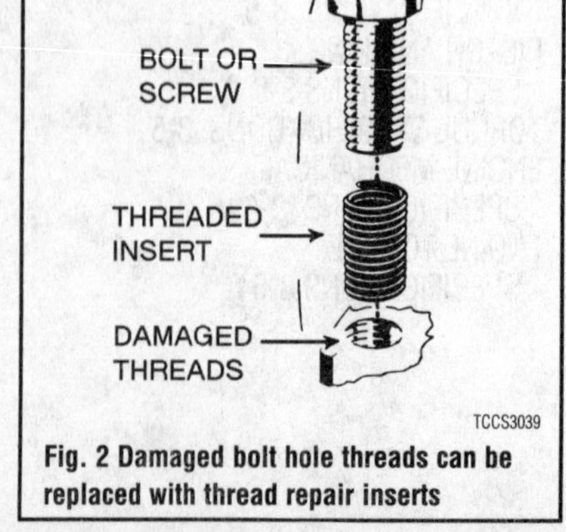

TCCS3039

Fig. 2 Damaged bolt hole threads can be replaced with thread repair inserts

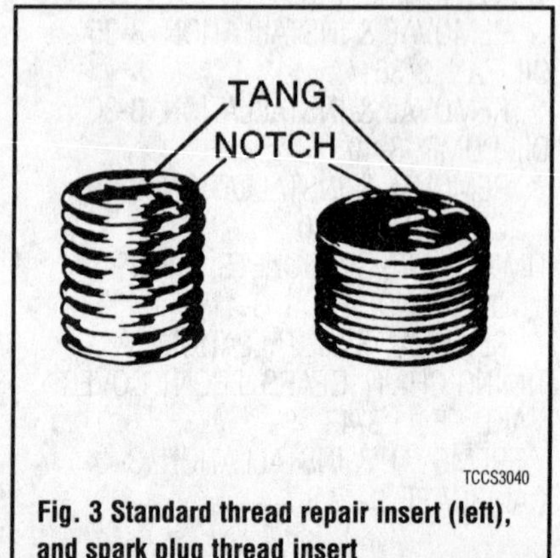

TCCS3040

Fig. 3 Standard thread repair insert (left), and spark plug thread insert

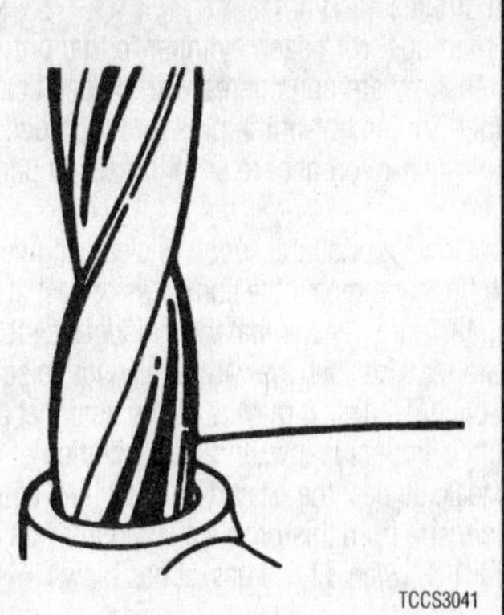

Fig. 4 Drill out the damaged threads with the specified size bit. Be sure to drill completely through the hole or to the bottom of a blind hole

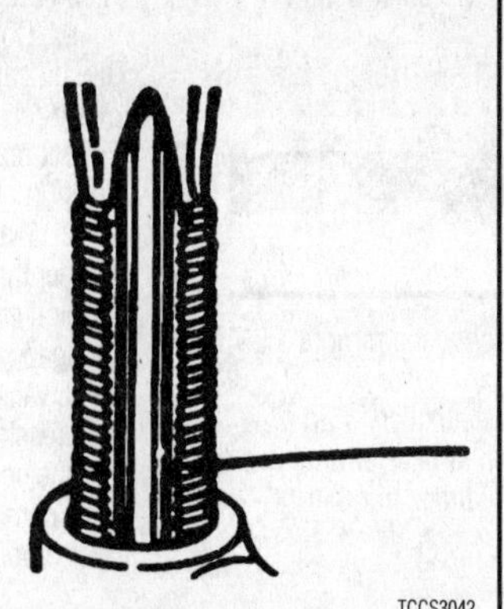

Fig. 5 Using the kit, tap the hole in order to receive the thread insert. Keep the tap well oiled and back it out frequently to avoid clogging the threads

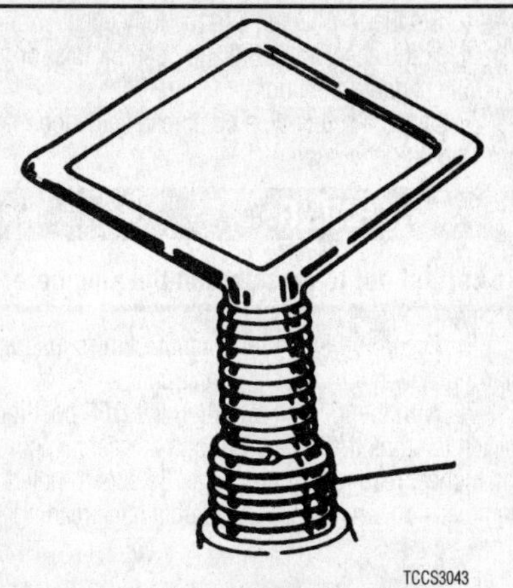

Fig. 6 Screw the insert onto the installer tool until the tang engages the slot. Thread the insert into the hole until it is ¼–½ turn below the top surface, then remove the tool and break off the tang using a punch

Checking Engine Compression

➧ **See Figures 7 and 8**

A noticeable lack of engine power, excessive oil consumption and/or poor fuel mileage measured over an extended period are all indicators of internal engine wear. Worn piston rings, scored or worn cylinder bores, blown head gaskets, sticking or burnt valves and worn valve seats are all possible culprits here. A check of each cylinder's compression will help you locate the problems.

A screw-in type compression gauge is more accurate that the type you simply hold against the spark plug hole. Although it takes slightly longer to use, it's worth the effort to obtain a more accurate reading.

1. Make sure the proper amount and viscosity of engine oil is in the engine crankcase, then make sure the battery is fully charged.
2. Warm-up the engine to normal operating temperature, then shut the engine **OFF**.
3. Thoroughly clean the cylinder head area around the spark plug ports, then remove all of the spark plugs.

Fig. 7 A screw-in type compression gauge is more accurate and easier to use without an assistant

Compression Pressure Limit Chart

Maximum PSI	Minimum PSI	Maximum PSI	Minimum PSI	Maximum PSI	Minimum PSI	Maximum PSI	Minimum PSI
134	101	164	123	194	145	224	168
136	102	166	124	196	147	226	169
138	104	168	126	198	148	228	171
140	105	170	127	200	150	230	172
142	107	172	129	202	151	232	174
144	108	174	131	204	153	234	175
146	110	176	132	206	154	236	177
148	111	178	133	208	156	238	178
150	113	180	135	210	157	240	180
152	114	182	136	212	158	242	181
154	115	184	138	214	160	244	183
156	117	186	140	216	162	246	184
158	118	188	141	218	163	248	186
160	120	190	142	220	165	250	187
162	121	192	144	222	166		

88153G01

Fig. 8 Find the indicated pressure from the highest reading cylinder in the Maximum PSI column and look one column to the right to find the Minimum PSI allowable for that engine

4. Set the throttle plate to the fully open (wide-open throttle) position. You can block the accelerator linkage open for this, or you can have an assistant hold the pedal to the floor.

5. Install a screw-type compression gauge into the no.1 spark plug hole until the fitting is snug.

⁂ WARNING

Be careful not to crossthread the plug hole.

6. According to the tool manufacturer's instructions, connect a remote starting switch into the starting circuit.

7. With the ignition switch in the **OFF** position, use the auxiliary start switch to crank the engine through at least five compression strokes and record the highest reading on the gauge. Be sure to note the approximate number of compression strokes needed to obtain the reading.

8. Repeat the test on each cylinder, cranking the engine approximately the same number of compression strokes each time.

9. Compare the highest readings from each cylinder to that of the others. The indicated compression pressures are considered within specification if the lowest reading cylinder is within 75 percent of the pressure recorded for the highest reading cylinder. For a quick-reference, refer to the accompanying compression pressure limit chart.

10. If a cylinder is unusually low, pour a tablespoon of clean engine oil into the cylinder through the spark plug hole and repeat the compression test. If the compression comes up after adding the oil, it means that the cylinder's piston rings are damaged or worn. If the pressure remains low, the valves may not be seating properly (a valve job is needed), or the head gasket may be blown near that cylinder. If compression in any two adjacent cylinders is low, and if the addition of oil doesn't help the compression, there is leakage past the head gasket. Oil and coolant water in the combustion chamber can result from this problem. There may be evidence of water droplets on the engine dipstick when a head gasket has blown.

GENERAL ENGINE SPECIFICATIONS

Year	Engine ID/VIN	Engine Displacement Liters (cc)	Fuel System Type	Net Horsepower @ rpm	Net Torque @ rpm (ft. lbs.)	Bore x Stroke (in.)	Compression Ratio	Oil Pressure @ rpm
1989	A	2.3 (2300)	MFI	88@4000	132@2600	3.78x3.13	9.0:1	40-60@2000
	E [1]	5.0 (4949)	MFI	225@4200	300@3200	4.00x3.00	9.0:1	40-60@2000
1990	A	2.3 (2300)	MFI	88@4000	132@2600	3.78x3.13	9.0:1	40-60@2000
	E [1]	5.0 (4949)	MFI	225@4200	300@3200	4.00x3.00	9.0:1	40-60@2000
1991	M	2.3 (2300)	MFI	105@4600	135@2600	3.78x3.13	9.5:1	40-60@2000
	E [1]	5.0 (4949)	MFI	225@4200	300@3200	4.00x3.00	9.0:1	40-60@2000
1992	M	2.3 (2300)	MFI	105@4600	135@2600	3.78x3.13	9.5:1	40-60@2000
	E [1]	5.0 (4949)	MFI	225@4200	300@3200	4.00x3.00	9.0:1	40-60@2000
1993	M	2.3 (2300)	MFI	105@4600	135@2600	3.78x3.13	9.5:1	40-60@2000
	E [1]	5.0 (4949)	MFI	235@4600	300@3200	4.00x3.00	9.0:1	40-60@2000

MFI - Multiport fuel injection

1 High output

88153C01

VALVE SPECIFICATIONS

Year	Engine ID/VIN	Engine Displacement Liters (cc)	Seat Angle (deg.)	Face Angle (deg.)	Spring Test Pressure (lbs. @ in.)	Spring Installed Height (in.)	Stem-to-Guide Clearance (in.) Intake	Stem-to-Guide Clearance (in.) Exhaust	Stem Diameter (in.) Intake	Stem Diameter (in.) Exhaust
1989	A	2.3 (2300)	45	44	128-142@ 1.12	1.53-1.59	0.0010-0.0027	0.0015-0.0032	0.3416-0.3423	0.3411-0.3418
	E	5.0 (4949)	45	44	1	1.75	0.0010-0.0027	0.0015-0.0032	0.3416-0.3423	0.3411-0.3418
1990	A	2.3 (2300)	45	44	128-142@ 1.12	1.53-1.59	0.0010-0.0027	0.0015-0.0032	0.3416-0.3423	0.3411-0.3418
	E	5.0 (4949)	45	44	1	2	0.0010-0.0027	0.0015-0.0032	0.3416-0.3423	0.3411-0.3418
1991	M	2.3 (2300)	45	44	128-142@ 1.12	1.49-1.55	0.0010-0.0027	0.0015-0.0032	0.3416-0.3423	0.3411-0.3418
	E	5.0 (4949)	45	44	1	2	0.0010-0.0027	0.0015-0.0032	0.3416-0.3423	0.3411-0.3418
1992	M	2.3 (2300)	45	44	128-142@ 1.12	1.49-1.55	0.0010-0.0027	0.0015-0.0032	0.3416-0.3423	0.3411-0.3418
	E	5.0 (4949)	45	44	1	2	0.0010-0.0027	0.0015-0.0032	0.3416-0.3423	0.3411-0.3418
1993	M	2.3 (2300)	45	44	128-142@ 1.12	1.49-1.55	0.0010-0.0027	0.0015-0.0032	0.3416-0.3423	0.3411-0.3418
	E	5.0 (4949)	45	44	1	2	0.0010-0.0027	0.0015-0.0032	0.3416-0.3423	0.3411-0.3418

1 Intake: 211-230@1.33
Exhaust: 200-226@1.15

2 Intake: 1.75-1.80
Exhaust: 1.58-1.64

88153C02

CAMSHAFT SPECIFICATIONS

All measurements given in inches.

Year	Engine ID/VIN	Engine Displacement Liters (cc)	Journal Diameter 1	2	3	4	5	Elevation In.	Ex.	Bearing Clearance	Camshaft End Play
1989	A	2.3 (2300)	1.7713-1.7720	1.7713-1.7720	1.7713-1.7720	1.7713-1.7720		0.4000	0.4000	0.0010-0.0030	0.0010-0.0070
	E	5.0 (4949)	2.0805-2.0815	2.0655-2.0665	2.0505-2.0515	2.0355-2.0365	2.0205-2.0215	0.2780	0.2780	0.0010-0.0030	0.0005-0.0055
1990	A	2.3 (2300)	1.7713-1.7720	1.7713-1.7720	1.7713-1.7720	1.7713-1.7720		0.4000	0.4000	0.0010-0.0030	0.0010-0.0070
	E	5.0 (4949)	2.0805-2.0815	2.0655-2.0665	2.0505-2.0515	2.0355-2.0365	2.0205-2.0215	0.2780	0.2780	0.0010-0.0030	0.0005-0.0055
1991	M	2.3 (2300)	1.7713-1.7720	1.7713-1.7720	1.7713-1.7720	1.7713-1.7720		0.2381	0.2381	0.0010-0.0030	0.0010-0.0070
	E	5.0 (4949)	2.0805-2.0815	2.0655-2.0665	2.0505-2.0515	2.0355-2.0365	2.0205-2.0215	0.2780	0.2780	0.0010-0.0030	0.0005-0.0055
1992	M	2.3 (2300)	1.7713-1.7720	1.7713-1.7720	1.7713-1.7720	1.7713-1.7720		0.2381	0.2381	0.0010-0.0030	0.0010-0.0070
	E	5.0 (4949)	2.0805-2.0815	2.0655-2.0665	2.0505-2.0515	2.0355-2.0365	2.0205-2.0215	0.2780	0.2780	0.0010-0.0030	0.0050-0.0055
1993	M	2.3 (2300)	1.7713-1.7720	1.7713-1.7720	1.7713-1.7720	1.7713-1.7720		0.2381	0.2381	0.0010-0.0030	0.0010-0.0070
	E	5.0 (4949)	2.0805-2.0815	2.0655-2.0665	2.0505-2.0515	2.0355-2.0365	2.0205-2.0215	0.2780 [1]	0.2780 [1]	0.0010-0.0030	0.0050-0.0055

NA - Not Available

1 Cobra: 0.2822 lift on intake and exhaust

88153C03

PISTON AND RING SPECIFICATIONS

All measurements are given in inches.

Year	Engine ID/VIN	Engine Displacement Liters (cc)	Piston Clearance	Ring Gap Top Compression	Ring Gap Bottom Compression	Ring Gap Oil Control	Ring Side Clearance Top Compression	Ring Side Clearance Bottom Compression	Ring Side Clearance Oil Control
1989	A	2.3 (2300)	0.0030-0.0038	0.0100-0.0200	0.0100-0.0200	0.0100-0.0490	0.0020-0.0040	0.0020-0.0040	SNUG
	E	5.0 (4949)	0.0030-0.0038	0.0100-0.0200	0.0100-0.0200	0.0150-0.0550	0.0020-0.0040	0.0020-0.0040	SNUG
1990	A	2.3 (2300)	0.0030-0.0038	0.0100-0.0200	0.0100-0.0200	0.0100-0.0490	0.0020-0.0040	0.0020-0.0040	SNUG
	E	5.0 (4949)	0.0030-0.0038	0.0100-0.0200	0.0100-0.0200	0.0150-0.0550	0.0020-0.0040	0.0020-0.0040	SNUG
1991	M	2.3 (2300)	0.0024-0.0034	0.0100-0.0200	0.0100-0.0200	0.0150-0.0490	0.0016-0.0033	0.0016-0.0033	SNUG
	E	5.0 (4949)	0.0030-0.0038	0.0100-0.0200	0.0100-0.0200	0.0150-0.0550	0.0020-0.0040	0.0020-0.0040	SNUG
1992	M	2.3 (2300)	0.0019-0.0029	0.0100-0.0200	0.0150-0.0250	0.0100-0.0400	0.0016-0.0033	0.0016-0.0033	SNUG
	E	5.0 (4949)	0.0030-0.0038	0.0100-0.0200	0.0100-0.0200	0.0150-0.0550	0.0020-0.0040	0.0020-0.0040	SNUG
1993	M	2.3 (2300)	0.0019-0.0029	0.0100-0.0200	0.0150-0.0250	0.0100-0.0400	0.0016-0.0033	0.0016-0.0033	SNUG
	E	5.0 (4949)	0.0012-0.0020	0.0100-0.0200	0.0180-0.0280	0.0100-0.0400	0.0020-0.0040	0.0020-0.0040	SNUG

88153C05

CRANKSHAFT AND CONNECTING ROD SPECIFICATIONS

All measurements are given in inches.

Year	Engine ID/VIN	Engine Displacement Liters (cc)	Crankshaft Main Brg. Journal Dia.	Crankshaft Main Brg. Oil Clearance	Crankshaft Shaft End-play	Crankshaft Thrust on No.	Connecting Rod Journal Diameter	Connecting Rod Oil Clearance	Connecting Rod Side Clearance
1989	A	2.3 (2300)	2.3982-2.3990	0.0008-0.0015	0.0030-0.0080	3	2.0464-2.0472	0.0008-0.0015	0.0035-0.0105
	E	5.0 (4949)	2.2482-2.2490	0.0004-0.0015	0.0040-0.0080	3	2.1228-2.1236	0.0008-0.0015	0.0100-0.0200
1990	A	2.3 (2300)	2.3982-2.3990	0.0008-0.0015	0.0030-0.0080	3	2.0464-2.0472	0.0008-0.0015	0.0035-0.0105
	E	5.0 (4949)	2.2482-2.2490	0.0004-0.0015	0.0040-0.0080	3	2.1228-2.1236	0.0008-0.0015	0.0100-0.0200
1991	M	2.3 (2295)	2.2051-2.2059	0.0008-0.0015	0.0030-0.0080	3	2.0462-2.0472	0.0008-0.0015	0.0035-0.0105
	E	5.0 (4949)	2.2482-2.2490	0.0004-0.0015	0.0040-0.0080	3	2.1228-2.1236	0.0008-0.0015	0.0100-0.0200
1992	M	2.3 (2295)	2.2051-2.2059	0.0008-0.0015	0.0030-0.0080	3	2.0462-2.0472	0.0008-0.0015	0.0035-0.0105
	E	5.0 (4949)	2.2482-2.2490	0.0004-0.0015	0.0040-0.0080	3	2.1228-2.1236	0.0008-0.0015	0.0100-0.0200
1993	M	2.3 (2295)	2.2051-2.2059	0.0008-0.0015	0.0030-0.0080	3	2.0462-2.0472	0.0008-0.0015	0.0035-0.0105
	E	5.0 (4949)	2.2482-2.2490	0.0004-0.0015	0.0040-0.0080	3	2.1228-2.1236	0.0008-0.0015	0.0100-0.0200

88153C04

TORQUE SPECIFICATIONS

All readings in ft. lbs.

Year	Engine ID/VIN	Engine Displacement Liters (cc)	Cylinder Head Bolts	Main Bearing Bolts	Rod Bearing Bolts	Crankshaft Damper Bolts	Flywheel Bolts	Manifold Intake	Manifold Exhaust	Spark Plugs	Lug Nut
1989	A	2.3 (2300)	[1]	[2]	[3]	103-133	56-64	[4]	[5]	5-10	85-105
	E	5.0 (4949)	[6]	60-70	19-24	70-90	75-85	[7]	18-24	5-10	85-105
1990	A	2.3 (2300)	[1]	[2]	[3]	103-133	56-64	[4]	[5]	5-10	85-105
	E	5.0 (4949)	[6]	60-70	19-24	70-90	75-85	[7]	18-24	5-10	85-105
1991	M	2.3 (2300)	[1]	[2]	[3]	114-151	56-64	[4]	[5]	5-10	85-105
	E	5.0 (4949)	[6]	60-70	19-24	70-90	75-85	[7]	18-24	5-10	85-105
1992	M	2.3 (2300)	[1]	[2]	[3]	114-151	56-64	[4]	[5]	5-10	85-105
	E	5.0 (4949)	[6]	60-70	19-24	70-90	75-85	[7]	18-24	5-10	85-105
1993	M	2.3 (2300)	[8]	[2]	[3]	114-151	56-64	[4]	[5]	7-10	85-105
	E	5.0 (4949)	[9]	60-70	19-24	70-90	75-85	[7]	26-32	7-10	85-105

NOTE: Always follow proper torque patterns

NOTE: Stretch bolts are used in all procedures that require rotating the fastener a certain number of degrees. The bolts stretch and cannot be reused. For reassembly, replace with new fasteners.

1 Step 1:50-60 ft. lbs.
Step 2: 80-90 ft. lbs.

2 Step 1: 50-60 ft. lbs.
Step 2: 75-85 ft. lbs.

3 Step 1: 25-30 ft. lbs.
Step 2: 30-36 ft. lbs.

4 Lower intake
Step 1: 5-7 ft. lbs.
Step 2: 20-29 ft. lbs.
Upper intake: 15-22 ft. lbs.

5 Step 1: 15-17 ft. lbs.
Step 2: 20-30 ft. lbs.
Stud bolts: 20-33 ft. lbs.

6 Step 1: 55-65 ft. lbs.
Step 2: 65-72 ft. lbs.

7 Lower intake
Step 1: 8 ft. lbs.
Step 2: 16 ft. lbs.
Step 3: 23-25 ft. lbs.
Upper intake: 12-18 ft. lbs.

8 Step 1: 52 ft. lbs.
Step 2: retighten to 52 ft. lbs.
Step 3: 80-100 degrees

9 Non-flanged head bolts
Step 1: 55-65 ft. lbs.
Step 2: 65-72 ft. lbs.
Flanged head bolts
Step 1: 25-35 ft. lbs.
Step 2: 45-55 ft. lbs.
Step 3: 85-95 degrees (1/4 turn)

88153C06

Engine

REMOVAL & INSTALLATION

✱✱ CAUTION

When draining the coolant, keep in mind that cats and dogs are attracted by ethylene glycol antifreeze, and are quite likely to drink any that is left in an uncovered container or in puddles on the ground. This will prove fatal in sufficient quantity. Always drain the coolant into a sealable container. Coolant should be reused unless it is contaminated or too old.

2.3L Engine

See Figures 9, 10 and 11

1. Disconnect the negative battery cable and relieve the fuel system pressure.
2. Drain the cooling system and the crankcase.
3. Mark the position of the hood on the hinges and remove the hood.
4. Remove the air cleaner outlet hose.
5. Disconnect the battery ground cable from the engine.
6. Remove the radiator upper and lower hoses.
7. Disengage the electrical connector to the cooling fan, then remove the fan and shroud assembly. If equipped with automatic transmission, disconnect the oil cooler lines from the radiator. Remove the radiator.
8. Disconnect the heater hose from the water pump (VIN A engine) or from the heater core (VIN M engine), whichever is easier.
9. Tag and disconnect the wires from the alternator and starter.
10. Disconnect the accelerator cable from the throttle body.
11. If equipped with air conditioning, remove the compressor from the mounting bracket and position it out of the way, leaving the refrigerant lines attached. BE SURE not to stress or damage the A/C lines.
12. If equipped with power steering, remove the pump and position out of the way, leaving the hoses attached.
13. Disconnect the flexible fuel line at the fuel rail and plug the fuel line.
14. Disconnect the coil primary wire, the oil pressure sending unit connector (VIN A engine), the water temperature sending unit connector and the injector wiring harness connectors from the main wiring harness.
15. Remove the starter, then remove the engine mount bolts.
16. Raise and safely support the vehicle using jackstands.
17. Remove the flywheel or converter housing upper retaining bolts.
18. Disconnect the muffler inlet pipe at the exhaust manifold. Disconnect the engine right and left mounts at the No. 2 crossmember pedestals. Remove the flywheel or converter housing cover.
19. If equipped with a manual transmission, remove the flywheel housing lower retaining bolts. If equipped with an automatic transmission, disconnect the converter from the flywheel and disconnect the transmission oil cooler lines, if attached to the engine at the pan rail. Remove the converter housing lower retaining bolts.

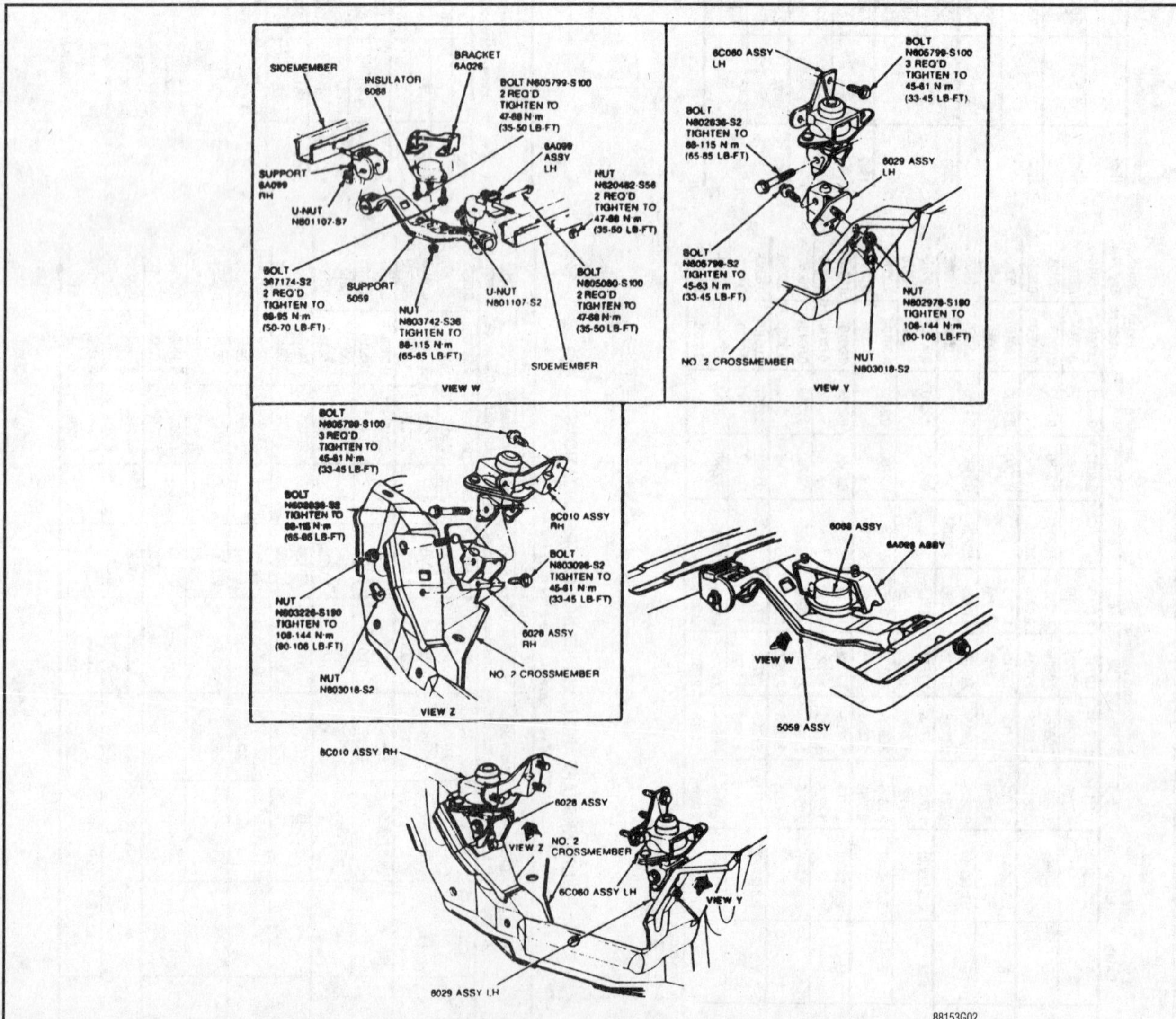

Fig. 9 Engine mounts—2.3L engine with the A4LD transmission (except convertible)

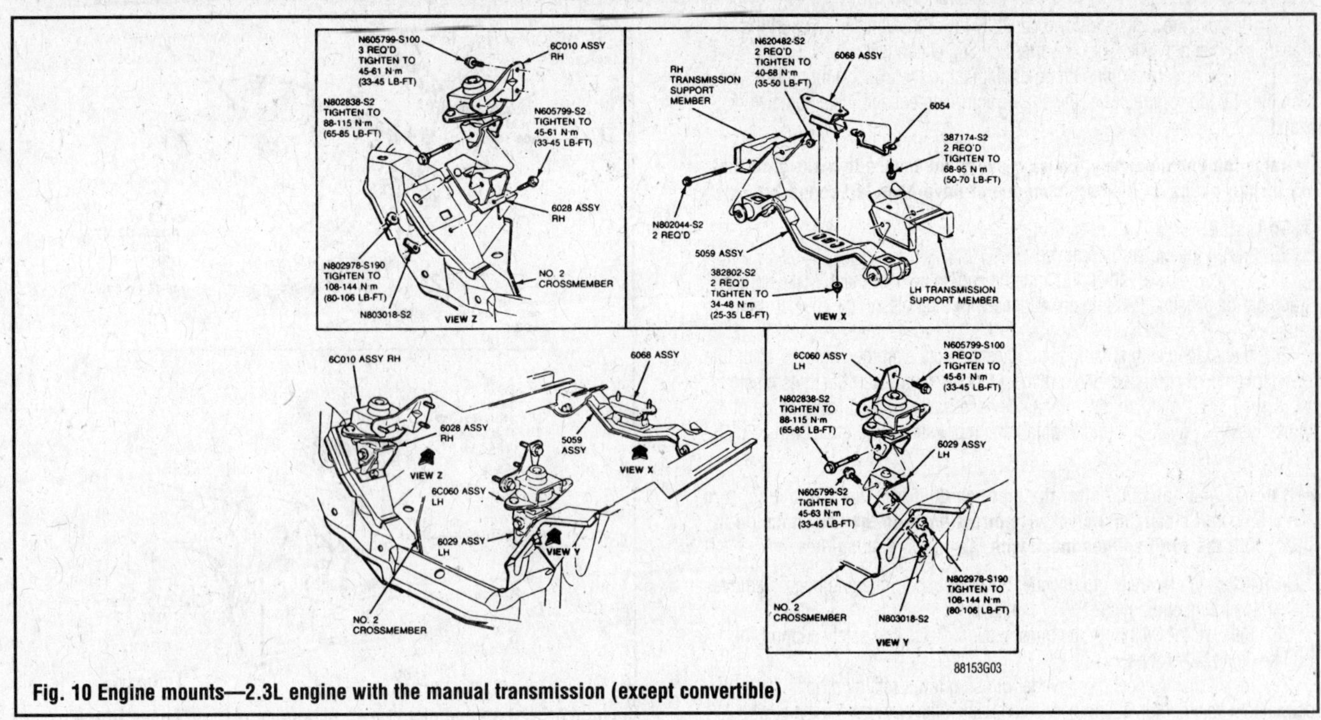

Fig. 10 Engine mounts—2.3L engine with the manual transmission (except convertible)

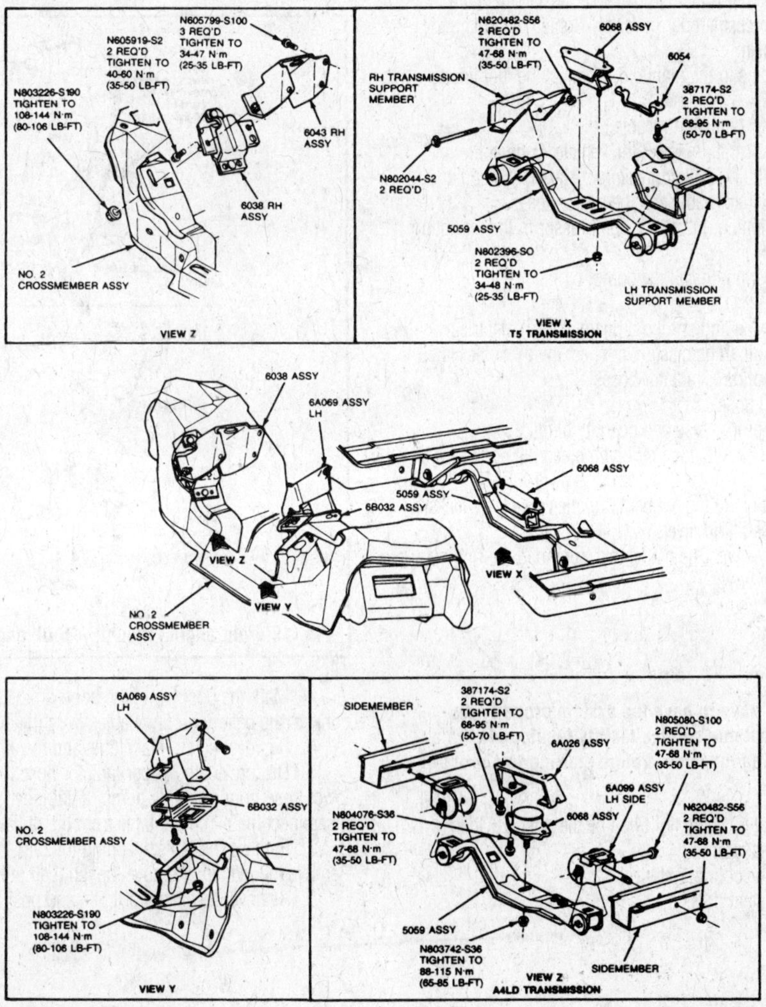

88153G04

Fig. 11 Engine mounts—2.3L engine (convertible)

20. Remove the jackstands and carefully lower the vehicle. Support the transmission and flywheel or converter housing with a jack.

21. Attach suitable engine lifting equipment to the existing lifting brackets. Carefully lift the engine out of the engine compartment and install on a work stand.

➡Raise the engine slowly, pausing every few inches to make sure that no wiring, hoses or lines are snagged or have been left connected.

To install:

22. Install the clutch, if removed.

23. Carefully lower the engine into the engine compartment. Make sure the studs on the exhaust manifold are aligned with the holes in the muffler inlet pipe.

24. If equipped with an automatic transmission, start the converter pilot into the crankshaft. If equipped with a manual transmission, start the transmission input shaft into the clutch disc. It may be necessary to adjust the position of the transmission in relation to the engine if the input shaft will not enter the clutch disc.

➡If the engine hangs up after the input shaft enters the clutch disc, turn the crankshaft slowly in a clockwise direction, with the transmission in gear, until the shaft splines mesh with the clutch disc splines.

25. Install the flywheel or converter housing upper retaining bolts. Remove the engine lifting equipment.

26. Remove the jack from the transmission. Raise and safely support the vehicle using jackstands.

27. Install the flywheel or converter housing lower retaining bolts. If equipped with an automatic transmission, attach the converter to the flywheel and tighten the retaining nuts to 20–34 ft. lbs. (27–46 Nm).

28. Install the flywheel or converter housing dust cover. Install the left and right engine mounts to the No. 2 crossmember pedestal. Tighten the nuts and bolts to 80–106 ft. lbs. (108–144 Nm).

29. Connect the muffler inlet pipe to the manifold. Connect the fuel line to the fuel rail.

30. Install the starter and connect the starter cable.

31. Remove the jackstands and carefully lower the vehicle. Engage the oil pressure and water temperature sending unit connectors. Connect the coil and alternator wires. Connect the accelerator cable and the heater hoses.

32. If equipped with air conditioning, install the compressor in the mounting bracket.

33. If equipped with power steering, install the pump.

34. Install the drive belt.

35. Install the radiator, cooling fan and shroud. Engage the fan electrical connector. If equipped with automatic transmission, connect the oil cooler lines to the radiator. Install the upper and lower radiator hoses.

36. Install the air cleaner outlet hose.

37. Fill the crankcase with the proper type and quantity of oil.

38. Connect the negative battery cable, then refill and bleed the cooling system.

39. Bring the engine to normal operating temperature, then check for leaks. Stop the engine and double check all fluid levels.

40. Align the hood on the hinges with the marks that were made during removal. Secure with the mounting bolts.

5.0L Engine

➧ See Figures 12, 13 and 14

➡If equipped with A/C you will have to have the system properly discharged and recovered by a reputable service facility (equipped with a refrigerant recovery and recycling machine) before starting this procedure.

1. Disconnect the negative battery cable, followed by the positive, then properly relieve the fuel system pressure.

2. Drain the crankcase and the cooling system.

3. Properly relieve the fuel system pressure.

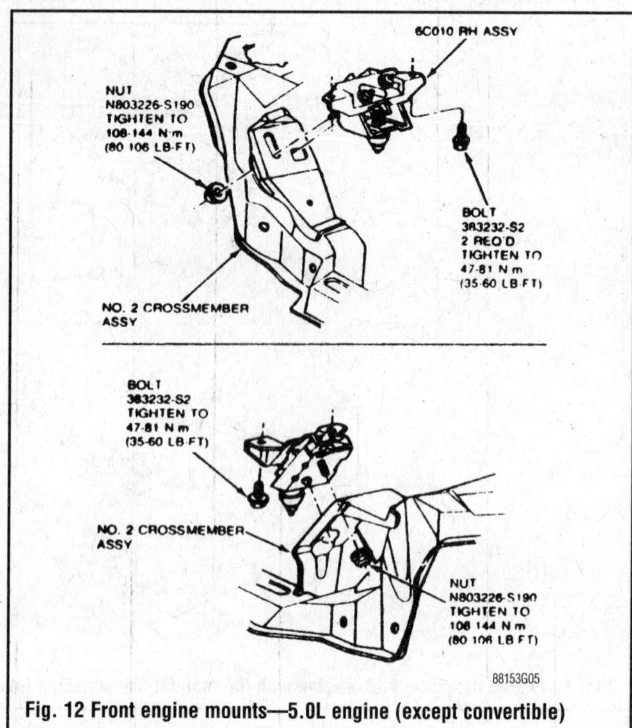

Fig. 12 Front engine mounts—5.0L engine (except convertible)

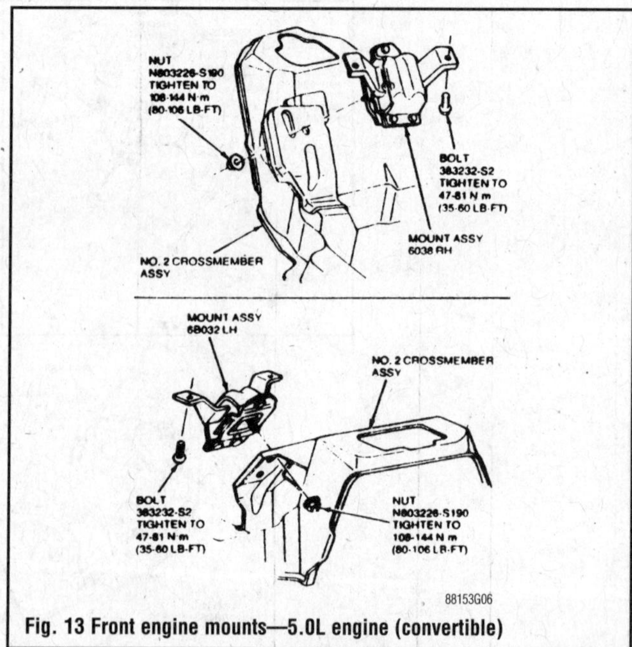

Fig. 13 Front engine mounts—5.0L engine (convertible)

4. Mark the position of the hood on the hinges and remove the hood. Disconnect the battery ground cables from the cylinder block.

5. Remove the air intake duct and the air cleaner, if engine mounted.

6. Disconnect the upper radiator hose from the thermostat housing and the lower hose from the water pump. If equipped with an automatic transmission, disconnect the oil cooler lines from the radiator.

7. Remove the bolts attaching the radiator fan shroud to the radiator. Remove the radiator. Remove the fan, belt pulley and shroud.

8. Remove the alternator bolts and position the alternator out of the way.

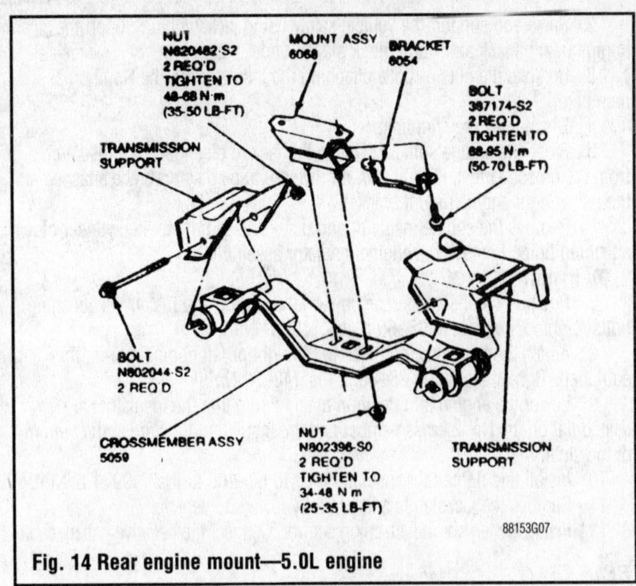

Fig. 14 Rear engine mount—5.0L engine

9. Disconnect the oil pressure sending unit wire from the sending unit. Disconnect the flexible fuel line at the fuel tank line. Plug the fuel tank line.

10. Disconnect the accelerator cable from the throttle body. Disconnect the Throttle Valve (TV) rod, if equipped with an automatic transmission. Disconnect the cruise control cable, if equipped.

11. Disconnect the throttle valve vacuum line from the intake manifold, if equipped.

12. Disconnect the transmission filler tube bracket from the cylinder block.

13. If equipped with air conditioning, disconnect the lines and electrical connectors at the compressor, then remove the compressor from the vehicle. Immediately plug the lines and the compressor fittings to prevent the entrance of dirt and moisture.

14. Disconnect the power steering pump bracket from the cylinder head. Remove the drive belt. Position the power steering pump out of the way in a position that will prevent the fluid from leaking.

15. Disconnect the power brake vacuum line from the intake manifold.

16. Disconnect the heater hoses from the heater tubes. Disengage the electrical connector from the coolant temperature sending unit.

17. Remove the converter housing-to-engine upper bolts.

18. Disconnect the wiring to the solenoid on the left rocker arm cover. Remove the wire harness from the left rocker arm cover and position the wires out of the way. Disconnect the ground strap from the block.

19. Disconnect the wiring harness at the two 10-pin connectors.

20. Raise and safely support the vehicle using jackstands. Disconnect the cable from the starter, then remove the starter motor from the engine.

21. Disconnect the muffler inlet pipes from the exhaust manifolds. Disconnect the engine support insulators from the chassis. Disconnect the downstream thermactor tubing and check valve from the right exhaust manifold stud, if equipped.

22. If equipped with an automatic transmission, disconnect the transmission cooler lines from the retainer and remove the converter housing inspection cover. Disconnect the flywheel from the converter and secure the converter assembly in the housing. Remove the remaining converter housing-to-engine bolts.

23. If equipped with a manual transmission, remove the flywheel housing retaining bolts.

24. Remove the jackstands and carefully lower the vehicle, then support the transmission. Attach engine lifting equipment and hoist the engine.

25. Raise the engine slightly and separate it from the transmission. Carefully lift the engine out of the engine compartment. Avoid bending or damaging the rear cover plate or other components. Install the engine on a workstand.

➡Raise the engine slowly, pausing every few inches to make sure that no wiring, hoses or lines are snagged or have been left connected.

To install:

26. Attach the engine lifting equipment and remove the engine from the workstand.

27. Lower the engine carefully into the engine compartment. Make sure the exhaust manifolds are properly aligned with the muffler inlet pipes.

28. If equipped with a manual transmission, start the transmission input shaft into the clutch disc. It may be necessary to adjust the position of the transmission in relation to the engine if the input shaft will not enter the clutch disc.

➡If the engine hangs up after the input shaft enters the clutch disc, turn the crankshaft slowly in a clockwise direction, with the transmission in gear, until the shaft splines mesh with the clutch disc splines.

29. If equipped with an automatic transmission, start the converter pilot into the crankshaft. Align the paint mark on the flywheel to the paint mark on the torque converter. Install the converter housing upper bolts, making sure the dowels in the cylinder block engage the converter housing.

30. Install the engine support insulator-to-chassis attaching fasteners and remove the engine lifting equipment.

31. Raise and support the vehicle safely using jackstands. Connect both muffler inlet pipes to the exhaust manifolds. Install the starter and connect the starter cable.

32. Remove the retainer holding the converter in the housing. Attach the converter to the flywheel. Install the converter housing inspection cover and install the remaining converter housing attaching bolts.

33. Remove the support from the transmission and lower the vehicle.

34. Connect the wiring harness at the two 10-pin connectors.

35. Connect the coolant temperature sending unit wire and connect the heater hoses. Connect the wiring to the metal heater tubes, engine coolant temperature, air charge temperature and oxygen sensors.

36. Connect the transmission filler tube bracket. Connect the manual shift rod and the retracting spring. Connect the throttle valve vacuum line, if equipped.

37. Connect the accelerator cable and TV cable. Connect the cruise control cable, if equipped.

38. Remove the plug from the fuel tank line, then connect the fuel line and the oil pressure sending unit wire.

39. Install the pulley, water pump belt and fan clutch assembly.

40. Position the alternator bracket and install the alternator bolts. Connect the alternator and ground cables. Adjust the drive belt tension.

41. Install the air conditioning compressor. Unplug and connect the refrigerant lines and engage the electrical connector to the compressor.

42. Install the power steering drive belt and power steering pump bracket. Connect the power brake vacuum line.

43. Install the fan on the water pump pulley. Place the shroud over the fan and install the radiator. Connect the radiator hoses and the transmission oil cooler lines. Position the shroud and install the bolts.

44. Connect the heater hoses to the heater tubes. Fill the crankcase with the proper type and quantity of engine oil. Adjust the transmission throttle linkage.

45. Install the air intake duct assembly.

46. Connect the negative battery cable, then fill and bleed the cooling system.

47. Bring the engine to normal operating temperature, then check for leaks.

48. Stop the engine and check all fluid levels.

49. Install the hood, aligning the marks that were made during removal.

50. If equipped, have the A/C system properly leak-tested, evacuated and charged.

Engine Mounts

REMOVAL & INSTALLATION

2.3L Engine

▸ See Figures 9, 10 and 11

FRONT

1. Disconnect the negative battery cable.
2. Raise and support the vehicle safely using jackstands. Support the engine using a wood block and jack placed under the engine.
3. Remove the through-bolts attaching both insulators to the No. 2 crossmember pedestal bracket. On the Mustang convertible, remove the nuts.
4. Disconnect the shift linkage.
5. Raise the engine sufficiently to disengage the insulator from the crossmember pedestal bracket.
6. Remove the bolts attaching the insulator and bracket assembly to the engine. Remove the insulator and bracket assembly.

To install:

7. Position the insulator and bracket assembly to the engine. Install the attaching bolts. Tighten to 33–45 ft. lbs. (45–61 Nm).
8. Lower the engine into position making sure that the insulators are seated flat on the No. 2 crossmember. Hand start the bolts, lower the engine completely, then tighten the through-bolts to 33–45 ft. lbs. (45–61 Nm).
9. On Mustang convertible, tighten the flange nut to 80–106 ft. lbs. (108–144 Nm).
10. Install the fuel pump shield attaching screw to left engine support, if equipped.
11. Install the shift linkage, then remove the jackstands and carefully lower the vehicle.
12. Connect the negative battery cable.

REAR

1. Disconnect the negative battery cable.
2. Raise and support the vehicle safely using jackstands.
3. Support the transmission with a jack and a wood block. Remove the nut(s) retaining the rear insulator to the crossmember.
4. Remove the two bolts and nuts retaining the crossmember to the body brackets. Remove the crossmember by raising the transmission slightly with the jack.
5. Remove the two bolts retaining the rear insulator to the transmission and remove the insulator and retainer. If equipped with automatic transmission, remove the two bolts retaining the rear insulator to the intermediate bracket.

To install:

6. Position the rear insulator and retainer on the transmission. Install the two retaining bolts and tighten to 50–70 ft. lbs. (68–95 Nm). If equipped with automatic transmission, tighten the two bolts to 33–45 ft. lbs. (46–61 Nm).
7. Install the crossmember to the body brackets. Tighten the retaining nuts and bolts to 35–50 ft. lbs. (48–68 Nm).
8. Lower the transmission and install the insulator to crossmember retaining nuts. Tighten to 25–35 ft. lbs. (34–47 Nm). If equipped with an automatic transmission, tighten the nut to 65–85 ft. lbs. (85–115 Nm).
9. Remove the jackstands and carefully lower the vehicle.
10. Connect the negative battery cable.

5.0L Engines

▸ See Figures 12, 13 and 14

FRONT

1. Disconnect the negative battery cable. Remove the fan shroud attaching screws.
2. Raise and support the vehicle safely using jackstands. Support the engine using a jack and wood block placed under the engine.
3. Remove the nuts or bolts attaching the insulators to the No. 2 crossmember.
4. Disconnect the shift linkage.
5. Raise the engine sufficiently with the jack to disengage the insulator from the crossmember. If equipped, remove the transmission brace attached at the left or right engine mount bracket.
6. Remove the engine insulator and bracket assembly to the cylinder block attaching bolts. Remove the engine insulator assembly.

To install:

7. Position the insulator assembly on the engine and install the attaching bolts. Tighten the bolts to 35–60 ft. lbs. (48–81 Nm).
8. Attach the transmission brace to the right or left engine mount, if equipped. Tighten the nut to 35–60 ft. lbs. (48–81 Nm).
9. Lower the engine into position making sure that the insulators are seated flat on the No. 2 crossmember and the insulator studs are at the bottom of the slots.
10. Install and tighten the insulator nuts to 80–105 ft. lbs. (109–142 Nm).
11. Remove the jackstands and carefully lower the vehicle.
12. Install the fan shroud attaching screws. Connect the negative battery cable.

REAR

1. Disconnect the negative battery cable.
2. Raise and support the vehicle safely using jackstands.
3. Support the transmission with a jack and wood block. Remove the two nuts attaching the insulator to the crossmember.
4. Remove the two bolts and nuts attaching the crossmember to the body brackets, then remove the crossmember by raising the transmission slightly with the jack.
5. Remove the two bolts attaching the rear insulator to the transmission, then remove the insulator and retainer.

To install:

6. Position the rear insulator and retainer on the transmission. Install the two attaching bolts and tighten to 50–70 ft. lbs. (68–95 Nm).
7. Install the crossmember to the body brackets. Tighten the attaching nuts to 35–50 ft. lbs. (48–68 Nm).
8. Lower the transmission and install the insulator to crossmember attaching nuts. Tighten to 25–35 ft. lbs. (34–48 Nm).
9. Remove the jackstands and carefully lower the vehicle, then connect the negative battery cable.

Rocker Arm (Camshaft/Valve) Cover

REMOVAL & INSTALLATION

2.3L Engine

▸ See Figure 15

1. Disconnect the negative battery cable for safety.
2. Disconnect the fresh air inlet hose at the crankcase oil filler cap.
3. Label for identification, then remove all wires and vacuum hoses interfering with the valve cover removal. On most distributor ignition motors (VIN A engines) you will have to tag and disconnect the spark plug wires to remove the valve cover.
4. Disconnect the accelerator cable at the throttle body. Remove the cable retracting spring. Remove the accelerator cable bracket from the upper intake manifold, then position the cable and bracket out of the way.
5. On the distributorless (VIN M) engine, the throttle body and Exhaust Gas Recirculation (EGR) supply tube may interfere with valve cover removal, if so they must be removed for access.
6. Loosen the retaining bolts, then remove the rocker arm cover from the engine.
7. Remove and discard the gasket.

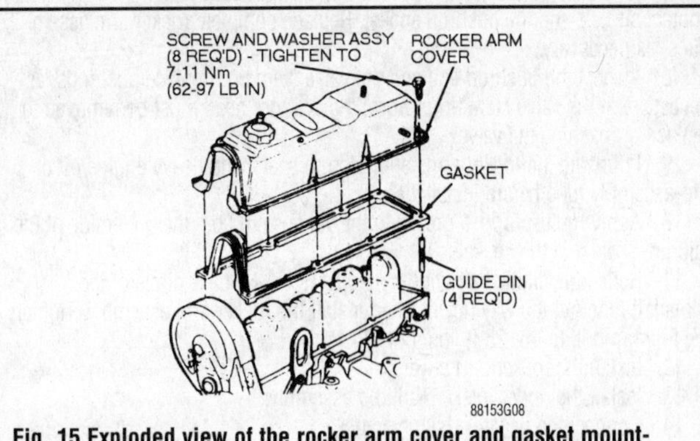

Fig. 15 Exploded view of the rocker arm cover and gasket mounting—2.3L engine

To install:

8. Clean the mating surfaces for the cover and head thoroughly. Keep any debris from falling into the engine.
9. Place the new gasket on the head with the locating tabs downward.
10. Place the valve cover on the head making sure the gasket is evenly seated. Tighten the bolts to 62–97 inch lbs. (7–11 Nm).
11. If removed, install the throttle body and the EGR supply tube.
12. Install the accelerator cable bracket, cable and cable retracting return spring.
13. On the distributor equipped VIN A engine, connect the spark plug wires as tagged during removal.
14. Connect the fresh air hose to the crankcase filler cap.
15. Connect the negative battery cable.

5.0L Engine

See Figures 16, 17, 18 and 19

1. Disconnect the negative battery cable for safety.
2. Remove the upper intake manifold assembly from the vehicle. For details, please refer to the intake manifold procedures found later in this section.
3. If you are removing the right rocker arm cover, disconnect the PCV closure tube from the oil fill stand pipe at the rocker arm cover.
4. Remove the Thermactor/secondary air bypass valve and air supply hoses, as necessary to gain clearance.
5. Loosen and remove the rocker arm cover bolts.
6. Lift off the cover from the engine. It may be necessary to break the cover loose by rapping on it with a rubber mallet. NEVER pry the cover off, as you could damage the gasket sealing surfaces!

To install:

7. Thoroughly clean the mating surfaces of both the cover and head.
8. Place the new gasket on the cover with the locating tabs engaging the slots.
9. Place the cover on the head making sure the gasket is evenly seated. Tighten the cover retaining bolts to 10–13 ft. lbs. (14–18 Nm) for 1989–92 vehicles or to 12–15 ft. lbs. (16–20 Nm) for 1993 vehicles. For 1989–92 vehicles, wait two minutes, then retighten the bolts to specification.
10. If removed for access, install the Thermactor/secondary air bypass valve and air supply hoses.
11. If you are installing the right rocker arm cover, connect the PCV closure tube to the oil fill stand pipe.
12. Install the upper intake manifold assembly.
13. Connect the negative battery cable.

Rocker Arms

REMOVAL & INSTALLATION

2.3L Engine

On this engine, the cam followers (rocker arms) are part of the hydraulic valve lash adjustment assembly. The hydraulic lash adjusters are placed at the fulcrum point of the rocker arms and act in a manner similar to hydraulic lifters

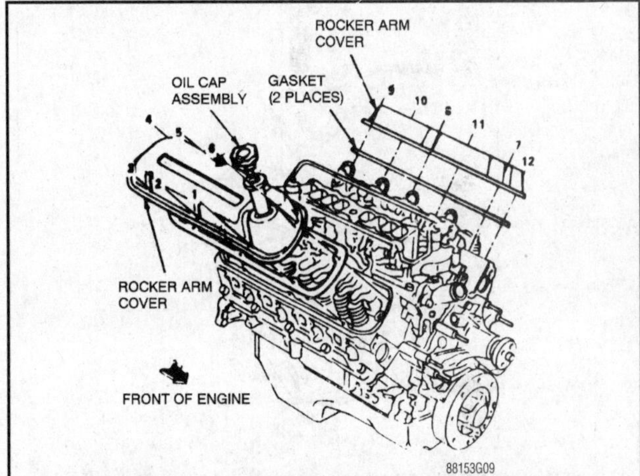

Fig. 16 Exploded view of the rocker arm covers and gasket mounting—5.0L engine

Fig. 17 Once access is cleared to the covers, loosen and remove the retaining bolts

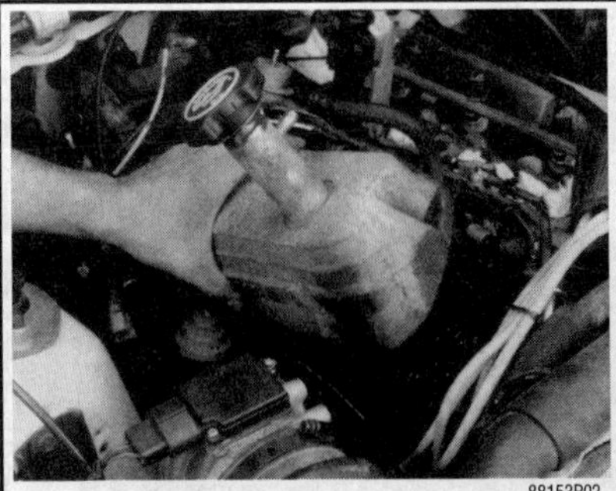

Fig. 18 Carefully break the gasket seal and remove the rocker arm cover from the engine

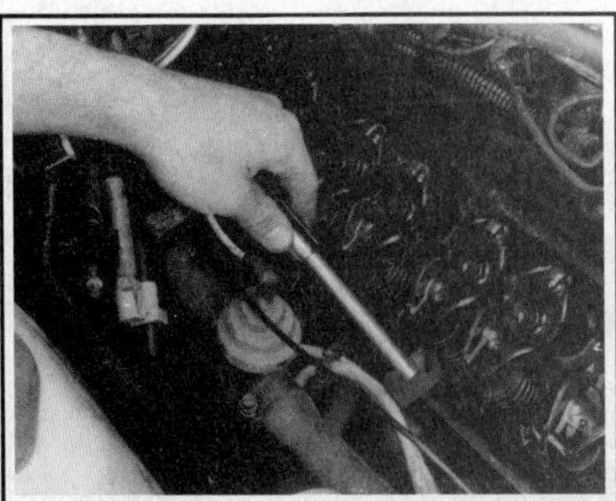

Fig. 19 Clean the gasket mating surfaces, taking care to keep debris out of the engine

in pushrod motors. If inspection or replacement is necessary, the rocker arms are removed as part of lash adjuster removal. For details, please refer to the Valve Lifter procedures found later in this section.

5.0L Engine

➧ See Figures 20, 21, 22 and 23

1. Disconnect the negative battery cable for safety.
2. Remove the upper intake manifold assembly. For details, please refer to the intake manifold procedures found later in this section.
3. Remove the rocker arm covers.
4. Except for the Cobra, loosen the rocker arm fulcrum bolt, then remove the bolt, fulcrum (seat), rocker arm and guide. KEEP ALL PARTS IN ORDER FOR INSTALLATION!

➡Label and/or arrange all rocker arm and fulcrum components to assure installation in their original locations.

5. On the Cobra, loosen the fulcrum bolt, then remove the bolt, roller rocker arm assembly and pedestal assembly.

To install:

6. Inspect the fulcrum bolts for damage. Replace any bolt on which damage is found.
7. Inspect the rocker arm and fulcrum seat or roller contact surfaces for wear and/or damage. Also check the rocker arm for wear on the valve stem tip contact surface and the pushrod socket. Replace complete rocker arm assemblies, as necessary.
8. Inspect the pushrod end and the valve stem tip. Replace pushrods, as necessary. If the valve stem tip is worn, the cylinder head must be removed to replace or machine the valve.
9. Lubricate the rocker arms and fulcrum seats with heavy engine oil or pre-assembly lube before installation.
10. Apply multi-purpose grease to the valve stem tips, the underside of the fulcrum seats and the sockets.
11. Rotate the crankshaft until the tappet is on the base circle of the camshaft lobe (all the way down), then install the rocker arm assembly. Tighten the fulcrum bolt to 18–25 ft. lbs. (24–34 Nm).
12. Install the rocker arm covers.
13. Install the upper intake manifold assembly.
14. Connect the negative battery cable.

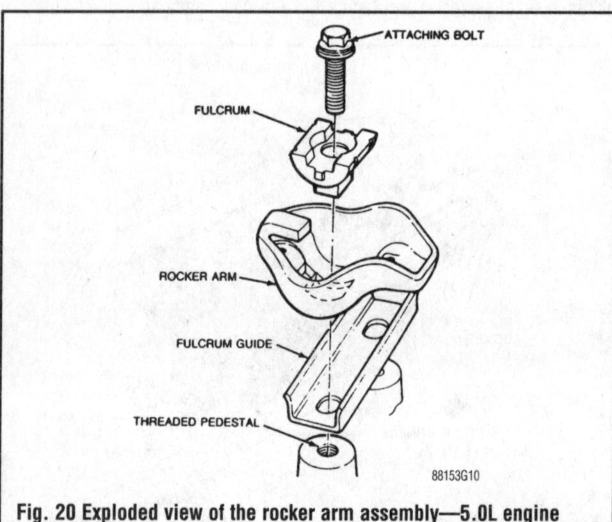

Fig. 20 Exploded view of the rocker arm assembly—5.0L engine (except Cobra)

Thermostat

REMOVAL & INSTALLATION

✲✲ CAUTION

When draining the coolant, keep in mind that cats and dogs are attracted by ethylene glycol antifreeze, and are quite likely to drink any that is left in an uncovered container or in puddles on the ground. This will prove fatal in sufficient quantity. Always drain the coolant into a sealable container. Coolant should be reused unless it is contaminated or too old.

2.3L Engine

➧ See Figures 24 and 25

1. Disconnect the negative battery cable for safety.
2. Open the radiator drain and allow the coolant to drain out so that the coolant level is below the coolant outlet elbow (which houses the thermostat).

➡On some models it will be necessary to remove the distributor cap, rotor and vacuum diaphragm in order to gain access to the thermostat housing mounting bolts.

3. On the distributorless (VIN M) engine, remove the upper radiator hose, saving the clamps for reuse during installation.
4. Disconnect the heater hose at the thermostat housing located on the left front lower side of the engine.
5. Remove the outlet elbow retaining bolts, then position the elbow sufficiently clear of the engine to provide access to the thermostat.

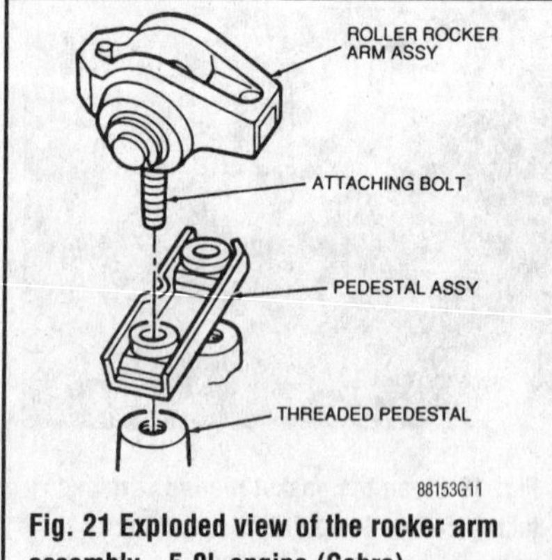

Fig. 21 Exploded view of the rocker arm assembly—5.0L engine (Cobra)

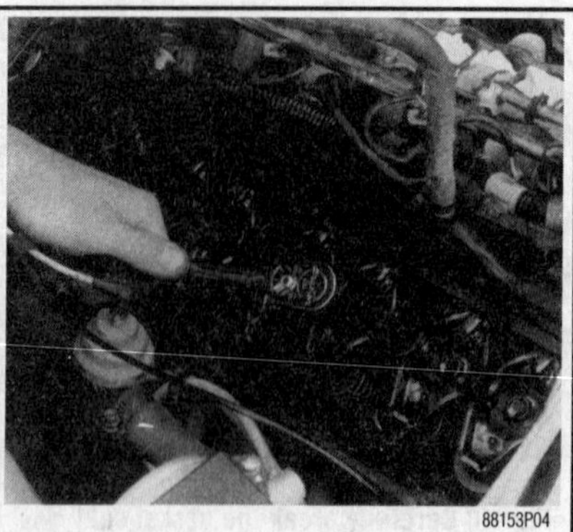

Fig. 22 Loosen and remove the fulcrum bolt . . .

Fig. 23 . . . then lift the rocker arm assembly from the engine

✲✲ WARNING

The thermostat is held into the housing by retaining flanges and must be removed by turning to align the flanges with the removal slots. DO NOT attempt to pry the thermostat free as this will result in thermostat or housing damage.

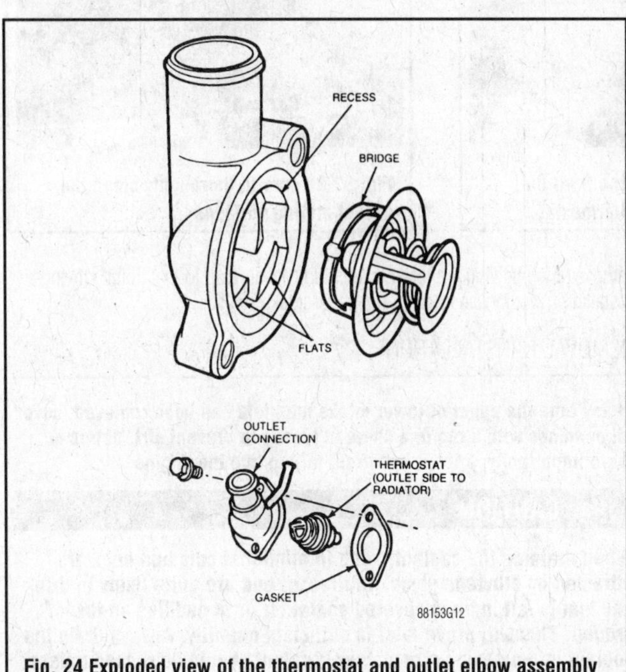

Fig. 24 Exploded view of the thermostat and outlet elbow assembly

6. Turn the thermostat counterclockwise in the housing until the thermostat is free, then remove it from the housing.
7. Remove the gasket.

To install:

8. Check the mating surfaces of the outlet elbow and the engine for traces of sealant, corrosion or damage. Clean the surfaces to assure a proper seal.

➡The water outlet casting contains a locking recess into which the thermostat is turned and locked. This is done to prevent the possibility of incorrect thermostat installation.

9. Position the gasket on the engine, then install the thermostat in the coolant elbow with the thermostat bridge section in the outlet casting.
10. Turn the thermostat clockwise to lock it in position on the flats which are cast into the outlet elbow. Visually inspect the installation to be assured of proper alignment. Be sure the full width of the heater outlet tube is visible within the thermostat port.

➡It is important that the rubber thermostat gasket be pressed and the correct thermostat installation alignment be made to provide coolant flow to the heater.

11. Install the outlet elbow and retaining bolts on the engine. Tighten the bolts to 14–21 ft. lbs. (19–28 Nm).
12. Connect the heater hose to the thermostat housing.
13. If removed (on VIN M engines), install the upper radiator hose using the clamps loosened earlier.
14. Connect the negative battery cable.
15. Refill the radiator. Run the engine at operating temperature and check for leaks. Recheck the coolant level.

5.0L Engine

➧ See Figures 26 thru 32

1. Disconnect the negative battery cable for safety.
2. Open the radiator drain and allow the coolant to drain out so that the coolant level is below the coolant outlet elbow which houses the thermostat.

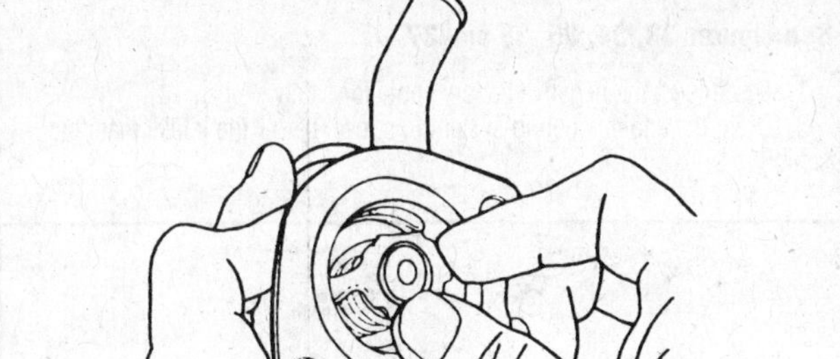

Fig. 25 The thermostat should be twisted clockwise into the locked position during installation

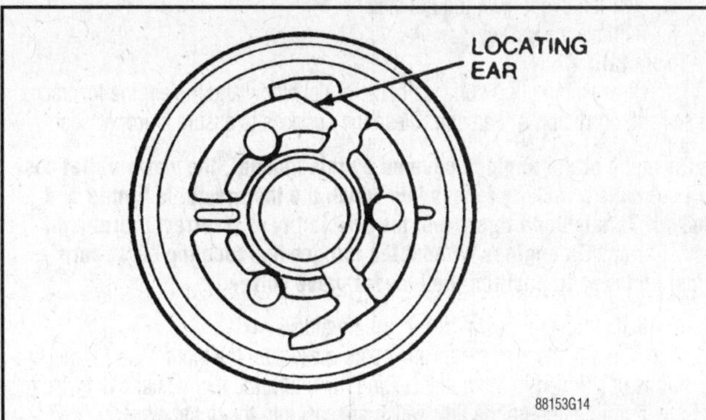

Fig. 26 Most of the engines covered by this manual utilize a thermostat equipped with locking ears to prevent improper installation

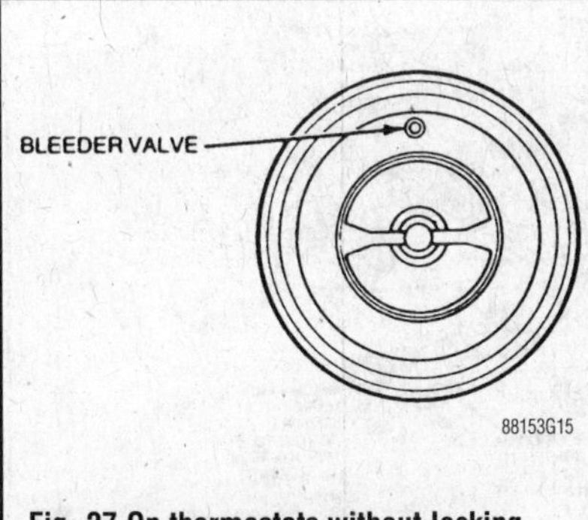

Fig. 27 On thermostats without locking ears you MUST make sure to position the bleeder valve at 12 o'clock

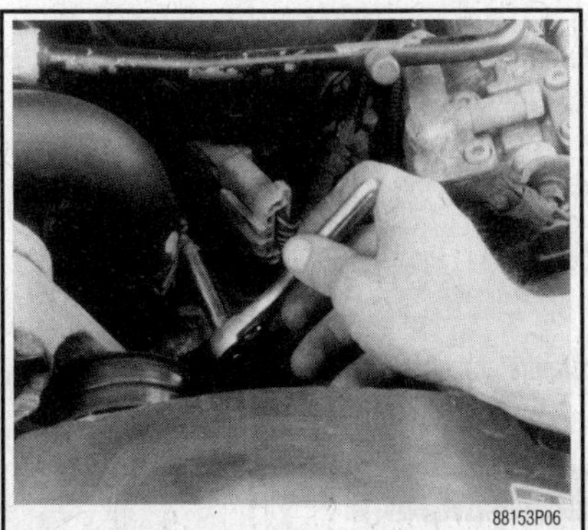

Fig. 28 Loosen the radiator hose retaining clamp . . .

Fig. 29 . . . then remove the upper radiator hose from the thermostat housing

88153P08

Fig. 30 Loosen and remove the housing retaining bolts (an open-end or box wrench is hand for this)

88153P09

Fig. 31 Separate the housing from the engine, then remove the thermostat

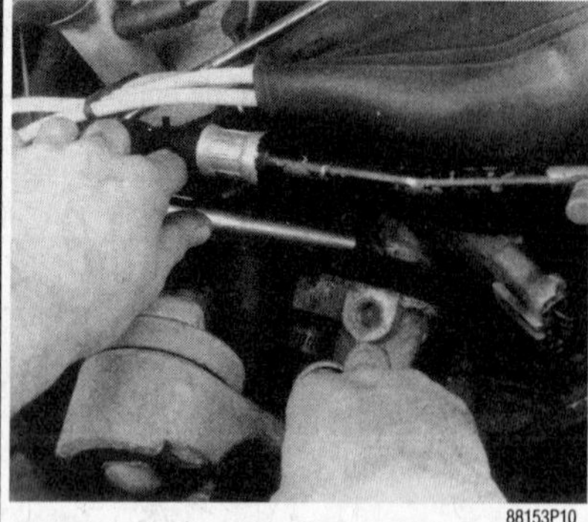
88153P10

Fig. 32 Be sure to thoroughly clean the gasket mating surfaces

3. Disconnect the bypass hose from the lower side of the thermostat housing. If access is difficult, hold off, it may be possible to separate the housing from the engine with this hose still attached, or it can be removed later when there is better access.
4. Disconnect the upper radiator hose at the thermostat housing.
5. If necessary for better access, remove the distributor cap and rotor.
6. Loosen and remove the thermostat housing retaining bolts, then carefully separate the housing from the engine.

✻✻ WARNING

On many of the engines covered by this manual, the thermostat is held into the housing by retaining flanges (locating ears) and must be removed by turning to align the flanges with the removal slots. DO NOT attempt to pry the thermostat free on these motors as this will result in thermostat or housing damage.

7. Turn the thermostat counterclockwise in the housing until the thermostat is free, then remove it from the housing.
8. Remove the gasket.

To install:

9. Check the mating surfaces of the outlet elbow and the engine for traces of sealant, corrosion or damage. Clean the surfaces to assure a proper seal.

➡On many of the engines covered by this manual, the water outlet casting contains a locking recess into which the thermostat is turned and locked. This is done to prevent the possibility of incorrect thermostat installation. On engines without the flanges and locating ears, care must be taken to position the bleeder valve correctly.

10. Install the thermostat in the coolant elbow.
   a. On models with the locating ears make sure the thermostat bridge section is positioned in the outlet casting, then turn the thermostat clockwise to lock it in position on the flats which are cast into the outlet elbow.
   b. On models equipped with a bleeder valve, position the thermostat with the valve at 12 o'clock (top) when viewed from the front of the engine.
11. Install the thermostat housing assembly and gasket, then tighten the bolts to 12–17 ft. lbs. (16–24 Nm).

➡If the bypass hose was removed later in the procedure than originally directed, be sure to reconnect it at that point of the installation in order to avoid difficulty later.

12. If removed for access, install the distributor cap and rotor.
13. Connect the upper radiator hose to the thermostat housing.
14. If removed and not installed earlier, connect the bypass hose to the lower side of the thermostat housing.
15. Connect the negative battery cable.
16. Refill the radiator. Run the engine at operating temperature and check for leaks. Recheck the coolant level.

Intake Manifolds

Both of the engines covered by this manual utilize an upper and lower intake manifold assembly. If necessary, only the upper intake manifold may be removed by following the intake manifold procedure up to that point. Obviously, installation would also begin at the upper intake steps.

REMOVAL & INSTALLATION

➡Any time the upper or lower intake manifold has been removed, cover all openings with a rag or a sheet of plastic to prevent dirt, debris or more importantly, a loose nut, from falling into the engine.

✻✻ CAUTION

When draining the coolant, keep in mind that cats and dogs are attracted by ethylene glycol antifreeze, and are quite likely to drink any that is left in an uncovered container or in puddles on the ground. This will prove fatal in sufficient quantity. Always drain the coolant into a sealable container. Coolant should be reused unless it is contaminated or too old.

2.3L Engine

➧ See Figures 33, 34, 35, 36 and 37

1. Disconnect the negative battery cable for safety.
2. Drain the engine cooling system to a level below the intake manifold assembly.

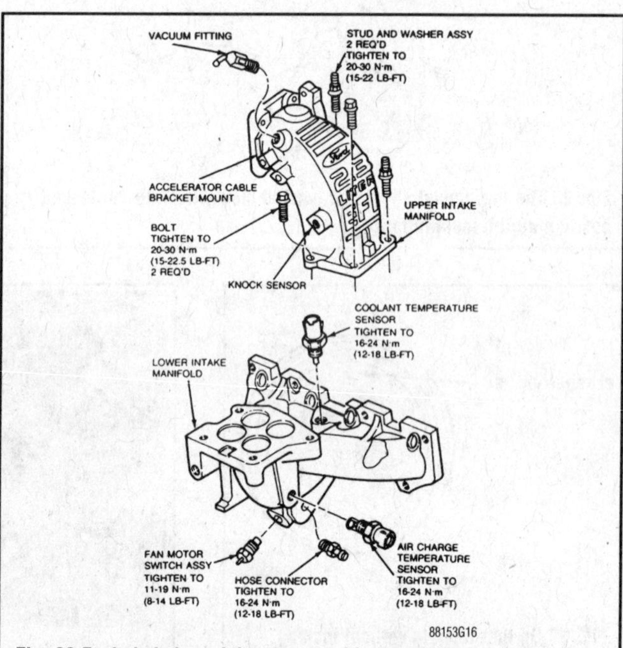

Fig. 33 Exploded view of the upper and lower intake manifold assembly—2.3L (VIN A) engine

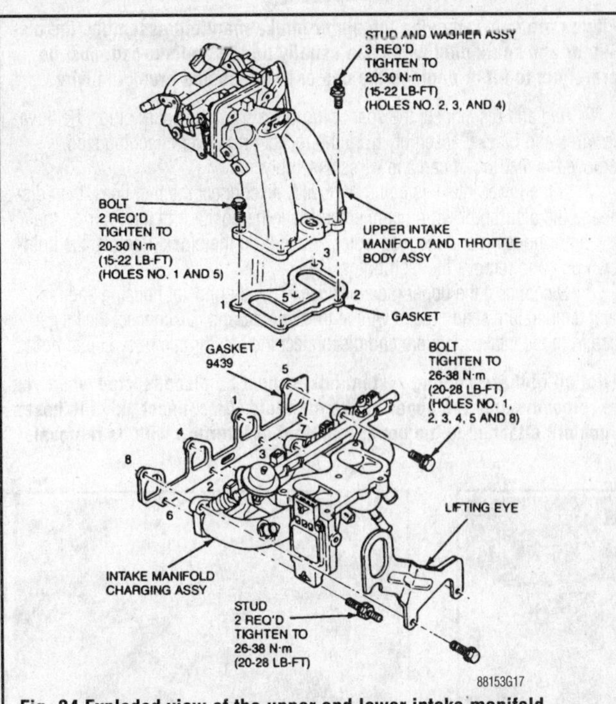

Fig. 34 Exploded view of the upper and lower intake manifold assembly with torque sequences—2.3L (VIN M) engine

CAUTION

Fuel lines on fuel injected vehicles will remain pressurized after the engine is shut off. Fuel pressure must be relieved before servicing the fuel system.

3. If you are removing the lower intake manifold (and not only removing the upper intake), properly relieve the fuel system pressure.
4. Tag and disengage the electrical connectors at the following:
   a. Idle Air Control (IAC) valve.
   b. Throttle Positioning (TP) sensor.
   c. Injector wiring harness.

➡On most vehicles the injector wiring harness should be unplugged at the main engine harness and the water temperature indicator sensor.

   d. Intake (charge) Air Temperature (IAT) sensor.
   e. Engine Coolant Temperature (ECT) sensor.
   f. EGR valve, if necessary.
   g. Fan switch, if necessary.
   h. Ignition control assembly on the distributorless (VIN M) engine.
5. Tag and disconnect the necessary vacuum lines.
6. Remove the throttle linkage shield. Disconnect the throttle linkage and, if equipped, the cruise control and kickdown cables. Unbolt the accelerator cable from the bracket and position the cable out of the way.
7. Disconnect the air intake hose and, on the distributorless (VIN M) engine, the crankcase vent hose.
8. Disconnect the PCV system hose from the fitting on the underside of the upper intake manifold.
9. Disconnect the water bypass hose at the lower intake manifold.
10. Loosen the EGR flange nut and disconnect the EGR tube.
11. Remove the engine oil dipstick bracket retaining bolt.
12. Remove the upper intake manifold retaining bolts and/or studs, then remove the upper intake manifold assembly.

➡Stop here if you are only removing the upper intake manifold assembly. Be sure to remove all old gasket material and to inspect the gasket mating surfaces before installation.

13. Disconnect the fuel lines from the fuel supply manifold.
14. Disengage the electrical connectors from the fuel injectors and move the harness aside.
15. Remove the fuel supply manifold retaining bolts and remove the manifold carefully. If desired, the injectors can be removed at this time by exerting a slight twisting/pulling motion.
16. Remove the lower intake manifold retaining bolts and remove the lower intake manifold. The front two bolts also secure an engine lift bracket.

To install:

17. Clean all gasket mating surfaces. Clean and oil the manifold bolt threads. Install a new intake manifold gasket.
18. Position the lower intake manifold to the head with the engine lift bracket. Install the manifold retaining bolts finger-tight.
19. Tighten the lower intake manifold retaining bolts, in sequence, in two steps, first to 5–7 ft. lbs. (7–10 Nm) and then to 20–29 ft. lbs. (26–38 Nm).

➡On the distributorless (VIN M) engine, the 3 bolts with stud heads should be placed in positions 2, 3, and 4 of the accompanying figure.

20. Install the fuel supply manifold and injectors. Engage the electrical wiring connectors to the injectors.
21. Install a new gasket and the upper intake manifold. Tighten the bolts to 15–22 ft. lbs. (20–30 Nm).
22. If the lower manifold was removed, connect the fuel lines to the fuel supply manifold.
23. Install the engine oil dipstick and retaining bolt.
24. Connect the EGR tube, water bypass line and PCV hose.
25. Engage the electrical connectors and vacuum lines to their original locations.
26. Connect the throttle linkage.
27. Connect the negative battery cable and cycle the ignition without starting the engine in order to build fuel system pressure. Turn the ignition key back and forth (from **ON** to **OFF**) at least 6 times, leaving the key **ON** for 5 seconds each time. Then check for fuel leaks.
28. Properly refill and bleed the cooling system.
29. Run the engine until normal operating temperature is reached and check for leaks.

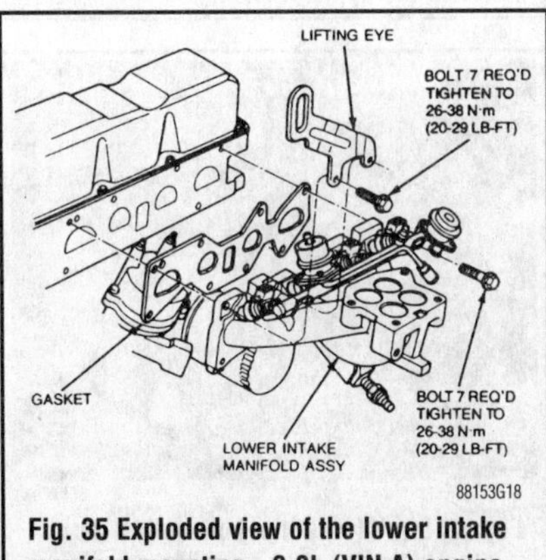

Fig. 35 Exploded view of the lower intake manifold mounting—2.3L (VIN A) engine

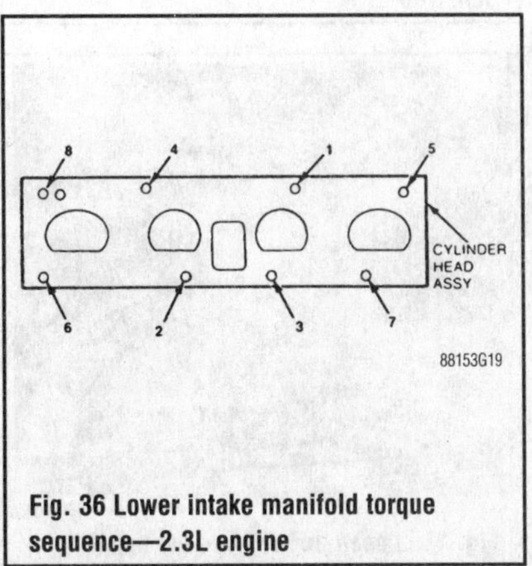

Fig. 36 Lower intake manifold torque sequence—2.3L engine

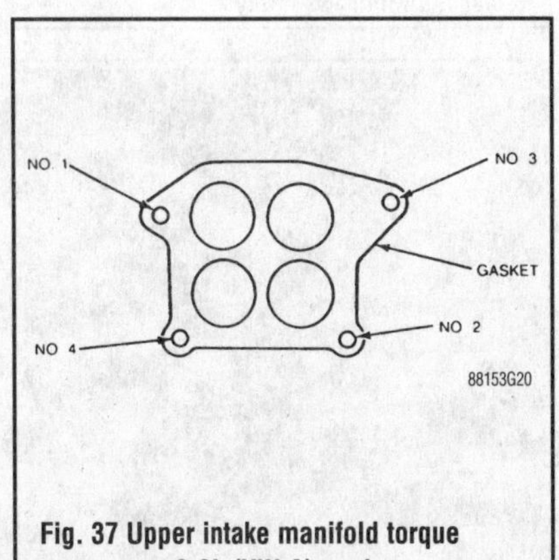

Fig. 37 Upper intake manifold torque sequence—2.3L (VIN A) engine

5.0L Engine

➧ See Figures 38 thru 64

1. Disconnect the negative battery cable for safety.
2. Drain the engine cooling system to a level below the manifold assembly.

✲✲ CAUTION

Fuel lines on fuel injected vehicles will remain pressurized after the engine is shut off. Fuel pressure must be relieved before servicing the fuel system.

3. If you are removing the lower intake manifold (and not only removing the upper intake), properly relieve the fuel system pressure.
4. Disconnect the accelerator cable and cruise control linkage, if equipped, from the throttle body. Disconnect the Throttle Valve (TV) cable, if equipped.
5. Tag and disconnect all accessible vacuum lines from their intake manifold fittings.

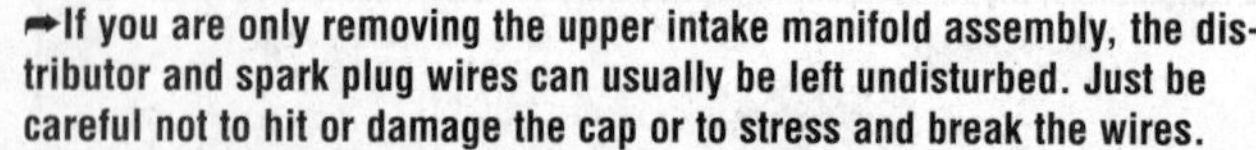

➥If you are only removing the upper intake manifold assembly, the distributor and spark plug wires can usually be left undisturbed. Just be careful not to hit or damage the cap or to stress and break the wires.

6. Tag and disconnect the spark plug wires from the spark plugs. Remove the wires and bracket assembly from the rocker arm cover attaching stud. Remove the distributor cap and wires assembly.
7. If the lower intake is being removed, disconnect the fuel lines, then disengage the distributor wiring connector. Mark the position of the rotor on the distributor housing and the distributor housing on the block. Remove the hold-down bolt and remove the distributor.
8. Disconnect the upper radiator hose at the thermostat housing and the water temperature sending unit wire at the sending unit. Disconnect the heater hose from the intake manifold and disconnect the two throttle body cooler hoses.

➥Not all of these cooling system hoses must be disconnected when you are removing only the upper intake manifold. Disconnect only the hoses which are attached to the upper manifold or interfere with its removal.

Fig. 38 Disconnect the accelerator cable linkage from the throttle body

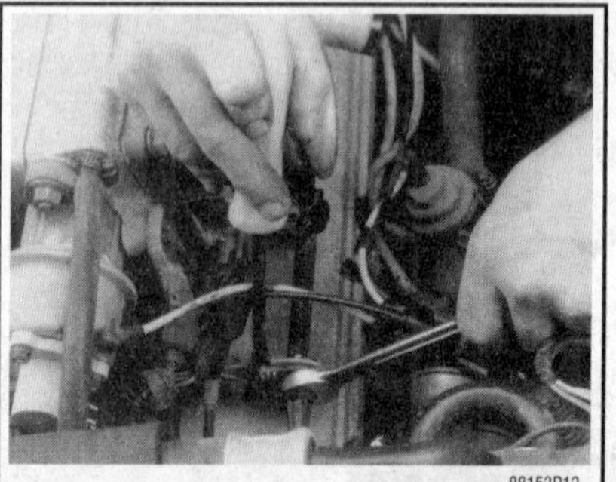

Fig. 39 Either free the cable from the bracket (as shown) or remove the bracket from the manifold

Fig. 40 Tag and disconnect the vacuum hoses from the throttle body . . .

Fig. 41 . . . and from the rest of the upper manifold assembly

Fig. 42 Don't forget the hoses on the "vacuum tree"

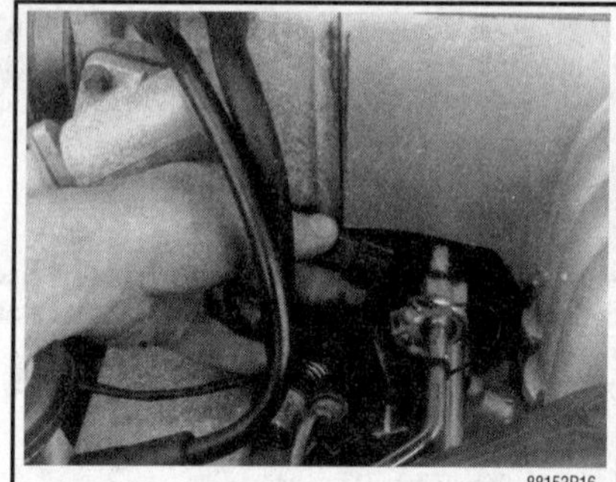

Fig. 43 Disengage any wiring that may interfere with upper or lower manifold removal (as applicable)

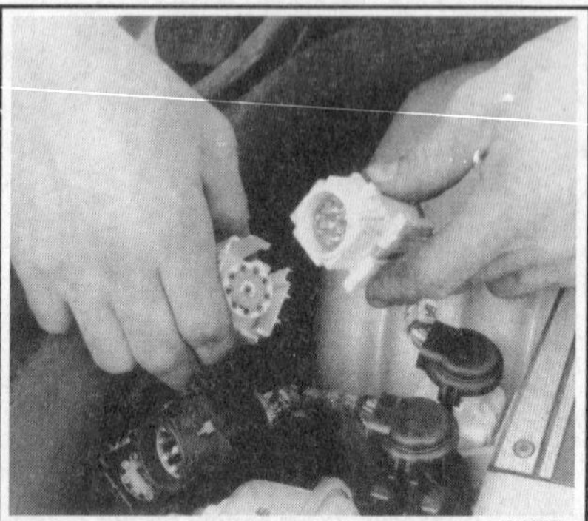

Fig. 44 Separate the multi-pin harnesses at the upper manifold assembly

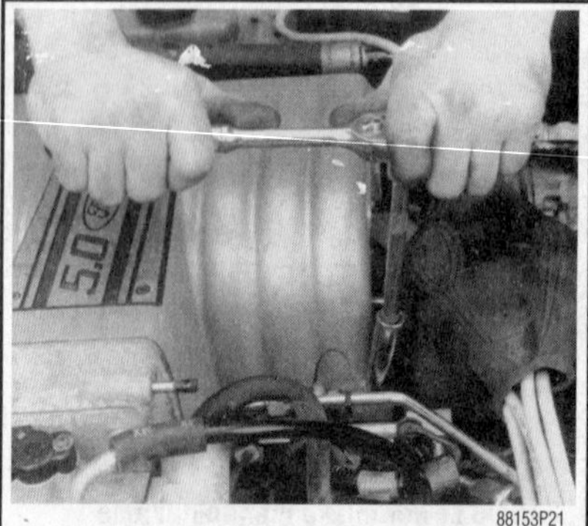

Fig. 45 Loosen and remove the upper intake manifold retaining bolts

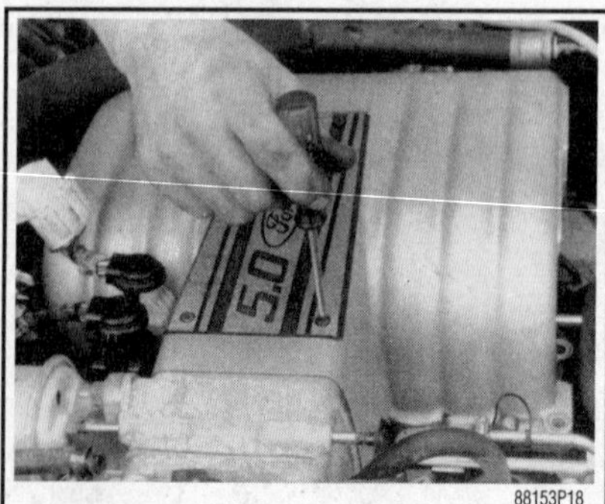

Fig. 46 Don't forget the bolts under the upper manifold cover, loosen the cover screws . . .

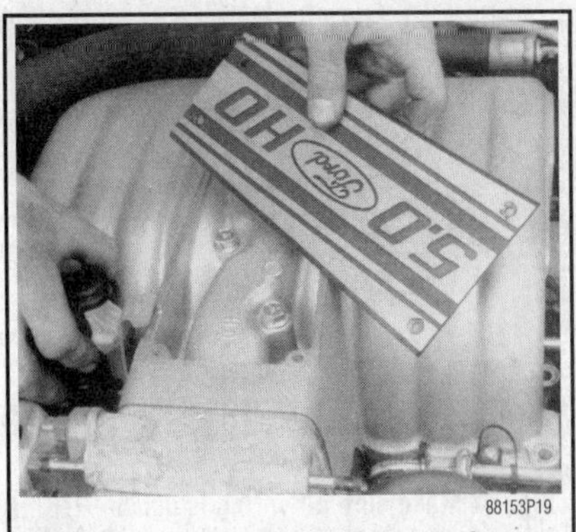

Fig. 47 . . . then remove the cover for access to the hidden manifold bolts

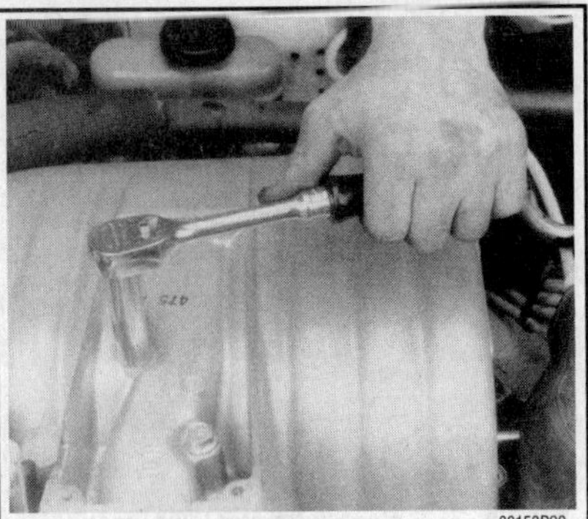

Fig. 48 Loosen and remove the remaining upper manifold bolts

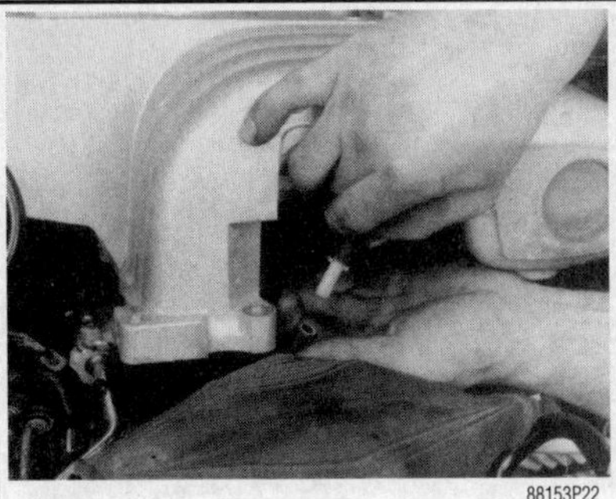

Fig. 49 Lift upward on the upper manifold for access, then disconnect the fuel evaporative purge hose

Fig. 50 Carefully lift and remove the upper manifold from the engine

Fig. 51 If the lower manifold is not being removed, clean the gasket mating surfaces at this time . . .

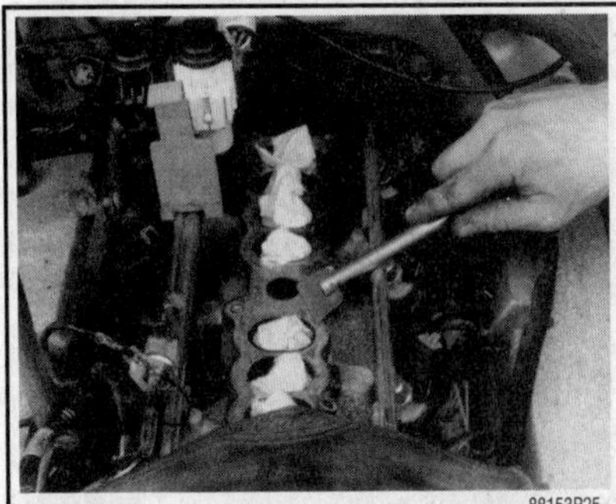

Fig. 52 . . . but be sure to cover the openings in the lower manifold to keep debris out of the engine

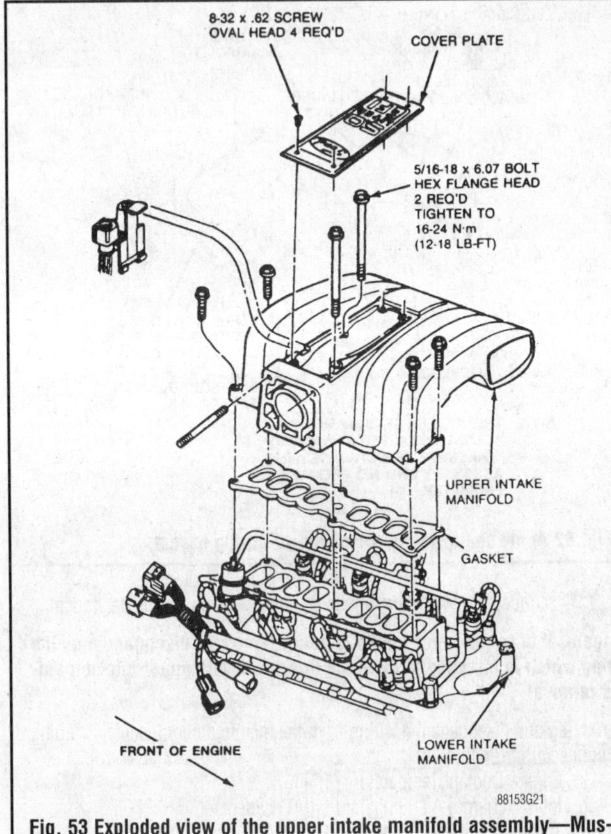

Fig. 53 Exploded view of the upper intake manifold assembly—Mustang 5.0L engine

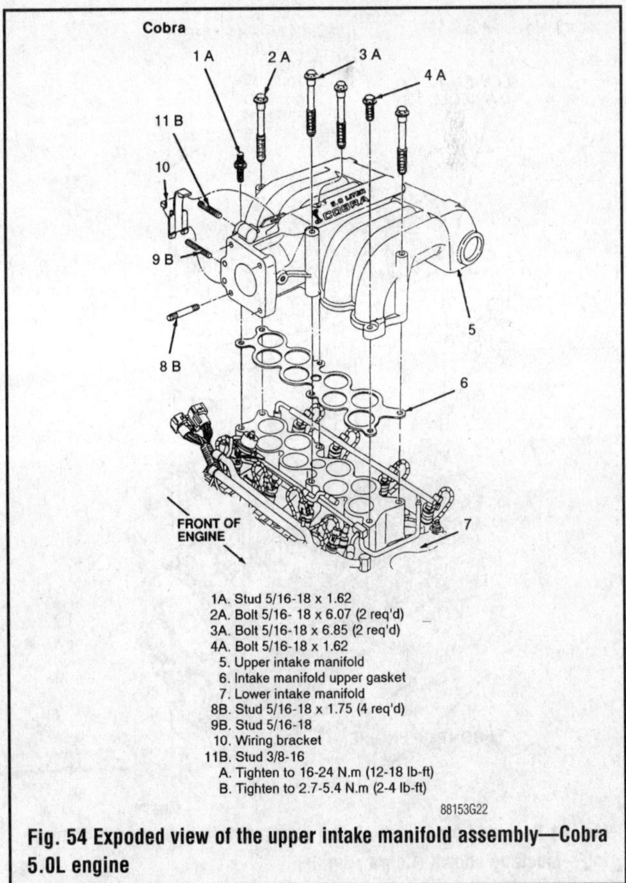

Fig. 54 Expoded view of the upper intake manifold assembly—Cobra 5.0L engine

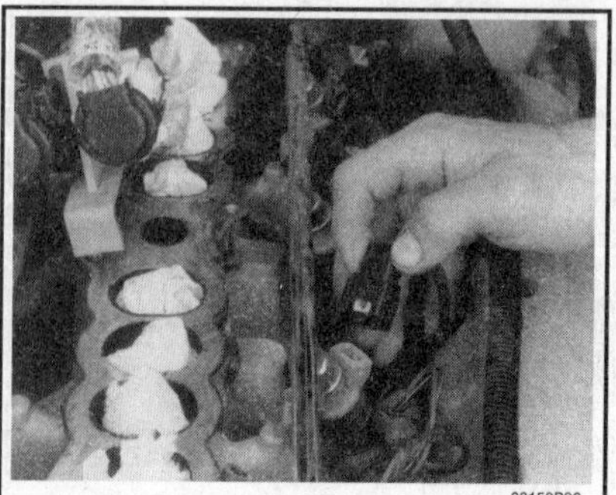

88153P26

Fig. 55 If the lower intake manifold is also being removed, unplug the injector wiring harness connectors . . .

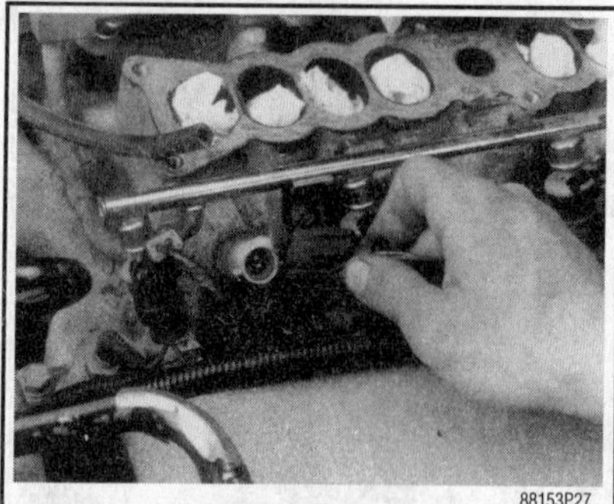

88153P27

Fig. 56 . . . along with any lower manifold wiring connectors which were not unplugged earlier

88153P28

Fig. 57 Make sure all wiring is disconnected from the lower manifold and nearby components

88153P29

Fig. 58 Loosen and remove the lower manifold retaining bolts

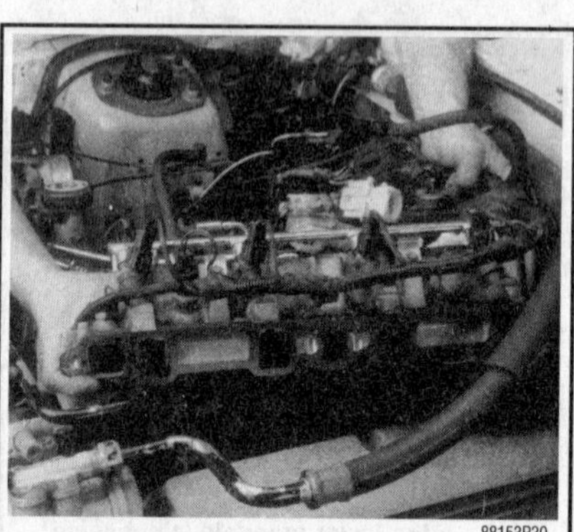

88153P30

Fig. 59 Then break the gasket seal by lifting the manifold from the engine

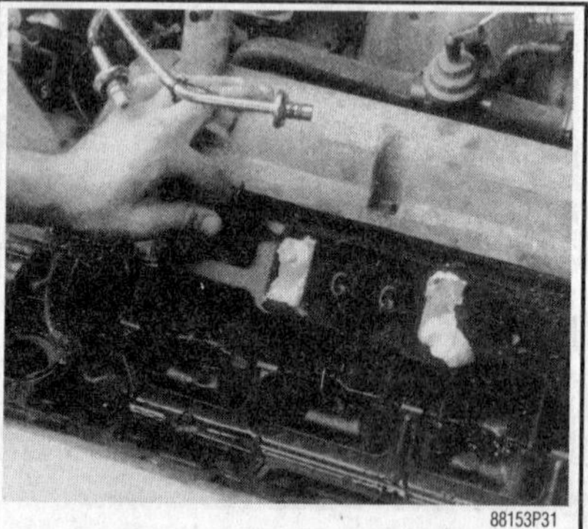

88153P31

Fig. 60 Again, keep debris from falling in the engine and remove the old gaskets

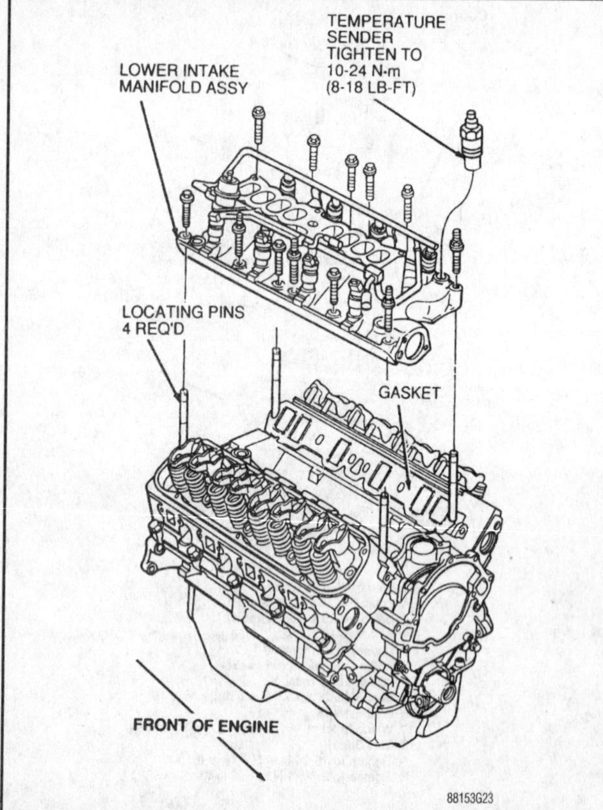

Fig. 61 Exploded view of the lower intake manifold assembly mounting—Mustang shown (Cobra similar)

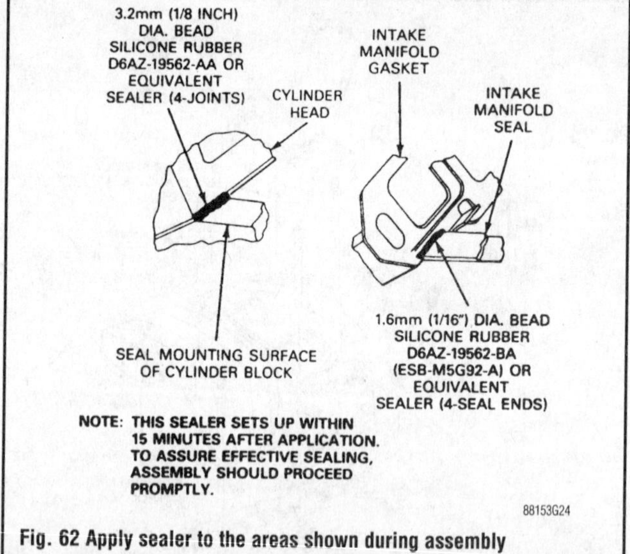

Fig. 62 Apply sealer to the areas shown during assembly

9. Disconnect the water pump bypass hose from the thermostat housing.

➡Again, if only the upper intake is being removed, disengage only the wiring which is attached to or which interferes with upper intake manifold removal.

10. Tag and disengage the wiring from the manifold components including the connectors from the:
   a. Engine Coolant Temperature (ECT).
   b. Intake (charge) Air Temperature (IAT) sensor.
   c. Throttle Position (TP) sensor.
   d. Idle Air Control (IAC) sensor.

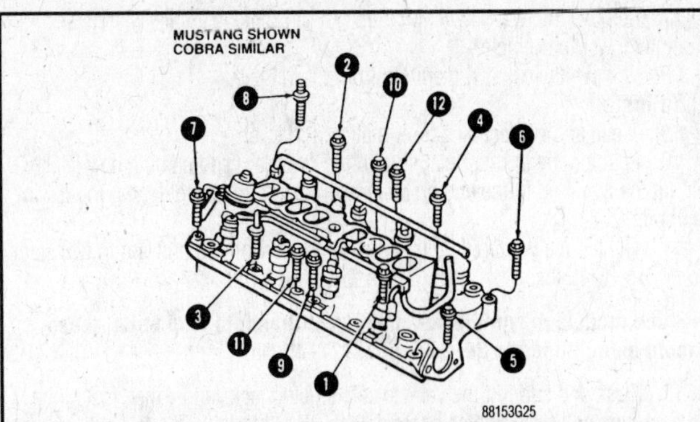

Fig. 63 Lower intake manifold torque sequence—Mustang shown (Cobra similar)

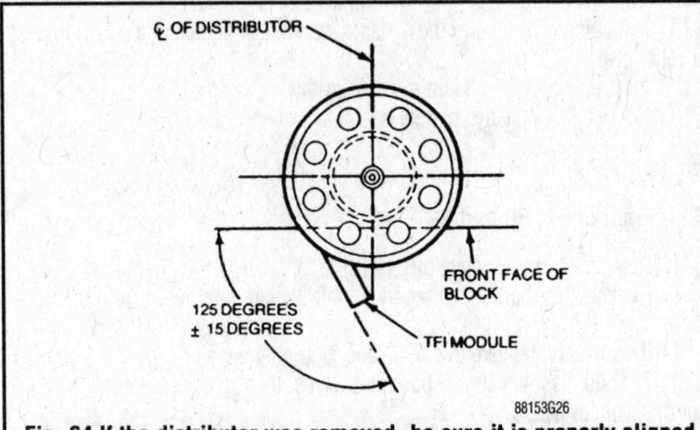

Fig. 64 If the distributor was removed, be sure it is properly aligned during installation

e. EGR sensors.
f. Injector wire connections.
g. Fuel charging assembly wiring.

11. Remove the PCV valve from the grommet at the rear of the lower intake manifold.
12. Disconnect the fuel evaporative purge hose from the plastic connector at the front of the upper intake manifold.
13. Remove the upper intake manifold cover plate and upper intake bolts. Remove the upper intake manifold.

➡Stop here if you are only removing the upper intake manifold assembly. Be sure to remove all old gasket material and to inspect the gasket mating surfaces before installation.

14. If equipped, remove the heater tube assembly from the lower intake manifold studs.
15. Remove the lower intake manifold retaining bolts and remove the lower intake manifold.

➡If it is necessary to pry the lower intake manifold away from the cylinder heads, be careful to avoid damaging the gasket sealing surfaces.

To install:

16. Clean all gasket mating surfaces. Apply a ⅛ in. (3mm) bead of silicone sealer to the points where the cylinder block rails meet the cylinder heads.
17. Position new seals on the cylinder block and new gaskets on the cylinder heads with the gaskets interlocked with the seal tabs. Make sure the holes in the gaskets are aligned with the holes in the cylinder heads.
18. Apply a 3/16 in. (5mm) bead of sealer to the outer end of each intake manifold seal for the full width of the seal. Make sure the silicone sealer will not fall into the engine and possibly block oil passages.
19. Using guide pins to ease installation, carefully lower the intake manifold into position on the cylinder block and cylinder heads.

➡After the intake manifold is in place, run a finger around the seal area to make sure the seals are in place. If the seals are not in place, remove the intake manifold and position the seals.

20. Make sure the holes in the manifold gaskets and the manifold are in alignment. Remove the guide pins.
21. Install the intake manifold attaching bolts and tighten, in 3 passes of the sequence:
    a. First tighten to 8 ft. lbs. (11 Nm).
    b. Then tighten to 16 ft. lbs. (22 Nm).
    c. Finally, tighten the bolts to 23–25 ft. lbs. (31–34 Nm).
22. Install the heater tube assembly to the lower intake manifold studs.
23. Install the water pump bypass hose on the thermostat housing. Install the hoses to the heater tubes. Connect the upper radiator hose.
24. Connect the fuel lines, then temporarily connect the negative battery cable. Cycle the ignition to pressurize the fuel system and check for leaks. Turn the ignition key back and forth (from **ON** to **OFF**) at least 6 times, leaving the key **ON** for 5 seconds each time. If no leaks are found, disconnect the negative battery cable and continue the installation.
25. If removed, install the distributor, aligning the housing and rotor with the marks that were made during removal. Install the distributor cap. Position the spark plug wires in the harness brackets on the rocker arm cover attaching stud and connect the wires to the spark plugs.

➡If the engine was moved with the distributor out, rotate the crankshaft until the No. 1 piston is at TDC of the compression stroke. Align the correct initial timing mark with the pointer, then position the distributor in the block with the rotor at the No. 1 firing position and install the hold-down clamp. For more information on distributor removal and installation, and for helpful hints on figuring out when the engine is at TDC, please refer to the distributor and timing procedures in Section 1 of this manual.

26. Install a new gasket and the upper intake manifold. Tighten the bolts to 12–18 ft. lbs. (16–24 Nm). Install the cover plate and connect the crankcase vent tube.
27. Connect the accelerator cable, TV cable and cruise control cable, as equipped, to the throttle body.
28. Engage the wiring connectors and vacuum lines as tagged during removal.
29. Connect the coolant hoses to the EGR spacer.
30. Install the air intake duct assembly and the crankcase vent hose.
31. Connect the negative battery cable, then fill and bleed the cooling system.
32. Run the engine to normal operating temperature and check for leaks.
33. Operate the engine at fast idle. When engine temperatures have stabilized, check the intake manifold bolt torque values.
34. If the lower intake was removed and/or the distributor was disturbed, check the ignition timing.

Exhaust Manifold

REMOVAL & INSTALLATION

➡Exhaust fasteners often rust in position and are easily rounded, broken or otherwise stripped. If possible allow the engine to thoroughly cool, then apply a penetrating lubricant to the retainers and allow it to soak in before removal.

✲✲ CAUTION

Use extra caution when working around rusted exhaust manifold fasteners, they can break loose or just plain break suddenly causing your hand and tools to jerk. Always position yourself properly to prevent a fall and be sure to pull on the wrench and not push on it.

2.3L Engine

➧ See Figures 65 and 66

1. Disconnect the negative battery cable for safety.
2. Remove the air cleaner and duct assembly.
3. Remove the EGR tube at the exhaust manifold and loosen the EGR valve.
4. Disconnect and, if necessary, remove the oxygen sensor from the exhaust manifold.

5. Remove the 8 exhaust manifold bolts, engine lifting eye and, if equipped, the heat shield.
6. Raise and support the vehicle safely using jackstands.

➡If the vehicle is supported at a level that allows access to both the top and bottom of the engine, you will not have to keep raising and lowering the vehicle for this procedure.

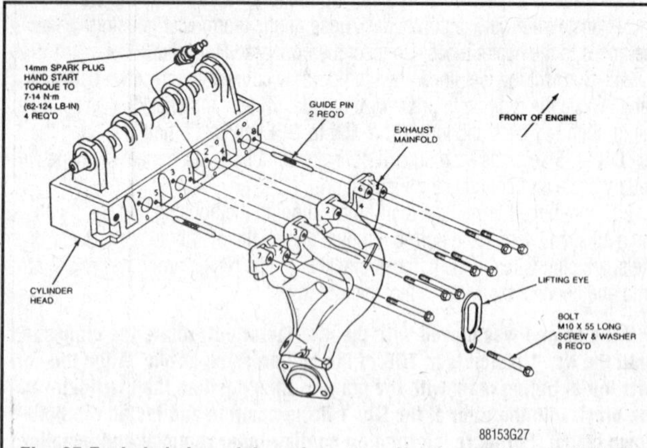

Fig. 65 Exploded view of the exhaust manifold assembly—2.3L (VIN A) engine

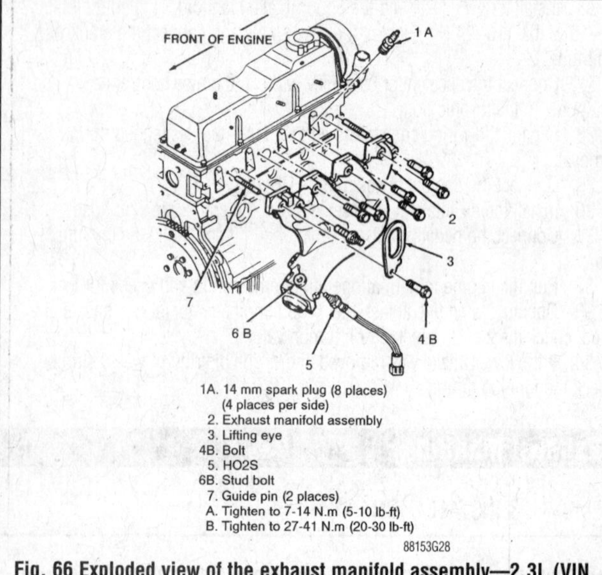

Fig. 66 Exploded view of the exhaust manifold assembly—2.3L (VIN M) engine

7. Remove the two exhaust pipe bolts, then remove the jackstands and carefully lower the vehicle.
8. Remove the exhaust manifold from the vehicle.

To install:

9. Clean and inspect all gasket mating surfaces.
10. Position the exhaust manifold to the cylinder head using a new gasket. Mount the manifold to the engine by threading and finger-tightening the retaining bolts.
11. Tighten the manifold bolts from the center working outward in two steps, first to 15–17 ft. lbs. (20–30 Nm), then to 20–30 ft. lbs. (27–41 Nm).

➡Some models may utilize as many as 3 manifold stud bolts, these should be tightened to 20–33 ft. lbs. (27–45 Nm).

12. Raise and support the vehicle safely using jackstands, then install the exhaust pipe bolts and tighten alternately to 25–34 ft. lbs. (36–46 Nm).
13. Remove the jackstands and carefully lower the vehicle.
14. If equipped, install the heat shield and tighten the retaining nuts to 20–29 ft. lbs. (27–41 Nm).
15. Connect and/or install the oxygen sensor, as applicable.
16. Install the EGR tube to the exhaust manifold and tighten the EGR tube at the EGR valve.
17. Install the air cleaner and duct assembly.
18. Connect the negative battery cable.

5.0L Engine

See Figures 67, 68 and 69

1. Disconnect the negative battery cable for safety.
2. Remove the Thermactor/secondary air injection hardware from the right exhaust manifold.
3. If necessary, remove the air cleaner and inlet duct.
4. Tag and disconnect the spark plug wires, then remove the spark plugs from the cylinder heads.
5. If necessary, disconnect the engine oil dipstick tube from the exhaust manifold stud.

➡If the vehicle is supported at a level that allows access to both the top and bottom of the engine, you will not have to keep raising and lowering the vehicle for this procedure.

6. Raise and support the vehicle safely using jackstands.
7. Disconnect the exhaust pipes from the exhaust manifolds.
8. If necessary, remove the engine oil dipstick tube by carefully tapping upward on the tube.
9. If necessary, disengage the oxygen sensor connector. If the manifold or sensor is being replaced, remove the sensor.
10. Unless upper engine access is possible in the current position, remove the jackstands and carefully lower the vehicle.
11. Remove the attaching bolts and washers, then remove the exhaust manifolds.

To install:

12. Clean and inspect all gasket mating surfaces.
13. Position the exhaust manifold to the cylinder head using a new gasket.

Fig. 67 On some models, it is necessary to remove the engine dipstick before the exhaust manifold

Fig. 68 From underneath the vehicle, loosen the exhaust pipe-to-manifold retainers

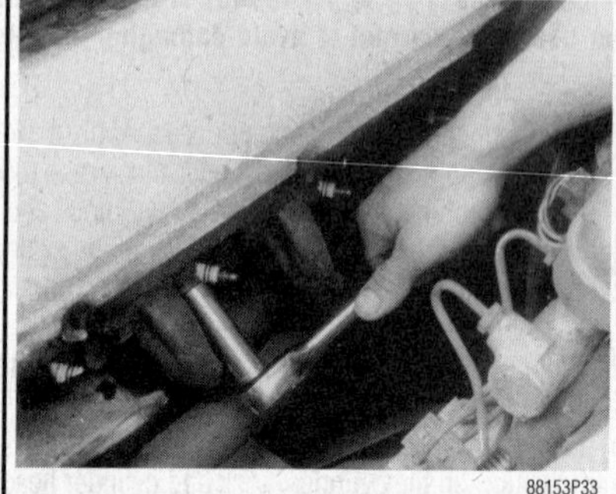

Fig. 69 Use a socket or box wrench on the manifold bolts—avoid open-end wrenches as these bolts are easily stripped

Retain the manifold to the engine by threading and finger-tightening the mounting bolts.

14. Working from the center to the ends, tighten the exhaust manifold attaching bolts to 18–24 ft. lbs. (24–32 Nm) for 1989–92 vehicles or to 26–32 ft. lbs. for 1993 vehicles.
15. If lowered for access, raise and support the vehicle safely using jackstands.
16. As applicable, install the engine oil dipstick tube, then install the oxygen sensor and engage the connector.
17. Position the exhaust pipes to the manifolds. Alternately tighten the exhaust pipe flange nuts to 20–30 ft. lbs. (27–41 Nm).
18. Remove the jackstands and carefully lower the vehicle.
19. Install the spark plugs and connect the spark plug wires.
20. If removed, install the Thermactor/air injection hardware to the right exhaust manifold.
21. If removed, install the air cleaner and inlet duct.
22. Connect the negative battery cable, then start the engine and check for exhaust leaks.

Radiator

REMOVAL & INSTALLATION

➧ See Figures 70 thru 79

✲✲ CAUTION

When draining the coolant, keep in mind that cats and dogs are attracted by ethylene glycol antifreeze, and are quite likely to drink any that is left in an uncovered container or in puddles on the ground. This will prove fatal in sufficient quantity. Always drain the coolant into a sealable container. Coolant should be reused unless it is contaminated or too old.

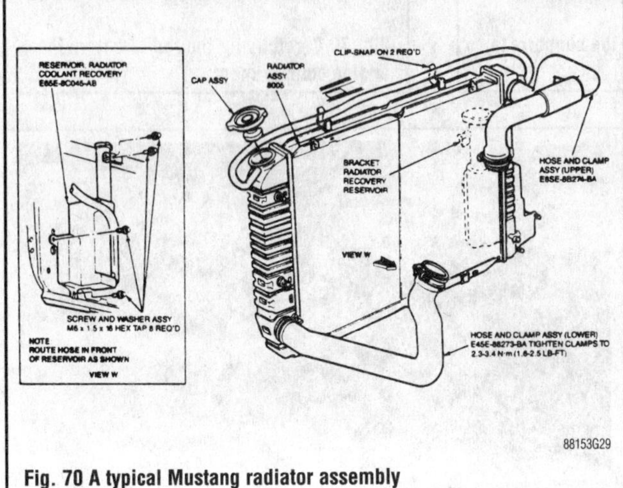

Fig. 70 A typical Mustang radiator assembly

1. Disconnect the negative battery cable for safety. On vehicles with an electric cooling fan, the fan could come on at any time.

➡Before draining the cooling system is a good time to decide if it is time to replace your coolant. If not, the drain pan must be clean and free of oil or other contaminants so that the coolant can be reused. For more information, please refer to the Fluids and Lubricants information in Section 1 of this manual.

2. Make sure the engine is cool, then remove the radiator cap and drain the engine cooling system into a suitable container.
3. Disconnect the upper, lower and coolant reservoir hoses at the radiator.
4. If equipped with an automatic transmission, disconnect the fluid cooler lines at the radiator. Depending on the year and model, your vehicle may used threaded fittings (on which a backup wrench should be used to prevent damage to the radiator) or quick-connect coupling fittings which require a special release tool.

➡On vehicles equipped with automatic transmissions and quick connect couplings, disconnect the fluid cooler lines at the radiator using oil cooler line quick connect coupling tool T82L-9500-AH or equivalent.

5. On the 2.3L engine, remove the electric cooling fan/shroud assembly.
6. On the 5.0L engine, remove the two upper fan shroud retaining bolts at the radiator support, lift the fan shroud sufficiently to disengage the lower retaining clips and lay the shroud back over the fan.
7. On some models the coolant overflow bottle is bolted to the radiator. If so, you can ease radiator removal by unbolting and removing the overflow bottle.
8. Remove the radiator upper support retaining bolts and remove the supports. Lift the radiator from the vehicle.

To install:

9. If a new radiator is to be installed, transfer the petcock from the old radiator to the new one. If equipped with automatic transmission and quick connect couplings, transfer the fluid cooler line fittings from the old radiator. Use a pipe sealant with Teflon® or equivalent oil resistant sealer.
10. Position the radiator assembly into the vehicle. Install the upper supports and the retaining bolts. If equipped with automatic transmission, connect the fluid cooler lines.
11. If removed, install the coolant overflow bottle.
12. On the 2.3L engine, install the electric cooling fan/shroud assembly.
13. On the 5.0L engine, place the fan shroud into the clips on the lower radiator support and install the two upper shroud retaining bolts. Position the shroud to maintain a minimum of 0.38 in. (9.7mm) clearance between the fan blades and the shroud.
14. Connect the radiator hoses. Close the radiator petcock.
15. Connect the negative battery cable, then fill and bleed the cooling system.
16. Run the engine to normal operating temperature. Check for coolant and transmission fluid leaks.

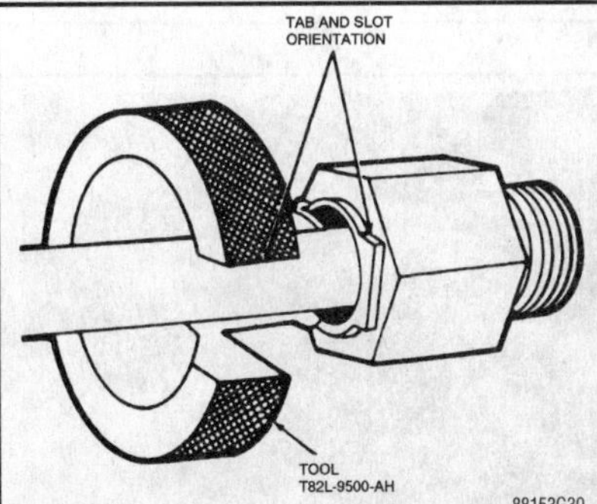

Fig. 71 Automatic transmission quick connect couplings are removed disengaged using a special fitting tool

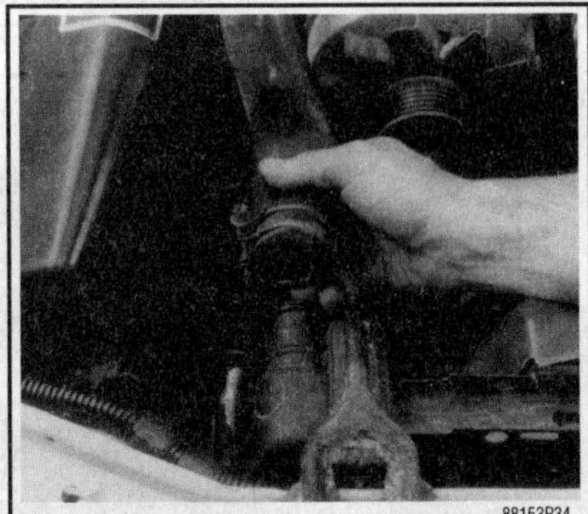

Fig. 72 Disconnect the hoses from the radiator

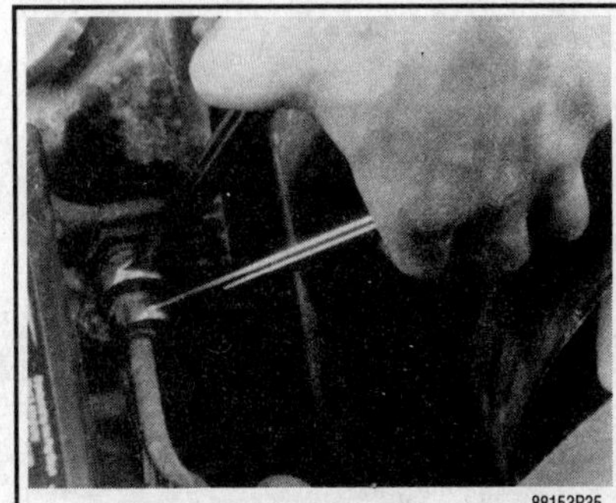

Fig. 73 On A/T vehicles, disconnect the cooler lines (threaded lines and a backup wrench shown)

88153P36

Fig. 74 Unbolt the fan shroud from the radiator

88153P37

Fig. 75 On some vehicles the coolant overflow bottle is bolted to the radiator . . .

88153P38

Fig. 76 . . . radiator removal on these vehicles may be easier if you first remove the bottle

88153P39

Fig. 77 Loosen and remove the radiator upper support retainer bolts . . .

88153P40

Fig. 78 . . . then remove the supports to free the radiator

88153P41

Fig. 79 Carefully lift the radiator from the engine compartment

17. Shut the engine **OFF**, then check the coolant and transmission fluid levels.

Engine Cooling Fan—Mechanical

All 5.0L engines covered by this manual are equipped with a belt driven engine cooling fan clutch and fan assembly. The 2.3L engines are instead equipped with a radiator mounted electric cooling fan.

REMOVAL & INSTALLATION

See Figures 80, 81 and 82

1. Disconnect the negative battery cable for safety.
2. Remove the fan shroud screws and move the shroud back away from the radiator.
3. Relieve the drive belt tension at the tensioner and slip the belt off one or more of the pulleys for free-play.

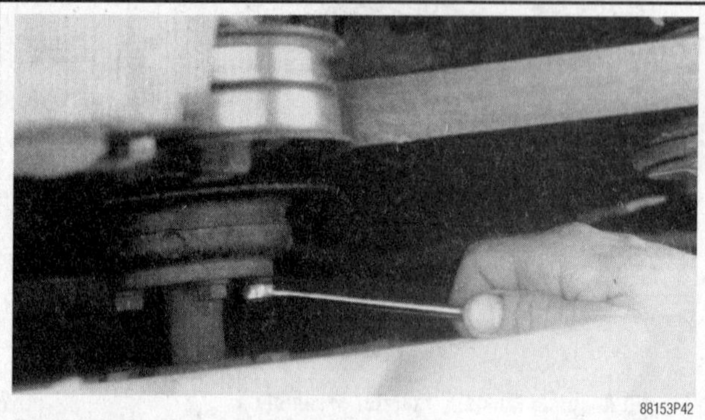
88153P42

Fig. 81 Use a box or open-end wrench to loosen the fan clutch-to-water pump hub retaining bolts

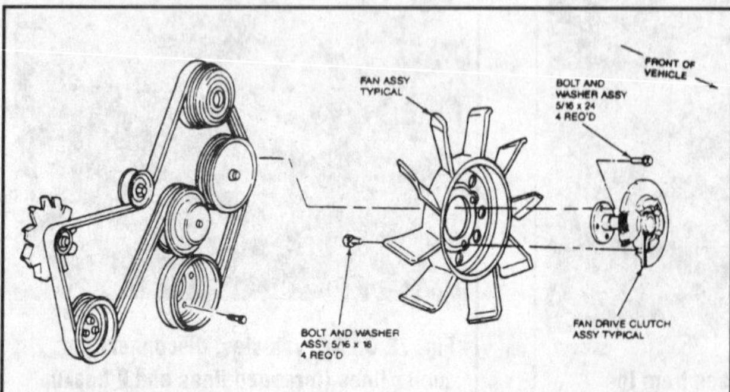

88153G31

Fig. 80 Exploded view of a typical Mustang 5.0L engine cooling fan and clutch mounting

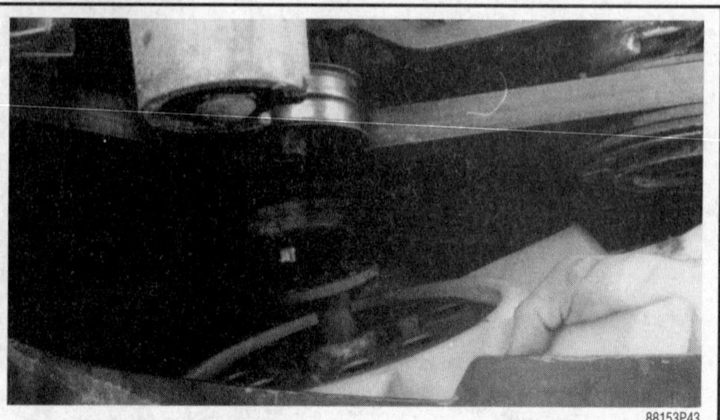
88153P43

Fig. 82 Once the bolts are removed, the clutch and fan assembly can be removed along with the fan shroud

4. Remove the bolts and washers retaining the fan clutch to the water pump hub.
5. Lift the clutch and fan assembly, along with the fan shroud from the engine compartment.
6. If necessary, remove the fan-to-clutch retaining bolts and separate the fan from the fan clutch.

** CAUTION

Examine the fan closely for cracks or separation. A damaged fan can cause serious personal injury or vehicle damage.

To install:

7. If separated, assemble the fan and fan clutch using the bolts and washers. Tighten the retaining bolts to 12–17 ft. lbs. (16–24 Nm).
8. Position the fan and clutch assembly inside the fan shroud, then lower them into the engine compartment. Position the shroud the best you can to keep it out of your way (an assistant can be very helpful for this).
9. Mount the fan clutch on the water pump hub by threading and finger-tightening the bolts and washers. Once all of the bolts are threaded and run-in, tighten them alternately and evenly to 15–22 ft. lbs. (20–30 Nm).
10. Using the belt tensioner, properly reposition the drive belt over all of the pulleys. Check for proper belt alignment.
11. Reposition the fan shroud. If necessary, adjust the shroud for equal clearance around the fan with a minimum clearance of 0.38 in. (9.6mm). Install and tighten the retaining screws.
12. Connect the negative battery cable.

Engine Cooling Fan—Electric

The 2.3L engines covered by this manual are equipped with a radiator mounted electric cooling fan. All 5.0L engines are instead equipped with a belt driven engine cooling fan clutch and fan assembly.

TESTING

See Figure 83

The single speed electric cooling fan is attached to the fan shroud behind the radiator. The system is wired to operate only with the ignition switch in the **RUN** position. The cooling fan is controlled either by a cooling fan control module (early models) or by a solid state Constant Control Relay Module (CCRM) and the engine control computer.

On early models, the cooling fan temperature switch will close at temperatures above 221°F (105°C) providing ground to the relay terminal which receives power from the ignition switch. At this point the relay will close the circuit from the fuse link providing voltage to the engine cooling fan. The A/C fan control relay and timing control circuit can also provide ground to the fan control relay. A wide-open throttle cut-out control is incorporated into the timing control.

On late models, the CCRM will energize the fan with power from the fuse link when it and the engine control module receive input from the temperature switch indicating that the engine coolant temperature has reached at least 221°F (105°C). It will stop the fan once the temperature drops below 200°F (90°C). They will also activate the cooling fan if the A/C is on and the vehicle speed does not provide a sufficient airflow (energizes fan below 43 mph/69 kmph and stops fan at or above 48 mph/77 kmph).

A quick check of the fan itself can be made by circumventing the control circuit and providing battery voltage directly to the motor. If the fan works with the control circuit by-passed, then the control circuit is at fault. If the fan still does not work, then the motor should be checked for binding or damage and repaired or replaced.

1. Disengage the electrical connector at the cooling fan motor.
2. Connect a jumper wire between the negative motor lead and ground.
3. Connect another jumper wire between the positive motor lead and the positive terminal of the battery.
4. If the cooling fan motor does not run, it should be replaced. If the motor works, the control circuit is the problem and must be repaired.

REMOVAL & INSTALLATION

See Figure 84

** CAUTION

The cooling fan is automatic and may start any time without warning. To avoid possible injury, always disconnect the negative battery cable when working near the electric cooling fan.

1. Disconnect the negative battery cable for safety.
2. Remove the fan wiring harness from the routing clip. Disconnect the wiring harness from the fan motor connector by pulling up on the single lock finger to separate the connectors.
3. Remove the mounting bracket attaching screws (usually 4) and remove the fan assembly from the vehicle.
4. If necessary, the fan and motor can be separated to replace either of the components:
   a. Remove the retaining clip from the end of the motor shaft and remove the fan.

➡A metal burr may be present on the motor after the retaining clip is removed. Deburring of the shaft may be required to remove the fan.

   b. Remove the nuts attaching the fan motor to the mounting bracket.

To install:

5. If separated for replacement, assembly the fan and motor:
   a. Position the motor on the shroud bracket and install the retaining nuts. Tighten the nuts to 49–62 inch lbs. (5.5–7.0 Nm).
   b. Install the fan on the motor shaft using the retaining clip.

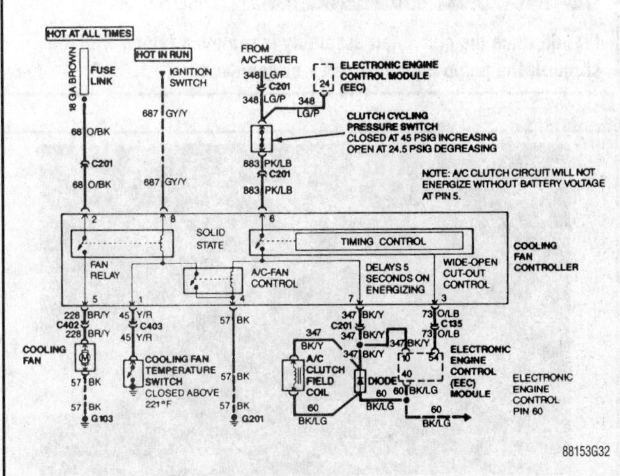

Fig. 83 Engine cooling fan electrical schematic—early model vehicles utilizing the cooling fan controller and relay

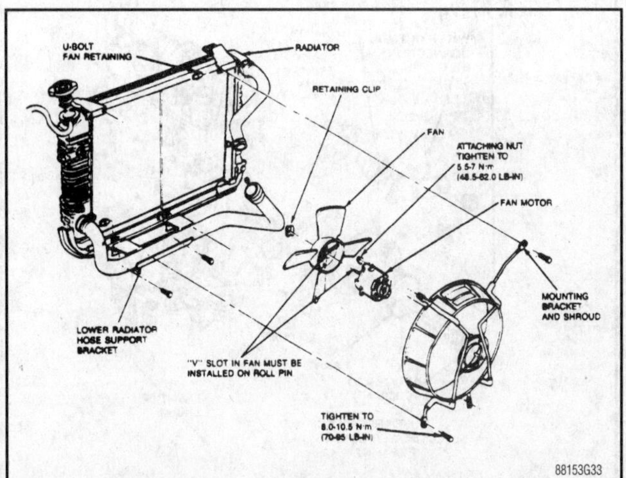

Fig. 84 Exploded view of the cooling fan, motor and shroud assembly—2.3L engine

6. Position the fan and shroud assembly in the vehicle, then install the mounting bracket retaining screws. Tighten the screws to 70–95 inch lbs. (8.0–10.5 Nm).
7. Engage the motor wiring connector to the harness. Make sure the lock finger on the connector snaps firmly into place.
8. Connect the negative battery cable.
9. Run the engine and check for proper fan operation.

Water Pump

REMOVAL & INSTALLATION

CAUTION

When draining the coolant, keep in mind that cats and dogs are attracted by ethylene glycol antifreeze, and are quite likely to drink any that is left in an uncovered container or in puddles on the ground. This will prove fatal in sufficient quantity. Always drain the coolant into a sealable container. Coolant should be reused unless it is contaminated or too old.

2.3L Engine

See Figure 85

1. Disconnect the negative battery cable for safety.
2. Drain the engine cooling system to a level below the water pump assembly.
3. Remove the four bolts retaining the pulley to the water pump shaft.
4. Remove the electric cooling fan and shroud assembly. For details, refer to the procedure found earlier in this section.
5. Remove the air conditioning and power steering belts, as equipped.
6. Remove the water pump pulley.
7. Disconnect the heater hose and lower radiator hose from the water pump.

A provision has been made in the inner timing belt cover to allow wrench clearance. Because of this, only the outer timing belt cover must be removed in order to replace the water pump.

8. Loosen the retaining bolt, then release the interlocking tabs and remove the outer timing belt cover.
9. Remove the water pump retaining bolts, then remove the water pump.

To install:

10. Thoroughly clean the mating surfaces of old gasket material and inspect them for damage.

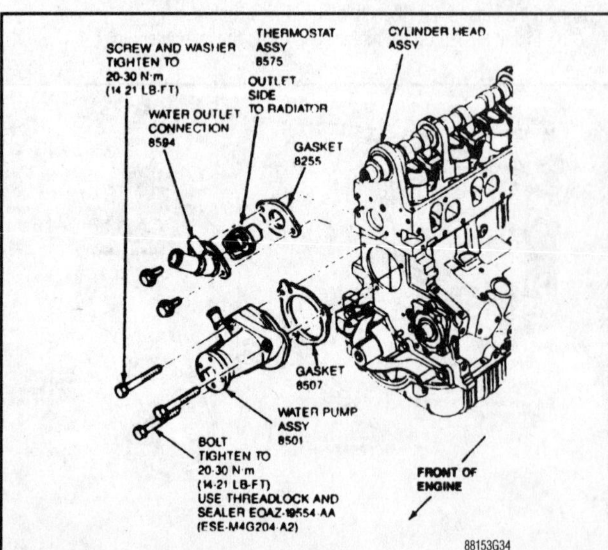

Fig. 85 Exploded view of the water pump assembly mounting—2.3L engine

11. Position the gasket to the water pump using contact cement.
12. Apply a pipe sealant with Teflon® to the 3 water pump retaining bolts, then position the pump to the engine and install the bolts. Tighten the bolts to 14–21 ft. lbs. (20–30 Nm)
13. Connect the lower radiator hose and the heater hose to the water pump.
14. Install the outer timing belt cover and tighten the retaining bolt to 6–9 ft. lbs. (8–12 Nm).
15. Position the water pump pulley over the pump hub and secure using the retaining bolts. Tighten the pulley retaining bolts to 15–22 ft. lbs. (20–30 Nm).
16. Position and install the power steering drive belt and, if equipped, the A/C drive belt.
17. Connect the negative battery cable, then refill and bleed the cooling system.
18. Operate the engine until normal operating temperatures have been reached and check for leaks.

5.0L Engine

See Figures 86 thru 93

1. Disconnect the negative battery cable for safety.
2. Drain the cooling system.
3. Remove the air inlet tube.
4. Remove the fan shroud attaching bolts and position the shroud over the fan.
5. Remove the fan and clutch assembly from the water pump shaft, then remove the clutch, fan and shroud from the vehicle.
6. Remove the accessory drive belt, then remove the water pump pulley.
7. Remove all accessory brackets that attach to the water pump.
8. Disconnect the lower radiator hose, heater hose and water pump bypass hose from the water pump.
9. Remove the water pump attaching bolts, then remove the water pump and discard the gasket.

To install:

10. Clean all old gasket material from the timing cover and water pump.
11. Apply a suitable waterproof sealing compound to both sides of a new gasket, then position the gasket on the timing cover.

Fig. 86 Once the clutch/fan assembly is removed (along with the shroud), the pump pulley can also be removed

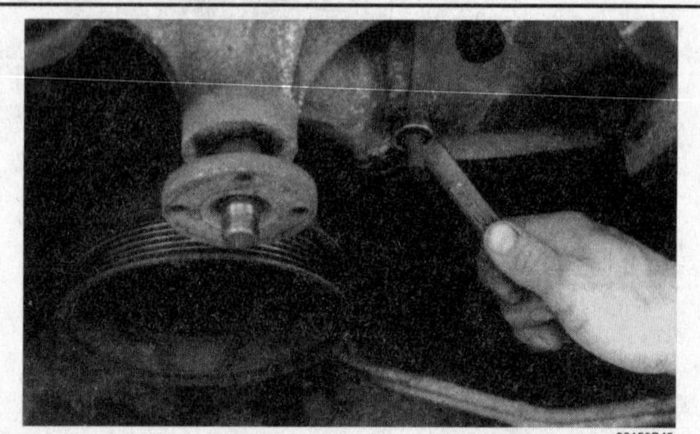

Fig. 87 Loosen and remove any accessory bracket retainers which attach to the water pump

Fig. 88 This A/C compressor bracket must also be unbolted from the A/C compressor . . .

Fig. 89 . . . and completely removed from the engine for access to the water pump

Fig. 90 Loosen the clamps and disconnect the hoses from the water pump assembly

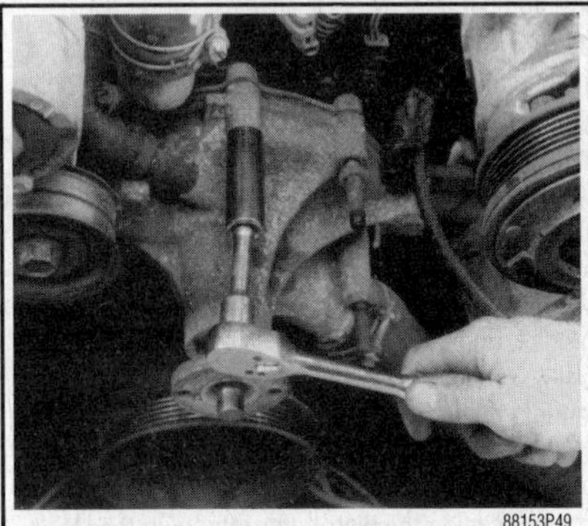

Fig. 91 Loosen and remove the water pump retaining bolts

Fig. 92 With the bolts removed, grasp the water pump and pull it from the engine to break the gasket seal

Fig. 93 To assure a proper seal, remove traces of the old gasket (being careful not to damage the surfaces)

12. Position the water pump carefully over the gasket (making sure not to dislodge it). Install and tighten the pump mounting bolts to 12–18 ft. lbs. (16–24 Nm).
13. Connect the hoses and accessory brackets to the water pump.
14. Install the pulley on the water pump shaft.
15. Install the shroud along with the clutch and fan assembly.
16. Route and install the accessory drive belt.
17. Connect the negative battery cable and refill the cooling system.
18. Run the engine and check for leaks.

Cylinder Head

REMOVAL & INSTALLATION

** CAUTION

When draining the coolant, keep in mind that cats and dogs are attracted by ethylene glycol antifreeze, and are quite likely to drink any that is left in an uncovered container or in puddles on the ground. This will prove fatal in sufficient quantity. Always drain the coolant into a sealable container. Coolant should be reused unless it is contaminated or too old.

2.3L Engine

See Figures 94 and 95

1. Disconnect the negative battery cable for safety.
2. Drain the cooling system and relieve the fuel system pressure.
3. Remove the air cleaner.

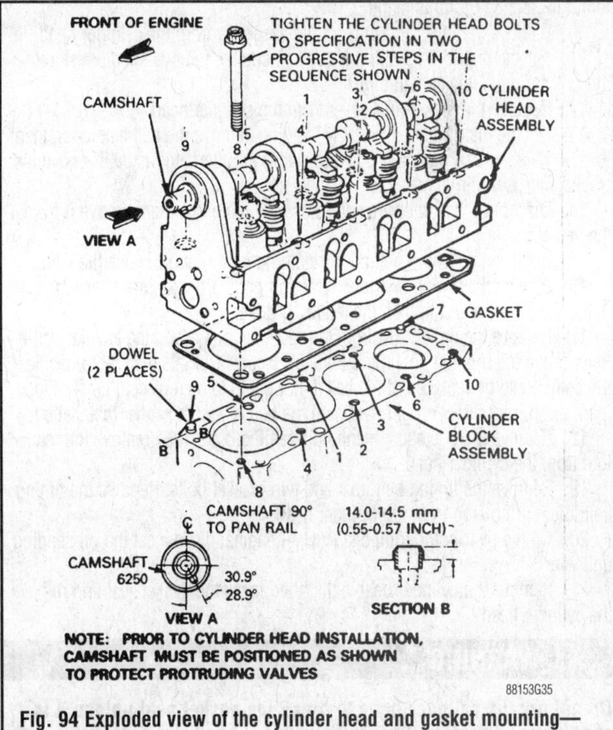

Fig. 94 Exploded view of the cylinder head and gasket mounting—2.3L engine

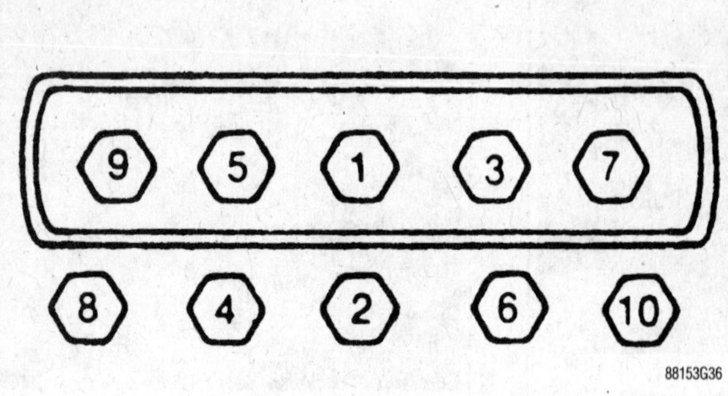

Fig. 95 Cylinder head bolt torque sequence—2.3L engine

➡Before removing the spark plug wires, check the configuration of your engine against the firing order diagrams found in Section 2 of this manual. If your engine is different in any way, make notations to the diagrams to assure proper installation. Also, be sure to tag all of the spark plug wires and the distributor cap or ignition coil pack terminals, as applicable.

4. Tag and remove the spark plug wires, then remove the spark plugs.
5. On the distributor equipped (VIN A) engine, remove the heater hose retaining screw from the rocker arm cover, then matchmark and remove the distributor assembly.
6. On the distributorless (VIN M) engine, tag and disconnect the engine and alternator harnesses.
7. Tag and disconnect the required vacuum hoses.
8. Remove the dipstick. On the distributorless (VIN M) engine, disconnect the dipstick tube from the bracket.
9. Remove the upper intake manifold and throttle body assembly (along with the EGR tube on distributorless VIN M engines). For details, please refer to the intake manifold procedure in this section and the throttle body procedure found in Section 5 of this manual.
10. Remove the lower intake manifold assembly from the cylinder head.
11. For the distributor equipped (VIN A) engine, remove the dipstick retaining bolt from the intake manifold.
12. Remove the rocker arm cover from the cylinder head.
13. For the distributorless (VIN M) engine, remove the belt tensioner, then loosen the alternator retaining bolt and swing the alternator aside. Remove the ribbed accessory drive belt.
14. Disconnect the upper radiator hose at both ends, then remove it from the vehicle.
15. Remove the timing belt cover retaining bolt(s) and remove the cover.
16. Loosen the timing belt idler retaining bolts. Position the idler in the unloaded position and tighten the retaining bolts.
17. Remove the timing belt from the camshaft pulley and the auxiliary pulley. Refer to the information on Timing Belts in Section 1 of this manual to decide if the belt should be replaced. If the belt is not going to be replaced, be sure to mark the current direction of rotation on the belt to assure proper installation.
18. Remove the 8 exhaust manifold retaining bolts, then remove the manifold from the cylinder head.
19. Remove the timing belt idler and two bracket bolts. Remove the timing belt idler spring stop from the cylinder head.
20. On the distributor equipped (VIN A) engine, disconnect the oil sending unit wire.
21. Remove the cylinder head bolts, then break the gasket seal and remove the cylinder head.

⁂ WARNING

Do not pry the cylinder head to break the gasket seal unless it is absolutely necessary. Prying the cylinder head can deform the soft metal and compromise the gasket mating surfaces.

To install:

22. Clean all gasket mating surfaces and blow the oil out of the cylinder head bolt block holes.
23. Check the cylinder head for flatness using a straightedge and a feeler gauge. If the head gasket surface is warped greater than 0.006 in. (0.152mm), it must be resurfaced. Do not grind off more than 0.010 in. (0.254mm) from the cylinder head.
24. Position a new cylinder head gasket on the engine. Rotate the camshaft so that the locating pin is approximately 30 degrees to the right of the 6 o' clock position when facing the front of the cylinder head (this places the pin about at the five o'clock position) to avoid damage to the valves and pistons.
25. If they are available, cut the heads off of two old cylinder head bolts to use as guide studs. Thread the studs into the engine block at opposite corners to use as guides.
26. Make sure the gasket is properly fit to the block, then set the head into place. Apply a non-hardening gasket sealer to the bolt threads and install the bolts finger-tight.
27. For 1989–92 vehicles, tighten the head bolts using 2 passes of the sequence, first to 50–60 ft. lbs. (68–81 Nm) and then to 80–90 ft. lbs. (108–122 Nm).
28. For 1993 vehicles, tighten the cylinder head bolts in 2 passes of the sequence to 52 ft. lbs. (70 Nm) and retighten to 52 ft. lbs. (70 Nm). Then, tighten the bolts an additional 90° plus or minus 10° in a third pass of the sequence. Although a torque angle meter is the best way to angle tighten bolts, you can get satisfactory results by painting or marking a line on the socket and watching it until a ¼ turn has been achieved.
29. On the distributor equipped (VIN A) engine, connect the oil sending unit wire.
30. Install the timing belt tensioner spring stop to the cylinder head.
31. Position the timing belt tensioner and tensioner spring to the cylinder head and install the retaining bolts. Rotate the tensioner against the spring with belt tensioner tool T74P–6254–A, or equivalent, and temporarily tighten.
32. Install the exhaust manifold using the 8 retaining bolts and a new gasket. For details, please refer to the Exhaust Manifold procedure found earlier in this section.
33. If equipped with a distributor, align the distributor rotor with the No. 1 plug location on the distributor cap and install.
34. Align the camshaft sprocket with the pointer and align the crankshaft pulley with the pointer on the timing belt cover.
35. Install the timing belt over the sprockets. If the belt is not being replaced, make sure you have installed it in the same direction of rotation as it was before removal.
36. Complete timing belt installation as detailed under the timing belt procedures located later in this section. Be sure to check belt tension and alignment, then to properly tighten the tensioner and pivot bolts.
37. Install the timing belt cover and tighten the retaining bolt(s) to 6–9 ft. lbs. (8–12 Nm).
38. Install the rocker arm cover and tighten the retaining bolts to 62–71 inch lbs. (7–11 Nm).
39. Install the lower intake manifold assembly. Tighten the bolts, in sequence, to 20–29 ft. lbs. (26–38 Nm).
40. Install the upper intake manifold and throttle body (along with the EGR tube assembly on VIN M engines). Tighten the upper intake-to-lower intake bolts to 15–22 ft. lbs. (20–30 Nm).
41. Install the upper radiator hose.
42. Connect the vacuum hoses as tagged during removal.
43. If removed, install the belt tensioner.
44. Position the alternator and install the drive belt.
45. Install the dipstick and, if applicable, secure the dipstick tube to the intake manifold using the retaining bolt.
46. On distributor equipped (VIN A) engines, install the distributor cap.
47. Install the spark plugs, then install the spark plug wires as tagged and noted during removal. Remember, that if your engine wiring didn't agree with the firing orders in Section 2, you should not try to make it agree now.
48. If not already installed, position and connect the engine and alternator wiring harnesses.
49. If equipped, install the heater hose retaining screw to the rocker arm cover.
50. Install the hose from the air cleaner to the throttle body.
51. Connect the negative battery cable, then fill and bleed the cooling system.
52. Bring the engine to normal operating temperature and check for leaks.
53. If equipped with distributor ignition, check the ignition timing.

5.0L Engine

➧ See Figures 96 thru 104

➡If the left cylinder head is being removed on vehicles equipped with A/C, the refrigerant system must be discharged and recovered using a suitable recovery station prior to starting the procedure. If you do not have the proper certification and access to the necessary equipment, take the vehicle to a service station and have the A/C system discharged before proceeding.

1. Disconnect the negative battery cable for safety.
2. Drain the cooling system and properly relieve the fuel system pressure.
3. Remove the upper and lower intake manifold assemblies, along with the throttle body. For details, please refer to the intake manifold procedures found earlier in this section.
4. If you are removing the left cylinder head:
   a. On vehicles equipped with A/C, properly discharge and recover the refrigerant from the air conditioning system, then remove the compressor.

✲✲ WARNING

Immediately cap or plug all openings to the air conditioning system in order to prevent system contamination and damage.

   b. If not done earlier, remove the drive belt from the power steering pump pulley, then disconnect the power steering pump bracket from the cylinder head. Position the pump out of the way in a position that will prevent the oil from draining out.
   c. Disconnect the oil level indicator tube bracket from the exhaust manifold stud, if necessary.
5. Remove the Thermactor/secondary air injection crossover tube from the rear of the cylinder heads.
6. If you are removing the right cylinder head:
   a. Disconnect the alternator or alternator and air pump mounting bracket from the cylinder head, as equipped.
   b. Remove the fuel line from the clip at the front of the cylinder head.
7. Raise and support the vehicle safely using jackstands. Disconnect the exhaust manifolds from the muffler inlet pipes, then remove the jackstands and carefully lower the vehicle.
8. Loosen the rocker arm fulcrum bolts so the rocker arms can be rotated to the side. Remove the pushrods and tag or arrange them in sequence so they may be installed in their original positions.

➡A piece of wood or cardboard may be drilled and labelled to help sort the pushrods and make sure they are only installed to the rocker arms and lifters from which they were removed.

9. Remove the cylinder head attaching bolts and the cylinder heads.Remove and discard the head gaskets.

➡It may be necessary to remove the exhaust manifolds for access to the lower head bolts. If so, be sure to thoroughly clean the gasket mating surfaces and to use new exhaust manifold gaskets upon installation.

10. Clean all gasket mating surfaces. Check the flatness of the cylinder head using a straightedge and a feeler gauge. The cylinder head must not be warped any more than 0.003 in. (0.076mm) in any 6 in. (152mm) span; 0.006 in. (0.152mm) overall. Machine if necessary. For details, please refer to the cylinder head inspection and refinishing procedures in this section.

To install:

11. Position the new cylinder head gasket over the dowels on the block. Position the cylinder heads on the block and install the head bolts.
12. For 1989–92 vehicles tighten the bolts, using 2 steps of the proper sequence. First tighten the bolts to 55–65 ft. lbs. (75–88 Nm), then to 65–72 ft. lbs. (88–98 Nm).

➡When the cylinder head bolts have been tightened following these procedures, it is not necessary (but it is permissible, if desired) to retighten the bolts after extended operation.

13. On 1993 vehicles, determine what type of head bolts are used in your engine. Standard non-flanged head bolts should be tightened using the same 2 steps and values as 1989–92 vehicles. Flanged hex head bolts should be tightened in three steps of the proper sequence. Start by tightening the bolts to

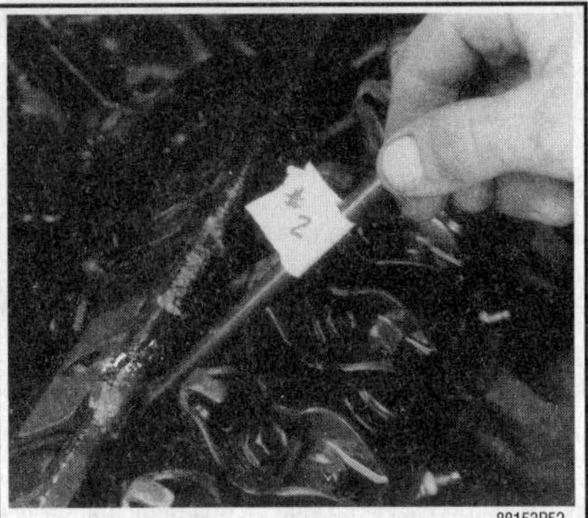
88153P52

Fig. 96 Label the pushrods to assure installation in the proper positions

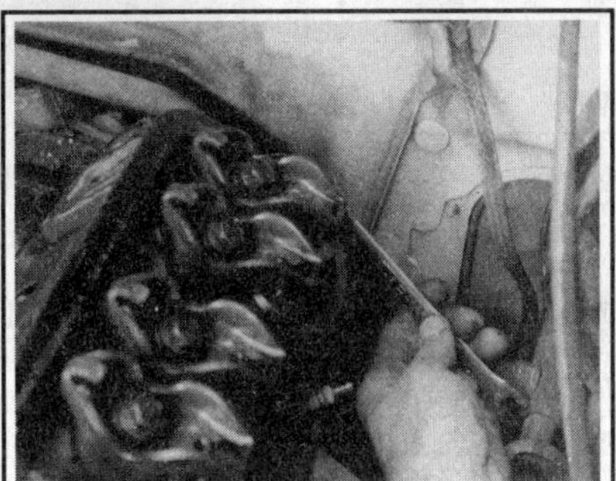
88153P53

Fig. 97 Remove the Thermactor/secondary air injection tube from the back of the cylinder heads

88153P54

Fig. 98 Loosen the cylinder head bolts using a breaker bar and socket

88153P55

Fig. 99 Lift the cylinder head from the block, breaking the gasket seal

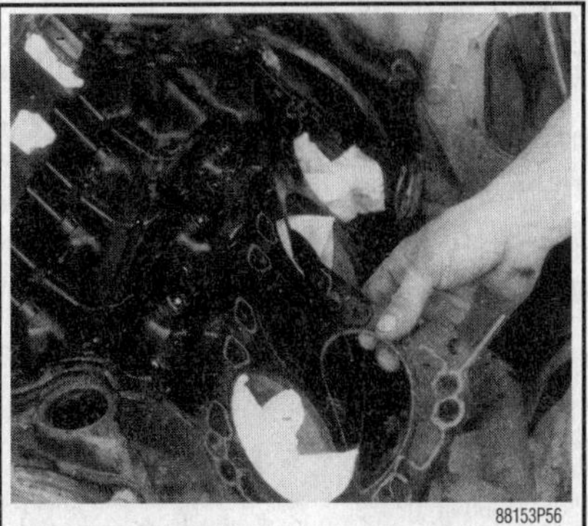
88153P56

Fig. 100 Remove the old gasket from the block

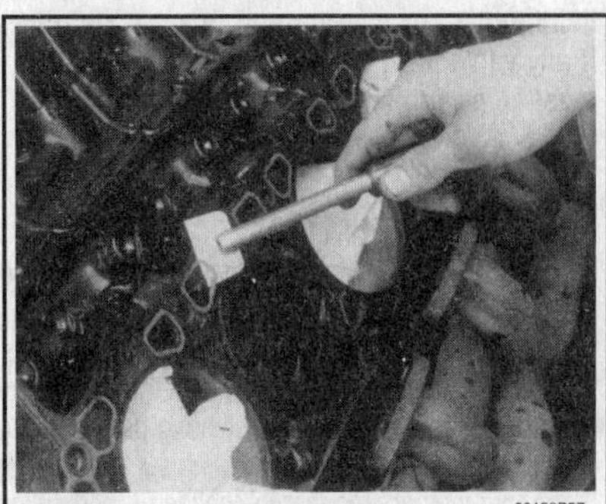
88153P57

Fig. 101 If you use a gasket scraper, be careful not to damage the surface and keep debris out of the cylinders

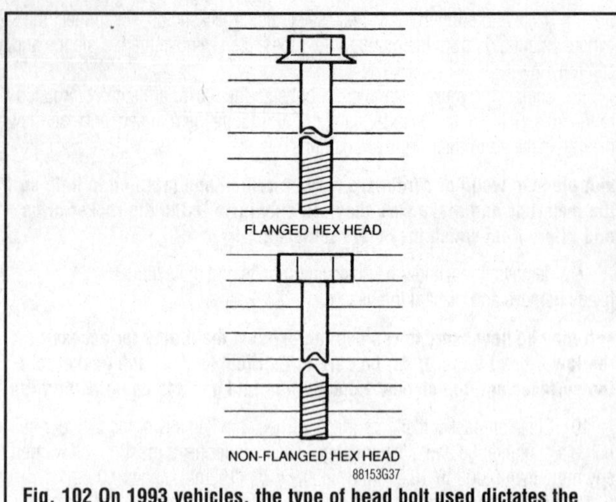

Fig. 102 On 1993 vehicles, the type of head bolt used dictates the proper torque values

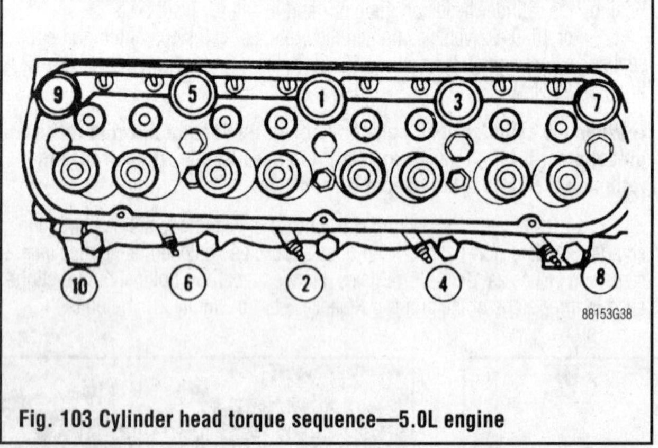

Fig. 103 Cylinder head torque sequence—5.0L engine

25–35 ft. lbs. (34–47 Nm), then tighten the bolts to 45–55 ft. lbs. (61–75 Nm). Finally, tighten all bolts an additional ¼ turn (85–95° if a torque angle meter is available).

14. If removed, install the exhaust manifolds using new gaskets.
15. Clean the pushrods, making sure the oil passages are clean. If you have access to compressed air, blow out the passages to be sure they are clear. Check the ends of the pushrods for wear. Visually check the pushrods for straightness or check for run-out using a dial indicator. Replace pushrods, as necessary.
16. Apply a suitable multi-purpose grease to the ends of the pushrods and install them in their original positions. Position the rocker arms over the pushrods and the valves.

➡If all the original valve train parts are reinstalled and no cylinder head milling was performed, a valve clearance check is not necessary. If any valve train components are replaced, a valve clearance check must be performed.

17. Raise and support the vehicle safely using jackstands. Connect the exhaust manifolds to the muffler inlet pipes, then remove the jackstands and carefully lower the vehicle.
18. If the right cylinder head was removed, reposition and install the alternator, or alternator and air pump bracket. Install the alternator assembly.
19. Install rocker arm covers using new gaskets.
20. If the left cylinder head was removed, reposition and install the A/C compressor and/or the power steering pump, as equipped.
21. Install the drive belt, making sure that the belt tensioner is maintaining the proper tension and that the belt is properly aligned on all of the pulleys.
22. Install the Thermactor/secondary air injection crossover tube at the rear of the cylinder heads.
23. Install the upper and lower intake manifold assemblies.

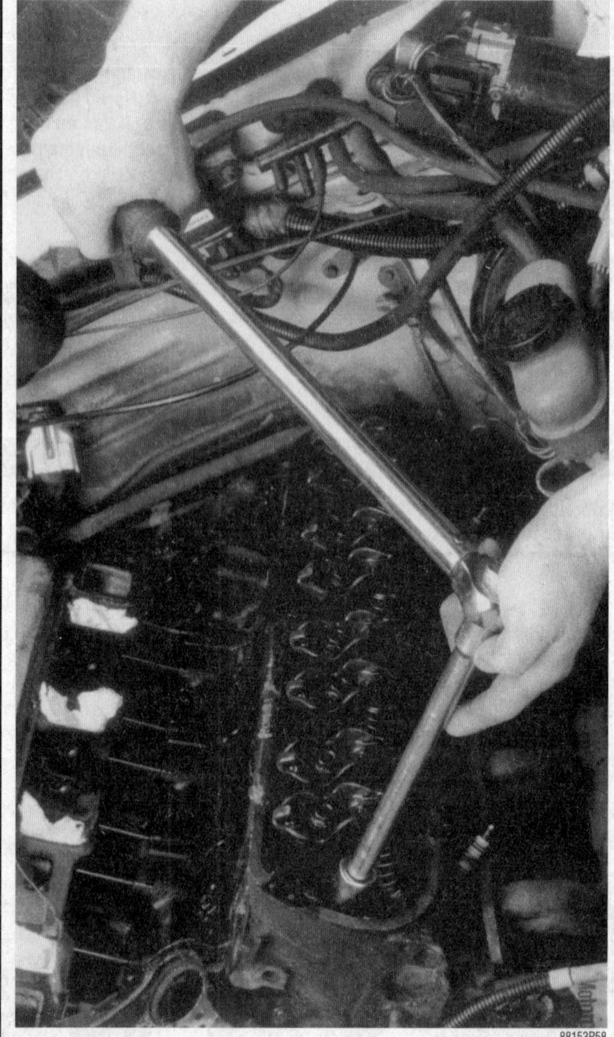

Fig. 104 Upon installation, tighten the cylinder head bolts in sequence using a torque wrench

24. Connect the negative battery cable, then fill and bleed the cooling system.
25. Bring to normal operating temperature. Check for leaks. Check all fluid levels.
26. If the A/C system was discharged, take the vehicle is a reputable service facility and have the refrigerant system leak-tested, evacuated and charged according to the proper procedures.

CLEANING AND INSPECTION

▸ See Figures 105, 106 and 107

1. With the valves installed to protect the valve seats, remove deposits from the combustion chambers and valve heads with a scraper and a wire brush. Be careful not to damage the cylinder head gasket surface. After the valves are removed, clean the valve guide bores with a valve guide cleaning tool. Using cleaning solvent to remove dirt, grease and other deposits, clean all bolts holes and be sure that all oil passages are.
2. Remove all deposits from the valves with a fine wire brush or buffing wheel.
3. Inspect the cylinder heads for cracks or excessively burned areas in the exhaust outlet ports.
4. Check the cylinder head gasket surfaces for cracks, burrs and nicks. Although burrs or nicks in this area can be dressed down using an oilstone, you should replace a head if it is cracked.

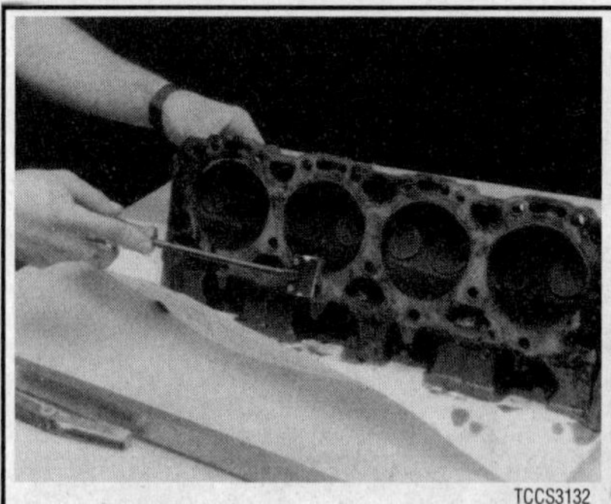
TCCS3132

Fig. 105 Use a gasket scraper to remove the bulk of the old head gasket from the mating surface . . .

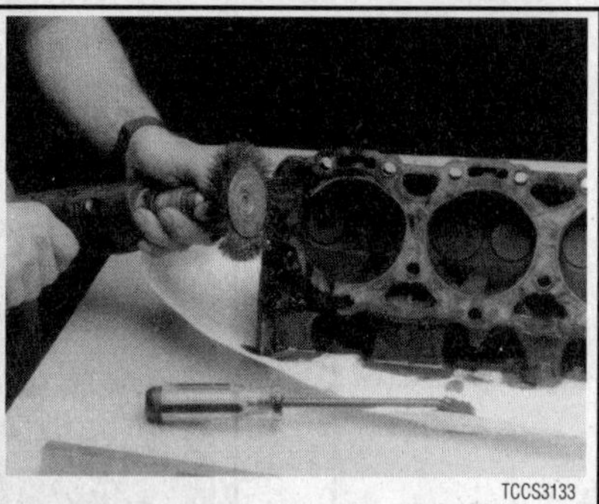
TCCS3133

Fig. 106 . . . then use an electric drill with a wire wheel to finish—but be careful NOT to damage the surface

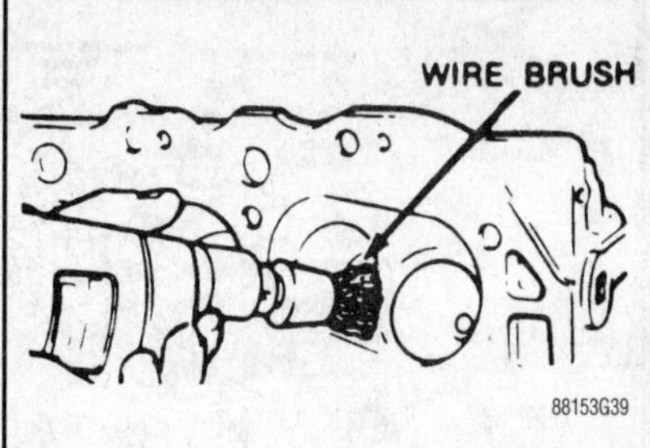

Fig. 107 Combustion chamber carbon can be removed with a drill and a wire brush—make sure the carbon is removed and not just burnished

5. On cylinder heads that incorporate valve seat inserts, check the inserts for excessive wear, cracks, or looseness.
6. If the cylinder head was removed to replace a blown head gasket, be sure to check the head for flatness and to determine if resurfacing is necessary.

RESURFACING

Cylinder Head Flatness

➧ See Figures 108, 109 and 110

When the cylinder head is removed, check the flatness of the cylinder head gasket surfaces. This is especially important if a head gasket was blown and cylinder head warpage is suspected.

1. Place a straightedge across the gasket surface of the cylinder head. Using feeler gauges, determine the clearance at the center of the straightedge.
2. If warpage exceeds 0.003 in. (0.076mm) in a 6 in. (152mm) span, or 0.006 in. (0.152mm) over the total length, the cylinder head must be resurfaced.
3. If necessary to refinish the cylinder head gasket surface, do not plane or grind off more than 0.254mm (0.010 in.) from the original gasket surface.

➡When milling the cylinder heads of V8 engines, the intake manifold mounting position is altered, and must be corrected by milling the manifold flange a proportionate amount. Consult an experienced machinist about this.

Valves and Springs

➡The valve springs and/or valve stem seals can be removed and installed with the cylinder head on the engine, provided that an air compressor and spark plug port fitting is available to keep the valves from falling into the combustion chambers. For details, please refer to the Valve Spring or Seal Replacement On Engine procedure found later in this section.

REMOVAL & INSTALLATION

➧ See Figures 111 thru 121

1. Block the head on its side, or install a pair of head-holding brackets made especially for valve removal.
2. Using a socket slightly larger than the valve stem and keys (keepers), place the socket over the valve stem and gently hit the socket with a plastic hammer to break loose any varnish buildup.
3. Remove the valve keys, retainer, spring shield and valve spring using a valve spring compressor (a threaded-jawed compressor or a locking C-clamp type is the easiest kind to use, but Ford recommends a lever-type on most of these engines).
4. Put the parts from each valve in a separate container numbered for the cylinder and valve being worked on; do not mix them with other parts removed.
5. Remove and discard the valve stem oil seals. A new seal will be used at assembly time.
6. Remove the valves from the cylinder head and place them, in order, through numbered holes punched in a stiff piece of cardboard or in a wooden valve holding rack.

➡The exhaust valve stems, on some engines, are equipped with small metal caps. Take care not to lose the caps. Make sure to reinstall them at assembly time. Replace any caps that are worn.

7. If a complete valve job is planned, use an electric drill and rotary wire brush to clean the intake and exhaust valve ports, combustion chamber and valve seats. In some cases, the carbon will need to be chipped away. Use a blunt pointed drift for carbon chipping. Be careful around the valve seat areas.

➡Cleaning the combustion chambers and valve seats with the valves removed is not recommended if a valve job is not being performed because of the possible danger to proper valve seal. For heads which are not getting a complete valve job, the cleaning performed earlier under Cylinder Head cleaning and inspection will suffice.

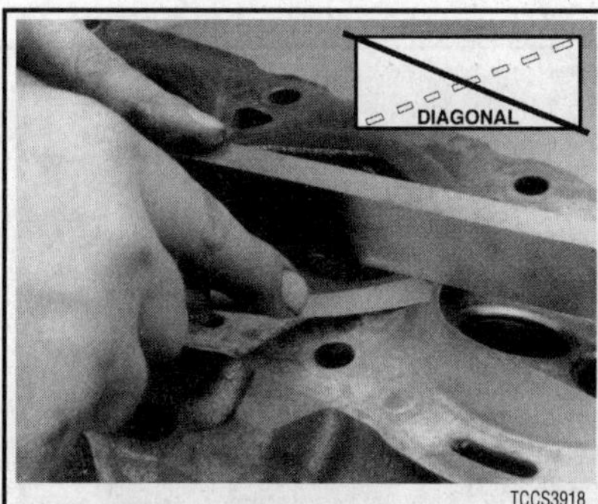

TCCS3918

Fig. 108 Use a feeler gauge and a straightedge to check for cylinder head flatness . . .

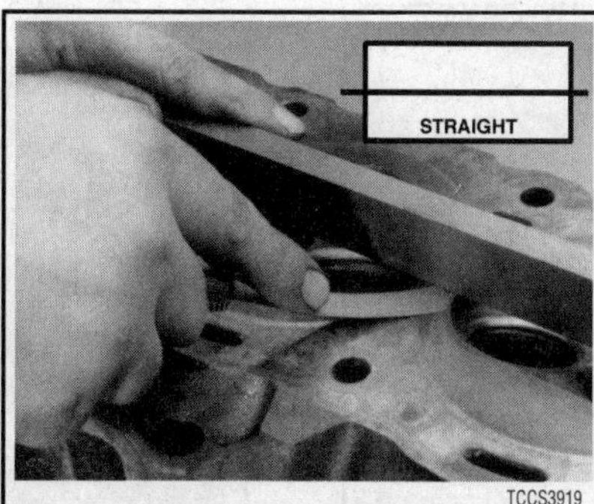

TCCS3919

Fig. 109 . . . be sure to check straight across the gasket mating surface and across both diagonals

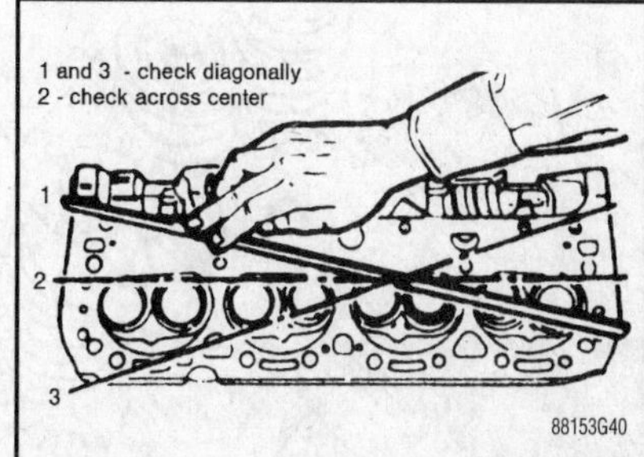

Fig. 110 Check the cylinder head for flatness or warpage across the gasket mating surface at these angles (straight and both diagonals)

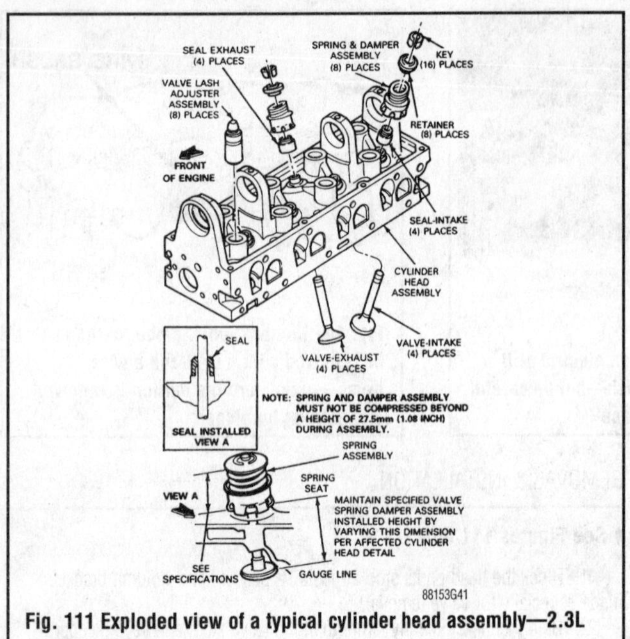

Fig. 111 Exploded view of a typical cylinder head assembly—2.3L (VIN M) engine shown

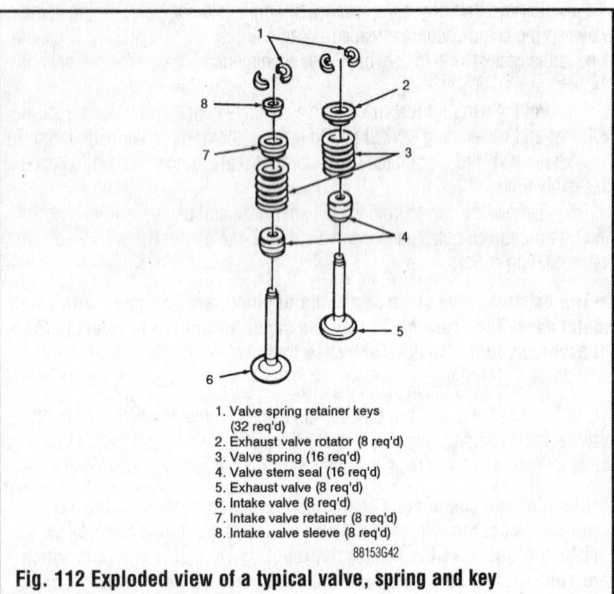

Fig. 112 Exploded view of a typical valve, spring and key (keeper/retainer) assembly—5.0L engine shown

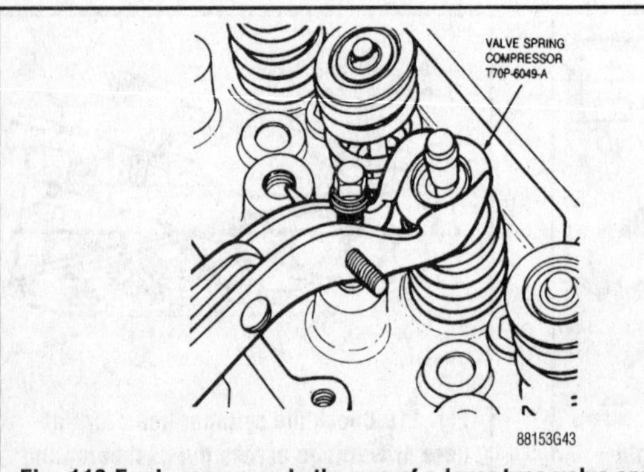

Fig. 113 Ford recommends the use of a lever type valve spring compressor such as this one for the 5.0L engine—but keep in mind this can be more difficult to use if the head is not mounted in a fixture

Fig. 114 Use a valve spring compressor tool (such as this threaded universal type) to relieve spring tension from the valve cap

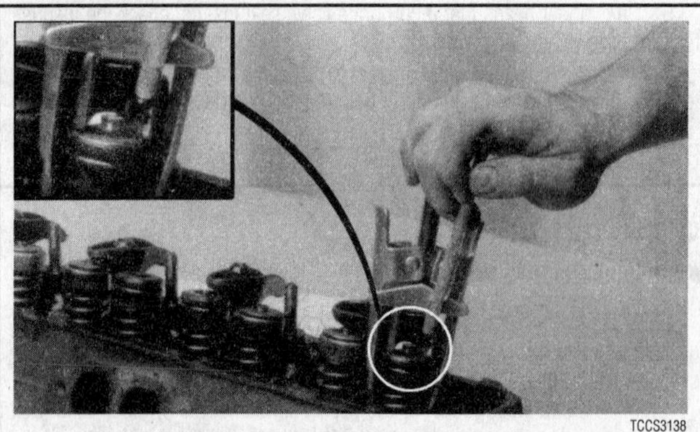

Fig. 115 A small magnet will help in removing the valve keys

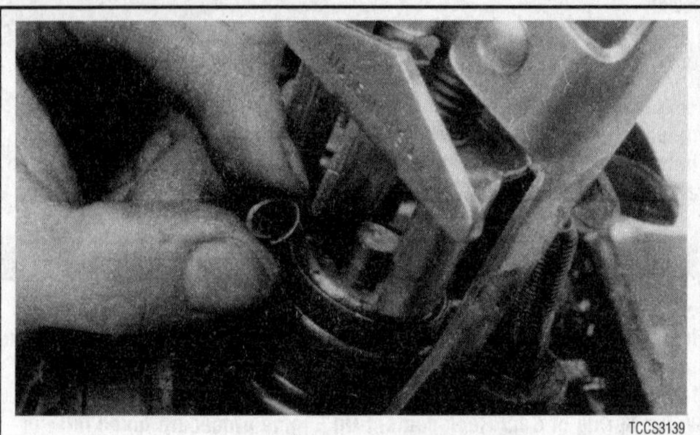

Fig. 116 Be VERY careful not to loose the valve keys

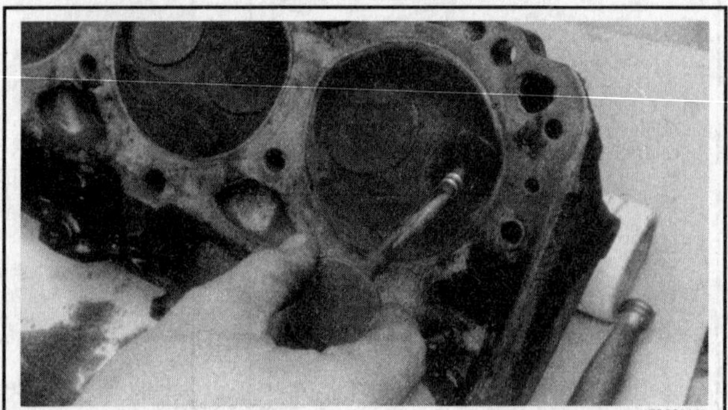

Fig. 117 Once the keys, spring and seal are removed, withdraw the valve from the head

Fig. 118 On heads which will undergo a complete valve job, use a wire wheel to clean the entire area of carbon deposits

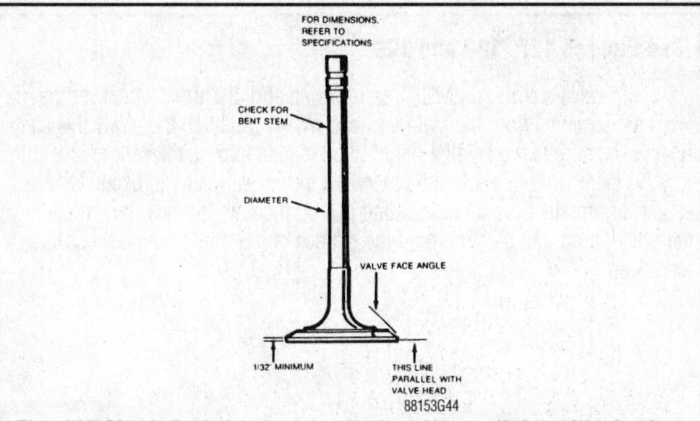

Fig. 119 Check the valve for wear or damage at all the critical valve dimensions

Fig. 120 A dial gauge can be used to check valve stem-to-guide clearance

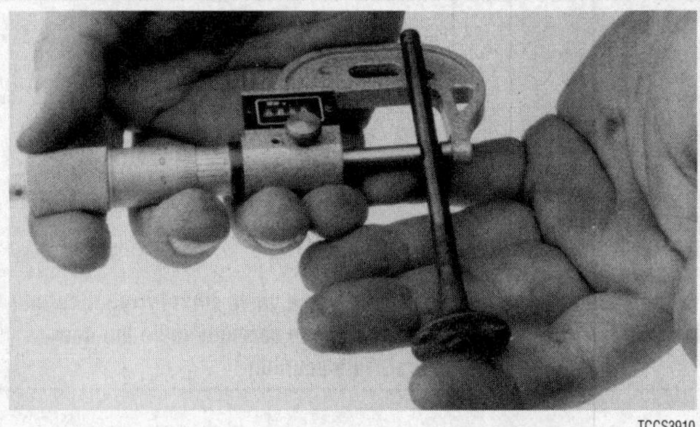

Fig. 121 Use a micrometer to check the valve stem diameter

8. Use a wire valve guide cleaning brush and safe solvent to clean the valve guides.
9. Clean the valves with a revolving wire brush. Heavy carbon deposits may be removed with the blunt drift.

➡When using a wire brush to clean carbon on the valve ports, valves etc., be sure that the deposits are actually removed, rather than burnished.

10. Wash and clean all valve springs, keepers, retaining caps etc., in safe solvent.
11. Clean the head with a brush and some safe solvent and wipe dry.
12. Check the head for cracks. Cracks in the cylinder head usually start around an exhaust valve seat because it is the hottest part of the combustion chamber. If a crack is suspected but cannot be detected visually, have the area checked with dye penetrant or other method by the machine shop.
13. After all cylinder head parts are reasonably clean, check the valve stem-to-guide clearance. If a dial indicator is not on hand, a visual inspection can give you a fairly good idea if the guide, valve stem or both are worn.
    a. Insert the valve into the guide until slightly away from the valve seat. Wiggle the valve sideways. A small amount of wobble is normal, excessive wobble means a worn guide or valve stem.
    b. If a dial indicator is on hand, mount the indicator so that the stem of the valve is at 90° to the valve stem, as close to the valve guide as possible. Move the valve off the seat, and measure the valve guide-to-stem clearance by rocking the stem back and forth to actuate the dial indicator.
    c. Measure the valve stem using a micrometer and compare to specifications to determine whether stem or guide wear is causing excessive clearance.
14. The valve guide, if worn, must be repaired before the valve seats can be resurfaced. Ford supplies valves with oversize stems to fit valve guides that are reamed to oversize for repair. The machine shop will be able to handle the guide reaming for you. In some cases, if the guide is not too badly worn, knurling may be all that is required.
15. Reface, or have the valves and valve seats refaced. The valve seats should be a true 45° angle. Remove only enough material to clean up any pits or grooves. Be sure the valve seat is not too wide or narrow. Use a 60° grinding wheel to remove material from the bottom of the seat to raise and a 30° grinding wheel to remove material from the top of the seat to narrow it.

➡Valve and Seat refacing are best left to the professional. The high degree of skill and specialty tools necessary, not to mention the importance of this work in relation to the performance of your engine after assembly should be reasons enough in this matter.

16. After the valves are refaced by machine, it may be necessary to hand lap them to the valve seat. Check with your machine shop to determine if the machining techniques used require, and the metals of the valve/seat will benefit from, hand lapping. If you determine that lapping is necessary, remember to clean the grinding compound off and check the position of face-to-seat contact after you are finished. Contact should be close to the center of the valve face. If contact is close to the top edge of the valve, narrow the seat; if too close to the bottom edge, raise the seat.
17. Valves should be refaced to a true angle of 44°. Remove only enough metal to clean up the valve face or to correct run-out. If the edge of a valve head, after machining, is 1/32 in. (0.8mm) or less replace the valve. The tip of the valve stem should also be dressed on the valve grinding machine, however, do not remove more than 0.010 in. (0.254mm).
18. After all valve and valve seats have been machined, check the remaining valve train parts (springs, retainers, keepers, etc.) for wear. Check the valve springs for straightness and tension.
19. Install the valves in the cylinder head, and if equipped, the metal caps.
20. Install new valve stem oil seals.
21. Install the valve keys, retainer, spring shield and valve spring using a valve spring compressor (again, threaded type or the locking C-clamp type is the easiest kind to use, especially if the head is off the engine and NOT secured in a holding fixture).
22. Check the valve spring installed height, shim or replace as necessary.

CHECKING VALVE SPRINGS

Spring Free Height and Squareness

See Figures 122, 123 and 124

If you have a caliper gauge, measure the free height of the spring. If a caliper gauge is unavailable, you can use a carpenter's square for both necessary measurements. Place the valve spring on a flat surface next to a carpenter's square. Measure the height of the spring, and rotate the spring against the edge of the square to measure distortion. If the spring height varies (by comparison) by more than 1/16 in. (1.6mm) or the distortion exceeds 1/16 in. (1.6mm), replace the spring.

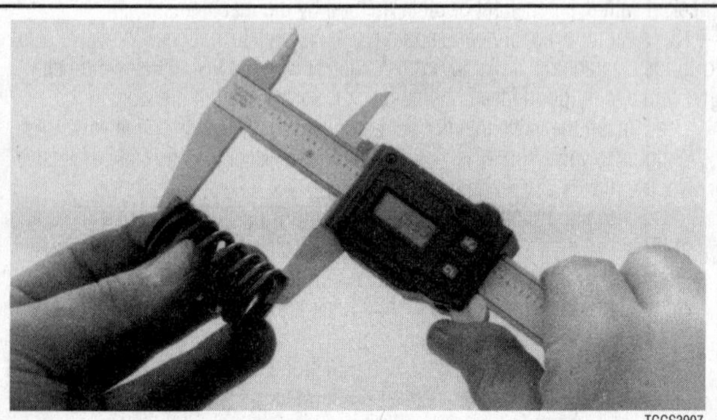

TCCS3907

Fig. 122 A caliper gauge can be used to check the valve spring free height

Spring Pressure

See Figure 125

Have the valve springs tested for spring pressure at the installed and compressed (installed height minus valve lift) height using a valve spring tester. Springs should be within one pound, plus or minus each other. Replace springs as necessary.

Spring Installed Height

See Figure 126

After installing the valve spring, measure the distance between the spring mounting pad and the lower edge of the spring retainer. Compare the measurement to specifications. If the installed height is greater than specification, add shim washers between the spring mounting pad and the spring. Use only washers designed for valve springs, available at most parts houses.

VALVE STEM OIL SEALS

See Figures 127, 128 and 129

The old valve stem seals MUST be removed and discarded whenever the valves are removed from the cylinder head. When installing the new valve stem oil seals, be sure that a small amount of oil is able to pass the seal to lubricate the valve stems and guide walls, otherwise, excessive wear will occur. New seals will normally have an installation cap on them which must be removed after positioning, but be sure to oil the surface of the cap to help ease seal installation.

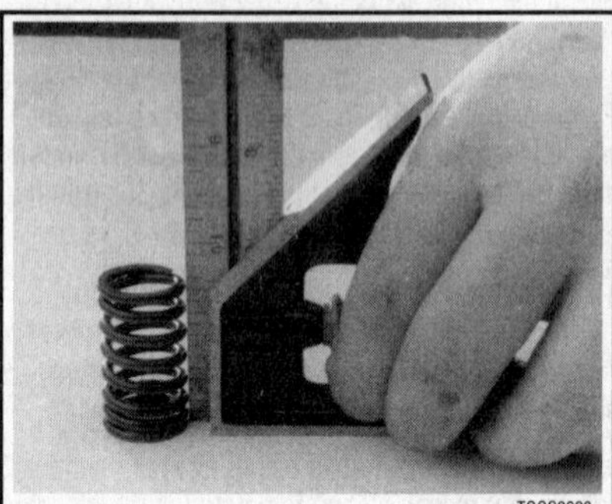

TCCS3908

Fig. 123 If a caliper gauge is unavailable, use a carpenter's square to measure the free height . . .

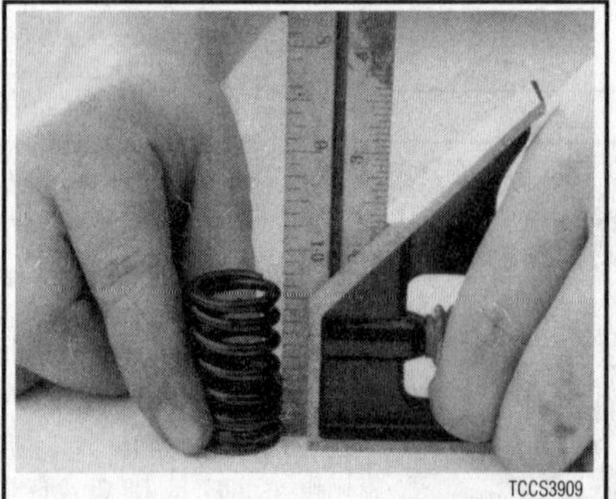

TCCS3909

Fig. 124 . . . then turn the spring by hand against the edge of the square to check for bending or distortion

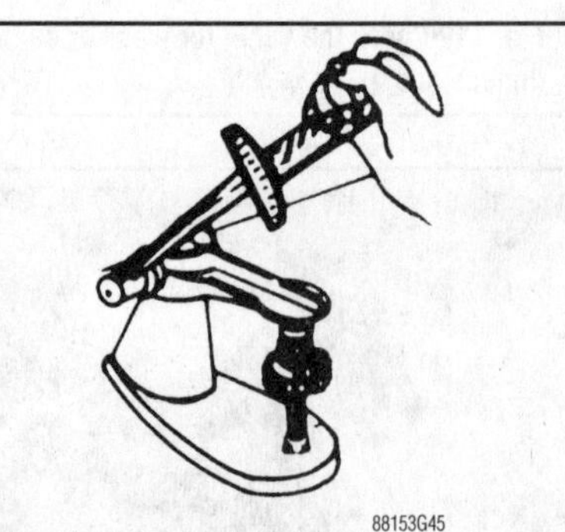

88153G45

Fig. 125 A machine shop will usually be able to check the spring pressure using a testing tool such as this one

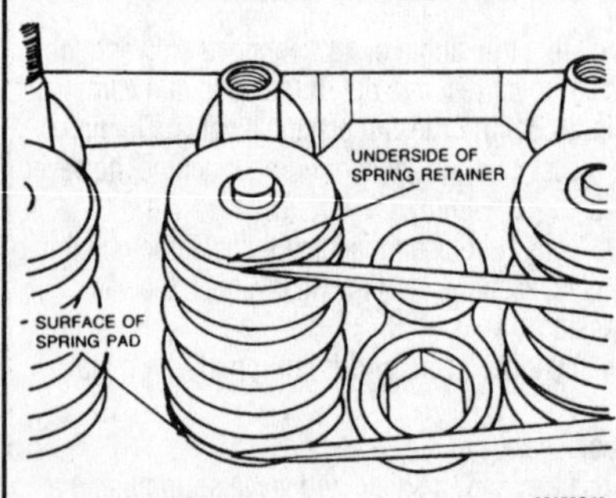

88153G46

Fig. 126 Measure the spring installed height from the surface of the spring pad to the underside of the spring retainer

TCCS3252

Fig. 127 The old valve stem seals must be removed and discarded whenever the valve is removed

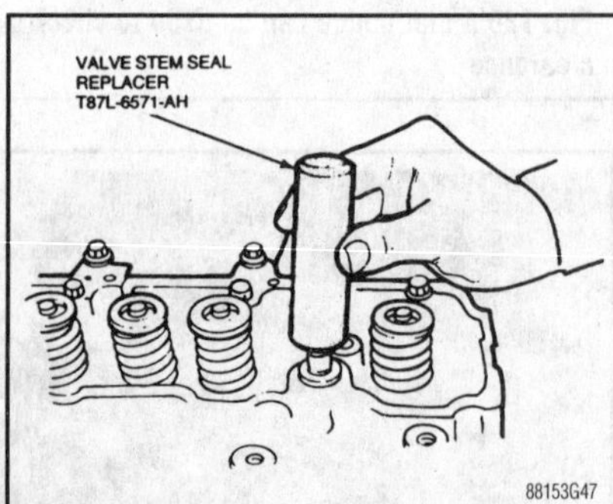

88153G47

Fig. 128 Use a valve stem installation tool such as this to carefully drive the new seals into position

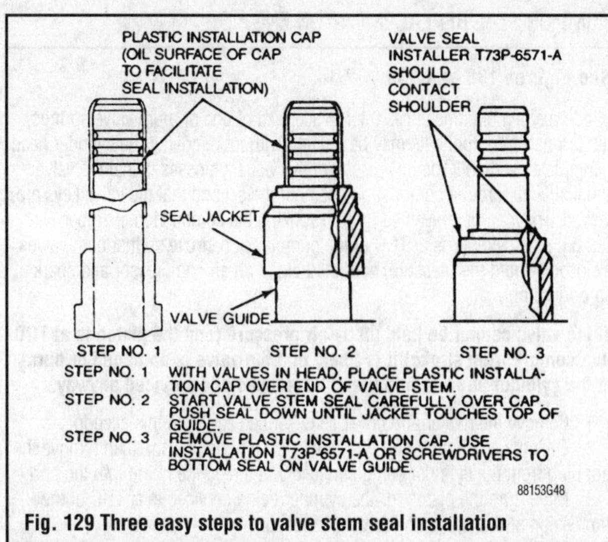

Fig. 129 Three easy steps to valve stem seal installation

VALVE AND SEAT REFACING

See Figures 130, 131, 132, 133 and 134

If the valve seat is damaged or burnt and cannot be serviced by refacing, it may be possible to have the seat machined and an insert installed. Likewise, a damaged valve face should be carefully examined to determine if refacing is possible, or if the valve should be replaced. Consult an automotive machine shop for their advice.

The high degree of precision in modern machining equipment, coupled with the extremely hard metals available for valves and seats today often make valve lapping unnecessary. But, it is best to consult with your machine shop to see if the techniques and materials used might benefit from lapping before final valve installation. If lapping is recommended use the following procedure along with their advise.

1. Invert the cylinder head so that the valve faces and combustion chambers are facing upward.
2. Lubricate the valve stems lightly with clean engine oil, then coat the valve seats with lapping compound. Install the valves into the cylinders as numbered, making sure no lapping compound enters the guide.
3. Moisten and attach the suction cup of a valve lapping tool to the valve head.

➡Valve lapping can also be accomplished by fastening the suction cup to a piece of drill rod mounted to an egg beater type drill. Proceed with the lapping, using the drill as the lapping tool, BUT due to the higher speeds involved when using a hand drill, care must be taken to avoid grooving the seat. Lift the tool and change the direction of rotation often.

4. Rotate the tool between your palms, changing position and lifting the tool often to prevent grooving. Lap the valve until a smooth polished seat is evident. You may have to add a bit more compound after some lapping is done.

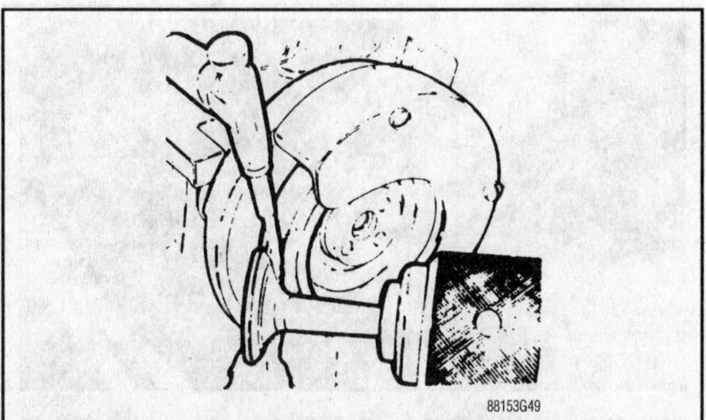

Fig. 130 Valve and seat refacing should be left to a reputable (and well equipped) machine shop

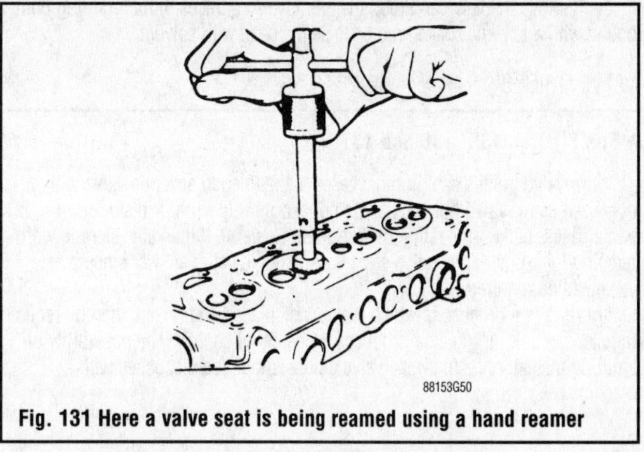

Fig. 131 Here a valve seat is being reamed using a hand reamer

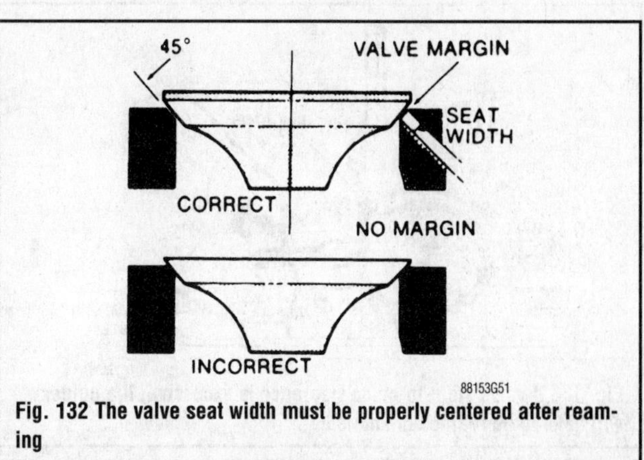

Fig. 132 The valve seat width must be properly centered after reaming

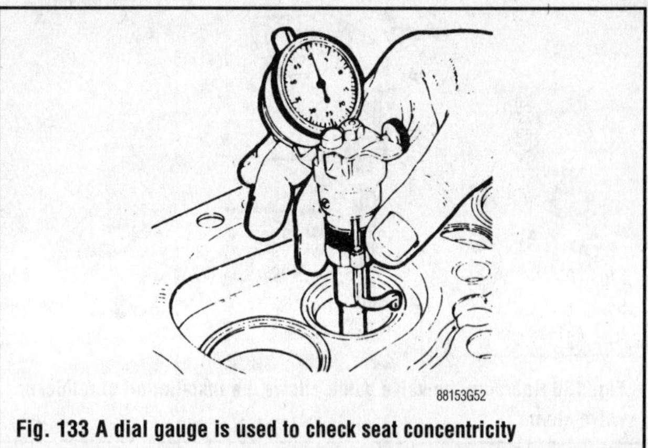

Fig. 133 A dial gauge is used to check seat concentricity

Fig. 134 If your machine shop advises it, you can finish the job by hand lapping the valves

5. Remove the valve and tool, then remove ALL traces of the grinding compound with a solvent-soaked rag or rinse the head with solvent.

VALVE GUIDES

See Figures 135, 136 and 137

Worn valve guides can, in most cases, be reamed to accept a valve with an oversized stem. Valve guides that are not excessively worn or distorted may, in some cases, be knurled rather than reamed. However, if the valve stem is worn reaming for an oversized valve stem is usually the better answer since a new valve will be required.

Knurling is a process in which metal is displaced and raised, thereby reducing clearance. Knurling also produces excellent oil control. The possibility of knurling instead of reaming the valve guides should be discussed with a machinist.

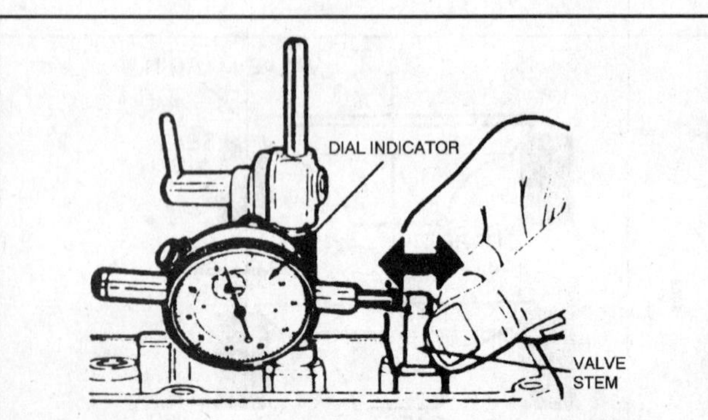

Fig. 135 If valve stem-to-guide clearance is excessive, the guides will have to be reamed or knurled

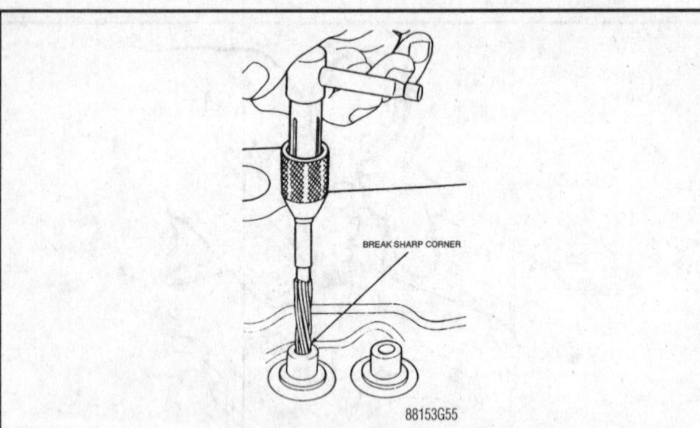

Fig. 136 Reaming the valve guide allows the installation of a thicker valve stem

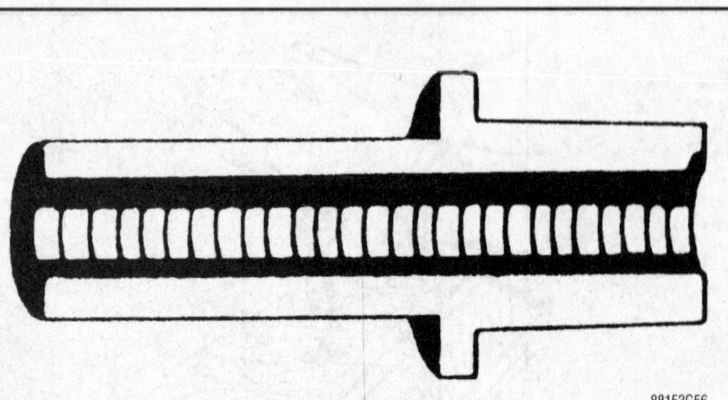

Fig. 137 Cross-section of a knurled valve guide—knurling allows reuse of a valve stem in a slightly worn guide

SPRING OR SEAL REPLACEMENT ON ENGINE

See Figures 138 and 139

Under certain circumstances the replacement of one or more valve springs, seals or related components may be desired without removing the cylinder head for complete overhaul. The only problem this usually posses is that the valve will usually fall into the combustion chamber the second that the valve keys are removed. This can be prevented by pressurizing the combustion chamber (assuming the cylinder is at TDC of the compression stroke so that both valves are closed to hold the pressure) with the help of an air compressor and spark plug port fitting.

➡If the valve cannot be held up by air pressure (and the piston is at TDC of the compression stroke) it is likely that the valve is damaged or burnt and the cylinder head should then be removed and serviced anyway.

1. Remove the rocker arm cover as described earlier in this section.
2. Obtain a spark plug port fitting for your air compressor, then remove the spark plug from the cylinder being serviced and thread the fitting into the port.
3. Make sure the piston for the cylinder being serviced is at TDC of the compression stroke and both valves are closed.
4. For the 2.3L engine, remove the rocker arm (cam follower) as described earlier in this section.
5. For the 5.0L engine, remove the rocker arm assemblies, as described earlier, then remove the pushrods for the cylinder being serviced. MAKE SURE that all parts are tagged or labelled to assure installation in the proper locations.
6. Pressurize the cylinder with a minimum of 140 psi (965 kpa) of compressed air.

➡Keep in mind that if air pressure forces the cylinder to the bottom of its travel, any release of air pressure will allow the valve(s) to fall into the cylinder, requiring cylinder head removal for retrieval. As this is exactly what we are trying to avoid with this procedure, a little bit of insurance in the form of a rubber band, tape or string wrapped around the end of the valve stem can help prevent this possibility and still allow enough room to work.

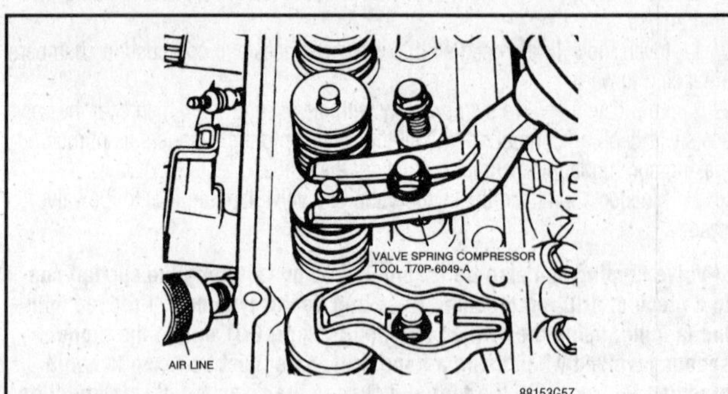

Fig. 138 Valve spring or stem seal replacement can be accomplished with the cylinder head installed if an air fitting is used to hold the valve in position

Fig. 139 Be careful not to loose the valve keys when working in the engine compartment like this

7. Using a suitable lever type spring compressor such as T88T-6565-BH for the 2.3L engine or T70P-6049-A for the 5.0L engine, depress the spring to free the valve keys (also known as locks or keepers). Carefully remove the locks and slowly release the spring tension, then remove the spring retainer.
8. Remove the valve spring and, if needed, the valve stem seal. Discard the components being replaced.
9. If the valve stem seal is being replaced, carefully drive the new seal into position.
10. Position the valve spring and retainer, then compress the spring using the lever tool and install the keys.
11. Carefully release the air pressure, then remove the spark plug adapter and reinstall the spark plug.
12. Install the pushrod and/or the rocker arm assembly (cam follower on the 2.3L engine), as applicable.

WARNING

Make sure the affected lash adjuster has been collapsed and released before rotating the camshaft on the 2.3L engine.

13. Install the rocker arm covers.
14. Run the engine and check for leaks/proper operation.

Valve Lifters

REMOVAL & INSTALLATION

2.3L Engine

See Figure 140

The 2.3L engine is equipped with hydraulic lash adjusters which, while not being exactly the same as a conventional hydraulic lifter, perform the same function to maintain proper valve train clearance. The hydraulic lash adjusters are placed at the fulcrum point of the cam followers (rocker arms) and act in a manner similar to hydraulic lifters in pushrod motors.

1. Disconnect the negative battery cable for safety.
2. Remove the rocker arm cover.
3. Rotate the camshaft so the base circle of the shaft is facing the cam follower to be removed.
4. Using valve spring compressor tool T88T–6565–BH or equivalent, compress the lash adjuster as required and/or depress the valve spring, if necessary, and slide the cam follower (rocker arm) over the lash adjuster and out.
5. Lift out the hydraulic lash adjuster.

To install:

6. Rotate the camshaft so the base circle of the shaft is facing the lash adjuster and cam follower to be installed. Place the hydraulic lash adjuster in position in the bore.
7. Using valve spring compressor tool T88T–6565–BH or equivalent, compress the lash adjuster, as necessary, to position the cam follower over the lash adjuster and the valve stem.
8. Before rotating the camshaft to the next position, make sure the lash adjuster just installed is fully compressed and released.
9. Install the rocker arm cover.
10. Connect the negative battery cable, then start the engine and check for leaks.

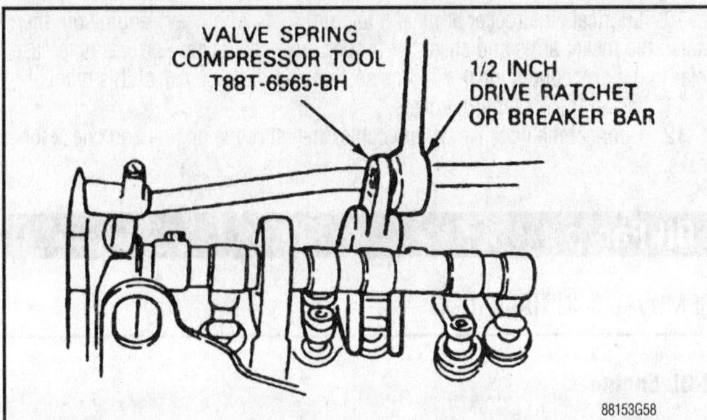

Fig. 140 The cam follower (rocker arm) and hydraulic lash adjuster are removed using a valve spring compressor tool

5.0L Engine

See Figures 141 thru 149

1. Disconnect the negative battery cable for safety.
2. Remove the rocker arm covers.
3. Loosen the rocker arm fulcrum bolts and rotate the rocker arms to the side.
4. Remove the valve pushrods and identify them so that they can be installed in their original position.
5. Remove the lifter guide retainer bolts. Remove the retainer and lifter guide plates. Identify the guide plates so they may be reinstalled in their original positions.

On roller lifters it is very important to note not only the original location, but the position as well to assure that the roller rotates in the same direction.

6. Using a magnet, remove the lifters and place them in a rack so that they can be installed in their original bores.

If the lifters are stuck in the bores due to excessive varnish or gum deposits, it may be necessary to use a claw-type tool to aid removal. When using a remover tool, rotate the lifter back and forth to loosen it from gum or varnish that may have formed on the lifter.

To install:

7. Lubricate the lifters and install them in their original bores. If new lifters are being installed, check them for free fit in their respective bores.
8. Install the lifter guide plates in their original positions, then install the guide plate retainer.
9. Install the pushrods in their original positions. Apply grease to the ends prior to installation.

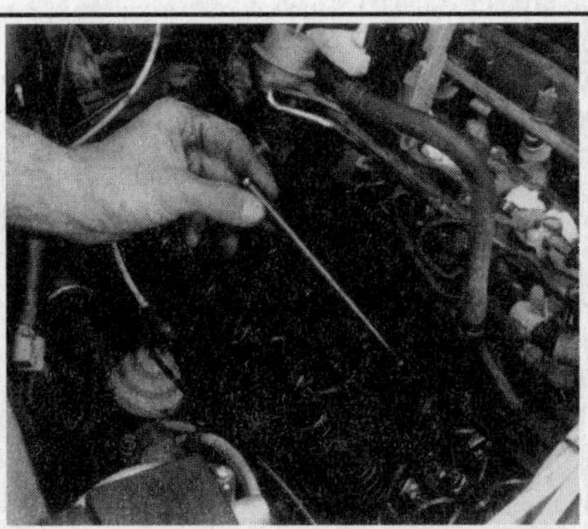

Fig. 141 Remove the pushrod for access to the lifter . . .

Fig. 142 . . . if more than one rod is being removed, tag each to assure proper installation

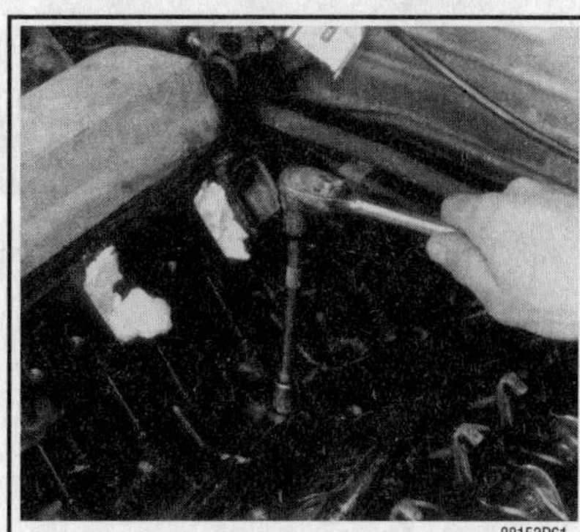

Fig. 143 Loosen and remove the bolts securing the lifter guide retainer . . .

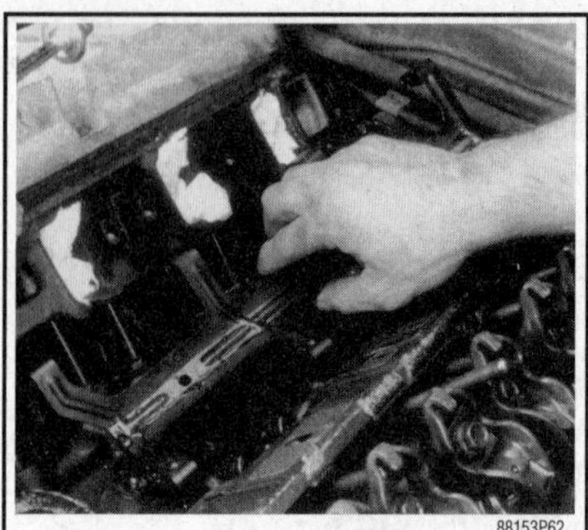
88153P62

Fig. 144 . . . then remove the retainer from the center of the block's lifter valley

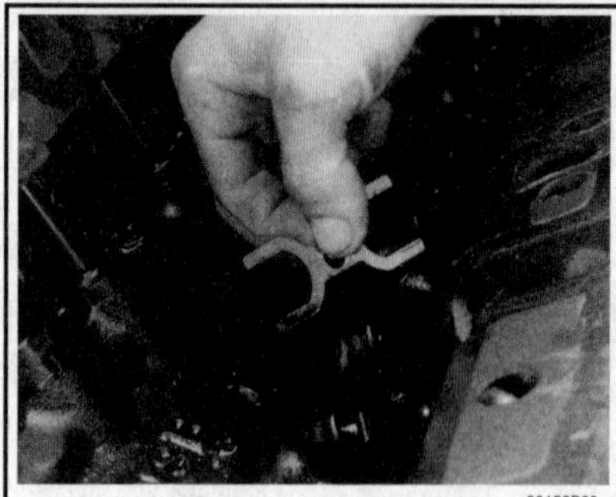
88153P63

Fig. 145 With the retainer removed, you can access the lifter guides—but be sure again, tag or arrange them

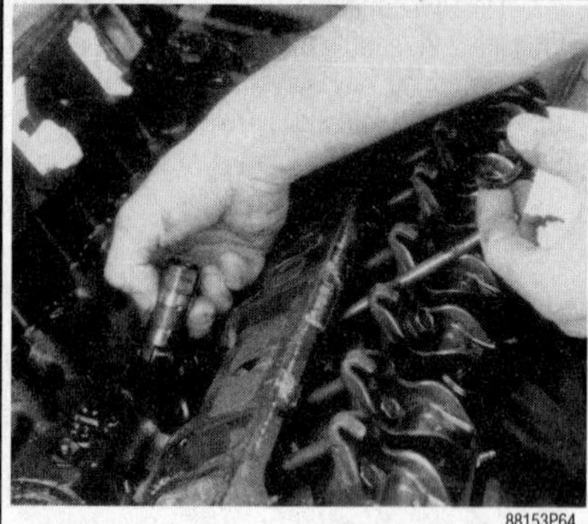
88153P64

Fig. 146 Finally, the lifter can be removed from its bore

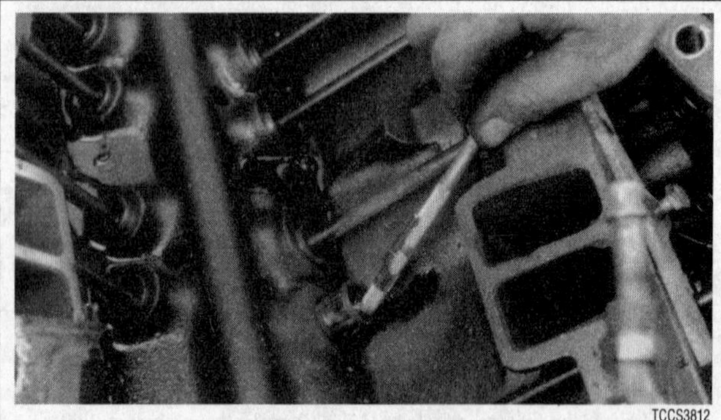
TCCS3812

Fig. 147 A magnet can be useful when removing lifters from their bores

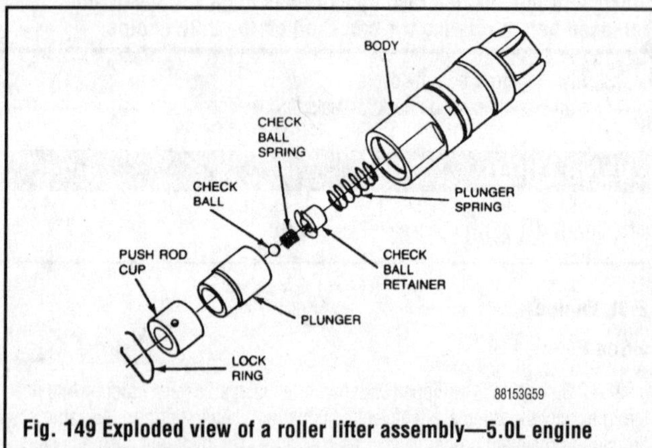

Fig. 149 Exploded view of a roller lifter assembly—5.0L engine

TCCS3813

Fig. 148 Stuck lifters can be freed using a slide hammer type lifter removal tool

10. Lubricate the rocker arms and fulcrum seats with heavy engine oil, then install the rocker arms and check for proper valve clearance. For details, please refer to the procedures located in this section and in Section 1 of this manual.
11. Install the rocker arm covers.
12. Connect the negative battery cable, then start the engine and check for leaks.

Oil Pan

REMOVAL & INSTALLATION

2.3L Engine

1989–90 MODELS

See Figure 150

1. Disconnect the negative battery cable for safety.
2. Drain the engine cooling system.
3. Remove the electric cooling fan and shroud assembly.
4. Disconnect the upper and lower cooling hoses from the radiator.
5. Raise and support the vehicle safely using jackstands.
6. Drain the crankcase and, if equipped, disconnect the low oil level sensor.
7. Except for on the convertible, remove the right and left engine support through-bolts.
8. On the convertible, remove the right and left engine support nuts.
9. Using a jack and a block of wood, raise the engine as high as it will go. Place wood blocks between the mounts and the crossmember pedestal brackets, then remove the jack.
10. Remove the shake brace.
11. Remove the sway bar retaining bolts and lower the sway bar.
12. Remove the starter motor assembly from the vehicle.
13. Remove the steering gear retaining bolts and carefully lower the gear.

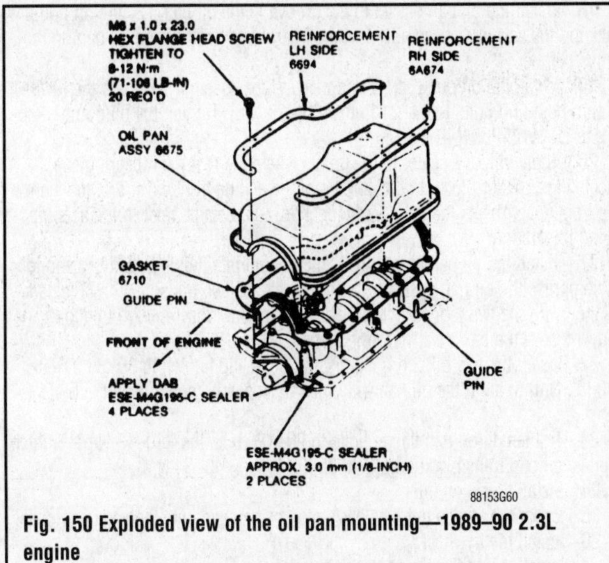

Fig. 150 Exploded view of the oil pan mounting—1989–90 2.3L engine

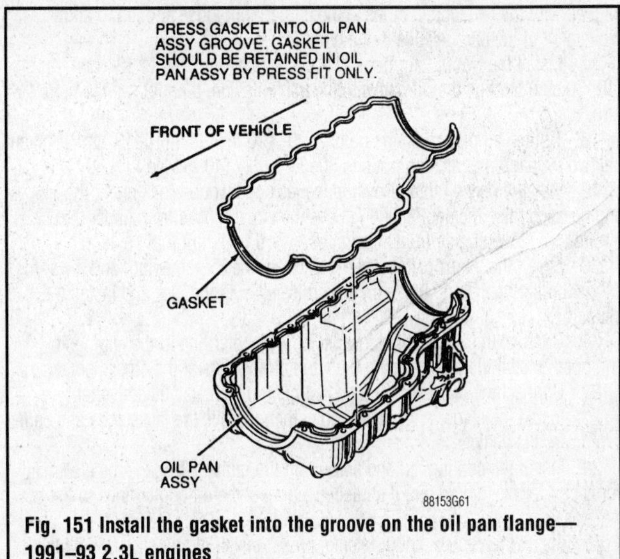

Fig. 151 Install the gasket into the groove on the oil pan flange—1991–93 2.3L engines

14. Remove the oil pan retaining bolts and allow the oil pan to drop to the crossmember. Rotate the crankshaft to position the No. 4 piston up in the cylinder bore so that the oil pan clears the crankshaft throw. Remove the oil pan from the vehicle.

To install:

15. Clean the oil pan and the gasket mating surfaces.
16. Remove and clean the oil pickup tube and screen assembly. After cleaning, reinstall.
17. Apply silicone sealer to the points where the rear main bearing cap meets the cylinder block, to the corners of the engine front cover and to where the front cover meets the cylinder block. Position the oil pan gasket to the cylinder block.
18. Position the oil pan and pan reinforcements to the cylinder block, then install the retaining bolts. Tighten to 71–106 inch lbs. (8–12 Nm).
19. Position and install the steering gear.
20. Position and install the starter motor assembly.
21. Raise the engine enough to remove the wood blocks. Lower the engine and remove the jack.
22. Install the shake brace.
23. Install the right and left engine through-bolts, except convertible, and tighten to 65–85 ft. lbs. (88–119 Nm). On convertibles, install the right and left engine support nuts, then tighten the nuts to 80–106 ft. lbs. (108–144 Nm).
24. Install the sway bar.
25. If equipped, connect the low oil level sensor.
26. Install a new oil filter.
27. Remove the jackstands and carefully lower the vehicle.
28. IMMEDIATELY, refill the engine crankcase to prevent an accidental attempt to start the engine with no oil.
29. Connect the radiator hoses.
30. Install the electric cooling fan and shroud assembly.
31. Connect the negative battery cable, then refill and bleed the engine cooling system.
32. Run the engine and check for leaks.

1991 MODELS

See Figures 151 and 152

1. Disconnect the negative battery cable for safety.
2. Remove the air cleaner outlet tube at the throttle body.
3. Remove the engine oil dipstick.
4. Remove the engine mount retaining nuts.
5. Remove the oil cooler lines at the radiator, if equipped. Disengage the electrical connector to the cooling fan and remove the cooling fan and shroud.
6. Raise and safely support the vehicle. Drain the crankcase.
7. Remove the starter cable from the starter and remove the starter.
8. Disconnect the exhaust manifold tube to the inlet pipe bracket. Disconnect the catalytic converter at the inlet pipe.

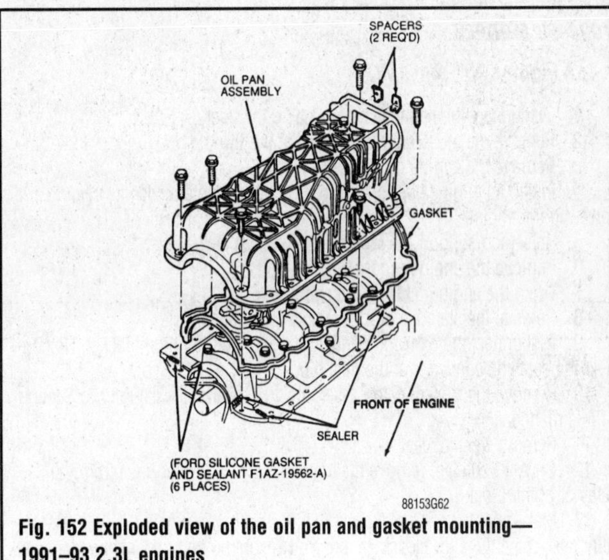

Fig. 152 Exploded view of the oil pan and gasket mounting—1991–93 2.3L engines

9. Remove the insulator and retainer assembly at the transmission. Remove the transmission mount retaining nuts to the crossmember. If equipped with an automatic transmission, remove the oil cooler lines from the retainer at the block.
10. Position a jack and a wood block under the engine. Raise the engine approximately 2.5 in. (63.5mm) high and place wood blocks between the mounts and crossmember.
11. Remove the jack and position it under the transmission. Raise the jack slightly to just unload the transmission mount.
12. Remove the oil pan retaining bolts and lower the pan to the chassis. Remove the oil pump drive and pickup tube assembly. Remove the oil pan with the oil pump.

To install:

13. Clean the oil pan and the gasket mating surfaces. Clean the oil pump pickup tube screen.
14. Install the oil pan gasket in the groove in the oil pan. Position the oil pan assembly on the crossmember and install the oil pump drive and pickup tube assembly.
15. Apply silicone sealer to the points where the rear main bearing cap meets the cylinder block, to the corners of the engine front cover and to where the front cover meets the cylinder block.
16. Install the oil pan assembly. Install the oil pan flange bolts tight enough to compress the oil pan gasket to the point that the two transmission holes are

aligned with the two tapped holes in the oil pan, but loose enough to allow movement of the pan, relative to the block.

17. Install the two oil pan/transmission bolts and tighten to 30–39 ft. lbs. (40–50 Nm) to align the oil pan with the transmission, then loosen the bolts ½ turn.

18. Tighten all oil pan flange bolts to 90–120 inch lbs. (10–13 Nm). Tighten the two oil pan/transmission bolts to 30–39 ft. lbs. (40–54 Nm).

19. Install a new oil filter. Position the jack and wood block under the engine, then raise the engine and remove the wood blocks from under the mounts. Shift the engine/transmission backward to its original position.

20. Install the insulator/bracket assembly to the crossmember and lower the engine on the insulators. Raise the transmission with the jack and install the insulator.

21. Connect the automatic transmission oil cooler line to the engine, if equipped. Install the transmission mount retaining nuts at the crossmember.

22. Connect the rear exhaust pipe just behind the catalytic converter.

23. Install the starter and starter cable, then remove the jackstands and carefully lower the vehicle.

24. Install the cooling fan and shroud on the radiator. Engage the electrical connector to the cooling fan. If equipped, connect the oil cooler lines to the radiator.

25. Install the engine mount retaining nuts. Install the dipstick and fill the crankcase with the proper type and quantity of engine oil.

26. Connect the negative battery cable, start the engine and check for leaks.

1992–93 MODELS

➧ See Figures 151 and 152

1. Disconnect the negative battery cable for safety.
2. Remove the air cleaner outlet tube at the throttle body.
3. Remove the engine oil dipstick.
4. Install an engine support fixture or other suitable device for raising and lowering the engine.
5. Raise and support the vehicle safely using jackstands.
6. Remove the engine mount through-bolts.
7. Drain the engine oil from the crankcase.
8. Remove the starter motor assembly from the vehicle.
9. Disconnect the exhaust manifold tube to the inlet pipe bracket. Disconnect the catalytic converter at the inlet pipe.
10. Remove the transmission assembly. For details, please refer to Section 7 of this manual.
11. Remove the flywheel.
12. On A/T vehicles, remove the transmission oil cooler lines from the retainer at the block.
13. Make sure the engine support fixture is still properly in position. Carefully raise the engine for clearance, but MAKE sure no components are damaged.
14. Remove the oil pan retaining bolts, then lower the pan to the chassis.
15. Remove the oil pump drive and pickup tube assembly, then lay the assembly in the oil pan.
16. Carefully remove the oil pan with the oil pump from the vehicle.

To install:

17. Clean the oil pan and the gasket mating surfaces. Clean the oil pump pickup tube screen.
18. Install the oil pan gasket to the groove in the oil pan. Lay the oil pump pickup tube and drive assembly in the oil pan, then position the oil pan on the crossmember.
19. Install the oil pump drive and pickup tube assembly. Tighten the oil pump mounting bolts to 14–21 ft. lbs. (19–29 Nm). Tighten the oil pump strap nut to 30–41 ft. lbs. (40–55 Nm).
20. Apply silicone sealer to the points where the rear main bearing cap meets the cylinder block, to the corners of the engine front cover and to where the front cover meets the cylinder block. For more details, refer to the accompanying illustration.
21. Install the oil pan assembly. Install the oil pan flange bolts tight enough to compress the oil pan gasket to the point that the two transmission holes are aligned with the two tapped holes in the oil pan, but loose enough to allow movement of the pan, relative to the block.
22. Install the two oil pan/transmission bolts and tighten to 30–39 ft. lbs. (40–50 Nm) to align the oil pan with the transmission, then loosen the bolts ½ turn.
23. Tighten all oil pan flange bolts to 90–120 inch lbs. (10–13 Nm). Tighten the two oil pan/transmission bolts to 30–39 ft. lbs. (40–54 Nm).
24. Install a new oil filter.
25. Lower the engine onto the back into position and onto the engine mounts.
26. Install the flywheel.
27. Install the transmission assembly.
28. Install the engine mount through-bolts and tighten to 65–85 ft. lbs. (88–115 Nm).
29. If equipped, connect the automatic transmission cooler lines to the retainer clip on the engine.
30. Connect the rear exhaust pipe just behind the catalytic converter, then connect the inlet pipe to the manifold assembly.
31. Install the starter motor assembly.
32. Remove the jackstands and carefully lower the vehicle.
33. IMMEDIATELY refill the engine crankcase to prevent an accidental attempt to start the motor with no oil in it. Install the engine oil dipstick.
34. Install the air cleaner outlet tube to the throttle body.
35. Connect the negative battery cable.
36. Start the engine and check for leaks.

5.0L Engine

➧ See Figure 153 thru 167

1. Disconnect the negative battery cable for safety.
2. Remove the air cleaner tube.
3. Remove the oil level indicator from the left side of the cylinder block.
4. Remove the fan shroud retaining bolts, then position the shroud over the fan.
5. Raise and support the vehicle safely using jackstands.
6. Drain the crankcase and remove the oil level sensor wiring from the oil pan.
7. Remove the starter motor assembly.
8. Remove the catalytic converter and muffler inlet pipes.
9. Remove the engine mount-to-No. 2 crossmember attaching bolts or nuts. Support the transmission and remove the No. 3 crossmember and rear insulator support assemblies.

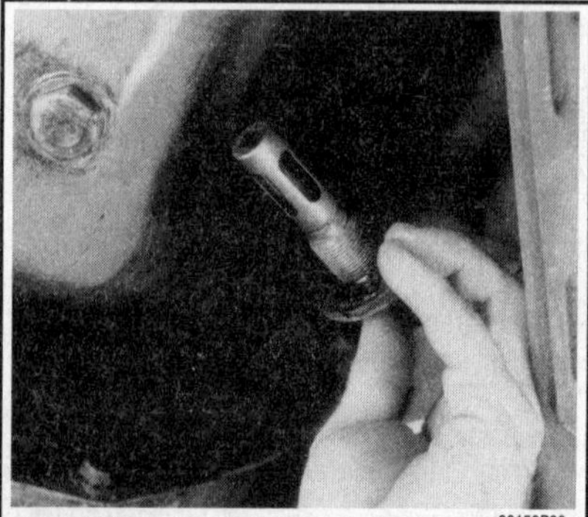

88153P98

Fig. 153 If necessary, the threaded oil level indicator is easily removed

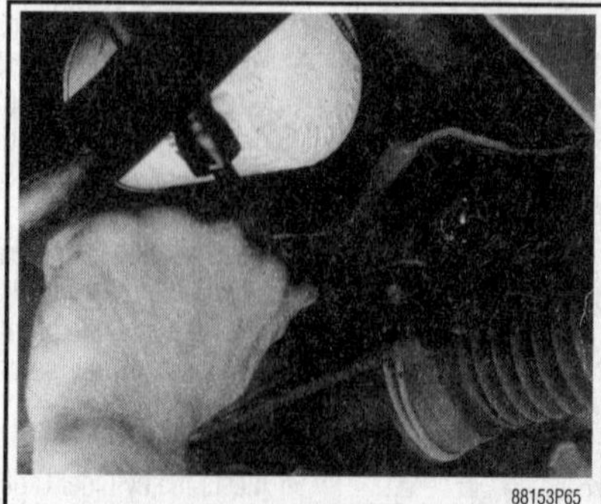

88153P65

Fig. 154 Loosen and remove the engine mount-to-No 2 crossmember attaching bolts or nuts . . .

88153P66

Fig. 155 . . . the tool you use (wrench, socket, extensions, etc) depends on the available access

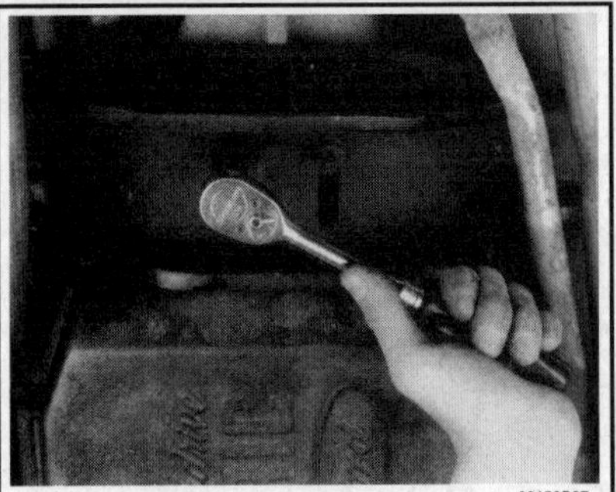

88153P67

Fig. 156 Support the transmission then remove the No. 3 insulator and rear support assemblies

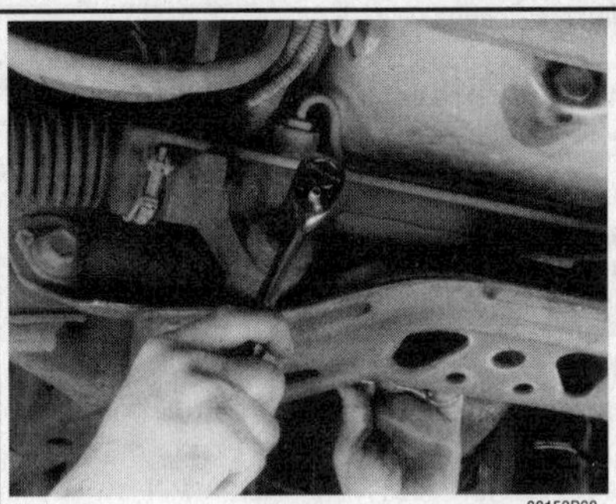

88153P68

Fig. 157 Using a backup wrench behind the crossmember, loosen the steering gear retaining bolts

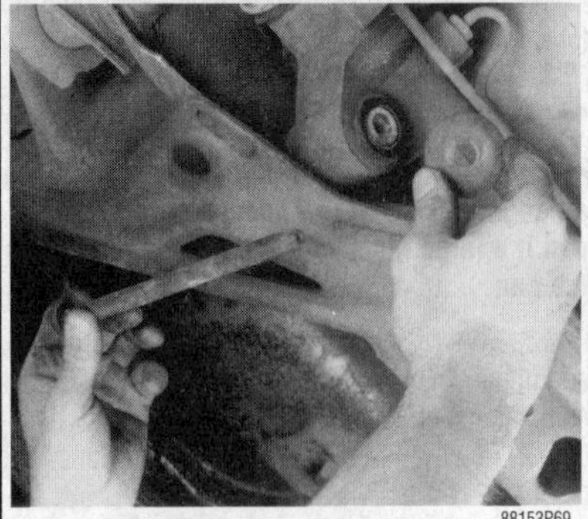

88153P69

Fig. 158 Remove the steering gear retaining through-bolts and washers

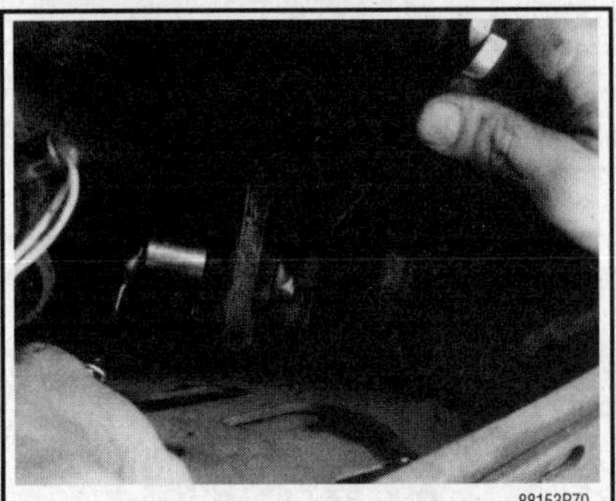

88153P70

Fig. 159 Because you are moving the steering gear, you will likely have to unbolt the input shaft from it

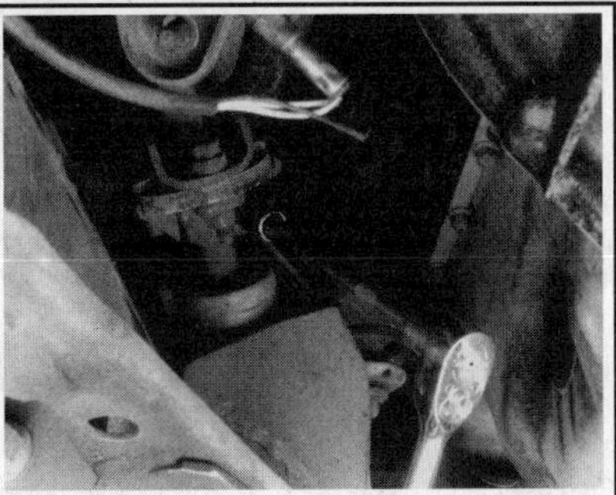

88153P71

Fig. 160 Again the tools you use will depend on the access you have to the fasteners

88153P72

Fig. 161 Once it is unbolted, reposition the steering gear out of the way

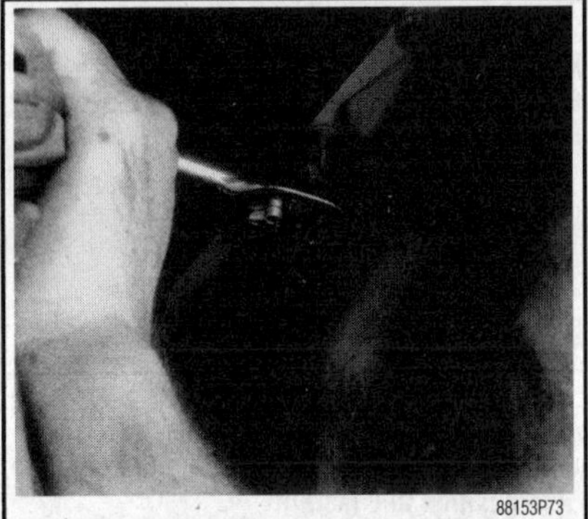

88153P73

Fig. 162 Loosen and remove the oil pan retaining bolts . . .

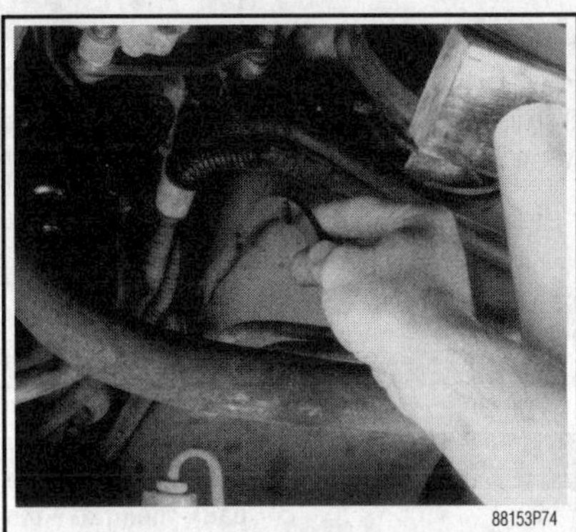

88153P74

Fig. 163 . . . and in this case, lower the pan reinforcements

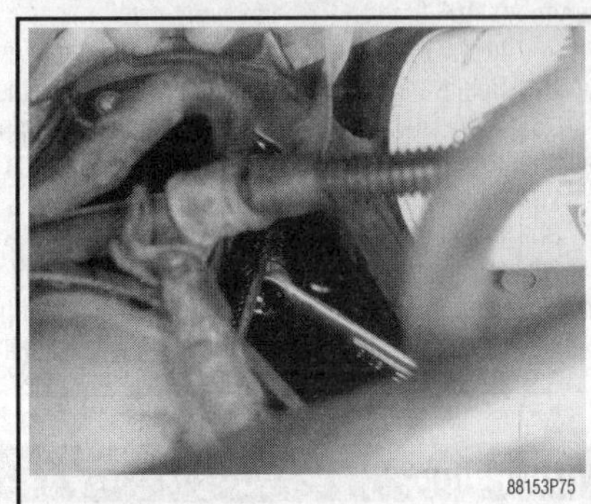

88153P75

Fig. 164 Lower the pan for access, then unbolt the oil pump and pickup tube assembly (lay it in the pan)

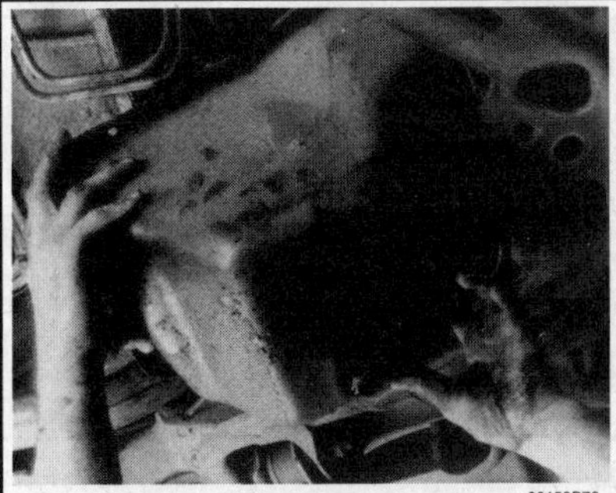

88153P76

Fig. 165 Carefully angle the pan (with the pump in it) over the crossmember and from the vehicle

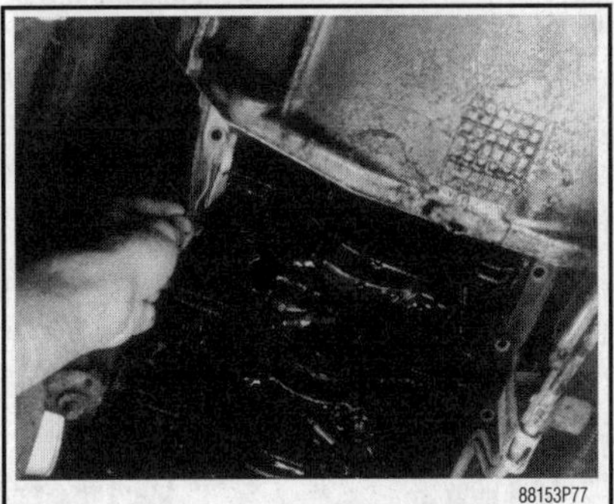

88153P77

Fig. 166 Once the oil pan is removed, check to see if the old gasket is still in place

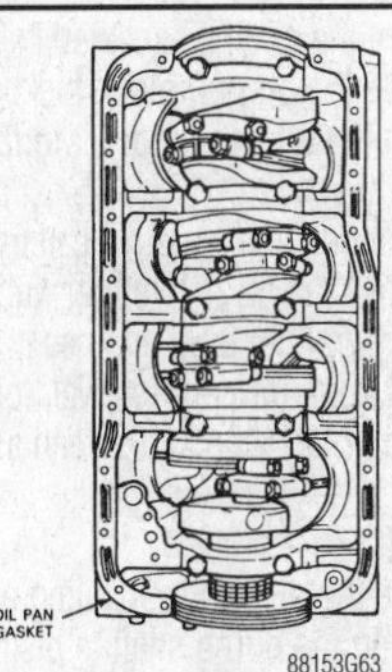

Fig. 167 On many of the engines covered by this manual, the gasket attaches to the block

10. Remove the steering gear attaching bolts and position the steering gear forward, out of the way.
11. Raise and support the engine to a position which allows clearance for oil pan removal.

➡**The best way to raise the engine is using an engine support fixture or an engine hoist. But, if necessary, a floor jack can be used under the oil pan if a large block of wood is used to distribute the load and protect the pan.**

12. With the engine raised, install wood blocks between the engine mounts and frame. Then, lower the engine onto the wood blocks. If you are using an engine hoist or support fixture, leave it in place for additional safety.
13. Remove the oil pan attaching bolts and lower the pan to the No. 2 crossmember.
14. Loosen the retaining bolts, then lower the oil pump and pickup tube assembly into the pan.
15. Remove the pan, along with the oil pump assembly, from the vehicle.

To install:

16. Clean the oil pan and the gasket mating surfaces.
17. Refer to the instructions included with the new oil pan gasket to determine if sealer is necessary for that type of gasket. Position the new gasket on the pan or block, as applicable.
18. With the oil pump and pickup tube assembly positioned in the oil pan, raise the pan onto the crossmember. Install the oil pump assembly.
19. With the pump properly secured, raise the oil pan into position and install the retaining bolts. Tighten the oil pan bolts to 71–106 inch lbs. (8–12 Nm) for 1989–92 vehicles or to 80–120 inch lbs. (9–14 Nm) for ¼ in. pan bolts and 12–18 ft. lbs. (16–24 Nm) for ⅝ in. pan bolts on 1993 vehicles.
20. Carefully raise the engine and remove the wood blocks, then lower the engine and remove the lifting device.
21. Install the engine mount-to-No. 2 crossmember attaching nuts or bolts. Tighten the retainers to 80–106 ft. lbs. (108–144 Nm).
22. Position the steering gear and install the retaining bolts.
23. Install the starter motor assembly.
24. Connect the oil level sensor wire to the oil pan.
25. Install the rear insulator and the No. 3 crossmember. Tighten the retainers to 80–106 ft. lbs. (108–144 Nm).
26. Install the catalytic converter and muffler inlet pipes.
27. Remove the jackstands and carefully lower the vehicle.
28. IMMEDIATELY refill the engine crankcase to prevent an accidental attempt to start the engine without oil in it. Install the oil level indicator.
29. Install the fan shroud.
30. Install the air cleaner tube.
31. Connect the negative battery cable, then start the engine and allow it to run for a few minutes. If there is no indication of oil pressure after the engine runs for a few seconds, shut it **OFF** and investigate the problem.
32. Check for leaks.

Oil Pump

REMOVAL & INSTALLATION

▶ **See Figures 168 and 169**

On most of the engines covered by this manual (except for the early model 2.3L engines), the oil pump and pickup tube assembly must be unbolted and positioned in the oil pan, in order to remove the pan while the engine is installed in the vehicle.

1. Disconnect the negative battery cable for safety.
2. Remove the oil pan, along with the oil pump and pickup tube assembly on all but early model 2.3L engines.
3. If not done for pan removal, loosen the retainers, then remove the oil pump pickup (inlet) tube and screen assembly, along with the oil pump assembly.

To install:

4. Prime the oil pump by filling either the inlet or outlet ports with engine oil and rotating the pump shaft to distribute the oil within the pump body.
5. Position the intermediate driveshaft into the distributor socket. With the shaft firmly seated in the distributor socket, the stop on the shaft should touch the roof of the crankcase. Remove the shaft and position the stop, as necessary.

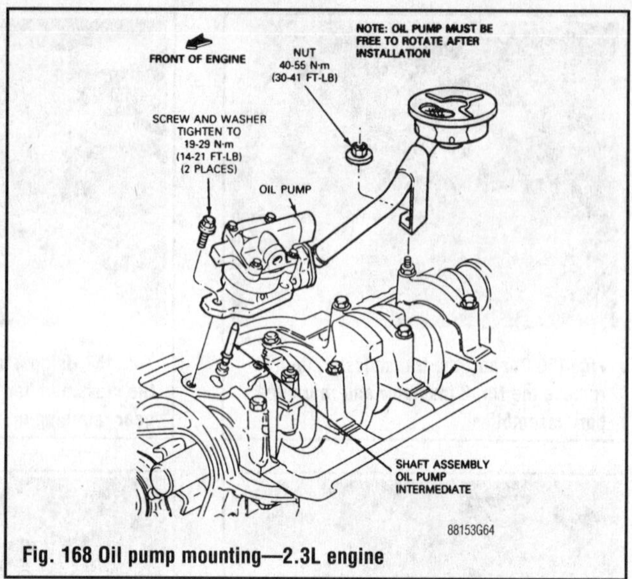

Fig. 168 Oil pump mounting—2.3L engine

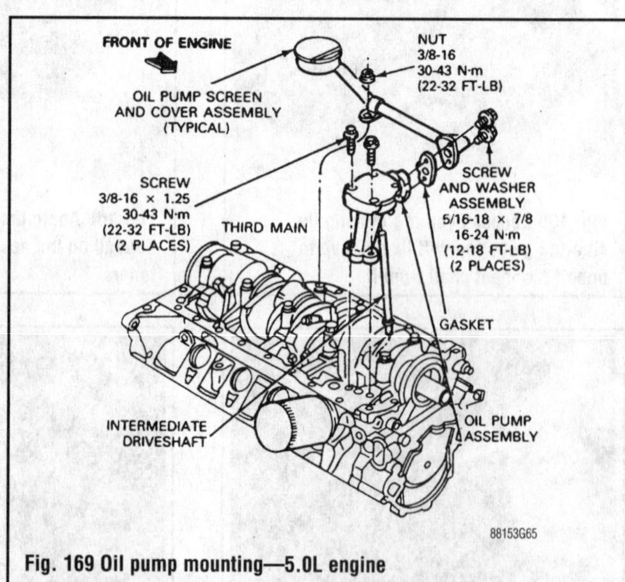

Fig. 169 Oil pump mounting—5.0L engine

➡**Remember, that on most vehicles covered by this manual, you will have to position the oil pan over the crossmember (with the pump in the pan), then raise the pump into position and install.**

6. Position a new gasket on the pump body, insert the intermediate shaft into the oil pump and install the pump and shaft as an assembly.

➡**Do not attempt to force the pump or shaft into position if it will not seat readily. The driveshaft hex may be misaligned with the distributor shaft. To align, rotate the intermediate shaft into a new position.**

7. Tighten the oil pump attaching screws to 14–21 ft. lbs. (19–29 Nm) on the 2.3L engine and 22–32 ft. lbs. (30–43 Nm) on the 5.0L engine.
8. If separated, clean and install the oil pump inlet tube and screen assembly.
9. Install the oil pan.
10. Connect the negative battery cable.

CHECKING

▶ **See Figures 170 and 171**

1. Wash all parts in solvent and dry them thoroughly with compressed air. Use a brush to clean the inside of the pump housing and the pressure relief valve chamber. Be sure all dirt and metal particles are removed.

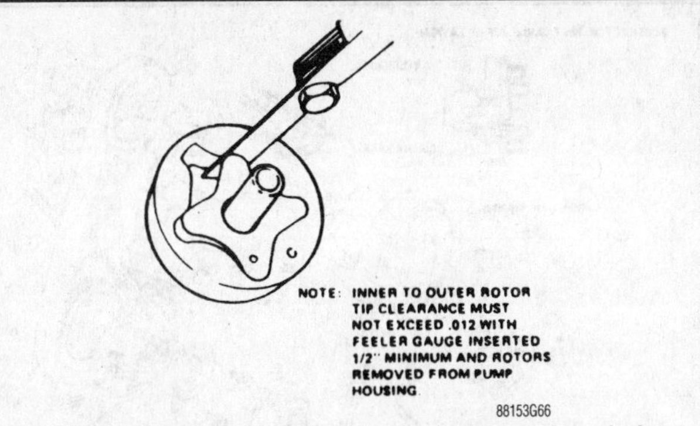

Fig. 170 Check the inner-to-outer rotor tip clearance using a feeler gauge

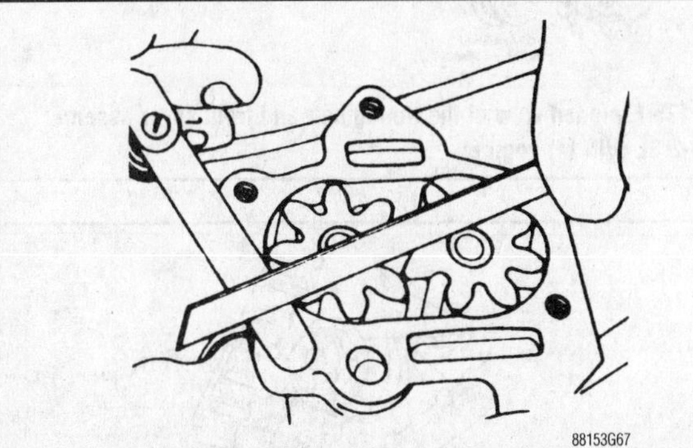

Fig. 171 Check rotor vertical clearance (end-play) using a straightedge and a feeler gauge

2. Check the inside of the pump housing and the inner and outer gears for damage or excessive wear.
3. Check the mating surface of the pump cover for wear. Minor scuff marks are normal, but if the cover, gears or housing surfaces are excessively worn, scored or grooved, replace the pump. Inspect the rotor for nicks, burrs or score marks. Remove minor imperfections with an oil stone.
4. Measure the inner-to-outer rotor tip clearance. With the rotor assembly removed from the pump and resting on a flat surface, the inner and outer rotor tip clearance must not exceed 0.012 in. (0.30mm) with the feeler gauge inserted 0.5 in. (13mm) minimum.
5. With the rotor assembly installed in the housing, place a straightedge over the rotor assembly and the housing. Measure the rotor end-play between the straightedge and both the inner and outer race. The maximum clearance must not exceed 0.005 in. (0.13mm).
6. Inspect the relief valve spring to see if it is collapsed or worn. Check the relief valve spring tension. Specifications are as follows:
   - 2.3L engine — 12.6–14.5 lbs. @ 1.20 in.
   - 5.0L engine — 10.6–12.2 lbs. @ 1.704 in.
7. If the spring tension is not within specification and/or the spring is worn or damaged, replace the pump.
8. Check the relief valve piston for scores and free operation in the bore.
9. Check the driveshaft-to-housing bearing clearance by measuring the OD of the shaft and the ID of the housing bearing. Clearance should be 0.0015–0.0030 in. (0.038–0.076mm).

➡Internal oil pump components are not serviced. If any component is out of specification, the entire pump must be replaced.

Timing Belt, Sprockets, Front Cover and Seals

The 2.3L engine, is the only engine covered by this manual to utilize a timing belt and sprockets (the 5.0L engine uses a timing chain and gear assembly instead). Because the timing belt is run dry (as opposed to a chain which is oiled) the front crankshaft, auxiliary shaft and camshaft seals are found underneath the belt, not in the timing cover as the crankshaft seal on timing chain motors.

➡Any time the timing cover is removed, the timing belt should be inspected for wear or damage to determine if it should be replaced. Please refer to Section 1 for more details concerning timing belt inspection.

REMOVAL & INSTALLATION

✻✻ CAUTION

When draining the coolant, keep in mind that cats and dogs are attracted by ethylene glycol antifreeze, and are quite likely to drink any that is left in an uncovered container or in puddles on the ground. This will prove fatal in sufficient quantity. Always drain the coolant into a sealable container. Coolant should be reused unless it is contaminated or too old.

Timing Belt Front Cover

See Figures 172 and 173

1. Disconnect the negative battery cable for safety.
2. Drain the cooling system to a level below the upper radiator hose and the thermostat housing.
3. Remove the automatic accessory drive belt tensioner and the drive belt(s).
4. Remove the four water pump pulley bolts, then remove the pulley for access.
5. Remove the upper radiator hose.
6. Remove the crankshaft pulley bolt and pulley. If difficulty is encountered, you may need to obtain a flywheel holding tool to keep the crankshaft from turn-

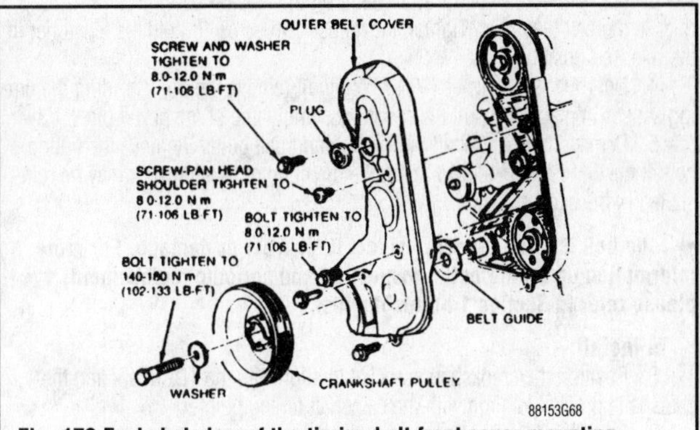

Fig. 172 Exploded view of the timing belt front cover mounting—2.3L (VIN A) engine

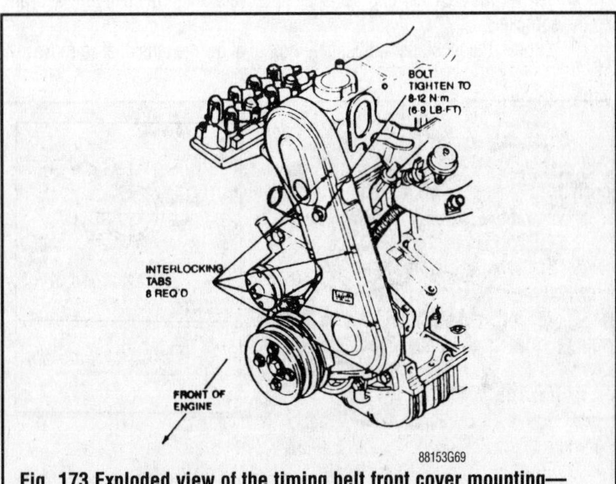

Fig. 173 Exploded view of the timing belt front cover mounting—2.3L (VIN M) engine

ing while loosening the bolt. Another method is to presoak the area with penetrating lubricant and allow it to sit overnight. A bolt which has been pretreated in this fashion will usually break loose easier.

7. Remove the thermostat housing and gasket.
8. Remove the timing belt outer cover retaining bolt(s). The VIN A engine is usually equipped with 4 bolts, while the VIN M engine only uses 1. Release the cover interlocking tabs (eight tabs on the VIN M engine), if equipped, and remove the cover.

To install:

9. Position the timing belt front cover. If equipped, snap the interlocking tabs into place.
10. Install the timing belt outer cover retaining bolt(s) and tighten to 71–106 inch lbs. (8–12 Nm).
11. Install the automatic drive belt tensioner.
12. Install the thermostat housing and a new gasket.
13. Install the upper radiator hose.
14. Install the crankshaft pulley and retaining bolt. Tighten the bolt to 103–133 ft. lbs. (140–180 Nm) for the VIN A engine (1989–90) or to 114–151 ft. lbs. (155–205 Nm) for the VIN M engine (1991–93).
15. Install the water pump pulley and the 4 retaining bolts.
16. Install the accessory drive belt(s).
17. Connect the negative battery cable, then properly refill the engine cooling system.
18. Run the engine and check for leaks.

Timing Belt and Tensioner

See Figures 174, 175, 176 and 177

1. Disconnect the negative battery cable for safety.
2. Remove the timing belt front cover.
3. Loosen the timing belt tensioner adjustment screw, position belt tensioner tool T74P–6254–A, or equivalent, on the tension spring roll pin and release the belt tensioner. Tighten the adjustment screw to hold the tensioner in the released position.
4. On 1991–93 vehicles (VIN M engine), remove the bolts holding the timing sensor in place and pull the sensor assembly free of the dowel pin.
5. Remove the crankshaft pulley, hub and belt guide. Remove the timing belt. If the belt is to be reused, mark the direction of rotation so it may be reinstalled in the same direction.

➡If the belt is to be reused, inspect it for wear or damage. For more information on timing belts, inspection and periodic replacement, please refer to Section 1 of this manual.

To install:

6. Position the crankshaft sprocket to align with the TDC mark and the camshaft sprocket to align with the camshaft timing pointer.
7. On 1989–90 vehicles, remove the distributor cap and set the rotor to the No. 1 firing position by turning the auxiliary shaft.
8. Install the timing belt over the crankshaft sprocket and then counterclockwise over the auxiliary and camshaft sprockets. Align the belt fore-and-aft on the sprockets.
9. Loosen the tensioner adjustment bolt to allow the tensioner to move against the belt. If the spring does not have enough tension to move the roller against the belt, it may be necessary to manually push the roller against the belt and tighten the bolt.
10. Remove a spark plug from each cylinder in order to relieve engine compression and to make sure the belt does not jump time during rotation in the next step.
11. Rotate the crankshaft two complete turns in the direction of normal rotation to remove the slack from the belt.
12. For 1992–93 (VIN M) engines, have an assistant hold the crankshaft pulley from turning (this can be done in a variety of ways including at the fly-

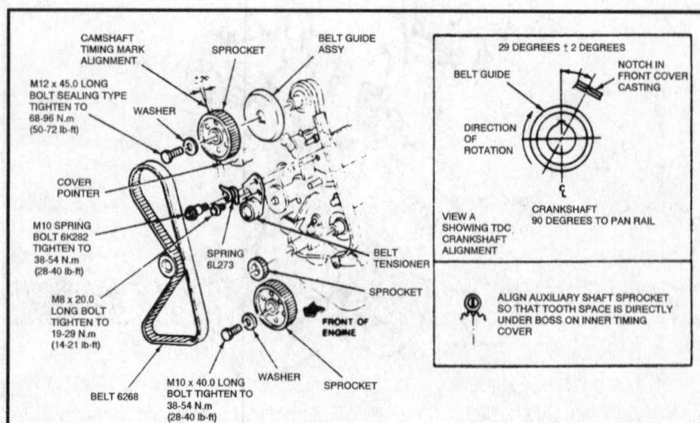

Fig. 174 Exploded view of the timing belt and sprocket assembly—2.3L (VIN A) engine

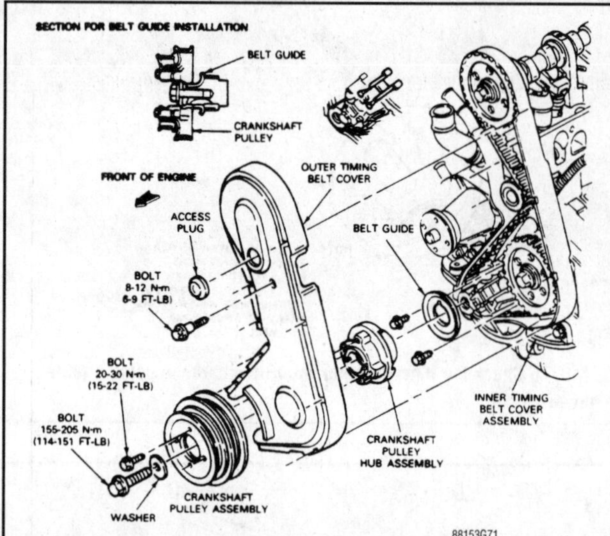

Fig. 175 Exploded view of the timing belt and front cover assembly—2.3L (VIN M) engine

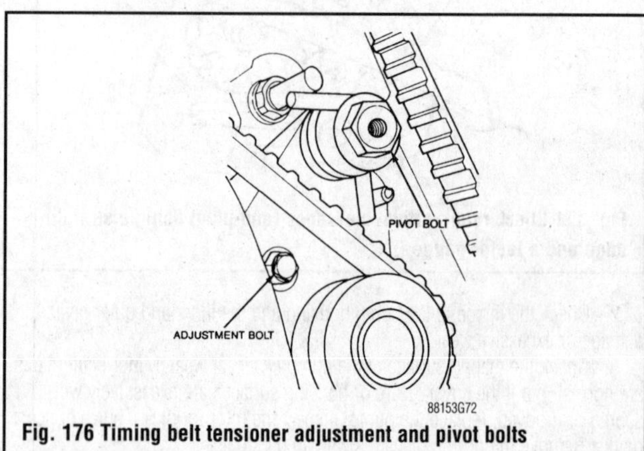

Fig. 176 Timing belt tensioner adjustment and pivot bolts

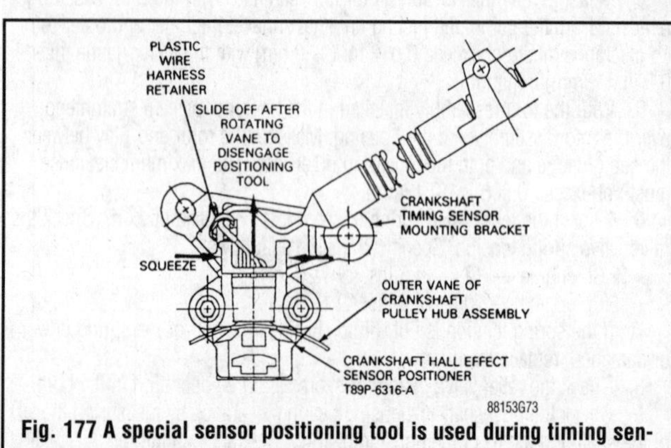

Fig. 177 A special sensor positioning tool is used during timing sensor installation—2.3L (VIN M) engine

wheel with a holding tool, or with a wrench and a prybar at the pulley bolts). Turn the camshaft sprocket counterclockwise using a torque wrench, until the torque setting reads 40 ft. lbs. (54 Nm), then while still holding both the camshaft and crankshaft from turning, tighten the tensioner adjustment and pivot bolts.

13. Tighten the tensioner adjustment bolt to 29–40 ft. lbs. (40–55 Nm) and pivot bolts to 14–22 ft. lbs. (20–30 Nm).
14. Recheck the alignment of the timing marks.
15. Install the crankshaft belt guide.
16. On 1989–90 vehicles, install the crankshaft pulley and tighten the retaining bolt to 103–133 ft. lbs. (140–180 Nm). On 1991–92 vehicles, proceed as follows:
    a. Install the timing sensor onto the dowel pin and tighten the two longer bolts to 14–22 ft. lbs. (20–30 Nm).
    b. Rotate the crankshaft 45 degrees counterclockwise, then install the crankshaft pulley and hub assembly. Tighten the bolt to 114–151 ft. lbs. (155–205 Nm).
    c. Rotate the crankshaft 90 degrees clockwise so the vane of the crankshaft pulley engages with timing sensor positioner tool T89P–6316–A, or equivalent. Tighten the two shorter sensor bolts to 14–22 ft. lbs. (20–30 Nm).
    d. Rotate the crankshaft 90 degrees counterclockwise, then remove the sensor positioner tool.
    e. Rotate the crankshaft 90 degrees clockwise and measure the outer vane-to-sensor air gap. The gap must be 0.018–0.039 in. (0.458–0.996mm).
17. Install the spark plug which was removed from each cylinder.
18. Install the timing belt front cover.
19. Connect the negative battery cable.
20. For distributor equipped (VIN A) engines, check the ignition timing.

Timing Sprockets

➧ See Figure 178

1. Disconnect the negative battery cable for safety.
2. Remove the timing belt front cover.
3. Remove the timing belt.
4. Remove the camshaft and auxiliary shaft sprocket retaining bolts, as necessary. A holding tool such as T74P-6256-B is extremely helpful here.
5. Remove the crankshaft, camshaft and auxiliary shaft sprockets, as necessary, using a suitable puller.

To install:

6. Install the crankshaft, camshaft and/or auxiliary shaft sprockets, as necessary.
7. While holding the sprocket from turning (using the holding tool), tighten the camshaft sprocket retaining bolt to 52–70 ft. lbs. (70–95 Nm) and/or the auxiliary sprocket retaining bolt to 28–40 ft. lbs. (38–54 Nm) for 1989–90 (VIN A) engines, or to 30–41 ft. lbs. (40–55 Nm) for 1991–93 (VIN M) engines.

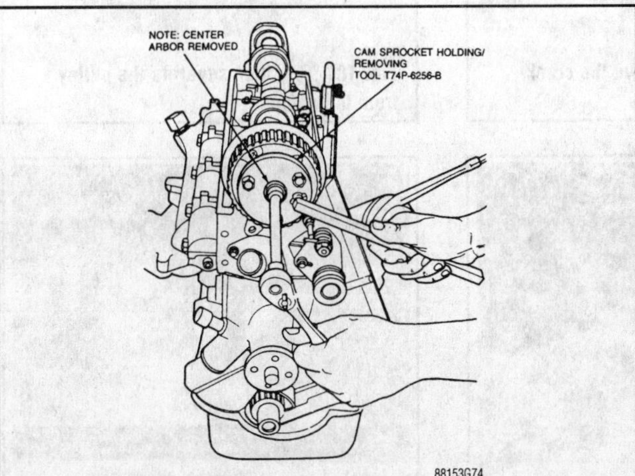

Fig. 178 The camshaft and auxiliary shaft sprockets are most easily removed or installed using a special holding tool

8. Install the timing belt.
9. Install the timing belt front cover.
10. Connect the negative battery cable.

Front Oil Seals

➧ See Figures 179 and 180

1. Disconnect the negative battery cable for safety.
2. Remove the timing belt front cover.
3. Remove the timing belt.
4. Remove the timing sprocket (crankshaft, camshaft and/or auxiliary shaft) under which the seal is being replaced.
5. Use seal remover tool T74P–6700–B, or an equivalent jawed seal puller, to remove the crankshaft, camshaft and/or auxiliary shaft seal(s). Position the tool so that the jaws are gripping the thin edge of the seal very tightly. Operate the jackscrew on the tool to remove the seal.

To install:

6. Lubricate the lips of the new seals with clean engine oil.
7. Use a threaded seal installer tool such as T74P–6150–A, or equivalent, to install the seals.
8. Install the timing sprocket(s).
9. Install the timing belt.
10. Install the timing belt front cover.
11. Connect the negative battery cable.

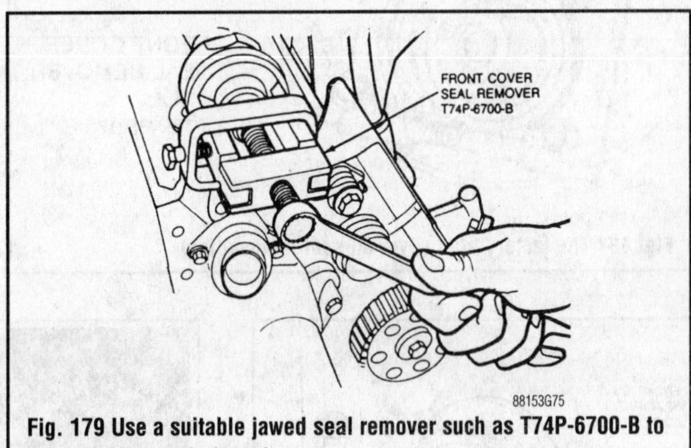

Fig. 179 Use a suitable jawed seal remover such as T74P-6700-B to remove the camshaft seal . . .

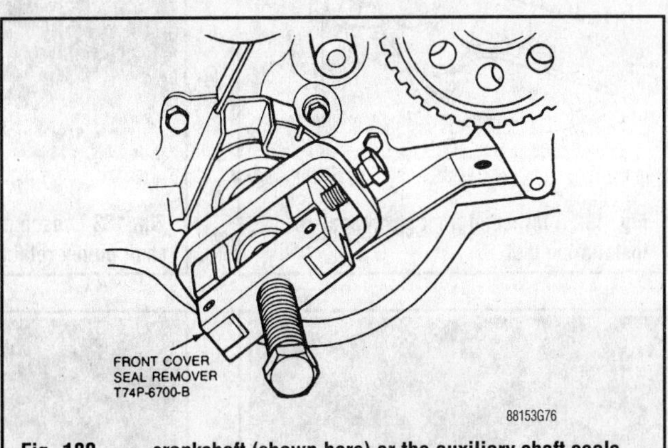

Fig. 180 . . . crankshaft (shown here) or the auxiliary shaft seals

Timing Chain, Gears, Front Cover and Seal

The 5.0L engine, is the only engine covered by this manual which uses a timing chain and gear assembly (the 2.3L engine uses a timing belt and sprockets). Because the timing chain is run wet (as opposed to belts which are run dry) the front crankshaft seal is found in the outer timing cover, and not underneath the cover as on timing belt motors.

REMOVAL & INSTALLATION

CAUTION

When draining the coolant, keep in mind that cats and dogs are attracted by ethylene glycol antifreeze, and are quite likely to drink any that is left in an uncovered container or in puddles on the ground. This will prove fatal in sufficient quantity. Always drain the coolant into a sealable container. Coolant should be reused unless it is contaminated or too old.

Front Cover Oil Seal

See Figures 181 thru 188

The front cover (crankshaft) oil seal may be replaced with the cover installed.

1. Disconnect the negative battery cable for safety.
2. Remove the fan shroud and position it back over the fan.

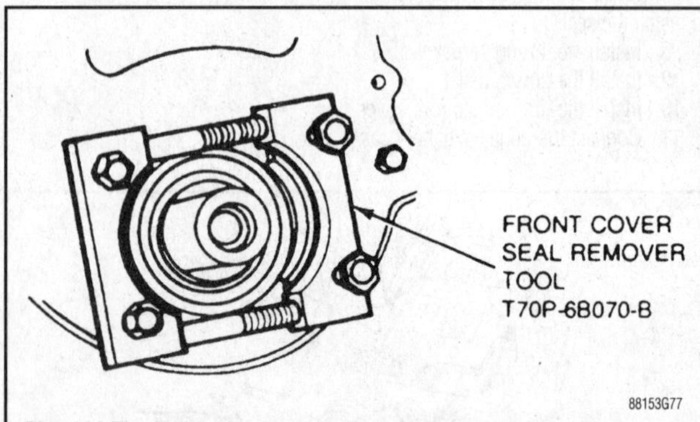

Fig. 181 The factory front cover oil seal removal tool

3. Remove the accessory drive belt.
4. Remove the fan/clutch assembly and shroud from the vehicle.
5. Remove the crankshaft pulley from the damper, then remove the damper retaining bolt. Remove the damper from the front of the crankshaft using a puller.
6. Use a suitable seal removal tool to remove the seal from the cover. The factory tool gets behind the metal flange similar to a bearing splitter tool and pulls the seal outward. Be careful not to damage the crankshaft or the seal bore in the timing chain cover.

To install:

7. Lubricate the seal lip with Lubriplate® or a clean multi-purpose grease, then install using a threaded seal installer.
8. Apply Lubriplate®, or a clean multi-purpose grease, to the sealing surface of the vibration damper. Then apply a small amount of silicone sealant to the keyway. Align the crankshaft damper keyway with the crankshaft key, then install the damper to the crankshaft. Do NOT hammer the damper on, carefully push the damper into position and, if difficulty is encountered, use the retaining bolt and washer to draw the damper into the fully seated position.
9. Tighten the damper retaining bolt to 70–90 ft. lbs. (95–122 Nm).
10. Install the crankshaft pulley.
11. Install the mechanical cooling fan/clutch assembly, along with the fan shroud.

Remember that the fan shroud must be lowered into the engine compartment along with the fan and clutch assembly as there will be insufficient clearance to accomplish this after the fan is installed.

12. Install the accessory drive belt.
13. Connect the negative battery cable.

Front (Timing Chain) Cover

See Figures 182 thru 195

1. Disconnect the negative battery cable for safety.
2. Drain the cooling system and the engine crankcase oil.
3. Remove the air inlet tube.

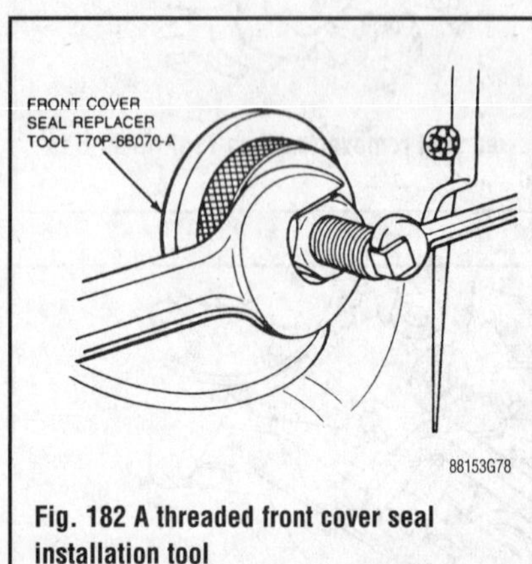

Fig. 182 A threaded front cover seal installation tool

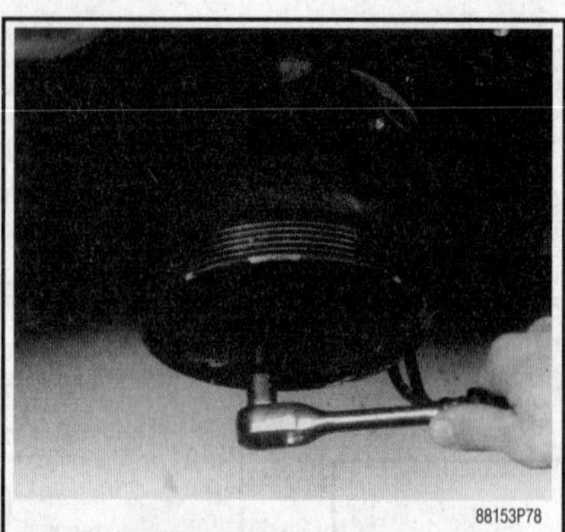

Fig. 183 Loosen and remove the crankshaft pulley retaining bolts . . .

Fig. 184 . . . then separate the pulley from the damper

Fig. 185 Loosen the crankshaft damper retaining bolt (a holding tool for the flywheel can be helpful here)

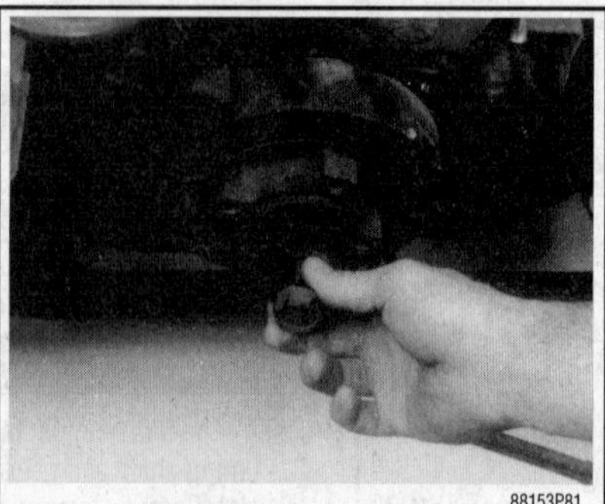

Fig. 186 Once loosened, unthread and remove the bolt and washer from the damper

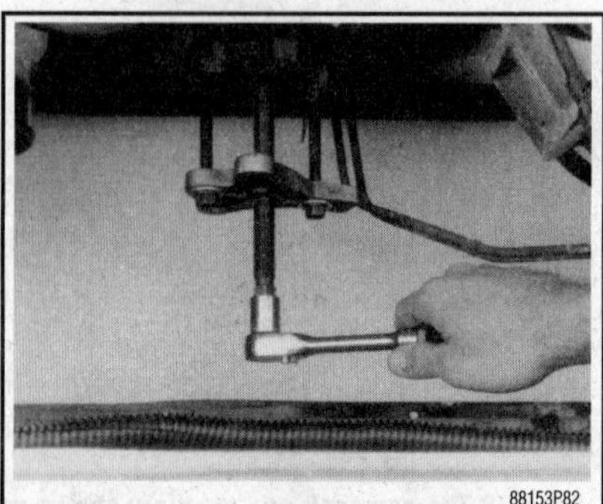

Fig. 187 Install a suitable threaded puller (NOT a jawed puller) to the crankshaft damper . . .

Fig. 188 . . . then thread the puller until the damper is free of the crankshaft

Fig. 189 Remove any accessory brackets which are attached to the water pump or front cover

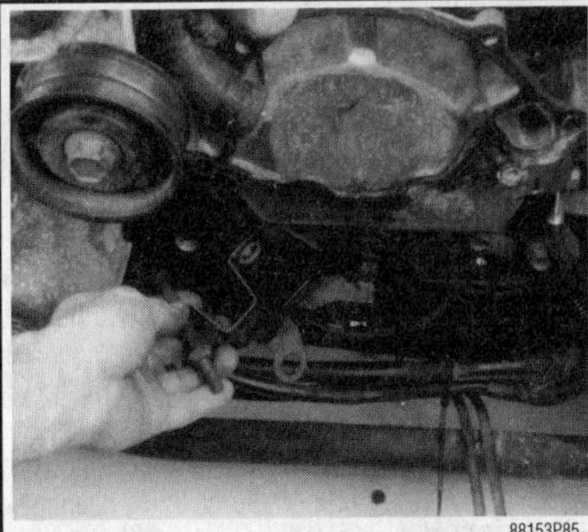

Fig. 190 In this case, a bracket had to be removed in order to reach another bracket

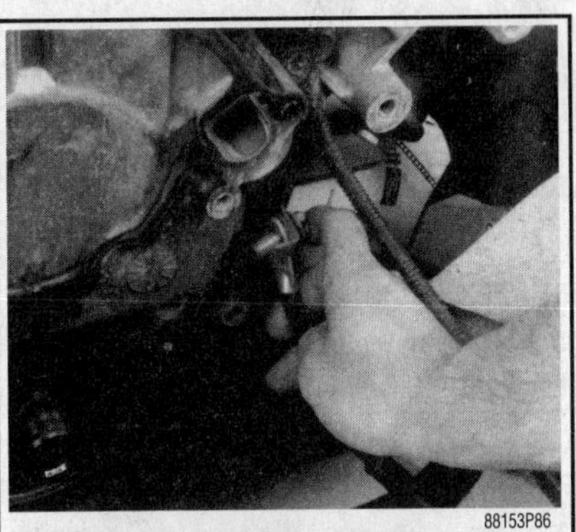

Fig. 191 Disconnect any wiring that would interfere with front cover removal

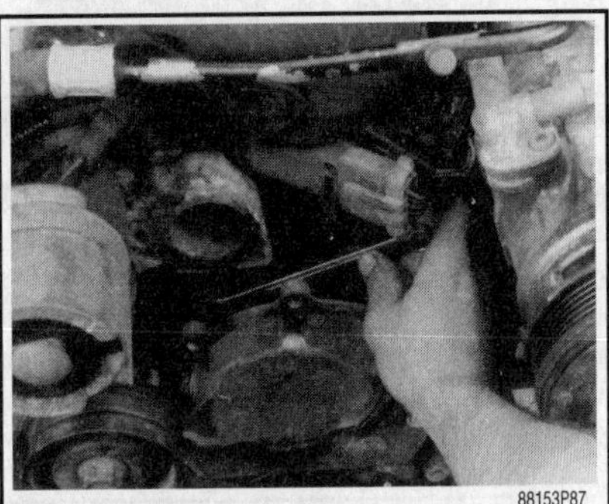

Fig. 192 Once ALL cover bolts (including at the oil pan) are removed, gently pry to break the gasket seal

Fig. 193 Remove the cover being careful to keep debris out of the oil pan

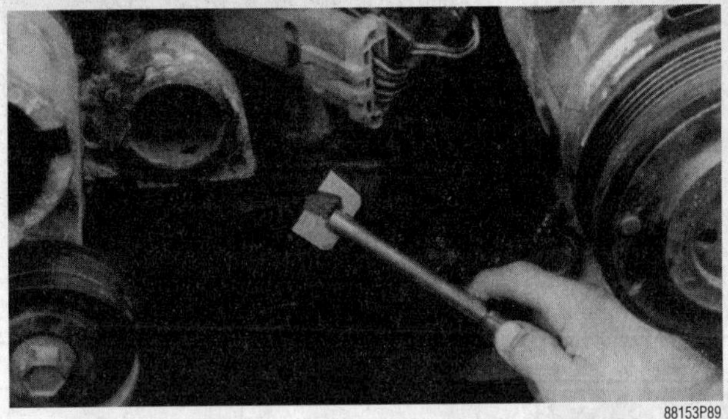

Fig. 194 Clean the gasket mating surfaces (again keeping debris OUT OF the oil pan)

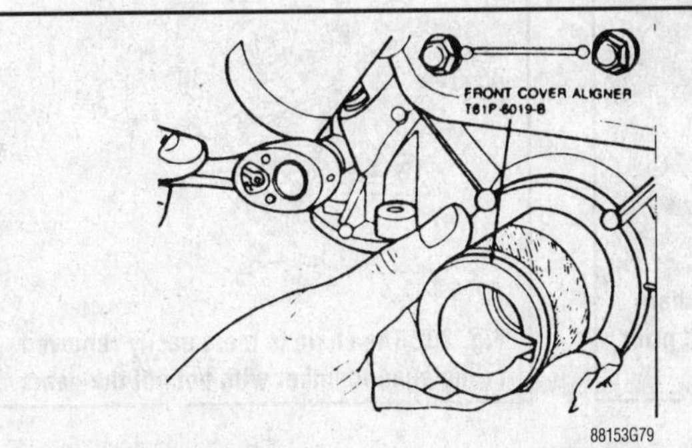

Fig. 195 A front cover alignment tool helps to align the bolt holes without having to move the cover so much that the gasket and sealant become dislodged

4. Remove the fan shroud attaching bolts and position the shroud over the fan.

5. Remove the fan and clutch assembly from the water pump shaft, then remove the clutch, fan and shroud from the vehicle.

6. Remove the accessory drive belt, then remove the water pump pulley.

7. Remove all accessory brackets that attach to the water pump.

8. Disconnect the lower radiator hose, heater hose and water pump bypass hose from the water pump.

9. Remove the crankshaft pulley from the crankshaft vibration damper. Remove the damper attaching bolt and washer, then remove the damper using a suitable threaded (NOT JAWED) puller.

10. Remove the oil pan-to-front cover attaching bolts. Use a thin-bladed knife to cut the oil pan gasket flush with the cylinder block face prior to separating the cover from the cylinder block.

➡Before removing the cover, verify that no other brackets or wires are attached.

11. Remove the cylinder front cover and water pump as an assembly.

➡Cover the front oil pan opening while the cover assembly is off to prevent foreign material from entering the pan.

To install:

12. If a new front cover is to be installed, remove the water pump from the old front cover and install it on the new front cover.

➡Ford recommends the installation of a new front cover seal whenever the cover has been removed. This is likely a precautionary measure to prevent you from having to disassemble the engine sufficiently to get at the seal, should it become worn or damaged. You will have to decide for yourself if the condition of your seal requires replacement.

13. Clean all gasket mating surfaces. If necessary, pry the old oil seal from the front cover and install a new one, using a seal installer.

14. Coat the gasket surface of the oil pan with sealer, cut and position the

required sections of a new gasket on the oil pan and apply silicone sealer at the corners. Apply sealer to a new front cover gasket, then install it on the block.

15. Position the front cover on the cylinder block. Use care to avoid seal damage or gasket dislocation. It may be necessary to force the cover downward to compress the pan gasket slightly. Use front cover aligner tool T61P–6019–B, or equivalent, to assist the operation.

16. Coat the threads of the front cover attaching screws with an oil resistant Teflon® pipe sealant and install. While pushing in on the alignment tool, tighten the oil pan-to-cover attaching screws to 12–18 ft. lbs. (16–24 Nm).

17. Tighten the front cover-to-cylinder block attaching bolts to 12–18 ft. lbs. (16–24 Nm). Remove the alignment tool.

18. Apply multi-purpose grease to the sealing surface of the vibration damper. Then apply a small amount of silicone sealant to the keyway. Align the crankshaft damper keyway with the crankshaft key, then install the damper to the crankshaft. Do NOT hammer the damper on, carefully push the damper into position and, if difficulty is encountered, use the retaining bolt and washer to draw the damper into the fully seated position.

19. Tighten the damper retaining bolt to 70–90 ft. lbs. (95–122 Nm).

20. Install the crankshaft pulley.

21. Before you go any further, REFILL THE ENGINE CRANKCASE with fresh, clean engine oil. DO IT NOW, DO NOT risk forgetting it later.

22. Connect the hoses and accessory brackets to the water pump.

23. Install the pulley on the water pump shaft.

24. Install the shroud along with the clutch and fan assembly.

25. Route and install the accessory drive belt.

26. Connect the negative battery cable and refill the cooling system.

27. Run the engine and check for leaks.

Timing Chain and Gears

See Figures 196 thru 202

1. Disconnect the negative battery cable for safety.
2. Remove the timing chain front cover.
3. Rotate the crankshaft until the timing marks on the gears are aligned.
4. Remove the camshaft retaining bolt, washer and eccentric. Slide both gears and the timing chain forward and remove them as an assembly.

To install:

5. Position the gears and timing chain on the camshaft and crankshaft simultaneously. Make sure the timing marks on the gears are aligned.

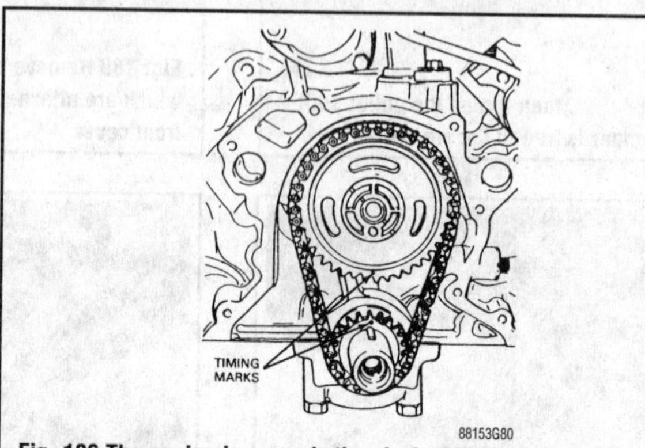

Fig. 196 The engine is properly timed when the timing marks are aligned at the point closest together on their travel

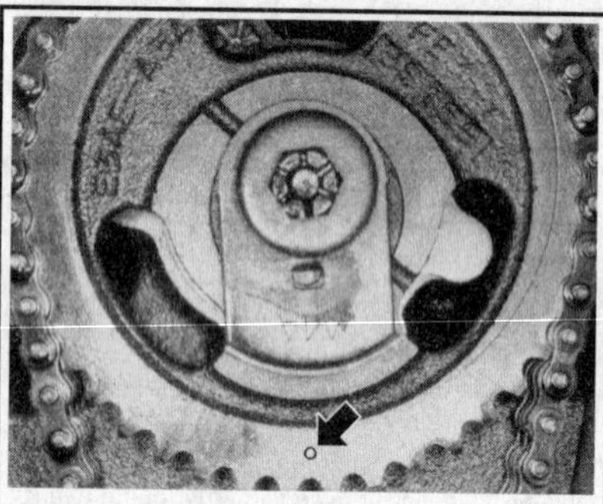

Fig. 197 Align the timing marks before chain and gear removal (here the cam mark is at the lowest point of travel)

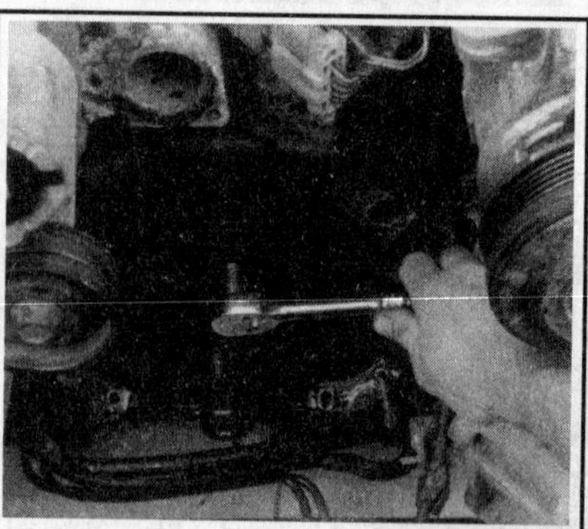

Fig. 198 With the marks aligned, loosen the camshaft gear retaining bolt

Fig. 199 Remove the gear retaining bolt and washer

Fig. 200 Then, remove the timing chain and gears as an assembly

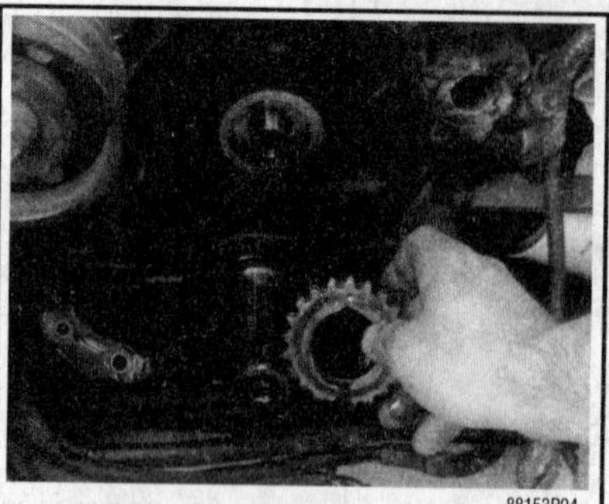

Fig. 201 This photo shows the crankshaft gear as the timing mark was oriented prior to removal

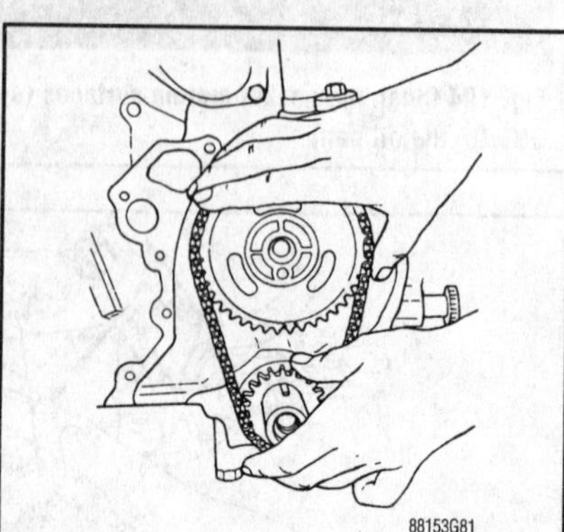

Fig. 202 The chain is most easily removed or installed together with both of the gears

6. Install the washer, eccentric (if equipped) and camshaft gear retaining bolt. Tighten the bolt to 40–45 ft. lbs. (54–61 Nm).
7. Install the timing chain front cover.
8. Connect the negative battery cable.

Camshaft

REMOVAL & INSTALLATION

CAUTION

When draining the coolant, keep in mind that cats and dogs are attracted by ethylene glycol antifreeze, and are quite likely to drink any that is left in an uncovered container or in puddles on the ground. This will prove fatal in sufficient quantity. Always drain the coolant into a sealable container. Coolant should be reused unless it is contaminated or too old.

2.3L Engine

See Figures 203 and 204

1. Disconnect the negative battery cable and drain the cooling system.
2. Remove the air intake and the throttle body.
3. Disconnect the radiator hoses. Remove the cooling fan and shroud assembly.
4. Tag and disconnect the spark plug wires, then position aside.
5. Tag and disengage the necessary electrical connectors and vacuum lines, positioning them aside for clearance.
6. Remove the rocker arm cover retaining bolts and the rocker cover.
7. Remove the timing belt front cover.
8. Remove the timing belt.
9. Compress the valve springs using valve spring compressor lever T88T–6565–BH, or equivalent, and remove the cam followers (rocker arms).
10. Remove the camshaft sprocket retaining bolt. Remove the camshaft sprocket using a suitable puller. Remove the camshaft seal using a seal removal tool.
11. Remove the two screws and the camshaft rear retainer.
12. Raise and support the vehicle safely using jackstands. Be sure to position the vehicle at a height which will allow access both above and below the engine.
13. Remove the right and left engine support bolts and nuts.
14. Position a block of wood and a jack under the engine. Raise the engine as high as it will go. Place blocks of wood between the engine mounts and chassis brackets. If the vehicle is supported at a height allowing access above and below the engine, you can leave the jack in position.

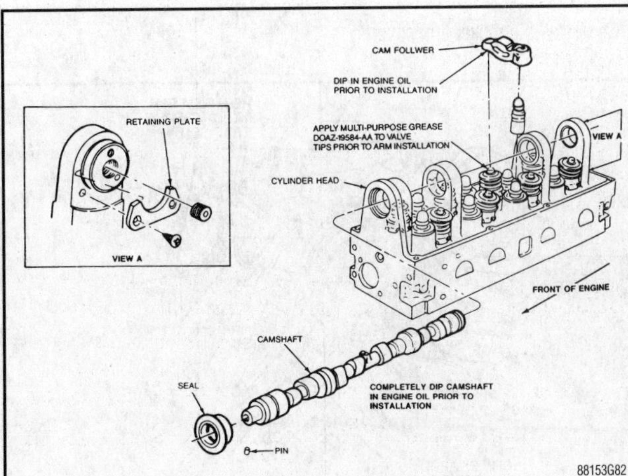

Fig. 203 Exploded view of the camshaft mounting—2.3L (VIN A) engine

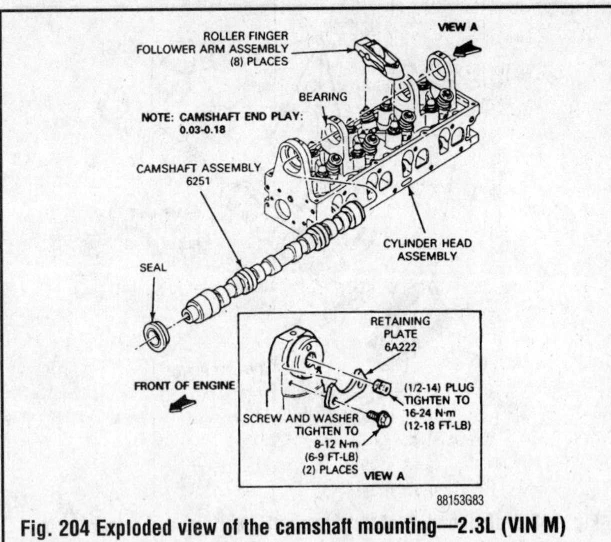

Fig. 204 Exploded view of the camshaft mounting—2.3L (VIN M) engine

15. Remove the camshaft slowly and carefully to prevent damage to the lobes, journals or bearings.
16. Inspect the lobes and bearings for damage or wear. Replace the camshaft and bearings, as necessary.

To install:

17. If camshaft bearing replacement is necessary, you will have to rent or buy a bearing removal and installation tool. Essentially the tool is a threaded rod with a pulling plate and nut, along with various size drivers to push the bearings out of or pull the bearings into position.
18. Make sure the threaded plug is in the rear of the camshaft. If you are replacing the camshaft, you may have to remove the plug from the old camshaftand install it in the new one.
19. Coat the camshaft lobes with multi-purpose grease and lubricate the journals with heavy engine oil before installation. An engine assembly lube can also be used. Carefully slide the camshaft through the bearings.
20. Install the camshaft rear retainer and tighten the two screws to 6–9 ft. lbs. (8–12 Nm). Install a new camshaft seal using a suitable seal installer.
21. Install the camshaft sprocket and tighten the retaining bolt to 52–70 ft. lbs. (70–95 Nm).
22. Install the timing belt.
23. Install the timing belt front cover.
24. Raise the engine with the jack and block of wood used earlier. Remove the blocks of wood, lower the engine and remove the jack.
25. Install the engine support bolts and nuts, then remove the jackstands and carefully lower the vehicle.
26. Install the rocker arm cover.
27. Engage the electrical connectors and vacuum lines as tagged earlier.
28. Connect the spark plug wires as tagged earlier.
29. Install the cooling fan and shroud assembly.
30. Connect the radiator hoses.
31. Install the throttle body and the air intake.
32. Connect the negative battery cable, then properly refill the engine cooling system.
33. Run the engine and check for leaks.
34. On the distributor equipped (VIN A) engine, check the ignition timing.

5.0L Engine

See Figure 205

If your vehicle is equipped with A/C, you will have to take the car to a service station to have the refrigerant discharged and recovered (using a proper recycling/recovery station) before beginning this procedure.

1. Properly discharge and recover the A/C refrigerant using a recovery station.
2. Disconnect the negative battery cable for safety.
3. Drain the cooling system and relieve the fuel system pressure.

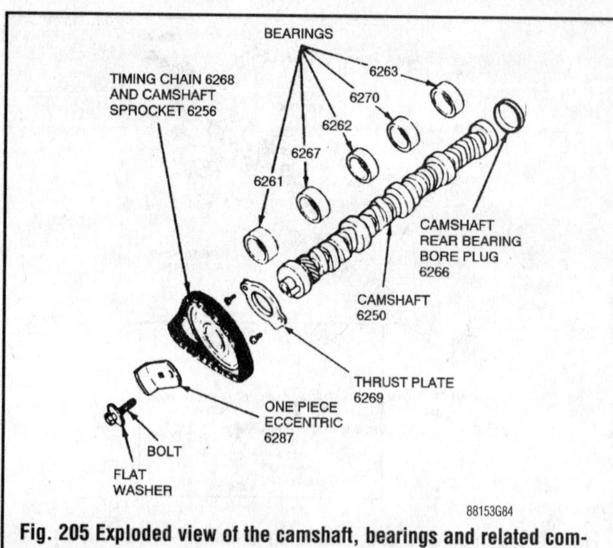

Fig. 205 Exploded view of the camshaft, bearings and related components—5.0L engine

4. Remove the radiator. If equipped with air conditioning, remove the condenser.
5. Remove the grille.
6. Remove the upper and lower intake manifold assembly.
7. Remove the rocker arm covers.
8. Remove the pushrods and lifters.

➡**Keep track of all valve train components. Any components which are to be reused, such as pushrods or lifters, must be reinstalled in their original locations. If necessary sort or label them during removal to assure installation in their correct positions.**

9. Remove the timing chain front cover.
10. Remove the timing chain and gears.
11. Remove the thrust plate. Remove the camshaft, being careful not to damage the bearing surfaces.

To install:

12. Lubricate the camshaft lobes and journals with heavy engine oil or a suitable engine assembly lube. An engine assembly lube is preferable if some time may pass before the job is completed and the engine is started. Install the camshaft, being careful not to damage the bearing surfaces while sliding it into position.
13. Install the camshaft thrust plate with the groove toward the cylinder block. Tighten the bolts to 9–12 ft. lbs. (12–16 Nm).
14. Check the camshaft play to determine whether or not the thrust plate must be replaced.
15. Install the lifters and pushrods.

➡**When reinstalling a camshaft, make sure the lifters and pushrods are installed in their original locations. If a new camshaft is being installed, new lifters and pushrods should be used.**

16. Install the timing chain and gears.
17. Install the engine front cover.
18. Install the rocker arm covers.
19. Install the upper and lower intake manifolds.
20. Install the grille. If equipped with air conditioning, install the condenser.
21. Install the radiator.
22. Connect the negative battery cable, then fill and bleed the engine cooling system.
23. Run the engine and check for leaks.

INSPECTION

Camshaft Lobe Lift

Camshaft lobe lift is the amount (measured in in. or mm) that the camshaft is capable of LIFITING the valve train components in order to open the valves. The lobe lift is a measure of how much taller the "egg shaped" portion of the camshaft lobe is above the base or circular portion of the shaft lobe. Lift is directly proportional to how far the valves can open and a worn camshaft (with poor lobe lift) cannot fully open the valves. The lobe lift therefore can be directly responsible for proper or poor engine performance.

Lobe lift can be measured in 2 ways, depending on what tools are available and whether or not the camshaft has been removed from the engine. The dial gauge can be used to measure the lift with the camshaft installed, while the micrometer is normally only used once the shaft has been removed from the engine.

DIAL GAUGE

➧ **See Figure 206**

On both the 2.3L and 5.0L engines, lobe lift may be checked with the camshaft installed. In both cases, a dial gauge is positioned somewhere on the valve train (pushrod, lifter, or camshaft itself) and the camshaft is then turned to measure the lift.

Check the lift of each lobe in consecutive order and make a note of the reading.

1. Remove the rocker arm cover for access to the camshaft (2.3L) or pushrods (5.0L).
2. On the 5.0L engine, either remove the rocker arms (remember to tag or arrange them for proper installation), or loosen their mounting and reposition them for access to the pushrods. Make sure the pushrod is in the valve tappet socket.
3. Install a dial indicator D78P–4201–B or equivalent. so that the actuating point of the indicator is in the pushrod socket (or the indicator ball socket adaptor tool 6565–AB is on the end of the pushrod) and in the same plane as the pushrod movement. On the 2.3L engine, the dial indicator may be directly placed on the camshaft.

➡**A remote starter can be used to turn the engine over during the next steps. If a remote starter is not available, remove the spark plugs (one from each cylinder on the 2.3L engine) in order to relieve engine compression and turn the engine over using a large wrench or socket on the crankshaft damper bolt. BE SURE to only turn the engine in the normal direction of rotation, especially on the 2.3L (TIMING BELT) engine.**

4. Turn the crankshaft over until the tappet is on the base circle of the camshaft lobe. At this position on the 5.0L engine, the pushrod will be at its lowest point of travel.
5. Zero the dial indicator. Continue to rotate the crankshaft slowly until the pushrod (or camshaft lobe) is in the fully raised position.
6. Compare the total lift recorded on the dial indicator with the elevation specification shown on the Camshaft Specification chart.

To check the accuracy of the original indicator reading, continue to rotate the crankshaft until the indicator reads zero. If the lift on any lobe is below specified wear limits listed, the camshaft and the valve tappet operating on the worn lobe(s) must be replaced.

7. When you are finished, install the rocker arms (5.0L engine) and check the valve clearance.
8. Install the rocker arm cover(s).

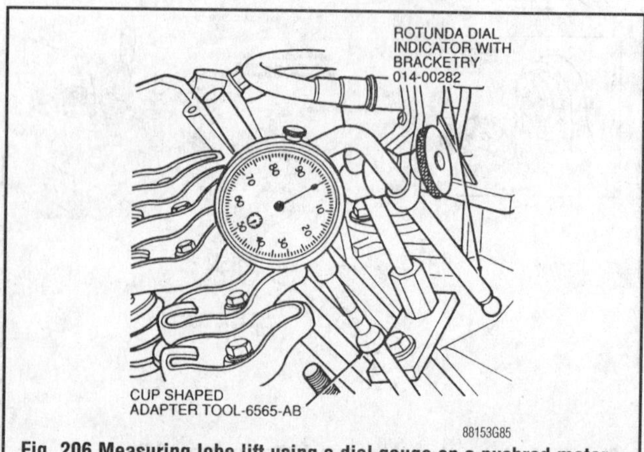

Fig. 206 Measuring lobe lift using a dial gauge on a pushrod motor such as the 5.0L engine

MICROMETER

◆ See Figures 207 and 208

A micrometer may used to measure camshaft lobe lift, but this is usually only after it has been removed from the engine. Once the rocker arm cover is removed from the 2.3L engine, access may be possible (though a little awkward) to measure the camshaft lobes using a micrometer.

In any case, 2 measurements are necessary for each lobe. Measurement **Y** or the total LOBE HEIGHT and measurement **X** or the total LOBE WIDTH. To find the lobe lift, you simply subtract **X** from **Y** (subtract the width from the height).

Note each measurement, then make your calculation to determine the lift. Note the final results and repeat the process on the remaining camshaft lobes. Finally, you should compare your results to the specifications charts and decide if a new camshaft is in your future.

Camshaft End-Play

➡On all gasoline V8 engines, prying against the aluminum-nylon camshaft sprocket, with the valve train load on the camshaft, can break or damage the sprocket. Therefore, the rocker arms must be loosened sufficiently to free the camshaft. After checking the camshaft end-play, check the valve clearance. Adjust if required (refer to the procedure in Section 1 of this manual for more details).

1. Push the camshaft toward the rear of the engine. Install a dial indicator (Tool D78P–4201–F, –G or equivalent) so that the indicator point is on the camshaft sprocket attaching screw.
2. Zero the dial indicator. Position a prybar between the camshaft gear and the block. Pull the camshaft forward and release it. Compare the dial indicator reading with the specifications.
3. If end-play is excessive, check the spacer for correct installation before it is removed. If the spacer is correctly installed, replace the thrust plate.
4. Remove the dial indicator.

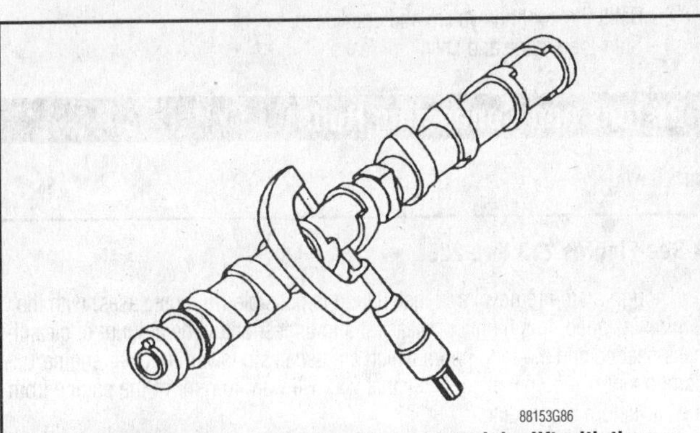

Fig. 207 A micrometer can be used to measure lobe lift with the camshaft removed from the engine

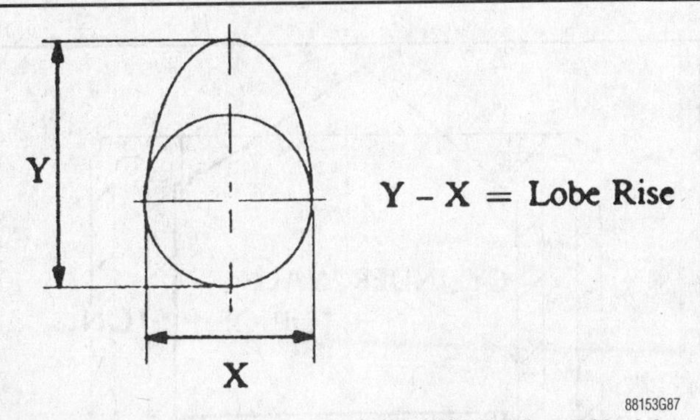

Fig. 208 Lobe lift is equal to Y (the lobe HEIGHT) minus X (the lobe WIDTH)

Auxiliary Shaft

REMOVAL & INSTALLATION

◆ See Figure 209

The 2.3L engine covered by this manual uses an auxiliary shaft (driven off the timing belt) to drive the oil pump and, on the VIN A engine, the distributor.

1. Disconnect the negative battery cable for safety.
2. Remove the front timing belt cover.
3. Remove the timing belt.
4. Remove the auxiliary shaft timing sprocket retaining bolt. Remove the sprocket using a puller.
5. On 1989–90 vehicles, remove the distributor.
6. Remove the auxiliary shaft cover and thrust plate.
7. Withdraw the auxiliary shaft from the block being careful not to damage the bearings.

To install:

8. Dip the auxiliary shaft in engine oil before installing. Slide the auxiliary shaft into the cylinder block, being careful not to damage the bearings.
9. Install the thrust plate. Tighten the thrust plate screws to 6–9 ft. lbs. (8–12 Nm).
10. Install a new gasket and auxiliary shaft cover. Tighten the cover screws to 6–9 ft. lbs. (8–12 Nm).

➡The auxiliary shaft cover and cylinder front cover share a common gasket. Cut off the old gasket around the cylinder cover and use half of the new gasket on the auxiliary shaft cover.

11. If equipped, insert the distributor.
12. Install the auxiliary shaft sprocket.
13. Align the timing marks and install the timing belt.
14. Install the timing belt cover.
15. Connect the negative battery cable.
16. On distributor equipped (VIN A) engines, be sure to check the ignition timing.

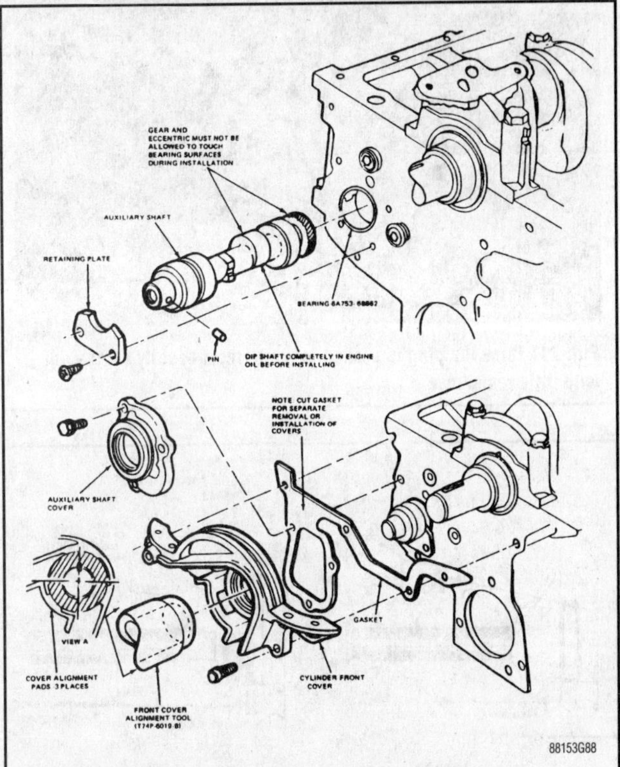

Fig. 209 Exploded view of the auxiliary shaft mounting—early model 2.3L (VIN A) shown (VIN M similar)

Core (Freeze) Plugs

REPLACEMENT

➧ See Figures 210, 211 and 212

Core plugs need replacement only if they are found to be leaking, are excessively rusty, have popped due to freezing or, if the engine is being overhauled.

If the plugs are accessible with the engine in the vehicle, they can be removed as is. If not, the engine will have to be removed.

1. If necessary, remove the engine and mount it on a work stand. If the engine is being left in the vehicle, drain the engine coolant and engine oil

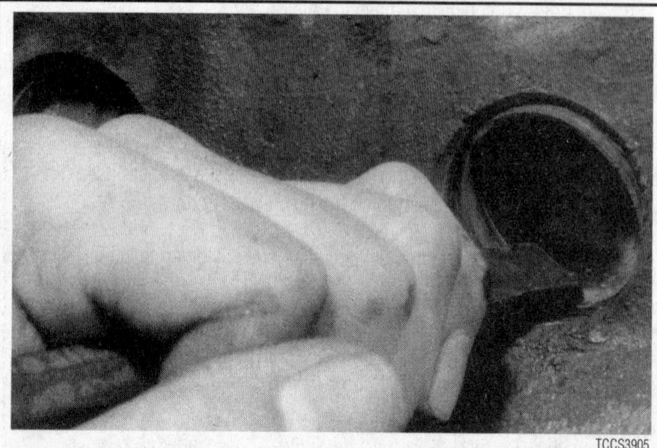

TCCS3905

Fig. 210 If you don't have a slide-hammer a chisel can usually cock the plug (BUT WEAR SAFETY GOGGLES)

TCCS3906

Fig. 211 Once the plug is cocked in the bore, it usually comes out with little resistance

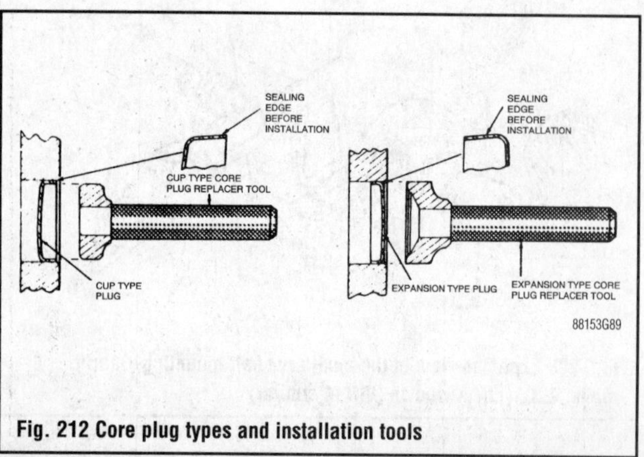

Fig. 212 Core plug types and installation tools

**** CAUTION**

When draining the coolant, keep in mind that your pets are attracted by ethylene glycol antifreeze, and are quite likely to drink any that is left in an uncovered container or in puddles on the ground. This will prove fatal in sufficient quantity. Always drain the coolant into a sealable container. Coolant should be reused unless it is contaminated or too old.

2. Remove anything blocking access to the plug or plugs to be replaced.
3. Drill or center-punch a hole in the plug. For large plugs, drill a ½ in. (13mm) hole; for small plugs, drill a ¼ in. (6mm) hole.
4. For large plugs, using a slide-hammer, thread a machine screw adapter or insert a 2-jawed puller adapter into the hole in the plug. Pull the plug from the block; for small plugs, pry the plug out with a pin punch.
5. Thoroughly clean the opening in the block, using steel wool or emery paper to polish the hole rim.
6. Coat the outer diameter of the new plug with sealer and place it in the hole.
   a. For cup-type core plugs: These plugs are installed with the flanged end outward. The maximum diameter of this type of plug is located at the outer edge of the flange. carefully and evenly, drive the new plug into place.
   b. For expansion-type plugs: These plugs are installed with the flanged end inward. The maximum diameter of this type of plug is located at the base of the flange. It is imperative that the correct type of installation tool is used with this type of plug. Under no circumstances is this type of plug to be driven in using a tool that contacts the crowned portion of the plug. Driving in this plug incorrectly will cause the plug to expand prior to installation. When installed, the trailing (maximum) diameter of the plug MUST be below the chamfered edge of the bore to create an effective seal. If the core plug replacing tool has a depth seating surface, do not seat the tool against a non-machined (casting) surface.
7. Install any removed parts and, if necessary, install the engine in the vehicle.
8. Refill the cooling system and crankcase.
9. Start the engine and check for leaks.

Pistons and Connecting Rods

REMOVAL

➧ See Figures 213 thru 220

Though piston removal and installation is possible (in most cases) with the engine installed, it is highly unpleasant and undesirable. The amount of cleanliness needed and the long hours which are usually involved in lower engine component overhaul make it likely that you will want to remove the engine from the car before proceeding.

2.3L Engine

1. Drain the cooling system and the crankcase.

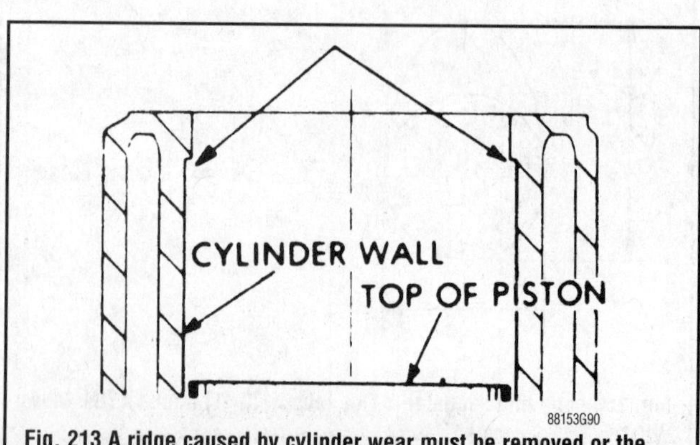

Fig. 213 A ridge caused by cylinder wear must be removed or the piston rings will catch on it and prevent removal (or break)

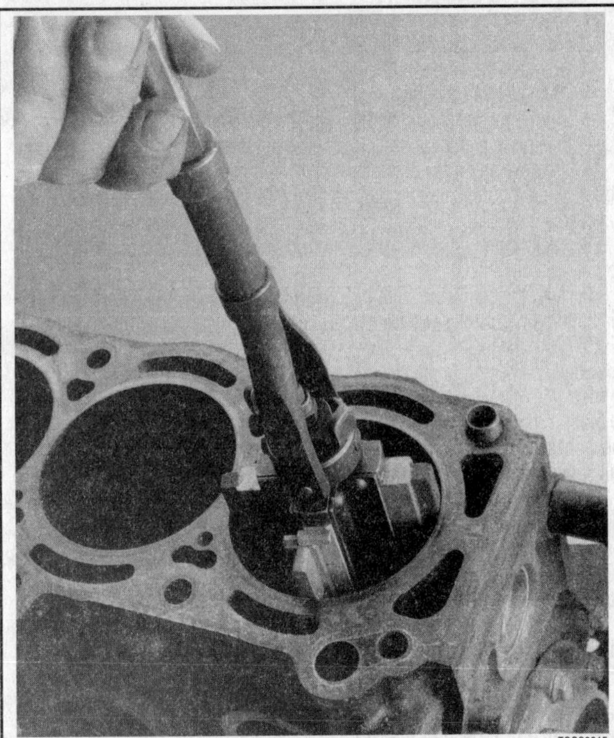

TCCS3915

Fig. 214 Remove the ridge from the cylinder bore using a ridge cutter

TCCS3916

Fig. 215 Follow the tool manufacturer's instructions closely, DO NOT remove too much metal

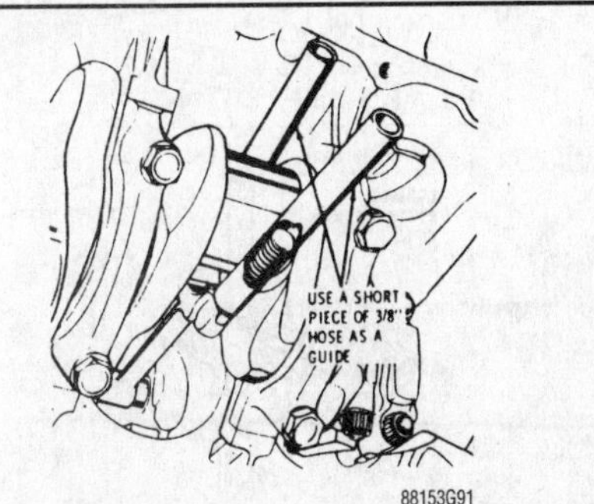

88153G91

Fig. 216 Make connecting rod bolt guides from short pieces of rubber tubing; they will protect the cylinder walls and the crankshaft journals from damage

TCCS3803

Fig. 217 Place rubber hose over the connecting rod studs to protect the crankshaft and cylinders . . .

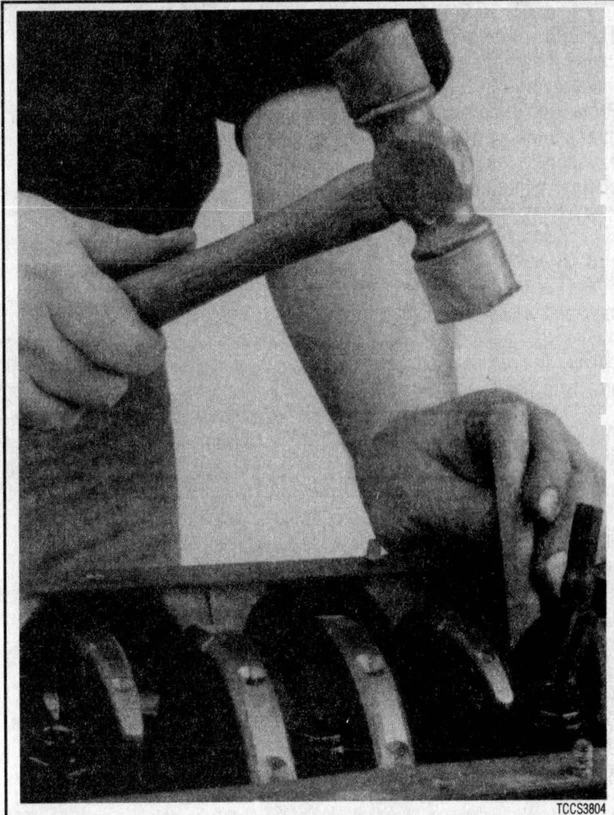

TCCS3804

Fig. 218 . . . then carefully tap the piston out of the bore using a wooden dowel

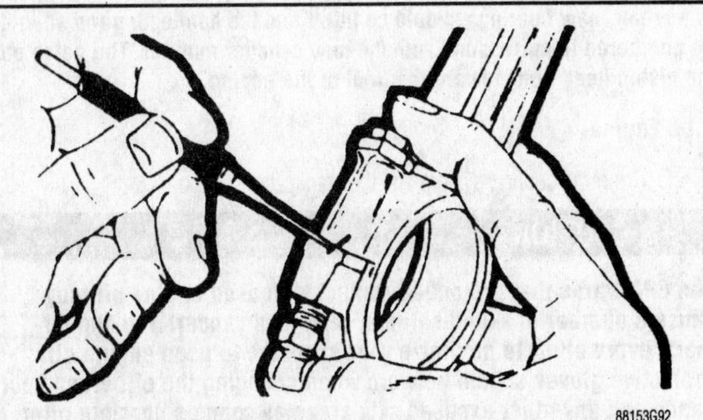

88153G92

Fig. 219 Connecting rods must be matchmarked to their caps to assure proper installation

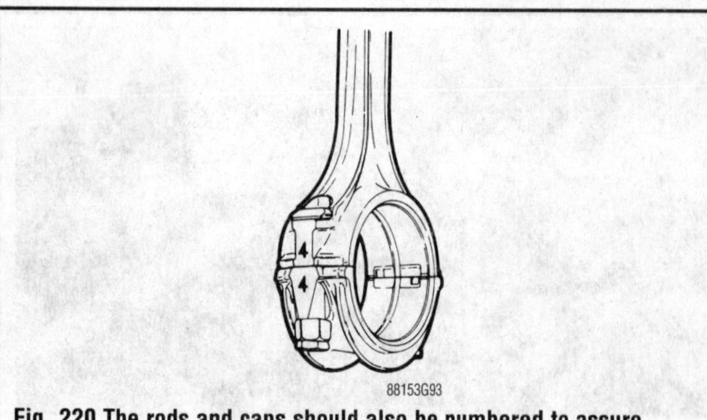

Fig. 220 The rods and caps should also be numbered to assure installation in the correct cylinder

CAUTION

The EPA warns that prolonged contact with used engine oil may cause a number of skin disorders, including cancer! You should make every effort to minimize your exposure to used engine oil. Protective gloves should be worn when changing the oil. Wash your hands and any other exposed skin areas as soon as possible after exposure to used engine oil. Soap and water, or waterless hand cleaner should be used.

2. Remove the cylinder head.
3. Remove the oil pan, the oil pump inlet tube and the oil pump.
4. Turn the crankshaft until the piston to be removed is at the bottom of its travel and place a cloth on the piston head to collect filings. Using a ridge reaming tool, remove any ridge of carbon or any other deposit from the upper cylinder walls where piston travel ends. Do not cut into the piston ring travel area more than 1/32 in. (0.8mm) while removing the ridge.
5. Mark all of the connecting rod caps so that they can be reinstalled in the original positions from which they are removed, then remove the connecting rod bearing cap. Also identify the piston assemblies as they, too, must be reinstalled in the same cylinder from which removed.
6. With the bearing caps removed, the connecting rod bearing bolts are potentially damaging to the cylinder walls during removal. To guard against cylinder wall damage, install 4 in. (101.6mm) or 5 in. (127mm) lengths of 3/8 in. (9.5mm) rubber tubing onto the connecting rod bolts. These will also protect the crankshaft journal from scratches when the connecting rod is installed, and will serve as a guide for the rod.
7. Squirt some clean engine oil into each cylinder before removing the pistons. Using a wooden hammer handle, push the connecting rod and piston assembly out of the top of the cylinder (pushing from the bottom of the rod). Be careful to avoid damaging both the crank journal and the cylinder wall when removing the rod and piston assembly.
8. Be sure to install the pistons in the cylinders from which they were removed.

➡The connecting rod and bearing caps are numbered from 1 to 4 beginning at the front of the engine. The numbers on the connecting rod and bearing cap must be on the same side when installed in the cylinder bore. If a connecting rod is ever transposed from one engine or cylinder to another, new bearings should be fitted and the connecting rod should be numbered to correspond with the new cylinder number. The notch on the piston head goes toward the front of the engine.

5.0L Engine

1. Drain the cooling system and the crankcase.

CAUTION

The EPA warns that prolonged contact with used engine oil may cause a number of skin disorders, including cancer! You should make every effort to minimize your exposure to used engine oil. Protective gloves should be worn when changing the oil. Wash your hands and any other exposed skin areas as soon as possible after exposure to used engine oil. Soap and water, or waterless hand cleaner should be used.

2. Remove the intake manifold.
3. Remove the cylinder heads.
4. Remove the oil pan.
5. Remove the oil pump.
6. Turn the crankshaft until the piston to be removed is at the bottom of its travel, then place a cloth on the piston head to collect filings.
7. Remove any ridge of deposits at the end of the piston travel from the upper cylinder bore, using a ridge reaming tool. Do not cut into the piston ring travel area more than 1/32 in. (0.8mm) when removing the ridge.
8. Make sure that all of the connecting rod bearing caps can be identified, so they will be reinstalled in their original positions.
9. Turn the crankshaft until the connecting rod that is to be removed is at the bottom of its stroke and remove the connecting rod nuts and bearing cap.
10. With the bearing caps removed, the connecting rod bearing bolts are potentially damaging to the cylinder walls during removal. To guard against cylinder wall damage, install 4 or 5 in. (102mm or 127mm) lengths of 3/8 in. (9.5mm) rubber tubing onto the connecting rod bolts. These will also protect the crankshaft journal from scratches when the connecting rod is installed, and will serve as a guide for the rod.
11. Squirt some clean engine oil into each cylinder before removing the piston assemblies. Using a wooden hammer handle, push the connecting rod and piston assembly out of the top of the cylinder (pushing from the bottom of the rod). Be careful to avoid damaging both the crankshaft journal and the cylinder wall when removing the rod and piston assembly.
12. If the bearings are to be replaced, remove the bearing inserts from the connecting rod and cap, then place the cap onto the piston/rod assembly from which it was removed.

➡The connecting rod and bearing caps are numbered from 1 to 4 in the right bank and from 5 to 8 in the left bank, beginning at the front of the engine. The numbers on the rod and cap must be on the same side when they are installed in the cylinder bore. Also, the largest chamfer at the bearing end of the rod should be positioned toward the crank pin thrust face of the crankshaft and the notch in the head of the piston faces toward the front of the engine.

Piston Ring and Wrist Pin

REMOVAL

➧ See Figures 221, 222, 223 and 224

All of the Ford gasoline engines covered in this guide utilize pressed-in wrist pins, which can only be removed by an arbor press. The piston/connecting rod assemblies should be taken to an engine specialist or qualified machinist for piston removal and installation.

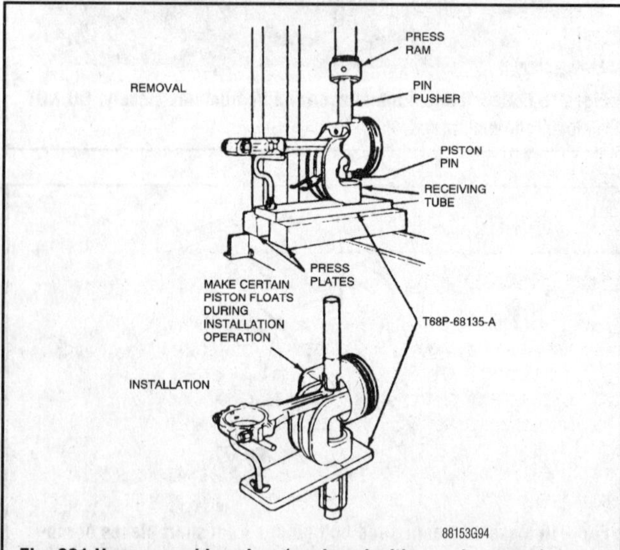

Fig. 221 Have a machine shop (equipped with an arbor press) remove or install the wrist pins from the pistons

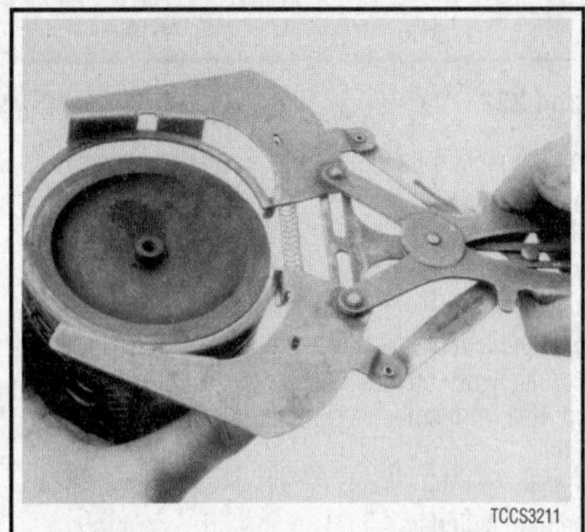

Fig. 222 Use a ring expander tool to remove the piston rings

Fig. 223 Clean the piston grooves using a ring groove cleaner

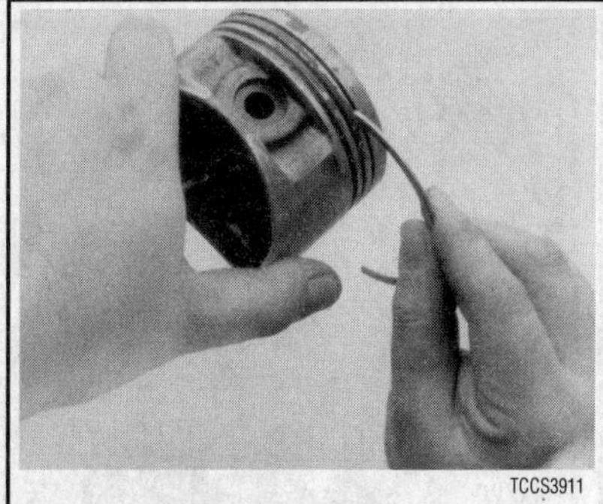

Fig. 224 You can use a piece of an old ring to clean the piston grooves, BUT be careful, the ring is sharp

A piston ring expander is necessary for removing the piston rings without damaging them; any other method (screwdriver blades, pliers, etc.) usually results in the rings being bent, scratched or distorted, or the piston itself being damaged. When the rings are removed, clean the ring grooves using an appropriate ring groove cleaning tool, using care not to cut too deeply. Thoroughly clean all carbon and varnish from the piston with solvent.

**** WARNING**

Do not use a wire brush or caustic solvent (acids, etc.) on pistons.

Inspect the pistons for scuffing, scoring, cracks, pitting, or excessive ring groove wear. If these are evident, the piston must be replaced.

The piston should also be checked in relation to the cylinder diameter. Using a telescoping gauge and micrometer, or a dial gauge, measure the cylinder bore diameter perpendicular (90°) to the piston pin, 2½ in. (64mm) below the cylinder block deck (surface where the block mates with the heads). Then, with the micrometer, measure the piston, perpendicular to its wrist pin on the skirt. the difference between the two measurements is the piston clearance. If the clearance is within specifications or slightly below (after the cylinders have been bored or hones), finish honing is all that is necessary. If the clearance is excessive, try to obtain a slightly larger piston to bring clearance to within specifications. If this is not possible, obtain the first oversize piston and hone (or if necessary, bore) the cylinder to size. Generally, if the cylinder bore is tapered 0.005 in. (0.127mm) or more or is out-of-round 0.003 in. (0.076mm) or more, it is advisable to rebore for the smallest possible oversize piston and rings.

After measuring, mark the pistons with a felt tip pen for reference and for assembly.

➡Cylinder honing and/or boring should be performed by a reputable, professional mechanic with the proper equipment. In some cases, clean-up honing can be done with the cylinder block in the vehicle, but most excessive honing and all cylinder boring must be done with the block stripped and removed from the vehicle.

MEASURING THE OLD PISTONS

See Figures 225, 226, 227, 228 and 229

Check used piston-to-cylinder bore clearance as follows:

1. Measure the cylinder bore diameter with a telescope gauge.
2. Measure the piston diameter. When measuring the pistons for size or taper, measurements must be made with the piston pin removed.
3. Subtract the piston diameter from the cylinder bore diameter to determine piston-to-bore clearance.
4. Compare the piston-to-bore clearances obtained with those clearances recommended. Determine if the piston-to-bore clearance is in the acceptable range.
5. When measuring taper, the largest reading must be at the bottom of the skirt.

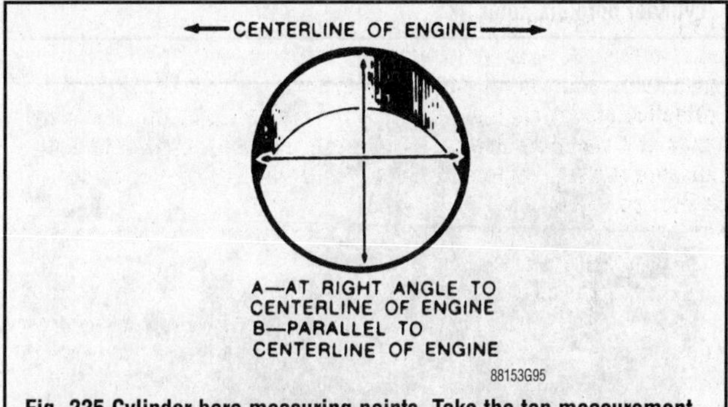

Fig. 225 Cylinder bore measuring points. Take the top measurement ½ in. (13mm) below the top of the block deck and the bottom measurement ½ in. (13mm) above the top of the piston when it is at BDC

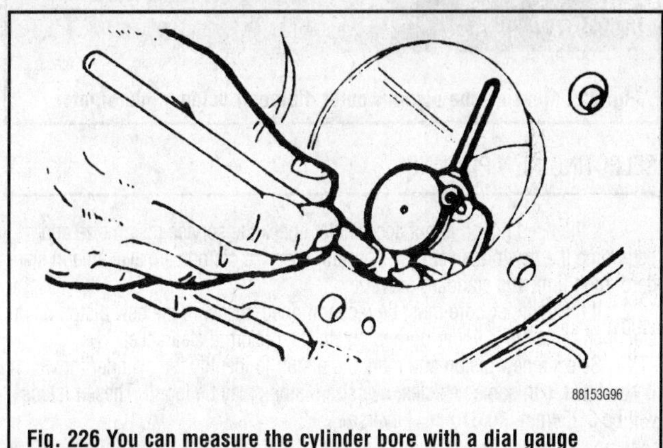

Fig. 226 You can measure the cylinder bore with a dial gauge

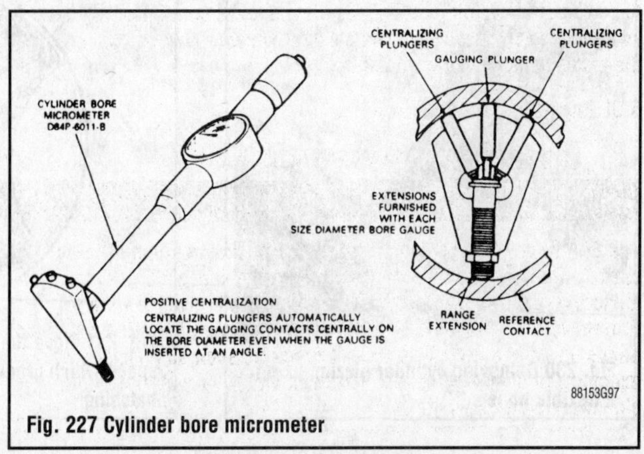

Fig. 227 Cylinder bore micrometer

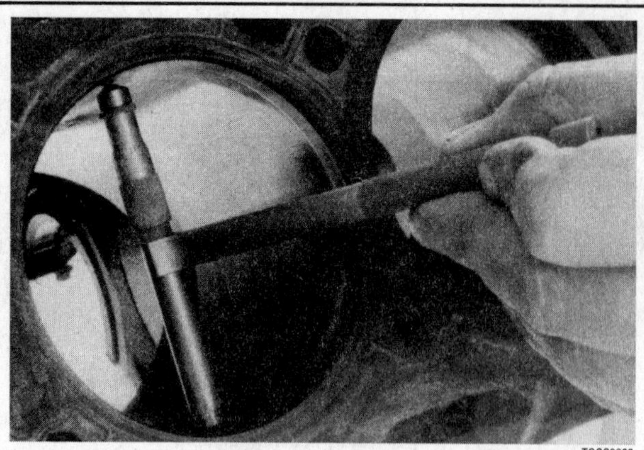
Fig. 228 A telescoping gauge may also be used to measure the cylinder bore diameter

Fig. 229 Measure the piston's outer diameter using a micrometer

SELECTING NEW PISTONS

1. If the used piston is not acceptable, check the service piston size and determine if a new piston can be selected. (Service pistons are available in standard, high limit and standard oversize.
2. If the cylinder bore must be reconditioned, measure the new piston diameter, then hone the cylinder bore to obtain the preferred clearance.
3. Select a new piston and mark the piston to identify the cylinder for which it was fitted. (On some vehicles, oversize pistons may be found. These pistons will be 0.254mm =[0.010 in.=] oversize).

CYLINDER HONING

See Figures 230, 231 and 232

1. When cylinders are being honed, follow the manufacturer's recommendations for the use of the hone.
2. Occasionally, during the honing operation, the cylinder bore should be thoroughly cleaned and the selected piston checked for correct fit.
3. When finish-honing a cylinder bore, the hone should be moved up and down at a sufficient speed to obtain a very fine uniform surface finish in a cross-hatch pattern of approximately 50–60° included angle. The finish marks should be clean but not sharp, free from embedded particles and torn or folded metal.
4. Permanently mark the piston for the cylinder to which it has been fitted and proceed to hone the remaining cylinders.

WARNING

Handle the pistons with care. Do not attempt to force the pistons through the cylinders until the cylinders have been honed to the correct size. Pistons can be distorted through careless handling.

5. Thoroughly clean the bores with hot water and detergent. Scrub well with a stiff bristle brush and rinse thoroughly with hot water. It is extremely essential that a good cleaning operation be performed. If any of the abrasive material is allowed to remain in the cylinder bores, it will rapidly wear the new rings and cylinder bores. The bores should be swabbed several times with light engine oil and a clean cloth and then wiped with a clean dry cloth. CYLINDERS SHOULD NOT BE CLEANED WITH KEROSENE OR GASOLINE! Clean the remainder of the cylinder block to remove the excess material spread during the honing operation.

PISTON RING END-GAP

See Figure 233

Piston ring end-gap should be checked while the rings are removed from the pistons. Incorrect end-gap indicates that the wrong size rings are being used; ring breakage could occur.

Compress the piston rings to be used in a cylinder, one at a time, into that cylinder. Squirt clean oil into the cylinder, so that the rings and the top two in. (51mm) of cylinder wall are coated. Using an inverted piston, press the rings approximately 1 in. (25mm) below the deck of the block. Measure the ring end-gap with the feeler gauge, and compare to the Ring Gap chart in this Section. Carefully pull the ring out of the cylinder and file the ends squarely with a fine file to obtain the proper clearance.

PISTON RING SIDE CLEARANCE CHECK AND INSTALLATION

See Figures 234, 235 and 236

Check the pistons to see that the ring grooves and oil return holes have been properly cleaned. Slide a piston ring into its groove, and check the side clear-

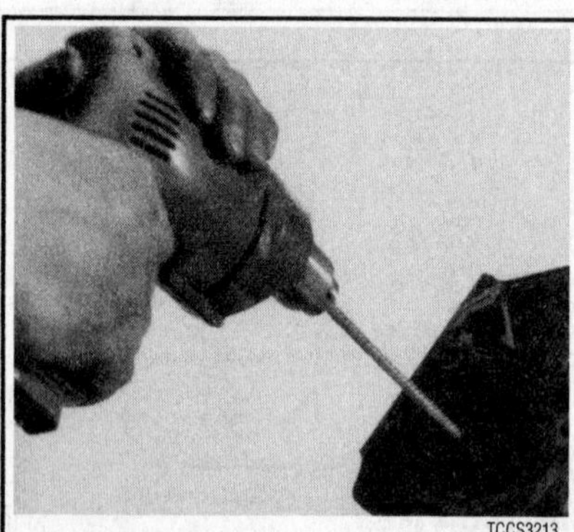
Fig. 230 Removing cylinder glazing using a flexible hone

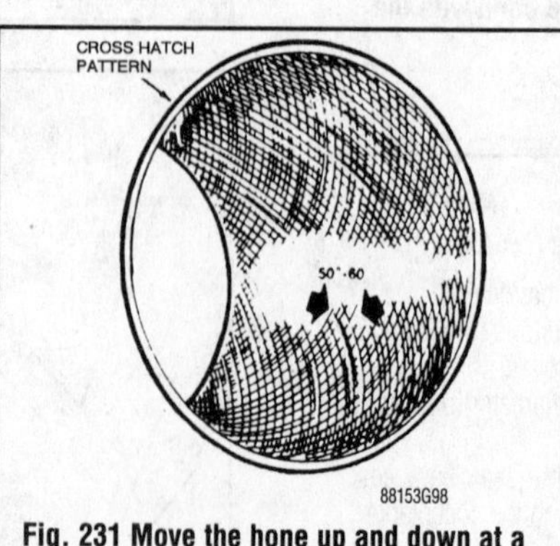

Fig. 231 Move the hone up and down at a speed which produces a 50–60° cross-hatching

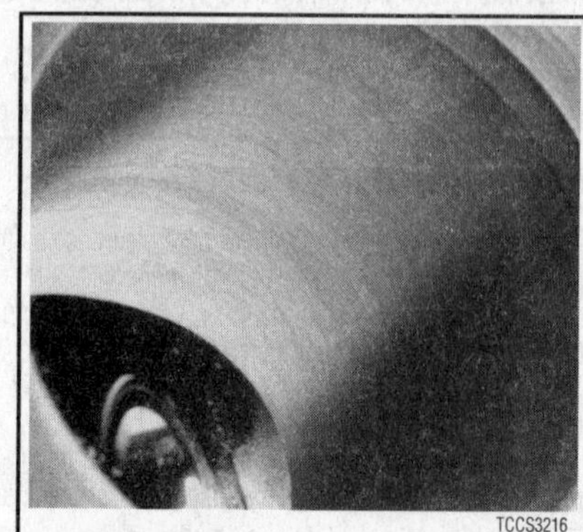
Fig. 232 A properly cross-hatched cylinder bore

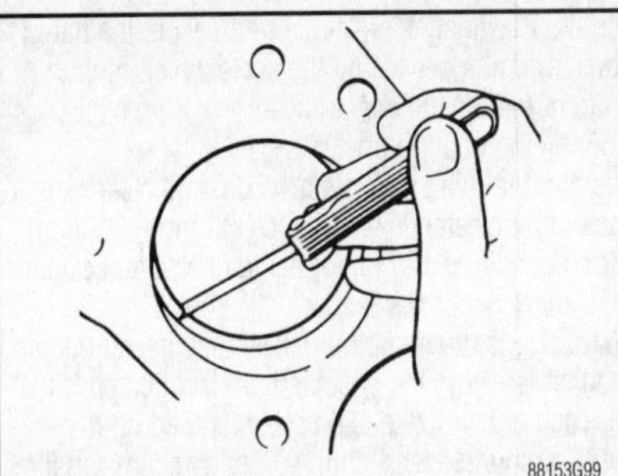

Fig. 233 Check the piston ring end-gap using a feeler gauge, with the ring positioned in the cylinder 1 in. (25mm) below the block deck

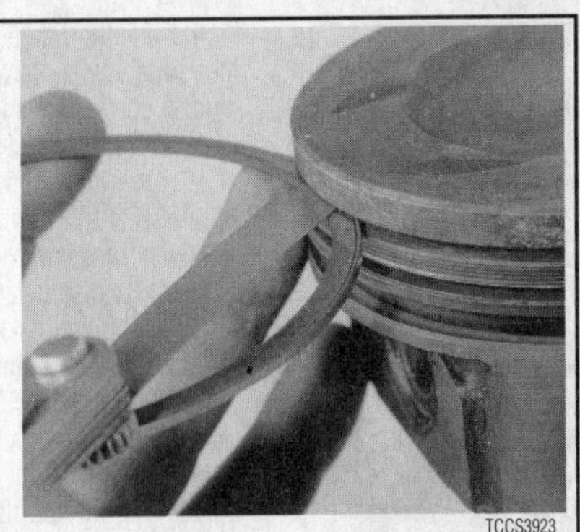

Fig. 234 Checking the ring-to-ring groove clearance

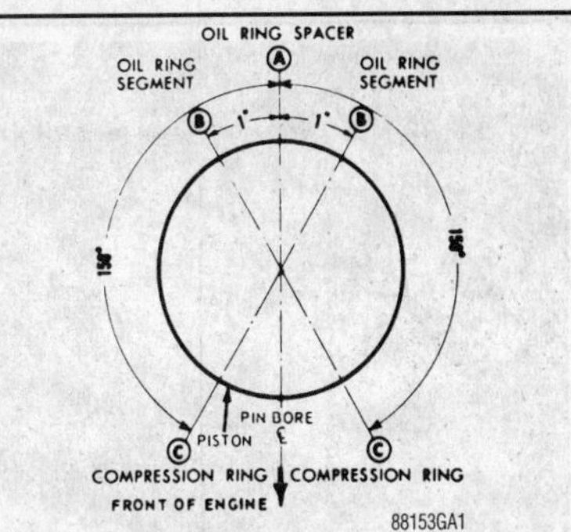

Fig. 235 Proper spacing of the piston ring gaps around the circumference of the piston

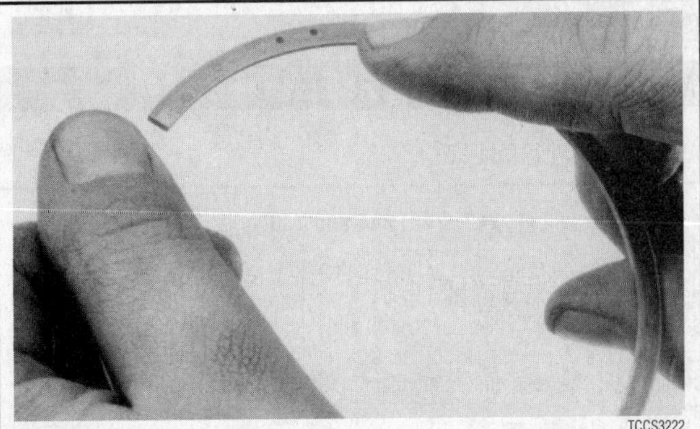

Fig. 236 Most rings are marked to show which side should face upward

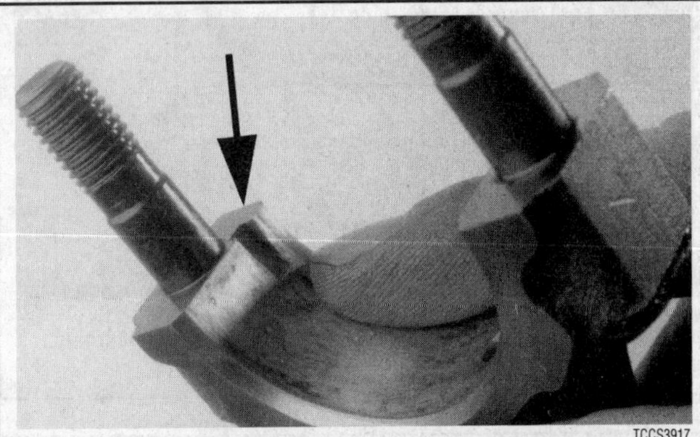

Fig. 237 A notch or tang is usually provided on the bearing cap to match a groove on the bearing insert

ance with a feeler gauge. Make sure you insert the gauge between the ring and its lower land (lower edge of the groove), because any wear that occurs forms a step at the inner portion of the lower land. If the piston grooves have worn to the extend that relatively high steps exist on the lower land, the piston grooves have worn to the extent that relatively high steps exist on the lower land, the piston should be replaced, because these will interfere with the operation of the new rings and ring clearance will be excessive. Piston rings are not furnished in oversize widths to compensate for ring groove wear.

Install the rings on the piston, lowest ring first, using a piston ring expander. There is a high risk of breaking or distorting the rings, or scratching the piston, if the rings are installed by hand or other means.

Position the rings on the piston as illustrated; spacing of the various piston ring gaps is crucial to proper oil retention and even cylinder wear. When installing new rings, refer to the installation diagram furnished with the new parts.

Connecting Rod Bearings

INSPECTION

➧ See Figure 237

Connecting rod bearings for the engines covered in this guide consist of two halves or shells which are interchangeable in the rod and cap. when the shells are placed in position, the ends extend slightly beyond the rod and cap surfaces so that when the rod bolts are torqued the shells will be clamped tightly in place to insure positive seating and to prevent turning. A tang holds the shells in place.

➡The ends of the bearing shells must never be filed flush with the mating surfaces of the rod and cap.

If a rod bearing becomes noisy or is worn so that its clearance on the crank journal is sloppy, a new bearing of the correct undersize must be selected and installed since there is a provision for adjustment.

✲✲ WARNING

Under no circumstances should the rod end or cap be filed to adjust the bearing clearance, nor should shims of any kind be used.

Inspect the rod bearings while the rod assemblies are out of the engine. If the shells are scored or show flaking, they should be replaced. If they are in good shape, check for proper clearance on the crank journal (see below). Any scoring or ridges on the crank journal means the crankshaft must be reground and fitted with undersized bearings, or replaced.

CHECKING BEARING CLEARANCE AND REPLACING BEARINGS

➧ See Figures 238, 239 and 240

➡Make sure connecting rods and their caps are kept together, and that the caps are installed in the proper direction.

Replacement bearings are available in the standard size, and in undersizes for reground crankshafts. Connecting rod-to-crankshaft bearing clearance is checked using Plastigage® at either the top or bottom of each crank journal. The Plastigage® has a range of 0 to 0.003 in. (0.076mm).

1. Remove the rod cap with the bearing shell. Completely clean the bearing shell and the crank journal, and blow any oil from the oil hole in the crankshaft.

➡The journal surfaces and bearing shells must be completely free of oil, because Plastigage® is soluble in oil.

2. Place a strip of Plastigage® lengthwise along the bottom center of the lower bearing shell, then install the cap with shell and tighten the bolt or nuts to specification. DO NOT TURN the crankshaft with the Plastigage® installed in the bearing.
3. Remove the bearing cap with the shell. The flattened Plastigage® will be found sticking to either the bearing shell or crank journal. Do not remove it yet.

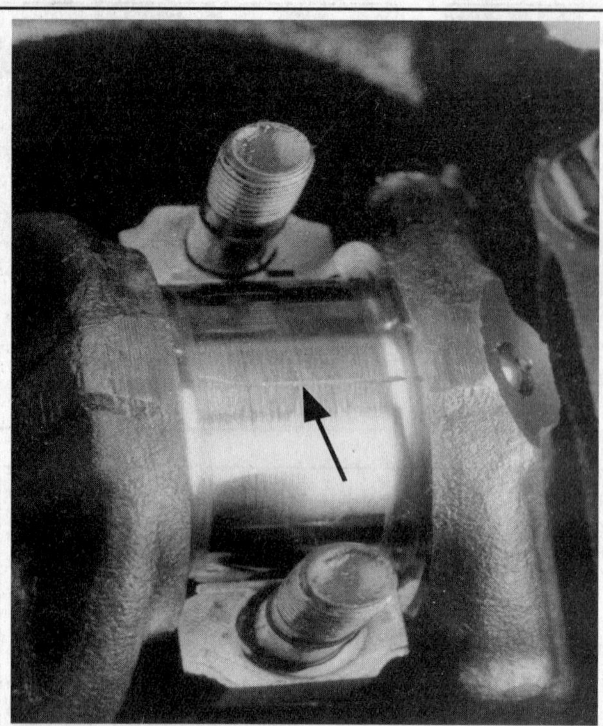

Fig. 238 Apply a strip of gauging material to the bearing journal, then install and torque the cap

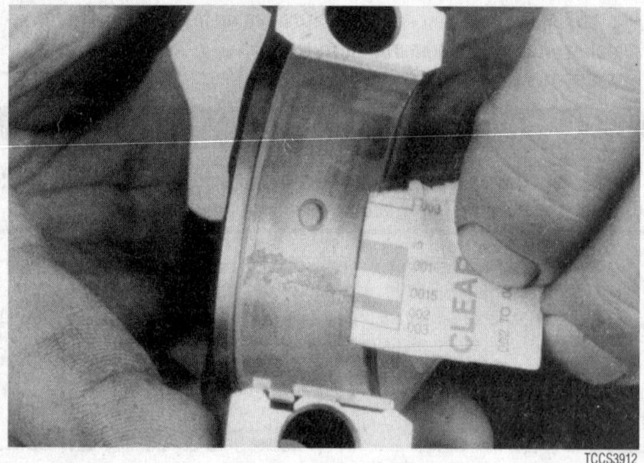

Fig. 239 After the cap is removed again, use the scale supplied with the gauge material to check clearances

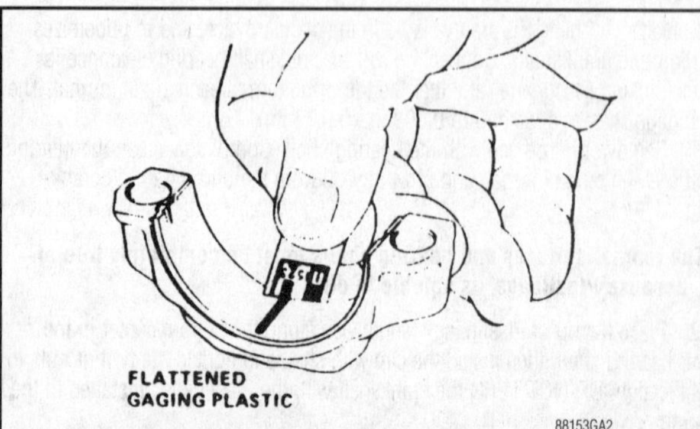

Fig. 240 The band width closest to the gauging material on the bearing represents the clearance

4. Use the printed scale on the Plastigage® envelope to measure the flattened material at its widest point. The number within the scale which most closely corresponds to the width of the Plastigage® indicates bearing clearance in thousandths of an inch or hundreths of a millimeter.
5. Check the specifications chart in this section for the desired clearance. It is advisable to install a new bearing if clearance exceeds 0.003 in. (0.076mm); however, if the bearing is in good condition and is not being checked because of bearing noise, bearing replacement is not necessary.
6. If you are installing new bearings, try a standard size, then each undersize in order until one is found that is within the specified limits when checked for clearance with Plastigage®. Each under size has its size stamped on it.
7. When the proper size shell is found, clean off the Plastigage® material from the shell, oil the bearing thoroughly, reinstall the cap with its shell and tighten the rod bolt nuts to specification.

➡With the proper bearing selected and the nuts torqued, it should be possible to move the connecting rod back and forth freely on the crank journal as allowed by the specified connecting rod end clearance. If the rod cannot be moved, either the rod bearing is too far undersize or the rod is misaligned.

Piston and Connecting Rod

ASSEMBLY & INSTALLATION

See Figures 241, 242, 243, 244 and 245

Install the connecting rod to the piston making sure piston installation notches and any marks on the rod are in proper relation to one another. Lubricate the wrist pin with clean engine oil and install the pin into the rod and piston assembly by using an arbor press as required. Install the wrist pin snaprings if equipped, and rotate them in their grooves to make sure they are seated.

1. Make sure the connecting rod big bearings (including end cap) are of the correct size and properly installed.
2. Fit rubber hoses over the connecting rod bolt to protect the crankshaft journals, as in the Piston Removal procedure. Coat the rod bearings with clean oil.
3. Before installing the piston/connecting rod assembly, be sure to clean all gasket mating surfaces, oil the pistons, piston rings and the cylinder walls with light engine oil.
4. Be sure to install the pistons in the cylinders from which they were removed:
    a. The connecting rod and bearing caps are numbered from 1 to 4 beginning at the front of the 2.3L engine. The numbers on the connecting rod and bearing cap must be on the same side when installed in the cylinder bore. If a connecting rod is ever transposed from one engine or cylinder to another, new bearings should be fitted and the connecting rod should be numbered to correspond with the new cylinder number. The notch on the piston head goes toward the front of the engine.
    b. On the 5.0L engine the connecting rod and bearing caps are numbered from 1 to 4 in the right bank and from 5 to 8 in the left bank, beginning at the front of the engine. The numbers on the rod and cap must be on the

Fig. 241 Most pistons are marked to indicate positioning (usually a mark means the side facing front)

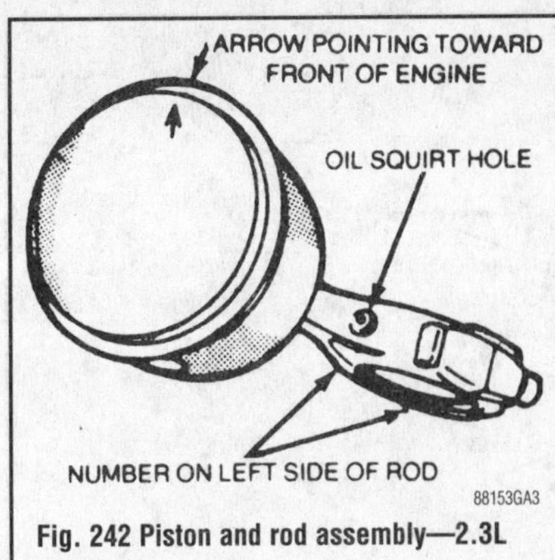

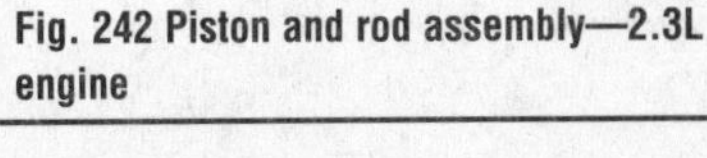

Fig. 242 Piston and rod assembly—2.3L engine

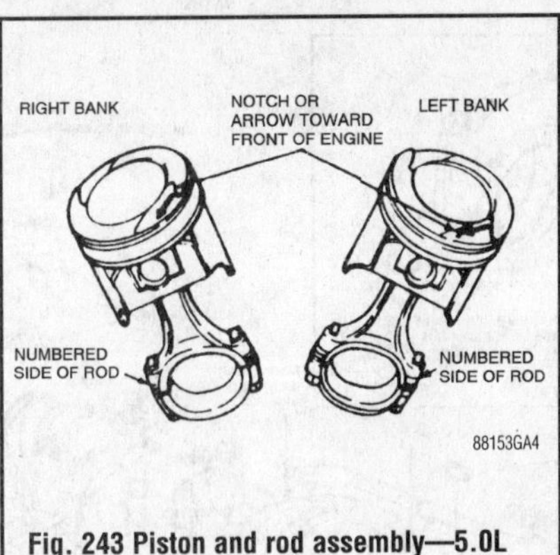

Fig. 243 Piston and rod assembly—5.0L engine

Fig. 244 Installing the piston into the block using a ring compressor and the handle of a hammer

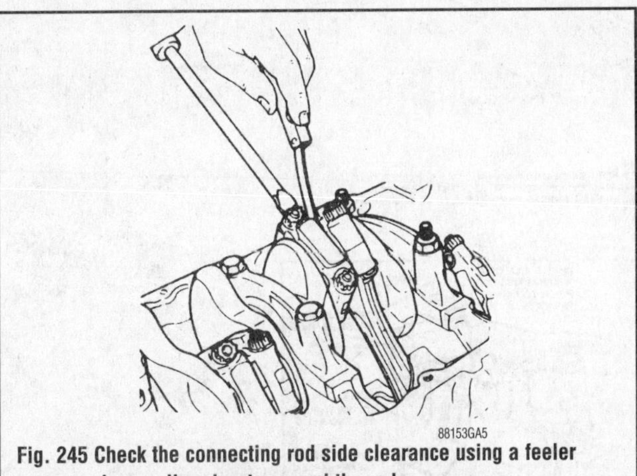

Fig. 245 Check the connecting rod side clearance using a feeler gauge and a small prybar to spread the rods

same side when they are installed in the cylinder bore. Also, the largest chamfer at the bearing end of the rod should be positioned toward the crank pin thrust face of the crankshaft and the notch in the head of the piston faces toward the front of the engine.

5. Make sure the ring gaps are properly spaced around the circumference of the piston. Make sure rubber hose lengths are fitted to the rod bolts. Fit a piston ring compressor around the piston and slide the piston and connecting rod assembly down into the cylinder bore, pushing it in with the wooden hammer handle. Push the piston down until it is only slightly below the top of the cylinder bore. Guide the connecting rods onto the crankshaft bearing journals carefully, using the rubber hose lengths, to avoid damaging the crankshaft.

6. From beneath the engine, coat each crank journal with clean oil. Pull the connecting rod, with the bearing shell in place, into position against the crank journal.

7. Remove the rubber hoses. Install the bearing cap and cap nuts and torque to specification.

➡When more than one rod and piston assembly is being installed, the connecting rod cap attaching nuts should only be tightened enough to keep each rod in position until all have been installed. This will ease the installation of the remaining piston assemblies.

8. Check the clearance between the sides of the connecting rods and the crankshaft using a feeler gauge. Spread the rods slightly with a small prytool to insert the gauge. If clearance is below the minimum tolerance, the rod may be machined to provide adequate clearance. If clearance is excessive, substitute an unworn rod, and recheck. If clearance is still outside specifications, the crankshaft must be welded and reground, or replaced.

9. Prime and install the oil pump and the oil pump intake tube, then install the oil pan.

10. Reassemble the rest of the engine in the reverse order of disassembly.

Crankshaft and Main Bearings

REMOVAL & INSTALLATION

See Figures 246 and 247

Engine Removed

1. With the engine removed from the vehicle and placed in a work stand, disconnect the spark plug wires from the spark plugs, then remove the wires and bracket assembly from the attaching stud on the rocker arm cover(s), if so equipped. On distributor ignition engines, disconnect the coil-to-distributor high tension lead at the coil, then remove the distributor cap and spark plug wires as an assembly. Remove the spark plugs to allow easy rotation of the crankshaft.
2. Remove the oil filter. Slide the water pump by-pass hose clamp (if so equipped) toward the water pump. Remove the alternator and mounting brackets.
3. Remove the crankshaft pulley from the crankshaft vibration damper. Remove the capscrew and washer from the end of the crankshaft. Use a universal puller such as Tool T58P–6316–D to remove the crankshaft vibration damper.
4. Remove the timing front cover and crankshaft timing belt or chain. Refer to timing covers and chain or belt procedures located earlier in this section.
5. Invert the engine on the work stand.
6. Remove the clutch pressure plate and disc (manual shift transmission).
7. Remove the flywheel and engine rear cover plate.
8. Remove the oil pan and gasket. Remove the oil pump.
9. Make sure all bearing caps (main and connecting rod) are marked so that they can be installed in their original locations. Turn the crankshaft until the connecting rod from which the cap is being removed is up (at the bottom of its normal travel), then remove the bearing cap. Push the connecting rod and piston assembly down into the cylinder. Repeat this procedure until all the connecting rod bearing caps are removed.
10. Remove the main bearing caps.
11. Carefully lift the crankshaft out of the block so that the thrust bearing surfaces are not damaged. Handle the crankshaft with care to avoid possible fracture to the finished surfaces.
12. Remove the rear journal seal from the block and rear main bearing cap.
13. Remove the main bearing inserts from the block and bearing caps.
14. Remove the connecting rod bearing inserts from the connecting rods and caps.
15. If the crankshaft main bearing journals have been refinished to a definite undersize, install the correct undersize bearings. Be sure the bearing inserts and bearing bores are clean. Foreign material under the inserts will distort the bearing and cause a failure.
16. Place the upper main bearing inserts in position in the bores with the tang fitting in the slot. Be sure the oil holes in the bearing inserts are aligned with the oil holes in the cylinder block.
17. Install the lower main bearing inserts in the bearing caps.
18. Clean the rear journal oil seal groove and the mating surfaces of the block and rear main bearing cap.

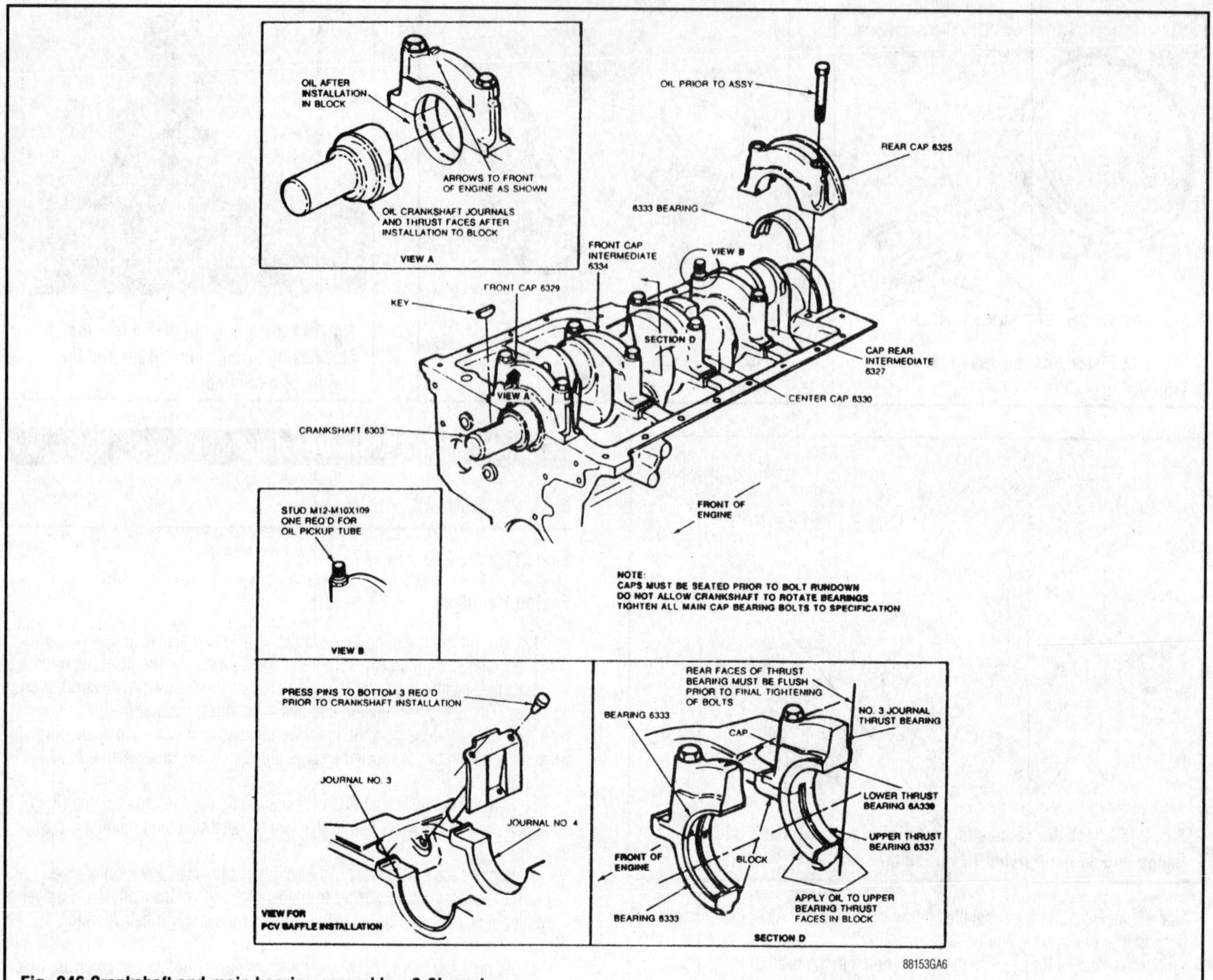

Fig. 246 Crankshaft and main bearing assembly—2.3L engine

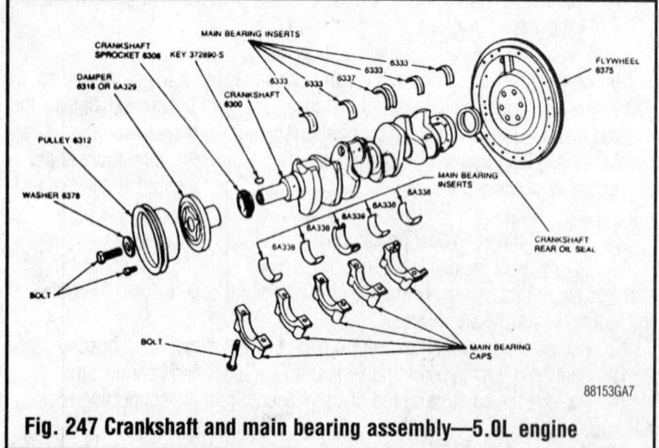

Fig. 247 Crankshaft and main bearing assembly—5.0L engine

19. Dip the lip-type seal halves in clean engine oil. Install the seals in the bearing cap and block with the undercut side of the seal toward the front of the engine.

➡This procedure applies only to engines with two piece rear main bearing oil seals. those having one piece seals (2.3L engine) will be installed after the crankshaft is in place.

20. Carefully lower the crankshaft into place. Be careful not to damage the bearing surfaces.

CHECKING MAIN BEARING CLEARANCES

See Figures 248, 249, 250, 251 and 252

1. Check the clearance of each main bearing by using the following procedure:
   a. Place a piece of Plastigage® or its equivalent, on bearing surface across the full width of the bearing cap and about ¼ in. (6mm) off center.
   b. Install the cap and tighten the bolts to specifications. Do not turn the crankshaft while Plastigage® is in place.

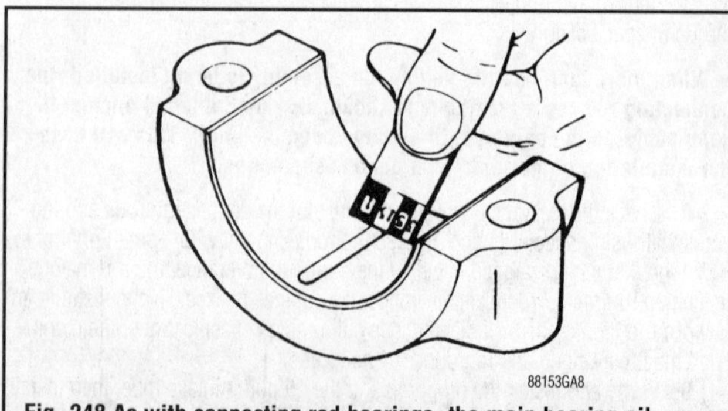

Fig. 248 As with connecting rod bearings, the main bearing oil clearance is checked using a gauging material which deforms based on the clearance between the two surfaces

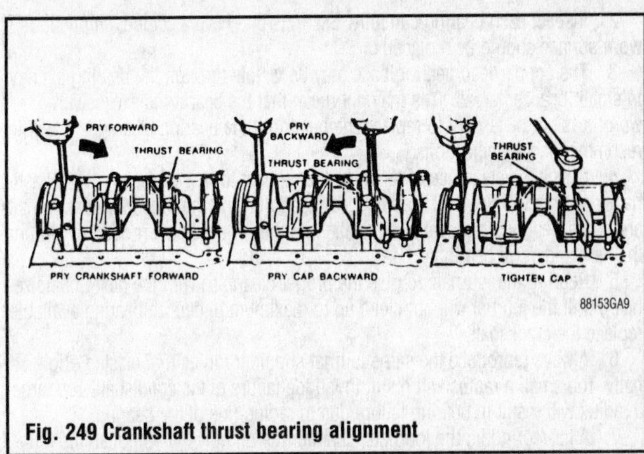

Fig. 249 Crankshaft thrust bearing alignment

Fig. 250 A dial gauge may be used to check crankshaft end-play

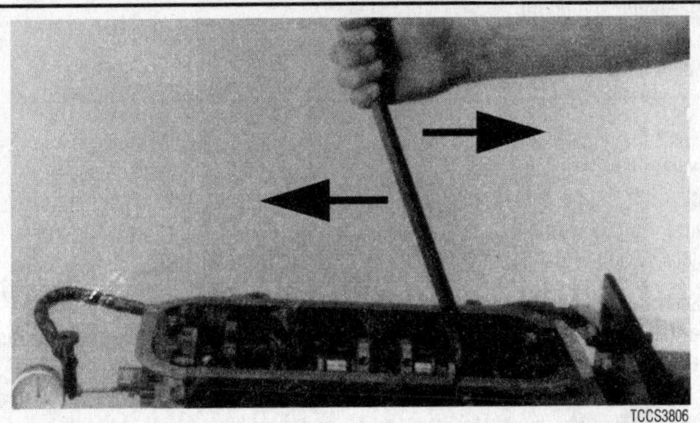

Fig. 251 Carefully pry the shaft back and forth while reading the dial gauge for play

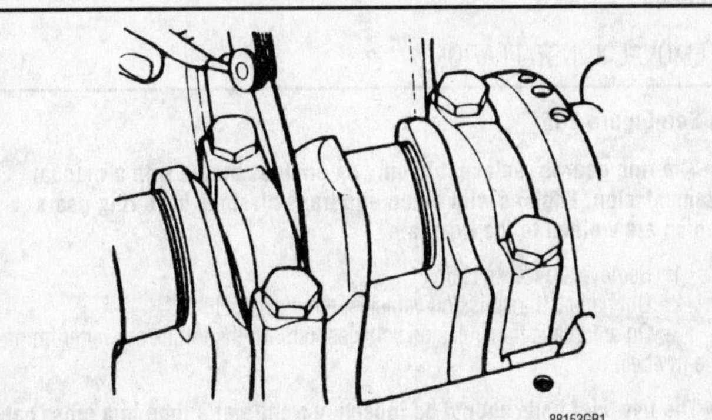

Fig. 252 Crankshaft end-play can also be checked using a feeler gauge

c. Remove the cap. Using the Plastigage® scale, check the width of the Plastigage® at the widest point to get the minimum clearance. Check at the narrowest point to get the maximum clearance. Difference between readings is the journal's taper.

d. If clearance exceeds the specified limits, try a 0.001 in. (0.0254mm) or 0.002 in. (0.051mm) undersize bearing in combination with the standard bearing. Bearing clearance must be within the specified limits. If standard and 0.002 in. (0.051mm) undersize bearings do not bring clearance within desired limits, refinish the crankshaft journal, then install undersize bearings.

➡Refer to Rear Main Oil Seal removal and installation, for special instructions in applying RTV sealer to rear main bearing cup.

2. Install all the bearing caps except the thrust bearing cap (no. 3 bearing on all except the 2.3L which use the no. 5 as the thrust bearing). Be sure the main bearing caps are installed in their original locations. Tighten the bearing cap bolts to specifications.
3. Install the thrust bearing cap with the bolts finger-tight.
4. Pry the crankshaft forward against the thrust surface of the upper half of the bearing.
5. Hold the crankshaft forward and pry the thrust bearing cap to the rear. This will align the thrust surfaces of both halves of the bearing.
6. Retain the forward pressure on the crankshaft. Tighten the cap bolts to specifications.
7. Check the crankshaft end-play using the following procedures:
   a. Force the crankshaft toward the rear of the engine.
   b. Install a dial indicator (tools D78P–4201–F, –G or equivalent) so that the contact point rests against the crankshaft flange and the indicator axis is parallel to the crankshaft axis.
   c. Zero the dial indicator. Push the crankshaft forward and note the reading on the dial.
   d. If the end-play exceeds the wear limit listed in the Crankshaft and Connecting Rod Specifications chart, replace the thrust bearing. If the end-play is less than the minimum limit, inspect the thrust bearing faces for scratches, burrs, nicks, or dirt. If the thrust faces are not damaged or dirty, then they probably were not aligned properly. Lubricate and install the new thrust bearing.
8. On engines with one piece rear main bearing oil seal (2.3L engine), coat a new crankshaft rear oil seal with oil, then install using Tool T65P–6701–A, or equivalent. Inspect the seal to be sure it was not damaged during installation.
9. Install new bearing inserts in the connecting rods and caps. Check the clearance of each bearing.
10. After the connecting rod bearings have been fitted, apply a light coat of engine oil to the journals and bearings.
11. Turn the crankshaft throw to the bottom of its stroke. Push the piston all the way down until the rod bearing seats on the crankshaft journal.
12. Install the connecting rod cap. Tighten the nuts to specification.
13. After the piston and connecting rod assemblies have been installed, check the side clearance with a feeler gauge between the connecting rods on each connecting rod crankshaft journal. Refer to Crankshaft and Connecting Rod specifications chart in this Section.
14. Install the timing chain and sprockets or gears, cylinder front cover, crankshaft pulley and adapter, following the steps under Cylinder Front Cover and Timing Chain Installation in this section.

Engine in the vehicle

➧ See Figures 253 and 254

1. With the oil pan, oil pump and spark plugs removed, remove the cap from the main bearing needing replacement and remove the bearing from the cap.
2. Make a bearing roll-out pin, using a bent cotter pin as shown in the illustration. Install the end of the pin in the oil hole in the crankshaft journal.
3. Rotate the crankshaft clockwise as viewed from the front of the engine. This will roll the upper bearing out of the block.
4. Lube the new upper bearing with clean engine oil, then insert the plain (un-notched) end between the crankshaft and the indented or notched side of the block. Roll the bearing into place, making sure that the oil holes are aligned. Remove the roll pin from the oil hole.
5. Lube the new lower bearing and install it in the main bearing cap. Install

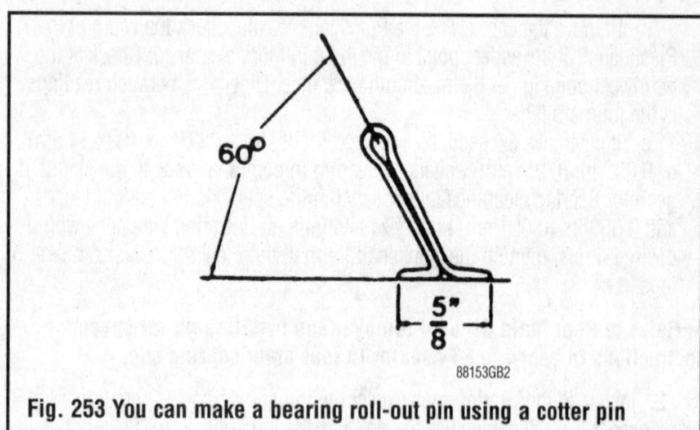

Fig. 253 You can make a bearing roll-out pin using a cotter pin

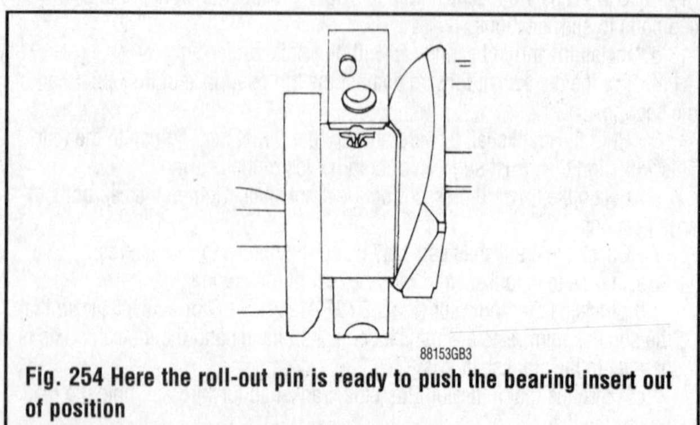

Fig. 254 Here the roll-out pin is ready to push the bearing insert out of position

the main bearing cap onto the block, making sure it is positioned in proper direction with the matchmarks in alignment.

6. Tighten the main bearing cap to specification.

➡See Crankshaft Installation for thrust bearing alignment.

CRANKSHAFT CLEANING AND INSPECTION

➡Handle the crankshaft carefully to avoid damage to the finished surfaces.

1. Clean the crankshaft with solvent, and blow out all oil passages with compressed air.
2. Use crocus cloth to remove any sharp edges, burrs or other imperfections which might damage the oil seal during installation or cause premature seal wear.

➡Do not use crocus cloth to polish the seal surfaces. A finely polished surface may produce poor sealing or cause premature seal wear.

3. Inspect the main and connecting rod journals for cracks, scratches, grooves or scores.
4. Measure the diameter of each journal in at least four places to determine if an out-of-round, taper or undersize condition exists.
5. On engines with manual transmissions, check the fit of the clutch pilot bearing in the bore of the crankshaft. A needle roller bearing and adapter assembly is used as a clutch pilot bearing. It is inserted directly into the engine crankshaft. The bearing and adapter assembly cannot be serviced separately. A new bearing must be installed whenever a bearing is removed.
6. Inspect the pilot bearing, when used, for roughness, evidence of overheating or loss of lubricant. Replace if any of these conditions are found.
7. Inspect the rear oil seal surface of the crankshaft for deep grooves, nicks, burrs, porosity, or scratches which could damage the oil seal lip during installation. Remove all nicks and burrs with crocus cloth.

Main Bearings

1. Clean the bearing inserts and caps thoroughly in solvent, and dry them with compressed air.

➡Do not scrape varnish or gum deposits from the bearing shells.

2. Inspect each bearing carefully. Bearings that have a scored, chipped, or worn surface should be replaced.
3. The copper/lead bearing base may be visible through the bearing overlay in small localized areas. This may not mean that the bearing is excessively worn. It is not necessary to replace the bearing if the bearing clearance is within recommended specifications.
4. Check the clearance of bearings that appear to be satisfactory with Plastigage® or its equivalent. Fit the new bearings following the procedure Crankshaft and Main Bearings removal and installation, they should be reground to size for the next undersize bearing.
5. Regrind the journals to give the proper clearance with the next undersize bearing. If the journal will not clean up to maximum undersize bearing available, replace the crankshaft.
6. Always reproduce the same journal shoulder radius that existed originally. Too small a radius will result in fatigue failure of the crankshaft. Too large a radius will result in bearing failure due to radius ride of the bearing.
7. After regrinding the journals, chamfer the oil holes, then polish the journals with a #320 grit polishing cloth and engine oil. Crocus cloth may also be used as a polishing agent.

COMPLETING THE REBUILDING PROCESS

Fill the oil pump with oil, to prevent cavitating (sucking air) on initial engine start up. Install the oil pump and the pickup tube on the engine. Coat the oil pan gasket as necessary, and install the gasket and the oil pan. Mount the flywheel and the crankshaft vibration damper or pulley on the crankshaft.

➡Always use new bolts when installing the flywheel. Inspect the clutch shaft pilot bushing in the crankshaft. If the bushing is excessively worn, remove it with an expanding puller and a slide hammer, and tap a new bushing into place.

Position the engine, cylinder head side up. Lubricate the lifters, and install them into their bores. Install the cylinder head, and tighten it as specified. Insert the pushrods (where applicable), and position the rocker arms.

Install the intake and exhaust manifolds. Mount all accessories and install the engine in the vehicle. Fill the radiator with coolant, and the crankcase with high quality engine oil.

BREAK-IN PROCEDURE

Start the engine, and allow it to run at low speed for a few minutes, while checking for leaks. Stop the engine, check the oil level, and fill as necessary. Restart the engine, and fill the cooling system to capacity. Check the ignition timing. Run the engine at low to medium speed (800–2,500 rpm) for approximately ½ hour. Road test the vehicle, and check again for leaks.

➡Some gasket manufacturers recommend not retorquing the cylinder head(s) due to the composition of the head gasket. Follow the directions in the gasket set.

Flywheel/Flexplate and Ring Gear

➡Flexplate is the term for a flywheel mated with an automatic transmission.

REMOVAL & INSTALLATION

▶ See Figure 255

➡The ring gear is replaceable only on engines mated with a manual transmission. Engines with automatic transmissions have ring gears which are welded to the flexplate.

1. Remove the transmission.
2. On manual transmission vehicles, remove the clutch.
3. On automatic transmission vehicles, remove the torque converter from the flywheel.

➡The flywheel bolts should be loosened a little at a time in a cross pattern to avoid warping the flywheel. Also, some vehicles will have an Orange bolt hole on the torque converter which should be matched with the Orange line on the flexplate for proper balance.

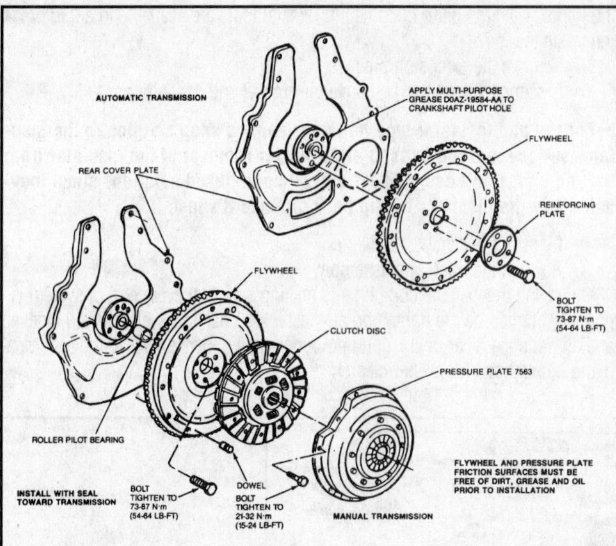

Fig. 255 Exploded view of a typical flywheel and flexplate mounting—2.3L shown

4. Loosen the flywheel bolts (gradually using several passes of a cross pattern) and remove the flywheel from the engine.

➡On vehicles with manual transmissions, replace the pilot bearing in the end of the crankshaft if removing the flywheel.

5. The flywheel should be checked for cracks and glazing. It can be resurfaced by a machine shop.
6. If the ring gear is to be replaced, drill a hole in the gear between two teeth, being careful not to contact the flywheel surface. Using a cold chisel at this point, crack the ring gear and remove it.
7. Polish the inner surface of the new ring gear and heat it in an oven to about 600°F (316°C). Quickly place the ring gear on the flywheel and tap it into place, making sure that it is fully seated.

** WARNING

Never heat the ring gear past 800°F (426°C), or the tempering will be destroyed.

To install:

8. Coat the threads of the flywheel bolts using a Teflon® based pipe sealant.
9. Install the flywheel on the end of the crankshaft. Tighten the bolts a little at a time, in a cross pattern, to the torque value shown in the Torque Specifications Chart.
10. Install the clutch or torque converter.
11. Install the transmission.

Rear Main Oil Seal

REPLACEMENT

See Figure 256

1. Disconnect the negative battery cable for safety.
2. Remove the flywheel or flexplate for access to the rear main seal.
3. Carefully punch 2 holes in the crankshaft rear oil seal on opposite sides of the crankshaft, just above the bearing cap to cylinder block split line. Install a sheet metal screw in each of the holes or use a small slide hammer to pry the crankshaft rear main oil seal from the block.

➡Use extreme caution not to scratch the crankshaft oil seal surface.

To install:

4. Clean the oil seal recess in the cylinder block and main bearing cap.
5. Coat the seal and the seal mounting surfaces with oil.
6. Position the seal on rear main seal installer T82L–6701–A, or equivalent, then position the tool and seal to the rear of the engine.
7. Alternate bolt tightening to seat the seal properly. The rear face of the seal must be within 0.005 in. (0.127mm) of the rear face of the block.
8. Install the flywheel or flexplate, as applicable.
9. Connect the negative battery cable.

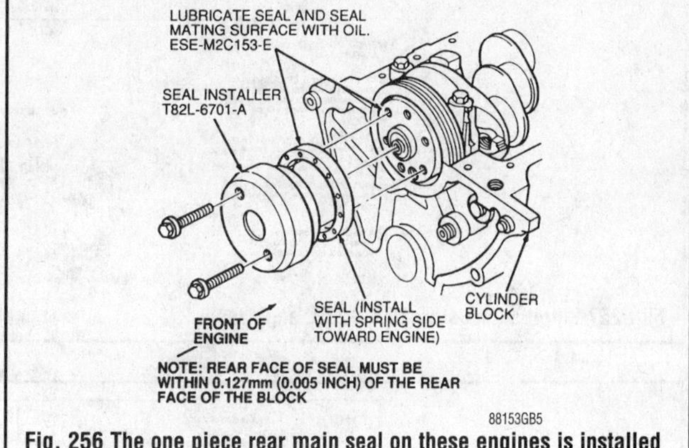

Fig. 256 The one piece rear main seal on these engines is installed with a special installation tool

EXHAUST SYSTEM

General Information

➡Safety glasses should be worn at all times when working on or near the exhaust system. Older exhaust systems will almost always be covered with loose rust particles which will shower you when disturbed. These particles are more than a nuisance and could injure your eye.

Whenever working on the exhaust system always keep the following in mind:

- Check the complete exhaust system for open seams, holes loose connections, or other deterioration which could permit exhaust fumes to seep into the passenger compartment.
- The exhaust system is usually supported by free-hanging rubber mountings which permit some movement of the exhaust system, but does not permit transfer of noise and vibration into the passenger compartment. Do not replace the rubber mounts with solid ones.
- Before removing any component of the exhaust system, ALWAYS squirt a liquid rust dissolving agent onto the fasteners for ease of removal. A lot of knuckle skin will be saved by following this rule. It may even be wise to spray the fasteners and allow them to sit overnight.

** CAUTION

Allow the exhaust system to cool sufficiently before spraying a solvent exhaust fasteners. Some solvents are highly flammable and could ignite when sprayed on hot exhaust components.

- Annoying rattles and noise vibrations in the exhaust system are usually caused by misalignment of the parts. When aligning the system, leave all bolts and nuts loose until all parts are properly aligned, then tighten, working from front to rear.
- When installing exhaust system parts, make sure there is enough clearance between the hot exhaust parts and pipes and hoses that would be adversely affected by excessive heat. Also make sure there is adequate clearance from the floor pan to avoid possible overheating of the floor.

Muffler, Catalytic Converter, Inlet and Outlet Pipes

➧ See Figures 257 and 258

REMOVAL & INSTALLATION

➡The following applies to exhaust systems using clamped joints. Some models, use welded joints at the muffler. These joints will, of course, have to be cut.

1. Raise and support the vehicle safely on jackstands.
2. Remove the U-clamps securing the muffler and outlet pipe.
3. Disconnect the muffler and outlet pipe bracket and insulator assemblies.
4. Remove the muffler and outlet pipe assembly. It may be necessary to heat the joints to get the parts to come off. Special tools are available to aid in breaking loose the joints.
5. Remove the extension pipe.
6. Disconnect the catalytic converter bracket and insulator assembly.

➡For rod and insulator type hangers, apply a soap solution to the insulator surface and rod ends to allow easier removal of the insulator from the rod end. Don't use oil-based or silicone-based solutions since they will allow the insulator to slip back off once it's installed.

7. Remove the catalytic converter.
8. Remove the inlet pipe assembly.
9. Install the exhaust components making sure that every part of system is properly aligned before tightening any fasteners. Make sure all tabs are indexed and all parts are clear of surrounding body panels. Please refer to the accompanying illustrations for proper clearances and alignment.

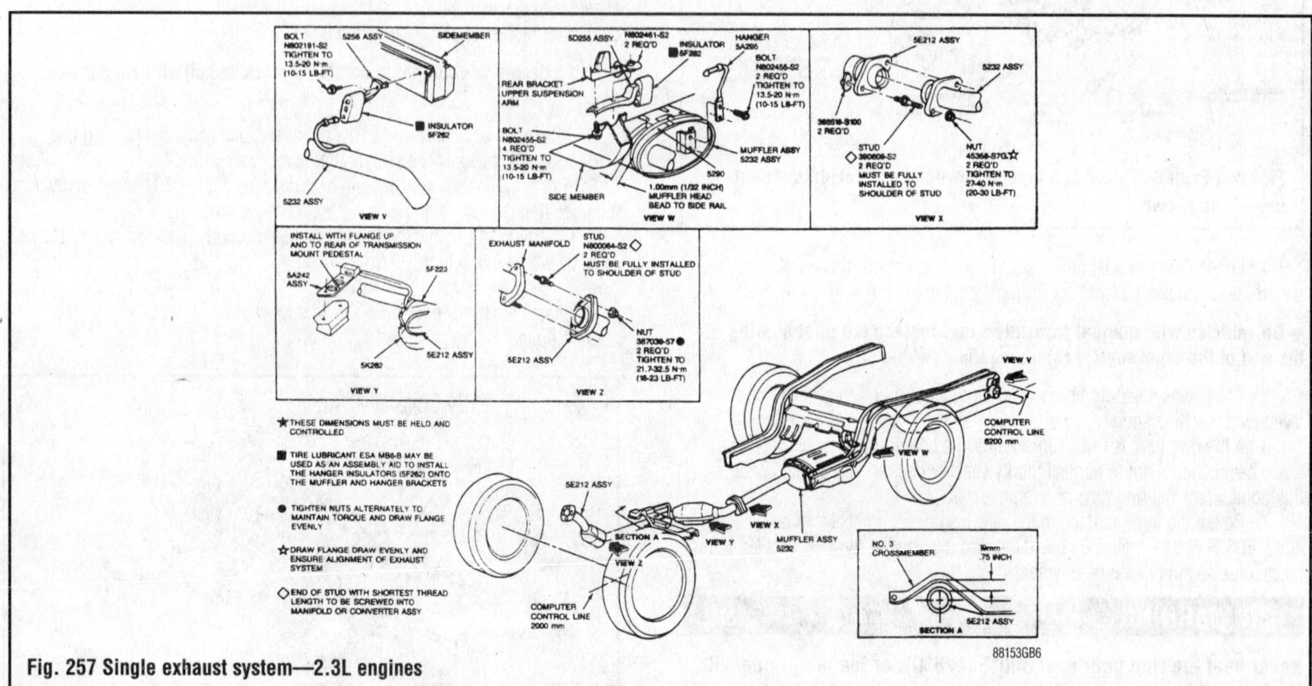

Fig. 257 Single exhaust system—2.3L engines

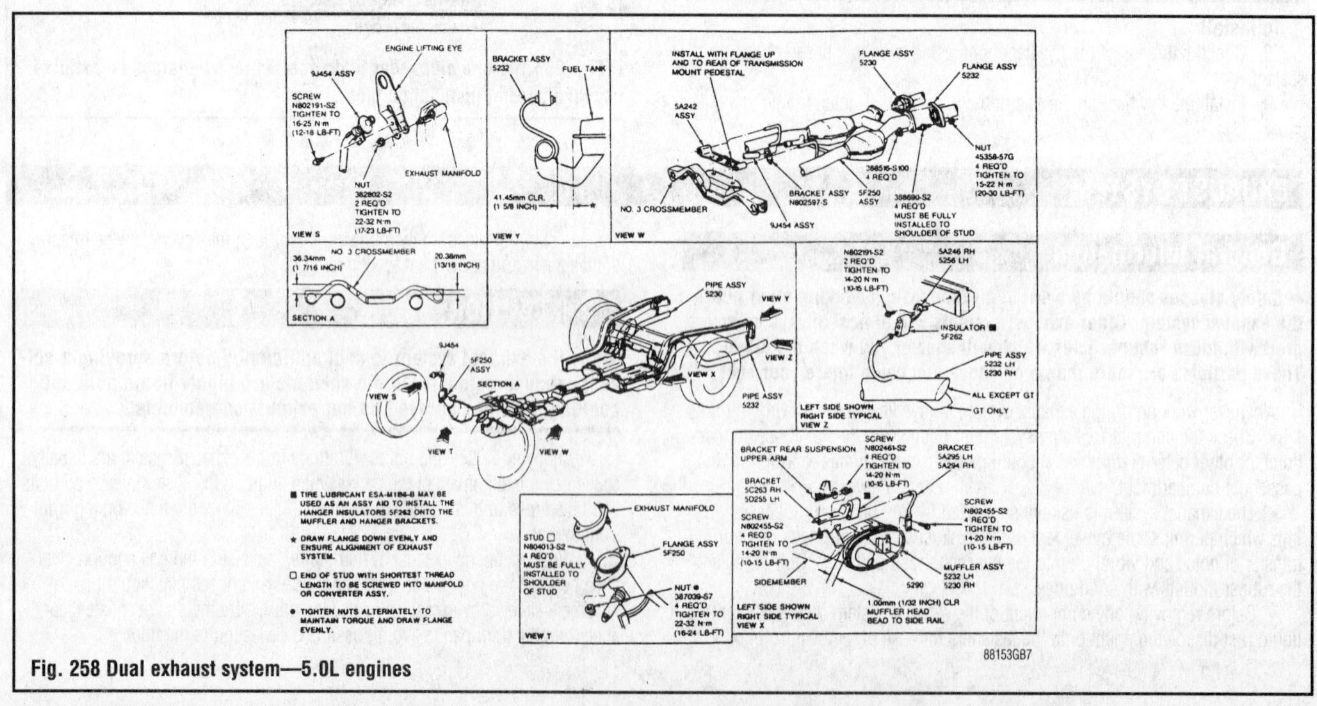

Fig. 258 Dual exhaust system—5.0L engines

ENGINE MECHANICAL SPECIFICATIONS

All specifications are given in inches

Component	2.3L Engine	5.0L Engine
Camshaft		
Maximum end-play:	0.0090[1]	0.0090[1]
Bearing diameter		
No. 1:	—	2.0825–2.0835
No. 2:	—	2.0675–2.0685
No. 3:	—	2.0525–2.0535
No. 4:	—	2.0375–2.0385
No. 5:	—	2.0225–2.0235
Journal diameter		
No. 1:	1.7713–1.7720	2.0805–2.0815
No. 2:	1.7713–1.7720	2.0655–2.0665
No. 3:	1.7713–1.7720	2.0505–2.0515
No. 4:	1.7713–1.7720	2.0355–2.0365
No. 5:		2.0205–2.0215
Bearing clearance:	0.0060[1]	0.0060[1]
Lobe lift		
Intake:	0.2381	0.2780[2]
Exhaust:	0.2381	0.2780[2]
Connecting rod		
Piston pin bore diameter:	0.9096–0.9012	0.9112–0.9096
Bearing oil clearance:	0.0008–0.0026[3]	0.008–0.0024[3]
Side clearance:	0.0140[1]	0.0230[1]
Crankshaft		
Connecting rod journal		
Diameter:	2.0462–2.0472	2.1228–2.1236
Out-of-round (max):	0.0006	0.0006
Taper (max):	0.0006	0.0006
Main bearing journal		
Diameter:	2.2059–2.2051[4]	2.2490–2.2482
Out-of-round (max):	0.0006	0.0006
Taper (max):	0.0006	0.0004
Main bearing oil clearance:	0.0008–0.0026[3]	0.0004–0.0021[3]
Crankshaft end-play:	0.0120[1]	0.0120[1]
Cylinder block		
Cylinder bore out-of-round limit:	0.0050	0.0050
Cylinder bore maximum taper:	0.0100	0.0100
Cylinder bore diameter:	3.7795–3.7825	4.0000–4.0048
Cylinder head		
Valve seat angle		
Intake:	45 degrees	45 degrees
Exhaust:	45 degrees	45 degrees
Valve guide bore diameter:	0.3433–0.3443	0.3433–0.3443
Hydraulic lifters		
Body diameter:	0.8422–0.8427	0.8740–0.8745
Clearance in block:	0.0007–0.0027	0.0007–0.0027
Collapsed tappet gap:	0.0350–0.0550	0.098–0.1980

88153C07

ENGINE MECHANICAL SPECIFICATIONS

All specifications are given in inches

Component	2.3L Engine	5.0L Engine
Oil pump		
Relief valve spring tension (lbs. at spec. length):	12.6–14.5 @ 1.20	10.6–12.2 @ 1.704
Driveshaft-to-housing bearing clearance:	0.0015–0.0030	0.0015–0.0030
Relief valve-to-bore clearance:	0.0015–0.0030	0.0015–0.0030
Rotor assembly end clearance (max):	0.0040	0.0040
Outer race-to-housing clearance:	0.001–0.0130	0.001–0.0130
Pistons		
Ring side clearance		
Compression (top):	0.0016–0.0033	0.002–0.004
Compression (bottom):	0.0016–0.0033	0.002–0.004
Ring width		
Compression (top):	0.0580–0.0590	0.0577–0.0587
Compression (bottom):	0.0580–0.0590	0.0577–0.0587
Piston-to-bore clearance:	0.0024–0.0034[5]	0.0030–0.0038[6]
Ring groove width		
Compression (top):	0.0600–0.0610	0.0600–0.0610
Compression (bottom):	0.0600–0.0610	0.0600–0.0610
Oil:	0.1596–0.1589	0.1587–0.1597
Piston pin length:	3.0100–3.0400	3.0100–3.0400
Piston pin diameter:	0.9118–0.9124	0.9119–0.9124
Piston-to-pin clearance:	0.0003–0.0005	0.0002–0.0004
Valves		
Face angle		
Intake:	44 degrees	44 degrees
Exhaust:	44 degrees	44 degrees
Head diameter		
Intake:	1.7300–1.7470	1.7700–1.7940
Exhaust:	1.4900–1.5100	1.4530–1.4680
Spring test pressure (lbs. @ spec. length)		
Intake:	64–74 @ 1.52	211-230 @ 1.33
Exhaust:	128–142 @ 1.12	200-226 @ 1.15
Spring installed height		
Intake:	1.4900–1.5500	1.7500–1.8000
Exhaust:	1.4900–1.5500	1.5800–1.6400
Spring free length		
Intake:	1.8770	2.0200
Exhaust:	1.8770	1.7900
Stem-to-guide clearance		
Intake:	0.0055[1]	0.0055[1]
Exhaust:	0.0055[1]	0.0055[1]
Stem diameter		
Intake:	0.3416–0.3423	0.3416–0.3423
Exhaust:	0.3411–0.3418	0.3411–0.3418

1. Specification is maximum wear limit
2. Cobra: 0.2822 lift on intake and exhaust
3. High end of specification represents max wear limit
4. Spec for Vin M; Vin A: 2.3990-2.3982
5. 1992-93: 0.0019-0.0029
6. 1993: 0.0012-0.0020

88153C08

ENGINE TORQUE SPECIFICATIONS

Component	English	Metric
Auxiliary shaft gear bolt		
2.3L engine	28–44 ft. lbs.	35–54 Nm
Auxiliary shaft thrust plate bolt		
2.3L engine	72–108 inch lbs.	8–12 Nm
Camshaft sprocket bolt		
2.3L engine	50–71 ft. lbs.	68-96 Nm
5.0L engine	40–45 ft. lbs.	54-61 Nm
Camshaft thrust plate		
2.3L engine	72–96 lbs.	8–12 Nm
5.0L engine	9–12 ft. lbs.	12-16 Nm
Connecting rod bearing cap nuts		
2.3L engine		
step 1:	25–30 ft. lbs.	34–41 Nm
step 2:	30–36 ft. lbs.	41–48 Nm
5.0L engine	19–24 ft. lbs.	25–33 Nm
Crankshaft pulley bolt		
2.3L engine		
1988–90	103–133 ft. lbs.	137–180 Nm
1991–92	114–151 ft. lbs.	155–205 Nm
5.0L engine	70–90 ft. lbs.	95–122 Nm
Cylinder Head bolt		
2.3L engine		
Except 1993		
step 1:	50–60 ft. lbs.	55–81 Nm
step 2:	80–90 ft. lbs.	108–122 Nm
1993		
Step 1:	52 ft. lbs.	70 Nm
Step 2:	Retighten to 52 ft. lbs.	Retighten to 70 Nm
Step 3:	80-100 degrees	80-100 degrees
5.0L engine		
Except 1993		
step 1:	55–65 ft. lbs.	75–88 Nm
step 2:	65–72 ft. lbs.	88–98 Nm
1993		
Non-flanged Head Bolts		
Step 1:	55-65 ft. lbs.	75-88 Nm
Step 2:	65-72 ft. lbs.	88-98 Nm
Flanged Head Bolts		
Step 1:	25-35 ft. lbs.	34-47 Nm
Step 2:	45-55 ft. lbs.	61-75 Nm
Step 3:	85-95 degrees (1/4 turn)	85-95 degrees (1/4 turn)
EGR valve		
2.3L engine	14–21 ft. lbs.	19–29 Nm
5.0L engine	15–22 ft. lbs.	20–30 Nm
EGR valve-to-spacer plate		
5.0L engine	12–18 ft. lbs.	16–24 Nm
EGR supply tube		
2.3L engine	9–12 ft. lbs.	12–16 Nm

88153C10

ENGINE TORQUE SPECIFICATIONS

Component	English	Metric
Engine mounts		
2.3L engine		
rear mount-to-trans bolts	35–45 ft. lbs.	41–61 Nm
front engine mount bolts	33–45 ft. lbs.	45–61 Nm
mount-to-body nuts	80–106 ft. lbs.	108–144 Nm
bracket-to-engine	30–42 ft. lbs.	40–60 Nm
5.0L engine		
rear mount-to-trans bolts	47–64 ft. lbs.	35–50 Nm
front engine mount bolts	15–22 ft. lbs.	20–30 Nm
mount-to-body bolts	35–50 ft. lbs.	47–67 Nm
bracket-to-engine	30–42 ft. lbs.	40–60 Nm
Exhaust flange-to-manifold nuts		
2.3L engine	35–48 ft. lbs.	46–65 Nm
5.0L engine	20–27 ft. lbs.	27–34 Nm
Exhaust Manifold		
2.3L engine		
step 1:	15–17 ft. lbs.	20–23 Nm
step 2:	20–30 ft. lbs.	27–41 Nm
5.0L engine	18–24 ft. lbs.	25–33 Nm
Exhaust manifold-to-heat shield nuts	15–22 ft. lbs.	20–30 Nm
Flywheel/flex plate-to-crankshaft bolts		
2.3L engine	56–64 ft. lbs.	76–87 Nm
5.0L engine	75–85 ft. lbs.	102–116 Nm
Flywheel-to-converter bolts	20–34 ft. lbs.	27–46 Nm
Fuel rail-to-intake manifold bolts		
2.3L engine	14–21 ft. lbs.	19–29 Nm
5.0L engine	70–105 ft. lbs.	8–12 Nm
Intake Manifold (Lower)		
2.3L engine		
Step 1:	5-7 ft. lbs.	7-9 Nm
Step 2:	20-29 ft. lbs.	27-41 Nm
5.0L HO engine		
Step 1:	8 ft. lbs.	11 Nm
Step 2:	16 ft. lbs.	22 Nm
Step 3:	23-25 ft. lbs.	31-34 Nm
Intake Manifold (Upper)		
2.3L engine	15–22 ft. lbs.	20–30 Nm
5.0L engine	12–18 ft. lbs.	16–24 Nm
Main bearing cap bolts		
2.3L engine		
step 1:	50–60 ft. lbs.	68–81 Nm
step 2:	75–85 ft. lbs.	102–116 Nm
5.0L engine	60–70 ft. lbs.	81–95 Nm
Oil filter adapter	15–22 ft. lbs.	20–30 Nm
Oil Pan-to-block		
2.3L engine	10–13 ft. lbs.	13–18 Nm
5.0L engine	9–11 ft. lbs.	12–15 Nm
Oil pan drain plug	15–25 ft. lbs.	20–34 Nm
Oil level low sensor	20–30 ft. lbs.	27–41 Nm
Oil pressure sending unit	12–16 ft. lbs.	16–22 Nm
Oil pump attaching bolts		
2.3L engine	14–21 ft. lbs.	19–29 Nm
5.0L engine	22–32 ft. lbs.	30–43 Nm

88153C11

ENGINE TORQUE SPECIFICATIONS

Component	English	Metric
Oil pump cover		
2.3L engine	90–130 inch lbs.	10–15 Nm
Rocker arm bolt		
5.0L engine	18–25 ft. lbs.	24–34 Nm
Rocker (Valve) cover		
2.3L engine	60–96 inch lbs.	7–11 Nm
5.0L engine	36–60 inch lbs.	4–7 Nm
Starter-to-block bolts	15–20 ft. lbs.	20–27 Nm
Thermostat housing		
2.3L engine	14–21 ft. lbs.	19–29 Nm
5.0L engine	15–22 ft. lbs.	20–30 Nm
Throttle body nuts	15–22 ft. lbs.	20–30 Nm
Timing belt tensioner bolt	14–19 ft. lbs.	19–29 Nm
Timing cover		
2.3L engine	72–108 inch lbs.	8–12 Nm
5.0L engine	12–18 ft. lbs.	16–24 Nm
Water pump		
2.3L engine	14–21 ft. lbs.	19–29 Nm
5.0L engine	12–18 ft. lbs.	16–24 Nm
Water pump pulley hub bolts		
2.3L engine	12–18 ft. lbs.	16–24 Nm
5.0L engine	36–47 ft. lbs.	48–64 Nm
Water pump tensioner bolt		
2.3L engine	35–48 ft. lbs.	47–65 Nm

88153C09

USING A VACUUM GAUGE

White needle = steady needle ***Dark needle = drifting needle***

The vacuum gauge is one of the most useful and easy-to-use diagnostic tools. It is inexpensive, easy to hook up, and provides valuable information about the condition of your engine.

Indication: Normal engine in good condition

Gauge reading: Steady, from 17-22 in./Hg.

Indication: Sticking valve or ignition miss

Gauge reading: Needle fluctuates from 15-20 in./Hg. at idle

Indication: Late ignition or valve timing, low compression, stuck throttle valve, leaking carburetor or manifold gasket.

Gauge reading: Low (15-20 in./Hg.) but steady

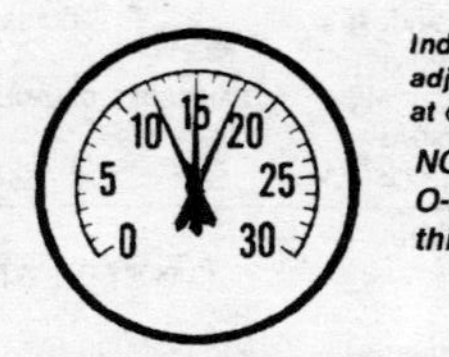

Indication: Improper carburetor adjustment, or minor intake leak at carburetor or manifold

NOTE: Bad fuel injector O-rings may also cause this reading.

Gauge reading: Drifting needle

Indication: Weak valve springs, worn valve stem guides, or leaky cylinder head gasket (vibrating excessively at all speeds).

NOTE: A plugged catalytic converter may also cause this reading.

Gauge reading: Needle fluctuates as engine speed increases

Indication: Burnt valve or improper valve clearance. The needle will drop when the defective valve operates.

Gauge reading: Steady needle, but drops regularly

Indication: Choked muffler or obstruction in system. Speed up the engine. Choked muffler will exhibit a slow drop of vacuum to zero.

Gauge reading: Gradual drop in reading at idle

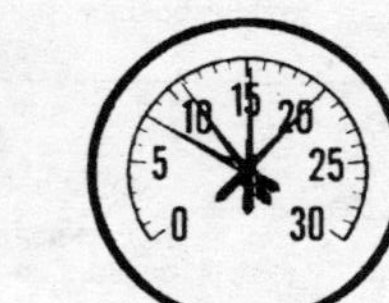

Indication: Worn valve guides

Gauge reading: Needle vibrates excessively at idle, but steadies as engine speed increases

TCCS3C01

Troubleshooting Engine Mechanical Problems

Problem	Cause	Solution
External oil leaks	· Cylinder head cover RTV sealant broken or improperly seated	· Replace sealant; inspect cylinder head cover sealant flange and cylinder head sealant surface for distortion and cracks
	· Oil filler cap leaking or missing	· Replace cap
	· Oil filter gasket broken or improperly seated	· Replace oil filter
	· Oil pan side gasket broken, improperly seated or opening in RTV sealant	· Replace gasket or repair opening in sealant; inspect oil pan gasket flange for distortion
	· Oil pan front oil seal broken or improperly seated	· Replace seal; inspect timing case cover and oil pan seal flange for distortion
	· Oil pan rear oil seal broken or improperly seated	· Replace seal; inspect oil pan rear oil seal flange; inspect rear main bearing cap for cracks, plugged oil return channels, or distortion in seal groove
	· Timing case cover oil seal broken or improperly seated	· Replace seal
	· Excess oil pressure because of restricted PCV valve	· Replace PCV valve
	· Oil pan drain plug loose or has stripped threads	· Repair as necessary and tighten
	· Rear oil gallery plug loose	· Use appropriate sealant on gallery plug and tighten
	· Rear camshaft plug loose or improperly seated	· Seat camshaft plug or replace and seal, as necessary
Excessive oil consumption	· Oil level too high	· Drain oil to specified level
	· Oil with wrong viscosity being used	· Replace with specified oil
	· PCV valve stuck closed	· Replace PCV valve
	· Valve stem oil deflectors (or seals) are damaged, missing, or incorrect type	· Replace valve stem oil deflectors
	· Valve stems or valve guides worn	· Measure stem-to-guide clearance and repair as necessary
	· Poorly fitted or missing valve cover baffles	· Replace valve cover
	· Piston rings broken or missing	· Replace broken or missing rings
	· Scuffed piston	· Replace piston
	· Incorrect piston ring gap	· Measure ring gap, repair as necessary
	· Piston rings sticking or excessively loose in grooves	· Measure ring side clearance, repair as necessary
	· Compression rings installed upside down	· Repair as necessary
	· Cylinder walls worn, scored, or glazed	· Repair as necessary

TCCS3C02

Troubleshooting Engine Mechanical Problems

Problem	Cause	Solution
Excessive oil consumption (cont.)	· Piston ring gaps not properly staggered	· Repair as necessary
	· Excessive main or connecting rod bearing clearance	· Measure bearing clearance, repair as necessary
No oil pressure	· Low oil level	· Add oil to correct level
	· Oil pressure gauge, warning lamp or sending unit inaccurate	· Replace oil pressure gauge or warning lamp
	· Oil pump malfunction	· Replace oil pump
	· Oil pressure relief valve sticking	· Remove and inspect oil pressure relief valve assembly
	· Oil passages on pressure side of pump obstructed	· Inspect oil passages for obstruction
	· Oil pickup screen or tube obstructed	· Inspect oil pickup for obstruction
	· Loose oil inlet tube	· Tighten or seal inlet tube
Low oil pressure	· Low oil level	· Add oil to correct level
	· Inaccurate gauge, warning lamp or sending unit	· Replace oil pressure gauge or warning lamp
	· Oil excessively thin because of dilution, poor quality, or improper grade	· Drain and refill crankcase with recommended oil
	· Excessive oil temperature	· Correct cause of overheating engine
	· Oil pressure relief spring weak or sticking	· Remove and inspect oil pressure relief valve assembly
	· Oil inlet tube and screen assembly has restriction or air leak	· Remove and inspect oil inlet tube and screen assembly. (Fill inlet tube with lacquer thinner to locate leaks.)
	· Excessive oil pump clearance	· Measure clearances
	· Excessive main, rod, or camshaft bearing clearance	· Measure bearing clearances, repair as necessary
High oil pressure	· Improper oil viscosity	· Drain and refill crankcase with correct viscosity oil
	· Oil pressure gauge or sending unit inaccurate	· Replace oil pressure gauge
	· Oil pressure relief valve sticking closed	· Remove and inspect oil pressure relief valve assembly
Main bearing noise	· Insufficient oil supply	· Inspect for low oil level and low oil pressure
	· Main bearing clearance excessive	· Measure main bearing clearance, repair as necessary
	· Bearing insert missing	· Replace missing insert
	· Crankshaft end-play excessive	· Measure end-play, repair as necessary
	· Improperly tightened main bearing cap bolts	· Tighten bolts with specified torque
	· Loose flywheel or drive plate	· Tighten flywheel or drive plate attaching bolts
	· Loose or damaged vibration damper	· Repair as necessary

TCCS3C03

Troubleshooting Engine Mechanical Problems

Problem	Cause	Solution
Connecting rod bearing noise	· Insufficient oil supply	· Inspect for low oil level and low oil pressure
	· Carbon build-up on piston	· Remove carbon from piston crown
	· Bearing clearance excessive or bearing missing	· Measure clearance, repair as necessary
	· Crankshaft connecting rod journal out-of-round	· Measure journal dimensions, repair or replace as necessary
	· Misaligned connecting rod or cap	· Repair as necessary
	· Connecting rod bolts tightened improperly	· Tighten bolts with specified torque
Piston noise	· Piston-to-cylinder wall clearance excessive (scuffed piston)	· Measure clearance and examine piston
	· Cylinder walls excessively tapered or out-of-round	· Measure cylinder wall dimensions, rebore cylinder
	· Piston ring broken	· Replace all rings on piston
	· Loose or seized piston pin	· Measure piston-to-pin clearance, repair as necessary
	· Connecting rods misaligned	· Measure rod alignment, straighten or replace
	· Piston ring side clearance excessively loose or tight	· Measure ring side clearance, repair as necessary
	· Carbon build-up on piston is excessive	· Remove carbon from piston
Valve actuating component noise	· Insufficient oil supply	· Check for: (a) Low oil level (b) Low oil pressure (c) Wrong hydraulic tappets (d) Restricted oil gallery (e) Excessive tappet to bore clearance
	· Rocker arms or pivots worn	· Replace worn rocker arms or pivots
	· Foreign objects or chips in hydraulic tappets	· Clean tappets
	· Excessive tappet leak-down	· Replace valve tappet
	· Tappet face worn	· Replace tappet; inspect corresponding cam lobe for wear
	· Broken or cocked valve springs	· Properly seat cocked springs; replace broken springs
	· Stem-to-guide clearance excessive	· Measure stem-to-guide clearance, repair as required
	· Valve bent	· Replace valve
	· Loose rocker arms	· Check and repair as necessary
	· Valve seat runout excessive	· Regrind valve seat/valves
	· Missing valve lock	· Install valve lock
	· Excessive engine oil	· Correct oil level

TCCS3C04

Troubleshooting Engine Performance

Problem	Cause	Solution
Hard starting (engine cranks normally)	• Faulty engine control system component	• Repair or replace as necessary
	• Faulty fuel pump	• Replace fuel pump
	• Faulty fuel system component	• Repair or replace as necessary
	• Faulty ignition coil	• Test and replace as necessary
	• Improper spark plug gap	• Adjust gap
	• Incorrect ignition timing	• Adjust timing
	• Incorrect valve timing	• Check valve timing; repair as necessary
Rough idle or stalling	• Incorrect curb or fast idle speed	• Adjust curb or fast idle speed (If possible)
	• Incorrect ignition timing	• Adjust timing to specification
	• Improper feedback system operation	• Refer to Chapter 4
	• Faulty EGR valve operation	• Test EGR system and replace as necessary
	• Faulty PCV valve air flow	• Test PCV valve and replace as necessary
	• Faulty TAC vacuum motor or valve	• Repair as necessary
	• Air leak into manifold vacuum	• Inspect manifold vacuum connections and repair as necessary
	• Faulty distributor rotor or cap	• Replace rotor or cap (Distributor systems only)
	• Improperly seated valves	• Test cylinder compression, repair as necessary
	• Incorrect ignition wiring	• Inspect wiring and correct as necessary
	• Faulty ignition coil	• Test coil and replace as necessary
	• Restricted air vent or idle passages	• Clean passages
	• Restricted air cleaner	• Clean or replace air cleaner filter element
Faulty low-speed operation	• Restricted idle air vents and passages	• Clean air vents and passages
	• Restricted air cleaner	• Clean or replace air cleaner filter element
	• Faulty spark plugs	• Clean or replace spark plugs
	• Dirty, corroded, or loose ignition secondary circuit wire connections	• Clean or tighten secondary circuit wire connections
	• Improper feedback system operation	• Refer to Chapter 4
	• Faulty ignition coil high voltage wire	• Replace ignition coil high voltage wire (Distributor systems only)
	• Faulty distributor cap	• Replace cap (Distributor systems only)
Faulty acceleration	• Incorrect ignition timing	• Adjust timing
	• Faulty fuel system component	• Repair or replace as necessary
	• Faulty spark plug(s)	• Clean or replace spark plug(s)
	• Improperly seated valves	• Test cylinder compression, repair as necessary
	• Faulty ignition coil	• Test coil and replace as necessary

TCCS3C05

Troubleshooting Engine Performance

Problem	Cause	Solution
Faulty acceleration (cont.)	• Improper feedback system operation	• Refer to Chapter 4
Faulty high speed operation	• Incorrect ignition timing	• Adjust timing (if possible)
	• Faulty advance mechanism	• Check advance mechanism and repair as necessary (Distributor systems only)
	• Low fuel pump volume	• Replace fuel pump
	• Wrong spark plug air gap or wrong plug	• Adjust air gap or install correct plug
	• Partially restricted exhaust manifold, exhaust pipe, catalytic converter, muffler, or tailpipe	• Eliminate restriction
	• Restricted vacuum passages	• Clean passages
	• Restricted air cleaner	• Cleaner or replace filter element as necessary
	• Faulty distributor rotor or cap	• Replace rotor or cap (Distributor systems only)
	• Faulty ignition coil	• Test coil and replace as necessary
	• Improperly seated valve(s)	• Test cylinder compression, repair as necessary
	• Faulty valve spring(s)	• Inspect and test valve spring tension, replace as necessary
	• Incorrect valve timing	• Check valve timing and repair as necessary
	• Intake manifold restricted	• Remove restriction or replace manifold
	• Worn distributor shaft	• Replace shaft (Distributor systems only)
	• Improper feedback system operation	• Refer to Chapter 4
Misfire at all speeds	• Faulty spark plug(s)	• Clean or relace spark plug(s)
	• Faulty spark plug wire(s)	• Replace as necessary
	• Faulty distributor cap or rotor	• Replace cap or rotor (Distributor systems only)
	• Faulty ignition coil	• Test coil and replace as necessary
	• Primary ignition circuit shorted or open intermittently	• Troubleshoot primary circuit and repair as necessary
	• Improperly seated valve(s)	• Test cylinder compression, repair as necessary
	• Faulty hydraulic tappet(s)	• Clean or replace tappet(s)
	• Improper feedback system operation	• Refer to Chapter 4
	• Faulty valve spring(s)	• Inspect and test valve spring tension, repair as necessary
	• Worn camshaft lobes	• Replace camshaft
	• Air leak into manifold	• Check manifold vacuum and repair as necessary
	• Fuel pump volume or pressure low	• Replace fuel pump
	• Blown cylinder head gasket	• Replace gasket
	• Intake or exhaust manifold passage(s) restricted	• Pass chain through passage(s) and repair as necessary
Power not up to normal	• Incorrect ignition timing	• Adjust timing
	• Faulty distributor rotor	• Replace rotor (Distributor systems only)

TCCS3C06

Troubleshooting Engine Performance

Problem	Cause	Solution
Power not up to normal (cont.)	• Incorrect spark plug gap	• Adjust gap
	• Faulty fuel pump	• Replace fuel pump
	• Faulty fuel pump	• Replace fuel pump
	• Incorrect valve timing	• Check valve timing and repair as necessary
	• Faulty ignition coil	• Test coil and replace as necessary
	• Faulty ignition wires	• Test wires and replace as necessary
	• Improperly seated valves	• Test cylinder compression and repair as necessary
	• Blown cylinder head gasket	• Replace gasket
	• Leaking piston rings	• Test compression and repair as necessary
	• Improper feedback system operation	• Refer to Chapter 4
Intake backfire	• Improper ignition timing	• Adjust timing
	• Defective EGR component	• Repair as necessary
	• Defective TAC vacuum motor or valve	• Repair as necessary
Exhaust backfire	• Air leak into manifold vacuum	• Check manifold vacuum and repair as necessary
	• Faulty air injection diverter valve	• Test diverter valve and replace as necessary
	• Exhaust leak	• Locate and eliminate leak
Ping or spark knock	• Incorrect ignition timing	• Adjust timing
	• Distributor advance malfunction	• Inspect advance mechanism and repair as necessary (Distributor systems only)
	• Excessive combustion chamber deposits	• Remove with combustion chamber cleaner
	• Air leak into manifold vacuum	• Check manifold vacuum and repair as necessary
	• Excessively high compression	• Test compression and repair as necessary
	• Fuel octane rating excessively low	• Try alternate fuel source
	• Sharp edges in combustion chamber	• Grind smooth
	• EGR valve not functioning properly	• Test EGR system and replace as necessary
Surging (at cruising to top speeds)	• Low fuel pump pressure or volume	• Replace fuel pump
	• Improper PCV valve air flow	• Test PCV valve and replace as necessary
	• Air leak into manifold vacuum	• Check manifold vacuum and repair as necessary
	• Incorrect spark advance	• Test and replace as necessary
	• Restricted fuel filter	• Replace fuel filter
	• Restricted air cleaner	• Clean or replace air cleaner filter element
	• EGR valve not functioning properly	• Test EGR system and replace as necessary
	• Improper feedback system operation	• Refer to Chapter 4

TCCS3C07

4 EMISSION CONTROLS

POSITIVE CRANKCASE VENTILATION SYSTEM

PCV Valve System

GENERAL INFORMATION

The PCV valve system vents crankcase gases into the engine air intake where they are burned with the fuel and air mixture. The PCV valve system keeps pollutants from being released into the atmosphere, and also helps to keep the engine oil clean, by ridding the crankcase of moisture and corrosive fumes. The PCV valve system consists of the PCV valve, it's mounting grommet, the nipple in the air intake and the connecting hoses. On some engine applications, the PCV valve system is connected with the evaporative emission system.

DESCRIPTION

See Figures 1, 2, 3 and 4

The PCV valve controls the amount of vapors pulled into the intake manifold from the crankcase and acts as a check valve by preventing air flow from entering the crankcase in the opposite direction. The PCV valve also prevents combustion backfiring from entering the crankcase in order to prevent detonation of the accumulated crankcase gases.

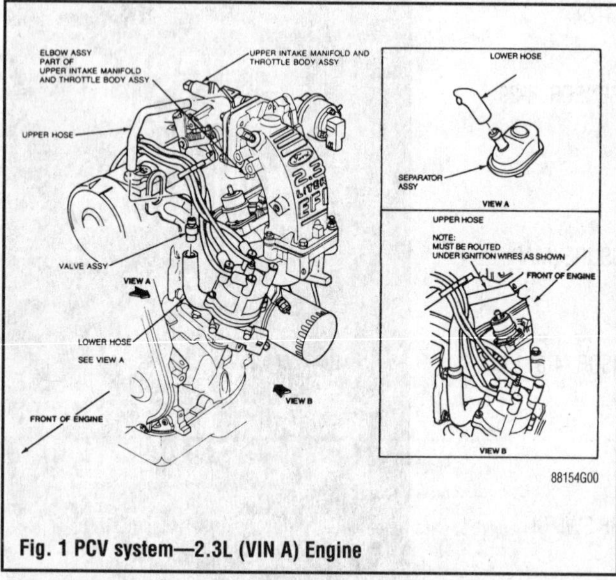

Fig. 1 PCV system—2.3L (VIN A) Engine

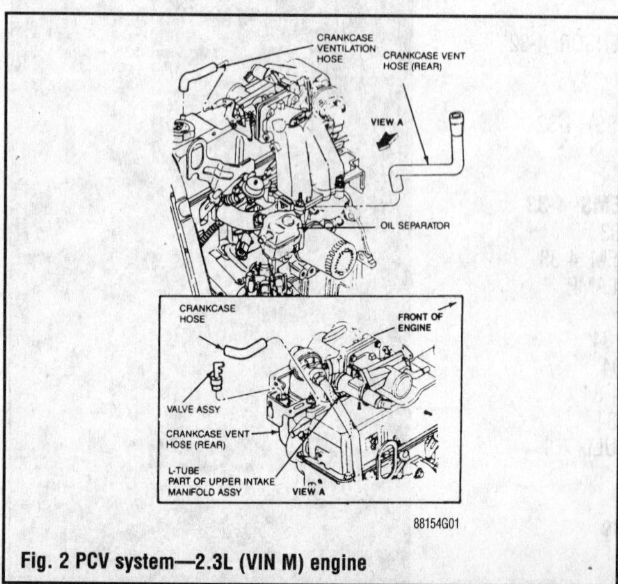

Fig. 2 PCV system—2.3L (VIN M) engine

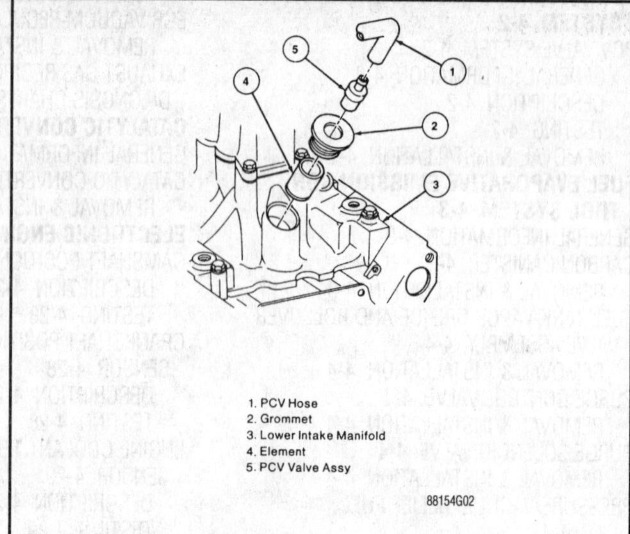

Fig. 3 PCV system—5.0L engine

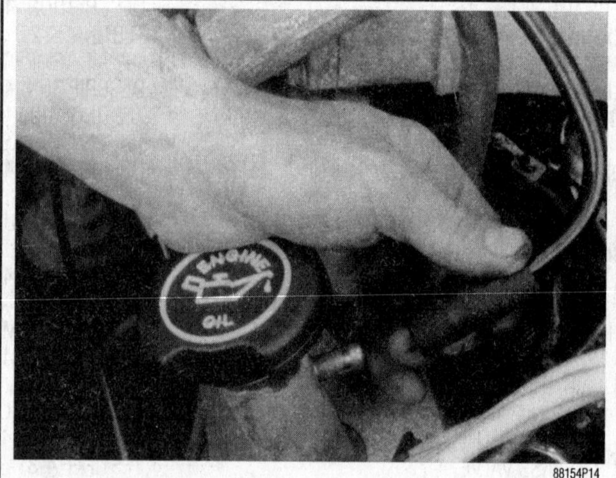

Fig. 4 This is where the crankcase vapors are drawn from the engine—5.0L engine

TESTING

1. Remove the PCV valve from the valve cover grommet. On the 5.0L engine, the PCV valve is located on top of the block by the firewall, while the 2.3L engines is mounted inline with the breather hose.
2. Shake the PCV valve. If the valve rattles when shaken, reinstall and proceed to Step 3. If the valve does not rattle, it is sticking and must be replaced.
3. Start the engine and bring it to normal operating temperature.
4. Disconnect the hose from the remote air cleaner or air outlet tube, the tube connecting the mass air flow meter and throttle body.
5. Place a stiff piece of paper over the hose end and wait 1 minute.
6. If vacuum holds the paper in place, the system is okay; reconnect the hose.
7. If the paper is not held in place, check for loose hose connections, vacuum leaks or blockage. Correct as necessary.

REMOVAL & INSTALLATION

1. Disconnect the vacuum hose from the PCV valve.
2. Remove the PCV valve from it's mounting grommet.
3. Installation is the reverse of the removal procedure.

FUEL EVAPORATIVE EMISSION CONTROL SYSTEM

General Information

Fuel vapors trapped in the sealed fuel tank are vented through the orifice vapor valve assembly in the top of the tank. The vapors leave the valve assembly through a single vapor line and continue to the carbon canister for storage until they are purged to the engine for burning.

Purging the carbon canister removes the fuel vapor stored in the carbon canister. The fuel vapor is purged via a purge port system, where the vapors flow from the carbon canister to the throttle body or via an EEC-IV controlled system, where the flow of vapors from the canister to the engine is controlled by a purge solenoid or vacuum controlled purge valve. Purging occurs when the engine is at operating temperature and, in most systems, off idle.

The evaporative emission control system consists of the carbon canister, fuel tank vapor orifice and rollover valve assembly, purge control valve and/or purge solenoid valve and the pressure/vacuum relief valve.

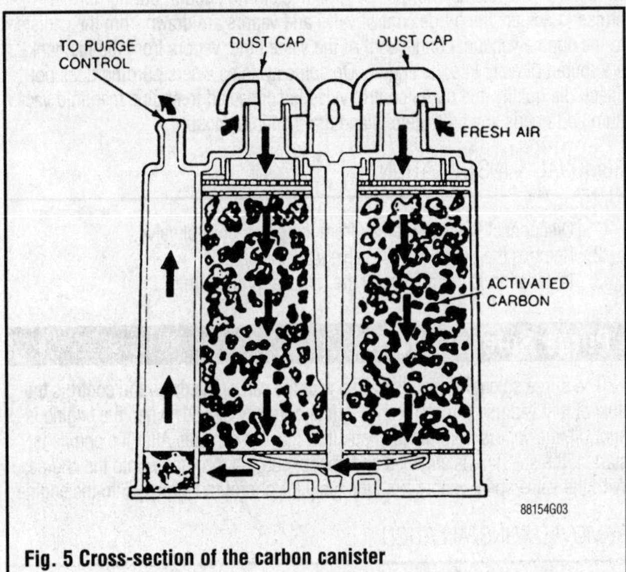

Fig. 5 Cross-section of the carbon canister

Carbon Canister

See Figures 5, 6 and 7

The fuel vapors from the fuel tank are stored in the carbon canister until the vehicle is operated, at which time, the vapors will purge from the canister into the engine for consumption. The carbon canister contains activated carbon, which absorbs the fuel vapor. The canister is located in the engine compartment or along the frame rail.

REMOVAL & INSTALLATION

1. Disconnect the vapor hoses from the carbon canister.
2. Remove the carbon canister attaching screws and remove the carbon canister.
3. Installation is the reverse of the removal procedure.

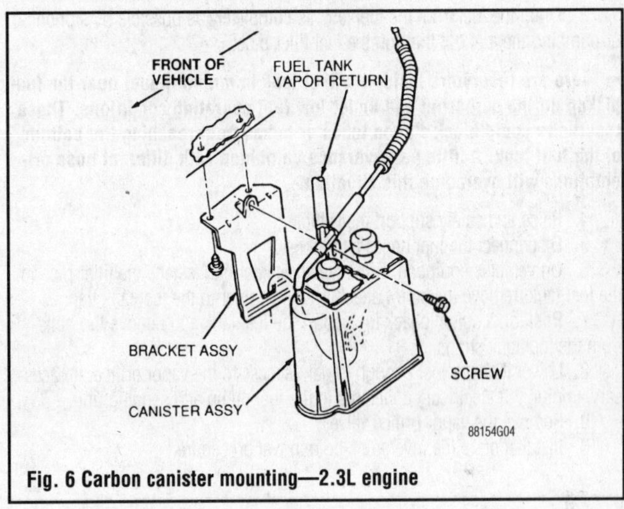

Fig. 6 Carbon canister mounting—2.3L engine

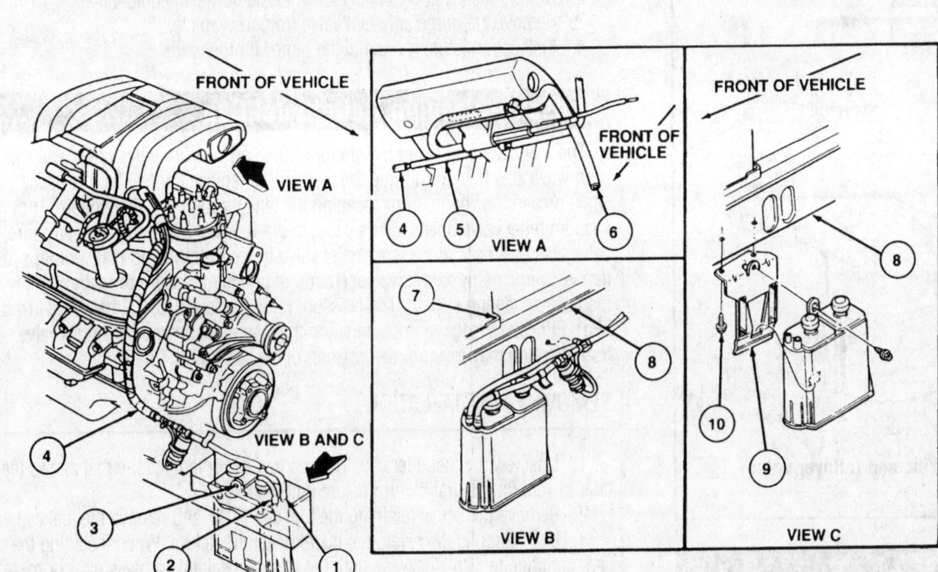

Fig. 7 Carbon canister mounting—5.0L engine

Fuel Tank Vapor Orifice And Rollover Valve Assembly

See Figure 8

Fuel vapor in the fuel tank is vented to the carbon canister through the vapor valve assembly. The valve is mounted in a rubber grommet at a central location in the upper surface of the fuel tank. A vapor space between the fuel level and the tank upper surface is combined with a small orifice and float shut-off valve in the vapor valve assembly to prevent liquid fuel from passing to the carbon canister. The vapor space also allows for thermal expansion of the fuel.

REMOVAL & INSTALLATION

1. Disconnect the negative battery cable.
2. Relieve the fuel system pressure as follows:
   a. Remove the fuel filler cap.
   b. Attach fuel pressure gauge T80L9974B or equivalent, to the fuel diagnostic valve on the fuel supply manifold.
   c. Relieve the fuel pressure into a suitable container.
   d. Remove the fuel pressure gauge.
3. Drain the fuel from the fuel tank as completely as possible by siphoning or pumping the fuel out through the fuel filler pipe.

There are reservoirs inside the fuel tank to maintain fuel near the fuel pickup during cornering and under low fuel operating conditions. These reservoirs could block siphon tubes or hoses from reaching the bottom of the fuel tank. A little perseverance combined with different hose orientations will overcome this situation.

4. Raise and safely support the vehicle.
5. Disconnect the fuel hoses and tubes.
6. On vehicles equipped with a metal retainer that fastens the filler pipe to the fuel tank, remove the screw attaching the retainer to the fuel tank flange.
7. Position a suitable jack to support the fuel tank and remove the bolts from the fuel tank straps.
8. Lower the tank just enough to gain access to the vapor orifice. If necessary, unplug the electrical connectors to the fuel pump and sending unit.
9. Remove the vapor orifice valve.
10. Installation is the reverse of the removal procedure.

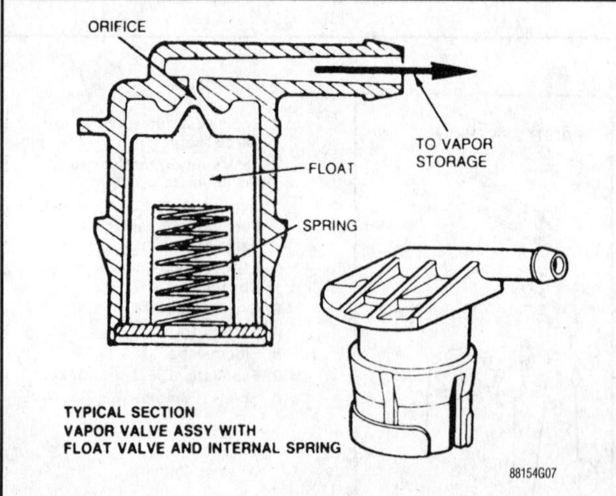

Fig. 8 Cross-section view of the vapor orific and rollover valve assembly

Purge Control Valve

See Figure 9

The purge control valve is in-line with the carbon canister and controls the flow of fuel vapors out of the canister.

When the engine is stopped, vapors from the fuel tank flow into the canister.

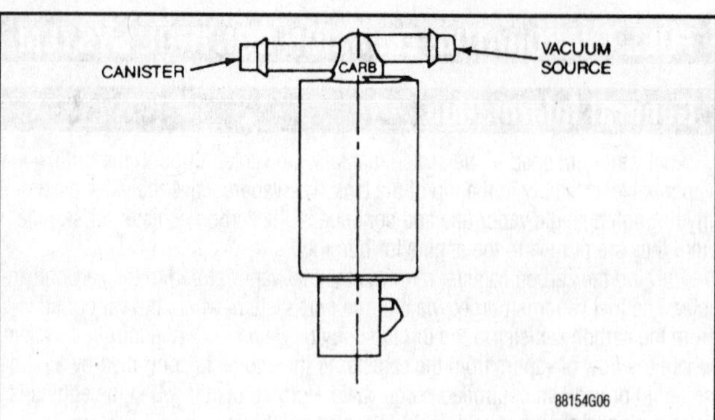

Fig. 9 Note which hose is connected to each side before removing the purge control valve

On controlled systems, the vacuum signal is strong enough during normal cruise to actuate the purge control valve and vapors are drawn from the canister to the engine vacuum connection. At the same time, vapors from the fuel tank are routed directly into the engine. On some systems where purging does not affect idle quality, the purge control valve is connected to engine manifold vacuum and opens any time there is enough manifold vacuum.

REMOVAL & INSTALLATION

1. Disconnect the vapor hoses from the purge control valve.
2. Remove the purge control valve from the vehicle.
3. Installation is the reverse of the removal procedure.

Purge Solenoid Valve

The purge solenoid valve is in-line with the carbon canister and controls the flow of fuel vapors out of the canister. It is normally closed. When the engine is shut off, the vapors from the fuel tank flow into the canister. After the engine is started, the solenoid is engaged and opens, purging the vapors into the engine. With the valve open, vapors from the fuel tank are routed directly into the engine.

REMOVAL & INSTALLATION

1. Disconnect the vapor hoses from the purge solenoid valve.
2. Unplug the electrical connector from the purge solenoid valve.
3. Remove the purge solenoid valve from the vehicle.
4. Installation is the reverse of the removal procedure.

Pressure/Vacuum Relief Fuel Cap

The fuel cap contains an integral pressure and vacuum relief valve. The vacuum valve acts to allow air into the fuel tank to replace the fuel as it is used, while preventing vapors from escaping the tank through the atmosphere. The vacuum relief valve opens after a vacuum of –0.5 psi (3.45 kPa). The pressure valve acts as a backup pressure relief valve in the event the normal venting system is overcome by excessive generation of internal pressure or restriction of the normal venting system. The pressure relief range is 1.6–2.1 psi (11.0–14.5 kPa). Fill cap damage or contamination that stops the pressure vacuum valve from working may result in deformation of the fuel tank.

REMOVAL & INSTALLATION

1. Unscrew the fuel filler cap. The cap has a pre-vent feature that allows the tank to vent for the first ¾ turn before unthreading.
2. Remove the screw retaining the fuel cap tether and remove the fuel cap.
3. Installation is the reverse of the removal procedure. When installing the cap, continue to turn clockwise until the ratchet mechanism gives off 3 or more loud clicks.

Evaporative Emission Diagnosis Chart

See Figures 10 and 11

Fuel Tank Evaporative Emission System

The following is a diagnostic guide for checking and/or servicing concerns of internal fuel tank pressure build-up. A typical concern may be a hissing sound as the fuel cap is removed for refueling.

The basic fuel tank venting system is typical for all vehicles.

The fuel evaporative emission system allows for controlled release of fuel tank pressure through a carbon vapor storage canister. Under normal operating conditions, this system will allow sufficient venting to prevent a build-up of internal fuel tank pressure.

Some operating conditions may cause temporary build-up of internal fuel tank pressure. Some of these conditions are:

- On warm or hot days, parking the vehicle after filling the fuel tank, the fuel is cool from underground storage and vaporizes rapidly when warmed.
- Parking after driving over rough roads, washboard, etc., after filling the fuel tank. Agitation of fuel increases vaporization.
- Parking after driving long distances in high temperature conditions.
- Climbing long grades, especially while towing a trailer, or while fully loaded.

A normally functioning evaporative emission system will relieve the pressure buildup.

No service is required if these conditions caused the customer concern. A blocked fuel evaporative emission system can cause abnormal fuel tank pressure and must be serviced. Refer to the chart for diagnosis and flow test.

PINPOINT TEST A: EVAPORATIVE EMISSIONS DIAGNOSIS

	TEST STEP	RESULT ▶	ACTION TO TAKE
A1	FUNCTIONAL TEST		
	• Test canister hose and inlet nipple for blockage. • **Are hoses or inlet blocked?**	Yes ▶ No ▶	REMOVE blockage. GO to **B1.**
A2	FUNCTIONAL TEST		
	• Test fuel evaporative emission system for blockage. • **Are all system passages open?**	Yes ▶ No ▶	REMOVE blockage or REPLACE component. GO to **B2.**
A3	VISUAL INSPECTION		
	• Inspect vapor tube and hoses for kinks or pinched areas. • **Are tube or hoses kinked or pinched?**	Yes ▶ No ▶	SERVICE or REPLACE tube or hoses. VERIFY service. GO to **A4.**
A4	VISUAL INSPECTION		
	• Inspect vapor hose routing between fuel tank and body for pinch. • **Is vapor hose pinched?**	Yes ▶ No ▶	LOOSEN fuel tank and reroute hose. VERIFY service. GO to **A5.**
A5	VISUAL INSPECTION		
	• Remove fuel tank. • Remove vapor separator valve. • Inspect valve for open air passage through orifice. • **Is air passage open?**	Yes ▶ No ▶	INSTALL valve in tank. INSTALL tank system test complete. REPLACE valve. VERIFY service.

88154G08

Fig. 10 Evaporative emissions diagnosis chart

PINPOINT TEST B: FLOW TEST—FUEL EVAPORATIVE SYSTEM

	TEST STEP	RESULT ▶	ACTION TO TAKE
B1	FLOW TEST		
	CAUTION: Do not use other high pressure air supplies. Will result in damage to canister. • Install hand pump and pressure gauge Rotunda 021-00014 Vacuum and Pressure Tester or equivalent in vapor hose at test point B1. • Hand pump to a maximum of 17.2 kPa (2.5 psi).	Pressure drop: Drops to zero immediately ▶ Holds pressure or leaks down slowly ▶	System flow OK, no servicing required. PERFORM Pinpoint Test Step **A3.**
B2	FLOW TEST		
	CAUTION: Failure to remove fuel cap may result in damage to fuel tank. • Remove fuel cap from fuel filler pipe. **CAUTION: Do not use other high pressure air supplies. May result in damage to fuel tank.** • Install hand pump and pressure gauge onto tee or canister nipple at test point B2. • Hand pump to a maximum of 17.2 kPa (2.5 psi). TEST POINT B2 WITH TEE / TEST POINT B1 WITH TEE / TEST POINT B2 WITHOUT TEE / VAPOR HOSE / VAPOR TUBE / TO FUEL TANK / CLOSE OFF LINE / TEST POINT B1 WITHOUT TEE / CARBON CANISTER	Pressure drop: Drops to zero immediately ▶ Holds pressure or leaks down slowly ▶	System OK, no servicing required. PERFORM Pinpoint Test Step **A4.**

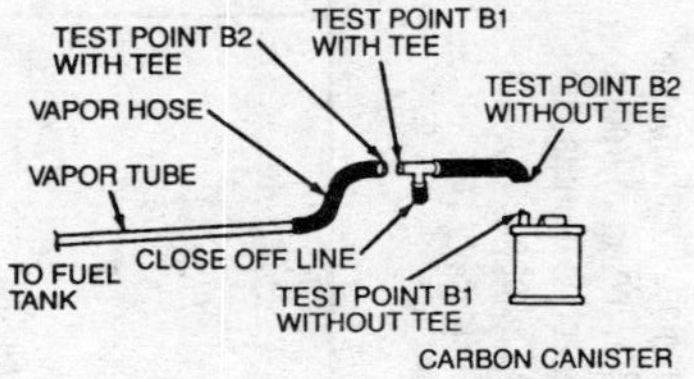

88154G09

Fig. 11 Evaporative emissions diagnosis chart—continued

EXHAUST EMISSION CONTROL SYSTEM

General Information

The exhaust emission control system begins at the air intake and ends at the tailpipe. Ford rear wheel drive vehicles are equipped with the following systems or components to manage exhaust emission control: thermostatic air inlet system, thermactor air injection system, exhaust gas recirculation system and exhaust catalyst. All vehicles do not share all systems or all components.

Thermostatic Air Inlet System

GENERAL INFORMATION

➧ **See Figures 12 and 13**

The thermostatic air inlet system is used on the 2.3L engine. The thermostatic air inlet system regulates the air inlet temperature by drawing air in from a cool air source as well as heated air from a heat shroud which is mounted on the exhaust manifold. The system consists of the following components: duct and valve assembly, heat shroud, bimetal sensor and the necessary vacuum lines and air ducts.

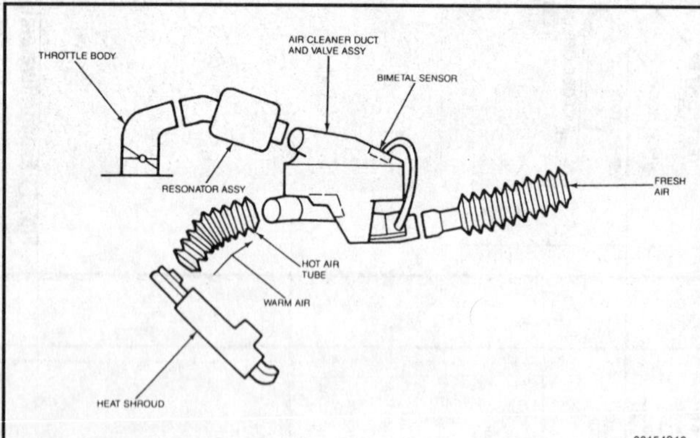

Fig. 12 The thermostatic air inlet system feeds warmed air to the engine—2.3L engine

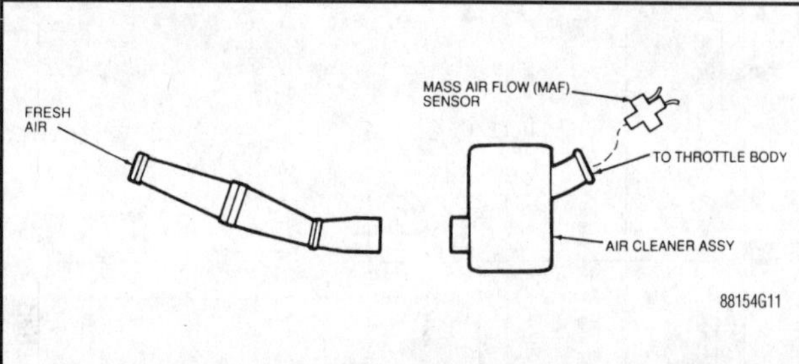

Fig. 13 The 5.0L Mustang does not use a thermostatic air system

Duct and Valve Assembly

The duct and valve assembly which regulates the air flow from the cool and heated air sources is attached to the air cleaner. The flow is regulated by means of a door that is operated by a vacuum motor. The operation of the motor is controlled by the bimetal sensor.

TESTING

1. If the duct door is in the "closed to fresh air" position, remove the hose from the air cleaner vacuum motor.
2. The door should go to the "open to fresh air" position. If it sticks or binds, service or replace, as required.
3. If the door is in the "open to fresh air" position, check the door by applying 8 in. Hg or greater of vacuum to the vacuum motor.
4. The door should move freely to the "closed to fresh air" position. If it binds or sticks, service or replace, as required.

➡**Make sure the vacuum motor is functional before changing the duct and valve assembly.**

REMOVAL & INSTALLATION

1. Disconnect the vacuum hose from the vacuum motor.
2. Separate the vacuum motor from the vacuum operated door and remove the vacuum motor.
3. Installation is the reverse of the removal procedure.

Bimetal Sensor

The core of the bimetal sensor is made of 2 different types of metals bonded together, each having different temperature expansion rates. At a given increase in temperature, the shape of the sensor core changes, bleeding off vacuum available at the vacuum motor. This permits the vacuum motor to open the duct door to allow fresh air in while shutting off full heat. The bimetal sensor is calibrated according to the needs of each particular application.

TESTING

1. Bring the temperature of the bimetal sensor below 75°F (24°C) and apply 16 in. Hg of vacuum with a vacuum pump at the vacuum source port of the sensor.
2. The duct door should stay closed. If not, replace the bimetal sensor.
3. The sensor will bleed off vacuum to allow the duct door to open and let in fresh air at or above the following temperatures:
   a. Brown: 75°F (24°C)
   b. Pink, black or red: 90°F (32.2°C)
   c. Blue, yellow or green: 105°F (40.6°C)

➡**Do not cool the bimetal sensor while the engine is running.**

REMOVAL & INSTALLATION

1. Remove the air cleaner housing lid to gain access to the sensor.
2. Disconnect the vacuum hoses from the sensor. It may be necessary to move the air cleaner housing to accomplish this.
3. Remove the sensor from the air cleaner housing.
4. Installation is the reverse of the removal procedure.

Thermactor Air Injection System

GENERAL INFORMATION

The Thermactor air injection system reduces the hydrocarbon and carbon monoxide content of the exhaust gases by continuing the combustion of unburned gases after they leave the combustion chamber. This is done by injecting fresh air into the hot exhaust stream leaving the exhaust ports or into the catalyst. At this point, the fresh air mixes with hot exhaust gases to promote further oxidation of both the hydrocarbons and carbon monoxide, thereby reducing their concentration and converting some of them into harmless carbon dioxide and water.

All Ford rear wheel drive vehicles, including the Mustang, equipped with the 5.0L engine have a managed air thermactor system. This system is utilized in electronic control systems to divert thermactor air either upstream to the exhaust manifold check valve or downstream to the rear section check valve and dual bed catalyst. The system will also dump thermactor air to atmosphere during some operating modes.

The Thermactor air injection system consists of the air supply pump, air bypass valve, check valves, air supply control valve, combination air bypass/air control valve, solenoid vacuum valve, thermactor idle vacuum valve and air pump resonator. Componentry will vary according to application.

AIR SUPPLY PUMP

The air supply pump is a belt-driven, positive displacement, vane-type pump that provides air for the thermactor system. It is available in 19 cu. in. (311cc) and 22 cu. in. (360cc) sizes, either of which may be driven with different pulley ratios for different applications. The pumps receive air from a remote silencer filter on the rear side of the engine air cleaner and is attached to the pumps' air inlet nipple or through an impeller-type centrifugal filter fan.

TESTING

1. Check the belt tension and adjust if needed.

➡Do not pry on the pump to adjust the belt. The aluminum housing is likely to collapse.

2. Disconnect the air supply hose from the bypass control valve.
3. The pump is operating properly if airflow is felt at the pump outlet and the flow increases as engine speed increases.
4. If the pump is not operating as described in Step 3 and the system is equipped with a silencer/filter, check the silencer/filter for possible obstruction before replacing the pump.

REMOVAL & INSTALLATION

1. Disconnect the negative battery cable.
2. Remove the drive belt from the air pump pulley.
3. Disconnect the air hose(s) from the air pump.
4. Remove the mounting bolts and if necessary the mounting brackets.
5. Remove the air pump from the vehicle.
6. Installation is the reverse of the removal procedure.

Air Bypass Valve

The air bypass valve supplies air to the exhaust system with medium and high applied vacuum signals when the engine is at normal operating temperature. With low or no vacuum applied, the pumped air is dumped through the silencer ports of the valve or through the dump port.

TESTING

1. Turn the ignition key **OFF**.
2. Remove the control vacuum line from the bypass valve.
3. Start the engine and bring to normal operating temperature.
4. Check for vacuum at the vacuum line. If there is no vacuum, check the solenoid vacuum valve assembly. If vacuum is present, inspect the air bypass valve.
5. Turn the engine **OFF** and disconnect the air hose at the bypass valve outlet.
6. Inspect the outlet for damage from the hot exhaust gas.
7. If the valve is damaged, replace it. If the valve is not damaged, check the bypass valve diaphragm.
8. Connect a vacuum pump to the bypass valve and apply 10 in. Hg of vacuum.
9. If the valve holds vacuum, leave the vacuum applied and proceed to Step 10. If the valve does not hold vacuum, it must be replaced.
10. Start the engine and increase the engine speed to 1500 rpm.
11. Check for air flow at the valve outlet, either audibly or by feel. If there is air flow, proceed to Step 12. If there is no air flow, replace the air bypass valve.
12. Release the vacuum applied by the vacuum pump and check that the air flow switches from the valve outlet to the dump port or silencer ports, either audibly or by feel.
13. If the air flow does not switch, replace the air bypass valve. If the air flow switches, the air bypass valve is okay, check the air supply control valve.

REMOVAL & INSTALLATION

1. Disconnect the negative battery cable.
2. Disconnect the air inlet and outlet hoses and the vacuum hose from the bypass valve.
3. Remove the bypass valve from the vehicle.
4. Installation is the reverse of the removal procedure.

Check Valve

➧ **See Figure 14**

The air check valve is a 1-way valve that allows thermactor air to pass into the exhaust system while preventing exhaust gases from passing in the opposite direction.

Fig. 14 Air check valves

TESTING

1. Turn the ignition key **OFF**.
2. Visually inspect the thermactor system hoses, tubes, control valve(s) and check valve(s) for leaks or external signs of damage, from the back flow of hot exhaust gases.
3. If the hoses and valves are okay, proceed to Step 4. If they are not, service or replace the damaged parts, including the check valve.
4. Remove the hose from the check valve inlet and visually check the inside of the hose for damage from hot exhaust gas.
5. If the hose is clean and undamaged, proceed to Step 6. If not, replace the hose and check valve.
6. Start the engine and listen for escaping exhaust gas from the check valve. Feel for the gas only if the engine temperature is at an acceptable level.
7. If any exhaust gas is escaping, replace the check valve.

REMOVAL & INSTALLATION

1. Disconnect the negative battery cable.
2. Disconnect the input hose from the check valve.
3. Remove the check valve from the connecting tube.
4. Installation is the reverse of the removal procedure.

Air Supply Control Valve

The air supply control valve directs air pump output to the exhaust manifold or downstream to the catalyst system depending upon the engine control strategy. It may also be used to dump air to the air cleaner or dump silencer.

TESTING

1. Turn the ignition key **OFF**.
2. Remove the hoses from the air control valve outlets and inspect the outlets for damage from hot exhaust gases.

3. If the air supply control valve is damaged, it must be replaced, then check the air check valve. If the air supply control valve is not damaged, proceed to Step 4.
4. Remove the vacuum line from the air supply control valve. Start the engine and bring to normal operating temperature, then shut the engine off.
5. Restart the engine and immediately check for vacuum at the hose. If vacuum was present at the start, proceed to Step 6. If vacuum was not present at the start, check the solenoid vacuum valve.
6. Start the engine and let it run. Check for the vacuum to change from high to low.
7. If the vacuum dropped to 0 within a few minutes after the engine started, proceed to Step 8. If not, check the solenoid vacuum valve.
8. Connect a vacuum pump to the air supply control valve and apply 10 in. Hg of vacuum.
9. If the valve holds vacuum, proceed to Step 10. If it does not hold vacuum, replace the air supply control valve.
10. Start the engine and bring to normal operating temperature. Make sure that air is being supplied to the air supply control valve.
11. If air is present, proceed to Step 12. If air is not present, check air pump operation.
12. Leave the engine running and apply 10 in. Hg of vacuum to the air supply control valve. Increase engine speed to 1500 rpm.
13. If air flow comes out of outlet A, proceed to Step 14. If not, replace the air supply control valve.
14. Leave the engine running. Vent the vacuum pump until there is 0 vacuum.
15. If the air flow switches from outlet A to outlet B, the air supply control valve is okay. If the air flow does not switch, replace the air supply control valve.

REMOVAL & INSTALLATION

1. Disconnect the negative battery cable.
2. Disconnect the air hoses and the vacuum line from the air control valve.
3. Remove the air control valve from the vehicle.
4. Installation is the reverse of the removal procedure.

Combination Air Bypass/Air Control Valve

The combination air control/bypass valve combines the secondary air bypass and air control functions. The valve is located in the air supply line between the air pump and the upstream/downstream air supply check valves.

The air bypass portion controls the flow of thermactor air to the exhaust system or allows thermactor air to be bypassed to atmosphere. When air is not being bypassed, the air control portion of the valve switches the air injection point to either an upstream or downstream location.

TESTING

1. Turn the ignition key **OFF**.
2. Remove the hoses from the combination air control valve outlets A and B and inspect the outlets for damage from hot exhaust gases.
3. If the valve appears damaged, replace it, then check the air check valve. If the valve is not damaged, proceed to Step 4.
4. Leave the hoses disconnected from the valve. Disconnect and plug the vacuum line to port D.
5. Start the engine and run at 1500 rpm. If air flow is present at the valve, proceed to Step 6. If it is not, check the air pump. If the air pump is okay, replace the combination air control valve.
6. Leave the engine running. Disconnect both vacuum lines to ports D and S.
7. Measure the manifold vacuum at both ports. If the proper vacuum is present, proceed to Step 8. If not, check the solenoid vacuum valve.
8. Turn the ignition key **OFF**. Reconnect the vacuum line to port D, but leave the vacuum line to port S disconnected and plugged.
9. Start the engine and run it at 1500 rpm. If air flow is present at outlet B, but not at outlet A, proceed to Step 10. If not, replace the combination air control valve and reconnect all hoses.
10. Turn the ignition key **OFF** and leave the vacuum line to port S disconnected and unplugged.
11. Apply 8–10 in. Hg of vacuum to port S on the combination valve. Start the engine and run at 1500 rpm. If air flow is present at outlet A, the combination valve is okay. If not, replace the combination air control valve.

➡If the combination valve is a bleed type, this will affect the amount of air flow.

REMOVAL & INSTALLATION

1. Disconnect the negative battery cable.
2. Disconnect the air hoses and vacuum lines from the valve.
3. Remove the valve from the vehicle.
4. Installation is the reverse of the removal procedure.

Solenoid Vacuum Valve Assembly

The normally closed solenoid valve assembly consists of 2 vacuum ports with an atmospheric vent. The valve assembly can be with or without control bleed. The outlet port of the valve is opened to atmospheric vent and closed to the inlet port when de-energized. When energized, the outlet port is opened to the inlet port and closed to atmospheric vent. The control bleed is provided to prevent contamination entering the solenoid valve assembly from the intake manifold.

TESTING

1. The ports should flow air when the solenoid is energized.
2. Check the resistance at the solenoid terminals with an ohmmeter. The resistance should be 51–108 ohms.
3. If the resistance is not as specified, replace the solenoid.

➡The valve can be expected to have a very small leakage rate when energized or de-energized. This leakage is not measurable in the field and is not detrimental to valve function.

REMOVAL & INSTALLATION

1. Disconnect the negative battery cable.
2. Disconnect the electrical connector and the vacuum lines from the solenoid valve.
3. Remove the mounting bolts and remove the solenoid valve.
4. Installation is the reverse of the removal procedure.

Air Pump Resonator

The air pump resonator reduces air dump noise during cold start and some cruise modes.

TESTING

1. Visually inspect the resonator for holes.
2. Remove the hoses and check for blocked or restricted ports.
3. Replace the resonator if it has holes or the ports are blocked or restricted.
4. Reconnect the hoses and install and tighten the clamps.

REMOVAL & INSTALLATION

1. Disconnect the negative battery cable.
2. Loosen the clamps and remove the hoses.
3. Remove the mounting bolts and remove the resonator.
4. Installation is the reverse of the removal procedure.

Exhaust Emission Control System Diagnosis Charts

System Descriptions

Secondary Air Injection (AIR) System

The Secondary Air Injection system is utilized in electronic control systems to divert secondary air either upstream to the exhaust manifold check valve or downstream to the rear section check valve and catalyst. The system will also dump secondary air to the atmosphere during some operating modes.

A Secondary Air Injection Diverter (AIRD) valve is used to direct the air either upstream or downstream.
A Secondary Air Injection Bypass (AIRB) valve is used to dump air to the atmosphere

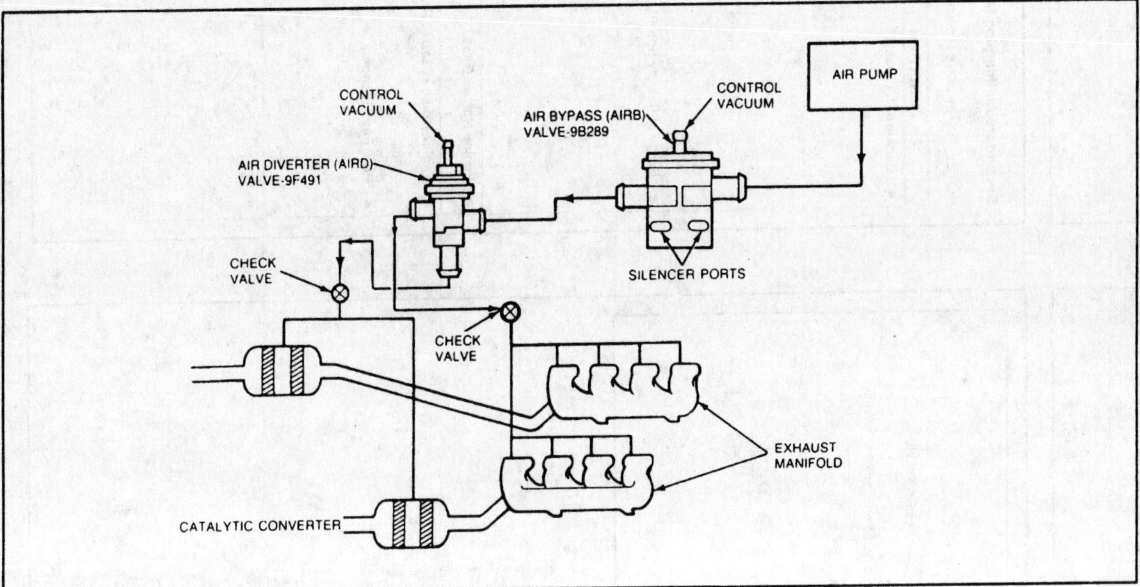

Typical Secondary Air Injection (AIR) System

88154G12

System Descriptions

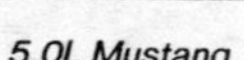

5.0L Mustang

88154G13

Diagnosis By Symptom

Secondary Air Injection (AIR) System

NOTE: Verify correct component type on the vehicle before proceeding.

CONDITION	POSSIBLE SOURCE	ACTION
• Backfire (Exhaust)	• AIRB valve malfunction. • AIRD valve malfunction. • Combination AIRB / AIRD valve malfunction. • AIRB / AIRD solenoid malfunction. • Exhaust manifolds or pipes loose.	• Perform AIRB valve diagnosis. Go to Pinpoint Test Step AIR7. • Perform AIRD valve diagnosis. Go to Pinpoint Test Step AIR12. • Perform combination valve diagnosis. Go to Pinpoint Test Step AIR19. • Perform solenoid diagnosis. Go to Pinpoint Test Step AIR27. • Inspect and tighten nuts or bolts to specification.
• Surge at Steady Speed	• AIRD valve malfunction. • Combination AIRB / AIRD valve malfunction. • AIRB / AIRD solenoid malfunction.	• Perform AIRD valve diagnosis. Go to Pinpoint Test Step AIR12. • Perform combination AIRB / AIRD valve diagnosis. Go to Pinpoint Test Step AIR19. • Perform solenoid diagnosis. Go to Pinpoint Test Step AIR27.
• Engine Noise - (Hiss)	• Secondary air hose leaks or disconnects.	• Visual inspection of hoses and connections.
• Engine Noise - (Rap or Roar)	• Secondary air hose or valves leak exhaust.	• Visual inspection of hoses and valves. Perform air check valve diagnosis.
• Poor Fuel Economy	• AIRD valve malfunction. • Combination AIRB / AIRD valve malfunction. • AIRB / AIRD solenoid valve malfunction. • Disconnected vacuum or electrical connections to secondary air injection components.	• Perform AIRD valve diagnosis. Go to Pinpoint Test Step AIR12. • Perform combination valve diagnosis. Go to Pinpoint Test Step AIR19. • Perform solenoid diagnosis. Go to Pinpoint Test Step AIR27. • Visual inspection.

88154G14

Diagnosis By Symptom

CONDITION	POSSIBLE SOURCE	ACTION
• Exhaust Smoke - (White)	• Disconnected vacuum or electrical connections to secondary air injection components.	• Visual inspection.
	• AIRB valve malfunction.	• Perform AIRB valve diagnosis. Go to Pinpoint Test Step AIR7.
	• AIRD valve malfunction.	• Perform AIRD valve diagnosis. Go to Pinpoint Test Step AIR12.
	• Combination AIRB / AIRD valve malfunction.	• Perform combination AIRB / AIRD valve diagnosis. Go to Pinpoint Test Step AIR19.
	• AIRB / AIRD solenoid malfunction.	• Perform AIRB / AIRD solenoid diagnosis. Go to Pinpoint Test Step AIR27.
• State Emission Test Failure	• Disconnected vacuum or electrical connections to secondary air injection components.	• Visual inspection.
	• AIRB valve malfunction.	• Perform AIRB valve diagnosis. Go to Pinpoint Test Step AIR7.
	• AIRD valve malfunction.	• Perform AIRD valve diagnosis. Go to Pinpoint Test Step AIR12.
	• Combination AIRB / AIRD valve malfunction.	• Perform combination AIRB / AIRD valve diagnosis. Go to Pinpoint Test Step AIR19.
	• AIRB / AIRD solenoid malfunction.	• Perform AIRB / AIRD solenoid diagnosis. Go to Pinpoint Test Step AIR27.
• Rolling Idle	• AIRB / AIRD solenoid malfunction.	• Perform AIRB / AIRD solenoid diagnosis. Go to Pinpoint Test Step AIR27.
	• Disconnected vacuum or electrical connections for secondary air injection components.	• Visual inspection.
	• AIRB valve malfunction.	• Perform AIRB valve diagnosis. Go to Pinpoint Test Step AIR7.
	• AIRD valve malfunction.	• Perform AIRD valve diagnosis. Go to Pinpoint Test Step AIR12.
	• Combination AIRB / AIRD valve malfunction.	• Perform combination AIRB / AIRD valve diagnosis. Go to Pinpoint Test Step AIR19.

88154G15

Diagnosis By Symptom

Secondary Air Injection (AIR) System Noise Test

CAUTION

Do not use a pry bar to move the air pump for belt adjustment.

NOTE: **The secondary air injection system is not completely noiseless. Under normal conditions, noise rises in pitch as engine speed increases. To determine if noise is the fault of the AIR system, disconnect the belt drive (only after verifying that belt tension is correct), and operate the engine. If the noise disappears, proceed with the following diagnosis.**

Diagnosis

CONDITION	POSSIBLE SOURCE	ACTION
• Excessive Belt Noise	• Loose belt.	• Tighten to specification using Tool T75L-9480-A or equivalent to hold belt tension and Belt Tension Gauge T63L-8620-A or equivalent. **CAUTION: Do not use a pry bar to move air pump.**
	• Seized pump.	• Replace pump.
	• Loose pulley.	• Replace pulley and / or pump if damaged. Tighten bolts to 13.6-17.0 N-m (120-150 lb-in).
	• Loose or broken mounting brackets or bolts.	• Replace parts as required and tighten bolts to specification.
• Excessive Mechanical Noise, Chirps, Squeaks, Clicks or Ticks	• Overtightened mounting bolt.	• Tighten to 34 N-m (25 lb-ft).
	• Overtightened drive belt.	• Same as loose belt.
	• Excessive flash on the air pump adjusting arm boss.	• Remove flash from the boss.
	• Distorted adjusting arm.	• Replace adjusting arm.
	• Pump or pulley mounting fasteners loose.	• Tighten fasteners to specification.

88154G16

Diagnosis By Symptom

CONDITION	POSSIBLE SOURCE	ACTION
• Excessive AIR System Noise (Putt-Putt, Whirring or Hissing)	• Leak in hose.	• Locate source of leak using soap solution and replace hoses as necessary.
	• Loose, pinched or kinked hose.	• Reassemble, straighten or replace hose and clamps as required.
	• Hose touching other engine parts.	• Adjust hose to prevent contact with other engine parts.
	• AIRB valve inoperative.	• Test the valve. Go to Pinpoint Test Step AIR7.
	• Check valve inoperative.	• Test the valve. Go to Pinpoint Test Step AIR33.
	• Restricted or bent pump outlet fitting.	• Inspect fitting and remove any flash blocking the air passage way. Replace bent fittings.
	• Air dumping through AIRB valve (at idle only).	• On many vehicles, the AIR system has been designed to dump air at idle to prevent overheating the catalyst. This condition is normal. Determine that the noise persists at higher speeds before proceeding.
	• Air dumping through AIRB valve (decel and cruise).	• On many vehicles, secondary air is dumped in the air cleaner or in remote silencer. Make sure hoses are connected and not cracked.
	• AIR pump resonator leaking or blocked.	• Check resonator for hole or restricted inlet / outlet tubes. Go to Pinpoint Test Step AIR6.
• Excessive Pump Noise - (Chirps, Squeaks and Ticks)	• Worn or damaged pump.	• Check the AIR system for wear or damage and make necessary corrections. Go to Pinpoint Test Step AIR3.
• Engine Noise - (Rap or Roar)	• Hose disconnected.	• Audible and visual inspection to assure all hoses are connected.
• State Emissions Test Failure	• Restricted hose.	• Inspect hoses for crimped and / or kinked hoses.
	• Plugged pulse air silencer.	• Remove inlet hose and inspect silencer inlet for dirt and foreign material. Clean or replace silencer as appropriate.
	• AIRD air valve malfunction (PAIR), leaking or restricted.	• Perform AIRD valve diagnosis. Go to Pinpoint Test Step AIR35.
	• AIRD valve malfunction (PAIR).	• Perform AIRD valve diagnosis. Go to Pinpoint Test Step AIR35.

88154G17

Functional Diagnosis: AIR Silencer/Filter (AIR Pump and PAIR Inlet)

TITLE — SYMBOL: SILN

Description

The AIR silencer is a combination silencer and PAIR filter for AIR pumps that are not equipped with an impeller-type centrifugal air filter fan or for PAIR systems. The air silencer is mounted in a convenient position in the engine compartment and is connected to the AIR pump or PAIR valve inlet by means of a flexible hose.

TO PUMP

Typical Air Silencer

AIR IN
NOTE: ON HEAVY DUTY TRUCKS, APPROXIMATELY THREE TIMES THIS SIZE.
TO PAIR VALVE OR DUAL AIR PUMP

Typical Air Silencer

	TEST STEP	RESULT	▶ ACTION TO TAKE
AIR1	VISUAL INSPECTION OF SILENCER / FILTER		
	• Key off. • Inspect silencer / filter for cracks or damage. • **Is silencer / filter damaged?**	Yes	▶ REPLACE silencer / filter. VERIFY drive concern.
		No	▶ GO to AIR2.
AIR2	CHECK FOR OBSTRUCTIONS		
	• Remove inlet hose (if so equipped). • Inspect inlet of silencer / filter for blockage (bugs, leaves, debris, etc.) • **Is inlet open?**	Yes	▶ RETURN to Diagnosis By Symptom for other possible causes.
		No	▶ REMOVE debris. VERIFY drive concern.

88154G18

Functional Diagnosis: AIR Pump

TITLE SYMBOL

Description

The AIR Pump is a belt-driven, positive displacement, vane-type pump that provides air for the Secondary Air Injection system. It is available in 19 and 22 cubic inch sizes, either of which may be driven with different pulley ratios for different applications. Pumps receive air from a remote silencer filter or from the clean air side of the engine air cleaner attached to the pump's air inlet nipple or through an impeller-type centrifugal filter fan.

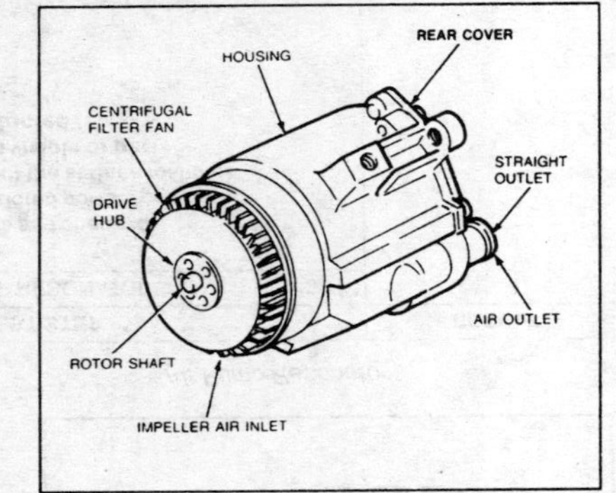

19 Cubic Inch AIR Pump — Car

TEST STEP		RESULT	▶	ACTION TO TAKE
AIR3	CHECK BELT TENSION			
	CAUTION: Do not pry on pump to adjust belt. The aluminum housing is likely to collapse. Refer to AIR Pump drive belt adjustment. • Key off. • Check belt tension and adjust to specification. • **Is belt tension adjusted properly?**	Yes No	▶ ▶	GO to AIR4. ADJUST to specification. GO to Functional Diagnosis AIR Pump Drive Belt Adjustment.
AIR4	CHECK AIR PUMP OPERATION			
	• Key off. • Disconnect air supply hose from AIRB valve. • Check air flow at the pump outlet. • **Does air flow increase as the engine speed increases?**	Yes No	▶ ▶	RETURN to Diagnosis by Symptom for other possible causes. **If equipped with Silencer/Filter:** GO to AIR5. **If not,** REPLACE AIR Pump.

88154G19

Functional Diagnosis: AIR Pump

TITLE SYMBOL

TEST STEP		RESULT	▶	ACTION TO TAKE
AIR5	CHECK SILENCER / FILTER FOR OBSTRUCTION			
	• **Remove inlet hose (if so equipped).** • **Inspect inlet of silencer / filter for blockage (bugs, leaves, debris, etc.).** • **Is inlet open?**	Yes No	▶ ▶	**REPLACE AIR Pump and VERIFY drive concern.** **REMOVE all debris and VERIFY drive concern.**

88154G20

Functional Diagnosis: AIR Pump Resonator

TITLE | SYMBOL

Description

The AIR Pump Resonator reduces air dump noise during cold start and some cruise modes.

Air Pump Resonator

TEST STEP		RESULT	▶	ACTION TO TAKE
AIR6	CHECK AIR PUMP RESONATOR			
	• Key off. • Remove hoses and check for blocked/restricted ports. • Visually inspect the surface for holes. • **Are any holes visible or ports blocked/restricted?**	Yes	▶	REPLACE resonator. INSTALL clamps to hoses and tighten to specification.
		No	▶	RETURN to Diagnosis By Symptom page.

88154G21

Functional Diagnosis: Secondary Air Injection Bypass (AIRB) Valves

TITLE | SYMBOL: AIRB AIRB AIRB AIRB

Description

There are two general groups of AIRB valves, normally closed and normally open. Normally closed valves supply air to the exhaust system with medium and high applied vacuum signals during normal (engine at normal operating temperature) modes. With low or no vacuum applied, the pumped air is dumped through the silencer ports of the valve or through the dump port.

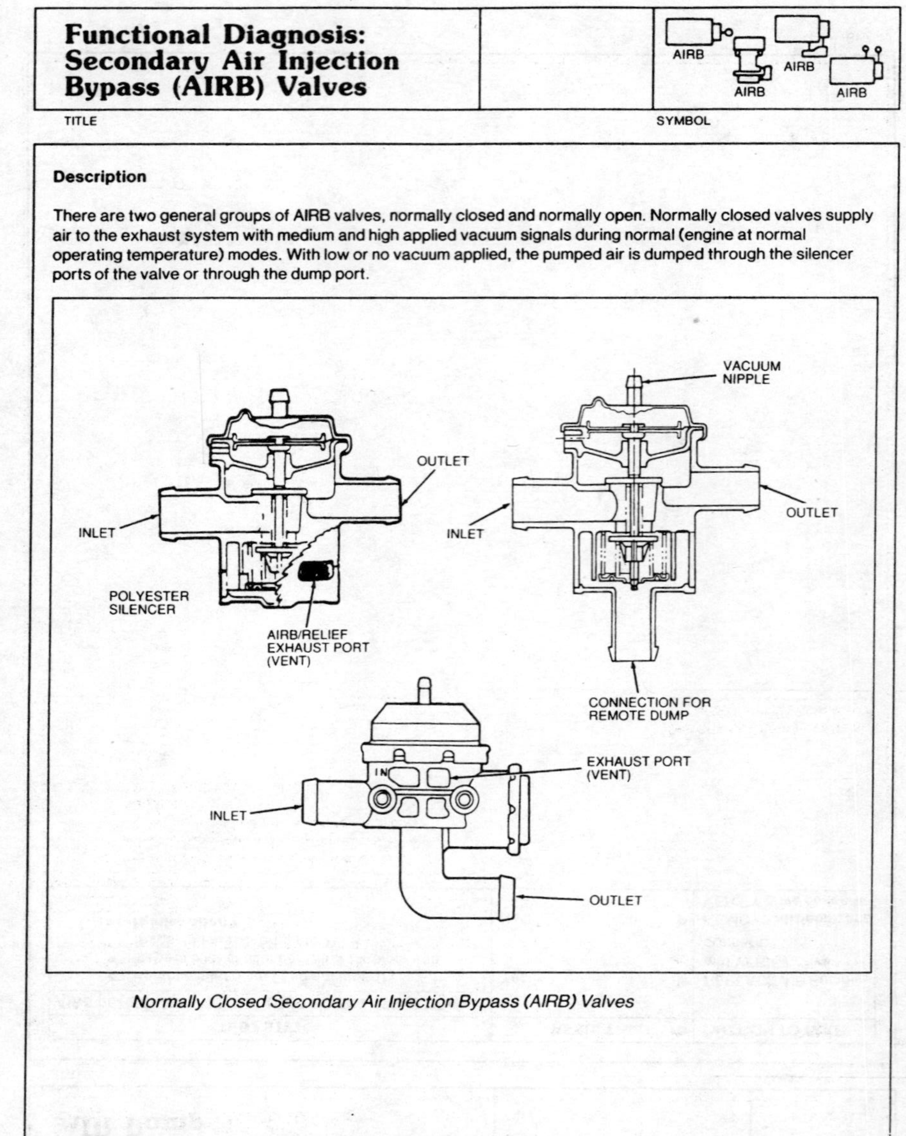

Normally Closed Secondary Air Injection Bypass (AIRB) Valves

88154G22

Functional Diagnosis: Secondary Air Injection Bypass (AIRB) Valves

TITLE — SYMBOL: AIRB

Normally Open AIRB Valves without Vacuum Vent

Heavy Truck Applications

Normally Open AIRB valves with a vacuum vent provide a dump of air when a minimum vacuum of about 34 kPa (10 in-Hg) is applied to the signal port. This prevents backfire during cold deceleration.

VACUUM NIPPLE (NOT SEEN)
AIR B/RELIEF EXHAUST PORTS (VENTS)
MOUNTING BOSS
INLET FROM AIR PUMP
OUTLET TO CHECK VALVE
ELBOW OUTLET

Normally Open Without Vacuum Vent

TEST STEP		RESULT	ACTION TO TAKE
AIR7	CHECK FOR VACUUM AT THE AIRB VALVE		
	• Key off. • Remove control vacuum line from AIRB valve. • Key on, engine running at normal operating temperature. • Check for vacuum at control vacuum line. • **Is vacuum present?**	Yes No	▶ GO to AIR8. ▶ GO to AIR27.
AIR8	INSPECT AIRB VALVE		
	• Key off. • Disconnect air hose at AIRB valve outlet. • Inspect AIRB valve outlet for damage from hot exhaust gas. • **Is AIRB valve damaged?**	Yes No	▶ REPLACE AIRB valve, then GO to AIR24 to inspect air check valve. ▶ GO to AIR9.
AIR9	CHECK AIRB VALVE DIAPHRAGM		
	• Connect auxiliary vacuum source to AIRB valve. • Apply 34 kPa (10 in-Hg) vacuum and trap. • **Does valve hold vacuum?**	Yes No	▶ LEAVE vacuum applied. GO to AIR10. ▶ REPLACE AIRB valve. VERIFY drive concern.

88154G23

Functional Diagnosis: Secondary Air Injection Bypass (AIRB) Valves

TITLE — SYMBOL: AIRB

TEST STEP		RESULT	ACTION TO TAKE
AIR10	CHECK AIRB OPERATION/FLOW		
	• Key on, engine running. • Increase engine speed to 1500 rpm. • Check for air flow at valve outlet (audibly or by feel). • **Is air flow present?**	Yes No	▶ GO to AIR11. ▶ REPLACE AIRB valve. VERIFY drive concern.
AIR11	CHECK AIRB OPERATION/DUMP		
	• Vent auxiliary vacuum source to zero. • Check that air flow switches from the valve outlet to the dump port or silencer ports (audibly or by feel). • **Does the air flow switch?**	Yes No	▶ GO to AIR12. ▶ REPLACE AIRB valve. VERIFY drive concern.

88154G24

Functional Diagnosis: Secondary Air Injection Diverter (AIRD) Valves

TITLE | SYMBOL: AIRD

Normally Open AIRD Valves Without Vacuum Vent

Description

The AIRD valve directs air pump output upstream to the exhaust manifold or downstream to the catalyst system depending upon the engine control strategy. The AIRD valve may also be used as a valve, directing air to the catalyst / exhaust system or to a remote air dump location depending on engine control strategy. A pressure relief valve also provides AIR pump protection in the event of excessive exhaust back pressure or system blockage.

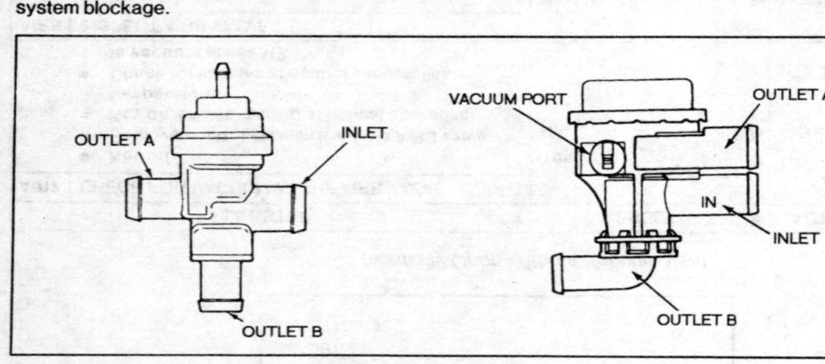

AIRD Valves Without Pressure Relief

AIRD Valve

88154G25

Functional Diagnosis: Secondary Air Injection Diverter (AIRD) Valves

TITLE | SYMBOL: AIRD

AIRD Valve

	TEST STEP	RESULT	▶ ACTION TO TAKE
AIR12	VISUALLY INSPECT AIRD VALVE		
	• Key off. • Remove hoses from AIRD valve outlets. • Inspect outlets for damage from hot exhaust gases. • **Is AIRD valve damaged?**	Yes No	▶ REPLACE AIRD valve, then GO to AIR24 for air check valve. ▶ GO to AIR13.
AIR13	CHECK FOR VACUUM AT AIRD VALVE		
	NOTE: **The next two test steps will require your attention to time.** • Key off. • Remove vacuum line from air supply control line. • Key on, engine running at normal operating temperature. • After engine has started, immediately check for vacuum. • **Was vacuum present at start?**	Yes No	▶ GO to AIR14. ▶ GO to AIR27 to VERIFY solenoid AIRD vacuum function.
AIR14	CHECK FOR VACUUM TO DROP		
	• Engine running. • Check for vacuum to change from high to low. • **Does vacuum drop to zero within a few minutes after engine was started?**	Yes No	▶ GO to AIR15. ▶ GO to AIR27.
AIR15	CHECK AIRD VALVE DIAPHRAGM		
	• Connect an auxiliary vacuum source to the AIRD valve. • Apply 34 kPa (10 in-Hg) vacuum and hold. • **Does valve hold vacuum?**	Yes No	▶ GO to AIR16. ▶ REPLACE AIRD valve. VERIFY drive concern.

88154G26

Functional Diagnosis: Secondary Air Injection Diverter (AIRD) Valves

TITLE | SYMBOL: AIRD

	TEST STEP	RESULT	►	ACTION TO TAKE
AIR16	CHECK FOR AIR SUPPLY AT AIRD VALVE			
	• Key on, engine running to normal operating temperature. • Verify that the air is being supplied to the AIRD valve. • **Is air present?**	Yes No	► ►	GO to AIR17. GO to AIR4 for AIR pump operation.
AIR17	CHECK FOR AIR AT OUTLET A			
	• Key on engine running. • Apply 34 kPa (10 in-Hg) of vacuum to AIRD valve. • Increase engine speed to 1500 rpm. • **Does air flow come out of outlet A?**	Yes No	► ►	GO to AIR18. REPLACE AIRD valve. VERIFY drive concern.
AIR18	CHECK FOR AIR AT OUTLET B			
	• Key on engine running. • Vent the auxiliary vacuum source to zero. • **Does air flow switch from outlet A to outlet B?**	Yes No	► ►	RETURN to Diagnosis By Symptom page. REPLACE AIRD valve. VERIFY drive concern.

88154G27

Functional Diagnosis: Combination AIRB/AIRD Valve

TITLE | SYMBOL

Description

The Combination AIRB / AIRD Valve combines the Secondary Air Injection Bypass (AIRB) and Air Diverter (AIRD) functions. The valve is located in the air supply line between the AIR pump and the upstream / downstream air supply check valves.

The AIRB portion controls the flow of secondary air to the exhaust system (air control portion of the valve) or allows secondary air to be bypassed to atmosphere. When air is not being bypassed, the air control portion of the valve switches the air injection point to either upstream or downstream location. This portion of the valve is called secondary air injection diverter (AIRD).

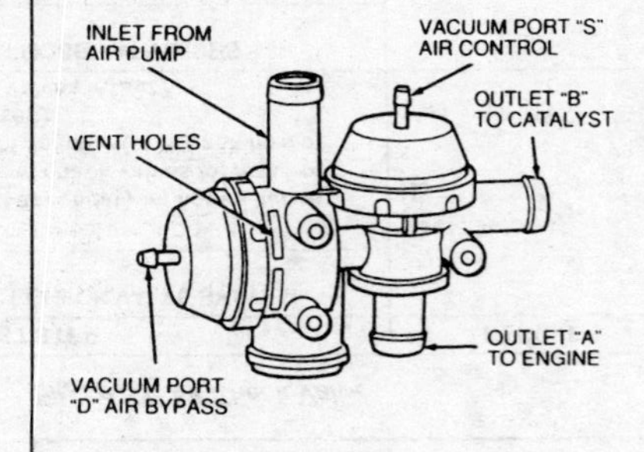

Combination AIRB / AIRD Valve

	TEST STEP	RESULT	►	ACTION TO TAKE
AIR19	VISUALLY INSPECT COMBINATION AIRB / AIRD VALVE			
	• Key off. • Remove hoses from combination air control valve outlets A and B. • Inspect outlets for damage from hot exhaust gases. • **Does valve appear to be damaged?**	Yes No	► ►	REPLACE combination AIRB / AIRD valve then GO to AIR24 to VERIFY check valve function. GO to AIR20.
AIR20	CHECK COMBINATION AIRB / AIRD VALVE			
	• Key off. • Outlet hoses A and B disconnected. • Disconnect and plug vacuum line to port D. • Start engine. • Maintain engine speed at 1500 rpm. • **Is air flow present at combination air control vents?**	Yes No	► ►	GO to AIR21. GO to AIR1 to verify AIR Pump function. If OK, REPLACE combination AIRB / AIRD valve.

88154G28

Functional Diagnosis: Combination AIRB/AIRD Valve

TITLE — SYMBOL

	TEST STEP	RESULT	▶ ACTION TO TAKE
AIR21	CHECK FOR MANIFOLD VACUUM		
	• Key on engine running. • Disconnect both vacuum lines to ports D and S. • Measure manifold vacuum at both ports. • **Is appropriate manifold vacuum present?**	Yes No	▶ GO to AIR22. ▶ GO to AIR27.
AIR22	CHECK COMBINATION AIRB / AIRD VALVE OPERATION		
	• Key off. • Reconnect vacuum line to port D. • Vacuum line to port S disconnected and plugged. • Start engine and idle at 1500 rpm. • **Is air flow present at outlet B and no air flow present at outlet A?**	Yes No	▶ GO to AIR23. ▶ REPLACE combination AIRB / AIRD valve. RECONNECT all hoses. VERIFY drive concern.
AIR23	CHECK COMBINATION AIRB / AIRD VALVE OPERATION		
	NOTE: **If the combination valve is a bleed type this will affect the amount of air flow.** • Key off. • S port vacuum line disconnected and unplugged. • Apply 27-34 kPa (8-10 in-Hg) vacuum to port S on the combination valve. • Start engine and idle at 1500 rpm. • **Is air flow present at outlet A?**	Yes No	▶ RETURN to Diagnosis by Symptom to address other possible causes. ▶ REPLACE combination AIRB / AIRD valve. VERIFY drive concern.

88154G29

Functional Diagnosis: Air Check Valve

TITLE — SYMBOL

INLET

Description

The Air Check Valve is a one-way valve that allows secondary air to pass into the exhaust system while preventing exhaust gases from passing in the opposite direction.

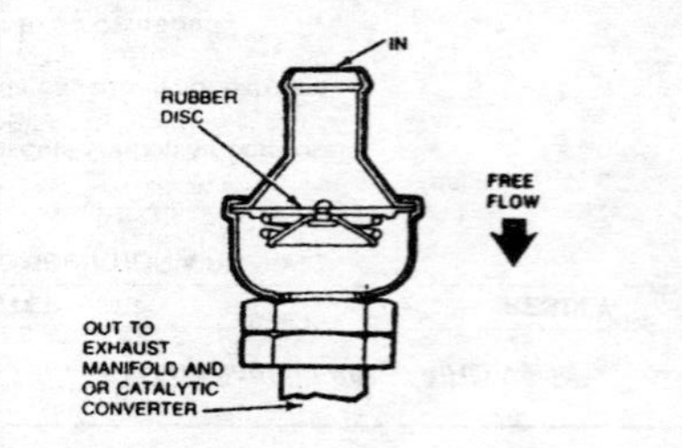

Figure 31: Air Check Valve

	TEST STEP	RESULT	▶ ACTION TO TAKE
AIR24	VISUALLY INSPECT CHECK VALVE SYSTEM (EXTERNALLY)		
	• Key off. • Visually inspect secondary air hoses, tubes, control valves and check valves for leaks or external signs of damage (from back flow of hot exhaust gases). • **Are hoses and valves intact?**	Yes No	▶ GO to AIR25. ▶ SERVICE or REPLACE damaged parts including check valve. VERIFY drive concern.
AIR25	VISUALLY INSPECT HOSES AT VALVES (INTERNALLY)		
	• Remove hose from check valve inlet. • Inspect inside the hose for damage from hot exhaust gas. • **Is the hose clean and undamaged?**	Yes No	▶ GO to AIR26. ▶ REPLACE hose and check valve. VERIFY drive concern.
AIR26	INSPECT CHECK VALVE FUNCTION		
	NOTE: **Check valve may "burble" as air is drawn in.** • Key on engine running. • Listen for escaping exhaust gas or feel for gas (only if engine temperature is at an acceptable level). • **Is any exhaust gas escaping?**	Yes No	▶ REPLACE check valve. VERIFY drive concern. ▶ RETURN to Diagnosis by Symptom to address other possible causes.

88154G30

Functional Diagnosis: Dual AIR Control Solenoids

TITLE		SYMBOL
Functional Diagnosis: Dual AIR Control Solenoids		SOL V

Description

The Dual Secondary Air Control Solenoid assembly consists of two normally closed vacuum solenoid(s) (AIRB and AIRD), one controlling the AIR Bypass (AIRB) valve and the other the AIR Diverter (AIRD) valve. Both are vented when de-energized, sourced by the intake manifold vacuum reservoir and controlled by the Powertrain Control Module (PCM). Also used on 2-wheel drive / 4-wheel drive vehicles and single solenoids for EGR shutoff.

Figure 32: Dual Secondary AIR Control Solenoids

NOTE: **The solenoids can be expected to have a very small leakage rate when energized or de-energized. This leakage is not measurable in the field and is not detrimental to solenoid function.**

Secondary Air Injection Strategy		
Secondary Air States	**AIRB Solenoid**	**AIRD Solenoid**
Upstream	On	On
Downstream	On	Off
Bypass	Off	Off

88154G31

Functional Diagnosis: Secondary Air Injection (AIR) Solenoid Assembly

TITLE		SYMBOL
Functional Diagnosis: Secondary Air Injection (AIR) Solenoid Assembly		SOL V

Description

Normally Closed

The Normally Closed Secondary Air Injection (AIR) Solenoid Assembly consists of two vacuum ports with an atmospheric vent. The solenoid assembly can be with or without control bleed. The outlet port of the solenoid is opened to atmospheric vent and closed to the inlet port when de-energized. When energized, the outlet port is opened to the inlet port and closed to atmospheric vent. The control bleed is provided to prevent contamination entering the solenoid assembly from intake manifold.

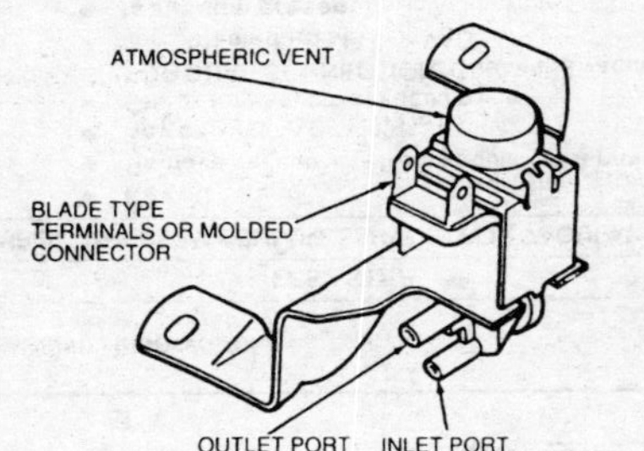

Typical Secondary Air Injection (AIR) Solenoid Assembly—Normally Closed

Solenoid Vacuum Valve Assembly

	TEST STEP	RESULT	▶ ACTION TO TAKE
AIR27	CHECK AIR SOLENOID		
	NOTE: **A rolling idle could be the result of a leaking AIR solenoid. Quick Test may also indicate Diagnostic Trouble Codes (DTCs) 41, 91, 44, 94, 311, 312, 313 or 314. If no rolling idle is present, go to Test Step AIR29.** • Start engine and run until its temperature is fully stabilized. • Turn the engine off. • Disconnect the vacuum hose at the AIR solenoid. • Plug the vacuum hose. • Restart engine. • After a few minutes of engine running the "rolling" idle should stop. • **Does rolling idle stop?**	Yes No	▶ REPLACE Secondary Air solenoid assembly. ▶ **For Rolling idle:** GO to Diagnosis by Symptom. **For DTC 311:** GO to AIR29.

88154G32

Functional Diagnosis: Secondary Air Injection (AIR) Solenoid Assembly

TITLE SYMBOL SOL V

TEST STEP	RESULT ▶	ACTION TO TAKE
AIR28 CHECK AIR SOLENOID		
• Start engine and run until its temperature is fully stabilized. • Turn engine off. • Disconnect the inlet port vacuum hose at the AIRD valve. • Plug the vacuum hose. • Run Engine Running Self-Test. • **Are any of the following DTCs present: 41, 91, 44, 94, 311, 312, 313 or 314?**	Yes ▶	address any DTC present.
	No ▶	REPLACE AIR solenoid assembly. RERUN Quick Test.

88154G33

Functional Diagnosis: Vacuum Reservoir

TITLE SYMBOL VRESER VRESER

Description

The Vacuum Reservoir (Figure 35) stores vacuum and provides "muscle" vacuum. It prevents rapid fluctuations or sudden drops in a vacuum signal such as those seen during an acceleration period.

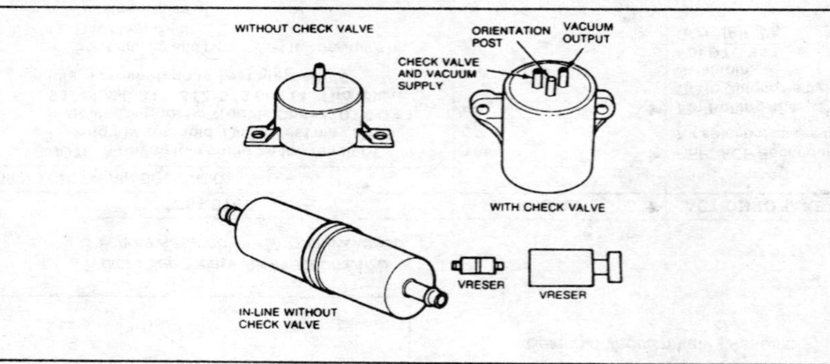

Vacuum Reservoirs

TEST STEP	RESULT ▶	ACTION TO TAKE
AIR29 CHECK VACUUM RESERVOIR FOR VACUUM		
• Key off. • Remove vacuum line from vacuum reservoir. • Key on, engine running. • Check for vacuum at vacuum line. FOR DUAL CONNECTION: Check the vacuum line port marked MAN or VAC. • **Is vacuum present?**	Yes ▶	**For Truck:** GO to AIR31. **For passenger car:** GO to AIR30.
	No ▶	SERVICE vacuum line for leaks, blockage, cracks, etc. VERIFY drive concern.
AIR30 CHECK RESERVOIR TO HOLD VACUUM		
• Key off. • Apply 51-67 kPa (15-20 in-Hg) vacuum to the reservoir port and hold. • **Is vacuum loss greater than 1.7 kPa (.5 in-Hg) after 60 seconds?**	No ▶	GO to Diagnosis By Symptom page.
	Yes ▶	REPLACE vacuum reservoir. VERIFY drive concern.

88154G34

Functional Diagnosis: Vacuum Reservoir

TITLE — SYMBOL: VRESER, VRESER

	TEST STEP	RESULT	▶ ACTION TO TAKE
AIR31	CHECK VACUUM RESERVOIR ABILITY TO HOLD VACUUM		
	• Key off. • Connect a vacuum gauge to the port that is NOT marked MAN or VAC. • **Does the vacuum gauge indicate applied vacuum?**	Yes No	▶ GO to AIR32. ▶ REPLACE vacuum reservoir. VERIFY drive concern.
AIR32	CHECK VACUUM RESERVOIR FUNCTION		
	• Key off. • Remove vacuum source from port marked MAN or VAC. • **Does vacuum gauge on the port indicate any vacuum loss?**	Yes No	▶ REPLACE reservoir. VERIFY drive concern. ▶ GO to Diagnosis By Symptom.

88154G35

Functional Diagnosis: Vacuum Check Valve

TITLE — SYMBOL: VCK-V

Description

A Vacuum Check Valve blocks airflow in one direction. It allows free air flow in the other direction. The check side of this valve will hold the highest vacuum seen on the vacuum side. If not, replace it.

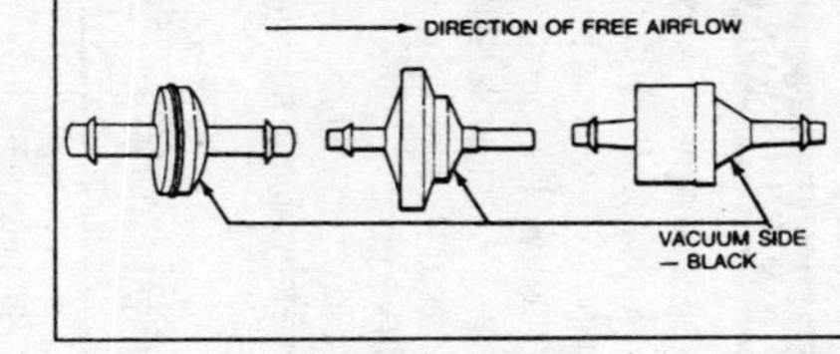

Vacuum Check Valve

	TEST STEP	RESULT	▶ ACTION TO TAKE
AIR33	CHECK AIR FLOW AT CHECK VALVE		
	• Key off. • Remove check valve from vacuum lines (note which direction check valve is installed). • Connect auxiliary vacuum source to black side of check valve. • Connect vacuum gauge to opposite side of check valve. • Apply 54 kPa (16 in-Hg) vacuum to black side. • **Does gauge indicate 54 kPa (16 in-Hg)?**	Yes No	▶ GO to AIR34. ▶ REPLACE Check Valve. VERIFY drive concern.
AIR34	VERIFY CHECK VALVE'S ABILITY TO HOLD VACUUM		
	• Key off. • Remove auxiliary vacuum source from the check valve. • **Does vacuum gauge reading remain above 50 kPa (15 in-Hg) for 10 seconds?**	Yes No	▶ GO to Diagnosis By Symptom to address other possible causes. ▶ REPLACE Check Valve. VERIFY drive concern.

88154G36

EXHAUST GAS RECIRCULATION SYSTEM

General Information

The Exhaust Gas Recirculation (EGR) system is designed to reintroduce exhaust gas into the combustion cycle, thereby lowering combustion temperatures and reducing the formation of nitrous oxide. There are 2 different EGR systems used on Ford rear wheel drive vehi-cles.

All 2.3L and 5.0L engines use the Electronic EGR valve (EEGR) system. In the EEGR system, EGR flow is controlled according to computer demands by means of an EGR Valve Position (EVP) sensor attached to the valve. The valve is operated by a vacuum signal from the electronic vacuum regulator which actuates the valve diaphragm. As supply vacuum overcomes the spring load, the diaphragm is actuated. This lifts the pintle off of it's seat allowing exhaust gas to recirculate. The amount of flow is proportional to the pintle position. The EVP sensor mounted on the valve sends an electrical signal of its position to the ECU.

Electronic EGR Valve

The electronic EGR valve is vacuum operated, lifting the pintle off of it's seat to allow exhaust gas to recirculate when the vacuum signal is strong enough. The EVP sensor which is mounted on top of the electronic EGR valve. The electronic EGR valve assembly is not serviceable. The EVP sensor and the EGR valve must be serviced separately.

REMOVAL & INSTALLATION

See Figures 15, 16, 17, 18 and 19

1. Disconnect the negative battery cable.
2. Disconnect the vacuum line from the EGR valve and the connector from the EVP sensor.
3. Remove the mounting bolts and remove the EGR valve.
4. Remove the EVP sensor from the EGR valve.
5. Installation is the reverse of the removal procedure. Be sure to remove all old gasket material before installation. Use a new gasket during installation.

EGR Vacuum Regulator (EVR)

The EVR is an electromagnetic device which controls vacuum output to the EGR valve. The EVR replaces the EGR solenoid vacuum vent valve assembly. An electric current in the coil induces a magnetic field in the armature which pulls on a disk, closing the vent to atmosphere. The ECU outputs a duty cycle to the EVR which regulates the vacuum level to the EGR valve. As the duty cycle is increased, an increased vacuum signal goes to the EGR valve. The vacuum source is manifold vacuum.

On the 2.3L engine, a current control thermistor device is also used to compensate for extreme temperature operation. The EVR and thermistor are serviced as an assembly.

REMOVAL & INSTALLATION

1. Disconnect the negative battery cable.
2. Unplug the electrical connector and the vacuum lines from the regulator.
3. Remove the regulator mounting bolts and remove the regulator.
4. Installation is the reverse of the removal procedure.

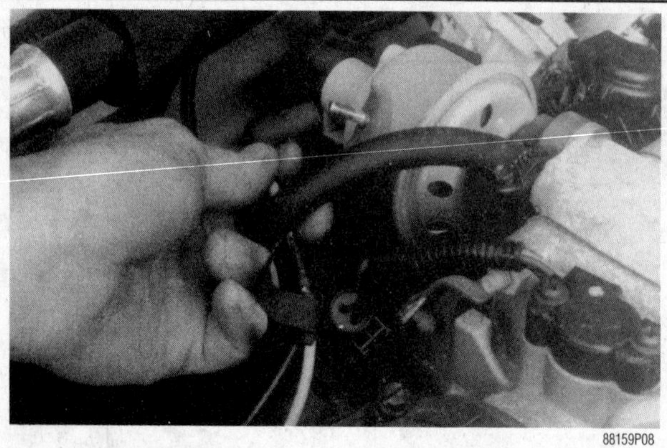

88159P08

Fig. 15 Check the condition of the vacuum line fitting as they can crack and leak

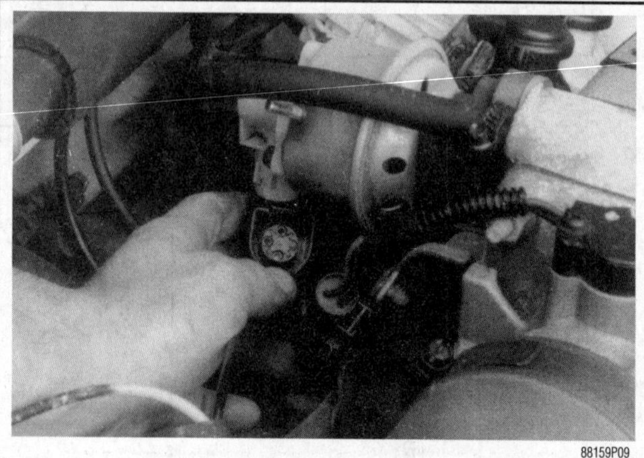

88159P09

Fig. 16 This is the electrical connector for the EVP sensor

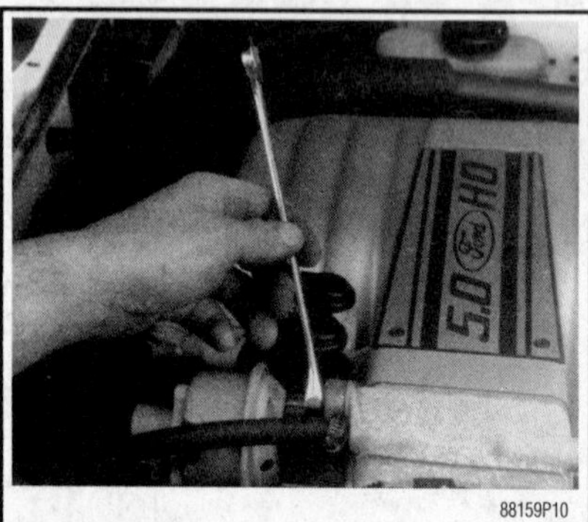

88159P10

Fig. 17 Loosen the two mounting nuts for the EGR valve

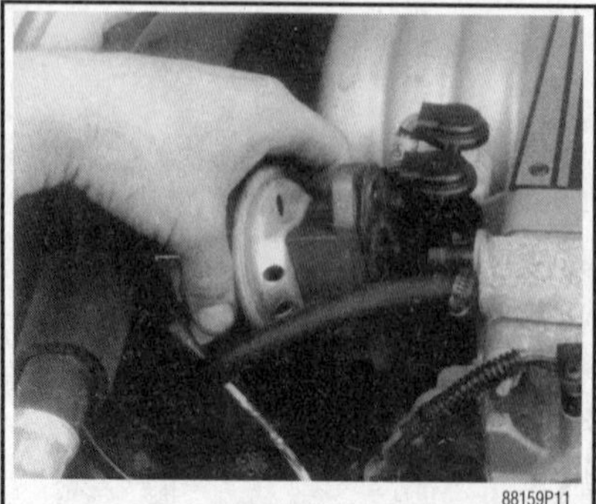

88159P11

Fig. 18 Pull the EGR valve straight back over the mounting studs

88159P12

Fig. 19 Replace the gasket each time the EGR valve is removed

Exhaust Gas Recirculation System Diagnosis Charts

EGR System Descriptions

EGR Valve Position (EVP) System

The EVP EGR Valve is required in EEC systems where EGR flow is controlled according to Powertrain Control Module (PCM) demands by means of an EGR Valve Position (EVP) sensor attached to the valve.

The valve is operated by a vacuum signal from the EGR Vacuum Regulator (EVR) Solenoid which actuates the valve diaphragm.

As supply vacuum overcomes the spring load, the diaphragm is actuated. This lifts the pintle off its seat allowing exhaust gas to recirculate (flow). The amount of flow is proportional to the pintle position. The EVP sensor mounted on the valve sends an electrical signal of its position to the PCM.

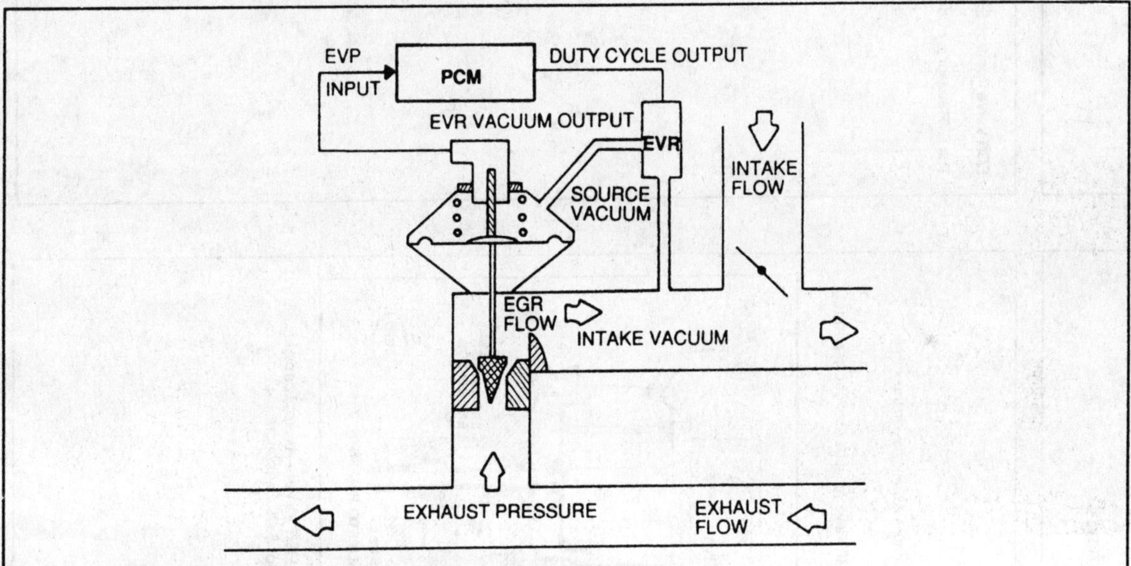

Typical EGR Valve Position (EVP) System

88154G37

EGR System Descriptions

System Components

EVP EGR Valve

The EGR valve for this system is a vacuum operated EGR valve which maintains a sonic flow in the valve seat / pintle area.

The EVP EGR valve assembly is not serviceable. The EVP sensor and EGR valve must be serviced separately.

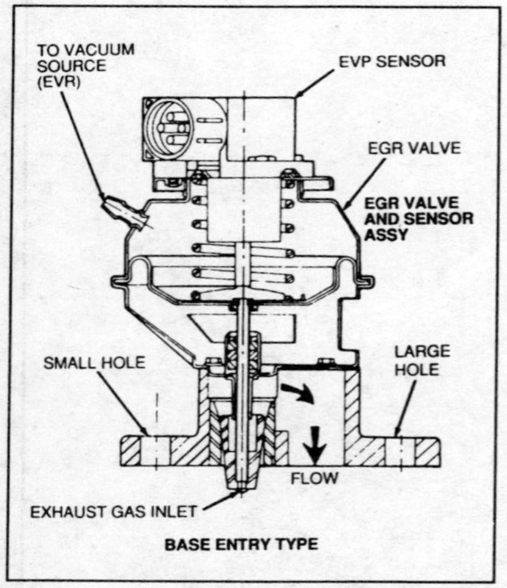

EVP EGR Valve—5.0L Passenger Car Only

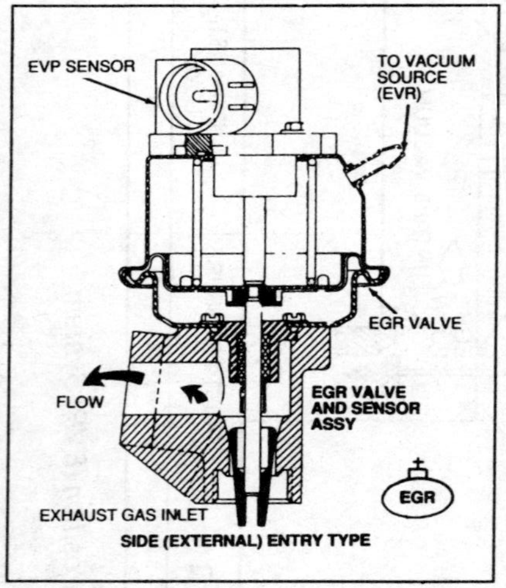

EVP EGR Valve—All Applications Except 5.0L Passenger Car

88154G38

EGR System Descriptions

EGR Valve Position (EVP) Sensor

The EVP sensor provides the EEC system with a signal indicating position of the EGR valve.

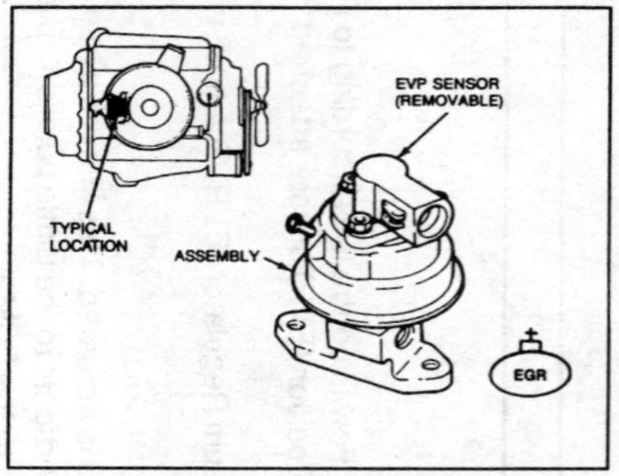

Figure 9: EGR Valve Position (EVP) Sensor

88154G39

EGR System Descriptions

EGR Vacuum Regulator (EVR) Solenoid

The EGR Vacuum Regulator (EVR) solenoid is an electromagnetic device which controls vacuum output to the EGR valve. An electric current in the coil induces a magnetic field in the armature which pulls on a disk closing the vent to atmosphere. The Powertrain Control Module (PCM) outputs a duty cycle to the EVR which regulates the vacuum level to the EGR valve. As the duty cycle is increased, so is the vacuum signal to the EGR valve. The vacuum source is manifold vacuum.

On some applications, a current control thermistor device is also used to compensate for extreme temperature operation. The EVR solenoid and thermistor are serviced as an assembly.

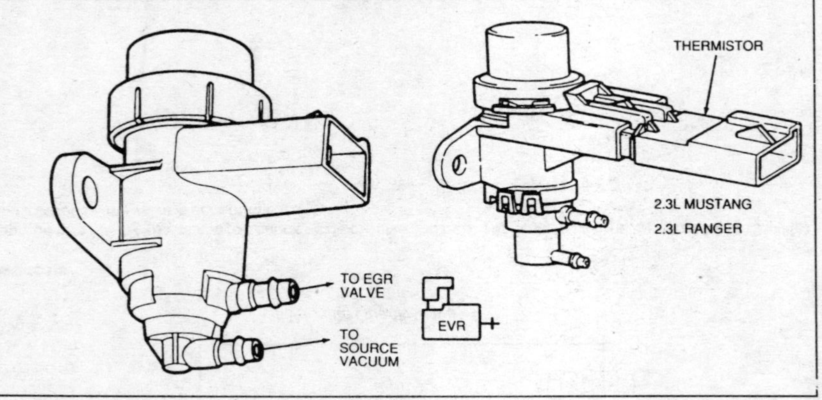

EGR Vacuum Regulator (EVR) Solenoid

88154G40

EGR System Descriptions

Vacuum Reservoir

The Vacuum Reservoir stores vacuum and provides "muscle" vacuum. It prevents rapid fluctuations or sudden drops in a vacuum signal such as those seen during an acceleration period.

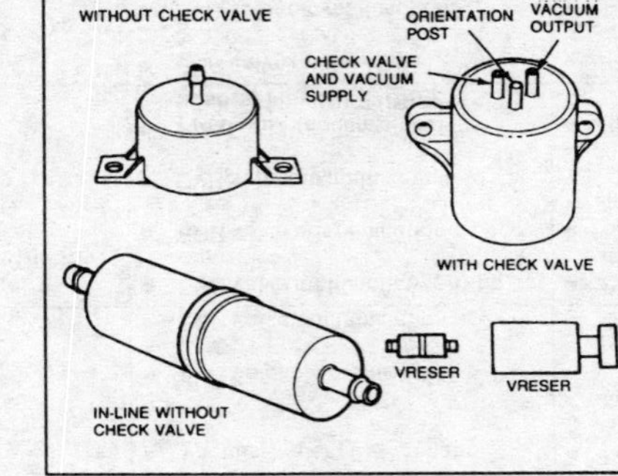

Vacuum Reservoirs

Diagnosis

When charged initially with 51-67 kPa (15-20 in-Hg) vacuum, vacuum loss shall not exceed 2 kPa (.5 in-Hg) in 60 seconds. If it does, replace the reservoir.

88154G41

EGR System Descriptions

Vacuum Check Valve

A vacuum check valve blocks airflow in one direction and frees airflow in the other direction. The check side of this valve will hold the highest vacuum seen on the vacuum side. If not, replace it.

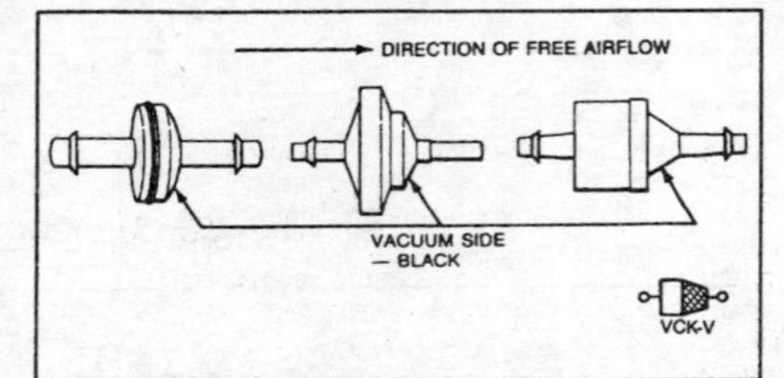

Vacuum Check Valve

Diagnosis

Apply 54 kPa (16 in-Hg) vacuum to "check" side of valve and trap. If vacuum remains above 50.6 kPa (15 in-Hg) for 10 seconds, the valve is acceptable.

88154G42

EGR System Diagnosis By Symptom

CONDITION	POSSIBLE SOURCE	ACTION
• Rough Idle Cold	• EGR valve malfunction.	
	• EGR flange gasket leaking.	• Replace flange gasket and tighten valve attaching nuts or bolts to specification.
	• EGR valve attaching nuts or bolts loose or missing.	• Replace flange gasket and tighten valve attaching nuts or bolts to specification.
	• Vacuum leak at EVP sensor.	• Replace O-ring seal and tighten EVP sensor attaching nuts to specification.
	• EVR solenoid malfunction.	
	• EGR valve contamination.	• Clean EGR valve.
• Rough Idle Hot	• EGR valve malfunction.	
	• EGR flange gasket leaking.	• Replace flange gasket and tighten valve attaching nuts or bolts to specification.
	• EGR valve attaching nuts or bolts loose or missing.	• Replace flange gasket and tighten valve attaching nuts or bolts to specification.
	• Vacuum leak at EVP sensor.	• Replace O-ring seal and tighten EVP sensor attaching nuts to specification.
	• EVR solenoid malfunction.	
	• EGR valve contamination.	• Clean EGR valve.
• Rough Running, Surge, Hesitation, Poor Part Throttle Performance—Hot	• EGR valve malfunction / erratic operation.	• Perform EGR valve functional diagnosis.
	• EGR valve contamination.	• Clean EGR valve and if necessary, replace EGR valve.
	• EVR solenoid malfunction.	
	• Pressure / Vacuum signal hose(s) leak (PFE / DPFE).	• Replace hose(s).
• Engine Stalls On Deceleration—Hot	• EGR valve malfunction.	• Perform EGR valve functional diagnosis.
	• EVR solenoid malfunction.	
	• EGR valve contamination.	• Clean EGR valve and if necessary, replace EGR valve.
• Engine Spark Knock or Ping	• EGR valve malfunction.	• Perform EGR valve functional diagnosis.
	• EGR valve attaching nuts or bolts loose or missing.	• Replace flange gasket and tighten valve attaching nuts or bolts to specification.
	• Blocked or restricted passages in valve or spacer (EVP).	• Clean passages in EGR spacer and EGR valve.

88154G43

EGR System Diagnosis By Symptom

CONDITION	POSSIBLE SOURCE	ACTION
• Engine Stalls At Idle—Cold	• EGR valve malfunction. • EGR flange gasket leaking. • EGR valve attaching nuts or bolts loose or missing. • EVR solenoid malfunction. • EGR valve contamination.	• Perform EGR valve functional diagnosis. • Replace flange gasket and tighten valve attaching nuts or bolts to specification. • Replace flange gasket and tighten valve attaching nuts or bolts to specification. • Clean EGR valve.
• Engine Stalls At Idle—Hot	• EGR valve malfunction. • EGR flange gasket leaking. • EGR valve attaching nuts or bolts loose or missing. • EGR valve contamination • Vacuum leak at EVP sensor. • EVR solenoid malfunction.	• Perform EGR valve functional diagnosis. • Replace flange gasket and tighten valve attaching nuts or bolts to specification. • Replace flange gasket and tighten valve attaching nuts or bolts to specification. • Clean EGR valve and if necessary, replace EGR valve. • Replace O-ring seal and tighten EVP sensor attaching nuts to specification.
• Engine Starts But Will Not Run—Engine Hard To Start Or Will Not Start	• EGR valve malfunction. • EGR flange gasket leaking. • EGR valve attaching nuts or bolts loose or missing. • EVR solenoid malfunction. • EGR valve contamination.	• Perform EGR valve functional diagnosis. • Replace flange gasket and tighten valve attaching nuts or bolts to specification. • Replace flange gasket and tighten valve attaching nuts or bolts to specification. • Clean EGR valve.

88154G44

EGR System Functional Diagnosis

TEST STEP	RESULT	▶ ACTION TO TAKE
EGR1 CHECK SYSTEM INTEGRITY		
• Check vacuum hoses and connections for looseness, pinching, leakage, splitting, blockage and proper routing. • Inspect EGR valve for loose attaching bolts or damaged flange gasket. • **Does system appear to be in good condition and vacuum hoses properly routed?**	Yes No	▶ GO to EGR2. ▶ SERVICE EGR system as required. RE-EVALUATE symptom.
EGR2 CHECK EGR VACUUM AT IDLE		
• Run engine until normal operating temperature is reached. • With engine running at idle, disconnect EGR vacuum supply at the EGR valve and check for a vacuum signal. NOTE: **The EVR solenoid has a constant internal leak. You may notice a small vacuum signal. This signal should be less than 3.4 kPa (1.0 in-Hg) at idle.** • **Is EGR vacuum signal less than 3.4 kPa (1.0 in-Hg) at idle?**	Yes No	▶ GO to EGR3. ▶ RECONNECT EGR vacuum hose. INSPECT EVR solenoid for leakage.
EGR3 CHECK EGR VALVE FUNCTION		
• Install a tachometer, Rotunda 059-00010 or equivalent. • Disconnect the Idle Air Control (IAC) solenoid (9F715) electrical connector. • Remove and plug the vacuum supply hose from the EGR valve nipple. • Start engine, idle with transmission in NEUTRAL, and observe idle speed. If necessary, adjust idle speed according to Section 9A. NOTE: **If the engine will not idle with IAC solenoid disconnected, provide an air bypass to the engine by slightly opening the throttle plate or by creating an intake vacuum leak. Do not exceed a typical idle rpm.** • Slowly apply 5-10 inches of vacuum to the EGR valve nipple using a hand vacuum pump, Rotunda 021-00014 or equivalent. • **Does idle speed drop more than 100 rpm with vacuum applied and return to normal (± 25 rpm) after the vacuum is removed?**	Yes No	▶ The EGR valve is OK. UNPLUG and RECONNECT the EGR valve vacuum supply hose. RECONNECT the IAC solenoid connector. ▶ INSPECT the EGR valve for blockage or contamination. CLEAN the valve using EGR valve cleaner. INSPECT valve for vacuum leakage. REPLACE if necessary.

88154G45

CATALYTIC CONVERTERS

General Information

Engine exhaust consists mainly of Nitrogen (N_2), however, it also contains Carbon Monoxide (CO), Carbon Dioxide (CO_2), Water Vapor (H_2O), Oxygen (O_2), Nitrogen Oxides (NOx) and Hydrogen, as well as various, unburned Hydrocarbons (HC). Three of these exhaust components, CO, NOx and HC, are major air pollutants, so their emission to the atmosphere has to be controlled.

The catalytic converter, mounted in the engine exhaust stream, plays a major role in the emission control system. The converter works as a gas reactor and it's catalytic function is to speed up the heat producing chemical reaction between the exhaust gas components in order to reduce the air pollutants in the engine exhaust. The catalyst material, contained inside the converter, is made of a ceramic substrate that is coated with a high surface area alumina and impregnated with catalytically active, precious metals.

Catalytic Converter

All Ford Mustang's use a 3-way catalyst and some also use this in conjunction with a conventional oxidation catalyst. The conventional oxidation catalyst, containing Platinum (Pt) and Palladium (Pd), is effective for catalyzing the oxidation reactions of HC and CO. The 3-way catalyst, containing Platinum (Pt) and Rhodium (RH) or Palladium (Pd) and Rhodium (RH), is not only effective for catalyzing the oxidation reactions of HC and CO, but it also catalyzes the reduction of NOx.

The catalytic converter assembly consists of a structured shell containing a ceramic, honeycomb construction. In order to maintain the converter's exhaust oxygen content at a high level to obtain the maximum oxidation for producing the heated chemical reaction, the oxidation catalyst sometimes requires the use of a secondary air source. This is provided by the thermactor air injection system.

The catalytic converter is protected by several devices that block out the air supply from the thermactor air injection system when the engine is laboring under one or more of the following conditions:

- Cold engine operation with rich choke mixture.
- Abnormally high engine coolant temperatures above 225°F (107°C), which may result from a condition such as an extended, hot idle on a hot day.
- Wide-open throttle.
- Engine deceleration.
- Extended idle operation.

REMOVAL & INSTALLATION

**** CAUTION**

Catalytic converters operate at extremely high temperatures. Do not attempt to remove the converter until it has been allowed to cool, or bodily injury may result.

1. Raise and safely support the vehicle.
2. Disconnect the secondary air supply tube from the fitting on the converter, if necessary.
3. Remove the retaining clamps or mounting bolts, as necessary and remove the converter.
4. Installation is the reverse of the removal procedure.

ELECTRONIC ENGINE CONTROLS

Camshaft Position (CMP) Sensor

DESCRIPTION

The Camshaft Position Sensor (CMP) is a single Hall effect magnetic switch which is activated by a single vane driven by the camshaft. The Engine Control Module (ECM) uses the information to calculate ignition and injection timing.

TESTING

See Figure 20

Three Wire Sensors

1. With the ignition **OFF**, disconnect the CMP sensor. With the ignition **ON** and the engine **OFF**, measure the voltage between sensor harness connector VPWR and PWR GND terminals (refer to the figure). If the reading is greater than 10.5V, the power circuit to the sensor is okay.
2. With the ignition **OFF**, install breakout box. Connect CMP sensor and ECM. Using DVOM on AC and scale set to monitor less than 5V, measure voltage between breakout box terminals 24 and 40 with the engine running at varying RPM. If the voltage reading varies more than 0.1V AC, the sensor is okay.

Two Wire Sensors

1. With the ignition **OFF**, install breakout box.
2. Connect CMP sensor and ECM.
3. Using DVOM on AC scale and set to monitor less than 5V, measure voltage between breakout box terminals 24 and 46 with the engine running at varying RPM. If the voltage reading varies more than 0.1V AC, the sensor is okay.

Crankshaft Position (CKP) Sensor

DESCRIPTION

The Crankshaft Position (CKP) sensor, located inside the front cover, is a variable reluctance sensor triggered by a trigger pulse wheel (36 minus 1 tooth). The sensor supplies a signal to the Engine Control Module (ECM) which is used to determine crankshaft position and crankshaft rpm.

TESTING

See Figure 21

Using DVOM on the AC scale and set to monitor less than 5V, measure voltage between the sensor Cylinder Identification (CID) terminal and ground. The

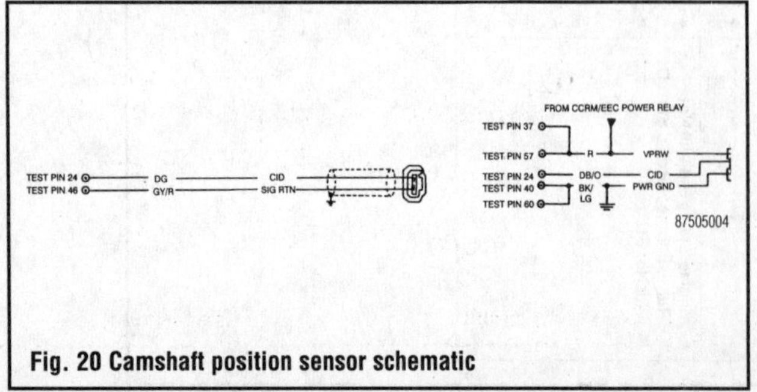

Fig. 20 Camshaft position sensor schematic

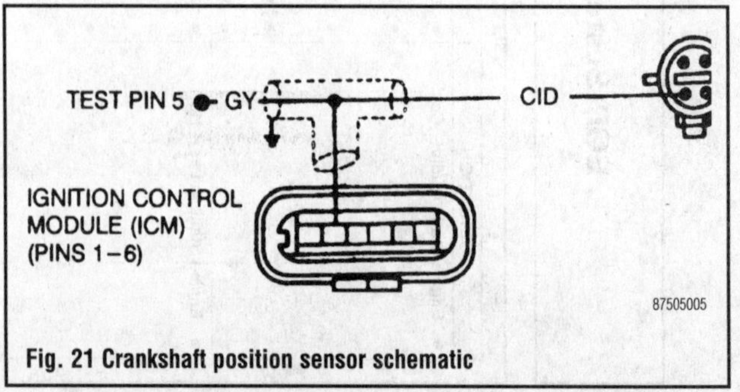

Fig. 21 Crankshaft position sensor schematic

sensor is okay if the voltage reading varies more than 0.1V AC with the engine running at varying RPM.

Engine Coolant Temperature (ECT) Sensor

DESCRIPTION

The Engine Coolant Temperature (ECT) sensor is a variable resistor which the Engine Control Module (ECM) uses to measure coolant temperature. The sensor's resistance decreases as the coolant temperature increases. The sensor is usually located in or near the thermostat housing.

TESTING

See Figurez 22 and 23

With ignition **OFF**, disconnect the ECT sensor. Measure the resistance across the sensor connector terminals. If the reading for a given temperature is about that shown in the table, the ECT sensor is okay.

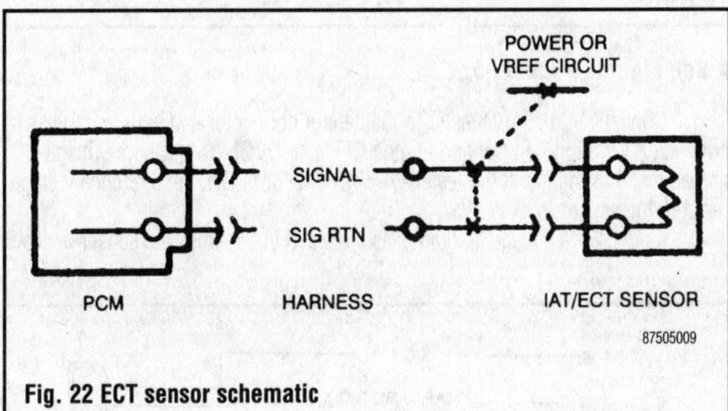

Fig. 22 ECT sensor schematic

Temperature—°F	Temperature—°C	Resistance—Ohms
248	120	1180
230	110	1550
212	100	2070
194	90	2800
176	80	3840
158	70	5370
140	60	7700
122	50	10,970
104	40	16,150
86	30	24,270
68	20	27,300
50	10	58,750

87505010

Fig. 23 ECT sensor performance chart

Exhaust Gas Recirculation (EGR) Valve Position (EVP) Sensor

DESCRIPTION

The Exhaust Gas Recirculation (EGR) Valve Position (EVP) system uses an electronic EGR valve to control the flow of exhaust gases. The Engine Control Module (ECM) monitors the flow by means of an EVP sensor and regulates the electronic EGR valve accordingly. The valve is operated by a vacuum signal from the EGR Vacuum Regulator (EVR) solenoid which actuates the valve diaphragm.

As the supply vacuum overcomes the spring load, the diaphragm is actuated. This lifts the pintle off its seat and allows exhaust gases to flow. The amount of flow is proportional to the pintle position. The EVP sensor, mounted on the valve, sends an electronic signal representing pintle position to the ECM.

TESTING

See Figure 24

1. Disconnect the EVP sensor connector. With the ignition **ON** and the engine **OFF**, measure the voltage between **VREF** and **SIG RTN** terminals of the EVP sensor harness connector. If the voltage is 4.0-6.0V, the power circuits to the sensor are okay.
2. Reconnect the EVP sensor. With the ignition **ON** and the engine **OFF**, measure the voltage between EVP sensor terminals EVP and **SIG RTN**. If the voltage reading is 0.67V or less, the sensor is okay.

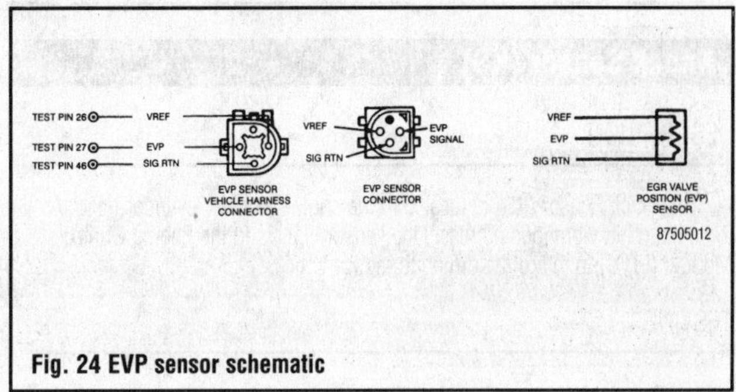

Fig. 24 EVP sensor schematic

Intake Air Temperature Sensor

DESCRIPTION

The Intake Air Temperature (IAT) sensor is a variable resistor which changes in response to intake air temperature. The resistance decreases as the surrounding air temperature increases. This temperature signal is sent to the Engine Control Module (ECM). The IAT sensor is located at the intake port or exit port of the air cleaner or in the intake manifold.

TESTING

See Figures 25 and 26

With ignition **OFF**, disconnect the IAT sensor. Measure the resistance across the sensor connector terminals. If the reading for a given temperature is about that shown in the table, the IAT sensor is okay.

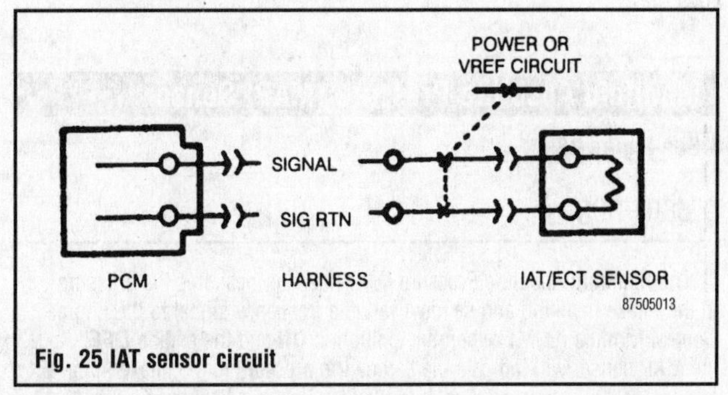

Fig. 25 IAT sensor circuit

Temperature—°F	Temperature—°C	Resistance—Ohms
248	120	1180
230	110	1550
212	100	2070
194	90	2800
176	80	3840
158	70	5370
140	60	7700
122	50	10,970
104	40	16,150
86	30	24,270
68	20	27,300
50	10	58,750

87505014

Fig. 26 IAT sensor performance chart

Knock Sensor (KS)

DESCRIPTION

The Knock Sensor (KS) is located in the engine block or cylinder head. As the detonation vibrations increase, the sensor signals to the Engine Control Module (ECM) to retard the timing to reduce knock.

TESTING

See Figure 27

1. With ignition **ON** and engine **OFF**, measure voltage between KS connector terminals. If voltage reading is 2.4-2.6V, the circuit between the ECM and KS is okay.
2. With engine running at idle and then at 3000 rpm, measure voltage using a DVOM on the AC setting between the KS terminals. If the AC voltage reading increases as the rpm increases, the sensor is okay.

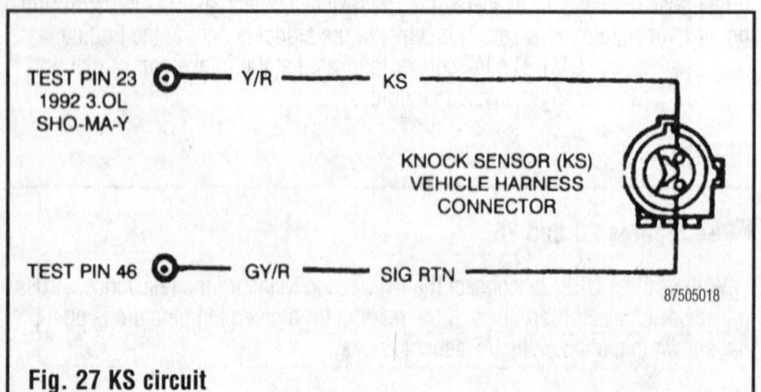

Fig. 27 KS circuit

Manifold Absolute Pressure (MAP) Sensor

See Figure 28

DESCRIPTION

The Manifold Absolute Pressure (MAP) sensor measures the pressure in the intake manifold and sends a variable frequency signal to the Engine Control Module (ECM). When the ignition is **ON** and the engine **OFF**, the MAP sensor will indicate the barometric pressure in the intake manifold.

Fig. 28 MAP sensors and BARO sensor look similar

TESTING

See Figures 29 and 30

1. Connect MAP/BARO tester to the sensor connector and sensor harness connector. With ignition ON and engine OFF, use DVOM to measure voltage across tester terminals. If the tester's 4-6V indicator is ON, the reference voltage input to the sensor is okay.
2. If the DVOM voltage reading is as indicated in the table, the sensor is okay.

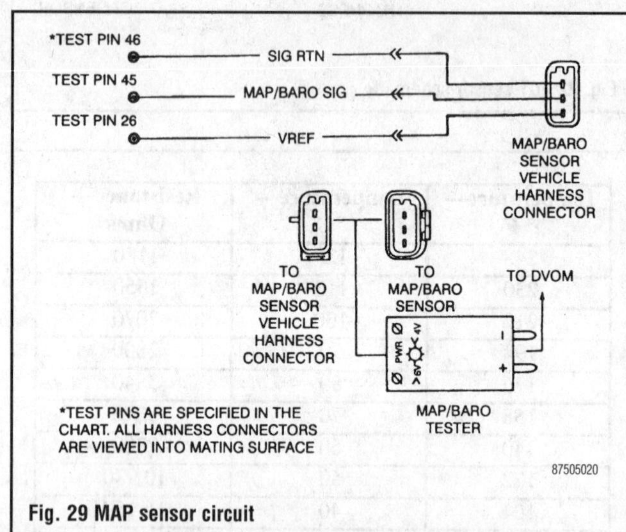

Fig. 29 MAP sensor circuit

Approximate Altitude (Feet)	Signal Voltage (±0.04V)
0	1.59
1000	1.56
2000	1.53
3000	1.50
4000	1.47
5000	1.44
6000	1.41
7000	1.39

87505021

Fig. 30 MAP sensor performance chart

Mass Air Flow (MAF) Sensor

➧ See Figures 31, 32 and 33

DESCRIPTION

The Mass Air Flow (MAF) sensor uses a hot wire sensing element to measure the amount of air entering the engine. Air passing over the hot wire causes it to cool. A cold wire is used to determine the ambient. The sensor compares the 2 elements and sends an analog voltage signal to the Engine Control Module (ECM). The ECM uses this signal to determine proper air/fuel mixture.

The MAF sensor is located between the air cleaner and the throttle body. The sensor hot wire sensing elements and housing are calibrated as a unit and must be serviced as a complete assembly.

TESTING

➧ See Figure 34 and 35

1. With engine running, use DVOM to verify there is at least 10.5V between terminals A and B of the MAF sensor connector. This indicates the power input to the sensor is okay.
2. With engine running, use DVOM to measure voltage between MAF sensor connector terminals C and D. If the readings are about as indicated in the table, the sensor is okay. The readings may vary based on vehicle load and temperature.

Oxygen Sensor (O_2S)

➧ See Figures 36, 37 and 38

DESCRIPTION

The Oxygen Sensor (O_2S) reacts to the oxygen in the exhaust gases and sends a voltage to the Engine Control Module (ECM) based on the reaction. A low voltage indicates too much oxygen in the exhaust or a lean conditions. A high voltage indicates not enough oxygen in the exhaust or a rich condition. The ECM uses this information to vary the air/fuel mixture. The oxygen sensor is located in the exhaust stream, ahead of the catalytic converter.

Most Ford vehicles use a heated oxygen sensor. The heated element keeps the sensor at proper operating temperature during all operating modes. Maintaining correct sensor temperature at all times allows the system to enter closed loop operation sooner and to remain in closed loop operation during periods of extended idle.

TESTING

1. Disconnect the O_2S. Measure resistance between the sensor connector terminals PWR and GND (heater). If the reading is 2-30 ohms, the sensor's heating element is okay.
2. With the O_2S connected and the engine running at normal operating temperature, measure voltage with DVOM between sensor connector terminals

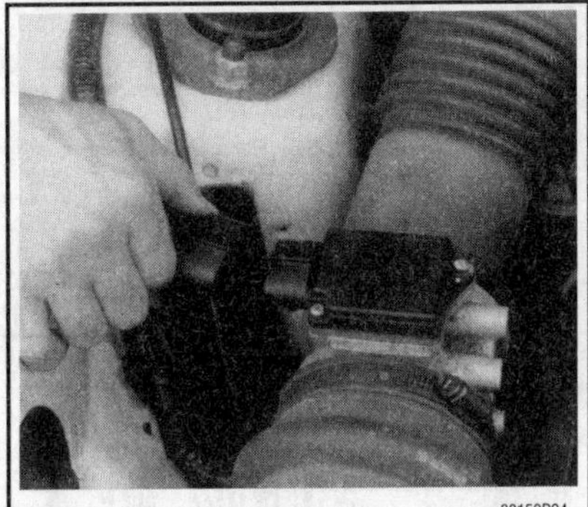

88159P04

Fig. 31 Pull the MAF sensor connector straight off to prevent damage to the pins

88159P05

Fig. 32 The MAF is suspended in the air inlet duct and held in place by hose clamps

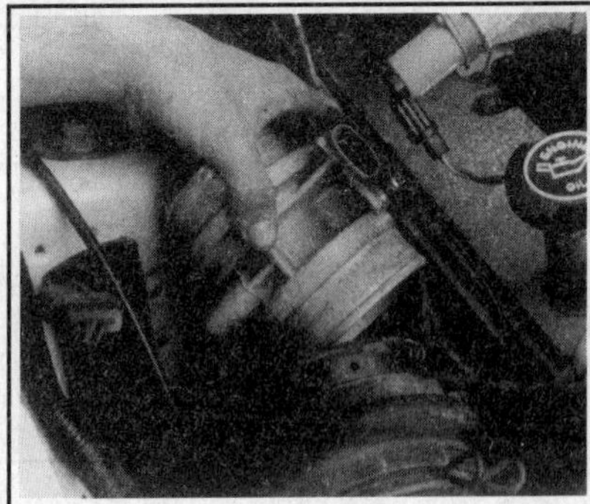

88159P06

Fig. 33 The MAF is removed by lossening the clamps and pulling the unit out

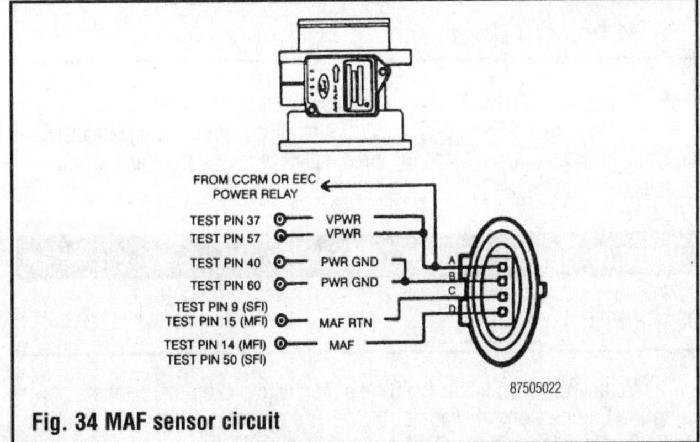

Fig. 34 MAF sensor circuit

Engine Condition	Signal Voltage—Sensor Terminals C and D
Idle	0.60V
20 mph	1.10V
40 mph	1.70V
60 mph	2.10V

87505023

Fig. 35 MAF sensor performance chart

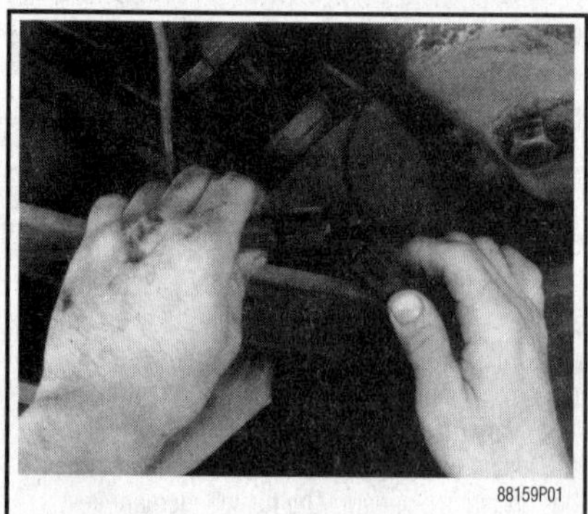
Fig. 36 The oxygen sensor connector is accessable from under the car

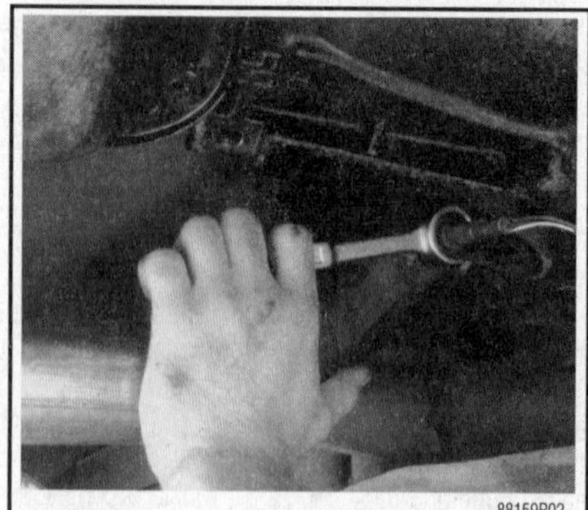
Fig. 37 This special oxygen sensor wrench grips most of the way around the sensor

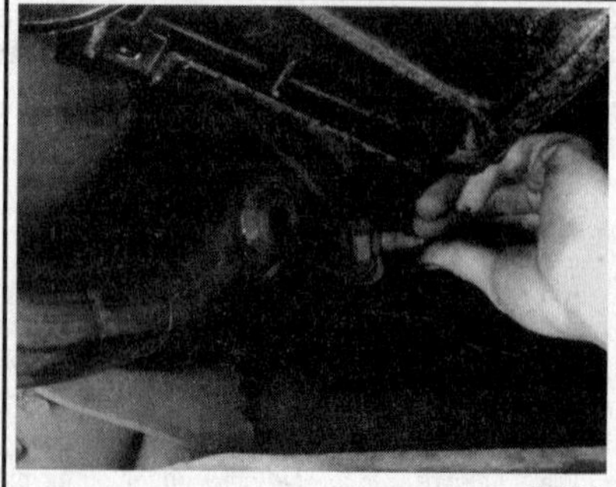
Fig. 38 Use approved anti-seize on the threads of the sensor. Non-approved anti-seize can contaminate the sensor

HO_2S and **SIG RTN**. If the voltage reading is 0-1.0V at idle and 0.5-1.0V when accelerating, the sensor is okay.

Power Steering Pressure Switch (PSPS)

DESCRIPTION

The Power Steering Pressure Switch (PSPS) opens as pressure increases. This sends a signal to the Engine Control Module (ECM) which adjust the idle speed to compensate for the additional load.

TESTING

▶ See Figure 39

Disconnect the PSPS. With engine idling, measure resistance between the PSPS connector terminals. If the resistance changes from less than 10 ohms to infinity (indicating open PSPS) when the steering wheel is turned from center to more than one half turn left or right, the PSPS is okay.

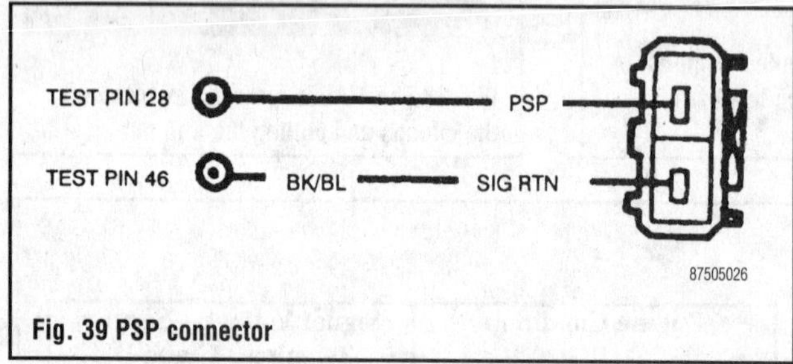

Fig. 39 PSP connector

Throttle Position (TP) Sensor

DESCRIPTION

The Throttle Position (TP) sensor is a potentiometer which provides a signal to the Engine Control Module (ECM) that is directly proportional to the throttle plate position.

The TP sensor is mounted to the throttle body and engages the throttle plate. As the throttle plate opens and closes, the resistance of the TP sensor changes and varies the output signal voltage accordingly.

TESTING

▶ See Figures 40 and 41

1. With ignition **ON** and engine **OFF**, measure voltage between sensor **VREF** and **SIG RTN** connector terminals. If voltage reading is 4.0-6.0V, the power circuits to the sensor are okay.

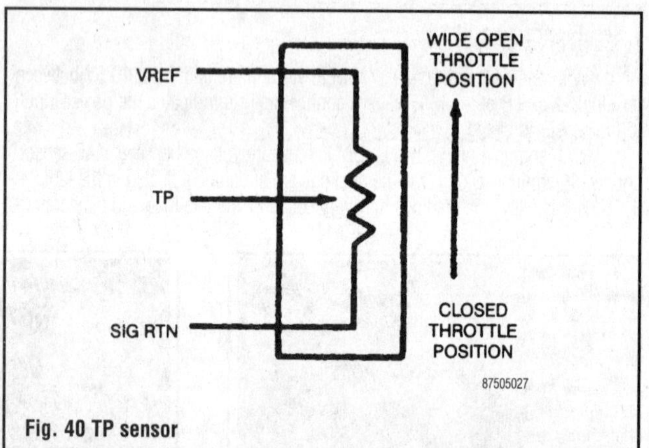

Fig. 40 TP sensor

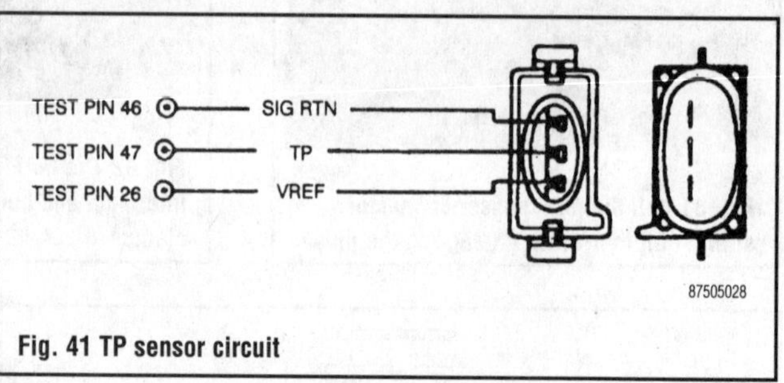

Fig. 41 TP sensor circuit

2. With ignition **ON** and engine **OFF**, use DVOM to measure voltage between sensor **SIG RTN** and TP connector terminals. If the voltage increases smoothly to greater than 3.5V as the throttle plate is moved from idle to wide open throttle, the sensor is okay.

Vehicle Speed Sensor (VSS)

DESCRIPTION

The Vehicle Speed Sensor (VSS) is a magnetic pickup that sends a signal to the Engine Control Module (ECM). The sensor measures the rotation of the transmission and the ECM determines the corresponding vehicle speed.

TESTING

▶ See Figures 42 and 43

With ignition **OFF**, disconnect VSS connector. Measure the resistance between the sensor connector terminals. If the resistance is 190–250 ohms, the sensor is okay.

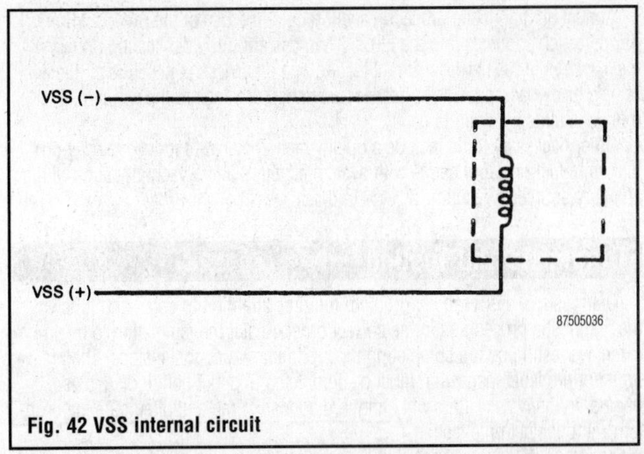

Fig. 42 VSS internal circuit

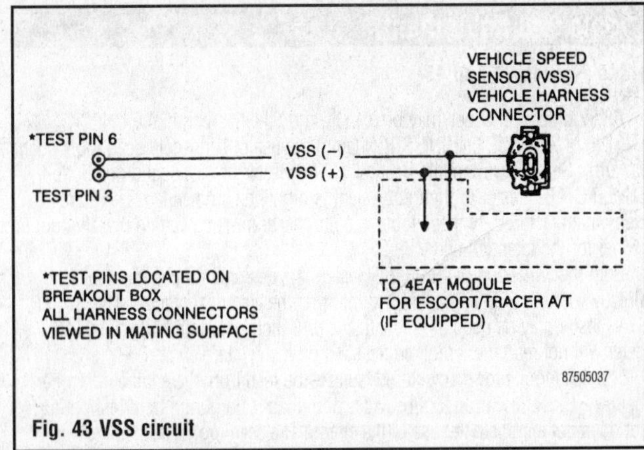

Fig. 43 VSS circuit

SELF DIAGNOSTIC SYSTEMS

General Description

Ford Mustang vehicles employ the 4th generation Electronic Engine Control system, commonly designated EEC-IV, to manage fuel, ignition and emissions on vehicle engines.

ENGINE CONTROL SYSTEM

The Engine Control Assembly (ECA) is given responsibility for the operation of the emission control devices, cooling fans, ignition and advance and in some cases, automatic transmission functions. Because the EEC-IV oversees both the ignition timing and the fuel injector operation, a precise air/fuel ratio will be maintained under all operating conditions. The ECA is a microprocessor or small computer which receives electrical inputs from several sensors, switches and relays on and around the engine.

Based on combinations of these inputs, the ECA controls outputs to various devices concerned with engine operation and emissions. The engine control assembly relies on the signals to form a correct picture of current vehicle operation. If any of the input signals is incorrect, the ECA reacts to what ever picture is painted for it. For example, if the coolant temperature sensor is inaccurate and reads too low, the ECA may see a picture of the engine never warming up. Consequently, the engine settings will be maintained as if the engine were cold. Because so many inputs can affect one output, correct diagnostic procedures are essential on these systems.

One part of the ECA is devoted to monitoring both input and output functions within the system. This ability forms the core of the self-diagnostic system. If a problem is detected within a circuit, the controller will recognize the fault, assign it an identification code, and store the code in a memory section. Depending on the year and model, the fault code(s) may be represented by two or three digit numbers. The stored code(s) may be retrieved during diagnosis.

While the EEC-IV system is capable of recognizing many internal faults, certain faults will not be recognized. Because the computer system sees only electrical signals, it cannot sense or react to mechanical or vacuum faults affecting engine operation. Some of these faults may affect another component which will set a code. For example, the ECA monitors the output signal to the fuel injectors, but cannot detect a partially clogged injector. As long as the output driver responds correctly, the computer will read the system as functioning correctly. However, the improper flow of fuel may result in a lean mixture. This would, in turn, be detected by the oxygen sensor and noticed as a constantly lean signal by the ECA. Once the signal falls outside the pre-programmed limits, the engine control assembly would notice the fault and set an identification code.

Additionally, the EEC-IV system employs adaptive fuel logic. This process is used to compensate for normal wear and variability within the fuel system. Once the engine enters steady-state operation, the engine control assembly watches the oxygen sensor signal for a bias or tendency to run slightly rich or lean. If such a bias is detected, the adaptive logic corrects the fuel delivery to bring the air/fuel mixture towards a centered or 14.7:1 ratio. This compensating shift is stored in a non-volatile memory which is retained by battery power even with the ignition switched **OFF**. The correction factor is then available the next time the vehicle is operated.

➡If the battery cable(s) is disconnected for longer than 5 minutes, the adaptive fuel factor will be lost. After repair it will be necessary to drive the car at least 10 miles to allow the processor to relearn the correct factors. The driving period should include steady-throttle open road driving if possible. During the drive, the vehicle may exhibit driveability symptoms not noticed before. These symptoms should clear as the ECA computes the correction factor. The ECA will also store Code 19 indicating loss of power to the controller.

Failure Mode Effects Management (FMEM)

The engine controller assembly contains back-up programs which allow the engine to operate if a sensor signal is lost. If a sensor input is seen to be out of range—either high or low—the FMEM program is used. The processor substitutes a fixed value for the missing sensor signal. The engine will continue to operate, although performance and driveability may be noticeably reduced. This function of the controller is sometimes referred to as the limp-in or fail-safe mode. If the missing sensor signal is restored, the FMEM system immediately returns the system to normal operation. The dashboard warning lamp will be lit when FMEM is in effect.

Hardware Limited Operation Strategy (HLOS)

This mode is only used if the fault is too extreme for the FMEM circuit to handle. In this mode, the processor has ceased all computation and control; the entire system is run on fixed values. The vehicle may be operated but performance and driveabilty will be greatly reduced. The fixed or default settings provide minimal calibration, allowing the vehicle to be carefully driven in for service. The dashboard warning lamp will be lit when HLOS is engaged. Codes cannot be read while the system is operating in this mode.

DASHBOARD WARNING LAMP (MIL)

The CHECK ENGINE or SERVICE ENGINE SOON dashboard warning lamp is referred to as the Malfunction Indicator Lamp (MIL). The lamp is connected to the engine control assembly and will alert the driver to certain malfunctions within the EEC-IV system. When the lamp is lit, the ECA has detected a fault and stored an identity code in memory. The engine control system will usually enter either FMEM or HLOS mode and driveability will be impaired.

The light will stay on as long as the fault causing it is present. Should the fault self-correct, the MIL will extinguish but the stored code will remain in memory.

Under normal operating conditions, the MIL should light briefly when the ignition key is turned **ON**. As soon as the ECA receives a signal that the engine is cranking, the lamp will be extinguished. The dash warning lamp should remain out during the entire operating cycle.

Tools and Equipment

▸ See Figures 44 and 45

Although stored codes may be read through the flashing of the CHECK ENGINE or SERVICE ENGINE SOON lamp, the use of hand-held scan tools such as Ford's Self-Test Automatic Readout (STAR) tester or the second generation SUPER STAR II tester or their equivalent is highly recommended. There are many manufacturers of these tools; the purchaser must be certain that the tool is proper for the intended use.

Both the STAR and SUPER STAR testers are designed to communicate directly with the EEC-IV system and interpret the electrical signals. The SUPER STAR tester may be used to read either 2 or 3 digit codes; the original STAR tester will not read the 3 digit codes used on many later vehicles.

The scan tool allows any stored faults to be read from the engine controller memory. Use of the scan tool provides additional data during troubleshooting but does not eliminate the use of the charts. The scan tool makes collecting information easier; the data must be correctly interpreted by an operator familiar with the system.

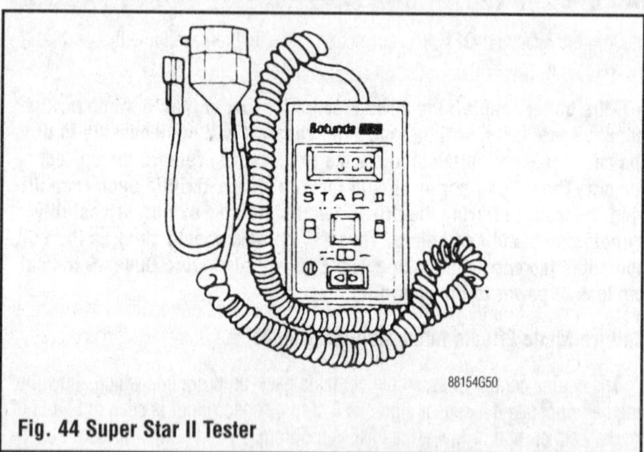

Fig. 44 Super Star II Tester

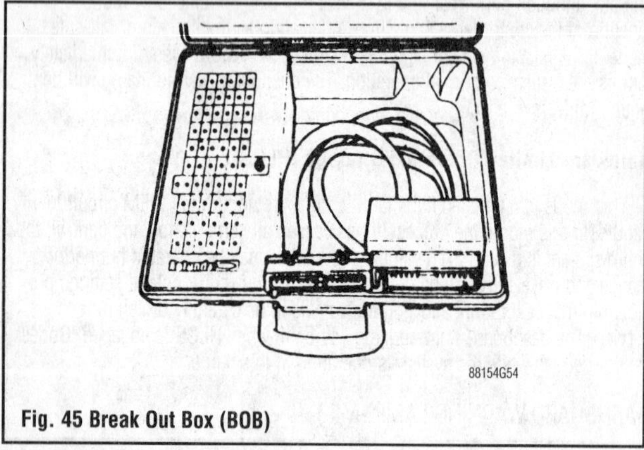

Fig. 45 Break Out Box (BOB)

ELECTRICAL TOOLS

The most commonly required electrical diagnostic tool is the Digital Multimeter, allowing voltage, ohmmage (resistance) and amperage to be read by one instrument. Many of the diagnostic charts require the use of a volt or ohmmeter during diagnosis.

The multimeter must be a high impedance unit, with 10 megohms of impedance in the voltmeter. This type of meter will not place an additional load on the circuit it is testing; this is extremely important in low voltage circuits. The multimeter must be of high quality in all respects. It should be handled carefully and protected from impact or damage. Replace the batteries frequently in the unit.

Additionally, an analog (needle type) voltmeter may be used to read stored fault codes if the STAR tester is not available. The codes are transmitted as visible needle sweeps on the face of the instrument.

Almost all diagnostic procedures will require the use of the Breakout Box, a device which connects into the EEC-IV harness and provides testing ports for the 60 wires in the harness. Direct testing of the harness connectors at the terminals or by back-probing is not recommended; damage to the wiring and terminals is almost certain to occur.

Other necessary tools include a quality tachometer with inductive (clip-on) pickup, a fuel pressure gauge with system adapters and a vacuum gauge with an auxiliary source of vacuum.

Diagnosis and Testing

Diagnosis of a driveability problem requires attention to detail and following the diagnostic procedures in the correct order. Resist the temptation to begin extensive testing before completing the preliminary diagnostic steps. The preliminary or visual inspection must be completed in detail before diagnosis begins. In many cases this will shorten diagnostic time and often cure the problem without electronic testing.

VISUAL INSPECTION

This is possibly the most critical step of diagnosis. A detailed examination of all connectors, wiring and vacuum hoses can often lead to a repair without further diagnosis. Performance of this step relies on the skill of the technician performing it; a careful inspector will check the undersides of hoses as well as the integrity of hard-to-reach hoses blocked by the air cleaner or other components. Wiring should be checked carefully for any sign of strain, burning, crimping or terminal pull-out from a connector.

Checking connectors at components or in harnesses is required; usually, pushing them together will reveal a loose fit. Pay particular attention to ground circuits, making sure they are not loose or corroded. Remember to inspect connectors and hose fittings at components not mounted on the engine, such as the evaporative canister or relays mounted on the fender aprons. Any component or wiring in the vicinity of a fluid leak or spillage should be given extra attention during inspection.

Additionally, inspect maintenance items such as belt condition and tension, battery charge and condition and the radiator cap carefully. Any of these very simple items may affect the system enough to set a fault.

READING FAULTS OR FAULT CODES

▸ See Figure 46

The EEC-IV system may be interrogated for stored codes using the Quick Test procedures. These tests will reveal faults immediately present during the test as well as any intermittent codes set within the previous 80 warm up cycles. If a code was set before a problem self-corrected (such as a momentarily loose connector), the code will be erased if the problem does not reoccur within 80 warm-up cycles.

The Quick Test procedure is divided into 2 sections, Key On Engine Off (KOEO) and Key On Engine Running (KOER). These 2 procedures must be performed correctly if the system is to run the internal self-checks and provide

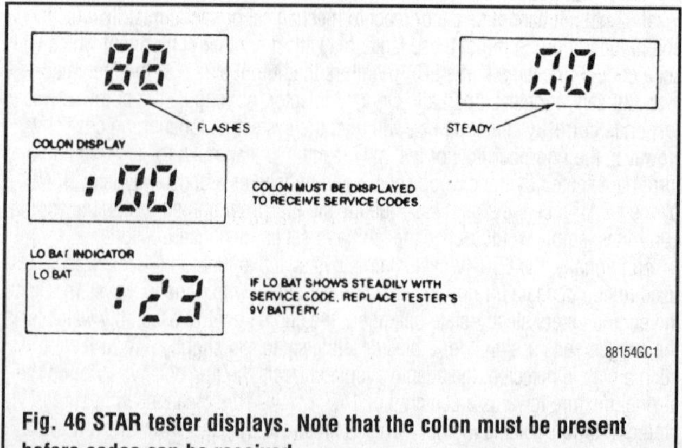

Fig. 46 STAR tester displays. Note that the colon must be present before codes can be received

accurate fault codes. Codes will be output and displayed as numbers on the hand scan tool, i.e. 23. If the codes are being read through the dashboard warning lamp, the codes will be displayed as groups of flashes separated by pauses. Code 23 would be shown as two flashes, a pause and three more flashes. A longer pause will occur between codes. If the codes are being read on an analog voltmeter, the needle sweeps indicate the code digits in the same manner as the lamp flashes.

In all cases, the codes 11 or 111 are used to indicate PASS during testing. Note that the PASS code may appear, followed by other stored codes. These are codes from the continuous memory and may indicate intermittent faults, even though the system does not presently contain the fault. The PASS designation only indicates the system passes all internal tests at the moment.

Once the Quick Test has been performed and all fault codes recorded, refer to the code charts. The charts direct the use of specific pinpoint tests for the appropriate circuit and will allow complete circuit testing.

CAUTION

To prevent injury and/or property damage, always block the drive wheels, firmly apply the parking brake, place the transmission in PARK or NEUTRAL and turn all electrical loads off before performing the Quick Test procedures.

Key On Engine Off Test

See Figure 47

1. Connect the scan tool to the self-test connectors. Make certain the test button is unlatched or up.
2. Start the engine and run it until normal operating temperature is reached.
3. Turn the engine **OFF** for 10 seconds.
4. Activate the test button on the STAR tester.
5. Turn the ignition switch **ON** but do not start the engine.
6. The KOEO codes will be transmitted. Six to nine seconds after the last KOEO code, a single separator pulse will be transmitted. Six to nine seconds after this pulse, the codes from the Continuous Memory will be transmitted.
7. Record all service codes displayed. Do not depress the throttle on gasoline engines during the test.

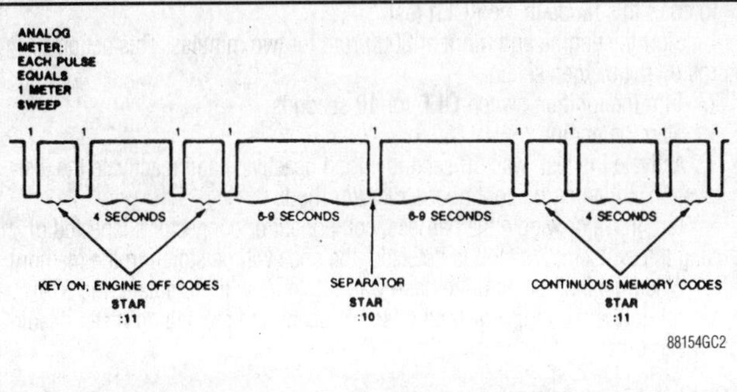

Fig. 47 Code transmission during KOEO test. Note that the continuous memory codes are transmitted after a pause and separator pause

Key On Engine Running Test

See Figure 48

1. Make certain the self-test button is released or de-activated on the STAR tester.
2. Start the engine and run it at 2000 rpm for two minutes. This action warms up the oxygen sensor.
3. Turn the ignition switch **OFF** for 10 seconds.
4. Activate or latch the self-test button on the scan tool.
5. Start the engine. The engine identification code will be transmitted. This is a single digit number representing ½ the number of cylinders in a gasoline engine. On the STAR tester, this number may appear with a zero, i.e., 20 = 2. The code is used to confirm that the correct processor is installed and that the self-test has begun.

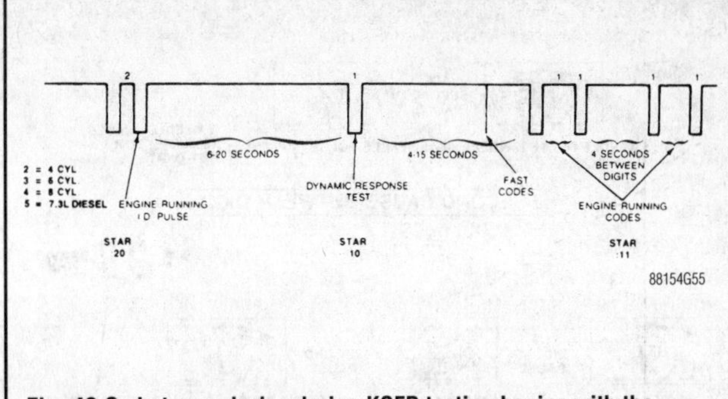

Fig. 48 Code transmission during KOER testing begins with the engine identification pulse and may include a dynamic response prompt

6. If the vehicle is equipped with a Brake On/Off (BOO) switch, the brake pedal must be depressed and released after the ID code is transmitted.
7. If the vehicle is equipped with a Power Steering Pressure Switch (PSPS), the steering wheel must be turned at least ½ turn and released within 2 seconds after the engine ID code is transmitted.
8. If the vehicle is equipped with the E40D transmission, the Overdrive Cancel Switch (OCS) must be cycled after the engine ID code is transmitted.
9. Certain Ford vehicles will display a Dynamic Response code 6,20 seconds after the engine ID code. This will appear as one pulse on a meter or as a 10 on the STAR tester. When this code appears, briefly take the engine to wide open throttle. This allows the system to test the throttle position, MAF and MAP sensors.
10. All relevant codes will be displayed and should be recorded. Remember that the codes refer only to faults present during this test cycle. Codes stored in Continuous Memory are not displayed in this test mode.
11. Do not depress the throttle during testing unless a dynamic response code is displayed.

Reading Codes With Analog Voltmeter

See Figures 49 and 50

In the absence of a scan tool, an analog voltmeter may be used to retrieve stored fault codes. Set the meter range to read DC 0–15 volts. Connect the positive lead of the meter to the battery positive terminal and connect the negative lead of the meter to the self-test output pin of the diagnostic connector.

Follow the directions given previously for performing the KOEO and KOER tests. To activate the tests, use a jumper wire to connect the signal return pin on the diagnostic connector to the self-test input connector. The self-test

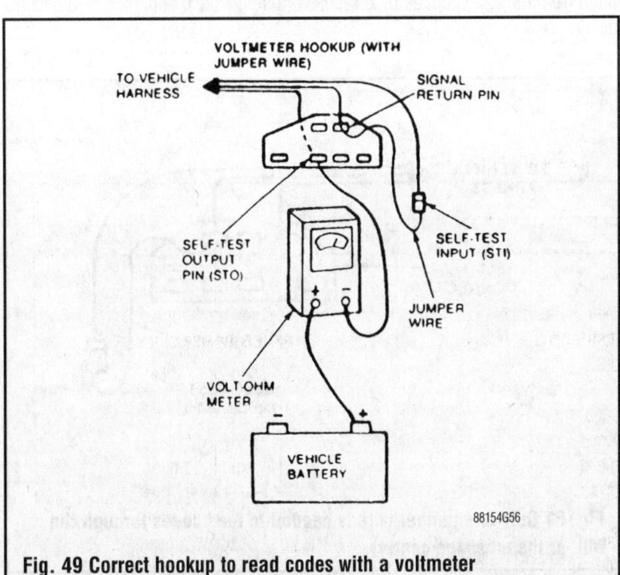

Fig. 49 Correct hookup to read codes with a voltmeter

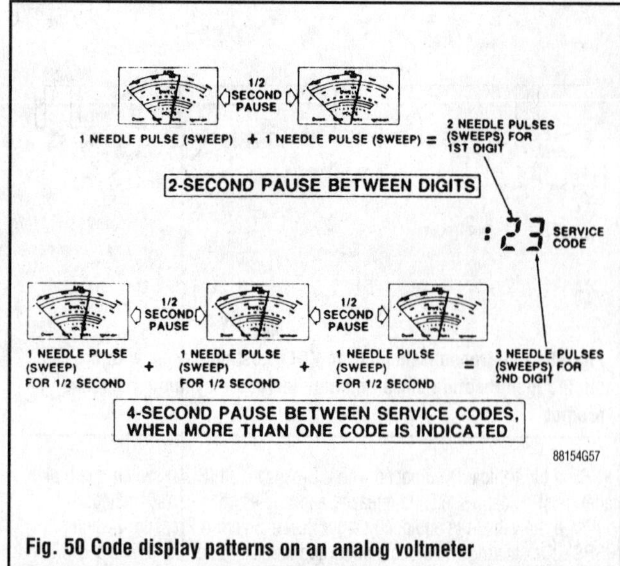

Fig. 50 Code display patterns on an analog voltmeter

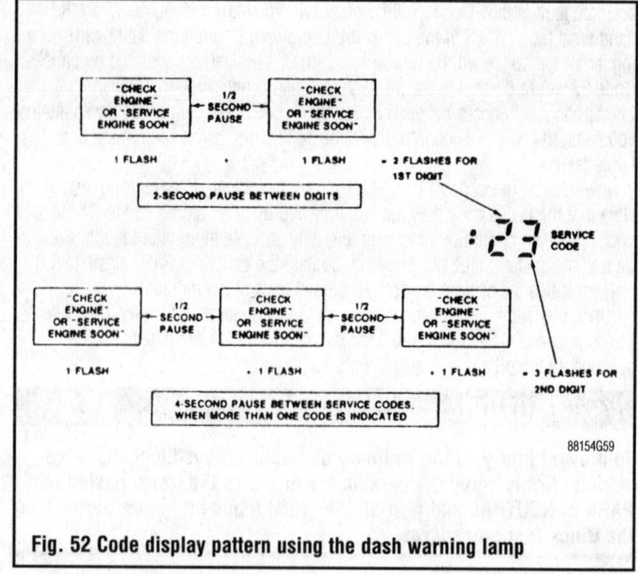

Fig. 52 Code display pattern using the dash warning lamp

input line is the separate wire and connector with or near the diagnostic connector.

The codes will be transmitted as groups of needle sweeps. This method may be used to read either 2 or 3 digit codes. The Continuous Memory codes are separated from the KOEO codes by 6 seconds, a single sweep and another 6 second delay.

Reading Codes With MIL

See Figures 51 and 52

The Malfunction Indicator Lamp (MIL) on the dashboard may also be used to retrieve the stored codes. This method displays only the stored codes and does not allow any system investigation. It should only be used in field conditions where a quick check of stored codes is needed.

Follow the directions given previously for performing the KOEO and KOER tests. To activate the tests, use a jumper wire to connect the signal return pin on the diagnostic connector to the self-test input connector. The self-test input line is the separate wire and connector with or near the diagnostic connector.

Codes are transmitted by place value with a pause between the digits; Code 32 would be sent as 3 flashes, a pause and 2 flashes. A slightly longer pause divides codes from each other. Be ready to count and record codes; the only way to repeat a code is to re-cycle the system. This method may be used to read either 2 or 3 digit codes. The Continuous Memory codes are separated from the KOEO codes by 6 seconds, a single flash and another 6 second delay.

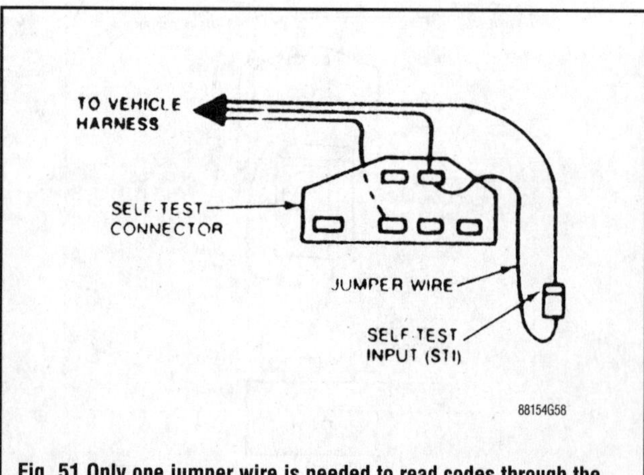

Fig. 51 Only one jumper wire is needed to read codes through the MIL or the message center

Other Test Modes

CONTINUOUS MONITOR OR WIGGLE TEST MODE

Once entered, this mode allows the technician to attempt to recreate intermittent faults by wiggling or tapping components, wiring or connectors. The test may be performed during either KOEO or KOER procedures. The test requires the use of either an analog voltmeter or a hand scan tool.

To enter the continuous monitor mode during KOEO testing, turn the ignition switch **ON**. Activate the test, wait 10 seconds, then deactivate and reactivate the test; the system will enter the continuous monitor mode. Tap, move or wiggle the harness, component or connector suspected of causing the problem; if a fault is detected, the code will be stored in the memory. When the fault occurs, the dash warning lamp will illuminate, the STAR tester will light a red indicator (and possibly beep) and the analog meter needle will sweep once.

To enter this mode in the KOER test:

1. Start the engine and run it at 2000 rpm for two minutes. This action warms up the oxygen sensor.
2. Turn the ignition switch **OFF** for 10 seconds.
3. Start the engine.
4. Activate the test, wait 10 seconds, then deactivate and reactivate the test; the system will enter the continuous monitor mode.
5. Tap, move or wiggle the harness, component or connector suspected of causing the problem; if a fault is detected, the code will be stored in the memory.
6. When the fault occurs, the dash warning lamp will illuminate, the STAR tester will light a red indicator (and possibly beep) and the analog meter needle will sweep once.

OUTPUT STATE CHECK

This testing mode allows the operator to energize and de-energize most of the outputs controlled by the EEC-IV system. Many of the outputs may be checked at the component by listening for a click or feeling the item move or engage by a hand placed on the case. To enter this check:

1. Enter the KOEO test mode.
2. When all codes have been transmitted, depress the accelerator all the way to the floor and release it.
3. The output actuators are now all ON. Depressing the throttle pedal to the floor again switches the all the actuator outputs OFF.
4. This test may be performed as often as necessary, switching between ON and OFF by depressing the throttle.
5. Exit the test by turning the ignition switch **OFF**,removing the jumper at the diagnostic connector or releasing the test button on the scan tool.

CYLINDER BALANCE TEST: SEFI ENGINES ONLY

The EEC-IV system allows a cylinder balance test to be performed on engines equipped with the Sequential Electronic Fuel Injection (SEFI) system. Cylinder balance testing identifies a weak or non-contributing cylinder.

1991-93 FORD EEC-IV VEHICLES 3-DIGIT QUICK TEST CODES—PASSENGER CARS

Service Codes / ENGINE (Liters) / FUEL SYSTEM	Quick Test Mode	2.3L OHC EFI	5.0L ① SEFI
111—System Pass	O/R/C	✓	✓
112—ACT sensor circuit grounded or reads 254°F	O/C	✓	✓
112—ACT sensor circuit grounded	O/R		
113—ACT sensor circuit open	O/R		
113—ACT sensor circuit open or reads −40°F	O/C	✓	✓
114—ACT outside test limits during KOEO or KOER tests	O/R	✓	✓
116—ECT outside test limits during KOEO or KOER tests	O/R	✓	✓
117—ECT sensor circuit grounded	O/C	✓	✓
118—ECT sensor circuit above maximum voltage or reads −40°F	O/C		✓
118—ECT sensor circuit open	O/C	✓	
121—Closed throttle voltage higher or lower than expected	O/R/C	✓	✓
122—TP sensor circuit below minimum voltage	O/C	✓	✓
123—TP sensor above maximum voltage	O/C	✓	✓
124—TP sensor voltage higher than expected, in range	C	✓	✓
125—TP sensor voltage lower than expected, in range	C	✓	✓
126—BP or MAP sensor higher or lower than expected	O/R/C	✓	
129—Insufficient MAF change during Dynamic Response test	R	✓	✓
136—HEGO shows system always lean (front)	R		
136—HEGO shows system always lean (left)	R		✓
137—HEGO shows system always rich (front)	R		
137—HEGO shows system always rich (left)	R		✓
139—No HEGO switching (front)	C		
139—No HEGO switching (left)	C		✓
144—No HEGO switching (right)	C		✓
144—No HEGO switching	C		
144—No HEGO switching detected	C	✓	
157—MAF sensor circuit below minimum voltage	C	✓	✓
158—MAF sensor circuit above maximum voltage	O/C	✓	✓
158—MAF sensor circuit above maximum voltage	O/R/C		
159—MAF higher or lower than expected during KOEO and KOER test	O/R	✓	✓
167—Insufficient TP change during Dynamic Response test	R	✓	✓
171—Fuel system at adaptive limit, HEGO unable to switch	C	✓	
171—Fuel system at adaptive limit, HEGO unable to switch (right)	C		
171—No HEGO switching; system at adaptive limit (rear)	C		
172—HEGO shows system always lean (rear)	R/C		
172—No HEGO switching seen; indicates lean	R/C	✓	
172—No HEGO switching seen; indicates lean (right)	R/C	✓	✓
173—HEGO shows system always rich (rear)	R/C		✓
173—No HEGO switching seen; indicates rich	R/C	✓	✓
173—No HEGO switching seen; indicates rich (right)	R/C		
174—HEGO switching time is slow (right)	C		✓
175—No HEGO switching; system at adaptive limit (front)	C		
175—No HEGO switching; system at adaptive limit (left)	C		✓
176—HEGO shows system always lean (front)	C		
176—HEGO shows system always lean (left)	C	✓	
177—HEGO shows system always lean (front)	C		
177—HEGO shows system always lean (left)	C		✓
178—HEGO switching time is slow (left)	C		✓
179—Fuel at lean adaptive limit at part throttle; system rich	C	✓	
179—System at lean adaptive limit at part throttle; system rich (rear)	C		
179—System at lean adaptive limit at part throttle; system rich (right)	C		✓
181—Fuel at rich adaptive limit at part throttle; system rich	C	✓	
181—System at rich adaptive limit at part throttle; system rich (rear)	C		
181—System at rich adaptive limit at part throttle; system rich (right)	C		✓
182—Fuel at lean adaptive limit at idle; system rich	C	✓	
182—System at lean adaptive limit at idle; system rich (rear)	C		
182—System at lean adaptive limit at idle; system rich (right)	C		✓
183—Fuel at rich adaptive limit at idle; system lean	C	✓	
183—System at rich adaptive limit at idle; system lean (rear)	C		
183—System at rich adaptive limit at idle; system lean (right)	C		✓
184—MAF higher than expected	C	✓	✓
185—MAF lower than expected	C	✓	✓
186—Injector pulse width higher than expected	C	✓	✓
187—Injector pulse width lower than expected	C	✓	✓
188—System at lean adaptive limit at part throttle; system rich (front)	C		
188—System at lean adaptive limit at part throttle; system rich (left)	C		✓
189—System at rich adaptive limit at part throttle; system rich (front)	C		
189—System at rich adaptive limit at part throttle; system rich (left)	C		✓
191—System at lean adaptive limit at idle; system rich (front)	C		
191—System at lean adaptive limit at idle; system rich (left)	C		✓
192—System at rich adaptive limit at idle; system rich (front)	C		
192—System at rich adaptive limit at idle; system rich (left)	C		✓
211—PIP circuit fault	C	✓	✓
212—Loss of IDM input to ECA or SPOUT circuit grounded	C	✓	✓
213—SPOUT circuit open	R	✓	✓
214—Cylinder identification circuit failure	C	✓	

88154G60

1991-93 FORD EEC-IV VEHICLES 3-DIGIT QUICK TEST CODES—PASSENGER CARS

Service Codes / ENGINE (Liters) / FUEL SYSTEM	Quick Test Mode	2.3L OHC EFI	5.0L ① SEFI
215—EEC processor detected Coil 1 primary circuit failure	C	✓	
216—EEC processor detected Coil 2 primary circuit fauilre	C	✓	
218—Loss of IDM signal, left side	C	✓	
219—Spark timing defaulted to 10°BTDC or SPOUT circ. open	C		
222—Loss of IDM signal, right side		✓	
223—Loss of dual plug inhibit control	C		
224—Erratic IDM input to rpocessor	C		
225—Knock not sensed during Dynamic Response test	R		
311—Thermactor air system inoperative (right)	R		✓
313—Thermactor air not bypassed during self-test	R		✓
314—Thermactor air system inoperative (left)	R		✓
326—PFE or DPFE circiut voltage lower than expected	R/C		
327—EVP or DPFE circuit below minimum voltage	O/R/C	✓	✓
328—EGR closed voltage lower than expected	O/R/C	✓	✓
332—Insufficient EGR flow detected	R/C	✓	✓
334—EGR closed voltage higher than expected	O/R/C	✓	✓
335—PFE or DPFE sensor voltage out of self-test range	O		
336—PFE sensor voltage higher than expected	R/C		
337—EVP or DPFE circuit above maximum voltage	O/R/C	✓	✓
341—Octane adjust service pin in use	O	✓	
411—Cannot control rpm during KOER low rpm check	R	✓	✓
412—Cannot control rpm during KOER high rpm check	R	✓	✓
452—Insufficient input from vehicle speed sensor	C	✓	✓
511—EEC processor ROM test failed	O	✓	✓
512—EEC processor Keep Alive Memory test failed	O		
512—EEC processor Keep Alive Memory test failed	C	✓	✓
513—Failure in EEC processor internal voltage	O		✓
519—Power steering pressure switch circuit open	O	✓	
521—Power steering pressure switch did not change state	R	✓	
522—Vehicle not in Park or Neutral during KOEO test	O	✓	✓
525—Vehicle in gear or A/C on during self-test	O		
528—Clutch switch circuit failure	C	✓	
536—Brake On/Off circuit failure/not actuated during KOER test	R/C	✓	
538—Insufficient rpm change during KOER Dynamic Response test	R	✓	✓
539—A/C on or Defroster on during KOEO test	O	✓	✓
542—Fuel pump secondary circuit failure: ECA to ground	O/C	✓	✓
543—Fuel pump secondary circuit failure: Batt to ECA	O/C	✓	✓
552—Air management 1 circuit failure	O		✓
556—Fuel pump primary circuit failure	O/C	✓	✓
558—EGR vacuum regulator circuit failure	O	✓	✓
563—High speed electro-drive fan circuit failure	O		
564—Electro-drive fan circiut failure	O	✓	
565—Canister purge circuit failure	O	✓	✓
566—3-4 shift solenoid circuit failure	O	✓	
621—Shift solenoid 1 circuit failure	O		
622—Shift solenoid 2 circuit failure	O		
624—EPC solenoid or driver circuit faiulre	O/C		
625—EPC driver open in ECA	O		
628—Lock-up solenoid failure: excessive clutch slippage	C		
629—Converter clutch control circuit failure	O	✓	
629—Lock-up solenoid failure	O		
634—MLP sensor voltage out of self-test range	C		
636—TOT sensor voltage out of self-test range	O/R		
637—TOT sensor circuit above maximum voltage	O/C		
638—TOT sensor circuit below maximum voltage	O/C		
639—Insufficient input from turbine speed sensor	R/C		
641—Shift solenoid 3 circuit failure	O		
645—Incorrect gear ratio obtained for 1st gear	C		
646—Incorrect gear ratio obtained for 2nd gear	C		
647—Incorrect gear ratio obtained for 3rd gear	C		
648—Incorrect gear ratio obtained for 4th gear	C		
649—EPC range failure	C		
651—EPC circuit failure	C		
998—Hard fault present	R	✓	✓

Codes not listed: Do not apply to vehicle being tested
No codes: Cannot perform self-test or cannot transmit codes
O—Key off, engine off test
R—Key on engine running test
C—Continuous codes
① Thunderbird and Cougar

88154G61

1989-93 FORD EEC-IV VEHICLES
2-DIGIT QUICK TEST CODES—PASSENGER CARS

Service Codes — ENGINE (Liters) / FUEL SYSTEM	Quick Test Mode	2.3L ① OHC EFI	5.0L SEFI (INC. MA)
11—System Pass	O/R/C	✓	✓
12—Rpm unable to achieve upper test limit	R	✓	✓
13—D.C. motor movement not detected	O		
13—Rpm unable to achieve lower test limit	R	✓	✓
13—D.C. motor did not follow dashpot	C		
14—PIP circuit failure	C	✓	✓
15—ECA read only memory test failed	O	✓	✓
15—ECA keep alive memory test failed	C	✓	✓
16—Idle rpm high with ISC off	R		
16—Idle too low to perform EGO test	R	✓	✓
17—Idle rpm low with ISC off	R		
18—SPOUT circuit open or spark angle word failure	R		✓
18—IDM circuit failure or SPOUT circuit grounded	C	✓	✓
19—Failure in ECA internal voltage	O	✓	✓
19—CID circuit failure	C		
19—Rpm dropped too low in ISC off test	R		
19—Rpm for EGR test not achieved	R		
21—ECT out of self-test range	O/R	✓	✓
22—BP sensor out of self-test range	O/C		✓
22—BP or map out of self-test range	O/R/C	✓	
23—TP out of self-test range	O/R	✓	✓
23—TP out of self-test range	O/R/C		
24—ACT sensor out of self-test range	O/R	✓	✓
25—Knock not sensed during dynamic test	R	✓	✓
26—VAF/MAF out of self-test range	O/R		✓
28—VAT out of self-test range	O/R		
29—Insufficient input from vehicle speed sensor	C		✓
31—PFE, EVP or EVR circuit below minimum voltage	O/R/C	✓	✓
32—EPT circuit voltage low (PFE)	R/C		
32—EVP voltage below closed limit	O/R/C		✓
32—EGR not controlling	R	✓	
33—EGR valve opening not detected	R/C		✓
33—EGR not closing fully	R	✓	
34—Defective PFE sensor or voltage out of range	O		
34—EPT sensor voltage high (PFE)	R/C		
34—EVP voltage above closed limit	O/R/C		✓
34—EGR opening not detected	R	✓	
35—PFE or EVP circuit above maximum voltage	O/R/C		✓
35—Rpm too low to perform EGR test	R	✓	
38—Idle tracking switch circuit open	C		
39—AXOD lock up failed	C		
41—HEGO sensor circuit indicates system lean	R	✓	✓③
41—No HEGO switching detected	R	✓	✓③
42—HEGO sensor circuit indicates system rich	R	✓	✓③
42—No HEGO switching detected—reads rich	C		
43—HEGO lean at wide open throttle	C		
44—Thermactor air system inoperative—right side	R		✓
45—Thermactor air upstream during self-test	R		✓
45—Coil 1 primary circuit failure	C		
46—Thermactor air not bypassed during self-test	R		✓
46—Coil 2 primary circuit failure	C		
47—Measured airflow low at base idle	R		
48—Coil 3 primary circuit failure	C		
48—Measured airflow high at base idle	R		
49—SPOUT signal defaulted to 10°BTDC or SPOUT open	C		
51—ECT/ACT reads −40°F or circuit open	O/C	✓	✓
52—Power steering pressure switch circuit open	O	✓	
52—Power steering pressure switch always open or closed	R		
53—TP circuit above maximum voltage	O/C	✓	✓
54—ACT sensor circuit open	O/C	✓	✓
55—Keypower circuit open	R		
56—VAF or MAF circuit above maximum voltage	O/C		✓
56—MAF circuit above maximum voltage	O/R/C		
57—Octane adjust service pin in use	O		
57—AXOD neutral pressure switch circuit failed open	C		
58—Idle tracking switch circuit open	O		
58—Idle tracking switch closed/circuit grounded	R		
58—VAT reads −40°F or circuit open	O/C		
59—Idle adjust service pin in use	O		
59—AXOD 4/3 pressure switch circuit failed open	C		
59—Low speed fuel pump circuit open—Battery to ECA	O/C		
59—AXOD 4/3 pressure switch failed closed	O		

88154G62

1989-93 FORD EEC-IV VEHICLES
2-DIGIT QUICK TEST CODES—PASSENGER CARS

Service Codes — ENGINE (Liters) / FUEL SYSTEM	Quick Test Mode	2.3L ① OHC EFI	5.0L SEFI (INC. MA)
61—ECT reads 254°F or circuit grounded	O/C	✓	✓
62—AXOD 4/3 or 3/2 pressure switch circuit grounded	O		
63—TP circuit below minimum voltage	O/C	✓	✓
64—ACT sensor input below test minimum or grounded	O/C	✓	✓
65—Never went to closed loop fuel control	C		
66—MAF sensor input below minimum voltage	C		✓
66—VAF sensor below minimum voltage	O/C		
66—MAF circuit below minimum voltage	R/C		
67—Neutral/drive switch open or A/C on	O	✓	✓
67—Clutch switch circuit failure	C		
67—Neutral/drive switch open or A/C on	O/R		
68—Idle tracking switch closed or circuit grounded	O		
68—Idle tracking switch circuit open	R		
68—AXOD transmission temperature switch failed open	O/R/C		
68—VAT reads 254°F or circuit grounded	O/C		
69—AXOD 3/2 pressure switch circuit failed closed	O		
69—AXOD 3/4 pressure switch circuit failed open	C		
70—ECA DATA communications link circuit failure	C		
71—Software re-initialization detected	C		
71—Idle tracking switch shorted to ground	C		
71—Cluster control assembly circuit failed	C		
72—Insufficient MAF/MAP change during dynamic test	R	✓	
72—Power interrupt or re-initialization detected	C		
72—Message Center control assembly circuit failed	C		
73—Insufficient throttle position change	O		
73—Insufficient TP change during dynamic test	R	✓	
74—Brake on/off switch failure or not actuated	R	✓	✓
75—Brake on/off switch circuit closed or ECA input open	R	✓	✓
76—Insufficient VAF change during dynamic test	R		
77—No WOT seen in self-test or operator error	R	✓	✓
79—A/C or defrost on during self-test	O		✓
81—IAS circuit failure	O		
81—Air management 2 circuit failure	O		✓
82—Air management 1 circuit failure	O		
82—Supercharger bypass circuit failure	O		
83—High-speed electro drive fan circuit failure	O		
83—Low speed primary fuel pump circuit failure	O/C		
84—EGR vacuum solenoid circuit failure	O	✓	✓
84—EGR vacuum regulator circuit failure	O/R		
85—Canister purge circuit failure	O/R		
85—Canister purge solenoid circuit failure	O		✓
85—Adaptive fuel lean limit reached	C		
86—3-4 shift solenoid circuit failure	O		
86—Adaptive fuel rich limit reached	C		
87—Fuel pump primary circuit failure	O/C		✓
87—Fuel pump primary circuit failure	O/C/R		
87—Fuel pump primary circuit failure	O	✓	
88—Electro drive fan circuit failure	O		
89—Converter clutch override circuit failure	O	✓	
89—Lock-up solenoid circuit failure	O		
91—HEGO sensor indicates system lean	R		✓④
91—No HEGO switching detected	C		✓④
92—HEGO sensor indicates system rich	R		✓④
93—TP sensor input low at maximum motor travel	O		
94—Thermactor air system inoperative—left side	R		✓
95—Fuel pump secondary circuit failure—ECA to ground	O/C		✓
96—Fuel pump secondary circuit failure—Battery to ECA	O/C		✓
96—High speed fuel pump circuit open	O/C		
98—Hard fault present	R	✓	✓
99—EEC has not learned to control idle: ignore codes 12 & 13	R		

No Codes: Cannot begin self-test or cannot transmit codes
Codes Not Listed: Do not apply to vehicle being tested
O—Key on, engine off test
R—Key on, engine running test
C—Continuous memory
① 1991-92: 3 digit codes
② Front HEGO
③ Right HEGO
④ Left HEGO
⑤ Rear HEGO

88154G63

Enter the cylinder balance test by depressing and releasing the throttle pedal within 2 minutes of the last code output in the KOER test. The idle speed will become fixed and engine rpm is recorded for later reference. The engine control assembly will shut off the fuel to the highest numbered cylinder (4 or 8), allow the engine to stabilize and then record the rpm. The injector is turned back on and the next one shut off and the process continues through cylinder No. 1.

The controller selects the highest rpm drop from all the cylinders tested, multiplies it by a percentage and arrives at an rpm drop value for all cylinders. For example, if the greatest drop for any cylinder was 150 rpm, the processor applies a multiple of 65% and arrives at 98 rpm. The processor then checks the recorded rpm drops, checking that each was at least 98 rpm. If all cylinders meet the criteria, the test is complete and the ECA outputs Code 90 indicating PASS.

If one cylinder did not drop at least this amount, then the cylinder number will be output instead of the 90 code. The cylinder number will be followed by a zero, so 30 indicates cylinder No. 3 did not meet the minimum rpm drop.

The test may be repeated a second time by depressing and releasing the throttle pedal within 2 minutes of the last code output. For the second test, the controller uses a lower percentage (and thus a lower rpm) to determine the minimum acceptable rpm drop. Again, either Code 90 or the number of the weak cylinder will be output.

Performing a third test causes the ECA to select an even lower percentage and rpm drop. If a cylinder is shown as weak in the third test, it should be considered non-contributing. The tests may be repeated as often as needed if the throttle is depressed within two minutes of the last code output. Subsequent tests will use the percentage from the third test instead of selecting even lower values.

CLEARING CODES

Continuous Memory Codes

These codes are retained in memory for 80 warm-up cycles. To clear the codes for the purposes of testing or confirming repair, perform the KOEO test. When the fault codes begin to be displayed, de-activate the test by either disconnecting the jumper wire (meter, MIL or message center) or releasing the test button on the hand scanner. Stopping the test during code transmission will erase the Continuous Memory. Do not disconnect the negative battery cable to clear these codes; the Keep Alive memory will be cleared and a new code, 19, will be stored for loss of ECA power.

Keep Alive Memory

The Keep Alive Memory (KAM) contains the adaptive factors used by the processor to compensate for component tolerances and wear. It should not be routinely cleared during diagnosis. If an emissions related part is replaced during repair, the KAM must be cleared. Failure to clear the KAM may cause severe driveability problems since the correction factor for the old component will be applied to the new component.

To clear the Keep Alive Memory, disconnect the negative battery cable for at least 5 minutes. After the memory is cleared and the battery reconnected, the vehicle must be driven at least 10 miles so that the processor may relearn the needed correction factors. The distance to be driven depends on the engine and vehicle, but all drives should include steady-throttle cruise on open roads. Certain driveability problems may be noted during the drive because the adaptive factors are not yet functioning.

VACUUM DIAGRAMS

➧ See Figures 53 thru 67

Following are vacuum diagrams for most of the engine and emissions package combinations covered by this manual. Because vacuum circuits will vary based on various engine and vehicle options, always refer first to the vehicle emission control information label, if present. Should the label be missing, or should the vehicle be equipped with a different engine from the vehicle's original equipment, refer to the diagrams below for the same or similar configuration.

If you wish to obtain a replacement emissions label, most manufacturers make the labels available for purchase. The labels can usually be ordered from a local dealer.

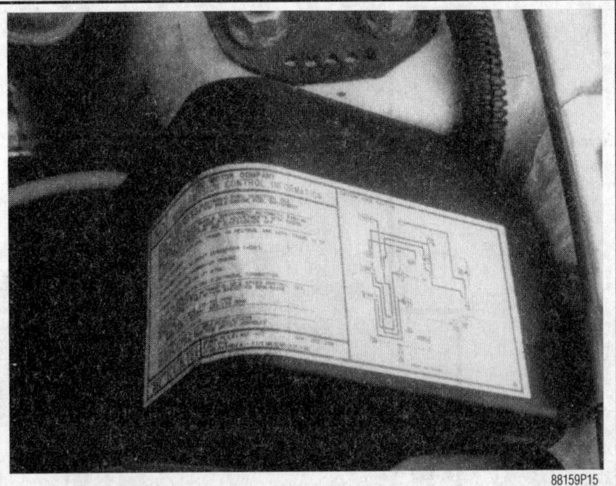

88159P15

Fig. 53 The vacuum diagram and emissions information is on a sticker under the hood of the car

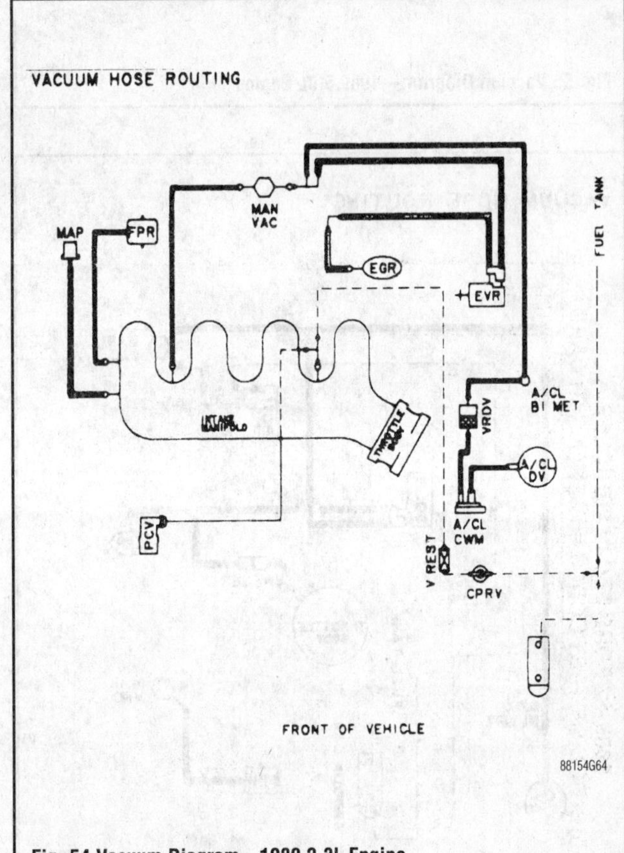

88154G64

Fig. 54 Vacuum Diagram—1989 2.3L Engine

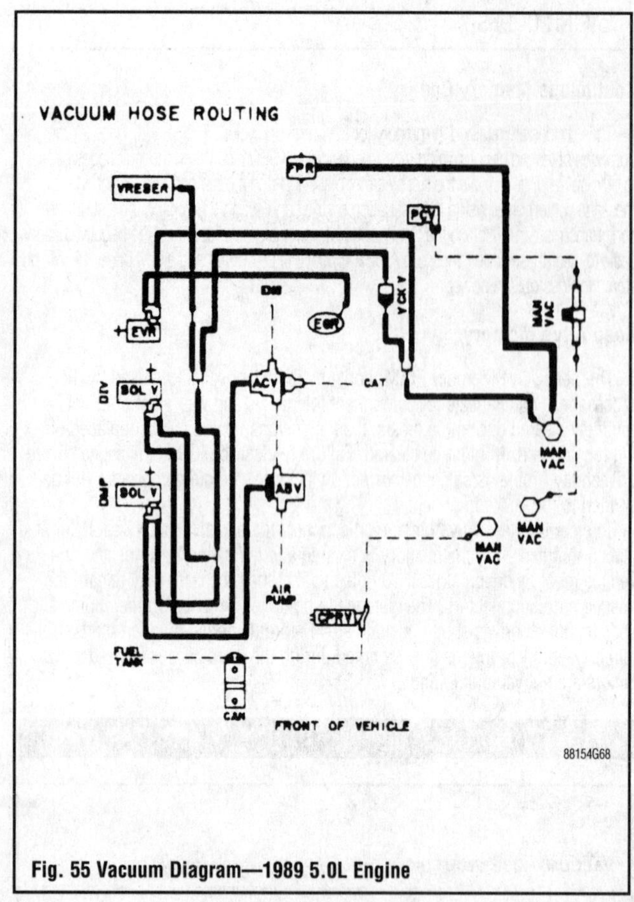

Fig. 55 Vacuum Diagram—1989 5.0L Engine

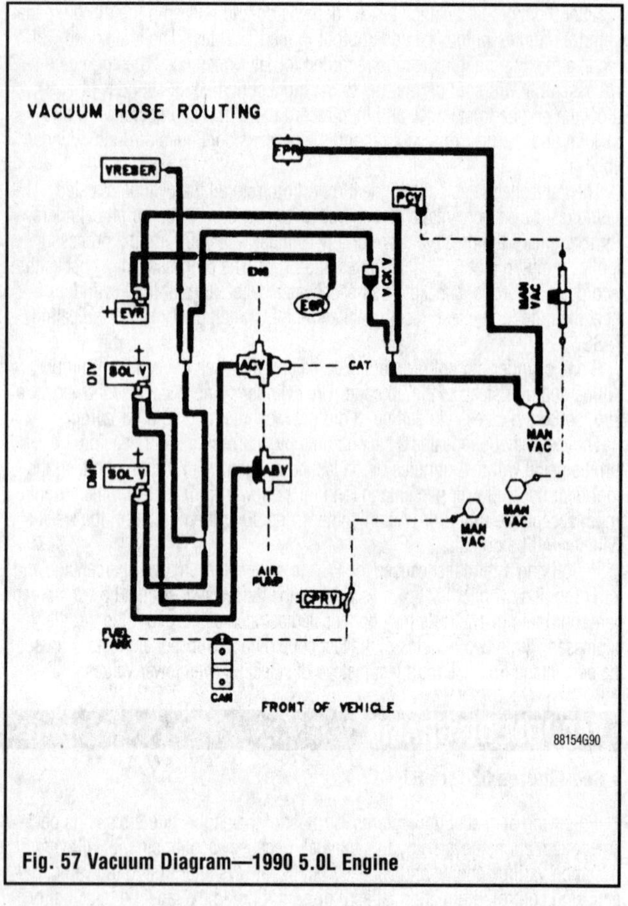

Fig. 57 Vacuum Diagram—1990 5.0L Engine

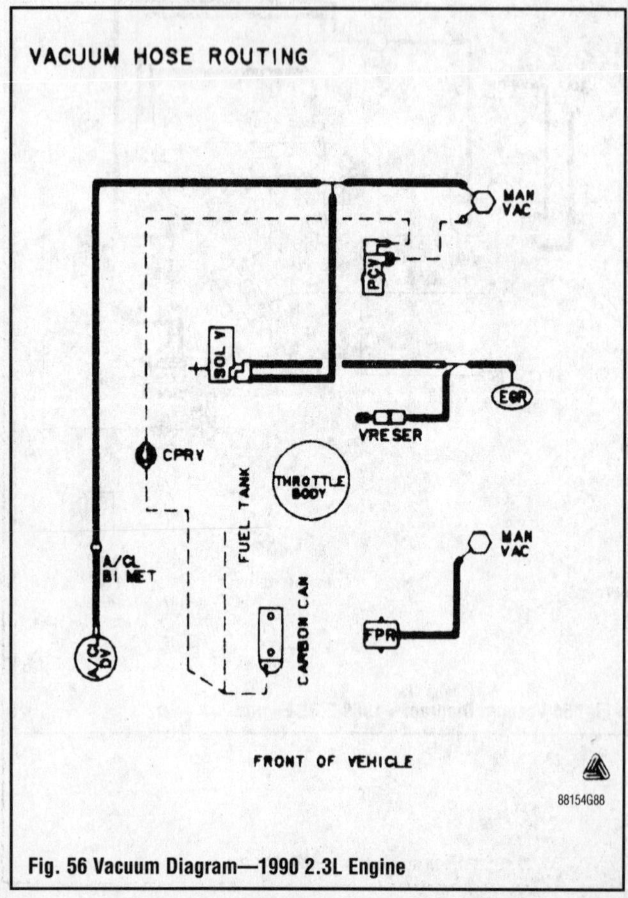

Fig. 56 Vacuum Diagram—1990 2.3L Engine

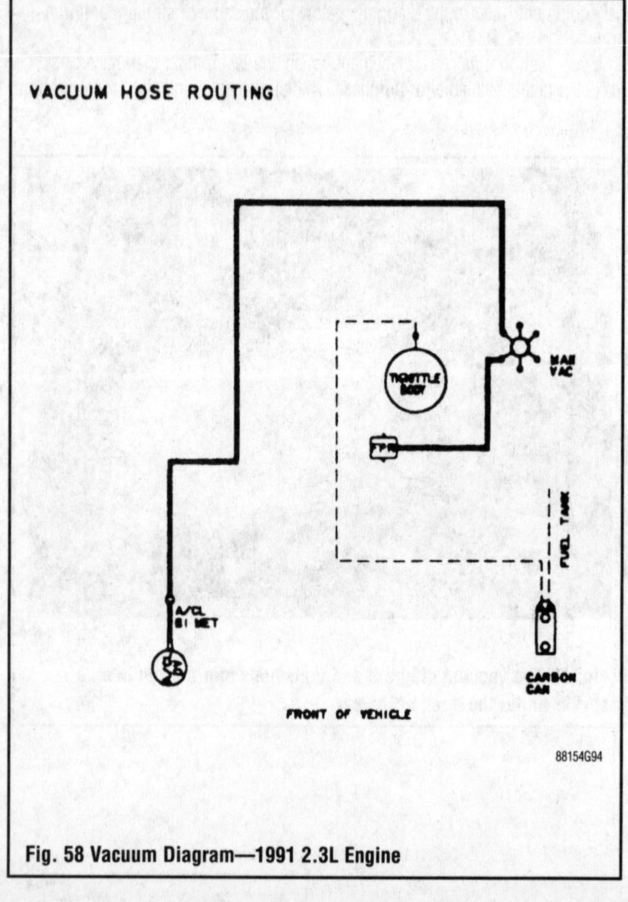

Fig. 58 Vacuum Diagram—1991 2.3L Engine

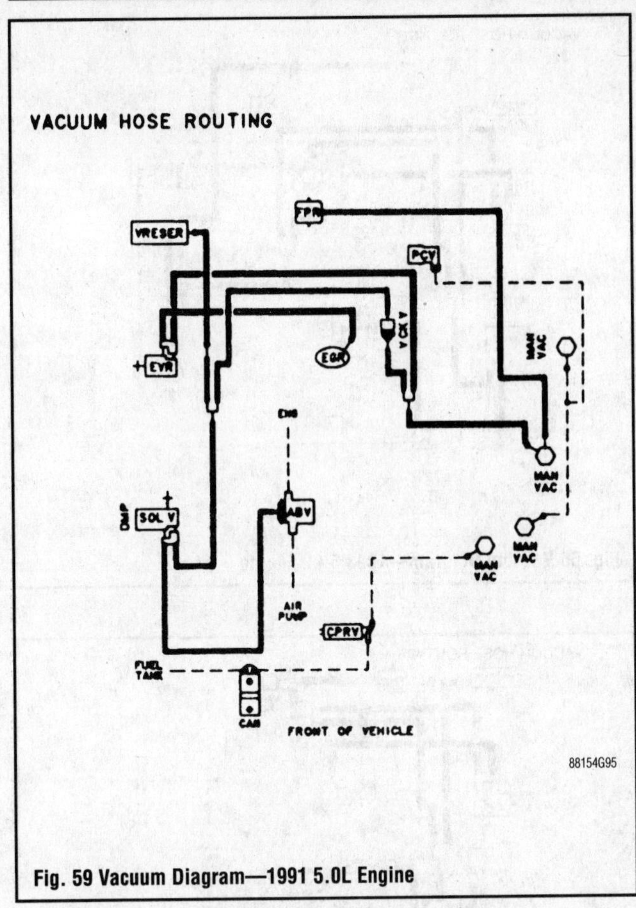

Fig. 59 Vacuum Diagram—1991 5.0L Engine

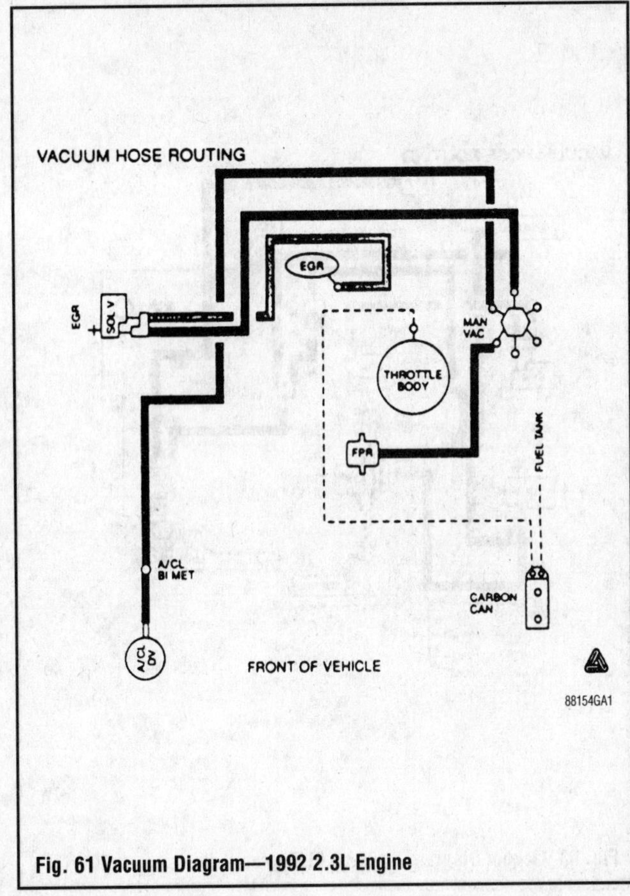

Fig. 61 Vacuum Diagram—1992 2.3L Engine

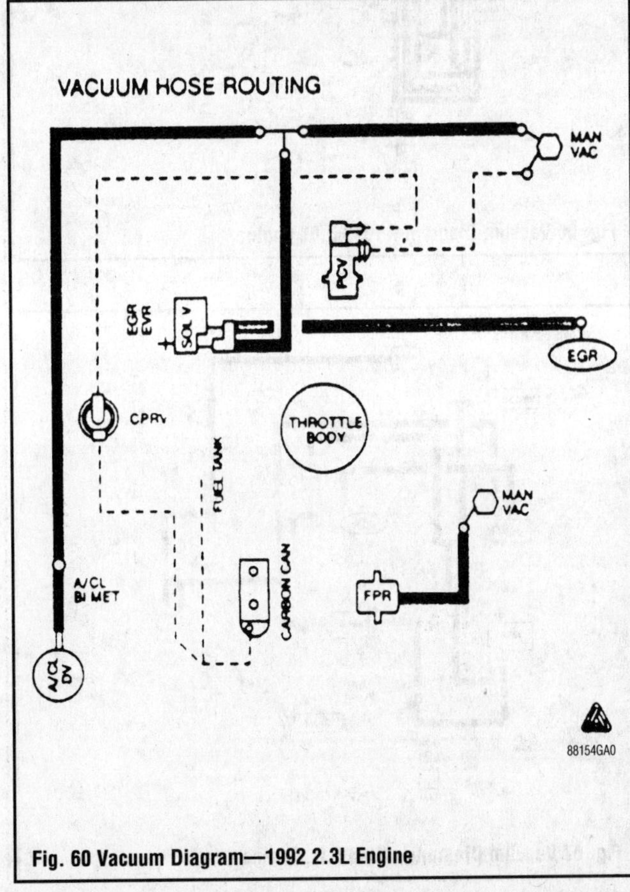

Fig. 60 Vacuum Diagram—1992 2.3L Engine

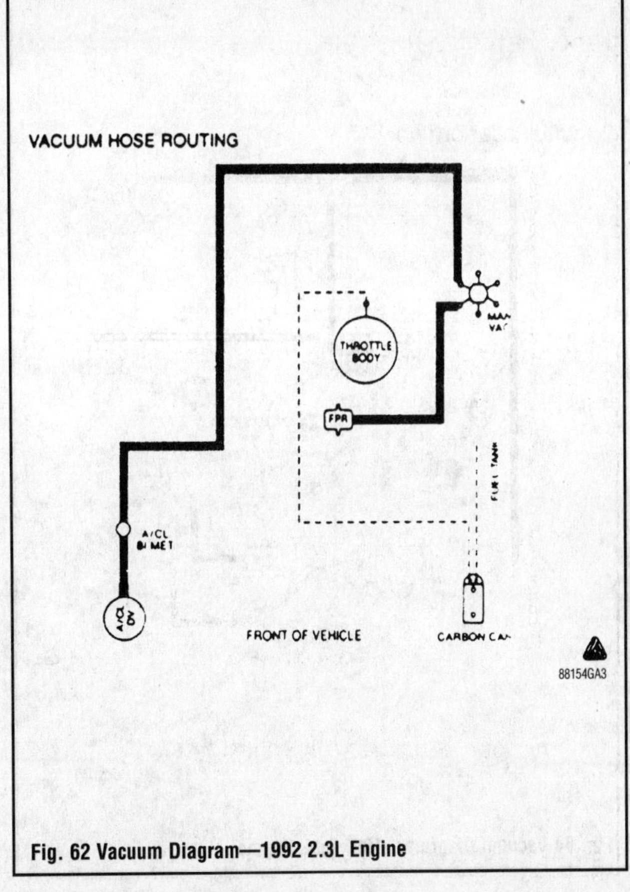

Fig. 62 Vacuum Diagram—1992 2.3L Engine

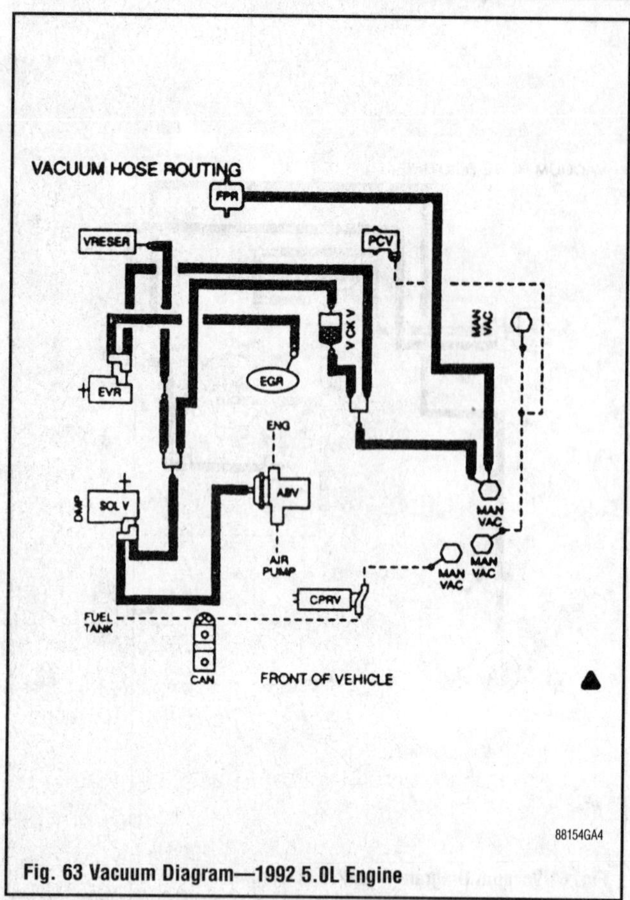

Fig. 63 Vacuum Diagram—1992 5.0L Engine

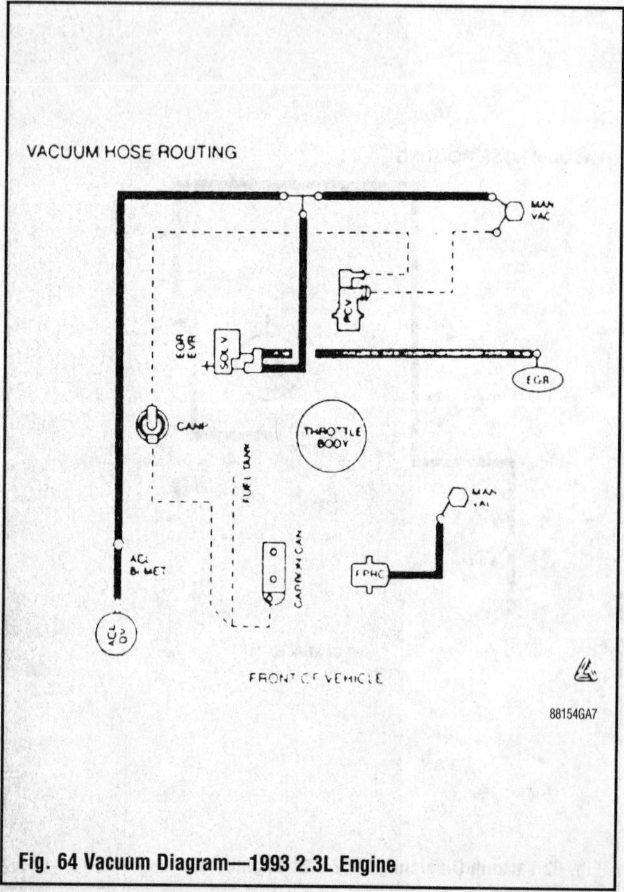

Fig. 64 Vacuum Diagram—1993 2.3L Engine

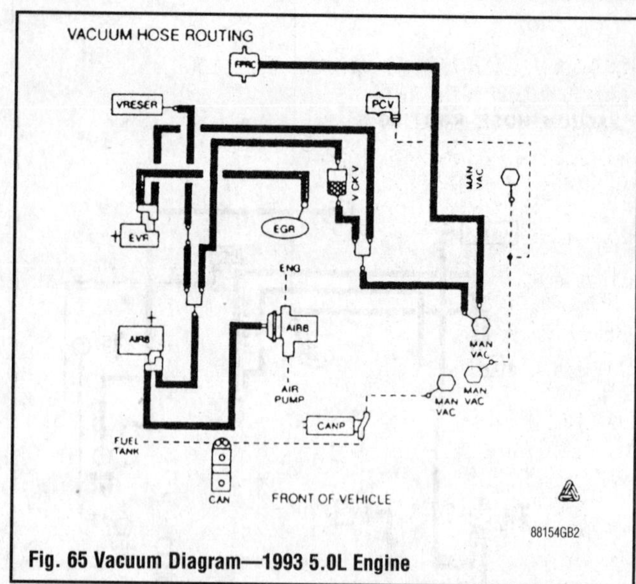

Fig. 65 Vacuum Diagram—1993 5.0L Engine

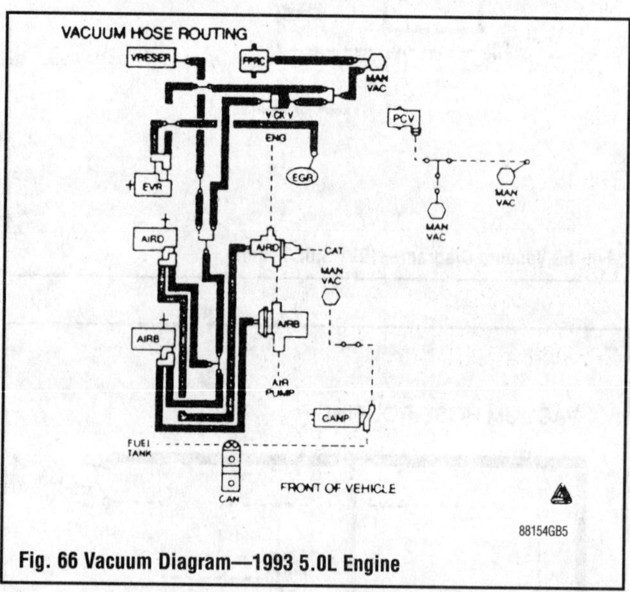

Fig. 66 Vacuum Diagram—1993 5.0L Engine

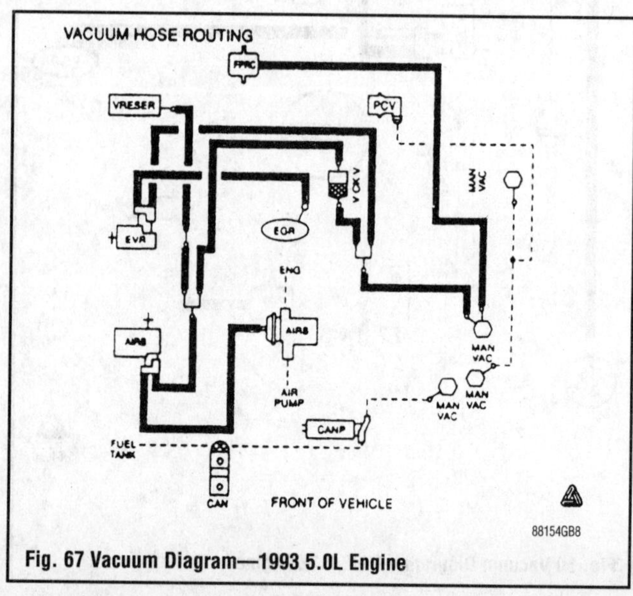

Fig. 67 Vacuum Diagram—1993 5.0L Engine

5

FUEL SYSTEM

BASIC FUEL SYSTEM DIAGNOSIS

When there is a problem starting or driving a vehicle, two of the most important checks involve the ignition and the fuel systems. The questions most mechanics attempt to answer first, "is there spark?" and "is there fuel?" will often lead to solving most basic problems. For ignition system diagnosis and testing, please refer to the information on engine electrical components and ignition systems found earlier in this manual. If the ignition system checks out (there is spark), then you must determine if the fuel system is operating properly (is there fuel?).

MULTI-POINT (EFI) AND SEQUENTIAL (SEFI) FUEL INJECTION SYSTEMS

Description and Operation

See Figures 1, 2, 3, 4 and 5

The Multi-point (EFI) and Sequential (SEFI) fuel injection sub-systems include a high pressure, in-line electric fuel pump, a low pressure, tank-mounted fuel pump, fuel charging manifold, pressure regulator, fuel filter and both solid and flexible fuel lines. The fuel charging manifold includes 4 or 8 electronically-controlled fuel injectors, each mounted directly above an intake port in the lower intake manifold. On the 4-cylinder EFI system, all injectors are energized simultaneously and spray once every crankshaft revolution, delivering a predetermined quantity of fuel into the intake air stream. On the V8 EFI engines, the injectors are energized in 2 banks of four, once each crankshaft revolution. On the SEFI system, each injector fires once every crankshaft revolution, in sequence with the engine firing order.

The fuel pressure regulator maintains a constant pressure drop across the injector nozzles. The regulator is referenced to intake manifold vacuum and is connected in parallel to the fuel injectors; it is positioned on the far end of the fuel rail. Any excess fuel supplied by the fuel pump passes through the regulator and is returned to the fuel tank via a return line.

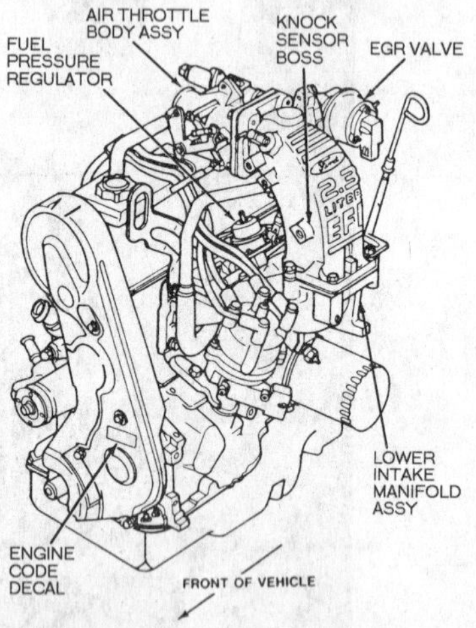

Fig. 1 General layout of the fuel injection system on the 2.3L engine

Fig. 2 Most of the fuel related parts are accesible from the top of the engine as shown on this 5.0L engine

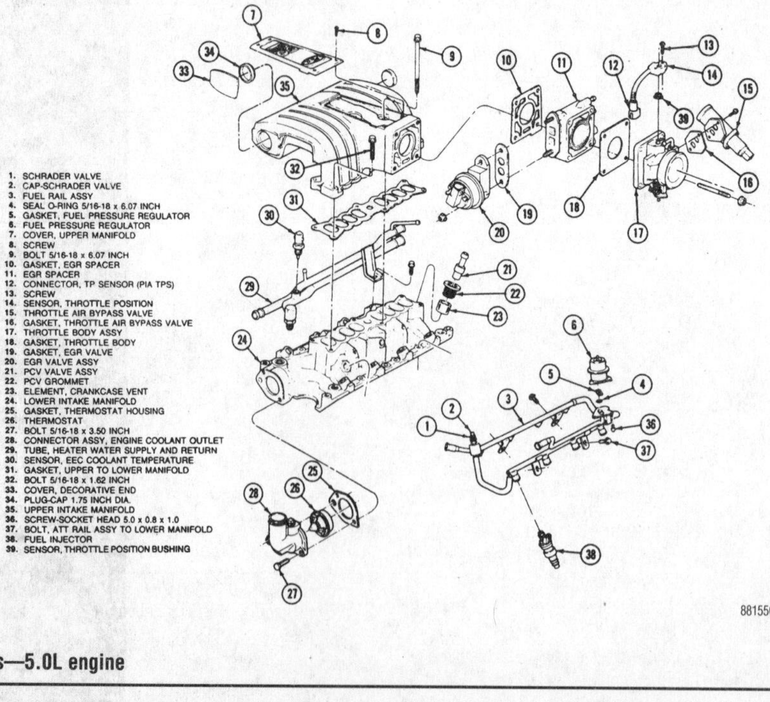

Fig. 3 Fuel supply components—5.0L engine

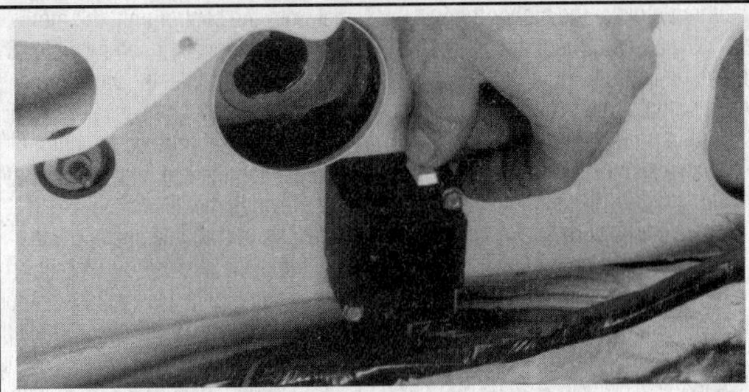

Fig. 4 The inertia switch is reset by pushing the buttom mounted on top. The switch is located behind the rear panel in the truck where the lights are

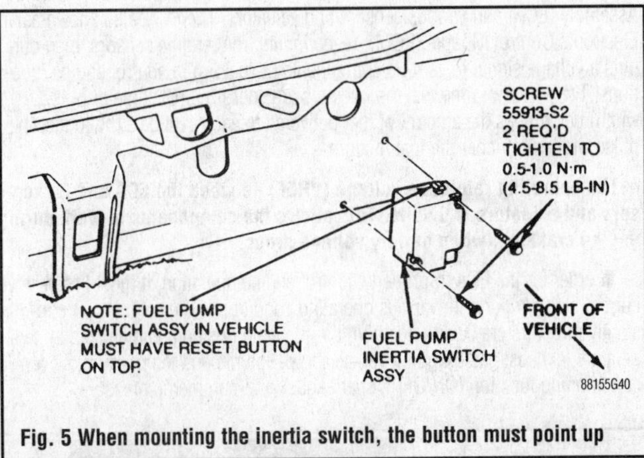

Fig. 5 When mounting the inertia switch, the button must point up

➡The pressure regulator reduces fuel pressure to 39–40 psi under normal operating conditions. At idle or high manifold vacuum condition, fuel pressure is further reduced to approximately 30 psi.

The fuel pressure regulator is a diaphragm-operated relief valve, in which the inside of the diaphragm senses fuel pressure and the other side senses manifold vacuum. Normal fuel pressure is established by a spring preload applied to the diaphragm. control of the fuel system is maintained through the EEC-IV control unit, although electrical power is routed through the fuel pump relay and an inertia switch. The fuel pump relay is normally located on a bracket somewhere above the Electronic Control Assembly (ECA) and the inertia switch is located in the trunk. The in-line fuel pump is usually mounted on a bracket at the fuel tank, or on a frame rail. Tank-mounted pumps can be either high- or low-pressure, depending on the model.

The inertia switch opens the power circuit to the fuel pump in the event of a collision. Once tripped, the switch must be reset manually by pushing the reset button on the assembly.

➡ Check that the inertia switch is reset before diagnosing power supply problems to the fuel pump.

FUEL SYSTEM COMPONENTS

Fuel Injectors

➧ See Figures 6, 7 and 8

The fuel injectors used with the EFI and SEFI system are electro-mechanical (solenoid) type, designed to meter and atomize fuel delivered to the intake ports of the engine. The injectors are mounted in the lower intake manifold and positioned so that their spray nozzles direct the fuel charge in front of the intake valves. The injector body consists of a solenoid-actuated pintle and needle-valve assembly.The control unit sends an electrical impulse that activates the solenoid, causing the pintle to move inward off the seat and allow the fuel to flow. The amount of fuel delivered is controlled by the length of time the injector is energized (pulse width), since the fuel flow orifice is fixed and the fuel pressure drop across the injector tip is constant. Correct atomization is achieved by contouring the pintle at the point where the fuel enters the pintle chamber.

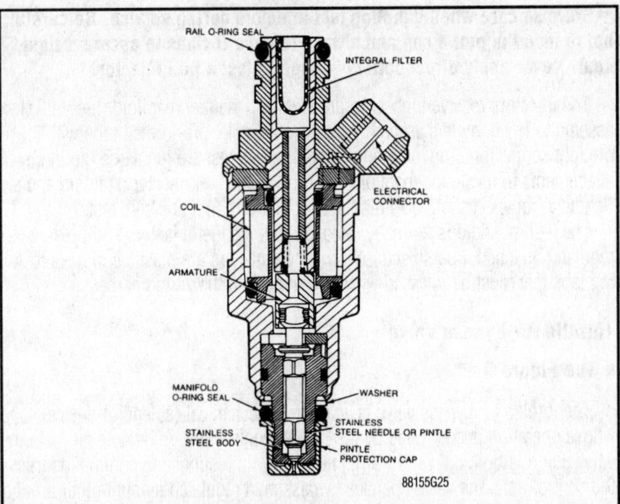

Fig. 6 The cross section of a fuel injector shows the precision construction that allows the injector to meter such fine quantities of fuel

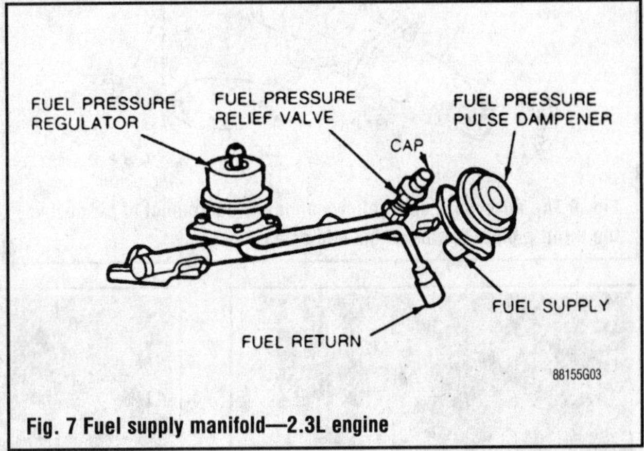

Fig. 7 Fuel supply manifold—2.3L engine

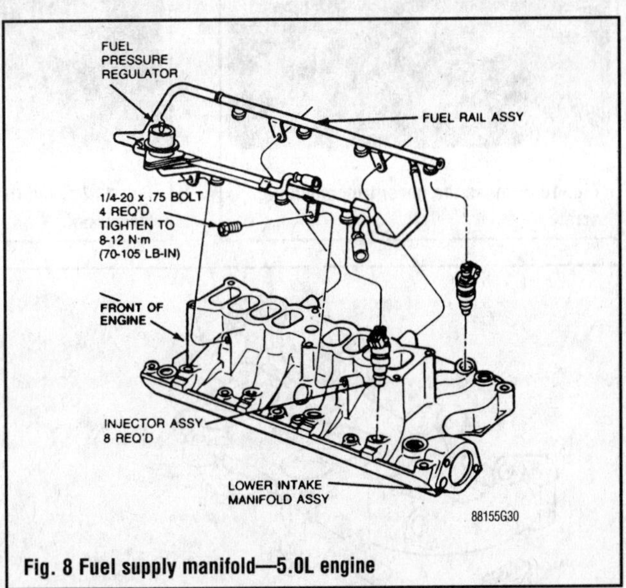

Fig. 8 Fuel supply manifold—5.0L engine

➡Exercise care when handling fuel injectors during service. Be careful not to lose the pintle cap and always replace O-rings to assure a tight seal. Never apply direct battery voltage to test a fuel injector.

The injectors receive high-pressure fuel from the fuel manifold (fuel rail) assembly. The complete assembly includes a single, pre-formed tube with four or eight connectors, the mounting flange for the pressure regulator, mounting attachments to locate the manifold and provide the fuel injector retainers and a Schrader® quick-disconnect fitting used to perform fuel pressure tests.

The fuel manifold is normally removed with the fuel injectors and pressure regulator attached. Fuel injector electrical connectors are plastic and have locking tabs that must be released when disconnecting the wiring harness.

Throttle Air Bypass Valve

➧ See Figure 9

The throttle air bypass valve is an electro-mechanical (solenoid) device whose operation is controlled by the EEC-IV control unit. A variable air metering valve controls both cold and warm idle air flow in response to commands from the control unit. The valve operates by passing a regulated amount of air around the throttle plate; the higher the voltage signal from the control unit, the more air is bypassed through the valve. In this manner, additional air can be added to the fuel mixture without moving the throttle plate. At curb idle, the valve provides smooth idle for various engine coolant temperatures, compensates for air conditioning load and compensates for transaxle load and no-load conditions. The valve also provides fast idle for start-up, replacing the fast idle cam, throttle kicker and anti-dieseling solenoid common to previous models.

There are no curb idle or fast idle adjustments. As in curb idle operation, the fast idle speed is proportional to engine coolant temperature. Fast idle kick-down will occur when the throttle is kicked. A time-out feature in the ECA will also automatically kick down fast idle to curb idle after approximately 15–25 seconds after coolant has reached approximately 160° F (71° C). The signal duty cycle from the ECA to the valve will be at 100% (maximum current) during the crank to provide maximum air flow to allow no-touch starting at any time (engine hot or cold).

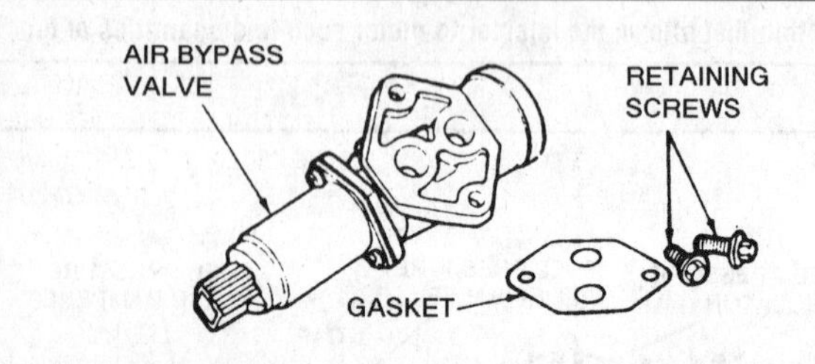

Fig. 9 The air bypass valve allows a measured amount of air past the throttle plate to control the idle speed

Electronic Engine Control

➧ See Figures 10, 11, 12, 13 and 14

The electronic engine control sub-system consists of the Electronic Control Assembly (ECA) and various sensors and actuators. The ECA, also known as an Electronic Control Module (ECM), reads inputs from engine sensors, then outputs a voltage signal to various components (actuators) to control engine functions. The period of time that the injectors are energized (ON time or pulse width) determines the amount of fuel delivered to each cylinder. The longer the pulse width, the richer the fuel mixture.

➡The operating reference voltage (VREF) between the ECA and its sensors and actuators is 5 volts. This allows the components to work during engine cranking, when battery voltage drops.

In order for the ECA to properly control engine operation, it must first receive current status reports on various operating conditions. The control unit constantly monitors crankshaft position, throttle plate position, engine coolant temperature, exhaust gas oxygen level, air intake volume and temperature, air conditioning function (ON/OFF), spark knock and barometric pressure.

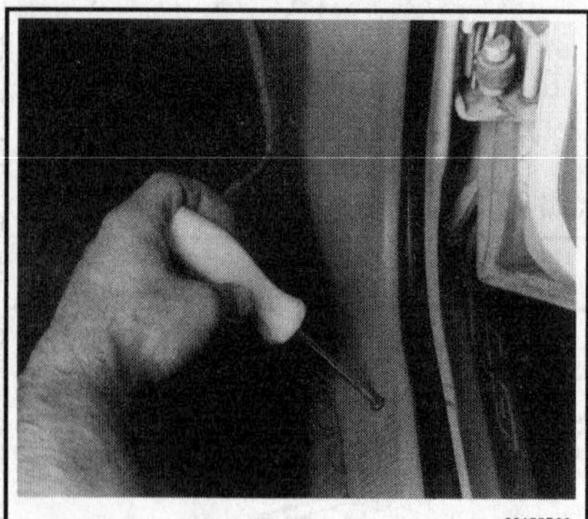

Fig. 10 Remove the lower trim mounting screw

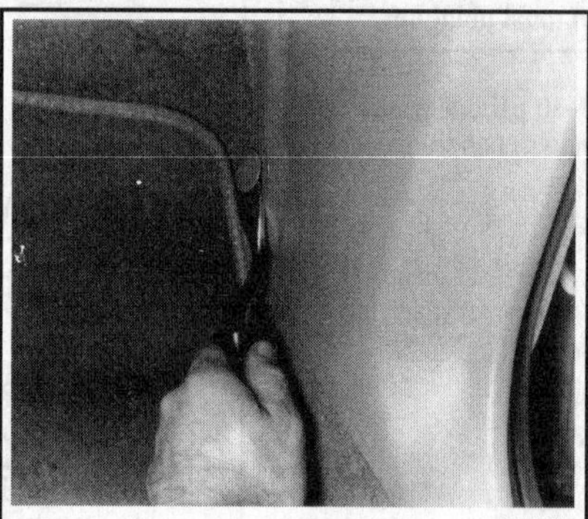

Fig. 11 Pry out the plastic fasteners on the kick panel

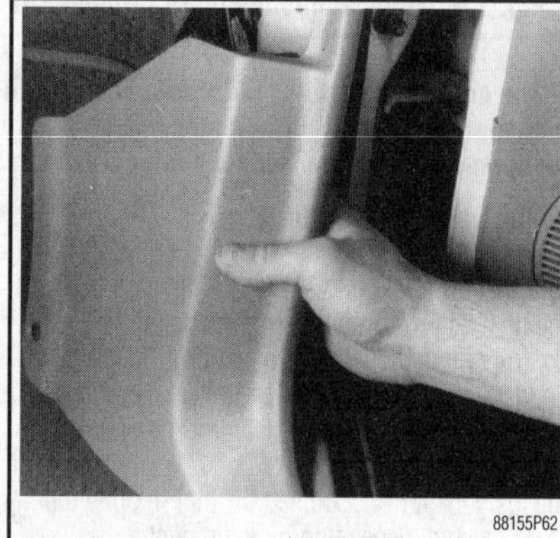

Fig. 12 Remove the kick panel

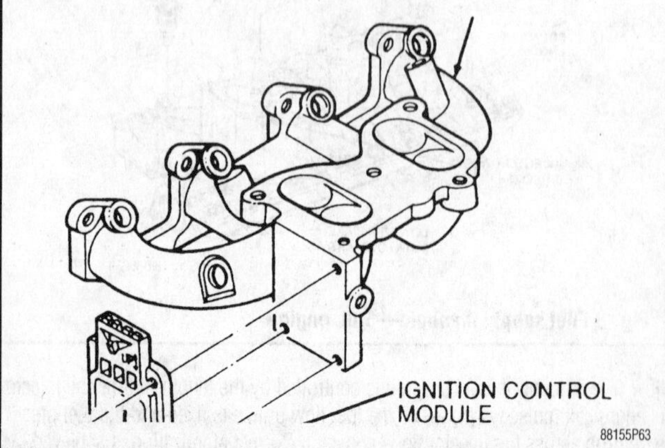

Fig. 13 Remove the insulation

Fig. 14 The computer is hidden in the passenger side kick panel

Universal Distributor

The primary function of the TFI-IV ignition system universal distributor is to direct the high secondary voltage to the spark plugs. In addition, it supplies crankshaft position and frequency information to the ECA using a Profile Ignition Pickup (PIP) sensor in place of the magnetic pickup or the crankshaft position sensor used on other models. This distributor does not have any mechanical or vacuum advance. The universal distributor assembly is adjustable for resetting base timing, if required, by disconnecting the SPOUT connector.

➡The PIP replaces the crankshaft position sensor found on other EEC-IV models.

The PIP sensor has an armature with four windows and four metal tabs that rotate past the stator assembly (Hall-effect switch). When a metal tab enters the stator assembly, a positive signal is sent to the ECA , indicating the 10°BTDC crankshaft position. The ECA calculates the precise time to energize the spark output signal to the TFI module. When the TFI module receives the spark output signal, it shuts off the coil primary current and the collapsing field energizes the secondary output.

➡Mis-adjustment of the base timing affects the spark advance in the same manner as a conventional, solid-state ignition system.

Thick Film Ignition (TFI-IV) Module

The TFI-IV module has six connector pins at the engine wiring harness that supply the following signals:

- Ignition switch in **RUN**.
- Engine cranking
- Tachometer
- PIP (crankshaft position to ECA)
- Spark advance (from ECA)
- Internal ground from the ECA to the distributor.

The TFI-IV module supplies the spark to the distributor through the ignition coil and calculates the duration. It receives its control signal from the ECA (spark output).

Distributorless Ignition System (DIS)

The DIS systems eliminate the need for a distributor by using multiple coils, which fire two spark plugs at the same time. This system uses either a dual-function crank sensor or a crank sensor and cam sensor. The cam sensor provides the cylinder identification (CID) signal, used to choose which coil to fire. The crank sensor provides a PIP signal for spark timing. The dual-function crank sensor provides both PIP and CID signals to the DIS module.

Distributorless Ignition System Module

The DIS module controls coil firing from the ECA commands similar to the way the TFI-IV module does. The DIS module functions include:

- Selection of coils
- Driving of coils
- Driving of tachometer
- PIP (crankshaft position to ECA)
- CID (cylinder identification)
- LOS (limited operating system base timing)

Throttle Position (TP) Sensor

➧ See Figure 15

The TP sensor is mounted on the throttle body. This sensor provides the ECA with a signal that indicates the angle of the throttle plate. The sensor output signal uses the 5-volt reference voltage previously described. From this input, the ECA controls:

1. Operating modes, which are Wide-Open Throttle (WOT), Part-Throttle (PT) and Closed-Throttle (CT).
2. Fuel enrichment at WOT.
3. Additional spark advance at WOT.
4. EGR cut-off during WOT, deceleration and idle.
5. Air conditioning cut-off at WOT (30 second maximum)
6. Cold start kick-down

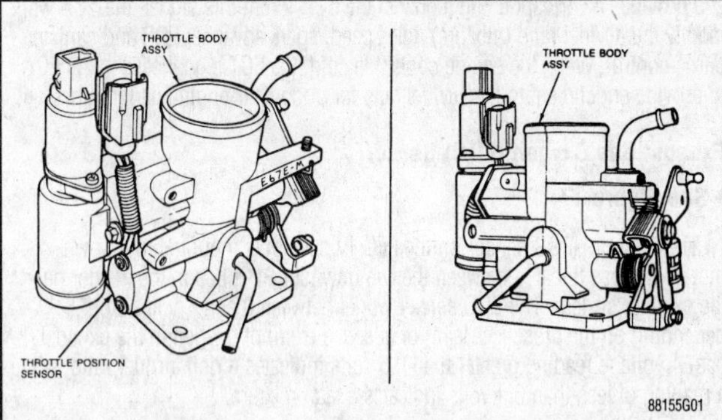

Fig. 15 The throttle position sensor mounts on the end of the throttle shaft on all engines

7. Fuel cut off during deceleration.
8. WOT de-choke during cranking or starting.

On the EEC-IV system, the TP sensor signal to the ECA only changes the spark timing during the WOT mode. As the throttle plate rotates, the TP sensor varies its voltage output. As the throttle plate moves from a closed position to a WOT position, the voltage output of the TP sensor will change from a low voltage (approximately 1.0 volt) to a high voltage (approximately 4.75 volts) If the TP sensor used is not adjustable it must be replaced if it is out of specification. The EEC-IV programming compensates for differences between sensors.

Engine Coolant Temperature (ECT) Sensor

➧ See Figure 16

The ECT sensor is located either in the heater supply tube, or in the lower intake manifold. The ECT sensor is a thermistor which changes resistance as a function of temperature. The sensor detects the temperature of the engine coolant

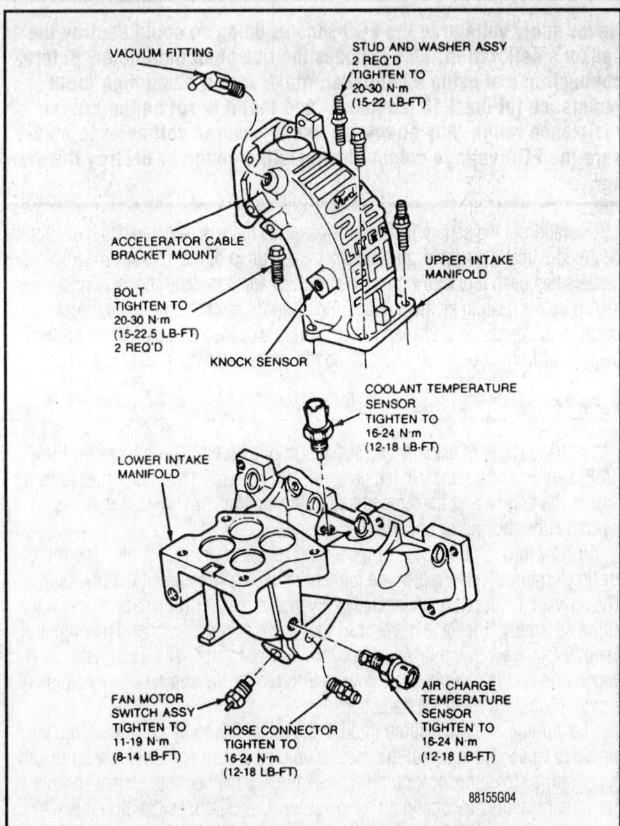

Fig. 16 The coolant temperature sensor will be placed in a coolant passage such as it is on this 2.3L engine. On the 5.0L engine it is in the heater water supply tube on the intake manifold

and provides a corresponding signal to the ECA. From this signal, the ECA will modify the air/fuel ratio (mixture), idle speed, spark advance, EGR and canister purge control. When the engine coolant is cold, the ECT signal causes the ECA to provide enrichment to the air/fuel ratio for good cold-engine performance.

Exhaust Gas Oxygen (EGO) Sensor

▸ See Figure 17

The EGO or HEGO sensor on the EEC-IV system is mounted in its own mounting boss, located between the two downstream tubes in the header near the exhaust system. The EGO sensor works between 0 and 1 volt output, depending on the presence (lean) or absence (rich) of oxygen in the exhaust gas. A voltage reading greater than 0.6 volts indicates a rich air/fuel ratio, while a reading of less than 0.4 volts indicates a lean mixture.

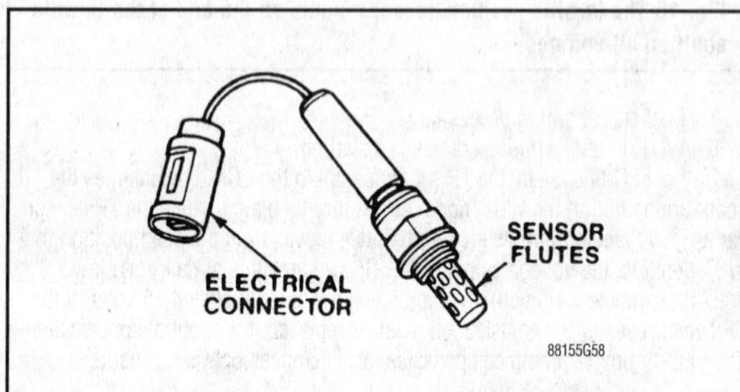

Fig. 17 The exhaust gas oxygen sensor reacts to the level of oxygen in the exhaust stream allowing the fuel injection to adjust the mixture

⁂ WARNING

Never apply voltage to the EGO sensor; doing so could destroy the sensor's calibration. This includes the use of an ohmmeter. Before connecting and using a voltmeter, make sure it has a high input resistance (at least 10 megohms) and that it is set on the proper resistance range. Any attempt to use a powered voltmeter to measure the EGO voltage output directly will damage or destroy the sensor.

Operation of the sensor is the same previous models. A difference that should be noted is that the rubber protective cap used on to of the sensor on earlier models has been replaced with a metal cap. In addition, later model sensors incorporate a heating element (HEGO) to bring the sensor up to operating temperature more quickly and keep it there during extended idle periods to prevent the sensor from cooling off and placing the system into open-loop operation.

Vane Meter

The vane meter is actually two sensors in one assembly—a Vane Air Flow (VAF) sensor and a Fane Air Temperature (VAT) sensor. This meter measures air flow to the engine and the temperature of the air stream. The vane meter is located either behind or under the air cleaner.

Air flow through the body moves a vane mounted on a pivot pin. The more air flowing through the meter, the further the vane rotates about the pivot pin. The air vane pivot pin is connected to a variable resistor (potentiometer) on top of the assembly. The vane meter uses the 5-volt reference signal. The output of the potentiometer to the ECA varies between 0 volts and VREF (5 volts), depending on the volume of air flowing through the sensor. A higher volume of air will produce a higher voltage output.

The volume of air measured through the meter has to be converted into an air-mass value. The mass of the specific volume of air varies with pressure and temperature. To compensate for these variables, a temperature sensor in front of the vane measures incoming air temperature. The ECA uses the air temperature and a programmed pressure value to convert the VAF signal into a mass airflow value. This value is used to calculate the fuel flow necessary for the optimum air/fuel ratio. The VAT also affects spark timing as a function of air temperature.

Air Conditioning Clutch Compressor (ACC) Signal

Any time battery voltage is applied to the A/C clutch, the same signal is also applied to the ECA. The ECA then maintains the engine idle speed with the throttle air bypass valve control solenoid to compensate for the added load created by the A/C clutch operation. Shutting down the air conditioning will have a reverse effect. The ECA will maintain the engine idle speed at 850–950 rpm.

Knock Sensor

The knock sensor is used to detect detonation. In situations of excessive knock, the ECA receives a signal from this sensor and retards the spark accordingly. It is mounted in the lower intake manifold at the rear of the engine.

Barometric (BAP) Sensor

▸ See Figure 18

The barometric pressure sensor is used to compensate for altitude variations. From this signal, the ECA modifies the air/fuel ratio, spark timing, idle speed and EGR flow. The barometric sensor is a design that produces a frequency based on atmospheric pressure (altitude). The sensor is mounted on the right fender apron.

Manifold Absolute Pressure (MAP) Sensor

The MAP sensor measures manifold vacuum and outputs a variable frequency. This gives the ECA information on engine load. It replaces the BAP sensor by providing the ECA updated barometric pressure readings during Key ON/Engine OFF and wide-open throttle. The MAP sensor output is used by the ECA to control spark advance, EGR flow and air/fuel ratio.

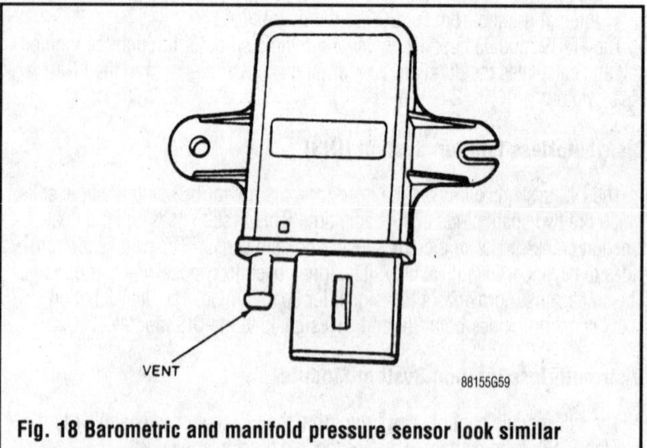

Fig. 18 Barometric and manifold pressure sensor look similar

EGR Shut-off Solenoid

The electrical signal to the EGR shut-off solenoid is controlled by the ECA. The signal is either ON or OFF. It is OFF during cold start, closed throttle or WOT. It is ON at all other times.

➡The canister purge valve is controlled by vacuum from the EGR solenoid. The purge valve is a standard valve and operates the same as in previous systems.

The solenoid is the same as the EGR control solenoid used on previous EEC systems. It is usually mounted on the left side of the firewall, in the engine compartment. The solenoid is normally closed, and the control vacuum from the solenoid is applied to the EGR valve.

Diagnosis and Testing

➡Testing for various fuel system components can be found in this section. For Self-Diagnostic system and access to Trouble Code Memory, please refer to the electronic control information found in Section 4 of this manual.

Fuel System Service Precautions

Safety is the most important factor when performing not only fuel system maintenance but any type of maintenance. Failure to conduct maintenance and repairs in a safe manner may result in serious personal injury or death. Work on a vehicle's fuel system components can be accomplished safely and effectively by adhering to the following rules and guidelines.

- To avoid the possibility of fire and personal injury, always disconnect the negative battery cable unless the repair or test procedure requires that battery voltage by applied.
- Always relieve the fuel system pressure prior to disconnecting any fuel system component (injector, fuel rail, pressure regulator, etc.) fitting or fuel line connection. Exercise extreme caution whenever relieving fuel system pressure to avoid exposing skin, face and eyes to fuel spray. Please be advised that fuel under pressure may penetrate the skin or any part of the body that it contacts.
- Always place a shop towel or cloth around the fitting or connection prior to loosening to absorb any excess fuel due to spillage. Ensure that all fuel spillage is quickly remove from engine surfaces. Ensure that all fuel-soaked cloths or towels are deposited into a flame-proof waste container with a lid.
- Always keep a dry chemical (Class B) fire extinguisher near the work area.
- Do not allow fuel spray or fuel vapors to come into contact with a spark or open flame.
- Always use a second wrench when loosening or tightening fuel line connections fittings. This will prevent unnecessary stress and torsion to fuel piping. Always follow the proper torque specifications.
- Always replace worn fuel fitting O-rings with new ones. Do not substitute fuel hose where rigid pipe is installed.

Relieving Fuel System Pressure

All EFI and SEFI fuel injected engines are equipped with a pressure relief valve located on the fuel supply manifold. Remove the fuel tank cap and attach fuel pressure gauge T80L–9974–A, or equivalent, to the valve to release the fuel pressure. If a pressure gauge is not available, disconnect the vacuum hose from the fuel pressure regulator and attach a hand vacuum pump. Apply about 25 in. Hg (84 kPa) of vacuum to the regulator to vent the fuel system pressure into the fuel tank through the fuel return hose. Note that this procedure will remove the fuel pressure from the lines, but not the fuel. Take precautions to avoid the risk of fire and use clean rags to soak up any spilled fuel when the lines are disconnected.

Fuel Line Fittings (Quick-Connects)

See Figures 19 thru 24

REMOVAL & INSTALLATION

➡Quick-connect (push type) fuel line fittings must be disconnected using proper procedure or the fitting may be damaged. There are two types of retainer used on the push connect fittings. Line sizes of 3/8 and 5/16 in. use a hairpin clip retainer. The 1/4 in. line connectors use a duck-bill clip retainer. In addition, some engines use spring-lock connections secured by a garter spring which requires special tool T81P–19623–G, or equivalent, for removal.

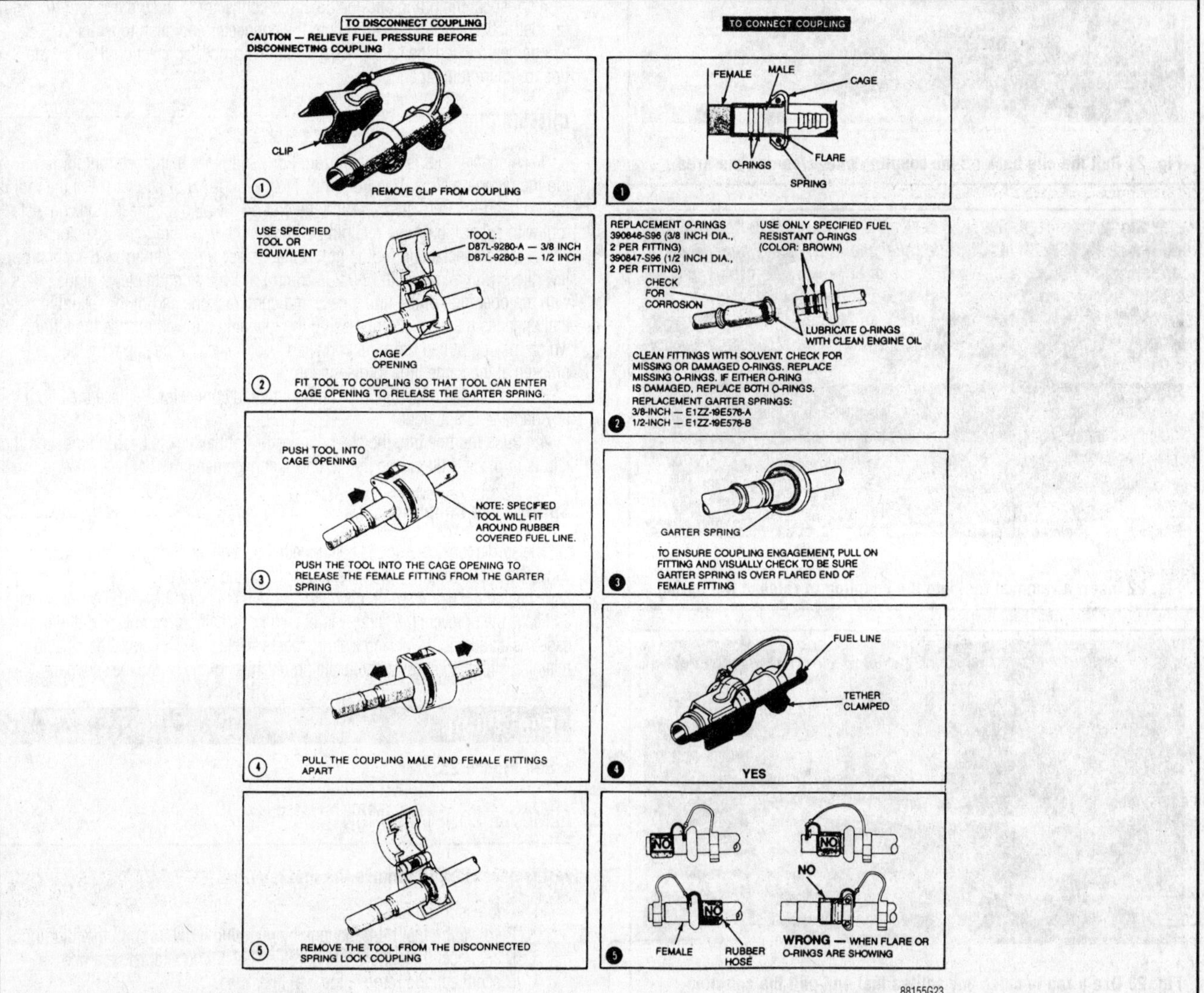

Fig. 19 Fuel line disconnection methods

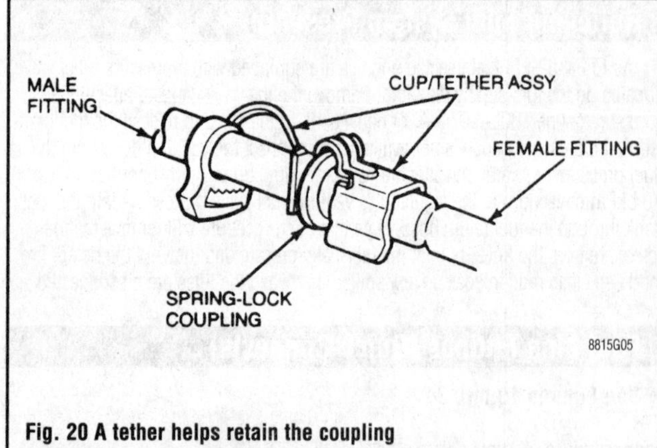

Fig. 20 A tether helps retain the coupling

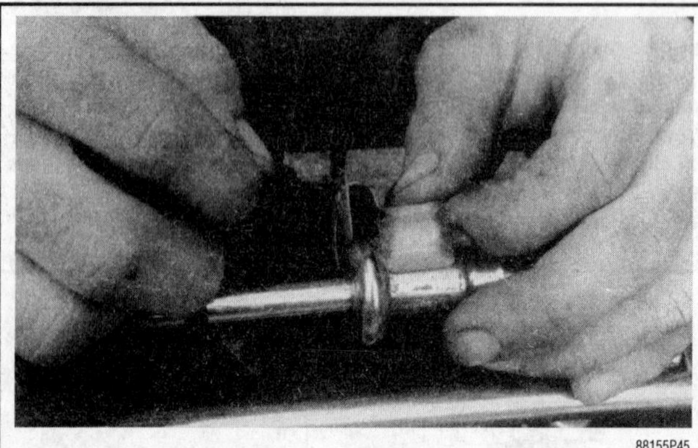

Fig. 21 Pull the clip back off the coupling after cleaning the area

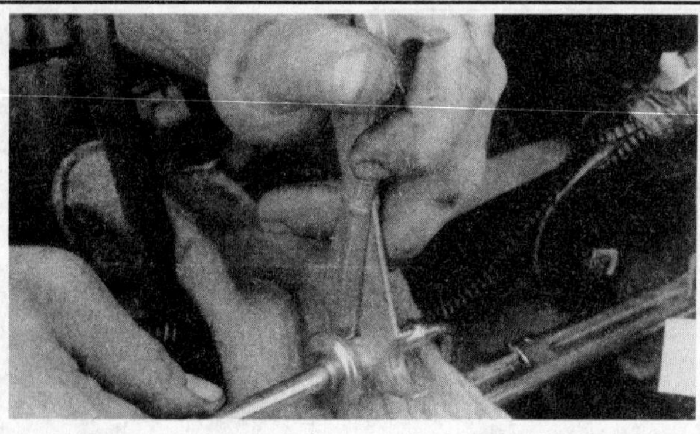

Fig. 22 Insert a removal tool into the coupling to release the spring

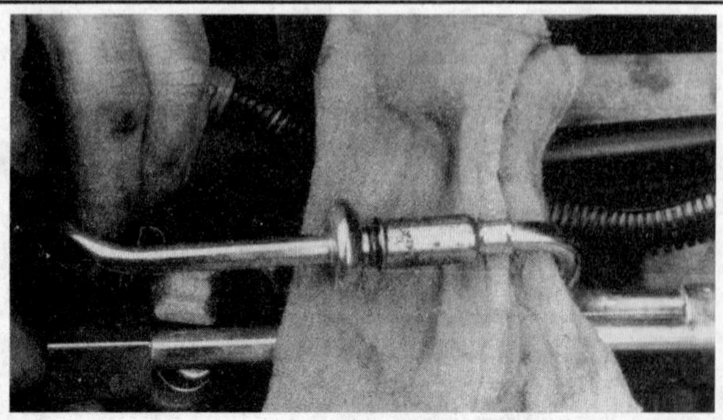

Fig. 23 Use a rag to catch any spilled fuel and pull the coupling apart

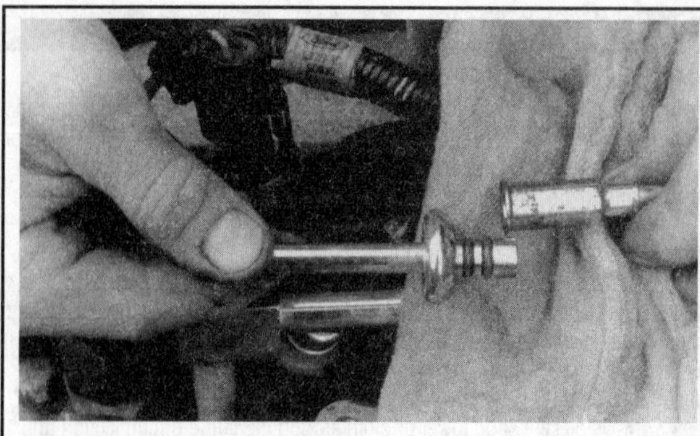

Fig. 24 Check the O-rings for damage and replace as necessary

Hairpin Clip

1. Clean all dirt and grease from the fitting. Spread the two clip legs about ⅛ in. (3mm) each to disengage from the fitting and pull the clip outward from the fitting. Use finger pressure only; do not use any tools.
2. Grasp the fitting and hose assembly and pull away from the steel line. Twist the fitting and hose assembly slightly while pulling, if the assembly sticks.
3. Inspect the hairpin clip for damage, replacing the clip if necessary. Reinstall the clip in position on the fitting.
4. Inspect the fitting and inside of the connector to ensure freedom from dirt or obstruction. Install the fitting into the connector and push together. A click will be heard when the hairpin snaps into the proper connection. Pull on the line to insure full engagement.

Duckbill Clip

1. A special tool is available from Ford and other manufacturers for removing the retaining clips. Use Ford tool T82L–9500–AH or equivalent. If the tool is not on hand, go onto step 2. Align the slot on the push connector disconnect tool with either tab on the retaining clip. Pull the line from the connector.
2. If the special clip tool is not available, use a pair of narrow 6-inch slip-jaw pliers with a jaw width of 0.2 in (5mm) or less. Align the jaws of the pliers with the openings of the fitting case and compress the part of the retaining clip that engages the case. Compressing the retaining clip will release the fitting, which may be pulled from the connector. Both sides of the clip must be compressed at the same time to disengage.
3. Inspect the retaining clip, fitting end and connector. Replace the clip if any damage is apparent.
4. Push the line into the steel connector until a click is heard, indicating the clip is in place. Pull on the line to check engagement.

Spring Lock Coupling

The spring lock coupling is held together by a garter spring inside a circular cage. When the coupling is connected together, the flared end of the female fitting slips behind the garter spring inside the cage of the male fitting. The garter spring and cage then prevent the flared end of the female fitting from pulling out of the cage. As an additional locking feature, most vehicles have a horseshoe-shaped retaining clip that improves the retaining reliability of the spring lock coupling.

Fuel Pump

➧ See Figure 25

REMOVAL & INSTALLATION

➡It is necessary to remove the fuel tank.

1. Depressurize the fuel system.
2. Remove the fuel from the tank by pumping it out through the filter tube.
3. Disconnect the supply fitting, return line fitting and the vent line.
4. Disconnect and remove the fuel filter tube.
5. Unplug the electrical connections to both the fuel sender and the fuel pump wiring harness.

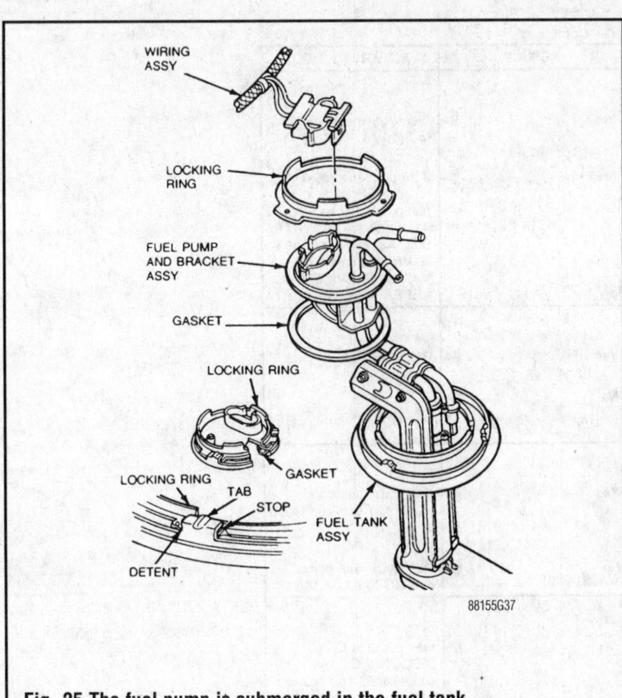

Fig. 25 The fuel pump is submerged in the fuel tank

6. Remove the fuel tank support straps and remove the fuel tank.
7. Remove any dirt that has accumulated around the fuel pump attaching flange, to prevent it from entering the tank during service.
8. Turn the fuel pump locking ring counter-clockwise using a locking ring removal tool and remove the locking ring.
9. Remove the fuel pump and bracket assembly.
10. Remove the seal gasket and discard it.

To install:

11. Put a light coating of heavy grease on a new seal ring to hold it in place during assembly. Install it in fuel tank ring groove.
12. Install the tank in the vehicle.
13. Install the electrical connector.
14. Install the fuel line fittings and tighten to 30–40 ft. lbs (40–54 Nm).
15. Install a minimum of 10 gallons of fuel and check for leaks.
16. Install a pressure gauge on the throttle body valve and turn the ignition **ON** for 3 seconds. Turn the key **OFF**, then repeat the key cycle five to ten times until the pressure gauge shows at least 30 psi. Reinspect for leaks at the fittings.
17. Remove the pressure gauge. Start the engine and check for fuel leaks.

TESTING

CAUTION

Fuel pressure must be relieved before attempting to disconnect any fuel lines.

The diagnostic pressure valve (Schrader valve) is located on the fuel rail on multi-point systems. This valve provides a convenient point for service personnel

FUEL PUMP DIAGNOSIS

	TEST STEP	RESULT	▶ ACTION TO TAKE
A1	CHECK STATIC FUEL PRESSURE		
	• Check for adequate fuel supply, fill as required.	Yes	▶ GO to **A3**.
	• Key OFF, install EFI and CFI fuel pressure gauge T80L-9974-B or equivalent on Shrader valve or engine fuel rails. Install test lead to FP lead of VIP test connector.	No	▶ GO to **A2**.
	VIP SELF TEST CONNECTOR; SIGNAL RETURN; SELF TEST OUT; FP (FUEL PUMP) LEAD (SHORT END OF CONNECTOR)		
	• Turn key to ON position. Ground test lead to run fuel pump.		
	• Refer to Fuel Pressure Specifications Chart in this Section. Is pressure within acceptable limits?		
A2	HYDRAULIC AND ELECTRICAL CIRCUIT CHECK		
	• Plugged fuel line filter (replace filter and check again for proper pressure)?	Yes	▶ If service was required and made. Pressure must be checked again REPEAT STEP **A1**.
	• Check for system leaks.		
	• Check for kinked/restricted fuel lines.	No	▶ If no service was required, REPLACE fuel pump. REPEAT STEP **A1**.
	• Low voltage to fuel pump (should be within 0.5 volts of battery voltage at pump connection)?		
	• Disconnect return fuel line and note if fuel is returning. If fuel is being returned, adjust or replace pressure regulator and check again for proper pressure.		
	• Inertia switch open? (Reset switch as required.)		
	• Wiring at fuel pump/tank connector loose or open?		
	• Fuel pump ground connection at chassis loose or damaged?		
	• Improper fuel pump relay operation (should operate when FP (test) lead is grounded with ignition switch in RUN position).		
	• EEC relay not operating if fuel pump relay is not operating.		
A3	CHECK VALVE TEST		
	• Remove ground from test lead and note pressure on gauge.	Yes	▶ GO to **A5**.
	• Does pressure remain within .14 kPa (2 psi) for 3 minutes after lead is ungrounded.	No	▶ GO to **A4**.

88155G38

FUEL PUMP DIAGNOSIS — Continued

	TEST STEP	RESULT	ACTION TO TAKE
A4	CIRCUIT LEAK CHECK		
	• Fuel lines or connectors leaking? • Disconnect fuel return line and plug engine side. • Momentarily activate fuel pump by grounding test lead. • Raise pressure to approximate operating pressure. • Repeat Step **A3**. If pressure holds, replace regulator and repeat Step **A3**.	Yes	▶ If service was made, GO to Step **A1**.
		No	▶ If no problems were found, REPLACE fuel pump and GO to Step **A1**. If unit still fails GO to Step **A3**, there may be a leaking fuel injector or fuel rail. SERVICE and REPEAT Step **A3**.
A5	ENGINE ON TEST		
	• If engine is equipped with fuel rail injectors, disconnect injectors and plug the vacuum line connected to the pressure regulator. • Start engine and run at idle. Fuel pressure should be as indicated in chart for Ignition On, Engine Off.	Yes	▶ GO to **A7**.
		No	▶ GO to **A6**.
A6	IDLE ENGINE SERVICE		
	• Fuel filter restricted? • Improper fuel pressure regulator adjustment? • Fuel line restricted? • Improper voltage to fuel pump (battery voltage at pump connections)?	Yes	▶ If damage has been found and serviced GO to **A1**.
		No	▶ REPLACE fuel pump and GO to **A1**.
A7	HIGH SPEED TEST		
	• With engine running at idle and vacuum line disconnected from pressure regulator if required from Step A5, note the fuel rail pressure. • Rapidly accelerate engine and watch fuel pressure. Does pressure remain within .35 kPa (5 psi) of starting pressure? **NOTE: Road test vehicle while monitoring pressure may give a better test under load conditions.**	Yes	▶ Fuel pump is OK. DISCONNECT test connections and connect vacuum and fuel lines as required.
		No	▶ GO to **A6**.

88155G39

to monitor fuel pressure, release the system pressure prior to maintenance, and to bleed out air which may become trapped in the system during pressure replacement. A pressure gauge with an adapter is required to perform pressure tests.

If the pressure tap is not installed or an adapter is not available, use a T-fitting to install the pressure gauge between the fuel filter line and the throttle body fuel inlet or fuel rail.

Testing fuel pressure requires the use of a special pressure gauge (T80L–9974–A or equivalent) that attaches to the diagnostic pressure tap fitting. Depressurize the fuel system before disconnecting any lines.

Throttle Body Assembly

See Figures 26 thru 33

REMOVAL & INSTALLATION

The following is a general procedure for throttle body removal. Certain components mentioned may not be used on all engines. Disconnection of the fuel supply line may not be necessary.

1. Disconnect the negative battery cable.
2. Remove the fuel cap to vent the tank pressure, then depressurize the fuel system at the pressure relief valve on the fuel rail
3. If the throttle body is coolant-warmed, drain the cooling system and disconnect the heater hoses at the throttle body.
4. Disconnect the push-connect fitting at the fuel supply line.
5. Disconnect the wiring harness at the throttle position sensor, air bypass valve and air charge temperature sensor.
6. Remove the air cleaner outlet tube between the air cleaner and throttle body by loosening the two clamps.
7. Remove the snow shield, if equipped, by removing the retaining nut on top of the shield and the bolts on the side.
8. Tag and disconnect the vacuum hoses at the vacuum fittings on the intake manifold.
9. Disconnect and remove the accelerator and speed control cables (if equipped) from the accelerator mounting bracket and throttle lever.
10. Remove the transmission throttle valve (TV) linkage from the throttle lever on automatic transmission models.

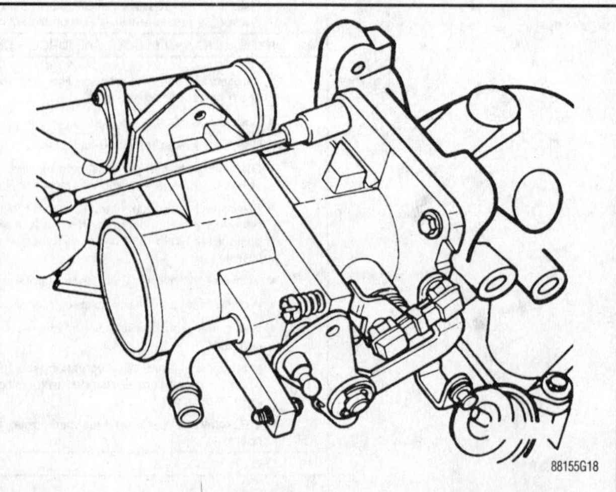

Fig. 26 The throttle body is held by 4 bolts to the upper intake manifold

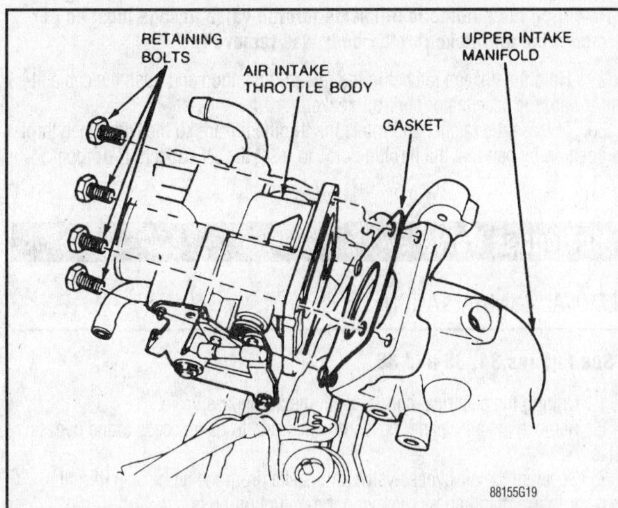

Fig. 27 When cleaning the gasket material from the surfaces, be careful not to nick the metal or drop anything into the manifold

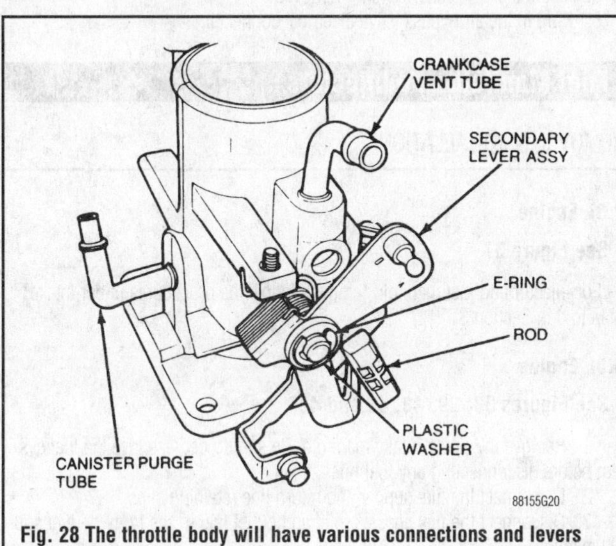

Fig. 28 The throttle body will have various connections and levers that perform various functions

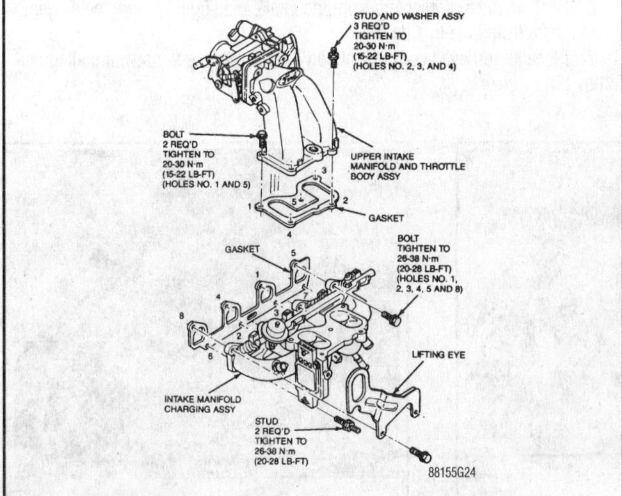

Fig. 29 The manifold is seperated into an upper and lower portion—2.3L (VIN M) engine

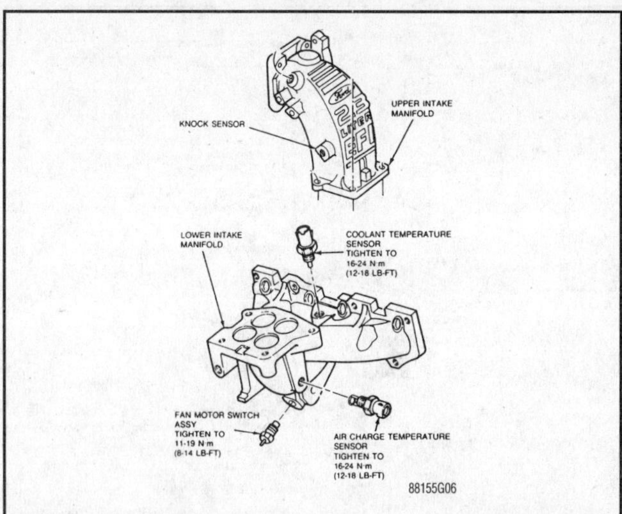

Fig. 30 The manifold is seperated into an upper and lower portion—2.3L (VIN A) engine

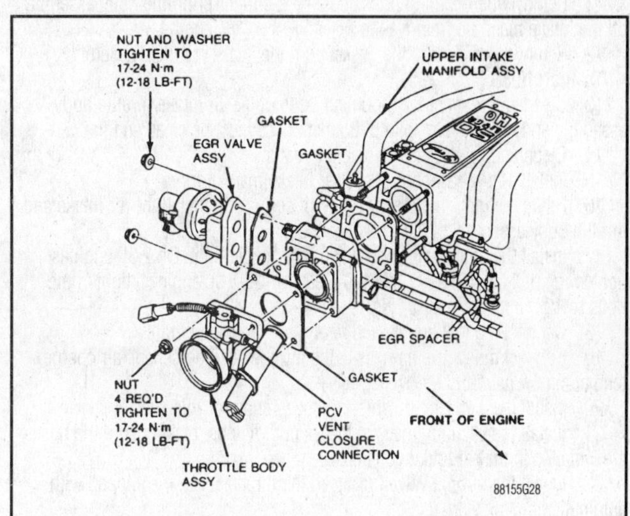

Fig. 31 The throttle body is only one item mounted at the upper manifold all held by the same four studs—5.0L engine

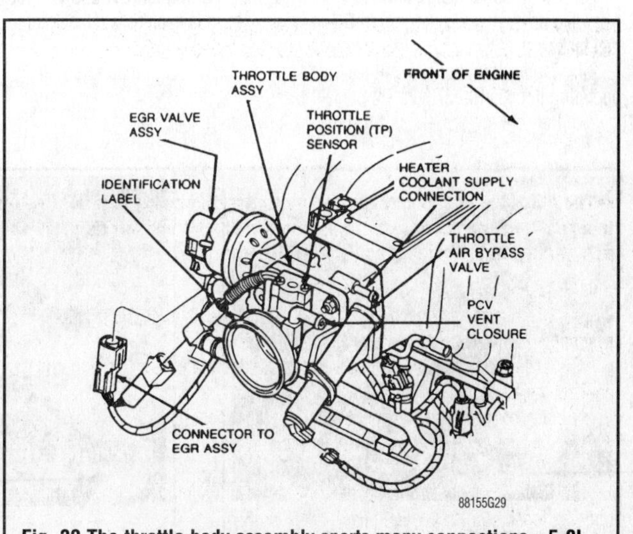

Fig. 32 The throttle body assembly sports many connections—5.0L engine

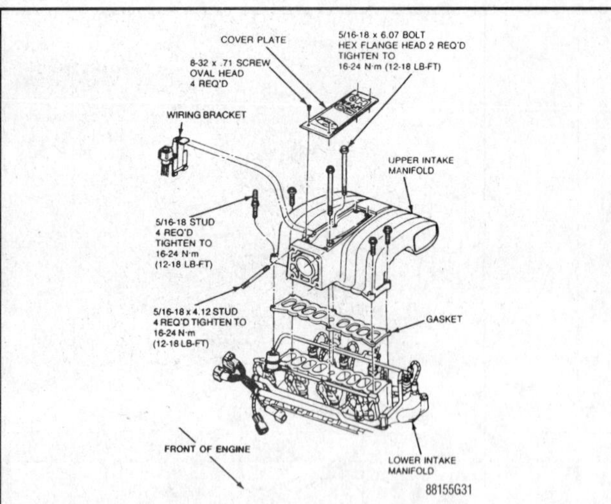

Fig. 33 The manifold is composed of two parts, upper and lower—5.0L engine

11. Remove the retaining bolts and lift the air intake/throttle body assembly off the intake manifold; remove the assembly from the engine.
12. Remove and discard the gasket from the intake manifold assembly.

To install:

13. Clean and inspect the mounting faces of the air intake/throttle body assembly and the intake manifold. Both surfaces must be clean and flat.
14. Clean and oil the manifold stud threads.
15. Install a new gasket on the lower intake manifold.
16. Using the guide pins as locators (if equipped), install the air intake and throttle body assembly to the intake manifold.
17. Install the studs and/or retaining bolts finger tight. On 2.3L engines, tighten the bolts to 15–22 ft. lbs. (20–30 Nm). On 5.0L engines, tighten the bolts to 12–18 ft. lbs. (17–24 Nm).
18. Connect the fuel supply and return lines to the fuel rail.
19. Connect the wiring harness to the throttle position sensor, air charge temperature sensor and air bypass valve.
20. Install the accelerator cable and speed control cable.
21. Install the vacuum hoses to the vacuum fittings, making sure the hoses are installed in their original positions.
22. Install the throttle valve linkage to the throttle lever, if equipped with automatic transmission.
23. Reconnect the negative battery cable.
24. Install the snow shield and air cleaner outlet tube.
25. Fill the cooling system if it was drained.
26. Build fuel pressure in the system by turning the ignition **ON** and **OFF** at least five times. Leave the ignition **ON** at least 5 seconds each time. Check for fuel leaks.
27. Replace the fuel cap and start the engine, allowing it to reach normal operating temperature. Check for coolant leaks.
28. Perform the EEC-IV self-test to check system functions.

➡Resetting the automatic transaxle throttle valve linkage must be performed if the air intake throttle body was removed.

29. Hold the linkage ratchet in the released position and push the cable fitting toward the accelerator control bracket.
30. Release the ratchet and rotate the throttle linkage to the wide-open throttle position by hand, at the throttle body, to reset the TV cable to the proper position.

Air Bypass Valve

REMOVAL & INSTALLATION

➧ See Figures 34, 35 and 36

1. Unplug the electrical connector at the air bypass valve.
2. Remove the air cleaner cover, if necessary, to gain access to the bypass valve.
3. Separate the air bypass valve and gasket from the air cleaner, throttle body, or intake manifold by removing the mounting bolts.

To install:

4. Install the air bypass valve and gasket to the air cleaner cover and tighten the retaining bolts to 72–102 inch lbs. (8–11.5 Nm)
5. Install the air cleaner cover, if removed.
6. Plug in the air bypass valve electrical connector.

Fuel Manifold and Injectors

REMOVAL & INSTALLATION

2.3L Engine

➧ See Figure 37

For injector and fuel manifold removal, follow the procedures under Intake Manifold in Section 3.

5.0L Engine

➧ See Figures 38, 39, 40, 41 and 42

1. Remove the upper intake manifold. Be sure to depressurize the fuel system before disconnecting any fuel lines.
2. Disconnect the fuel supply and return line retaining clips.
3. Disconnect the fuel chassis inlet and outlet fuel hoses from the fuel supply manifold.
4. Remove the four fuel supply manifold retaining bolts.
5. Carefully disengage the fuel rail assembly from the fuel injectors by lifting and gently rocking the rail.
6. Remove the fuel injectors from the intake manifold by lifting while gently rocking them from side to side
7. Place all removed components on a clean surface to prevent contamination by dirt or grease.

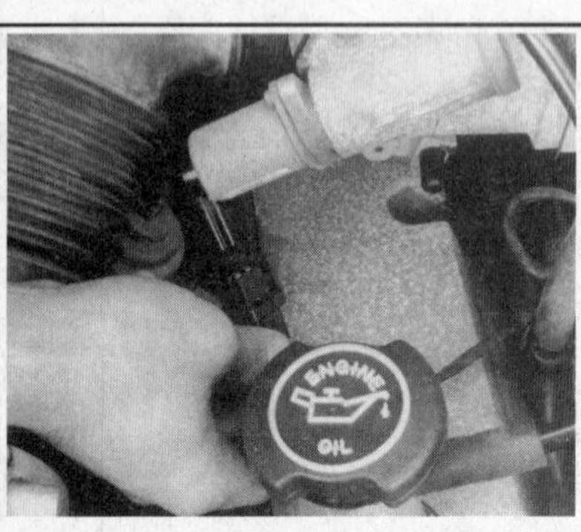

88159P65

Fig. 34 Disconnect the harnes from the valve and check the pins for damage

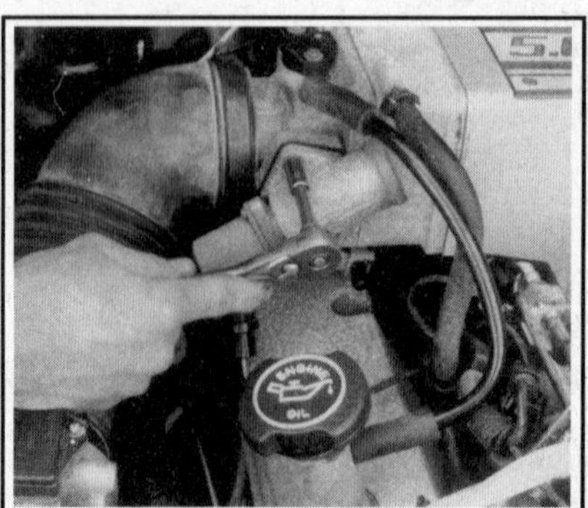

88159P66

Fig. 35 The air bypass valve is held by the two bolts

88159P67

Fig. 36 Replace the gasket whenever the air bypass valve is removed

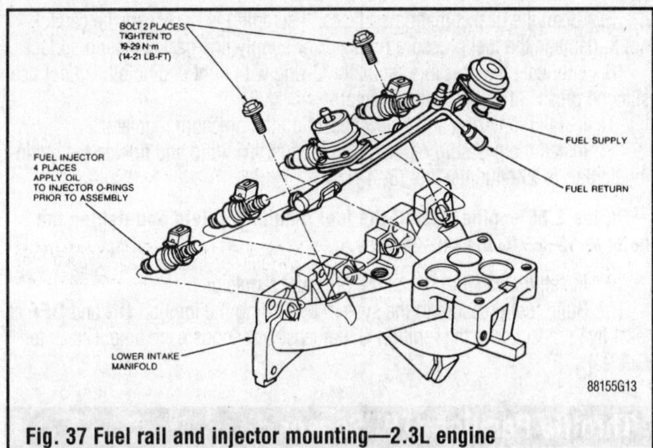

Fig. 37 Fuel rail and injector mounting—2.3L engine

Fig. 38 Disconnect the injector harnesses before proceding with the removal

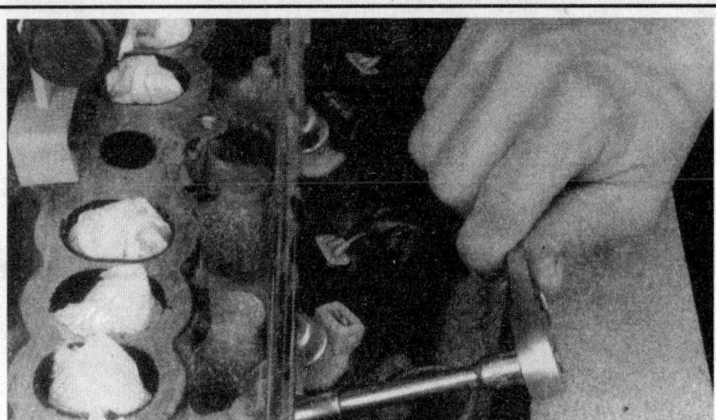

Fig. 39 Remove the fuel rail bolts. Be careful not to drop them into the mainfold openings

Fig. 40 Sometimes the injectors will come out with the fuel rail easier than keeping them in the manifold

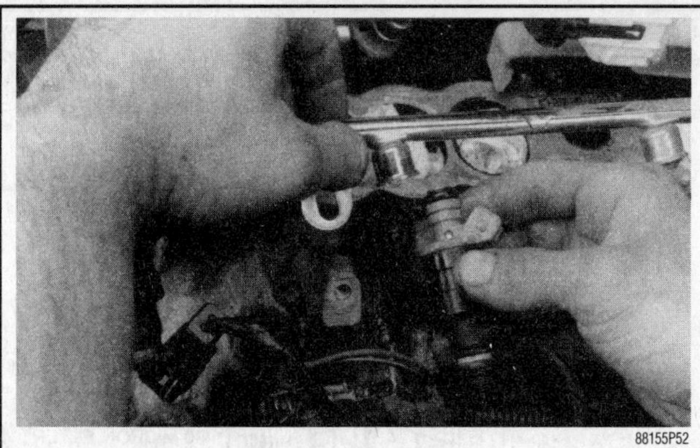

Fig. 41 Remove the injector by gently twisting

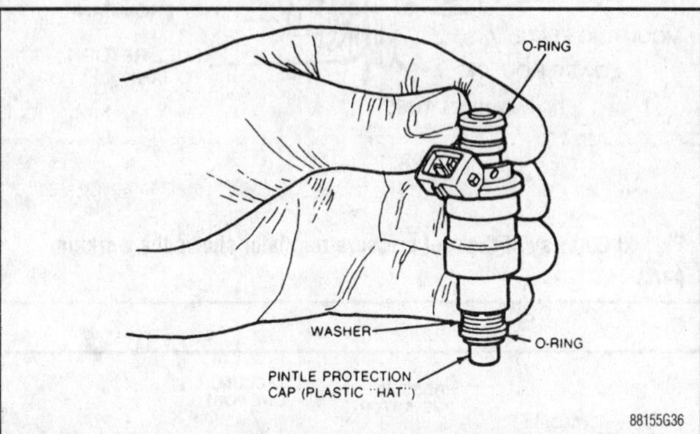

Fig. 42 Inspect the injector for damage and replace the O-rings before installation

➡Never use silicone grease; it will clog the injector. All injectors and the fuel rail must be handled with extreme care to prevent damage to sealing areas and sensitive fuel metering orifices.

8. Examine the injector O-rings for deterioration damage, replacing them as needed.
9. Make sure the injector caps are clean and free from contamination or damage.

To install:

10. Lubricate all O-rings with clean engine oil, then install the injectors into the fuel rail using a light twisting/pushing motion.
11. Carefully install the fuel rail assembly and injectors into the lower intake manifold. Make certain to correctly position the insulators. Push down on the fuel rail to make sure the O-rings are seated.
12. Hold the fuel rail assembly in place and install the retaining bolts finger tight. Then tighten the bolts to 15–22 ft. lbs (20–30 Nm).
13. Connect the fuel supply and return lines.
14. Connect the fuel injector wiring harness at the injectors.
15. Connect the vacuum line to the fuel pressure regulator, if removed.
16. Install the air intake and throttle body assembly.
17. Run the engine and check for fuel leaks.

Fuel Pressure Regulator

➧ See Figures 43 thru 48

REMOVAL & INSTALLATION

1. Depressurize the fuel system; remove shielding as needed.
2. Remove the vacuum line at the pressure regulator.
3. Remove the three Allen® retaining screws from the regulator housing.
4. Remove the pressure regulator assembly, gasket and O-ring. Discard the gasket and check the O-ring for signs of cracks or deterioration.

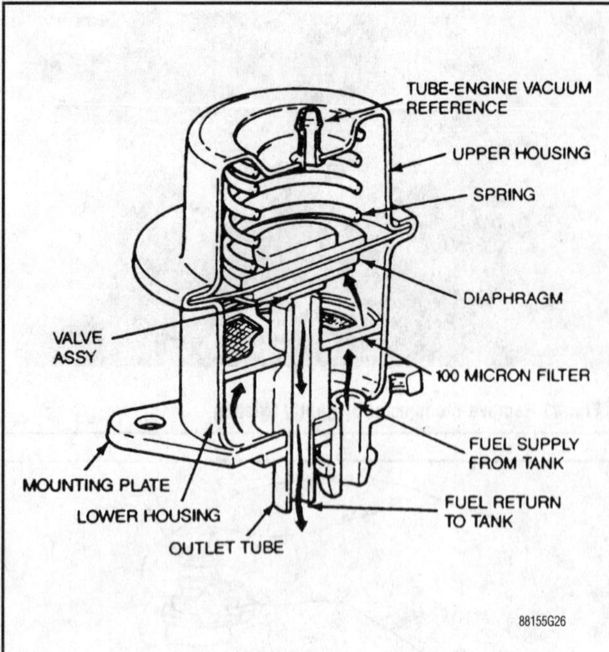

Fig. 43 Cutaway of the fuel pressure regulator shows the working parts

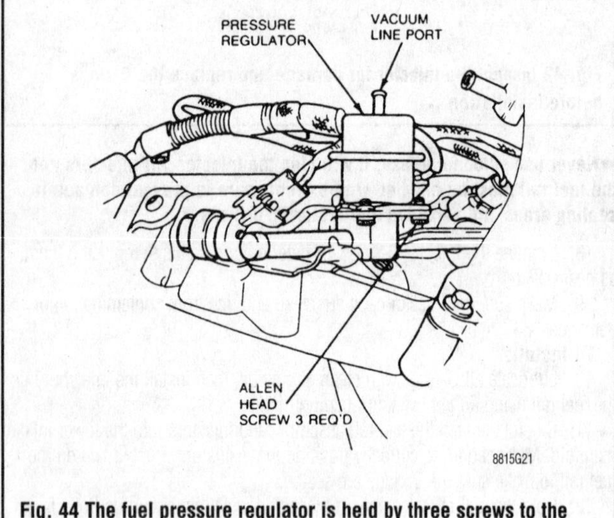

Fig. 44 The fuel pressure regulator is held by three screws to the fuel rail

5. Clean the gasket mating surfaces. If scraping is necessary, be careful not to damage the fuel pressure regulator or supply line gasket mating surfaces.
6. Lubricate the pressure regulator O-ring with light engine oil. Do not use silicone grease; it will clog the injectors.
7. Install the O-ring and a new gasket on the pressure regulator.
8. Install the pressure regulator on the fuel manifold and tighten the retaining screws to 27–40 inch lbs. (3–4 Nm).

➡On the 2.3L engine, install the fuel manifold shield and tighten the bolts to 15–22 ft. lbs (20–30 Nm).

9. Install the vacuum line at the pressure regulator.
10. Build fuel pressure in the system by turning the ignition **ON** and **OFF** at least five times. Leave the ignition **ON** at least 5 seconds each time. Check for fuel leaks.

Throttle Position (TP) Sensor

REMOVAL & INSTALLATION

▶ See Figure 49

2.3L Engine

1. Unplug the throttle position sensor electrical connector.
2. Remove the screw retaining the TP sensor electrical connector to the air throttle body, if equipped.
3. Scribe alignment marks on the air throttle body and TP sensor to indicate proper alignment during installation.

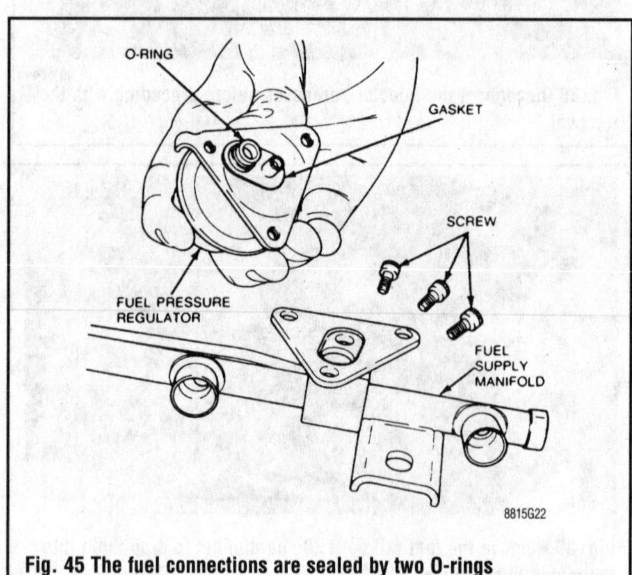

Fig. 45 The fuel connections are sealed by two O-rings

Fig. 46 Be ready for any spilled fuel that may come out when the regulator is removed. A rag underneath the unit would help catch any dripping fuel

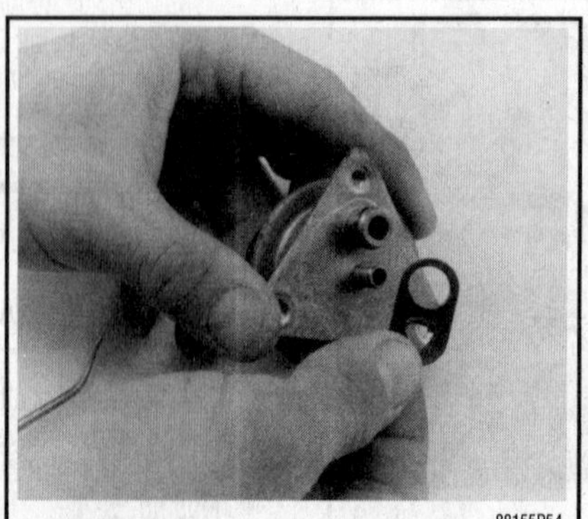

Fig. 47 Inspect the gasket for damage and replace as necessary

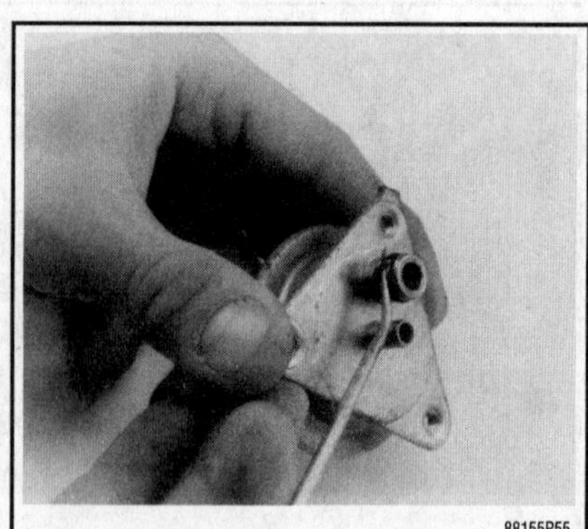

Fig. 48 eplace the O-rings if there is any sign of damage

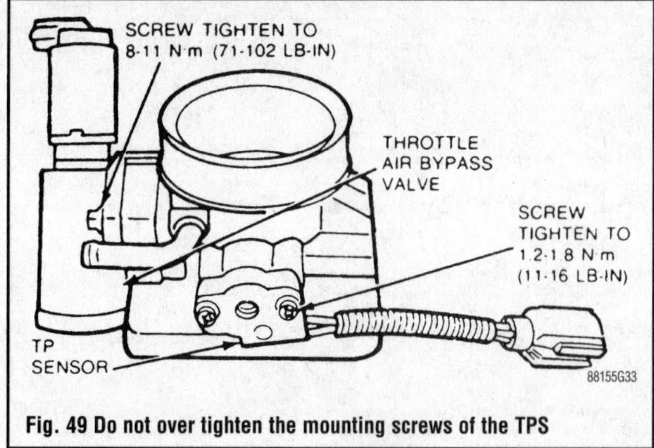

Fig. 49 Do not over tighten the mounting screws of the TPS

4. Remove the TP sensor retaining screws, then remove the TP sensor and gasket from the throttle body.

To install:

5. Position the TP sensor so that the wiring harness is parallel to the venturi bores. Place the TP sensor and gasket on the throttle body, making sure the rotary tangs on the sensor are aligned with the throttle shaft blade. Slide the rotary tangs into position over the throttle shaft blade, then rotate the throttle position sensor clockwise only to its installed position as shown by the scribed marks made earlier

➡Slide the rotary tangs into position over the throttle shaft blade, then rotate the throttle position sensor clockwise only to its installed position. Failure to install the TP sensor in this manner may result in excessive idle speeds.

6. Once the scribe marks are aligned, install the retaining screws and tighten them to 14–16 inch lbs. (1.6–1.8 Nm).
7. Position the electrical connector over the locating dimple, if equipped, then secure to the throttle body with the retaining screw.
8. Inspect the connector terminals for corrosion, damage and bent pins and repair as necessary. Replace any cracked or burned terminals. Plug in the TP sensor electrical connector, start the engine and check the idle speed. On the rotary TP sensor with round mounting holes, no further TP sensor adjustment is possible. On sensors with oblong mounting holes, proceed with the adjustment procedure.

5.0L Engine

1. Unplug the throttle position sensor electrical connector.
2. Remove the screw retaining the TP sensor connector to the air throttle body, if equipped.
3. Scribe alignment marks on the air throttle body and TP sensor to indicate proper alignment during installation.
4. Remove the TP sensor retaining screws, then remove the sensor and gasket from the throttle body.
5. The throttle position sensor bushing, if equipped, must be reused.

To install:

6. Install the bushing with the larger diameter facing outward.
7. Install the TP sensor on the throttle shaft and rotate it counter-clockwise 10–20 degrees to align the screw holes.
8. Install the pair of retaining screws and tighten them to 11–16 inch lbs. (1.2–1.8 Nm).
9. Cycle the throttle lever to wide open throttle. It should return without interference.
10. Plug in the TP sensor electrical connector, start the engine and check the idle speed. On the TP sensor with round mounting holes, no further adjustment is possible. On the sensor with oblong mounting holes, proceed to the adjustment procedure.

ADJUSTMENT

Adjustable TP Sensors Only

1. Make sure the ignition switch is **OFF.** Install an EEC-IV breakout box such as Rotunda T83L–50 EEC-IV or equivalent.
2. Using a digital volt/ohmmeter (10 megohms impedance), connect the positive lead to Pin 47 and the negative lead to Pin 46. Set the DVOM on the 20-volt scale.
3. Turn the ignition key **ON** but do not start the engine.
4. Loosen the mounting screws slightly and rotate the TP sensor until the meter reads the minimum specified voltage. Maximum voltage on all engines is 4.84 volts.
   - 2.3L engine: 0.34 volts
   - 5.0L engine: 0.20 volts
5. Tighten the TP sensor screws to the correct torque.
6. While watching the DVOM, move the throttle to the wide-open position, then back to idle. For proper operation, the DVOM should move from the minimum voltage to the maximum specified voltage and back to minimum during throttle operation.

FUEL TANK

Tank Assembly

➧ See Figures 50, 51 and 52

REMOVAL & INSTALLATION

1. Disconnect the negative battery cable and relieve the fuel system pressure.
2. Siphon or pump as much fuel as possible out through the fuel filler pipe.

➡Fuel injected vehicles have reservoirs inside the fuel tank to maintain fuel near the fuel pick-up during cornering or low-fuel operation. These reservoirs could block siphon hoses or tubes from reaching the bottom of the fuel tank. Repeated attempts, using different hose orientations, can overcome this obstacle.

3. Raise and safely support the vehicle.
4. Disconnect the fuel fill and vent hoses connecting the filler pipe to the tank. Disconnect one end of the vapor crossover hose at the rear, over the driveshaft.
5. On vehicles equipped with a metal retainer fastening the filler pipe to the fuel tank, remove the screw holding the retainer to the fuel tank flange.
6. Disconnect the fuel lines and the electrical connections to the fuel tank sending unit. On some vehicles, these are inaccessible on top of the tank. In this case, they must be disconnected with the tank partially lowered.
7. Place a safety support under the fuel tank and remove the bolts from the fuel tank straps. Allow the straps to swing out of the way. Be careful not to deform the fuel tank.
8. Partially remove the tank and disconnect the fuel lines and electrical connection from the sending unit if required.
9. Remove the tank from the vehicle.

To install:

10. Raise the fuel tank into position in the vehicle. Attach the fuel lines and sending unit electrical connector, if necessary before the tank is in its final position.
11. Lubricate the fuel filler pipe with water-based tire mounting lubricant. Install the tank onto the filler pipe, then bring the tank into final position. Be careful not to deform the tank.
12. Bring the tank straps around the tank and start the retaining nut or bolt. Align the tank with the straps. If equipped, mane sure the fuel tank shields are installed with the straps and are positioned correctly.
13. Check the hoses and wiring on top of the tank. Make sure they are correctly routed and will not be pinched between the tank and body.
14. Tighten the fuel tank strap retaining nuts or bolts to 20–30 ft. lbs. (28–40 Nm).
15. If not already attached, connect the fuel hoses and lines. Make sure the fuel supply, fuel return (if present) and the vapor vent attachments are made properly. If not already attached, connect the sending unit.
16. Lower the vehicle. Replace the fuel that was drained from the tank. Check all connections for leaks.

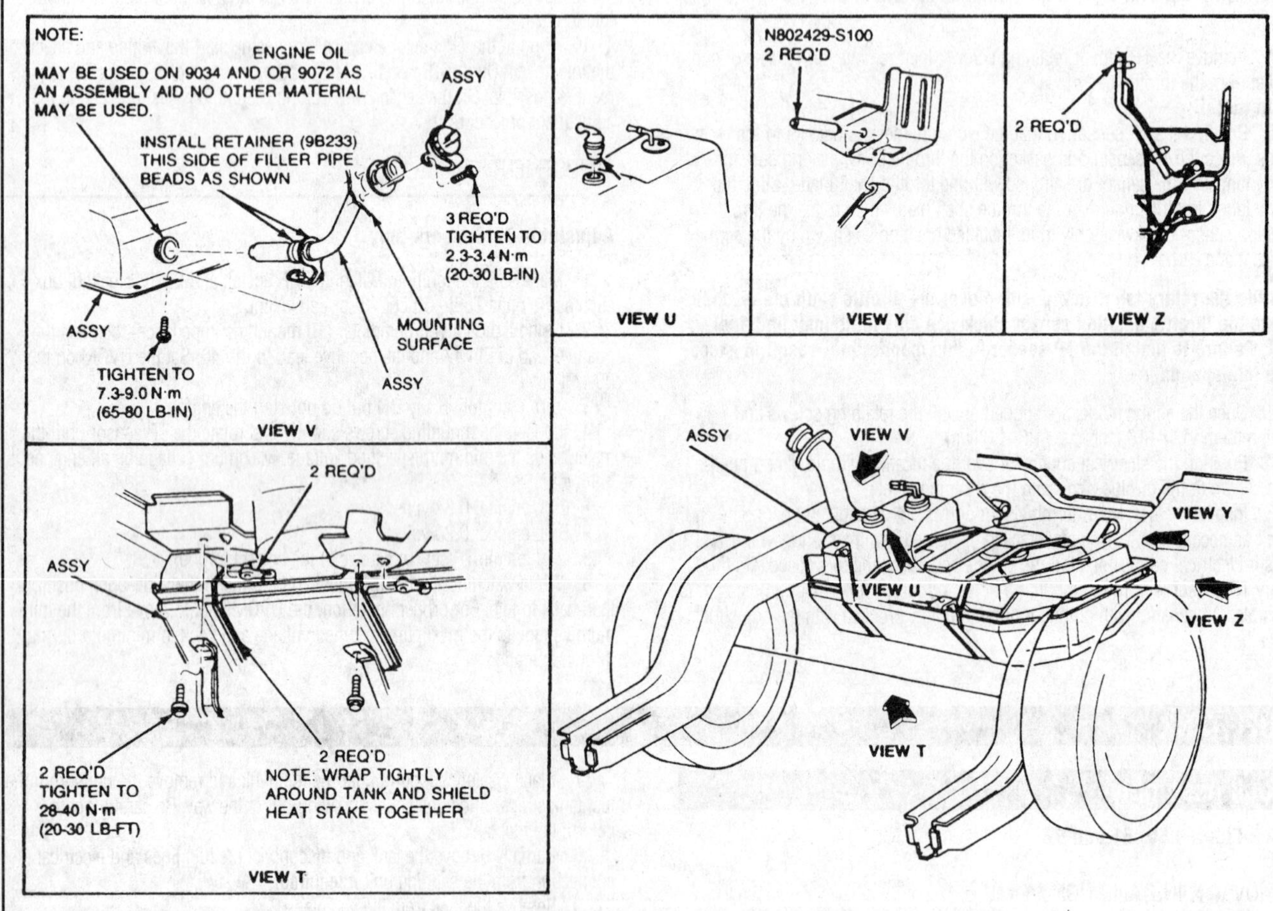

Fig. 50 Fuel tank mounting method

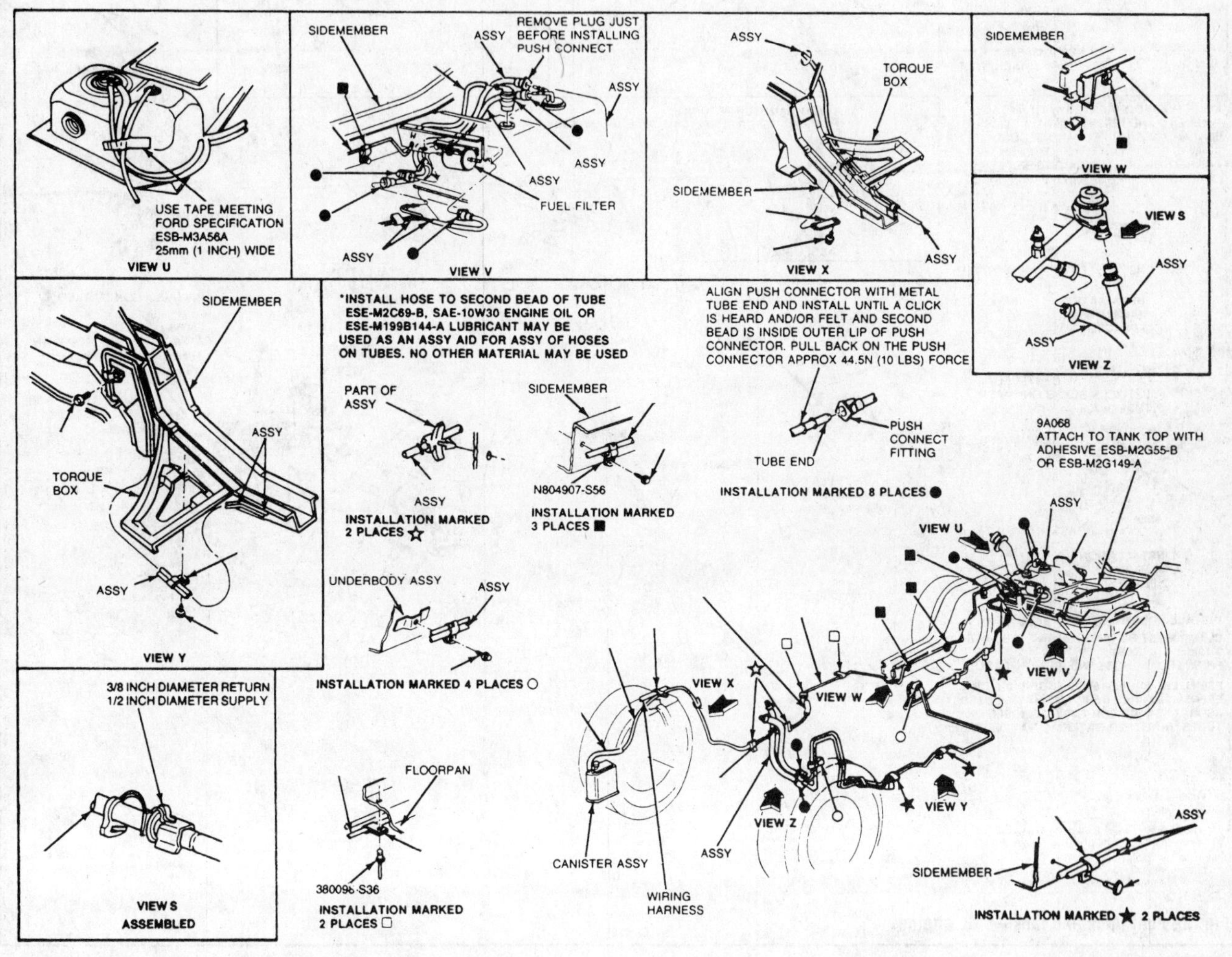

Fig. 51 Fuel lines and tank—2.3L engine

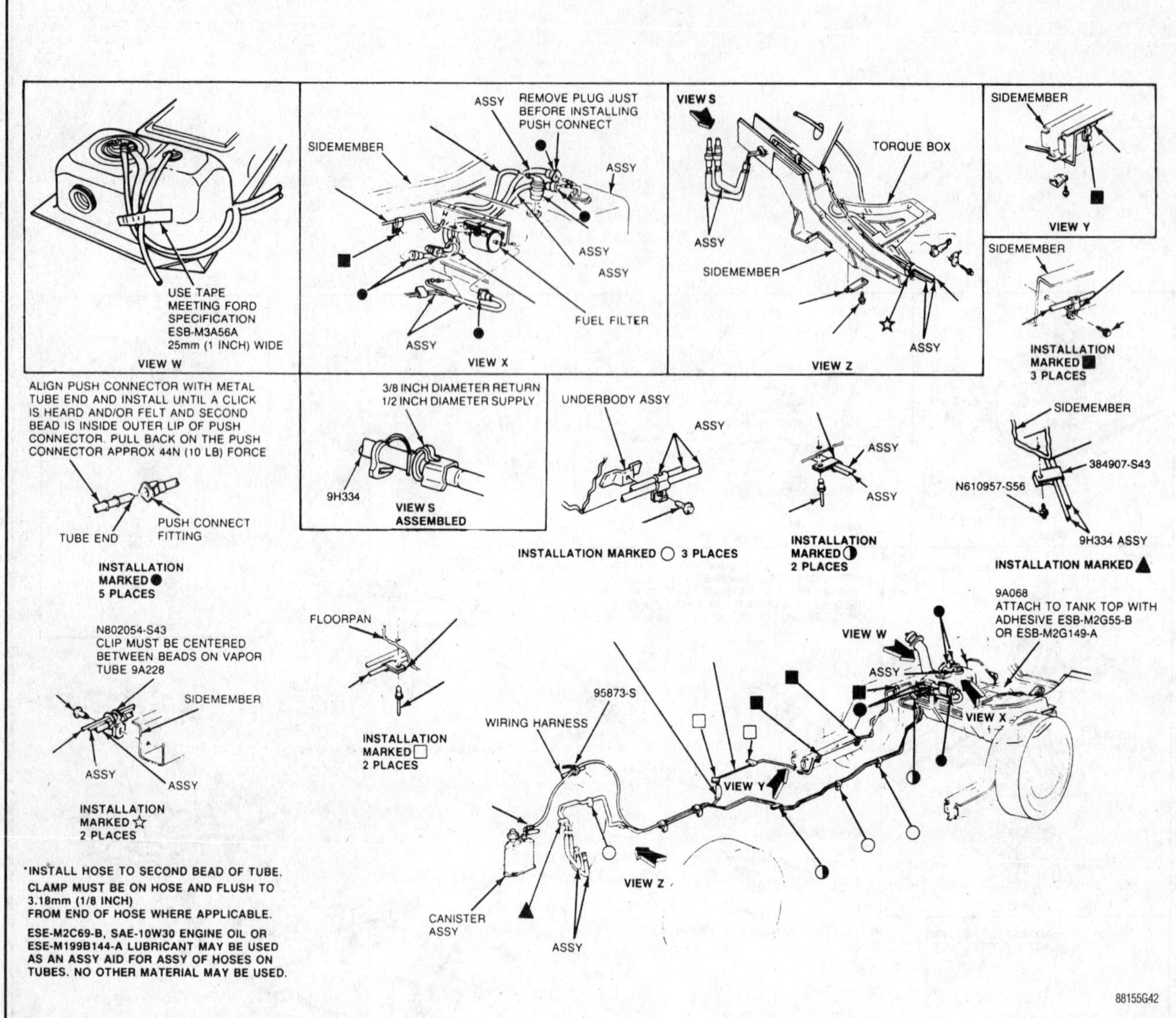

Fig. 52 Fuel lines and tank—5.0L engine

6 CHASSIS ELECTRICAL

UNDERSTANDING AND TROUBLESHOOTING ELECTRICAL SYSTEMS

Basic Electrical Theory

➧ See Figure 1

For any 12 volt, negative ground, electrical system to operate, the electricity must travel in a complete circuit. This simply means that current (power) from the positive (+) terminal of the battery must eventually return to the negative (-) terminal of the battery. Along the way, this current will travel through wires, fuses, switches and components. If, for any reason, the flow of current through the circuit is interrupted, the component fed by that circuit will cease to function properly.

Perhaps the easiest way to visualize a circuit is to think of connecting a light bulb (with two wires attached to it) to the battery—one wire attached to the negative (-) terminal of the battery and the other wire to the positive (+) terminal. With the two wires touching the battery terminals, the circuit would be complete and the light bulb would illuminate. Electricity would follow a path from the battery to the bulb and back to the battery. It's easy to see that with longer wires on our light bulb, it could be mounted anywhere. Further, one wire could be fitted with a switch so that the light could be turned on and off.

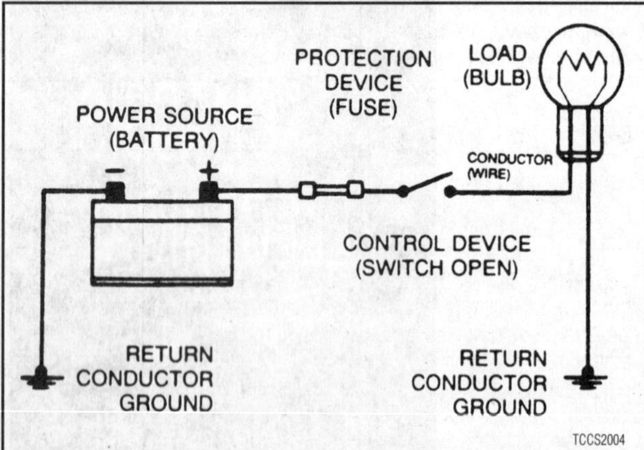

Fig. 1 This example illustrates a simple circuit. When the switch is closed, power from the positive (+) battery terminal flows through the fuse and the switch, and then to the light bulb. The light illuminates and the circuit is completed through the ground wire back to the negative (-) battery terminal. In reality, the two ground points shown in the illustration are attached to the metal frame of the vehicle, which completes the circuit back to the battery

The normal automotive circuit differs from this simple example in two ways. First, instead of having a return wire from the bulb to the battery, the current travels through the frame of the vehicle. Since the negative (-) battery cable is attached to the frame (made of electrically conductive metal), the frame of the vehicle can serve as a ground wire to complete the circuit. Secondly, most automotive circuits contain multiple components which receive power from a single circuit. This lessens the amount of wire needed to power components on the vehicle.

HOW DOES ELECTRICITY WORK: THE WATER ANALOGY

Electricity is the flow of electrons—the subatomic particles that constitute the outer shell of an atom. Electrons spin in an orbit around the center core of an atom. The center core is comprised of protons (positive charge) and neutrons (neutral charge). Electrons have a negative charge and balance out the positive charge of the protons. When an outside force causes the number of electrons to unbalance the charge of the protons, the electrons will split off the atom and look for another atom to balance out. If this imbalance is kept up, electrons will continue to move and an electrical flow will exist.

Many people have been taught electrical theory using an analogy with water. In a comparison with water flowing through a pipe, the electrons would be the water and the wire is the pipe.

The flow of electricity can be measured much like the flow of water through a pipe. The unit of measurement used is amperes, frequently abbreviated as amps (a). You can compare amperage to the volume of water flowing through a pipe. When connected to a circuit, an ammeter will measure the actual amount of current flowing through the circuit. When relatively few electrons flow through a circuit, the amperage is low. When many electrons flow, the amperage is high.

Water pressure is measured in units such as pounds per square inch (psi); The electrical pressure is measured in units called volts (v). When a voltmeter is connected to a circuit, it is measuring the electrical pressure.

The actual flow of electricity depends not only on voltage and amperage, but also on the resistance of the circuit. The higher the resistance, the higher the force necessary to push the current through the circuit. The standard unit for measuring resistance is an ohm. Resistance in a circuit varies depending on the amount and type of components used in the circuit. The main factors which determine resistance are:

- Material—some materials have more resistance than others. Those with high resistance are said to be insulators. Rubber materials (or rubber-like plastics) are some of the most common insulators used in vehicles as they have a very high resistance to electricity. Very low resistance materials are said to be conductors. Copper wire is among the best conductors. Silver is actually a superior conductor to copper and is used in some relay contacts, but its high cost prohibits its use as common wiring. Most automotive wiring is made of copper.
- Size—the larger the wire size being used, the less resistance the wire will have. This is why components which use large amounts of electricity usually have large wires supplying current to them.
- Length—for a given thickness of wire, the longer the wire, the greater the resistance. The shorter the wire, the less the resistance. When determining the proper wire for a circuit, both size and length must be considered to design a circuit that can handle the current needs of the component.
- Temperature—with many materials, the higher the temperature, the greater the resistance (positive temperature coefficient). Some materials exhibit the opposite trait of lower resistance with higher temperatures (negative temperature coefficient). These principles are used in many of the sensors on the engine.

OHM'S LAW

There is a direct relationship between current, voltage and resistance. The relationship between current, voltage and resistance can be summed up by a statement known as Ohm's law.

Voltage (E) is equal to amperage (I) times resistance (R): $E=I \times R$

Other forms of the formula are $R=E/I$ and $I=E/R$

In each of these formulas, E is the voltage in volts, I is the current in amps and R is the resistance in ohms. The basic point to remember is that as the resistance of a circuit goes up, the amount of current that flows in the circuit will go down, if voltage remains the same.

The amount of work that the electricity can perform is expressed as power. The unit of power is the watt (w). The relationship between power, voltage and current is expressed as:

Power (w) is equal to amperage (I) times voltage (E): $W=I \times E$

This is only true for direct current (DC) circuits; The alternating current formula is a tad different, but since the electrical circuits in most vehicles are DC type, we need not get into AC circuit theory.

Electrical Components

POWER SOURCE

Power is supplied to the vehicle by two devices: The battery and the alternator. The battery supplies electrical power during starting or during periods when the current demand of the vehicle's electrical system exceeds the output capacity of the alternator. The alternator supplies electrical current when the engine is running. Just not does the alternator supply the current needs of the vehicle, but it recharges the battery.

The Battery

In most modern vehicles, the battery is a lead/acid electrochemical device consisting of six 2 volt subsections (cells) connected in series, so that the unit is capable of producing approximately 12 volts of electrical pressure. Each subsection consists of a series of positive and negative plates held a short distance apart in a solution of sulfuric acid and water.

The two types of plates are of dissimilar metals. This sets up a chemical reaction, and it is this reaction which produces current flow from the battery when its positive and negative terminals are connected to an electrical load . The power removed from the battery is replaced by the alternator, restoring the battery to its original chemical state.

The Alternator

On some vehicles there isn't an alternator, but a generator. The difference is that an alternator supplies alternating current which is then changed to direct current for use on the vehicle, while a generator produces direct current. Alternators tend to be more efficient and that is why they are used.

Alternators and generators are devices that consist of coils of wires wound together making big electromagnets. One group of coils spins within another set and the interaction of the magnetic fields causes a current to flow. This current is then drawn off the coils and fed into the vehicles electrical system.

GROUND

Two types of grounds are used in automotive electric circuits. Direct ground components are grounded to the frame through their mounting points. All other components use some sort of ground wire which is attached to the frame or chassis of the vehicle. The electrical current runs through the chassis of the vehicle and returns to the battery through the ground (-) cable; if you look, you'll see that the battery ground cable connects between the battery and the frame or chassis of the vehicle.

➡It should be noted that a good percentage of electrical problems can be traced to bad grounds.

PROTECTIVE DEVICES

➧ See Figure 2

It is possible for large surges of current to pass through the electrical system of your vehicle. If this surge of current were to reach the load in the circuit, the surge could burn it out or severely damage it. It can also overload the wiring, causing the harness to get hot and melt the insulation. To prevent this, fuses, circuit breakers and/or fusible links are connected into the supply wires of the electrical system. These items are nothing more than a built-in weak spot in the system. When an abnormal amount of current flows through the system, these protective devices work as follows to protect the circuit:

- Fuse—when an excessive electrical current passes through a fuse, the fuse "blows" (the conductor melts) and opens the circuit, preventing the passage of current.
- Circuit Breaker—a circuit breaker is basically a self-repairing fuse. It will open the circuit in the same fashion as a fuse, but when the surge subsides, the circuit breaker can be reset and does not need replacement.
- Fusible Link—a fusible link (fuse link or main link) is a short length of special, high temperature insulated wire that acts as a fuse. When an excessive electrical current passes through a fusible link, the thin gauge wire inside the link melts, creating an intentional open to protect the circuit. To repair the circuit, the link must be replaced. Some newer type fusible links are housed in plug-in modules, which are simply replaced like a fuse, while older type fusible links must be cut and spliced if they melt. Since this link is very early in the electrical path, it's the first place to look if nothing on the vehicle works, yet the battery seems to be charged and is properly connected.

CAUTION

Always replace fuses, circuit breakers and fusible links with identically rated components. Under no circumstances should a component of higher or lower amperage rating be substituted.

SWITCHES & RELAYS

➧ See Figures 3 and 4

Switches are used in electrical circuits to control the passage of current. The most common use is to open and close circuits between the battery and the various electric devices in the system. Switches are rated according to the amount of amperage they can handle. If a sufficient amperage rated switch is not used in a circuit, the switch could overload and cause damage.

Some electrical components which require a large amount of current to operate use a special switch called a relay. Since these circuits carry a large amount of current, the thickness of the wire in the circuit is also greater. If this large wire were connected from the load to the control switch, the switch would have to carry the high amperage load and the fairing or dash would be twice as large to accommodate the increased size of the wiring harness. To prevent these problems, a relay is used.

Relays are composed of a coil and a set of contacts. When the coil has a current passed though it, a magnetic field is formed and this field causes the contacts to move together, completing the circuit. Most relays are normally open, prevent-

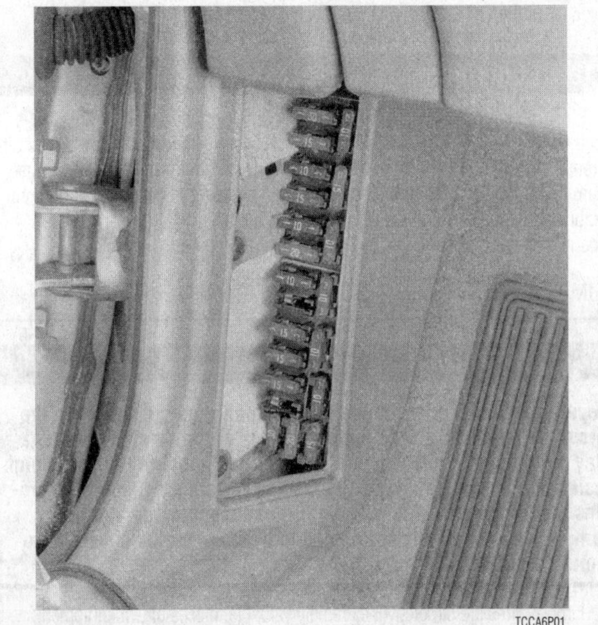

TCCA6P01

Fig. 2 Most vehicles use one or more fuse panels. This one is located on the driver's side kick panel

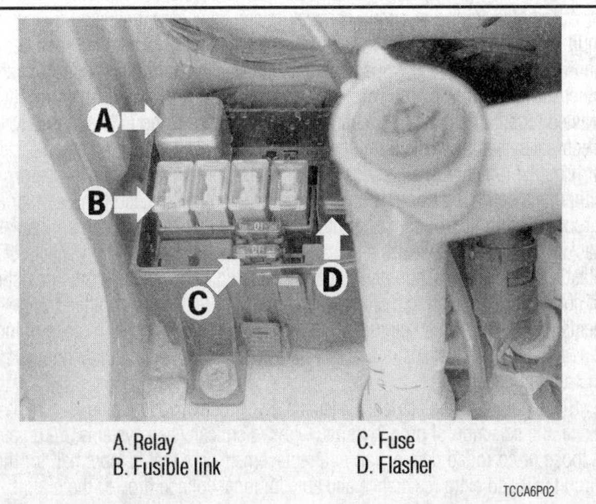

A. Relay
B. Fusible link
C. Fuse
D. Flasher

TCCA6P02

Fig. 3 The underhood fuse and relay panel usually contains fuses, relays, flashers and fusible links

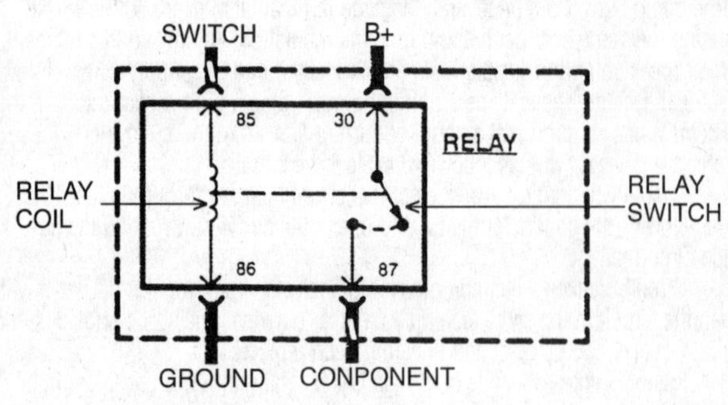

Fig. 4 Relays are composed of a coil and a switch. These two components are linked together so that when one operates, the other operates at the same time. The large wires in the circuit are connected from the battery to one side of the relay switch (B+) and from the opposite side of the relay switch to the load (component). Smaller wires are connected from the relay coil to the control switch for the circuit and from the opposite side of the relay coil to ground

ing current from passing through the circuit, but they can take any electrical form depending on the job they are intended to do. Relays can be considered "remote control switches." They allow a smaller current to operate devices that require higher amperages. When a small current operates the coil, a larger current is allowed to pass by the contacts. Some common circuits which may use relays are the horn, headlights, starter, electric fuel pump and other high draw circuits.

LOAD

Every electrical circuit must include a "load" (something to use the electricity coming from the source). Without this load, the battery would attempt to deliver its entire power supply from one pole to another. This is called a "short circuit." All this electricity would take a short cut to ground and cause a great amount of damage to other components in the circuit by developing a tremendous amount of heat. This condition could develop sufficient heat to melt the insulation on all the surrounding wires and reduce a multiple wire cable to a lump of plastic and copper.

WIRING & HARNESSES

The average vehicle contains meters and meters of wiring, with hundreds of individual connections. To protect the many wires from damage and to keep them from becoming a confusing tangle, they are organized into bundles, enclosed in plastic or taped together and called wiring harnesses. Different harnesses serve different parts of the vehicle. Individual wires are color coded to help trace them through a harness where sections are hidden from view.

Automotive wiring or circuit conductors can be either single strand wire, multi-strand wire or printed circuitry. Single strand wire has a solid metal core and is usually used inside such components as alternators, motors, relays and other devices. Multi-strand wire has a core made of many small strands of wire twisted together into a single conductor. Most of the wiring in an automotive electrical system is made up of multi-strand wire, either as a single conductor or grouped together in a harness. All wiring is color coded on the insulator, either as a solid color or as a colored wire with an identification stripe. A printed circuit is a thin film of copper or other conductor that is printed on an insulator backing. Occasionally, a printed circuit is sandwiched between two sheets of plastic for more protection and flexibility. A complete printed circuit, consisting of conductors, insulating material and connectors for lamps or other components is called a printed circuit board. Printed circuitry is used in place of individual wires or harnesses in places where space is limited, such as behind instrument panels.

Since automotive electrical systems are very sensitive to changes in resistance, the selection of properly sized wires is critical when systems are repaired. A loose or corroded connection or a replacement wire that is too small for the circuit will add extra resistance and an additional voltage drop to the circuit.

The wire gauge number is an expression of the cross-section area of the conductor. Vehicles from countries that use the metric system will typically describe the wire size as its cross-sectional area in square millimeters. In this method, the larger the wire, the greater the number. Another common system for expressing wire size is the American Wire Gauge (AWG) system. As gauge number increases, area decreases and the wire becomes smaller. An 18 gauge wire is smaller than a 4 gauge wire. A wire with a higher gauge number will carry less current than a wire with a lower gauge number. Gauge wire size refers to the size of the strands of the conductor, not the size of the complete wire with insulator. It is possible, therefore, to have two wires of the same gauge with different diameters because one may have thicker insulation than the other.

It is essential to understand how a circuit works before trying to figure out why it doesn't. An electrical schematic shows the electrical current paths when a circuit is operating properly. Schematics break the entire electrical system down into individual circuits. In a schematic, usually no attempt is made to represent wiring and components as they physically appear on the vehicle; switches and other components are shown as simply as possible. Face views of harness connectors show the cavity or terminal locations in all multi-pin connectors to help locate test points.

CONNECTORS

▶ See Figures 5 and 6

Three types of connectors are commonly used in automotive applications—weatherproof, molded and hard shell.

- Weatherproof—these connectors are most commonly used where the connector is exposed to the elements. Terminals are protected against moisture and dirt by sealing rings which provide a weathertight seal. All repairs require the use of a special terminal and the tool required to service it. Unlike standard blade type terminals, these weatherproof terminals cannot be straightened once they are bent. Make certain that the connectors are properly seated and all of the sealing rings are in place when connecting leads.
- Molded—these connectors require complete replacement of the connector if found to be defective. This means splicing a new connector assembly into the harness. All splices should be soldered to insure proper contact. Use care when probing the connections or replacing terminals in them, as it is possible to create a short circuit between opposite terminals. If this happens to the wrong terminal pair, it is possible to damage certain components. Always use jumper wires between connectors for circuit checking and NEVER probe through weatherproof seals.
- Hard Shell—unlike molded connectors, the terminal contacts in hard-shell connectors can be replaced. Replacement usually involves the use of a special terminal removal tool that depresses the locking tangs (barbs) on the connector terminal and allows the connector to be removed from the rear of the shell. The connector shell should be replaced if it shows any evidence of burning, melting, cracks, or breaks. Replace individual terminals that are burnt, corroded, distorted or loose.

Test Equipment

Pinpointing the exact cause of trouble in an electrical circuit is most times accomplished by the use of special test equipment. The following describes different types of commonly used test equipment and briefly explains how to use them in diagnosis. In addition to the information covered below, the tool manufacturer's instructions booklet (provided with the tester) should be read and clearly understood before attempting any test procedures.

JUMPER WIRES

**** CAUTION**

Never use jumper wires made from a thinner gauge wire than the circuit being tested. If the jumper wire is of too small a gauge, it may overheat and possibly melt. Never use jumpers to bypass high resistance loads in a circuit. Bypassing resistances, in effect, creates a short circuit. This may, in turn, cause damage and fire. Jumper wires should only be used to bypass lengths of wire or to simulate switches.

Jumper wires are simple, yet extremely valuable, pieces of test equipment. They are basically test wires which are used to bypass sections of a circuit. Although jumper wires can be purchased, they are usually fabricated from lengths of standard automotive wire and whatever type of connector (alligator clip, spade connector or pin connector) that is required for the particular application being tested. In cramped, hard-to-reach areas, it is advisable to have insulated boots over the jumper wire terminals in order to prevent accidental grounding. It is also advisable to include a standard automotive fuse in any jumper wire. This is commonly referred to as a "fused jumper". By inserting an in-line fuse holder between a set of test leads, a fused jumper wire can be used for bypassing open circuits. Use a 5 amp fuse to provide protection against voltage spikes.

Jumper wires are used primarily to locate open electrical circuits, on either the ground (-) side of the circuit or on the power (+) side. If an electrical component fails to operate, connect the jumper wire between the component and a good ground. If the component operates only with the jumper installed, the ground circuit is open. If the ground circuit is good, but the component does not operate, the circuit between the power feed and component may be open. By moving the jumper wire successively back from the component toward the power source, you can isolate the area of the circuit where the open is located. When the component stops functioning, or the power is cut off, the open is in the segment of wire between the jumper and the point previously tested.

You can sometimes connect the jumper wire directly from the battery to the "hot" terminal of the component, but first make sure the component uses 12 volts in operation. Some electrical components, such as fuel injectors or sensors, are designed to operate on about 4 to 5 volts, and running 12 volts directly to these components will cause damage.

TEST LIGHTS

➧ See Figure 7

The test light is used to check circuits and components while electrical current is flowing through them. It is used for voltage and ground tests. To use a 12 volt test light, connect the ground clip to a good ground and probe wherever necessary with the pick. The test light will illuminate when voltage is detected. This does not necessarily mean that 12 volts (or any particular amount of voltage) is present; it only means that some voltage is present. It is advisable before using the test light to touch its ground clip and probe across the battery posts or terminals to make sure the light is operating properly.

✲✲ WARNING

Do not use a test light to probe electronic ignition, spark plug or coil wires. Never use a pick-type test light to probe wiring on computer controlled systems unless specifically instructed to do so. Any wire insulation that is pierced by the test light probe should be taped and sealed with silicone after testing.

Like the jumper wire, the 12 volt test light is used to isolate opens in circuits. But, whereas the jumper wire is used to bypass the open to operate the load, the 12 volt test light is used to locate the presence of voltage in a circuit. If the test light illuminates, there is power up to that point in the circuit; if the test light does not illuminate, there is an open circuit (no power). Move the test light in successive steps back toward the power source until the light in the handle illuminates. The open is between the probe and a point which was previously probed.

The self-powered test light is similar in design to the 12 volt test light, but contains a 1.5 volt penlight battery in the handle. It is most often used in place of a multimeter to check for open or short circuits when power is isolated from the circuit (continuity test).

The battery in a self-powered test light does not provide much current. A weak battery may not provide enough power to illuminate the test light even when a complete circuit is made (especially if there is high resistance in the circuit). Always make sure that the test battery is strong. To check the battery, briefly touch the ground clip to the probe; if the light glows brightly, the battery is strong enough for testing.

➡A self-powered test light should not be used on any computer controlled system or component. The small amount of electricity transmitted by the test light is enough to damage many electronic automotive components.

MULTIMETERS

Multimeters are an extremely useful tool for troubleshooting electrical problems. They can be purchased in either analog or digital form and have a price range to suit any budget. A multimeter is a voltmeter, ammeter and ohmmeter (along with other features) combined into one instrument. It is often used when testing solid state circuits because of its high input impedance (usually 10 megaohms or more). A brief description of the multimeter main test functions follows:

- Voltmeter—the voltmeter is used to measure voltage at any point in a circuit, or to measure the voltage drop across any part of a circuit. Voltmeters usually have various scales and a selector switch to allow the reading of different voltage ranges. The voltmeter has a positive and a negative lead. To avoid damage to the meter, always connect the negative lead to the negative (-) side of the circuit (to ground or nearest the ground side of the circuit) and connect the positive lead to the positive (+) side of the circuit (to the power source or the nearest power source). Note that the negative voltmeter lead will always be black and that the positive voltmeter will always be some color other than black (usually red).
- Ohmmeter—the ohmmeter is designed to read resistance (measured in ohms) in a circuit or component. Most ohmmeters will have a selector switch which permits the measurement of different ranges of resistance (usually the selector switch allows the multiplication of the meter reading by 10, 100, 1,000 and 10,000). Some ohmmeters are "auto-ranging" which means the meter itself will determine which scale to use. Since the meters are powered by an internal battery, the ohmmeter can be used like a self-powered test light. When the ohmmeter is connected, current from the ohmmeter flows through the circuit or component being tested. Since the ohmmeter's internal resistance and voltage are known values, the amount of current flow through the meter depends on the resistance of the circuit or component being tested. The ohmmeter can also be used to perform a continuity test for suspected open circuits. In using the meter for making continuity checks, do not be concerned with the actual resistance readings. Zero resistance, or any ohm reading, indicates continuity in the circuit. Infinite resistance indicates an opening in the circuit. A high resistance reading where there should be none indicates a problem in the circuit. Checks for short circuits are made in the same manner as checks for open circuits, except that the circuit must be isolated from both power and normal ground. Infinite resistance indicates no continuity, while zero resistance indicates a dead short.

TCCA6P03

Fig. 5 Hard shell (left) and weatherproof (right) connectors have replaceable terminals

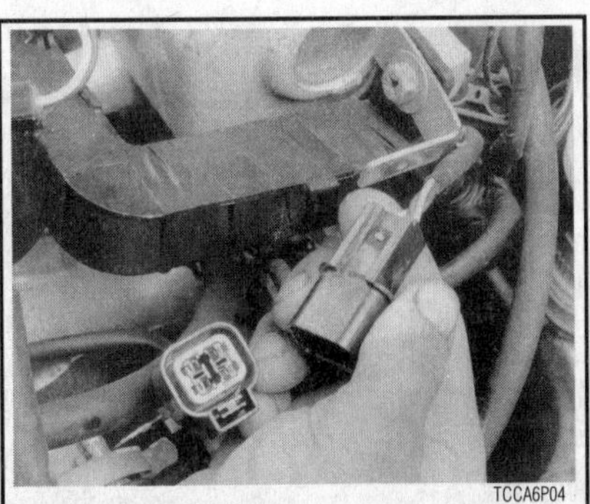
TCCA6P04

Fig. 6 Weatherproof connectors are most commonly used in the engine compartment or where the connector is exposed to the elements

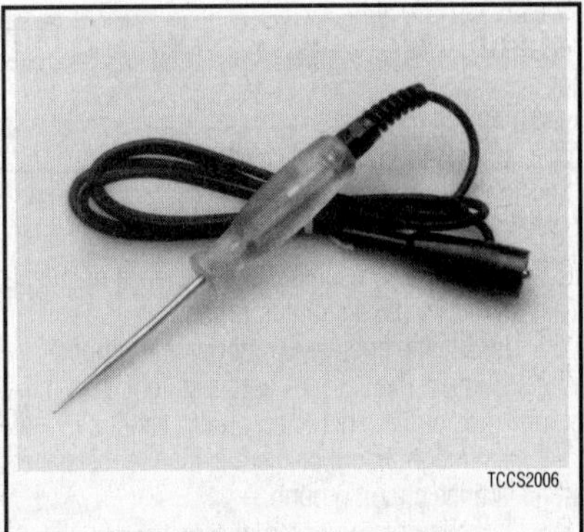
TCCS2006

Fig. 7 A 12 volt test light is used to detect the presence of voltage in a circuit

**** WARNING**

Never use an ohmmeter to check the resistance of a component or wire while there is voltage applied to the circuit.

- Ammeter—an ammeter measures the amount of current flowing through a circuit in units called amperes or amps. At normal operating voltage, most circuits have a characteristic amount of amperes, called "current draw" which can be measured using an ammeter. By referring to a specified current draw rating, then measuring the amperes and comparing the two values, one can determine what is happening within the circuit to aid in diagnosis. An open circuit, for example, will not allow any current to flow, so the ammeter reading will be zero. A damaged component or circuit will have an increased current draw, so the reading will be high. The ammeter is always connected in series with the circuit being tested. All of the current that normally flows through the circuit must also flow through the ammeter; if there is any other path for the current to follow, the ammeter reading will not be accurate. The ammeter itself has very little resistance to current flow and, therefore, will not affect the circuit, but it will measure current draw only when the circuit is closed and electricity is flowing. Excessive current draw can blow fuses and drain the battery, while a reduced current draw can cause motors to run slowly, lights to dim and other components to not operate properly.

Troubleshooting Electrical Systems

When diagnosing a specific problem, organized troubleshooting is a must. The complexity of a modern automotive vehicle demands that you approach any problem in a logical, organized manner. There are certain troubleshooting techniques, however, which are standard:

- Establish when the problem occurs. Does the problem appear only under certain conditions? Were there any noises, odors or other unusual symptoms? Isolate the problem area. To do this, make some simple tests and observations, then eliminate the systems that are working properly. Check for obvious problems, such as broken wires and loose or dirty connections. Always check the obvious before assuming something complicated is the cause.
- Test for problems systematically to determine the cause once the problem area is isolated. Are all the components functioning properly? Is there power going to electrical switches and motors. Performing careful, systematic checks will often turn up most causes on the first inspection, without wasting time checking components that have little or no relationship to the problem.
- Test all repairs after the work is done to make sure that the problem is fixed. Some causes can be traced to more than one component, so a careful verification of repair work is important in order to pick up additional malfunctions that may cause a problem to reappear or a different problem to arise. A blown fuse, for example, is a simple problem that may require more than another fuse to repair. If you don't look for a problem that caused a fuse to blow, a shorted wire (for example) may go undetected.

Experience has shown that most problems tend to be the result of a fairly simple and obvious cause, such as loose or corroded connectors, bad grounds or damaged wire insulation which causes a short. This makes careful visual inspection of components during testing essential to quick and accurate troubleshooting.

Testing

OPEN CIRCUITS

See Figure 8

This test already assumes the existence of an open in the circuit and it is used to help locate the open portion.

1. Isolate the circuit from power and ground.
2. Connect the self-powered test light or ohmmeter ground clip to the ground side of the circuit and probe sections of the circuit sequentially.
3. If the light is out or there is infinite resistance, the open is between the probe and the circuit ground.
4. If the light is on or the meter shows continuity, the open is between the probe and the end of the circuit toward the power source.

SHORT CIRCUITS

➡Never use a self-powered test light to perform checks for opens or shorts when power is applied to the circuit under test. The test light can be damaged by outside power.

1. Isolate the circuit from power and ground.
2. Connect the self-powered test light or ohmmeter ground clip to a good ground and probe any easy-to-reach point in the circuit.
3. If the light comes on or there is continuity, there is a short somewhere in the circuit.
4. To isolate the short, probe a test point at either end of the isolated circuit (the light should be on or the meter should indicate continuity).
5. Leave the test light probe engaged and sequentially open connectors or switches, remove parts, etc. until the light goes out or continuity is broken.
6. When the light goes out, the short is between the last two circuit components which were opened.

VOLTAGE

This test determines voltage available from the battery and should be the first step in any electrical troubleshooting procedure after visual inspection. Many electrical problems, especially on computer controlled systems, can be caused by a low state of charge in the battery. Excessive corrosion at the battery cable terminals can cause poor contact that will prevent proper charging and full battery current flow.

1. Set the voltmeter selector switch to the 20V position.
2. Connect the multimeter negative lead to the battery's negative (-) post or terminal and the positive lead to the battery's positive (+) post or terminal.
3. Turn the ignition switch **ON** to provide a load.
4. A well charged battery should register over 12 volts. If the meter reads below 11.5 volts, the battery power may be insufficient to operate the electrical system properly.

VOLTAGE DROP

See Figure 9

When current flows through a load, the voltage beyond the load drops. This voltage drop is due to the resistance created by the load and also by small resistances created by corrosion at the connectors and damaged insulation on the wires. The maximum allowable voltage drop under load is critical, especially if there is more than one load in the circuit, since all voltage drops are cumulative.

1. Set the voltmeter selector switch to the 20 volt position.
2. Connect the multimeter negative lead to a good ground.
3. Operate the circuit and check the voltage prior to the first component (load).
4. There should be little or no voltage drop in the circuit prior to the first component. If a voltage drop exists, the wire or connectors in the circuit are suspect.
5. While operating the first component in the circuit, probe the ground side of the component with the positive meter lead and observe the voltage readings. A small voltage drop should be noticed. This voltage drop is caused by the resistance of the component.
6. Repeat the test for each component (load) down the circuit.
7. If a large voltage drop is noticed, the preceding component, wire or connector is suspect.

RESISTANCE

See Figures 10 and 11

**** WARNING**

Never use an ohmmeter with power applied to the circuit. The ohmmeter is designed to operate on its own power supply. The normal 12 volt electrical system voltage could damage the meter!

1. Isolate the circuit from the vehicle's power source.
2. Ensure that the ignition key is **OFF** when disconnecting any components or the battery.
3. Where necessary, also isolate at least one side of the circuit to be checked, in order to avoid reading parallel resistances. Parallel circuit resistances will always give a lower reading than the actual resistance of either of the branches.

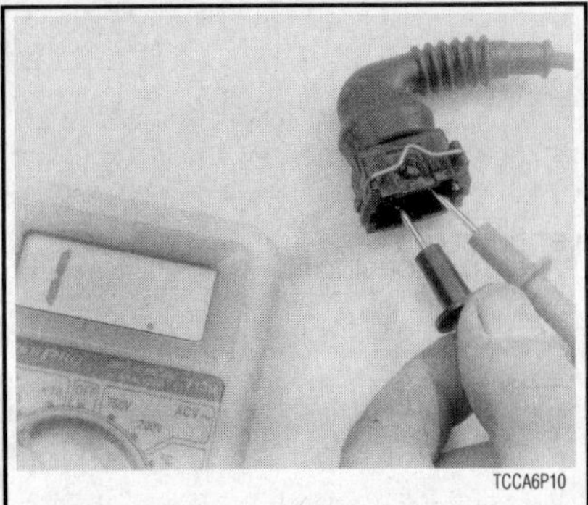

Fig. 8 The infinite reading on this multimeter indicates that the circuit is open

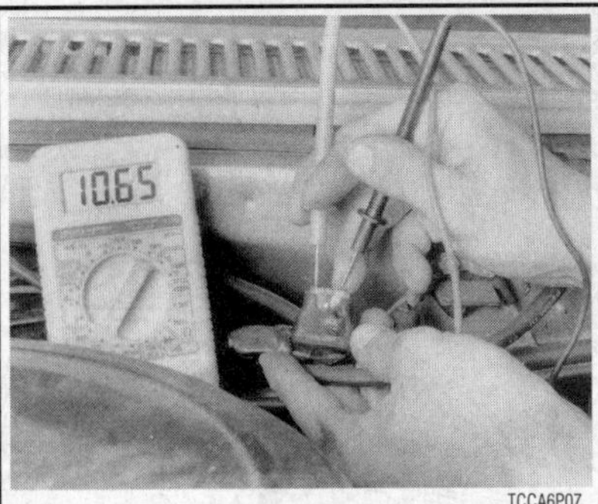

Fig. 9 This voltage drop test revealed high resistance (low voltage) in the circuit

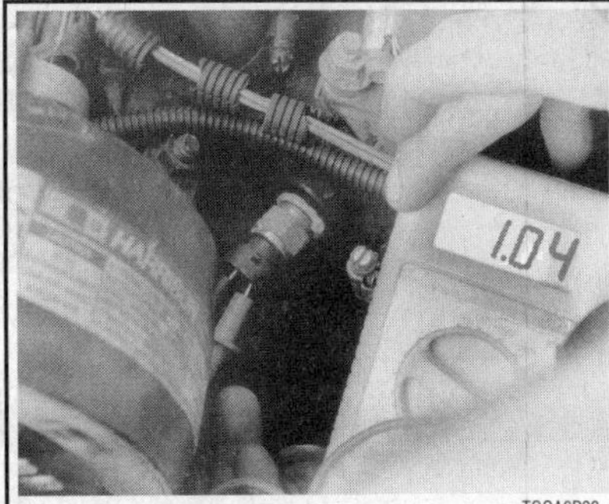

Fig. 10 Checking the resistance of a coolant temperature sensor with an ohmmeter. Reading is 1.04 kilohms

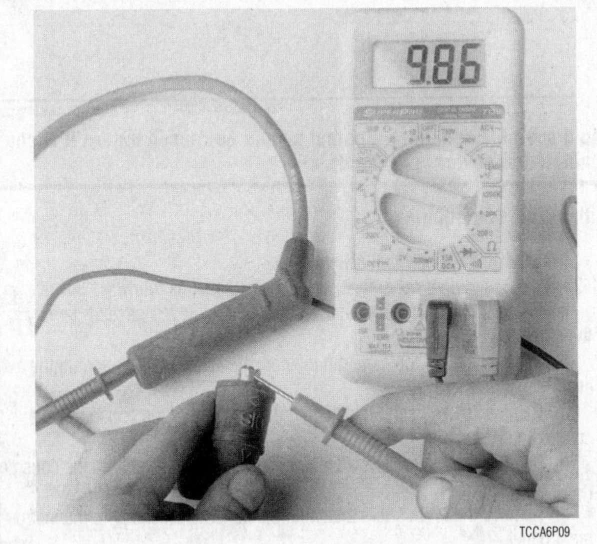

Fig. 11 Spark plug wires can be checked for excessive resistance using an ohmmeter

4. Connect the meter leads to both sides of the circuit (wire or component) and read the actual measured ohms on the meter scale. Make sure the selector switch is set to the proper ohm scale for the circuit being tested, to avoid misreading the ohmmeter test value.

Wire and Connector Repair

Almost anyone can replace damaged wires, as long as the proper tools and parts are available. Wire and terminals are available to fit almost any need. Even the specialized weatherproof, molded and hard shell connectors are now available from aftermarket suppliers.

Be sure the ends of all the wires are fitted with the proper terminal hardware and connectors. Wrapping a wire around a stud is never a permanent solution and will only cause trouble later. Replace wires one at a time to avoid confusion. Always route wires exactly the same as the factory.

➡If connector repair is necessary, only attempt it if you have the proper tools. Weatherproof and hard shell connectors require special tools to release the pins inside the connector. Attempting to repair these connectors with conventional hand tools will damage them.

Add-On Electrical Equipment

The electrical system in your vehicle is designed to perform under reasonable operating conditions without interference between components. Before any additional electrical equipment is installed, it is recommended that you consult your dealer or a reputable repair facility that is familiar with the vehicle and its systems.

If the vehicle is equipped with mobile radio equipment and/or mobile telephone, it may have an effect upon the operation of any on-board computer control modules. Radio Frequency Interference (RFI) from the communications system can be picked up by the vehicle's wiring harnesses and conducted into the control module, giving it the wrong messages at the wrong time. Although well shielded against RFI, the computer should be further protected by taking the following measures:

- Install the antenna as far as possible from the control module. For instance, if the module is located behind the center console area, then the antenna should be mounted at the rear of the vehicle.
- Keep the antenna wiring a minimum of eight inches away from any wiring running to control modules and from the module itself. NEVER wind the antenna wire around any other wiring.
- Mount the equipment as far from the control module as possible. Be very careful during installation not to drill through any wires or short a wire harness with a mounting screw.
- Insure that the electrical feed wire(s) to the equipment are properly and tightly connected. Loose connectors can cause interference.
- Make certain that the equipment is properly grounded to the vehicle. Poor grounding can damage expensive equipment.

HEATER AND AIR CONDITIONER

Blower Motor

REMOVAL & INSTALLATION

➧ See Figure 12

1. Disconnect the negative battery cable. Loosen the glove compartment assembly by squeezing the sides together to disengage the retainer tabs.
2. Let the glove compartment and door hang down in front of instrument panel and remove blower motor cooling hose.
3. Disconnect electrical wiring harness. Remove four screws attaching motor to housing. Pull motor and wheel out of housing.
4. Installation is the reverse of the removal procedure.

Blower Motor Resistor

REMOVAL & INSTALLATION

➧ See Figures 13 thru 19

1. Disconnect the negative battery cable.
2. Disconnect the blower motor resistor wiring harness.
3. Remove the two screws that attach the resistor board to the evaporator case and remove the resistor assembly.
4. Installation is the reverse of the removal procedure.

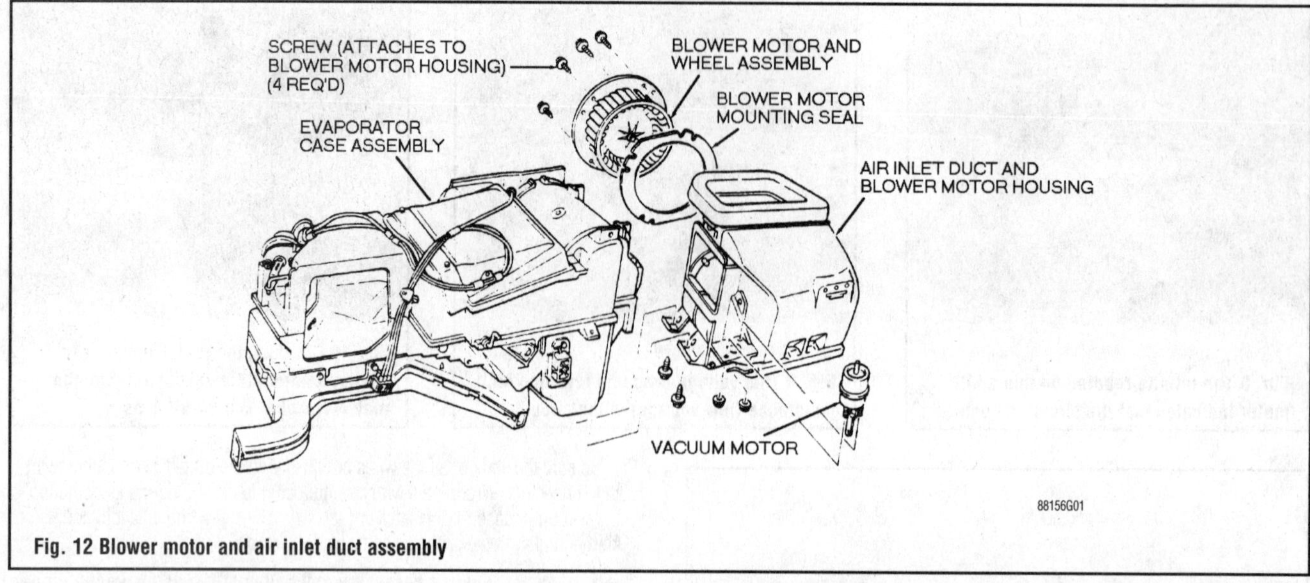

Fig. 12 Blower motor and air inlet duct assembly

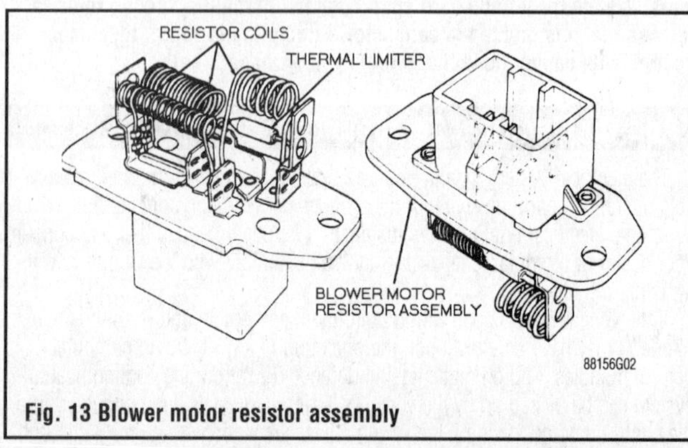

Fig. 13 Blower motor resistor assembly

Heater Core

REMOVAL & INSTALLATION

➧ See Figure 20

⁂ CAUTION

When draining the coolant, keep in mind that cats and dogs are attracted to ethylene glycol antifreeze, and are likely to drink any that is left in an uncovered container or in puddles on the ground. This will prove fatal in sufficient quantity. Always drain the coolant into a sealable container. Coolant should be reused unless it is contaminated or several years old.

Without Air Conditioning

1. Disconnect the negative battery cable.
2. Remove the floor console and instrument panel as follows:
   a. Remove the four screws that attach the console top panel assembly to the console assembly.
   b. Lift the console top panel off the console assembly and unplug the two electrical connectors.
   c. Remove the two screws attaching the rear end of the console to the console panel support.
   d. Remove the four screws attaching the console assembly to the console panel front support.
   e. Remove the four screws attaching the console assembly to the instrument panel.
   f. Lift the console assembly off of the transmission tunnel.

➡The console assembly includes a snap-in finish panel which conceals the heater control assembly attaching screws. To gain access to these screws, it is necessary to remove the floor console

   g. Disconnect all underhood wiring from the main wiring harness. Disengage the rubber grommet seal from the dash panel and push the wiring harness and connectors into the passenger compartment.
   h. Remove the three bolts attaching the steering column opening cover and reinforcement panel. Remove the cover.
   i. Remove the steering column opening reinforcement by removing the two bolts. Remove the two bolts retaining the lower steering column opening reinforcement and remove the reinforcement.

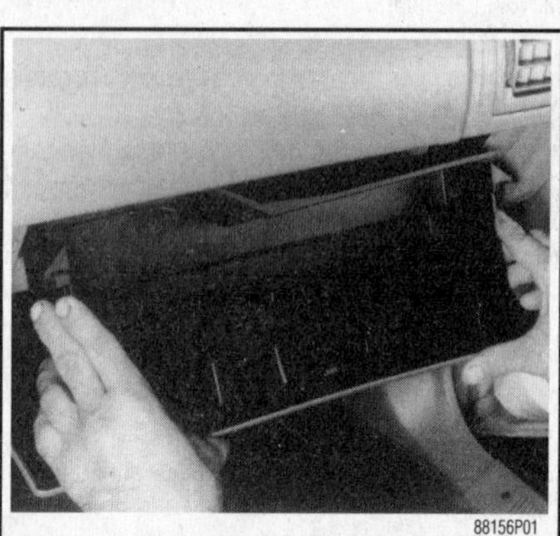

Fig. 14 Push in the sides of the glove compartment door to allow it to drop down

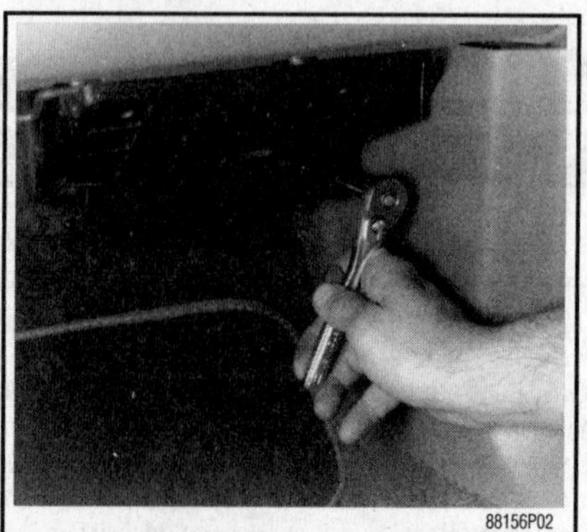

Fig. 15 This cover may need to be removed to reach the blower motor

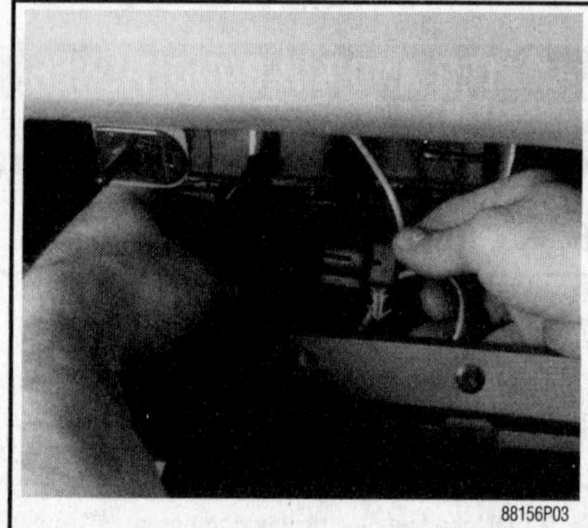

Fig. 16 The blower motor wiring may be held by a push in tab

88156P04

Fig. 17 The motor cooling hose pushes onto its fitting

88156P05

Fig. 18 Note that the mounting flange has locator tabs in it allowing it to fit in only one orientation

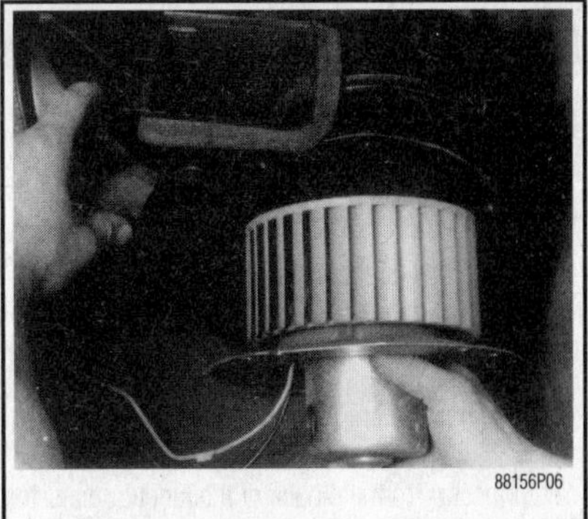

88156P06

Fig. 19 Check the fan blades for damage and for debris in the housing

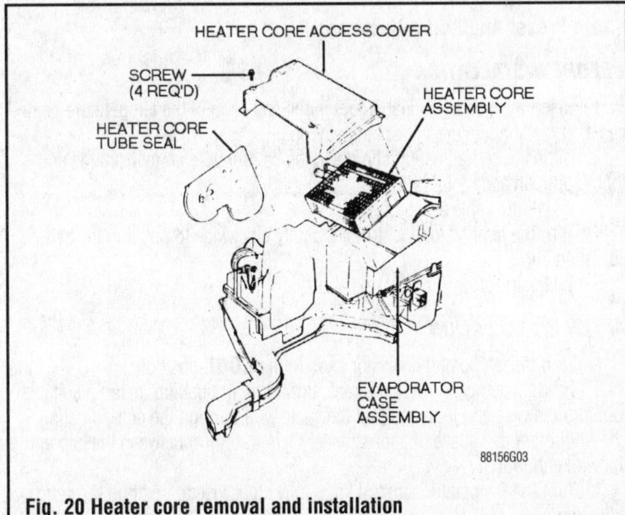

Fig. 20 Heater core removal and installation

j. Remove the six steering column retaining nuts. Two are retaining the hood release mechanism and four retain the column to the lower brake pedal support. Lower the steering column to the floor.

k. Remove the steering column upper and lower shrouds and disconnect the wiring from the multi-function switch.

l. Remove the brake pedal support nut and snap out the defroster grille.

m. Remove the screws from the speaker covers. Snap out the speaker covers. Remove the front screws retaining the right and left scuff plates at the cowl trim panel. Remove the right and left side cowl trim panels.

n. Disconnect the wiring at the right and left cowl sides. Remove the cowl side retaining bolts, one on each side.

o. Open the glove compartment door and flex the glove compartment bin tabs inward. Drop down the glove compartment door assembly.

p. Remove the five cowl top screw attachments. Gently pull the instrument panel away from the cowl. Disconnect the speedometer cable and wiring.

3. Drain the coolant from the cooling system and remove the hoses from the heater core. Plug the hoses and the core.

4. Remove the screw attaching the air inlet duct and blower housing assembly support bracket to the cowl top panel.

5. Disconnect the black vacuum supply hose from the in-line vacuum check valve in the engine compartment.

6. Disconnect the blower motor wire harness from the resistor and motor head.

7. Working under the hood, remove the two nuts retaining the heater assembly to the dash panel.

8. In the passenger compartment, remove the screw attaching the heater assembly support bracket to the cowl top panel. Remove the one screw retaining the bracket below the heater assembly to the dash panel.

9. Carefully pull the heater assembly away from the dash panel and remove from the vehicle.

10. Remove the four heater core access cover attaching screws and remove the access cover from the case.

11. Lift the heater core and seal from the case. Remove the seal from the heater core tubes.

To install:

12. Install the heater core tube seal on the heater core tubes. Inspect the heater core sealer in the heater case and replace, if necessary.

13. Install the heater core in the case with the seals on the outside of the case. Position the heater core access cover on the case and install the four attaching screws.

14. Position the heater assembly in the vehicle. Install the screw attaching the heater assembly support bracket to the cowl top panel.

15. Check the heater assembly drain tube to ensure it is through the dash panel and is not pinched or kinked.

16. Working under the hood, install the two nuts retaining the heater assembly to the dash panel. Install the air inlet duct and blower housing support bracket attaching screw. Install one screw to the retainer bracket below the heater assembly to the dash panel.

17. Connect the blower motor ground wire to ground and the harness to the resistor and blower motor lead.

18. Connect the black vacuum supply hose to the vacuum check valve in the engine compartment.

19. Install the instrument panel and floor console by reversing the removal procedure.

20. Connect the heater hoses to the heater core and fill the cooling system. Check the system for proper operation.

With Air Conditioning

1. Disconnect the negative battery cable and drain the cooling system.

2. Discharge the refrigerant from the air conditioning system according to the proper procedure.

3. Remove the evaporator case assembly.

➡Whenever an evaporator case is replaced, it will be necessary to replace the suction accumulator/drier.

4. Remove the four heater core access cover attaching screws and remove the cover from the case.

5. Lift the heater core and seal from the case. Remove the seal from the heater core tubes.

To install:

6. Install the heater core tube seal on the heater core tubes.

7. Inspect the heater core sealer in the evaporator case. Replace with suitable caulking cord, if necessary.

8. Install the heater core in the case with the seals on the outside of the case. Position the heater core access cover on the case and install the four attaching screws.

9. Install the evaporator case.

10. Fill the cooling system. Leak test, evacuate and charge the refrigerant system according to the proper procedure. Observe all safety precautions.

11. Connect the negative battery cable and check the system for proper operation.

Control Panel

REMOVAL & INSTALLATION

See Figure 21

1. Disconnect the negative battery cable.
2. Remove the snap-in trim moulding in the floor console to expose the four control assembly attaching screws. Remove the four screws attaching the control assembly to the instrument panel.
3. Roll the control out of the opening in the console. Unplug the fan switch connectors and temperature control cable. Remove the vacuum hose and electrical connector from the back of the function selector knob. Disconnect the control assembly illumination bulbs.
4. Remove the control assembly.

To install:

5. Connect the temperature cable to the geared arm on the temperature control.
6. Install the electrical connector at the following locations: blower switch, control assembly illumination bulbs and function selector switch.
7. Install the vacuum harness connector for the function selector knob.
8. Roll the control assembly into position against the instrument panel and install the four attaching screws.
9. Snap the console trim moulding into position, connect the negative battery cable and check the system for proper operation.

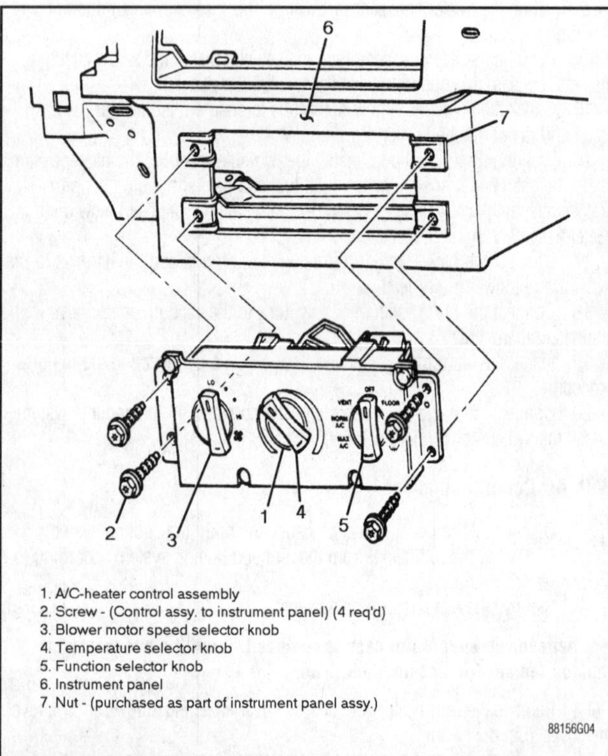

Fig. 21 Heater control assembly

Control Cables

ADJUSTMENT

See Figure 22

The temperature control cable is self-adjusting with the movement of the temperature selector knob to its fully clockwise position in the red band on the face of the control assembly. To prevent kinking of the control wire, a preset adjustment should be made before attempting to perform the self-adjustment operation. The preset adjustment may be performed either with the cable installed in the vehicle or before cable installation.

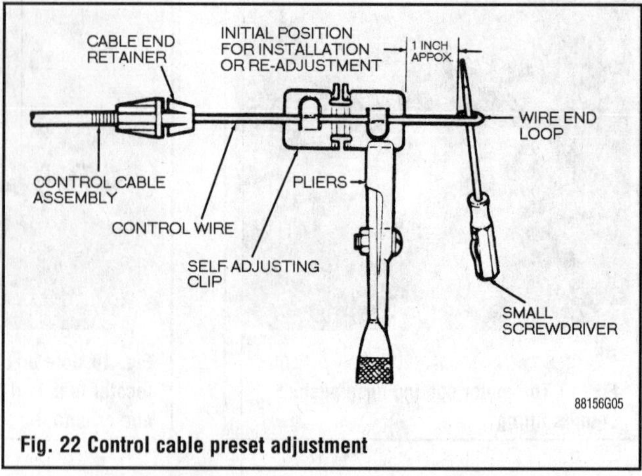

Fig. 22 Control cable preset adjustment

Cable Preset And Self-Adjustment

BEFORE INSTALLATION

1. Insert the end of a suitable tool in the end-loop of the temperature control cable, at the temperature door crank arm end.
2. Slide the self-adjusting clip down the control wire, away from the end loop, approximately 1 in. (25mm).
3. Install the cable assembly.
4. Turn the temperature control knob fully clockwise to position the self-adjusting clip.
5. Check for proper control operation.

AFTER INSTALLATION

1. Turn the temperature selector knob to the **COOL** position.
2. Hold the temperature door crank arm firmly in position, insert a suitable tool into the wire end loop and pull the cable wire through the self-adjusting clip until there is a space of approximately 1 in. (25 mm) between the clip and the wire end loop.
3. Turn the temperature control knob fully clockwise to position the self-adjusting clip.
4. Check for proper control operation.

REMOVAL & INSTALLATION

1. Disconnect the negative battery cable.
2. Remove the control assembly from the instrument panel.
3. Disengage the temperature control cable from the cable actuator on the control assembly. Disconnect the temperature cable from the plenum temperature blend door crank arm and cable mounting bracket.
4. Note the cable routing and remove the cable from the vehicle.

To install:

5. Check to ensure the self-adjusting clip is at least 1 in. (25 mm) from the end loop of the control cable.
6. Route the cable behind the instrument panel and connect the control cable to the mounting bracket on the plenum. Install the self-adjusting clip on the temperature blend door crank arm.
7. Engage the cable end with the cable actuator on the control assembly. Install the control assembly in the instrument panel.
8. Turn the temperature control knob all the way to the right, to the **WARM** position, to position the self-adjusting clip on the control cable. Check the temperature control knob for proper operation.
9. Connect the negative battery cable and check the system for proper operation.

Electric Cooling Fan

TESTING

1. Disconnect the electrical connector at the cooling fan motor.
2. Connect a jumper wire between the negative motor lead and ground.

3. Connect another jumper wire between the positive motor lead and the positive terminal of the battery.
4. If the cooling fan motor does not run, it must be replaced.

REMOVAL & INSTALLATION

2.3L Engine

1. Disconnect the negative battery cable.
2. Remove the fan wiring harness from the routing clip. Unplug the wiring harness from the fan motor connector by pulling up on the single lock finger.
3. Remove the four mounting bracket attaching screws and remove the fan assembly from the vehicle.
4. Remove the retaining clip from the end of the motor shaft and remove the fan.

➡A metal burr may be present on the motor after the retaining clip is removed. Deburring of the shaft may be required to remove the fan.

5. Remove the nuts attaching the fan motor to the mounting bracket.
6. Installation is the reverse of the removal procedure. Tighten the fan motor-to-mounting bracket attaching nuts to 48–62 inch lbs. (5.5–7.0 Nm) and the mounting bracket attaching screws to 70–95 inch lbs. (8.0–10.5 Nm).

A/C Vacuum Motors

OPERATION

The vacuum motors operate the doors which in turn direct the airflow through the system. A vacuum selector valve, controlled by the function control lever, distributes the vacuum to the various door vacuum motors.

REMOVAL & INSTALLATION

➧ See Figure 23

Panel/Defrost Door Vacuum Motor

1. Disconnect the negative battery cable.
2. Remove the instrument panel according to the following procedure:
   a. Remove the four screws that attach the floor console top panel assembly to the floor console assembly.
   b. Lift the console top panel off the console assembly and unplug the two electrical connectors.
   c. Remove the two screws attaching the rear end of the console to the console panel support assembly.

Fig. 23 Check the vacuum motor fittings for leaks and deterioration

   d. Remove four screws attaching the console assembly to the console panel front support.
   e. Remove the four screws attaching the console assembly to the instrument panel.
   f. Lift the console assembly off of the transmission tunnel.

➡The console assembly includes a snap-in finish panel which conceals the heater and air conditioning control assembly attaching screws. To gain access to these screws, it is necessary to remove the floor console.

   g. Disconnect all underhood wiring from the main wiring harness. Disengage the rubber grommet seal from the dash panel and push the wiring harness and connectors into the passenger compartment.
   h. Remove the three bolts attaching the steering column opening cover and reinforcement panel. Remove the cover.
   i. Remove the steering column opening reinforcement by removing the two bolts. Remove the two bolts retaining the lower steering column opening reinforcement and remove the reinforcement.
   j. Remove the six steering column retaining nuts; two retain the hood release mechanism and four retain the column to the lower brake pedal support. Lower the steering column to the floor.
   k. Remove the steering column upper and lower shrouds and disconnect the wiring from the multi-function switch.
   l. Remove the brake pedal support nut and snap out the defroster grille.
   m. Remove the screws from the speaker covers. Snap out the speaker covers. Remove the front screws retaining the right and left scuff plates at the cowl trim panel. Remove the right and left side cowl trim panels.
   n. Disconnect the wiring at the right and left cowl sides. Remove the cowl side retaining bolts, one on each side.
   o. Open the glove compartment door and flex the glove compartment bin tabs inward. Drop down the glove compartment door assembly.
   p. Remove the five cowl top screw attachments. Gently pull the instrument panel away from the cowl. Disconnect the speedometer cable and wire connectors.
3. Remove the spring nut retaining the panel/defrost door vacuum motor arm to the door shaft.
4. Remove the two nuts retaining the vacuum motor to the mounting bracket. Remove the vacuum motor from the mounting bracket and disconnect the vacuum hose.

To install:

5. Position the vacuum motor to the mounting bracket and door shaft. Install two nuts to attach the panel/defrost vacuum motor to the mounting bracket.
6. Connect the vacuum hose to the panel/defrost vacuum motor.
7. Install the instrument panel by reversing the removal procedure.
8. Connect the negative battery cable.

Floor/Defrost Door Vacuum Motor

1. Disconnect the negative battery cable and drain the cooling system.
2. Discharge the refrigerant from the air conditioning system according the to proper procedure.
3. Remove the instrument panel according to the following procedure:
   a. Remove the four screws that attach the floor console top panel to the floor console assembly.
   b. Lift the console top panel assembly off the console and disconnect the two electrical connectors.
   c. Remove the two screws attaching the rear end of the console to the console panel support assembly.
   d. Remove four screws attaching the console assembly to the console panel front support.
   e. Remove the four screws attaching the console assembly to the instrument panel.
   f. Lift the console assembly off of the transmission tunnel.

➡The console assembly includes a snap-in finish panel which conceals the heater and air conditioning control assembly attaching screws. To gain access to these screws, it is necessary to remove the floor console.

   g. Disconnect all underhood wiring from the main wiring harness. Disengage the rubber grommet seal from the dash panel and push the wiring harness and connectors into the passenger compartment.

h. Remove the three bolts attaching the steering column opening cover and reinforcement panel. Remove the cover.

i. Remove the steering column opening reinforcement by removing two bolts. Remove the two bolts retaining the lower steering column opening reinforcement and remove the reinforcement.

j. Remove the six steering column retaining nuts; two retain the hood release mechanism and four retain the column to the lower brake pedal support. Lower the steering column to the floor.

k. Remove the steering column upper and lower shrouds and disconnect the wiring from the multi-function switch.

l. Remove the brake pedal support nut and snap out the defroster grille.

m. Remove the screws from the speaker covers. Snap out the speaker covers. Remove the front screws retaining the right and left scuff plates at the cowl trim panel. Remove the right and left side cowl trim panels.

n. Disconnect the wiring at the right and left cowl sides. Remove the cowl side retaining bolts, one on each side.

o. Open the glove compartment door and flex the glove compartment bin tabs inward. Drop down the glove compartment door assembly.

p. Remove the five cowl top screw attachments. Gently pull the instrument panel away from the cowl. Disconnect the speedometer cable and wiring.

4. Disconnect the liquid line and the accumulator/drier inlet tube from the evaporator core at the dash panel. Cap the refrigerant lines and evaporator core tube to prevent the entrance of dirt and excessive moisture.
5. Disconnect the heater hoses from the heater core tubes and plug the hoses and tubes.
6. Remove the screw attaching the air inlet duct and blower housing assembly support brace to the cowl top panel.
7. Disconnect the black vacuum supply hose from the in-line vacuum check valve in the engine compartment. Disconnect the blower motor wires from the wire harness and disconnect the wire harness from the blower motor resistor.
8. Working under the hood, remove the two nuts retaining the evaporator case to the dash panel. Inside the passenger compartment, remove the two screws attaching the evaporator case support brackets to the cowl top panel.
9. Remove the one screw retaining the bracket below the evaporator case to the dash panel. Carefully pull the evaporator case away from the dash panel and remove the evaporator case assembly from the vehicle.
10. Remove the two nuts that attach the vacuum motor to the case and disconnect the vacuum hose from the motor.
11. Remove the spring nut that attaches the motor crank arm to the shaft and remove the motor.

To install:

12. Position the motor and install the spring nut that attaches the motor crank arm to the shaft.
13. Connect the vacuum hose to the motor and install the two nuts that attach the vacuum motor to the case.
14. Position the evaporator case assembly in the vehicle. Install the screws attaching the evaporator case support brackets to the cowl top panel. Check the evaporator case drain tube to ensure it is through the dash panel and is not pinched or kinked.
15. Install one screw retaining the bracket below the evaporator case to the dash panel. Working under the hood, install the two nuts retaining the evaporator case to the dash panel. Tighten the four nuts and two screws in the engine compartment. Tighten the two screws in the passenger compartment and the two support bracket attaching screws.
16. Connect the blower motor wire harness to the resistor and blower motor. Connect the black vacuum supply hose to the vacuum check valve in the engine compartment.
17. Using new O-rings lubricated with clean refrigerant oil, connect the liquid line and suction accumulator inlet to the evaporator core tubes. Tighten each connection using a backup wrench to prevent component damage.
18. Install the instrument panel by reversing the removal procedure.
19. Connect the heater hoses to the heater core and fill the cooling system.
20. Connect the negative battery cable. Leak test, evacuate and charge the refrigerant system according to the proper procedure. Observe all safety precautions.
21. Check the system for proper operation.

Outside/Recirculating Door Vacuum Motor

1. Remove the glove compartment. Disconnect the vacuum hose from the vacuum motor.
2. Remove the motor arm retainer from the outside/recirculating door shaft.
3. Remove the two nuts retaining the vacuum motor to the mounting bracket and remove the motor.
4. Installation is the reverse of the removal procedure.

CRUISE CONTROL

Control Switches

REMOVAL & INSTALLATION

➡Please refer to the Steering Wheel removal and installation procedure in Section 8 for control switches which are located in the steering wheel. Extreme caution must be observed with vehicles equipped with air bags!

Speed Sensor

REMOVAL & INSTALLATION

➧ See Figure 24

1. Raise the vehicle and support safely on jackstands.
2. Remove the bolt retaining the speed sensor mounting clip to the transmission.
3. Remove the sensor and the drive gear from the transmission.
4. Uplug the electrical connector and disconnect the speedometer cable from the speed sensor.
5. Remove the speedometer cable by pulling it out of the sensor.

➡DO NOT remove the spring retainer clip with the speedometer cable in the sensor.

6. Remove the drive gear retainer. Remove the drive gear from the sensor.

To Install:

7. Position the drive gear to the speed sensor. Install the gear retainer.
8. Plug in the electrical connector.

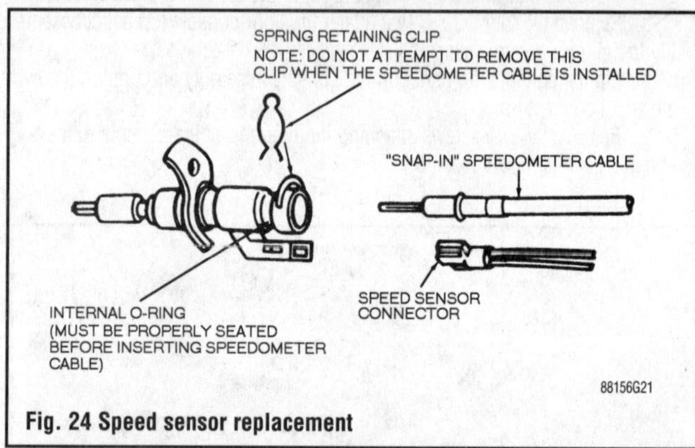

Fig. 24 Speed sensor replacement

9. Check that the O-ring is properly seated in the sensor housing. Snap the speedometer cable onto the sensor housing.
10. Insert the sensor assembly into the transmission. Install the retaining bolt. Lower the vehicle.

Amplifier

REMOVAL & INSTALLATION

➧ See Figure 25

The amplifier is located inside the passenger compartment, on the left hand side cowl panel around the parking brake.

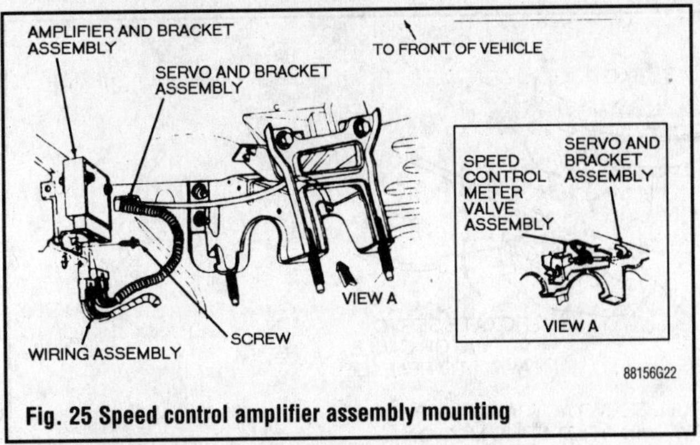

Fig. 25 Speed control amplifier assembly mounting

1. Disconnect the negative battery cable.
2. Remove the screws retaining the amplifier assembly to the mounting bracket.
3. Unplug the two electrical connectors at the amplifier.

To Install:

4. Plug in the two electrical connectors at the amplifier.
5. Position the amplifier assembly on the mounting bracket and install the retaining screws.
6. Connect the negative battery cable.

Servo

REMOVAL & INSTALLATION

See Figures 26 and 27

1. Disconnect the negative battery cable.
2. Disconnect the servo wiring at the amplifier, and disconnect the white stripe vacuum hose from the dump valve in the passenger compartment.
3. Disconnect the speed control actuator cable from the accelerator cable.
4. Remove the grommet and wiring from the passenger compartment.
5. Raise the vehicle and support safely on jackstands.

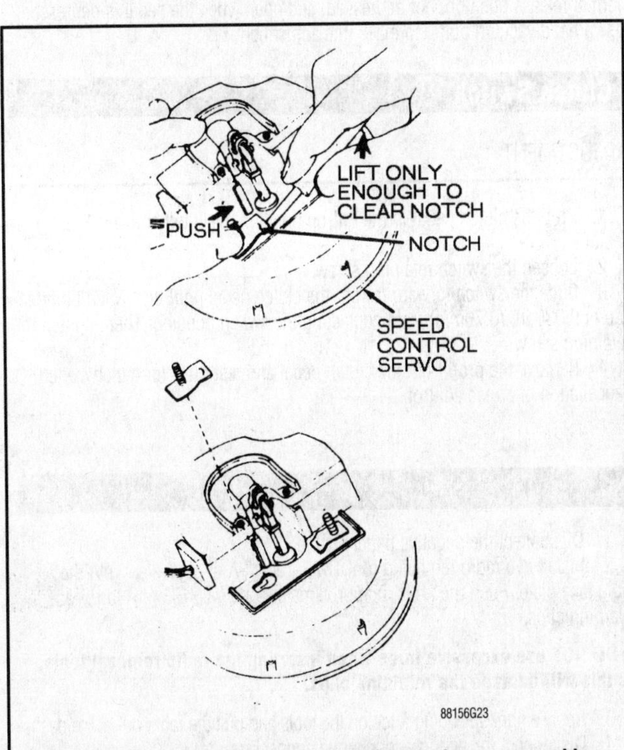

Fig. 26 Removing the nuts from the speed control servo assembly

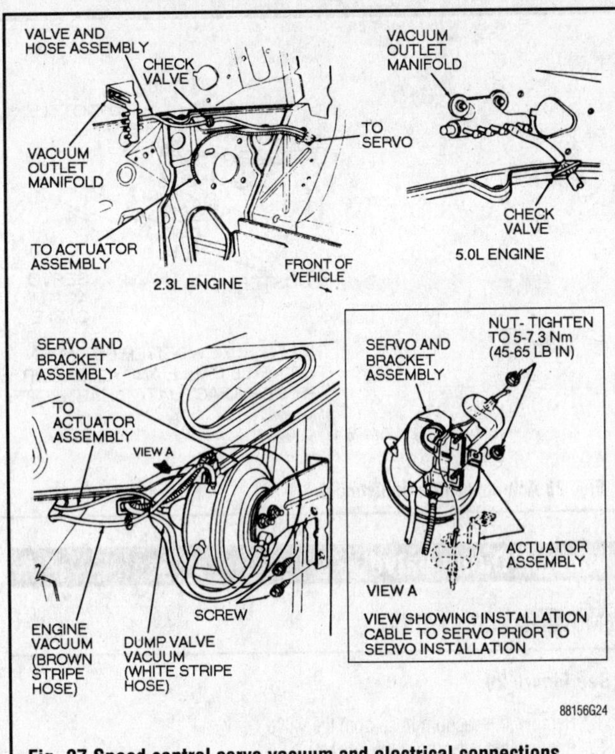

Fig. 27 Speed control servo vacuum and electrical connections

6. Remove the left front tire.
7. Remove the inner fender splash shield.
8. Remove the brown stripe vacuum hose from the servo assembly.
9. Remove the two screws from the servo bracket to the A-pillar.
10. Remove the two nuts from the actuator cable cover at the servo. Remove the cable and the cover. Remove the rubber boot.
11. Remove the two nuts retaining the servo to the mounting bracket.
12. If the servo is being replaced, remove the two bolt assemblies from the front of the servo.

To Install:

13. Install the two bolts to the front of the servo.
14. Install the two nuts retaining the servo to the mounting bracket. Tighten to 45–65 inch lbs. (5–7 Nm).
15. Install the rubber boot.
16. Attach the actuator cable to the servo plunger. Install the cable cover to the servo with two nuts. Tighten to 45–65 inch lbs. (5–7 Nm).
17. Install the servo and bracket to the A-pillar with two screws.
18. Insert the servo connector and dump valve hose through the grommet hole in the passenger compartment. Fully seat the wire harness and the hose assembly into the hole.
19. Attach the brown strip vacuum hose to the servo. Adjust the servo boot to protect the servo.
20. Install the inner fender splash shield.
21. Install the tire and tighten the lug bolts to 85–105 ft. lbs. (115–142 Nm).
22. Lower the vehicle.
23. Connect the servo wiring at the amplifier in the passenger compartment.
24. Attach the servo vacuum hose with the white strip to the dump valve in the passenger compartment.
25. Connect the speed control actuator cable to the speedometer cable. Connect the negative battery cable.

ACTUATOR CABLE LINKAGE ADJUSTMENT

See Figure 28

1. Remove the cable retaining clip.
2. Push the cable through the adjuster until a slight tension is felt.
3. Insert the cable retaining clip and snap into place.

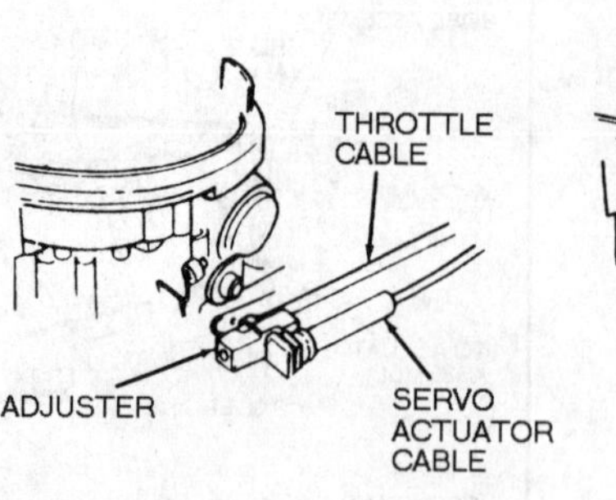

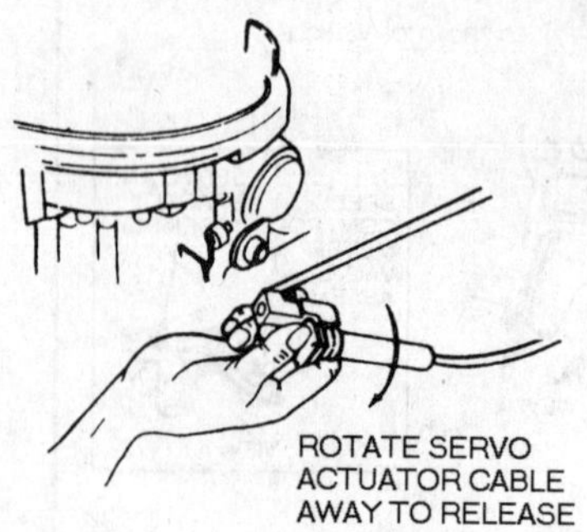

Fig. 28 Actuator cable adjustment

Vacuum Dump Valve

REMOVAL & INSTALLATION

See Figure 29

1. Remove the vacuum hose from the valve.
2. Remove the valve from the bracket.

To Install:

3. Install the valve to the bracket.
4. Connect the vacuum hose.
5. Adjust the valve.

ADJUSTMENT

See Figure 30

The vacuum dump valve is movable in its mounting bracket. It should be adjusted so that it is closed, no vacuum leaks, when the brake pedal is in its normal release position, not depressed, and open when the pedal is depressed. Use a hand vacuum pump to make this adjustment.

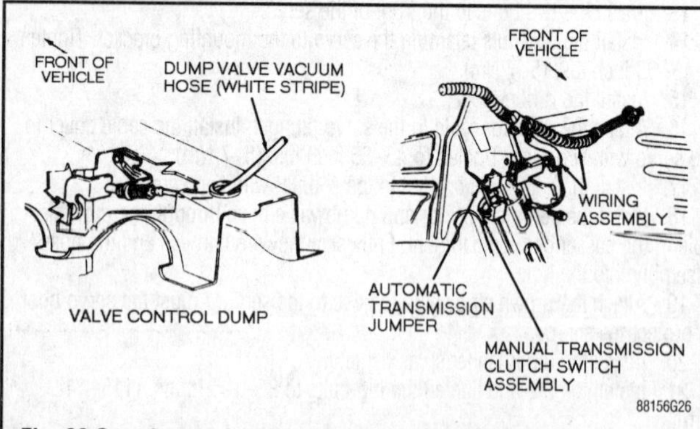

Fig. 29 Speed control vacuum dump valve replacement

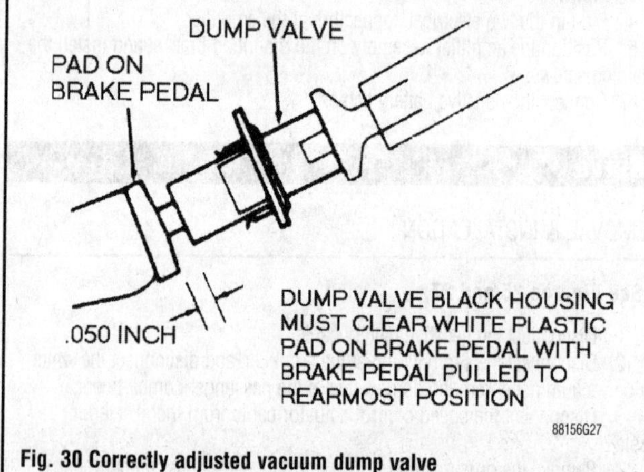

Fig. 30 Correctly adjusted vacuum dump valve

Clutch Switch

ADJUSTMENT

1. Prop the clutch pedal in the full-up position, pawl fully released from the sector.
2. Loosen the switch retaining screw.
3. Slide the switch forward toward the clutch pedal until the switch plunger cap is 0.030 in. (0.76mm) from contacting the switch housing. Then, tighten the retaining screw.
4. Remove the prop from the clutch pedal and test drive for clutch switch cancellation of cruise control.

ENTERTAINMENT SYSTEMS

Radio/Tape Player

REMOVAL & INSTALLATION

See Figure 31

These vehicles have DIN-standard radios; a special tool T87P-19061-A or equivalent is required to release the clips and remove the radio from the vehicle.

1. Disconnect the negative battery cable.
2. Install two radio removing tool T87P-19061-A or equivalent into the radio face plate. Push the tools in approximately one inch (25mm) to release the retaining clips.

DO NOT use excessive force when inserting the radio removal tools, as this will damage the retaining clips.

3. Apply a light spreading force on the tools and pull the radio out of the dash.
4. Disconnect the wiring and antenna connectors.

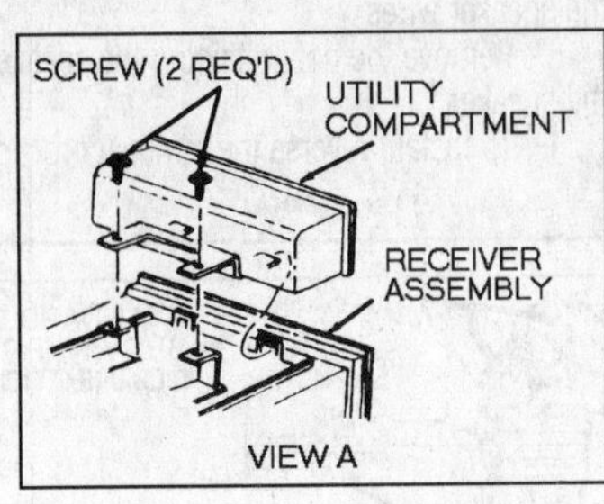

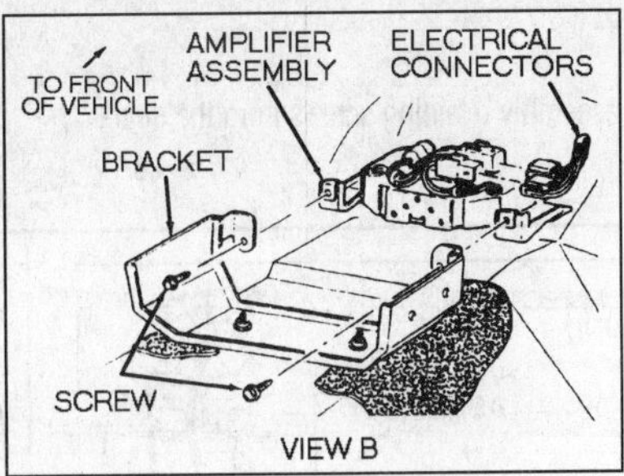

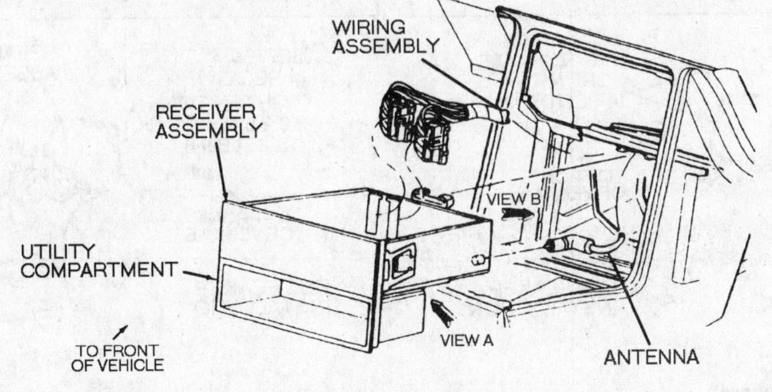

Fig. 31 Radio and amplifier mounting locations

To Install:

5. Connect the wiring and antenna connectors to the radio.
6. Slide the radio into the instrument panel ensuring that the rear radio bracket is engaged on the upper support rail.
7. Connect the negative battery cable. Check the radio for proper operation.

Amplifier

➧ See Figure 31

REMOVAL & INSTALLATION

1. Disconnect the negative battery cable.
2. Remove the radio as outlined previously.
3. Remove the two screws retaining the amplifier to the tunnel bracket.
4. Unplug the electrical connectors and remove the amplifier.
5. To install, reverse the removal procedures.

Speakers

REMOVAL & INSTALLATION

Instrument Panel Mounted

➧ See Figures 32, 33, 34 and 35

1. Remove the retaining screw at the side of the instrument panel.
2. Use a fabricated hook to disengage the clips and remove the speaker grills.
3. Remove the speaker retaining screws. Lift the speaker and disconnect the speaker wires.
4. To install, reverse the removal procedure.

Door Mounted

➧ See Figure 36

1. Remove the door trim panel.
2. Remove the three speaker retaining screws.
3. Lift the speaker and disconnect the speaker wires.

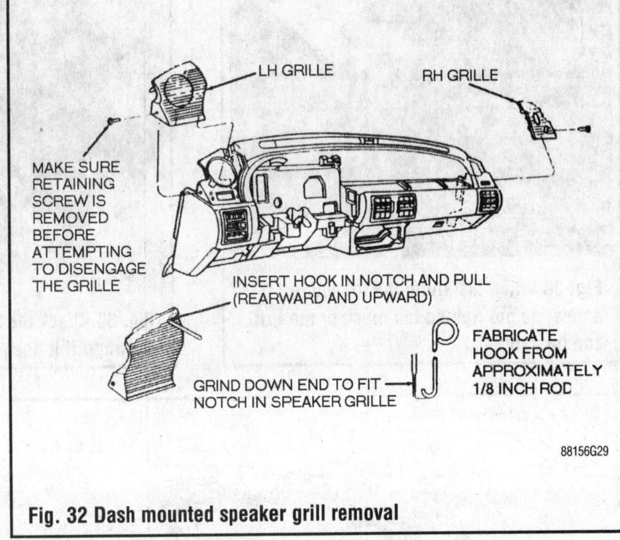

Fig. 32 Dash mounted speaker grill removal

To Install:

4. Connect the speaker wires, position the speaker to the door side panel and install the retaining screws.
5. Push the lock clip into the hole in the door inner panel and check the speaker operation.
6. Install the door trim panel.

Rear Mounted

2-DOOR

➧ See Figure 37

1. From within the luggage compartment, disconnect the speaker wiring.
2. Remove the speaker cover, speaker retaining nuts and the speaker from the underside of the package shelf.
3. To install, reverse the removal procedure.

3-DOOR

See Figure 38

1. Remove the speaker and grille assembly retaining screws from the quarter trim panel.
2. Lift the speaker and the grille assembly from the trim panel. Disconnect the speaker wires.
3. Remove the nuts retaining the speaker to the grille assembly and remove the speaker.
4. To install, reverse the removal procedures.

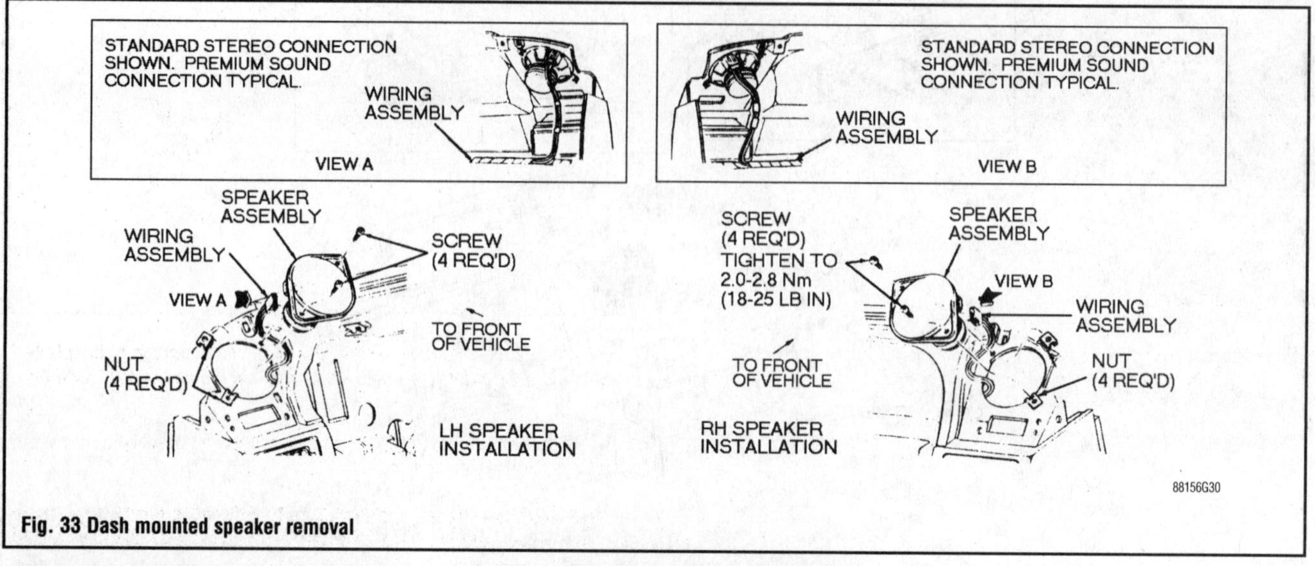

Fig. 33 Dash mounted speaker removal

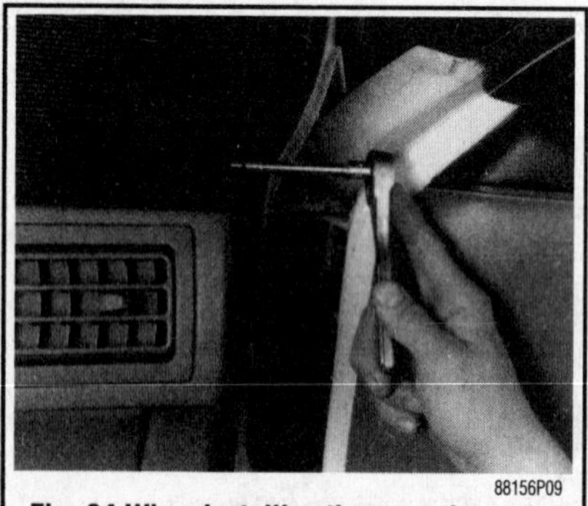

Fig. 34 When installing the mounting screw, do not tighten too much or the grill can be damaged

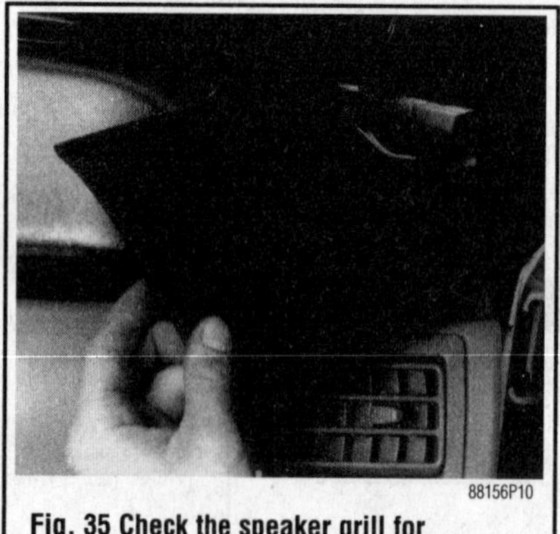

Fig. 35 Check the speaker grill for warpage if it does not fit back properly

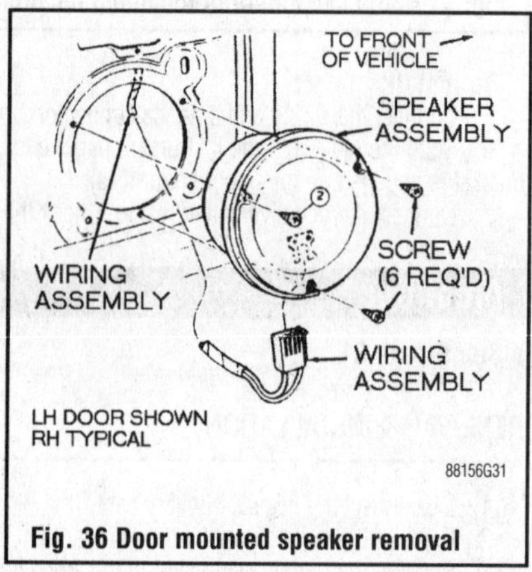

Fig. 36 Door mounted speaker removal

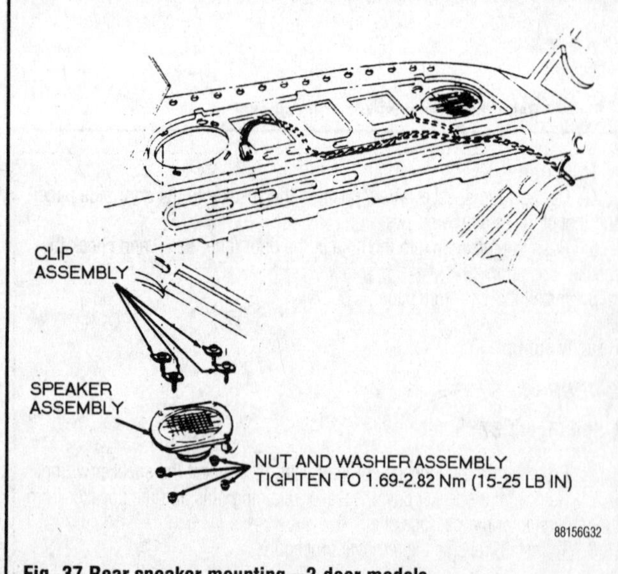

Fig. 37 Rear speaker mounting—2-door models

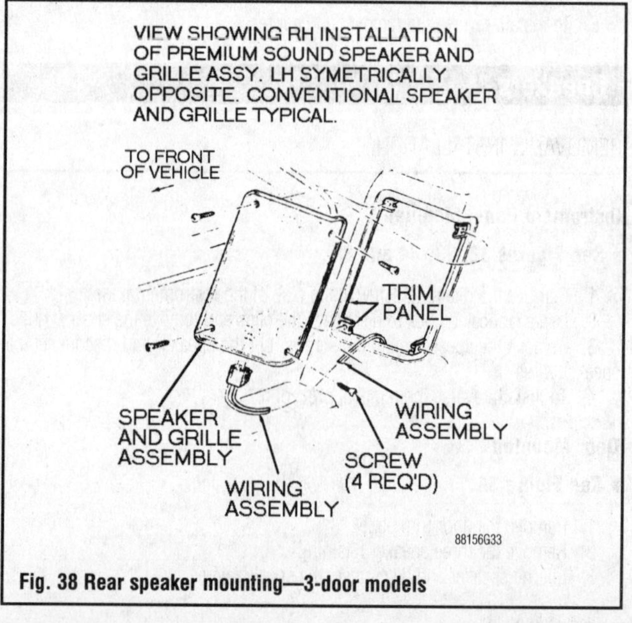

Fig. 38 Rear speaker mounting—3-door models

WINDSHIELD WIPERS AND WASHERS

Wiper Arm

REMOVAL & INSTALLATION

See Figures 39 and 40

Raise the blade end of the arm off of the windshield and move the slide latch away from the pivot shaft. This will unlock the wiper arm from the pivot shaft and hold the blade end of the arm off of the glass at the same time. The wiper arm can now be pulled off of the pivot shaft without the aid of any tools.

When installing the wiper arm, the arm must be positioned properly. There is a measurement which can be made to determine the proper blade positioning. With the wiper motor in the PARK position, install the arm so that the distance between the blade-to-arm saddle and the lower windshield molding is as shown in the accompanying figure.

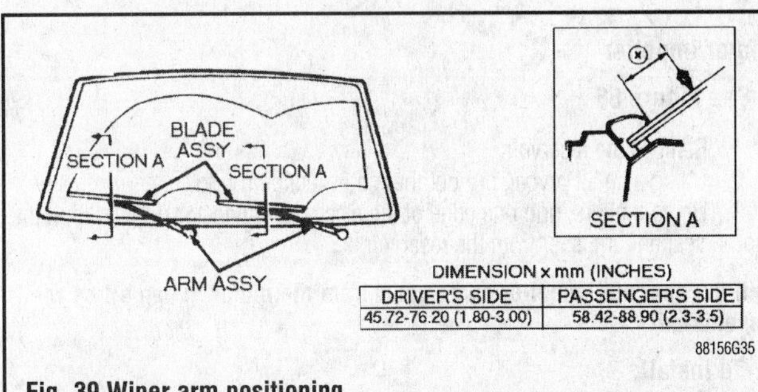

Fig. 39 Wiper arm positioning

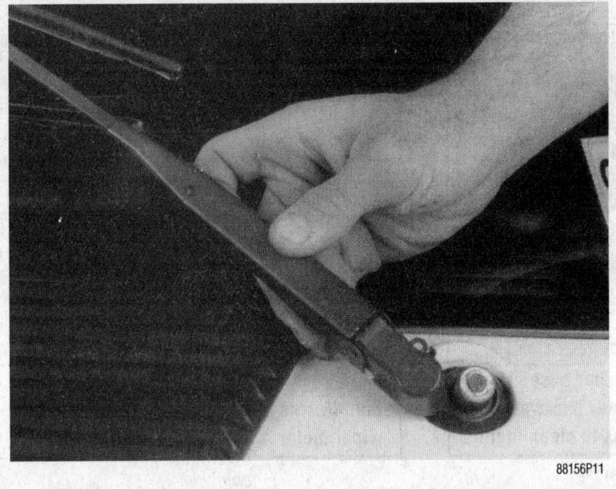

Fig. 40 Slide the latch away from the arm and the assembly can be pulled off without using any tools

Wiper Blade

REMOVAL & INSTALLATION

See Figure 41

1. Cycle arm and blade assembly to a position on the windshield where removal of blade assembly can be performed without difficulty. Turn ignition key off at desired position.
2. With the blade assembly resting on windshield, grasp either end of the wiper blade frame and pull away from windshield, then pull blade assembly from pin.

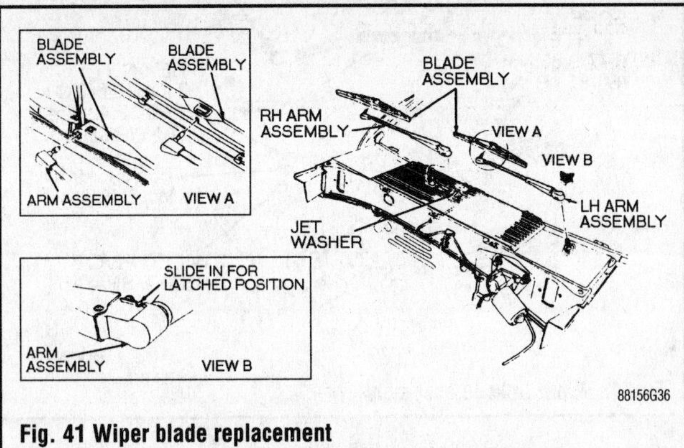

Fig. 41 Wiper blade replacement

➡Rubber element extends past frame. To prevent damage to the blade element, be sure to grasp blade frame and not the end of the blade element.

3. To install, push blade assembly onto pin until fully seated. Be sure blade is securely attached to the wiper arm.

Wiper Motor

REMOVAL & INSTALLATION

See Figures 42 thru 51

1. Disconnect the negative battery cable.
2. Remove both wiper arm and blade assemblies.
3. Remove the cowl grille attaching screws and lift the cowl grille slightly.
4. Disconnect the washer nozzle hose and remove the cowl grille assembly.
5. Remove the wiper linkage clip from the motor output arm.
6. Unplug the wiper motor's wiring connector.
7. Remove the wiper motor's three attaching screws and remove the motor.

To Install:

8. Install the motor and attach the three attaching screws. Tighten to 60–85 inch lbs.
9. Plug in wiper motor's wiring connector.
10. Install wiper linkage clip to the motors output arm.
11. Connect the washer nozzle hose and install the cowl assembly and attaching screws.
12. Install both wiper arm assemblies.
13. Connect negative battery cable.

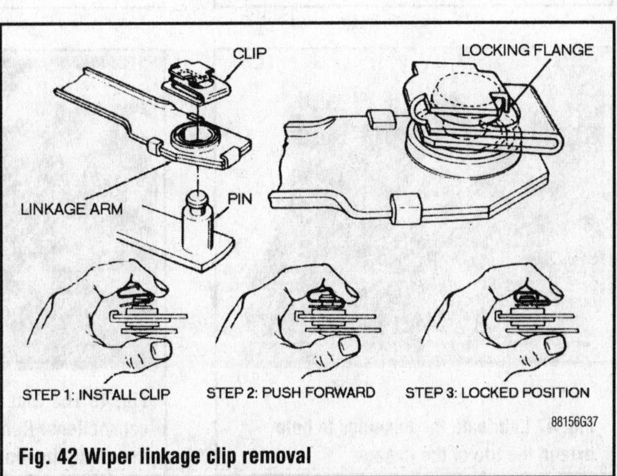

Fig. 42 Wiper linkage clip removal

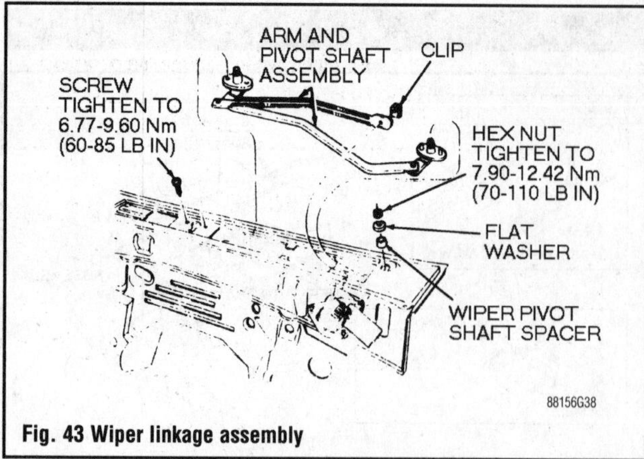

Fig. 43 Wiper linkage assembly

Wiper Linkage

REMOVAL & INSTALLATION

1. Disconnect the battery ground cable.
2. Remove both wiper arm assemblies.
3. Remove the cowl grille attaching screws and lift the cowl grille slightly.
4. Disconnect the washer nozzle hose and remove the cowl grille assembly.
5. Remove the wiper linkage clip from the motor output arm and pull the linkage from the output arm.
6. Remove the pivot body to cowl screws and remove the linkage and pivot shaft assembly (three screws on each side). The left and right pivots and linkage are independent and can be serviced separately.

To Install:

7. Attach the linkage and pivot shaft assembly to cowl with attaching screws.
8. Replace the linkage to the output arm and attach the linkage clip.
9. Connect the washer nozzle hose and cowl grills assembly.
10. Attach cowl grille attaching screws.
11. Replace both wiper arm assemblies.
12. Connect battery ground cable.

Washer Reservoir and Pump Motor

REMOVAL & INSTALLATION

Reservoir

➧ See Figure 52

1. Disconnect the wiring at the pump motor. Use a small screwdriver to unlock the connector tabs.
2. Remove the washer hose.
3. Remove the reservoir attaching screws or nuts and lift the assembly from the vehicle.

Motor/Impeller

➧ See Figure 53

1. Remove the reservoir.
2. Using a small prybar, pry out the motor retaining ring.
3. Using a pliers, grip one edge of the electrical connector ring and pull the motor, seal and impeller from the reservoir.

➡If the seal and impeller come apart from the motor, it can all be re-assembled.

To install:

4. Take the time to clean out the reservoir before installing the motor.
5. Coat the seal with a dry lubricant, such as powdered graphite or spray Teflon®. This will aid assembly.

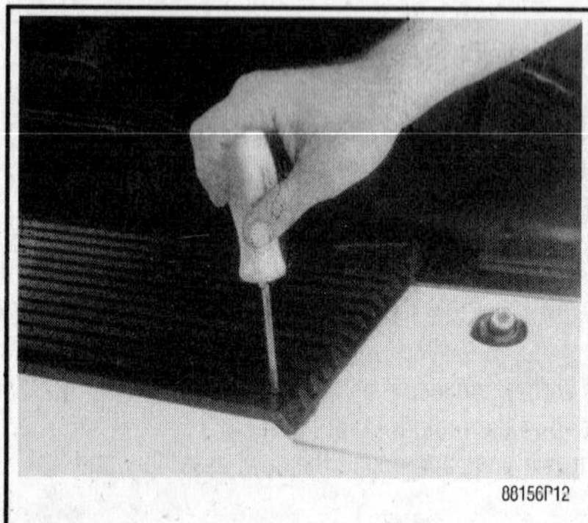

Fig. 44 Remove the screws to allow removal of the cowl grill

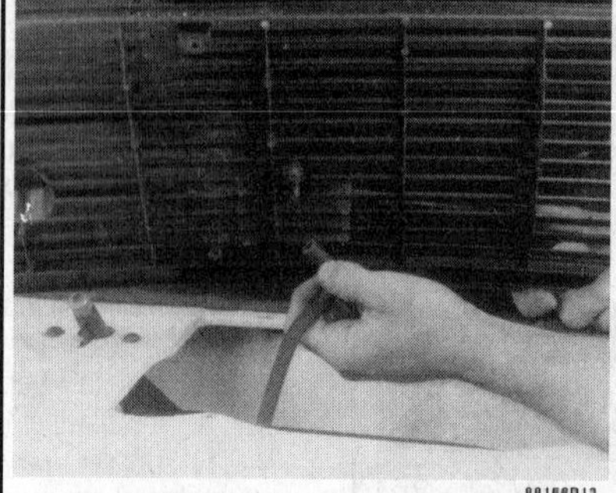

Fig. 45 Disconnect the washer hose. This is a good time to force water backwards through the washer nozzles to clean them

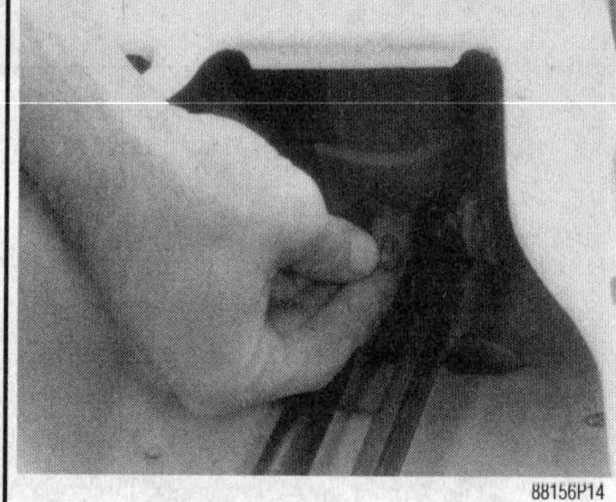

Fig. 46 This clips holds the linkage to the wiper motor

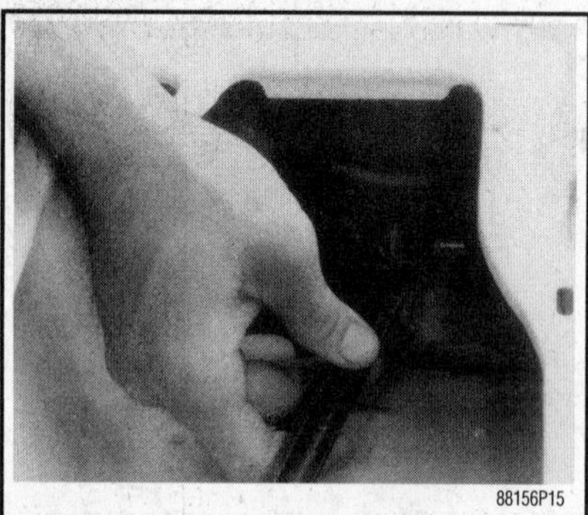

Fig. 47 Lubricate the bushings to help extend the life of the linkage

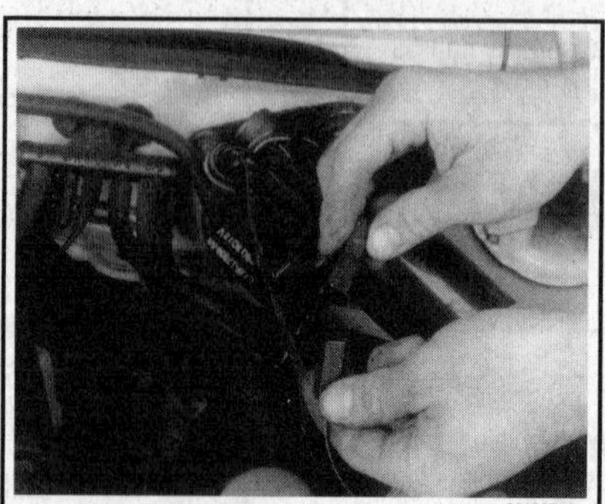

Fig. 48 The wiper motor has two electrical connections. Remember this one when installing the motor

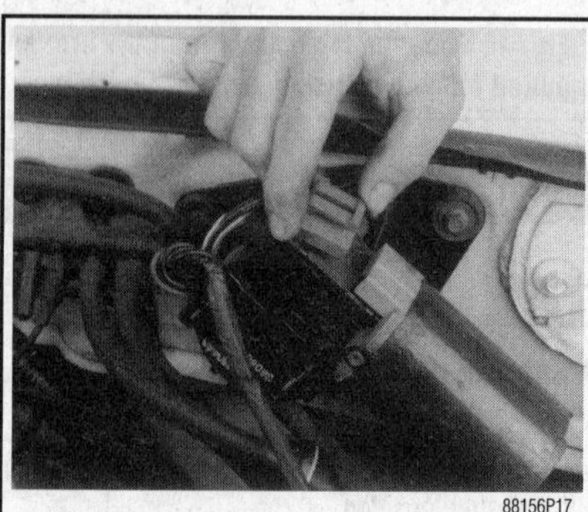

Fig. 49 Pull back the latch before trying to disconnect the harness from the motor

6. Align the small projection on the motor end cap with the slot in the reservoir and install the motor so that the seal seats against the bottom of the motor cavity.

7. Press the retaining ring into position. A 1 in. (25mm), 12-point socket or length of 1 in. (25mm) tubing, will do nicely as an installation tool.

8. Install the reservoir and connect the wiring.

➡It's not a good idea to run a new motor without filling the reservoir first. Dry-running will damage a new motor.

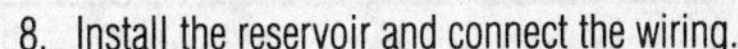

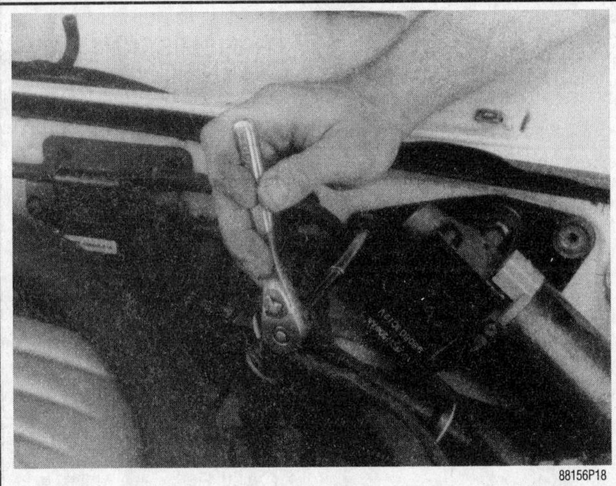

88156P18

Fig. 50 The wiper motor is suspended in these rubber mounts. Do not overtighten the bolts or the mounts will be crushed

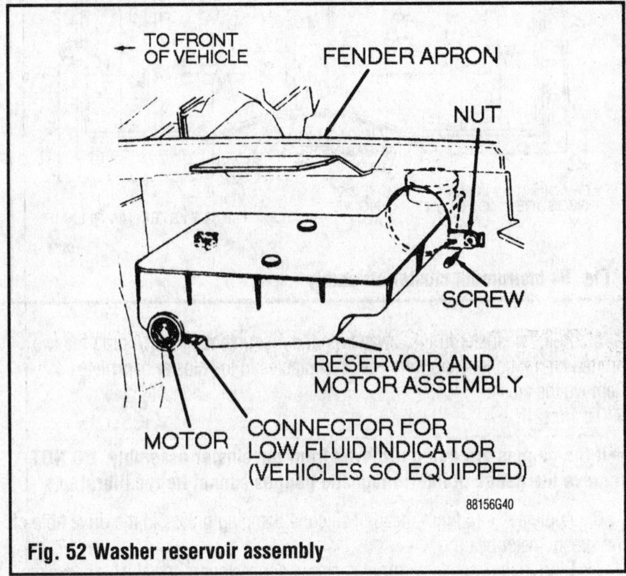

Fig. 52 Washer reservoir assembly

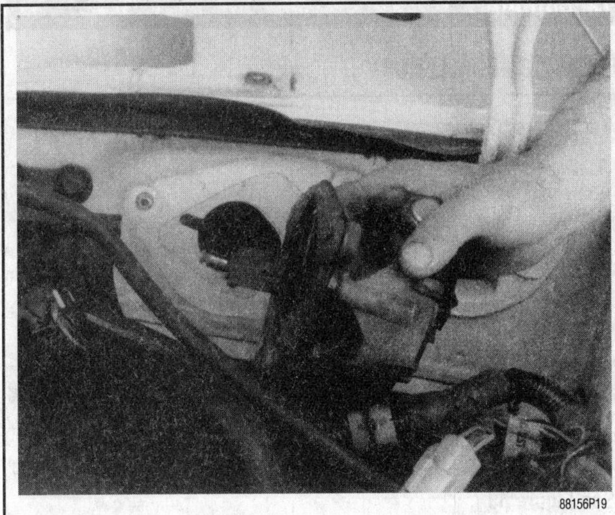

88156P19

Fig. 51 Check the gasket around the motor before installing

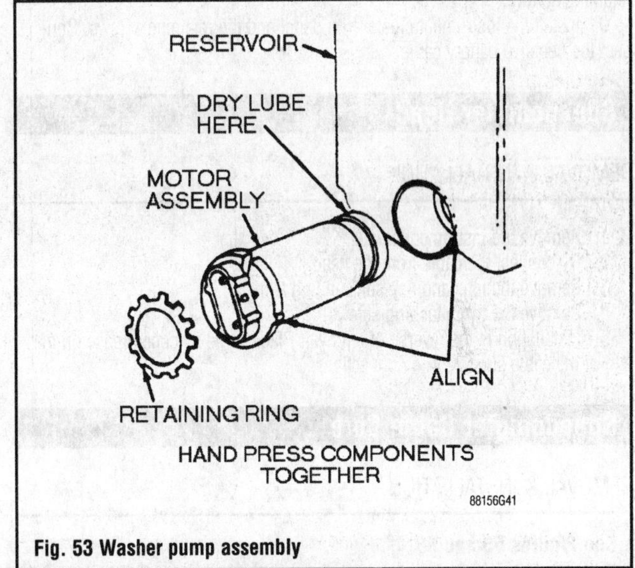

Fig. 53 Washer pump assembly

INSTRUMENTS AND SWITCHES

Precautions

Electronic modules, such as instrument clusters, powertrain controls and sound systems are sensitive to static electricity and can be damaged by static discharges which are below the levels that you can hear snap or detect on your skin. A detectable snap or shock of static electricity is in the 3,000 volt range. Some of these modules can be damaged by a charge of as little as 100 volts.

The following are some basic safeguards to avoid static electrical damage:

- Leave the replacement module in its original packing until you are ready to install it.
- Avoid touching the module connector pins.
- Avoid placing the module on a non-conductive surface.
- Use a commercially available static protection kit. These kits contain such things as grounding cords and conductive mats.

Instrument Cluster

REMOVAL & INSTALLATION

▶ See Figure 54

1. Disconnect the negative battery cable.
2. Remove the switch assembly on the right and left-hand sides of the cluster.
3. Remove the upper and lower retaining screws from the instrument cluster trim cover. Remove the trim cover.
4. Pull the cluster away from the instrument panel. Release the speedometer cable by pressing on the flat surface of the plastic connector located behind the instrument cluster.

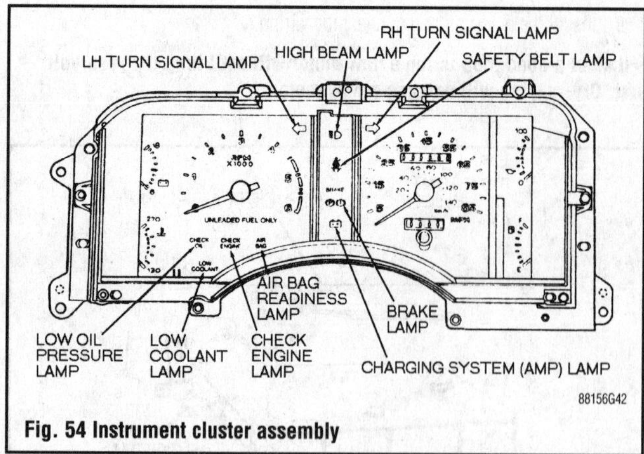

Fig. 54 Instrument cluster assembly

5. Pull the cluster further away from the instrument panel. Unplug the two printed circuit connectors from their receptacles in the cluster backplate. Remove the cluster.

To Install:

➡If the gauges are being removed from the cluster assembly. DO NOT remove the gauge pointer; magnetic gauges cannot be recalibrated.

6. Apply a 3/16 (4.6mm) bead of silicone damping grease in the drive hole of the speedometer head.
7. Plug in the two cluster printed circuit connectors to the cluster backplate.
8. Position the instrument cluster to the instrument panel and install the retaining screws.
9. Install the instrument cluster trim panel and the retaining screws. Connect the negative battery cable.

Speedometer Head

REMOVAL & INSTALLATION

1. Remove the instrument cluster.
2. Disconnect the cable from the head.
3. Remove the lens and any surrounding trim.
4. Remove the two attaching screws.
5. Installation is the reverse of removal. Place some silicone grease on the end of the cable core prior to connection.

Speedometer Cable Core

REMOVAL & INSTALLATION

See Figures 55 and 56

1. Reach up behind the cluster and release the cable by depressing the quick disconnect tab and pulling the cable away.
2. Remove the cable from the casing. If the cable is broken, raise the vehicle on a hoist and disconnect the cable from the transmission.

➡On vehicles equipped with a transmission mounted speed sensor, remove the speedometer cable by pulling it out of the speed sensor. DO NOT attempt to remove the spring retainer clip with the speedometer in the sensor. To install the cable, snap it into the sensor.

3. Remove the cable from the casing.
4. To remove the casing from the vehicle pull it through the floor pan.

To Install:

5. To replace the cable, slide the new cable into the casing and connect it at the transmission.
6. Route the cable through the floor pan and position the grommet in its groove in the floor.
7. Push the cable onto the speedometer head.

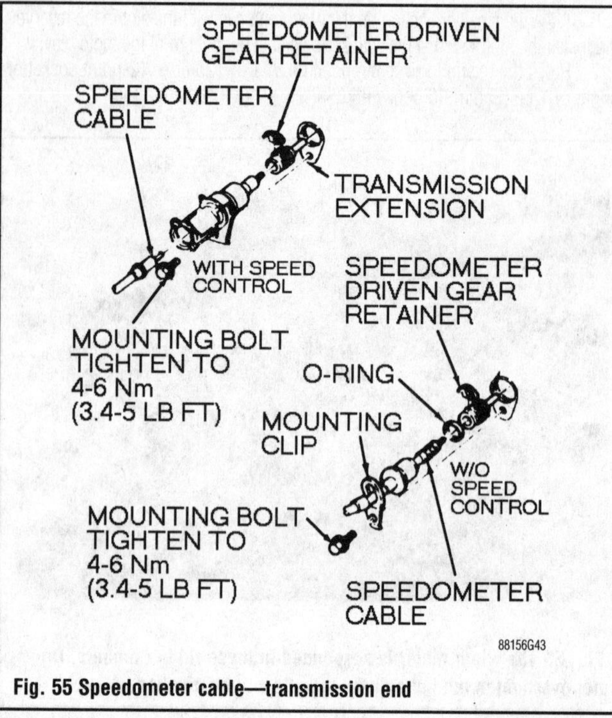

Fig. 55 Speedometer cable—transmission end

Tachometer

REMOVAL & INSTALLATION

See Figure 57

1. Disconnect the negative battery cable.
2. Remove the instrument cluster.
3. Remove the cluster mask and lens.
4. Remove the tachometer by prying the dial away from the cluster backplate. The tachometer is retained by clips.
5. Installation is the reverse of removal. Make sure the clips are properly seated.

Fuel Gauge

REMOVAL & INSTALLATION

See Figure 58

1. Disconnect the negative battery cable.
2. Remove the instrument cluster.
3. Remove the cluster mask and lens.
4. Remove the fuel/oil pressure gauge assembly.
5. Installation is the reverse of removal.

Windshield Wiper Switch

REMOVAL & INSTALLATION

See Figure 59

1. Disconnect the negative battery cable.
2. Remove the steering column shrould attaching screws.
3. Grasp the top and bottom of the shrould and separate.
4. Remove the two wiper switch attaching bolts and remove the switch assembly. Push the wire connector off the wiper switch with a flat screwdriver.
5. To install, reverse the removal procedures.

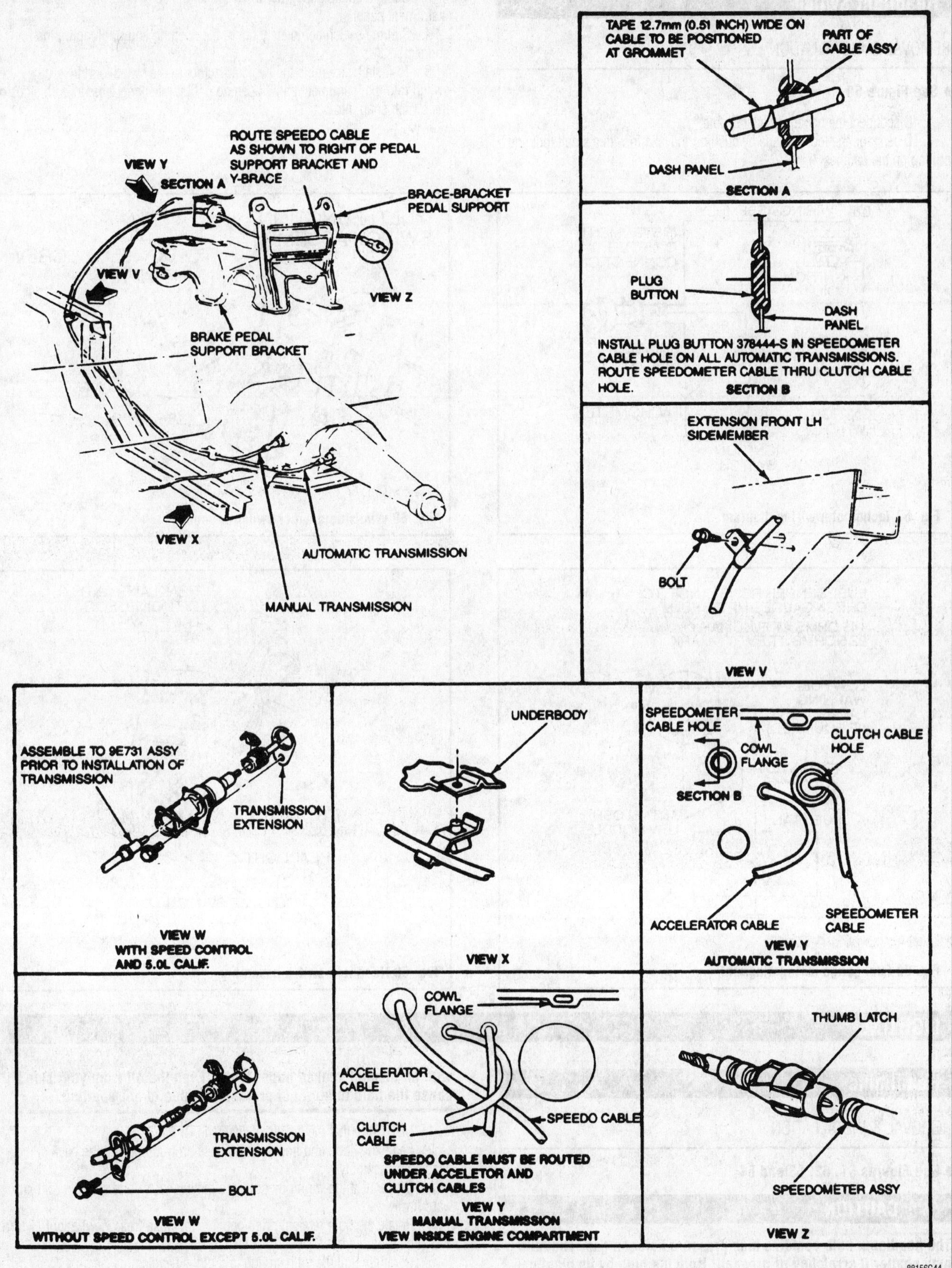

Fig. 56 Speedometer cable replacement

Headlight Switch

REMOVAL & INSTALLATION

➧ **See Figure 60**

1. Disconnect the negative battery cable.
2. Disengage the locking tabs by pushing the tabs in with a small tool and pulling on the paddles.
3. Using a suitable tool, pry the right hand side of the switch out of the instrument panel.
4. Pull the switch completely out of the opening and unplugging the two connectors.
5. To install, assemble the two connectors to the switch and insert the switch into the instrument panel opening until the locking tabs on both sides of the switch snap into place.

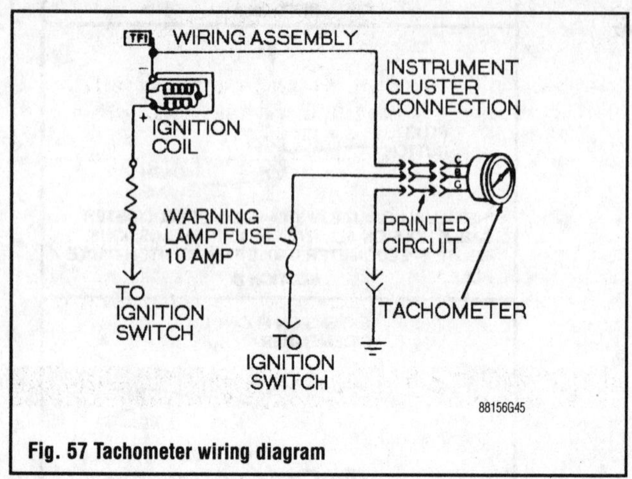

Fig. 57 Tachometer wiring diagram

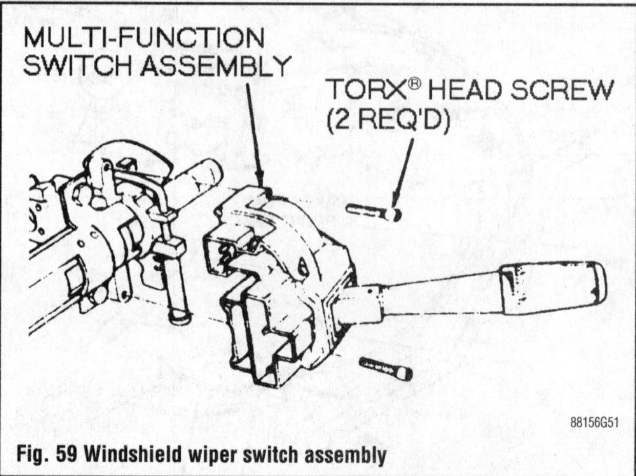

Fig. 59 Windshield wiper switch assembly

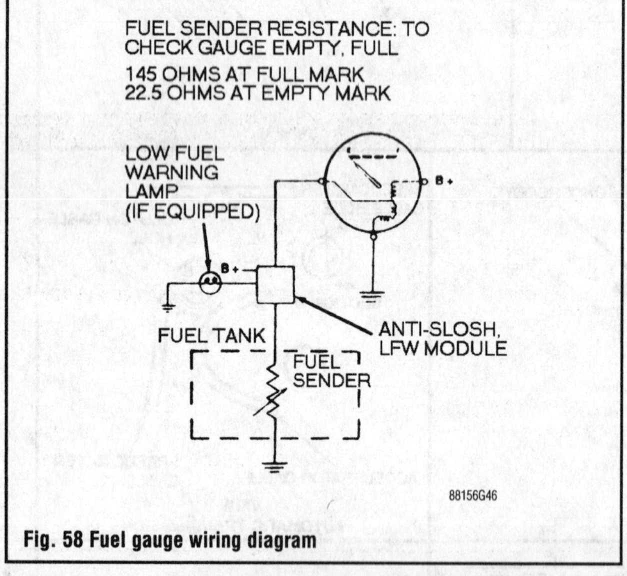

Fig. 58 Fuel gauge wiring diagram

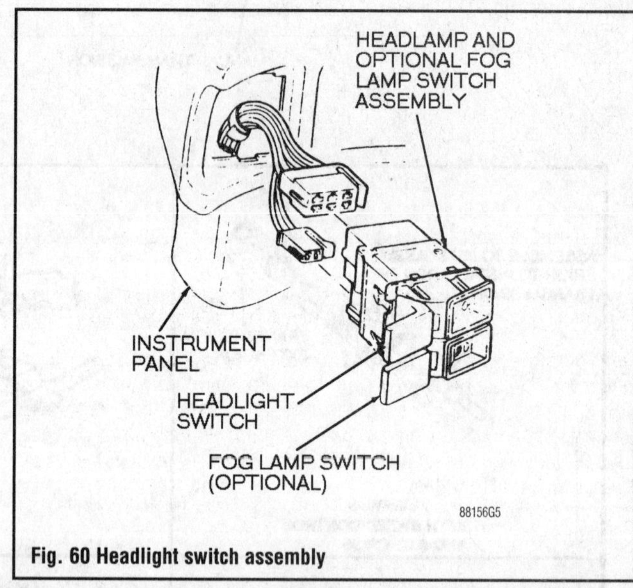

Fig. 60 Headlight switch assembly

LIGHTING

Headlights

REMOVAL & INSTALLATION

➧ **See Figures 61, 62, 63 and 64**

CAUTION

The headlamp bulb contains high pressure halogen gas. The bulb may shatter if scratched or dropped! Hold the bulb by its plastic base only. If you touch the glass portion with your fingers, or if any dirt or oily deposits are found on the glass, it must be wiped clean with an alcohol soaked paper towel. Even the oil from your skin will cause the bulb to burn out prematurely due to hot-spotting.

1. Make sure that the headlight switch is **OFF**.
2. Raise the hood and find the bulb base protruding from the back of the headlamp assembly
3. Disconnect the wiring by grasping the connector and snapping it rearward firmly.
4. Rotate the bulb retaining ring counterclockwise (rear view) about ⅛ turn and slide it off the bulb base. Don't lose it; it's re-usable.
5. Carefully pull the bulb straight out of the headlamp assembly. Don't rotate it during removal.

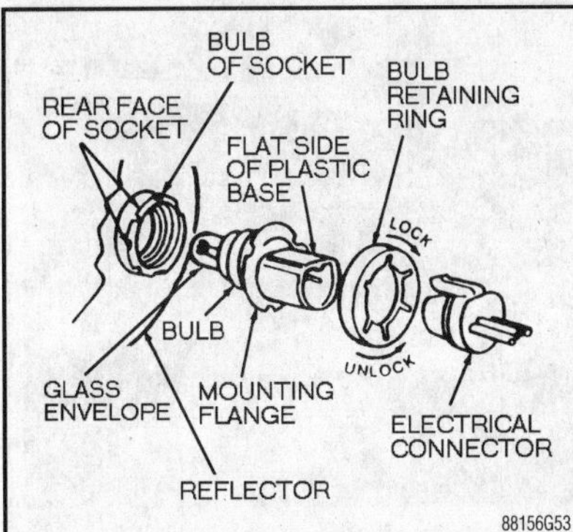

Fig. 61 Exploded view of the headlight bulb components

Fig. 62 Reach behind the radiator support to get at the headlight and twist the ring to release the socket

Fig. 63 Pull up the bulb but do not touch the surface otherwise you will need to clean it with alcohol

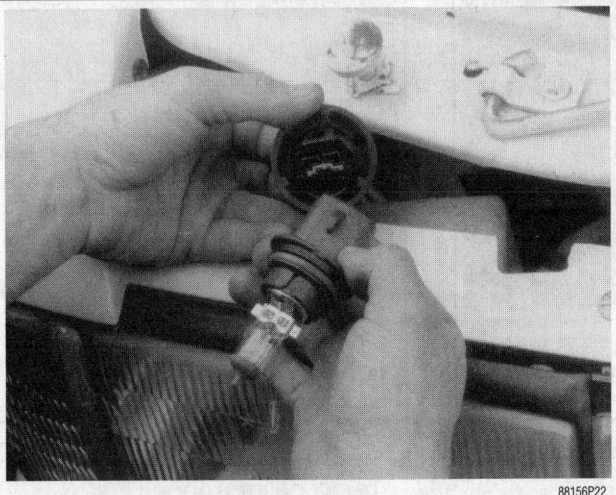

Fig. 64 Seperate the bulb and socket by grasping the bulb at the base, not the glass

**** WARNING**

Don't remove the old bulb until you are ready to immediately replace it! Leaving the headlamp assembly open, without a bulb, will allow foreign matter such as water, dirt, leaves, oil, etc. to enter the housing. This type of contamination will cut down on the amount and direction of light emitted, and eventually cause premature blow-out of the bulb.

To install:

6. With the flat side of the bulb base facing upward, insert it into the headlamp assembly. You may have to turn the bulb slightly to align the locating tabs. Once aligned, push the bulb firmly into place until the bulb base contacts the mounting flange in the socket.
7. Place the retaining ring over the bulb base, against the mounting flange and rotate it clockwise to lock it. It should lock against a definite stop when fully engaged.
8. Snap the electrical connector into place. A definite snap will be felt.
9. Turn the headlights on a check that everything works properly.

HEADLIGHT ADJUSTMENT

➡Before making any headlight adjustments, perform the following steps for preparation:

1. Make sure all tires are properly inflated.
2. Take into consideration any faulty wheel alignment or improper rear axle tracking.
3. Make sure there is no load in the vehicle other than the driver.
4. Make sure all lenses are clean.

Each headlight is adjusted by means of two screws located at the 12 o'clock and 9 o'clock positions on the headlight underneath the trim ring. Always bring each beam into final position by turning the adjusting screws clockwise so that the headlight will be held against the tension springs when the operation is completed.

Parking Lamps

REMOVAL & INSTALLATION

▸ See Figure 65

1. Remove the socket from the rear of the lamp housing.
2. Replace the bulb.
3. Installation is the reverse of removal.

Rear Lamps

REMOVAL & INSTALLATION

▸ See Figures 66 thru 71

➡Two types of rear sockets are used; the standard plastic socket and the three-tab socket.

1. Remove the socket from the rear of the lamp housing by turning it counterclockwise to the stop.
2. Replace the bulb.
3. Installation is the reverse of removal. Index the smallest tab for locating the three locking tabs then press the socket into the lamp housing and rotate clockwise to the stop.

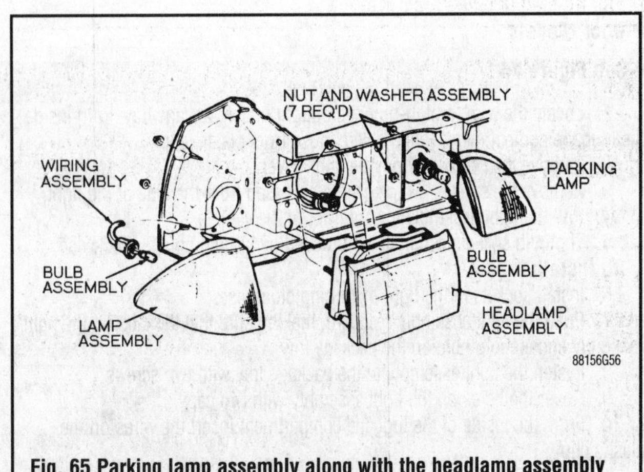

Fig. 65 Parking lamp assembly along with the headlamp assembly

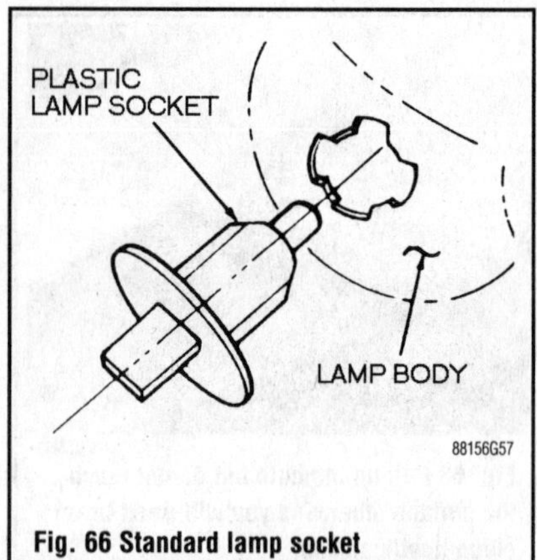

Fig. 66 Standard lamp socket

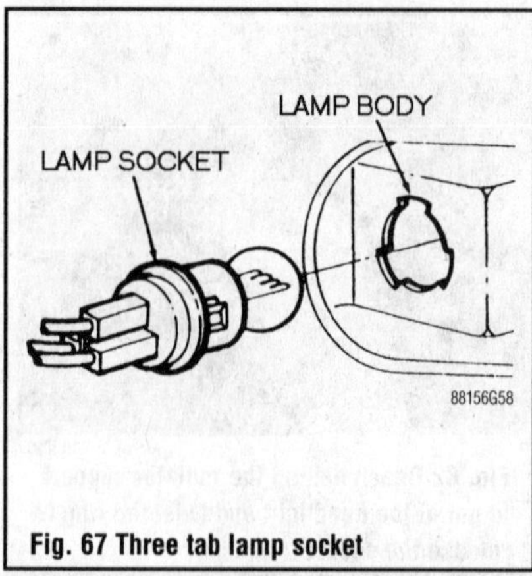

Fig. 67 Three tab lamp socket

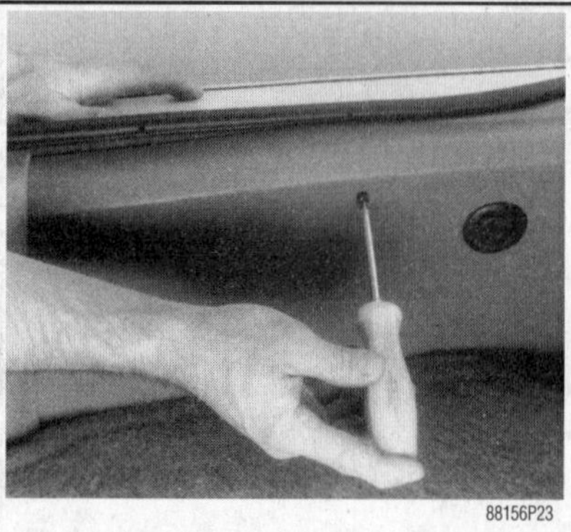

Fig. 68 The rear panel needs to be removed from the trunk area to expose the rear lights

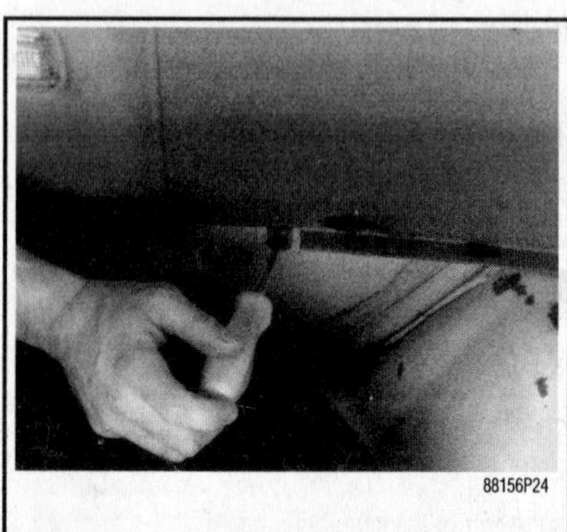

Fig. 69 Don't forget the lower panel screws

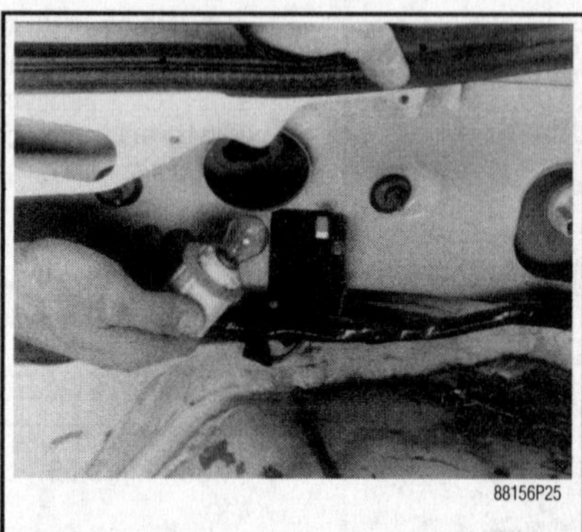

Fig. 70 Twist and pull to remove the sockets

88156P26

Fig. 71 The bulbs have a bayonet mount so they need to be pushed down before twisting to remove

License Plate Lights

REMOVAL & INSTALLATION

➧ See Figures 72, 73, 74 and 75

1. Open the trunk lid or vehicle hatch.
2. Remove the license lamp screws and lens.
3. Remove the socket and bulb, and pull the bulb out of the socket.
4. To install, reverse the removal procedure.

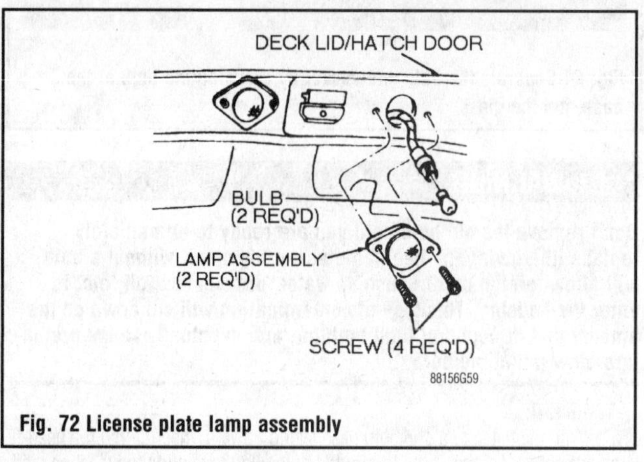

Fig. 72 License plate lamp assembly

High-Mount Brake Light

REMOVAL & INSTALLATION

2-Door Models

➧ See Figure 76

1. Locate the wire to high-mount stoplight under package tray, from inside the luggage compartment. Pull the wire loose from plastic clip.
2. Remove the two caps from the light cover.
3. Remove the screws, which can be accessed from the side of the light.
4. Pull the light assembly toward front of the vehicle.
5. The bulb sockets can then be removed by turning counterclockwise.

To Install:

6. Install sockets in the light by turning clockwise.
7. Push the light assembly rearward, making sure that the tabs on the light assembly engage into hole on the package tray.
8. Fasten the light assembly to the package tray with two screws.
9. Cover the holes on the light assembly with two caps.
10. From the inside of the luggage compartment insert the wires on the plastic clip.

3-Door Models

➧ See Figures 77, 78, 79 and 80

1. Remove the two screws from the light assembly.
2. The light can then be pulled rearward from spoiler.
3. Disengage the wiring harness strain relief clip by pulling straight out from light.
4. The bulb sockets can then be removed by gently twisting and pulling straight out of the light.

To Install:

5. Install the sockets in the light ensuring they are seated.
6. Insert the wiring harness strain relief clip.
7. Align the light mounting holes with U-nut in the spoiler.
8. Fasten the light to the spoiler with two screws.

88156P27

Fig. 73 Once the screws are removed the entire light assembly will drop out of the opening

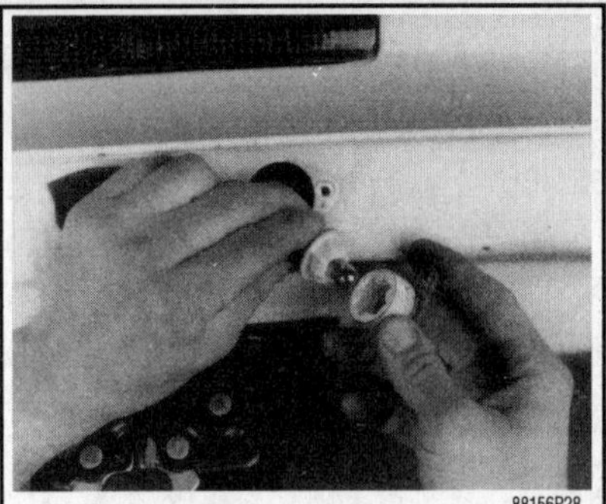
88156P28

Fig. 74 Twist and pull the socket out of the light assembly

88156P29

Fig. 75 The bulb has a tab base so it pulls straight out

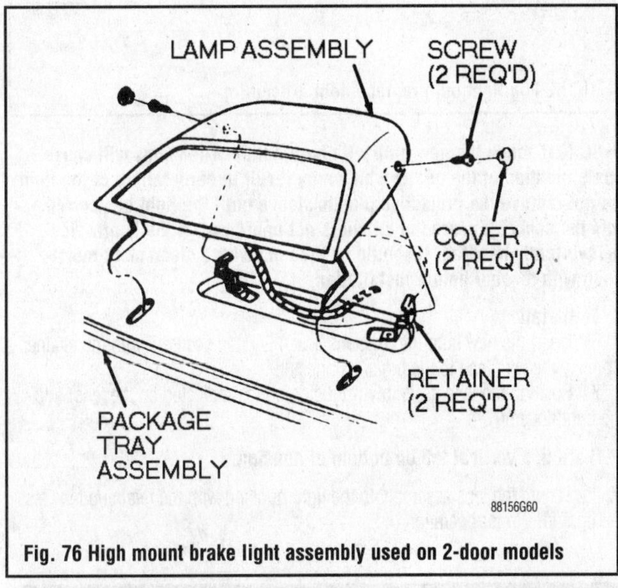

Fig. 76 High mount brake light assembly used on 2-door models

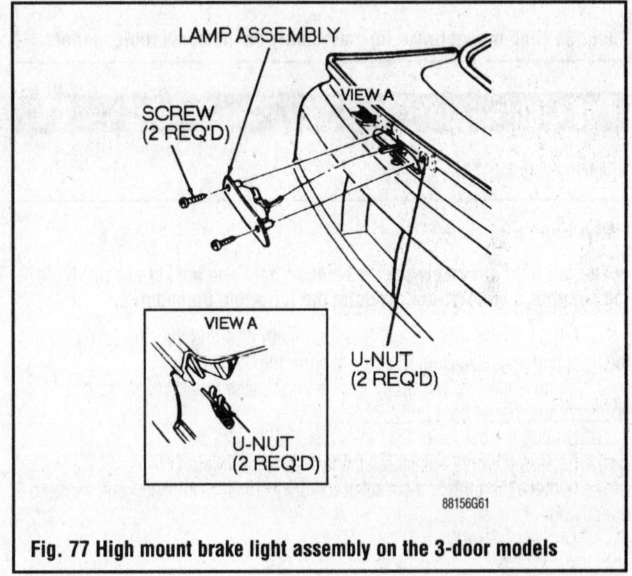

Fig. 77 High mount brake light assembly on the 3-door models

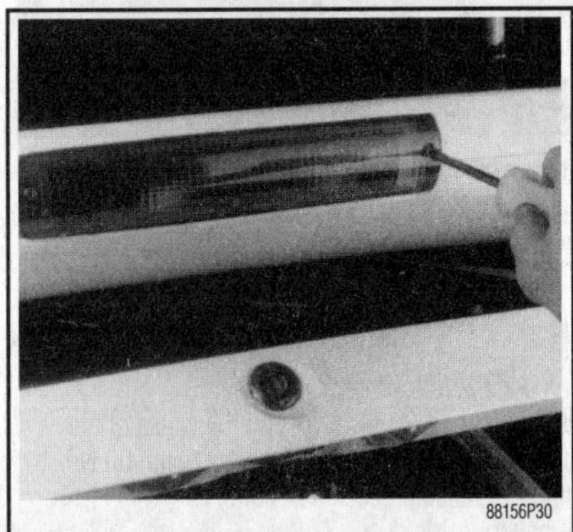
88156P30

Fig. 78 The third brake light is held to the spoiler by these two screws

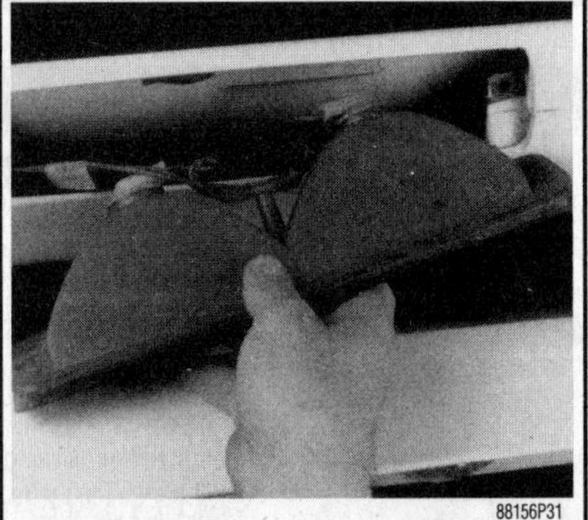
88156P31

Fig. 79 The brake lights are actually two bulb and reflector assemblies in one

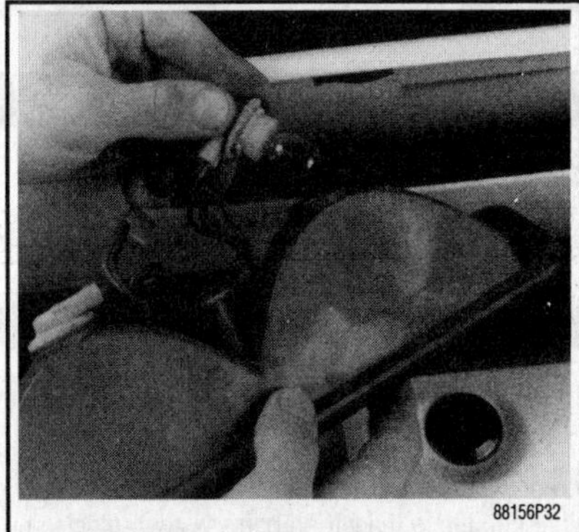
88156P32

Fig. 80 The bulbs pull out of the sockets and have tab type bases

Convertible Models

See Figure 81

1. Remove the luggage crossbar.
2. Remove the two screws which can be accessed from the top of the light.
3. The light can then be lifted from the deck lid.
4. Disengage the wiring harness strain relief clip by pulling it straight out from the light.
5. The bulb sockets can then be remove by gently twisting and pulling it straight out of the light.

To Install:

6. Ensure the rubber seal is positioned properly on the light.
7. Install the sockets in the light ensuring they are seated.
8. Insert the wiring harness strain relief clip.
9. Align the light mounting holes with plastic nuts in the deck lid.
10. Fasten the light to the deck lid with two screws.
11. Install the luggage rack crossbar.

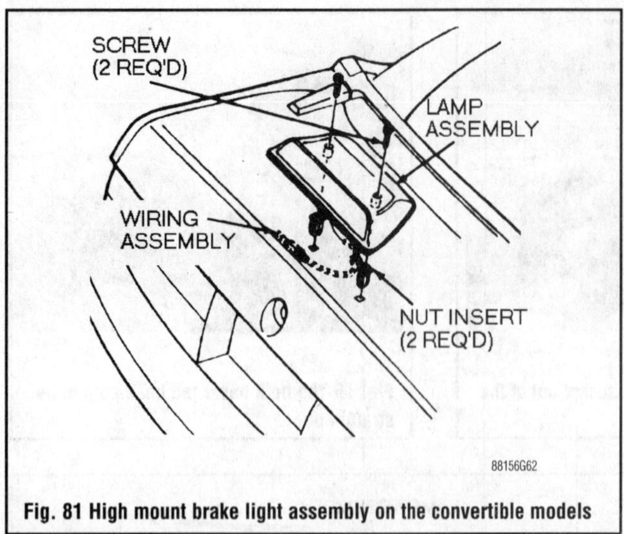

Fig. 81 High mount brake light assembly on the convertible models

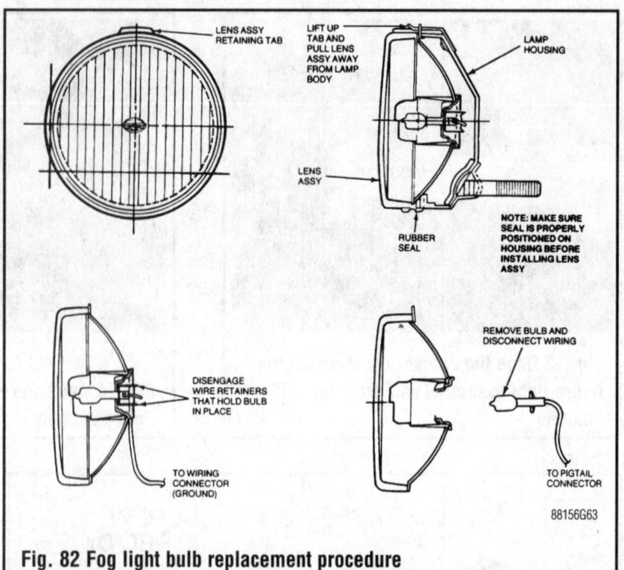

Fig. 82 Fog light bulb replacement procedure

Fog Lights

REMOVAL & INSTALLATION

See Figure 82

The fog light assembly uses a halogen bulb and socket assembly. In the event of a bulb failure, perform the following procedures.

1. Lift up on the lens assembly retaining tab retaining the lens assembly to the light housing. Use caution to avoid dropping the lens.
2. Remove the lens assembly from the light housing and turn it to gain access to the rear of light body.
3. Unplug the bulb wire lead from the pigtail connector.
4. Release the bulb socket retainer from the locking tab.
5. Remove the bulb and socket assembly from light body and pull the bulb directly out of the socket.

DO NOT touch the new bulb with bare hands. The stains will cause contamination of the quartz which may result in early failure of the light. Do not remove the protective plastic sleeve until the light is inserted into the socket. Ensure the circuit is not energized. If the quartz was inadvertently handled, it should be cleaned with a clean cloth moistened with alcohol before installation.

To Install:

6. Insert the new bulb into the lens assembly and secure it with the retainer. Connect the wire lead to the pigtail connector.
7. Position the lens assembly right side up (as indicated on the lens) into the light housing.

There is a vertical tab on bottom of housing.

8. Secure the lens assembly to the light housing with the retaining tab. Test the light for proper operation.

CIRCUIT PROTECTION

Fuses

See Figures 83, 84 and 85

The fuse panel is located on the driver's side under the instrument panel.

Circuit Breakers

See Figures 86 and 87

Two circuits are protected by circuit breakers located in the fuse panel: the power windows (20 amp) and the windshield wiper circuit (8.25 amp). Three other circuits in the wiring harness are protected by circuit breakers: the headlights (22 amp) located in the headlight switch, the power seats and door locks (20 amp) located at the starter relay, and the convertible top (25 amp) located in the lower instrument panel reinforcement. The breakers are self-resetting.

Turn Signal and Hazard Flasher Locations

See Figures 88 and 89

Two flasher units are used. One is used for the turn signal circuit and the other is for the hazard warning circuit. The turn signal flasher is mounted on the instrument panel reinforcement above the fuse panel. The hazard warning flasher is mounted in the fuse panel.

Fuse Link

The fuse link is a short length of special, Hypalon (high temperature) insulated wire, integral with the engine compartment wiring harness and should not be confused with standard wire. It is several wire gauges smaller than the circuit which it protects. Under no circumstances should a fuse link replacement repair be made using a length of standard wire cut from bulk stock or from another wiring harness.

To repair any blown fuse link use the following procedure:

1. Determine which circuit is damaged, its location and the cause of the open fuse link. If the damaged fuse link is one of three fed by a common No. 10 or 12 gauge feed wire, determine the specific affected circuit.
2. Disconnect the negative battery cable.
3. Cut the damaged fuse link from the wiring harness and discard it. If the fuse link is one of three circuits fed by a single feed wire, cut it out of the harness at each splice end and discard it.
4. Identify and procure the proper fuse link and butt connectors for attaching the fuse link to the harness.
5. To repair any fuse link in a 3-link group with one feed:
   a. After cutting the open link out of the harness, cut each of the remaining undamaged fuse links close to the feed wire weld.
   b. Strip approximately ½ in. (13mm) of insulation from the detached ends of the two good fuse links. Then insert two wire ends into one end of a butt connector and carefully push one stripped end of the replacement fuse link into the same end of the butt connector and crimp all three firmly together.

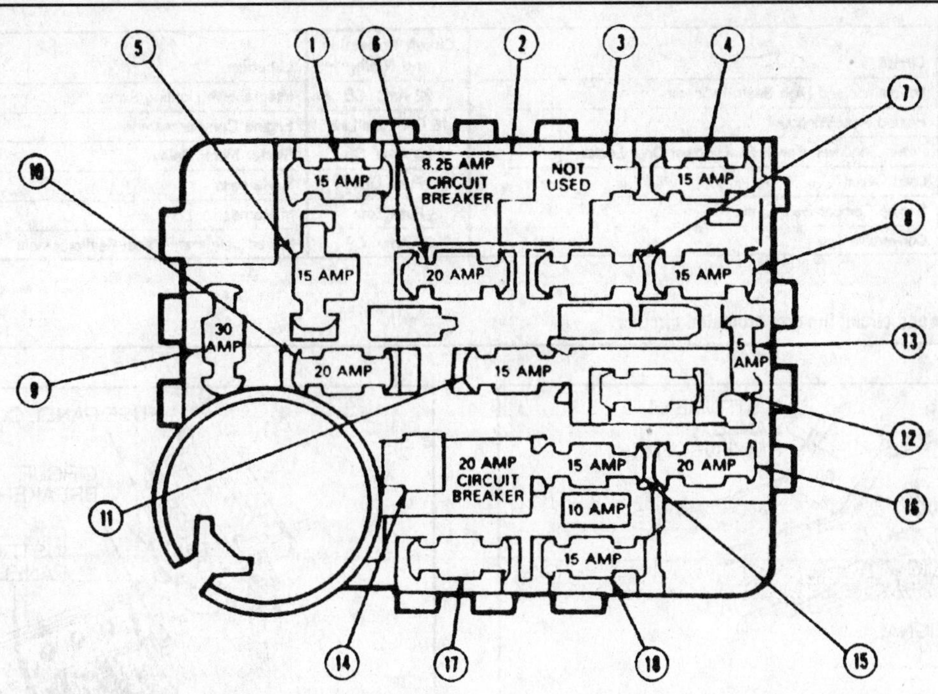

Cavity Number	Fuse Rating	Color	Circuit Protected
1	15 Amp	Lt. Blue	Stoplamps, Hazard Warning Lamps, Speed Control
2	8.25 Amp C. B		Windshield Wiper, Windshield Washer Pump, Interval Wiper, Washer Fluid Level Indicator
3	Spare		Not Used
4	15 Amp	Red	Tail Lamps, Parking Lamps, Side Marker Lamps, Instrument Cluster Illumination Lamps, License Lamps
5	15 Amp	Lt. Blue	Turn Signal Lamps, Backup Lamps, Fluids Module, Heated Rear Window Relay
6	20 Amp	Yellow	A/C Clutch, Heated Rear Window Control, Luggage Compartment Lid Release, Speed Control Module, Clock/Radio Display, A/C Throttle Positioner, Day/Night Illumination Relay
7	Spare		Not Used
8	15 Amp	Lt. Blue	Courtesy Lamps, Key Warning Buzzer, Fuel Filler Door Release, Radio, Power Mirror
9	30 Amp	Lt. Green	Heater Blower Motor
10	20 Amp	Yellow	Flash-To-Pass, Low Oil Warning Relay
11	15 Amp	Lt. Blue	Radio, Tape Player, Premium Sound, Graphic Equalizer
12	Spare		Not Used
13	5 Amp	Tan	Instrument Cluster Illumination Lamps, Radio, Climate Control, Ash Receptacle Lamps, Floor "PRNDL" Lamp
14	20 Amp C B		Power Windows 15 Amp Fuse
15	15 Amp	Lt. Blue	Fog Lamps
16	20 Amp	Yellow	Horn, Cigar Lighter
17	Spare		Not Used
18	15 Amp	Lt Blue	Warning Indicator Lamps, Throttle Solenoid Positioner, Low Fuel Module, Dual Timer Buzzer, Tachometer, Engine Idle Track Relay, Fluids Module Display

88156G64

Fig. 83 Fuse panel assembly and circuit locations

88156P33

Fig. 84 The fuse panel cover pulls off

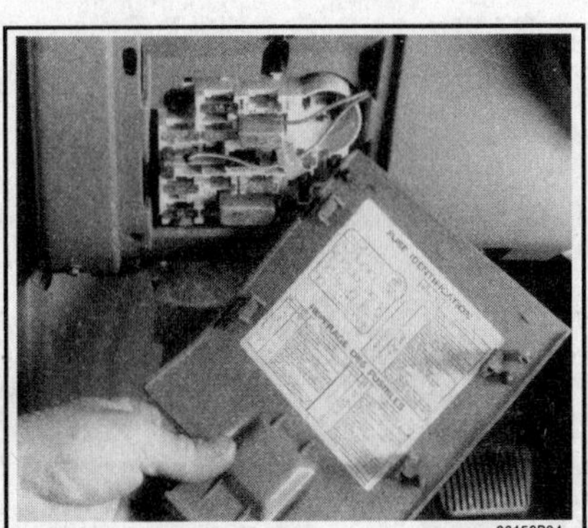

88156P34

Fig. 85 The fuse identification chart is on the back of the panel cover

88156P35

Fig. 86 The circuit brakers pull straight out similar to the fuses

Circuit	Circuit Protection and Rating	Location
Headlamps and High Beam Indicator	22 Amp CB	Integral with Lighting Switch
Heated Rear Window	16 GA Fuse Link	Engine Compartment
Power Windows, Power Seat, Power Door Locks	20 Amp. CB	Starter Motor Relay
Load Circuit	Fuse Link	In Harness
Engine Compartment Lamp	Fuse Link	In Harness
Convertible Top	25 Amp CB	Lower Instrument Panel-Reinforcement

88156G65

Fig. 87 Fusible link and circuit breaker protected circuits

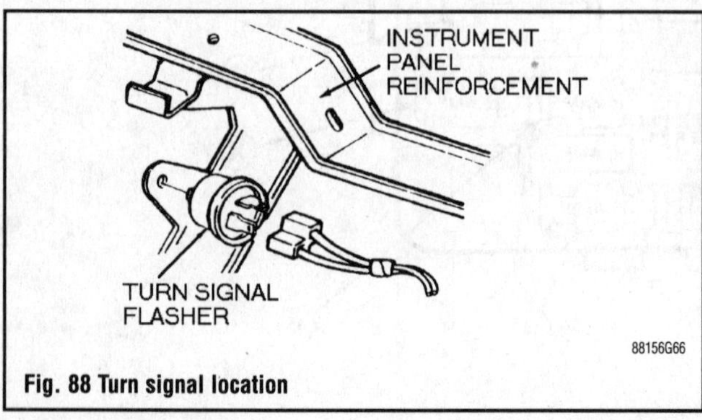

Fig. 88 Turn signal location

➡Care must be taken when fitting the three fuse links into the butt connector as the internal diameter is snug for three wires. Make sure to use a proper crimping tool. Pliers, side cutters, etc. will not apply the proper crimp to retain the wires and withstand a pull test.

c. After crimping the butt connector to the three fuse links, cut the weld portion from the feed wire and strip approximately ½ in. (13mm) of insulation from the cut end. Insert the stripped end into the open end of the butt connector and crimp firmly.

d. To attach the remaining end of the replacement link, strip approximately ½ in. (13mm) of insulation from the wire end of the circuit from which the blown fuse was removed, and firmly crimp a butt connector or equivalent to the stripped wire. Then, insert the end of the replacement link into the other end of the butt connector and crimp firmly.

e. Using rosin core solder with a consistency of 60 percent tin and 40 percent lead, solder the connectors and the wires at the repairs and insulate with electrical tape.

6. To replace any fuse link on a single circuit in a harness, cut out the damaged portion, strip approximately ½ in. (13mm) of insulation from the two wire ends and attach the appropriate replacement fuse link to the stripped wire ends with two proper size butt connectors. Solder the connectors and wires and insulate the tape.

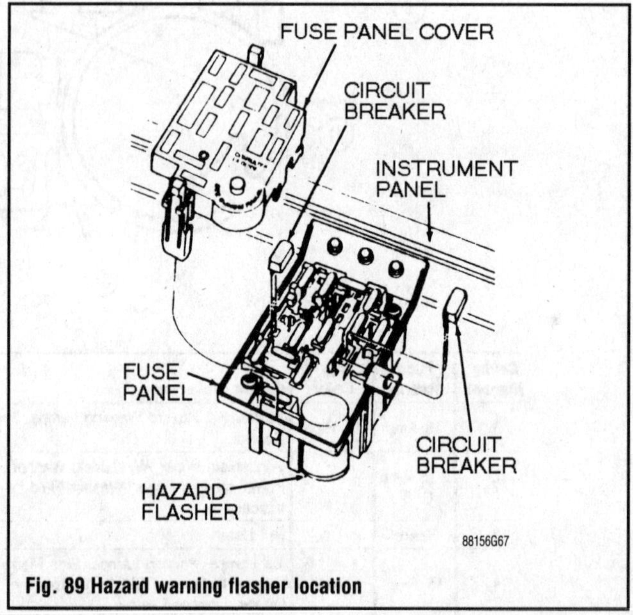

Fig. 89 Hazard warning flasher location

7. To repair any fuse link which has an eyelet terminal on one end such as the charging circuit, cut off the open fuse link behind the weld, strip approximately ½ in. (13mm) of insulation from the cut end and attach the appropriate new eyelet fuse link to the cut stripped wire with an appropriate size butt connector. Solder the connectors and wires at the repair and insulate with tape.

8. Connect the negative battery cable to the battery and test the system for proper operation.

➡Do not mistake a resistor wire for a fuse link. The resistor wire is generally longer and has print stating, "Resistor: don't cut or splice."

WIRING DIAGRAMS

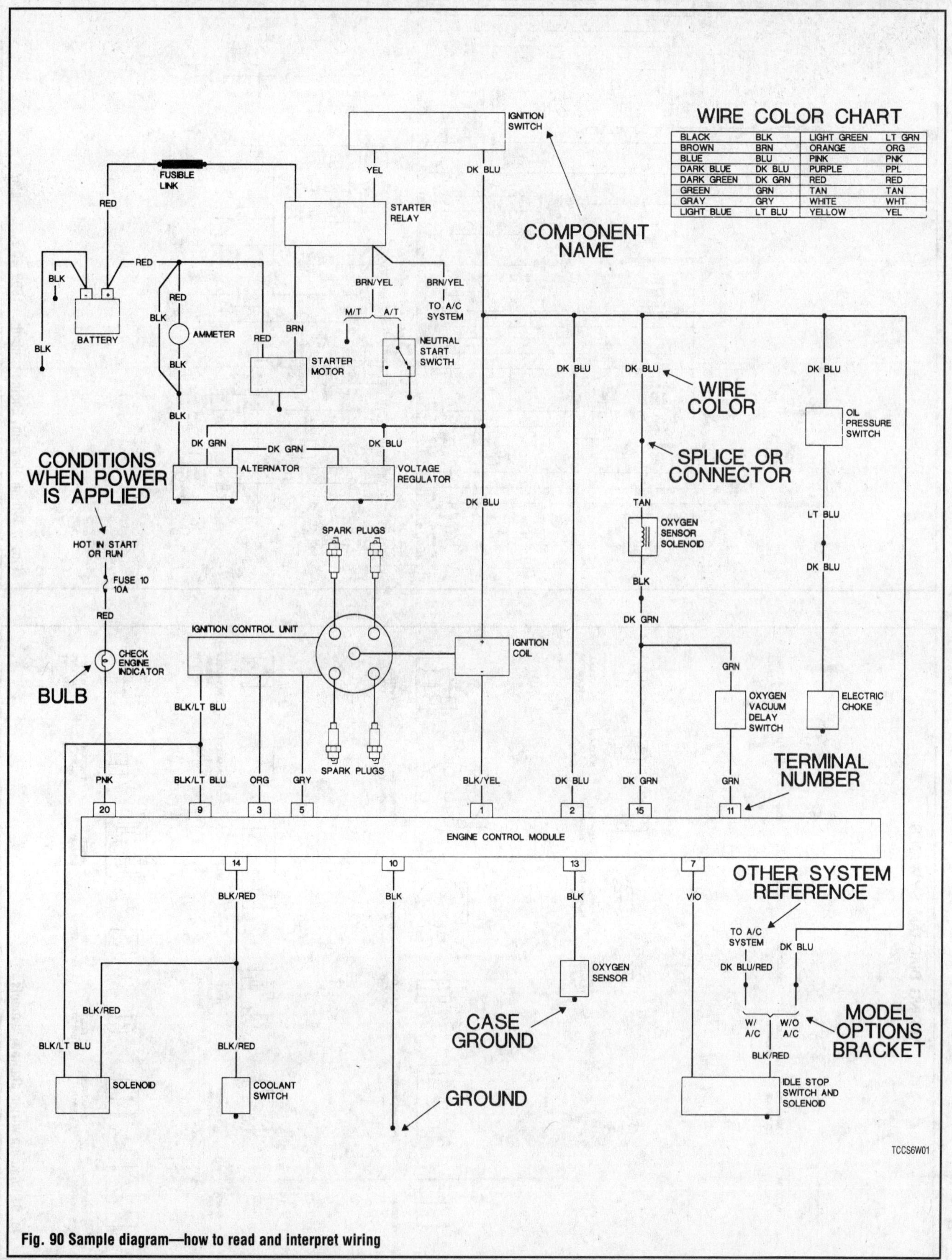

Fig. 90 Sample diagram—how to read and interpret wiring

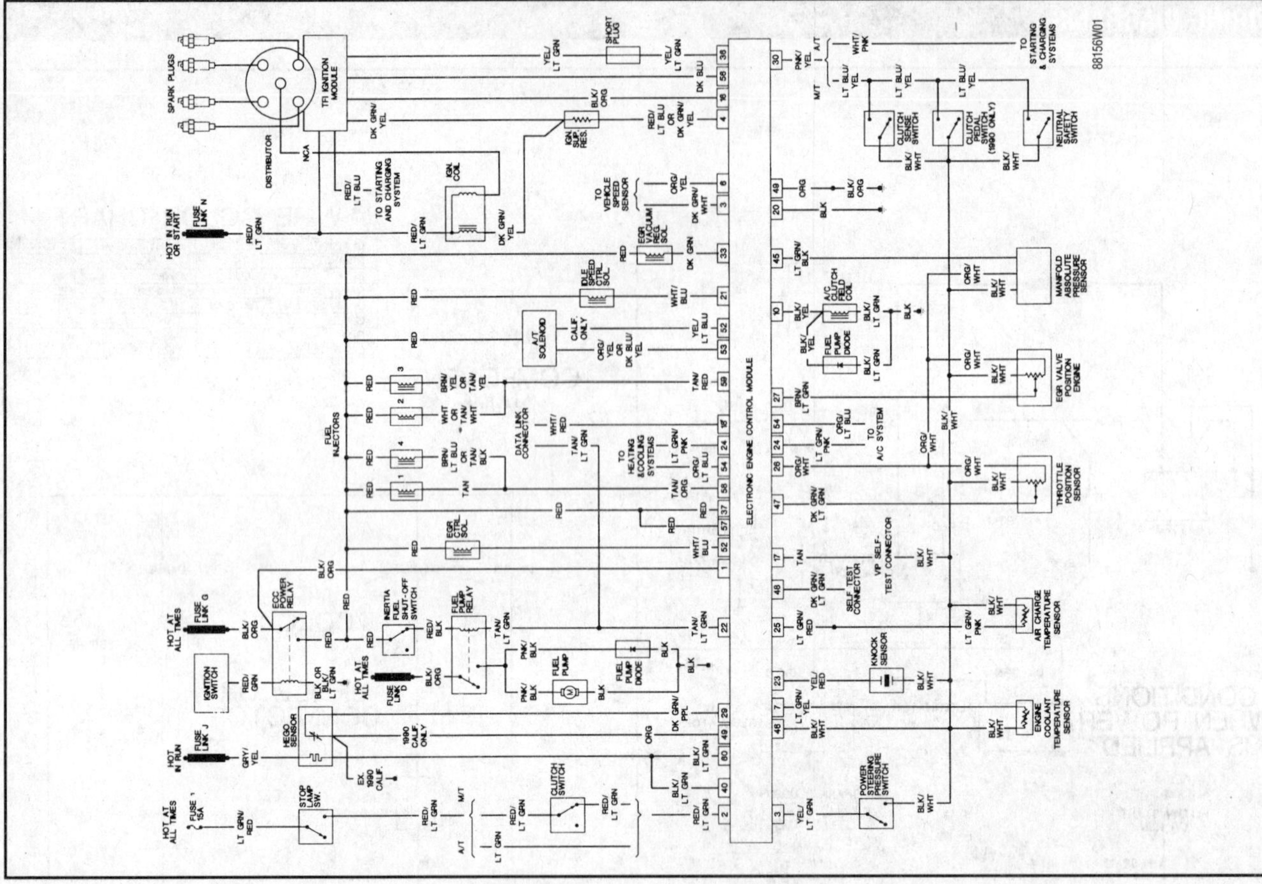

88156W01

Fig. 92 Wiring diagram, Engine controls—1989–90 2.3L engine

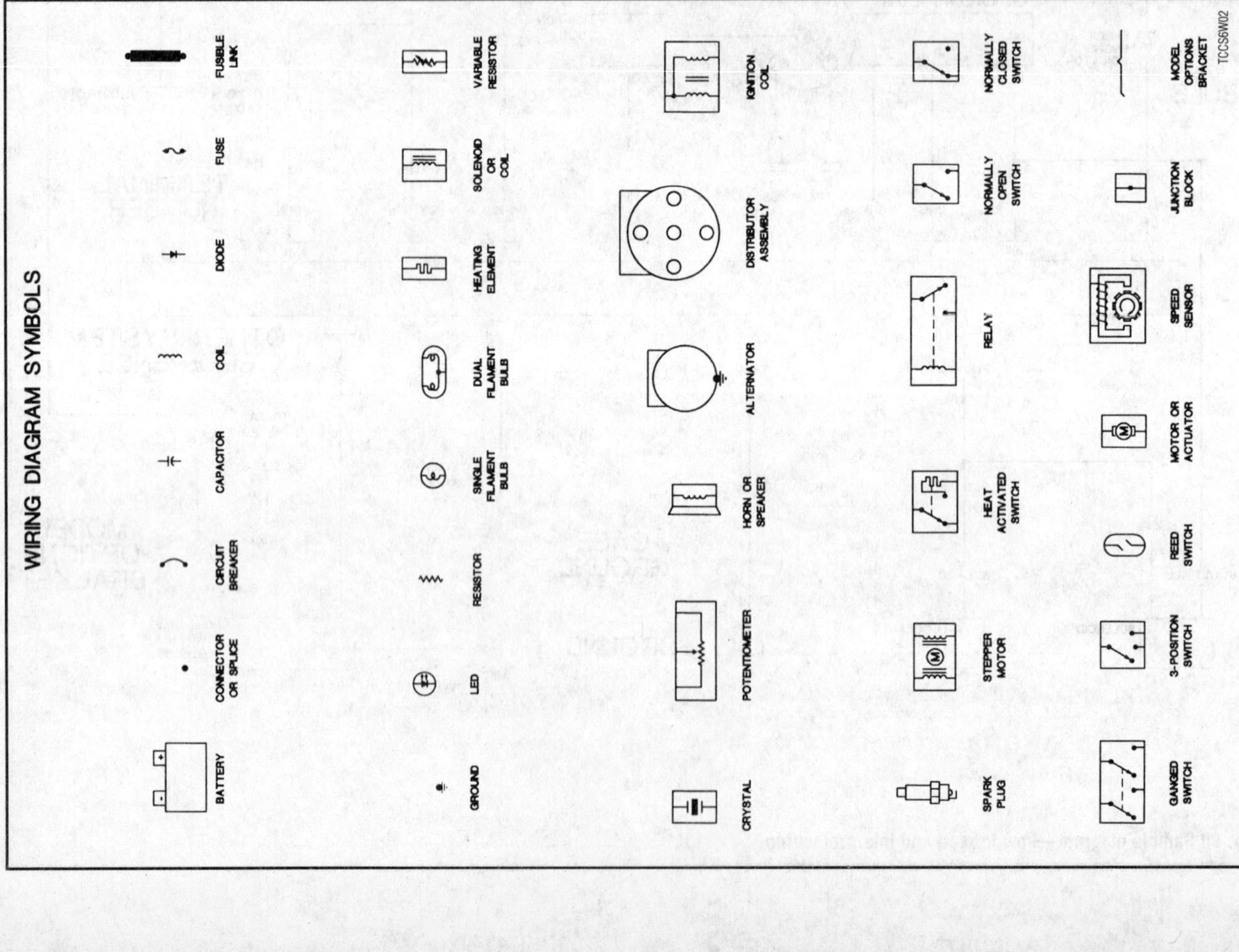

WIRING DIAGRAM SYMBOLS

BATTERY

CONNECTOR OR SPLICE

CIRCUIT BREAKER

CAPACITOR

COIL

DIODE

FUSE

FUSIBLE LINK

GROUND

LED

RESISTOR

SINGLE FILAMENT BULB

DUAL FILAMENT BULB

HEATING ELEMENT

SOLENOID OR COIL

VARIABLE RESISTOR

CRYSTAL

POTENTIOMETER

HORN OR SPEAKER

ALTERNATOR

DISTRIBUTOR ASSEMBLY

IGNITION COIL

SPARK PLUG

STEPPER MOTOR

HEAT ACTIVATED SWITCH

RELAY

NORMALLY OPEN SWITCH

NORMALLY CLOSED SWITCH

GANGED SWITCH

3-POSITION SWITCH

REED SWITCH

MOTOR OR ACTUATOR

SPEED SENSOR

JUNCTION BLOCK

MODEL OPTIONS BRACKET

TCCS6W02

Fig. 91 Common wiring diagram symbols

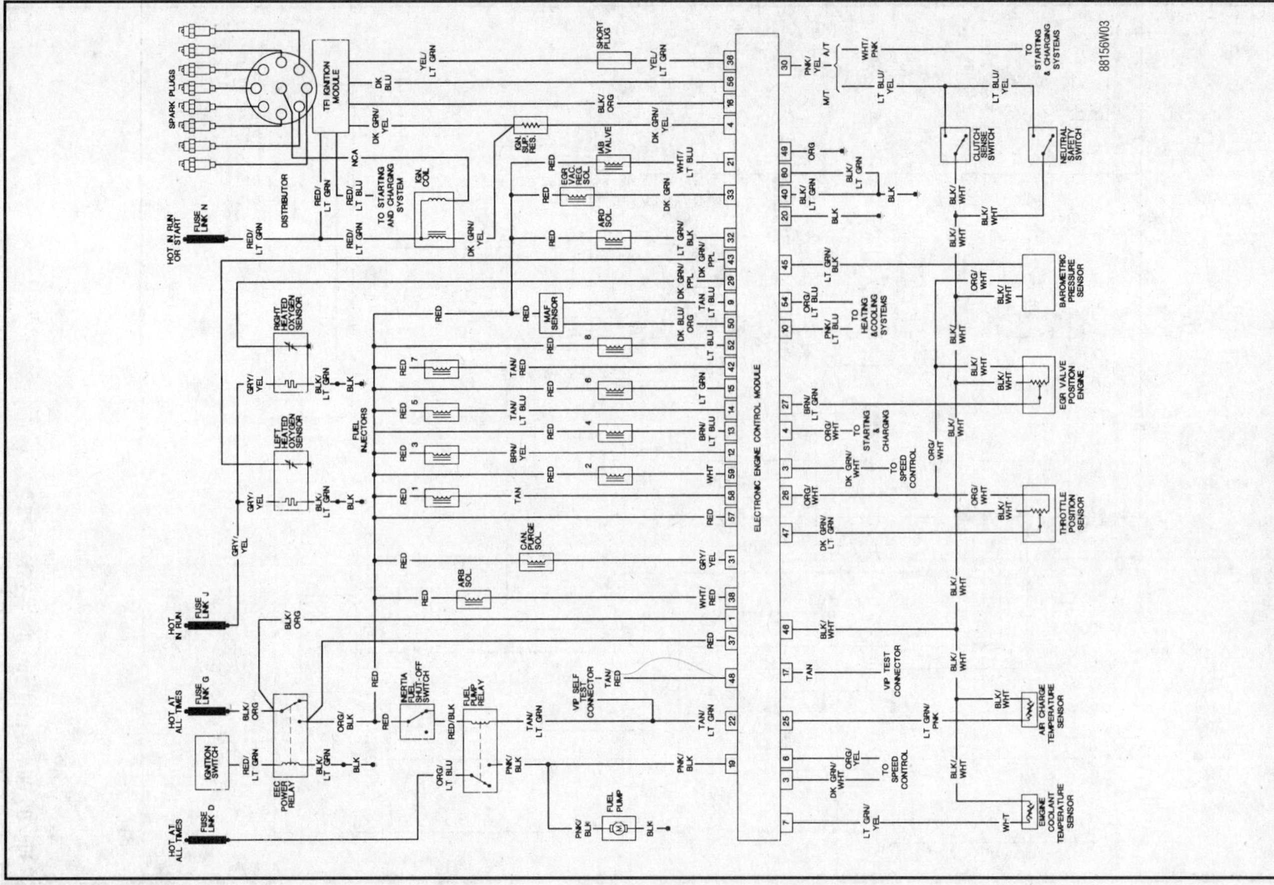

88156W03

Fig. 94 Wiring diagram, Engine controls—1989–90 5.0L engine

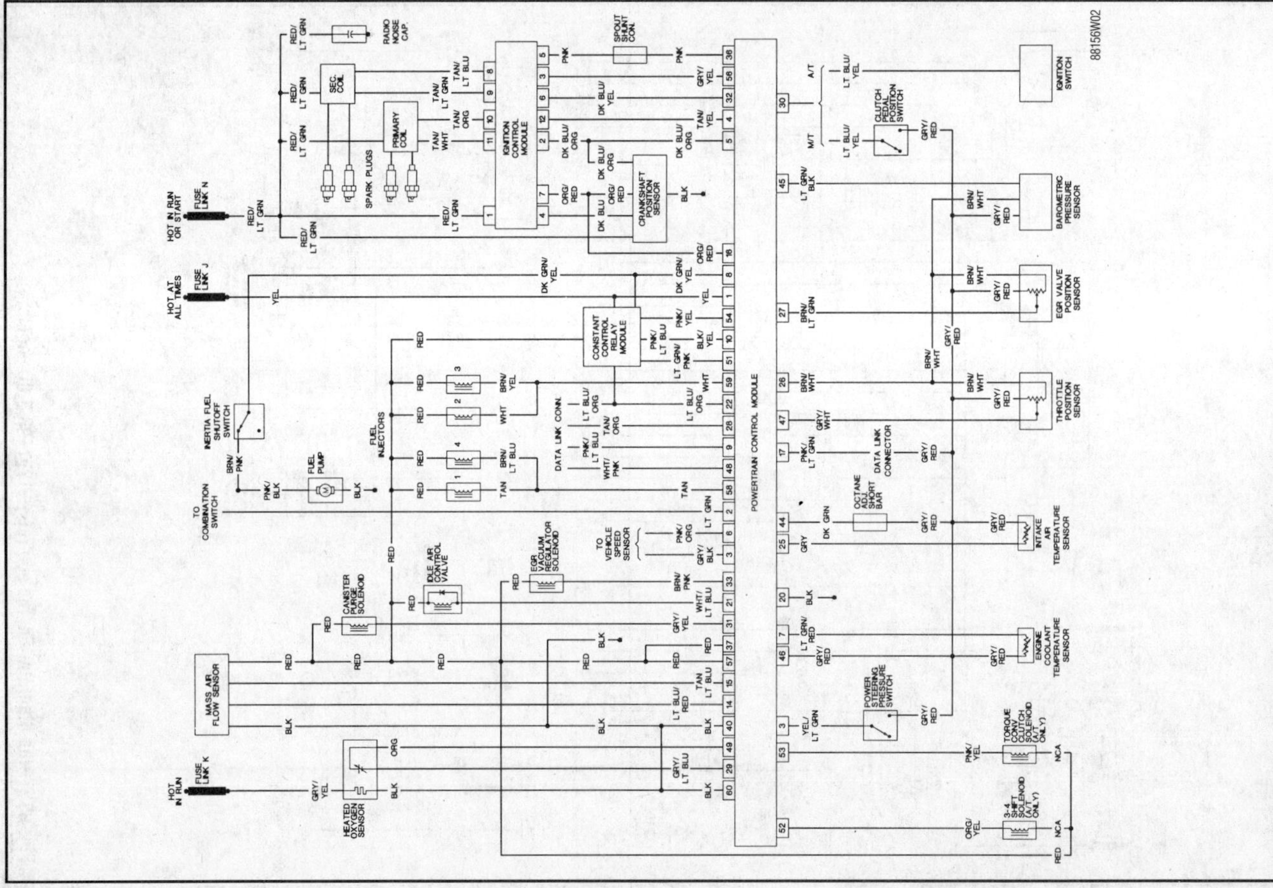

88156W02

Fig. 93 Wiring diagram, Engine controls—1991–93 2.3L engine

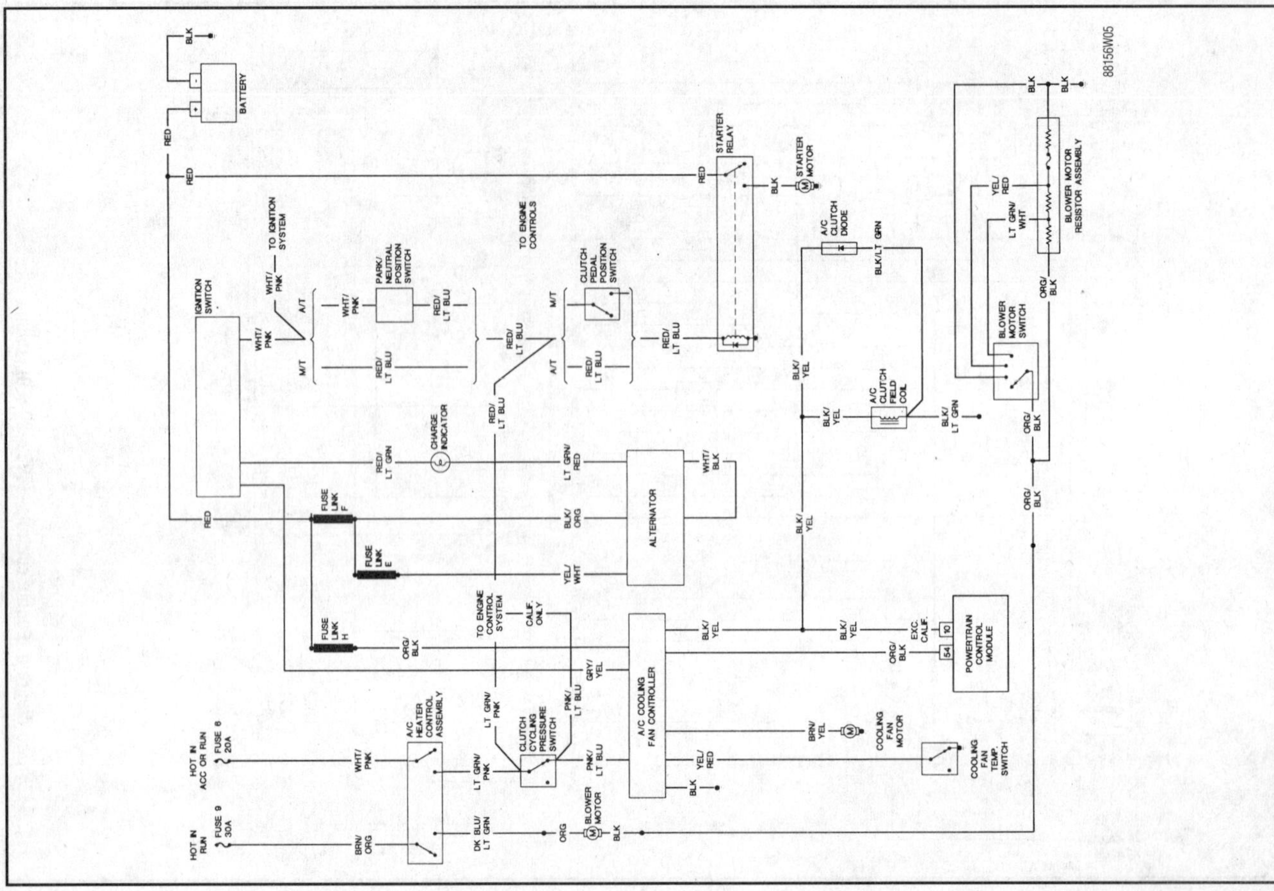

Fig. 96 Wiring diagram, Body—1989–90 2.3L engine

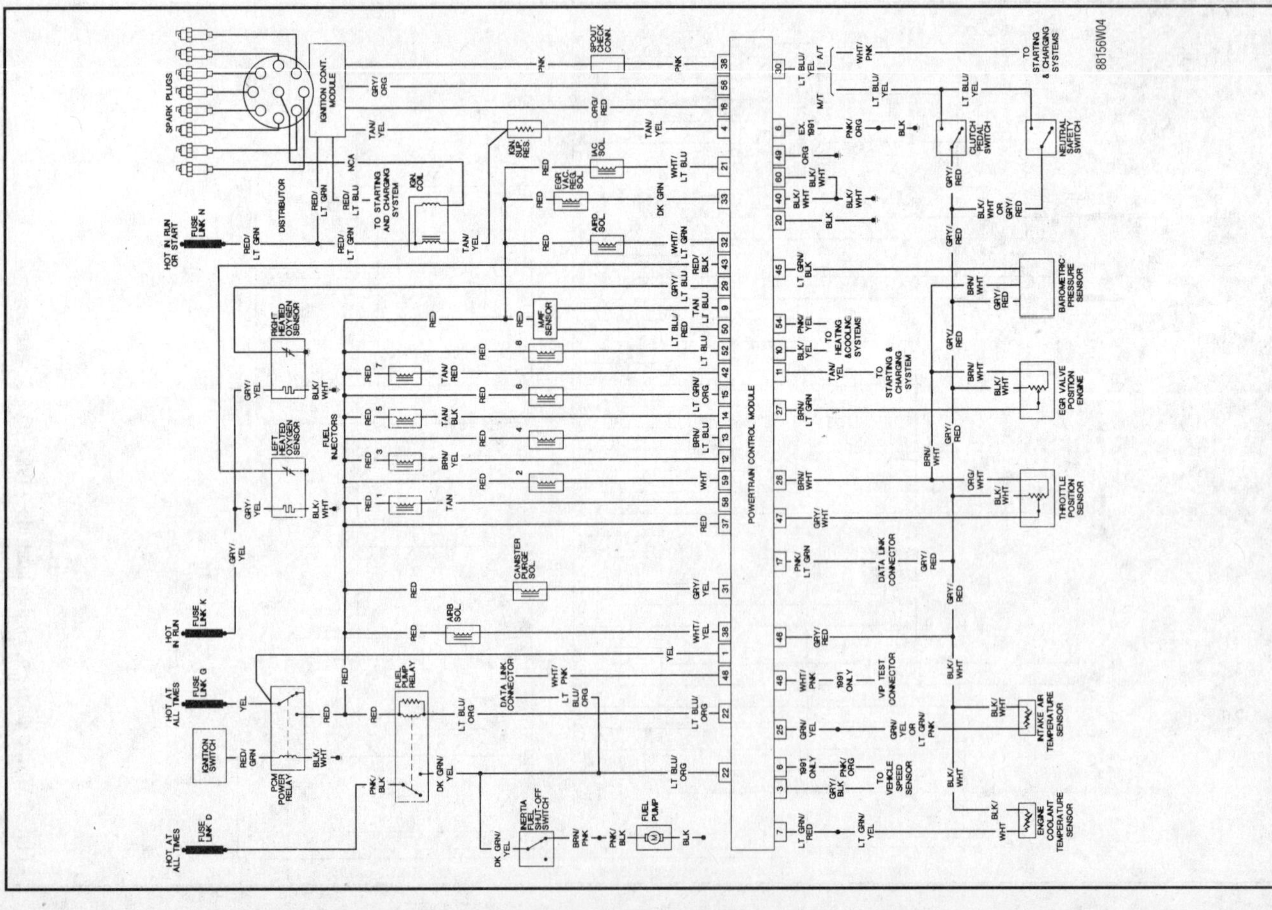

Fig. 95 Wiring diagram, Engine controls—1991–93 5.0L engine

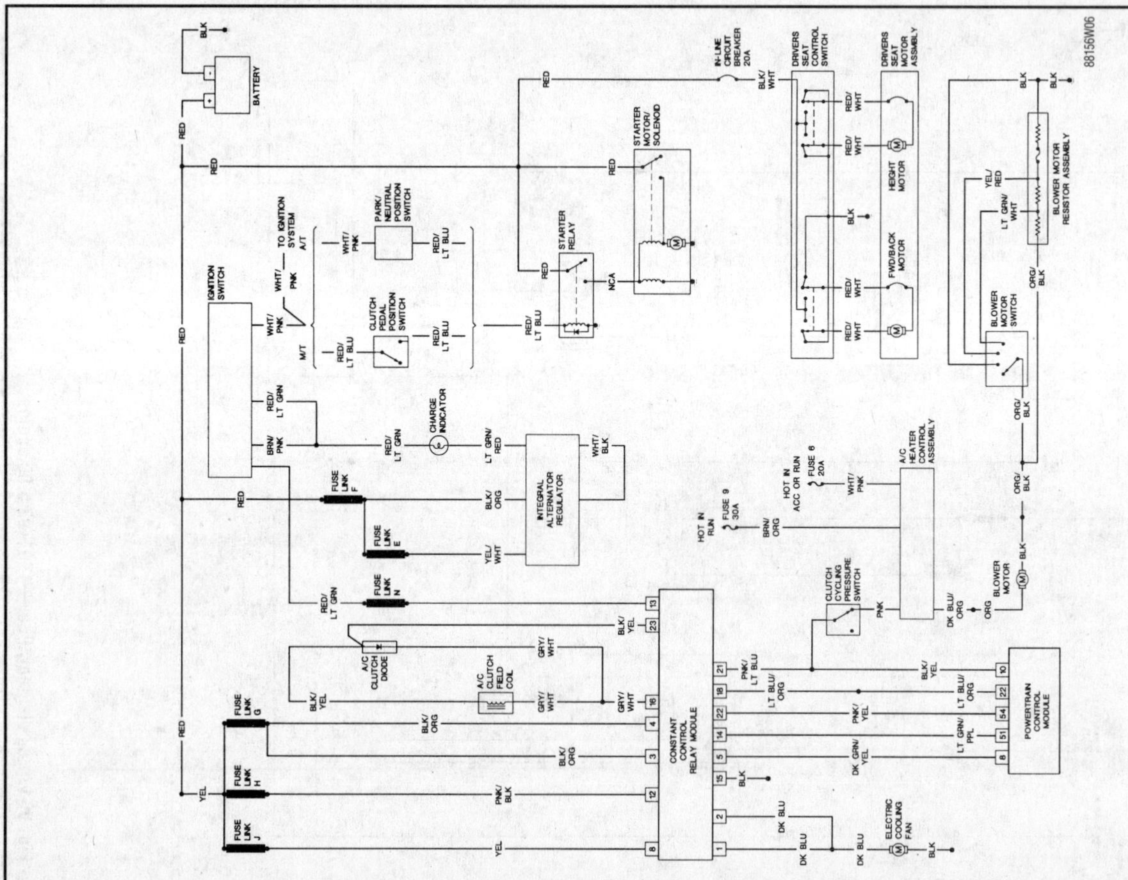

88156W07

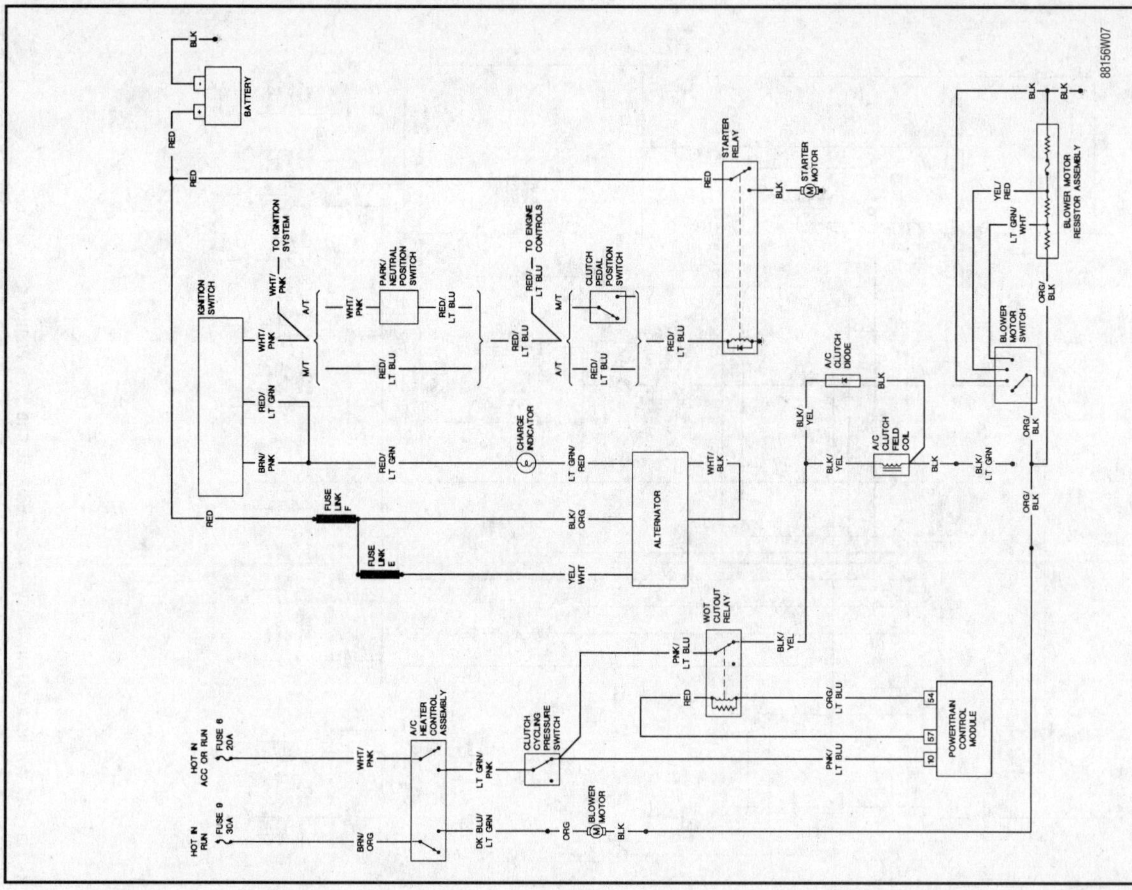

Fig. 98 Wiring diagram, Body—1989–90 5.0L engine

88156W06

Fig. 97 Wiring diagram, Body—1991–93 2.3L engine

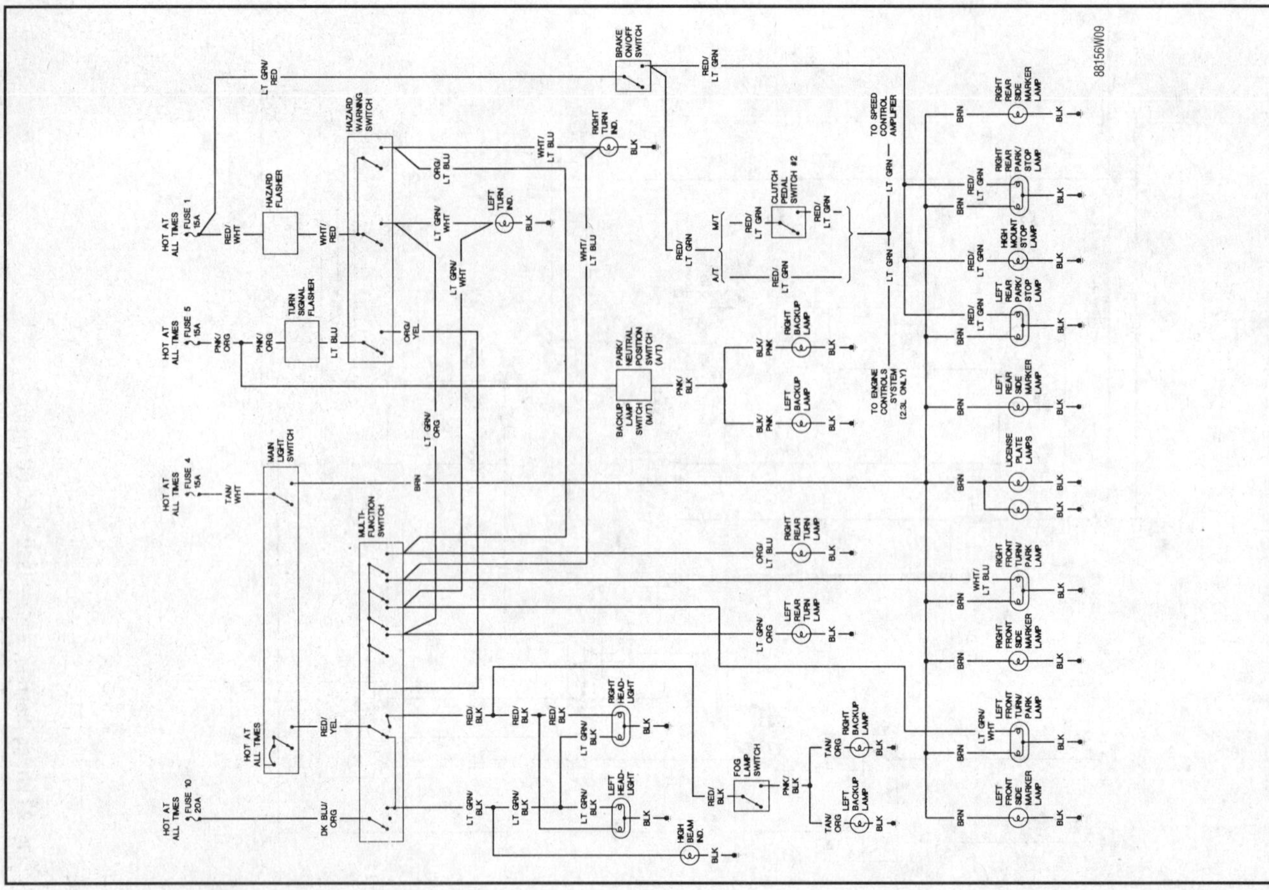

Fig. 100 Wiring diagram, Body—1989–93 2.3L and 5.0L engine

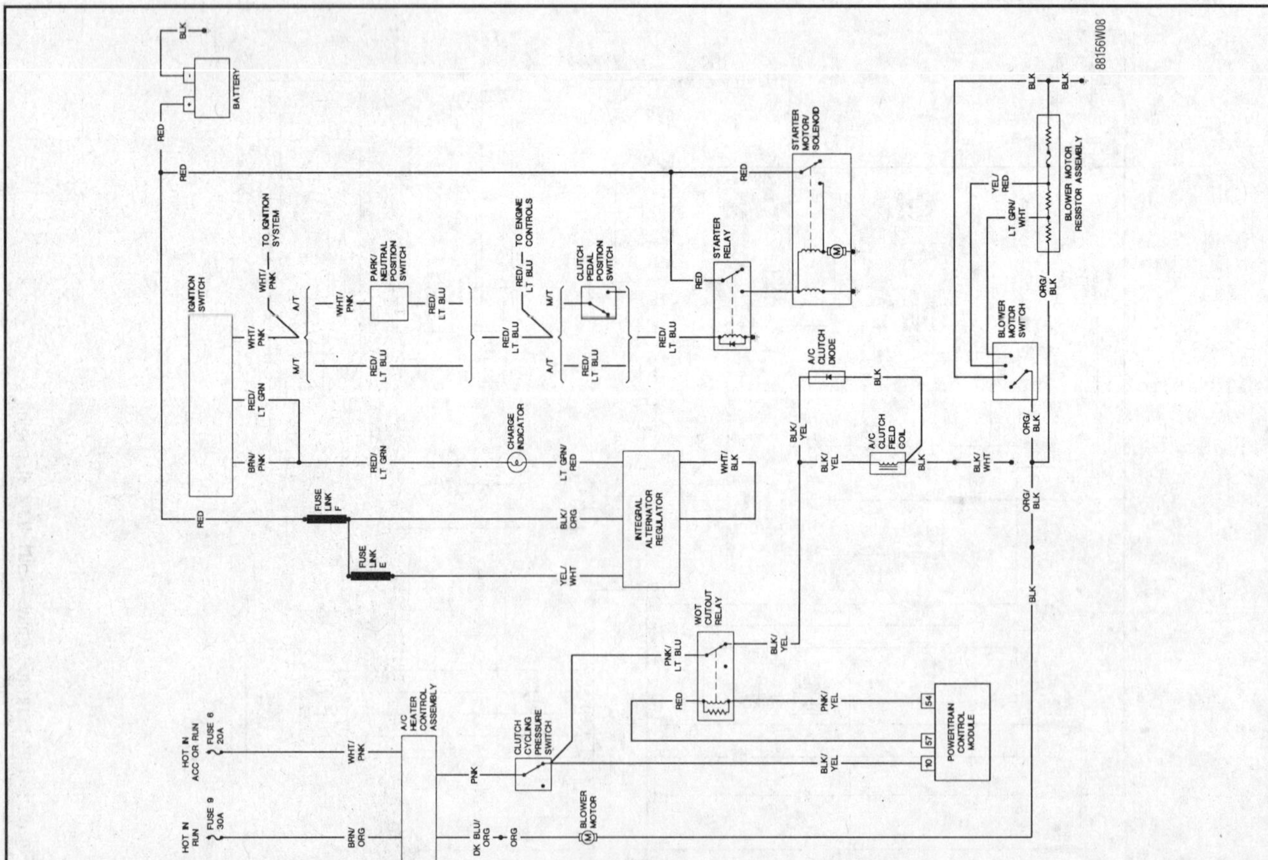

Fig. 99 Wiring diagram, Body—1991–93 5.0L engine

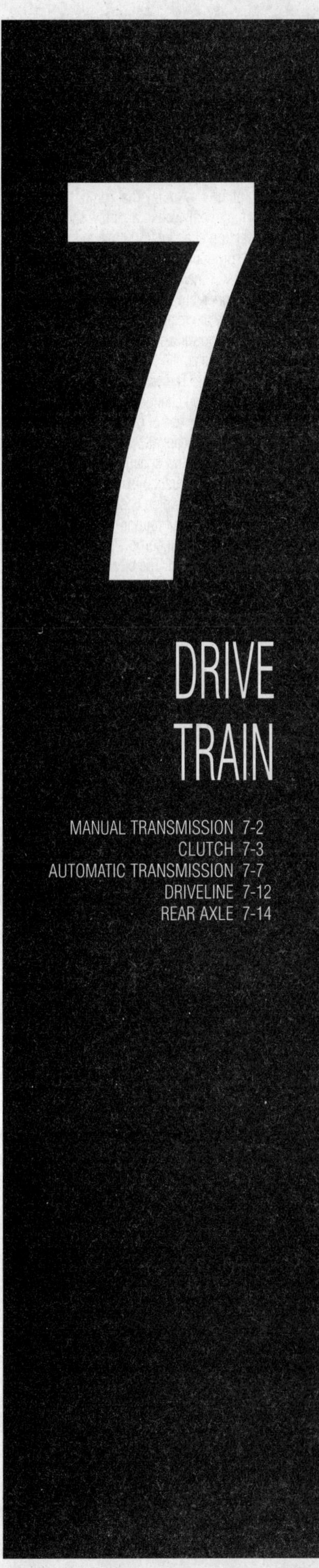

7 DRIVE TRAIN

MANUAL TRANSMISSION

Understanding the Manual Transmission

Because of the way an internal combustion engine breathes, it can produce torque (or twisting force) only within a narrow speed range. Most overhead valve pushrod engines must turn at about 2500 rpm to produce their peak torque. Often by 4500 rpm, they are producing so little torque that continued increases in engine speed produce no power increases.The torque peak on overhead camshaft engines is, generally, much higher, but much narrower.The manual transmission and clutch are employed to vary the relationship between engine RPM and the speed of the wheels so that adequate power can be produced under all circumstances. The clutch allows engine torque to be applied to the transmission input shaft gradually, due to mechanical slippage. The vehicle can, consequently, be started smoothly from a full stop.The transmission changes the ratio between the rotating speeds of the engine and the wheels by the use of gears. 4-speed or 5-speed transmissions are most common. The lower gears allow full engine power to be applied to the rear wheels during acceleration at low speeds.The clutch driveplate is a thin disc, the center of which is splined to the transmission input shaft. Both sides of the disc are covered with a layer of material which is similar to brake lining and which is capable of allowing slippage without roughness or excessive noise.The clutch cover is bolted to the engine flywheel and incorporates a diaphragm spring which provides the pressure to engage the clutch. The cover also houses the pressure plate. When the clutch pedal is released, the driven disc is sandwiched between the pressure plate and the smooth surface of the flywheel, thus forcing the disc to turn at the same speed as the engine crankshaft.The transmission contains a mainshaft which passes all the way through the transmission, from the clutch to the driveshaft. This shaft is separated at one point, so that front and rear portions can turn at different speeds.Power is transmitted by a countershaft in the lower gears and reverse. The gears of the countershaft mesh with gears on the mainshaft, allowing power to be carried from one to the other. Countershaft gears are often integral with that shaft, while several of the mainshaft gears can either rotate independently of the shaft or be locked to it. Shifting from one gear to the next causes one of the gears to be freed from rotating with the shaft and locks another to it. Gears are locked and unlocked by internal dog clutches which slide between the center of the gear and the shaft. The forward gears usually employ synchronizers; friction members which smoothly bring gear and shaft to the same speed before the toothed dog clutches are engaged.

Identification

All vehicles covered by this manual that are equipped with a manual transmission use the Ford T50D 5-speed overdrive transmission.

Shift Lever and Boot Assembly

REMOVAL & INSTALLATION

See Figure 1

1. Remove the shift knob by rotating it counterclockwise.
2. Remove the console trim and lift the boot over the shift lever.

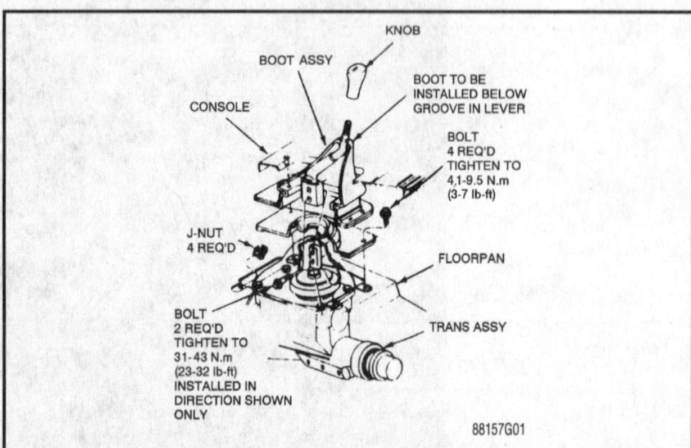

Fig. 1 Exploded view of the transmission shift lever mounting

3. Remove the two bolts retaining the shift lever to the transmission.

To install:

4. Position the shift lever to the transmission, then install the two retaining bolts and tighten to 23–32 ft. lbs. (31–43 Nm).

➡Shift lever bolts must only be installed in one direction, from the left side of the shift lever.

5. Install the console trim and the shift boot.
6. Install the shift knob by screwing it into place. When tension is felt, rotate it an additional 180 degrees to align the graphics on the knob.

Backup Light Switch

REMOVAL & INSTALLATION

1. Place the shift lever in Neutral.
2. Raise and support the vehicle safely using jackstands.
3. Be sure to block the wheels remaining on the ground. If the front end is being raised, firmly set the parking brake.
4. Unplug the electrical connector at the switch.
5. Unscrew the switch from the transmission extension housing.

To install:

6. Thread the new switch into position and tighten to 60 inch lbs. (7 Nm).
7. Connect the switch wiring.
8. Remove the jackstands and carefully lower the vehicle.
9. Put the transmission in gear and firmly set the parking brake, then remove the wheel blocks.

Transmission

REMOVAL & INSTALLATION

1. Disconnect the negative battery cable for safety.
2. Firmly set the parking brake and block the drive wheels, then raise and support the front of the vehicle safely using jackstands.
3. Matchmark the driveshaft for reassembly. Disconnect the driveshaft from the rear U-joint flange. Slide the driveshaft off the transmission output shaft, then install an extension housing seal installation tool into the extension housing to prevent lubricant from leaking.

➡If a seal tool is not available, place a plastic bag over the extension housing and secure it with one or more rubber bands. This will help prevent a mess of transmission fluid.

4. Remove the bolts and remove the catalytic converter.
5. Remove the two nuts attaching the rear transmission support to the crossmember, then remove the retaining bolts.
6. Use a jack to support the engine and transmission assembly. Always use a block of wood to spread the load and prevent damage to the engine and drivetrain components.
7. Remove the two nuts from the crossmember bolts. Remove the bolts, then raise the jack slightly and remove the crossmember.
8. Lower the transmission to expose the two bolts securing the shift handle to the shift tower. Remove the two nuts and bolts, then remove the shift handle.
9. Disconnect the wiring harness from the backup lamp switch. On the 5.0L engine, disconnect the Neutral sensing switch.
10. Remove the bolt from the speedometer cable retainer, then remove the speedometer driven gear from the transmission.
11. Remove the four bolts that secure the transmission to the flywheel housing.
12. Remove the transmission and jack rearward until the transmission input shaft clears the flywheel housing. If necessary, lower it enough to obtain clearance for removing the transmission.

⁂ WARNING

Do NOT depress the clutch while the transmission is removed. To prevent this it is usually wise to either block the pedal in the upward position or to tie it up to the steering column.

To install:

13. Make sure the mounting surface of the transmission and flywheel housing are clean and free of dirt, paint and burrs.
14. Install two guide pins in the flywheel housing lower mounting bolt holes. Raise the transmission, then move it forward onto the guide pins until the input shaft splines enter the clutch hub splines and the case is positioned against the flywheel housing.
15. Install the two upper bolts holding the transmission to the flywheel housing. Snug the bolts, then remove the guide pins. Install the two lower bolts, then tighten all the bolts to 45–65 ft. lbs. (61–88 Nm).
16. Raise the transmission with a jack until the shift handle can be secured to the shift tower. Install tighten the attaching bolts and washers, then tighten them to 23–32 ft. lbs. (31–43 Nm).
17. Connect the speedometer cable to the extension housing and tighten the attaching screw.
18. Raise the rear of the transmission with the jack and install the transmission support. Install and tighten the attaching bolts to 36–50 ft. lbs. (48–68 Nm).
19. With the transmission extension housing resting on the engine rear support, install the attaching bolts and tighten them to 25–35 ft. lbs. (38–48 Nm).
20. Connect the backup lamp switch wiring harness. On the 5.0L engine, connect the neutral sensing switch to the wiring harness.
21. Install the catalytic converter. Tighten the attaching bolts to 20–30 ft. lbs. (27–41 Nm).
22. Remove the extension housing installation tool and slide the forward end of the driveshaft over the transmission output shaft. Connect the driveshaft to the rear U-joint flange. Make sure the matchmarks align. Tighten the U-bolt nuts to 42–57 ft. lbs. (56–77 Nm).
23. Fill the transmission with the proper type and quantity of fluid. For details, please refer to the Fluid and Lubricant information in Section 1 of this manual.
24. Remove the jackstands, then carefully lower the vehicle. Check the shift and crossover motion for full shift engagement and smooth crossover operation.

➡Remember to remove the wheel blocks before attempting to move the vehicle.

CLUTCH

⁂ CAUTION

The clutch driven disc often contains asbestos, which has been determined to be a cancer-causing agent Never clean clutch surfaces with compressed air. Avoid inhaling any dust from any clutch surface. When cleaning clutch surfaces, use a commercially-available brake cleaning fluid.

Understanding the Clutch

The purpose of the clutch is to disconnect and connect engine power at the transmission. A vehicle at rest requires a lot of engine torque to get all that weight moving. An internal combustion engine does not develop a high starting torque (unlike steam engines) so it must be allowed to operate without any load until it builds up enough torque to move the vehicle. To a point, torque increases with engine rpm. The clutch allows the engine to build up torque by physically disconnecting the engine from the transmission, relieving the engine of any load or resistance.The transfer of engine power to the transmission (the load) must be smooth and gradual; if it weren't, drive line components would wear out or break quickly. This gradual power transfer is made possible by gradually releasing the clutch pedal. The clutch disc and pressure plate are the connecting link between the engine and transmission. When the clutch pedal is released, the disc and plate contact each other (the clutch is engaged) physically joining the engine and transmission. When the pedal is pushed in, the disc and plate separate (the clutch is disengaged) disconnecting the engine from the transmission.Most clutch assemblies consists of the flywheel, the clutch disc, the clutch pressure plate, the throw out bearing and fork, the actuating linkage and the pedal. The flywheel and clutch pressure plate (driving members) are connected to the engine crankshaft and rotate with it. The clutch disc is located between the flywheel and pressure plate, and is splined to the transmission shaft. A driving member is one that is attached to the engine and transfers engine power to a driven member (clutch disc) on the transmission shaft. A driving member (pressure plate) rotates (drives) a driven member (clutch disc) on contact and, in so doing, turns the transmission shaft.There is a circular diaphragm spring within the pressure plate cover (transmission side). In a relaxed state (when the clutch pedal is fully released) this spring is convex; that is, it is dished outward toward the transmission. Pushing in the clutch pedal actuates the attached linkage. Connected to the other end of this is the throw out fork, which hold the throw out bearing. When the clutch pedal is depressed, the clutch linkage pushes the fork and bearing forward to contact the diaphragm spring of the pressure plate. The outer edges of the spring are secured to the pressure plate and are pivoted on rings so that when the center of the spring is compressed by the throw out bearing, the outer edges bow outward and, by so doing, pull the pressure plate in the same direction – away from the clutch disc. This action separates the disc from the plate, disengaging the clutch and allowing the transmission to be shifted into another gear. A coil type clutch return spring attached to the clutch pedal arm permits full release of the pedal. Releasing the pedal pulls the throw out bearing away from the diaphragm spring resulting in a reversal of spring position. As bearing pressure is gradually released from the spring center, the outer edges of the spring bow outward, pushing the pressure plate into closer contact with the clutch disc. As the disc and plate move closer together, friction between the two increases and slippage is reduced until, when full spring pressure is applied (by fully releasing the pedal) the speed of the disc and plate are the same. This stops all slipping, creating a direct connection between the plate and disc which results in the transfer of power from the engine to the transmission. The clutch disc is now rotating with the pressure plate at engine speed and, because it is splined to the transmission shaft, the shaft now turns at the same engine speed.The clutch is operating properly if:

1. It will stall the engine when released with the vehicle held stationary.
2. The shift lever can be moved freely between 1st and reverse gears when the vehicle is stationary and the clutch disengaged.

Self-Adjusting Clutch Assembly

➧ See Figure 2

The clutch free-play is adjusted automatically by a built-in clutch control mechanism. This devise allows the clutch controls to self-adjust during normal operation.

The system consists of a spring-loaded gear quadrant, a spring-loaded pawl and a clutch cable which is spring-loaded to preload the release lever bearing. This compensates for movement of the release lever, as the clutch disc wears. The pawl, located at the top of the clutch pedal, engages the gear quadrant when the clutch pedal is depressed and pulls the cable through its continuously adjusted stroke. Clutch cable adjustments are not required because of this feature.

CHECKING ADJUSTMENT

The self-adjusting feature should be checked every 5000 miles (8000 km). This is accomplished by insuring that the clutch pedal travels to the top of its upward position. Grasp the clutch pedal with your hand or put your foot under the clutch pedal, pull up on the pedal until it stops. Very little effort is required (about 10 lbs./4.5 Kg). Finally, depress the clutch pedal and listen for an audible "click." If you hear a sound, the clutch was in need of adjustment, and it has just adjusted itself.

REMOVAL & INSTALLATION

Self-Adjusting Assembly

➧ See Figure 3

1. Disconnect the negative battery cable for safety.
2. Remove the steering wheel, using puller T67L–3600–A or equivalent.

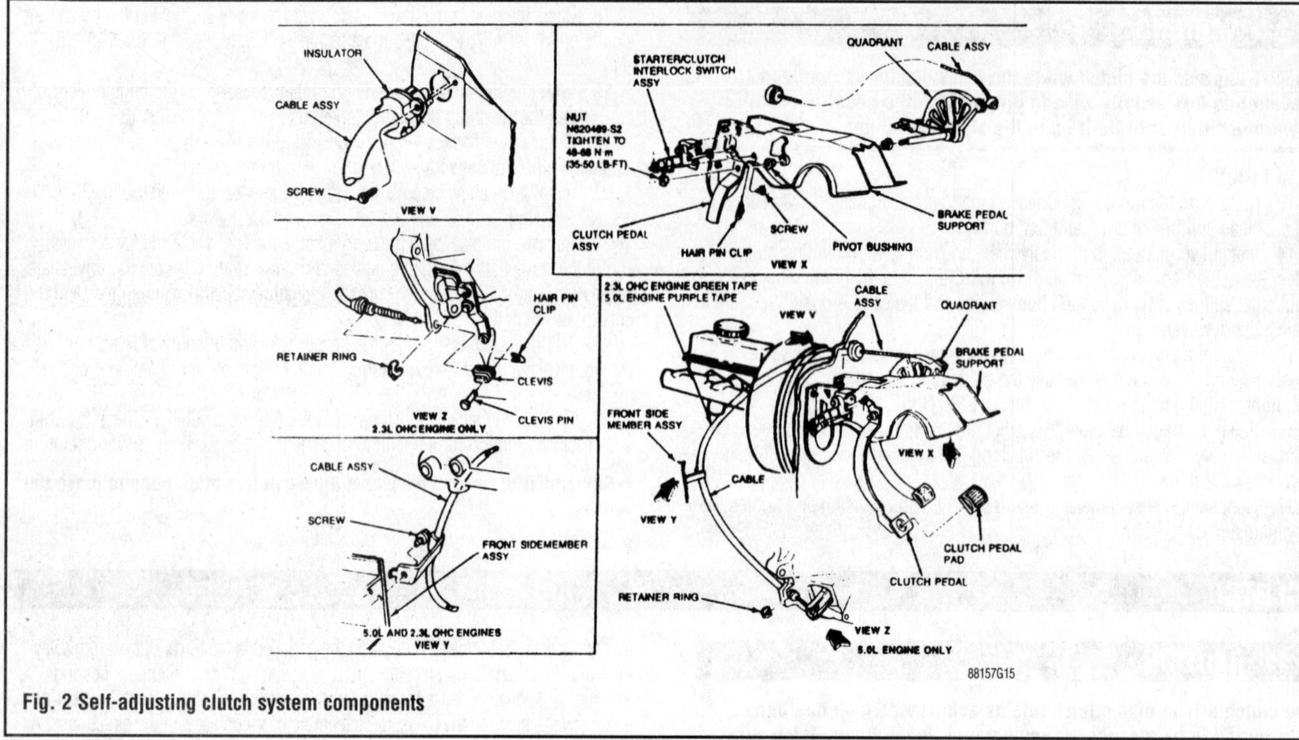

Fig. 2 Self-adjusting clutch system components

3. Remove the lower dash panel section to the left of the steering column.
4. Remove the shrouds from the steering column.
5. Disconnect the brake lamp switch and the master cylinder pushrod from the brake pedal.
6. Rotate the clutch quadrant forward and unhook the clutch cable from the quadrant. Allow the quadrant to slowly swing rearward.
7. Remove the bolt holding the brake pedal support bracket lateral brace to the left side of the vehicle.
8. Unplug all electrical connectors from the steering column.
9. Remove the four nuts that hold the steering column to the brake pedal support bracket and lower the steering column to the floor.
10. Remove the four booster nuts that hold the brake pedal support bracket to the dash panel.
11. Remove the bolt holding the brake pedal support bracket to the underside of the instrument panel, then remove the brake pedal support bracket assembly from the vehicle.
12. Remove the clutch pedal shaft nut and the clutch pedal as outlined.
13. Slide the self-adjusting mechanism out of the brake pedal support bracket.

To install:

14. Remove the self-adjusting mechanism shaft bushings from either side of the brake pedal support bracket and replace, if worn.
15. Lubricate the self-adjusting mechanism shaft with motor oil and install the mechanism into the brake pedal support bracket.
16. Position the quadrant towards the top of the vehicle. Align the flats on the shaft with the flats in the clutch pedal assembly; install the retaining nuts. Tighten them to 32–50 ft. lbs. (43–68 Nm).
17. Position the brake pedal support bracket assembly beneath the instrument panel, aligning the holes with the studs in the dash panel. Loosely install the four nuts. Install the bolt through the support bracket into the instrument panel and tighten to 13–25 ft. lbs. (18–34 Nm).
18. Tighten the four booster nuts that hold the brake pedal support bracket to the dash panel to 13–25 ft. lbs. (18–34 Nm).
19. Connect the brake lamp switch and the master cylinder pushrod to the brake pedal.
20. Attach the clutch cable to the quadrant.
21. Position the steering column onto the four studs in the support bracket and start the four nuts, but do not tighten them.
22. Engage the steering column electrical connectors.
23. Install the steering column shrouds.
24. Install the brake pedal support lateral brace.
25. Now tighten the steering column attaching nuts to 20–37 ft. lbs. (27–50 Nm).
26. Install the lower dash panel section.
27. Install the steering wheel.
28. Connect the negative battery cable.
29. Check the steering column for proper operation.
30. Depress and raise the clutch pedal several times to adjust the cable.

Quadrant Pawl, Self-Adjusting

See Figure 3

1. Remove the self-adjusting mechanism.
2. Remove the two hairpin clips that hold the pawl and quadrant on the shaft assembly.
3. Remove the quadrant and quadrant spring.
4. Remove the pawl spring.
5. Remove the pawl.

To install:

6. Lubricate the pawl and quadrant pivot shafts with M1C75B or equivalent grease.

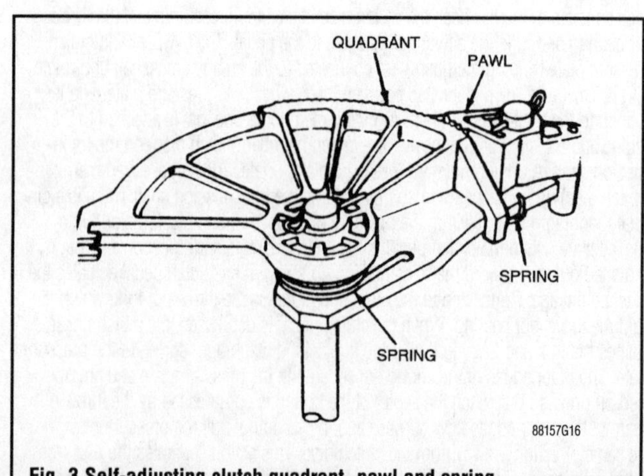

Fig. 3 Self-adjusting clutch quadrant, pawl and spring

7. Install the pawl. Position the teeth of the pawl toward the long shaft and the spring hole at the end of the arm. Do not position the spring hole beneath the arm.
8. Insert the straight portion of the spring into the hole, with the coil up.
9. Keeping the straight portion in the hole, rotate the spring 180 degrees to the left and slide the coiled portion of the spring over the boss.
10. Hook the bent portion of the spring under the arm.
11. Install the retainer clip on the opposite side of the spring.
12. Place the quadrant spring on the shaft, with the bent portion of the spring in the hole in the arm.
13. Place the lubricated quadrant on the shaft, aligning the projection at the bottom of the quadrant to a position beneath the arm of the shaft assembly. Push the pawl up so the bottom tooth of the pawl meshes with the bottom tooth of the quadrant.
14. Install the quadrant retaining pin.
15. Grasp the straight end of the quadrant spring with pliers and position it behind the ear of the quadrant.
16. Install the self-adjusting mechanism.
17. Install the clutch pedal assembly.

Starter/Clutch Interlock Switch

See Figure 4

The starter/clutch switch is designed to prevent starting the engine unless the clutch pedal is fully depressed. The switch is connected between the ignition witch and the starter motor relay coil; it maintains an open circuit with the clutch pedal up (engaged).

The switch is designed to self-adjust automatically the first time the clutch pedal is pressed to the floor. The self-adjuster consists of a two-piece clip, snapped together over a serrated rod. When the plunger or rod is extended, the clip bottoms out on the switch body and allows the rod to ratchet over the serrations to a position determined by the clutch pedal travel limit. In this way, the switch is set to close the starter circuit when the clutch is pressed all the way to the floor (disengaged).

CHECKING CONTINUITY AND ADJUSTMENT

1. Disengage the inline wiring connector at the jumper harness.
2. Using a self-powered test lamp or a continuity tester, check that the switch is open with the clutch pedal up, and closed at approximately 1 in. (25mm) from the pedal's full-downward position.
3. If the switch does not operate, check to see if the self-adjusting clip is out of position on the rod. It should be near the end of the rod.
4. If the clip is out of place, remove and reposition the clip to about 1 in. (25mm) from the end of the rod.
5. Reset the switch by pressing the clutch pedal to the floor.
6. Recheck the switch for continuity in both positions. If the switch is damaged, replace it.

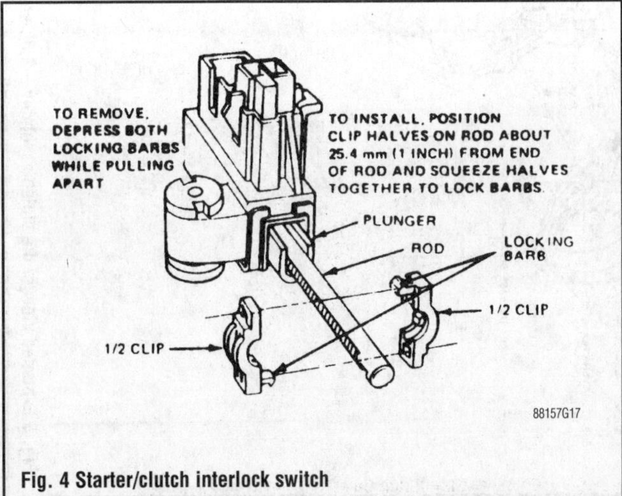

Fig. 4 Starter/clutch interlock switch

REMOVAL & INSTALLATION

1. Disengage the wiring connector.
2. Remove the retaining pin from the clutch pedal.
3. Remove the switch bracket attaching screw.
4. Lift the switch and bracket assembly upward to disengage the tab from the pedal support.
5. Move the switch outward to disengage the actuating rod eyelet from the clutch pedal pin and remove the switch from the vehicle.

To install:

WARNING

Always install the switch with the self-adjusting clip about 1 inch (25mm) from the end of the rod. The clutch pedal must be fully up (clutch engaged). Otherwise, the switch may be misadjusted.

6. Place the eyelet end of the rod onto the pivot pin.
7. Swing the switch assembly around to line up the hole in the mounting boss with the hole in the bracket.
8. Install the attaching screw.
9. Install the retaining pin in the pivot pin.
10. Connect the wiring harness.

Clutch Pedal Assembly

REMOVAL & INSTALLATION

1. Remove the starter/clutch interlock switch.
2. Remove the clutch pedal attaching nut.
3. Pull the clutch pedal off the clutch pedal shaft.

To install:

4. Align the square hole of the clutch pedal with the clutch pedal shaft and push the clutch pedal on.
5. Install the pedal attaching nut and tighten it to 32–50 ft. lbs. (43–68 Nm).
6. Install the starter/clutch interlock switch.

Clutch Cable Assembly

REMOVAL & INSTALLATION

1. Lift the clutch pedal to its upward-most position to disengage the pawl and quadrant. Push the quadrant forward, unhook the cable from the quadrant and allow it to slowly swing rearward.
2. Open the hood and remove the screw that holds the cable assembly isolator to the dash panel.
3. Pull the cable through the dash panel and into the engine compartment. On 5.0L engines, remove the cable bracket screw from the fender apron.
4. Raise and support the vehicle safely using jackstands.
5. Remove the dust cover from the bell housing.
6. Remove the clip retainer holding the cable assembly to the bell housing.
7. Slide the ball on the end of the cable assembly through the hole in the clutch release lever and remove the cable.
8. Remove the dash panel isolator from the cable.

To install:

9. Install the dash panel isolator on the cable assembly.
10. Insert the cable through the hole in the bell housing and through the hole in the clutch release lever. Slide the ball on the end of the cable assembly away from the hole in the clutch release lever.
11. Install the clip retainer that holds the cable assembly to the bell housing.
12. Install the dust shield on the bell housing.
13. Push the cable assembly into the engine compartment and lower the vehicle. On 5.0L engines, install the cable bracket screw in the fender apron.
14. Push the cable assembly into the hole in the dash panel and secure the isolator with a screw.

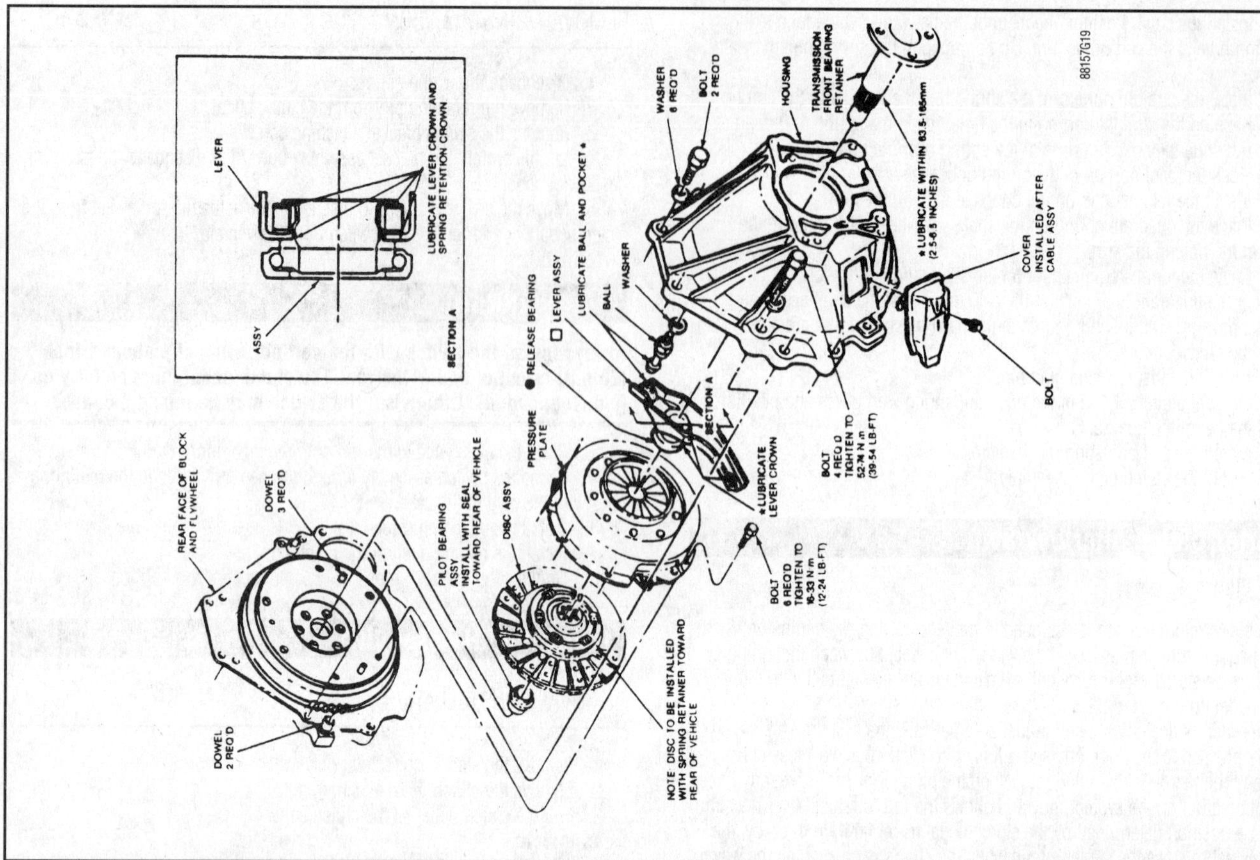

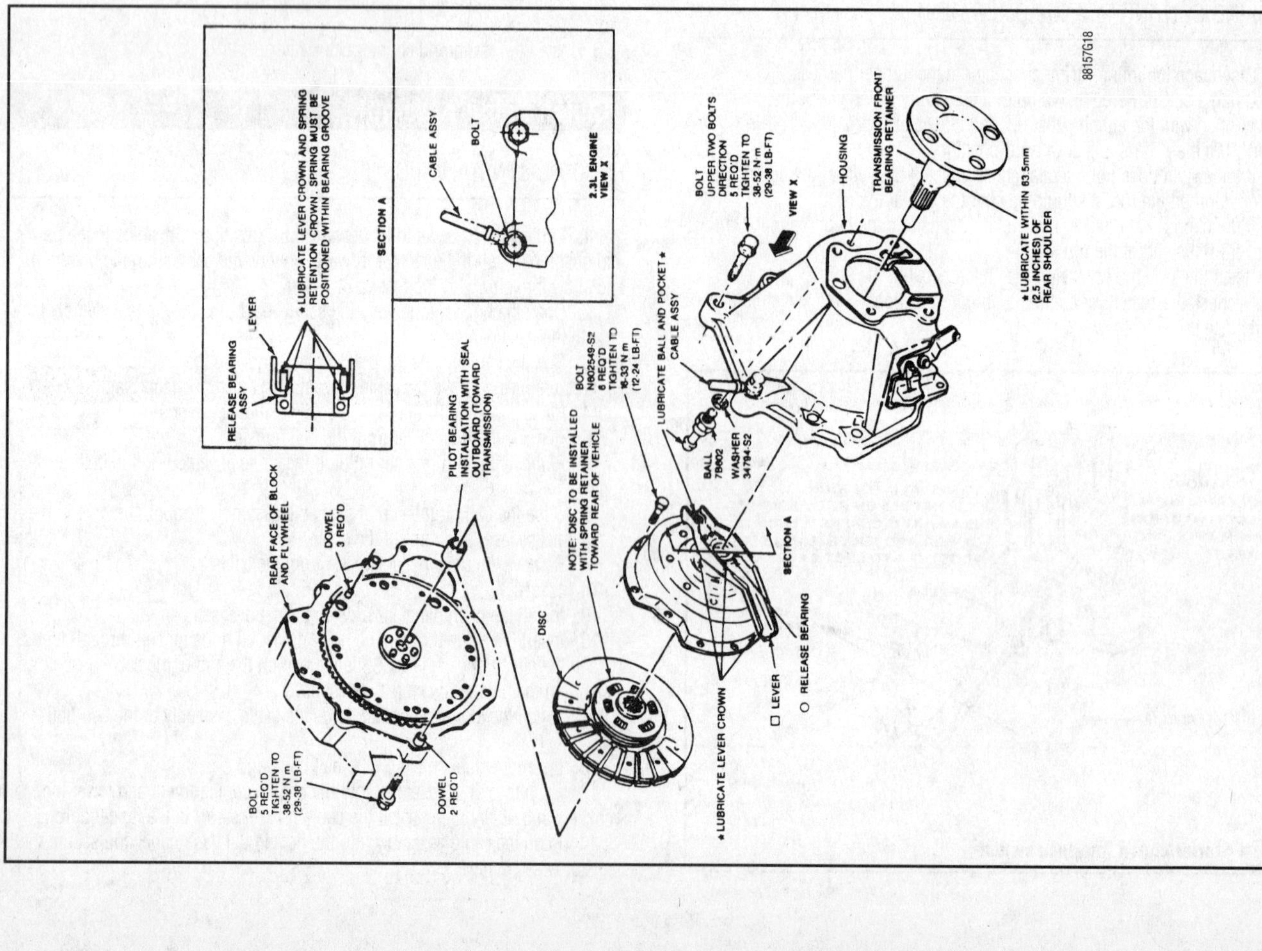

Fig. 5 Exploded view of the clutch assembly—2.3L engine

Fig. 6 Exploded view of the clutch assembly—5.0L engine

15. Install the cable assembly by lifting the clutch pedal to disengage the pawl and quadrant. Then, pushing the quadrant forward, hook the end of the cable over the rear of the quadrant.

16. Depress the clutch cable several times to adjust the cable.

Driven Disc and Pressure Plate

REMOVAL & INSTALLATION

See Figures 5, 6, 7, 8 and 9

1. Disconnect the negative battery cable for safety.
2. Lift the clutch pedal to its upward-most position to disengage the pawl and quadrant. Push the quadrant forward, unhook the cable from the quadrant and allow it to slowly swing rearward.
3. Raise and support the vehicle safely using jackstands. Remove the dust shield.
4. Disconnect the cable from the release lever. Remove the retaining clip and remove the clutch cable from the flywheel housing.
5. Remove the starter and the bolts holding the engine rear plate to the lower part of the flywheel housing.
6. Remove the transmission, then remove the flywheel housing.
7. Remove the clutch release lever from the housing by pulling it through the window in the housing until the retainer spring is disengaged from the pivot. Remove the release bearing from the release lever.
8. Loosen the pressure plate cover attaching bolts evenly, to release spring tension gradually and avoid distorting the cover. If the same pressure plate and cover are to be re-installed, mark the cover and flywheel so that the pressure plate can be installed in its original position. Remove the pressure plate and clutch disc from the engine.
9. Inspect the flywheel for scoring, cracks or other damage. Machine or replace as necessary. Inspect the pilot bearing for damage and free movement. Replace as necessary.

To install:

10. If removed, install the flywheel. Make sure the mating surfaces of the flywheel and the crankshaft flange are clean prior to installation. Tighten the flywheel bolts to 56–64 ft. lbs. (73–87 Nm) on 2.3L engines or to 75–85 ft. lbs. (102–115 Nm) on 5.0L engines.
11. Position the clutch disc and pressure plate assembly on the flywheel. The three dowel pins on the flywheel must be properly aligned with the pressure plate. Bent, damaged or missing dowels must be replaced. Start the pressure plate bolts, but do not tighten them.
12. Align the clutch disc using a disc alignment tool inserted into the pilot bearing. Alternately tighten the bolts a few turns at a time, until they are all tight. Then, tighten all the bolts to 12–24 ft. lbs. (17–32 Nm) and remove the alignment tool.
13. Apply a light coat of multi-purpose grease to the release lever pivot pocket, the release lever fork and the flywheel housing pivot ball. Fill the grease groove of the release bearing hub with the same grease. Clean all excess grease from the inside bore of the bearing hub.
14. Install the release bearing on the release lever and install the lever in the flywheel housing.
15. Install the flywheel housing. Tighten the bolts to 28–38 ft. lbs. (38–52 Nm) on the 2.3L engine or to 38–55 ft. lbs. (52–74 Nm) on the 5.0L engine.
16. Install the remaining components.
17. Remove the jackstands and carefully lower the vehicle.
18. Depress and lift the clutch several times to allow the self-adjusting mechanism to properly set the free-play.
19. Connect the negative battery cable, then check for proper clutch operation.

TCCS7116

Fig. 7 Loosen the pressure plate bolts evenly (using a crosswise pattern) to gradually release the spring tension . . .

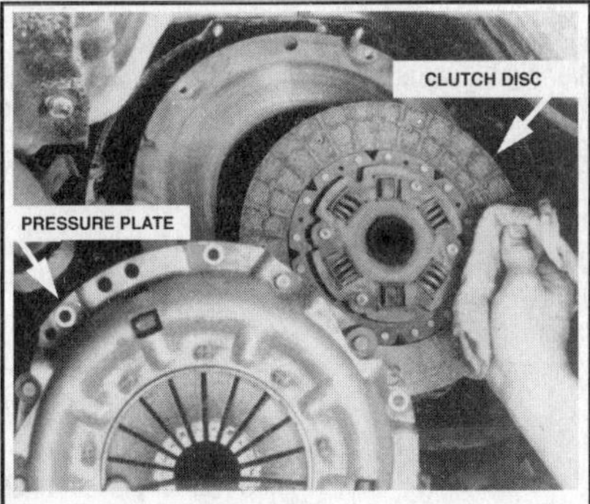

TCCS7118

Fig. 8 . . . then remove the pressure plate and clutch disc from the engine

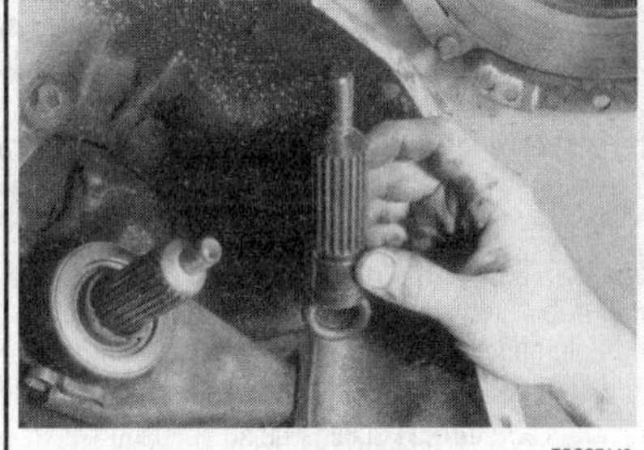

TCCS7142

Fig. 9 A clutch alignment arbor of the same size, shape and (most importantly) spline pattern as the transmission input shaft is needed for installation

AUTOMATIC TRANSMISSION

Understanding the Automatic Transmission

The automatic transmission allows engine torque and power to be transmitted to the rear wheels within a narrow range of engine operating speeds. It will allow the engine to turn fast enough to produce plenty of power and torque at very low speeds, while keeping it at a sensible rpm at high vehicle speeds (and it does this job without driver assistance). The transmission uses a light fluid as the medium for the transmission of power. This fluid also works in the operation of various hydraulic control circuits and as a lubricant. Because the transmission fluid performs all of these functions, trouble within the unit can easily travel from one part to another.

TORQUE CONVERTER

See Figure 10

The torque converter replaces the conventional clutch. It has three functions:

1. It allows the engine to idle with the vehicle at a standstill, even with the transmission in gear.

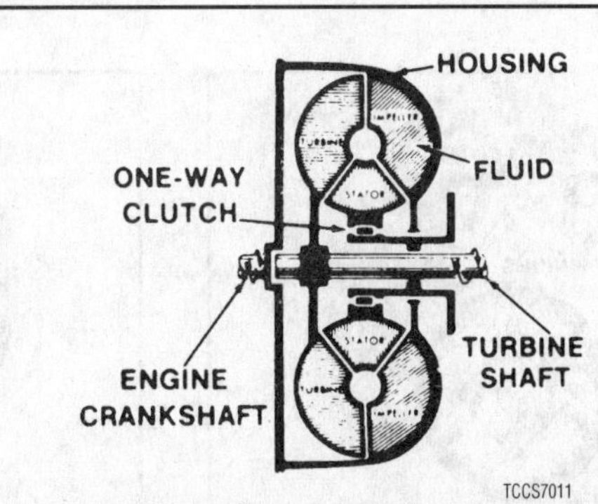

TCCS7011

Fig. 10 The torque converter housing is rotated by the engine's crankshaft, and turns the impeller—The impeller then spins the turbine, which gives motion to the turbine shaft, driving the gears

2. It allows the transmission to shift from range-to-range smoothly, without requiring that the driver close the throttle during the shift.

3. It multiplies engine torque to an increasing extent as vehicle speed drops and throttle opening is increased. This has the effect of making the transmission more responsive and reduces the amount of shifting required.

The torque converter is a metal case which is shaped like a sphere that has been flattened on opposite sides. It is bolted to the rear end of the engine's crankshaft. Generally, the entire metal case rotates at engine speed and serves as the engine's flywheel.

The case contains three sets of blades. One set is attached directly to the case. This set forms the torus or pump. Another set is directly connected to the output shaft, and forms the turbine. The third set is mounted on a hub which, in turn, is mounted on a stationary shaft through a one-way clutch. This third set is known as the stator.

A pump, which is driven by the converter hub at engine speed, keeps the torque converter full of transmission fluid at all times. Fluid flows continuously through the unit to provide cooling.

Under low speed acceleration, the torque converter functions as follows:

The torus is turning faster than the turbine. It picks up fluid at the center of the converter and, through centrifugal force, slings it outward. Since the outer edge of the converter moves faster than the portions at the center, the fluid picks up speed.

The fluid then enters the outer edge of the turbine blades. It then travels back toward the center of the converter case along the turbine blades. In impinging upon the turbine blades, the fluid loses the energy picked up in the torus.

If the fluid was now returned directly into the torus, both halves of the converter would have to turn at approximately the same speed at all times, and torque input and output would both be the same.

In flowing through the torus and turbine, the fluid picks up two types of flow, or flow in two separate directions. It flows through the turbine blades, and it spins with the engine. The stator, whose blades are stationary when the vehicle is being accelerated at low speeds, converts one type of flow into another. Instead of allowing the fluid to flow straight back into the torus, the stator's curved blades turn the fluid almost 90° toward the direction of rotation of the engine. Thus the fluid does not flow as fast toward the torus, but is already spinning when the torus picks it up. This has the effect of allowing the torus to turn much faster than the turbine. This difference in speed may be compared to the difference in speed between the smaller and larger gears in any gear train. The result is that engine power output is higher, and engine torque is multiplied.

As the speed of the turbine increases, the fluid spins faster and faster in the direction of engine rotation. As a result, the ability of the stator to redirect the fluid flow is reduced. Under cruising conditions, the stator is eventually forced to rotate on its one-way clutch in the direction of engine rotation. Under these conditions, the torque converter begins to behave almost like a solid shaft, with the torus and turbine speeds being almost equal.

PLANETARY GEARBOX

See Figures 11, 12 and 13

The ability of the torque converter to multiply engine torque is limited. Also, the unit tends to be more efficient when the turbine is rotating at relatively high speeds. Therefore, a planetary gearbox is used to carry the power output of the turbine to the driveshaft.

Planetary gears function very similarly to conventional transmission gears. However, their construction is different in that three elements make up one gear system, and, in that all three elements are different from one another. The three elements are: an outer gear that is shaped like a hoop, with teeth cut into the inner surface; a sun gear, mounted on a shaft and located at the very center of the outer gear; and a set of three planet gears, held by pins in a ring-like planet carrier, meshing with both the sun gear and the outer gear. Either the outer gear or the sun gear may be held stationary, providing more than one possible torque multiplication factor for each set of gears. Also, if all three gears are forced to rotate at the same speed, the gearset forms, in effect, a solid shaft.

Most automatics use the planetary gears to provide various reductions ratios. Bands and clutches are used to hold various portions of the gearsets to the transmission case or to the shaft on which they are mounted. Shifting is accomplished, then, by changing the portion of each planetary gearset which is held to the transmission case or to the shaft.

SERVOS AND ACCUMULATORS

See Figure 14

The servos are hydraulic pistons and cylinders. They resemble the hydraulic actuators used on many other machines, such as bulldozers. Hydraulic fluid enters the cylinder, under pressure, and forces the piston to move to engage the band or clutches.

The accumulators are used to cushion the engagement of the servos. The transmission fluid must pass through the accumulator on the way to the servo. The accumulator housing contains a thin piston which is sprung away from the discharge passage of the accumulator. When fluid passes through the accumulator on the way to the servo, it must move the piston against spring pressure, and this action smooths out the action of the servo.

HYDRAULIC CONTROL SYSTEM

The hydraulic pressure used to operate the servos comes from the main transmission oil pump. This fluid is channeled to the various servos through the shift valves. There is generally a manual shift valve which is operated by the transmission selector lever and an automatic shift valve for each automatic upshift the transmission provides.

➡Many new transmissions are electronically controlled. On these models, electrical solenoids are used to better control the hydraulic fluid. Usually, the solenoids are regulated by an electronic control module.

There are two pressures which affect the operation of these valves. One is the governor pressure which is effected by vehicle speed. The other is the modulator pressure which is effected by intake manifold vacuum or throttle position. Governor pressure rises with an increase in vehicle speed, and modulator pressure rises as the throttle is opened wider. By responding to these two pressures, the shift valves cause the upshift points to be delayed with increased throttle opening to make the best use of the engine's power output.

Most transmissions also make use of an auxiliary circuit for downshifting. This circuit may be actuated by the throttle linkage the vacuum line which actuates the modulator, by a cable or by a solenoid. It applies pressure to a special downshift surface on the shift valve or valves.

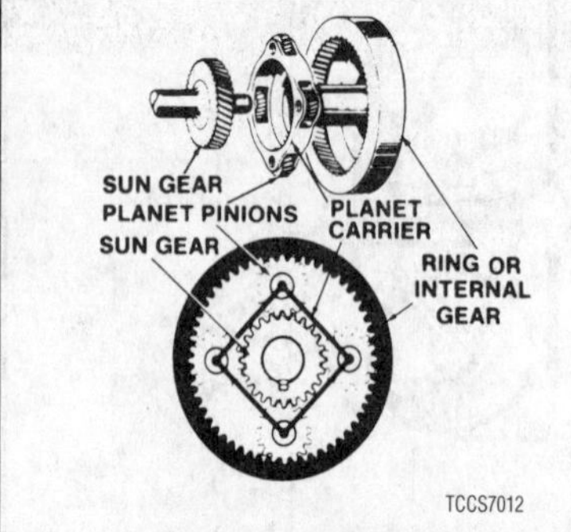

Fig. 11 Planetary gears work in a similar fashion to manual transmission gears, but are composed of three parts

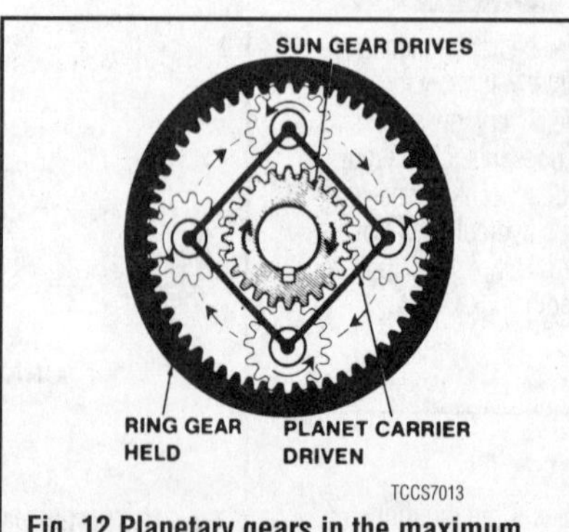

Fig. 12 Planetary gears in the maximum reduction (low) range. The ring gear is held and a lower gear ratio is obtained

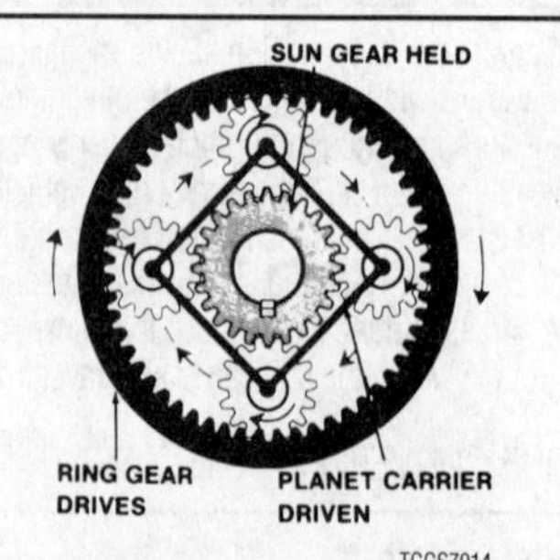

Fig. 13 Planetary gears in the minimum reduction (drive) range. The ring gear is allowed to revolve, providing a higher gear ratio

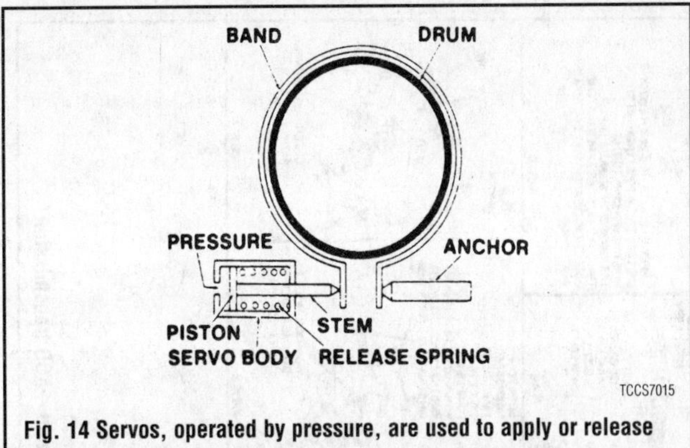

Fig. 14 Servos, operated by pressure, are used to apply or release the bands, to either hold the ring gear or allow it to rotate

The transmission modulator also governs the line pressure, used to actuate the servos. In this way, the clutches and bands will be actuated with a force matching the torque output of the engine.

Transmission Identification

➧ **See Figures 15 and 16**

All Mustangs are equipped with a Vehicle Certification Label attached to the left side door lock post. The transmission code is located in the space marked TR on the label. For more information regarding serial number identification, please refer to Section 1 of this manual or see your local parts dealer.

There are two automatic transmissions used in the Mustangs covered in this manual, the AOD and the A4LD. Additional information is located on the tag attached to the transmission case such as service ID, level, and build date.

Adjustments

SHIFT LINKAGE

Solid or Cable Link Types

➧ **See Figures 17 and 18**

1. Place the transmission shift lever in OVERDRIVE. Be certain the selector is tight against the rearward stop.
2. Raise the vehicle and loosen the manual lever shift rod retaining nut or the manual lever shift calbe retaining nut, whichever is applicable. Move the transmission lever to the OVERDRIVE position. OVERDRIVE is the third detent from the full counterclockwise position.

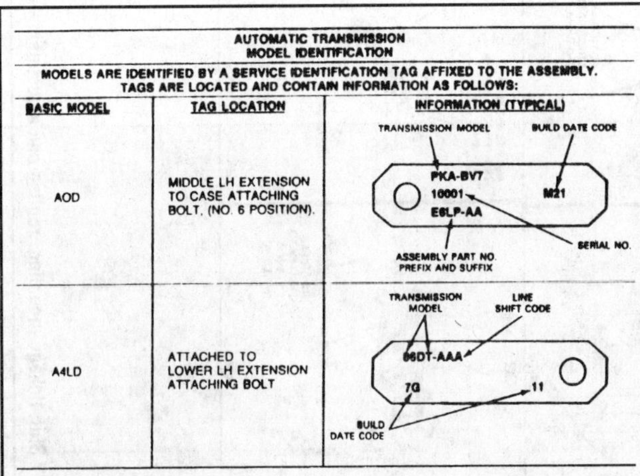

AUTOMATIC TRANSMISSION MODEL IDENTIFICATION

MODELS ARE IDENTIFIED BY A SERVICE IDENTIFICATION TAG AFFIXED TO THE ASSEMBLY. TAGS ARE LOCATED AND CONTAIN INFORMATION AS FOLLOWS:

BASIC MODEL	TAG LOCATION	INFORMATION (TYPICAL)
AOD	MIDDLE LH EXTENSION TO CASE ATTACHING BOLT. (NO. 6 POSITION).	TRANSMISSION MODEL: PKA-BV7; SERIAL NO.: 10001; ASSEMBLY PART NO. PREFIX AND SUFFIX: E6LP-AA; BUILD DATE CODE: M21
A4LD	ATTACHED TO LOWER LH EXTENSION ATTACHING BOLT	TRANSMISSION MODEL / LINE SHIFT CODE: 86DT-AAA; BUILD DATE CODE: 7G, 11

88157G20

Fig. 15 Automatic transmissions may be identified using the ID tags attached to the housing assembly

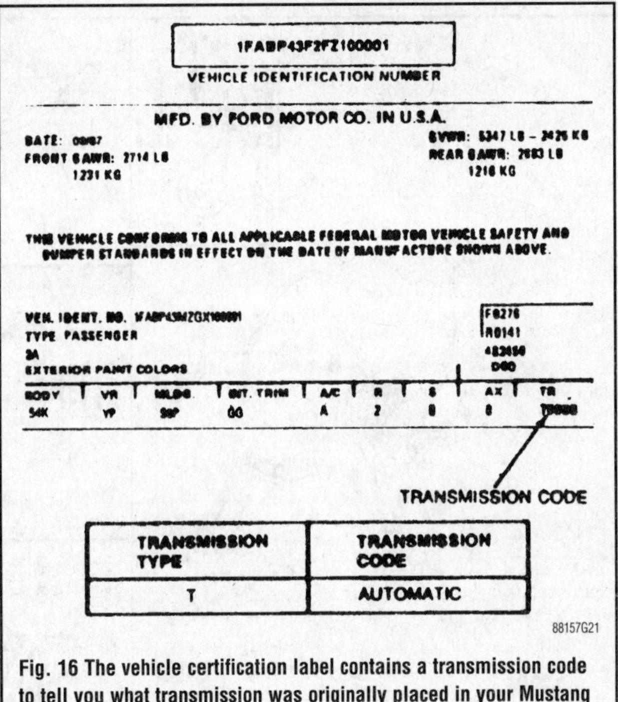

Fig. 16 The vehicle certification label contains a transmission code to tell you what transmission was originally placed in your Mustang

3. With the shift lever and the transmission manual lever in position, tighten the retaining nut to 10–19 ft. lbs. (13–27 Nm).
4. Check transmission operation for all selector lever detent positions.

THROTTLE VALVE (TV) CABLE

AOD Transmission

➧ **See Figure 19**

ADJUSTMENT WITH ENGINE OFF

1. Set the parking brake and put the selector lever in **N**.
2. Remove the protective cover from the cable.
3. Make sure that the throttle lever is at the idle stop. If it isn't, check for binding or interference. NEVER attempt to adjust the idle stop.
4. Make sure the cable is free of sharp bends or is not rubbing on anything throughout its entire length.
5. Lubricate the TV lever ball stud with chassis lube.
6. Unlock the locking tab at the throttle body by prying with a small, flat tool.
7. Install a spring on the TV control lever, to hold it in the rearmost-travel position. The spring must exert at least 10 lbs. (4.5 Kg) of force on the lever.
8. Rotate the transmission outer TV lever 10–30 degrees and allow it to return.
9. Push down on the locking tab until flush.
10. Remove the retaining spring from the lever.

Neutral Start Switch

REMOVAL & INSTALLATION

➧ **See Figure 20**

➡The neutral safety switch on the A4LD and AOD transmissions is not adjustable.

1. Disconnect the negative battery cable.
2. Raise and support the front of the car safely using jackstands.
3. Disconnect the switch harness by pushing the harness straight up, off the switch, with a long screwdriver underneath the rubber plug section.
4. Using special tool socket T74P–77247–A, or equivalent, on a ratchet extension at least 9½ inches long, unscrew the switch. To use the tool, position it over the switch and reach around the rear of the transmission, over the extension housing.

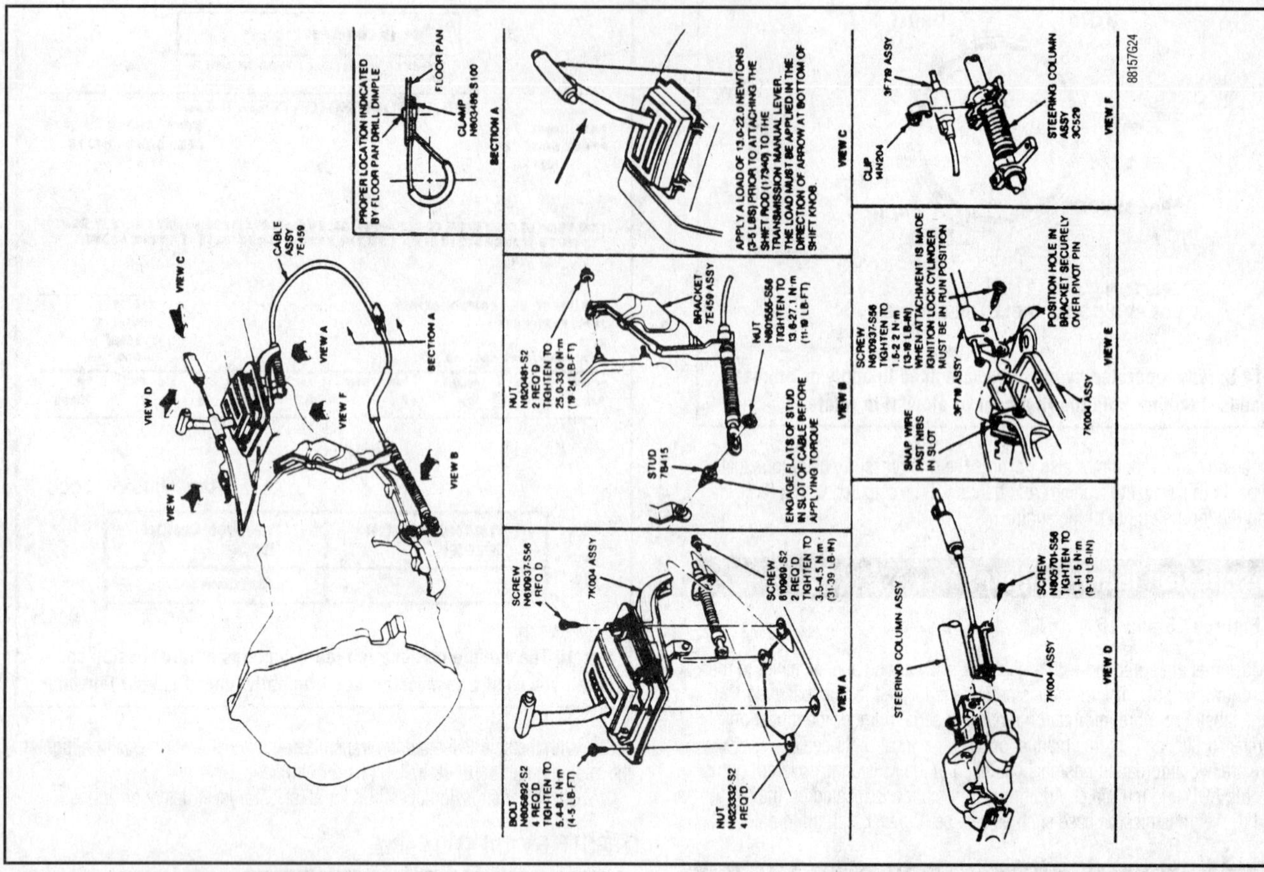

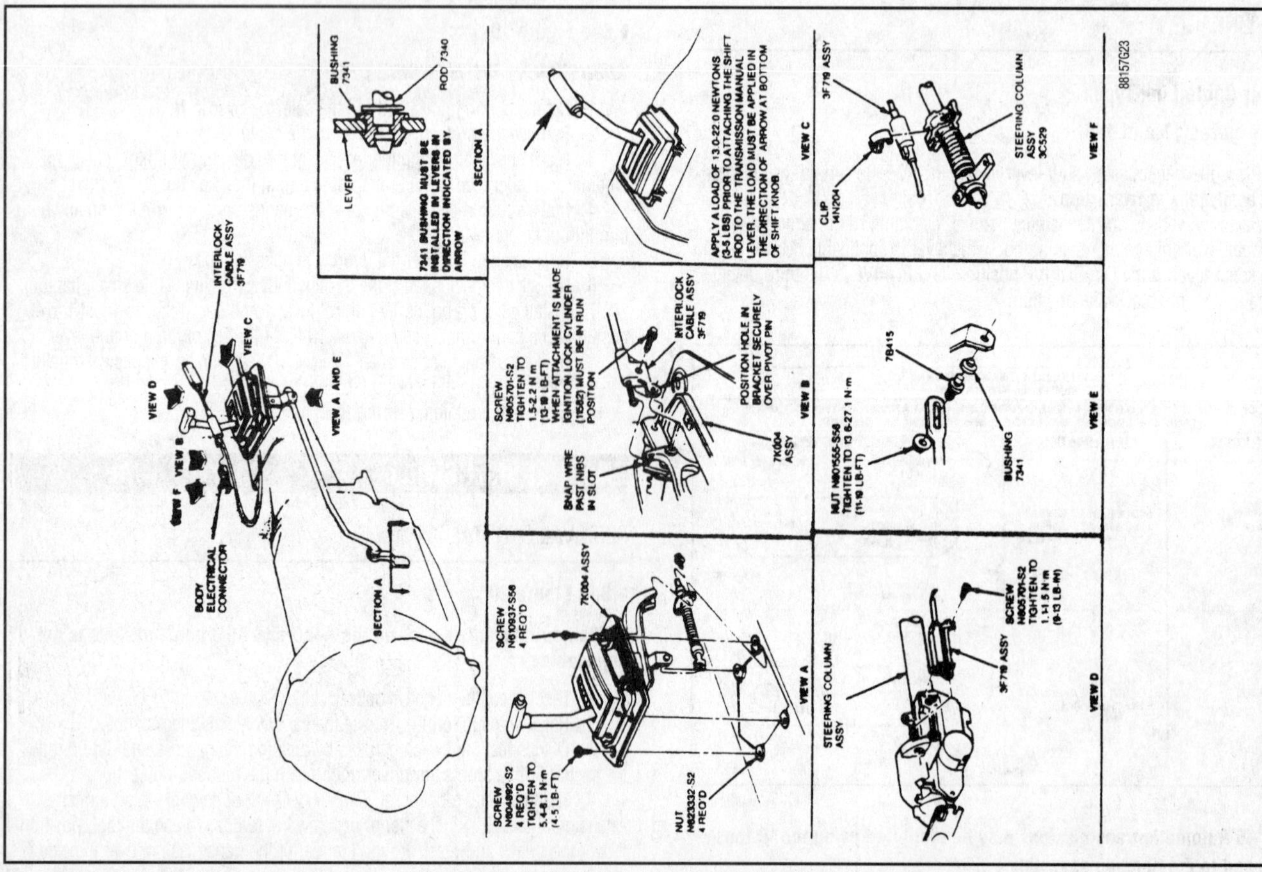

Fig. 17 Shift linkage mounting, routing and adjustment—A4LD transmission

Fig. 18 Shift linkage mounting, routing and adjustment—AOD transmission

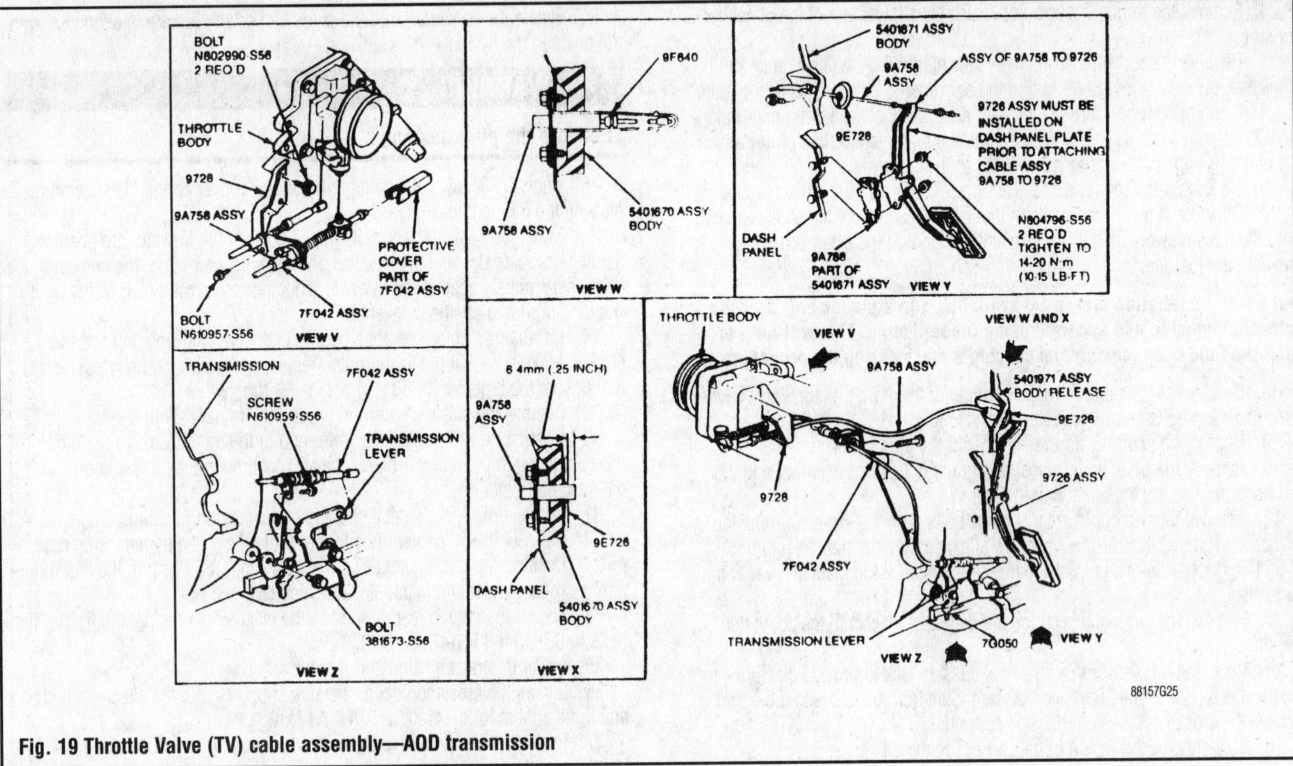

Fig. 19 Throttle Valve (TV) cable assembly—AOD transmission

To install:

➡Always use a new O-ring when installing the switch to assure of a proper seal.

5. Make sure the O-ring is in position on the switch, then carefully thread the switch into position by hand.
6. Tighten the switch to 11 ft. lbs. (15 Nm).
7. Engage the switch wiring.
8. Remove the jackstands and carefully lower the vehicle.
9. Connect the negative battery cable.
10. Verify proper switch operation.

Vacuum Modulator

REMOVAL & INSTALLATION

➧ See Figure 21

1. Disconnect the hose from the vacuum diaphragm.
2. Remove the vacuum diaphragm retaining bolt and clamp. DO NOT pry or bend the clamp. Pull the vacuum diaphragm from the transmission case.
3. Remove the vacuum diaphragm control rod from the transmission case.

To install:

4. Install the vacuum diaphragm control rod in the transmission case.
5. Push the vacuum diaphragm into the case. Secure the retaining clamp and bolt. Tighten the bolt to 80–106 inch lbs. (9–12 Nm).
6. Install the hose to the vacuum diaphragm.

Transmission

REMOVAL & INSTALLATION

➧ See Figure 22

1. Disconnect the negative battery cable for safety.
2. Raise and support the vehicle safely using jackstands.
3. Place a drain pan under the transmission fluid pan. Starting at the rear of the pan and working toward the front, loosen the attaching bolts and allow the fluid to drain. Finally, remove all of the pan attaching bolts except two at the front, to allow the fluid to further drain. With the fluid drained, install two bolts on the rear side of the pan to temporarily hold it in place.

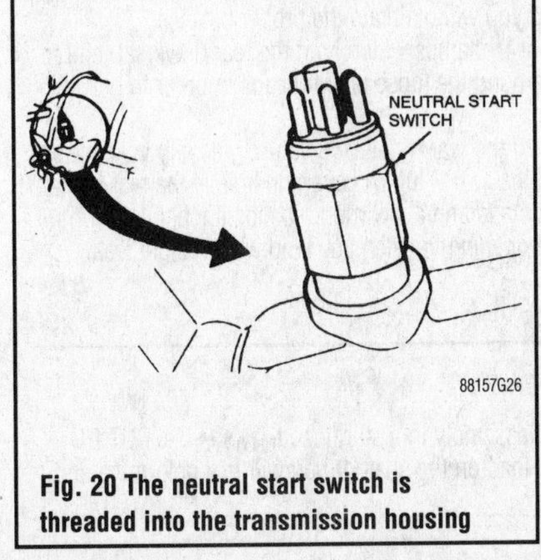

Fig. 20 The neutral start switch is threaded into the transmission housing

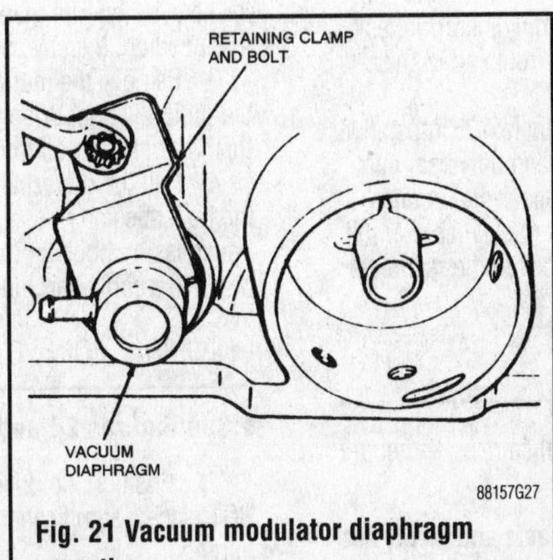

Fig. 21 Vacuum modulator diaphragm mounting

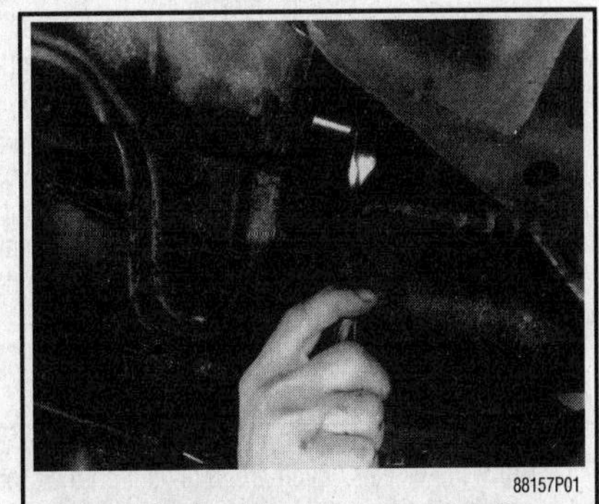

Fig. 22 The lower converter housing-to-engine bolts are easy to access using a socket and ratchet driver

4. Remove the torque converter cover from the lower end of the converter housing.

5. Remove the converter-to-flywheel attaching nuts. Place a wrench on the crankshaft pulley attaching bolt to turn the converter to gain access to the nuts.

6. If equipped with a torque converter drain plug, place a drain pan under the converter to catch the fluid. With the wrench on the crankshaft pulley attaching bolts, turn the converter to gain access to the converter drain plug and remove the plug. After the fluid has been drained, reinstall the plug.

7. Disconnect the driveshaft from the rear axle and slide the shaft rearward from the transmission. Install a seal installation tool in the extension housing to prevent fluid leakage.

➡If a seal installation tool is not available, slip a plastic bag over the extension housing and secure it using rubber bands. This will help to keep the fluid from leaking and causing a mess during the procedure.

8. Disconnect the cable from the terminal or the starter motor. Remove the three attaching bolts and remove the starter motor.

9. Unplug the neutral start switch wires at the plug connector.

10. Remove the bolts holding the rear mount to the crossmember and the two bolts holding the crossmember to the frame.

11. Remove the two engine rear support bolts from the extension housing.

12. Disconnect the Throttle Valve (TV) linkage from the transmission TV lever. Disconnect the manual linkage from the transmission manual lever at the transmission.

13. Remove the two bolts securing the bellcrank bracket to the converter housing.

14. Raise the transmission with a transmission jack to provide clearance to remove the crossmember. Remove the rear mount from the crossmember and remove the crossmember from the side supports.

15. Lower the transmission to gain access to the oil cooler lines.

16. Disconnect each oil line from the fittings on the transmission.

17. Disconnect the speedometer cable from the extension housing.

18. Remove the bolt that secures the transmission fluid filler tube to the cylinder block. Lift the filler tube and the dipstick from the transmission.

19. Secure the transmission to the jack with a chain.

20. Remove the bolts between the converter housing and the cylinder block.

21. Carefully move the transmission and converter assembly away from the engine and, at the same time, lower the jack to clear the underside of the vehicle.

22. Remove the converter and mount the transmission in a holding fixture.

To install:

23. Position the converter on the transmission, making sure the converter drive flats are fully engaged in the pump gear by rotating the converter.

24. With the converter properly installed, place the transmission on the jack. Secure the transmission to the jack with a safety chain.

25. Rotate the converter until the studs and drain plug are in alignment with the holes in the flywheel.

⁂ WARNING

Lubricate the pilot bushing.

26. Align the yellow balancing marks on the converter and flexplate on models with the 5.0L engine.

27. Move the converter and transmission assembly forward into position, using care not to damage the flywheel and the converter pilot. The converter must rest squarely against the flywheel. This indicates that the converter pilot is not binding in the engine crankshaft.

28. Install and tighten the bolts between the converter housing and the engine. Make sure that the vacuum line retaining clips are properly positioned and tighten the bolts to 40–50 ft. lbs. (54–68 Nm).

29. Remove the safety chain from around the transmission.

30. Install a new O-ring on the lower end of the transmission filler tube. Insert the tube in the transmission case and secure the tube to the engine with the attaching bolts.

31. Connect the speedometer cable to the extension housing.

32. Connect the oil cooler lines to the right side of the transmission case.

33. Position the crossmember on the side supports. Position the rear mount on the crossmember and install the attaching bolt and nut.

34. Secure the engine rear support to the extension housing and tighten the bolts to 35–40 ft. lbs. (47–54 Nm).

35. Lower the transmission and remove the jack.

36. Secure the crossmember to the side supports with the attaching bolts and tighten them to 35–40 ft. lbs. (47–54 Nm).

37. Position the bellcrank to the converter housing and install the two attaching bolts.

38. Connect the TV linkage to the transmission TV lever. Connect the manual linkage to the manual lever at the transmission.

39. Secure the converter-to-flywheel nuts and tighten them to 20–30 ft. lbs. (27–41 Nm).

40. Install and secure the converter housing access cover.

41. Secure the starter motor in place with the bolts. Connect the cable to the terminal on the starter. Engage the neutral start switch wires at the plug connector.

42. Connect the driveshaft to the rear axle.

43. Adjust the shift linkage as required.

44. Adjust the throttle linkage.

45. Lower the vehicle.

46. Fill the transmission to the correct level. Start the engine and shift the transmission to all ranges, then recheck the fluid level.

DRIVELINE

Driveshaft and U-joints

➧ See Figure 23

The driveshaft is the means by which the power from the engine and transmission (which are in the front of the car) can be transferred to the differential, rear axles and finally to the rear wheels. The driveshaft assembly incorporates two universal joints, one at each end, and a slip yoke (at the front end of the assembly), which fits into the back of the transmission.

All driveshafts are balanced when installed in a car. It is, therefore, imperative that before applying undercoat to the chassis, the driveshaft and universal joint assembly be completely covered or removed to prevent the accidental application of undercoating to the surfaces and the subsequent loss of balance. For this same reason, it is also a good idea to matchmark the driveshaft to the rear axle drive pinion flange before removal.

DRIVESHAFT REMOVAL

1. Block the wheels which are to remain on the ground, then raise and support the vehicle safely.

➡If the front end is raised, be sure to block the drive wheels and firmly set the parking brake before lifting the vehicle. If the rear is raised, then the front wheels MUST be blocked, but the parking brake will be of no use. Also, keep in mind that lifting the vehicle at the rear may help prevent transmission fluid from leaking out of the transmission extension housing.

2. Matchmark the relationship of the rear driveshaft yoke and the drive pinion flange of the axle. If the original yellow marks are visible, there is no need for new marks. The marks facilitate installation of the assembly in its exact original position, thereby assuring you will maintain the proper balance.

3. Remove the four bolts or U-clamps which hold the rear universal joint to the pinion flange. Wrap tape around the loose bearing caps in order to prevent them from falling off the spider.

4. Pull the driveshaft toward the rear of the vehicle until the slip yoke clears the transmission housing and the seal. Plug or cover the hole at the rear of the transmission housing (a plastic bag and a few rubber bands are helpful for this) or place a container under the opening to catch any fluid which might leak.

UNIVERSAL JOINT OVERHAUL

➧ See Figures 24 and 25

1. Position the driveshaft assembly in a sturdy soft-jawed vise, BUT DO NOT place a significant clamp load on the shaft or you will risk deforming and ruining it.

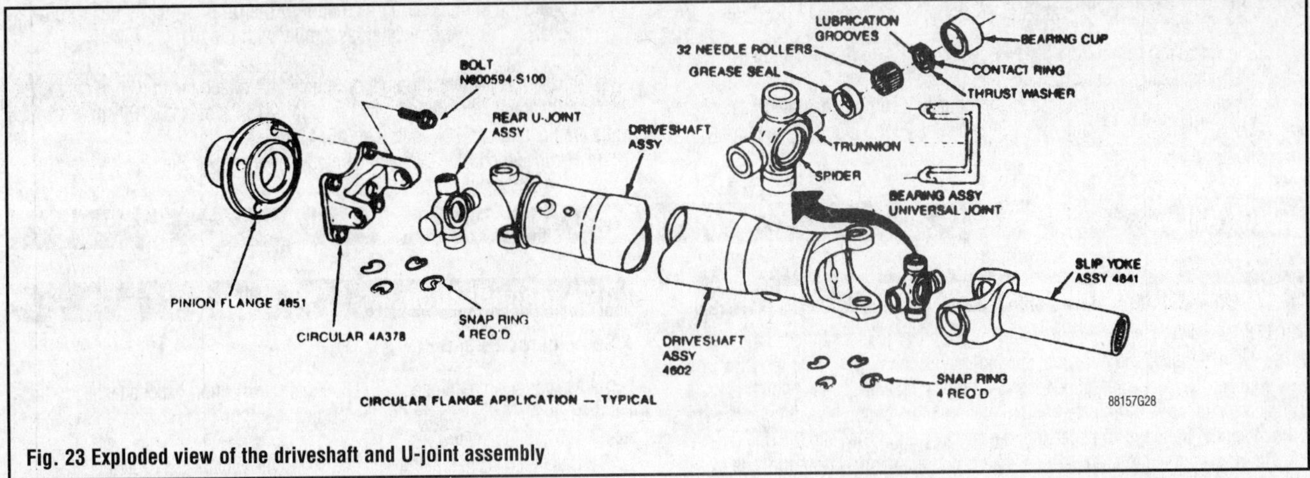

Fig. 23 Exploded view of the driveshaft and U-joint assembly

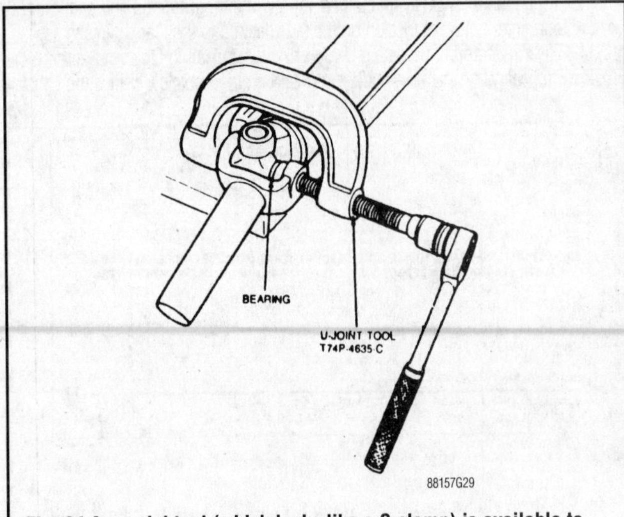

Fig. 24 A special tool (which looks like a C-clamp) is available to remove or install U-joints—removal shown here

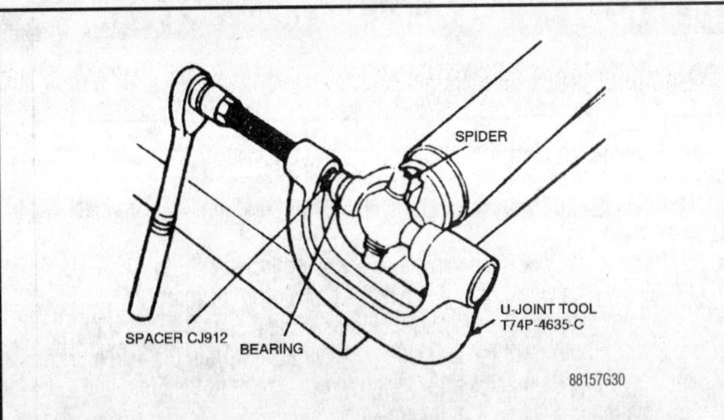

Fig. 25 The tool comes with special drivers or spacers such as the spacer shown here that is used when installing the U-joint

2. Remove the snaprings which retain the bearings in the slip yoke (front only) and in the driveshaft (front and rear).

➡A U-joint removal and installation tool (which looks like a large C-clamp) is available to significantly ease the task, but it is very possible to replace the U-joints using an arbor press or a large vise and a variety of sockets.

3. Using a large vise or an arbor press along with a socket smaller than the bearing cap (on one side) and a socket larger than the bearing cap (on the other side), drive one of the bearings in toward the center of the universal joint, which will force the opposite bearing out.

➡The smaller socket is used as a driver here, as it can pass through the opening of the U-joint or slip yoke flange. The larger socket is used to support the other side of the flange so that the bearing cap has room to exit the flange (into the socket).

4. As each bearing is forced far enough out of the universal joint to be accessible, grip it with a pair of pliers and pull it from the driveshaft yoke. Drive the spider in the opposite direction in order to make the opposite bearing accessible and pull it free with a pair of pliers. Use this procedure to remove all the bearings from both universal joints.
5. After removing the bearings, lift the spider from the yoke.
6. Thoroughly clean all dirt and foreign matter from the yokes on both ends of the driveshaft.

⁂ WARNING

When installing new bearings in the yokes, it is advisable to use an arbor press or the special C-clamp tool. If this tool is not available, the bearings should be driven into position with extreme care, as a heavy jolt on the needle bearings can easily damage or misalign them. This will greatly shorten their life and hamper their efficiency.

7. Start a new bearing into the yoke at the rear of the driveshaft.
8. Position a new spider in the rear yoke and press the new bearing ¼ in. (6mm) below the outer surface of the yoke.
9. With the bearing in position, install a new snapring.
10. Start a new bearing into the opposite side of the yoke. Press the bearing until the opposite bearing, which you have just installed, contacts the inner surface of the snapring.
11. Install a new snapring on the second bearing. It may be necessary to grind the surface of the second snapring.
12. Reposition the driveshaft in the vise, so that the front universal joint is accessible.
13. Install the new bearings, new spider and new snaprings in the same manner as you did for the remaining joint.
14. Position the slip yoke on the spider. Install new bearings, nylon thrust bearings and snaprings.
15. Check both reassembled joints for freedom of movement, If misalignment of any part is causing a bind, a sharp rap on the side of the yoke with a brass hammer should seat the bearing needle and provide the desired freedom of movement. Care should be exercised to firmly support the shaft end during this operation, as well as to prevent blows to the bearings themselves. Under no circumstance should the driveshaft be installed in a car if there is any binding in the universal joints.

DRIVESHAFT INSTALLATION

1. Carefully inspect the rubber seal on the output shaft and the seal in the end of the transmission extension housing. Replace them if they are damaged.
2. Examine the lugs on the axle pinion flange and replace the flange if the lugs are shaved or distorted.

3. Coat the yoke spline with special-purpose lubricant. The Ford part number for this product is B8A–19589–A.

4. If installed to prevent fluid leakage, remove the plug or cover from the rear of the transmission housing.

5. Insert the yoke into the transmission housing and onto the transmission output shaft. Make sure that the yoke assembly does not bottom on the output shaft with excessive force.

6. Locate the alignment marks made (or the original marks noted) during removal. Install the driveshaft assembly with the marks properly aligned.

7. Install the U-bolts and nuts or bolts which attach the universal joint to the pinion flange. Tighten the U-bolt nuts to 8–15 ft. lbs. (11–20 Nm). Flange bolts are tightened to 70–95 ft. lbs. (95–130 Nm).

8. Remove the jackstands and carefully lower the vehicle.

REAR AXLE

Understanding Drive Axles

The drive axle is a special type of transmission that reduces the speed of the drive from the engine and transmission and divides the power to the wheels. Power enters the axle from the driveshaft via the companion flange, which is mounted on the drive pinion shaft. From there, the drive pinion shaft (which turns at engine/transmission speed) and gear carry the power into the differential. The gear on the end of the pinion shaft drives a large ring gear, the axis of rotation of which is 90 degrees away from that of the pinion. The pinion and gear reduce the gear ratio of the axle, and change the direction of rotation to turn the axle shafts which drive both wheels. The axle gear ratio is found by dividing the number of pinion gear teeth into the number of ring gear teeth.

The ring gear drives the differential case. The case provides the two mounting points for the ends of a pinion shaft, on which are mounted two pinion gears. These pinion gears drive the two side gears, each attached to the inner end of an axle shaft.

By driving the axle shafts through this arrangement, the differential allows the outer drive wheel to turn faster that the inner drive wheel in a turn.

The main drive pinion and the side bearings, which bear the weight of the differential case, are shimmed to provide proper bearing preload, and to position the pinion and ring gears properly.

WARNING

The proper adjustment of the relationship of the ring and pinion gears is critical. It should be attempted only by those with both the proper equipment and experience.

Limited-slip differentials include clutches which tend to link each axle shaft to the differential case. Clutches may be engaged either by spring action or by pressure produced by the torque on the axles during a turn. When turning on dry pavement, the effects of the clutches are overcome and each wheel turns at the required speed. When slippage occurs at the either wheel, however, the clutches will transmit some of the power to the wheel with the greater amount of traction. Because of the clutches, limited-slip units often require a special lubricant.

Determining Axle Ratio

The drive axle is said to have a certain axle ratio (meaning the amount which the rear axle reduces the turning speed of the engine/transmission as it transmits this motion to the rear wheels. This number is actually comparison of the number of gear teeth on the ring gear and pinion gear. For example, a 4.11 rear means that there are 4.11 teeth on the ring gear for every tooth on the pinion gear. Put another way, the driveshaft must turn 4.11 times to turn the rear wheels once. Actually, on a 4.11 rear, there might be 37 teeth on the ring gear and 9 on the pinion gear. By dividing the number of teeth on the pinion gear into the number of teeth on the ring gear, the numerical axle ratio is obtained. This also provides a good method of ascertaining exactly what axle ratio with which you car is equipped.

Another, less accurate but quicker method of determining gear ratio is to jack up and support the car so that BOTH rear wheels are off the ground. Make a chalk mark on the rear wheel and driveshaft, then place the transmission in Neutral and turn the rear wheel one complete turn (exactly). While turning the rear wheel, count the number of turns that the driveshaft makes (an assistant makes this a little easier). The number of turns made by the driveshaft (during one complete rotation of the rear wheel) is an approximation of the rear axle ratio. Again, if the driveshaft turned just a little bit more than 4 times, you have a 4.11 or similar gear ratio.

Axle Identification

➧ See Figures 26 and 27

All Mustangs are equipped with a Vehicle Certification Label attached to the left door post. The axle code (for the original equipment) is located in the space marked AX on the label.

Basically two different rear axles are used in the Mustangs covered by this manual: the Integral Carrier, 7.5 inch ring gear and the Integral Carrier, 8.8 inch ring gear. But, each may be available in a variety of configurations and gear ratios.

Additional information is located on the tag attached to the rear axle such as ring gear size, gear ratio and build date. The Drive Axle Application Chart in Section 1 will provide gear ratios from the code you obtain on the Vehicle Certification Label.

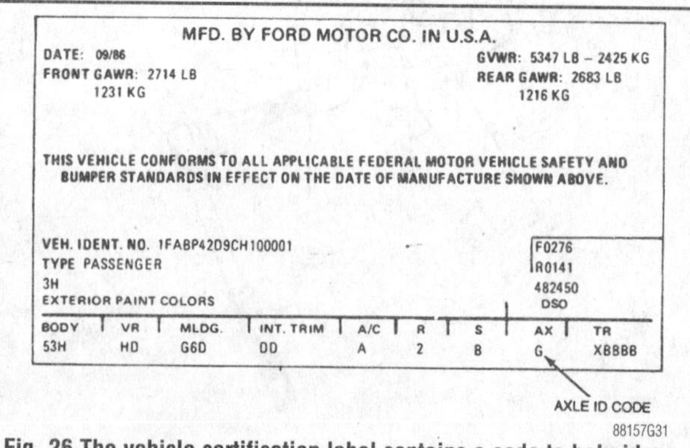

Fig. 26 The vehicle certification label contains a code to help identify the car's original axle

Rear Axle Shaft, Bearing and Seal

REMOVAL & INSTALLATION

➧ See Figures 28 thru 40

1. Block the front wheels, then loosen the lug nuts on the rear wheel that is being removed.

2. Raise and support the vehicle safely using jackstands.

3. Remove the wheel, then remove the brake drum or rotor.

4. If equipped, remove the anti-lock brake speed sensor.

5. Clean all dirt from the area of the carrier cover. Drain the axle lubricant by removing the housing cover. For details, please refer to the Fluid and Lubricant information in Section 1 of this manual.

6. Remove the differential pinion shaft lock bolt and pinion shaft.

7. Push the flanged end of the axle shafts toward the center of the vehicle (to create the necessary play and free the C-lock), then remove the C-lock from the button end of the axle shaft.

8. Slowly withdraw the axle shaft from the housing, being careful not to damage the oil seal (unless you are replacing it anyway).

9. If the seal is being replaced (or if you damaged it on the way out) insert a wheel bearing and seal replacement tool, such as T85L–1225–AH or equivalent, in the bore and position it behind the bearing so the tangs on the tool engage the bearing outer race. Remove the bearing and seal as a unit, using an impact slide hammer.

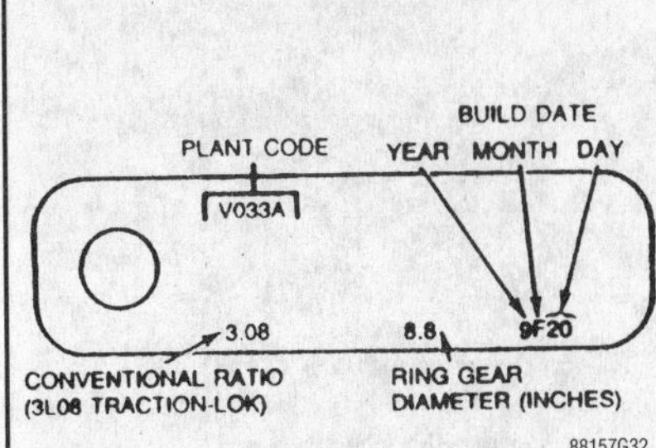

Fig. 27 Each rear axle should be equipped with a tag that gives build and ratio information

Fig. 28 Remove the brake drum (shown) or rotor for access to the axle shaft

Fig. 29 On drum brake vehicles, no other brake components must be removed

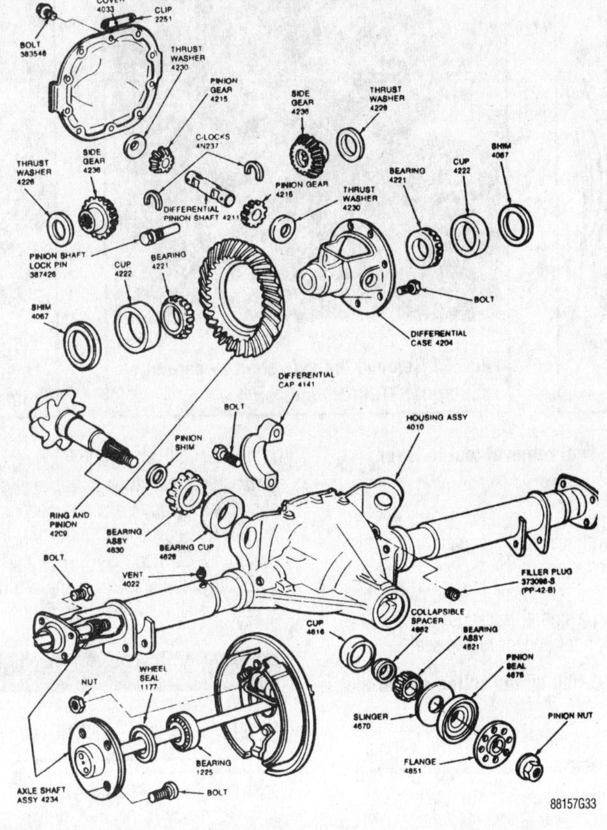

Fig. 30 Exploded view of the rear axle assembly

Fig. 31 Remove the rear axle housing cover and allow the fluid to drain

Fig. 32 Loosen the pinon shaft lock bolt using a socket and a ratchet

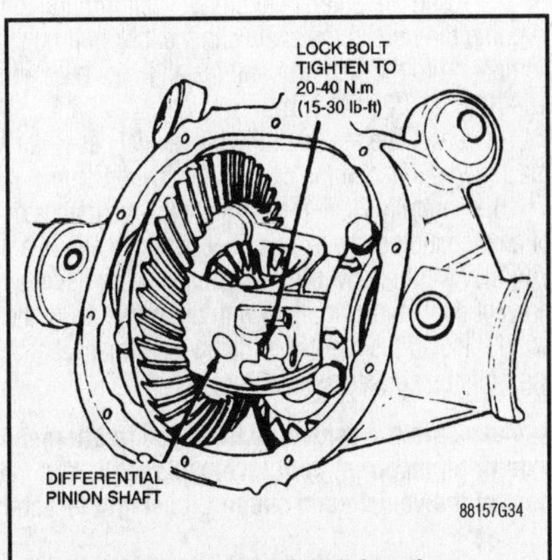

Fig. 33 Rear pinon lock bolt location

88157P06

Fig. 34 Remove the pinon shaft lock bolt . . .

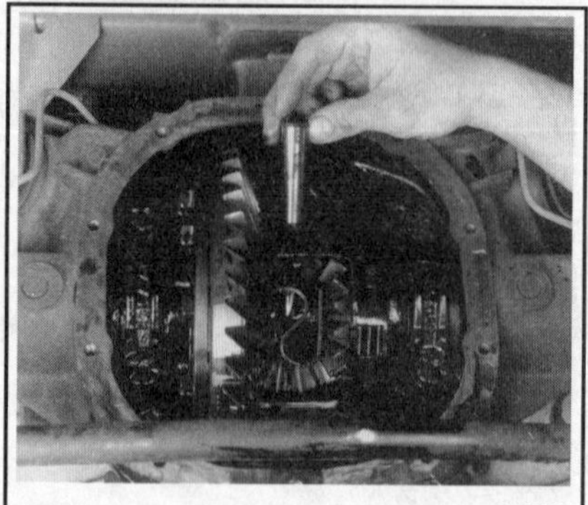
88157P07

Fig. 35 . . . then withdraw the pinon shaft from the differential

88157P08

Fig. 36 After pushing inward slightly on the axle shaft, withdraw the C-clip

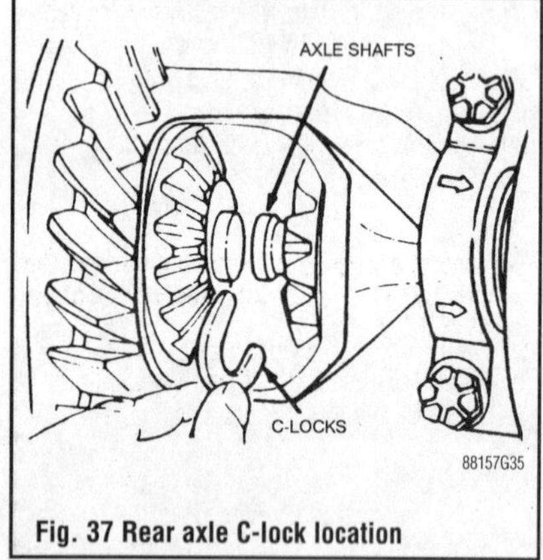

88157G35

Fig. 37 Rear axle C-lock location

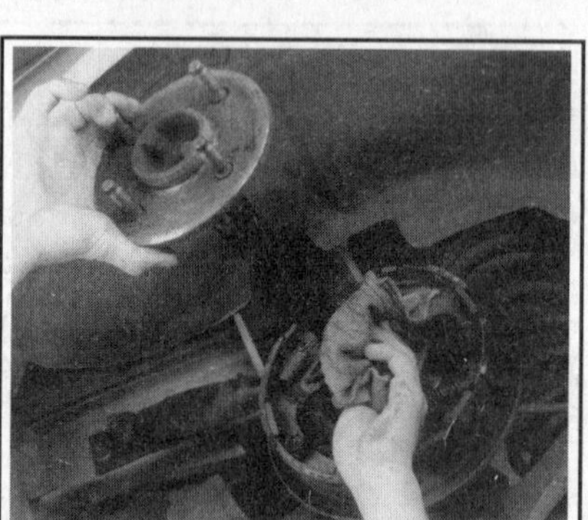
88157P09

Fig. 38 Remove the axle shaft by carefully pulling it STRAIGHT outward

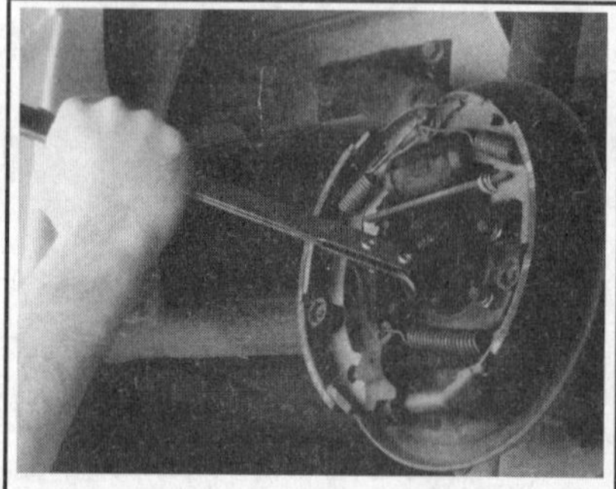
88157P10

Fig. 39 If the bearing is not being removed, use a lever-type seal puller to remove the old seal . . .

➡If only the seal is being replaced, use a seal removal tool to lever ONLY THE SEAL from the axle housing.

To install:

10. If removed, lubricate the new bearing with rear axle lubricant. Install the bearing into the housing bore with a bearing installer.

11. If removed, install a new axle seal using a seal installer. Essentially, the installation tool is a driver of the right diameter; a smooth socket or piece of pipe can also be used as a driver, just be careful not to damage the seal.

➡Check for the presence of an axle shaft O-ring on the spline end of the shaft; install one if none is found.

12. Carefully slide the axle shaft STRAIGHT into the axle housing, without damaging the bearing or seal assembly. Start the splines into the side gear and push firmly until the shaft splines engage. It may be necessary to rotate the axle slightly to align the splines.

13. Install the C-lock, then pull outward slightly on the axle shaft and make sure the C-lock seats in the counterbore of the differential side gear.

14. Insert the differential pinion shaft through the case and pinion gears, aligning the hole in the shaft with the lock bolt hole. Apply a suitable locking compound to the lock bolt and install in the case and pinion shaft. Tighten to 15–30 ft. lbs. (20–41 Nm).

15. Cover the inside of the differential case with a shop rag and clean the machined surface of the carrier and cover. Remove the shop rag.

16. Carefully clean the gasket mating surfaces of the cover and axle housing of any remaining gasket or sealer. A putty knife is a good tool to use for this. You may want to cover the differential gears using a rag or piece of plastic to prevent contaminating them with dirt or pieces of the old gasket.

17. Install the rear cover using a new gasket and sealant. Tighten the retaining bolts using a crosswise pattern.

➡Make sure the vehicle is level before attempting to add fluid to the rear axle or an incorrect fluid level will result. You may have to lift all four corners of the vehicle and support it using 4 jackstands in order to do this.

18. Refill the rear axle housing using the proper grade and quantity of lubricant as detailed earlier in this section. Install the filler plug, operate the vehicle and check for any leaks.

19. If removed, install the anti-lock speed sensor and tighten the retaining bolt to 40–60 inch lbs. (5–7 Nm).

20. Install the brake calipers and rotors or the brake drums, as applicable.

21. Install the wheel, then remove the jackstands and carefully lower the vehicle.

Pinion Seal

REMOVAL & INSTALLATION

➧ See Figures 41 and 42

1. Raise and support the vehicle safely using jackstands.

2. Matchmark the rear driveshaft yoke and the companion flange so they may be reassembled in the same way to maintain balance.

3. Disconnect the driveshaft from the rear axle companion flange, remove the driveshaft from the extension housing. Plug or cover the extension housing to prevent leakage. A plastic bag and a few rubber bands works well to cover the housing.

4. Install an inch/pound torque wrench on the pinion nut and record the torque required to maintain rotation of the pinion through several revolutions.

5. While holding the companion flange with holder tool No. T78P–4851–A, or equivalent, remove the pinion nut.

6. Clean the area around the oil seal and place a pan under the seal.

7. Mark the companion flange in relation to the pinion shaft so the flange can be installed in the same position.

8. Remove the rear axle companion flange using tool No. T65L–4851–B, or equivalent.

9. Pry the seal out of the housing using a prytool.

To install:

10. Clean the oil seal seat surface and install the seal in the carrier using seal replacer tool T79P–4676–A, or equivalent. Apply lubricant to the lips of the seal.

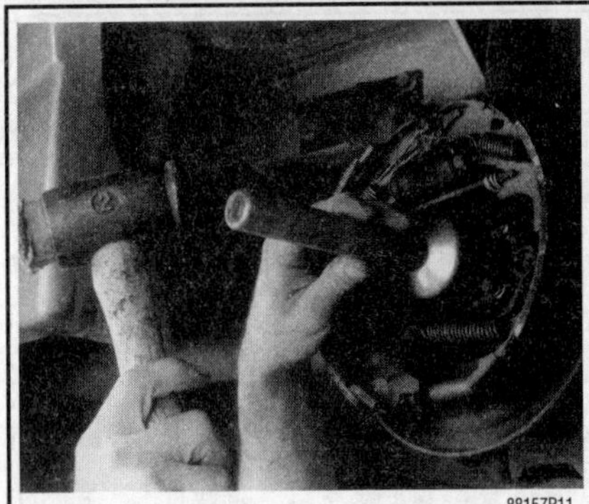
88157P11

Fig. 40 . . . then use a suitable seal installer or driver to install the new seal

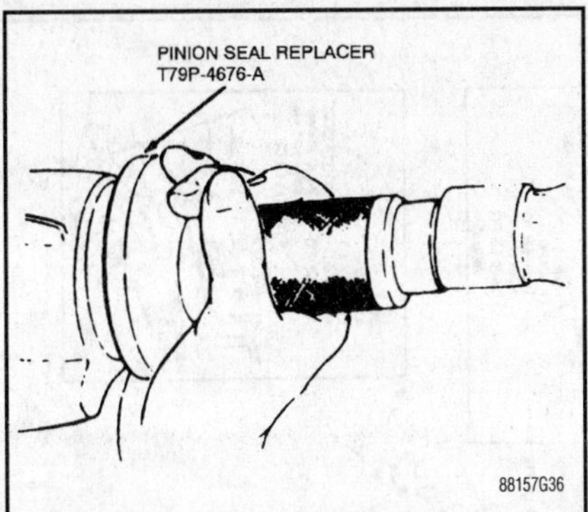

Fig. 41 A new pinion shaft seal should be installed using a suitable driver

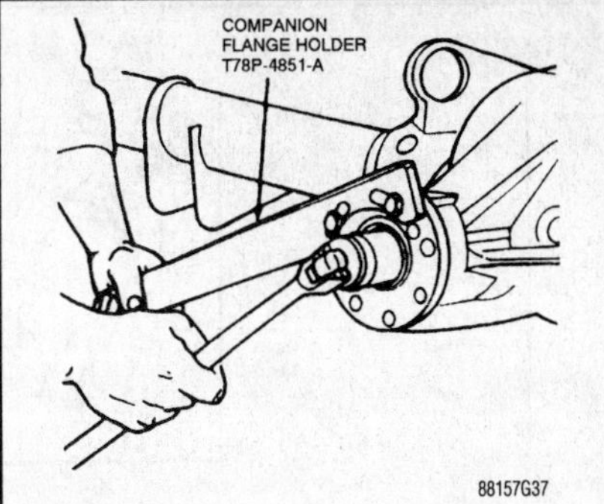

Fig. 42 A holding fixture tool is necessary when loosening or tightening the pinion shaft nut

11. Apply a small amount of lubricant to the companion flange splines, align the marks on the flange and on the pinion shaft and install the flange.
12. Install a new nut on the pinion shaft and apply lubricant on the washer side of the nut.
13. Hold the flange with the holder tool while tightening the nut. Rotate the pinion to ensure proper seating and take frequent pinion bearing torque preload readings until the original recorded reading (before disassembly) is obtained.
14. If the original recorded preload is less than the minimum specification of 170 ft. lbs. (230 Nm), on the 7.5 in diameter ring gear axle or 140 ft. lbs. (190 Nm) on the 8.8 in. diameter ring gear axle, tighten the nut to specification. If the preload is higher than specification, tighten to the original reading as recorded.

➡Under no circumstance should the pinion nut be backed off to reduce preload. If reduced preload is required, a new collapsible pinion spacer and pinion nut should be installed.

15. Remove the plug or cover from the transmission extension housing and install the front end of the driveshaft on the transmission output shaft.
16. Connect the rear end of the driveshaft to the axle companion flange, aligning the scribed marks. Tighten the four bolts to 71–95 ft. lbs. (95–130 Nm).

➡Remember that when you check fluid in the rear axle or the manual transmission, the car MUST be level. If it is necessary to raise and support the vehicle for access, then it must be supported at all four corners.

17. Add rear axle lubricant to the carrier to a level ¼–7⁄16 in. (6–15mm) below the bottom of the fill hole. Install the filler plug and tighten to 15–30 ft. lbs. (20–41 Nm).
18. Make sure the axle vent is not plugged with debris.
19. Remove the jackstands and carefully lower the vehicle.

Axle Housing

REMOVAL & INSTALLATION

➧ See Figures 43 and 44

1. Raise and support the vehicle safely using jackstands. Position additional jackstands under the rear frame crossmember.
2. Remove the cover and drain the axle lubricant.
3. Remove the wheel and tire assemblies.
4. Remove the brake drums or brake rotors.
5. Remove the lock bolt from the pinion shaft and remove the shaft.
6. If equipped, remove the anti-lock brake sensors before removing the axle shafts.
7. Push the axle shafts inward to remove the C-locks and remove the axle shafts.
8. If necessary, remove the bolt attaching the brake junction block to the rear cover.
9. Remove the brake lines from the clips and position it out of the way.
10. If equipped with drum brakes, remove the four retaining nuts from each backing plate and wire the backing plate to the underbody.
11. Matchmark the driveshaft yoke and companion flange. Disconnect the driveshaft at the companion flange and wire it to the underbody.
12. Support the axle housing with jackstands. Disengage the brake line from the clips that retain the line to the axle housing.
13. Disconnect the axle vents from the rear axle housing.

➡Some axle vents may be secured to the housing assembly through the brake junction block. At assembly, a thread lock/sealer must be applied to ensure retention.

14. Disconnect the lower shock absorber studs from the mounting brackets on the axle housing. If equipped, disconnect the quad shock from the quad shock bracket.
15. Disconnect the upper arms from the mountings on the axle housing ear brackets.
16. Lower the axle housing assembly until the coil springs are released and lift out the coil springs.
17. Disconnect the suspension lower arms at the axle housing.
18. Lower the axle housing and remove it from the vehicle.

To install:

19. Position the axle housing under the vehicle and raise the axle with a hoist or jack. Connect the lower suspension arms to their mounting brackets on the axle housing. Do not tighten the bolts and nuts at this time.
20. Reposition the rear coil springs.
21. Raise the housing into position.
22. Connect the upper arms to the mounting ears on the housing. Tighten the nuts and bolts to 70–100 ft. lbs. (95–135 Nm). Tighten the lower arm bolts to 70–100 ft. lbs. (95–135 Nm).
23. Install the axle vent and the brake line to the clips that retain the line to the axle housing.
24. If equipped with drum brakes, install the brake backing plates on the axle housing flanges.
25. Connect the lower shock absorber studs to the mounting bracket on the axle housing. If equipped, connect the quad shock to the quad shock bracket.
26. Connect the driveshaft to the companion flange and tighten the bolts to 70–95 ft. lbs. (95–130 Nm).
27. Slide the rear axle shafts into the housing until the splines enter the side gear. Push the axle shafts inward and install the C-lock at the end of each shaft spline. Pull the shafts outboard until the C-lock enters the recess in the side gears.
28. Install the pinion shaft and the pinion shaft lock bolt. Tighten to 15–30 ft. lbs. (20–41 Nm).
29. Install the anti-lock sensor, if it was removed.
30. Install the rear brake drums or rotors and calipers.
31. Install the rear carrier cover.
32. Install the brake junction block on the carrier cover and tighten to 10–18 ft. lbs. (14–24 Nm).
33. Properly refill the rear axle with lubricant. Remember that the vehicle MUST be level to assure a proper amount of fluid is added.
34. Remove the jackstands and carefully lower the vehicle.

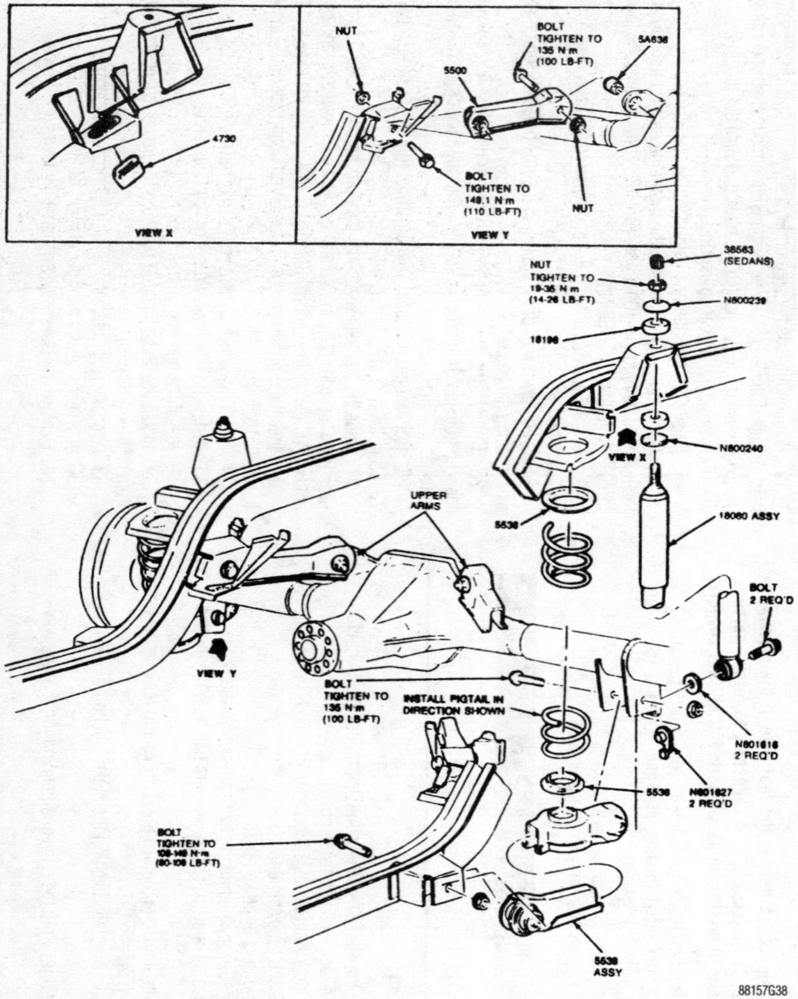

88157G38

Fig. 43 Exploded view of the rear axle assembly mounting—7.5 in. ring gear axle housing

88157G39

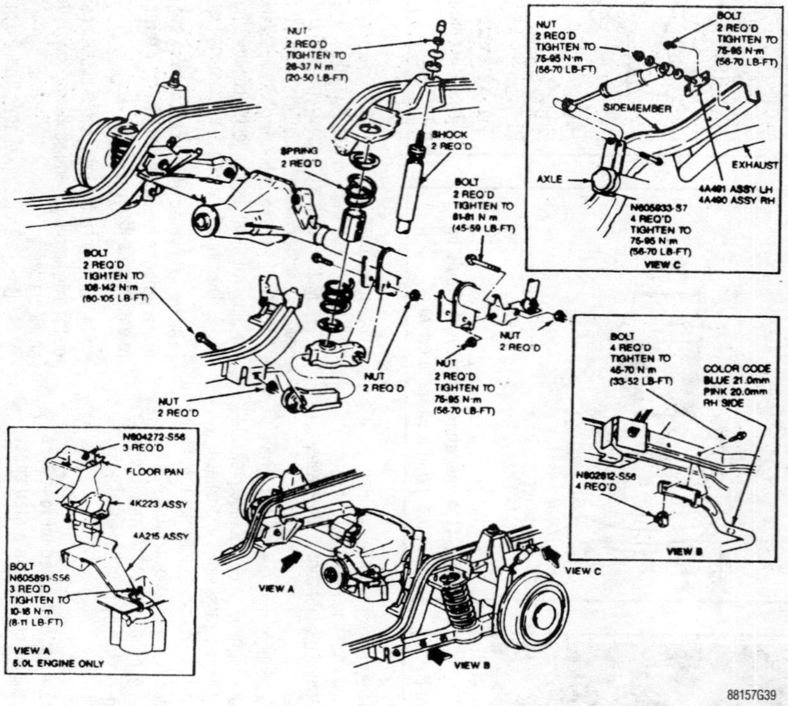

Fig. 44 Exploded view of the rear axle assembly mounting—8.8 in. ring gear axle housing

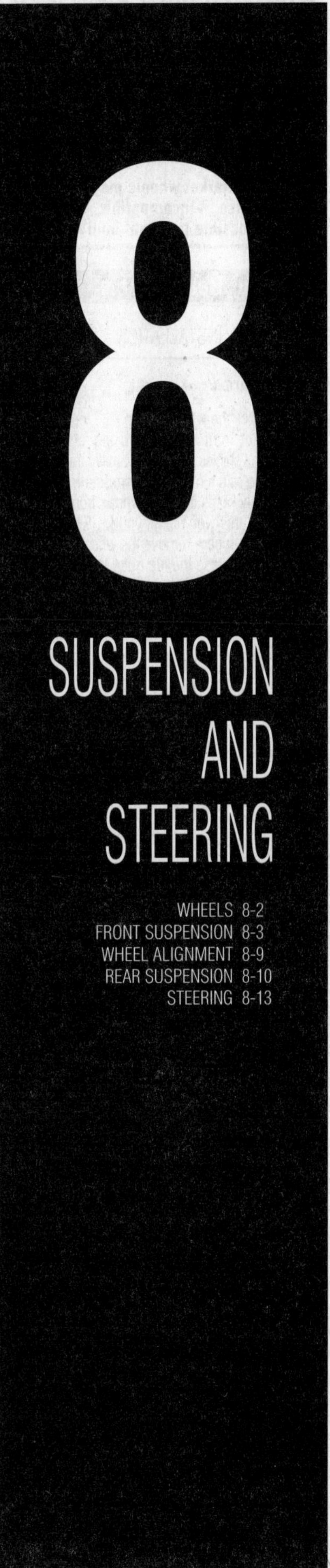

8 SUSPENSION AND STEERING

WHEELS

CAUTION

Some aftermarket wheels may not be compatible with these vehicles. The use of incompatible wheels may result in equipment failure and possible personal injury! Use only approved wheels!

Front or Rear Wheels

REMOVAL & INSTALLATION

See Figure 1

1. Block the wheel(s) opposite the wheel(s) being raised.
2. If the front wheels are being raised, firmly set the parking brake.
3. On vehicles with an automatic transmission, place the selector lever in **P**. On vehicles with a manual transmission, place the transmission in gear. Remember that this only keeps the drive wheels from turning, so if you are raising the rear of the vehicle, this won't help, you MUST block the front wheels in this case.
4. If equipped, remove the wheel cover.
5. Break loose the lug nuts. If a nut is stuck, never use heat to loosen it, otherwise damage to the wheel and bearings may occur. If the nuts are seized, one or two heavy hammer blows directly on the end of the bolt/nut head usually loosens the rust. Be careful as continued pounding will likely damage the brake drum or rotor.
6. Raise the vehicle (using a jack at one of the proper jacking points—see Jacking in Section 1 for details) until the tire is clear of the ground. Support the vehicle safely using jackstands.
7. Remove the lug nuts, then remove the tire and wheel assembly.

To install:

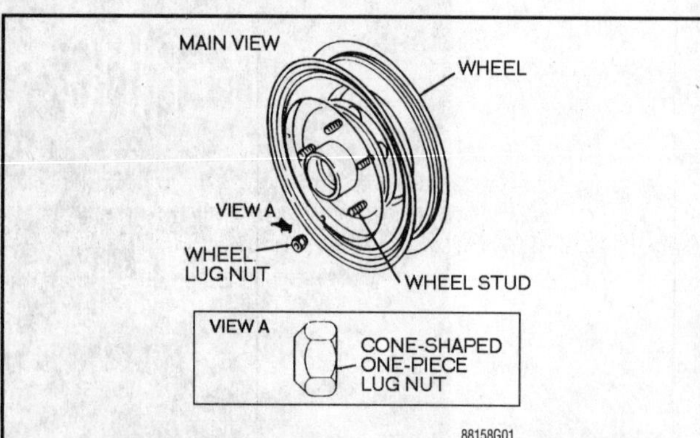

Fig. 1 Be sure to install the lug nuts with the cone-shaped portion facing towards the wheel

8. Make sure the wheel and hub mating surfaces, as well as the wheel lug studs, are clean and free of all foreign material. Always remove rust from the wheel mounting surfaces and the brake rotors/drums. Failure to do so may cause the lug nuts to loosen in service or could help the wheel to rust onto the rotor/drum making removal even more difficult next time.
9. Position the wheel on the hub or drum and hand-tighten the lug nuts. Make sure that the coned ends face inward.
10. Tighten all the lug nuts, in a crisscross pattern, until they are snug.
11. Remove the supports and carefully lower the vehicle. Tighten the lug nuts, in a crisscross pattern to 85–105 ft. lbs. (115–142 Nm). Always use a torque wrench to achieve the proper lug nut torque and prevent stretching the wheel studs.
12. Repeat the torque pattern to assure proper wheel tightening.
13. If equipped, install the hub cab or wheel cover.

INSPECTION

Check the wheels for any damage. They must be replaced if they are bent, dented, heavily rusted, have elongated bolt holes, or have excessive lateral or radial runout. Wheels with excessive runout may cause a high-speed vehicle vibration.

Replacement wheels must be of the same load capacity, diameter, width, offset and mounting configuration as the original wheels. Using the wrong wheels may affect wheel bearing life, ground and tire clearance, or speedometer and odometer calibrations.

Wheel Lug Nut Stud

REPLACEMENT

Front Wheels

See Figures 2 and 3

USING A PRESS

1. Remove the wheel.
2. Remove the hub and rotor assembly along with the wheel bearings. For details, please refer to the wheel bearing procedures found in Section 1 or in this section, but DO NOT remove the inner bearing seal unless you are removing the bearing to inspect or repack it.
3. Place the hub/rotor assembly in a press, supported by the hub surface. NEVER rest the assembly on the rotor!
4. Press the stud from the hub.
5. Position the new stud in the hub and align the serrations. Make sure it is square and press it into place.

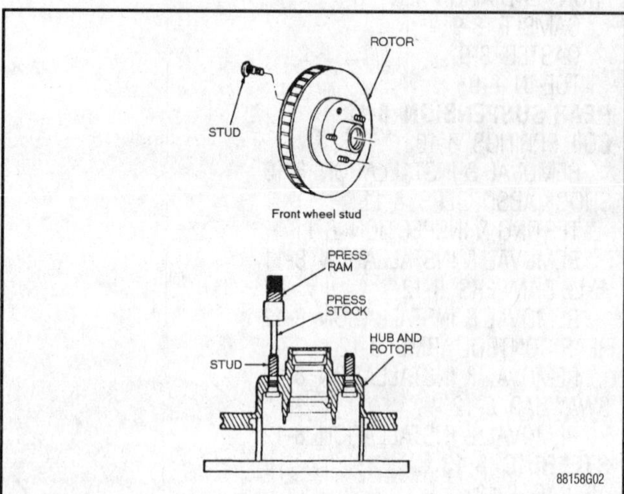

Fig. 2 A press can be used to easily free old studs from the hub and rotor assembly

USING A HAMMER AND DRIVER

1. Remove the wheel.
2. Remove the hub and rotor assembly along with the wheel bearings. For details, please refer to the wheel bearing procedures found in Section 1 or in this Section, but DO NOT remove the inner bearing seal unless you are removing the bearing to inspect or repack it.
3. Support the hub/rotor assembly on a flat, hard surface, resting the assembly on the hub. NEVER rest the assembly on the rotor!
4. Position a driver, such as a drift or broad punch, on the outer end of the stud and drive it from the hub.
5. Turn the assembly over, coat the serrations of the new stud with liquid soap, position the stud in the hole, aligning the serrations, and, using the drift and hammer, drive it into place until fully seated.

If installation of the new stud is difficult, you can also draw the stud into position using the lug nut and a stack of washers. Align the serra-

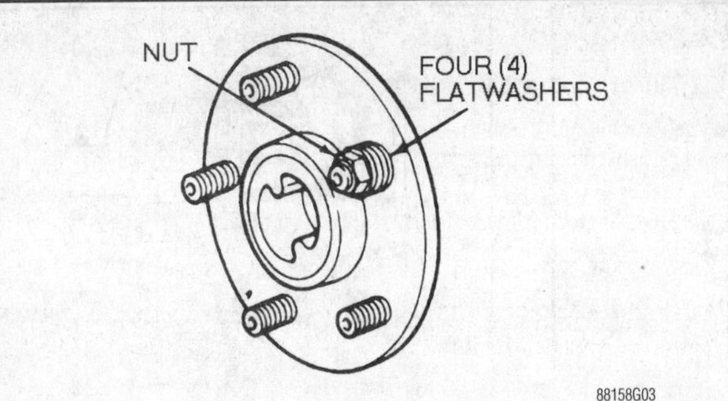

Fig. 3 One method of installing replacement studs is to draw it in place using a stack of washers and the lug nut (flat side toward the washers)

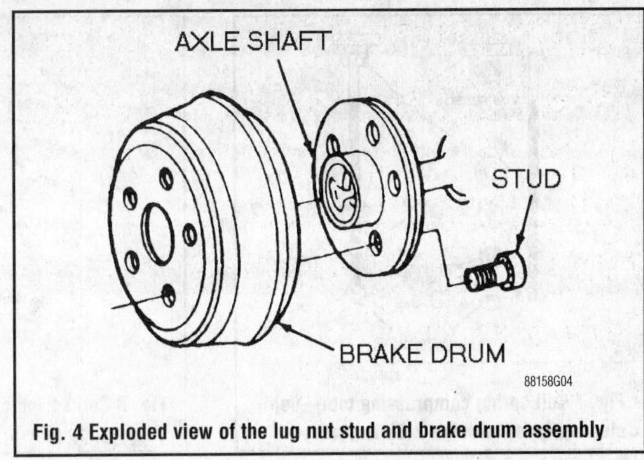

Fig. 4 Exploded view of the lug nut stud and brake drum assembly

tions of the new stud in the rotor, then place a short stack of washers over the stud. Thread the lug nut onto the stud (with the flat side facing the washers) until the stud threads pass through the nut (you may have to remove some of the washers, but make sure enough threads are through to prevent stripping the new stud). Tighten the lug nut against the washers and the threads will pull the stud into position in the hub.

Rear Wheels

➧ See Figures 3, 4 and 5

1. Remove the wheel.
2. Remove the drum or rotor from the axle shaft or hub studs.
3. Using a large C-clamp and socket, press the stud from the drum or rotor.
4. Coat the serrated part of the stud with liquid soap and place it in the hole. Align the serrations.
5. Place three or four flat washers on the outer end of the stud and thread a lug nut on the stud with the flat side against the washers. Tighten the lug nut until the stud is drawn all the way in.

✱✱ WARNING

Do not use an impact wrench!

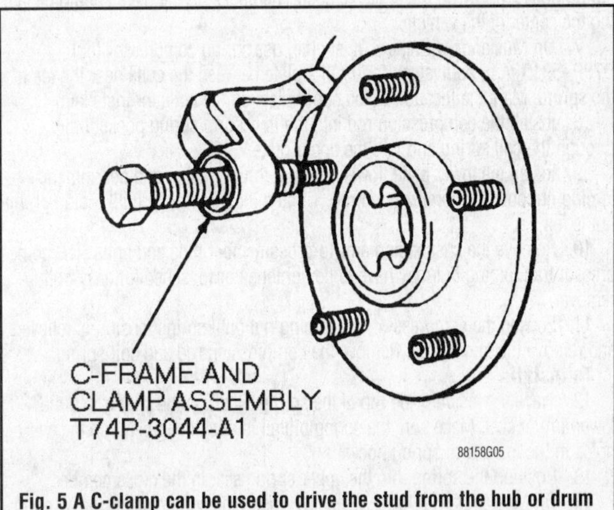

Fig. 5 A C-clamp can be used to drive the stud from the hub or drum

FRONT SUSPENSION

➧ See Figure 6

Coil Springs

✱✱ CAUTION

Always use extreme caution when working with coil springs. Always use the proper spring compression tools, since the springs are VERY strong and if pressure is released suddenly (and without control) serious personal injury could result. Also, ALWAYS be sure the vehicle is very well supported when working around springs.

REMOVAL & INSTALLATION

➧ See Figures 7, 8 and 9

➡This procedure REQUIRES the use of a coil spring compression tool. This tool can usually be rented for a one time use, otherwise it can be purchased from your local parts store.

1. Raise and support the vehicle safely using jackstands, but allowing the control arms to hang free.
2. Remove the wheel and tire assembly.
3. Remove the brake caliper. Suspend the caliper with a length of wire; DO NOT let the caliper hang by the brake hose.
4. Disconnect the tie rod end from the steering spindle and disconnect the stabilizer link from the lower arm.

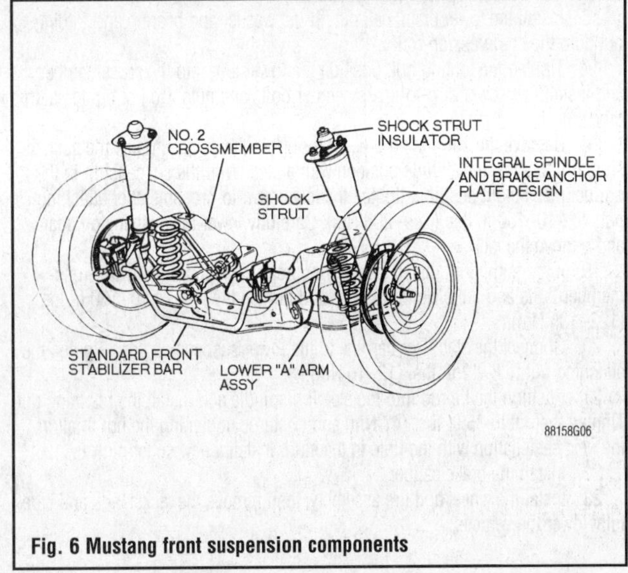

Fig. 6 Mustang front suspension components

5. If necessary, remove the steering gear (rack and pinion) bolts and reposition the gear so the suspension arm bolt can be removed.
6. On Mustangs equipped with the 2.3L engine, use spring compressor tool T82P–5310–A or equivalent to place the upper plate in position into the

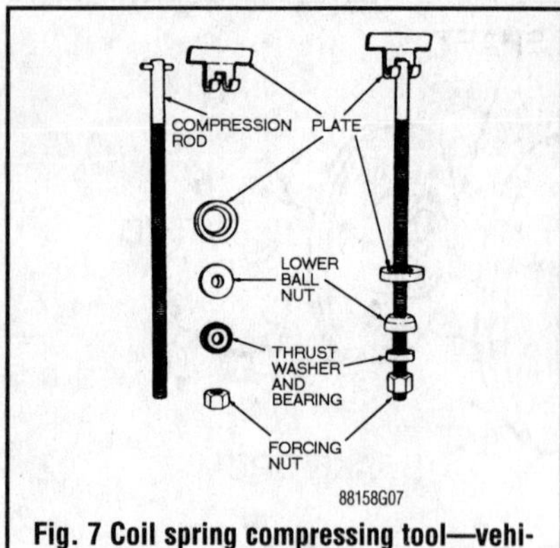

Fig. 7 Coil spring compressing tool—vehicles equipped with the 2.3L engine

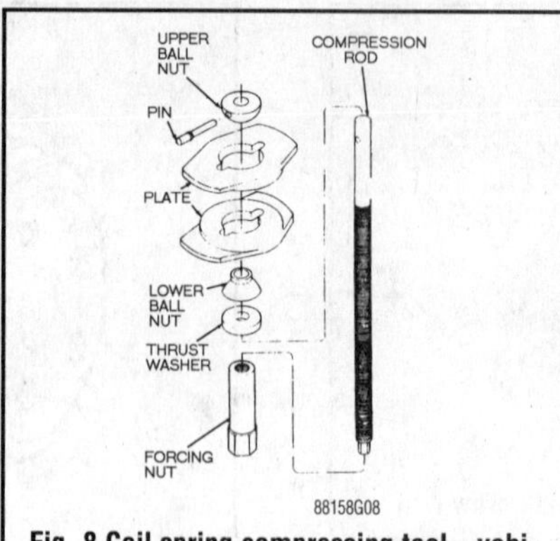

Fig. 8 Coil spring compressing tool—vehicles equipped with the 5.0L engine

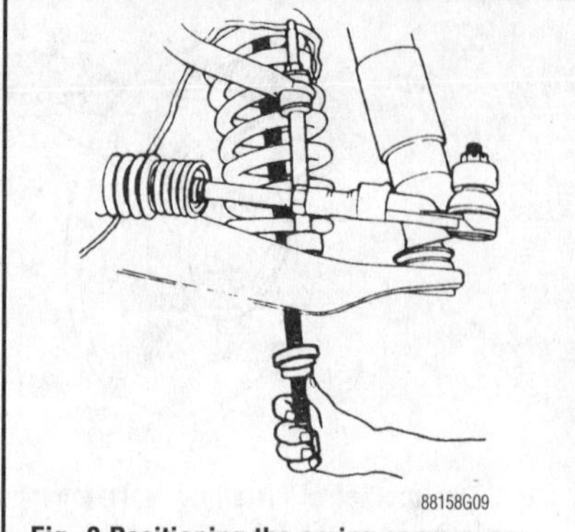

Fig. 9 Positioning the spring compressor tool into the coil

spring pocket cavity on the crossmember. The hooks on the plate should be facing the center of the vehicle.

7. On Mustangs with the 5.0L engine, use spring compressor tool D78P–5310–A or equivalent, to install a plate between the coils near the toe of the spring. Mark the location of the upper plate on the coils for installation.
8. Install the compression rod into the lower arm spring pocket hole, through the coil spring and into the upper plate.
9. Install the lower plate, lower ball nut, thrust washer and bearing and forcing nut onto the compression rod. Tighten the forcing nut until a drag on the nut is felt.
10. Remove the suspension arm-to-crossmember nuts and bolts. The compressor tool forcing nut may have to be tightened or loosened for easy bolt removal.
11. Loosen the compression rod forcing nut until spring tension is relieved and remove the forcing nut. Remove the compression rod and coil spring.

To install:

12. Place the insulator on top of the spring. Position the spring into the lower arm pocket. Make sure the spring pigtail is positioned between the two holes in the lower arm spring pocket.
13. Position the spring into the upper spring seat in the crossmember.
14. On Mustangs with the 2.3L engine, insert the compression rod through the control arm and spring, then hook it to the upper plate. The upper plate is installed with the hooks facing the center of the vehicle.
15. On Mustangs with the 5.0L engine, install the upper plate between the coils in the location marked during removal.
16. Install the lower plate, ball nut, thrust washer and bearing and forcing nut onto the compression rod.
17. Tighten the forcing nut, position the lower arm into the crossmember and install new lower arm-to-crossmember bolts and nuts. Do not tighten at this time.
18. Remove the spring compressor tool from the vehicle. Raise the suspension arm to a normal attitude position with a jack. With the suspension in the normal ride-height position, tighten the lower arm-to-crossmember attaching nuts to 110–150 ft. lbs. (149–203 Nm). Carefully lower the suspension again and remove the jack.
19. If repositioning, install the steering gear (rack and pinion)-to-crossmember bolts and nuts. Hold the bolts and tighten the nuts to 90–100 ft. lbs. (122–135 Nm).
20. Connect the stabilizer bar link to the lower suspension arm. Tighten the attaching nut to 8–12 ft. lbs. (12–16 Nm).
21. Position the tie rod into the steering spindle and install the retaining nut. Tighten the nut to 35 ft. lbs. (47 Nm) and continue tightening the nut to align the next castellation with the hole in the stud. Install a new cotter pin.
22. Install the brake caliper.
23. Instal the wheel and tire assembly, then remove the jackstands and carefully lower the vehicle.

MacPherson Strut

➧ **See Figures 10 and 11**

TESTING & INSPECTION

Bounce Test

Each strut can be tested by bouncing the corner of the vehicle until maximum up and down movement is obtained. Let go of the vehicle and watch. It should stop bouncing in 1–2 bounces. If not, the strut should be inspected for damage and possibly replaced.

Strut Mounts

Check the strut mountings for worn or defective grommets, loose mounting nuts, interference or missing bump stops. If no apparent defects are noted, check the strut for hydraulic leaks.

Checking for Hydraulic Leaks

Disconnect each strut lower mount and pull down on the strut until it is fully extended. inspect for leaks in the seal area. Strut fluid is very thin and has a

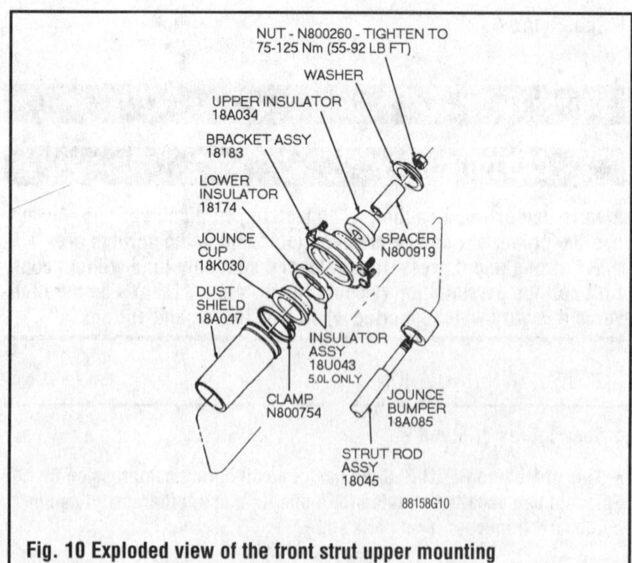

Fig. 10 Exploded view of the front strut upper mounting

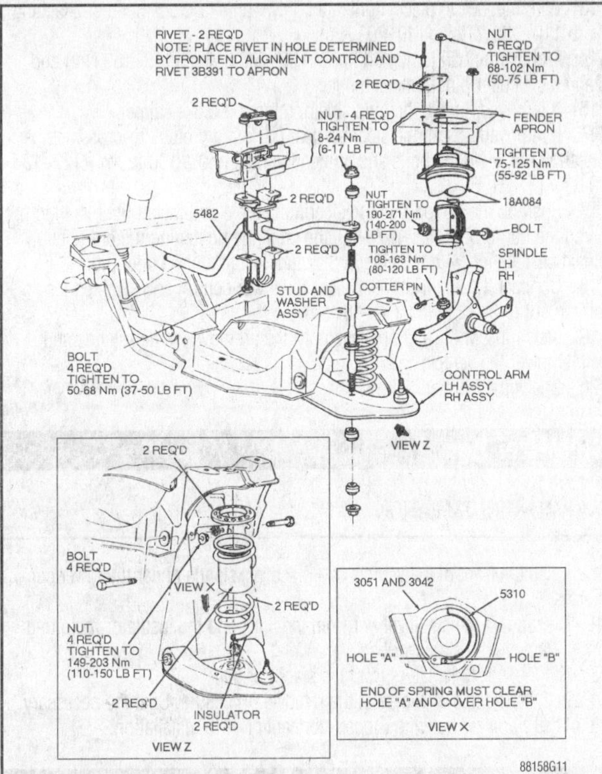

Fig. 11 Exploded view of the front suspension assembly—including front strut

characteristic odor and dark brown color. Don't confuse the glossy paint on some struts with leaking fluid. A slight trace of fluid is a normal condition; they are designed to seep a certain amount of fluid past the seals for lubrication. If you are in doubt as to whether the fluid on the strut is coming from the strut itself or from some other source, wipe the seal area clean and manually operate the strut (refer to the procedure later in this section). Fluid will appear if the unit is leaking.

Manually Operating the Struts

It may be necessary to fabricate a holding fixture for certain types of strut absorbers. If a suspected problem is in the front struts, disconnect both front strut lower mountings.

Grip the lower end of the strut and pull down (rebound stroke) and then push up (compression stroke). The control arms will limit the movement of front struts during the compression stroke. Compare the rebound resistance of both struts and compare the compression resistance. Usually any strut showing a noticeable difference will be the one at fault.

If the strut has internal noises, extend the strut fully then exert an extra pull. If a small additional movement is felt, this usually means a loose piston, and the strut should be replaced. Other noises that are cause for replacing struts are a squeal after a full stroke in both directions, a clicking noise on fast reverse and a lag at reversal near mid-stroke.

REMOVAL & INSTALLATION

➧ See Figures 12, 13 and 14

1. Disconnect the negative battery cable.
2. Place the ignition switch in the unlocked position to permit free movement of the front wheels.
3. Raise the vehicle by the lower control arms until the wheels are just off the ground. From the engine compartment, remove and discard the three upper mount retaining nuts. Do not remove the pop-rivet holding the camber plate in position.
4. Continue to raise the front of the vehicle by the lower control arms and position jackstands under the frame jacking pads, rearward of the wheels.
5. Remove the wheel and tire assembly, then remove the brake caliper. Support the caliper with a length of wire; do not let the caliper hang by the brake hose.

➡To help assure that wheel alignment is not changed, place matchmarks on the strut and spindle (steering knuckle) before removal. If the strut is being replaced, carefully transfer the marks to the new part.

6. Remove the two lower nuts that attach the strut to the spindle, leaving the bolts in place. Carefully remove both spindle-to-strut bolts, push the bracket free of the spindle and remove the strut.
7. Compress the strut to clear the upper mount of the body mounting pad. If necessary, remove the upper mount and jounce bumper.

To install:

8. If removed, install the upper mount and jounce bumper.
9. Position the three upper mount studs into the body mounting pad and camber plate, then start three new nuts.
10. Compress the strut and position into the spindle. Install two new lower retaining bolts and hand start the nuts. Remove the suspension load from the control arms by lowering the vehicle. Tighten the lower retaining nuts to 140–200 ft. lbs. (190–271 Nm).
11. Raise the suspension control arms (to position the suspension at normal ride height) and tighten the upper mount retaining nuts to 40–55 ft. lbs. (54–75 Nm).
12. Install the brake caliper.
13. Install the wheel and tire assembly.
14. Remove the jackstands and carefully lower the vehicle to the ground.
15. Check the front end alignment and adjust, as necessary.

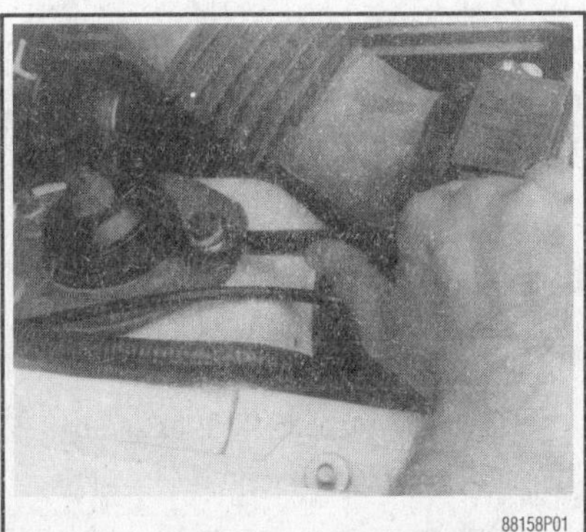

Fig. 12 Loosen the three upper mount retaining nuts

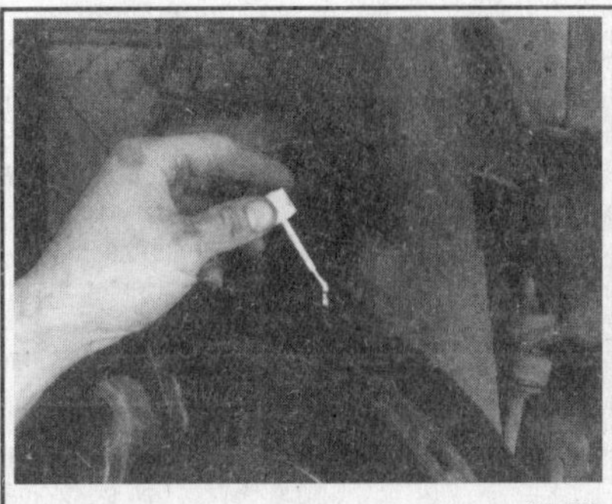

Fig. 13 Matchmark the strut and spindle (knuckle) to assure proper wheel alignment is maintained . . .

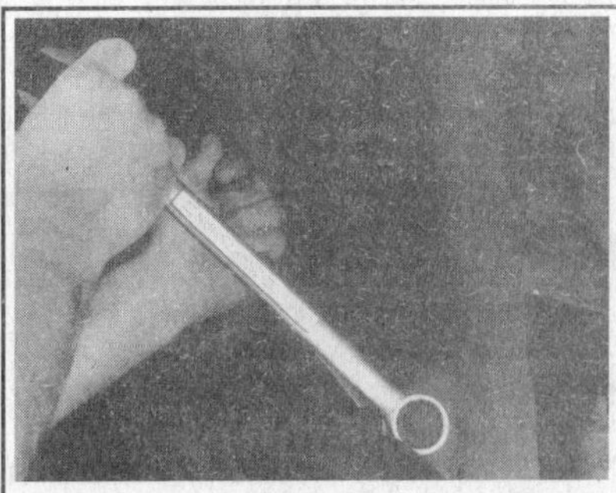

Fig. 14 . . . then loosen the strut lower fasteners (a backup wrench is necessary to keep the nuts/bolts from spinning)

Lower Ball Joints

INSPECTION

See Figure 15

1. Support the vehicle in a normal driving position with the ball joints loaded.
2. Wipe the wear indicator and ball joint cover checking surface clean.
3. The checking surface should project outside the cover. If the checking surface is inside the cover, replace the lower arm assembly.

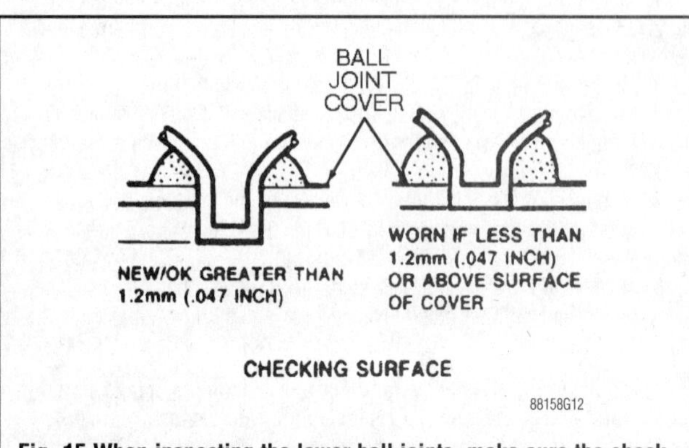

Fig. 15 When inspecting the lower ball joints, make sure the checking surface protrudes outside the cover

REMOVAL & INSTALLATION

The ball joint is an integral part of the lower control arm. If the ball joint is defective, the entire lower control arm must be replaced. For more details, please refer to the Lower Control Arm removal and installation procedure.

Lower Control Arm

REMOVAL & INSTALLATION

1. Raise and support the vehicle safely using jackstands, but be sure to allow the control arms to hang free.
2. Remove the wheel and tire assembly.
3. If necessary, remove the brake caliper and suspend with a length of wire; do not let the caliper hang by the brake hose. Remove the brake rotor and dust shield.
4. Disconnect the tie rod end from the steering spindle. Disconnect the stabilizer bar link from the lower arm.
5. If necessary for suspension arm bolt removal, remove the steering gear (rack and pinion) bolts and lower the gear out of the way to provide clearance.
6. Remove the cotter pin and loosen the lower ball joint stud nut 1–2 turns. Do not remove the nut at this time. Tap the spindle boss sharply to relieve the stud pressure.
7. Install a suitable spring compressor and compress the coil spring so it is free in the seat.
8. Remove and discard the ball joint nut and raise the entire strut and spindle assembly. Wire out of the way to obtain working room.
9. Remove and discard the suspension arm-to-crossmember nuts and bolts. Remove the lower control arm and coil spring.

To install:

10. Position the coil spring into the lower arm pocket. Make sure the spring pigtail is positioned between the two holes in the pocket.
11. Position the lower arm to the crossmember and install new arm-to-crossmember bolts and nuts. Do not tighten at this time.
12. Raise the control arm with a jack to a normal attitude position and remove the spring compressor.
13. With the jack in place, tighten the lower arm-to-crossmember attaching nuts to 110–150 ft. lbs. (149–203 Nm).
14. Tighten the ball joint stud nut to 100–120 ft. lbs. (136–163 Nm) and install a new cotter pin. Remove the jack.
15. If removed, install the dust shield, rotor and brake caliper.
16. If removed, install the steering gear (rack and pinion)-to-crossmember bolts and nuts. Hold the bolts and tighten the nuts to 90–100 ft. lbs. (122–136 Nm).
17. Position the tie rod into the steering spindle and install the retaining nut. Tighten the nut to 35 ft. lbs. (47 Nm) and continue tightening the nut to align the next castellation with the hole in the stud. Install a new cotter pin.
18. Connect the stabilizer bar link to the lower control arm. Tighten the retaining nut to 9–12 ft. lbs. (12–16 Nm).
19. Install the wheel and tire assembly, then remove the jackstands and carefully lower the vehicle.
20. Check the front end alignment.

Stabilizer Bar

REMOVAL & INSTALLATION

1. Raise the front of the vehicle and place jackstands under the lower control arms.
2. Disconnect the stabilizer bar from the links and the insulator mounting clamps. Remove the stabilizer bar.
3. Cut the worn insulators from the stabilizer bar.
4. Installation is the reverse of the removal procedure. Coat the necessary parts of the stabilizer bar with rubber lubricant prior to installation.

Spindle (Steering Knuckle)

REMOVAL & INSTALLATION

1. Raise and support the front end on jackstands placed under the frame rails.
2. Remove the wheels.
3. Remove the calipers and suspend them out of the way.
4. Remove the hub and rotor assemblies.
5. Remove the rotor dust shields.
6. Unbolt the stabilizer links from the control arms.
7. Using a separator, disconnect the tie rod ends from the spindle.
8. Remove the cotter pin and loosen the ball joint stud nut a few turns. Don't remove it at this time!
9. Using a hammer, tap the spindle boss sharply to relieve stud pressure.
10. Support the lower control arm with a floor jack, compress the coil spring and remove the stud nut.
11. Remove the two bolts and nuts attaching the spindle to the strut. Compress the strut until working clearance is obtained.
12. Remove the spindle.

To install:

13. Place the spindle on the ball joint stud, and install the stud nut, but don't tighten it yet.
14. Lower the strut until the attaching holes are aligned with the holes in the spindle. Install two new bolts and nuts.
15. Tighten the ball stud nut to 80–120 ft. lbs. (108–163 Nm) and install the cotter pin.
16. Tighten the strut-to-spindle attaching nuts to 140–200 ft. lbs. (190–271 Nm).
17. Install the stabilizer links. Torque the nuts to 6–17 ft. lbs. (8–23 Nm).
18. Lower the floor jack.
19. Attach the tie rod ends and torque the nuts to 35–47 ft. lbs. (47–64 Nm).
20. Install the rotor dust shields.
21. Install the hub and rotor assemblies.
22. Reposition and secure the brake calipers.
23. Install the wheels.
24. Remove the jackstands and carefully lower the vehicle.

Front Wheel Bearings

ADJUSTMENT

➧ See Figure 16

1. Raise and safely support the front of the vehicle using jackstands.
2. Remove the wheel or hub cover and grease cap.
3. Remove the cotter pin and nut retainer.
4. Loosen the adjusting nut three turns and rock the wheel back and forth a few times to release the brake pads from the rotor.
5. While rotating the wheel and hub assembly in a clockwise direction, tighten the adjusting nut to 17–25 ft. lbs. (23–24 Nm).
6. Back off the adjusting nut one-half turn, then retighten to 10–28 inch lbs. (1.1–3.2 Nm).
7. Install the nut retainer and a new cotter pin. Check the wheel rotation. If it is noisy or rough, the bearings need to be cleaned, repacked or replaced.
8. Lower the vehicle. Before driving, pump the brake pedal several times to restore the proper brake pedal travel.

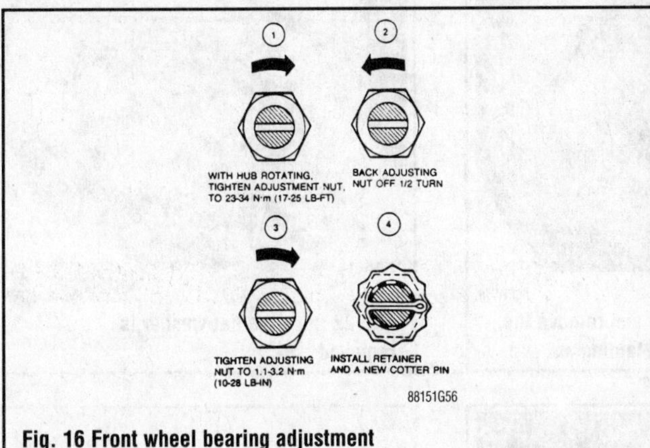

Fig. 16 Front wheel bearing adjustment

REMOVAL & INSTALLATION

➧ See Figures 17 thru 28

Before handling the bearings, learn these rules.

You should ALWAYS:

- Remove all dirt from the housing before exposing the bearing.
- Treat a used bearing as gently as you would a new one.
- Work with clean tools in clean surroundings.
- Use clean, dry canvas or plastic gloves.
- Always use clean, fresh solvents and lubricants.
- Place the bearings on clean paper to dry.
- Cover disassembled bearings to prevent rust and contamination by dirt.
- Use clean rags when necessary.
- Keep the bearings in oiled, moisture-proof paper when they are to be stored or out of service for more than a short period.
- Clean the inside of the housing before replacing the bearing.

You should NEVER:

- Work in dirty surroundings.
- Use dirty, chipped or damaged tools.
- Work on wooden surfaces or use wooden mallets.
- Handle the bearings with dirty or wet hands.
- Use gasoline for cleaning anything.
- Use compressed air to spin-dry the bearings. They will be damaged.
- Spin the bearings before cleaning them.
- Use dirty rags or cotton waste to wipe bearings.
- Allow the bearing to be scratched, dropped or nicked during service.

1. Loosen the lug nuts on the wheel(s) being removed, then raise and support the vehicle safely using jackstands.
2. Remove the wheel and tire assembly. Remove the caliper and suspend it with a length of wire; do not allow it to hang by the hose.
3. CAREFULLY Pry off the dust cap, making sure not to distort the flange. Tap out and discard the cotter pin. Remove the nut retainer.
4. Loosen and remove the adjusting nut, along with the flat washer (the outer bearing cone and roller assembly may come off at this time.
5. Being careful not to drop the outer bearing (if it is still in the hub), pull off the brake disc and wheel hub assembly.
6. Remove the inner grease seal using a seal removal tool. If necessary, a small prybar may be used, but be VERY CAREFUL not to damage the bearing or the race. Remove the inner wheel bearing.
7. Clean the wheel bearings with solvent and inspect them for pits, scratches and excessive wear. Wipe all the old grease from the hub and inspect the bearing races. If either bearings or races are damaged, the bearing races must be removed; new bearings and races should then be installed as a set.
8. If the bearings are to be replaced, drive out the races from the hub using a brass drift.
9. Make certain the spindle, hub and bearing assemblies are clean prior to installation.

To install:

10. If the bearing races were removed, install new ones using a bearing race installer (a suitably sized round driver).
11. Pack the bearings with a bearing packer. If done by hand, take great care to force as much grease as possible between the rollers and the cages, scoop the grease in from the top and bottom of the bearing cages.
12. Coat the inner surface of the hub and bearing races with grease.
13. Install the inner bearing in the hub. Lubricate the lip of the new seal with grease, then being careful not to distort it, install the oil seal with the lip facing the bearing. Drive the seal in until its outer edge is even with the edge of the hub. A seal installer is best to use for this, but any suitably sized and SMOOTH EDGED round driver can be used, including a piece of plastic pipe or a socket.
14. Install the hub/disc assembly on the spindle; being careful not to damage the oil seal.
15. Install the outer bearing, flat washer and spindle nut.
16. Properly adjust the wheel bearings. For details, refer to the procedure and the illustration found earlier in this section.
17. Install the grease cap, taking care not to distort or damage the cap, but also making sure it is fully seated.
18. Install the caliper.
19. Install the wheel and tire assembly.
20. Remove the jackstands and carefully lower the vehicle.

✲✲ CAUTION

BE SURE to pump the brake pedal to seat the pads before attempting to move the vehicle.

88151P62

Fig. 17 Carefully remove the grease cap from the wheel hub and disc

88151P63

Fig. 18 Straighten the ends of the cotter pin . . .

88151P64

Fig. 19 . . . then remove the cotter pin from the spindle

88151P65

Fig. 20 Remove the castellated nut retainer . . .

88151P66

Fig. 21 . . . then loosen and remove the wheel bearing and hub retaining nut

88151P67

Fig. 22 Once the flat washer is removed . . .

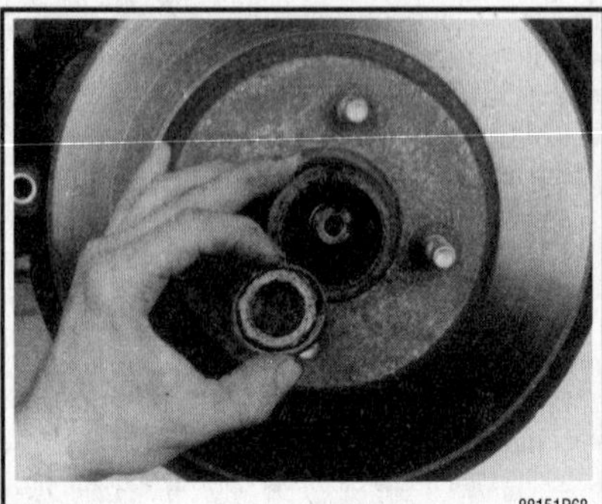

88151P68

Fig. 23 . . . the outer bearing is usually free for removal (or it sometimes just fall right out)

88151P69

Fig. 24 Remove the hub and disc assembly (along with the inner bearing) from the spindle

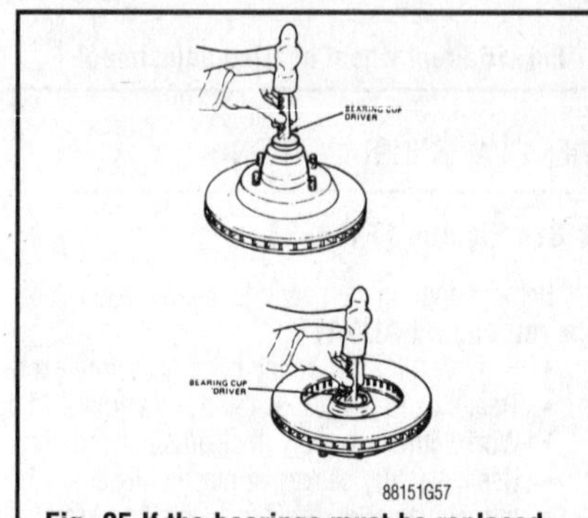

88151G57

Fig. 25 If the bearings must be replaced, new races must be installed using appropriately sized drivers

TCCS8033

Fig. 26 Thoroughly pack the bearing with fresh, high temperature wheel bearing grease before installation

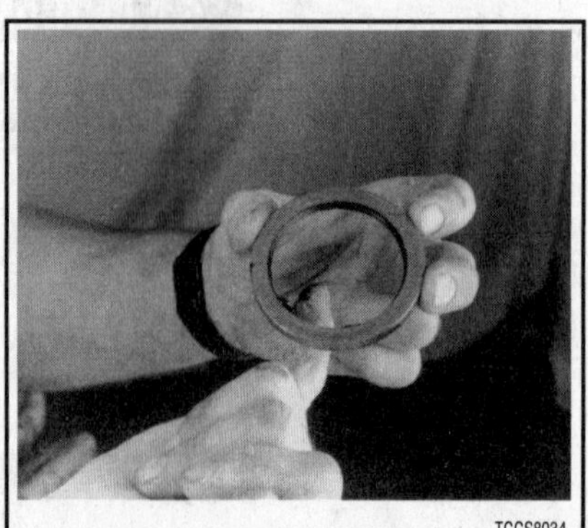

TCCS8034

Fig. 27 Apply a thin coat of fresh grease to the new seal's inner bearing lip

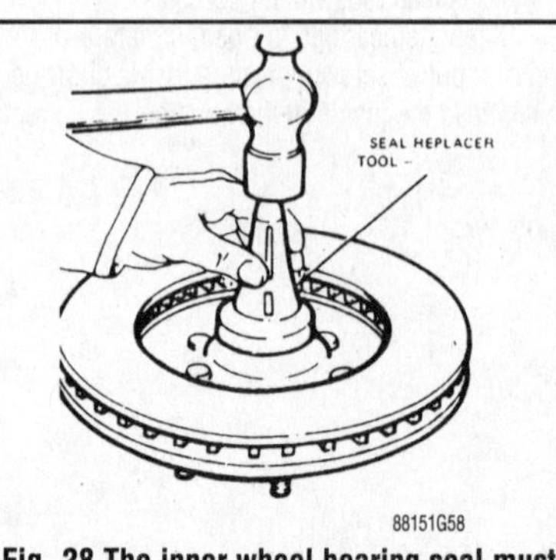

88151G58

Fig. 28 The inner wheel bearing seal must also be driven in place using an installation tool

WHEEL ALIGNMENT

Front End Alignment

If the tires are worn unevenly, if the vehicle is not stable on the highway or if the handling seems uneven in spirited driving, wheel alignment should be checked. If an alignment problem is suspected, first check tire inflation and look for other possible causes such as worn suspension and steering components, accident damage or unmatched tires. Repairs may be necessary before the wheels can be properly aligned. Wheel alignment requires sophisticated equipment and should only be performed at a properly equipped shop.

The following conditions should be met before checking the wheel alignment:

- The spare tire, jack and jack handle should all be installed in their normal positions. All other loads should be removed from the vehicle.
- The front seats should be moved to the rear-most setting.
- All tires should be checked and inflated to the proper cold pressure specification.
- All excessive rod dirt, deposits and mud should be removed from the undercarriage.

CAMBER

See Figure 29

Looking at the wheels from the front of the vehicle, camber adjustment is the tilt of the wheel. When the wheel is tilted in at the top, this is called negative camber. When you are driving the vehicle through a turn, a slight amount of negative camber helps maximize contact of the outside tire with the road. Too much negative camber makes the vehicle unstable in a straight line.

On Ford Mustangs, the camber is adjusted by removing the pop-rivet in the camber plate. Loosen the 3 nuts which hold the strut mount to the body apron, then move the top of the strut to the desired position. Once the strut is in position, the top nuts should be tightened to 40–55 ft. lbs. (54–75 Nm) and a new pop-rivet should be installed.

CASTER

See Figure 30

Wheel alignment is defined by three different adjustments in three planes. Looking at the vehicle from the side, caster angle describes the steering axis rather than a wheel angle. The steering knuckle is attached to the strut at the top and the control arm at the bottom. The wheel pivots around the line between these points to steer the vehicle. When the upper point is tilted back, this is described as positive caster. Having a positive caster tends to make the wheels self-centering, increasing directional stability. Excessive positive caster makes the wheels hard to steer, while an uneven caster will cause a pull to one side. Caster is usually determined by the suspension components (in a fixed position by body geometry) and is usually not adjustable.

TOE-IN

See Figures 31 and 32

Looking down at the wheels from above the vehicle, toe alignment is the distance between the front of the wheels relative to the distance between the back of the same wheels. If the wheels are closer at the front, they are said to be toed-in or to have a negative toe. A small amount of negative toe enhances directional stability and provides a smoother ride on the highway.

Toe-In Adjustment

See Figures 31 and 32

1. Turn the steering wheel, from left to right, several times and center.

If car has power steering, start the engine before centering the steering wheel.

2. Secure the centered steering wheel with a steering wheel holder, or any device that will keep it centered.
3. Release the tie rod end bellows clamps so the bellows will not twist while an

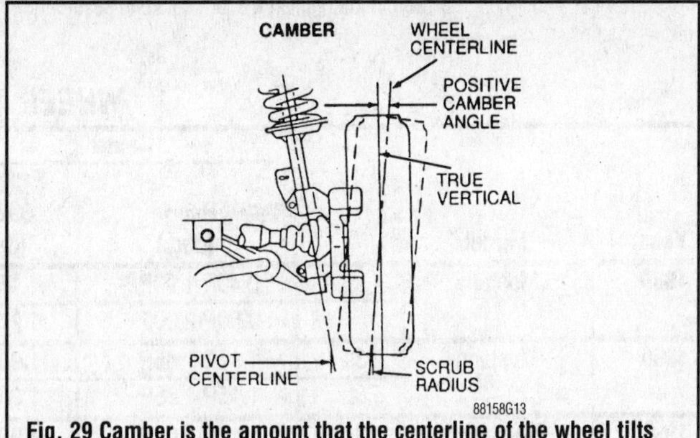

Fig. 29 Camber is the amount that the centerline of the wheel tilts inward or outward from true vertical

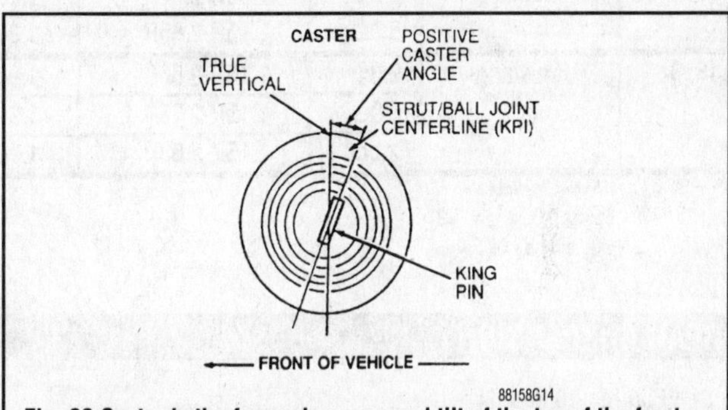

Fig. 30 Caster is the forward or rearward tilt of the top of the front-wheel spindle

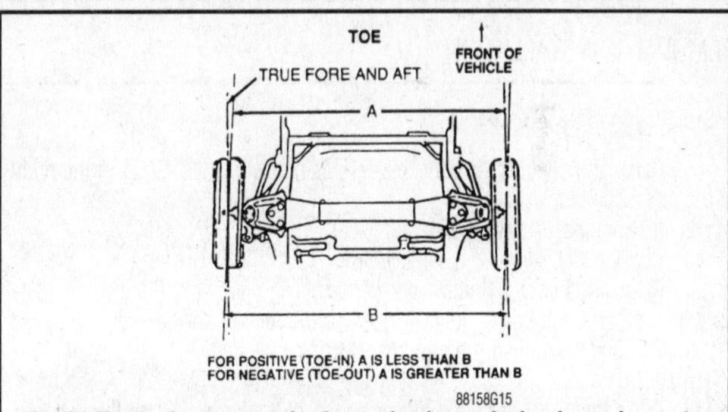

Fig. 31 Toe is the amount the front wheels are facing inward or outward with the steering wheel in the center position

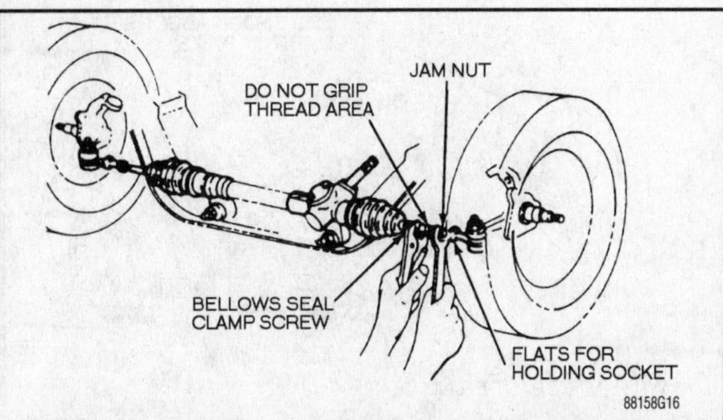

Fig. 32 Toe is adjusted at the tie rod ends using a threaded adjuster turnbuckle

adjustment is made. Loosen the jam nuts on the tie rod ends. Adjust the left and right connector sleeves until each wheel has one-half of the desired toe setting.

4. After the adjustment has been made, tighten the jam nuts and secure the bellows clamps.

5. Release the steering wheel lock and check for steering wheel center. Readjust, if necessary until the steering wheel is centered, and the toe is within specs.

WHEEL ALIGNMENT

Year	Model		Caster Range (deg.)	Caster Preferred Setting (deg.)	Camber Range (deg.)	Camber Preferred Setting (deg.)	Toe-in (in.)	Steering Axis Inclination (deg.)
1989	Mustang	1	0.40P-1.90P	1.15P	0.85N-0.65P	0.10N	0.19P	15.72
		2	0.50P-2.00P	1.27P	0.60N-0.90P	0.14P	0.19P	15.72
1990	Mustang	2.3L	1.15P-2.65P	1.90P	1.25N-0.25P	0.50N	0.12N	15.72
		5.0L	1.15P-2.65P	1.90P	1.35N-0.15P	0.60N	0.12N	15.72
1991	Mustang	2.3L	1.15P-2.65P	1.90P	1.25N-0.25P	0.50N	0.12N	15.72
		5.0L	1.15P-2.65P	1.90P	1.35N-0.15P	0.60N	0.12N	15.72
1992	Mustang	2.3L	1.15P-2.65P	1.90P	1.25N-0.25P	0.50N	0.12N	15.72
		5.0L	1.15P-2.65P	1.90P	1.35N-0.15P	0.60N	0.12N	15.72
1993	Mustang	2.3L	1.15P-2.65P	1.90P	1.25N-0.25P	0.50N	0.12N	NA
		5.0L	1.15P-2.65P	1.90P	1.35N-0.15P	0.60N	0.12N	NA
		Cobra	1.15P-2.65P	1.90P	1.35N-0.15P	0.60N	0	NA

NA: Not Available
1 Except 5.0L engine - GT
2 5.0L engine - GT

88158C01

REAR SUSPENSION

➧ See Figures 33 and 34

Coil Springs

REMOVAL & INSTALLATION

➧ See Figures 33 and 34

1. Raise and support the vehicle safely using jackstands. Support the body at the rear body crossmember.
2. If equipped, remove the stabilizer bar.
3. Support the axle with a suitable jack.
4. Place another jack under the lower arm axle pivot bolt. Remove and discard the bolt and nut. Lower the jack slowly until the coil spring load is relieved.
5. Remove the coil spring and insulator from the vehicle.

To install:

6. Place the upper spring insulator on top of the spring. Place the lower spring insulator on the lower arm.

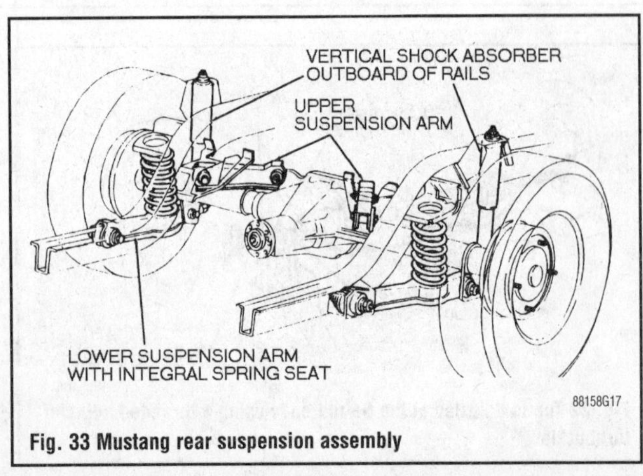

Fig. 33 Mustang rear suspension assembly

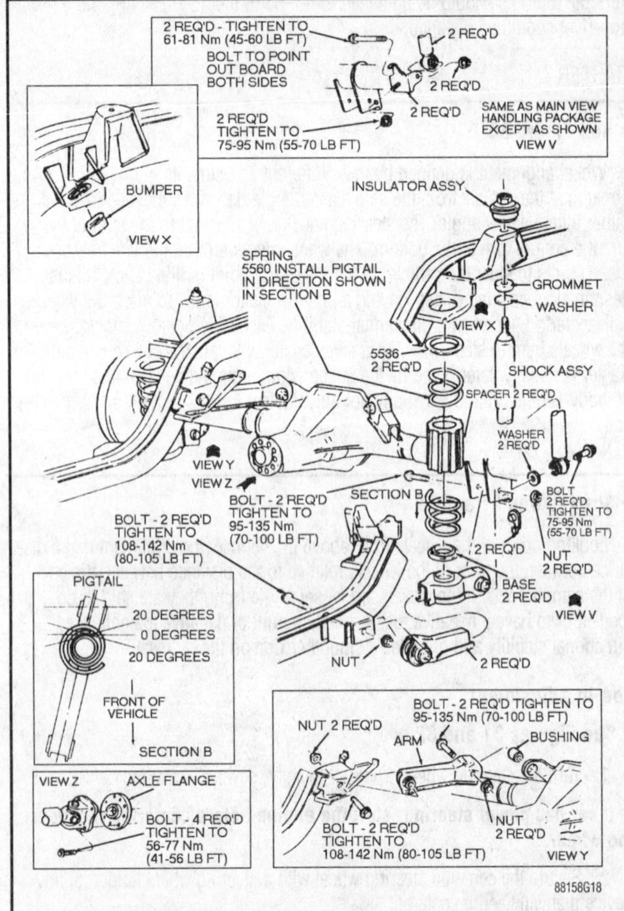

Fig. 34 Exploded view of the rear suspension assembly

7. Position the coil spring on the lower arm spring seat, so the pigtail on the lower arm is at the rear of the vehicle and pointing toward the left side of the vehicle.
8. Slowly raise the jack until the arm is in position. Insert a new rear pivot bolt and nut, with the nut facing outward. Do not tighten at this time.
9. Raise the axle to curb height. Tighten the lower arm-to-axle pivot bolt to 70–100 ft. lbs. (95–135 Nm).
10. If equipped, install the stabilizer bar.
11. Remove the crossmember supports and carefully lower the vehicle.

Shock Absorbers

TESTING & INSPECTION

Bounce Test

Each shock absorber can be tested by bouncing the corner of the vehicle until maximum up and down movement is obtained. Let go of the vehicle and watch. It should stop bouncing in 1–2 bounces. If not, the shock should be inspected for damage and possibly replaced.

Shock Mounts

Check the shock mountings for worn or defective grommets, loose mounting nuts, interference or missing bump stops. If no apparent defects are noted, check the shock for hydraulic leaks.

Checking for Hydraulic Leaks

Disconnect each shock lower mount and pull down on the shock until it is fully extended. inspect for leaks in the seal area. Shock absorber fluid is very thin and has a characteristic odor and dark brown color. Don't confuse the glossy paint on some shocks with leaking fluid. A slight trace of fluid is a normal condition; they are designed to seep a certain amount of fluid past the seals for lubrication. If you are in doubt as to whether the fluid on the shock is coming from the shock itself or from some other source, wipe the seal area clean and manually operate the shock (refer to that procedure later in this section). Fluid will appear if the unit is leaking.

Manually Operating the Shocks

It may be necessary to fabricate a holding fixture for certain types of shock absorbers. If a suspected problem is in the front shocks, disconnect both front shock lower mountings.

Grip the lower end of the shock and pull down (rebound stroke) and then push up (compression stroke). The control arms will limit the movement of front shocks during the compression stroke. Compare the rebound resistance of both shocks and compare the compression resistance. Usually any shock showing a noticeable difference will be the one at fault.

If the shock has internal noises, extend the shock fully then exert an extra pull. If a small additional movement is felt, this usually means a loose piston and the shock should be replaced. Other noises that are cause for replacing shocks are a squeal after a full stroke in both directions, a clicking noise on fast reverse and a lag at reversal near mid-stroke.

REMOVAL & INSTALLATION

▸ See Figures 35, 36, 37, 38 and 39

➡Some Ford Mustangs use Torx® head bolts to retain the shocks at the lower mounts. Check to make sure you have the proper drivers before beginning this procedure.

1. Raise the vehicle and support it safely using jackstands under the rear axle housing.
2. Open the luggage compartment, or on Mustang 3-door models, open the hatch door.
3. Remove the trim panels, as necessary, to gain access to the shock absorber.
4. Remove the shock absorber retaining nut washer and insulator.

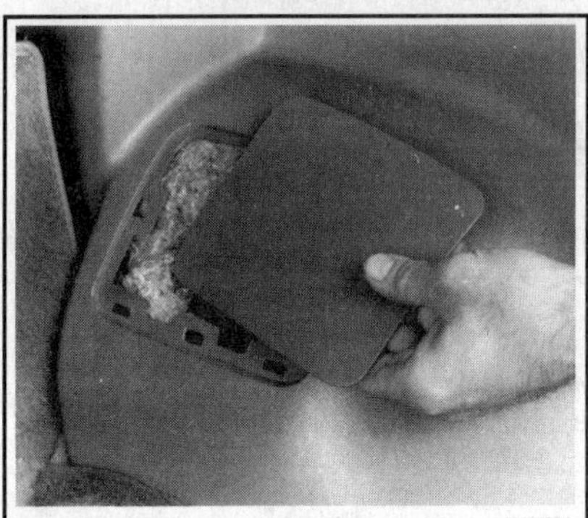
88158P04
Fig. 35 Remove the trim panel cover for access to the top of the shock

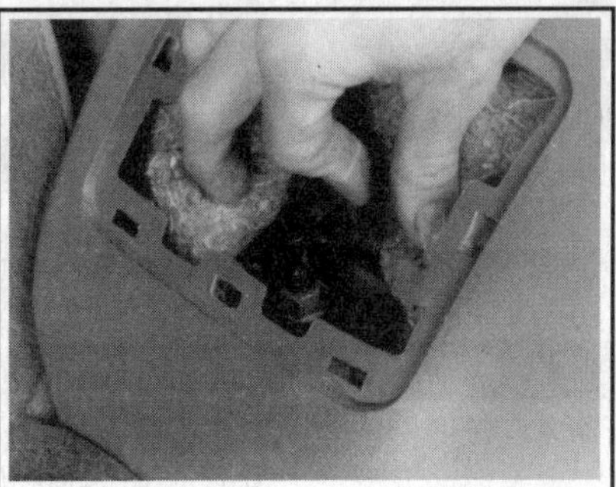
88158P05
Fig. 36 You may have to pull back the sound deadening insulation to see the shock

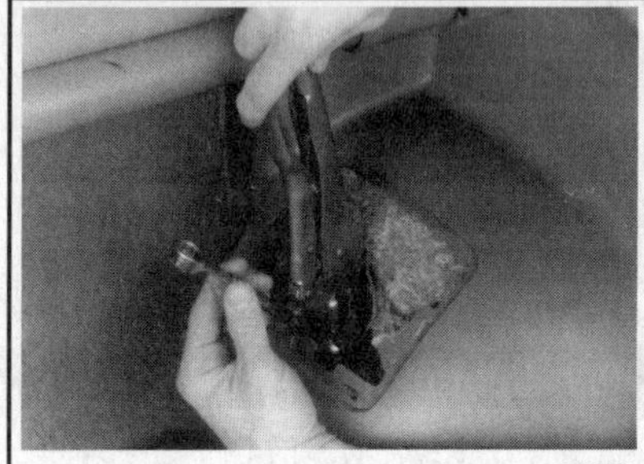
88158P06
Fig. 37 Loosen the top mounting nut—you may have to use an open-end wrench so you can keep the top of the shock from spinning

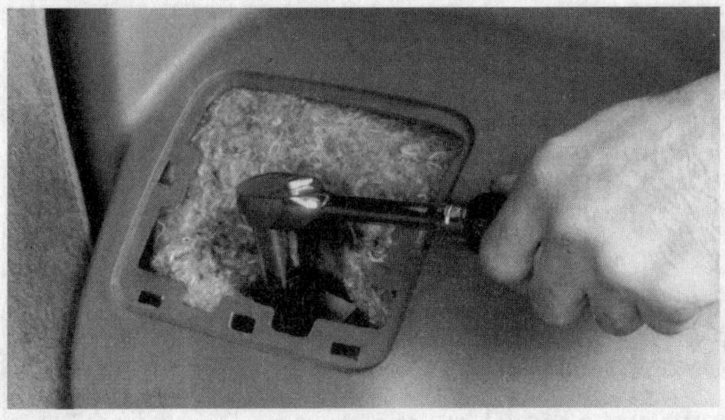
88158P07
Fig. 38 Once loosened, the top mounting nut is quickly removed using a ratchet and deep-well socket

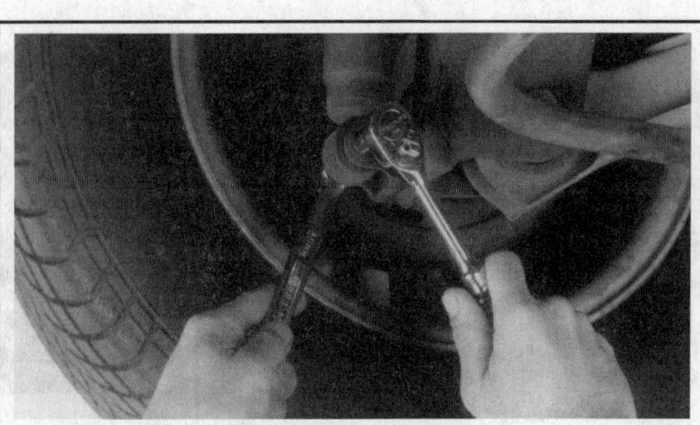
88158P08
Fig. 39 Loosen and remove the lower mounting fasteners, then remove the shock from the vehicle

5. Remove the shock absorber bolt, washer and nut at the lower arm and remove the shock absorber.

➡**Vehicles are equipped with gas pressurized shock absorbers which will extend unassisted.**

To install:

6. Prime the new shock absorber as follows:
   a. With the shock absorber right side up, extend it fully.
   b. Turn the shock upside down and fully compress it.
   c. Repeat the previous two steps at least three times to make sure any trapped air has been expelled.
7. Place the inner washer and insulator on the upper retaining stud and position the stud through the shock tower mounting hole.
8. Attach the lower end of the shock absorber with the retaining bolt and nut. Tighten the bolt to 55–70 ft. lbs. (75–95 Nm).
9. Install the upper insulator, washer and retaining nut and tighten to 27 ft. lbs. (37–47 Nm).
10. Remove the jackstands and carefully lower the vehicle.

Axle Dampers

REMOVAL & INSTALLATION

➧ **See Figures 40, 41 and 42**

Models equipped with the handling suspension package are equipped with an axle damper (a horizontal shock absorber for the rear axle).

1. Loosen the lug nuts on the wheel which is being removed (on the same side as the axle damper).
2. Raise and support the rear of the vehicle safely.
3. Remove the tire and wheel assembly.
4. Loosen and remove the front retaining pivot bolt (damper-to-rear axle). A backup wrench should be used to keep the fasteners from spinning.
5. Loosen and remove the rear axle damper retaining nut (damper-to-frame rail).
6. Remove the damper from the vehicle.

To install:

7. Position the damper to the vehicle and loosely install the fasteners.
8. Tighten the rear retaining nut and then the front retaining bolt to 57–75 ft. lbs. (76–103 Nm).
9. Install the tire and wheel assembly.
10. Remove the jackstands and carefully lower the vehicle.

Rear Control Arms

REMOVAL & INSTALLATION

Upper Arm

➡**For safety, even if only one arm needs to be replaced, the other arm should be replaced as well.**

1. Raise and support the vehicle safely using jackstands at the rear crossmember.
2. Remove and discard the upper arm pivot bolts and nuts, then remove the control arm.

To install:

3. Place the upper arm into the bracket of the body side rail. Install a new pivot bolt and nut with the nut facing outboard. Do not tighten at this time.
4. Using a jack, raise the suspension until the upper arm-to-axle pivot hole is in position with the hole in the axle bushing. Install a new pivot bolt and nut with the nut facing inboard.
5. Raise the suspension to curb height. Tighten the front upper arm bolt to 70–100 ft. lbs. (95–135 Nm) and the rear upper arm bolt to 80–105 ft. lbs. (108–142 Nm).
6. Remove the jackstand and carefully lower the vehicle.

Lower Arm

➡**For safety, even if only one arm needs to be replaced, the other arm should be replaced as well.**

1. Raise and support the vehicle safely using jackstands at the rear crossmember.
2. If equipped, remove the stabilizer bar.
3. Place a jack under the lower arm-to-axle pivot bolt. Remove and discard the bolt and nut. Lower the jack slowly until the coil spring can be removed.
4. Remove and discard the lower arm-to-frame pivot bolt and nut. Remove the lower arm.

To install:

5. Position the lower arm assembly into the front arm bracket. Install a new pivot bolt and nut with the nut facing outwards. Do not tighten at this time.
6. Position the coil spring on the lower arm spring seat, so the pigtail on the lower arm is at the rear of the vehicle and pointing toward the left side of the vehicle.
7. Slowly raise the jack until the arm is in position. Insert a new rear pivot bolt and nut with the nut facing outward. Do not tighten at this time.
8. Raise the axle to curb height. Tighten the lower arm front bolt to 80–105 ft. lbs. (108–142 Nm) and the rear bolt to 70–100 ft. lbs. (95–135 Nm).
9. If equipped, install the stabilizer bar.
10. Remove the jackstands from the crossmember and carefully lower the vehicle.

Sway Bar

REMOVAL & INSTALLATION

➧ **See Figure 43**

1. Raise and support the vehicle using jackstands.
2. Remove and discard the 4 bolts and stamped nuts attaching the stabilizer bar to the brackets in the lower control arms.
3. Remove the stabilizer bar from the vehicle.

➡**If the bar is being reinstalled, be sure to note the proper orientation. If necessary, mark one side to indicate which end should be installed on the passenger side of the vehicle.**

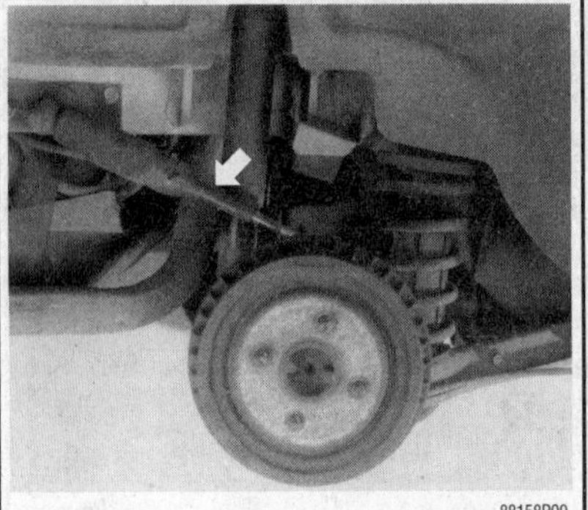

88158P09

Fig. 40 Remove the tire and wheel assembly for access to the axle damper

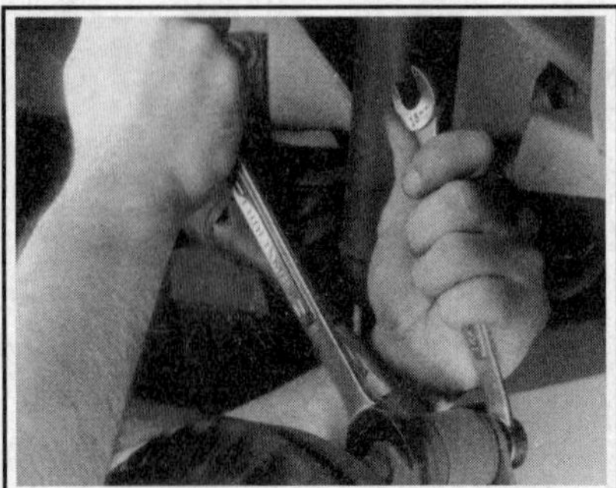

88158P10

Fig. 41 Use a backup wrench when loosening the front retaining pivot bolt from the axle

88158P11

Fig. 42 A wrench or socket and driver can be used to loosen the rear damper retaining nut

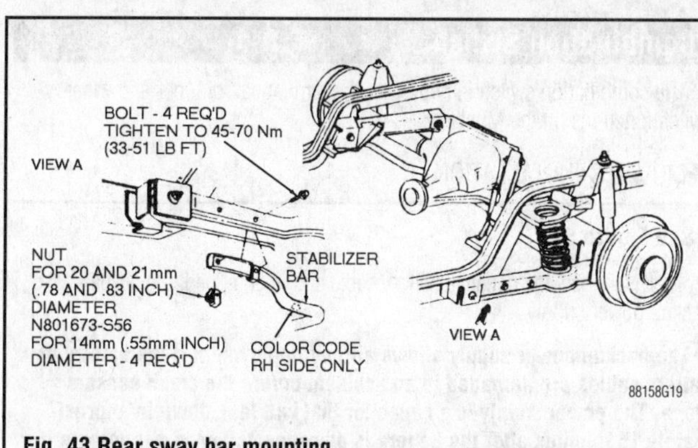

Fig. 43 Rear sway bar mounting

To install:

➡The stabilizer bar should only be installed in one direction. A color code is provided on new parts to indicate which end should be installed on the passenger side. Improper installation (reversing sides) will provide insufficient clearance between the control arm and bar during vehicle operation.

4. Install 4 NEW stamped nuts on the stabilizer bar over each retaining hole.
5. Align the 4 holes in the stabilizer bar with the holes in the lower control arm bracket holes.
6. Install 4 NEW bolts and tighten to 33–51 ft. lbs. (45–70 Nm).
7. Remove the jackstands and carefully lower the vehicle.
8. Visually inspect the bar to make sure there is adequate clearance between the bar and lower arm.

STEERING

Air Bag

DISARMING

1. Disconnect the negative battery cable and the backup power supply.

➡The backup power supply allows air bag deployment if the battery or battery cables are damaged in an accident before the crash sensors close. The power supply is a capacitor that will leak down in approximately 15 minutes after the battery is disconnected or in one minute if the battery positive cable is grounded. The backup power supply must be disconnected before any air bag related service is performed.

2. Remove the four nut and washer assemblies retaining the driver air bag module to the steering wheel.
3. Disengage the driver air bag module connector and attach a jumper wire to the air bag terminals on the clockspring.
4. If equipped with a passenger air bag, open the glove compartment and rotate all the way down, past the stops. Disengage the passenger air bag connector and attach a jumper wire to the air bag terminals on the wiring harness side of the passenger air bag module connector.
5. Reverse these steps to arm the air bag assembly only AFTER all work has been finished.

Steering Wheel

✲✲ CAUTION

If equipped with an air bag, the negative battery cable and air bag backup power supply must be disconnected, before working on the system. Failure to do so may result in deployment of the air bag and possible personal injury.

REMOVAL & INSTALLATION

With Air Bag

➧ See Figure 44

1. Center the front wheels to the straight ahead position.
2. Disconnect the negative battery cable and air bag backup power supply to disarm the air bag assembly.

➡The backup power supply allows air bag deployment if the battery or battery cables are damaged in an accident before the crash sensors close. The power supply is a capacitor that will leak down in approximately 15 minutes after the battery is disconnected or in one minute if the battery positive cable is grounded. The backup power supply must be disconnected before any air bag related service is performed.

3. Remove the four air bag module retaining nuts and lift the module off the steering wheel.
4. Disengage the electrical connector from the air bag module and remove the module.

✲✲ CAUTION

When carrying a live air bag, make sure the bag and trim cover are pointed away from the body. In the unlikely event of an accidental deployment, the bag will then deploy with minimal chance of injury. In addition, when placing a live air bag on a bench or other surface, always face the bag and trim cover up, away from the surface. This will reduce the motion of the air bag if it is accidentally deployed.

5. If equipped, disengage the cruise control wire harness from the steering wheel.

➡Before removing the steering wheel be sure to matchmark the wheel and steering shaft to assure installation in the proper position.

6. Remove and discard the steering wheel fastener. Remove the steering wheel using a suitable puller. Route the contact assembly wire harness through the steering wheel as the wheel is lifted off the shaft.

➡Do not use a knock-off type steering wheel puller or strike the retaining bolt with a hammer. This could cause damage to the steering shaft bearing.

To install:

7. Make sure the front wheels are in the straight ahead position.
8. Route the contact assembly wire harness through the steering wheel opening at the 3 o'clock position and install the steering wheel on the steering shaft. The steering wheel and shaft alignment marks should be aligned. Make sure the air bag contact wire is not pinched.

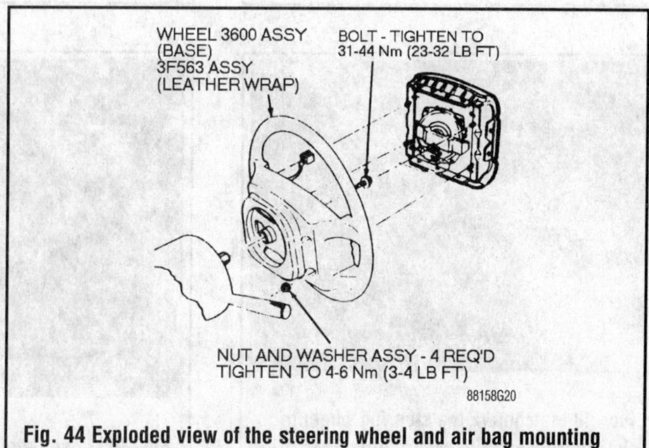

Fig. 44 Exploded view of the steering wheel and air bag mounting

9. Install a new steering wheel retaining bolt and tighten to 23–33 ft. lbs. (31–48 Nm).
10. If equipped, connect the cruise control wire harness to the wheel and snap the connector assembly into the steering wheel clip. Make sure the wiring does not get trapped between the steering wheel and contact assembly.
11. Connect the air bag wire harness to the air bag module and install the module to the steering wheel. Tighten the module retaining nuts to 3–4 ft. lbs. (4–6 Nm).
12. Connect the air bag backup power supply and negative battery cable. Verify the air bag warning indicator.

Without Air Bag

See Figures 45 thru 50

1. Disconnect the negative battery cable.
2. Remove the horn pad and cover assembly. Disengage the horn electrical connector.
3. If equipped, disconnect the cruise control switch electrical connector.

➡Before removing the steering wheel be sure to matchmark the wheel and steering shaft to assure installation in the proper position.

4. Remove and discard the steering wheel fastener. Remove the steering wheel using a suitable puller.

➡Do not use a knock-off type steering wheel puller or strike the retaining bolt with a hammer. This could cause damage to the steering shaft bearing.

To install:

5. Align the index marks on the steering wheel and shaft and install the steering wheel.
6. Install a new steering wheel retaining bolt and tighten to 30 ft. lbs. (41 Nm).
7. If equipped, engage the cruise control electrical connector.
8. Engage the horn electrical connector and install the horn pad and cover.
9. Connect the negative battery cable.

Combination Switch

The combination switch incorporates the turn signal, dimmer and wiper switch functions on the Mustang.

REMOVAL & INSTALLATION

See Figure 51

1. Disconnect the negative battery cable and, if equipped, the air bag backup power supply.

➡The backup power supply allows air bag deployment if the battery or battery cables are damaged in an accident before the crash sensors close. The power supply is a capacitor that will leak down in approximately 15 minutes after the battery is disconnected or in one minute if the battery positive cable is grounded. The backup power supply must be disconnected before any service is performed on or around the air bag.

2. Remove the shroud retaining screws, then remove the upper and lower shrouds.
3. Remove the switch retaining screws and lift up the switch assembly.
4. With the wiring exposed, carefully lift the connector retainer tabs and disengage the connectors.
5. Installation is the reverse of the removal procedure. Tighten the attaching bolts to 18–26 ft. lbs. (2–3 Nm).

Ignition Lock

REMOVAL & INSTALLATION

See Figure 52

1. Disconnect the negative battery cable and, if equipped, the air bag backup power supply.

88158P12

Fig. 45 Loosen and remove the retainers holding the horn pad to the steering wheel

88158P13

Fig. 46 Lift the horn pad for access to the wiring (you can leave the pad wiring attached if you like, then remove the wheel and pad as an assembly)

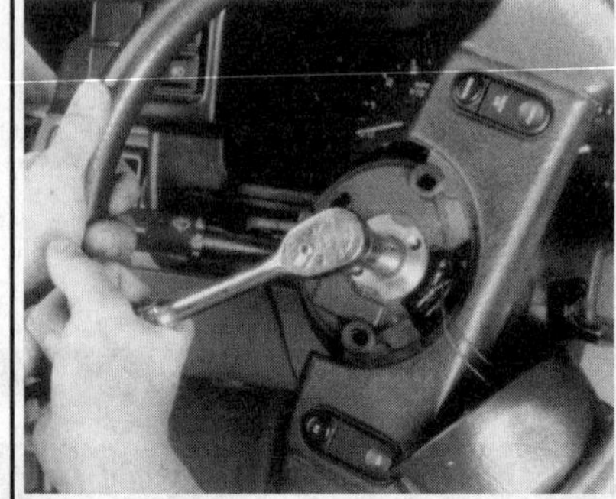

88158P14

Fig. 47 Loosen the steering wheel retaining nut

88158P15

Fig. 48 Matchmark the steering wheel to the steering shaft to assure proper installation

88158P16

Fig. 49 Loosen the steering wheel using a suitable puller

88158P17

Fig. 50 Remove the steering wheel (and in this case the horn cap) from the steering column

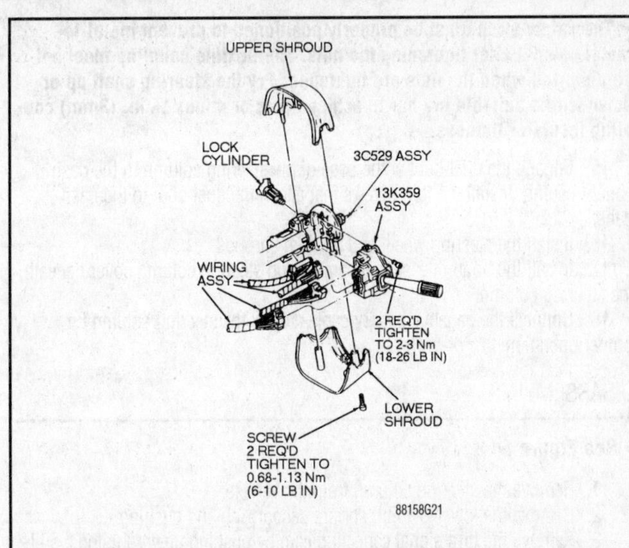

Fig. 51 Exploded view of the combination switch assembly mounting

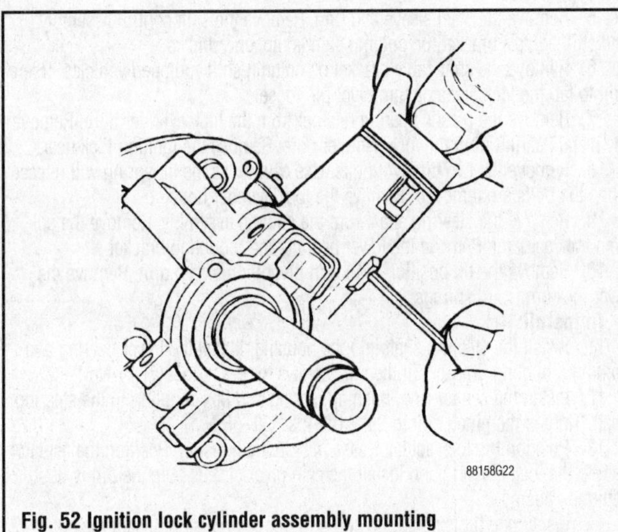

Fig. 52 Ignition lock cylinder assembly mounting

➡The backup power supply allows air bag deployment if the battery or battery cables are damaged in an accident before the crash sensors close. The power supply is a capacitor that will leak down in approximately 15 minutes after the battery is disconnected or in one minute if the battery positive cable is grounded. The backup power supply must be disconnected before any service is performed on or around the air bag.

2. On Mustangs equipped with a tilt column, remove the upper extension shroud by unsnapping the shroud retaining clip at the 9 o'clock position.
3. Remove the trim shroud halves by removing the attaching screws. Remove the electrical connector from the key warning switch.
4. Turn the ignition to the **RUN** position.
5. Place a ⅛ in. (3mm) diameter wire pin or small drift punch in the hole in the casting surrounding the lock cylinder and depress the retaining pin while pulling out on the lock cylinder to remove it from the column housing.

To install:

6. Turn the lock cylinder to the **RUN** position and depress the retaining pin. Insert the lock cylinder into its housing in the lock cylinder casting.
7. Make sure that the cylinder is fully seated and aligned in the interlocking washer before turning the key to the **OFF** position. This action will permit the cylinder retaining pin to extend into the hole in the lock cylinder housing.
8. Using the ignition key, rotate the cylinder to ensure the correct mechanical operation in all positions.
9. Connect the negative battery cable and check for proper operation in **P** or **N**. Also make sure that the start circuit cannot be actuated in **D** or **R** positions and that the column is locked in the **LOCK** position.
10. Connect the key warning buzzer electrical connector and install the trim shrouds, if required.

Ignition Switch

REMOVAL & INSTALLATION

1. Disconnect the negative battery cable and, if equipped, the air bag backup power supply.

➡The backup power supply allows air bag deployment if the battery or battery cables are damaged in an accident before the crash sensors close. The power supply is a capacitor that will leak down in approximately 15 minutes after the battery is disconnected or in one minute if the battery positive cable is grounded. The backup power supply must be disconnected before any service is performed on or around the air bag.

2. On all vehicles with a tilt column, remove the upper extension shroud by unsnapping the shroud from the retaining clips at the 9 o'clock position.
3. Remove the steering column shroud.
4. Disengage the electrical connector from the ignition switch.
5. Rotate the ignition key lock cylinder to the **RUN** position.
6. Remove the two screws attaching the ignition switch.
7. Disengage the ignition switch from the actuator pin and remove the switch.

To install:

8. Adjust the new ignition switch by sliding the carrier to the **RUN** position.
9. Check to ensure that the ignition key lock cylinder is in the **RUN** position. The **RUN** position is achieved by rotating the key lock cylinder approximately 90 degrees from the **LOCK** position.
10. Install the ignition switch onto the actuator pin.
11. Align the switch mounting holes and install the attaching screws. Tighten the screws to 50–69 inch lbs. (5.6–7.9 Nm).
12. Engage the electrical connector to the ignition switch.
13. Connect the negative battery cable. Check the ignition switch for proper function in **START** and **ACC** positions. Make sure the column is locked in the **LOCK** position.
14. Install the remaining components in the reverse order of removal.

Steering Column

REMOVAL & INSTALLATION

See Figure 53

➡The backup power supply allows air bag deployment if the battery or battery cables are damaged in an accident before the crash sensors close. The power supply is a capacitor that will leak down in approximately 15 minutes after the battery is disconnected or in one minute if the battery positive cable is grounded. The backup power supply must be disconnected before any service is performed on or around the air bag.

1. Disconnect the negative battery cable. If equipped with an air bag, disconnect the air bag backup power supply.

➡If equipped with an air bag, do not remove the steering column wheel and air bag module as an assembly unless the column is locked or the steering shaft is secured to keep it from turning. This will avoid damage to the clockspring assembly.

2. Remove the two nuts that attach the flexible coupling to the flange on the steering input shaft. Disengage the safety strap and bolt assembly from the flexible coupling. If equipped with column shift, disconnect the transmission shift rod from the transmission control selector lever.
3. If equipped with column shift, remove the shift linkage grommet and replace with new using shift linkage insulator tool T67P–7341–A or equivalent.

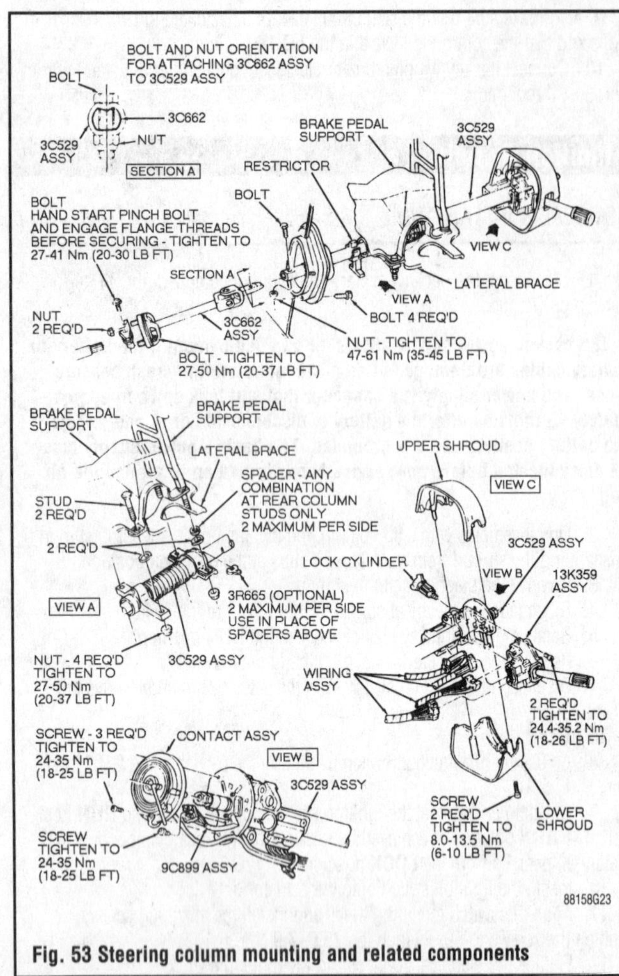

Fig. 53 Steering column mounting and related components

4. Remove the steering wheel and the steering column trim shrouds.
5. Remove the steering column cover and hood release mechanism directly under the column.
6. Disengage the electrical connectors to the steering column switches.
7. If equipped with column shift, loosen the four nuts holding the column to the brake pedal support, allowing the column to be lowered enough for access to the shift indicator lever and cable assembly.

➡Be careful not to lower the column too far, so the plastic lever or cable is not damaged due to the weight of the column.

8. If equipped with column shift, reach between the steering column and instrument panel and gently lift the shift indicator cable off the cleat on the shift indicator lever. Remove the shift indicator cable clamp from the steering column tube.
9. Remove the four screws that attach the dust boot to the dash panel.
10. Remove the four attaching nuts holding the column to the brake pedal support. Lower the column to clear the four mounting bolts and pull the column out, so the U-joint assembly will pass through the clearance hole in the dash panel.

To install:

11. Install the steering column by inserting the U-joint assembly through the opening in the dash panel. Be careful not to damage the column during installation.
12. Align the four bolts on the brake pedal support with the mounting holes on the column collar and bracket. If equipped with floor shift, attach the nuts and tighten to 20–37 ft. lbs. (27–50 Nm). On column shift, attach the nuts loosely, so the column will hang with a clearance between the column and instrument panel.
13. Engage the electrical connectors to the steering column switches.
14. Engage the safety strap and bolt assembly to the flange on the steering gear (rack and pinion) input shaft. Install the two nuts that attach the steering column lower shaft and U-joint assembly to the flange on the steering gear input shaft. Tighten the nuts to 20–37 ft. lbs. (27–50 Nm).

➡The safety strap must be properly positioned to prevent metal-to-metal contact after tightening the nuts. The flexible coupling must not be distorted when the nuts are tightened. Pry the steering shaft up or down with a suitable pry bar to achieve plus or minus ⅛ in. (3mm) coupling insulator flatness.

15. Engage the dust boot at the base of the steering column to the dash panel opening. Install the four screws that attach the dust boot to the dash panel.
16. Install the steering wheel and the trim shrouds.
17. Install the hood release mechanism and steering column cover beneath the steering column.
18. Connect the negative battery cable. Check the steering column for proper operation.

DISASSEMBLY

➧ See Figure 54

1. Remove the steering column from the vehicle.
2. Remove the lower U-joint, spring, sensor ring and bushing.
3. Remove the turn signal canceling cam by pushing upward using a suitable tool. Note the direction of the flush surface.
4. Remove the ignition switch assembly. Remove the upper snapring and coil spring.
5. Remove the steel sleeve and ring. Remove the shift control assembly and shift control bracket, on column shift equipped vehicles.
6. Remove the shift cable bracket on column shift equipped vehicles. Use a drift to tap the lock actuator cam pivot pin loose.
7. Remove the plastic bearing retainer from the lock cylinder bore. Remove the metal bearing from the lock cylinder bore. Remove the ignition lock gear.
8. Remove the two tilt pivot bolts. Use caution as the tilt spring will release when the bolts are removed. Remove the lock cylinder housing.
9. Remove the steering shaft from the column assembly. Remove the column lock actuator. Remove the lower bearing and mounting bracket.
10. Remove the tilt position lever arm pivot pin using a drift. Remove the lever lock arms and springs.

To install:

11. Install the steering shaft into the housing. Install the lower bearing and column mounting bracket. Tighten the screws to 5–8 ft. lbs. (7–11 Nm).
12. Install the sensor ring, bushing, spring and flex coupling to the steering shaft. Tighten the pinch bolt to 29–41 ft. lbs. (39–56 Nm).
13. Position the lock actuator assembly in the housing. Position the actuator cam in the lock housing and install the cam pivot pin. Be sure the pin is flush with the housing.
14. Install one tilt lever spring and arm into the housing. Install the outer lever spring and arm with the pivot pin. Tap the pin in place while driving out the drift.
15. Support the housing in a vise and drive the pin flush with the housing. Position the two nuts or spacers to hold the tilt lock arms away from the housing.
16. Position the tilt spring on the lock housing. With an assistant, install the lock housing and pivot bolts. Torque them to 14–20 ft. lbs. (19–27 Nm). Lube the pivot bolts with grease before installation.
17. Install the steel sleeve and ring gear over the steering shaft and onto the upper bearing.
18. Install the spring and a new snapring on the top side of the spring using a ¾ in. X 2¼ in. (19mm X 57mm) PVC pipe. Install the turn signal cancel cam, flush surface UP.
19. Install the ignition switch. Align the pin from the switch with the slot in the lock/column assembly. Position the slot in the assembly with the index mark on the casting. Torque the retaining screws 5–8 inch lbs. (0.6–0.9 Nm).
20. Install the ignition lock gear. Coat the gear with grease before installation.
21. Install the metal bearing. Coat the metal bearing with grease before installation.
22. Install the plastic bearing retainer. Install the shift control tube assembly. Coat the bushings with grease prior to installation. Torque the retaining screws 5–8 ft. lbs. (7–11 Nm)
23. Install the shift cable bracket on the lower column bearing assembly.
24. Install the steering column in the vehicle.

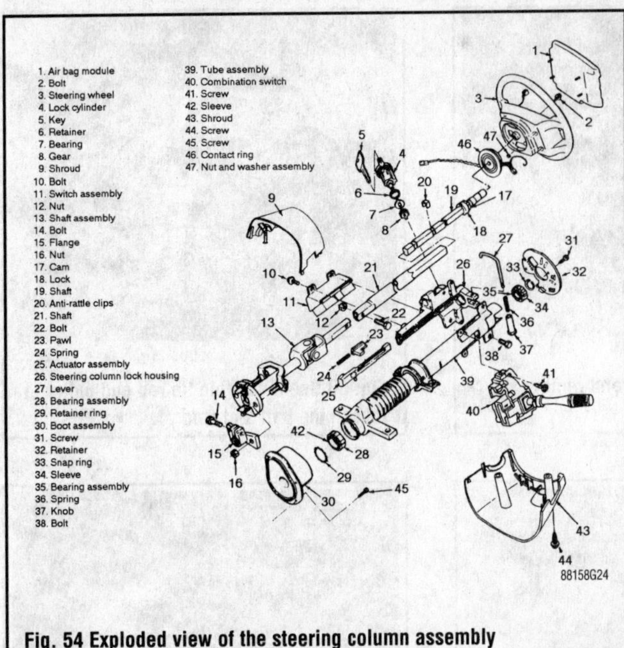

Fig. 54 Exploded view of the steering column assembly

Power Steering Rack and Pinion

ADJUSTMENT

Rack Yoke Plug Clearance

➧ See Figure 55

The rack yoke plug clearance adjustment is not a normal service adjustment. It is only required when the input shaft and valve assembly is removed.

1. Clean the exterior of the steering rack thoroughly.
2. Install two long bolts and washers through the bushings and attach the rack to a bench mounted holding fixture T57L–500–B or equivalent.
3. Do not remove the external pressure lines, unless they are leaking or damaged. If the lines are removed, install new seals. If the lines are damaged, they must be replaced.
4. Drain the power steering fluid by rotating the input shaft lock-to-lock twice using pinion shaft torque adapter tool T74P–3504–R or equivalent. Cover the ports on the valve housing with a shop cloth while draining the gear to avoid possible oil spray.

Fig. 55 A dial or deflecting beam torque wrench is necessary for steering rack yoke plug clearance adjustment

5. Insert an inch pound torque wrench with a maximum capacity of 30–60 inch lbs. (3.4–6.8 Nm) into the pinion shaft torque adapter tool. Position the adapter and wrench on the input shaft splines.
6. Loosen the yoke plug locknut with pinion housing locknut wrench T78P–3504–H or equivalent. Loosen the yoke plug with a ¾ in. socket wrench.
7. With the rack at the center of travel, tighten the yoke plug to 45–50 inch lbs. (5.0–5.6 Nm). Clean the threads of the yoke plug prior to tightening to prevent a false reading.
8. Back off the yoke plug approximately ⅛ turn, 44 degrees minimum to 54 degrees maximum until the torque required to initiate and sustain rotation of the input shaft is 7–18 inch lbs. (0.8–2.0 Nm) for base power steering or 7–24 inch lbs. (0.8–3.0 Nm) for handling package.
9. Place pinion housing yoke locknut wrench T78P–3504–H or equivalent, on the yoke plug locknut. While holding the yoke plug, tighten the locknut to 44–66 ft. lbs. (60–89 Nm).

➡Do not allow the yoke plug to move while tightening or the preload will be affected.

10. Install the steering rack in the vehicle.

REMOVAL & INSTALLATION

1. Disconnect the negative battery cable. Turn the ignition switch to the **RUN** position.
2. Raise and support the vehicle safely using jackstands. Position a drain pan to catch the fluid from the power steering lines.
3. Remove the one bolt retaining the flexible coupling to the input shaft.
4. Remove the front wheel and tire assemblies. Remove the cotter pins and nuts from the tie rod ends and separate the tie rod studs from the spindles.
5. Remove the two nuts, insulator washers and bolts retaining the steering rack to the crossmember. Remove the front rubber insulators.
6. Position the rack to allow access to the hydraulic lines and disconnect the lines.
7. Remove the steering rack.

To install:

8. Install new plastic seals on the hydraulic line fittings.
9. Install the rack on the mounting spikes and install the hydraulic lines. Tighten the fittings to 10–15 ft. lbs. (14–20 Nm) on 1989 vehicles and 20–25 ft. lbs. (27–33 Nm) on 1990–93 vehicles.

➡The hoses are designed to swivel when properly tightened. Do not attempt to eliminate looseness by over-tightening the fittings.

10. Install the front rubber insulators. Make sure all rubber insulators are pushed completely inside the gear housing before installing the mounting bolts.
11. Insert the input shaft into the flexible coupling. Install the mounting bolts, insulator washers and nuts. Tighten the nuts to 30–40 ft. lbs. (41–54 Nm) while holding the bolts. Install and tighten the flexible coupling bolt to 20–30 ft. lbs. (28–40 Nm).
12. Connect the tie rod ends to the spindle arms and install the retaining nuts. Tighten to 35–47 ft. lbs. (48–63 Nm). After tightening, tighten the nuts to their nearest cotter pin castellation and install new cotter pins.
13. Remove the jackstands and carefully lower the vehicle.
14. Turn the ignition switch to **OFF** and connect the negative battery cable.
15. Fill the power steering system with the proper type and quantity of fluid.
16. If the tie rod ends were loosened, check and adjust the front end alignment.

Tie Rod Ends

REMOVAL & INSTALLATION

➧ See Figures 56 thru 69

➡If a steering boot or inner rod is damaged on the rack and pinion assembly, they are easily replaced after tie rod end removal. DO NOT allow a torn boot to go unattended as steering rack damage will likely occur.

1. Raise and support the vehicle safely using jackstands.
2. Remove the cotter pin and nut from the tie rod end ball stud. Disconnect

88158P18

Fig. 56 Remove the cotter pin from the tie rod ball stud . . .

88158P19

Fig. 57 . . . then loosen and remove the castellated nut

88158P20

Fig. 58 Use a suitable tie rod end puller to loosen the ball and stud . . .

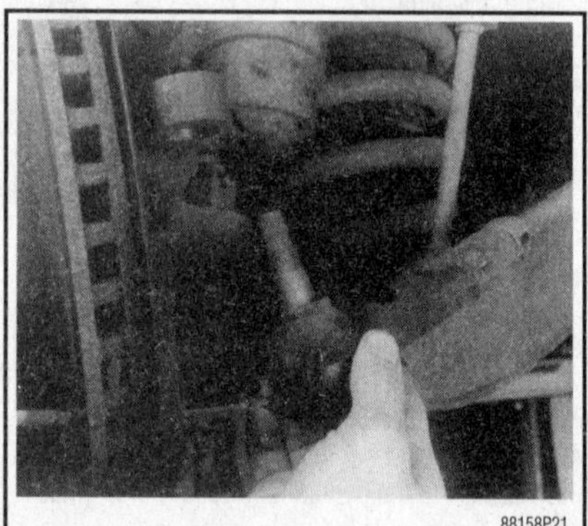

88158P21

Fig. 59 . . . then free the assembly from the knuckle

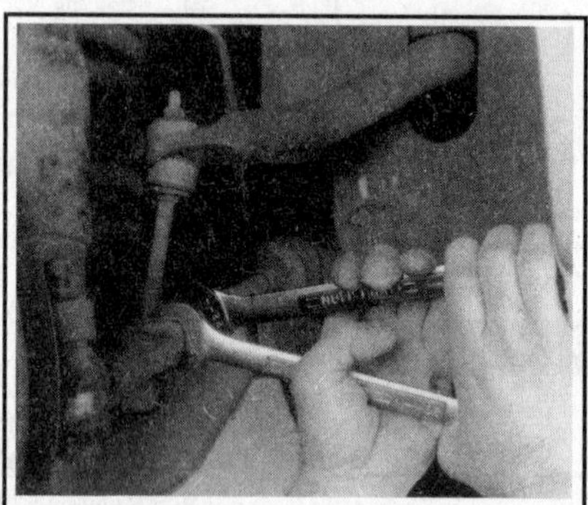

88158P22

Fig. 60 If necessary, loosen the jam nut to free the tie rod end . . .

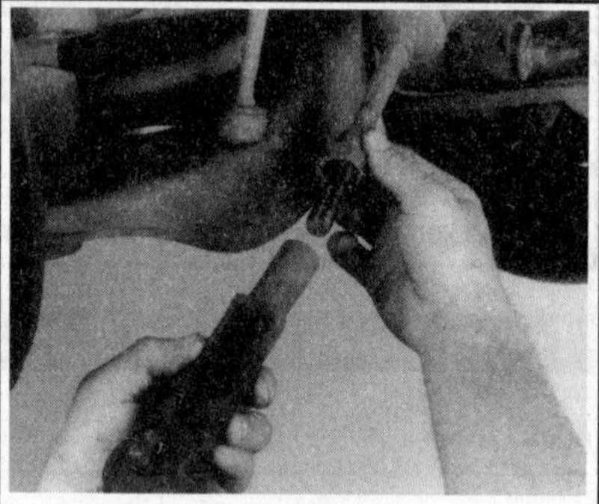

88158P23

Fig. 61 . . . then thread the end from the rack's inner rod

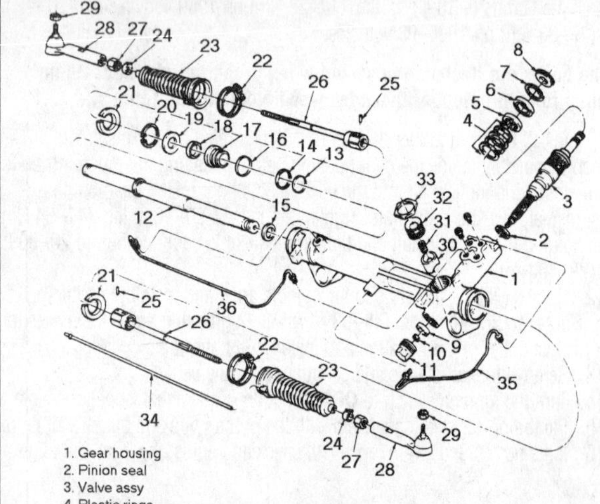

1. Gear housing
2. Pinion seal
3. Valve assy
4. Plastic rings
5. Input shaft bearing
6. Input shaft seal
7. Snap ring - Seal retainer
8. Input shaft dust seal
9. Pinion bearing
10. Pinion bearing locknut
11. Pinion bearing plug
12. Rack assy
13. Backup o-ring - Rubber
14. Piston seal - Plastic
15. Inner rack seal
16. Rack bushing o-ring
17. Rack bushing
18. Outer rack seal
19. Housing end plate
20. Snap ring
21. Travel restrictors
22. Inner bellows clamp
23. Bellows
24. Outer bellows clamp
25. Spiral pin
26. Tie rod assy
27. Jam nut
28. Tie rod end assy
29. Castellated nut
30. Rack yoke
31. Yoke spring
32. Yoke plug
33. Yoke plug locknut
34. Breather tube
35. Right turn transfer tube
36. Left turn transfer tube

88158G26

Fig. 62 Exploded view of the power steering rack and pinion assembly (including tie rod ends)

the tie rod end from the spindle using ball stud remover tool 3290–D or equivalent.

3. Holding the tie rod end with a wrench, loosen the tie rod jam nut. Grip the tie rod end with pliers and remove the assembly from the tie rod, but first note the depth to which the tie rod was located by using the jam nut as a marker.

➡On some rack assemblies, the jam nut DOES NOT have to be touched, as the tie rod end can be unthreaded once the ball stud is free. On these assemblies, leaving the jam nut undisturbed will prevent you from having to make alignment marks for installation purposes. BUT, if a tie rod is replaced, you should still check toe-in after installation.

To install:

4. Clean the tie rod threads.
5. Thread the new tie rod end onto the tie rod to the same depth as the removed tie rod end.
6. Place the tie rod end ball stud into the spindle and install the nut. Make sure the front wheels are in the straight ahead position.
7. Tighten the nut to 35 ft. lbs. (48 Nm) and continue tightening the nut to align the next castellation of the nut with the cotter pin hole in the stud. Install a new cotter pin.
8. Check and, if necessary, set the toe to specification. Tighten the jam nut to 35–50 ft. lbs. (48–68 Nm).

Power Steering Pump

REMOVAL & INSTALLATION

➧ See Figure 70

1. Disconnect the negative battery cable.
2. Disconnect the fluid return hose at the reservoir and drain the fluid into a container.

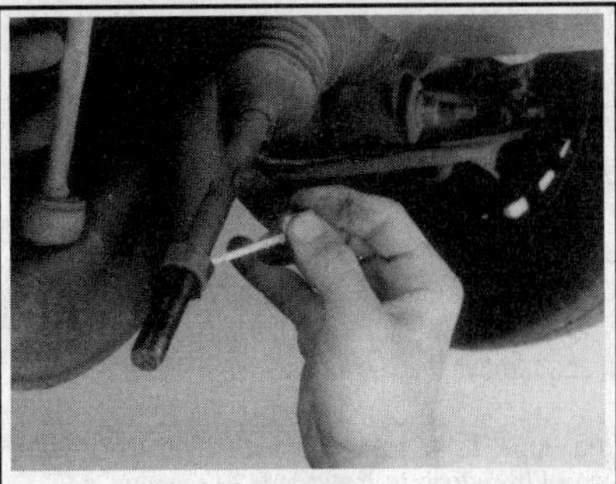

Fig. 63 If the steering rack boot or inner rod must be replaced, mark the jam nut positioning on the inner rod . . .

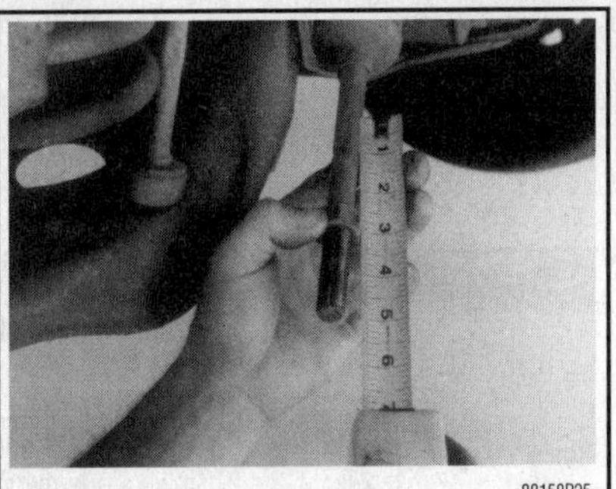

Fig. 64 . . . or you can measure the position of the jam nut in relation to the inner rod threads

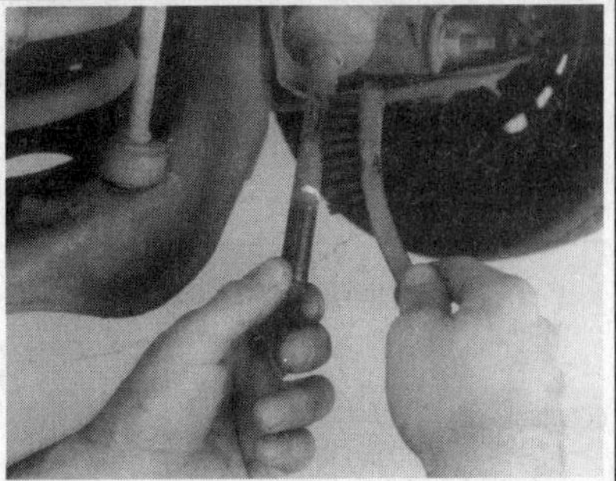

Fig. 65 Clean the inner rod threads thoroughly to prevent damage (and to make installation easier)

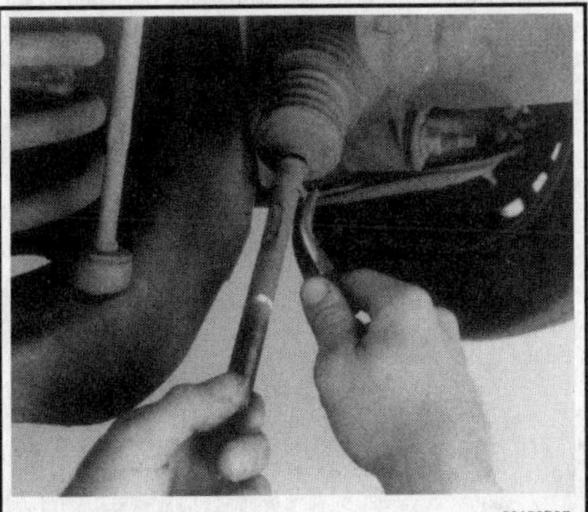

Fig. 66 Remove the steering rack outer boot clamp . . .

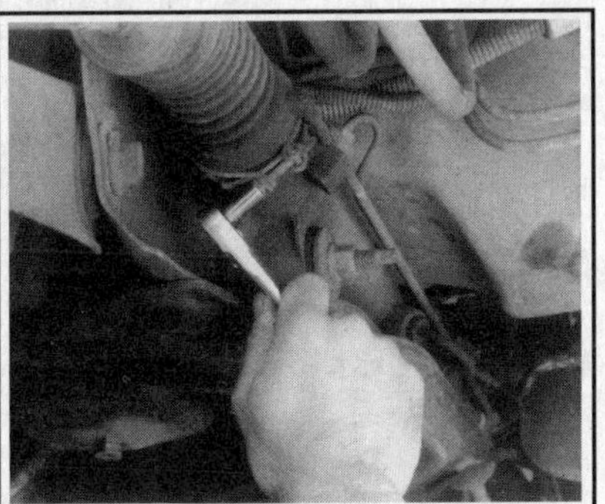

Fig. 67 . . . followed by the inner boot clamp

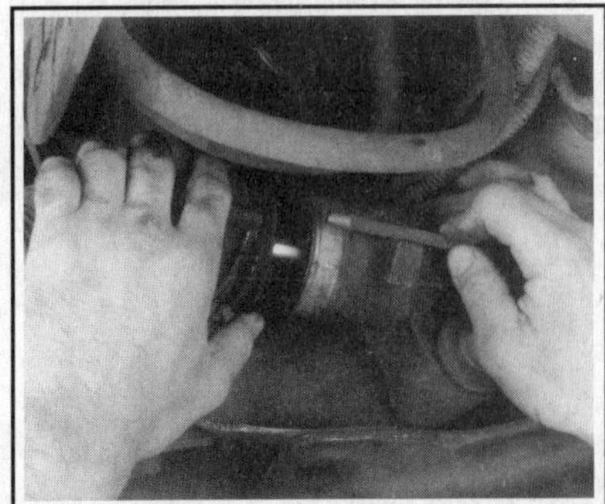

Fig. 68 Carefully slide the boot off of the steering rack . . .

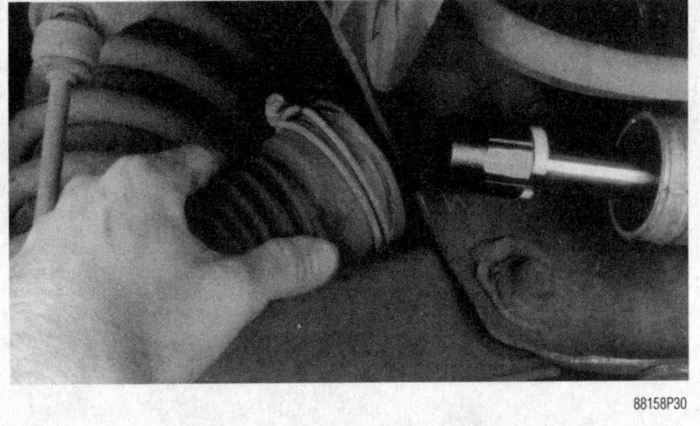

Fig. 69 . . . then remove the boot and inner rod from the vehicle

3. Remove the pressure hose from the pump and, if necessary, drain the fluid into a container. Do not remove the fitting from the pump.
4. Remove the pump mounting bracket. Disconnect the belt from the pulley and remove the pump.
5. On engines with the fixed pump system, remove the pulley before removing the pump.

To install:

6. On non-fixed pump systems, install the pulley on the pump, if removed.
7. Place the pump on the mounting bracket and install the bolts at the front of the pump. Tighten to 30–45 ft. lbs. (40–62 Nm).
8. On fixed pump systems, install the pulley.
9. Place the belt on the pump pulley.
10. Install the pressure hose to the pump fitting. Tighten the tube nut with a tube nut wrench rather than with an open-end wrench. Tighten to 20–25 ft. lbs. (27–34 Nm).

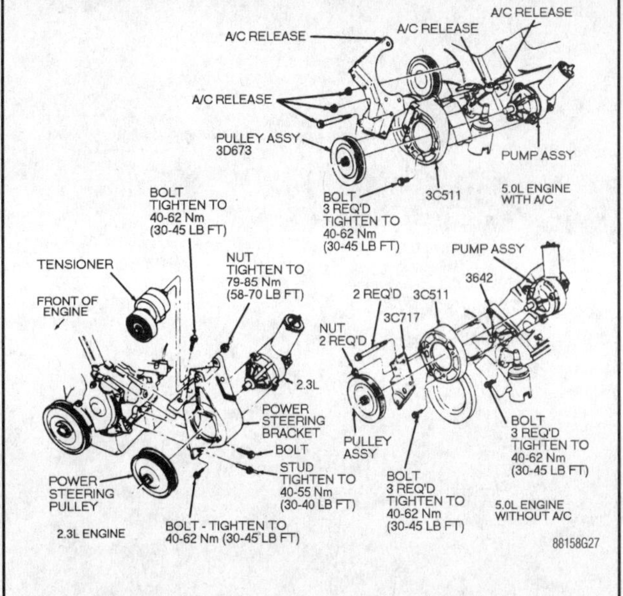

Fig. 70 Exploded view of the power steering pump mounting

➡Do not overtighten this fitting. Swivel and/or end-play of the fitting is normal and does not indicate a loose fitting. Over-tightening the tube nut can collapse the tube nut wall, resulting in a leak and requiring replacement of the entire pressure hose assembly. Use of an open-end wrench to tighten the nut can deform the tube nut hex which may result in improper torque and may make further servicing of the system difficult.

11. Connect the return hose to the pump and tighten the clamp. Fill the reservoir with the proper type and quantity of fluid.
12. Connect the negative battery cable and properly bleed the power steering system.

SYSTEM BLEEDING

1. Disconnect the ignition coil and raise the front wheels off the floor.
2. Fill the power steering fluid reservoir.
3. Crank the engine with the starter and add fluid until the level remains constant.
4. While cranking the engine, rotate the steering wheel from lock-to-lock.

➡The front wheels must be off the floor during lock-to-lock rotation of the steering wheel.

5. Check the fluid level and add fluid, if necessary.
6. Connect the ignition coil wire. Start the engine and allow it to run for several minutes.
7. Rotate the steering wheel from lock-to-lock.
8. Shut off the engine and check the fluid level. Add fluid, if necessary.
9. If air is still present in the system, purge the system of air using power steering pump air evacuator tool 021–00014 or equivalent, as follows:
    a. Make sure the power steering pump reservoir is full to the FULL COLD mark on the dipstick.
    b. Tightly insert the rubber stopper of the air evacuator assembly into the pump reservoir fill neck.
    c. Apply 15 in. Hg maximum vacuum on the pump reservoir for a minimum of three minutes with the engine idling. As air purges from the system, vacuum will fall off. Maintain adequate vacuum with the vacuum source.
    d. Release the vacuum and remove the vacuum source. Fill the reservoir to the FULL COLD mark.
    e. With the engine idling, apply 15 in. Hg vacuum to the pump reservoir. Slowly cycle the steering wheel from lock-to-lock every 30 seconds for approximately five minutes. Do not hold the steering wheel on the stops while cycling. Maintain adequate vacuum with the vacuum source as the air purges.
    f. Release the vacuum and remove the vacuum source. Fill the reservoir to the FULL COLD mark.
    g. Start the engine and cycle the steering wheel. Check for oil leaks at all connections. In severe cases of aeration, it may be necessary to repeat Steps 9b–9f.

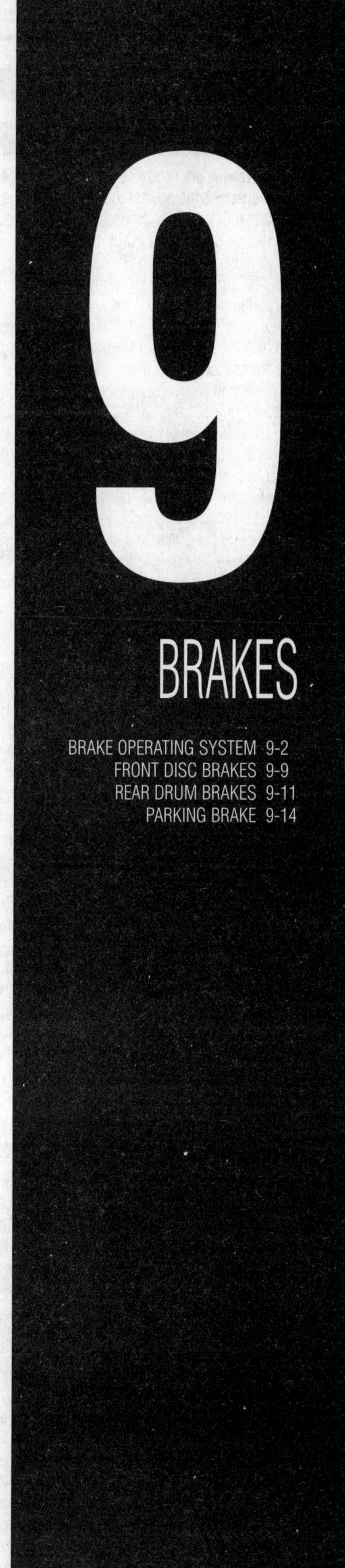

9 BRAKES

BRAKE OPERATING SYSTEM

Basic Operating Principles

Hydraulic systems are used to actuate the brakes of all modern automobiles. The system transports the power required to force the frictional surfaces of the braking system together from the pedal to the individual brake units at each wheel. A hydraulic system is used for two reasons.

First, fluid under pressure can be carried to all parts of an automobile by small pipes and flexible hoses without taking up a significant amount of room or posing routing problems.

Second, a great mechanical advantage can be given to the brake pedal end of the system, and the foot pressure required to actuate the brakes can be reduced by making the surface area of the master cylinder pistons smaller than that of any of the pistons in the wheel cylinders or calipers.

The master cylinder consists of a fluid reservoir along with a double cylinder and piston assembly. Double type master cylinders are designed to separate the front and rear braking systems hydraulically in case of a leak. The master cylinder coverts mechanical motion from the pedal into hydraulic pressure within the lines. This pressure is translated back into mechanical motion at the wheels by either the wheel cylinder (drum brakes) or the caliper (disc brakes).

Steel lines carry the brake fluid to a point on the vehicle's frame near each of the vehicle's wheels. The fluid is then carried to the calipers and wheel cylinders by flexible tubes in order to allow for suspension and steering movements.

In drum brake systems, each wheel cylinder contains two pistons, one at either end, which push outward in opposite directions and force the brake shoe into contact with the drum.

In disc brake systems, the cylinders are part of the calipers. At least one cylinder in each caliper is used to force the brake pads against the disc.

All pistons employ some type of seal, usually made of rubber, to minimize fluid leakage. A rubber dust boot seals the outer end of the cylinder against dust and dirt. The boot fits around the outer end of the piston on disc brake calipers, and around the brake actuating rod on wheel cylinders.

The hydraulic system operates as follows: When at rest, the entire system, from the piston(s) in the master cylinder to those in the wheel cylinders or calipers, is full of brake fluid. Upon application of the brake pedal, fluid trapped in front of the master cylinder piston(s) is forced through the lines to the wheel cylinders. Here, it forces the pistons outward, in the case of drum brakes, and inward toward the disc, in the case of disc brakes. The motion of the pistons is opposed by return springs mounted outside the cylinders in drum brakes, and by spring seals, in disc brakes.

Upon release of the brake pedal, a spring located inside the master cylinder immediately returns the master cylinder pistons to the normal position. The pistons contain check valves and the master cylinder has compensating ports drilled in it. These are uncovered as the pistons reach their normal position. The piston check valves allow fluid to flow toward the wheel cylinders or calipers as the pistons withdraw. Then, as the return springs force the brake pads or shoes into the released position, the excess fluid reservoir through the compensating ports. It is during the time the pedal is in the released position that any fluid that has leaked out of the system will be replaced through the compensating ports.

Dual circuit master cylinders employ two pistons, located one behind the other, in the same cylinder. The primary piston is actuated directly by mechanical linkage from the brake pedal through the power booster. The secondary piston is actuated by fluid trapped between the two pistons. If a leak develops in front of the secondary piston, it moves forward until it bottoms against the front of the master cylinder, and the fluid trapped between the pistons will operate the rear brakes. If the rear brakes develop a leak, the primary piston will move forward until direct contact with the secondary piston takes place, and it will force the secondary piston to actuate the front brakes. In either case, the brake pedal moves farther when the brakes are applied, and less braking power is available.

All dual circuit systems use a switch to warn the driver when only half of the brake system is operational. This switch is located in a valve body which is mounted on the firewall or the frame below the master cylinder. A hydraulic piston receives pressure from both circuits, each circuit's pressure being applied to one end of the piston. When the pressures are in balance, the piston remains stationary. When one circuit has a leak, however, the greater pressure in that circuit during application of the brakes will push the piston to one side, closing the switch and activating the brake warning light.

In disc brake systems, this valve body also contains a metering valve and, in some cases, a proportioning valve. The metering valve keeps pressure from traveling to the disc brakes on the front wheels until the brake shoes on the rear wheels have contacted the drums, ensuring that the front brakes will never be used alone. The proportioning valve controls the pressure to the rear brakes to lessen the chance of rear wheel lock-up during very hard braking.

Warning lights may be tested by depressing the brake pedal and holding it while opening one of the wheel cylinder bleeder screws. If this does not cause the light to go on, substitute a new lamp, make continuity checks, and, finally, replace the switch as necessary.

The hydraulic system may be checked for leaks by applying pressure to the pedal gradually and steadily. If the pedal sinks very slowly to the floor, the system has a leak. This is not to be confused with a springy or spongy feel due to the compression of air within the lines. If the system leaks, there will be a gradual change in the position of the pedal with a constant pressure.

Check for leaks along all lines and at wheel cylinders. If no external leaks are apparent, the problem is inside the master cylinder.

DISC BRAKES

Instead of the traditional expanding brakes that press outward against a circular drum, disc brake systems utilize a disc (rotor) with brake pads positioned on either side of it. An easily-seen analogy is the hand brake arrangement on a bicycle. The pads squeeze onto the rim of the bike wheel, slowing its motion. Automobile disc brakes use the identical principle but apply the braking effort to a separate disc instead of the wheel.

The disc (rotor) is a casting, usually equipped with cooling fins between the two braking surfaces. This enables air to circulate between the braking surfaces making them less sensitive to heat buildup and more resistant to fade. Dirt and water do not drastically affect braking action since contaminants are thrown off by the centrifugal action of the rotor or scraped off the by the pads. Also, the equal clamping action of the two brake pads tends to ensure uniform, straight line stops. Disc brakes are inherently self-adjusting. There are three general types of disc brake:

1. A fixed caliper.
2. A floating caliper.
3. A sliding caliper.

The fixed caliper design uses two pistons mounted on either side of the rotor (in each side of the caliper). The caliper is mounted rigidly and does not move.

The sliding and floating designs are quite similar. In fact, these two types are often lumped together. In both designs, the pad on the inside of the rotor is moved into contact with the rotor by hydraulic force. The caliper, which is not held in a fixed position, moves slightly, bringing the outside pad into contact with the rotor. There are various methods of attaching floating calipers. Some pivot at the bottom or top, and some slide on mounting bolts. In any event, the end result is the same.

DRUM BRAKES

Drum brakes employ two brake shoes mounted on a stationary backing plate. These shoes are positioned inside a circular drum which rotates with the wheel assembly. The shoes are held in place by springs. This allows them to slide toward the drums (when they are applied) while keeping the linings and drums in alignment. The shoes are actuated by a wheel cylinder which is mounted at the top of the backing plate. When the brakes are applied, hydraulic pressure forces the wheel cylinder's actuating links outward. Since these links bear directly against the top of the brake shoes, the tops of the shoes are then forced against the inner side of the drum. This action forces the bottoms of the two shoes to contact the brake drum by rotating the entire assembly slightly (known as servo action). When pressure within the wheel cylinder is relaxed, return springs pull the shoes back away from the drum.

Most modern drum brakes are designed to self-adjust themselves during application when the vehicle is moving in reverse. This motion causes both shoes to rotate very slightly with the drum, rocking an adjusting lever, thereby causing rotation of the adjusting screw. Some drum brake systems are designed to self-adjust during application whenever the brakes are applied. This on-board adjustment system reduces the need for maintenance adjustments and keeps both the brake function and pedal feel satisfactory.

POWER BOOSTERS

Virtually all modern vehicles use a vacuum assisted power brake system to multiply the braking force and reduce pedal effort. Since vacuum is always available when the engine is operating, the system is simple and efficient. A vacuum diaphragm is located on the front of the master cylinder and assists the driver in applying the brakes, reducing both the effort and travel he must put into moving the brake pedal.

The vacuum diaphragm housing is normally connected to the intake manifold by a vacuum hose. A check valve is placed at the point where the hose enters the diaphragm housing, so that during periods of low manifold vacuum brakes assist will not be lost.

Depressing the brake pedal closes off the vacuum source and allows atmospheric pressure to enter on one side of the diaphragm. This causes the master cylinder pistons to move and apply the brakes. When the brake pedal is released, vacuum is applied to both sides of the diaphragm and springs return the diaphragm and master cylinder pistons to the released position.

If the vacuum supply fails, the brake pedal rod will contact the end of the master cylinder actuator rod and the system will apply the brakes without any power assistance. The driver will notice that much higher pedal effort is needed to stop the car and that the pedal feels harder than usual.

Vacuum Leak Test

1. Operate the engine at idle without touching the brake pedal for at least one minute.
2. Turn off the engine and wait one minute.
3. Test for the presence of assist vacuum by depressing the brake pedal and releasing it several times. If vacuum is present in the system, light application will produce less and less pedal travel. If there is no vacuum, air is leaking into the system.

System Operation Test

1. With the engine **OFF**, pump the brake pedal until the supply vacuum is entirely gone.
2. Put light, steady pressure on the brake pedal.
3. Start the engine and let it idle. If the system is operating correctly, the brake pedal should fall toward the floor if the constant pressure is maintained.

Power brake systems may be tested for hydraulic leaks just as ordinary systems are tested.

**** WARNING**

Clean, high quality brake fluid is essential to the safe and proper operation of the brake system. You should always buy the highest quality brake fluid that is available. If the brake fluid becomes contaminated, drain and flush the system, then refill the master cylinder with new fluid. Never reuse any brake fluid. Any brake fluid that is removed from the system should be discarded.

Adjustments

DRUM BRAKES

The drum brakes are self-adjusting and require manual adjustment only after the brake shoes have been replaced or when the length of the adjusting screw has been changed while performing some other service operation, such as removing the brake drum.

To adjust the brakes, follow these procedures:

Drum Installed

See Figure 1

1. Raise and support the rear end on jackstands.
2. Remove the rubber plug from the adjusting slot on the backing plate.
3. Insert a brake adjusting tool into the slot and engage the lowers possible tooth on the starwheel. Move the end of the tool downward; this moves the starwheel tooth upward and expands the adjusting screw. Repeat this operation until the brakes lock the wheel.

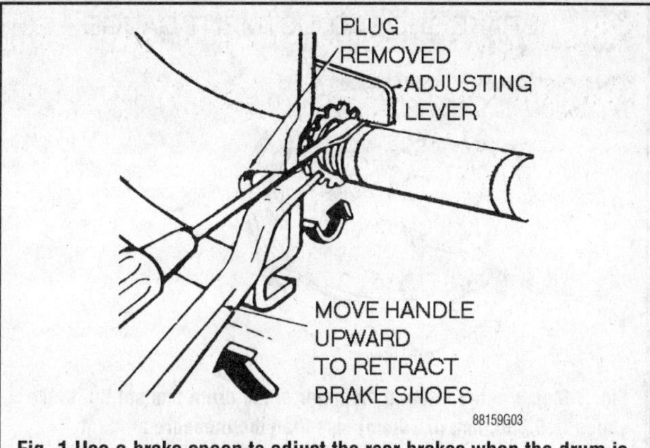

Fig. 1 Use a brake spoon to adjust the rear brakes when the drum is still installed

4. Insert a small tool or piece of stiff wire into the adjusting slot. Use it to push the automatic adjusting lever out and free of the starwheel and hold it there.
5. Engage the topmost tooth on the starwheel with the adjuster tool. Move the end of the tool upward (driving the tooth of the wheel downward) to contract the adjusting screw. Back off the starwheel until the brakes unlock and the wheel spins freely with a minimum of drag. Keep track of the number of turns that the starwheel is backed off or the number of strokes taken with the brake tool
6. Repeat the process for the brakes on the other side. The starwheel adjuster must be backed off the same number of turns as the first side to prevent side-to-side brake pull.
7. Remove the safety stands and lower the vehicle. Road test the vehicle.
8. When the brakes are adjusted, make several stops while backing the vehicle. This will equalize the brakes at both wheels.

Drum Removed

See Figures 2 and 3

**** CAUTION**

Brake friction material may contain asbestos, which has been determined to be a cancer causing agent. Never clean the brake surfaces with compressed air! Avoid inhaling any dust from any brake surface! When cleaning brake surfaces, use a commercially available brake cleaning fluid.

1. Make sure the shoe-to-contact pad areas are clean and well lubricated.
2. Use an inside caliper to check the inner diameter of the drum. Measure across the diameter of the assembled brake shoes at their widest point.
3. Turn the adjusting screw so that the diameter of the shoes is 0.030 in. (0.76mm) less than the brake drum inner diameter.
4. Install the drum.

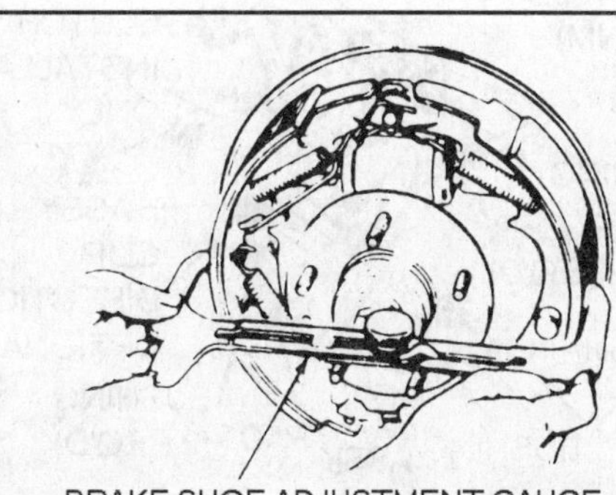

Fig. 2 Measure the installed brake shoes to determine the proper adjustment

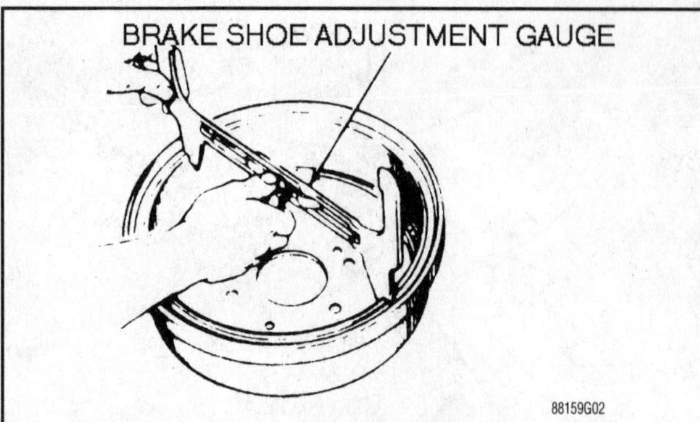

Fig. 3 Measure the internal diameter of the drum and set the brake shoes to 0.030 inch (0.76mm) less than the measure amount

Stoplight Switch

REMOVAL & INSTALLATION

➧ **See Figure 4**

1. Disconnect the negative battery cable.
2. Unplug the wire harness at the connector from the switch mounted at th brake pedal. The locking tab must be lifted before the connector can be removed.
3. Remove the hairpin retainer, slide the stoplight switch, the pushrod and the nylon washers and bushings away from the pedal and remove the switch.

➡Since the switch side-plate nearest the brake pedal is slotted, it is not necessary to remove the brake master cylinder pushrod and washer from the brake pedal pin.

To install:

4. Position the switch so the U-shaped side is nearest the pedal and directly over/under the pin. Slide the switch down or up, trapping the master cylinder pushrod and black bushing between the switch side plates. Push the switch and pushrod assembly firmly toward the brake pedal arm.
5. Assemble the outside white plastic washer to the pin and install the hairpin retainer to trap the whole assembly.
6. Assemble the wire harness connector to the switch. Check the switch for proper operation. Connect the negative battery cable.

➡The stoplight switch wire harness must be long enough to travel with the switch during full-pedal stroke. If the wire length is insufficient, reroute the harness or service, as required.

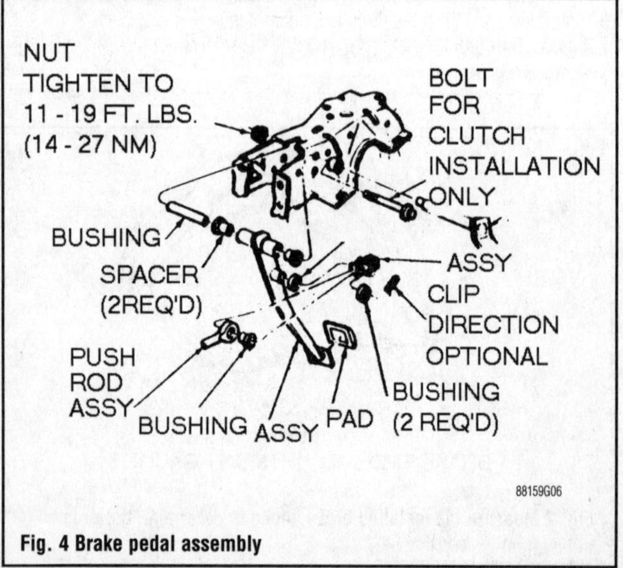

Fig. 4 Brake pedal assembly

Brake Pedal

➧ **See Figure 4**

REMOVAL & INSTALLATION

1. Remove the brake light switch.
2. Slide the pushrod and spacer from the pedal pin.
3. If the vehicle is equipped with speed control, the speed control bracket may be left in place.
4. On vehicles with manual transmission:
   a. Disconnect the clutch cable from the clutch pedal.
   b. Remove the pedal and bushings.
5. On vehicles with automatic transmission:
   a. Remove the spring retainer and bushing from the brake pedal shaft.
   b. From the other end, pull out the shaft and remove the pedal.
   c. Remove the bushings and spring washer from the pedal.

To install:

6. For automatic transmission:
   a. Install the bushings and spring washer on the pedal.
   b. Install the pedal.
   c. Install the spring retainer and bushing on the brake pedal shaft.
7. For manual transmission:
   a. Install the pedal and bushings.
   b. Reposition the clutch pedal.
   c. Install the clutch cable.
8. Slide the pushrod and spacer onto the pedal pin.
9. Install the brake light switch.

Master Cylinder

REMOVAL & INSTALLATION

➧ **See Figures 5, 6, 7, 8 and 9**

1. Disconnect the negative battery cable.
2. Tag and remove the brake lines from the primary and secondary outlet ports of the master cylinder.
3. Unplug the brake warning indicator connector.
4. Remove the nuts attaching the master cylinder to the brake booster assembly.
5. Slide the master cylinder forward and upward from the vehicle.

To install:

6. Before installation, bench bleed the new master cylinder:
   a. Mount the new master cylinder in a holding fixture. Be careful not to damage the housing.

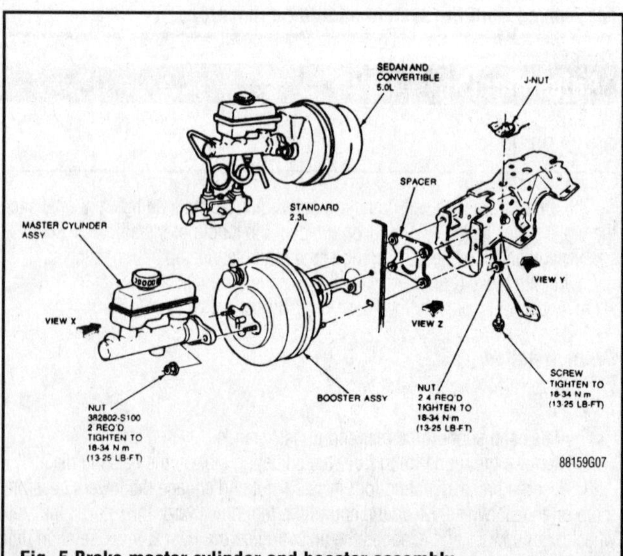

Fig. 5 Brake master cylinder and booster assembly

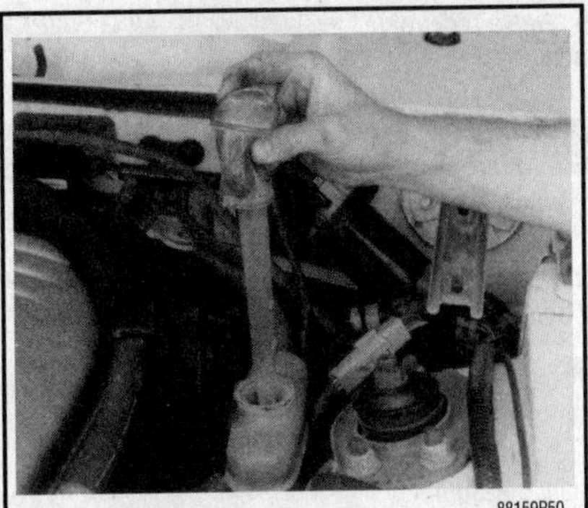
88159P50

Fig. 6 Remove as much of the brake fluid from the reservoir using a clean syringe

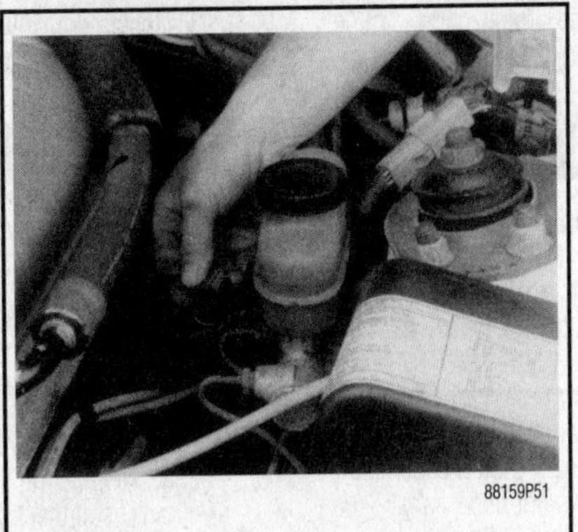
88159P51

Fig. 7 Disconnect the fluid level sensor

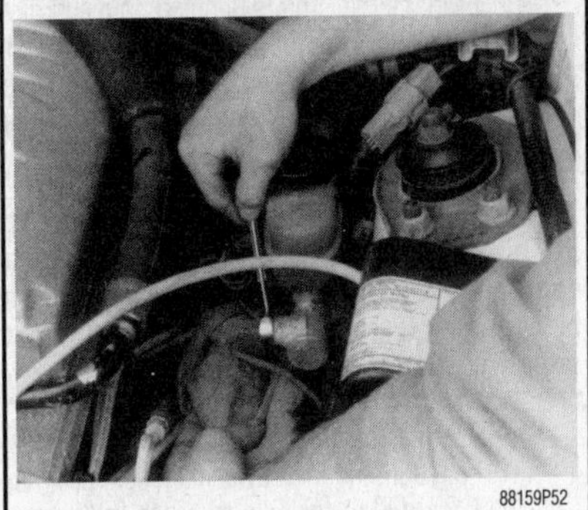
88159P52

Fig. 8 Clean the fittings and loosen the hydraulic lines

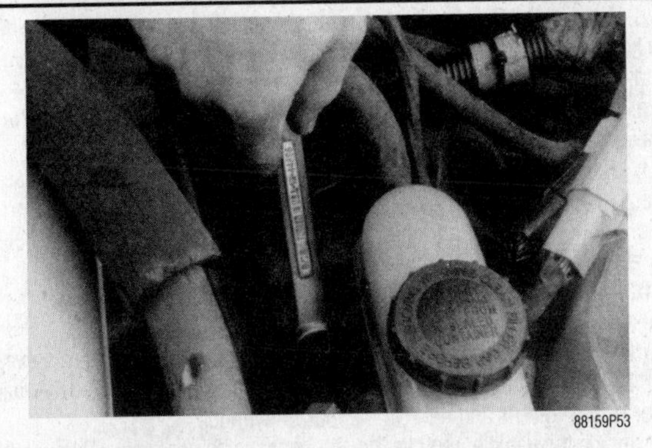
88159P53

Fig. 9 The master cylinder is held by a nut on each side

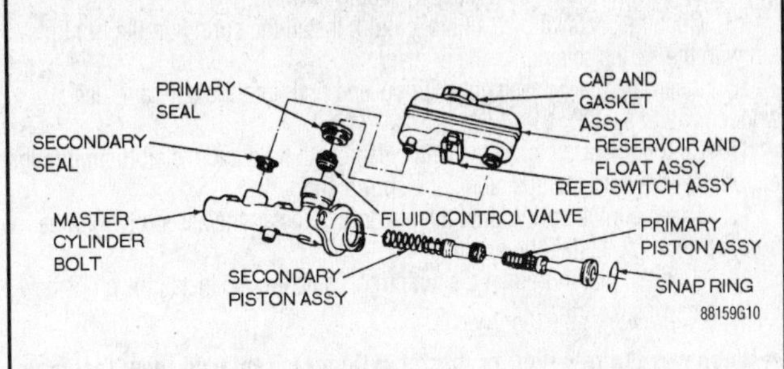

Fig. 10 Exploded view of the master cylinder showing all the replacable parts

b. Fill the master cylinder reservoir with clean brake fluid.

c. Insert a small tool into the booster pushrod cavity; press the master cylinder pushrod in slowly. Place a container under the master cylinder to catch the fluid being expelled from the outlet ports.

d. Place a finger tightly over each outlet port and allow the master cylinder piston to return.

7. Repeat the procedure until clear fluid only is expelled from the master cylinder. Plug the outlet ports and remove the cylinder from the holding fixture.
8. Mount the master cylinder on the booster.
9. Attach the brake fluid lines to the master cylinder.
10. Connect the brake warning indicator wiring.
11. Bleed the system. Operate the brakes several times, then check for external hydraulic leaks. Connect the negative battery cable.

OVERHAUL

See Figures 10, 11 and 12

The most important thing to remember when rebuilding the master cylinder is cleanliness. Work in clean surroundings with clean tools. Use clean cloth or paper for drying purposes. Have plenty of clean alcohol and brake fluid on hand to clean and lubricate the internal components. There are service repair kits available for overhauling the master cylinder.

1. Remove the master cylinder from the vehicle and drain the brake fluid.
2. Pry the reservoir off the master cylinder with a large, flat tool.
3. Mount the cylinder in a vise so that the outlets are up; remove the seal from the hub.
4. Remove The proportioning valve from the cylinder.
5. Remove the stopscrew from the bottom of the master cylinder.
6. Depress the primary piston and remove the snapring from the bottom of the bore.
7. Use compressed air to remove the secondary piston assembly. Cover the bore opening with a cloth to prevent damage to the piston.
8. To remove the primary piston, use compressed air in the outlet port at the blind end and plug the other port.

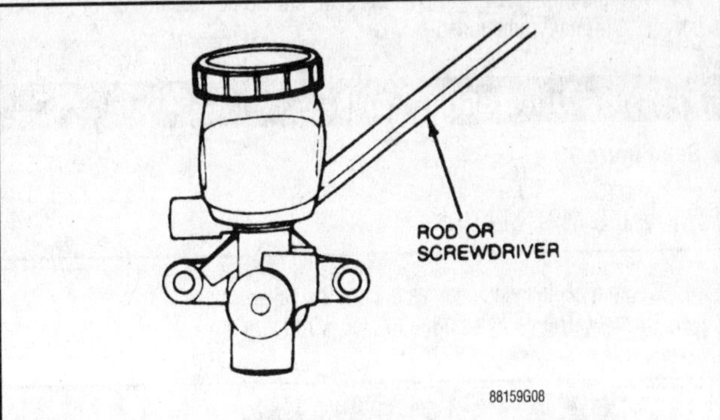

Fig. 11 Remove the reservoir by gently prying it out of the mounting grommets

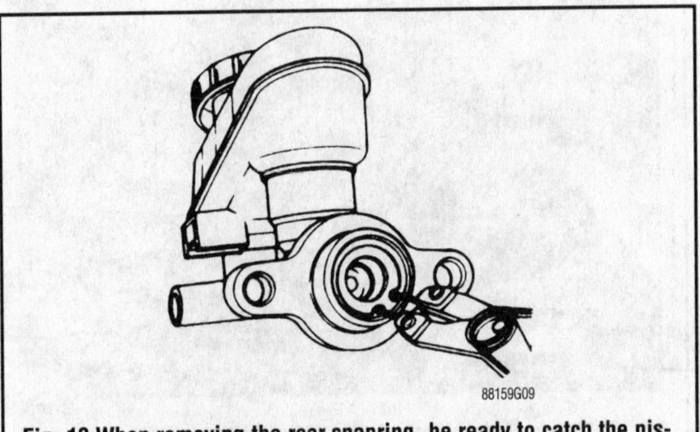

Fig. 12 When removing the rear snapring, be ready to catch the piston as it is spring loaded

9. Clean the metal parts in brake fluid and discard the rubber parts.

10. Inspect the bore for damage or wear and check the pistons for damage. Also check the pistons for proper clearance in the bore.

**** CAUTION**

Do not hone the cylinder bore. If the bore is pitted or deeply scored, the master cylinder assembly must be replaced. If any evidence of contamination is found in the master cylinder, the entire hydraulic system should be flushed and refilled with clean brake fluid. Blow out all passages with compressed air.

11. If the master cylinder is not damaged, it may be serviced with a rebuilding kit. The rebuilding kit may contain secondary and primary piston assemblies instead of just rubber seals. In this case, seal installation is not necessary.

12. Clean all parts in isopropyl alcohol.

13. Install new secondary seals in the two grooves in the flat end of the front piston. The lips of the seals will be facing away from each other.

14. Install a new primary seal and the seal protector on the opposite end of the front piston with the lips of the seal facing outward.

15. Coat the seals with clean brake fluid. Install the spring on the front piston with the spring retainer in the primary seal.

16. Insert the piston assembly, spring-end first, into the bore and use a wooden rod to seat it.

17. Coat the rear piston seals with clean brake fluid and install them into the piston grooves with the lips facing the spring end.

18. Assemble the spring onto the piston and install the assembly into the bore, spring first. Install the snapring.

19. Hold the piston train at the bottom of the bore and install the stopscrew. Install a new seal on the hub.

➡Whenever the reservoir or master cylinder is replaced, new reservoir grommets should be used.

20. Coat the new grommets with clean brake fluid and insert them into the master cylinder. Bench-bleed the cylinder or install and bleed the cylinder on the car.

21. Press the reservoir into place. A snap should be felt, indicating that the reservoir is properly positioned.

Pressure Differential Valve

➧ See Figure 13

REMOVAL & INSTALLATION

1. Disconnect the electrical leads from the valve.
2. Unscrew The valve from the master cylinder.
3. Install the valve in the reverse order of removal.
4. Bleed the master cylinder.

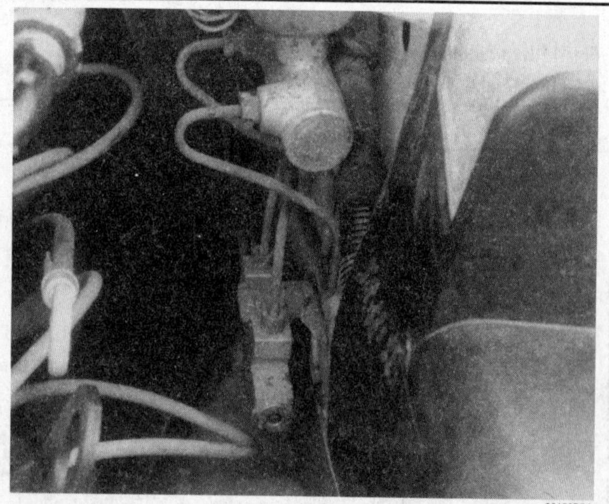

88159P54

Fig. 13 The pressure differential valve is located beneath the master cylinder

Power Brake Booster

REMOVAL & INSTALLATION

➧ See Figure 5

1. Disconnect the negative battery cable and remove the air cleaner.
2. Remove the cruise control actuator cable and cruise control servo.
3. If equipped with the 2.3L engine:
   a. Relieve the fuel system pressure.
   b. Disconnect the accelerator cable from the throttle body. Remove the screw that secures the accelerator cable to the accelerator shaft bracket and remove the cable from the bracket.
   c. Remove the screws that secure the accelerator shaft bracket to the manifold and rotate the bracket toward the engine. Remove the horn.
   d. Unplug the two manifold injector connectors located near the oil dipstick retaining bracket. Disconnect the two fuel hoses to the fuel supply manifold.
   e. Remove the three bolts holding the oil dipstick bracket to the upper intake manifold. Remove the dipstick and bracket.
   f. Remove the windshield wiper motor and remove the vacuum hoses directly over the brake booster at the dash panel vacuum tee.
   g. Remove the bolt holding the clutch cable stand. Move the bracket to the side rail at the fender inner panel.
   h. Move the cruise control cable, if equipped, to the side to clear the booster.
4. Disconnect the manifold vacuum hose from the booster check valve.
5. Disconnect the brake lines from the master cylinder. Remove the master cylinder retaining nuts and remove the master cylinder.
6. Inside the vehicle, remove the stoplight switch connector. Remove the switch retaining pin and slide the switch off the brake pedal pin just far enough for the outer arm to clear the pin, then remove the switch. Be careful not to damage the switch.
7. Remove the booster retaining nuts. If necessary, remove the cowl top intrusion bolt.
8. If equipped with cruise control, remove and set aside the control amplifier, mounted on the lower outboard booster stud.
9. Slide the booster pushrod, washers and bushing off the brake pedal pin. Remove the booster.
10. Installation is the reverse of the removal procedure. Tighten the booster mounting nuts and the master cylinder retaining nuts to 13–25 ft. lbs (18–34 Nm). If the brake lines were disconnected, bleed the brake system.

BRAKE BOOSTER PUSHROD ADJUSTMENT

➧ See Figures 14 and 15

The pushrod has an adjustment screw to maintain the correct relationship between the booster control valve plunger and the master cylinder piston. If the plunger is too long, it will prevent the master cylinder piston from completely

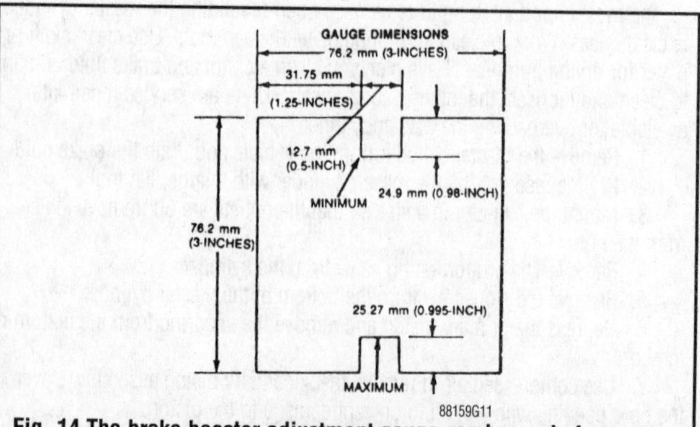

88159G11

Fig. 14 The brake booster adjustment gauge can be made from a piece of metal or cardboard sheet cut to these dimensions

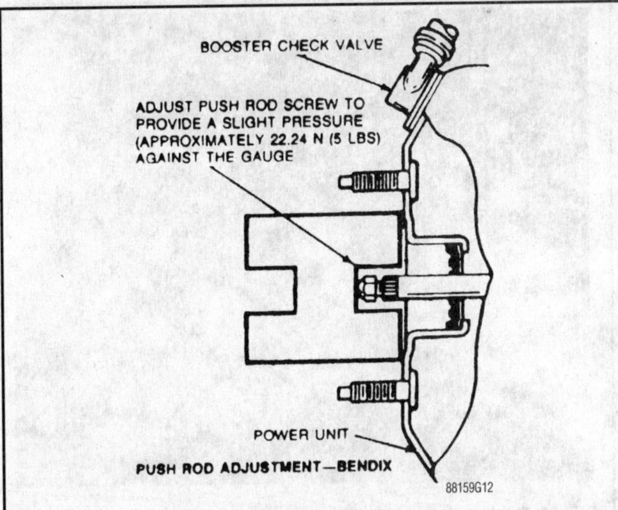

Fig. 15 Place the adjustment gauge over the pushrod and screw or unscrew the end to get the correct measurement

releasing pressure, causing the brakes to drag. If the plunger is too short, it will cause excessive pedal travel and an undesirable clunk in the booster area. Remove the master cylinder for access to the booster pushrod.

To check the adjustment of the screw, fabricate a gauge (from cardboard, following the dimensions in the illustration) and place it against the master cylinder mounting surface of the booster body. Adjust the pushrod screw by turning it until the end of the screw just touches the inner edge of the slot in the gauge. Install the master cylinder and bleed the system.

Brake Hoses and Lines

➧ See Figure 16

HYDRAULIC BRAKE LINE CHECK

The hydraulic brake lines and brake linings are to be inspected at the recommended intervals in the maintenance schedule. Follow the steel tubing from the master cylinder to the flexible hose fitting at each wheel. If a section of the tubing is found to be damaged, replace the entire section with tubing of the same type, size, shape and length.

✻✻ CAUTION

Copper tubing should never be used in the brake system. Use only SAE J526 or J527 steel tubing.

When installing anew section of brake tubing, flush clean brake fluid or denatured alcohol through to remove any dirt or foreign material from the line. Be sure to flare both ends to provide sound, leak-proof connections.

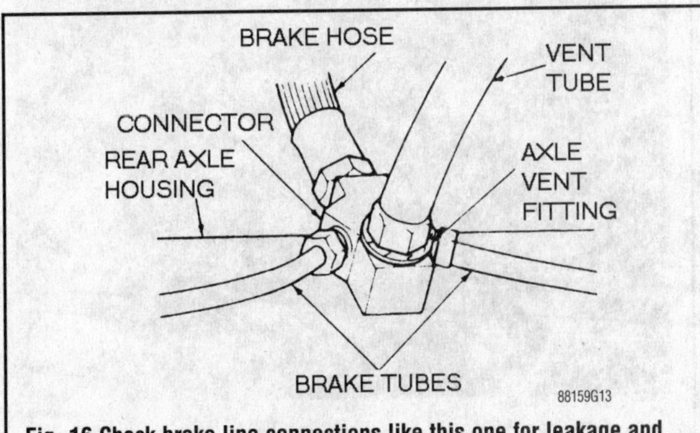

Fig. 16 Check brake line connections like this one for leakage and damage

✻✻ CAUTION

Double-flare brake lines; never install a new line with only a single flare.

When bending the tubing to fit the under-body contours, be careful not to kink or crack the line. tighten all hydraulic connections to 10–15 ft. lbs (14–20 Nm).

Check the flexible brake hoses that connect the steel tubing to each wheel cylinder. Replace the hose if it shows any signs of softening, cracking or other damage. When installing a new front brake hose, position the hose to avoid contact with other chassis parts. Place a new copper gasket over the hose fitting and thread the hose assembly into the front wheel cylinder. A new rear brake hose must be positioned clear of the exhaust pipe or shock absorber. Thread the hose into the rear brake tube connector. When installing either a new front or rear brake hose, engage the opposite end of the hose to the bracket on the frame. Install the horseshoe retaining clip and connect the tube to the hose with the tube fitting nut.

Always bleed the system after hose or line replacement. Before bleeding, make sure that the master cylinder is topped up with high-temperature, extra heavy duty fluid of at least SAE 70R3 (DOT 3) quality.

FLARING A BRAKE LINE

Using a Split-Die Flaring Tool

➧ See Figures 17 and 18

1. Use a tubing cutter to cut the required length of line.
2. Square the end with a file and chamfer the end.
3. Place the tube in the proper size die hole and position it so that it is flush with the die face. Lock the line with the wing nut.
4. The punches included with most tools are marked to identify the sequence of flaring. Such marks are usually OP.1 and OP. 2 or something similar.

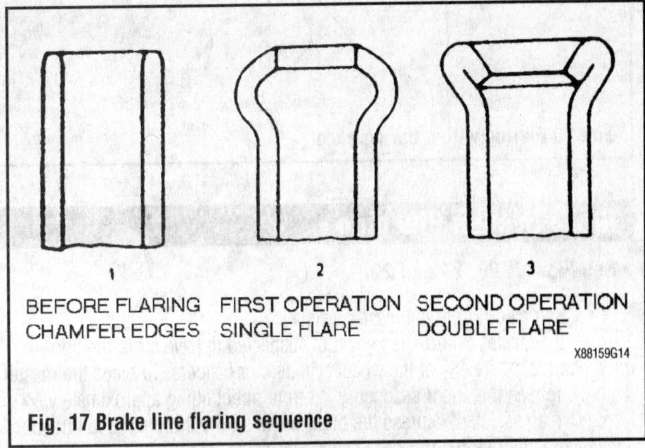

Fig. 17 Brake line flaring sequence

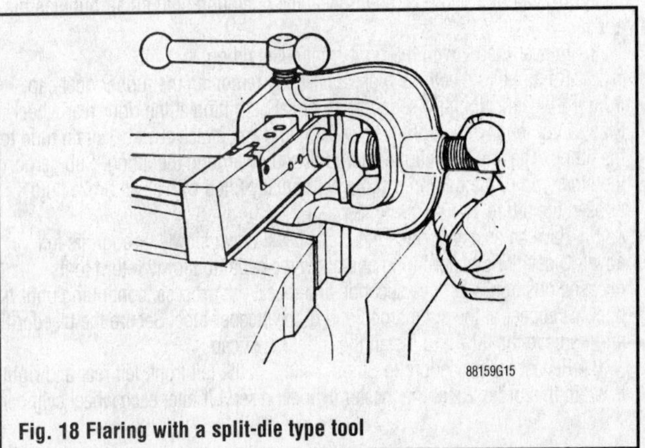

Fig. 18 Flaring with a split-die type tool

5. Slide the OP.1 punch into position and tighten the screw to form a single flare.
6. Remove the screw and position the OP.2 punch. Tighten the screw to form the double flare.
7. Remove the punch and release the line from the die.
8. Inspect the finished flare for cracks or uneven flare form. If the flare is not perfect, cut it off and re-flare the end.

Using a Flaring Bar Tool

▶ See Figure 19

1. Use a tubing cutter to cut the required length of line.
2. Square the end with a file and chamfer the end.
3. Insert the tube into the proper size hole in the bar, until the end of the tube sticks out as far as the thickness of the adapter above the bar, or, depending on the tool, even with the bar face.
4. Fit the adapter onto the tube and slide the bar into the yoke. Lock the bar in position with the tube beneath the yoke screw.
5. Tighten the yoke screw and form the single flare.
6. Release the yoke screw and remove the adapter.
7. Install the second adapter and form the double flare.
8. Release the screw and remove the tube. Inspect the finished flare for cracks or uneven flare form. If the flare is not perfect, cut it off and re-flare the end.

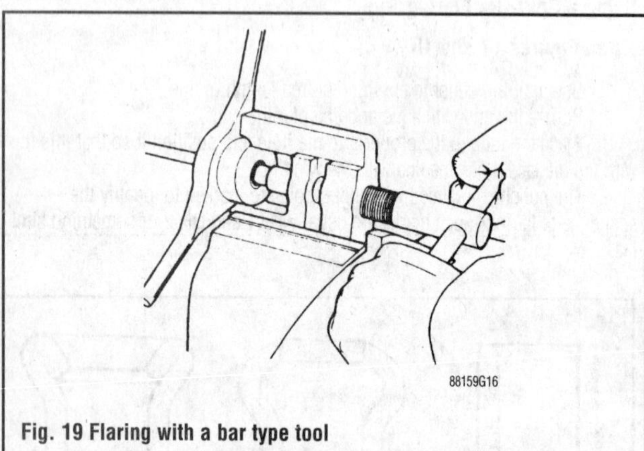

Fig. 19 Flaring with a bar type tool

Brake System Bleeding

▶ See Figures 20, 21 and 22

1. Clean all dirt from the master cylinder.
2. If the master cylinder is known or suspected to have air in the bore, it must be bled before any of the wheel cylinders or calipers. To bleed the master cylinder, loosen the upper secondary left front outlet fitting approximately ¾ turn. Have an assistant depress the brake pedal slowly through its full travel. Close the outlet fitting and let the pedal return slowly to the fully-released position. Wait five seconds, then repeat the operation until all air bubbles disappear.
3. Repeat Step 2 with the right-front outlet fitting.
4. Continue to bleed the brake system by removing the rubber dust cap from the wheel cylinder bleeder fitting or caliper fitting at the right-rear wheel. Place a box-end wrench on the bleeder fitting and attach a rubber drain tube to the fitting. The end of the tube should fit snugly around the fitting. Submerge the other end of the tube in a container partially filled with clean brake fluid. Loosen the fitting ¾ turn.
5. Have an assistant push the brake pedal down slowly through its full travel. Close the bleeder fitting and allow the pedal to slowly return to its released position. Wait five seconds and repeat the process, continuing until no bubbles appear at the submerged end of the bleeder tube. Secure the bleeder fitting, remove the tube and install the rubber dust cap.
6. Repeat the procedure in Steps 4 and 5 at the left front, left rear and right front, in this order. Refill the master cylinder reservoir after each wheel cylinder

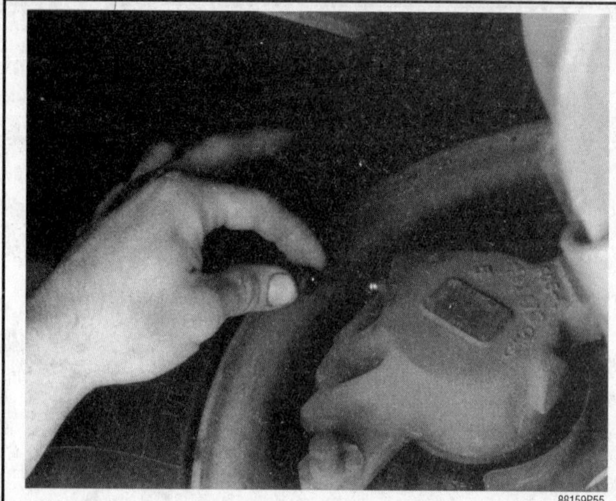

Fig. 20 The bleeders may have these protective caps on them. Be sure to replace them to keep dirt out of the bleeder assemblies

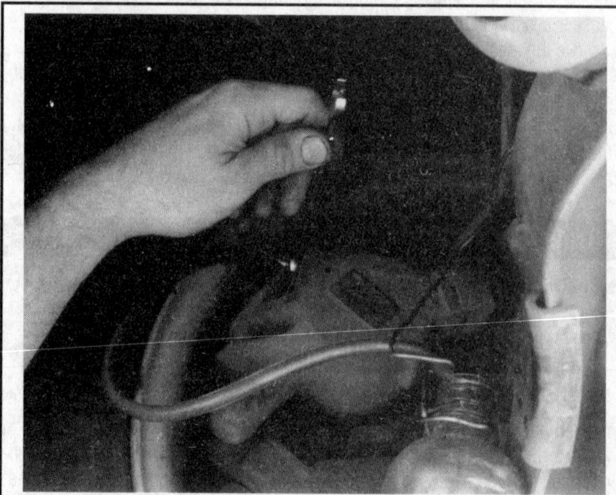

Fig. 21 Bleeding the front caliper

Fig. 22 Bleeding the rear wheel cylinder

or caliper has been bled; install the master cylinder cover and gasket. When bleeding is completed, the fluid level should be filled to the maximum level indicated on the reservoir.

7. Always make sure the disc brake pistons are returned to their normal positions by depressing the brake pedal several times until normal pedal travel is established. If the pedal feels spongy, repeat the bleeding procedure.

FRONT DISC BRAKES

➧ See Figure 23

** CAUTION

Brake linings may contain asbestos which has been determined to be a cancer-causing agent. Never clean brake surfaces with compressed air. Avoid inhaling any dust from any brake surface. When cleaning brake surfaces, use a commercially available brake cleaning fluid.

Brake Pads

REMOVAL & INSTALLATION

➧ See Figure 24

1. Remove and discard half of the brake fluid in the master cylinder reservoir.
2. Raise and safely support the vehicle. Remove the front wheel(s).
3. Remove the caliper locating pins and remove the caliper from the anchor plate and rotor. Do not disconnect the brake hose.
4. Remove the outer brake pad from the caliper assembly and remove the inner brake pad from the caliper piston.
5. Inspect the brake rotor for scoring and wear. Replace or machine the disc as necessary.
6. Suspend the caliper inside the fender housing with a length of wire. do not let the caliper hang by the brake hose.

To install:

7. Use a large C-clamp to push the caliper piston back into its bore.
8. Install the inner brake pad, then the outer; make sure the clips are engaged in the caliper piston.
9. Install the caliper and lower the vehicle.
10. Pump the brake pedal prior to moving the vehicle to seat the brake pads. Refill the master cylinder.

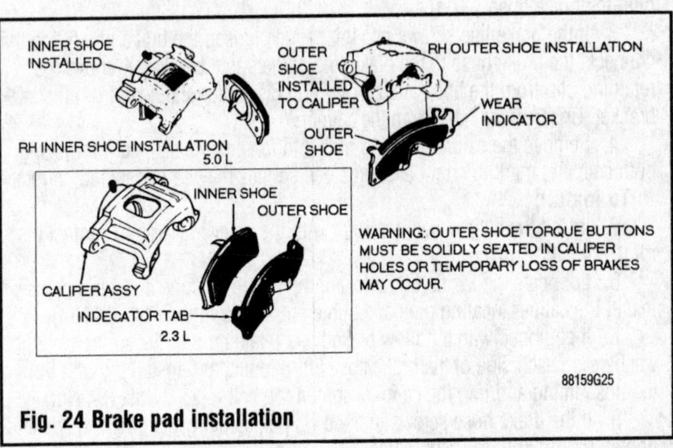

Fig. 24 Brake pad installation

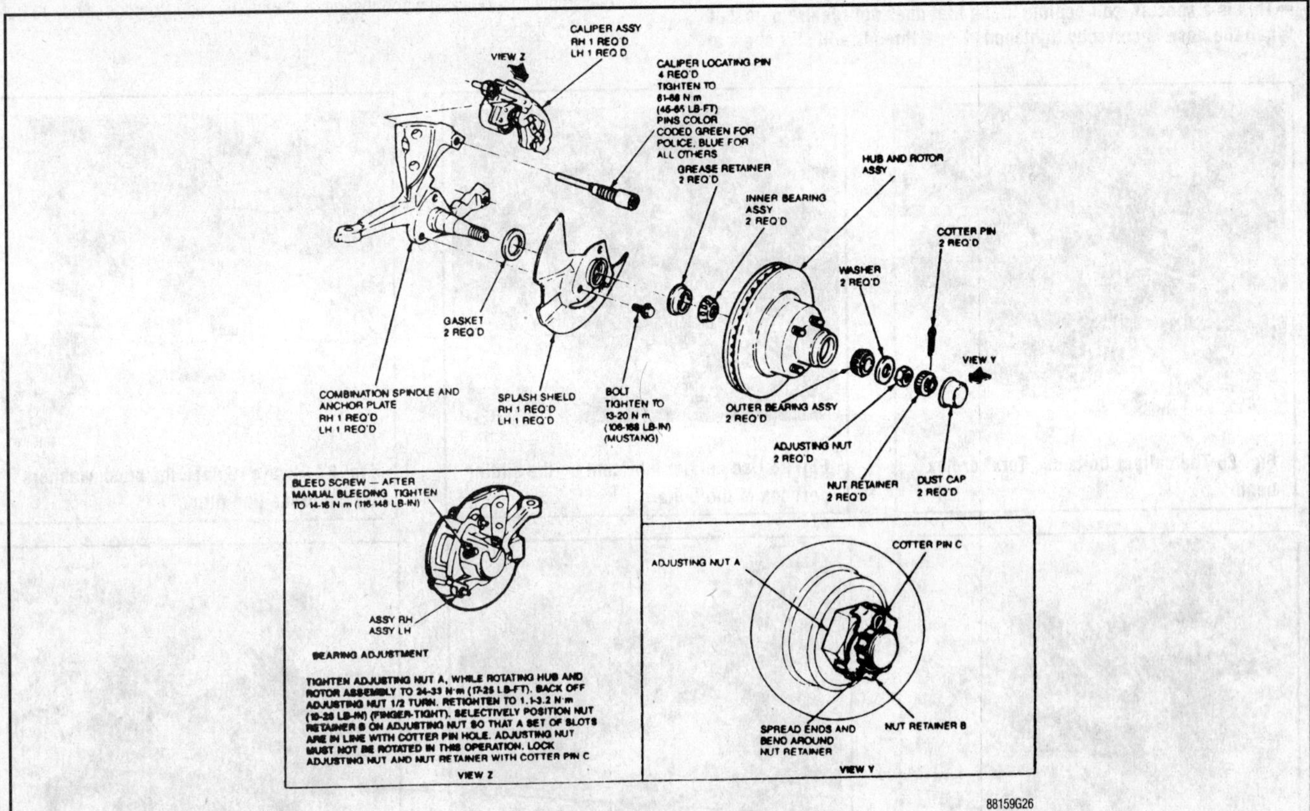

Fig. 23 Front disc brake components

INSPECTION

Remove the brake pads and measure the thickness of the lining. If the lining at any point on the pad is less than 0.125 in (3.175 mm), replace the pad. Also replace the pad if it shows any cracking, separation, or contamination from oil or grease.

Brake Caliper

REMOVAL & INSTALLATION

See Figures 25, 26 and 27

1. Raise and safely support the vehicle. Remove the front wheel(s).
2. If equipped with a hollow brake hose retaining bolt, remove the bolt and plug the brake hose.
3. If the brake line screws into the caliper, loosen the brake line fitting that connects the brake hose to the brake line at the frame bracket. Remove the retaining clip from the hose and bracket and disengage the hose from the bracket. Unscrew the hose from the caliper.
4. Remove the caliper locating pins and remove the caliper. If removing both calipers, mark the right and left sides so they may be reinstalled correctly.

To install:

5. Install the caliper over the rotor with the outer brake shoe against the rotor's braking surface.
6. Lubricate the inside of the locating pin with silicone dielectric grease. Install the caliper locating pins and tighten to 45–65 ft. lbs. (61–88 Nm).
7. If equipped with a hollow brake hose retaining bolt, install new copper washers on each side of the brake hose fitting outlet and install the bolt through the hose fitting and into the caliper. Tighten the bolt to 25 ft. lbs. (34 Nm).
8. If the brake hose screws into the caliper, carefully start the threads and tighten to 20–30 ft. lbs. (28–41 Nm).

➡This is a special, self-sealing fitting that does not require a gasket. When the hose is correctly tightened, 1 or 2 threads will still show at the caliper. It is not necessary for the hose fitting to be flush with the caliper for a good seal; do not overtighten.

9. Bleed the brake system, install the wheel and lower the vehicle.
10. To position the brake pads, apply the brake pedal several times before moving the vehicle.

OVERHAUL

See Figures 28, 29, 30 and 31

1. Clean the outside of the caliper in alcohol after removing it from the vehicle and removing the brake pads.
2. Drain the caliper through the inlet port.
3. Roll some thick shop cloths or rags and place them between the piston and the outer legs of the caliper.
4. Apply compressed air to the caliper inlet port until the piston comes out of the bore. Use low air pressure to avoid having the piston pop out too rapidly and possibly causing injury
5. If the piston becomes cocked in the bore and will not come out, use a soft mallet to tap it straight. Do not use a sharp tool or attempt to pry the piston out. Once straightened, reapply the compressed air.
6. Remove the boot from the piston and remove the seal from the caliper bore.
7. Clean the piston and caliper in alcohol.
8. Lubricate the piston seal with clean brake fluid, and position the seal in the groove in the cylinder bore.
9. Coat the outside of the piston and both of the beads of the dust boot with clean brake fluid. Insert the piston through the dust boot until the boot is around the bottom (closed end) of the piston.
10. Hold the piston and dust boot directly above the caliper bore and use your fingers to work the bead of the dust boot into the groove near the top of the cylinder bore.
11. After the bead is seated in the groove, press straight down on the piston until it bottoms in the bore. Be careful not to cock the piston. If necessary, use a C-clamp with a block of wood inserted between the clamp and the piston to bottom the piston.

88159P58

Fig. 25 The caliper bolts use Torx® or hex head

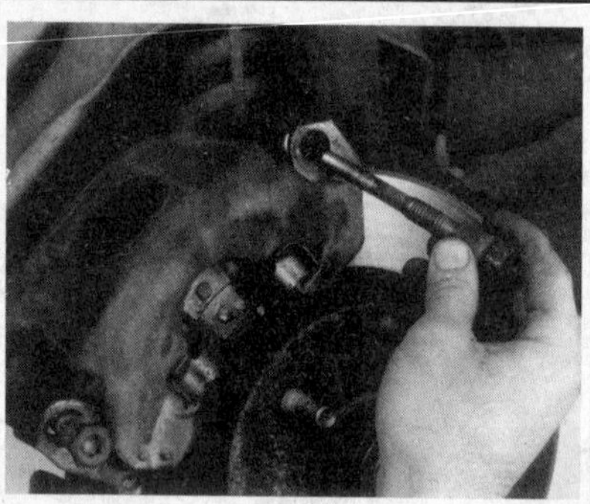
88159P59

Fig. 26 Use caliper lubricant on the sliding portions of the bolts

88159P60

Fig. 27 Always replace the crush washers on the brake line fitting

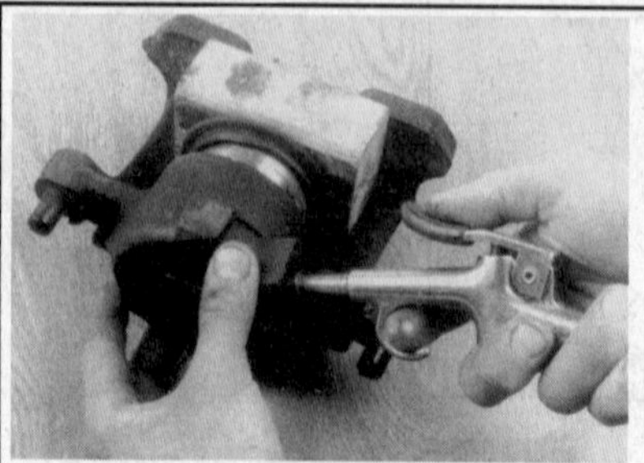
88159P61

Fig. 28 Use compressed air to force the piston from the caliper. Use a block of wood to prevent it from ejecting out of the caliper

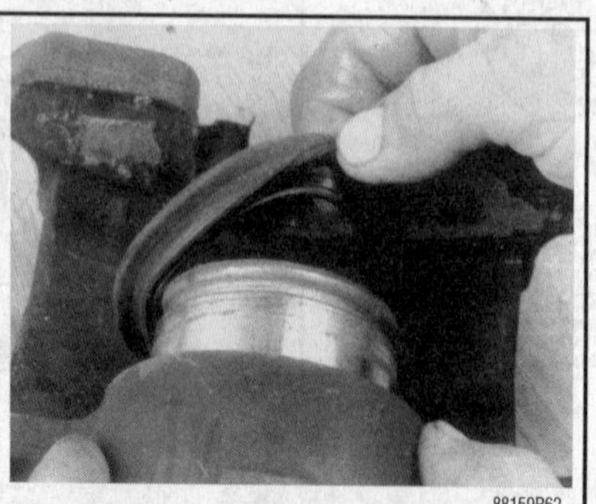
88159P62

Fig. 29 The dust boot groove must be clean and free of corrosion for the boot to seal tightly

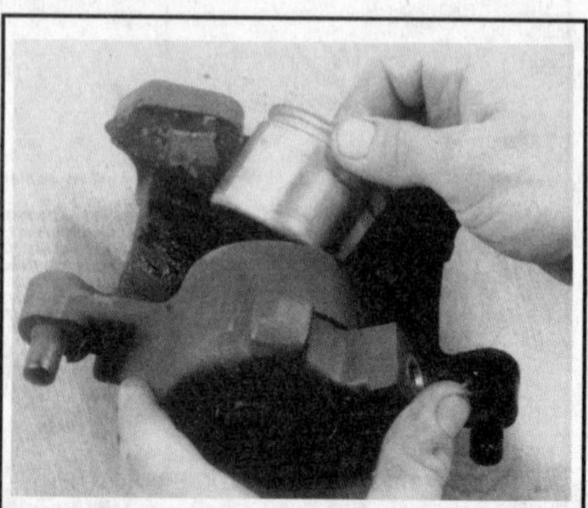
88159P63

Fig. 30 Check the piston for corrosion and pitting

88159P64

Fig. 31 Replace the piston seal as a matter of course when rebuilding a caliper

12. Install the brake pads and the caliper. Bleed the hydraulic system and re-center the pressure differential valve. Do not drive the vehicle until a firm brake pedal is achieved.

Brake Rotor

REMOVAL & INSTALLATION

1. Raise and safely support the vehicle. Remove the wheel.
2. Remove the caliper but do not disconnect the brake hose. Suspend the caliper inside the fender with wire. Do not allow the caliper to hang by the hose.
3. Remove the grease cap from the hub and remove the cotter pin, locknut, adjusting nut and flat washer.
4. Remove the outer bearing cone and roller assembly; remove the hub and rotor assembly.
5. Inspect the rotor for scoring and wear. Replace or machine as necessary. If machining, observe the minimum thickness specification.
6. Installation is the reverse of removal. Make sure the grease in the hub is clean and adequate. Adjust the wheel bearings.

INSPECTION

➧ See Figures 32 and 33

If the rotor is deeply scarred or has shallow cracks, it may be refinished on a brake lathe.

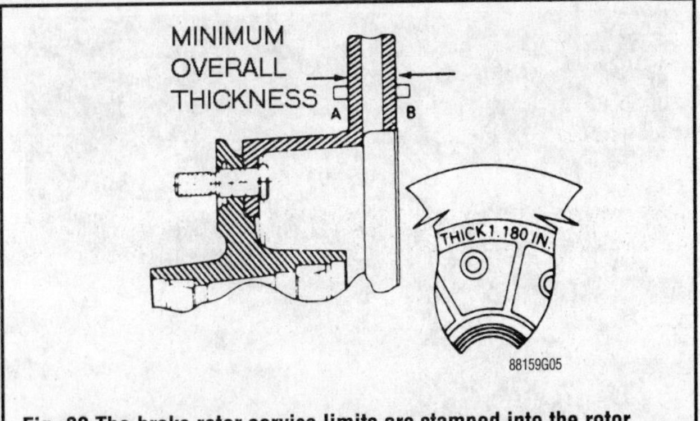

88159G05

Fig. 32 The brake rotor service limits are stamped into the rotor

88159P65

Fig. 33 Check the rotor for deep grooves and scoring

A minimum thickness of 0.972 in (24.68 mm) must be maintained on 5.0L vehicles, and 0.810 in. (20.5 mm) must be maintained on 2.3L vehicles. If the damage cannot be corrected by grinding to these minimums, the rotor must be replaced.

The finished braking surfaces of the rotor must be parallel within 0.007 in (0.18 mm) and lateral run-out must not be more than 0.003 in. (0.076 mm) on the inboard surface in a 5 inch (127 mm) radius.

REAR DRUM BRAKES

⁂ CAUTION

Brake linings contain asbestos, which has been determined to be a cancer-causing agent. Never clean the brake surfaces with compressed air. Avoid inhaling dust from any brake surface. When cleaning brake surfaces, use a commercially available brake cleaning fluid.

Rear Brake Drum

REMOVAL & INSTALLATION

➧ See Figures 34 and 35

1. Raise and safely support the vehicle.
2. Remove the wheel and tire assembly.
3. Remove the drum retaining nuts and remove the brake drum.

➡If the drum will not come off, pry the rubber plug from the backing plate. Insert a narrow rod through the hole in the backing plate and dis-

88159P66

Fig. 34 Back off the brake shoe adjustment and the drum should slide right off

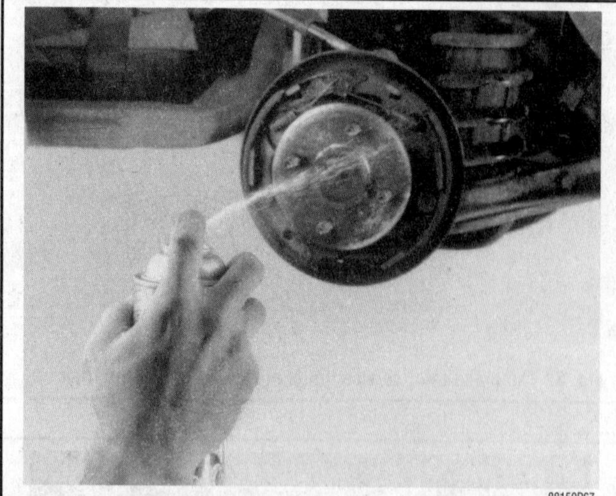

Fig. 35 Clean the surface of the hub flange. A small amount of anti-sieze compound will prevent the drum from corroding to the hub

engage the adjusting lever from the adjusting screw. While holding the adjustment lever away from the screw, back off the adjusting screw with a brake adjusting tool.

4. Inspect the brake drum for scoring and wear. Replace or machine as necessary. If machining, observe the maximum diameter specification.
5. Installation is the reverse of removal.

INSPECTION

See Figure 36

Check that there are no cracks or chips in the braking surface. Excessive bluing indicates overheating and a replacement drum is needed. The drum can be machined to remove minor damage and to establish a rounded surface on a warped drum. Never exceed the maximum oversize of the drum when machining the braking surface. The minimum inside diameter is stamped on the rim of the drum.

Rear Brake Shoes

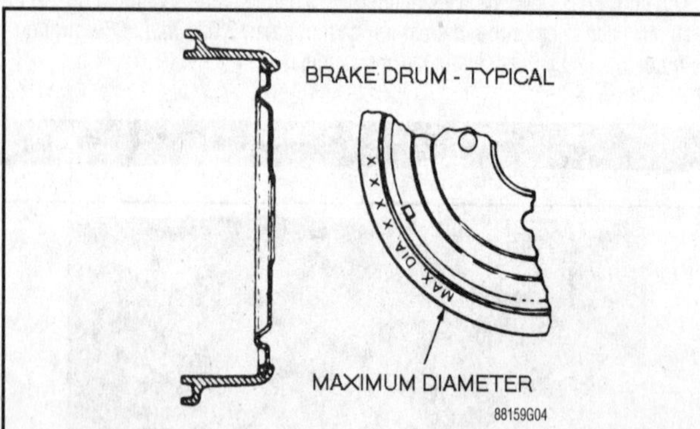

Fig. 36 The brake drum maximum diameter will be stamped into the drum

REMOVAL & INSTALLATION

See Figures 37 thru 47

1. Raise and safely support the vehicle. Remove the rear wheels. Remove the brake drum.
2. Remove the shoe anchor springs and unhook the cable eye from the anchor pin. Remove the anchor pin plate.

Fig. 37 Release the return springs with a tool made for that purpose

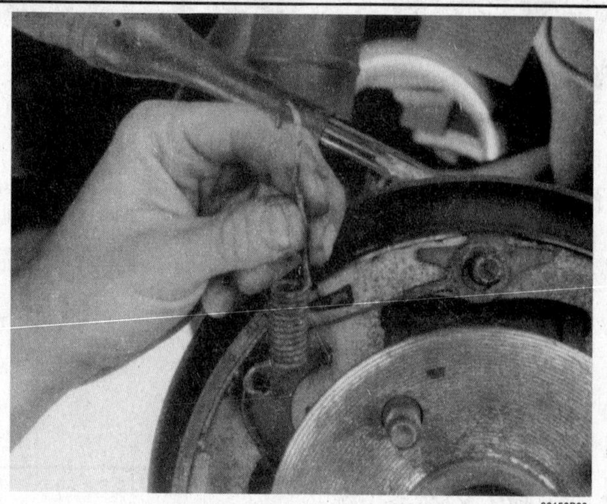

Fig. 38 Check the return springs for damage or elongation

Fig. 39 Remove the cable from the assembly keeping note of its routing

88159P71

Fig. 40 Note the orientaion of the plate

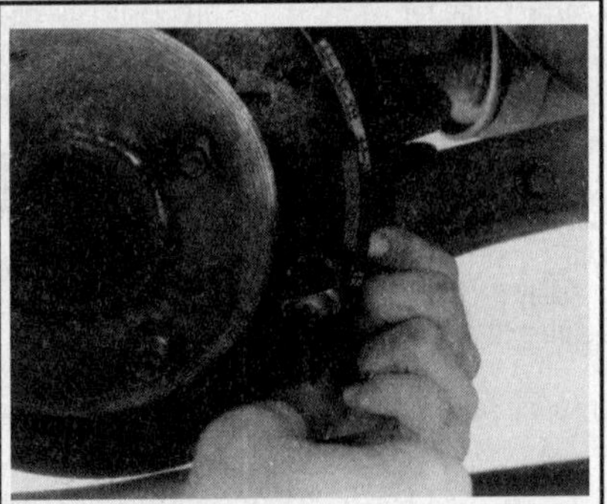
88159P72

Fig. 41 Release the holddown springs with a tool made for that purpose

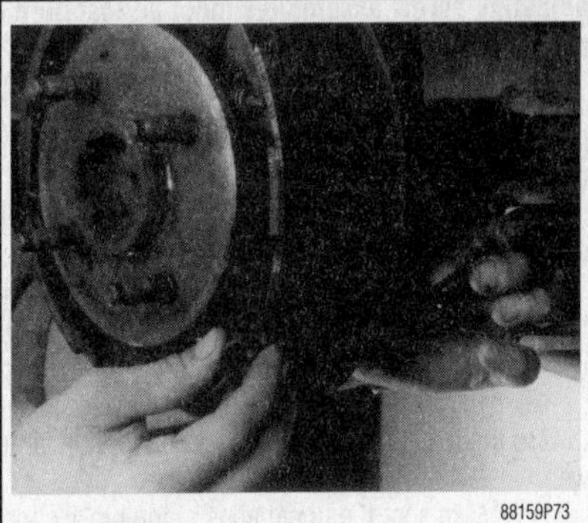
88159P73

Fig. 42 Pull the pin out from the rear of the backing plate

88159P74

Fig. 43 The shoes can be removed at this stage

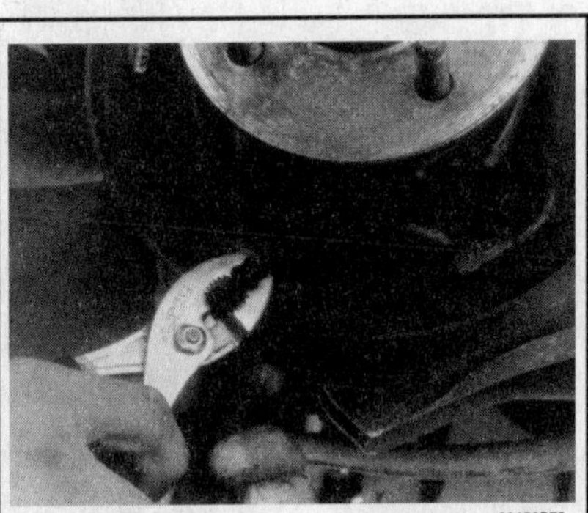
88159P75

Fig. 44 The lever needs to be removed from the parking brake cable

88159P77

Fig. 45 Do not lose the spring on the bar

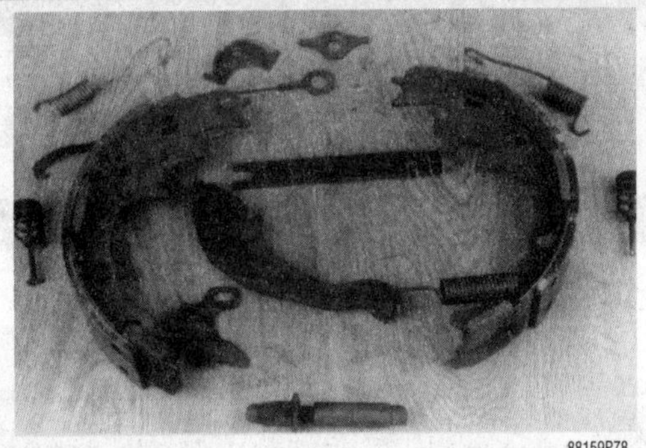
88159P78

Fig. 46 This is a good reason to do only one side at a time. The multitude of parts can be daunting to reassemble from memory

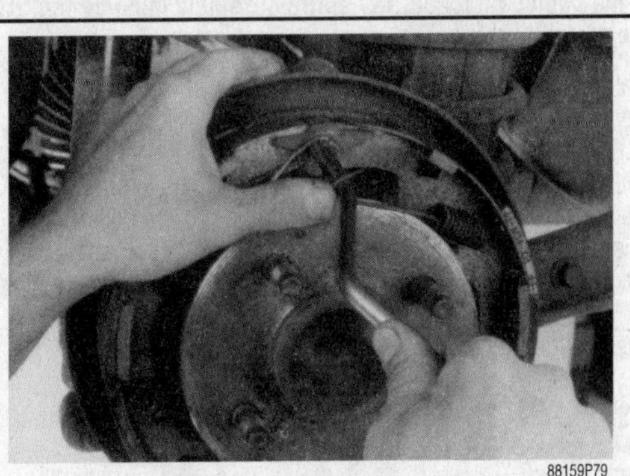
88159P79

Fig. 47 Use the proper tool to reassemble the return springs on the post. This tool makes the job easier and safer

3. Remove the shoe hold-down springs, shoes adjusting screw, pivot nut, socket and automatic adjustment parts.
4. Remove the parking brake link, spring and retainer. Disconnect the parking brake cable from the parking brake lever.
5. After removing the rear brake secondary shoe, disassemble the parking brake lever from the shoe by removing the retaining clip and spring washer.

To install:

6. Before installing the rear brake shoes, assemble the parking brake lever to the secondary shoe and secure it with the spring washer and retaining clip.
7. Apply a light coating of caliper slide grease at the points where the brake shoes contact the backing plate. Be careful not to get any lubricant on the brake linings.
8. Position the brake shoes on the backing plate. The primary shoe (with the short lining) faces the front of the vehicle; the secondary, to the rear. Secure the assembly with the hold-down springs. Install the parking brake link, spring and retainer. Back off the parking brake adjustment, then connect the parking brake cable to the parking brake lever.
9. Install the anchor pin plate on the anchor pin. Place the cable eye over the anchor pin with the crimped side toward the drum. Install the primary shoe to the anchor pin.
10. Install the cable guide on the secondary shoe web with the flanged hole fitted into the hole in the secondary shoe web. Thread the cable around the cable guide groove.

➡The cable must be positioned in the groove and not between the guide and the shoe web.

11. Install the secondary shoe anchor spring. Make sure the cable eye is not cocked or binding on the anchor pin when installed. All parts should be flat on the anchor pin.
12. Apply a thin coat of lubricant to the threads and the socket end of the adjusting screw. Turn the adjusting screw into the pivot nut to the limit of the threads, then back it off one-half turn.

➡Make sure the socket end of the adjusting screw, stamped with R or L, is correctly installed to the right or left side of the vehicle. The

adjusting screw assemblies must be installed on the correct side for proper brake adjustment.

13. Place the adjusting socket on the screw and install the assembly between the shoe ends with the adjusting screw toothed wheel nearest the secondary shoe.
14. Place the cable hook into the hole in the adjusting lever. The adjusting levers are stamped with R or L to indicate correct installation.
15. Position the hooked end of the adjuster spring completely into the large hole in the primary shoe web. Connect the loop end of the spring to the adjuster lever hole.
16. Pull the adjuster lever, cable and automatic adjuster spring down and toward the rear, engaging the pivot hook in the large hole of the secondary shoe web.
17. Make sure the upper ends of the brake shoes are seated against the anchor pin and the shoes are centered on the backing plate.
18. Adjust the brakes, using brake adjustment gauge D18L–1103–A or equivalent.
19. Install the brake drum, install the wheel and lower the vehicle.
20. Apply the brakes several times while backing the vehicle. After each stop, the vehicle must be moved forward.

Wheel Cylinder

REMOVAL & INSTALLATION

➧ See Figures 48 and 49

1. Remove the wheel and remove the brake drum.
2. Remove the brake shoe assembly.
3. Disconnect the brake line from the wheel cylinder at the backing plate.
4. Remove the wheel cylinder attaching bolts and the wheel cylinder.
5. Installation is the reverse of removal. Tighten the brake cylinder attaching bolts to 10—20 ft. Lbs. (14–28 Nm)
6. Bleed the brake system.

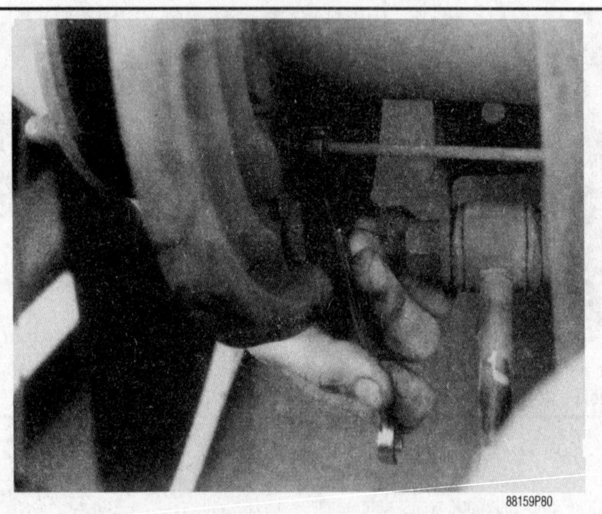
88159P80

Fig. 48 Clean the brake line fitting before trying to loosen it

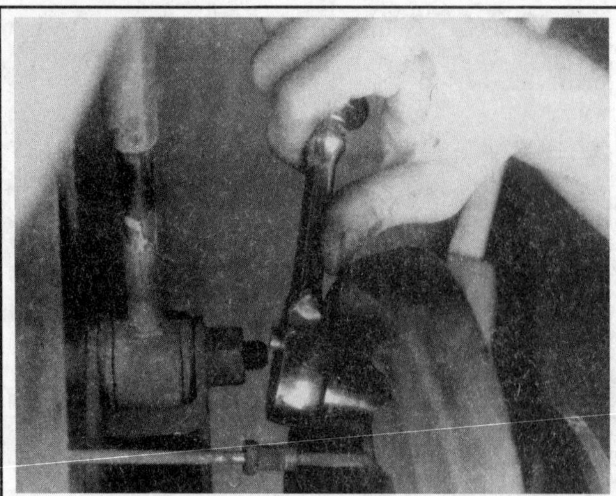
88159P81

Fig. 49 The wheel cylinder is held by two bolts on the rear of the backing plate

PARKING BRAKE

Parking Brake Cable

➧ See Figure 50

ADJUSTMENT

1. Make sure the parking brake is fully released.
2. Place the transmission in **N**. Raise and safely support the vehicle.
3. Tighten the adjusting nut against the cable equalizer, causing rear wheel brake drag. Loosen the adjusting nut until the brakes are fully released; the wheel should spin with no drag.
4. Lower the vehicle and check the operation of the parking brake.

REMOVAL & INSTALLATION

➧ See Figures 51 and 52

1. Place the parking brake control in the released position. Release the cable tension as follows:
   a. Remove the floor console.
   b. With an assistant inside, raise and safely support the vehicle.
   c. Have another assistant pull the equalizer rearward approximately 1–2½ inches to rotate the self-adjuster reel backward.
   d. Insert a steel lockpin through the holes in the lever and control assembly. This locks the ratchet wheel in the cable-release position.

➡Do not remove the lockpin until the cables are connected to the equalizer. Pin removal releases the tension in the ratchet wheel, causing the spring to unwind and release its tension. If the pin is removed without the cables attached, the entire assembly must be removed to reset the spring tension.

2. Remove the rear cables from the equalizer.
3. Remove the cable snap fitting from the body. Remove the retaining clip that attaches the cable to the underbody.
4. Remove the wheels and remove the brake drums.
5. Remove the self-adjuster springs from the backing plates.
6. Disconnect the cable ends from the parking brake levers, compress the cable retainer springs and pull the cable ends from the backing plates.
7. Installation is the reverse of removal. Adjust the parking brake.

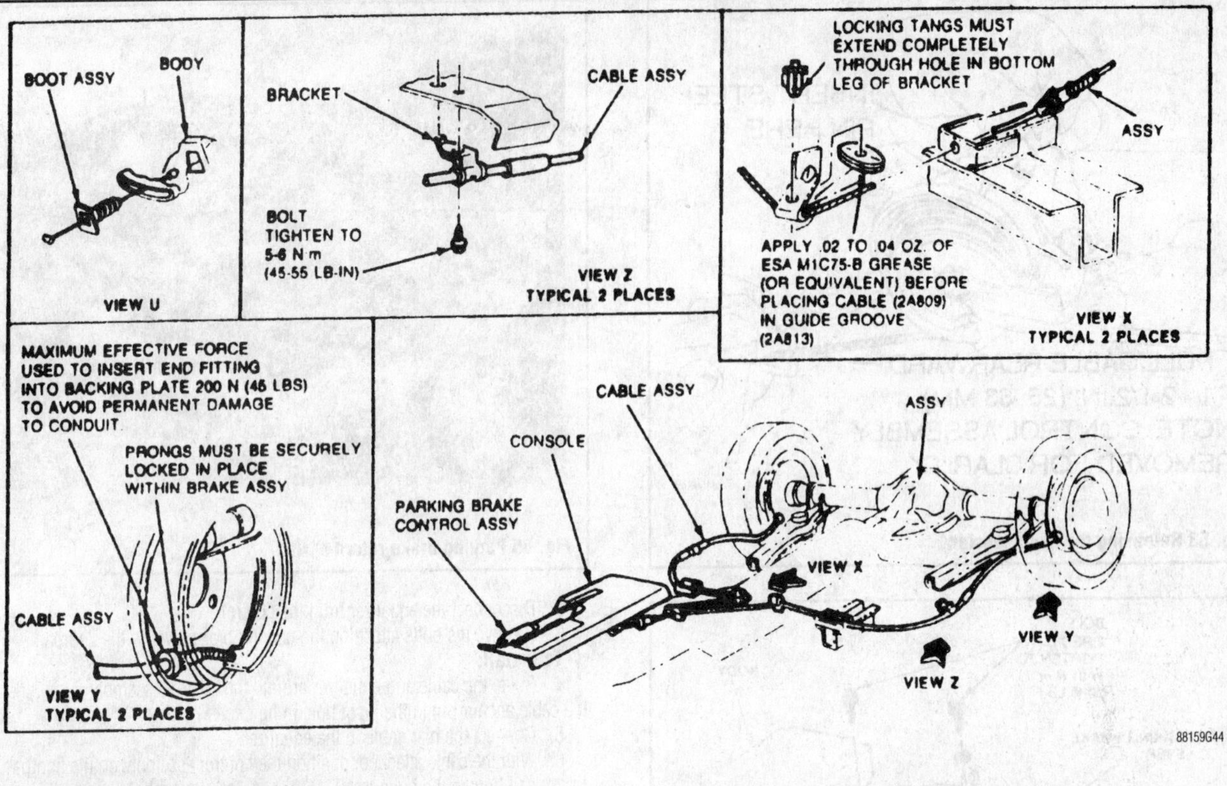

Fig. 50 Parking brake cable assemblies

Fig. 51 The cable has to be disconnected from the brake lever before it can be pulled through

Fig. 52 Slide a box end wrench over the cable and press it against the tab to release the cable housing from the backing plate

Parking Brake Lever

See Figures 53, 54 and 55

REMOVAL & INSTALLATION

1. Place the parking brake control in the released position. Release the cable tension as follows:
   a. Remove the floor console.
   b. With an assistant inside, raise and safely support the vehicle.
   c. Have another assistant pull the equalizer rearward approximately 1–2½ inches to rotate the self-adjuster reel backward.
   d. Insert a steel lockpin through the holes in the lever and control assembly. This locks the ratchet wheel in the cable-release position.

Do not remove the lockpin until the cables are connected to the equalizer. Pin removal releases the tension in the ratchet wheel, causing the spring to unwind and release its tension. If the pin is removed without the cables attached, the entire assembly must be removed to reset the spring tension.

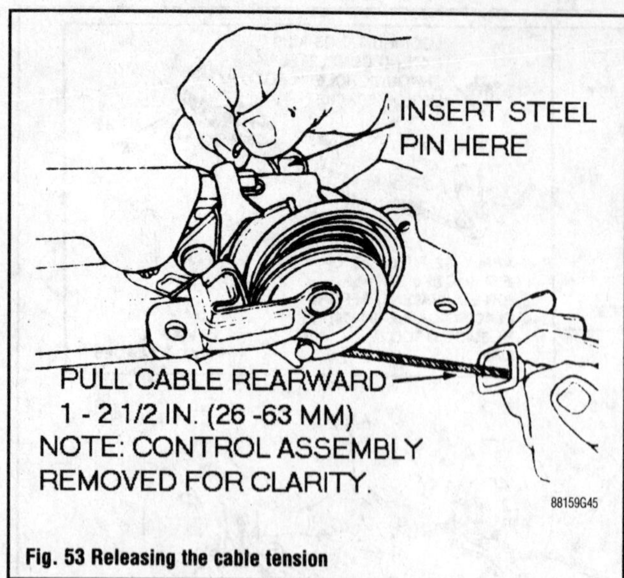

Fig. 53 Releasing the cable tension

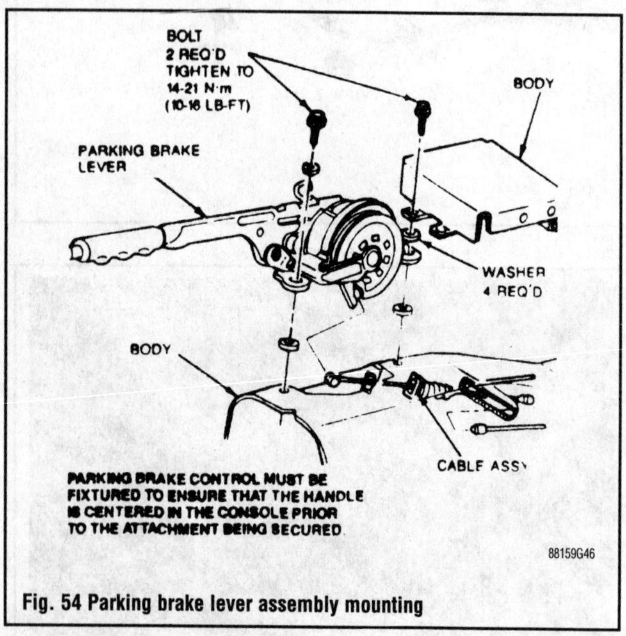

Fig. 54 Parking brake lever assembly mounting

Fig. 55 Parking brake return spring

2. Disconnect the equalizer from the control.
3. Remove the bolts attaching the parking brake lever to the floorpan.

To install:

4. Route the cable and equalizer around the control assembly pulley. Install the cable anchor pin in the pivot hole in he ratchet.
5. Connect the rear cable to the equalizer.
6. With the cable attached, position the control assembly on the floorpan. Install and tighten the bolts to 10–16 ft. Lbs. (12–21 Nm).
7. Remove the lockpin from the control assembly to reset the tension.
8. Apply the parking brake several times. Make certain that the brakes apply and that the BRAKE warning lamp on the instrument panel lights when the lever is engaged.
9. Install the console.

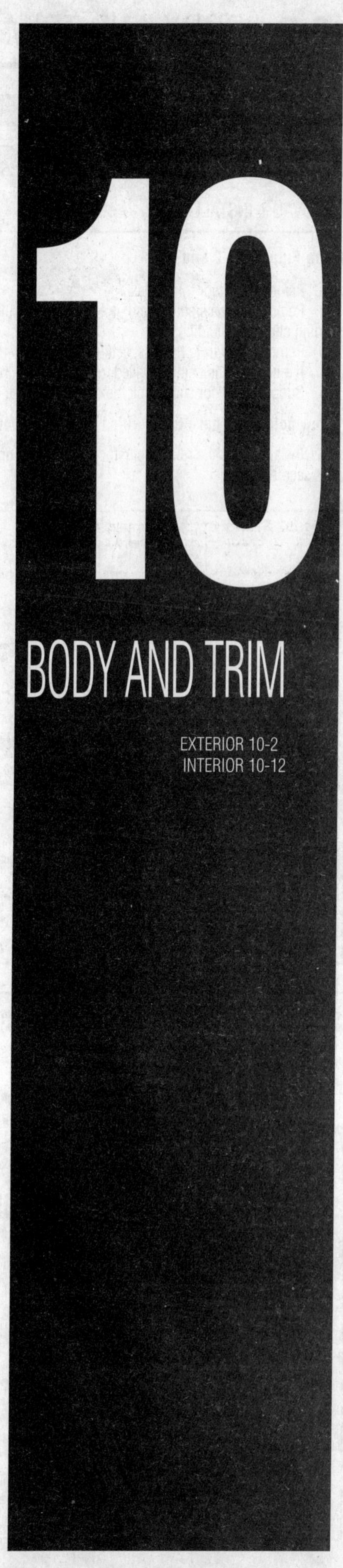
10
BODY AND TRIM
EXTERIOR 10-2
INTERIOR 10-12

EXTERIOR

Doors

REMOVAL & INSTALLATION

➧ **See Figures 1, 2 and 3**

1. Remove the door trim panel.
2. Remove the watershield, and, if a new door is being installed, save all the molding clips and moldings.
3. Remove the wiring harness, actuator and speakers.
4. If a new door is being installed, remove all window and lock components.
5. Support the door and unbolt the hinges from the door.

➡New holes may have to be drilled in a replacement door for the trim.

6. Installation is the reverse of removal. Align the door and tighten the hinge bolts securely.

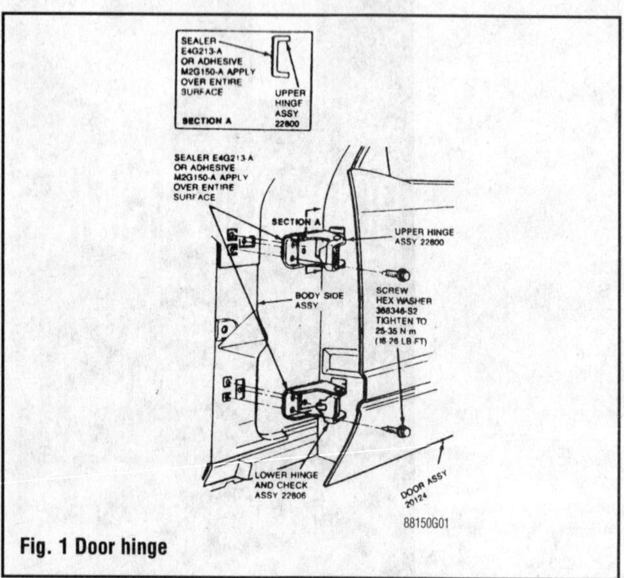

Fig. 1 Door hinge

ADJUSTMENT

➧ **See Figures 1, 2, 3 and 4**

➡Loosen the hinge-to-door bolts for lateral adjustment only. Loosen the hinge-to-body bolts for both lateral and vertical adjustment.

1. Determine which hinge bolts are to be loosened and back them out just enough to allow movement.
2. To move the door safely, use a padded pry bar. When the door is in the proper position, tighten the bolts to 24 ft. lbs. (33 Nm), then check door operation. There should be no binding or other interference when the door is either closed or opened.
3. Door closing adjustment can also be affected by the position of the lock striker plate. Loosen the striker plate bolts and move the striker plate just enough to permit proper closing and locking of the door.

Hood

REMOVAL & INSTALLATION

➧ **See Figures 5, 6, 7 and 8**

1. Open and support the hood.
2. Matchmark the hood-to-hinge positions.
3. Have an assistant support the hood while you remove the hinge-to-hood bolts.

⁂ WARNING

An assistant is needed to keep the hood from sliding back and damaging the windshield once the bolts are removed.

4. Once the bolts are removed, carefully lift the hood (with the help | or your assistant) and position it aside. You may wish to place the hood on a soft protective surface such as carpet remnants or some clean rags.
5. Installation is the reverse of removal.

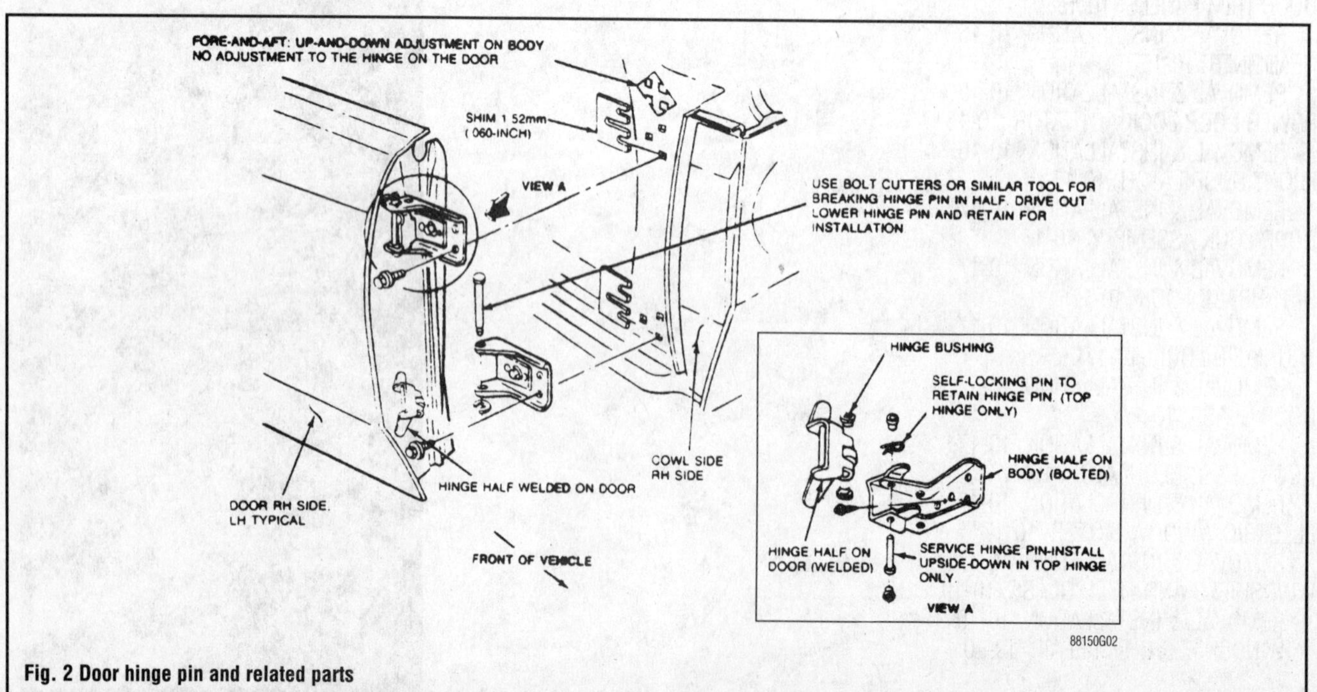

Fig. 2 Door hinge pin and related parts

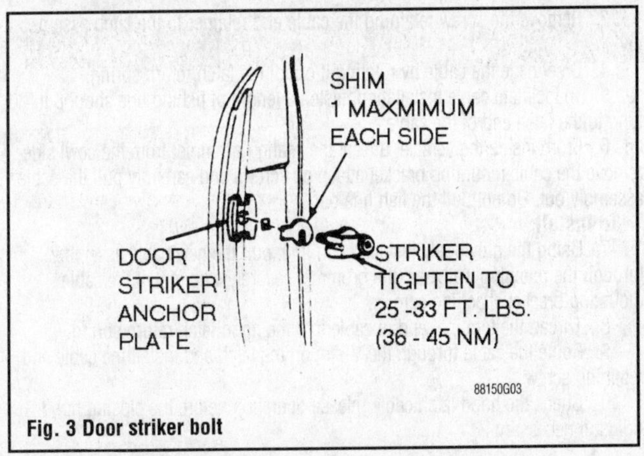

Fig. 3 Door striker bolt

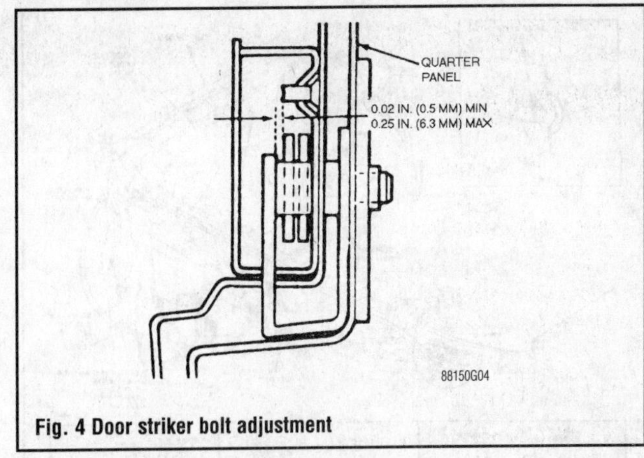

Fig. 4 Door striker bolt adjustment

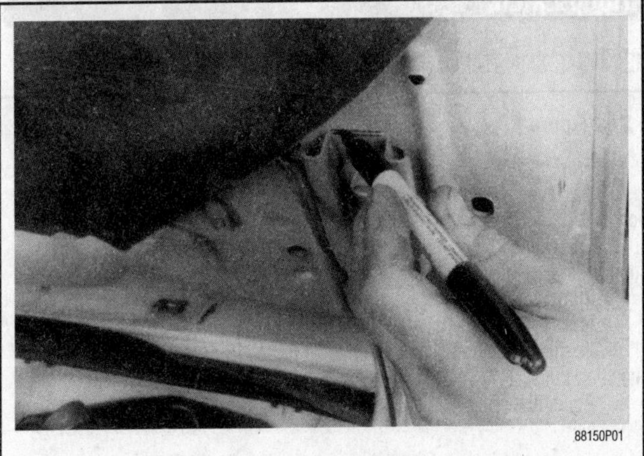

Fig. 5 Matchmark the hood to the hinges before removal, this will greatly ease installation and alignment

Fig. 6 While an assistant supports the hood, loosen and remove the retaining bolts

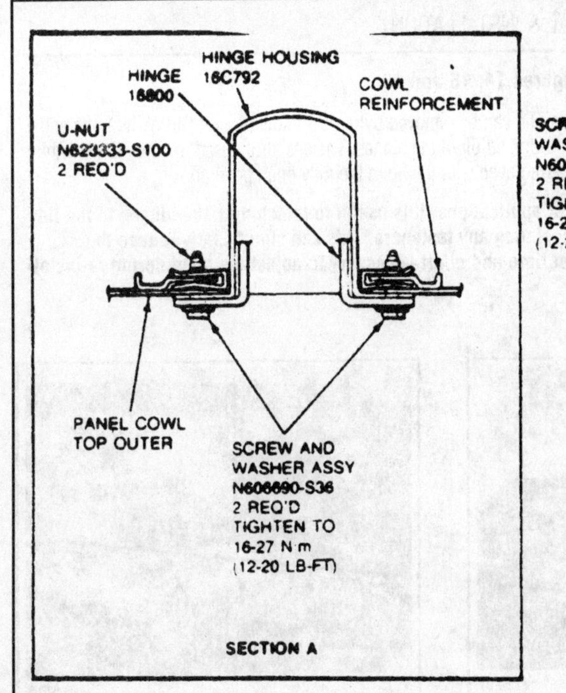

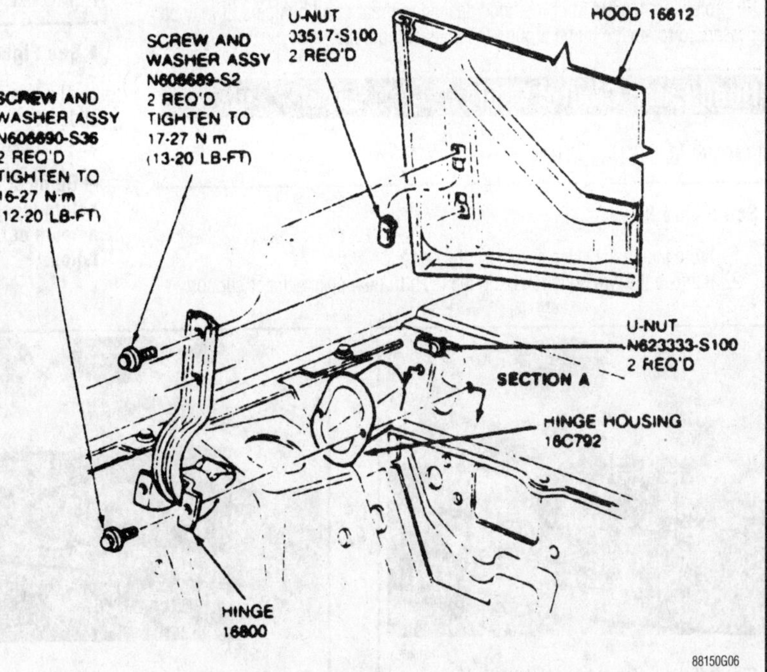

Fig. 7 Hood hinge assembly

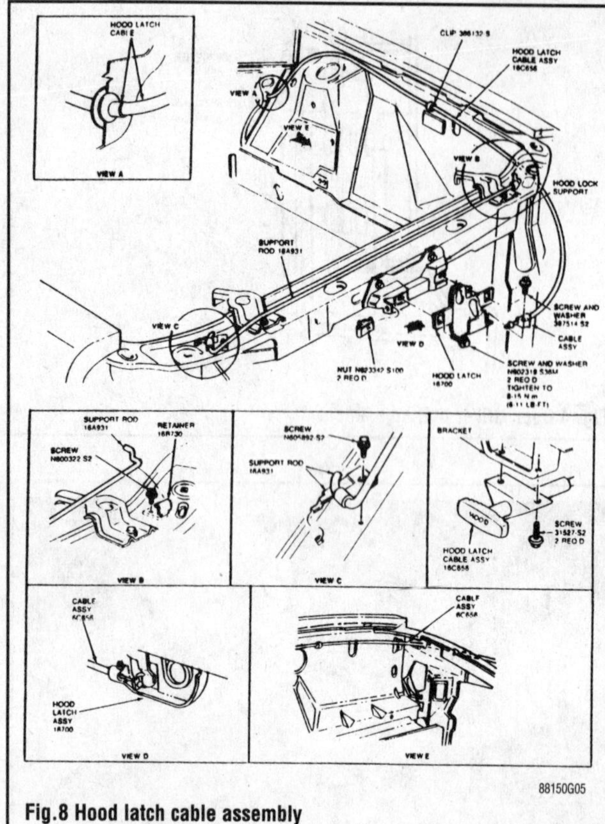

88150G05

Fig.8 Hood latch cable assembly

ALIGNMENT

➧ See Figure 7

1. Side-to-side and fore-aft adjustments can be made by loosening the hood-to-hinge attachment bolts, then positioning the hood as necessary.
2. Hood vertical fit can be adjusted by raising or lowering the hinge-to-fender reinforcement bolts.
3. To ensure a snug fit of the hood against the rear hood bumpers, it may be necessary to rotate the hinge around the 3 attaching bolts.

Hood Latch Control Cable

REMOVAL & INSTALLATION

➧ See Figure 8

1. From inside the vehicle, release the hood.
2. Remove the two bolts retaining the latch to the upper radiator support.
3. Remove the screw retaining the cable end retainer to the latch assembly.
4. Disengage the cable by rotating it out of the latch return spring.
5. To facilitate cable installation, fasten a length of fishing line about 8 ft. long to the latch end of the cable.
6. From inside the vehicle, unseat the sealing grommet from the cowl side, remove the cable mounting bracket attaching screws and carefully pull the cable assembly out. Do not pull the fish line out.

To install:

7. Using the previously installed fish line, pull the new cable assembly through the retaining wall, seat the grommet securely, and install the cable mounting bracket attaching screws.
8. Thread the terminal end of cable into the hood latch return spring.
9. Route the cable through the V-slot on the latch and install the cable end retaining screw.
10. Check the hood latch cable release operation before the closing hood. Adjust if necessary.

Hood Latch

REMOVAL & INSTALLATION

➧ See Figure 8

1. From inside the vehicle release the hood.
2. Remove the two bolts retaining the latch to the upper radiator support.
3. Remove the two bolts retaining the hood latch assembly to the radiator support, then remove the latch.

To install:

4. Engage the hood latch to the control cable.
5. Position the hood latch to the radiator support, then install the two attaching bolts.
6. Adjust the hood latch and tighten the attaching bolts to 7–10 ft. lbs. (9–14 Nm).

Trunk Lid/Hatch Door

➧ See Figures 9, 10, 11, 12 and 13

REMOVAL & INSTALLATION

➧ See Figures 14, 15 and 16

The trunk lid can be removed by removing the hinge-to-trunk lid bolts and sliding the trunk lid off of the hinges. The gas struts used to support the trunk lid must be removed with the lid in the fully open position.

➡On most applications, it is useful to matchmark the hinges to the lid before loosening any fasteners. This can significantly reduce the amount of time and effort necessary to adjust the hood during re-installation.

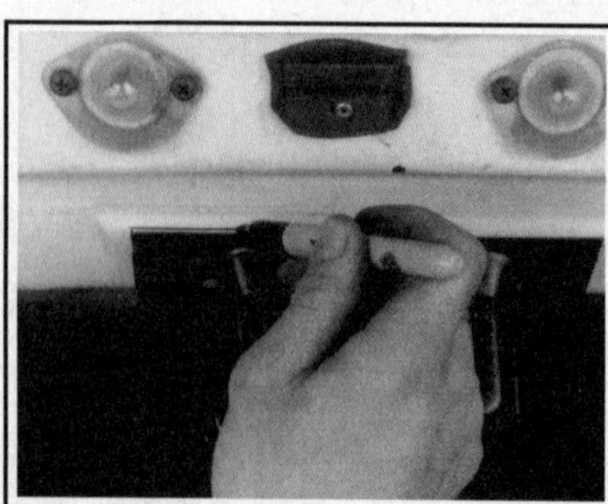

88150P03

Fig. 9 If the hatch lid or latch/striker requires replacement or adjustment, always start by marking a reference line . . .

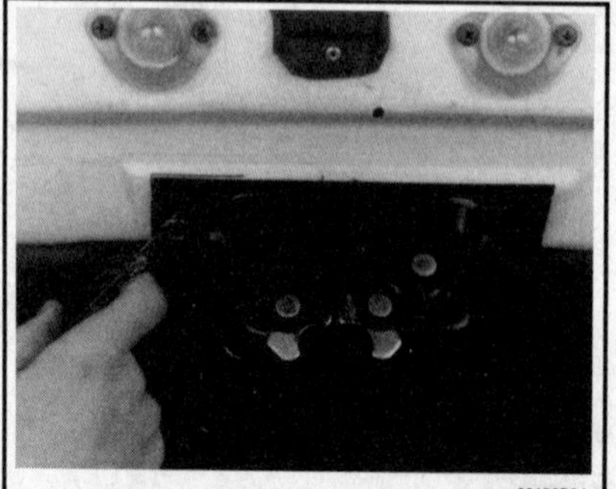

88150P04

Fig. 10 . . . then loosen and remove the component's retaining bolts (such as this latch from a 3 door hatch lid)

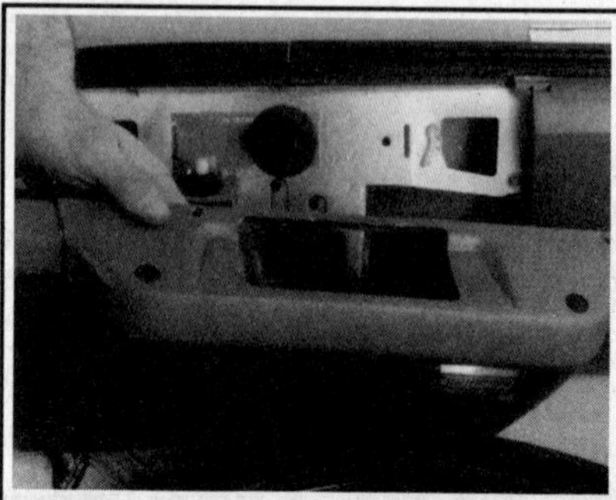

88150P05

Fig. 11 If the striker must be replaced you will first have to remove a trim panel for access . . .

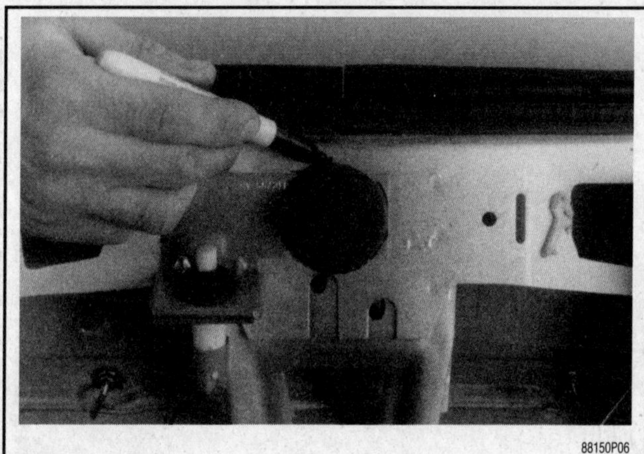
88150P06

Fig. 12 . . . again draw an orientation line for reference . . .

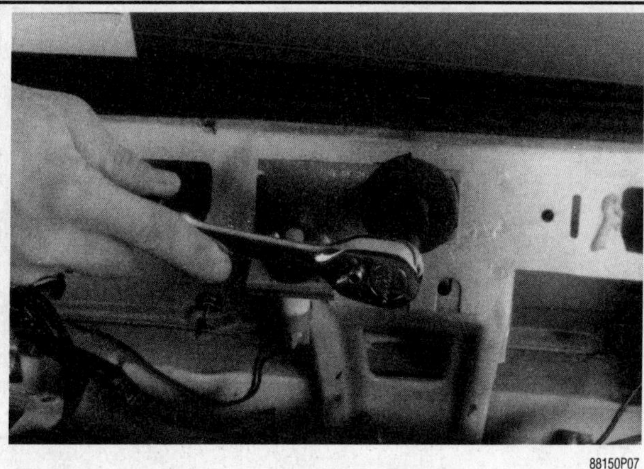
88150P07

Fig. 13 . . . then loosen and remove the striker

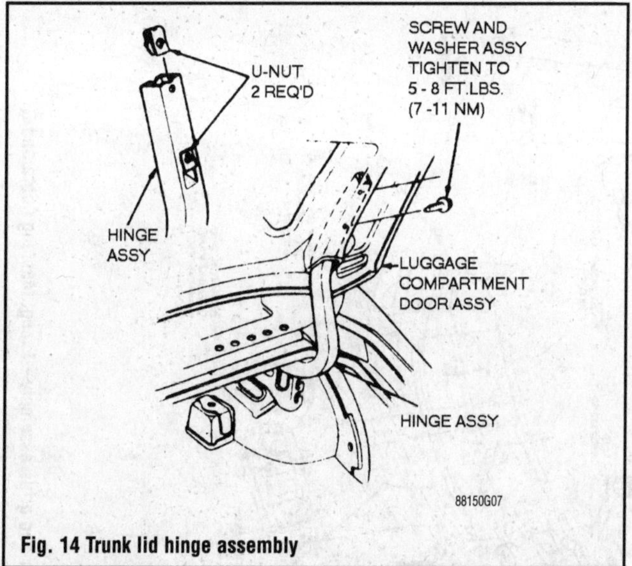

88150G07

Fig. 14 Trunk lid hinge assembly

ALIGNMENT

Fore-aft fit may be adjusted by loosening the hinge-to-lid bolts and positioning the lid as necessary.

Vertical fit can be adjusted by adding or deleting shims located between the the hinges and trunk lid.

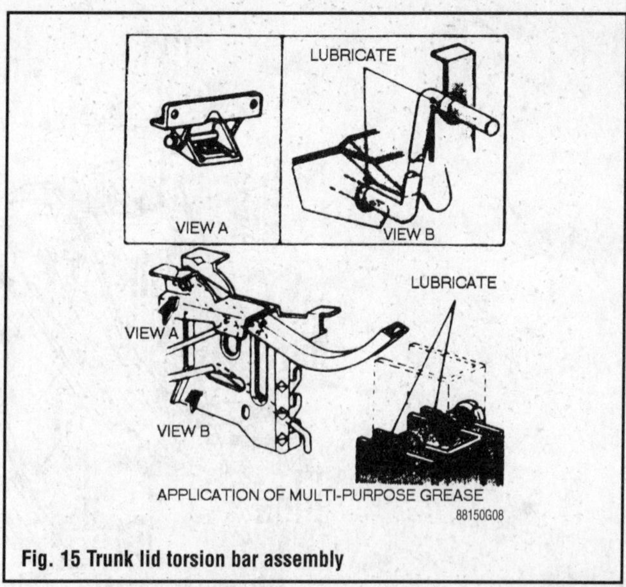

88150G08

Fig. 15 Trunk lid torsion bar assembly

Liftgate Support Cylinder

REMOVAL & INSTALLATION

➧ **See Figure 16**

1. Open the liftgate and temporarily support it.
2. The lift cylinder end fitting is a spring-clip design and removal is accomplished by sliding a small prybar under it, then prying up to remove it from the ball stud.
3. Remove the support cylinder.

To install:

4. Install each cylinder to the C-pillar and the liftgate bracket ball socket by pushing the cylinder's locking wedge onto the socket.
5. Close the liftgate. Check the support cylinder operation.

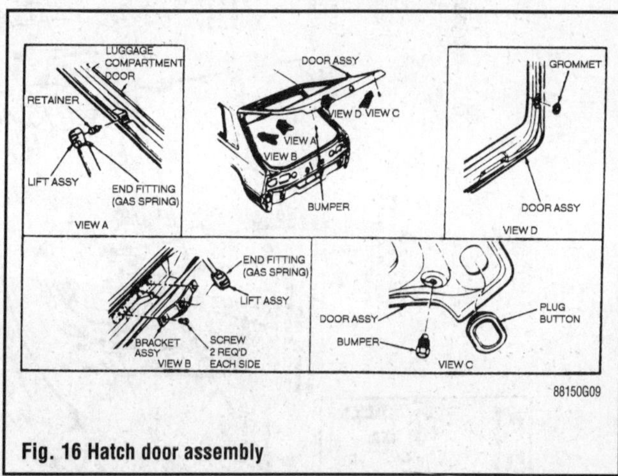

88150G09

Fig. 16 Hatch door assembly

Front Bumper

REMOVAL & INSTALLATION

➧ **See Figures 17 and 18**

➡ **On most models, the front facia/bumper cover must be removed before bumper removal. The facia is usually fastened on both sides and along its entire length.**

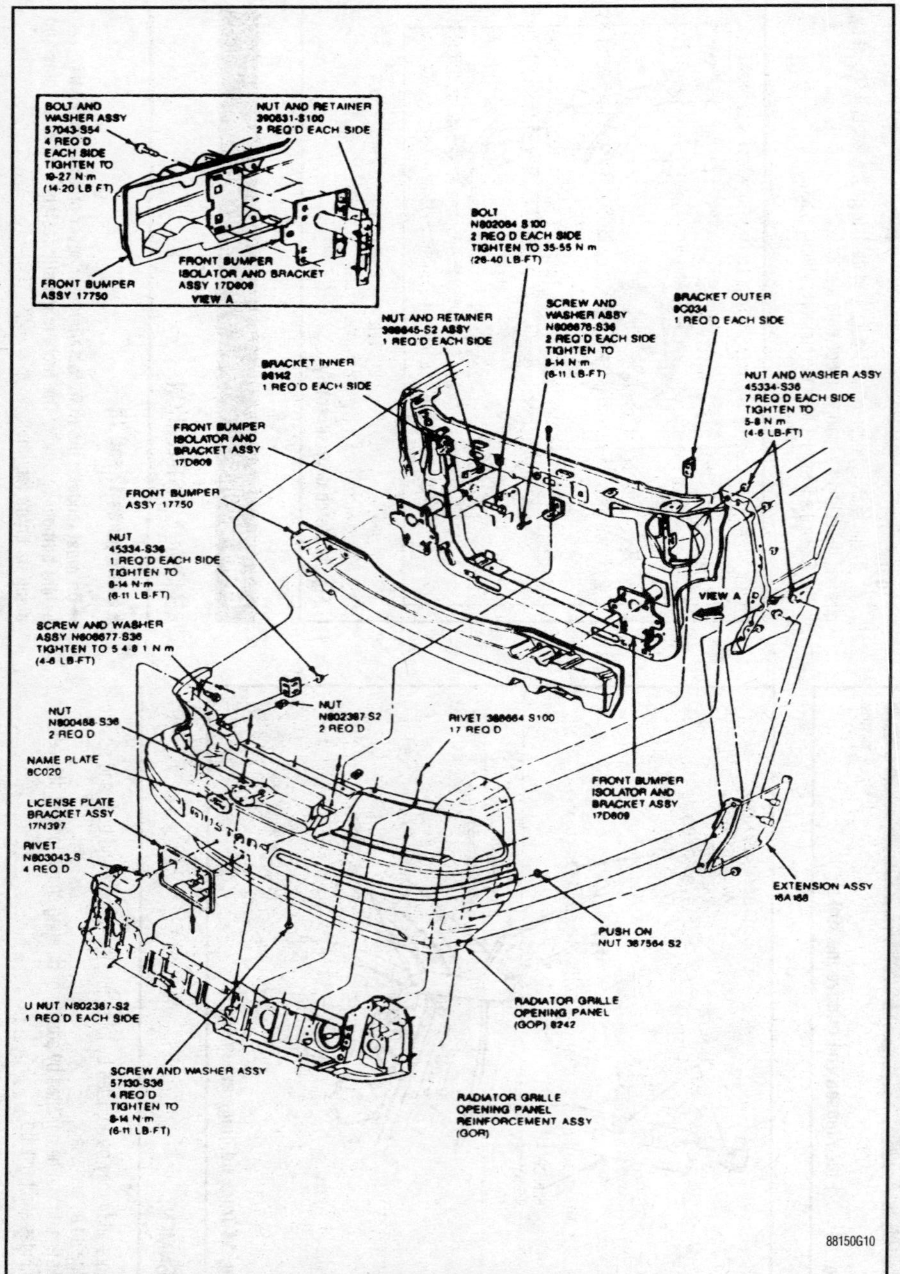

Fig. 17 Front bumper and grille assembly—Except Mustang Cobra and GT

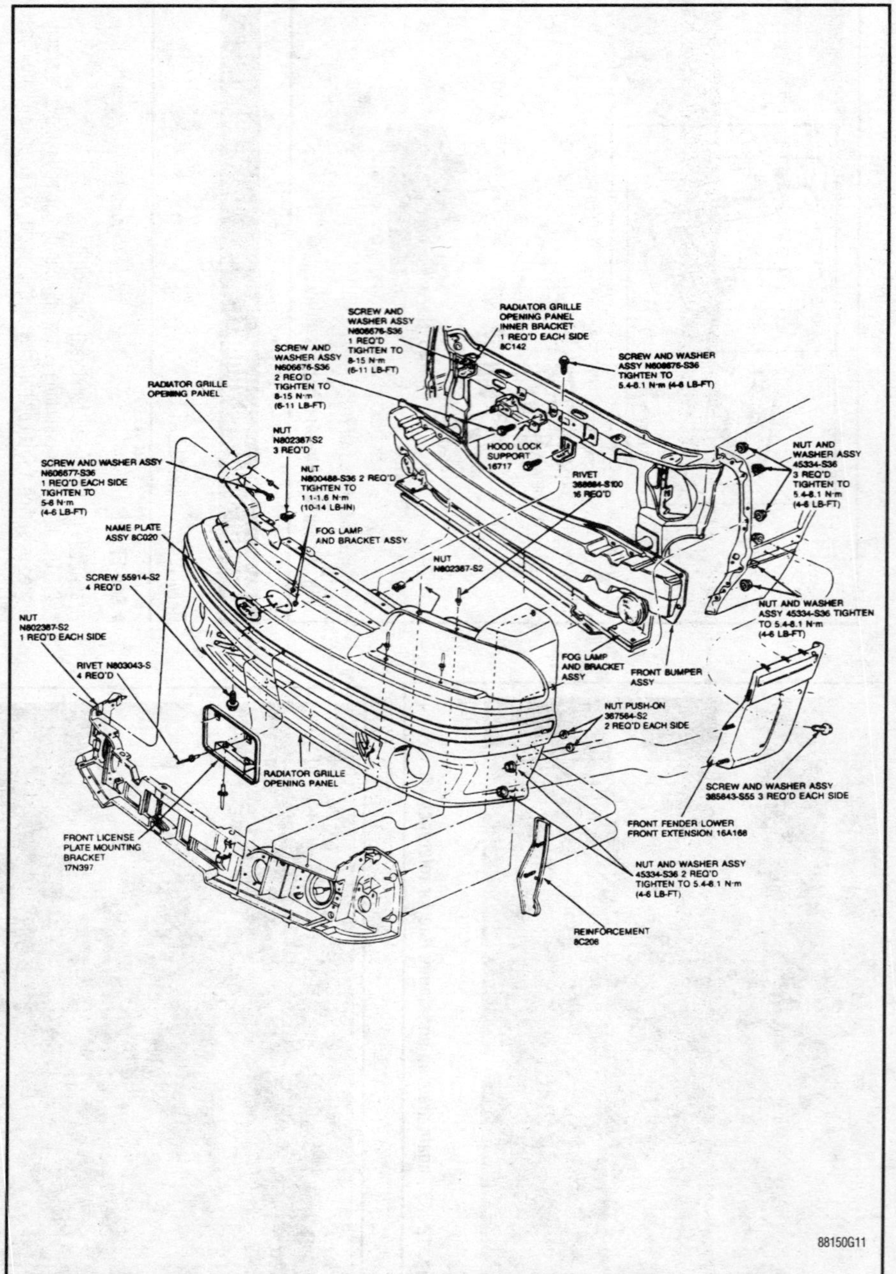

Fig. 18 Front bumper and grille assembly—Mustang GT (Cobra similar)

1. The bumper is freed by removing the 8 attaching bolts.
2. Squeeze the bumper pad retaining tabs with pliers and push them through their holes until the pads are removed.
3. Installation is the reverse of removal. Tighten the bracket-to-bumper bolts to 14–20 ft. lbs. (19–27 Nm) and the isolator-to-reinforcement bolts to 25–38 ft. lbs. (34–51 Nm).

Rear Bumpers

REMOVAL & INSTALLATION

See Figures 19, 20, 21 and 22

1. Remove the 6 pushpins retaining the cover to the bottom of the reinforcement. The pushpins must be destroyed to remove them.
2. Remove the nuts or bolts attaching the cover to the body.
3. Remove the 6 isolator-to-bracket bolts and remove the bumper.
4. Installation is the reverse of removal. Tighten the bolts to 20 ft. lbs. (27 Nm).

Grille

REMOVAL & INSTALLATION

See Figures 17 and 18

1. Remove the license plate bolts or rivets.
2. Remove the lower grille-to-radiator support screws.
3. Remove the upper grille-to-support brackets.
4. Remove the grille-to-fender nuts and detach the reinforcement assembly.

88150P08

Fig. 19 Although the rear bumper bolts are easily accessed from beneath the vehicle . . .

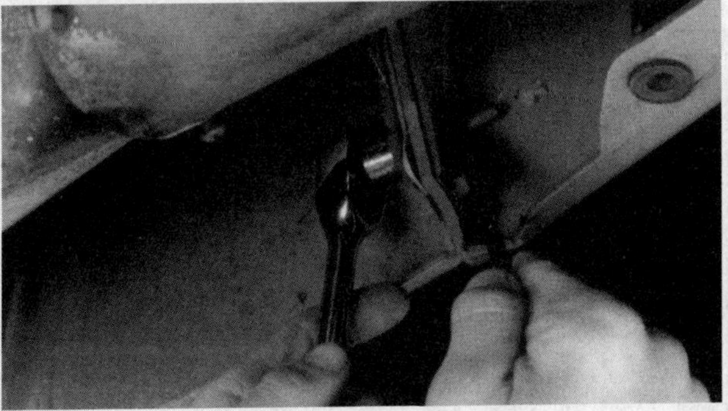

88150P09

Fig. 20 . . . don't attempt bumper removal until the cover is unbolted from the body and grille assembly—Except Mustang Cobra and GT

5. Remove the headlamp side marker, park and turn lamps from the reinforcement.
6. Remove the 2 pushnuts per side attaching the lower corner reinforcement assembly.
7. Drill out the grille-to-reinforcement rivets and remove the grille.
8. Installation is the reverse of removal.

Outside Mirror

REMOVAL & INSTALLATION

Right Hand Standard (Manual) Type

1. Remove the inside sail cover.
2. Remove the nut and washer assemblies and lift the mirror off the door.

To install:

3. Install the mirror on door.
4. Install and tighten the nut and washer assemblies.
5. Install the inside sail cover.

Left Hand Remote Control

See Figure 23

1. Pull the nob assembly to remove it from the control shaft.
2. Remove the interior sail cover retainer screw and remove the cover.
3. Loosen the setscrew retaining the control assembly to the sail cover.
4. Remove the mirror attaching nuts, washers and grommet. Remove the mirror and the control assembly.

To install:

5. Seat the grommet in the outer door panel and position the mirror to the door. Install the attaching nuts and washers, then tighten to 25–39 inch lbs. (3–4 Nm).
6. Route the control mechanism through the door and position to the sail trim panel. Tighten the setscrew to 2–6 inch lbs. (0.2–0.7 Nm).
7. Position the sail cover to the door and install the retaining screw.
8. Position the rubber knob onto the control shaft and push to install.

Power Outside Mirrors

See Figure 24

Outside mirrors that are frozen must be thawed prior to adjustment. Do not attempt to free-up the mirror by pressing the glass assembly.

1. Disconnect the negative battery cable.
2. Remove the one screw retaining the mirror mounting hole cover and remove the cover.
3. Remove the door trim panel.
4. Disconnect the mirror assembly wiring connector. Remove the necessary wiring guides.
5. Remove the three mirror retaining nuts on the sail mirrors, two on door mirrors. Remove the mirror while guiding the wiring and connector through the hole in the door.

To install:

6. Install the mirror assembly by routing the connector and wiring through the hole in the door. Attach with the three retaining nuts on the sail mirrors, two on the door mirrors. Tighten the retaining nuts.
7. Engage the mirror wiring connector and install the wiring guides.
8. Replace the mirror mounting hole cover and install one screw.
9. Replace the door trim panel.
10. Connect the negative battery cable.

Antenna

REMOVAL & INSTALLATION

See Figures 25 and 26

1. Remove the radio and disconnect the antenna cable at the radio by pulling it straight out of the set.
2. Remove the right-hand cowl side trim panel.

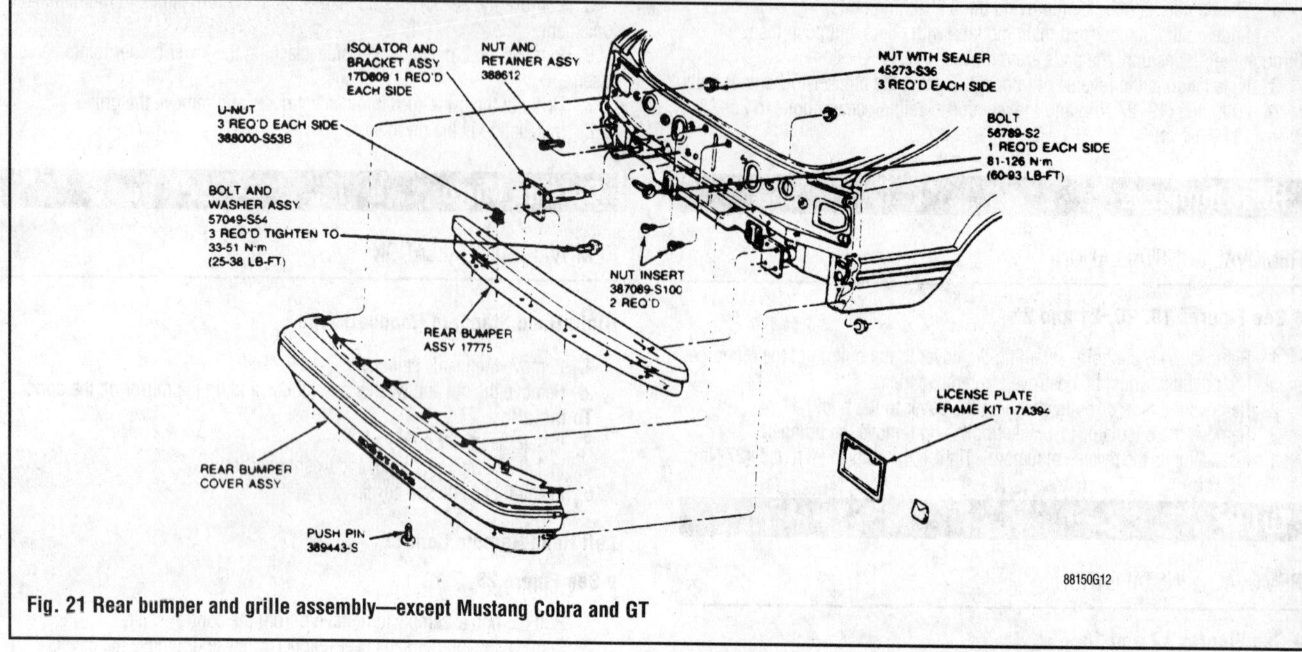

Fig. 21 Rear bumper and grille assembly—except Mustang Cobra and GT

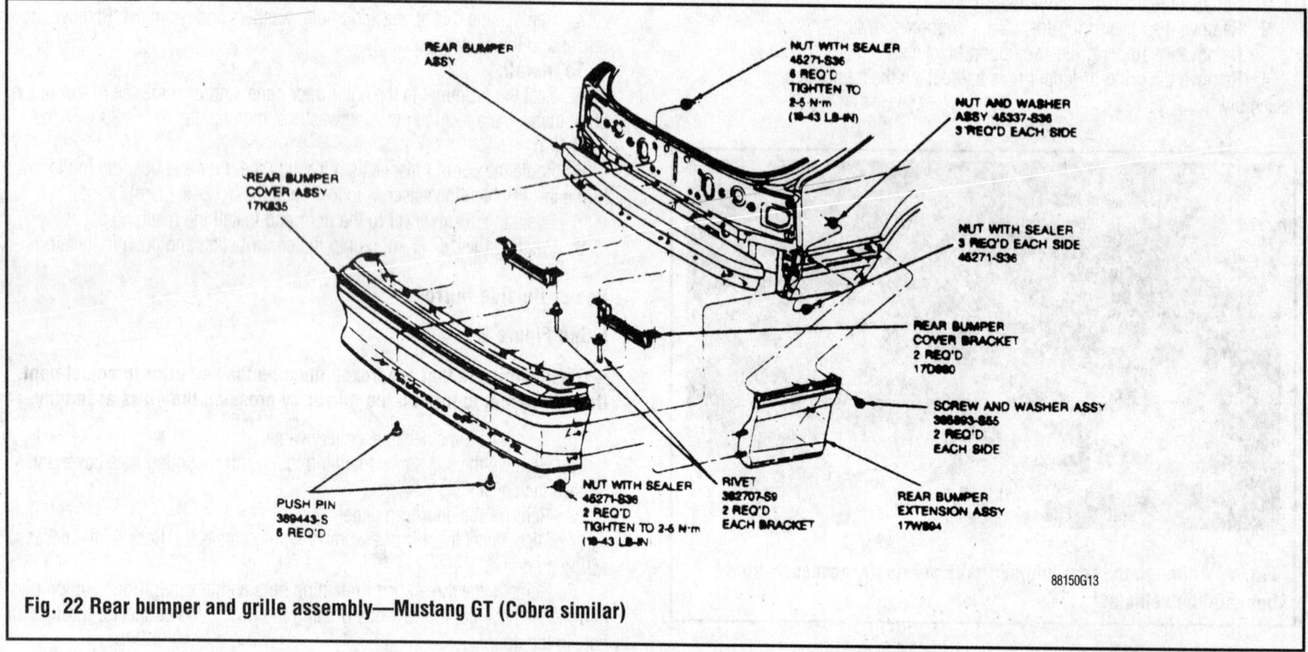

Fig. 22 Rear bumper and grille assembly—Mustang GT (Cobra similar)

3. Remove the antenna cable clip holding the antenna cable to the heater plenum.
4. Remove the antenna cap and antenna base retaining screws, then pull the cable through the holes in the door hinge pillar and fender. Remove the antenna assembly.

To install:

5. With the right-hand door open, position the antenna assembly in the fender opening, put the gasket in position on the antenna and install the antenna base to the fender.
6. Pull the antenna lead through the door hinge pillar opening. Seat the grommet by pulling the cable from inside the vehicle.
7. Route the cable behind the heater plenum and attach the locating clip. Connect the lead to the rear of the radio.
8. Install the right side cowl trim panel. Install the radio.

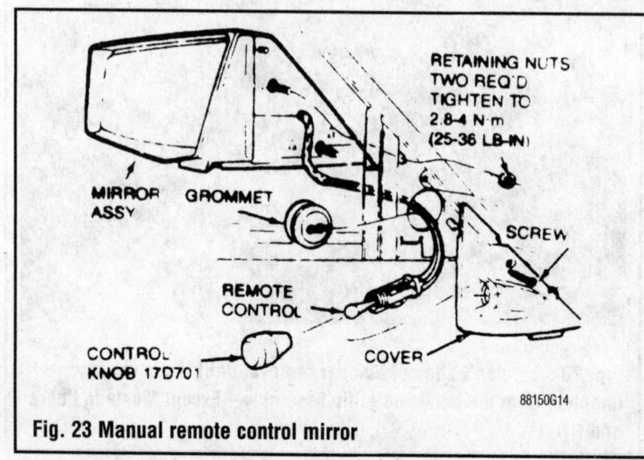

Fig. 23 Manual remote control mirror

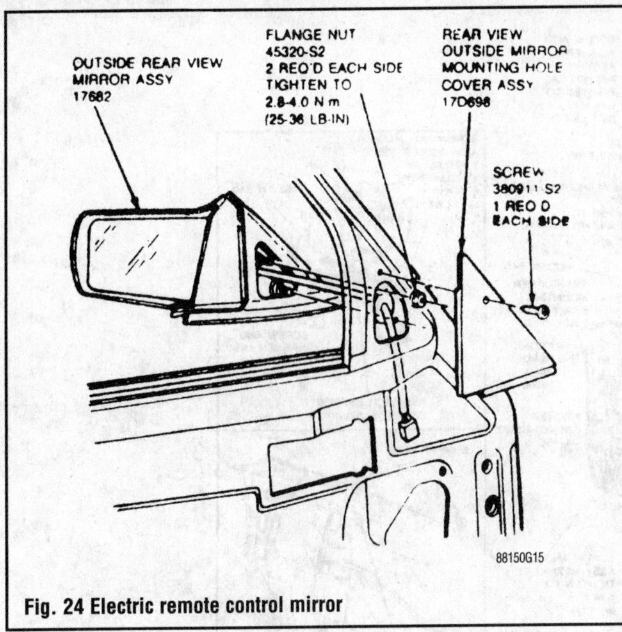

Fig. 24 Electric remote control mirror

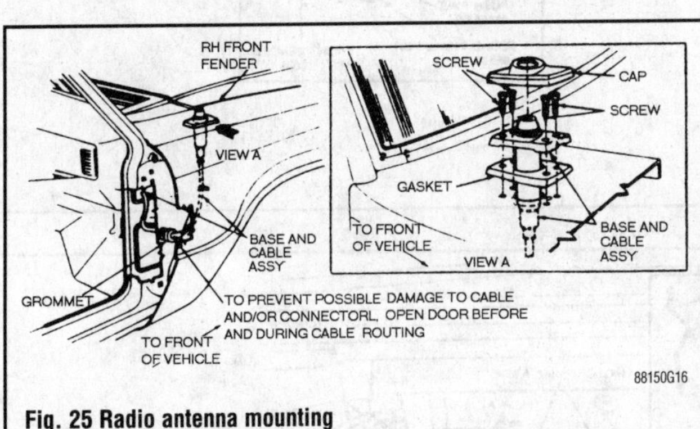

Fig. 25 Radio antenna mounting

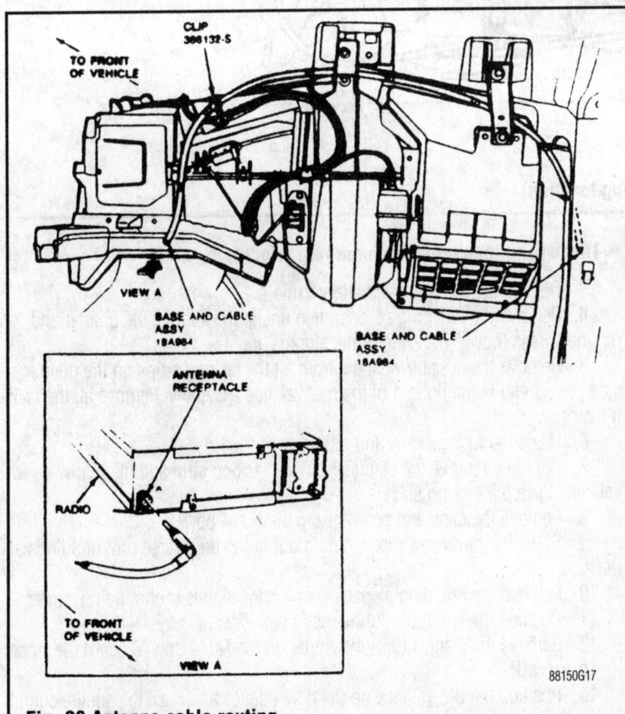

Fig. 26 Antenna cable routing

Fenders

REMOVAL & INSTALLATION

See Figure 27

1. Remove the front bumper assembly.
2. Remove the screws retaining the grille opening reinforcement panel to the fender. Remove the screws retaining the upper front fender mounting bracket to the fender.
3. Remove the screws retaining the front fender mounting bracket to the fender. Remove the screws retaining the lower rear fender to the side of the body.
4. Remove the bolts retaining the upper and lower front fender. Remove the three retaining bolts from the catwalk area of the fender apron. Remove the fender from the vehicle.
5. Installation is the reverse of the removal procedure.

Convertible Top

MOTOR REPLACEMENT

See Figures 28 and 29

Motor and Pump

1. Open the top to the fully raised position.
2. Disconnect the negative battery cable.
3. Disconnect the wires at the pump motor.
4. Vent the reservoir by removing, then reinstalling the filler plug. The plug is located on the top of the reservoir.

The reservoir must be vented to equalize pressure. This will minimize the possibility of hydraulic fluid spraying all over when the hoses are disconnected.

5. Place rags beneath the hose connections. Disconnect the hoses, then plug the open fittings and lines.
6. Remove the retaining nuts and washers, then remove the motor and pump assembly from the floorpan. Be careful not to loose any of the rubber grommets.

To install:

7. Remove any plugs from the lines and fittings, then connect the lines to the pump.
8. Install the assembly to the floorpan. Check that all rubber grommets are in the proper position.
9. Connect the wires at the pump motor.
10. Connect the negative battery cable.
11. Operate the top assembly 2–3 times to bleed any air from the system, and check the fluid level in the reservoir. The fluid should not be less that ¼ in. (6mm) below the filler opening. The top must be up when the fluid level is checked.
12. Position the retaining clips on the rear folding top compartment support wire, then install the retaining screws.

Motor Assembly

1. Remove the rear seat back, quarter trim panel and front shoulder belt retractor.
2. Disconnect the motor-to-switch connector.
3. Remove the three motor attaching bolts and remove the motor and regulator from the panel.
4. For motor service, remove the bracket and seal from the motor by removing the three bracket retaining screws and one seal retaining screw.
5. To install, reverse the removal procedures. Tighten the motor assembly to 54–62 inch lbs. (6–7 Nm).

TOP REPLACEMENT

Rear Window Valance

See Figure 30

1. Disengage the right and left top latches by rotating the handles inward.
2. Raise the top and put 4–6 inch blocks under the front of the top.

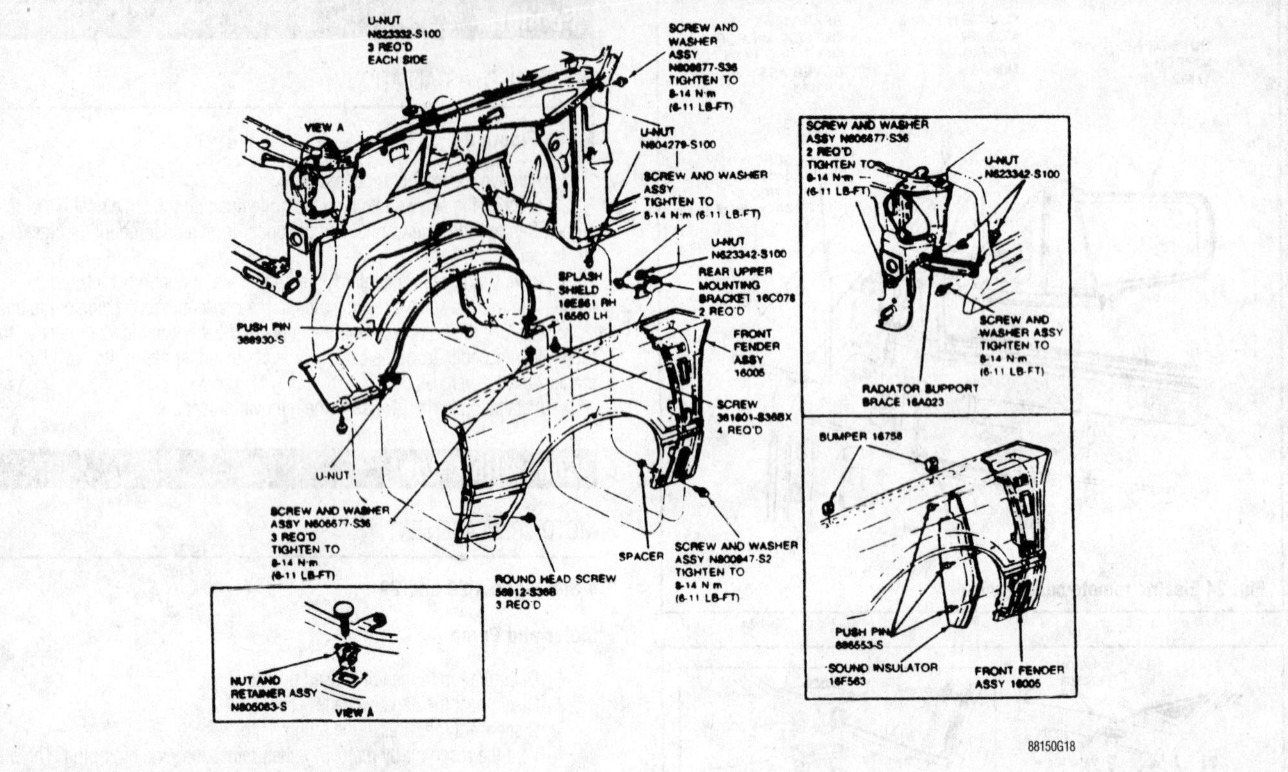

Fig. 27 Exploded view of the front fender assembly

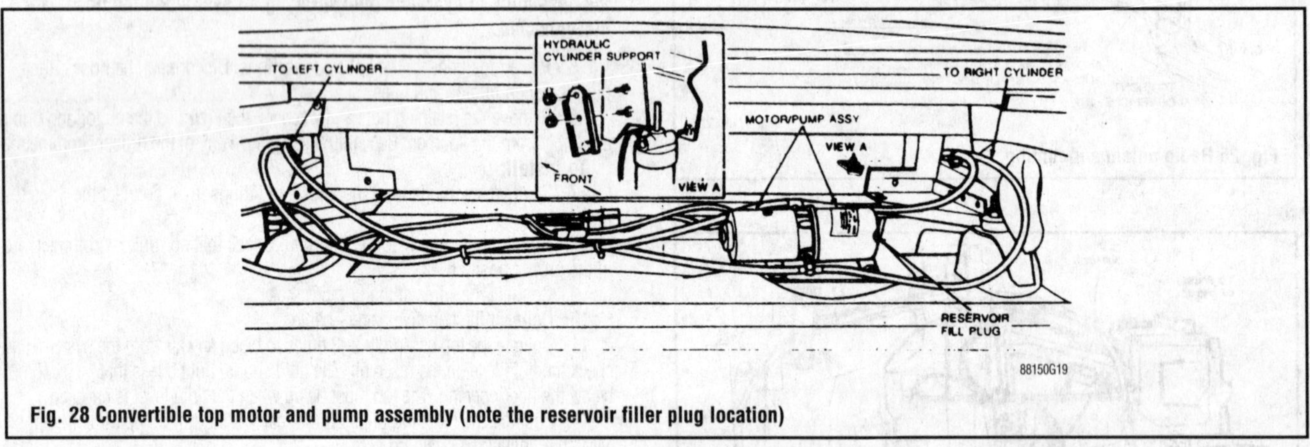

Fig. 28 Convertible top motor and pump assembly (note the reservoir filler plug location)

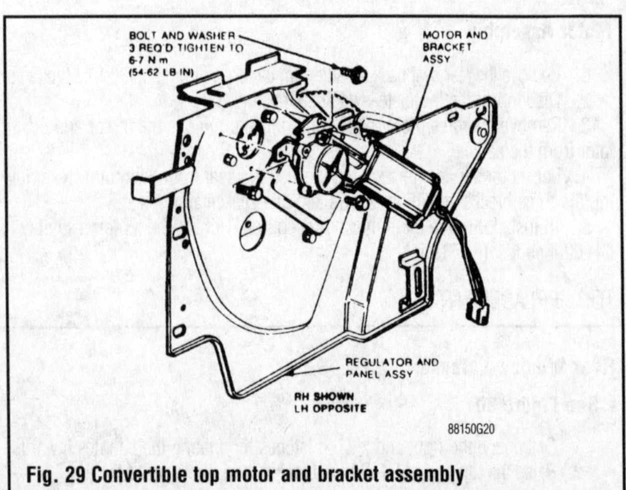

Fig. 29 Convertible top motor and bracket assembly

➡This will relieve tension on the rear window.

3. Disconnect the negative battery cable.
4. Remove the retaining screws, then unclip the sling at the quarter and rear belt areas. Lower the sling to the storage area.
5. Remove the nut and washers from all the tacking strips on the quarter side panels and at the bottom of the rear valance assembly. Remove all the tacking strips.
6. Unzip the rear window and put aside.
7. Carefully remove the staples from the tacking strip and the rear window valance. Save the tacking strip.
8. Remove the caps and screws from the No. 4 bow.
9. Slide the transverse roof molding out of the transverse roof molding carrier.
10. Remove the retaining staples from the transverse roof molding carrier.
11. Position the left and right quarter sides forward.
12. Remove the staples from the zipper on the No. 4 bow. Discard the zipper

To install:

13. Position the old valance on the new valance and trace the square cutout holes onto the new valance.

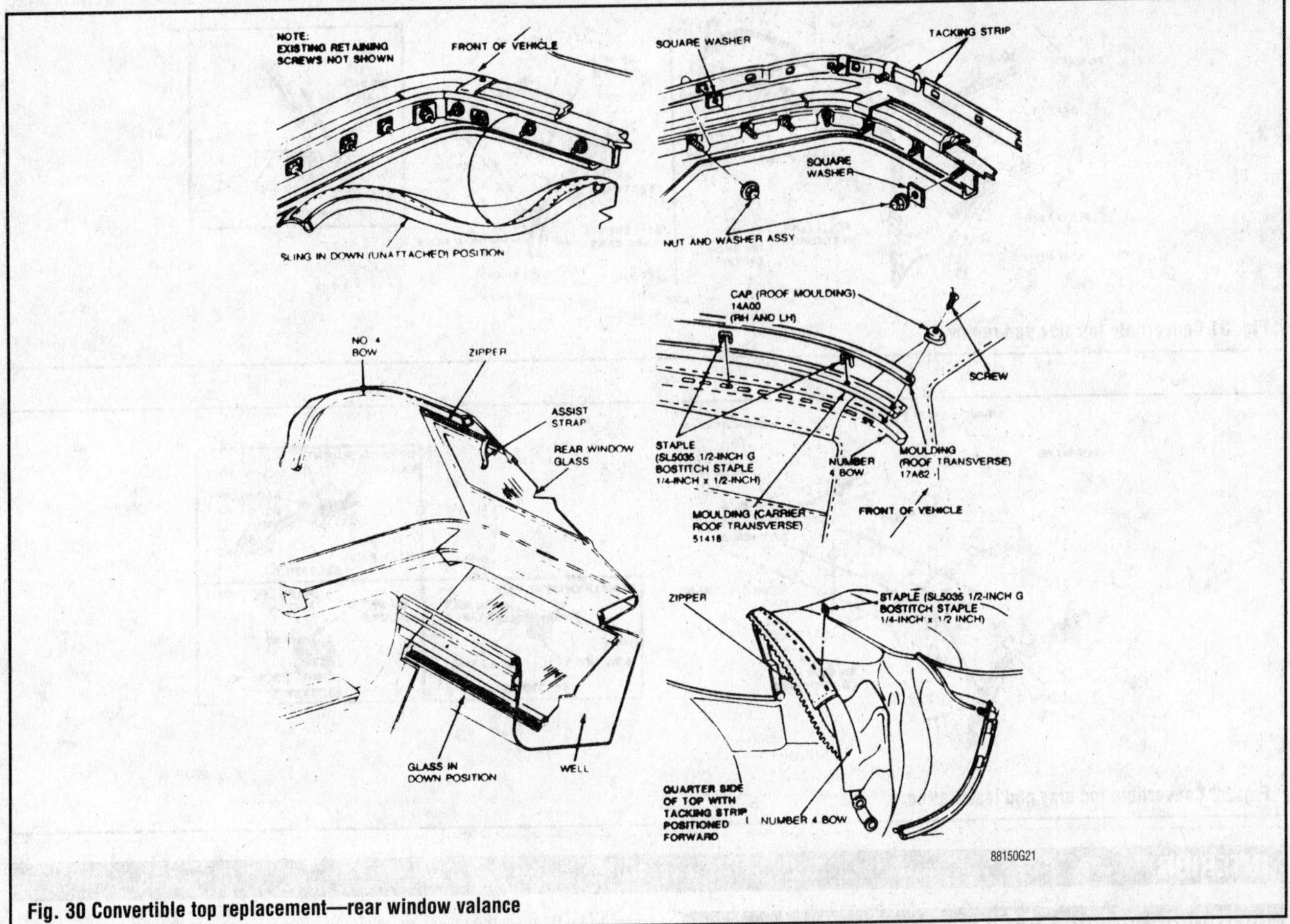

Fig. 30 Convertible top replacement—rear window valance

14. Staple the tacking strip to the new valance using a staple gun and ¼ in. x 5⁄16 in. (6mm–8mm) staples.

➡**Staples should be shot in a row with a minimal gap of ¼ in. (6mm) between each staple.**

15. Measure end-to-end on the No. 4 bow, then mark the centerline with a grease pencil.
16. Measure end-to-end on the valance, then mark the centerline with a grease pencil on the zipper of the valance.
17. Position the zipper of the valance on the No. 4 bow, aligning the centerline of the valance with the centerline of the No. 4 bow.
18. Staple the zipper portion of the valance to the No. 4 bow using a staple gun and ¼ x ½ in. (6mm–13mm) staples.

➡**Staples should be shot in a row with a minimal gap of ¼ in. (6mm) between each staple.**

19. Trim off excess material on the zipper.
20. Move the right and left quarter sides back into proper position.
21. Position the roof transverse carrier molding above the convertible top material on the No. 4 bow, then staple using a staple gun and ¼ in. x ½ in. (6mm–13mm) staples.

➡**Use RTV sealer on the top of the transverse roof carrier to prevent leaks where stapled.**

22. Slide the transverse roof molding into the transverse roof molding carrier, then attach with roof molding caps and screws.
23. Install the rear window valance in the proper position and zip closed.
24. Finger-tighten the nut and washer assemblies for the tacking strips on the quarter side panels and at the bottom of the rear window assembly.
25. Remove the blocks used to relieve tension, then open the latches, lower the top into position and lock the latches closed.
26. Adjust and secure all tacking strips on the quarter side panels and at the bottom of the rear window valance assembly.

➡**Be certain that the rear window valance has no visible sags or buckles.**

27. Cling on the sling well and attach with the retaining screws.
28. Connect the negative battery cable.
29. Raise and lower the top and confirm proper operation.

Top Stay Pad

➧ **See Figures 31 and 32**

1. Remove the top, quarter stay pad and rear window valance.
2. Remove the stay pad staples at bow No. 1 and bow No. 2.
3. Separate the inside and outside flaps, remove the needle pad and reinforcement pad.
4. Remove the staples attaching the stay pad at each corner and to the bows 2, 3, and 4, then remove the stay pad.

To install:

5. Remove the needle and reinforcement pads from the stay pad. Fold the stay pad closed, then position the pad against the offset of the bows and staple each corner with ¼ in. (6mm) staples.
6. Open the stay pad and staple at bows 2, 3, and 4 with ⅜ in. (10mm) staples.
7. Position the reinforcement in the stay pad and staple at bow No. 1 with ¼ in. (6mm) staples. Stretch the reinforcement and staple at bows 2, 3, and 4 with ⅜ in. (10mm) staples.
8. Apply adhesive to the exposed side of the reinforcement pad and to both sides of the needle pad.
9. Position the needle pad on the stay pad at the edge of bow No. 4 and just short of bow No. 1.
10. Apply adhesive to the inside surface of the stay pad flaps. Fold the flap against the needle pad and apply adhesive to the edge. Fold the outside flap over the inside flap and staple at bow No. 1 with ¼ in. (6mm) staples and at bow No. 4 with ⅜ in. (10mm) staples.
11. Install the vinyl cover.

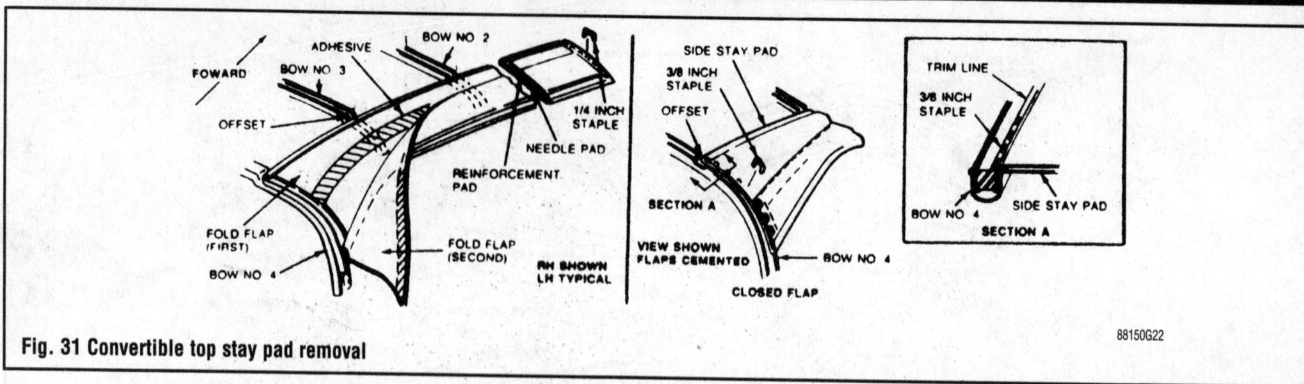

Fig. 31 Convertible top stay pad removal

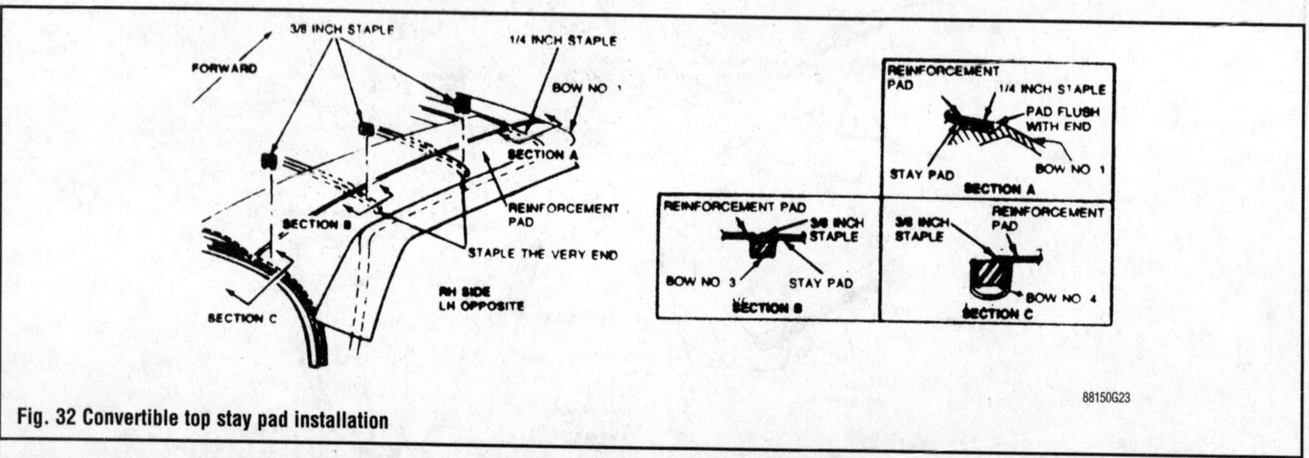

Fig. 32 Convertible top stay pad installation

INTERIOR

Instrument Panel and Pad

REMOVAL & INSTALLATION

See Figures 33 and 34

CAUTION

Some vehicles are equipped with air bags. Before attempting to service air bag-equipped vehicles, be sure that the system is properly disarmed and all safety precautions are taken. Serious personal injury and vehicle damage could result if this note is disregarded.

1. Disconnect the negative battery cable.
2. Disconnect all electrical connectors from the steering column assembly.
3. Remove the three bolts retaining the steering column opening cover and reinforcement panel. Remove the panel.
4. Remove the two bolts retaining the lower steering column opening reinforcement and remove the reinforcement.
5. Remove the floor console.
6. Remove the six nuts retaining the steering column to the instrument panel (two are retaining the hood release mechanism and four are retaining the column to lower brake pedal support). Lower the steering column to the floor.
7. Remove the steering column upper and lower shrouds, then disconnect the wiring from the combination switch.
8. Remove the brake pedal support nut.
9. Snap out the defroster grille.
10. Remove the screws from the speaker covers. Snap out the speaker covers.
11. Remove the front screws retaining the right-hand and left-hand scuff plates at the cowl trim panel.
12. Remove the right-hand and left-hand side cowl trim panels.
13. Disconnect the wiring at right-hand and left-hand cowl sides.
14. Remove the cowl side retaining bolts (one each side).
15. Open the glove compartment door and flex the glove compartment bin tabs inward. Drop down the glove compartment door assembly.
16. Remove the five cowl top screw attachments.
17. Gently pull the instrument panel away from cowl. Disconnect the air conditioning controls, speedometer cable and wire connectors.
18. If instrument panel is being replaced, transfer all components, wiring and hardware to new instrument panel.

To install:

19. Position the instrument panel in place. Engage the electrical connections. Install the instrument panel upper screws. Install the instrument panel lower screws.
20. Install the lower brace and tighten the bolts. Install the radio speaker grilles.
21. Using all openings, install all the instrument panel electrical connections, air conditioning outlets, air conditioning control cables, antenna wires and anything else that may have been removed.
22. Continue the installation in the reverse order of the removal procedure.
23. Check for proper operation of the air bag indicator. Check for proper operation of all components.

Console

REMOVAL & INSTALLATION

See Figures 35 thru 41

1. Disconnect the negative battery cable.
2. Remove the gearshift opening panel and console floor bracket retaining screws.
3. Remove the two access covers at the rear of the console assembly, in order to expose the console mounting screws. Remove the screws.
4. Remove the rear access panel and the three console-to-floor bracket retaining screws.

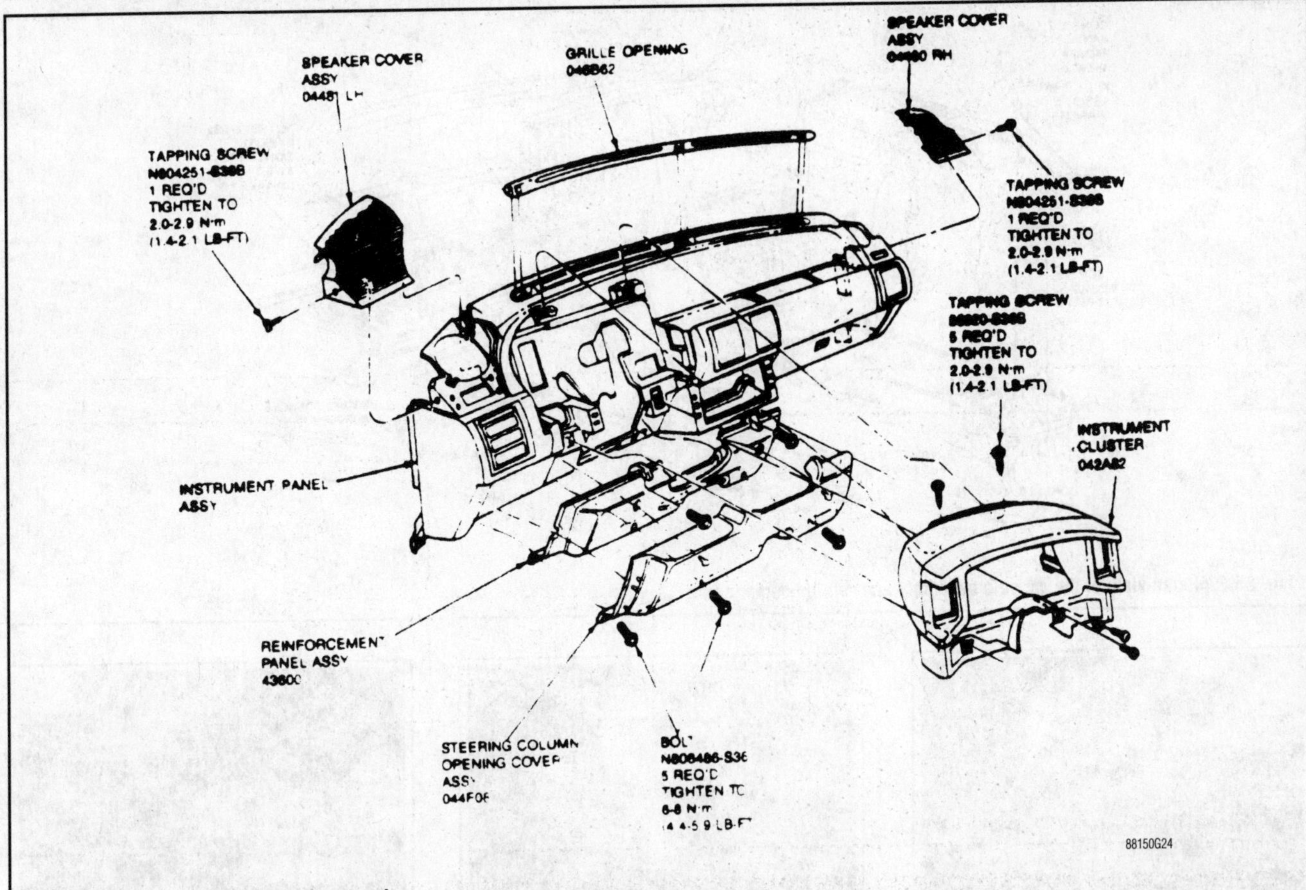

Fig. 33 Instrument panel trim pad removal

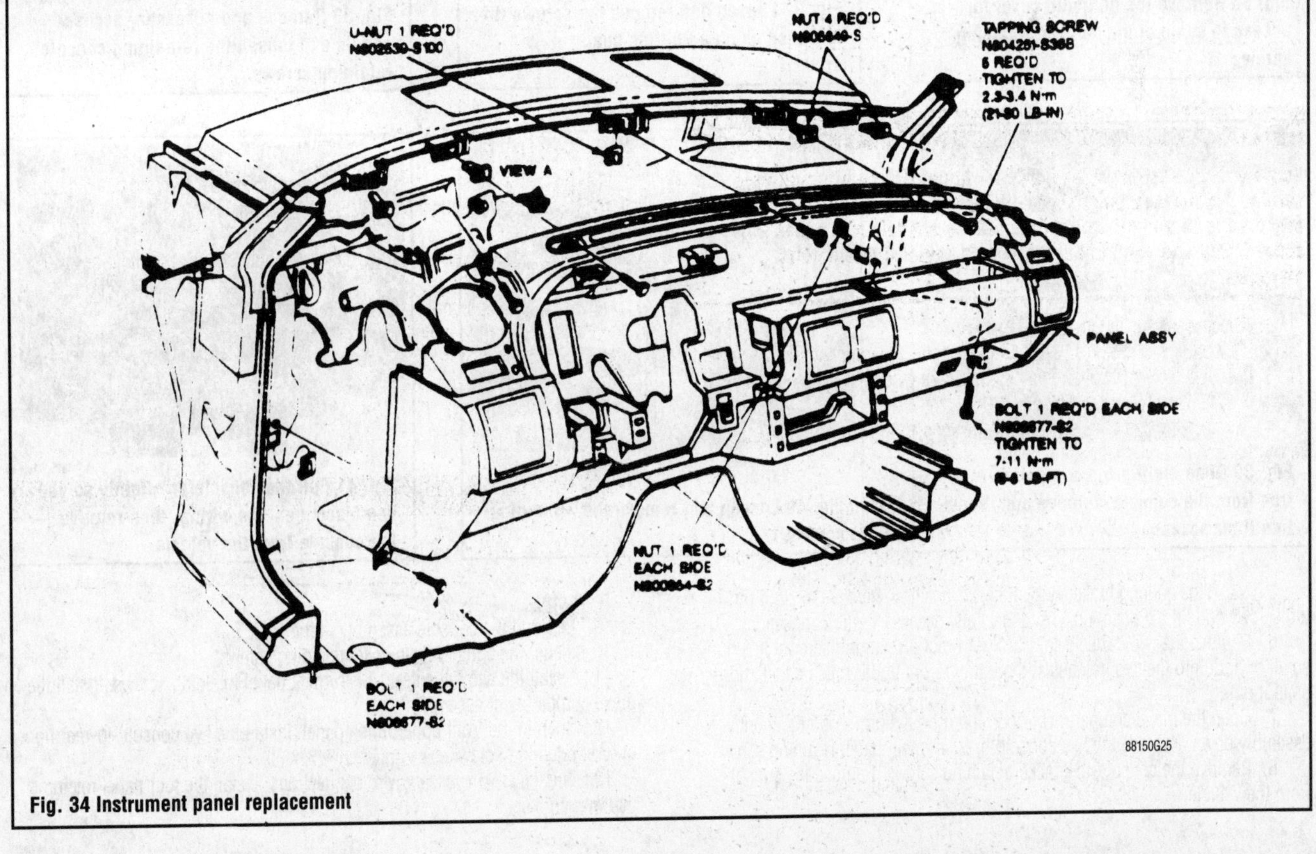

Fig. 34 Instrument panel replacement

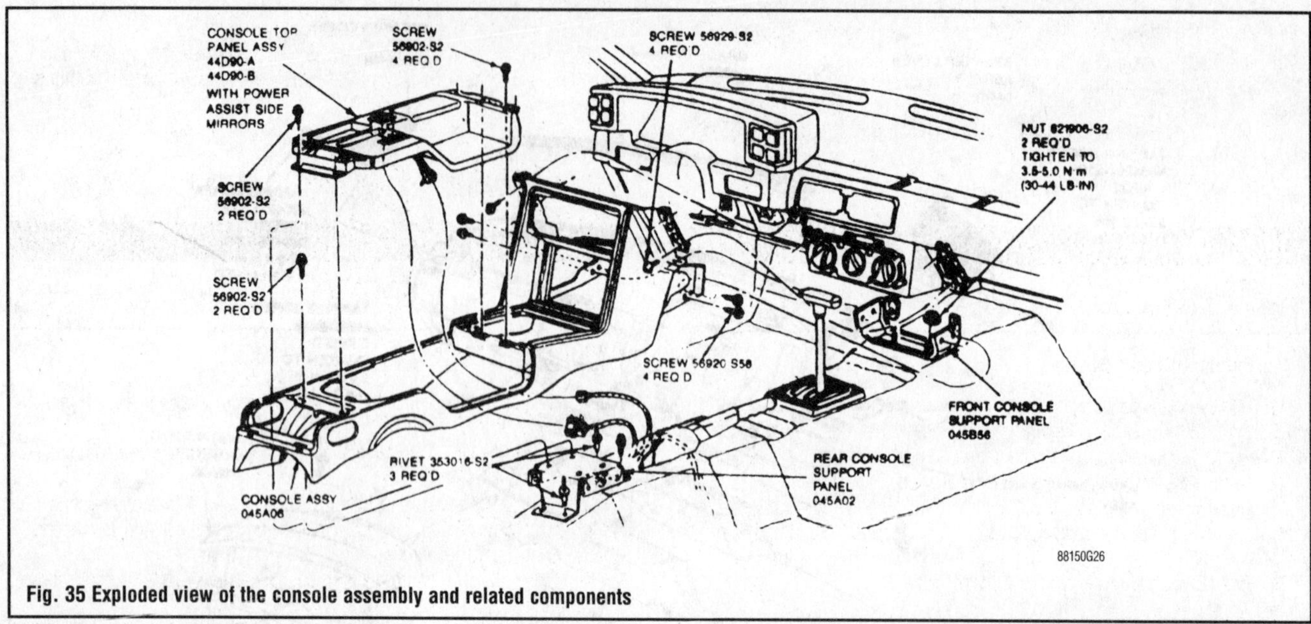

Fig. 35 Exploded view of the console assembly and related components

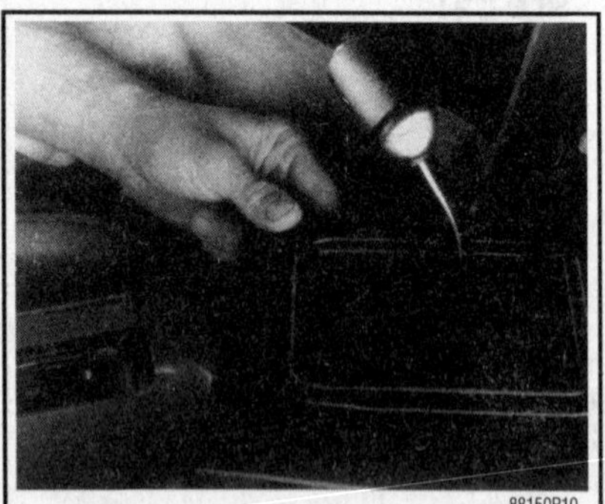

88150P10

Fig. 36 Remove the gearshift cover for access to some of the console retaining screws

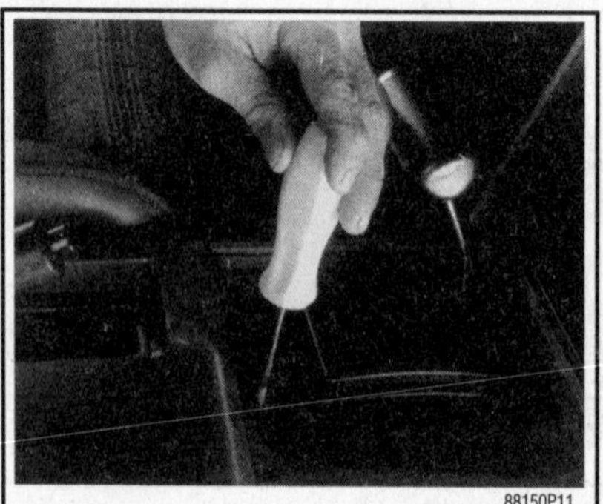

88150P11

Fig. 37 Loosen and remove the screws (in this case using a Phillips head screwdriver)

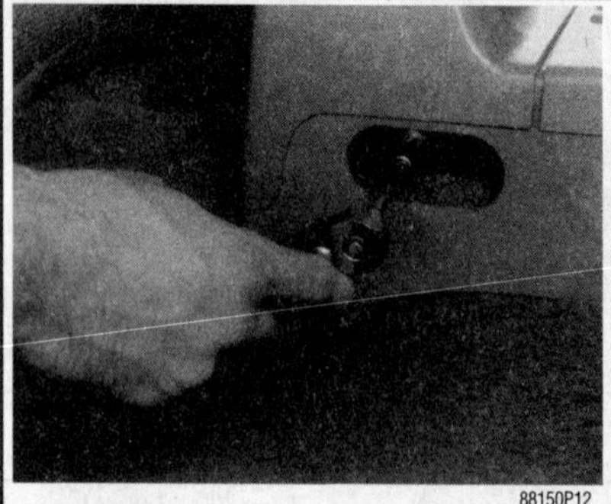

88150P12

Fig. 38 Remove and necessary access panels and loosen the remaining console retaining screws

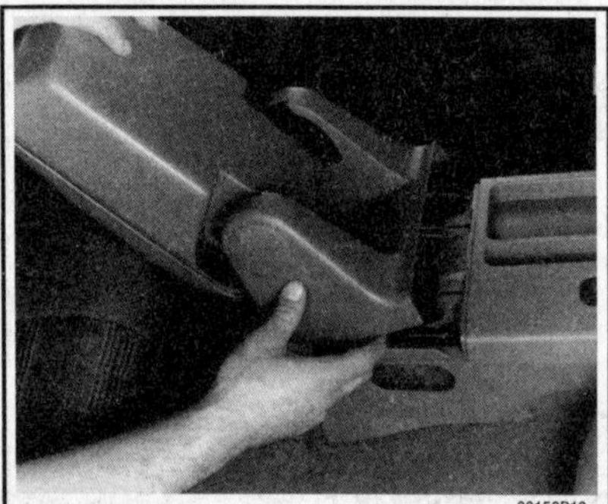

88150P13

Fig. 39 Once the flip-top compartment is free from the console, remove and reposition it for access

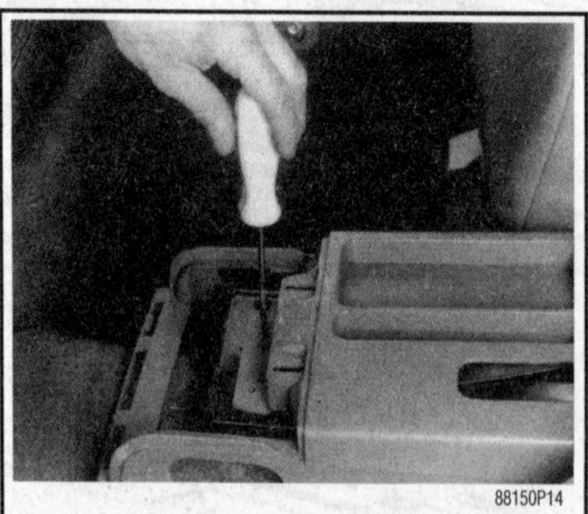

88150P14

Fig. 40 Loosen and remove the remaining screws

88150P15

Fig. 41 Pull the console up slightly so you can disconnect the wiring, then remove the console from the vehicle

5. Move the parking brake lever in the UP position. Remove the four retaining screws and lift the panel up. Disconnect any necessary wire connections.
6. Remove the two console-to-rear floor bracket retaining screws. Insert a small prytool into the two notches at the bottom front upper finish panel and snap it out.
7. Open the glove compartment door and drop the glove compartment assembly down. Remove the two console-to-instrument panel retaining screws.
8. Remove the console-to-bracket retaining screws. Remove the console from the vehicle.

To install:

9. Position the console assembly in the vehicle.
10. Install the console-to-bracket retaining screws.
11. Install the two console-to-instrument panel retaining screws. Install the glove compartment assembly.
12. Snap in the front upper finish panel. Install the two console-to-rear floor bracket retaining screws..
13. Engage any necessary wire connections. Install the four panel retaining screws..

14. Install the rear access panel and the three console-to-floor bracket retaining screws.
15. Install the gearshift opening panel and console floor bracket retaining screws.
16. Install the console mounting screws. Install the two access covers at the rear of the console assembly.
17. Connect the negative battery cable.

Door Trim Panels

REMOVAL & INSTALLATION

See Figures 42 thru 51

1. Remove the window handle retaining screw, then remove the handle.
2. Remove the door latch handle retaining screw, then remove the handle.
3. Remove the screws from the armrest door pull cup area.
4. Remove the retaining screws from the armrest.
5. On cars with power door locks and/or power windows, remove the retaining screws and power switch cover assembly. Remove the screws holding the switch housing.
6. Remove the mirror remote control bezel nut.
7. Remove the door trim panel retaining screws.
8. With a flat, wooden spatula, pry the trim retaining clips from the door panel. These clips can be easily torn from the trim panel, so be very careful to pry as closely as possible to the clips.
9. Pull the panel out slightly and disconnect all wiring.
10. If a new panel is being installed, transfer all necessary parts.
11. Installation is the reverse of removal.

Headliner

REMOVAL & INSTALLATION

See Figure 52

1. Disconnect the negative battery cable. Remove the front seats. Remove the rear seats.
2. Remove the sun visors. Remove the sun visor arm clip retaining screws, remove the arm clip.
3. If equipped, remove the roof console. Remove all dome and reading lights. Snap out the assist strap trim covers. Remove the retaining screws and remove the straps from their mountings.
4. Remove the center body pillar inside finish panel. Remove the coat hooks.

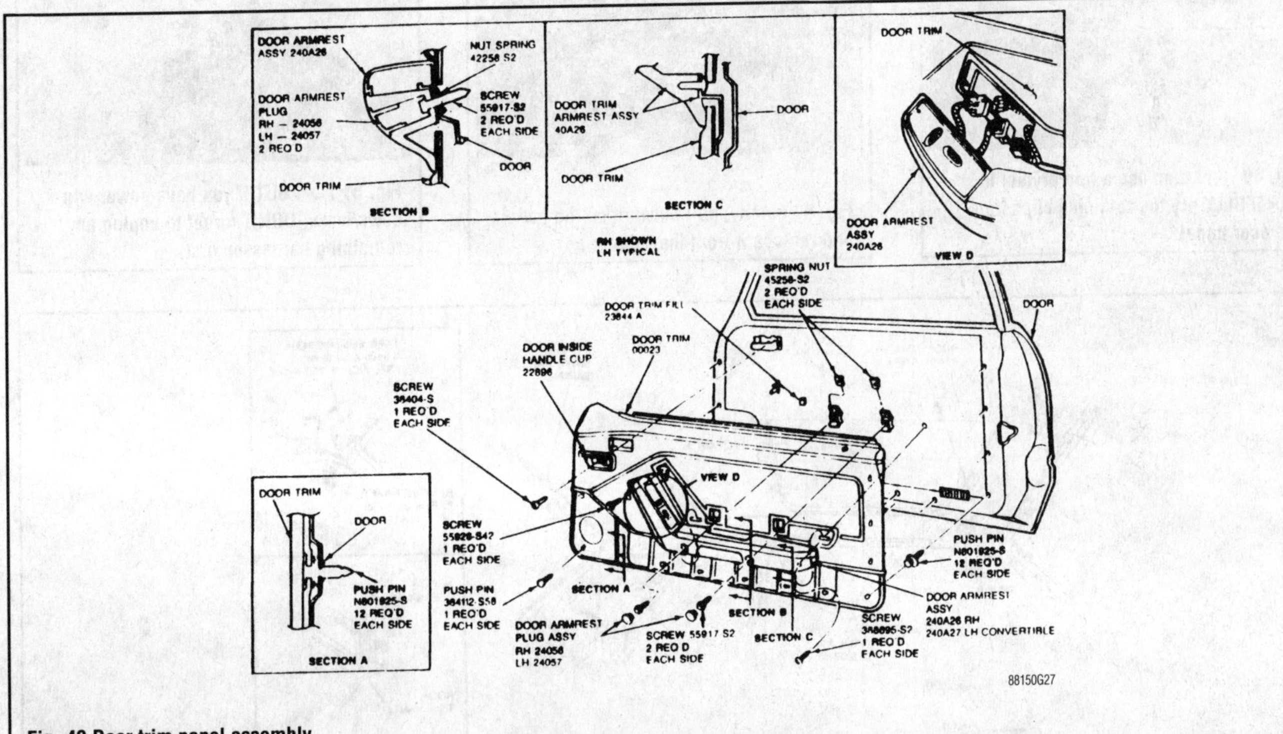

Fig. 42 Door trim panel assembly

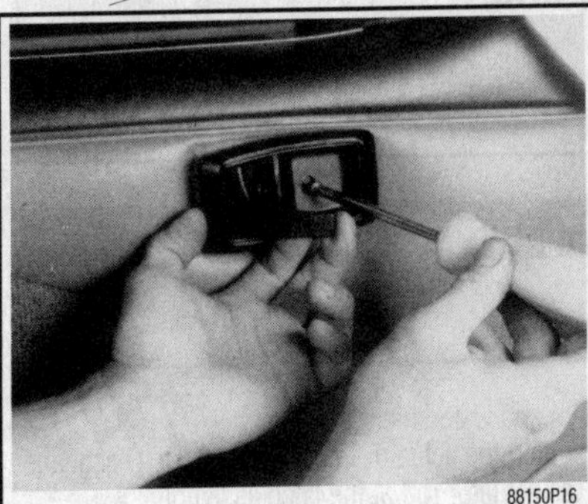

Fig. 43 Remove the door handle retainer, then remove the handle assembly

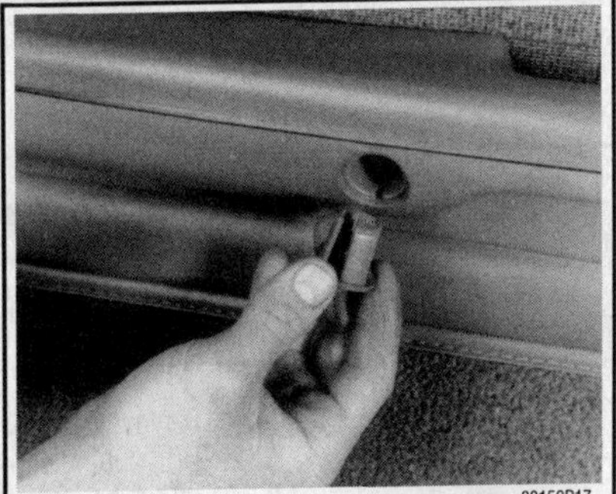

Fig. 44 To access the armrest retaining screws you may have to remove snap-in covers such as this one . . .

Fig. 45 . . . then loosen and remove the screw(s)

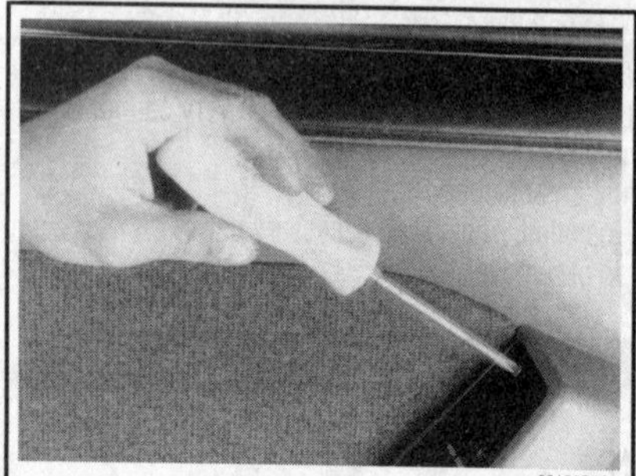
88150P19

Fig. 46 On vehicles with power windows and locks, the trim panel must be removed to access the wiring . . .

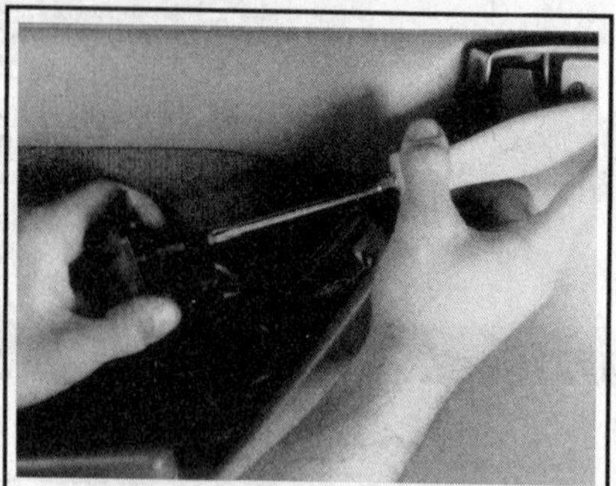
88150P20

Fig. 47 . . . tilt the panel upward and disconnect the harness from the switches

88150P21

Fig. 48 Loosen and remove the remaining door panel fasteners . . .

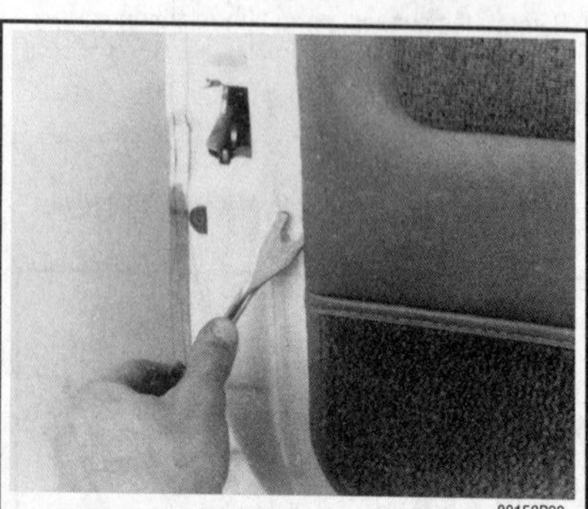
88150P22

Fig. 49 . . . then use a thin prytool to CAREFULLY pry the retaining clips from the door panel

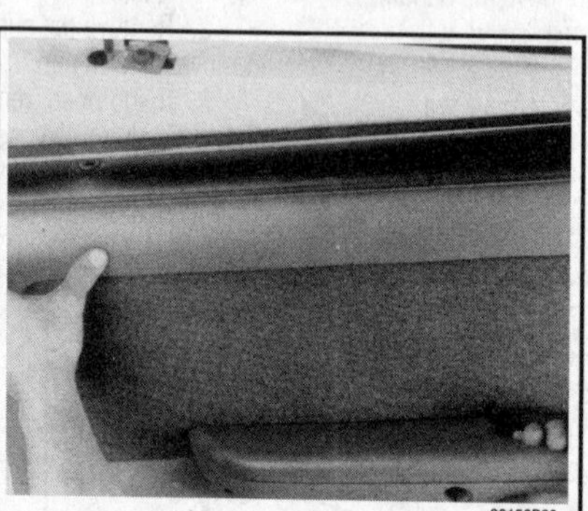
88150P23

Fig. 50 Finally, pull outward on the panel and remove it from the vehicle . . .

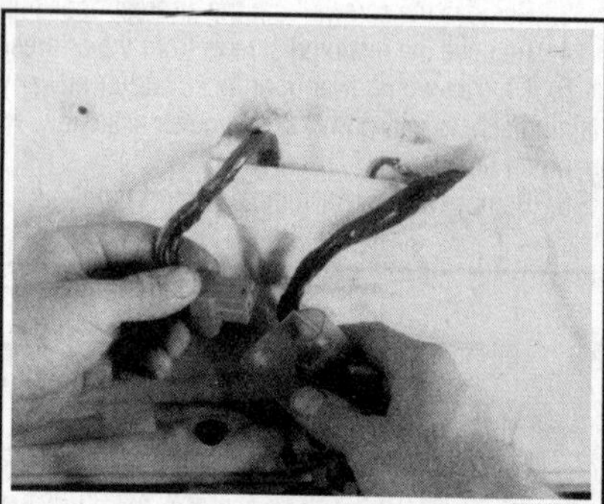
88150P24

Fig. 51 . . . BUT if you have power windows/locks, DON'T forget to unplug any remaining harnesses first

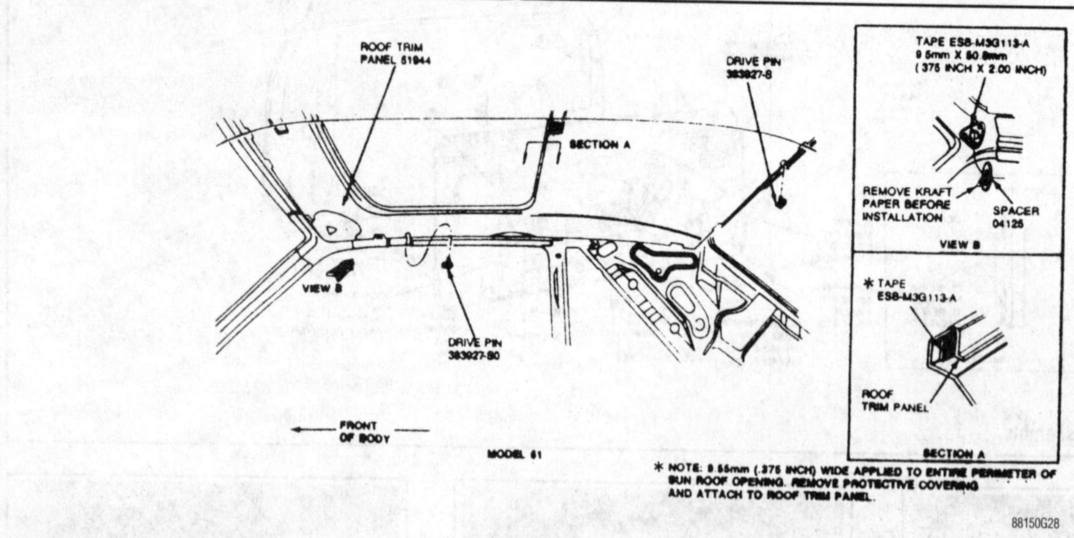

Fig. 52 Headliner installation

5. Remove the rear roof side trim panel.
6. Remove the roof side inner molding, the liftgate header rail garnish molding and the upper rear corner pillar finish panel.
7. Remove the quarter trim panel. Remove the headliner from the vehicle.

To install:

8. Position the headliner assembly in the vehicle. Install the proper trim panels and moldings.
9. Install the sun visors.
10. Install the front seats. Install the rear seats.

Power Door Lock Actuator

REMOVAL & INSTALLATION

1. Remove the door trim panel and watershield.
2. Drill out the pop-rivet attaching the actuator motor to the door. Disengage the wiring at the connector and the actuator rod at the latch assembly.

To install:

3. Attach the actuator motor rod to the door latch and connect the wire to the actuator connector.

4. Install the door actuator motor to the door with a pop-rivet or equivalent.
5. Install the door trim panel and watershield.

Front Door Latch

REMOVAL & INSTALLATION

➧ See Figure 53

1. Remove the door trim panel and the watershield.
2. Check all the connections of the remote control link and the rod. Service if necessary.
3. Remove the remote control assembly and the link clip.
4. Remove the clip attaching the control assembly and the link clip.
5. Remove the clip from the actuator motor, if so equipped.
6. Remove the clip attaching the push-button rod to the latch.
7. Remove the clip attaching the outside door handle rod to the latch assembly.
8. Remove the three screws attaching the latch assembly to the door.
9. Remove the latch assembly (with the remote control link lock cylinder rod) and anti-theft shield from the door cavity.

To install:

10. Install the new bushings and clips onto the new latch assembly. Install the anti-theft shield, remote control link and the lock cylinder rod onto the latch assembly levers.
11. Position the latch (with the link and rod) onto the door cavity, aligning the screw holes in the latch and door. Install the three screws and tighten to 36–72 inch lbs. (4–8 Nm).
12. Attach the outside door handle rod to the latch with a clip.
13. Attach the push-button rod to the latch assembly with clip.
14. Remove the clip from the actuator motor (if so equipped).
15. Attach the lock cylinder rod to the lock cylinder with clip.
16. Install the remote control assembly (and the link clip).
17. Open and close the door to check the latch assembly operation.
18. Install the watershield and the door trim panel.

Door Lock Assembly

REMOVAL & INSTALLATION

➡When a lock cylinder must be replaced, replace both sides in a set to avoid carrying an extra set of keys.

1. Remove the door trim panel and watershield.
2. Remove the clip attaching the lock cylinder rod-to-lock cylinder.
3. Pry the lock cylinder out of the slot in the door.

To install:

4. Work the lock cylinder assembly into the outer door panel.
5. Install the cylinder retainer into the slot and push the retainer onto the lock cylinder.
6. Connect the lock cylinder rod to the lock cylinder and install the clip. Lock and unlock the door to check for proper operation.
7. Install the watershield and door trim panel.

Hatchback Lock

REMOVAL & INSTALLATION

➧ See Figure 54

1. Open the hatchback door.
2. Remove the screws retaining the latch assembly.
3. Remove the pop-rivet and retainer. The lock cylinder must be removed with the retainer.
4. Installation is the reverse of the removal procedure. Tighten the latch retaining screws to 7–10 inch lbs. (0.8–1.0 Nm). Adjust the striker plate and tighten to 20–28 ft. lbs. (27–38 Nm).

Trunk Lid Lock

REMOVAL & INSTALLATION

➧ See Figure 55

1. Remove the latch retaining screws. Remove the latch.
2. Remove the retainer clip by drilling out the rivet with a ¼ in. (6mm) drill. Remove the lock support.
3. Remove the lock cylinder retainer as you remove the lock cylinder.
4. Installation is the reverse of the removal procedure. Tighten the retaining screws 6–10 ft. lbs. (8–14 Nm).

Door Glass

REMOVAL & INSTALLATION

➧ See Figure 56

1. Remove the door trim panel and watershield.
2. Remove the screw attaching each glass rear stabilizer to the inner panel, and remove the stabilizer.
3. Loosen the 2 screws that attach the door glass front run retainer to the inner door panel.
4. Lower the glass to gain access to the glass bracket rivets.
5. Drill out the glass bracket attaching rivets and push out the rivets.

⁂ WARNING

Before removing the rivets, insert a suitable block support between the door outer panel and the glass bracket to stabilize the glass during rivet removal.

6. Remove the glass.
7. Installation is the reverse of removal. Replace the rivets with ¼–20 1 in. nuts and bolts. When the glass is operating properly, tighten the bolts to 20 inch lbs. (2 Nm).

Door Glass Regulator

REMOVAL & INSTALLATION

➧ See Figure 57

1. Remove the trim panel and watershield.
2. Prop the window glass in the full up position.
3. Disconnect the window motor wiring if so equipped.
4. Drill out the 3 rivets (manual windows) or 4 rivets (electric windows), attaching the regulator to the inner door panel.
5. Remove the upper screw and washer and the lower nut and washer, attaching the run and bracket to the inner door panel. Slide the run tube up between the door belt and glass. It's a good idea to cover the glass with a protective cloth.
6. Remove the regulator slide from the glass bracket and remove the regulator through the door access hole.
7. Installation is the reverse of removal. Replace the rivets with ¼–20 1 in. bolts and nuts.

Electric Window Motor

REMOVAL & INSTALLATION

1. Raise the window to the full up position, if possible. If glass cannot be raised and is in a partially down or in the full down position, it must be supported so that it will not fall into door well during the motor removal.
2. Disconnect the negative (–) battery cable.
3. Remove the door trim panel and watershield.

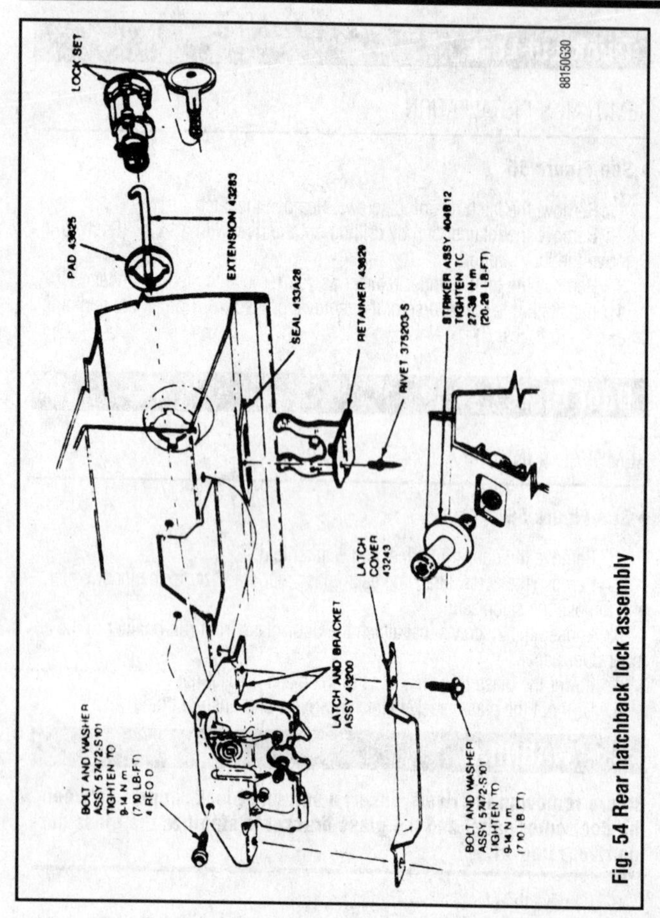

Fig. 54 Rear hatchback lock assembly

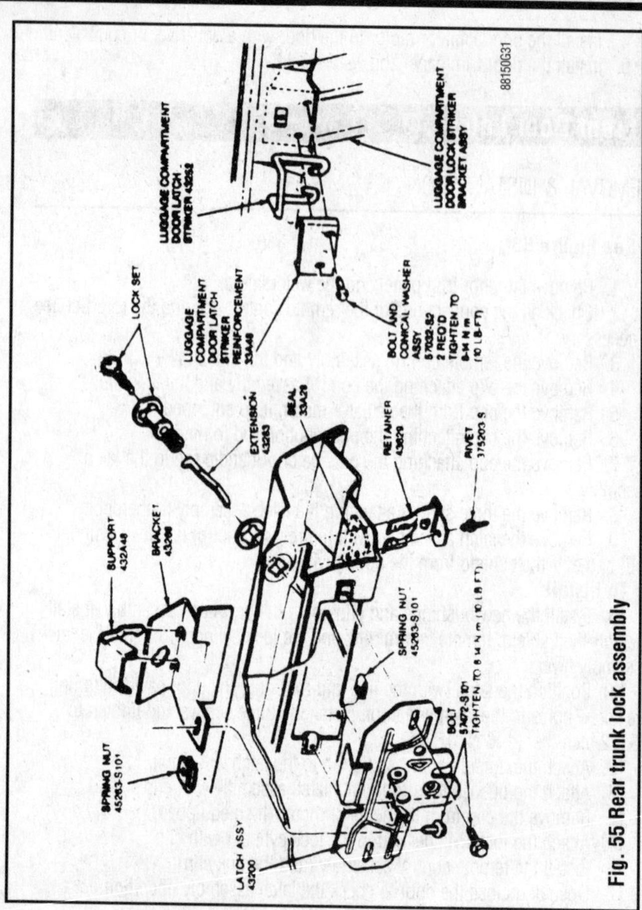

Fig. 55 Rear trunk lock assembly

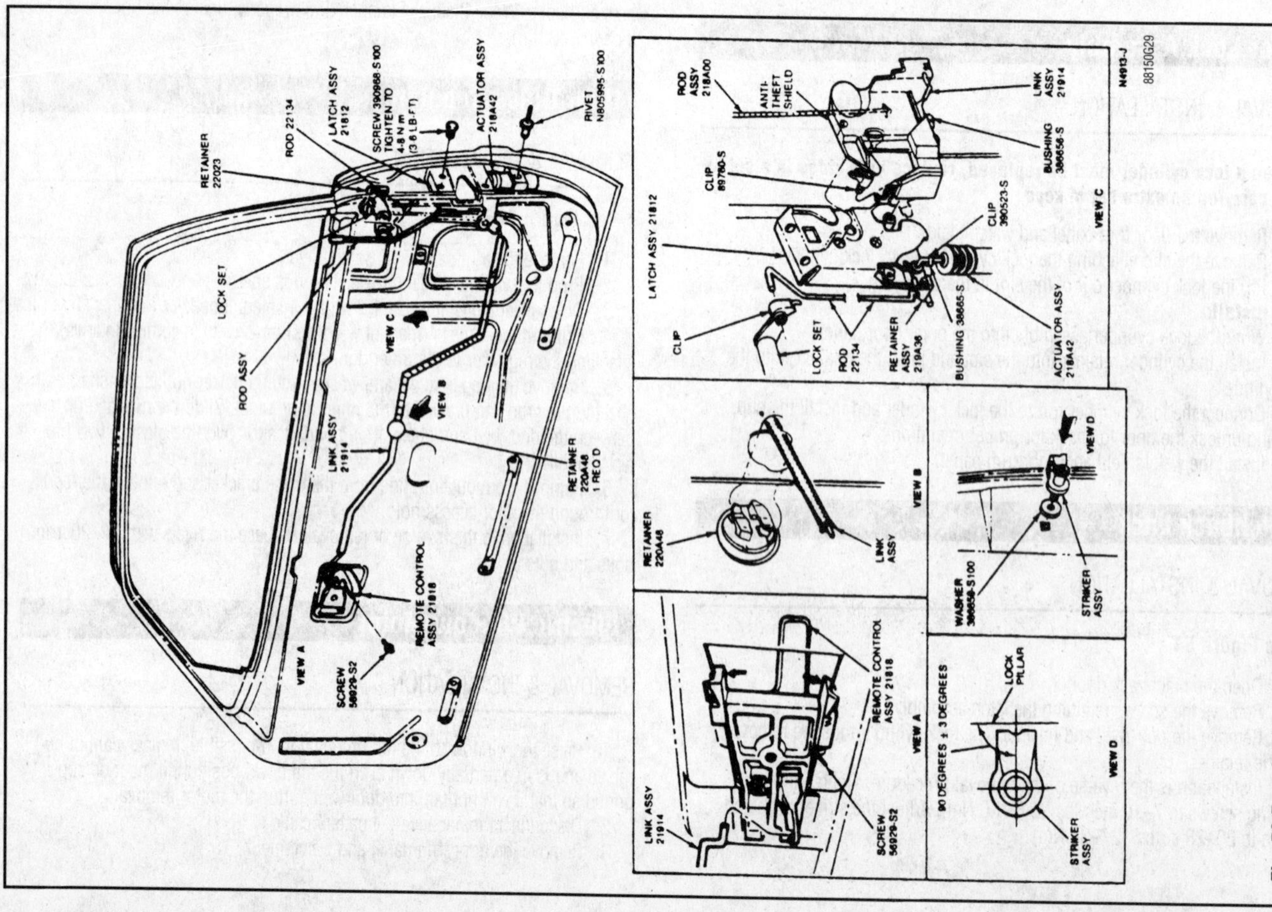

Fig. 53 Door latch assembly and related components

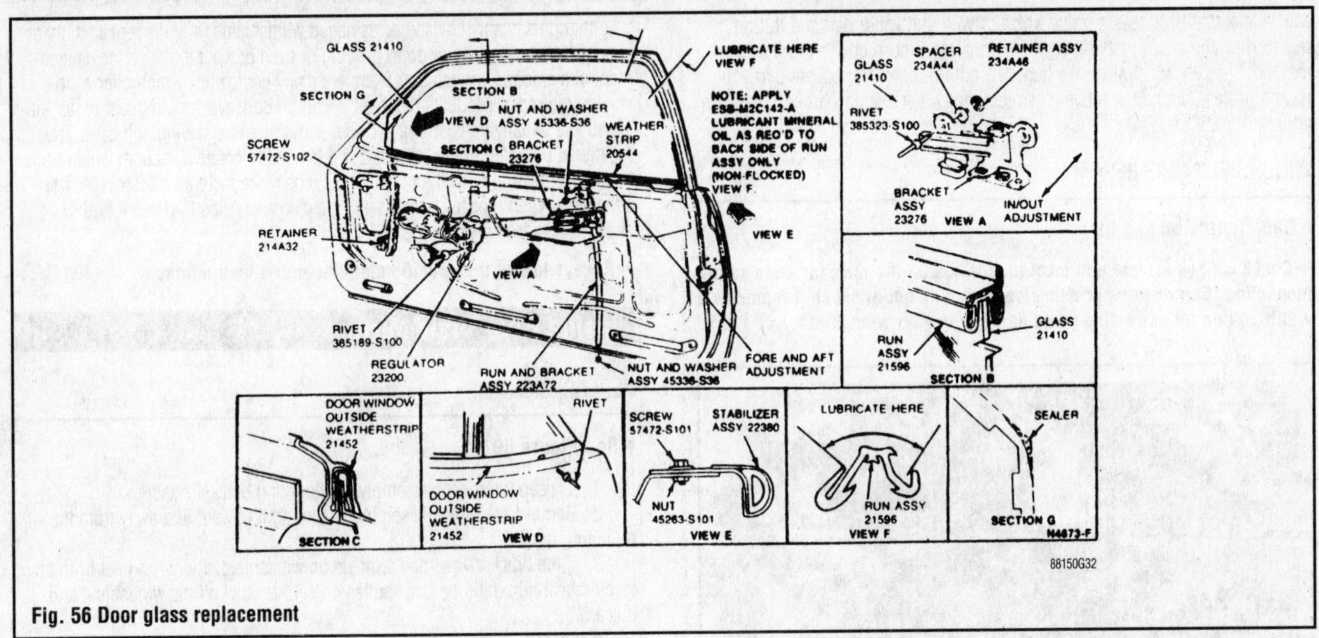

Fig. 56 Door glass replacement

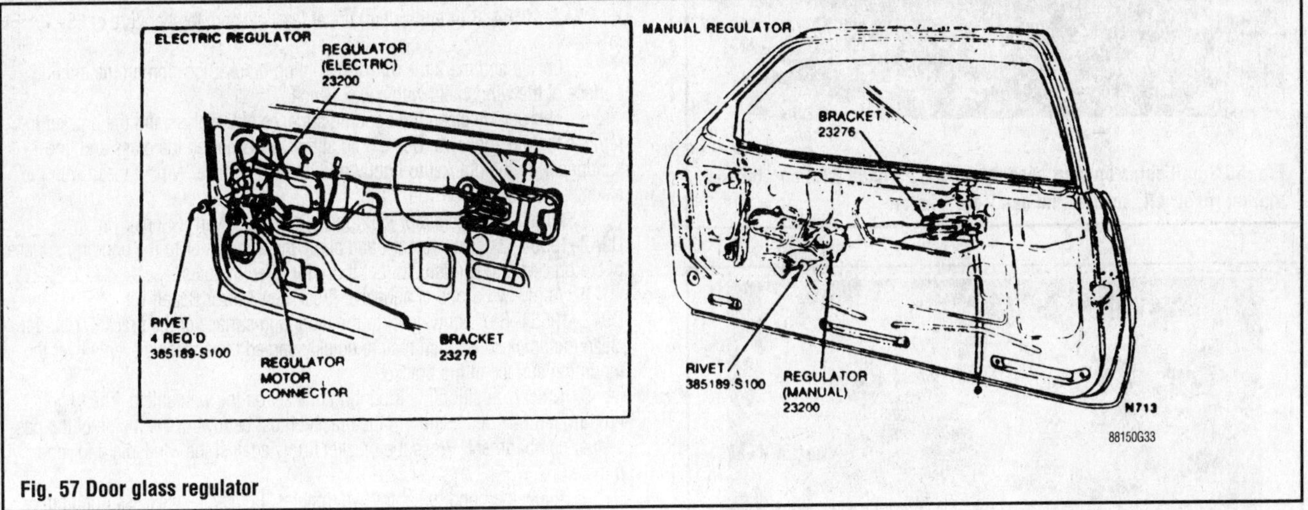

Fig. 57 Door glass regulator

4. Remove the three motor mounting screws, then disengage the motor and drive drive assembly from the regulator quadrant gear.

To install:

5. Install the new motor and drive assembly. Tighten the three motor mounting screws to 50–85 inch lbs. (6–10 Nm).
6. Connect the window motor wiring leads.
7. Connect the negative (–) battery cable.
8. Check the power window for proper operation.
9. Install the door trim panel and the watershield.

➡**Verify that all the drain holes at bottom of doors are open to prevent water accumulation over the motor.**

Windshield and Fixed Glass

REMOVAL & INSTALLATION

If your windshield, or other fixed window, is cracked or chipped, you may decide to replace it with a new one yourself. However, there are two main reasons why replacement windshields and other window glass should be installed only by a professional automotive glass technician: safety and cost.

The most important reason a professional should install automotive glass is for safety. The glass in the vehicle, especially the windshield, is designed with safety in mind in case of a collision. The windshield is specially manufactured from two panes of specially-tempered glass with a thin layer of transparent plastic between them. This construction allows the glass to "give" in the event that a part of your body hits the windshield during the collision, and prevents the glass from shattering, which could cause lacerations, blinding and other harm to passengers of the vehicle. The other fixed windows are designed to be tempered so that if they break during a collision, they shatter in such a way that there are no large pointed glass pieces. The professional automotive glass technician knows how to install the glass in a vehicle so that it will function optimally during a collision. Without the proper experience, knowledge and tools, installing a piece of automotive glass yourself could lead to additional harm if an accident should ever occur.

Cost is also a factor when deciding to install automotive glass yourself. Performing this could cost you much more than a professional may charge for the same job. Since the windshield is designed to break under stress, an often life saving characteristic, windshields tend to break VERY easily when an inexperienced person attempts to install one. Do-it-yourselfers buying two, three or even four windshields from a salvage yard because they have broken them during installation are common stories. Also, since the automotive glass is designed to prevent the outside elements from entering your vehicle, improper installation can lead to water and air leaks. Annoying whining noises at highway speeds from air leaks or inside body panel rusting from water leaks can add to your stress level and subtract from your wallet. After buying two or three windshields, installing them and ending up with a leak that produces a noise while driving and water damage during rainstorms, the cost of having a professional do it correctly the first time may be much more alluring. We here at Chilton, therefore, advise that you have a professional automotive glass technician service any broken glass on your vehicle.

WINDSHIELD CHIP REPAIR

See Figures 58 and 59

Check with your state and local authorities on the laws for state safety inspection. Some states or municipalities may not allow chip repair as a viable option for correcting stone damage to your windshield.

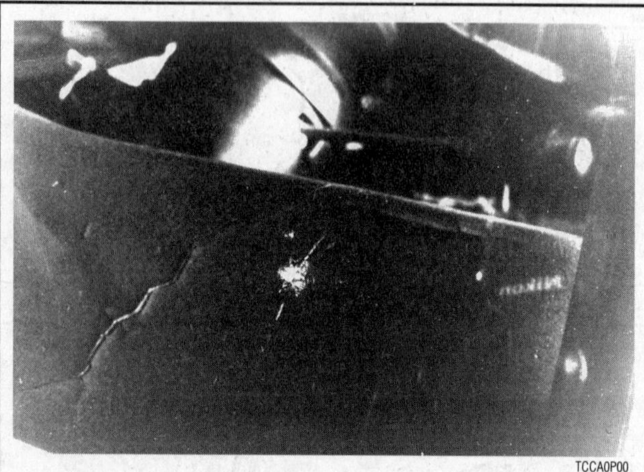

Fig. 58 Small chips on your windshield can be fixed with an aftermarket repair kit, such as the one from Loctite®

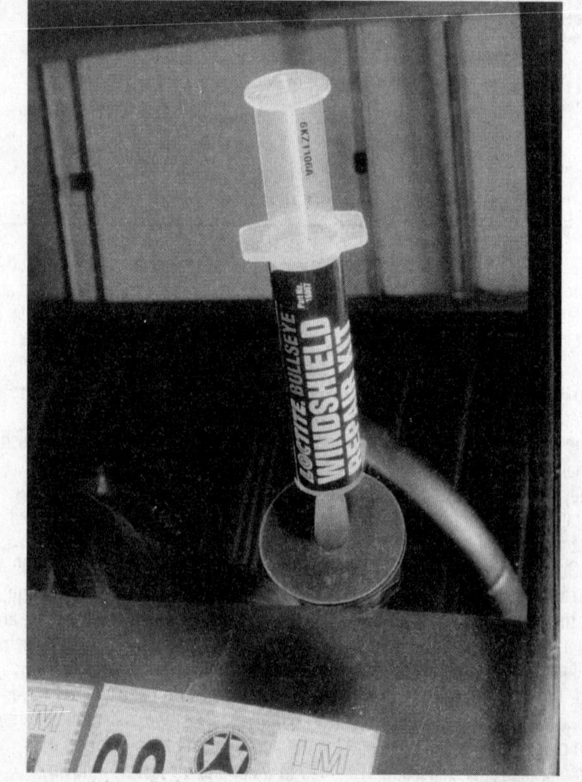

Fig. 59 Most kits use a self-stick applicator and syringe to inject the adhesive into the chip or crack

Although severely cracked or damaged windshields must be replaced, there is something that you can do to prolong or even prevent the need for replacement of a chipped windshield. There are many companies which offer windshield chip repair products, such as Loctite's® Bullseye™ windshield repair kit. These kits usually consist of a syringe, pedestal and a sealing adhesive. The syringe is mounted on the pedestal and is used to create a vacuum which pulls the plastic layer against the glass. This helps make the chip transparent. The adhesive is then injected which seals the chip and helps to prevent further stress cracks from developing

Always follow the specific manufacturer's instructions.

Inside Rear View Mirror

REPLACEMENT

See Figure 60

1. Loosen the mirror assembly-to-mounting bracket setscrew.
2. Remove the mirror assembly by sliding it upward and away from the mounting bracket.
3. If the bracket vinyl pad remains on windshield, apply low heat from an electric heat gun until the vinyl softens. Peel the vinyl off the windshield and discard.

To install:

4. Make sure the glass, bracket, and adhesive kit, (Rear view Mirror Repair Kit D9AZ–19554–B or equivalent) are at least at room temperature of 65–75° F (18–24° C).
5. Locate and mark the mirror mounting bracket location on the outside surface of the windshield with a wax pencil.
6. Thoroughly clean the bonding surfaces of the glass and the bracket to remove the old adhesive. Use a mild abrasive cleaner on the glass and fine sandpaper on the bracket to lightly roughen the surface. Wipe it clean with the alcohol-moistened cloth.
7. Crush the accelerator vial (part of rear view Mirror Repair Kit D9AZ–19554–B or equivalent), and apply the accelerator to the bonding surface of the bracket and windshield. Let it dry for three minutes.
8. Apply two drops of adhesive (Rear view Mirror Repair Kit D9AZ–19554–B or equivalent) to the mounting surface of the bracket. Using a clean toothpick or wooden match, quickly spread the adhesive evenly over the mounting surface of the bracket.
9. Quickly position the mounting bracket on the windshield. The 3/8 in. (10mm) circular depression in the bracket must be toward the inside of the passenger compartment. Press the bracket firmly against the windshield for one minute.
10. Allow the bond to set for five minutes. Remove any excess bonding material from the windshield with an alcohol dampened cloth.
11. Attach the mirror to the mounting bracket and tighten the setscrew to 10–20 inch lbs. (1–2 Nm).

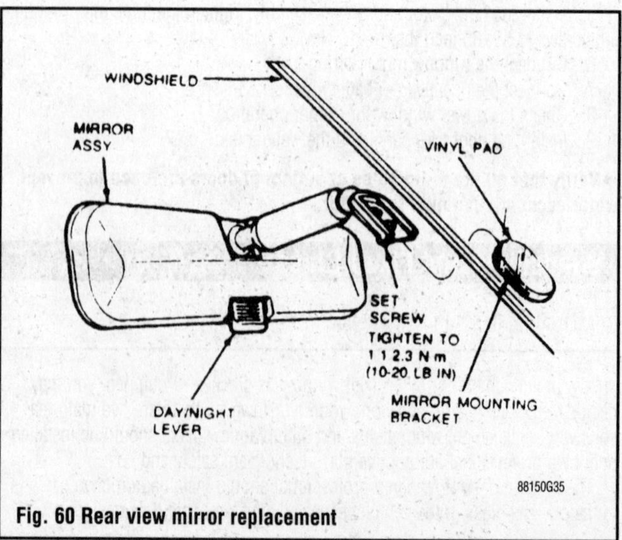

Fig. 60 Rear view mirror replacement

Front Bucket Seats

REMOVAL & INSTALLATION

➧ See Figure 61

1. Remove the plastic shield retaining screws and remove the shield.
2. Remove the bolts and nut and washer assemblies retaining the seat tracks to the floor.
3. Remove the seat and track assembly from the vehicle and place on a clean working area.

➡Use care when handling the seat and track assembly. Dropping the assembly or sitting on the seat not secured in the vehicle may result in damaged components.

4. Remove the seat track-to-seat cushion attaching screws. Remove the seat cushion and assist spring from the tracks.
5. If the seat tracks are being replaced, transfer the assist springs and spacers, if so equipped, to the new track assembly.

To install:

6. Mount the seat tracks to the seat cushion.
7. Install the seat track-to-seat cushion retaining screws.
8. Place the seat assembly into the vehicle and ensure proper alignment.
9. Install the screws, studs, plastic shields, and nut and washer assemblies.

Rear Seats

REMOVAL & INSTALLATION

Seat Cushion

➧ See Figure 62

1. Apply knee pressure to the lower portion of the rear seat cushion. Push rearward to disengage the seat cushion from the retainer brackets.

To install:

2. Position the seat cushion assembly into the vehicle.
3. Place the seat belts on top of the cushion.
4. Apply knee pressure to the lower portion of the seat cushion assembly. Push rearward and down to lock the seat cushion into position.
5. Pull the rear seat cushion forward to be certain it is secured into its floor retainer.

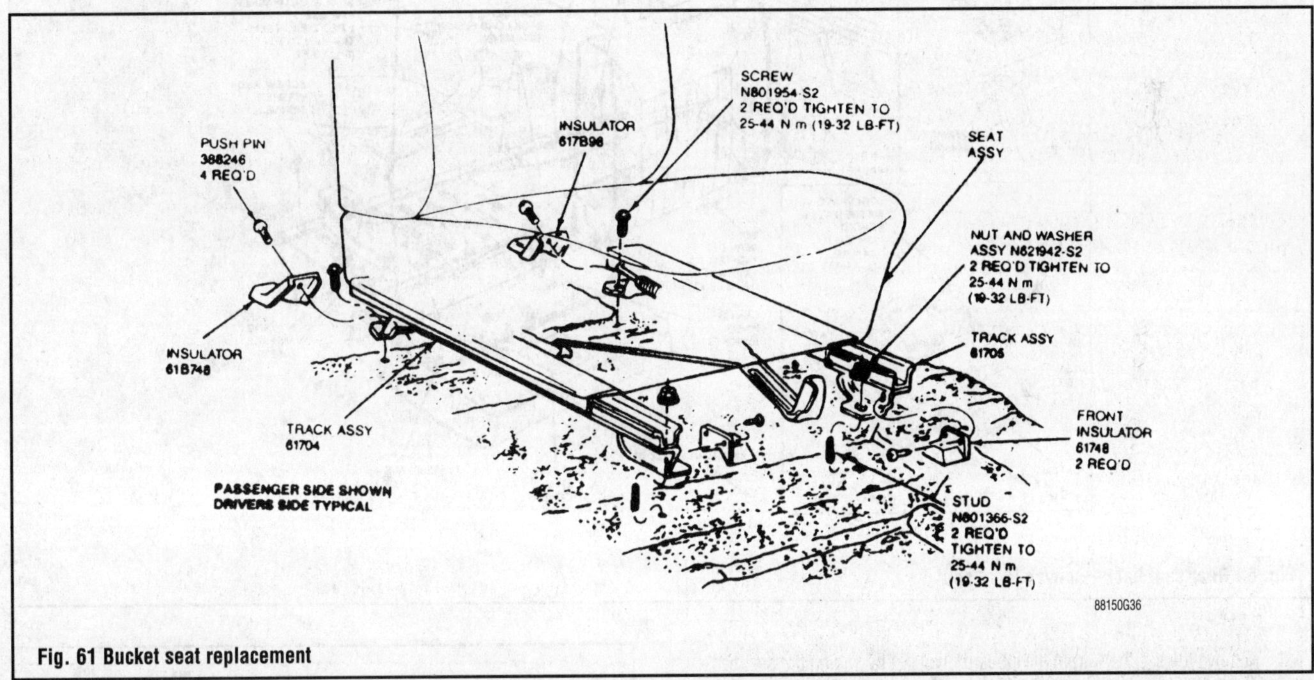

Fig. 61 Bucket seat replacement

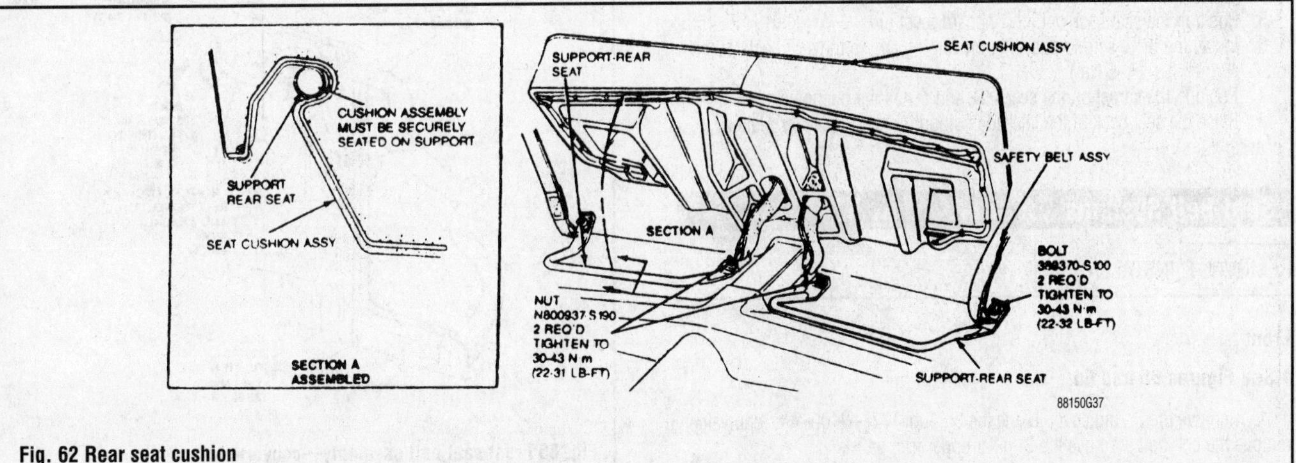

Fig. 62 Rear seat cushion

Seat Back Rest

➧ **See Figure 63**

1. Remove the rear seat cushion.
2. Remove the seat back bracket attaching bolts.
3. Grasp the seat back assembly at the bottom and lift it up to disengage the hanger wire from the retainer brackets.

To install:

4. Position the seat back in the vehicle so that the hanger wires are engaged with the retaining brackets.
5. Install the seat back bolts and tighten to 5–7 ft. lbs. (7–9 Nm).
6. Install the rear seat cushion.

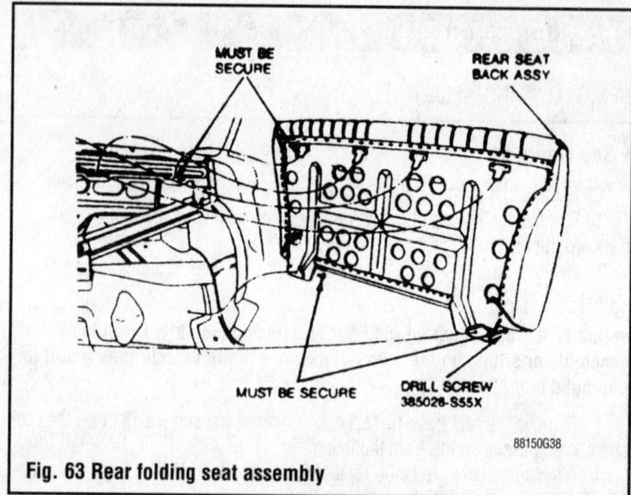

Fig. 63 Rear folding seat assembly

Split Folding Rear Seat Back

➧ **See Figure 64**

1. Fold the seat back down.
2. Carefully pry up the five pushpins to disengage the carpet from the seat back.
3. Remove the three screws attaching the folding arm to the seat back.

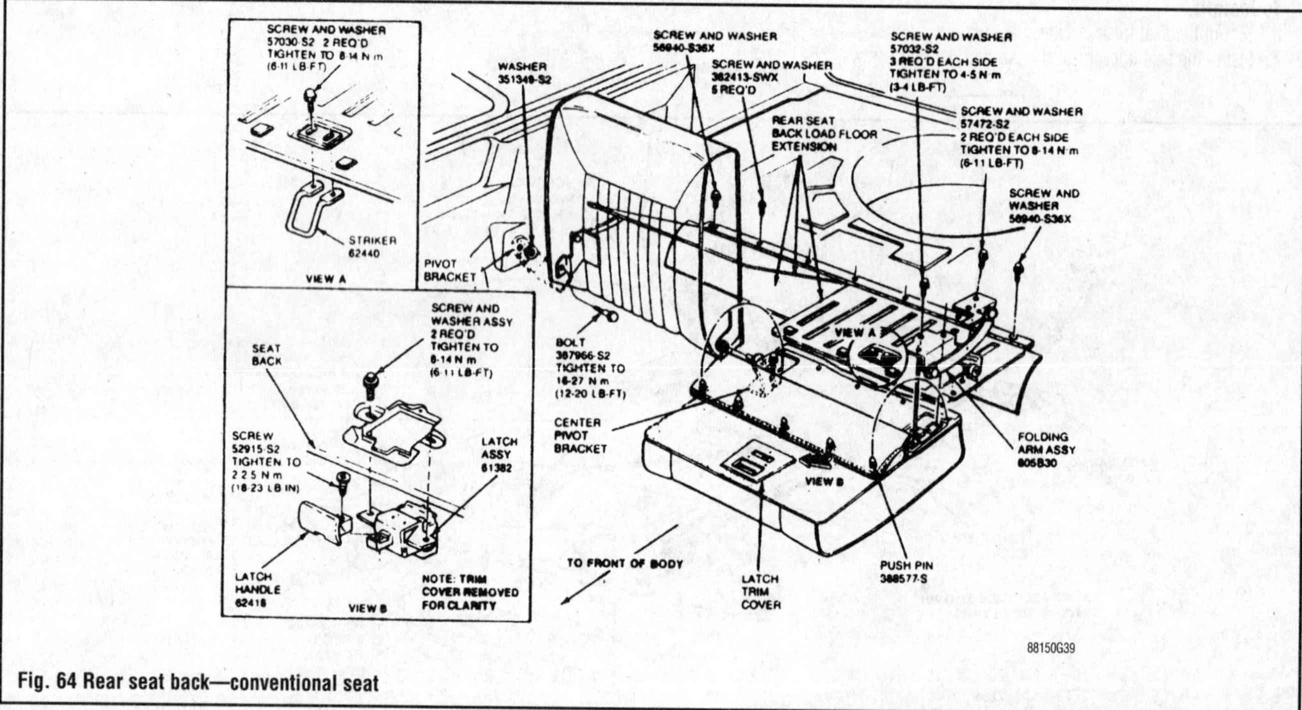

Fig. 64 Rear seat back—conventional seat

4. Remove the seat back from the inboard pivot pin by sliding the seat back toward the outboard side of the vehicle.

To install:

5. Position the seat back onto the inboard pivot pin.
6. Install the three screws attaching the folding arm to the seat back. Tighten to 36–48 inch lbs. (4–5 Nm).
7. Position the carpet on the seat back and install the pushpins.
8. Raise the seat back to the latched position. Adjust the striker plate as necessary.

Seat Belt Systems

REMOVAL & INSTALLATION

Front

➧ **See Figures 65 and 66**

1. Remove the D-ring cover. Using the bit, tool T77L–2100–A or equivalent, remove the belt bolt. Remove the B–pillar upper trim panel.

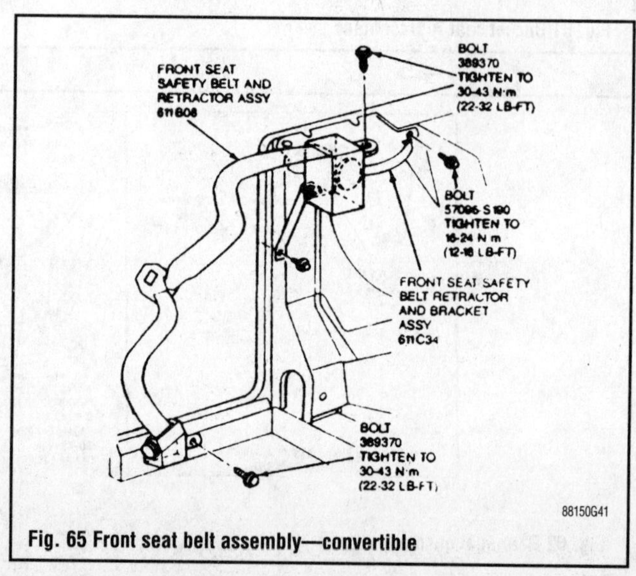

Fig. 65 Front seat belt assembly—convertible

2. Remove the scuff plate retaining screws and panel. Remove the belt through the slot in the upper center trim panel.

3. Remove the belt anchor to sill bolt and rubber washer. Remove the belt retractor bolt. Remove the web guide retaining screw and slide the guide rearward to remove it from the B-pillar.

4. Remove the outboard safety belt assembly from the vehicle. Remove the nut from the inboard buckle assembly. On the left side disconnect the buzzer wire and pry off the locator.

5. Pull the buckle upward and remove it from the seat.

6. Installation is the reverse of the removal procedure.

Rear

➧ See Figures 67, 68 and 69

1. Remove the rear seat back and cushion.
2. Remove the angel wing trim and package tray trim.
3. Remove the buckle end anchor nuts. Remove the buckle end belts.
4. Remove the retaining bolt to both rear seat retractors. Remove the retractors.
5. Installation is the reverse of the removal procedure.

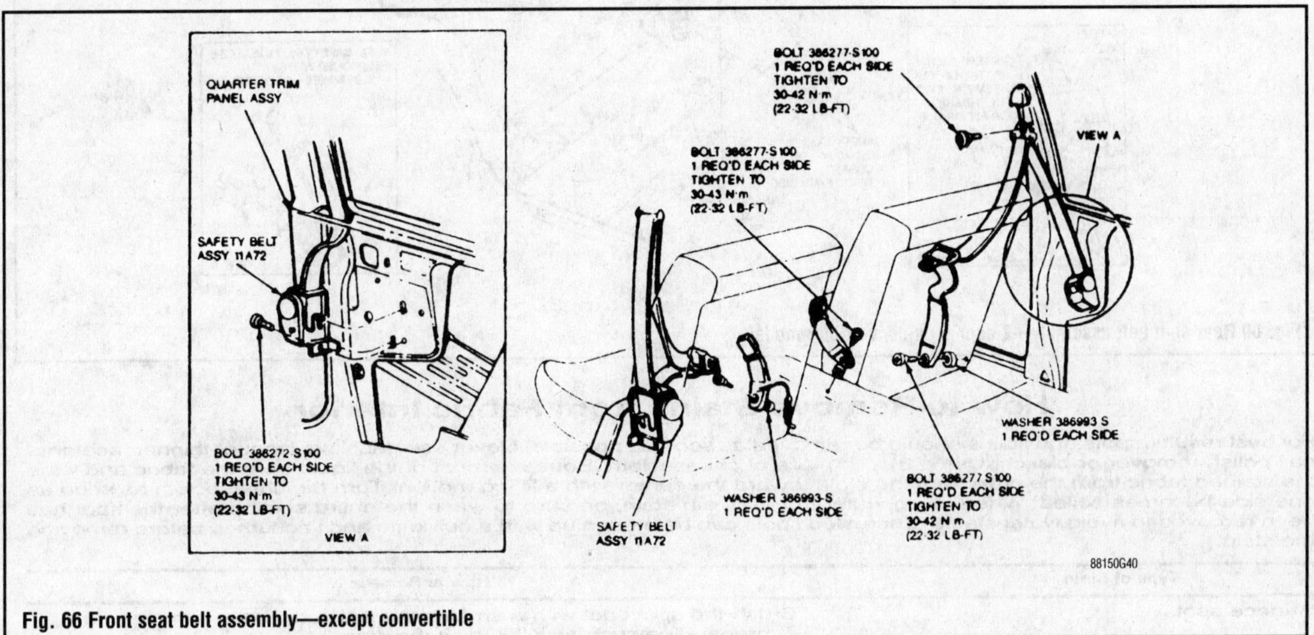

Fig. 66 Front seat belt assembly—except convertible

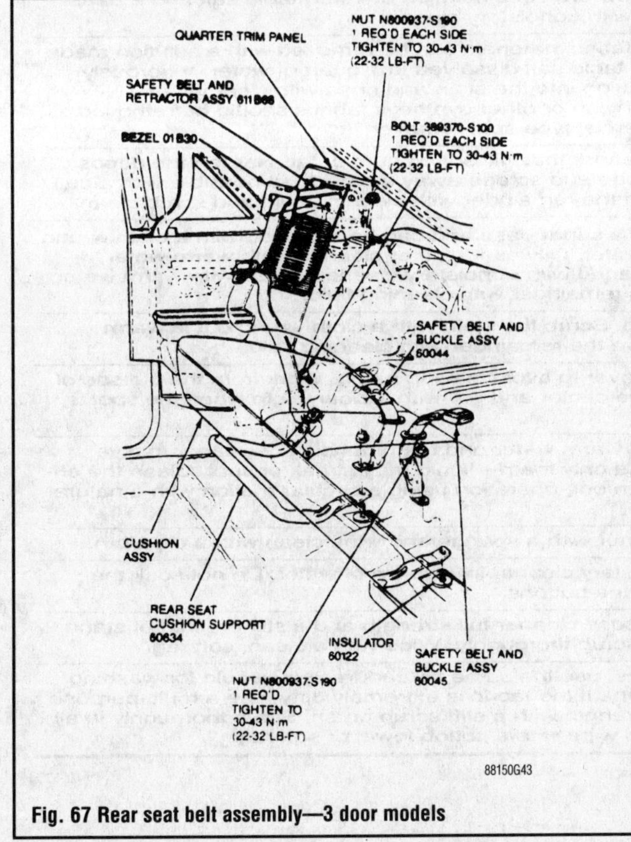

Fig. 67 Rear seat belt assembly—3 door models

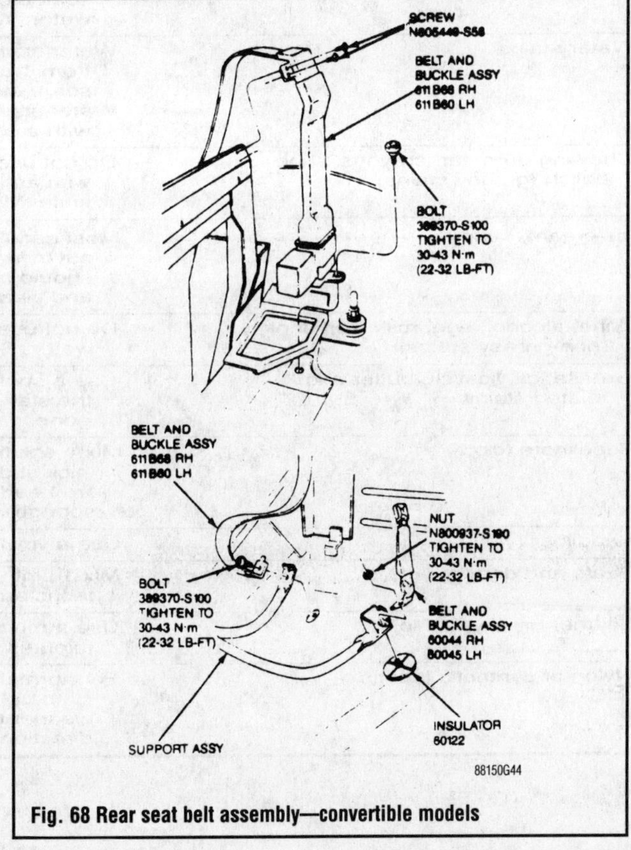

Fig. 68 Rear seat belt assembly—convertible models

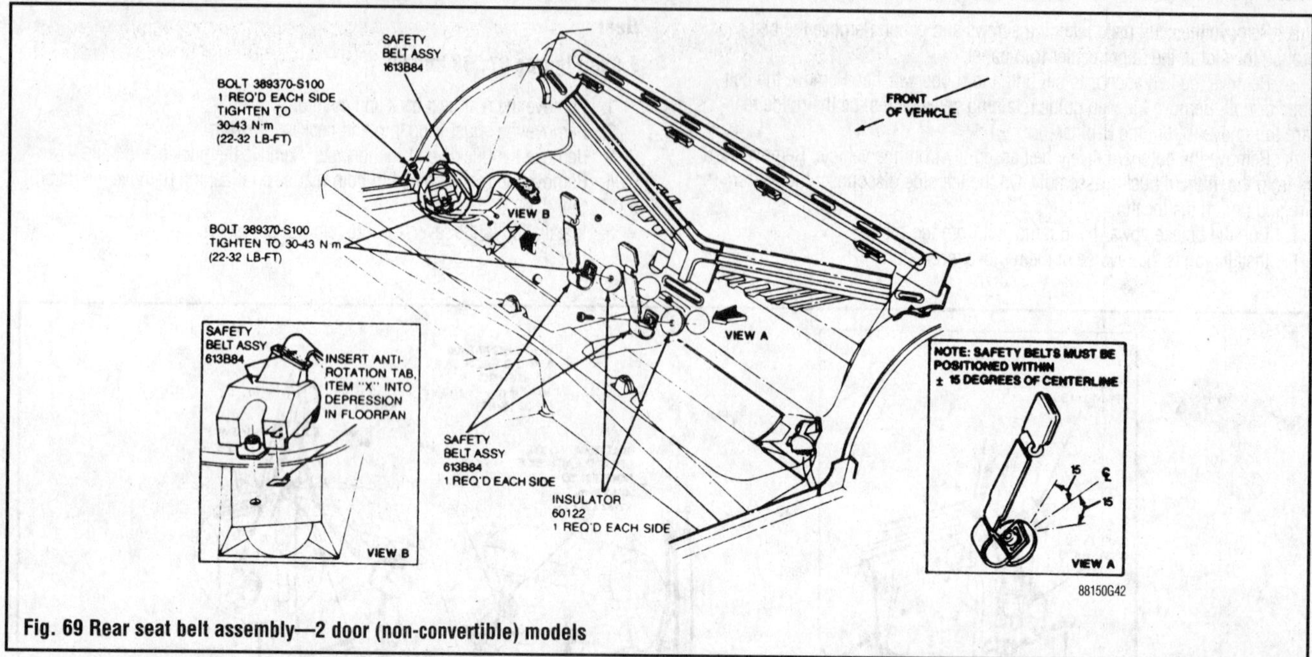

Fig. 69 Rear seat belt assembly—2 door (non-convertible) models

How to Remove Stains from Fabric Interior

For best results, spots and stains should be removed as soon as possible. Never use gasoline, lacquer thinner, acetone, nail polish remover or bleach. Use a 3' x 3" piece of cheesecloth. Squeeze most of the liquid from the fabric and wipe the stained fabric from the outside of the stain toward the center with a lifting motion. Turn the cheesecloth as soon as one side becomes soiled. When using water to remove a stain, be sure to wash the entire section after the spot has been removed to avoid water stains. Encrusted spots can be broken up with a dull knife and vacuumed before removing the stain.

Type of Stain	How to Remove It
Surface spots	Brush the spots out with a small hand brush or use a commercial preparation such as K2R to lift the stain.
Mildew	Clean around the mildew with warm suds. Rinse in cold water and soak the mildew area in a solution of 1 part table salt and 2 parts water. Wash with upholstery cleaner.
Water stains	Water stains in fabric materials can be removed with a solution made from 1 cup of table salt dissolved in 1 quart of water. Vigorously scrub the solution into the stain and rinse with clear water. Water stains in nylon or other synthetic fabrics should be removed with a commercial type spot remover.
Chewing gum, tar, crayons, shoe polish (greasy stains)	Do not use a cleaner that will soften gum or tar. Harden the deposit with an ice cube and scrape away as much as possible with a dull knife. Moisten the remainder with cleaning fluid and scrub clean.
Ice cream, candy	Most candy has a sugar base and can be removed with a cloth wrung out in warm water. Oily candy, after cleaning with warm water, should be cleaned with upholstery cleaner. Rinse with warm water and clean the remainder with cleaning fluid.
Wine, alcohol, egg, milk, soft drink (non-greasy stains)	Do not use soap. Scrub the stain with a cloth wrung out in warm water. Remove the remainder with cleaning fluid.
Grease, oil, lipstick, butter and related stains	Use a spot remover to avoid leaving a ring. Work from the outisde of the stain to the center and dry with a clean cloth when the spot is gone.
Headliners (cloth)	Mix a solution of warm water and foam upholstery cleaner to give thick suds. Use only foam—liquid may streak or spot. Clean the entire headliner in one operation using a circular motion with a natural sponge.
Headliner (vinyl)	Use a vinyl cleaner with a sponge and wipe clean with a dry cloth.
Seats and door panels	Mix 1 pint upholstery cleaner in 1 gallon of water. Do not soak the fabric around the buttons.
Leather or vinyl fabric	Use a multi-purpose cleaner full strength and a stiff brush. Let stand 2 minutes and scrub thoroughly. Wipe with a clean, soft rag.
Nylon or synthetic fabrics	For normal stains, use the same procedures you would for washing cloth upholstery. If the fabric is extremely dirty, use a multi-purpose cleaner full strength with a stiff scrub brush. Scrub thoroughly in all directions and wipe with a cotton towel or soft rag.

88150C01

GLOSSARY

AIR/FUEL RATIO: The ratio of air-to-gasoline by weight in the fuel mixture drawn into the engine.

AIR INJECTION: One method of reducing harmful exhaust emissions by injecting air into each of the exhaust ports of an engine. The fresh air entering the hot exhaust manifold causes any remaining fuel to be burned before it can exit the tailpipe.

ALTERNATOR: A device used for converting mechanical energy into electrical energy.

AMMETER: An instrument, calibrated in amperes, used to measure the flow of an electrical current in a circuit. Ammeters are always connected in series with the circuit being tested.

AMPERE: The rate of flow of electrical current present when one volt of electrical pressure is applied against one ohm of electrical resistance.

ANALOG COMPUTER: Any microprocessor that uses similar (analogous) electrical signals to make its calculations.

ARMATURE: A laminated, soft iron core wrapped by a wire that converts electrical energy to mechanical energy as in a motor or relay. When rotated in a magnetic field, it changes mechanical energy into electrical energy as in a generator.

ATMOSPHERIC PRESSURE: The pressure on the Earth's surface caused by the weight of the air in the atmosphere. At sea level, this pressure is 14.7 psi at 32°F (101 kPa at 0°C).

ATOMIZATION: The breaking down of a liquid into a fine mist that can be suspended in air.

AXIAL PLAY: Movement parallel to a shaft or bearing bore.

BACKFIRE: The sudden combustion of gases in the intake or exhaust system that results in a loud explosion.

BACKLASH: The clearance or play between two parts, such as meshed gears.

BACKPRESSURE: Restrictions in the exhaust system that slow the exit of exhaust gases from the combustion chamber.

BAKELITE: A heat resistant, plastic insulator material commonly used in printed circuit boards and transistorized components.

BALL BEARING: A bearing made up of hardened inner and outer races between which hardened steel balls roll.

BALLAST RESISTOR: A resistor in the primary ignition circuit that lowers voltage after the engine is started to reduce wear on ignition components.

BEARING: A friction reducing, supportive device usually located between a stationary part and a moving part.

BIMETAL TEMPERATURE SENSOR: Any sensor or switch made of two dissimilar types of metal that bend when heated or cooled due to the different expansion rates of the alloys. These types of sensors usually function as an on/off switch.

BLOWBY: Combustion gases, composed of water vapor and unburned fuel, that leak past the piston rings into the crankcase during normal engine operation. These gases are removed by the PCV system to prevent the buildup of harmful acids in the crankcase.

BRAKE PAD: A brake shoe and lining assembly used with disc brakes.

BRAKE SHOE: The backing for the brake lining. The term is, however, usually applied to the assembly of the brake backing and lining.

BUSHING: A liner, usually removable, for a bearing; an anti-friction liner used in place of a bearing.

CALIPER: A hydraulically activated device in a disc brake system, which is mounted straddling the brake rotor (disc). The caliper contains at least one piston and two brake pads. Hydraulic pressure on the piston(s) forces the pads against the rotor.

CAMSHAFT: A shaft in the engine on which are the lobes (cams) which operate the valves. The camshaft is driven by the crankshaft, via a belt, chain or gears, at one half the crankshaft speed.

CAPACITOR: A device which stores an electrical charge.

CARBON MONOXIDE (CO): A colorless, odorless gas given off as a normal byproduct of combustion. It is poisonous and extremely dangerous in confined areas, building up slowly to toxic levels without warning if adequate ventilation is not available.

CARBURETOR: A device, usually mounted on the intake manifold of an engine, which mixes the air and fuel in the proper proportion to allow even combustion.

CATALYTIC CONVERTER: A device installed in the exhaust system, like a muffler, that converts harmful byproducts of combustion into carbon dioxide and water vapor by means of a heat-producing chemical reaction.

CENTRIFUGAL ADVANCE: A mechanical method of advancing the spark timing by using flyweights in the distributor that react to centrifugal force generated by the distributor shaft rotation.

CHECK VALVE: Any one-way valve installed to permit the flow of air, fuel or vacuum in one direction only.

CHOKE: A device, usually a moveable valve, placed in the intake path of a carburetor to restrict the flow of air.

CIRCUIT: Any unbroken path through which an electrical current can flow. Also used to describe fuel flow in some instances.

CIRCUIT BREAKER: A switch which protects an electrical circuit from overload by opening the circuit when the current flow exceeds a predetermined level. Some circuit breakers must be reset manually, while most reset automatically.

COIL (IGNITION): A transformer in the ignition circuit which steps up the voltage provided to the spark plugs.

COMBINATION MANIFOLD: An assembly which includes both the intake and exhaust manifolds in one casting.

COMBINATION VALVE: A device used in some fuel systems that routes fuel vapors to a charcoal storage canister instead of venting them into the atmosphere. The valve relieves fuel tank pressure and allows fresh air into the tank as the fuel level drops to prevent a vapor lock situation.

COMPRESSION RATIO: The comparison of the total volume of the cylinder and combustion chamber with the piston at BDC and the piston at TDC.

CONDENSER: 1. An electrical device which acts to store an electrical charge, preventing voltage surges. 2. A radiator-like device in the air conditioning system in which refrigerant gas condenses into a liquid, giving off heat.

CONDUCTOR: Any material through which an electrical current can be transmitted easily.

CONTINUITY: Continuous or complete circuit. Can be checked with an ohmmeter.

COUNTERSHAFT: An intermediate shaft which is rotated by a mainshaft and transmits, in turn, that rotation to a working part.

CRANKCASE: The lower part of an engine in which the crankshaft and related parts operate.

CRANKSHAFT: The main driving shaft of an engine which receives reciprocating motion from the pistons and converts it to rotary motion.

CYLINDER: In an engine, the round hole in the engine block in which the piston(s) ride.

CYLINDER BLOCK: The main structural member of an engine in which is found the cylinders, crankshaft and other principal parts.

CYLINDER HEAD: The detachable portion of the engine, usually fastened to the top of the cylinder block and containing all or most of the combustion chambers. On overhead valve engines, it contains the valves and their operating parts. On overhead cam engines, it contains the camshaft as well.

DEAD CENTER: The extreme top or bottom of the piston stroke.

DETONATION: An unwanted explosion of the air/fuel mixture in the combustion chamber caused by excess heat and compression, advanced timing, or an overly lean mixture. Also referred to as "ping".

DIAPHRAGM: A thin, flexible wall separating two cavities, such as in a vacuum advance unit.

DIESELING: A condition in which hot spots in the combustion chamber cause the engine to run on after the key is turned off.

DIFFERENTIAL: A geared assembly which allows the transmission of motion between drive axles, giving one axle the ability to turn faster than the other.

DIODE: An electrical device that will allow current to flow in one direction only.

DISC BRAKE: A hydraulic braking assembly consisting of a brake disc, or rotor, mounted on an axle, and a caliper assembly containing, usually two brake pads which are activated by hydraulic pressure. The pads are forced against the sides of the disc, creating friction which slows the vehicle.

DISTRIBUTOR: A mechanically driven device on an engine which is responsible for electrically firing the spark plug at a predetermined point of the piston stroke.

DOWEL PIN: A pin, inserted in mating holes in two different parts allowing those parts to maintain a fixed relationship.

DRUM BRAKE: A braking system which consists of two brake shoes and one or two wheel cylinders, mounted on a fixed backing plate, and a brake drum, mounted on an axle, which revolves around the assembly.

DWELL: The rate, measured in degrees of shaft rotation, at which an electrical circuit cycles on and off.

ELECTRONIC CONTROL UNIT (ECU): Ignition module, module, amplifier or igniter. See Module for definition.

ELECTRONIC IGNITION: A system in which the timing and firing of the spark plugs is controlled by an electronic control unit, usually called a module. These systems have no points or condenser.

END-PLAY: The measured amount of axial movement in a shaft.

ENGINE: A device that converts heat into mechanical energy.

EXHAUST MANIFOLD: A set of cast passages or pipes which conduct exhaust gases from the engine.

FEELER GAUGE: A blade, usually metal, or precisely predetermined thickness, used to measure the clearance between two parts.

FIRING ORDER: The order in which combustion occurs in the cylinders of an engine. Also the order in which spark is distributed to the plugs by the distributor.

FLOODING: The presence of too much fuel in the intake manifold and combustion chamber which prevents the air/fuel mixture from firing, thereby causing a no-start situation.

FLYWHEEL: A disc shaped part bolted to the rear end of the crankshaft. Around the outer perimeter is affixed the ring gear. The starter drive engages the ring gear, turning the flywheel, which rotates the crankshaft, imparting the initial starting motion to the engine.

FOOT POUND (ft. lbs. or sometimes, ft.lb.): The amount of energy or work needed to raise an item weighing one pound, a distance of one foot.

FUSE: A protective device in a circuit which prevents circuit overload by breaking the circuit when a specific amperage is present. The device is constructed around a strip or wire of a lower amperage rating than the circuit it is designed to protect. When an amperage higher than that stamped on the fuse is present in the circuit, the strip or wire melts, opening the circuit.

GEAR RATIO: The ratio between the number of teeth on meshing gears.

GENERATOR: A device which converts mechanical energy into electrical energy.

HEAT RANGE: The measure of a spark plug's ability to dissipate heat from its firing end. The higher the heat range, the hotter the plug fires.

HUB: The center part of a wheel or gear.

HYDROCARBON (HC): Any chemical compound made up of hydrogen and carbon. A major pollutant formed by the engine as a byproduct of combustion.

HYDROMETER: An instrument used to measure the specific gravity of a solution.

INCH POUND (inch lbs.; sometimes in.lb. or in. lbs.): One twelfth of a foot pound.

INDUCTION: A means of transferring electrical energy in the form of a magnetic field. Principle used in the ignition coil to increase voltage.

INJECTOR: A device which receives metered fuel under relatively low pressure and is activated to inject the fuel into the engine under relatively high pressure at a predetermined time.

INPUT SHAFT: The shaft to which torque is applied, usually carrying the driving gear or gears.

INTAKE MANIFOLD: A casting of passages or pipes used to conduct air or a fuel/air mixture to the cylinders.

JOURNAL: The bearing surface within which a shaft operates.

KEY: A small block usually fitted in a notch between a shaft and a hub to prevent slippage of the two parts.

MANIFOLD: A casting of passages or set of pipes which connect the cylinders to an inlet or outlet source.

MANIFOLD VACUUM: Low pressure in an engine intake manifold formed just below the throttle plates. Manifold vacuum is highest at idle and drops under acceleration.

MASTER CYLINDER: The primary fluid pressurizing device in a hydraulic system. In automotive use, it is found in brake and hydraulic clutch systems and is pedal activated, either directly or, in a power brake system, through the power booster.

MODULE: Electronic control unit, amplifier or igniter of solid state or integrated design which controls the current flow in the ignition primary circuit based on input from the pick-up coil. When the module opens the primary circuit, high secondary voltage is induced in the coil.

NEEDLE BEARING: A bearing which consists of a number (usually a large number) of long, thin rollers.

OHM: (Ω) The unit used to measure the resistance of conductor-to-electrical flow. One ohm is the amount of resistance that limits current flow to one ampere in a circuit with one volt of pressure.

OHMMETER: An instrument used for measuring the resistance, in ohms, in an electrical circuit.

OUTPUT SHAFT: The shaft which transmits torque from a device, such as a transmission.

OVERDRIVE: A gear assembly which produces more shaft revolutions than that transmitted to it.

OVERHEAD CAMSHAFT (OHC): An engine configuration in which the camshaft is mounted on top of the cylinder head and operates the valve either directly or by means of rocker arms.

OVERHEAD VALVE (OHV): An engine configuration in which all of the valves are located in the cylinder head and the camshaft is located in the cylinder block. The camshaft operates the valves via lifters and pushrods.

OXIDES OF NITROGEN (NOx): Chemical compounds of nitrogen produced as a byproduct of combustion. They combine with hydrocarbons to produce smog.

OXYGEN SENSOR: Use with the feedback system to sense the presence of oxygen in the exhaust gas and signal the computer which can reference the voltage signal to an air/fuel ratio.

PINION: The smaller of two meshing gears.

PISTON RING: An open-ended ring with fits into a groove on the outer diameter of the piston. Its chief function is to form a seal between the piston and cylinder wall. Most automotive pistons have three rings: two for compression sealing; one for oil sealing.

PRELOAD: A predetermined load placed on a bearing during assembly or by adjustment.

PRIMARY CIRCUIT: the low voltage side of the ignition system which consists of the ignition switch, ballast resistor or resistance wire, bypass, coil, electronic control unit and pick-up coil as well as the connecting wires and harnesses.

PRESS FIT: The mating of two parts under pressure, due to the inner diameter of one being smaller than the outer diameter of the other, or vice versa; an interference fit.

RACE: The surface on the inner or outer ring of a bearing on which the balls, needles or rollers move.

REGULATOR: A device which maintains the amperage and/or voltage levels of a circuit at predetermined values.

RELAY: A switch which automatically opens and/or closes a circuit.

RESISTANCE: The opposition to the flow of current through a circuit or electrical device, and is measured in ohms. Resistance is equal to the voltage divided by the amperage.

RESISTOR: A device, usually made of wire, which offers a preset amount of resistance in an electrical circuit.

RING GEAR: The name given to a ring-shaped gear attached to a differential case, or affixed to a flywheel or as part of a planetary gear set.

ROLLER BEARING: A bearing made up of hardened inner and outer races between which hardened steel rollers move.

ROTOR: 1. The disc-shaped part of a disc brake assembly, upon which the brake pads bear; also called, brake disc. 2. The device mounted atop the distributor shaft, which passes current to the distributor cap tower contacts.

SECONDARY CIRCUIT: The high voltage side of the ignition system, usually above 20,000 volts. The secondary includes the ignition coil, coil wire, distributor cap and rotor, spark plug wires and spark plugs.

SENDING UNIT: A mechanical, electrical, hydraulic or electro-magnetic device which transmits information to a gauge.

SENSOR: Any device designed to measure engine operating conditions or ambient pressures and temperatures. Usually electronic in nature and designed to send a voltage signal to an on-board computer, some sensors may operate as a simple on/off switch or they may provide a variable voltage signal (like a potentiometer) as conditions or measured parameters change.

SHIM: Spacers of precise, predetermined thickness used between parts to establish a proper working relationship.

SLAVE CYLINDER: In automotive use, a device in the hydraulic clutch system which is activated by hydraulic force, disengaging the clutch.

SOLENOID: A coil used to produce a magnetic field, the effect of which is to produce work.

SPARK PLUG: A device screwed into the combustion chamber of a spark ignition engine. The basic construction is a conductive core inside of a ceramic insulator, mounted in an outer conductive base. An electrical charge from the spark plug wire travels along the conductive core and jumps a preset air gap to a grounding point or points at the end of the conductive base. The resultant spark ignites the fuel/air mixture in the combustion chamber.

SPLINES: Ridges machined or cast onto the outer diameter of a shaft or inner diameter of a bore to enable parts to mate without rotation.

TACHOMETER: A device used to measure the rotary speed of an engine, shaft, gear, etc., usually in rotations per minute.

THERMOSTAT: A valve, located in the cooling system of an engine, which is closed when cold and opens gradually in response to engine heating, controlling the temperature of the coolant and rate of coolant flow.

TOP DEAD CENTER (TDC): The point at which the piston reaches the top of its travel on the compression stroke.

TORQUE: The twisting force applied to an object.

TORQUE CONVERTER: A turbine used to transmit power from a driving member to a driven member via hydraulic action, providing changes in drive ratio and torque. In automotive use, it links the driveplate at the rear of the engine to the automatic transmission.

TRANSDUCER: A device used to change a force into an electrical signal.

TRANSISTOR: A semi-conductor component which can be actuated by a small voltage to perform an electrical switching function.

TUNE-UP: A regular maintenance function, usually associated with the replacement and adjustment of parts and components in the electrical and fuel systems of a vehicle for the purpose of attaining optimum performance.

TURBOCHARGER: An exhaust driven pump which compresses intake air and forces it into the combustion chambers at higher than atmospheric pressures. The increased air pressure allows more fuel to be burned and results in increased horsepower being produced.

VACUUM ADVANCE: A device which advances the ignition timing in response to increased engine vacuum.

VACUUM GAUGE: An instrument used to measure the presence of vacuum in a chamber.

VALVE: A device which control the pressure, direction of flow or rate of flow of a liquid or gas.

VALVE CLEARANCE: The measured gap between the end of the valve stem and the rocker arm, cam lobe or follower that activates the valve.

VISCOSITY: The rating of a liquid's internal resistance to flow.

VOLTMETER: An instrument used for measuring electrical force in units called volts. Voltmeters are always connected parallel with the circuit being tested.

WHEEL CYLINDER: Found in the automotive drum brake assembly, it is a device, actuated by hydraulic pressure, which, through internal pistons, pushes the brake shoes outward against the drums.

MASTER
INDEX